A CULTURAL HISTORY OF MODERN CHINESE LITERATURE

This is an illustrated cultural history of the emergence of modern literature in China from the late nineteenth century through the early years of the Chinese Republic, the 1930s, and the war period, ending in 1949. Wu Fuhui takes an interdisciplinary approach to the topic, drawing in book production, translation, popular and elite texts, international influences, and political history. Presented here in English translation for the first time, Wu argues that this was a transformative period in Chinese literature informed both by developments in China's domestic history and the dynamics of global circulation and encounter.

WU FUHUI is a scholar of the history of modern Chinese literature and has published widely on this topic. He is the former director of the Research Room of the National Museum of Modern Chinese Literature, deputy president of the Modern Chinese Literature Association, and chief editor of the journal *Modern Chinese Literature Studies*.

THE CAMBRIDGE CHINA LIBRARY

The Cambridge China Library is a series of new English translations of books by Chinese scholars that have not previously been available in the West. Covering a wide range of subjects in the arts and humanities, the social sciences, and the history of science, the series aims to foster intellectual debate and to promote closer cross-cultural understanding by bringing important works of Chinese scholarship to the attention of Western readers.

A CULTURAL HISTORY OF MODERN CHINESE LITERATURE

WU FUHUI

Peking University, Beijing

WITH AN INTRODUCTION BY DAVID DER-WEI WANG

Edward C. Henderson Professor of Chinese Literature, Harvard University

TRANSLATED BY RUI MA

CAMBRIDGE
UNIVERSITY PRESS

CAMBRIDGE
UNIVERSITY PRESS

University Printing House, Cambridge CB2 8BS, United Kingdom

One Liberty Plaza, 20th Floor, New York, NY 10006, USA

477 Williamstown Road, Port Melbourne, VIC 3207, Australia

314–321, 3rd Floor, Plot 3, Splendor Forum, Jasola District Centre, New Delhi – 110025, India

79 Anson Road, #06–04/06, Singapore 079906

Cambridge University Press is part of the University of Cambridge.

It furthers the University's mission by disseminating knowledge in the pursuit of
education, learning, and research at the highest international levels of excellence.

www.cambridge.org
Information on this title: www.cambridge.org/9781107069497
DOI: 10.1017/9781107706828

Originally published by Peking University Press as The Development of Modern Chinese Literature in 2010
(9787301079867)

© Peking University Press 2010

This updated edition is published by Cambridge University Press with the permission of Peking University Press
under the China Book International programme.

For more information on the China Book International programme, please visit

www.chinabookinternational.org

Cambridge University Press retains copyright in its own contributions to this English translation edition

© Cambridge University Press 2020

First published 2020

Printed in the United Kingdom by TJ International Ltd. Padstow Cornwall

A catalogue record for this publication is available from the British Library.

Library of Congress Cataloging-in-Publication Data
NAMES: Wu, Fuhui, author. | Ma, Myra, Translator. | Wang, Dewei, author of introduction.
TITLE: A cultural history of modern Chinese literature / Fuhui Wu, Peking University, Beijing ;
with an introduction by David Der-wei Wang, Edward C. Henderson Professor of
Chinese Literature, Harvard University ; translated by Myra Ma.
OTHER TITLES: Zhongguo xian dai wen xue fa zhan shi. English
DESCRIPTION: Cambridge, United Kingdom ; New York : Cambridge University Press, 2020. | Series: The
Cambridge China library | Includes bibliographical references and index.
IDENTIFIERS: LCCN 2019043934 (print) | LCCN 2019043935 (ebook) | ISBN 9781107069497 (hardback) |
ISBN 9781107706828 (ebook)
SUBJECTS: LCSH: Chinese literature – 20th century – History and criticism.
CLASSIFICATION: LCC PL2302 .W725513 2020 (print) | LCC PL2302 (ebook) | DDC 895.1/006–dc23
LC record available at https://lccn.loc.gov/2019043934
LC ebook record available at https://lccn.loc.gov/2019043935

ISBN 978-1-107-06949-7 Hardback

CONTENTS

FIGURES

MAPS

TABLES

INTRODUCTION TO THE ENGLISH EDITION

Literary history is a unique phenomenon in modern China as a scholarly undertaking, a pedagogical vehicle, a political statement, and even a cultural industry. Particularly since 1949, hundreds of literary histories have been published on any subject one can think of. This phenomenon bespeaks not only a civilization deeply ingrained in the linkage between literariness (*wen*) and historicity (*shi*) but also a state apparatus that continuously strives to reauthenticate the meaning of past and present in narrative terms. As such, literary history has been institutionalized to embody a coherent account of canonical figures, masterpieces, mandated movements, and events, and an articulation of national characteristics and party lines. Literary history is a "history" encapsulated in literary forms.

In this context, *A Cultural History of Modern Chinese Literature* is an extraordinary project. In forty chapters, the book describes the dynamics of Chinese literature from the late-nineteenth century (the late-Qing dynasty), to the founding of the People's Republic of China in 1949, a crucial time in China's search for modernity. Its author, Professor Wu Fuhui (b. 1939), is a veteran Chinese scholar known for his encyclopedic knowledge and critical engagement. For years, Wu has explored new approaches to literary history vis-à-vis the extant paradigm; *A Cultural History of Modern Chinese Literature* represents his efforts at their most provocative.

For readers unfamiliar with modern Chinese literature, two aspects of Wu's project should be noted. First, in traditional China, literature refers to a much broader spectrum of humanistic exercises, as ornament, belles lettres, scholarly discipline, cultural upbringing, and above all, civilization. Literature underwent drastic transformations in the nineteenth century to become "literature" as we understand the word to mean today. Still, the belief in literature as a manifestation of the world at large remained intact even during the radical days of socialist China.

Secondly, the Chinese "modern" refers not only to a concept of temporality in response to Western stimuli ranging from industrialization to nationalism, urbanization, and psychologized subjectivity, but also to an indigenous intervention with the global imposition of a progressive agenda. At stake here is the political landscape that compelled the Chinese to conceive of and act out the modern in a unique manner. Especially in Chinese communist discourse, literature development is made to parallel political periodization. Thus, the "modern" era (*xiandai*) is taken to mean a time from 1911 (the founding of the Republic of China) to 1949, one that overcame the "early modern" era (*jindai*, the final decades of the Qing dynasty), and anticipated the "contemporary" era (*dangdai*), which spans from 1949 to date and presumably the infinite future.

A Cultural History of Modern Chinese Literature tackles these complexities. It proposes that we rethink issues such as the periodization of "modern" Chinese literature, the conceptualization of Chinese "literature," and the feasibility of "literary history." In the main, it ventures to view Chinese literary moderniza-tion as a long and sprawling process traceable to the last decades of the nine-teenth century. Instead of a monolithic timetable, it acknowledges the arrival of the modern at any given historical juncture as a competition of new pos-sibilities, where the result does not necessarily reflect the best or even any one of the possibilities.

Such an approach is no small feat given the environment in which Professor Wu wrote this book. Wu's task comes as part of the endeavor of "rewriting literary history" launched by People's Republic of China scholars in the last decade of the modern century. As his preface indicates, Wu benefited from the new models developed by fellow scholars, such as Professor Yan Jiayan's attention to the "ecology" of literary production at both public and per-sonal levels; Professor Chen Sihe's consideration of the continued negotiation between avant-garde impulses and the yearning for normalcy and stabilization; Professor Yang Yi's mapping of the "literary cartography" of modern China; and Professor Fan Boqun's campaign for the coexistence of both elite and popular literature. Based on these models, Wu develops his own framework which highlights the tapestry-like networking of both mainstream and non-mainstream literatures, both material and textual productions.

A Cultural History of Modern Chinese Literature comprises four parts, each of which has a different thematic strain. Part I ushers us into the moment prior to the rise of modern Chinese literature, when the vernacular language emerged to become the dominant role in place of the classical language in literary communication, and the rising print culture changed the mode of cultural production as well as the identity of literati for good. Part II features the May Fourth movement (1919) as the main force that drastically changed the "structure of feeling" of Republican China, giving rise to a new *habitus* of literary culture in the name of enlightenment. Part III follows up by describing the golden time of post–May Fourth literature, when multiple subjects, styles, cliques, and events interacted with each other to form a polyphonic scene of articulation. Part IV focuses on the Second Sino-Japanese War (1937–1945) and

the civil war (1946–1949), a time that witnessed the devastation and regeneration of literature amid foreign aggression, nationalist campaign, and communist revolution.

While Professor Wu's book may first appear to have followed the conventional format of narrative, a careful reader will quickly discover his unconventional design. For one thing, in addition to textual narrative, it is enriched
with numerous illustrations, photographs, charts, chronologies, and maps. The
pictorial data is presented in such a way as to direct – even distract – the reader
to a different horizon of knowledge, in which the textual and the visual, the
streamlined narrative and the seemingly inexhaustible statistic account, supplement as much as redefine each other's premise of intelligibility. As a result, the
"master narrative" about the rise and development of modern Chinese literature has undergone a subtle shakeup. This shakeup and its critical implication
can be described in the following aspects.

To begin with, Wu starts the timeline of his history not with the May
Fourth era, the official harbinger of Chinese literary modernization, but with
the final decades of the late-Qing dynasty. The three terms of periodizing
modern Chinese history, "early modern," "modern," and "contemporary," are
encoded with political messages. Conventional wisdom sees the "early modern" as a moment when the old literary and political order was falling apart
– a decadent, transitional period awaiting the outburst of the May Fourth. Wu
disagrees. He indicates in the first part of his history that while May Fourth
set in motion a series of paradigm changes, the conception, production, and
dissemination of literature during the last decades of the Qing demonstrated a
vigor and variety that could hardly be confined to the parameters prescribed
by May Fourth discourse. The May Fourth may have discovered as many pos-
sibilities as it obscured, or even eliminated, that which had once thrived in the
late Qing.

One finds equally inspiring observations in Part IV, which deals with wartime literature and its consequences. In contrast with the standard discourse
that stresses a literature leading inevitably toward the 1949 revolution, Wu
downplays the linear factor of history, juxtaposing instead six sites, Chongqing,
Yan'an, Kunming, Guilin, Shanghai, and even Hong Kong and Taiwan in
which distinct environments, ideologies, and literatures generated an unlikely
heteroglossia. Only from such a perspective, Wu contends, can one better appreciate the tension between aspirations and apprehensions, historical necessity
and contingency, on the eve of the communist victory.

The second aspect that distinguishes Wu's book is his emphasis on the material aspect of literary production. The first chapter starts with an overview
of the print industry in late-Qing Shanghai. As Wu notes, this was a period
that saw literature conceptualized, practiced, circulated, and assessed in ways
unprecedented in Chinese history. Imported printing technology, innovative

marketing tactics, increased literacy, widening readership, a boom in the diversity of forms of media and translation, and the advent of professional writers, all created fields of literary production and consumption that in preceding centuries would hardly have been imaginable.

Throughout Wu's history, one comes to learn issues ranging from the economic circumstances of a professional writer to market demand versus censorship, from ideological contestations to theatrical and cinematic adaptations. Literature, as he would have it, is not so much a discursive exercise as it is a field of cultural production charged with extraliterary factors. One would have assumed that in a socialist culture these material factors should have taken precedence over those oriented to superstructure. The fact is, however, that Wu may well be among the very few who refuses to pay only lip service to the socialist formula and instead truly explores the intricate relationships between the material and the discursive circumstances. For instance, in each of the four parts in his history, Wu foregrounds a specific year (1903; 1921; 1936; 1948) with a detailed chart of events and publications of the year, thus literally illustrating the complexity of the time in discussion. The implication, to be sure, is that any given year could generate such a kaleidoscopic view of literature in relation to society.

Wu's third contribution is in presenting modern Chinese literature as a continued interplay among discourses, media spheres, and political platforms otherwise seemingly independent of, or even hostile to, each other. In other words, he is aiming an ecological vista through which the indigenous and the foreign, the popular and the elite, the hegemonic and the subversive are brought into play. In the wake of May Fourth, realism was hailed as the magic form that can expose social injustice and invoke humanist compassion. Wu reminds us that realist discourse aside, modern Chinese readers were equally drawn to the "Mandarin Ducks and Butterfly fiction" – middle-brow literature "for comfort" – and avant-garde writing in both modernist and socialist terms. More importantly, just as writers and readers alike do not always hold on to one specific trend or position, literary discourses can transgress each other's boundaries. Thus, Wu describes the way in which the poets of Nanshe utter their revolutionary zeal by composing in the conservative form of classical style poetry; popular literature in Shanghai and populist literature in Yan'an share the same ground of engaging the mass in opposition to the elite May Fourth discourse.

Last but not least, Wu contends that modern Chinese literature is part of the national and global circulation of discourses and practices of modernity. This circulation comes about through travel, both in the sense of physical mobility and conceptual, affective, and technological transmutation through space and time. Whereas late-Qing literati moved to Shanghai and other metropolises to make a living, in the May Fourth era, young writers from all over China traveled to Beijing and Shanghai for enlightenment. During the Second Sino-Japanese War, hundreds of thousands of literati joined the exodus to the hinterland while progressive youth took the pilgrimage to Yan'an for communist baptism.

Travel leads to transculturation: the linguistic, cultural, and intellectual interactions between continents, nations, societies, institutions, and communities. The most important medium of transculturation is, without a doubt, translation, through which China and other civilizations encounter and produce new forms of knowledge, feeling, and power exchange. Throughout the twentieth century, as Wu points out, from Lin Shu's entrepreneurial, collaborative "translation" of foreign literature to Guo Moruo's leftist rendition of Goethe's *Faust*, from the wild popularity of Soviet fiction during the early years of Socialist China to the fever of consuming modernist literature in high societies, translation has been the venue where language has been refashioned and thoughts negotiated. Sherlock Holmes, *La Dame aux Camélias*, and Werther became household names. Whereas Shakespeare's plays were all translated by Zhu Shenghao in exile during the wartime, Nicolai Ostrovsky's *How the Steel Was Tempered* captured the heart of revolutionary youth in Yan'an.

To conclude, a few more words about the author. Wu Fuhui belongs to the generation of scholars who went through almost all the ups and downs of New China. He started out being a high school teacher in 1959, and did not enroll in the graduate program of Chinese literature at Peking University until 1978, two years after the end of the Great Cultural Revolution. Despite the lag of educational time, he received the best possible training from scholars such as Wang Yao and Yan Jiayan. Whereas Wang Yao published the first modern Chinese literary history after the founding of the PRC, Yan Jiayan was among the forerunners of "rewriting literary history" in the New Era of the 1980s. In other words, Wu took up where his mentors left off in the enterprise of literary history.

In 1987, together with Qian Liqun and Wen Rumin, who later became leading scholars in their own right, Wu Fuhui edited *Three Decades of Modern Chinese Literature*, a landmark of the revisionist engagement of modern literary history. All along Wu had planned to write a literary history illustrating his own critical viewpoint, and his wish was realized when the Chinese edition of *A Cultural History of Modern Chinese Literature* came out in 2010. The way in which Wu entered the academic sphere amid political turmoil, working with the key figures of contemporary Chinese literary studies, and becoming an outstanding figure, points to the volatile progress and surprising consequences of literary history in contemporary China. Now with the English translation of his history to be published by Cambridge University Press, Professor Wu Fuhui is finally able to share his insights of and reflections on the twists and turns of modern Chinese history with readers worldwide.

David Der-wei Wang

PREFACE

I have opened up a plot of raw land in my own academic garden: writing an experimental illustrated history of modern Chinese literature. Now I have finally finished it and present it to my readers.

For me, the journey toward the completion of this book has not been a smooth one. It started from the publication plans of two publishing houses, one in Beijing and the other in Shanghai, whose editors asked me to write a history of modern Chinese literature with illustrations closely related to text. The plans were worthy and ambitious, but in front of the harsh reality, both were put aside for reasons unrelated to me, and seemed abandoned forever. But it turned out to be a blessing in disguise. Unbeknown to me, after the plans were hung up, we entered a new era in which the writing of literary history is going through significant changes. If this book had been completed several years ago, it would probably have been some clichéd literary historical narrative with some awkwardly inserted illustrations and maps. It may have seemed like something new, but actually the innovations would have been very superficial. This book, although it is far from perfect and its illustrations and tables not so very remarkable, can be seen as a literary history with brand new concepts, and it might be bold to say that one can find an emergent framework of literary history writing – the future in embryo – in this book.

I discussed the emerging change of ideas of literary history with young teachers of Shanghai University, where I gave lectures last winter. Later they compiled their recording of my speech and entitled it "The New Trend in the Research of Modern Chinese Literature," which will be included in my symposium *Through the Multifaceted Prism* to be published soon. There I have described in detail five new perceptive observations on literary history raised recently: the literary "ecology" view of Yan Jiayan (严家炎); the view of Fan Boqun (范伯群) on the "mutual development" of genteel and popular literature; "avant-garde versus normalcy" proposed by Chen Sihe (陈思和); the effort of "remapping Chinese literature" by Yang Yi (杨义); as well as my own shallow views elaborated in *Literature and Art Forum* (《文艺争鸣》) on deconstructing and disintegrating "mainstream" literary historical narratives and writing a literary history "concertedly compiled with distinctive points of view." These ideas are by no means discrete and unrelated to each other; on the contrary, they are interconnected and constitute mutually complementary visions, from which we can see the consensus of the "coexistence of various views" and a "broad scope of literary history." This shows that people throughout the entire academic circle have come to the stage to rewrite Chinese literary history. Negligible and unnoticed as it is, we can see a trend that will surely make an impact on future scholars in this field of study.

Certainly, I have developed and gradually defined my own concept of literary history in the academic environment where different ideas and viewpoints interact with, argue against, and meanwhile influence each other. I remember an analogy made by Professor Wang Yao (王瑶), which he has repeated many times, that there are generally two methods of doing scholarly work. The first one focuses on a central viewpoint, like the vinyl disc circling around a single stylus on the phonograph, hence a main tune. The second method features disorganized parts, something like the front and back parts when you try to knit a woolen sweater or a scarf. Professor Wang says the first method represents an advanced standpoint, while the second one is also very important, and we cannot afford to neglect it. Since the founding of the People's Republic of China, our literary history has been centered around either "revolution" or "modernity"; do we really need to write another literary history with "postmodernism" or "nation-state" as its guiding ideology? In my opinion, ever since the concept of "twentieth-century Chinese literature" was raised, we have been doing a kind of deconstructing work, and it is still not the time for summing up and drawing a conclusion. "Deconstruction" and "summing up" are traditional Chinese methodologies I am used to. Specifically, summing up would cohere literary history into an imagined complete structure, while deconstructing would challenge the existing structure and break it into heterogeneous parts. Borrowing Wang's analogy between scholarship and knitting, I think a mosaic literary history may better suit today's academic climate. Similarly, on the interconnection and interaction between "revolution" and "modernity" in Chinese literary history, we can bridge their antithetical relationship with such notions as "coexistence", "transition," and "building-up." At the time when Chinese literature was building up modernity, motley literary expressions were absolutely necessary; and since revolution was a historical process that accelerated the modernization of Chinese literature, there were many turns and twists in the process. Such building up and transitions created an even more complex and varied literary history, and thus there were multiple literary genres, including, broadly, left-wing literature, market-oriented literature, Beijing school literature, and Shanghai school literature. None of these four dominated the literary world in any single period, for each had its own reader group, and each fell into a distinct category: political literature, commercial literature, or belles lettres. These categories were not isolated from each other, but interconnected, with the border frequently crossed. For example, left-wing political literature relied heavily on the book market of Shanghai, and Beijing school literature disapproved of political literature but was itself not divorced from social life and social reality (not belles lettres in its truest sense). This was a multifaceted literary scene unprecedented ever since Chinese literature took form, and it was no doubt a "modern" one. No literary genre had become the truly dominating one in the literary landscape, which remains true even to this day.

I have been exploring a multifaceted understanding and writing of literary history, which is still ongoing today. Nevertheless, I have accepted the request of Peking University Press to write a new literary history, thus putting my thoughts and ideas into shape. Without much to draw on for guidance in the process, I have to learn from my contemporaries. For example, Yan Jiayan's "literary ecology" theory suggests that a literary history cannot disregard people's lifestyles, nor can it leave aside authors' states of mind and the social and cultural context directly connected with such states of mind. Fan Boqun's theory of "mutual development" of genteel and popular literature serves as both a reminder and inspiration for me, and though I don't think popular literature and avant-garde literature can be paralleled in a literary history, I seriously considered how to integrate popular literature into urban citizen literature, which became a popular literature with an avant-garde edge when the Shanghai school emerged, so that the line between the two was not that clear-cut any more. This is the reason why Chen Sihe proposed "avant-garde" and "normalcy" as two interacting literary formats. Thus I analyzed typical avant-garde works in my literary history, and at the same time, while giving full attention to the normalcy clue of popular culture, I tried to extend the latter by including both rural popular literature and urban popular literature. Yang Yi's view on a broader literary map helped me enrich the single-dimensional viewpoints on Chinese literature into a multidimensional, open, and networked literary landscape. In this sense, I think this literary history can be seen as a history of literary development of the period in question.

The title "A Cultural History of Modern Chinese Literature" is used to distinguish this book from literary history written by others in the past, and it is also used in memory of my personal experience. Immediately after the end of the "Cultural Revolution," I registered for the entrance examination for graduate studies in modern Chinese literature, only to find, just one month before the exam, that Professor Wang Yao had added some questions on ancient Chinese literature. Time pressed and I had no other reference book available, so I crammed myself with Liu Dajie's *History of the Development of*

Chinese Literature, which was "contaminated" in the late 1960s.[1] But more importantly, in writing this book, I have given full play to the sense of "development" of Chinese literature; that is, everything related to literary works and authors is put back into the ever-changing historical "context." The release, publication, spread, reception, and evolvement of literary works are given special attention, and the social–cultural environment in which literary works took shape is given more importance than ever before. The change of literary venues, the living conditions of authors, their migration, and material and spiritual lifestyle are unfolded in detail at certain key historical points. I give an account of various literary associations and schools as well as their links with the modern mass media, such as newspapers, magazines, literary supplements, and book series, thus trying to restore the original ecology in which literature happened. Then there were extensions of modern literature, like the tentacles of an octopus, related with readers through literary criticism, with world literature of all times through translation, and with other contemporary art forms through films. And the formation and evolvement of modern vernacular and its use in literature should be considered in the close reading of works of the modern literary canon. Then I try to construct major literary periods in the book, bring readers to the literary scene of the time with something like chronicles of literary events. I certainly know the real "original ecology" is nonexistent, since either major periods or major events are choices made by me as a chronicler of literary history. But this chronological method that tries to bring us closer to the mode of creation and evolvement of literature, unexhausted as it is, plays a special role in the restoration of real literary history, which has been distorted and misinterpreted.

Since this book focuses on the development of modern Chinese literature, it shall be open-ended and ever-extending, and nobody has the right to put an end to it. I am writing a single-volume literary history, and with illustrations added, the space is quite limited. And since scholars have already expanded the literary history of this period into a much broader one, I must find some key points that may best represent each period. In this book, I consciously cut down narratives about authors and try not to cover all their literary works, but give a detailed analysis of typical representative works, in which process the lack and neglect of some major authors and works are unavoidable. Maybe this is a writing method worth trying, and this book may provide both a positive and negative experience for future scholars who try to write ever more concise and focused literary histories.

All literary histories shall be based on the results of academic research available at the time they are written, and it is by no means an easy task for a single

---

[1] Liu Dajie (刘大杰) revised his book in the late 1960s to suit the ideology of the "Cultural Revolution". – Translator's note

writer. All quotations are referenced, as well as the sources of various tables and figures. The References at the end of the book list all books I have actually referred to in writing my literary history, whose purpose is nothing but to express my acknowledgment to the authors whose books I have read. I remember when I coauthored the book *Thirty Years in Modern Chinese Literature* (《中国现代文学三十年》), we were not very confident in our textual research, and thus invited several experts from Beijing to check our manuscript, but later we found there were still some errors and omissions throughout that book. Now I have written this book independently, and besides so many quotations and references, there are such a large number of chronologies, tables, figures, and records of events, and I can imagine, with fear and awe, how many mistakes there must be in this book. I am looking forward to experts' and readers' generous criticism and advice.

Selecting illustrations was another difficulty in writing this book. Different from collecting and selecting photos of popular literature, there are too few illustrations for some literary material and too many for others. For example, I tried to select the portraits of authors produced at the same time of the publication of their representative works, and besides photos, I tried to find caricatures, self-portraits, and group photos, which are a bit harder to find. Sometimes it is also difficult to find the magazines in which the literary works were first published, as well as authors' manuscripts of their representative works. And then there are the authors' former residences and gathering places, maps, and pictures of literary characters hand-drawn by authors, the newspapers and magazines in which literary works were published as well as their advertisements, and posters or photos of scenes from various plays and films; in a word, a fine, new, and complete collection of such illustrations is not an easily accomplished task. The illustration collection and selection was especially difficult at the later stage of writing; some were not determined even after the writing was finished. I hereby express my sincere gratitude to the National Museum of Modern Chinese Literature, where I have been working for a long time, for some of the illustrations it has provided, and for the help of some of my colleagues and students.

Many thanks are extended to the publishing house of my alma mater, especially to my editor Gao Xiuqin for her invitation to write this book, without which this book would never have been possible, not to say in such a great time. She allowed me full freedom in writing and revising my manuscript, including the captions of the illustrations. During the entire process while I have been so particular with text and picky about illustrations, her tremendous patience and encouragement have been invaluable. Then she agreed that the book shall be completed in 2009, so that it may finally come out at the beginning of a new decade. My thanks also go to my editors-in-charge, Zhu Jing and Ding Chao, whose generosity has been limitless, allowing me to express my own ideas in my own style freely and independently. Their careful proof-reading and correction have ensured there is no major error in the final copy. It is my great honor that the publishing of this book has coincided with the thirtieth anniversary of Peking University Press.

This book does not intend to create a new paradigm for a new-type literary history; it is rather a "warm-up" heralding the new-type literary history, and a preparation for new possibilities open to future literary historians. In writing this book I have fulfilled one of my dreams. In the past decade, I had many dreams, some wonderful dreams and some terrible nightmares. In the former I seemed to have been rejuvenated and still have so many new plans in writing and something else, and I seemed to see our society more just and prosperous, and young people growing up lively and healthily. In the latter I seemed to have been forced back to the place I drifted in my own youth, lost and hurt. It seems that some of my dreams in literature have been fulfilled, some broken, and some reborn. This book is my dream fulfilled, despite its endless imperfections.

After all, a literary scholar cannot live without dreams.

Nov. 12, 2009, during snow in Beijing

Outside my window, the trees are covered in whiteness

This book was first produced by the Peking University Peiwin Education Company, and then went through two printings in traditional Chinese, in which process the errors and omissions were corrected. Now that the book is going through the second printing in simplified Chinese, thanks to the efforts of editors-in-charge Gao Xiuqin, Zhu Jing, and Ding Chao, and especially the detailed work by editor Huang Weizheng, there is an overall revision to the entire book, including the material, text, notes, pictures, and tables. I have always been looking forward to a complete and finer written literary history to be published on the mainland and satisfy its readers, and am so happy to see it now. Life is short, and it is never easy to accomplish something one really aspires to, be it great or small. For me, the revision of this literary history is one of my accomplishments. My heartfelt thanks to all.

Wu Fuhui
On the Chinese Lunar New Year's Day of 2015

Promise of New Opportunities

第一章 孕育新机

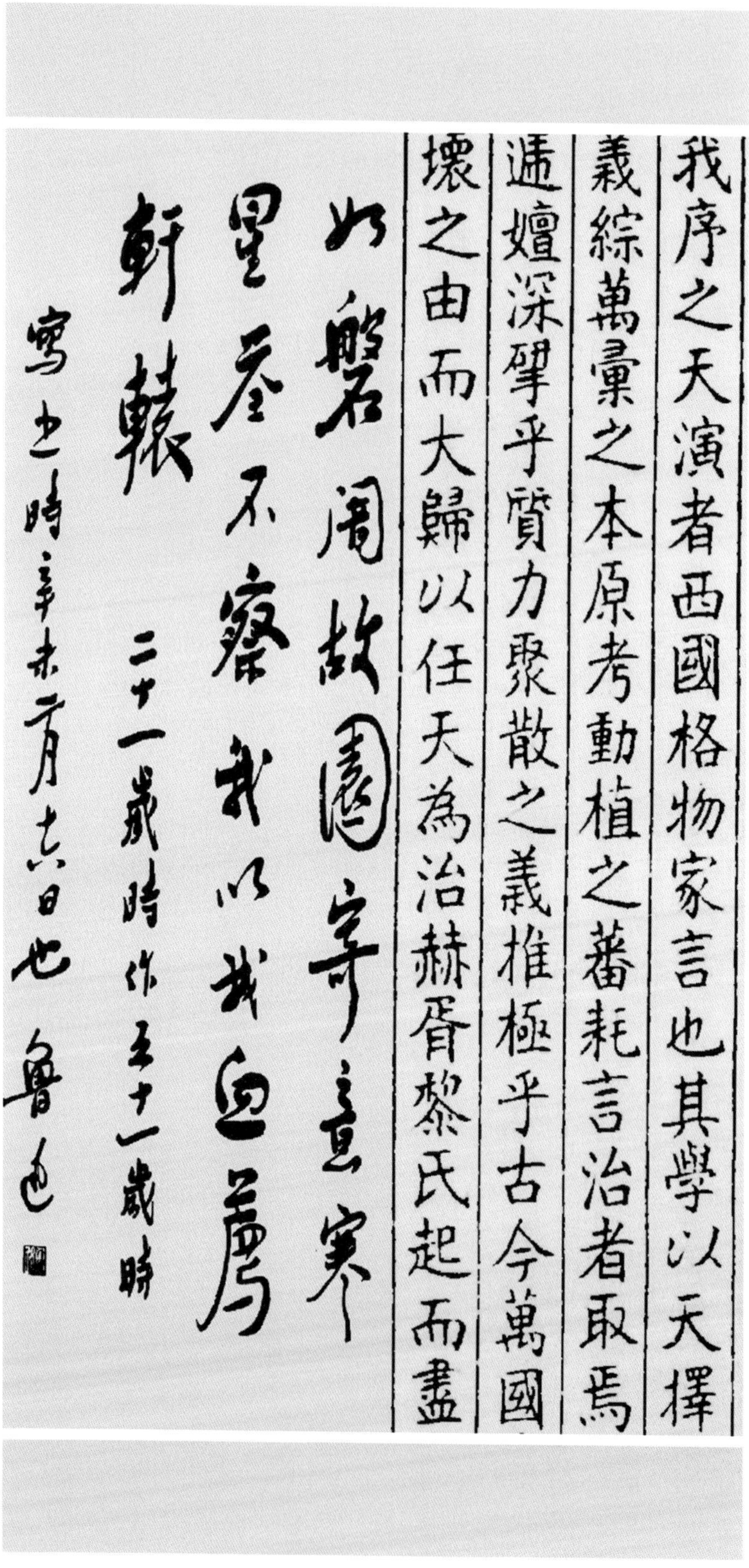
我序之天演者西國格物家言也其學以天擇
義綜萬彙之本原考動植之蕃耗言治者取焉
遞嬗深擘乎質力聚散之義推極乎古今萬國
壞之由而大歸以任天為治赫胥黎氏起而盡
如磐闇故園寄意寒
星荃不察我以我血薦
軒轅
二十一歲時作 五十一歲時
寫之時辛未二月十六日也 魯迅

ONE

WANGPING STREET – FUZHOU ROAD

The Changing Scene of Chinese Literature

T HE REASON WHY I'VE CHOSEN TO START RECOUNTING the story of China's modern literature with its earliest newspaper street, Shanghai's Wangping Street (望平街) (similar to London's Fleet Street), is to emphasize that from its very outset the country's modern literature, yet to continue for more than 100 years, took place within a new range of contexts totally different from those of classical Chinese literature. Besides economic development, the most important factors for literary activities among these contexts involved drastic transformation in the intellectual circle as well as social and cultural reconstruction, both of which were best represented by the rise of modern journalism and the publishing industry.

1.1. Map of Shanghai District in the Ming dynasty (1368–1644)

1.2. Wangping Street (today's Fuzhou Road and Shandong Middle Road) was lined with newspaper offices and publishing houses

Tushanwan (土山湾) is a place-name that should be familiar to us, but has probably been obscured from historical memory: it was the predecessor of Wangping Street. After the Western powers won the Opium War, some French Catholic missionaries came to Shanghai, settled in Xujiahui (徐家汇), and built a church (the one that is still standing there today, St. Ignatius Cathedral, rebuilt in 1910), monastery, public school, library, museum, observatory and orphanage, among other things, around nearby Tushanwan. The name Xujiahui (literally, "Xu's junction") has far-reaching significance. On the one hand, this area was originally the property of the family of Xu Guangqi (徐光启, 1562–1633), Minister of Rites of the late Ming dynasty, a Chinese scientist and Catholic convert who, under the influence of the Italian Jesuit priest Matteo Ricci (1552–1610), started the Chinese people's centuries-long journey to learn Western science and technologies. Xu was buried in Xujiahui after his death, and his descendants lived in the district for generations. (The mother of the famous Soong sisters was a descendant of Xu. Soong Ching-ling [宋庆龄, 1893–1981], the second of the sisters, and her parents are all buried in Xujiahui. The parents of Xie Wanying [谢婉莹, 1900–1999], the modern Chinese writer better known by her pseudonym Bing Xin [冰心], are also buried there.) On the other hand, it was

1.3. Bird's-eye view of the area around the church in Xujiahui, where modern civilization was first introduced to China. City and countryside already appear to be merging

1.4. Western-style sketching class at Tushanwan Painting Studio (土山湾画馆), the earliest institution to teach Western fine arts in China. Many modern Chinese painters hailed from here

here that Western church culture found its way into China. Western church culture, so to speak, was as much modern as it was colonial. The church originally built its crafts factory, and its painting and printing studio, to provide job opportunities for the orphans raised in the Tushanwan Orphanage, but no one had expected it to become the birthplace of modern Chinese painting and the origin of the country's modern printing and publishing industry.

The popular belief holds that Dianshizhai Lithographic Studio (点石斋石印局) was the first printing institution to abandon ancient Chinese block printing and adopt lithography in 1879, but actually, it was through hiring Qiu Zi'ang (邱子昂), a technician from Tushanwan Printing Shop (土山湾印刷所), that Dianshizhai acquired the technique. Tushanwan Printing Shop adopted lithography in 1876, three years earlier than Dianshizhai. And it was doubtless the very first institution in China to adopt the collotype printing technique, nearly thirty years earlier than the Commercial Press (商务印书馆), which did not adopt this technique until 1907.

The boss of Dianshizhai Lithographic Studio, Ernest Major, founded one of the earliest Chinese newspapers in modern China, *Shun Pao* (《申报》, literally "Shanghai Newspaper"). Before the Qing dynasty ended, he sold the newspaper to Chinese owners, having turned it into a well-established commercial newspaper. *Shun Pao* put an end to the history of missionary-run religious-oriented Chinese newspapers. Being a commercial newspaper, it incorporated cultural and literary content, and enjoyed such a great popularity that citizens of Shanghai considered *Shun Pao* their only newspaper and called it "*Shun Pao Zhi*," something like "*the* Paper." When *Shun Pao* was launched in 1872, its office was located at the junction of Hankou (汉口路) and Jiangxi (江西路) roads, and in 1882, it moved two blocks westward to 309 Hankou Road at the corner of Shandong Road (山东路), and thus was on Wangping

Street. Also known as Temple Street (庙街) and Maijiaquan (麦家圈), Wangping Street (a north–south street located where today's Shandong Middle Road (north section) is, and based on traditional Chinese measure, its length was no more than fifty or sixty *zhang*[1]) became the center of a major cultural network consisting of newspaper offices and publishing houses. This certainly had something to do with the fact that Wangping Street was immediately adjacent to Baoshan Street (宝善街, also known as Guangdong Road or Fifth Avenue) and Fuzhou Road (福州路, also known as Fourth Avenue and which later became a famous cultural street), both extremely prosperous during the late-Qing period. At that time, when people came across Yangjing Creek (洋泾浜) by boat to the urban section of Shanghai, they would first come to these busy streets. For example, at the beginning of *The Sing-Song Girls of Shanghai* (《海上花列传》), when Zhao Puzhai (赵朴斋, a character in the novel) came to Shanghai to learn business, the very first place he arrived was the red-light district around Fifth and Fourth avenues. At that time, the modern printing technique had already been introduced into China, and people, having just been inspired and enlightened by the Self-Strengthening movement (洋务运动, aka Westernization movement) and Reform movement (维新思潮), recognized the importance of newspapers in promoting intellect and spreading new ideas. The great progress of the modern printing industry, as well as the concentration of newspaper offices, thus made Wangping Street and Fuzhou Road the birthplace of modern Chinese newspapers and journals.

1.5. Façade of the *Shun Pao* office during the late-Qing dynasty

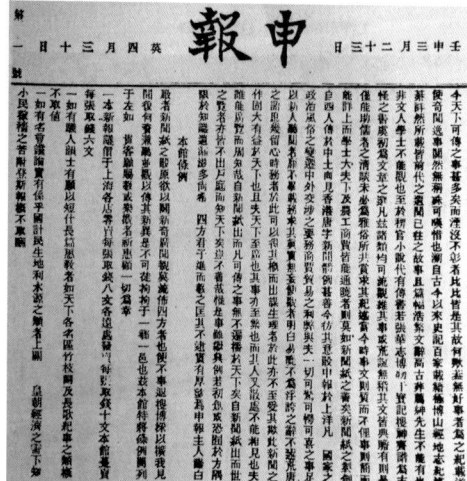

1.6. Inaugural issue of *Shun Pao*, April 30, 1872

---

[1]   *Zhang* (丈): a traditional Chinese measurement of length equal to 10 *chi* (尺), or 3.58 metres (11 feet 9 inches). – Translator's note

On account of the length of time that has elapsed, the rise and fall of newspapers due to fierce competition and their frequently moving in and out, it is extremely difficult to trace the specific locations of newspaper offices along Wangping Street during the late-Qing period, but let me try to give a general picture of the thriving newspapers at that time. According to the information

1.7. Printing machine used to print *Shun Pao* in its early days

available so far, by the time the Republic of China (ROC) was founded, there were over twenty newspaper offices on this street. The less popular ones included *Minli Bao* (《民立报》), *Tianduo Bao* (《天铎报》), *Minqiang Bao* (《民强报》), the *Chinese People's Newspaper* (《中华民报》), the *Pacific Newspaper* (《太平洋报》), *Jing Bao* (《晶报》), the *Shanghai Pictorial* (《上海画报》) and the *Asian Daily* (《亚西亚报》), etc. Then came more influential newspapers, including *Shun Pao*, *News Report* (《新闻报》), the *Current Affairs Newspaper* (《时务报》), the *Su Newspaper* (《苏报》) and the *Eastern Times* (《时报》). *News Report* was launched in 1893, originally at Wangping Street, but later moved to 274 Hankou Road nearby. It was the only newspaper that could rival *Shun Pao*. The *Current Affairs Newspaper* was launched in 1896, with its office located at Fuzhou Road. As Liang Qichao (梁启超, 1873–1929) was its editor-in-chief, the newspaper disseminated Reformation ideas, making it popular all over the country. The *Su Newspaper* was also launched in 1896, first at Fuzhou Road, then moving to 20 Hankou Road. It was known for the notorious "*Su Newspaper* case" brought by the Qing imperial court against its editorial staff for articles written by Zhang Taiyan (章太炎, 1868–1936) and Zou Rong (邹容, 1885–1905) that advocated revolution to overthrow the Qing. The *Eastern Times* was launched in 1904, with its office at 6 Wangping Street, later moving to Chessboard Street (棋盘街, now Henan Middle Road 河南中路). Its founder, Di Baoxian (狄葆贤, 1873–1941), had a peculiar pagoda-style office building built, which became the feature of many historical pictures (see Figure 1.9). The de facto head of the newspaper was Liang Qichao, who made daring innovations in news reports, and established new columns such as Fiction and Entertainment, which formed the earliest literary supplement unique to the *Eastern Times*. In his article "Looking Back Over Seventeen Years" (《十七年的回顾》), Hu Shi (胡适, 1891–1962) mentioned how the *Eastern Times* "became China's first daily newspaper that opened a 'supplement paper' with literary interest,"

1.8. *Eastern Times* office, located in Wangping Street during the late-Qing period

and this "supplement paper" later became the literary supplement of the newspaper. The *Eastern Times* later became increasingly successful in terms of sales and popularity, and was one of the three major newspapers in Shanghai, the other two being *Shun Pao* and *News Report*. Then there was the *Shenzhou Daily* (《神州日报》) launched by Yu Youren (于右任, 1879–1964) in 1907 at 161 Wangping Street, and two other newspapers launched by Yu Youren later in 1909, the *Minhu Daily* (《民呼日报》) and the *Minyu Daily* (《民吁日报》), which both had their offices at 160 Wangping Street. Another well-known newspaper, the *China Times* (《时事报》), was published in 1907, with its office at Wangping Street. Its Chinese name was later changed to 《时事新报》, "*New Current Affairs*".

There is a bamboo twig ballad (竹枝词, a literary form adapted from folk songs) about the busy metropolitan scene of

1.9. South end of Wangping Street (at the corner of Shandong Road and Fuzhou Road), with a view of the pagoda-style building of the *Eastern Times* office, which was quite a visual spectacle

Shanghai dedicated to this thriving newspaper street: "Every piece of news goes all over the city from Wangping Street, which is lined with newspaper offices on the east and west sides. Nearby were some shops doing other business, which have had to move to other places and put up new signs." Following the market rules, those who engaged in other business had to move, while the newspapers not originally headquartered on Wangping Street made every attempt to get a foothold along the street, or to at least open an outlet

1.10. Until the 1920s, Wangping Street was busy every morning with vendors buying newspapers and journals wholesale

or sales venue there. This shows the attractiveness of this cultural center. At that time, every day before daybreak, vendors would gather along Wangping Street to buy newspapers wholesale, making it an extremely busy and exciting place. On the days when breaking news happened at home or abroad, people could not wait to see the "special editions" of newspapers, making the street even more busy and crowded.

Certainly, not all modern Chinese newspapers were launched in Shanghai. In chronological terms, Southeast Asia was in fact the birthplace of Chinese newspapers. For example, the *Universal Circulating Herald* (《循环日报》), launched in Hong Kong in 1874, was the very first major newspaper successfully launched by a Chinese national, and its founder, Wang Tao (王韬, 1828–1897), was thus hailed as the "Father of China's Newspaper Industry" by Lin Yutang (林语堂, 1895–1976). In Tianjin, the largest commercial port in North China, the *National News Report* (《国闻报》) was launched in 1897, with Yan Fu (严复, 1854–1921) as one of its founders, and *Ta Kung Pao* (《大公报》) was launched in 1902. In Beijing, the *Pekingese Daily News* (《京话日报》) was launched in 1904. Nevertheless, Wangping Street was the only place in China where so many newspaper offices amassed. This evidenced the rapid growth of Shanghai as a modern metropolis, and that Wangping Street, as a national

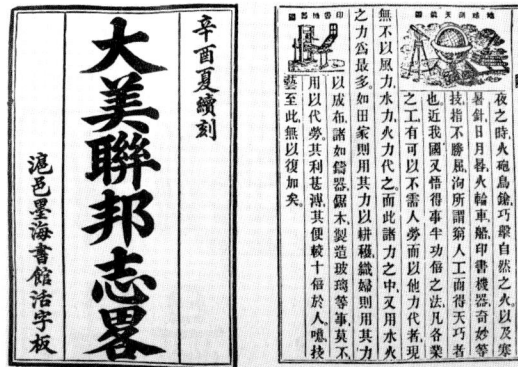

1.11. *A Short Account of the Commonwealth of America* (《大美联邦志略》), a book printed using movable type by the London Missionary Society Press (Mohai Shuguan) in Shanghai

newspaper center, played a significant role in shaping a new literary scene in which modern Chinese literature burgeoned during the late-Qing period.

Besides newspaper offices, the thriving printing industry also resulted in the concentration of publishing houses around Wangping Street and Fuzhou Road (the Chinese terms *shu-ju* [书局, literally "book bureau"] and *shu-guan* [书馆, literally "book house"] meant publishing institutions whose front shops sold books). China's first modern publishing house was London Missionary Society Press (*Mohai Shuguan* 墨海书馆), founded in the old town of Shanghai in 1843 by Walter H. Medhurst (1796–1857), an English Congregationalist missionary to China, and it was moved to Maijiaquan two years later. At first the publishing institution printed and published *The Bible* and other religious texts, while later it hired Wang Tao and others to translate Western literary, historic, and scientific books. In 1857, Mohai Shuguan launched the monthly magazine *Shanghai Serial* (《六合丛谈》), the earliest Chinese magazine issued in mainland China.

Then there were translation and publishing institutions, which played a significant role in introducing Western ideas as well as literary and scientific learnings to China, but they were initially run by the government, such as the Imperial Interpreters College (京师同文馆) founded in 1862 and the Shanghai Foreign-Language School (广方言馆) founded in 1863. The Translation Division of the Jiangnan Machinery Manufacturing Company (江南制造局翻译馆) was founded in 1868, only to be merged into the Shanghai Foreign-Language School one year later. Thus even when government-run translation and publishing institutions were taken into consideration, Shanghai was still the publishing center of the country. Dianshizhai Lithographic Studio was established in 1876, and when it finally decided to reprint the *Kangxi Dictionary* (《康熙字典》), as many as 100,000 copies went to press in a matter of months! This encouraged other publishers, with Hongwen Shuju (鸿文书局) and Hongbaozhai Lithographic Printing House (鸿宝斋石印书局) being established successively along Wangping Street and Fuzhou Road, respectively. Seeing the huge profit earned by printing books and magazines, large-scale publishing institutions financed by domestic venture capital funds finally took shape in Shanghai. In 1897, Chinese capitalists Xia Ruifang (夏瑞芳, 1871–1914), Xia Cuifang (夏粹芳), and Bao Xian'en (鲍咸恩, 1861–1910)[2] raised funds and founded the Commercial Press in Dechang Alley (德昌里), Jiangxi Road, and later established its distribution agency in Chessboard Street, making huge profits by publishing textbooks.

---

[2]   According to the translator's research, the founders of the Commercial Press should be Xia Ruifang, Bao Xianchang (鲍咸昌), and Bao Xian'en, the latter two being brothers. Cuifang (粹芳) is the literary name (字) of Xia Ruifang; that is, Xia Ruifang and Xia Cuifang are two names for the same person. – Translator's note

Later, the Commercial Press had its own printing factories and translation department, and gradually became the largest publishing company in China. The Commercial Press attached great importance to the publishing of newspapers and magazines, including literary journals. A number of magazines were launched and published during this time, including *Oriental Magazine* (《东方杂志》), *Ladies' Journal* (《妇女杂志》), *Education Magazine* (《教育杂志》), *Student Magazine* (《学生杂志》), *Juvenile Magazine* (《少年杂志》), and *Fiction Monthly* (《小说月报》). *Oriental Magazine* was launched in 1904 and remained active for over forty years until its demise in

1.12. Commercial Press distribution agency in its early days (Henan Road, Shanghai). It saw rapid development soon after its inception

1948, during which time publication was suspended and resumed from time to time. It was a comprehensive magazine, and had such literary columns as Fiction, Collected Talks (丛谈), Literary Garden (文苑), and Miscellaneous Essays (杂纂) as early as the late-Qing period. *Fiction Monthly*, on the other hand, was a literary journal. Launched in 1910, it was originally a stronghold of the so-called Mandarin Duck (Love Birds) and Butterfly literary school (鸳鸯蝴蝶派), though it changed later. Thus we can see that from its very outset, China's modern publishing industry developed in close association with modern Chinese literature. Moreover, many publishing institutions along Chessboard Street and Fuzhou Road specialized in literary books. Saoye Shanfang (扫叶山房), which was founded in the Ming dynasty and enjoyed a long history, moved its office to the area from Suzhou. Datong Translation Bureau (大同译书局, founded in 1897) was well-known for its books promoting Reformation ideas; its *The Revolutionary Army* (《革命军》) by Zou Rong was reprinted over twenty times and altogether 1.1 million copies were sold. Kwong Chi Book Co. (广智书局, founded in 1898) published such books as *Bizarre Happenings Eyewitnessed over Two Decades* (《二十年目睹之怪现状》) and the translated novel *The Lady of the Camellias* (*La Dame aux*

1.13. The impressive Commercial Press building on Fourth Avenue, Shanghai, during the 1930s

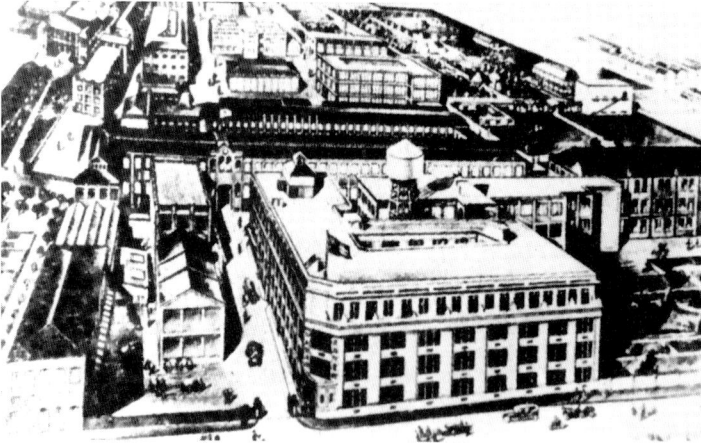

1.14. Bird's-eye view of the Commercial Press, which would later experience great development

Camélias). The People's Study Society (群学社) launched the magazine *All-Story Monthly* (《月月小说》); Guangyi Press (广益书局, founded in 1900) published popular fiction, and Qunyi Book Company (群益书社, founded in 1907) published *Short Stories from Abroad* (《域外小说集》), translated by the Zhou brothers, as well as the magazine *New Youth* (《新青年》), which was to be extremely popular in the years to come. All in all, by the time the Xinhai Revolution (辛亥革命) broke out, there were as many as sixty-eight bookshops along Fuzhou Road, most of which sold literary books and magazines.

The rapid development of the modern publishing industry in Shanghai could be seen as a sign that China's literary scene had already begun to change during the late-Qing period. Modern Chinese metropolises took shape under the pressure of foreign influences, of which Beijing and Shanghai represented two widely different situations. Beijing was a city featuring a conservative political atmosphere; with its corrupt bureaucratic system and people's sensitivity to the political climate, as well as the medley of old and new consumption patterns and lifestyles, the city was an endless mine of material to be exposed and satirized in literature. Beijing was among the earliest Chinese cities to establish new-style schools, imitated by people all over the country, which trained "qualified talents" in modern literature. After the imperial examination system was abolished in 1905, readers and authors trained in the new-style educational system gradually came to the foreground. Shanghai, on the other hand, became China's largest commercial metropolis under the influence of foreign concession, where Chinese and foreign people lived together, had trade relations, and invested heavily in industries, enabling Western civilization to find its way into the city at a faster pace. The cultural landscape of Shanghai and local people's lifestyle changed and became widely different from those in the inland parts of the country. The modern printing industry promoted newspaper and book publication, accelerated and lowered the cost of information and knowledge dissemination, and enlarged its reader group, which was a reason why Reformists always launched newspapers, established new-style schools, and promoted new learning concurrently. Almost all pioneers in modern Chinese literature had some kind of connection with newly launched newspapers and magazines, including Yan Fu, Xia Zengyou (夏曾佑, 1862–1924), Wang Tao, Huang Zunxian (黄遵宪, 1848–1905), and Liang Qichao, to name just a few, and they gave vent to their ideas and literary expressions in newspapers and magazines. Yan Fu, who was famous for translating *Evolution and Ethics, and other Essays* by the English biologist T. H. Huxley (1825–1895), launched the *National News Report*, and his Chinese translation of *Evolution and Ethics, and other Essays* was serialized in the *Collection of the National News* (《国闻汇编》) before the separate edition was published. The serialization of this book was an epoch-making event that inspired Chinese people and permanently changed their perspective on the world. According to Lu Xun's (鲁迅) recollection on his schooldays in Nanjing: "Whenever I had some spare time, I would, as usual, eat pancakes, peanuts, hot peppers and read *Evolution and Ethics, and other Essays*. Wow! Now I knew there was a person called Huxley sitting in his study and thinking in this way, and his thought was so new to me! I read on and on without a break, and came to know competition, natural selection, Socrates, Plato, and Stoicism," and he read it so carefully that he could even recite some of the passages,[3] which is evidence of the profound influence of this book on Chinese people. In 1897, Yan Fu and Xia Zengyou published an essay entitled "On the Origin of the Fiction Department of This Publishing House" (《本馆附印说部缘起》), an important document incorporating the Western theories of evolution and human nature into fiction writing. The case of Liang Qichao was even more obvious: Liang strongly rejected the Westernizationists' tendency to oppose literature to practical learnings and regard literature as something endangering the nation; on the contrary, he integrated new ideas into the new literary genre, and was sensitive enough to incorporate literature into the modern knowledge and information dissemination system (newspapers and magazines), and crafted the well-known slogans of "poetry revolution" (诗界革命), "literary revolution" (文界革命), and "fiction revolution" (小说界革命).

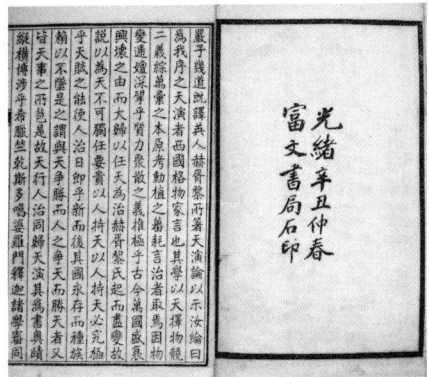

1.15. First page of the Chinese edition of *Evolution and Ethics and other Essays* (printed in the Xinchou year of the Guangxu era)

---

3   Lu Xun: "Trivial Notes," *Dawn Blossoms Plucked at Dusk* (《朝花夕拾》), collected in *Complete Works of Lu Xun* (《鲁迅全集》), Vol. 2. Beijing: People's Literature Press, 1981, p. 296.

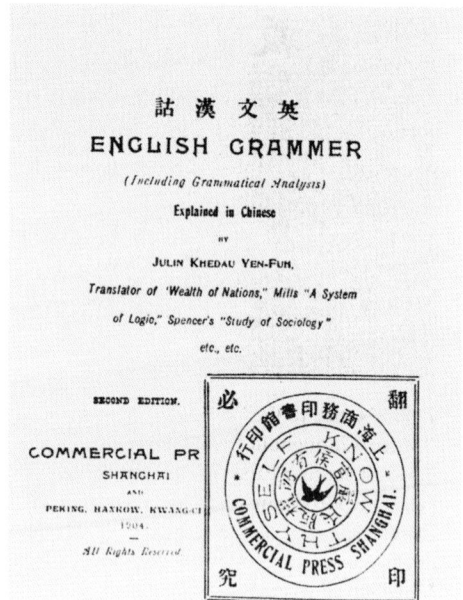

1.16. Yan Fu (front) and his associates

1.17. *English Grammar*, annotated by Yan Fu, published by the Commercial Press in 1904. On the bottom right corner is China's earliest "copyright stamp" used for copyright protection

The large circulation of newspapers and magazines greatly increased the readership of literature, and the intended target audience of literary writings changed. The newly established author payment system also helped by partially emancipating literary authors so that they did not have to find an official career; they could make a living with their intellectual skills. It was the relatively independent status of authors that finally gave rise to the modern profession of authorship. The earliest extant material on author payment is the "Notice to Well-Known Painters Throughout the Country on Contributing Paintings to Our News Reports" (《请各处名手专画新闻启》), published several times in *Shun Pao* during June 1884. The notice was short, and I hereby copy the entire text as follows:

> This publishing house produces several issues of its pictorial each month, and its circulation has greatly increased. However, there are so many news stories happening outside this city, and besides those that have been published in *Shun Pao*, a number of stories cannot be published in the pictorial due to the lack of paintings. Therefore, this publishing house hereby gives this notice to all painters throughout the country: whenever you see anything amazing happen, please paint it with fresh dark ink on a piece of white paper, and write the story on a separate piece of paper. In case we find it vivid and intriguing enough to be published in our pictorial, the painter will gain a payment of two silver dollars. The painting thus contributed will not be returned, no matter if it is used or not. The name

1.18. "Notice to Well-Known
Painters Throughout the Country
on Contributing Paintings to Our
News Reports," published in *Shun
Pao* on June 4, 1884; the earliest
public announcement of payment for
contributing writings and paintings

1.19. Example of a *Shun Pao* spread, issued during
the ninth year of Emperor Guangxu's reign
(1883). Type No. 4 characters are set lengthways
and printed single-sided on thinner, better-
quality Sailian paper (赛连纸). On these pages
there are essays, poems and bamboo twig ballads,
etc. This could be considered the origin of future
newspaper literary supplements

and address of the painter shall be provided. A receipt shall be given
upon our receiving the painting, and once it is published in the pictorial,
the painter shall cash out his money with the receipt. In case the painting is not published, the receipt shall be deemed as invalid to avoid any
misunderstanding or confusion. Please kindly contribute your work or
comments on it.

This was China's very first public notice inviting contributions that included
payment rates. In general, however, there were agreed market rates of remuneration for authors and painters, and the payment was not necessarily announced
as a fixed rate like this one. For example, Bao Tianxiao (包天笑, 1875–1973),
a representative author of the Mandarin Duck and Butterfly literary school,
worked for both the *Eastern Times* and *Forest of Fiction* (《小说林》) in 1906
(the thirty-second year of Emperor Guangxu's reign). According to his memoir:

> As for the rate of remuneration for fiction writing, in Shanghai the stand-
> ard rate was two silver dollars per thousand characters, and fictions of this
> level needed no revision. Some gained one silver dollar or even as low
> as half a silver dollar per thousand characters, for their fictions usually
> needed revisions. … Later they raised the rate of remuneration for my
> fictions to three silver dollars per thousand characters. … By that time Mr.
> Lin Qinnan (林琴南, 1852–1924) had been translating and writing fic-
> tions for the Commercial Press and other publishing institutions, and the
> Commercial Press paid him five silver dollars per thousand characters.[4]

---

[4] Bao Tianxiao: "Working For *Forest of Fiction*," *Memoirs of the Bracelet Shadow Chamber*
(《钏影楼回忆录·在小说林》), Hong Kong: Dahua Publishing House, 1971, pp. 324–325.

These generally agreed rates of remuneration were subject to fluctuations according to market demand. Obviously, this was possible only when newspapers and magazines became daily reading material for the general public in major cities, and their emergence per se formed an important part of the context of modern Chinese literature. By that time, China's earliest modern professional writers were ready for the exciting new opportunities ahead.

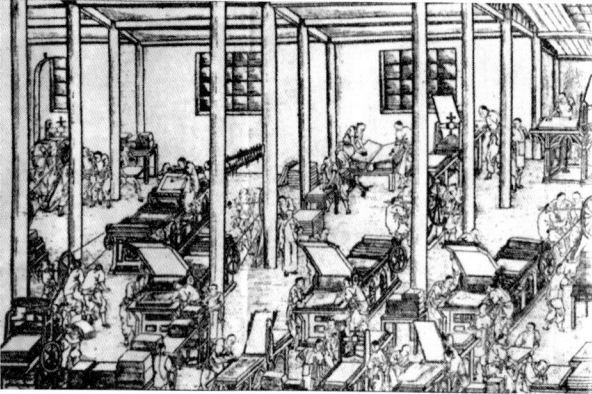

1.20. Interior of Dianshizhai Lithographic Studio, which was quite a large-scale printing house by that time

TWO

VERNACULAR NEWSPAPERS AND THE TRANSFORMATION OF WRITTEN LITERARY LANGUAGE

LANGUAGE IS THE MEDIUM OF LITERATURE, AND THUS the reform of the Chinese language became a prerequisite for the modern transformation of Chinese literature. By the late-Qing period, people still used classical Chinese language in their poetic and prose writings. It was at that time that the status of classical Chinese language as the country's orthodox written language was effectively challenged.

The crisis facing the classical Chinese language was closely related to the overall social environment. With the intrusion of Western civilization into every aspect of Chinese people's everyday lives, from material items to social institutions to their spiritual life, from sound, light, chemistry, and electricity to politics, law, literature, and art, Chinese people were confronted with an explosion of vocabularies from the "language of new learning," like *huo-che* (火车, train), *lun-chuan* (轮船, ship), *dian-deng* (电灯, electric lamp), *dian-bao* (电报, telegraph), *yang-qi* (氧气, oxygen), *qun-xue* (群学, sociology), and *ba-li-men* (巴力门, Chinese transliteration of 'parliament'), to name just a few. China had had its vernacular fictions since ancient times, but they had largely been marginalized and had no impact on the general literary landscape (though they would shortly afterward). Since poetry had been the dominant genre in classical Chinese literature, poets were among the first to feel the pressure to reform the Chinese language. From Gong Zizhen (龚自珍, 1792–1841) of the early eighteenth century[1] to Huang Zunxian, poets of the Qing dynasty had long since emphasized the individual and emotional experience in their poetic expression and borrowed new vocabularies that represented new things and new knowledge. The Reformist poets who advocated "poetry of new learning" (新学之诗), such as Tan Sitong (谭嗣同, 1865–1898) and Xia Zengyou, incorporated a great number of loan words and allusions to Confucian, Buddhist, and Christian scriptures into their classical poems, giving them a fresh albeit weird look. An example of this is the third of Tan Sitong's "Three Poems on Hearing Preachings in Jinling" (《金陵听说法诗三首》): "Those at the head of the assembly observe the entire world, / Uttering praises by virtue of the Buddha's power. / Even though betrayal happens in the Dharma field, / Souls can be saved in the ocean of Buddha nature. / Confucius virtues divide people like castes, / And the Buddhist assemblies are thus as lively as parliaments. / Now we see the land and water of our country, / They are as real as āmalaka fruit in one's palms." (而为上首普观察，承佛威神说偈言。一任法田卖人子，独从性海救灵魂。纲伦惨以喀私德，法会盛于巴力门。大地山河今领取，庵摩罗果掌中论。) And Xia Zengyou's representative work of this kind read: "The world was so cold during the Ice Age, / When the flood spread vast the regions of the land divided. / Human races were then alienated in front of the Tower of Babel, / And since then they are divided like stars apart in the sky." (冰期世界太清凉，洪水茫茫下土方。巴别塔前分种教，人天从此感参商。) Later Liang Qichao explained this poem, saying that "the Ice Age and flood are geological terms. The Tower of Babel comes from a story told in the Old Testament on the separation of Shem, Ham, and Japheth." (See *Poetry Talks from the Ice-Drinking Studio* [《饮冰室诗话》].[2]) This kind of poetry, as well as their explanations, seem hard to understand for today's readers, but they manifested the fact that the classical Chinese prosody that had been used for over a thousand years was finally endangered by the explosion of loan words. These imported foreign words rolled in like an irresistible tidal wave, carrying everything along with them. Indeed, if you understand that words that are now indispensable to our everyday life, such as *gan-bu* (干部, cadre), *wu-tai* (舞台, stage), *jin-bu* (进步, progress), *mu-di* (目的, purpose), *dai-biao* (代表, representative),

2.1. Tan Sitong, looking courageous and heroic

---

[1]   Should be "the early nineteenth century." – Translator's note
[2]   Liang Qichao: *Poetry Talks from the Ice-Drinking Studio*, Beijing: People's Literature Press, 1959.

tuan-ti (团体, group), *zu-zhi* (组织, institution), *she-hui* (社会, society), *ying-xiang* (影响, influence), *chong-tu* (冲突, conflict), and *peng-zhang* (膨胀, expand), were all borrowed from Japanese vocabulary during the inflow of loan words 100 years ago, I believe you will accept the clumsiness of the "poetry of new learning" with more grace.

The increasing use of loan words actually loosened the structure of classical Chinese sentences. Here, again, modern newspapers and magazines played a vital role. When people like Wang Tao and Liang Qichao wrote articles for newspapers and magazines, their target audience was the general reading public, so they were immediately faced with the need to vernacularize classical Chinese texts. For this purpose, in their classical Chinese writings, they avoided using difficult one-character words and added a large number of new two-character words, which were increasingly popular in society. This was by no means a small adjustment, for even though the structure of classical Chinese sentences remained largely unchanged, they became simpler and easier to understand. An example was the classical text Liang Qichao wrote when he fled to Japan after the failure of the Wuxu Reform (戊戌变法):

2.2. First issue of *Qingyi Bao* (《清议报》, *China Discussion*), in which Liang Qichao published his article "On the Transitional Period" (《过渡时代论》)

> That a country in the transitional period is like the fish *kun* changing itself into the giant bird *peng*, flying southward and covering a distance of 90,000 *li*; or it is like all waters flowing into the sea despite so many bends and turns. With its impressive manner it has tremendous promise ahead; with its vital essence the country shows its ambition to become a great nation. Its current energy is as great as the power of 10,000 bulls, and who could stop it from going forward? Its future is as brilliant as gold and who could restrain it from shining through? Therefore, the transitional period is actually a huge stage for virtuous men of outstanding talent, and it is the road to success for many countries that have transformed from declining to growing, from being bullied to revitalization, from enslavement to liberation, from poverty to prosperity. How great the transitional period is![3]

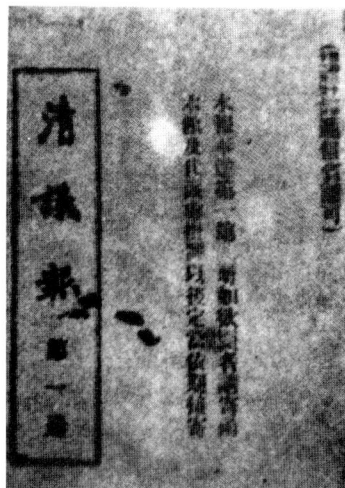

2.3. Table of contents of the first issue of the *China Vernacular Newspaper* (《中国白话报》)

---

[3]   Liang Qichao: "On the Transitional Period," *Complete Works of Liang Qichao* (《梁启超全集》), Beijing: Beijing Press, 1999, p. 464.

In Liang Qichao's passage, such words as "transitional period" (过渡时代), "outlook" (目的), "stage" (舞台), and "nation" (民族) were all imported from foreign languages. With these words incorporated into the essay, written in alternated rhymed and nonrhymed prose styles, the text is easy to understand even for today's readers. Now that the Chinese written language had evolved to such an extent, it was indeed well-prepared for the "transition" into a modern vernacular style. This was a very important preparation, and it will be discussed in detail in the section dedicated to Liang Qichao later in this book (Chapter 4).

Meanwhile, toward the end of the nineteenth century, an upsurge of newspaper launches swept over the country. This time there was a new tide of vernacular newspapers, which further promoted the development of modern vernacular language and helped it become the formal written language of Chinese text during the May Fourth period.

Now we know there were over 200 vernacular newspapers launched from the late-Qing period to the Xinhai Revolution (辛亥革命). These newspapers were launched all over the country, but most of the major ones were launched in Shanghai. There were more than forty vernacular newspapers, including those whose names included "vernacular newspaper" and "slang newspaper," half of which were published in the area around Shanghai's Fuzhou Road and Wangping Street. Interestingly, some newspapers indicated their regional attribution in their names, such as *Ningbo Vernacular Newspaper* (《宁波白话报》), *Huzhou Vernacular Newspaper* (《湖州白话报》), and *Anhui Vernacular Newspaper* (《安徽白话报》), but they were actually published in Shanghai, which showed Shanghai's undoubted status as China's modern publishing center. Vernacular newspapers made up a large proportion of newspapers in Beijing, but other than this, Beijing lagged far behind Shanghai in launching and publishing newspapers, partly because the so-called vernacular language was evolved from the Mandarin of the Qing dynasty, which was based on the Beijing dialect, making such newspapers very popular in Beijing. These vernacular newspapers were more like magazines in their format; indeed, earlier in the history of modern newspapers and magazines, these two were not clearly divided, so we have to read them one by one to tell whether they were technically newspapers or magazines. For those that are available for reading today, most had a thirty-two page format, and there were more periodicals published every ten days, semimonthly, or monthly than daily ones. As for their contents, almost all of them had the sections "Discourses" (演说), "Headline News" (要闻), and "Miscellaneous" (杂俎), roughly equivalent to "Editorials," "Current Events," and "Supplements" in modern Chinese newspapers. Compared with major classical Chinese newspapers, these vernacular newspapers seemed trivial and not worthy of mention, and very few of them have been preserved till today (their dissemination and collection was more or less similar to that of Red Guard publications from the Cultural Revolution). But it was these vernacular newspapers that preached and advocated the use of vernacular language and created a vigorous atmosphere all over the country to promote the use of the vernacular.

Nowadays it is generally agreed that China's earliest vernacular newspaper was *Min Bao* (《民报》, *People's Newspaper*), which was launched by the established *Shun Pao* Office. On the second day after its launch, an introduction to this newspaper was published in the *North China Daily News* (《字林西报》) in Shanghai, which read: "We now see the inaugural issue of a new newspaper published by the *Shun Pao* Office, called *Min Bao*, and it is sold at five pence per copy. The newspaper is characterized by its vernacular language, and therefore readers may easily understand its contents. A space is left at the end of each sentence, and a vertical line or dotted line is drawn beside each proper name as an indication of this status. The newspaper is sold at no more than half a copper coin per copy, making it accessible to those who cannot afford or understand *Shun Pao*, such as craftsmen, manual workers, or assistants of small shops, etc. The newspaper will be issued daily."[4] From this introduction we see that the vernacular nature of this newspaper was closely related to its intended target audience. Another of the earliest was the *Renditions Vernacular Newspaper* (《演义白话报》), which was launched along the Fuzhou Road in November 1897, and the article "An Introductory Note to the Vernacular Newspaper" (《白话报小引》) published in its inaugural issue explained the purpose of this kind of newspaper. The text read: "If ordinary Chinese people want to succeed and not to suffer the unfavorable situation any more, they must learn about foreign countries

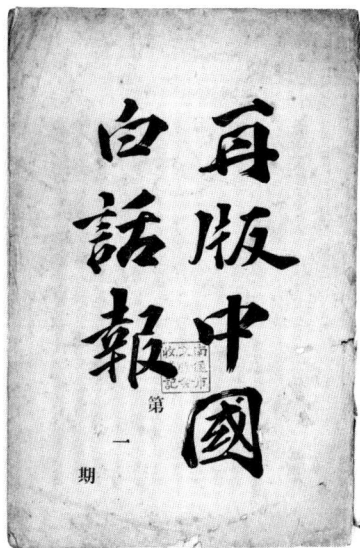

2.4. Reprint of the first issue of the *China Vernacular Newspaper*. Evidence that the newspaper was very popular among readers

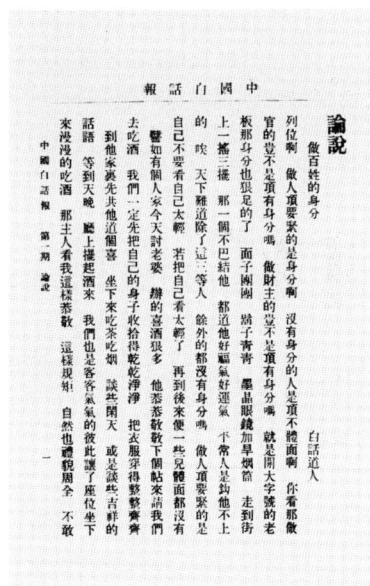

2.5. Layout of the first page of the main body of the first issue of the *China Vernacular Newspaper*

---

4   Quoted from "Vernacular Newspapers of Sixty Years Ago" (《六十年前的白话报》), *Sequel to Research Material on Shanghai* (《上海研究资料续集》), compiled by Shanghai Tongshe (上海通社, Society of Shanghai Natives), Shanghai: Shanghai Bookstore Publishing House, 1984, p. 321.

and international affairs; if they want to learn about foreign countries and international affairs, they must read newspapers; and if they want to read newspapers, they must read vernacular ones which are easy to understand."[5] These were indeed vernacular Chinese texts. In May 1898 Qiu Tingliang (裘廷梁, 1857–1943) and his niece Qiu Yufang (裘毓芳, 1871–1904) launched *Wuxi Vernacular Newspaper* (《无锡白话报》), and Qiu Tingliang's "Foreword to *Wuxi Vernacular Newspaper*" was also published in its inaugural issue, which was quite elegant, more or less like Liang Qichao's style, but also easy to understand. He argued:

> To seek our national interest, we shall try to enlighten every member of our country, so that scholars, farmers, business people, and workers can all use their talents to serve the country, and then China can compete with Western powers. … In order to enlighten people, we shall start with opening public schools to educate them, and the second best way is to let them read newspapers. How can newspapers be understood by everybody? Let's start with vernacular newspapers.[6]

The year 1904 saw the launch of two vernacular newspapers, one in the northern part and one in the southern part of the country. The editor's opening statement in Suzhou's *Vernacular Newspaper of Wu County* (《吴郡白话报》) claimed that "[This newspaper] will, gradually, let all of you know the common sense and plain learnings as well as current affairs of the world."[7] And that of the *Pekingese Daily News* (《京话日报》) claimed: "The purpose of this newspaper is to import Western civilization, improve Chinese customs, and enlighten the majority of people in our society. Therefore Beijing dialect is used throughout this newspaper, and we intend to teach simple lessons and report important news with clear and simple language, which can be understood and appreciated by all."[8] In a word, this was the sole purpose of most vernacular newspapers; they did not mention anything about creating a better written language to better suit the needs of modern society. In fact, the founders of vernacular newspapers at that time had three purposes: firstly, like all reform advocates, they intended to invigorate the Chinese nation, resist foreign invasion, and enlighten ordinary people. These were their original ideas. To illustrate this, Qiu Tingliang once wrote an article entitled "On Vernacular

---

[5]   Quoted from Chen Yushen (陈玉申, 1961–): *A History of the Newspaper Industry of the Late Qing Dynasty* (《晚清报业史》), Jinan: Shandong Pictorial Publishing House, 2003, p. 109.

[6]   Quoted from Chen Yushen: *A History of the Newspaper Industry of the Late Qing Dynasty*, p. 110.

[7]   Quoted from *Compiled Contents of Modern Chinese Periodicals* (《中国近代期刊编目汇录》), Book 2, Vol. 3, compiled by Shanghai Municipal Library, Shanghai: Shanghai People's Press, 1981, p. 1178.

[8]   Quoted from Chen Yushen: *A History of the Newspaper Industry of the Late Qing Dynasty*, p. 152.

Language as the Foundation of Social Reform" (《论白话为维新之本》)[9]. Secondly, for this purpose, they advocated a new form of written language for the general public, the "vernacular," and thus people's oral language tended to be similar to the written language in newspapers. And thirdly, not everyone had the ideal to "unify oral and written forms of language"; for most intellectuals, the vernacular was used so the general public could better understand written language. Therefore, most vernacular advocates of that time used two sets of language: they wrote vernacular for common people and classical Chinese for their fellow intellectuals. An interesting example was that of Peng Yizhong (彭翼仲, 1864–1921), who launched *Pekingese Daily News* to "enlighten the majority of people," launching another newspaper, *Zhonghua Bao* (《中华报》, *China Newspaper*) to "enlighten officials," which used classical Chinese. Vernacular newspapers originated from civil society, and when "everybody participated in the Reform" and Empress Dowager Cixi gave her conditional approval for "constitutional monarchy," officially run vernacular newspapers began to mushroom. This is obvious by looking at such names as "Preliminary Constitutional Vernacular Newspaper" (预备立宪白话报) and "Local Self-Government Vernacular Newspaper" (地方自治白话报). Later the government promoted the "national language," and the state educational department put emphasis on education in the national language. Thus some people say it was through the "joint efforts of non-official intellectuals and the government" that "the transformation of classical Chinese language into national language and vernacular language was accomplished."[10]

2.6. Table of contents of the first issue of the *Anhui Colloquial Newspaper* (《安徽俗话报》)

2.7. Front cover of the first issue of the *Anhui Colloquial Newspaper*

[9] Qiu Tingliang: "On Vernacular Language as the Foundation of Social Reform," *China Vernacular Newspaper with Official Pronunciations* (《中国官音白话报》 (known as *Wuxi Vernacular Newspaper* for the first five issues), August 27, 1898, Issues 19 and 20.

[10] Wang Feng (王风): "On the Relationship between Literary Revolution and National Language Movement" (《文学革命与国语运动之关系》), *Studies on Modern Chinese Literature* (《中国现代文学研究丛刊》), 2001, Issue 3.

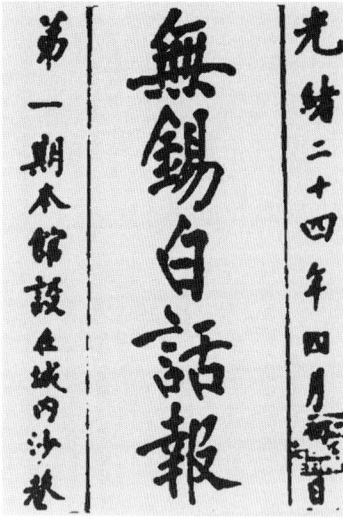

2.8. First issue of the *Wuxi Vernacular Newspaper*

In order to implement the principle to reform the written language and make it understandable for the general public, people needed a term for this language, and they used "*bai-hua*" (白话, literally, "plain language; vernacular"), which was readily available throughout the Chinese literary tradition. The material of this vernacular language consisted of ancient vernacular language (represented by *hua-ben* [话本], vernacular novels of the Song dynasty, and recorded prose), and then it drew its material from the spoken language of ordinary people of that time. Therefore, some vernacular newspapers used the general term "vernacular" to include local dialects, colloquial language, and slang expressions. Certainly, in drawing material from local dialects, most vernacular newspapers did not go too far in this direction, their guideline being to make it understood by people of the province in question. The reason for this was that in the late-Qing period, besides the vernacular movement, there was a Chinese Latinization movement (汉字拼音化运动).

The Chinese Latinization movement started after the ban on maritime trade had been lifted. At that time, some Chinese intellectuals saw the outside world and became aware that all rich and powerful Western countries attached great importance to education. Comparing the Chinese characters with alphabetic languages, they realized that to promote universal education in China, one of the major challenges involved Chinese characters, which was extremely difficult because the written characters belonged to a system totally different from that of oral language. Therefore, Liang Qichao and Tan Sitong proposed to reform Chinese characters. From *A Primer at a Glance: Chinese New Phonetic Script in the Amoy Dialect* (《一目了然初阶》), put forward by Lu Gangzhang (卢戆章, 1854–1928) in 1892, various Latinization schemes were proposed successively, their original purpose being the same: creating a Latinized Chinese writing system to substitute for Chinese characters, making it easier for common people to read and write. However, despite all their painstaking efforts, altering the pictographic Chinese characters seemed a mission impossible. The reformists' aim to create a new Latinized Chinese language was never achieved, but in the process, they agreed on a new goal: to unify the phonetics of Chinese oral language and establish a unified national language. In 1918, the Ministry of Education of the Republic of China officially published the Phonetic Alphabet of Chinese characters. Soon after that, the term "national language" emerged among Latinization advocates. It turned out that this term has a great vitality, which later evolved into the National Language movement (国语运动) and even the Common Language movement (普通话运动) and was inherently linked with the "literature of national language"

(国语的文学) proposed by Hu Shi during the May Fourth New Cultural movement. During the late-Qing period, this term actually became a kind of vital force of the vernacular movement, so that the "unification of written and spoken forms" and the "unification of phonetics of Chinese oral language" were not truly antagonistic. Here in the term "unification of written and spoken forms," the "spoken form" did not mean that of dialects or slang, but the spoken language with unified phonetics. And this could explain why so many vernacular newspapers published throughout the country did not lead to an overwhelming use of local dialects, which would have virtually "divided" the Chinese language.

At that time, the vernacular was increasingly used in literary works. However, since the evolution of a written language could not occur overnight, it was a common practice to mix classical Chinese and the vernacular in literary works. Most scholar-officials or intellectuals applauded reforms and advocated new learning, but classical Chinese still dominated their poetic or prose writings. Vernacular newspapers had been extremely popular, but even for those who wrote in the vernacular, their logic and reasoning of writing were still "characteristic of classical Chinese, and we know the vernacular writings of that time were actually vernacular translation of what the authors thought in classical Chinese," as Zhou Zuoren (周作人, 1885–1967) pointed out in his writing, taking as an example the one who wrote the introduction for *Comments on Female Education* (《女诫注释》, one of the *Vernacular Book Series* [《白话丛书》]).[11] It was totally different from the vernacular used after the May Fourth movement. Therefore, both the "revival" of the Tongcheng School of the Ancient Classics movement (桐城古文派), supported by Zeng Guofan (曾国藩, 1811–1872), as well as its later disciples (including Wu Rulun [吴汝纶, 1840–1903] and Lin Shu [林纾, also known as Lin Qinnan]), and the Tongguang-style (同光体) poets (represented by Chen Sanli [陈三立, 1852–1937], father of Chen Yinke [陈寅恪, 1890–1969]) were seemingly quite influential in literary circles, but they were actually spent forces.

2.9. Title page of *The Tale of Heroic Sons and Daughters* (《儿女英雄传》) by Wen Kang (文康, dates unknown, of the Qing dynasty) (illustrated, with commentary, edition)

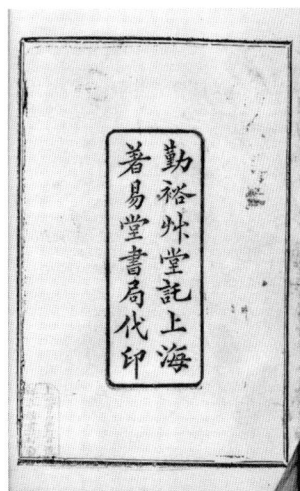

2.10. Copyright page of *The Tale of Heroic Sons and Daughters* (illustrated, with commentary, edition)

[11] Zhou Zuoren: *On the Origins of China's New Literature* (《中国新文学的源流》), Beijing: Humanities Bookstore, 1932, p. 97.

The use of the vernacular had been a traditional practice in ancient Chinese fictions. For example, in the novel *The Tale of Heroic Sons and Daughters* (its original name was *Comments on the Tale of Heroic Sons and Daughters* [《儿女英雄传评话》]), the first sentence of the first chapter read: "The general idea of *The Tale of Heroic Sons and Daughters* will be explained clearly in this 'prologue and first chapter,' and will not be reiterated anymore. What story is this book trying to tell? And who are the characters? Of which dynasty? Please be at ease and let me recount the details from the beginning."[12] It seemed natural to use vernacular Chinese here. Later, the four great exposure novels of the late Qing also used vernacular Chinese. The beginning of *A Revelation of Official Circles* (《官场现形记》 (first edition published 1903) read: "It is said that in Chaoyi District of Tongzhou Prefecture of Shaanxi, around 30 *li* to the south of the town, there was a village, in which no other people lived except two big families, the Zhao's and the Fang's."[13] And the beginning of *Bizarre Happenings Eyewitnessed over Two Decades* (《二十年目睹之怪现状》) (separate edition first published 1906) read: "Shanghai was a place where businesspeople gathered and Chinese and foreign people lived together, and thus it was crowded and busy with cargo ships going to and fro. Seeing that there were so many rich people in Shanghai, many prostitutes from Suzhou and Yangzhou swarmed into the city and lived around the Fourth Avenue, talking loudly about their business and competing with gorgeous beauty."[14] All are quite easy to understand. But classical Chinese novels persisted until much later. For example, Su Manshu (苏曼殊, 1884–1918), nicknamed "love monk" or "poet monk," who was born nearly twenty years later than Li Boyuan (李伯元, 1867–1906, author of *A Revelation of Official Circles*) and Wu Jianren (吴趼人, 1866–1910, author of *Bizarre Happenings Eyewitnessed over Two Decades*), wrote novels in classical Chinese. In his representative work, *The Lone Swan* (《断鸿零雁记》), which had a far-reaching influence on Chinese literary history, when the narrator, who had already become a Buddhist monk, heard his long-lost mother order him to marry, he felt sad, and the narration goes like this: "I gave it many thoughts and found it hard to comfort myself, when I heard the wind wailing among the woods beyond the hills. I could not help trembling with sadness and anxiety, and recited what the Buddha said: 'Ardently

---

[12] See Chapter 1, "A Hermit of the West Mountain Lecturing to a Talented Student behind Closed Doors, an Old Man Was the First to Come to the Southern Palace" (隐西山闭门课骥子 捷南宫垂老占龙头) of Wen Kang: *The Tale of Heroic Sons and Daughters*, Tianjin: Baihua Literature and Arts Press, 2003, p. 10.

[13] See the first chapter of Li Boyuan: *A Revelation of Official Circles*, Beijing: People's Literature Press, 1957, p. 1.

[14] The first chapter of Wu Jianren: *Bizarre Happenings Eyewitnessed over Two Decades*, Beijing: People's Literature Press, 1981, p. 1.

contemplate the four primary elements (earth, water, fire, and wind) that comprise the body. Each has its own name, while each is devoid of the self.' Alas, I do hope my beloved mother would not drive her son to be a mute sheep!"[15] Comparing Su Manshu with the authors of exposure fiction, we can see that his perceptions, as well as his literary techniques, were so much more modern. The passage just given, for example, portrayed in great detail the psychological stress felt by the first-person narrator, a young Buddhist monk who had fallen in love, and thus caught between his self-consciousness, the Buddhist teachings, and his mother's desire for him to get married. While in the later novels written by those of the Mandarin Duck and Butterfly literary school, that is, by the group of writers who used a lot of vernacular in their novels, we can see their perceptions were not as modern as Su's. Therefore, when exploring the

2.11. Portrait of Su Manshu, a handsome young man at that time, wearing a Western-style suit

literary works of this transitional period featuring a mixed use of classical and vernacular Chinese language, we should avoid a biased understanding

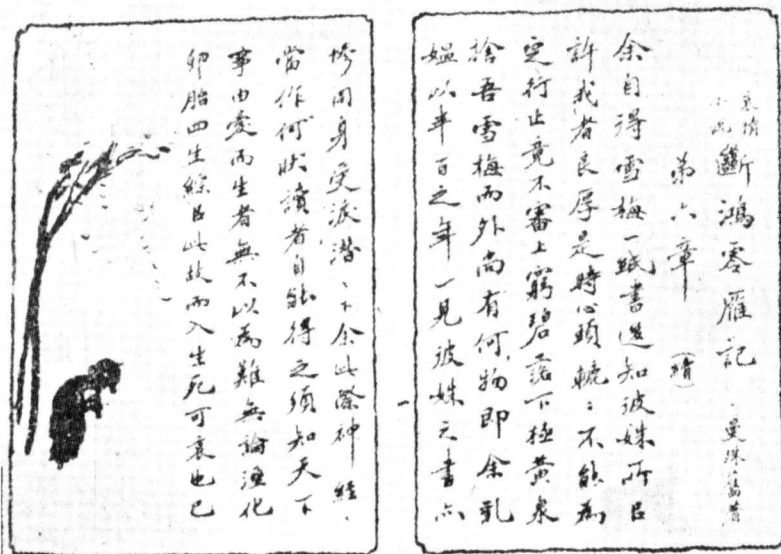

2.12. Page of the first edition of Su Manshu's *The Lone Swan*

[15] Su Manshu: *The Lone Swan, Collected Novels of Su Manshu* (《苏曼殊小说集》), Hangzhou: Zhejiang People's Press, 1981, p. 29.

2.13. Sun Yat-sen's inscription for Su Manshu, who was referred to by Dr. Sun as a "revolutionary monk," from which we can see that those who wrote in classical Chinese language did not necessarily have decadent old ideas

of the relationship between the use of language and the author's literary ideas and expressions. Another case that should be given special attention is that, as already mentioned, newspapers and magazines were among the first to advocate the use of vernacular Chinese, but on the other hand, it was in newspapers and magazines that classical Chinese remained for the longest period, so much so that even today classical Chinese is often used in news reports in newspapers and magazines in Hong Kong and Taiwan. And even today, people still tend to associate writing in classical Chinese with a high level of learning. Meanwhile, it is true that people tend to use easy-to-understand language when writing to friends and families, which means unintentionally, people admit that using vernacular language helps convey a sense of intimacy. A convincing example of this is *Home Letters of Zeng Guofan* (《曾国藩家书》), which is still quite popular today. It seemed that Zeng Guofan did not want to use the Tongcheng-style classical Chinese when writing to his family. Look at this passage written in 1871:"I see the children of the family are all weak and make little progress in learning, and teach them six points of health preserving: the first is walking a thousand steps after meals; the second is washing their feet before sleep; the third is avoiding being angry and annoyed; the fourth is often sitting quietly; the fifth is often practicing archery (this may help them gain bearing and strength, so the children in the family are encouraged to practice more), and the sixth is eating plain rice early in the morning without any other dish."[16] The writing here is quite clear and easy to understand. Indeed, at that time, people did have this dualistic attitude toward the use of classical and vernacular language.

Earlier in the Republican period, the term "classical written language" (*guo-wen*, 国文) was replaced by the term "national oral language" (*guo-yu*, 国语) in school textbooks, which meant the domination of classical Chinese

[16] Tang Haoming's Comments on *Home Letters of Zeng Guofan* (Vol. 2),"To My Brothers Cheng and Yuan, the 23rd Day of the Tenth Month of the Tenth Year under Emperor Tongzhi's Reign" (《致澄弟沅弟 同治十年十月二十三日》), Changsha:Yuelu Press, 2002, p. 434.

had really come to an end. In 1920, the Ministry of Education gave an explicit order that Chinese textbooks in vernacular must be used for the first and second grades of primary school. It was with the support of the national educational system that the achievement of the vernacular movement was finally acknowledged and the vernacular universalized. Interestingly, in 1912, Xu Zhenya (徐枕亚, 1889–1937), an earlier author of the Mandarin Duck and Butterfly literary school, published his novel *Jade Pear Spirit* (《玉梨魂》), and the tragic love story was extremely popular among readers. Xu did not show any decadent old ideas in this novel, for his tragic love story was similar to that of the May Fourth period, but his writing featured an alternation of rhymed and nonrhymed prose styles. Even in 1928, this linked-chapter novel written in classical Chinese was still reprinted by some publishing houses, and it was from then on that this writing style truly lost its readership base. Therefore, we can make a rough estimate that the 1930s were the final point of decline for mass readers of classical Chinese literary works.

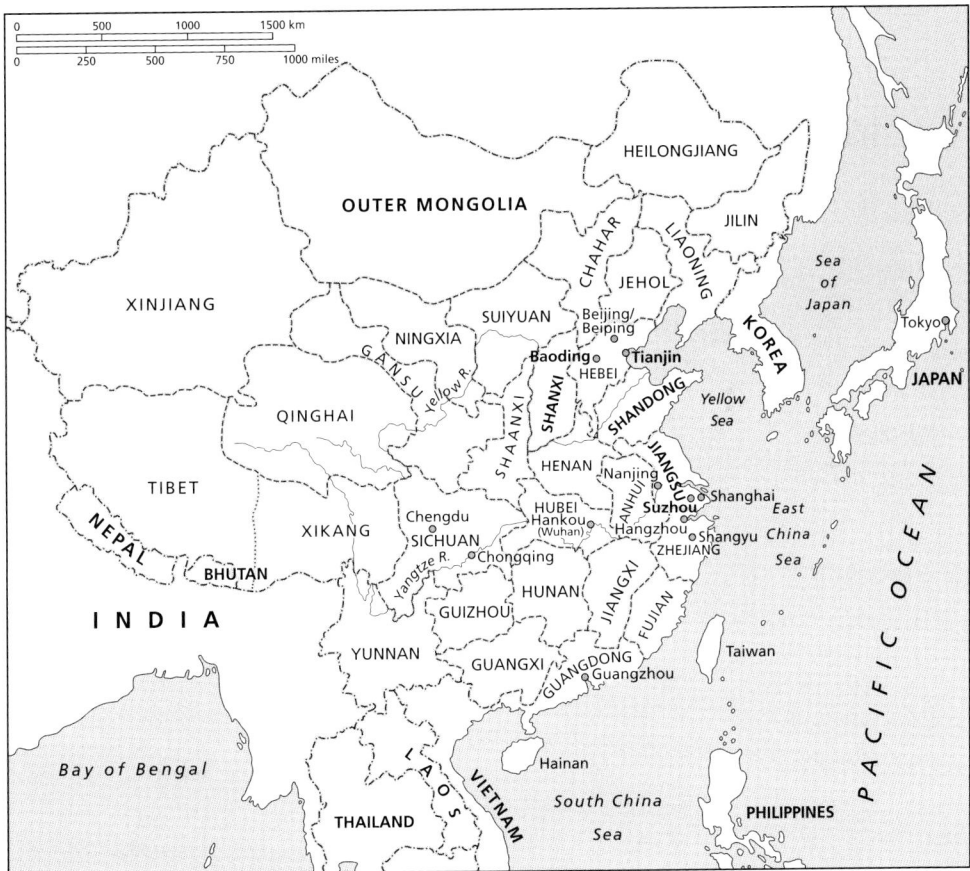

MAP 2.1. Distribution of vernacular newspapers and magazines nationwide (I)

TABLE 2.1 *Vernacular newspapers and magazines nationwide (I)*

Name of the newspaper or magazine	Time of launch	Type	Founder or editorial writer	Address of the headquarters of place of publication	Notes
Ili Vernacular Newspaper (伊犁白话报)	1910		Feng Temin (冯特民)	Ili (Xinjiang)	Published in Chinese, Manchu, Mongolian, and Uygur languages
Tibetan Vernacular Newspaper (西藏白话报)	1907		Lian Yu (联豫), Zhang Yintang (张荫棠)	Lhasa	Lian Yu and Zhang Yintang were officials of the Qing dynasty who had been sent abroad
Guilin Vernacular Newspaper (桂林白话报)				Guilin	
Jiangxi Popular Education Magazine (江西通俗教育杂志)	Feb. 1915			Nanchang	Later changed into *Jiangxi Popular Ten-Daily* (江西通俗旬报)
Jiangxi New Vernacular Newspaper (江西新白话报)				Jiangxi	
Mongolian Vernacular Newspaper (蒙古白话报)				Mongolia	
Bell Vernacular Newspaper (钟声白话报)	Nov. 1907			Harbin	Originally called *A Chime Vernacular Newspaper* (一声钟白话报)
Heilongjiang Vernacular Daily (黑龙江白话日报)	1908	Daily	Han Lianqing (韩莲青)	Harbin	A daily newspaper published by the Office of *Heilongjiang Gazette* (published every ten days)

(continued)

TABLE 2.1 *(continued)*

Name of the newspaper or magazine	Time of launch	Type	Founder or editorial writer	Address of the headquarters of place of publication	Notes
Jilin Vernacular Newspaper (吉林白话报)	Aug. 4, 1907	Published every two days	An Jingquan (安镜全)	Changchun (Changchun Prefecture)	The newspaper distribution agency was based within the East Gate Official Newspaper Agency of the capital city of Jilin Province
Popular Vernacular Newspaper (通俗白话报)	1908	Published every ten days	Library of Fengtian Academic Society (奉天学务公所图书科)	Fengtian (today's Shenyang)	The same name as the *Popular Vernacular Newspaper* first released in 1907
Self-Government Vernacular Newspaper (自治白话报)	1908		Guan Luosheng (管洛声)	Fengtian (Shenyang)	Guan Luosheng was then Head of the Autonomous Bureau of Fengtian Province
Haicheng Vernacular Lecturing Newspaper (海城白话演说报)	Oct. 1906		Guan Luosheng	Haicheng (Liaoning)	Guan Luosheng was then Prefect of Haicheng
Phonetic Alphabet Newspaper in Official Language (拼音字母官话报)	1904			Baoding	
Zhili Vernacular Newspaper (直隶白话报)	Feb. 4, 1905	Fortnightly	Wu Yue (吴樾)	Baoding	
Northern Zhili Newspaper on Agriculture (北直农话报)	Nov. 1905	Fortnightly	Zhang Jiajun (张家隽), He Chengyuan (贺澄源), etc.	Baoding	

(continued)

TABLE 2.1 *(continued)*

Name of the newspaper or magazine	Time of launch	Type	Founder or editorial writer	Address of the headquarters of place of publication	Notes
Local Vernacular Newspaper (地方白话报)	Dec. 16, 1906	Fortnightly; later published every ten days	Wang Faqin (王法勤)	Baoding	Published by the Local Newspaper Agency
Beiyang Official Language Newspaper (北洋官话报)	1905		Beiyang Official Newspaper Bureau	Tianjin	Supplement of the *Beiyang Official Newspaper* (北洋官报)
Zhuyuan Vernacular Newspaper (竹园白话报)	1907		Probably Ding Guorui (丁国瑞)	Tianjin	
Tientsin Police Affairs Vernacular Newspaper (天津警务白话报)	1908		Tientsin Police Newspaper Agency	Tianjin	
Tientsin Vernacular Newspaper (天津白话报)	Jan. 1910	Daily	Tientsin Vernacular Newspaper Agency	Tianjin	
Chinese Medicine Vernacular Newspaper (中国医药白话报)	1912			Tianjin	
Vernacular Afternoon Newspaper (白话午报)	1917	Daily	Vernacular Afternoon Newspaper Agency	Tianjin	
Tientsin Vernacular Daily (天津白话日报)				Tianjin	
Morning Bell Vernacular Newspaper (晨钟白话报)				Tianjin	

(continued)

TABLE 2.1 (continued)

Name of the newspaper or magazine	Time of launch	Type	Founder or editorial writer	Address of the headquarters of place of publication	Notes
Shanxi Vernacular Lecturing Newspaper (山西白话演说报)	1905		Shanxi Jin Newspaper Bureau	Taiyuan	Supplement of the *Jin Newspaper* (晋报)
Jinyang Vernacular Newspaper (晋阳白话报)	Oct. 9, 1906		Wang Yongbin (王用宾), Jing Dingcheng (景定成), Jing Yaoyue (景耀月)	Taiyuan	Reconstructed from the *Jin Academic Journal* (晋学报)
Shanxi Vernacular Newspaper (山西白话报)				Shanxi	
Understandable-to-All Vernacular Newspaper (妇孺易知白话报)	May 1905		Yuan Shuding (袁书鼎)	Shandong (or Ningyang County, not quite clear)	
Jinan Vernacular Daily (济南白话日报)	Feb. 23, 1906	Daily	Wang Ne (王讷)	Jinan	
Official Language Daily (官话日报)	Mar. 1906	Daily	Li Mingpu (李明浦), Hou Fengchen (侯丰臣)	Within the Official Language Newspaper Agency in Jinan	The name was later changed to *Government by the People Daily* (民治日报)
Wuxi Vernacular Newspaper	May 20, 1898	Published every five days; later fortnightly	Qiu Tingliang, Qiu Yufang	Wuxi	The name was changed to the *Chinese Vernacular Journal in Mandarin Pronunciation* (中国官音白话报) after five issues were published
Chang Newspaper (常报)				Jiangsu	

(continued)

TABLE 2.1 *(continued)*

Name of the newspaper or magazine	Time of launch	Type	Founder or editorial writer	Address of the headquarters of place of publication	Notes
Suzhou Vernacular Newspaper (苏州白话报)	Oct. 12, 1901	Weekly	Bao Tianxiao	In the opening of Shapi Lane, Hulong Street, Suzhou	Woodblock printed
Wu County Vernacular Newspaper	Jan. 31, 1904	Fortnightly	Wujun Vernacular Newspaper Agency	Suzhou	Printed in Shanghai
Jiangsu Vernacular Newspaper (江苏白话报)	Sep. 19, 1904	Monthly	Qinnan Academic Society (琴南学社)	Changshu (Jiangsu)	Printed in Shanghai
Taicang Vernacular Newspaper (太仓白话报)	Oct. 1908			Taicang (Jiangsu)	
Vernacular Newspaper of Xijin Educational Board (锡金教育会白话报)	Oct. 1908	Monthly	Xijin Educational Board	Wuxi	"Xijin" is the former appellation of Wuxi
Rugao County Government Popular Newspaper (如皋县公署通俗报)	1913	Weekly	Rugao County Government Office	Rugao (Jiangsu)	
Rugao Vernacular Newspaper (如皋白话报)	Dec. 1915	(Improvement) Fortnightly	Rugao Vernacular Newspaper Agency	Rugao (Jiangsu)	
Anhui Colloquial Newspaper	Mar. 31, 1904	Fortnightly	Chen Duxiu (陈独秀), Wang Mengzou (汪孟邹)	Anqing, soon moved into Wuhu Scientific Library	

(continued)

TABLE 2.1 *(continued)*

Name of the newspaper or magazine	Time of launch	Type	Founder or editorial writer	Address of the headquarters of place of publication	Notes
Pili Vernacular Newspaper (霹雳白话报)	Nov. 5, 1912		Anhui Popular Education Newspaper Agency	Anqing	Some say this newspaper was launched in August 1912, and later its name was changed to *Popular Education Newspaper* (通俗教育报)
Henan Vernacular Lecturing Newspaper (河南白话演说报)	1906	Published every five days	Bian Province Official Newspaper Agency (汴省官报局)	Kaifeng	

MAP 2.2. Distribution of vernacular newspapers and magazines nationwide (II)

TABLE 2.2 *Vernacular newspapers and magazines nationwide (II)*

Name of the newspaper or magazine	Time of launch	Type	Founder or editorial writer	Address of the headquarters of place publication	Notes
Popular Newspaper (通俗报)	May 1898		Pan Qingyin (潘清荫)	Chongqing	
Official and Popular Vernacular Newspaper (正俗白话报)				Sichuan	
Enlightenment Popular Newspaper (启蒙通俗报)	1902	Fortnightly; later monthly	Fu Qiaocun (傅樵邨)	Chengdu	
New Popular Newspaper (通俗新报)	Mar. 11, 1909	Daily	New Popular Newspaper Agency	Chengdu	
New Vernacular (Newspaper) (新白话【报】)	Dec. 1903	Monthly	Dan Dang (担当, pseudonym of a native of Jiangxi studying in Japan) etc.	Tokyo, Japan	Released by the Shanghai Puyi Book Company (普益书局)
Jiangxi Vernacular Newspaper (江西白话报)	1903		Zhang Shiying (张世膺)	Tokyo, Japan	There was a fortnightly edition published in Jiujiang in the same year, whose details were not clear
Vernacular (白话)	Sep. 24, 1904	Monthly	Qiu Jin (秋瑾) from the Public Speech Practice Association of Chinese Students in Japan	Tokyo, Japan	Released and sold by the office of *Forest of Fiction*, Shanghai
The First Shanxi Dialect Newspaper (第一晋话报)	July 1905	Monthly	The Association of Chinese Students in Japan with Shanxi Origin	Tokyo, Japan	

(continued)

TABLE 2.2 *(continued)*

Name of the newspaper or magazine	Time of launch	Type	Founder or editorial writer	Address of the headquarters of place publication	Notes
History of Shanxi (晋乘)	Sep. 15, 1907	Irregularly	Jing Dingcheng, Jing Yaoyue	Tokyo, Japan	Discontinued in 1908
Yunnan Dialect Newspaper (滇话报)	Dec. 1907	Monthly		Tokyo, Japan	
Yunnan Dialect (滇话)	Apr. 1908	Monthly	Liu Zhonghua (刘钟华), Li Changchun (李长春)	Tokyo, Japan	Launched by students from Yunnan studying in Japan
Today's Education Journal (教育今语杂志)	Mar. 1910		Zhang Taiyan (章太炎), Tao Chengzhang (陶成章)	Tokyo, Japan	Launched when the United Allegiance Society (同盟会) was split and the Restoration Society was founded
Hubei Vernacular Newspaper (湖北白话报)	Apr. 1904				
Popular Vernacular Newspaper	May 1907		Li Yadong (李亚东), Chen Shaowu (陈少武)	Hanyang	
New Popular Newspaper	1907		Xu Zixin (徐自新)	Hankou	
Popular Newspaper of Hunan and Hubei (两湖通俗报)	1908		Yang Dixiang (杨涤湘)	Wuchang	
Constitutional Vernacular Newspaper (宪政白话报)	Jan. 1910	Weekly	Zhang Guorong (张国溶, president)	Hankou	Presided over by Hankou Constitutional Government Society (汉口宪政同志会)

(continued)

TABLE 2.2 *(continued)*

Name of the newspaper or magazine	Time of launch	Type	Founder or editorial writer	Address of the headquarters of place publication	Notes
Dajiang Vernacular Newspaper (大江白话报)	Dec. 14, 1910		Zhan Dabei (詹大悲, editor-in-chief)	Hankou	Launched by Mei Baoji (梅宝玑) and others, its named was later changed to the *Dajiang Newspaper* (大江报)
Hubei Local Self-Government Vernacular Newspaper (湖北地方自治白话报)	1910				
Dajiang Vernacular Newspaper	Jan. 3, 1911		Hu Shi'an (胡石庵)	Hankou	Ordered to discontinue on Aug. 11 of the same year; there was another newspaper with the same name
Wuchang Vernacular Newspaper (武昌白话报)				Wuchang	
Pinghu Vernacular Newspaper (平湖白话报)	1897		Chen Weijian (陈惟俭), Cai Bohua (蔡伯华)	Pinghu (Zhejiang)	
Shaoxing Vernacular Newspaper (绍兴白话报)	July 9, 1903	Published every ten days; later every five days	Chen Gongxia (陈公侠), Wang Ziyu (王子余), Cai Guoqing (蔡国卿)	Shaoxing	Discontinued in 1908
Nanxun Popular Newspaper (南浔通俗报)	Jan. 1904	Fortnightly		Nanxun (Zhejiang)	Printed in Shanghai
Vernacular Daily (白话日报)	1900		Lin Wanli (林万里), Wang Shuming (汪叔明)	Hangzhou	

(continued)

TABLE 2.2 *(continued)*

Name of the newspaper or magazine	Time of launch	Type	Founder or editorial writer	Address of the headquarters of place publication	Notes
Awakening Citizens' Newspaper (觉民报)	1900			Gongbu, Hangzhou	
Hangzhou Vernacular Newspaper (杭州白话报)	June 20, 1901	Published every ten days	Xiang Lansheng (项兰生), Hu Xiulu (胡修庐), Sun Yizhong (孙翼中)	Hangzhou	Lu Xun visited the newspaper office in 1903
Illustrated Lecturing Newspaper (图画演说报)	Jan. 9, 1902	Monthly		Hangzhou	The illustrations were woodcut and the texts were printed with moveable type
Zhejiang Vernacular Newspaper (浙江白话报)	Nov. 12, 1909		Xu Zuqian (许祖谦)	Hangzhou	There was a vernacular pictorial launched as a supplement of this newspaper
New Vernacular Newspaper (白话新报)	Nov. 17, 1909	Daily	Hang Xinzhai (杭辛斋), Xu Zuqian	Hall of Benevolence and Honesty (仁信堂), Commercial Center, Hangzhou	There was a newspaper of the same name in Beijing
Zhejiang New Vernacular Newspaper (浙江白话 新报)	Feb. 15, 1910	Daily	Hang Xinzhai	Youshengguan Alley, Hangzhou	Founded by merging the *Zhejiang Vernacular Newspaper* and the *New Vernacular Newspaper*
Vernacular Alarm Bell Newspaper (白话省钟报)	Aug. 24, 1911		Vernacular Alarm Bell Newspaper Office	Sanyuanfang (三元坊), Hangzhou	
Shaoxing Vernacular Newspaper	Mar. 15, 1910	Published every ten days		Shaoxing Printing Bureau, Dingjia Alley outside Shaoxing City Gate	The same name as the *Shaoxing Vernacular Newspaper* of 1903

(continued)

TABLE 2.2 *(continued)*

Name of the newspaper or magazine	Time of launch	Type	Founder or editorial writer	Address of the headquarters of place publication	Notes
Hunan Popular Newspaper (湖南通俗报)				Hunan	
Popular Education Newspaper (通俗教育报)				Hunan	
Slang Newspaper (俚语报)	June 1898		Chen Zhenrui (陈贞瑞)	Hengyang	
Slang Daily (俚语日报)	1903	Daily	Song Haiwen (宋海闻)	West Gongyuan Street, Changsha	Closed down in 1905
Hunan Vernacular Newspaper (湖南白话报)	Apr. 29, 1903	Daily		Changsha	
Hunan Popular Lecturing Newspaper (湖南演说通俗报)	May 1903		Hunan Popular Lecturing Newspaper Office	Changsha	
Ningxiang Local Self-Government Vernacular Newspaper (宁乡地方自治白话报)	Sep. 1910	Monthly	Ningxiang Local Self-Government Preparation Office	Ningxiang (Hunan)	
Hunan Local Self-Government Vernacular Newspaper (湖南地方自治白话报)	Mar. 1910	Monthly	Hunan Local Self-Government Preparation Office	Changsha	

(continued)

TABLE 2.2 *(continued)*

Name of the newspaper or magazine	Time of launch	Type	Founder or editorial writer	Address of the headquarters of place publication	Notes
Changsha Local Self-Government Vernacular Newspaper (长沙地方自治白话报)	Aug. 1910	Monthly	Changsha Local Self-Government Preparation Office	Changsha	
Diplomatic Slang Newspaper (外交俚语报)				Changsha	
Fujian Vernacular Newspaper (福建白话报)	Oct. 9, 1904	Fortnightly	Fujian Vernacular Newspaper Office	Fuzhou	The distribution headquarters were located in Shanghai
Popular Education Magazine (通俗教育杂志)	1914			Fujian	
Fujian Colloquial Newspaper (福建俗话报)				Fujian	
Chaozhou Vernacular Newspaper (潮州白话报)	Sep. 20, 1903	Monthly	Yang Shouyu (杨守愚), Zhuang Yiwu (庄一梧)	Prefectural city of Chaozhou (Guangdong)	
Women and Children's Newspaper (妇孺报)	May 1904	Monthly	Guangzhou Primary Education Book Bureau (广州蒙学书局)	Shuangmendi, Guangzhou	
Sound of Tides (潮声)	Apr. 24, 1906	Fortnightly	Zeng Xingcun (曾杏邨)	Shantou (Guangdong)	
Guangdong Vernacular Newspaper (广东白话报)	May 31, 1907	Published every ten days; later weekly	Presumably Huang Boyao (黄伯耀), Huang Shizhong (黄世仲)	Guangzhou	

(continued)

TABLE 2.2 *(continued)*

Name of the newspaper or magazine	Time of launch	Type	Founder or editorial writer	Address of the headquarters of place publication	Notes
Lingnan Vernacular Journal (岭南白话杂志)	Feb. 9, 1908	Weekly	Ou Boming (欧博明), Huang Yaogong (黄耀公)	Lingnan Vernacular Journal Office, Shuangmendi, Guangzhou	The headquarters were located in the Po Wan Building, Hollywood Road, Hong Kong
Women and Children's Daily (妇孺日报)	1908	Daily	Chen Cheng (陈诚)	Panyu (Guangdong)	

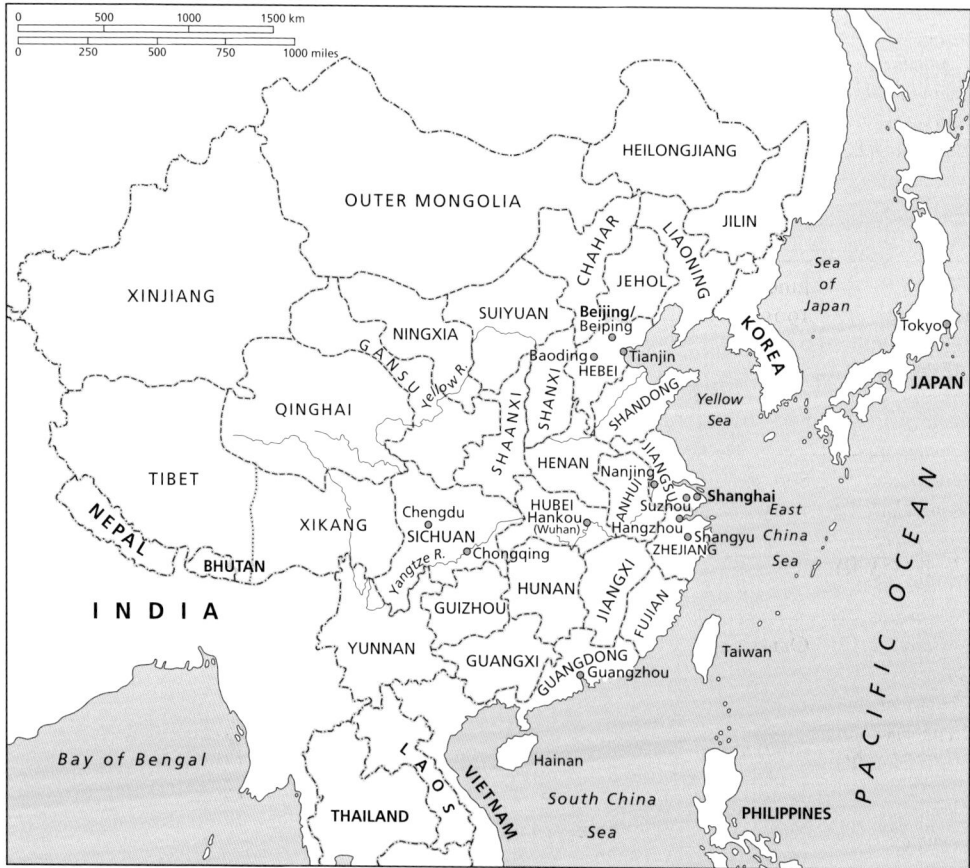

MAP 2.3. Distribution of vernacular newspapers and magazines nationwide (III)

TABLE 2.3 *Vernacular newspapers and magazines nationwide (III)*

Name of the newspaper or magazine	Time of launch	Type	Founder or editorial writer	Address of the headquarters of place of publication	Notes
Peking Dialect Newspaper (京话报)	Aug. 15, 1901	Published every ten days	Huang Xiubo (黄秀伯)	Beijing	Discontinued in December of the same year
Enlightenment Pictorial (启蒙画报)	June 1902	Daily; later fortnightly; then every ten days	Peng Yizhong	Beijing Enlightenment Pictorial Office	
Pekingese Daily News	Aug. 16, 1904	Small-scale daily	Peng Yizhong	Wudaomiao Road, Beijing	Suspended and resumed publication several times; finally closed in 1923
Common Peking Dialect Newspaper (普通京话报)	Apr. 1905			Beijing	Founded by someone whose surname is Zhu (朱), a member of the Society for Learning Japanese (东文学社)
Peking Woman's Newspaper (北京女报)	June 28, 1905	Daily	Zhang Zhanyun (张展云)	Beijing	The preparation office was located at Yangrou Lane, Yanshou Temple Street outside Qianmen Gate
Military Vernacular Newspaper (军事白话报)	Sep. 30 1905			Beijing	Closed down by Yuan Shikai less than half a month after it was launched
Military Strategy Vernacular Newspaper (兵学白话报)	Oct. 1905	Daily	Bureau of Military Training	Beijing	
Vernacular Common Learning Newspaper (白话普通学报)	Oct. 1905	Weekly		Fangjin Alley within Chongwen Gate, Beijing	

(continued)

TABLE 2.3 *(continued)*

Name of the newspaper or magazine	Time of launch	Type	Founder or editorial writer	Address of the headquarters of place of publication	Notes
Vernacular Enlightenment Newspaper (白话开通报)	Dec. 1905	Daily		Beijing	Appended to the *Jintai Serial Newspaper* (金台组报)
Peking Official Language Newspaper (北京官话报)	1905			Beijing	Appended to the *Peking Newspaper* (北京报)
Peking Dialect Public Newspaper (京话广报)	Sep. 30, 1906		Peking Daily Office	Beijing	
Constitution Vernacular Newspaper (宪法白话报)	Oct. 4, 1906		Jin Tiangen (金天根)	Beijing	
Orthodox Patriotism Newspaper (正宗爱国报)	Nov. 16, 1906	Daily	Ding Guozhen (丁国珍), Wang Zizhen (王子贞), Wen Yitang (文益堂)	Beijing	Over 2,000 issues were published before it was discontinued in 1913
Invention Vernacular Newspaper (发明白话报)	Nov. 1906		Chen Xiongfan (陈雄藩)	Beijing	Its original name was *Alarm Newspaper* (警报)
Peking Dialect News (京话实报)	Second half of 1906		Tan Tianchi (谭天池)	Beijing	
Peking Dialect News Story (京话汇报)	1906			Beijing	
Vernacular Public Service Newspaper (白话公益报)	1906			Beijing	
Peking Dialect Official Report (京话公报)	1906			Beijing	

(continued)

TABLE 2.3 *(continued)*

Name of the newspaper or magazine	Time of launch	Type	Founder or editorial writer	Address of the headquarters of place of publication	Notes
Central Vernacular Newspaper (中央白话报)	1906			Beijing	
Vernacular Citizens' Newspaper (白话国民报)	Dec. 20, 1906	Daily	Chun Linzhou (春麟洲)	West end of North Beiliu Alley, outside the Xuanwu Gate, Beijing	
Beijing Dialect Times (京话时报)	1907		Juxing Beijing Newspaper Office	Beijing	Launched by someone whose surname was Wang
Datong Vernacular Newspaper (大同白话报)	1908		Datong Vernacular Newspaper Office	Beijing	Its office was located in Beijing
Capital Vernacular Daily (京都白话日报)	1908	Daily	Wang Zizhen	Beijing	
Capital Daily (京都日报)	1908	Daily	Xiao Delin (萧德霖)	Capital Daily Office, Beijing	Also known as *Official Language Capital Daily* (官话京都日报)
Elementary Politics and Law Newspaper (法政浅说报)	May 1911	Published every ten days	Bai Jun (白鋆)	Beijing	
Women's Vernacular Ten-Daily (女子白话旬报)	Oct. 21, 1912	Published every ten days; later fortnightly	Tang Qunying (唐群英,), Shen Nanya (沈南雅), etc.	Beijing	Later changed to fortnightly and its name was changed to *Women's Vernacular Newspaper*
Mass Power Newspaper (群强报)	May 29, 1912	Daily	Ji Kunhou (纪昆侯, aka Hou Dehui [侯德辉])	Beijing	Discontinued in July 1937

(continued)

TABLE 2.3 *(continued)*

Name of the newspaper or magazine	Time of launch	Type	Founder or editorial writer	Address of the headquarters of place of publication	Notes
Peking Dialect News Report (京话真报)	1912			Beijing	
Daily Vernacular (日报白话报)	1912			Beijing	
Citizens' Vernacular Newspaper (牖民白话报)	1912			Beijing	
Vernacular Republic Pictorial (白话共和画报)	1912			Beijing	
Elementary Talks of Republican Practice Newspaper (共和实进浅说报)	1912			Beijing	
Vernacular Evening (白话晚报)	1912			Tianjin	
Vernacular Newspaper of Central News (中央新闻附白话报)	1912			Beijing	
Minduo Vernacular Newspaper (民铎白话报)	1912			Beijing	
Peking Vernacular Newspaper (北京白话报)	1912			Beijing	
Vernacular Alarm (白话当头棒)	1912			Beijing	

(continued)

TABLE 2.3 *(continued)*

Name of the newspaper or magazine	Time of launch	Type	Founder or editorial writer	Address of the headquarters of place of publication	Notes
New Citizen Vernacular Newspaper (新民白话报)	1912			Beijing	
Elementary Talks City Newspaper (浅说市报)	1912			Beijing	
Vernacular New Citizen Newspaper (白话新民报)	1912			Beijing	
Beijing Dialect Citizens' Newspaper (京话民报)	1912			Beijing	
Free Bell Vernacular Newspaper (自由钟白话报)	1912			Beijing	
Law and Politics Vernacular Newspaper (法政白话报)	Feb. 6, 1913		Law Newspaper and Magazine Office (法律书报社)	Tangzi Lane, Fenfang Liuli Street, Beijing	Released by the branch of Law Newspaper and Magazine Office
Patriotism Vernacular Newspaper (爱国白话报)	July 30, 1913	Daily	Ma Taipu (马太朴)	Beijing	Discontinued on Feb. 26, 1922
Vernacular Express News (白话捷报)	Aug. 3, 1913	Daily	Wen Zhixian (文治贤)	Beijing	Discontinued on Aug. 22, 1914
Tibetan Vernacular Newspaper (藏文白话报)	1913	Monthly		Beijing	
Mongolian Vernacular Newspaper (蒙文白话报)	1913			Beijing	Presumably published on Jan. 27

(continued)

TABLE 2.3 *(continued)*

Name of the newspaper or magazine	Time of launch	Type	Founder or editorial writer	Address of the headquarters of place of publication	Notes
Elementary Talks of Industry (实业浅说)	1915	Fortnightly	Ministry of Agriculture and Commerce, Beijing	Beijing	
Official Phonetic Alphabet Newspaper (官话注音字母报)	Apr. 1916	Fortnightly	Phonetic Alphabet Newspaper Office	Beijing	
Chinese Characters Lecturing Newspaper (广仓学演说报)	July 1916	Monthly	Society of Studies of Chinese Characters (广仓学窘)	Beijing	
Public Speech Newspaper (公言报)	Sep. 1, 1916	Daily	Lin Xie (林獬, also known as Lin Baishui [林白水])	Beijing	Discontinued on July 22, 1920
Vernacular Strong Nation Newspaper (白话国强报)	Jan. 1918	Daily	Vernacular Strong Nation Newspaper Office	Beijing	Discontinued on Apr. 18, 1925
Vernacular News Report (实事白话报)	1918		Vernacular News Report and Entertainment Newspaper Office	Beijing	Its name was later changed to *Vernacular News Report and Entertainment Newspaper* (实事白话游艺报)
Peking Vernacular Newspaper	July 1919	Daily	Ren Pusheng (任朴生)	Beijing	Discontinued on Sep. 5, 1938
Vernacular News Report	Feb. 8, 1920	Daily	Dai Lansheng (戴兰生)	Beijing	Discontinued on Aug. 30, 1932
New Vernacular Newspaper				Beijing	

(continued)

TABLE 2.3 *(continued)*

Name of the newspaper or magazine	Time of launch	Type	Founder or editorial writer	Address of the headquarters of place of publication	Notes
Renewed Newspaper (从新报)			Tan Peiting (谭佩亭)	Beijing	
Peking Dialect News				Beijing	
Exhortation Vernacular Newspaper (劝兴白话报)				Beijing	
Peking and Tientsin Vernacular Newspaper (京津白话报)				Beijing	
Official Language Simplified Chinese Newspaper (官话简字报)				Beijing	
Simple Newspaper (简字报)				Beijing	
Official Language Beijing News Report (官话北京实报)				Beijing	
Public Service Newspaper (公益报)			Wen Shiquan (文实权)	Beijing	Not clear whether it was the *Vernacular Public Service Newspaper* of 1906
Capital Public Newspaper (京师公报)			Wen Shiquan	Beijing	

(continued)

TABLE 2.3 *(continued)*

Name of the newspaper or magazine	Time of launch	Type	Founder or editorial writer	Address of the headquarters of place of publication	Notes
Evolution Newspaper (进化报)			Cai Youmei (蔡友梅)	Beijing	This newspaper paid special attention to the livelihood of descendants of the Eight Banners
Official Language Political Newspaper (官话政报)			Li Zhongti (李仲悌)	Beijing	
Capital Vernacular Newspaper (神京白话报)			Rong Guang (荣光)	Beijing	
New Beijing Newspaper (北京新报)			Yang Manqing (杨曼青)	Beijing	
Peking Official Language Newspaper				Beijing	
Orthodox Vernacular Newspaper (正宗白话报)				Beijing	
Min Bao	Mar. 30, 1876	Daily	*Shun Pao* Office	Wangping Street at the crossroads of Hankou and Jiangxi roads, Shanghai	The first vernacular newspaper in China
Primary Education Newspaper (蒙学报)	Oct. 26, 1897	Published every ten days	Wang Kangnian (汪康年)	Chaozongfang, Wangping Street and Hankou Road, Shanghai	
Renditions Vernacular Newspaper	Nov. 7, 1897	Literary daily	Zhang Bochu (章伯初), Zhang Zhonghe (章仲和)	Huifu Alley, Fuzhou Road, Shanghai	

(continued)

TABLE 2.3 *(continued)*

Name of the newspaper or magazine	Time of launch	Type	Founder or editorial writer	Address of the headquarters of place of publication	Notes
Women's Learning Newspaper (女学报)	July 24, 1898	Published every ten days	Kang Tongwei (康同薇), Li Huixian (李惠仙), Qiu Yufang	Wenyuanfang, outside the West Gate, Shanghai	China's first women's newspaper, seeking to promote vernacular
Popular Newspaper	July 12, 1899	Daily	Popular Newspaper Office	Printing Bureau of Hanyang Book Company, Sixth Avenue, Shanghai	The same name as the *Popular Newspaper* launched in 1898
Suzhou Vernacular Newspaper	Aug. 5, 1902			Within Scholar's Hall (文翰斋), Wangping Street, Shanghai	Using the Wu dialect; the same name as the woodblock-printed *Suzhou Vernacular Newspaper*
Mass Wisdom Vernacular Newspaper (智群白话报)	Jan. 1903	Monthly	Biansu Daoren (砭俗道人), Tang Ziquan (唐孜权)	Shanghai Civilization Translation, Editing, and Printing Bureau (上海文明编译印书局)	Tang Ziquan was its general manager
Ningbo Vernacular Newspaper	Nov. 23, 1903	Published every ten days	Ningbo Residents Association in Shanghai	Shanghai	Released by Ningbo Residents Association in Shanghai
China Vernacular Newspaper	Dec. 19, 1903	Fortnightly; later published every ten days	Baihua Daoren (白话道人, another alias of Lin Xie, or Lin Baishui)	Shanghai	Discontinued in Oct. 1904
Huzhou Vernacular Newspaper	May 15, 1904	Fortnightly	Huzhou Vernacular Newspaper Office (Zhejiang)	Shanghai	The sales headquarters is Shanghai Kaiming Bookstore

(continued)

TABLE 2.3 (continued)

Name of the newspaper or magazine	Time of launch	Type	Founder or editorial writer	Address of the headquarters of place of publication	Notes
Hunan Vernacular Newspaper	1904			Shanghai	
Primary Learning Vernacular Newspaper (初学白话报)	1904			Shanghai	
Children's Learning (童蒙易知草)	1905			Shanghai	
The Struggle Ten-Daily (竞业旬报)	Oct. 28, 1906	Published every ten days	Fu Junjian (傅君剑)	Shanghai	Published by the Society for Striving to Accomplish our Tasks (竞业协会)
Preliminary Constitutional Official Language Newspaper (预备立宪官话报)	Dec. 16, 1906	Monthly	Zhuang Jingzhong (庄景仲)	Shanghai	Founded by the Preliminary Constitutional Society
New China Vernacular Newspaper (新中国白话报)	1907			Shanghai	
National Vernacular Daily (国民白话日报)	July 28, 1908	Daily	Presumably Fan Hongxian (范鸿仙)	Shanghai National Vernacular Daily Office	Hu Shi claimed he contributed articles to this newspaper
Anhui Vernacular Newspaper	Oct. 5, 1908	Published every ten days	Li Duo (李铎), Li Xieshu (李燮枢, courtesy name: Xinbai [辛白]), etc.	Shanghai	After the newspaper office was burnt down in a fire, publication resumed in September the next year, with "New" added to its name

(continued)

TABLE 2.3 *(continued)*

Name of the newspaper or magazine	Time of launch	Type	Founder or editorial writer	Address of the headquarters of place of publication	Notes
Vernacular Fiction (白话小说)	Oct. 20, 1908	Monthly	Laoxia Yusheng (姥下余生)	Shanghai Vernacular Fiction Editorial Office	
Yangtze River Vernacular Newspaper (扬子江白话报)	Jan. 1909		Launched by Yangtze River Vernacular Newspaper Office	Shanghai	The same name as *Yangtze River Vernacular Newspaper* launched in 1904
Lecturing Newspaper (演说报)	1912	Daily	Shanghai Lecturing Newspaper Office	Shanghai	
Popular Education Newspaper	Mar. 18, 1913	Monthly	Shanghai Popular Education Newspaper Office	Shanghai	
China Vernacular Newspaper	May 22, 1915	Published every ten days	Lin Xie (Lin Baishui)	Shanghai	Lin Xie resumed publication of the newspaper he launched in 1903 with the same name
Popular Magazine (通俗杂志)	Aug. 1915	Fortnightly	Shanghai Popular Magazine Editorial Office	Shanghai	
Chaozhou Vernacular Newspaper				Shanghai	The Newspaper Office was in Shanghai
New Vernacular Newspaper (新白话报)				Shanghai	
Enlightening People Patriotic Newspaper (启民爱国报)				Shanghai	

(continued)

TABLE 2.3 *(continued)*

Name of the newspaper or magazine	Time of launch	Type	Founder or editorial writer	Address of the headquarters of place of publication	Notes
Illustrated Novel Magazine (小说画报)	1917	Monthly	Bao Tianxiao	Shanghai Civilization Book Company (上海文明书局)	
Healthcare Vernacular Newspaper (卫生白话报)	1908	Monthly	Shanghai Healthcare Vernacular Newspaper Office	Shanghai	
Shanghai Vernacular Newspaper (上海白话报)	Nov. 2, 1910	Daily	Xie Huichan (谢慧禅)	86 Stone Alley, Second Avenue, Shanghai	

(*Sources*: Cai Lesu [蔡乐苏]: "Over 170 Vernacular Newspapers during the Late Qing and Early Republican Period" [《清末民初的一百七十余种白话报刊》], in Ding Shouhe [丁守和] ed., *An Overview of Periodicals during the Xinhai Revolution* [《辛亥革命时期期刊介绍》], Beijing: People's Press, 1983; Fang Hanqi [方汉奇]: *History of China's Newspapers and Magazines in Early Modern Times* [《中国近代报刊史》], Taiyuan: Shanxi Education Press, 1991; Li Nan [李楠]: *Tabloids in Shanghai During the Late Qing and Early Republican Period* [《晚清民国时期上海小报》], Beijing: People's Literature Press, etc.)

THREE

EARLIEST INTELLECTUALS WITH A GLOBAL OUTLOOK

3.1. This sketch, "China and the Western Powers," illustrating how China was divided by the Western powers, appeared in the very first issue of *China's New Magazine* (《中国新报》), which was one of many such sketches trying to provoke Chinese people's sense of crisis about the country's territorial integrity

Filled with a sense of crisis that China would be divided by Western powers, the progressive intellectuals of the late-Qing period began turning their eyes to the outside world. From the sketches of China's situation appearing in newspapers and magazines during this period, we can feel the eagerness for

independence and self-reliance of the general public and progressive intellectuals. Meanwhile, understanding the world better and breaking through the
old knowledge system became the consensus of many pioneer reformers. Lin
Zexu (林则徐, 1785–1850) was one of the earliest of them. In order to "contain
barbarian foreigners" and "keep barbarian foreigners away," he presided over
the translation and editing of the *Record of the Four Continents* (《四洲志》).
Lin's peers Wei Yuan (魏源, 1794–1857) and Gong Zizhen also advocated
practical statecraft together with Lin. Entrusted by Lin, Wei Yuan compiled
the *Illustrated Records of the Maritime Nations* (《海国图志》) based on the
Record of the Four Continents and other Chinese and foreign documents. Wei
Yuan proposed to "learn the advanced technology from foreign nations with
the purpose to contain them," in which the word "learn" shall be given great
importance, because it was indeed not easy for such a brilliant civilization as
China to admit that it should "learn" from barbarian foreigners. Gong Zizhen,
as a poet of great influence, wrote poems to expose and attack corrupt Qing
society and to rejuvenate Chinese people, which was quite forward-looking in
that historical period. The three of them all paid much attention to studies on
human and historical geography of the world and China's border areas. Then
there were Wang Tao and Huang Zunxian, who were born later than Lin, Wei,
and Gong but were the first to go abroad, and together with Liang Qichao and
others who were a bit younger than them, they formed the earliest intellectual
(writer) group with a global outlook.

Wang Tao lived quite an extraordinary life. He had petitioned the Qing government on strategies for cracking down on the Taiping Heavenly Kingdom
(太平天国), to which a deaf ear was turned. Later when he returned home to
see his sick mother, he offered advice to the generals of the Taiping Heavenly
Kingdom on how to occupy Shanghai, which was later brought to light, causing him to be listed as wanted by the Qing court. He fled to Hong Kong
in 1862 with the help of his British friends. His earlier political views were
obviously utilitarian, which he sold to whoever took him in. However, his
life in exile for twenty-two years made him what he was known for. From
1867 to 1870 he was hired to translate books in Britain, during which time
he had the opportunity to travel in Europe. In 1879 he traveled in Japan, and
it was there that he met Huang Zunxian for the first time. Earlier in his life,
in 1849, when he was still in China, Wang had begun working at the London
Missionary Society Press of Shanghai at the invitation of Walter H. Medhurst.
Since Medhurst was the foreigner who had founded the very first Chinese
magazine and the very first modern publishing house in China, Wang was
fortunate to become one of the earliest to play a role in China's modern publishing industry and translation. Working at the London Missionary Society
Press for more than a decade, Wang read extensively about natural science

and cultural studies of the West, opening his horizons to a world not known to most Chinese people of the time. In Hong Kong, he assisted James Legge of the Anglo-Chinese College to translate classical Chinese scriptures into English, and later he traveled between Hong Kong and the United Kingdom with Legge. In 1874, after Legge returned home to teach Chinese studies in Oxford, Wang Tao raised funds to buy the printing equipment from Anglo-Chinese College and launched *Universal Circulating Herald*, the first Chinese language newspaper launched by a Chinese national. He published political comments on the newspaper for a dozen years, echoing the political views of Kang Youwei and Liang Qichao, and became one of the most influential figures advocating reformation.

3.2. Portrait of Wang Tao

Wang Tao's transformation from a refined scholar and feudal scholar-official into a new-style newspaperman, writer, and publicist represented the spirit of the time. Well-versed in learnings of both ancient and modern times, he failed in his political career but became a professional writer for the general readership. At that time, his political comments were quite different from his "petitions" submitted to the Qing government, because it was no longer necessary for him to be loyal to anybody, and with his views to be read by the general public, he became less scrupulous in expressing his opinions and spared no efforts in introducing new concepts and ideas from the West. He was even earlier than Liang Qichao to write in a freer classical Chinese style, making him indeed the pioneer of "newspaper style." He wrote several notebook fictions in classical Chinese language, including *Carefree Jottings of a Songjiang Recluse* (《淞隐漫录》), *False Words of a Man in a Hidden Cave* (《遁窟谰言》) and *Anecdotes on the Song River Bank* (《淞滨琐话》). *Carefree Jottings of a Songjiang Recluse* was serialized in the *Dianshizhai Illustrated Magazine* (《点石斋画报》, released by the *Shun Pao* Office), whose chief editor, Wu Youru (吴友如), created illustrations for the text. Through these fictional writings one saw in Wang Tao a real Shanghai-school literary scholar. These fictions were combinations of news reports, folklores, and anecdotes, written to entertain urban residents or express his own thoughts and feelings, corresponding to the author's promiscuous life in Shanghai. In a sense, Wang's fictions were unprecedented in depicting people and scenes of the modern metropolis. He was also among the first to write overseas travelogues, extant ones including *Jottings of My Roamings* (《漫游随录》) and *A Travel to Japan* (《扶桑游记》).

As an exile from China, Wang Tao went abroad seven years earlier than Guo Songtao (郭嵩焘, 1818–1891), the first Chinese ambassador to the United

3.3. "Overseas Beauties" from
Carefree Jottings of a Songjiang Recluse
by Wang Tao, drawn by Wu Youru

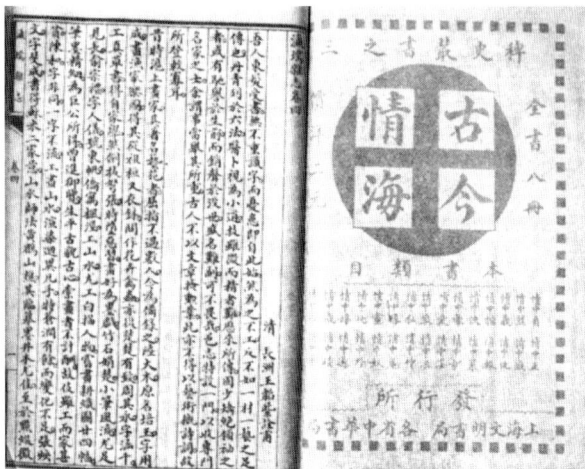

3.4. Book advertisements inserted into Wang Tao's *Miscellaneous
Records of Foreign Lands* (《瀛壖杂志》) (ROC edition)

Kingdom. Wang traveled around Shanghai in 1847, only four years after its opening as a trading port, and he lived there for fourteen years after joining the London Missionary Society Press. He then lived for quite a long time in Hong Kong. As well-read and well-traveled a person as he was, according to his travelogue, he felt "my eyes were immediately opened and what I saw seemed almost like a different universe" once he landed in the south of France, evidence that one had to see Western civilization with one's own eyes. Here is his first impression of Marseilles:

> Two days later we arrived in Marseilles, a large seaport of France. It was then that I began to know the busy and bustling market as well as splendid buildings of foreign countries. The buildings were seven or eight stories high, grand in style and exquisite in decorations, so much so that I doubted I had been in heaven, and indeed, even heaven was eclipsed by what was in front of me. The streets were wide and busy, the lights bright and blazing. The richness and extravagance of furniture and displays in my hotel room were just beyond words. A carriage had been ordered and waited there whenever we wanted to go out, for which a fixed rate was charged so that one need not worry about being overcharged. I went around the market together with Xia Wen (夏文), where I saw a large variety of goods and prosperous people. So many merchants gathered there, making it one of the largest markets even in France.[1]

---

[1] Wang Tao: *Jottings of My Roamings and A Travel to Japan*, Changsha: Hunan People's Press, 1982, p. 80.

Constrained by the traditional Chinese writing style, Wang Tao could not be very specific in describing the streets, but upon arrival in Europe, he became aware of such details as the height of buildings, brightness of lights at night, the pricing of hackney-coaches, the varieties of merchandise on the market, and the crowds of business people, which was quite exceptional. He did hunt for novelties in Europe and recorded them in his travelogues, but he paid attention to the municipal governance, was enthusiastic about visiting museums in each city, and took an interest in the relationships between men and women, as well as female education. At that time Wang Tao had also shown an interest in the relationship between the living conditions of cities and their citizens. He described the road management in London: "The streets are as wide as six or seven *zhang*, paved with smooth stones on both sides. The central part of some streets is paved with logs for the easier and less noisy passage of carriages. Each morning, a sprinkler scatters water on the roads to get rid of the dust and clean the streets. Long drains are dug under the street to drain sewage." He described the tap water supplies: "There are spring pipes inside the walls of households, which can be turned on and off with a tap. Turning on the tap, one sees water pouring out, and there is no need to worry about a shortage of water." He also recorded the households being illuminated with gas: "People do not use oil and candles alone to illuminate at night; a gas pipe is placed within the wall of each household, from which people can turn on the gas and use

3.5. University of London during the mid-nineteenth century

3.6. La Scala Opera House, Milan, Italy. One of the pictures collected by Kang Youwei as he traveled around the world (the words in the margin were handwritten by Kang)

3.7. Milan Cathedral, Italy. Another picture collected by Kang Youwei as he traveled around the world (the words in the margin were also handwritten by Kang)

it conveniently."[2] These were quite careful recordings of details. He also visited the library of the Museum of London and wrote about it in his travelogue:

> The library has a huge collection of books, including no less than 520,000 titles of maps and books of ancient and modern times. There are many rooms connected to each other within the library, in which rows of huge bookshelves and large volumes are kept in neat condition. Books are also categorized according to country and placed in perfect order. The librarian in charge of Chinese books is Degler, who is fluent in Chinese and lived in Tianjin for five years. The front hall of the library is the reading room, where there are rows of tables and chairs that may accommodate several hundred people. Pens and ink are provided on the tables, and the reading room is circled with iron rings. Each day there are more than 100 men and women reading in the room; they come early in the morning and return home late in the evening. All books are available for reading, but people are not allowed to take them out.[3]

In a word, Wang Tao's travel notes about Europe represented the highest level of the earliest modern Chinese intellectuals going abroad. He enjoyed great freedom drawing on Western civilization, although his attention to women was seen as a kind of pleasure seeking. However he did set a high standard in facilitating exchange between Chinese and Western cultures, and he did so with dignity and grace.

There were other people who, like Wang Tao, wrote overseas travelogues, diaries, and memoirs, including Rong Hong (容閎, 1828–1912, better known as Yung Wing), Guo Songtao, Xue Fucheng (薛福成, 1838–1894), and Li Shuchang (黎庶昌, 1837–1897), but these were the earliest diplomats of modern China.

---

[2] Wang Tao: *Jottings of My Roamings and A Travel to Japan*, pp. 103–104.
[3] Wang Tao: *Jottings of My Roamings and A Travel to Japan*, p. 105.

Of them, Rong Hong was the first to go abroad. In 1847 he received a grant to study in the United States, and later he was admitted to Yale University, thus becoming the very first Chinese graduate from a top university in the United States. He was then recruited as a staff member by Zeng Guofan, and was appointed as Vice Ambassador to the United States. Rong Hong accomplished two major tasks: first, he participated in the planning of the Jiangnan Manufacturing Bureau and went to the United States to purchase machinery for the bureau; and second, he persuaded the Qing court to send a total of 120 boys (in four detachments) to study in the United States under the Chinese Educational Mission from 1872, a process in which he supervised the selection of candidates. The mission was later sabotaged by the conservative

3.8. Portrait of Rong Hong in his youth

group within the government and was aborted in 1881 (the year Lu Xun was born), but some of the children did make great achievements, including Zhan Tianyou (詹天佑), the chief engineer responsible for the construction of the Peking–Kalgan Railway, and Tang Shaoyi (唐绍仪), the first Premier of the Republic of China. In 1909 Rong Hong wrote about his experience in English and published the book *My Life in China and America*, which was translated into Chinese by Yun Tieqiao (恽铁樵) and Xu Fengshi (徐凤石) in 1915 and published by the Commercial Press as 《西学东渐记》. In the book Rong Hong recorded what he saw in the United States in the mid-nineteenth

3.9. First batch of children, including Zhan Tianyou, sent for education in the United States by the Qing court. Rong Hong was responsible for their selection

century as well as his personal experiences, including an anecdote that in order to be admitted to Yale, he almost accepted the condition to become a missionary. The book was quite an inspiring read.

Guo Songtao was the most senior of this group; a classmate of Zeng Guofan from Yuelu Academy (岳麓书院) and his sworn brother, he was candid and outspoken and thus incurred enmity in official circles. It was not until 1876–1879 that Guo was appointed as an ambassador to the United Kingdom and France, during which time Yan Fu was studying in United Kingdom, and they became friends despite an age difference of forty years. He was a member of the Westernization Group but was a bit more progressive in his political views. He had no good luck as an ambassador. He was tricked by Empress Dowager Cixi to go on a mission to apologize for an incident where people from the British Embassy were killed in Yunnan, but was condemned as a traitor even before he began the mission. Later when he published his diaries written during the fifty days' journey to London with the title *A Record of an Envoy's Journey to the West* (《使西纪程》), it evoked anger all over the country. Zhang Peilun (张佩纶), Zhang Ailing's (张爱玲) grandfather, petitioned the court to remove Guo from his official position, and eventually the print blocks of his book were ordered to be destroyed. Therefore, his diaries on traveling in Europe written in his last two years as an ambassador were not printed, and it was not until 1984, nearly a century later, that the diaries were published with the title *Diaries Written in London and Paris* (《伦敦与巴黎日记》), based on his manuscripts.[4] *A Record of an Envoy's Journey to the West* was accused of acknowledging that Western countries also had 2,000 years of civilization and comparing Western civilization with China's. His subordinate, Vice Ambassador Liu Xihong (刘锡鸿), called Guo "traitor" behind his back and listed three accusations against him, which were indeed weird, and I might as well copy them here: "Firstly, he draped a foreigner's coat over his shoulders when visiting the London battery, which he should not have done even though it was freezing. Secondly, he stood up voluntarily when meeting the ruler of Brazil. How can an ambassador from the Heavenly Dynasty pay respect to the ruler of such a small country? Thirdly, he imitated foreigners and read the concert program when listening to music at Buckingham Palace."[5] In fact, Guo Songtao went on diplomatic mission at the age of fifty-eight (he celebrated his sixtieth birthday in London) and traveled over 80,000 *li* to and from Europe. From his diaries we can see that when he visited the countries, he was quite earnest in exploring the education, ship management, and public law about not killing captives, and tried to learn more about the religions and prison management of European countries. He

---

[4]   Guo Songtao, *Diaries Written in London and Paris*. Changsha: Yuelu Press, 1984.
[5]   The impeachment by Liu Xihong is quoted from "On Guo Songtao"(《论郭嵩焘》) by Zhong Shuhe (钟叔河), collected in Guo Songtao's *Diaries Written in London and Paris*.

even went as far as identifying the national flag, navy flag, and flags of commercial ships of each European country, which he did for nothing but the interest of his own country and people.

Like Guo Songtao, Xue Fucheng also paid attention to the prison management in foreign countries and wrote this in his *Diaries Written on Mission to Britain, France, Italy, and Belgium* (《出使英法义比四国日记》). At that time, prison management in China was extremely poor and life there was a real torture, so in his diaries, Xue Fucheng described prisons in Paris like this: "[The prisoners] are paid to work; the wages are their personal gains and shall not be confiscated. They may spend it to buy food, and some even

3.10. Copperplate portrait of Guo Songtao

have savings. … In winter, coal is used to keep the cells warm. This prison spends 30,000 francs each winter to buy coal." Xue Fucheng was a staff member under Zeng Guofan and was one of the "Four Assistants of Zeng Guofan," another being Li Shuchang. Before he went abroad, Xue felt Guo Songtao's "generous praises of the state governance and mores of Western countries" were "overstatements," but when he was appointed as Ambassador to Britain, France, Italy, and Belgium during the four and a half years from 1890 to 1894 and saw the Western countries with his own eyes, he began "to believe what the Assistant Minister [referring to Guo Songtao] said, which shall be closely examined through the parliaments, schools, prisons, hospitals, and streets." He also went into great detail about the streets of Paris, as well as the Eiffel Tower, which he had climbed soon after it was constructed and described with a literary delicacy: "Each story higher, one can find everything down on the ground one time smaller, and at the top of the tower, the entire city of Paris is under you. It seems you have ridden on the wind and been isolated from the world." When he again climbed the tower several years later, he calculated the tower's gains based on the statistics of initial investment and cost, number of visitors, ticket income, and stock profit, and figured out the reason why Western countries could "acquire so much wealth." Xue Fucheng took an interest in business profit, but he was also renowned for his literary talent. He was praised for the concise and vivid description in his diaries of oil paintings and wax figures he saw in Paris, which were often included in textbooks on literary writing.

Another of the "Four Assistants of Zeng Guofan," Li Shuchang went to the United Kingdom with Guo Songtao in 1867. From the following year, he was frequently transferred between the embassies of Germany, France, and Spain, until he was promoted as Ambassador to Japan in 1881. He wrote down his experience in Europe in a book entitled *Miscellaneous Records of the West*

(《西洋杂志》). The book was called "Miscellaneous Records" because it was not, like the diaries of the above diplomats, organized in a chronological or geographical order, but was devoted to the social customs of European countries, and was a combination of travelogue, correspondence, and geographic essays. Li Shuchang had a unique point of view when observing European society. For example, he paid less attention to political exchanges between countries, and gave more detailed information about the etiquette and customs of each country, including such significant matters as the reception of letters of credence, dress codes for certain ceremonies, ceremonial military reviews, and assembling of parliament, through to such trivial matters as engagement and marriage, and how to host a dance party at home. "Celebrating Child Birth in Advance" (《预贺生子》) and "Verification of the Newborn" (《生子女取证》) were interesting records about how the Queen of Spain received congratulations from ministers in the court and foreign officials when she was five months pregnant; on the day she gave birth, the ministers and ambassadors were invited to wait outside the delivery room, and the newborn was placed on a silver tray and taken out of the delivery room to be verified. Li also wrote down his experience of a hydrogen-balloon ride. What is also worth mentioning is his passion for human geography. Seeing the czar's attempt to expand Russian territory, Li Shuchang proposed to travel and conduct geographical examinations in the Siberian area of Russia, for which he translated and collected geographical material and wrote essays, of which "An Outline of the Route from Beijing to Mongolia and then to the Capital of Russia" (《由北京出蒙古中路至俄都路程考略》) and "An Outline of the Route from the Asian Region of Russia to Ili and Other Places" (《由亚西亚俄境西路至伊犁等处路程考略》) were collected in his book. These were not just a mechanical cluttering of documentation. As an example, here is his outline of the entire route:

> One should go by paddle steamer to travel from Shanghai to Tianjin, then change to a Chinese sailboat from Tianjin to Tongzhou, and use a string of mules to go from Tongzhou to Beijing. From Beijing to Zhangjiakou (Kalgan in Mongolian) one should go by sedan chair carried by mules. Then one should ride a camel from Zhangjiakou to Khyaagta, and from Khyaagta to the Russian train station one should take a Russian four-wheeler.[6]

He also wrote down detailed instructions about how to go through the desert in Mongolia and how to hire a carriage:

> One may ride a camel or horse to go through the desert in Mongolia, and Mongolian-style saddles shall be used if one chooses to ride a horse. One may start the journey in July (the seventh month of the Western calendar,

[6]   Li Shuchang, *Miscellaneous Records of the West*, Changsha: Yuelu Press, 1985, p. 549.

which is the end of the fifth month or beginning of the sixth month of the traditional Chinese calendar), when the grass grows high and can be used to feed the pack animals. If one goes fast and changes horse every day, he may go through the desert in twelve days, but it is quite a tough journey, for it is 800 miles long, which is 2,400 *li*. (Chapter 1)

…

One has to travel by night and day from Khyaagta to the capital of Russia, and everything one needs on the road may be purchased in Khyaagta. The most important things one should purchase there are tea and sugar, and one should change [silver coins] into copper coins, which will be used to buy trivial stuff and give the carriage drivers as tips. One should obtain an official passport before the journey and submit it to the Russian minister, who will affix an official seal on it. One should take as few belongings as possible, and the packages shall not be too large lest they hurt the camel or horse, and small packages are easier to be put on and taken off the carriage. (Chapter 1)[7]

It seemed that only an intellectual who had received both traditional Chinese education on the art of government and Western-style practical training could write such texts.

Those who wrote overseas travelogues and diaries can be divided into several categories. The earliest were translators and secretaries going abroad with foreigners, such as Luo Sen (罗森) and Bin Chun (斌椿), whose texts were no more than superficial scribblings of what they saw outside the national border. Then there were the above-mentioned diplomats, who recorded their observations for later reference. The third category were nonofficial individuals, such as Xu Jianyin (徐建寅, 1845–1901), Li Gui (李圭, 1842–1903), and Qian Shan Shili (钱单士厘, 1856–1943), who had unique perspectives in their description of the outside world.

At seventeen years of age, Xu Jianyin was taken by his father, Xu Shou (徐寿), to work at Anqing Arsenal, founded by Zeng Guofan, where they independently manufactured China's very first ship, *Huanghu* (黄鹄号). Then Xu Shou and his son manufactured even more warships and cannons, for which they also prepared gunpowder and nitric acid. In 1879, when Xu Jianyin was working at Shandong

3.11. Block-printed edition of Li Shuchang's *Miscellaneous Records of the West*, in which "杂志" is part of the title and not its usual meaning, "magazine"

---

7   Li Shuchang, *Miscellaneous Records of the West*, p. 550.

Machinery Bureau, he was selected by Li Hongzhang (李鸿章, 1823–1901), a Chinese politician, general, and diplomat of the late-Qing dynasty, to be sent to Germany to purchase warships for the North China Navy and took the chance to travel around Europe. He was among the few first-class engineering experts in China. *Miscellaneous Records of My Voyages to Europe* (《欧游杂录》) was a faithful record of his visits to more than eighty factories and research institutes in Germany, France, and the United Kingdom, and it was indeed different from those of the diplomats. For example, he frequently traveled between Paris and Berlin, but he paid no attention to the streets; instead, he once went to a public bathroom, and later wrote in great detail about the exact size of the bathtub, even including the number of steps one took from the bathtub down to the ground. Needless to say, as an engineer, he kept a careful record of the appearance, structure, and performance of each Western machine he saw. He went to Europe to learn from foreigners, and during his trip he became aware of the fact that the equipment imported by China was actually good enough, but the products made in China were inferior to those made in foreign countries. According to Xu Jianyin: "I have seen the equipment used by gunpowder manufacturers in Germany, which is not as good as the equipment used in manufacturing bureaus in Tianjin, Nanjing, Jinan, and Shanghai, but why is the gunpowder made here in Germany better than the gunpowder made in China? The reason is that people here are extremely careful when conducting experiments and in measuring tension, speed, and weight, etc., and try their best to eliminate errors whenever they are found. There is no other secret to success."[8] Here Xu went beyond general talks about technological improvement and pointed out the gap in management personnel between China and foreign countries, which was why his field trip was superior to others. He became aware of the difference in administrative abilities, the gap in terms of "people" instead of "equipment." He surely could not imagine that later in the First Sino-Japanese War, the largest and most cutting-edge warships bought during this trip, *Zhenyuan* (镇远号) and *Dingyuan* (定远号), would be defeated by the Japanese warships that were far more inferior to them in every aspect and sunk in the Yellow Sea. The competitions in science and technology between countries around the world were eventually determined by people's abilities and capabilities. During his trip to Berlin, Xu Jianyin saw the latest scientific miracle, a robot, in an exhibition of wax figures. Here is his report on the robot:

> A new wax figure has come to the yard. His appearance and clothing are like those of a living person, and he can write at a desk. On his feet there are wheels, so that he can be pushed and placed wherever one likes.

---

[8]   Xu Jianyin: *Miscellaneous Records of My Voyages to Europe*, Changsha: Yuelu Press, 1985, p. 701.

Turning down his clothes, one can see complex gears and wheels on his chest, and thus see through his mechanism. Turning on the power, the wax figure will use one hand to press the paper and use another to write. If you write numbers on his palm and knock on it, he will make the calculation and write down the answer, though he cannot speak the answer. Its performance is just beyond imagination.[9]

For a Chinese individual of more than 100 years ago who was still wearing their hair in a queue, this was something truly incredible.

New Record of My Voyage around the Globe (《环游地球新录》) was written by Li Gui during his voyage around the globe after his trip to the World Exposition in Philadelphia as a representative of China's business and commerce circle. Li Gui was found competent by H. E. Hobson, the Englishman who was the Inspector of Ningbo Customs Office, and appointed as the latter's secretary (in the late-Qing period, the customs officials of many provinces were Englishmen, including the Inspector-General of Chinese Maritime Customs Service, Robert Hart). He made this trip ten years after that, when the World Exposition was held in the United States as part of the celebration of the 100th anniversary of the Declaration of Independence. Li Gui's book

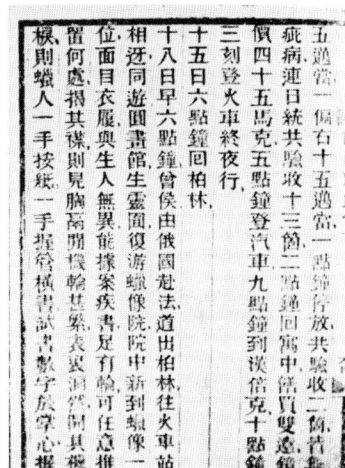

3.12. Description of robots in *Miscellaneous Records of My Voyages to Europe*

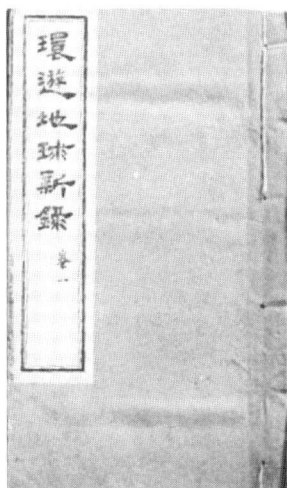

3.13. Li Gui's *New Record of My Voyage around the Globe*

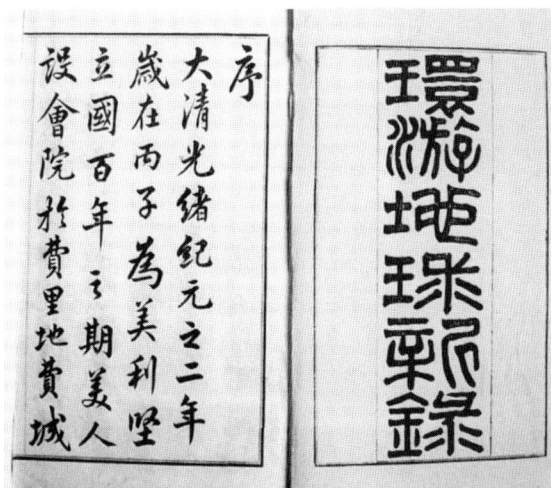

3.14. Li Gui's *New Record of My Voyage around the Globe* and its foreword written by Li Hongzhang

9 Ibid., p. 777.

first described the fair's pavilions and halls, especially the US Pavilion and the China Pavilion, then it recorded the author's journey around the United States and Europe after the Expo, and finally recounted the author's eastbound voyage around the globe. During the Expo, he admired and praised the 1,500-horse-power Corliss steam engine, which was indeed a colossal invention of the time. Bearing China's specific conditions in mind, Li Gui paid special attention to the agricultural machineries exhibited at the fair, and observed that China's neighbor, Japan, ordered eighteen kinds of agricultural machineries at the fair (naturally, the Great Qing would not do such a humiliating thing). As for the paintings of female nudes displayed in the gallery, Li's understanding was quite enlightened: "It is actually easier to paint beauties in clothes but more difficult to paint them nude, for one should pay great attention to the nuanced veins and lines on the nude body, and the subtlest defects would show. The same is true for stone carvings and copper sculptures. So the use of nudes epitomizes the painters' and sculptors' artistic achievements, not deliberate presentation of disagreeable works."[10] This was much earlier than the uproar over nude models being used at Liu Haisu's Shanghai Art School, and Li's viewpoint was much more up to date. Then, seeing the work of Chinese children (selected by Rong Hong) studying in the United States displayed at the fair, and that more than 100 Chinese children were coming to the fair and were received by the president of the United States, Li wrote the section entitled "On the Children Coming to the Fair" (《书幼童观会事》), noting "I saw the children visiting the halls and pavilions, where they felt quite comfortable and at home in front of so many people. They were mostly dressed like Westerners, and only their jackets were Chinese-style. They were quite close to us, with their style of speech quite Western-like. The smaller ones followed their female teachers, with whom they talked fluently about things at the fair. They looked like intimate mothers and sons." He concluded that "the children trained in Western learnings will have a bright future."[11] It was indeed not so easy for people of that time to show such admiration for the advanced state of foreign education.

3.15. Opening Ceremony of the World Exposition, Philadelphia, on May 10, 1876. The colossal machine in the picture is the 1,500-horsepower Corliss steam engine

[10] Li Gui: *New Record of My Voyage around the Globe*, Changsha: Yuelu Press, 1985, p. 232.
[11] Ibid., p. 298–299.

On his trip to the United States, Li Gui had started from China and headed eastward, and afterward he continued east until finally he had gone around the globe. This was something he felt very proud of, so he published his "A Diary of My Travels to the East" (《东行日记》) in *Shun Pao* under the pseudonym "Global Traveler" (环游地球客). At that time, "very few" Chinese people believed "the earth is a globe moving around the sun. It is not the sun but the earth that is moving." Even Li himself was doubtful of this. Now that he had traveled around the world, he finally believed the theory, for as he said: "if the earth were square, and if it is the sun instead of the earth that is moving, how can I have started eastward from Shanghai and finally returned to Shanghai? For I have never turned westward during this 82351-*li* voyage. The reason is that the earth is a globe and there are actually no such directions as east and west on a globe."[12] This can be seen as a metaphor of Chinese intellectuals seeking truth from the outside world.

Qian Shan Shili was the wife of diplomat Qian Xun (钱恂) and sister-in-law of Qian Xuantong (钱玄同). In order to accompany and visit her husband, she had been to Japan and countries in Europe, and thus became one of the earliest Chinese women to travel overseas immediately after getting out of their private chamber. Qian Shan Shili's *A Record of My Journeys in 1903* (《癸卯旅行记》) was about her eighty-day journey from Vladivostok through Manchuria and Siberia, and then by train to Moscow and Saint Petersburg. Her literary style was feminine and elegant; take her description of the scenery near Lake Baikal for example:

> At dawn, from time to time I had a glimpse of water through the hills and trees, and I knew this was the world's largest freshwater lake, Lake Baikal (it was called White Sea in ancient China and was once called Chrysanthemum Sea during the Yuan dynasty). After the train passed Verkhneudinsk, there were dense forests and mountain ranges; the scene was beautiful, and the road extremely tough. But tough and perilous as it was, the trip was a pleasure, and we did not feel terrible. This reminded me of Su Wu (苏武) who herded sheep around the sea (referring to Lake Baikal) in the north with his eminent moral integrity. I knew he must have lived a very difficult life due to severe cold and hunger, but who could say he never enjoyed living with his family in such a secluded and peaceful place?[13]

3.16. Picture of Qian Shan Shili. As simple as her appearance was, she was one of the earliest Chinese women to travel abroad

---

[12] Li Gui: *New Record of My Voyage around the Globe*, p. 313.

[13] Qian Shan Shili: *A Record of My Journeys in 1903*, Changsha: Yuelu Press, 1985, pp. 734–735.

From a woman's perspective, she did not write about patriotism, but held that it was not a bad thing for Su Wu to live in retirement in such a quiet place. The book was first published in Japan in 1904 and caused a stir there. She described Russia under the autocratic rule of the czar as a backward but vast and beautiful country. Since she had traveled in Japan and Europe, she was keenly aware of the shortcomings of Russia, especially the carelessness, arrogance, and dishonesty of officials, as well as people's ineffectiveness under high pressure, things like that. The Siberian Railway displayed in the Russia Pavilion at the Paris Exposition was highly praised as cutting-edge, but traveling on the railway, she found managerial flaws everywhere. The route they took on the train to Russia was one from nomad communities through agricultural society to industrial society, making it a historical landscape of Eurasia. It was certainly unusual for a woman from feudal China to unfold such a landscape in front of us.

Such can be seen as a typical literary phenomenon, to widen one's horizon by traveling abroad and recording the experience with "travelogues." These travelogues were not written purely for the sake of traveling or entertainment; the writers tried to express their political views in them. Then there were those written a bit later, at the beginning of the twentieth century, including Kang Youwei's *Traveling in Italy* (《意大利游记》) and *Traveling in France* (《法兰西游记》, later combined into *Traveling in Eleven Countries in Europe* (《欧洲十一国游记》), and Liang Qichao's *Traveling around the New Continent* (《新大陆游记》), which were better known. Certainly, the

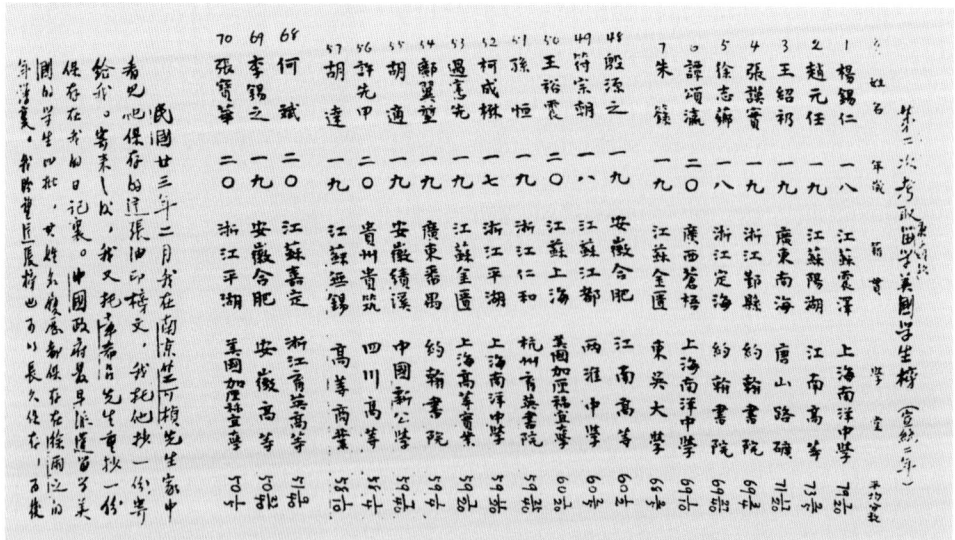

3.17. List (written from memory) of candidates for the Chinese Educational Mission in the second year of the Xuantong era (1910). The second was Zhao Yuanren and the fifty-fifth was Hu Shi. They were successors of the youths sent abroad under the same mission mentioned earlier in this chapter

person who made the greatest achievement in writing about the world with poetry and prose was Huang Zunxian, who will be discussed in the next chapter as a major member of Liang Qichao's "new literary style" movement. However, one or two generations of Chinese intellectuals had been abroad before Huang Zunxian, and if we draw a map of all their traveling routes, including the Russian railway route taken by Qian Shan Shili and her husband, the sea route to the United Kingdom taken by Wang Tao and Guo Songtao, the sea route to the United States taken by Rong Hong, the land and sea route to Europe taken by Xue Fucheng and Xu Jianyin, and the global sea route taken by Li Gui, we can see that all together, they had covered quite a large area around the world. These people originally belonged to the Westernization Group; while enlightened about science and democracy after traveling abroad, they got to know something about modern civil management, legal systems, humanity, education, science and technology, and political systems, and began to show some tendencies of the Reformation Group. These people were loyal to the Qing court and opposed Sun Yat-sen's revolution, but at that time they were indeed the most sensible intellectuals in China. They were the predecessors of Hu Shi and his peers.

FOUR

THE POLITICALLY MOTIVATED "NEW LITERARY STYLE" MOVEMENT

THE MILESTONE THAT MARKED THE BEGINNING OF MODERN Chinese literature was the May Fourth New Cultural movement, and the "new literary style" initiated by Liang Qichao could be seen as the preparation by late-Qing literary scholars for the advent of modern literature. To name the most distinguished figure of this literary period, albeit not a writer in the purely literary sense, it shall be the man who promoted the reformation of both the Chinese language and various literary genres, who was among the first to wear both Western-style business suits and Mandarin jackets, the advocate of social reformation, Liang Qichao (1873–1929). Liang was younger than most social reformers of the late-Qing period. He was born thirty-two years after Gong Zizhen passed away, was twenty-five years younger than Huang Zunxian and nearly twenty years younger than Yan Fu. He once wrote about his birthdate like this: "I was born on the twenty-sixth of the first lunar month of the Kuiyou year under Emperor Tongzhi's reign, ten years after the Taiping Heavenly Kingdom uprising had been put down in Jinling, one year after the grand academician of Qing, Zeng Guofan, passed away, three years after the eruption of the Franco-Prussian War, and the year when the Italian parliament declared the creation of the Kingdom of Italy in Rome (which was actually on Feb. 18, 1861)."[1] This was quite a compelling presentation of his universal outlook and breadth of vision.

---

[1] Liang Qichao: "Self-Account at the Age of 30" (《三十自述》), *Selected Works of Liang Qichao* (《梁启超选集》), Shanghai: Shanghai People's Press, 1984, p. 375.

The ideas of "reformation" and "innovation" that we are familiar with today were actually expressed by the term "revolution" during Liang's time. At first Liang followed his tutor Kang Youwei and assisted Emperor Guangxu in the latter's doomed reformation, and then he advocated constitutionalism, and later applauded the republic form of government, taking on such important positions as chief justice, president of Monetary Bureau, and minister of finance in the Republic of China. Then he realized that he should play a vital role in running newspapers, writing articles and doing academic research. He created the slogans "literary revolution," "poetry revolution," and "fiction revolution," which were political as well as literary. Liang made great achievements in all four literary genres, namely prose, poetry, novel, and drama; however his main focus was not on literary creation but on initiating and interpreting various literary movements during this transitional period.

Liang Qichao seized on the opportunity of classical written-style Chinese being watered down to initiate his "literary revolution," and in promoting the revolution, he invented a literary style that was most influential at that time. He did write in classical written-style Chinese, but it was different from the style of the past. People gave various names to the style: it was called "newspaper style" because his writings were different from treatises and were written for newspapers and magazines; it was called "current affairs style" because Liang was editor-in-chief of *Journal of Current Affairs* in Shanghai; and when he fled to Japan after the failure of the Wuxu Reform and launched *New Citizen* (《新民丛报》) in 1902, it was called "new citizen style." In general, it was

4.1. Young Liang Qichao, wearing a Western-style business suit; the inscription on the picture reads "One writer is stronger than 100,000 soldiers"

4.2. Middle-aged Liang Qichao, just turning forty-seven

4.3. Liang Qichao in his later years, wearing a Mandarin jacket

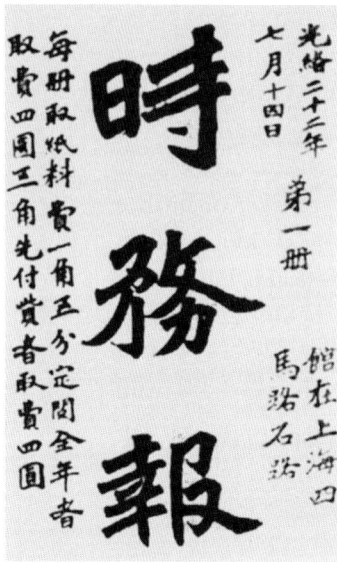

4.4. Inaugural issue of *Journal of Current Affairs* (published every ten days), founded by Liang Qichao, Wang Kangnian, and others in Shanghai in 1896, which had a circulation of over 10,000 and contributed greatly to promoting the Reformation movement

called the "new literary style." Liang Qichao had explained this style from the perspective of literary writing, and perhaps no one had ever made it clearer than himself:

I have long disliked the prose writing style of the Tongcheng School. Since childhood I learned the style of late Han, Wei, and Jin dynasties, which was quite reserved and concise. After shaking off the restraints of the old style, I always write in an easy and clear one, sometimes using slang, verses, and loan words, without constraints to my free expression of ideas. My fellow scholars try to imitate me and call it "new literary style," while those of the older generation abhor it and criticize it as vulgar. However, since my writings are well organized and often show heartfelt emotions, they are especially appealing to readers.[2]

Here he meant an understandable written-style Chinese, mixed with slang, verses, and loan words (including borrowed words and expressions). Thanks to the unity between written and spoken language, this style facilitated logical and convincing argument, and one could hardly stop when finding something to say. This style was thus best for introducing new words and concepts and enlightening people. Political propaganda in this style may have a conceptual and emotional impact on readers. Let's look at Liang's major work "On the Young China" (《少年中国说》, 1900), which best exemplifies this style. The essay begins with:

The Japanese are used to calling our China the old empire, over and over again. They might get this idea from the Westerners. Alas! Is China indeed old? Liang Qichao says: Oh, what kind of understanding is this! What kind of understanding is this! I have a young China in my heart.[3]

Here he came straight to the point at the beginning, with his opinion clearly expressed, showing a strong tendency toward political commentary. The next paragraph starts with "Talking about whether a country is old or young, let's

[2]   Liang Qichao: *Intellectual Trends in the Ching [Qing] Period: Confucius Philosophy* (《清代学术 概论·儒家哲学》), Tianjin: Tianjin Classics Publishing House, 2003, p. 77.
[3]   Liang Qichao: "On the Young China", *Selected Works of Liang Qichao*, Shanghai: Shanghai People's Press, 1984, p. 122.

first see the age-related features of people," and the whole paragraph expounds the analogy between "people" and "countries":

> old people are always tired of things, while young people are always fond of things. Those who are tired of things may find nothing to do, while those who are fond of things often find nothing cannot be done. Old people are like the setting sun, while young people are like the rising sun; old people are like lean cows, while young people are like newborn tigers; old people are like monks, while young people are like heroes; old people are like dictionaries, while young people are like dramas; old people are like opium, while young people are like brandy; old people are like an aerolite departing from a planet, while young people are like a coral island embraced by the sea; old people are like the pyramids in the desert of Egypt, while young people are like the newly built railroad in Siberia; old people are like late autumn willows, while young people are like early spring grass; old people are like a stagnant water pond, while young people are like the headstream of the Yangtze River. All these are differences between old people and young people. Liang Qichao says people are like this, and so are countries.[4]

The writing is intense and the rhythm fast, like wave after wave of seawater. The analogies are not only clear and understandable but contain deep meanings. The overall theme is clearly presented, and the specific words and sentences can be pondered over. Some words of foreign origin, such as brandy, planet, aerolite, Egypt, pyramid, Siberia, and railroad, may look common today, but considering this essay was written more than 100 years ago, one can truly sense the enthusiasm of Liang to embrace new things from the outside world. Certainly, to readers of later generations this style may be too elaborate and weak in logic and thus not characteristic of profound reasoning, but at that time Liang Qichao had argued with Yan Fu, translator of *Evolution and Ethics* (who introduced the theory of evolution to China and influenced Lu Xun and a whole generation of Chinese intellectuals), about this style. Yan did not think that Chinese literature needed a "revolution," stressing that his translation was not to be read by "those illiterate from the backstreets and remote rural areas," but by "those who are going to read even more ancient Chinese classics."[5] Liang bluntly criticized Yan as "in too ardent pursuit of depth and gentility, and painstakingly imitating the pre-Qin style," and he insisted the purpose of writing should be "spreading enlightened ideas among ordinary people, instead of achieving literary immortality for oneself."[6]

---

[4] Ibid., pp. 122–123.

[5] See "Letter to Liang Qichao" (《与梁启超书》) (2), *Collection of Yan Fu* (《严复集》), Beijing: Zhonghua Book Company, 1986, Vol. 3, pp. 516–517.

[6] See Liang Qichao's review of Yan Fu's translation of Adam Smith's *The Wealth of Nations* in the inaugural issue of *New Citizen*.

And so it was that Liang's new concept considered acceptance by general readers as the real purpose of writing.

Certainly, Liang Qichao won the support of most people of his time. Talking about how their own thinking and writing styles took shape, many people born at the end of the nineteenth century and who became known during the May Fourth movement mentioned Liang's extremely popular "new literary style." Hu Shi once said: "Mr. Liang showed his strong and sincere emotions in his easy and smooth essays, so that readers could not help following him and thinking like him."[7] Recalling Liang Qichao's influence on him, Guo Moruo (郭沫若) even said "young people of twenty years ago, be they proponents or opponents of Liang, arguably every one of them was influenced by his thoughts or writings."[8] And according to Mao Zedong's (毛泽东) conversation with Edgar Snow about his experience at the First Normal School of Hunan, his Chinese teacher scorned his writing style (imitating Liang Qichao): "He ridiculed my essays, dismissing them as written in a journalist style. He thought little of my model Liang Qichao, mocking at Liang as semi-learned."[9] These were specific examples showing that Liang's "new literary style" was actually a precedent of the May Fourth style, and that both were of the same tradition. During Liang Qichao's time, classical written-style Chinese was already largely weakened, and he vernacularized it by introducing into it his own themes and techniques. From the time Liang proposed the "literary revolution," he insisted on two principles. Firstly, the purpose of reforming the literary style was to spread enlightened ideas and cultivate "new citizens." The concept of "new citizens" raised by Liang Qichao was different from the "development of individual man" proposed by Lu Xun in 1908 in his "On Cultural Extremes" (《文化偏至论》), but they were somewhat related. Secondly, all established styles, ancient or modern, Chinese or foreign, should not become set frames and scaffolding, and the "gap between written and oral language presentations" should be bridged. Liang Qichao once said: "When written and spoken forms of Chinese are unified, new words and expressions of spoken Chinese may be immediately incorporated into written Chinese. New nouns and new artistic conceptions may find their place in the written language, which may thus keep abreast of the times. On the other hand, when written and spoken forms of Chinese are separated, the new words and expressions in spoken Chinese cannot be incorporated into the written language, or what are incorporated cannot be explained, or what are explained cannot be used easily and freely.

---

[7]   See Hu Shi: *An Autobiographical Account at Forty* (《四十自述》), Shanghai: East Asian Library Press, 1941, p. 100.

[8]   See Guo Moruo: *My Childhood* (《少年时代》), Shanghai: Petrel Bookstore, 1947, p. 126.

[9]   Edgar Snow (dictated): *The Autobiography of Mao Tse-tung*, translated by Wang Heng, Beijing: People's Liberation Army Art Press, 2001, pp. 26–27.

Therefore, even if there is an opportunity for the language to be updated, it is shackled."[10] Obviously, the goal he wanted to achieve through his "new literary style," the "unification of written and spoken forms of Chinese," was generally interrelated with the May Fourth vernacular movement a dozen years later. The difference was that Liang's time was a transitional period from written-style Chinese to vernacular Chinese, and his "new literary style" represented the spirit of reformation, while the May Fourth vernacular movement claimed to abandon the outdated classical written-style Chinese.

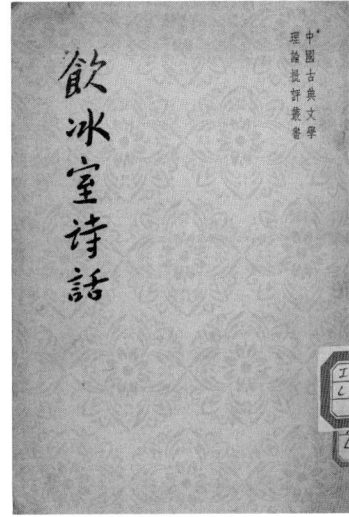

4.5. *Poetry Talks from the Ice-Drinking Studio*

What really fell into the category of literary movement were "poetry revolution" and "fiction revolution." Liang proposed the term "poetry revolution" in the essay "Traveling around Hawaii" (《夏威夷游记》) written in 1899. Before that, like Tan Sitong and Xia Zengyou, he had gone through a kind of transitional period of "poetry of new learning." After the *Journal of Pure Critique* (《清议报》) was launched, Liang began a literary column called Random Notes on Poetry and Prose (诗文辞随录), in which he published a number of Huang Zunxian's poems together with his own criticism. Later he started the column Tidy Sound of Poetry (诗界潮音集) in *New Citizen*, published *Poetry Talks from the Ice-Drinking Studio* there, and wrote the column Miscellaneous Ballads (杂歌谣) in the journal *New Fiction* (《新小说》); all could be seen as his efforts to promote poetic innovation. At that time, Liang Qichao had already thought about the malpractice of piling up new terms in the "poetry of new learning," saying: "A revolution is destined to happen in the transitional period, while the revolution should be a spiritual instead of a formal one. Recently, people of our party like to talk about poetry revolution, but if a revolution means piling up new nouns, how is it different from the Reformation of the Manchu government? Only if one can promote new artistic conceptions within the old frame may the spirit of revolution be truly realized."[11] Therefore, Liang proposed two standards for the poetry revolution, new words and expressions, and new artistic conceptions, and he gave the latter more weight. He himself wrote literati poetry and promoted the folk-ballad style; in his old age, he wrote some vernacular poems and occasionally wrote some vernacular discourses.

---

[10] Liang Qichao: "On Progress" (《论进步》), Section 11, *About New Citizens* (《新民说》), *Selected Works of Liang Qichao*, Shanghai: Shanghai People's Press, 1984, p. 236.

[11] Liang Qichao: *Poetry Talks from the Ice-Drinking Studio*, p. 51.

When he became friends with Liang Qichao, Huang Zunxian (1848–1905) was already elderly, but both had a global outlook and aspiration for reformation. In the very first of his autobiographical *Assorted Quatrains of 1899* (《己亥杂诗》), Huang wrote: "I hail from north, south, east, and west; / All my life I've been known as a man of wind and waves; / I spent half a century wandering the world's continents; / And will remain at home for another fifty springs!" (我是东西南北人，平生自号风波民。百年过半洲游四，留得家园五十春。) In an adieu poem written for his Japanese friends, Huang wrote: "In the past we were enemies in the same boat, / While today we are wandering people from neighboring countries. / Along the 23,000-*li* road ahead of us, we are people from north, south, east, and west." (昔日同舟多敌国，而今四海总比邻。更行二万三千里，等是东西南北人。) (the fifth of "Adieu Poems for My Japanese Friends on the Order to Assume the Position of Consul General in San Francisco" [《奉命为美国三富兰西士果总领事留别日本诸君子》]) A poet who liked to call himself "a person from north, south, east, and west," Huang had thirteen or fourteen years' experience of traveling abroad: from 1877 to 1882 he worked as a counsellor in Japan, and from 1882 to 1885 he was transferred to San Francisco to take the position of Consul General, which he did not resume after returning home to visit his family as he stayed at home to write a 40-volume, 500,000-character *Treatise on Japan* (《日本国志》), a document compiled based on the idea of reformation, which Emperor Guangxu later publicly announced he wanted to read when he sought help in the time of emergency in the year of Wuxu Reform. From 1890 to 1891 Huang went on a diplomatic mission to Europe with Xue Fucheng, and from 1891 to 1894 he was transferred to the position of Consul General to Singapore. Before the Wuxu Reform, he had two opportunities to go on diplomatic missions in Germany and Japan, respectively, but both aborted for some reason. Even so, he was the late-Qing literary scholar with the longest and most rewarding overseas experience. Thanks to such experience, he wrote 200 poems collected as *Poems on Miscellaneous Subjects from Japan* (《日本杂事诗》), and of the nearly 700 poems in his anthology *Assorted Poetry from the Hut Within the Human Realm* (《人境庐诗草》), one third were about his travels abroad, such as "I Composed This Poem Gazing at the Moon from a Ship in the Pacific Ocean on the Night of the Mid-Autumn Festival" (《八月十五夜太平洋舟中望月作歌》), "Assorted Poetry on Singapore" (《新加坡杂诗》), "The Great London Fog" (《伦敦大雾行》), "On the Ancient Pillar of Egypt" (《埃及国古柱》), "On the Closure of Educational Mission in America" (《罢美国留学感赋》), and "On Foreign Guests" (《番客篇》), etc. What's more important than these poetic lines, however, was that such overseas experience helped him develop a unique literary and poetic style, through which we can see his broad knowledge of world history and enlightened and critical outlook, as well as the perspective he gained from looking at China from the outside world. On the one hand, he felt that China was no more than a country within the huge world, not as significant as Chinese people boasted, which he did not realize until after traveling abroad. An example of this can be seen in "(Three Poems on) My Feelings of Events" (《感事（三首）》): "China has been there since the ancient times, / And all around it there were barbarian and savage nations. / While we did not know that there were eight continents outside China covering over 21,000 miles, / Where there are great nations with 2,000-year history." (芒芒九有古禹域，南北东西尽戎狄。岂知七万余里大九洲，竟有二千年来诸大国。) Traveling across the Pacific Ocean to the United States, his bosom was suddenly opened wide. In "Assorted Feelings on Traveling Overseas" (《海行杂感》), he wrote: "The Nine Provinces are small and the Three Islands look tiny, / Indeed, we human beings shall turn our eyes to the whole universe." (九点烟微三岛小，人间世要纵婆娑。) "Nine Provinces" meant China and "Three Islands" referred to Japan, and both became small when looking from the Pacific. Then he wrote: "Stars are flashing all over the sky, / And the boundary between the world and the universe blurs. / If there are people traveling across the Milky Way, / I believe they must feel the earth is but a small ball." (星星世界遍诸天，不计三千与大千。倘亦乘槎中有客，回头望我地球圆。) Even the earth is not that large any more. Huang Zunxian was indeed among the very few in the late-Qing period with such great ambitions and aspirations. On the other hand, whatever Huang Zunxian wrote about China, he could shift his focus from specific events to a larger picture of society. Besides these overseas poems, he also wrote many patriotic poems, which were regarded by many as "epics." Huang Zunxian was born after the First Opium War and died just before the Xinhai Revolution, and his lifetime was an eventful period for China: the annexation of the Liuqiu Islands by Japan; the Sino-French War; the first Sino-Japanese War of 1894; the Wuxu Reform; and the Gengzi Incident were all mentioned in his poems, and he sometimes even wrote a sequence of poems to express his patriotic sentiments. In some of them he expressed his cares and worries frankly, such as "Songs of Liuqiu" (《琉球歌》), "Songs of General Feng" (《冯将军歌》), and "On the Eight-Nation Alliance's Invasion of Beijing on July 21" (《七月二十一日八国联军入犯京师》), while in others he used analogies to show such feelings implicitly, such as in the following lines in "Watching the Moon on the River on the Thirteenth Night of the Fifth Lunar Month" (《五月十三夜江行望月》): "I shed so many tears that they might fill the East Sea, / And today the moon is again round. / The river is still the same as in the past, / But the world has changed such a lot." (洒泪填东海，而今月一圆，江流仍此水，世界竟何年。) Here the poet seemed to write about the moon and the river, but actually he was thinking about the humiliation of China's defeat by Japan in the maritime war of 1894. These lines in "Climbing

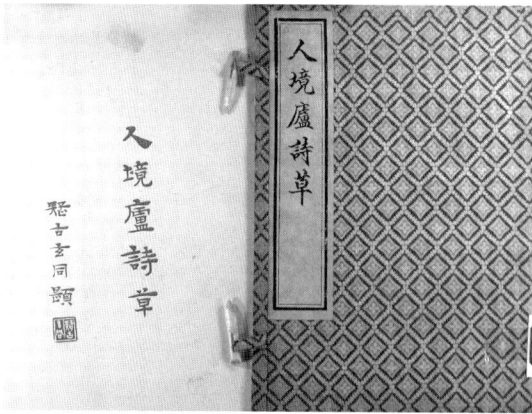

4.6. *Assorted Poetry from the Hut Within the Human Realm*

the Tower of Huanghe" (《上黄鹤楼》): "Watching the water flowing east at the top of Huanghuji, / The rails remain unchanged and the autumn scene is the same as the past." (矶头黄鹄日东流，又此阑干又此秋。) The poet had climbed the tower in the past, but this time he heard the news that Taiwan had been ceded to Japan. And these lines in "Climbing the Tower of Yueyang" (《上岳阳楼》): "Be aware that suddenly Qin is overwhelmed by other strong powers, / And it is hard to define the Chinese border when drawing maps." (当心忽压秦头日，画地难分禹迹州。) It seems that as he was climbing the tower, he thought of the fact that the Yangtze River and Hunan Province were ceded to England through the competition of Western powers and felt so sad for his own country. All these showed Huang's deep feelings of love and sense of duty toward China.

Huang's overseas poems were also called "New World Poetry" by Qiu Fengjia (邱逢甲, 1864–1912), another late-Qing poet from Taiwan, who regarded Huang as a Columbus-like figure in the world of Chinese poetry. The term "New World Poetry" was an even more straightforward way to say that Huang and his fellow poets helped open up Chinese people's horizons to the outside world. In his "Preface to *Poems on Miscellaneous Subjects from Japan*" (《日本杂事诗自序》), Huang made it clear that the purpose of these poems was to correct Chinese scholar–officials' prejudices and their "ignorance and negligence" toward the world. Basically, "New World Poetry" reflected a late-nineteenth-century Chinese intellectual's approach to novelties of the world, and such a "Chinese perspective" had the following four characteristics. Firstly, it emphasized the newness of what Huang saw in foreign countries. In "Departure of Today (Four Poems)" (《今别离（四首）》), for example, he wrote about four new things of his time, namely the ship, telegraph, camera, and time zones. These were also mentioned by other intellectuals, but Huang Zunxian sought to contrast the speed brought about by these modern technologies with the grief of parting that had been felt by human beings since ancient times: "The mountains and rivers have been there since the ancient times, / So were carriages and boats that took our friends away. / Those who went away in old-style carriages and boats, / May still choose their way and their whereabouts. / On today's ships and trains however, / One feels ever deeper and more urgent grief of parting." (古亦有山川，古亦有车舟，车舟载离别，行止犹自由。今日舟与车，并力生离愁。) "The leaver has

4.7. The Hut within the Human Realm, former residence of Huang Zunxian, in Meizhou, Guangdong Province

disappeared over the horizon, / While the one left behind has not yet returned. / I try to have one more look at his departing friend, / But the only thing in sight is the thick fog on the sea." (送者未及返，君在天尽头，望影倏不见，烟波杳悠悠。) The artistic conception of these poems was thus much higher. Secondly, the poet sought to show his grief and indignation through these poems. The insult toward his nation's dignity was a reality too harsh to be accepted, and he felt it difficult to calm down without writing such poems as "Lament For Weihai" (《悲威海》) and "Driven-Out Guests" (《逐客篇》). Thirdly, Huang sought to promote new ideas so that they could be learned and adopted by the Chinese people. Such anxiety to learn from foreigners can be seen from the fact that he wrote a number of poems on the Meiji Restoration in succession. "In Donggou" (《东沟行》) was about what he had learned from the failure of China in the maritime war of 1894: "People say that strongly built ships were not as good as fast ships, / While I think one is doomed to fail without competent leaders and soldiers." (人言船坚不如疾，有器无人终委敌。) In this Huang had outpaced those of the Westernization Group. And fourthly, his poems showed higher ideals. In "Climbing the Iron Tower in Paris" (《登巴黎铁塔》), for example, he expressed his ideal to ride balloons and fly into the sky with the help of science. "Dwarfing all peaks under my feet, / I feel that the five continents are so small that they can be held by a hand. / Now that I am climbing to the top of the tower, / No wonder I am dreaming of flying in the sky." (一览小天下，五洲如在掌。既登绝顶高，更作凌风想。) And he wrote of his political ideal when watching the sun rise over the sea during a diplomatic mission in the forty-ninth of *Assorted Quatrains of 1899*: "The red, red sun is now rising in the east, / And seawater on the horizon has become a rainbow. / From now on the yellow people should be selected to hold the sun, / In the east of the East Sea of Japan." (赫赫红轮上大空，摇天海绿化为虹。从今要约黄人捧，此是扶桑东海东。) "Reclining Buddha of Ceylon" (《锡兰岛卧佛》), which was highly praised by Liang Qichao, boasted "an unprecedented poetic structure" in that it contained "a history of India," "a history of Buddhism," "a theory on the relationship between religion and politics," and "a theory on religions on the earth," and its message was quite profound.

It was the shared political and literary values that made Huang Zunxian a friend of Liang Qichao, who was more than twenty years younger than him. Originally summoned by Zhang Zhidong (张之洞) from his diplomatic mission to return home to pursue the westernization cause, Huang spoke frankly and loudly in a Western style to Zhang at their first meeting; Zhang was quite dissatisfied with this and thus refused to appoint him to important positions. Because Huang Zunxian remained out of office for many years, he had a chance to meet Liang Qichao. The two first met each other in Shanghai in 1898. Huang and others raised funds to publish the *Journal of Current Affairs* and asked Liang Qichao to be the editor-in-chief. During the time when Huang Zunxian took the position of judicial commissioner of Hunan Province and assisted Chen Baozhen to carry out political reformation in Hunan, he asked Liang Qichao to come to Hunan to preside over the Study Hall for Current Affairs. After the Wuxu Reform failed, Liang Qichao fled to Japan and Huang Zunxian was placed under house arrest in Shanghai. He refused to be rescued by his Japanese friends and was later removed from office and sent to his hometown to live in retirement. After two years' separation, he finally resumed correspondence with Liang. Huang thought very highly of Liang's "new literary style," claiming that "the *Journal of Pure Critique* was much better than the *Journal of Current Affairs*, and now the *New Citizen* is a hundred times better than *Journal of Pure Critique*. The writings are so exciting and the thought profound. The essays reflect what everybody has on their mind but nobody has ever written like this, and even those with stony hearts should be moved. These are the most powerful words since the ancient times."[12] The "poetry revolution" proposed by Liang Qichao was a major revolutionary movement to promote the transition from classical Chinese poetry to modern Chinese poetry, and Huang Zunxian was regarded by Liang as an excellent example of the "poetry revolution." Huang's ideal in poetry writing was to "discard

---

[12] Huang Zunxian: "Letter to Liang Qichao (Ninth Correspondence), I" 《致梁启超书（九通）•一》, *Collection of Huang Zunxian*, 《黄遵宪集》 Vol. 2, Tianjin: Tianjin People's Press, 2003, p. 490.

ancient people's dross and break free from the restraints set by ancient people," to write about "things not seen by ancient people and realms not opened in ancient times … one should think about something above poetry and write about people in one's poetry," and "one should not be bound by conventional style but should have one's own style." In his early days Huang once claimed that "my pen should reflect what I say and what I think; how can I be bound by an ancient style," and in his old age he made some efforts to write popular poems and songs, including "Songs of the Army" (《出军歌》, eight songs), "School Songs of Kindergartens" (《幼稚园上学歌》, ten songs), "Chorus Songs for Primary School Students" (《小学校学生相和歌》, nineteen songs). He also learned to write folk songs, such as "What Is Said by Five Birds" (《五禽言》, five songs) and "Ballads" (《山歌》, six

4.8. Inaugural issue of Liang Qichao's *New Fiction*

songs), etc.[13] These poetic assertions agreed with the goals of the "poetry revolution," and therefore, Liang constantly published and promoted Huang Zunxian's poems in his own newspapers and journals, saying that "one should read the poems of Gongdu (公度, Huang Zunxian's courtesy name), for they open a unique realm and boast a unique style in the twentieth-century poetic world." "Reading four of Huang Gongdu's 'Songs of the Army' makes me extremely happy … His spirit is no doubt glorious, lively, vigorous, and profound, and the words and expressions he uses have never been used in the past 2,000 years. It is the highest achievement of the poetry revolution." Indeed, Huang Zunxian's literary achievements would have been out of the question if he had not become a person with an international outlook, and it is this that made the two perfect friends for each other.

As for the "fiction revolution," Liang Qichao fully participated in every aspect of this movement; he proposed the slogan, edited, wrote, and translated novels, and elaborated modern theories on this specific literary genre. In 1912 he launched *New Fiction* (《新小说》) in Tokyo, which was the first journal in Chinese history to specialize in fiction, and was the very first of four major fiction journals in the late Qing. However, we should always bear in mind that Liang Qichao's ultimate goal in launching the journal was political reform and intellectual enlightenment, and the fiction was used as a means to achieve this goal, and thus he had never entertained the idea of "art for art's sake." On the contrary, what he promoted was a kind of political fiction. Even in translation, he chose *The Adventure of a Beauty* (《佳人奇遇》), which

---

[13] See *Collection of Huang Zunxian*, Vol. 1, Tianjin: Tianjin People's Press, 2003.

4.9. Second issue of *New Fiction*, the journal Liang Qichao used as a means to promote the "fiction revolution"

was by no means a masterpiece in Japanese literary history, and wrote "Translator's Foreword to *The Adventure of a Beauty*," whose title was later changed to "Foreword to the Publication of Political Novels in Translation" (《译印政治小说序》) and itself became one of his important essays on literary theories. In the foreword he wrote: "Political novels contributed the most to the political progress of the United States, United Kingdom, Germany, France, Austria, Italy, and Japan. Just as a British elite once proposed: 'Novels shall be used to enlighten common people.'"[14] From this we can see that Liang put much emphasis on the political function of novels. His essay "On the Relationship between Novels and Governance of Society" (《论小说与群治之关系》), which was published in the inaugural issue of *New Fiction*, was even better known, and the discourse at the beginning and end of the essay is familiar to many:

In order to empower people of a country, one must first vitalize the country's novels. Therefore, new novels are necessary to promote morality, ameliorate religions, reform politics, invigorate customs, and enhance education, as well as fundamentally change people's spirit and characters. Why is that? Because novels have an incredible power to dominate human nature.

4.10. Liang Qichao's handwritten copy of the remaining stone inscription on Mount Tai written by Li Si (李斯, 284–208BC), a prime minister of the Qin dynasty

4.11. Example of Liang Qichao's handwriting

[14] Liang Qichao: "Foreword to the Publication of Political Novels in Translation," *Journal of Pure Critique*, 1898, Issue 1.

> Therefore today's reform of social governance must start from the fiction revolution. A new society is impossible without new novels.[15]

Such overemphasis on the role of fiction was in itself an improper practice, if it were not for making the point that "the novel is the supreme form of literature."[16] Some people even claim that the phenomenon of literature and art serving nothing but political purposes, a practice dominating the latter half of the twentieth century, shall be attributed to Liang Qichao. This is certainly an exaggeration of Liang's role in this, for the idea that one should "write to convey truth" had been a long-held tradition in China for several thousand years, and it is unfair to put the blame on Liang Qichao alone. Liang Qichao's viewpoint was certainly biased when he saw literature and art as a political tool, but it was not wrong to emphasize the role of novels in shaping the national spirit. In addition, the novel literary genre was traditionally not given enough attention; largely used to tell historical stories to ordinary people, novels were not on a par with poetry and essays in ancient Chinese literature. In proposing that the novel was the "supreme" literary genre, Liang Qichao did a kind of pioneering work, and at least partly thanks to his efforts, the novel has indeed become the foremost form of literature since the twentieth century.

Liang Qichao also wrote the type of novel he himself promoted. His only political novel, *A Future Record of New China* (《新中国未来记》), was published in the inaugural issue of *New Fiction*, and it was said that his original purpose in launching this journal was to publish this literary work. The narration of the novel "started from the Boxer Uprising and ended at the fiftieth year from today," but it was not finished, and only five chapters were actually written. The existing text was about a fictional event, the Shanghai Expo in 1962 to celebrate the fiftieth anniversary of the Reform movement, and then flashed back to several decades earlier when members of the reformist group, Huang Keqiang (黄克强) and Li Qubing (李去病), returned home from Europe and contacted their comrades to promote reform, and they had some quarrels and debates. From the remaining text, we can see that the author had not even started to develop the first fictional plot he originally designed – "a province in the southern part of China announced independence, and people of exceptional abilities from all over the country assisted the independent cause and helped it to establish a republic and constitutional government" – this was not even mentioned.[17] The novel was arguably a typical example of the

---

[15] Liang Qichao: "On the Relationship between Novels and Governance of Society," *Critical Material on Theories of the Twentieth-Century Chinese Novel* (《二十世纪中国小说理论资料》), Vol. 1, Beijing: Peking University Press, 1997, pp. 50, 53–54.

[16] Ibid., p. 51.

[17] Editorial Office of New Fiction: "New Fiction, China's Only Literary Journal" (《中国唯一之文学报〈新小说〉》), *Critical Material on Theories of the Twentieth-Century Chinese Novel*, Vol. 1, Beijing: Peking University Press, 1997, p. 61.

"new fiction" advocated by Liang Qichao, for it gave expression to the new thoughts and visions of Chinese political reformers of his time in the old form of a linked-chapter novel, and the narration was a mixture of speeches, news reports, constitutions, treatises, and fictional plots, seeking to combine the old with the new. Liang Qichao knew that the novel was exotic even by the traditional Chinese standard of "collection of tales." After the novel was serialized in his journal for two or three chapters, he wrote: "While it seems like a collection of tales, it is not; and while it seems like a treatise, it is not; so I don't know what genre it is, and I can't help laughing at myself." But he insisted on writing in this way, because "I wish to express my political opinions and discuss national affairs, and its form could not but differ somewhat from ordinary fictions."[18] Thus the literary genre of "political novel" was consciously coined by Liang, and because they did not abide by literary rules, it was hard for political novels published in *New Fiction* to survive and be sustainable, and the ground was eventually lost to urban popular fiction writers like Wu Jianren and Zhou Guisheng (周桂笙).

Looking back we can see that throughout the literary history of the past century, it was a repeated practice to add new outlooks, new knowledge, and new images to old literary forms, which time and again echoed Liang's slogan to "introduce new conceptions in old styles." Later examples included the Mandarin Duck and Butterfly literary school, which enjoyed enduring popularity, and the earlier anti-Japanese literature, which advocated putting "new wine in old bottles." On the other hand, the May Fourth movement opened a totally new literary landscape, in which writers created totally new literature. Therefore, Liang Qichao did make preparations for vernacular May Fourth fiction and poetry writing, but the essence of his "literary revolution" was actually *reformation* instead of *revolution*, and was by no means comparable to May Fourth literature.

Later Liang Qichao withdrew from the political arena and devoted himself to teaching and academic research at China Public School, Nankai University, and Tsinghua University. Figure 4.12 is a group photo of Liang Qichao, Wang Guowei (王国维), and several others, which was taken when they were working as supervisors at Tsinghua University Research Institute. Liang had been a supervisor at the Institute for nearly ten years and enjoyed working there. He was quite erudite in traditional Chinese learning, and could draw new spirit and methods from Western science, so his *Intellectual Trends in the Ching [Qing] Period* (《清代学术概论》), *A History of Scholarship in China over the Last*

---

[18] Liang Qichao: "Introduction to *A Future Record of New China*" (《〈新中国未来记〉绪言》), *Critical Material on Theories of the Twentieth-Century Chinese Novel*, Vol. 1, Beijing: Peking University Press, 1997, p. 55.

4.12. Group photo of Wang Guowei (third from the left) and Liang Qichao (fifth from the left), both supervisors at the Tsinghua University Research Institute, and others in 1925. The academic authoritativeness of this institute was and is still considered the highest in modern Chinese history

Three Hundred Years (《中国近三百年学术史》), *Research Methods for Chinese History* (《中国历史研究法》) and others were profound academic works and showed a critical position. Some people thought that Liang Qichao, as a literary critic, actually corrected his earlier understanding that novels should be a tool for social reformation and began to pay more attention to the emotional expression and artistic values of literary works.[19] For such a major figure in the intellectual circle of China's transitional period as Liang, this remark perfectly matches his characteristic of constantly changing his ideas with time and in keeping with the historical trends. He was a prolific writer, and wrote the forty-volume *Collected Essays from the Ice-Drinker's Studio* (《饮冰室合集》) over his lifetime. He died because the doctors at Peking Union Medical College Hospital made an incorrect diagnosis and adopted the wrong treatment. When he was severely ill, he once said that "soldiers shall die on the battlefield and scholars

4.13. Group photo of Liang Qichao, his third daughter Liang Sizhuang, and his daughter-in-law Lin Huiyin, taken around 1925 when they climbed the Great Wall together. Lin showed quite an obvious Western style in this photo

[19] Xia Xiaohong (夏晓虹): "From 'Saving the Nation with Literature' to 'Emotion-Oriented Literature'" (《从'文学救国'到'情感中心'》), *Awakening and Transmission: Liang Qichao's Literary Path* (《觉世与传世——梁启超的文学道路》), Shanghai: Shanghai People's Press, 1991, Chapter 2.

shall die in the lecture room."[20] He was the father of Liang Sicheng (梁思成), a scholar in ancient Chinese architecture, and father-in-law of Lin Huiyin (林徽因), an architect and literary writer. There were a great number of valuable photos taken by them together, and this, I think, can be seen as an inseparable connection between Liang Qichao and modern Chinese literature.

4.14. Group photo of Liang Qichao and Indian poet Tagore, who was visiting China in 1924, and others

[20] Ding Wenjiang (丁文江): *A First Draft of the Long Version of Master Liang Rengong's Chronological History, Volume II* (《梁任公先生年谱长编初稿下》), Taipei: World Books (世界书局), 1972, p. 780.

FIVE

A CHRONICLE OF LITERARY EVENTS IN THE YEAR 1903 (AN ERA OF LITERARY ACCUMULATION)

THE YEAR 1903 WITNESSED A LARGE NUMBER OF MAJOR literary events, characteristic of a period that was to pave the way for modern Chinese literature. Having experienced a series of catastrophes in the years of Jiawu (1894), Wuxu (1898), and Gengzi (1901), the Qing Empire was precipitated into ruin, and thus its ideological shackles became looser than ever. The national salvation and anti-Manchu trends and literary movements mutually fed on each other, and literary authors and scholars began to play a role in the literary centers of Shanghai and Japan. At that time, Liang Qichao was caught between conservative and progressive values, but he still held an outstanding position in intellectual and literary circles, and the propaganda and agitation writings by writers such as Zou Rong and Chen Tianhua (陈天华) had already caused an undeniable stir at home and abroad. Lu Xun was still a student seeking to express himself by means of literature, but he had already made his voice heard. The launching and circulation of modern newspapers and magazines witnessed one high point after another and even more were thriving. Such newspapers and magazines, including the newspapers founded by reformists and revolutionaries, as well as the journals and magazines founded by Chinese students studying abroad, were instrumental in shaping modern Chinese literature. Many vernacular newspapers of the late Qing were launched, and there were increasingly more fiction journals; all four of the major exposure novels of this period that are well-known today emerged this year. Obviously, the booming of revolutionary and democratic literature and the transition of late-Qing fictions into a modern form were two major focal points of the literary scene in 1903. And throughout the entire late-Qing period, the literary accumulation leading to modernity involved both a reforming trend promoted by literary elites and a progressive movement implemented by urban literary authors through modern mass media. And then there were modern dramas, and many world literary works were introduced to China through translation, so that Chinese modern literature finally became a part of world literature.

The first literary center of the late Qing was Shanghai. Shanghai's rise as an emerging metropolis, the rapid development of the modern publishing industry, and its foreign concession served as a kind of shelter for free speech, all contributing to the newspaper and printing boom, as well as the emergence of the earliest professional writers and modern urban readership. Even before Wangping Street became modern China's newspaper street, Huifu Alley of Fourth Avenue and the roads beside the small garden in Bao'an Alley of Guangdong Avenue, were lined with major newspaper agencies from all over the country. It was estimated that around the period of 1902–1904, the number of vernacular newspapers and magazines edited, printed, and published in Shanghai nearly equaled that of all other places in the country combined. Then a dozen entertaining tabloids were launched around this time, with the first being *Entertainment* (《游戏报》), launched by Li Boyuan in 1897, all published in Shanghai. It was in these tabloids that many literary works were first published. Of the four major late-Qing fiction journals that will be discussed later in this part, three were launched in Shanghai, namely *Illustrated Fictions* (《绣像小说》), *All-Story Monthly* (《月月小说》), and *Forest of Fiction* (《小说林》), and the only one published in Japan was *New Fiction*. Other fiction journals at the time included *New New Fiction* (《新新小说》), *New World Novel Journal* (《新世界小说社报》), *Fiction Weekly* (《小说七日报》), *Fiction Times* (《小说时报》), *Ten-Day Fiction* (《十日小说》), and *Fiction Monthly* (《小说月报》), all published in Shanghai and circulated across the country. At that time, many Chinese intellectuals lived in Shanghai, most of whom were newspapermen, publishers, and novelists. Except for a few, those involved in this chronicle of literary events were all living and working in Shanghai and Japan (Yan Fu had been living as a recluse for a total of seven years after the Boxer Uprising). Another congregation point of Chinese literary scholars from the late Qing to the Republican period was Tokyo and nearby Yokohama. The period saw a sharp increase in the number of Chinese students studying in Japan, which reached several thousand in 1903, and increased to 10,000 in 1906. After the Wuxu Reform failed, many progressive intellectuals moved eastward, thus the map of distribution of such intellectuals was imperceptibly changed. Therefore, most Chinese people carrying out literary and artistic activities in Japan had the "revolutionary" tendency. There were idle people from rich families, like those mentioned in the novel by Pingjiang Buxiaosheng (平江不肖生, aka Xiang Kairan, 向恺然), *Private Records of Studying in Japan* (《留东外史》), who claimed to be studying in Japan at either the state's or their own expense but did not study hard or do any business, and neither did they have anything to do with literature. The Japanese government had an ambiguous relationship with the Qing government, but it was outside the latter's control, which was why Zou Rong, Chen Duxiu, and their fellow students dared to cut off the queue of Yao Wenfu (姚文甫), the supervisor of Chinese students in Japan appointed by the Qing government, and hung it outside the Chinese Student House. According to Zhou Zuoren who went to Japan a bit later: "It had been a while since Chinese students from different provinces began launching their own journals, and the earliest were launched by students from Hunan, Hubei, Jiangsu, and Zhejiang provinces."[1] Considering the popularity of *Journal of Pure Critique*, *New Citizen*, and *New Fiction* within China, which were all edited by Liang Qichao in Yokohama, we can see the strong influence of Japan as a literary center of that time. Recalling his studying in Japan with his brother Lu Xun, Zhou Zuoren repeatedly mentioned that they were indebted to *New Fiction*, saying that Lu Xun "did not attach great importance to literature when he first went to Japan. Maybe it was after he read Liang Rengong's *New Fiction* and his essay 'On the Relationship between Novels and the Governance of Society' that he began to be influenced by the latter"; and "when I was studying in Nanjing, my literary readings were none other

5.1. Main entrance of Sendai Medical School, where Lu Xun studied medicine

---

[1] Zhou Zuoren: "81. Henan: New Life, I" (八一 河南——新生甲编), *Memoirs from the Hall of Wisdom* (《知堂回想录》), Hong Kong: Sanyu Book and Stationery Company, 1980, p. 217. "Rengong" (任公) was the pseudonym of Liang Qichao. – Translator's note

than those published in Liang Rengong's *New Fiction*."[2] "Studying in Nanjing" referred to the period when he studied at Jiangnan Naval Academy, where he could read every issue of *New Fiction* published in Yokohama, evidence of the fact that Japan was a stronghold of Chinese literature. At that time there were frequent communications and connections between Tokyo, Yokohoma, and Shanghai, and many Chinese students' journals were edited in Shanghai, printed in Japan, and then carried back to be published in Shanghai. At that time, people did not need to apply for visas, and one could travel between both countries simply by buying a passage ticket, which made it possible for the coexistence of both literary centers.

TABLE 5.1 *Chronicle of literary events in 1903*

Date	Major literary event
Jan. 29	A (Lunar) New Year gathering was held at the Chinese Student House in Tokyo, which was attended by more than 1,000 students, including young Zhou Shuren (Lu Xun). Zou Rong, Ma Junwu (马君武), and others delivered speeches to criticize the corruption and betrayal of the Qing court
	At that time, Lu Xun was studying in the Jiangnan Class of the General Program of Kobun Institute, his fellow schoolmates including Xu Shouchang (许寿裳), Chen Tianhua, and Huang Xing (黄兴)
Jan. 29	*Hubei Students* (《湖北学生界》) was launched in Tokyo. Its name was changed to *The Sounds of Han* (《汉声》) after six issues had been published. It was founded by Liu Chengyu (刘成禺) and other Chinese students from Hubei, and it was the earliest journal launched by Chinese students in Japan
January	Chen Feishi (陈匪石) translated "The Last Lesson" by Alphonse Daudet, which was published in the *Hunan Education Journal* (《湖南教育杂志》)
Feb. 17	*Zhejiang Tide* (《浙江潮》, published monthly) was launched in Tokyo. Its chief editors were Sun Jiangdong (孙江东) and Jiang Baili (蒋百里), both Chinese students studying in Japan, and it was taken over by Xu Shouchang from the fifth issue
Feb. 20	Liang Qichao departed from Yokohoma and began his travels to North America (Canada and the United States). Later he wrote *Traveling around the New Continent*
March	Ma Xiangbo (马相伯) founded Aurora College (震旦学院) at the former site of Xujiahui Observatory in Shanghai
March	Zhang Taiyan began teaching at the Shanghai Patriotic Society (上海爱国学社)

(continued)

---

[2]   Zhou Zuoren: "73. Preparing to Launch a Journal" (七三——筹备杂志), *Memoirs from the Hall of Wisdom*, Hong Kong: Sanyu Book and Stationery Company, 1980, pp. 195–197. "Rengong" (任公) was the pseudonym of Liang Qichao. – Translator's note

TABLE 5.1 (continued)

Date	Major literary event
March	Lu Xun became the first in the Jiangnan Class to cut off his queue, and he had a picture taken of his new appearance and sent it to his family and friends back home. Later he wrote the line "My heart has no escape but to care like darting arrows" (灵台无计逃神矢) on the picture before giving it to Xu Shouchang
Spring	Wang Guowei became a lecturer at Tongzhou Normal School (通州师范学校), teaching philosophy, psychology, ethics, and other courses, where he devoted himself to the research of Kant and Schopenhauer
Apr. 8	Yan Fu's *Biography of Adam Smith* (《斯密亚丹传》) was published in issue 27 of the *Lujiang Newspaper* (《鹭江报》)
Apr. 8	Hu Binxia (胡彬夏) and others founded the Mutual Love Society (共爱会) in Tokyo, which was China's earliest women's association promoting equal gender rights
Apr. 26	The *Universal Progressive Journal* (《广益丛报》, published every ten days) was launched in Chongqing
Apr. 27	*Jiangsu* (《江苏》, published monthly) was launched in Tokyo by Qin Yuliu (秦毓鎏) and others from the Japanese Jiangsu Fellow Association
Apr. 27	The Anglo-Chinese School in Tientsin (天津中西学堂) changed its name to Peiyang University (北洋大学)
Apr. 29	Chinese students gathered in Japan to protest against Russia casting its greedy eyes on China's three northeastern provinces. Zou Rong, Chen Tianhua, Su Manshu, and others joined the Anti-Russian Volunteer Army (拒俄义勇队) organized by Chinese student associations
April	Li Boyuan's *A Revelation of Official Circles* began to be serialized in *World Vanity Fair* (《世界繁华报》), with the last installment published in December 1905
May 6	The novel of China's "new citizen" (referring to Liang Qichao), *The Legend of New Rome* (《新罗马传奇》), began to be serialized in the third issue of *Universal Progressive Journal*, with the last installment published in 1905 in issue 64
May 27	*Illustrated Fictions* (published fortnightly) was launched in Shanghai by Li Boyuan. It was discontinued in 1906
May 27	Li Boyuan's novel *Short History of Civilization* (《文明小史》) began to be serialized in the inaugural issue of *Illustrated Fictions*, with the last installment published in 1905 in issue 56
Sep. 5	The Owner of the Hut within the Human Realm (referring to Huang Zunxian) published his poem "Driven-Out Guests" (《逐客篇》) in issue 37 of *New Citizen*
Sep. 11	Zhang Taiyan published his poems "To Zou Rong from Prison" (《狱中赠邹容》), "On Learning of Shen Yuxi's Death in Prison" (《狱中闻沈禹希见杀》), and "On Learning of the Arrest of Someone from Hunan in Prison" (《狱中闻湘人某被捕有感》) in issue 7 of *Zhejiang Tide*

(continued)

TABLE 5.1 *(continued)*

Date	Major literary event
Sep. 21	Liu E (刘鹗) began publishing the first thirteen chapters of his *Travels of Lao Ts'an* (《老残游记》) in installments in *Illustrated Fictions* (issues 9–18)
September	The first two parts of Sun Yusheng's (孙玉声) novel *Dreams in Shanghai* (《海上繁华梦》) were published by the *Forest of Laughter Daily* (《笑林报》) Office in Shanghai
Oct. 5	Wu Jianren's novel *Bizarre Happenings Eyewitnessed over Two Decades* began to be serialized in issue 8 of *New Fiction*, with the last installment published in 1906 in issue 24
Oct. 5	Wu Jianren's novel *Annals of Sorrow* (《痛史》) began to be serialized in issue 8 of *New Fiction*, with the last installment published in 1906 in issue 24
Oct. 8	Su Manshu and Chen Duxiu cooperated on the translation of Victor Hugo's *Les Misérables* (with its title translated into 《惨世界》, literally, "The Miserable World"), and it was published in the *National Daily* (《国民日报》)
Oct. 10	Lu Xun published his "On Radium" (《说鈤》) and "A Brief Outline of Chinese Geology" (《中国地质略论》) in issue 8 of *Zhejiang Tide*
October	Lu Xun translated the science fiction novel *From the Earth to the Moon* by the French writer Jules Verne, which was published by Evolution Publishing in Tokyo
Autumn and Winter	Chen Tianhua's *Fiercely Looking Back* (《猛回头》, storyteller ballads) and *Alarm Bells* (《警世钟》, vernacular prose) were published successively in Tokyo
Nov. 7	The Peking Translation Academy (北京译学馆) was opened
November	The first two chapters of Jin Songcen's (金松岑) novel *A Flower in a Sinful Sea* (《孽海花》) were published in issue 8 of *Jiangsu*. Its last chapters (from the seventh) were completed by Zeng Pu (曾朴)
November	*Tales from Shakespeare* (《莎士比亚故事集》), translated by Lin Shu and others, was published
November	Lu Xun, referred by Xu Shouchang and others, joined the Zhejiang Study Society (浙学会), the precursor of the Anti-Qing Restoration Society (光复会)
November	*Ningbo Vernacular Newspaper* (published every ten days) was launched in Shanghai and released by the Ningbo Fellow Association in Shanghai
November	*Awakening Citizens* (《觉民》, published monthly) was launched in Songjiang, with its editor-in-chief being Gao Xu (高旭)
Dec. 8	Lu Xun translated the first two chapters of Jules Verne's science fiction novel *Journey to the Center of the Earth* (《地底旅行》), and the translated work was published in installments in issues 10, 11, and 12 of *Zhejiang Tide*
Dec. 15	*Alarming News about Russian Actions* (《俄事警闻》) was launched by the Society of Anti-Russian Comrades (对俄同志会), organized by Cai Yuanpei (蔡元培) and others, with its editor-in-chief being Wang Xiaoxu (王小徐)

(continued)

TABLE 5.1 *(continued)*

Date	Major literary event
Dec. 19	The *China Vernacular Newspaper* (published fortnightly, later every ten days) was launched in Shanghai, with its editor-in-chief being Lin Xie
Dec. 19	*Record of the Su Newspaper Case* (《苏报案记事》, aka *Record in Prison in the Year of Kuimao* [《癸卯大狱记》]) was published
December	Liu Yazi (柳亚子, 1887–1958) joined the China Education Society (中国教育会), went to study at the Shanghai Patriotic Society, and began his revolutionary and propaganda activities. He published "Biography of Zheng Chenggong" (《郑成功传》), "On China's Constitution" (《中国立宪问题》) and "Three Hundred Years' History of Taiwan" (《台湾三百年史》), and other works in *Jiangsu*
December	The *New Vernacular Newspaper* (published monthly) was launched in Tokyo and released by the Shanghai Puyi Book Company
This year	Huang Zunxian began living as a recluse in the "Hut within the Human Realm" in his hometown, Jiaying of Guangdong Province, less than one year before he died
This year	Lin Shu worked as a transcriber at the Translation Bureau of the Imperial University of Peking while he taught at Jintai Academy (金台书院) and Wucheng School (五城学堂) in Beijing
This year	Lengxue (冷血, referring to Chen Jinghan [陈景韩]) translated the first two volumes of *Talking about Detection* (《侦探谈》), which was published by Shizhong Bookstore (时中书局)
This year	Shanghai Dawen Publishing House (达文社) organized the translation and published *Strange Tales from Overseas* (《海外奇谈》) by Shakespeare, which was the earliest Chinese translation of Charles Lamb's *Tales from Shakespeare*
This year	Ji Yihui (戢翼翚) translated Pushkin's *The Captain's Daughter*, with its Chinese title being 《俄国情史》, literally, "A Romance of Russia," which was published by Kaiming Bookstore (开明书店)
End of this year	Su Manshu became a Buddhist monk in Huizhong, Guangdong Province

Whether in Shanghai or Tokyo, it was the intellectual and cultural atmosphere that was essential for the modern transition of Chinese literature. In 1903, specifically, Chinese intellectuals and scholars in these literary centers could enjoy the freedom to criticize the corrupt official circle of the Qing Empire. Bao Tianxiao told an interesting story about this. Once in Shanghai, he went with his friend Chen Peiren (陈佩忍, his name was Qubing [去病], and Peiren was his courtesy name), an editor of the *Great Stage of the Twentieth Century* (《二十世纪大舞台》), to interview Wang Xiaonong (汪笑侬), a renowned actor from Beijing. However, when they met the actor they did not achieve the original intention of their interview. "Peiren wanted him to

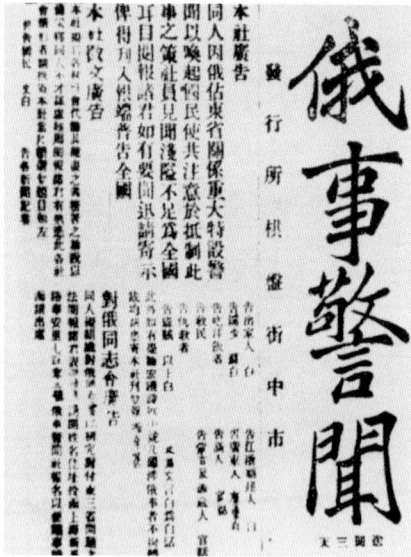

5.2. First issue of *Alarming News about Russian Actions*, launched by Cai Yuanpei in the late-Qing period, which disclosed the crisis of the Chinese nation. See the entry on Dec. 15 in Table 5.1

talk about the dramatic reform, but he shifted the topic to the politics in Beijing and bitterly reviled the official circle in the capital, even including those nobilities and court officials."[3] This practice of "criticizing officialdom" once being away from Beijing and entering Shanghai was characteristic of that period, and newspapers, magazines, and novels written during that period contributed immensely to the collapse of the Qing court. The Su Newspaper Case was an example of Shanghai's newspapers having the audacity to oppose Empress Dowager Cixi. The *Su Newspaper* was originally launched by a Chinese national residing in Japan, and later it was taken over by Chen Fan (陈范) of the South Society (南社). From May to July 1903, with the support of the China Education Society, founded by Cai Yuanpei and revolutionary students who had returned from Japan, the newspaper published a number of radical essays written by Zhang Shizhao (章士钊), Zhang Taiyan, and Zhang Ji (张继) to push forward and give support to student unrest, including

5.3. Photo of Lu Xun, taken when he graduated from the Kobun Institute in 1904

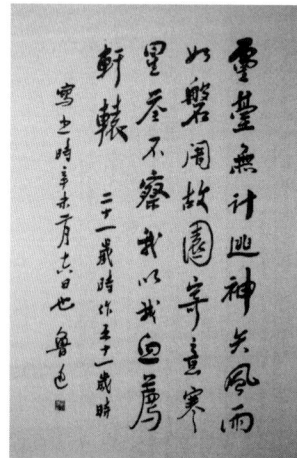

5.4. Lu Xun's handwritten poem "Self-Inscription on a Small Photograph," with its last line demonstrating his ambitions

[3]   Bao Tianxiao: "The Spring Willow Society and Others" (春柳社及其他), *Memoirs of the Bracelet Shadow Chamber* (《钏影楼回忆录》), Hong Kong: Dahua Press, 1971, p. 399.

5.5. *Su Newspaper*, launched in 1896 (the twenty-second year under Emperor Guangxu's reign). It was originally launched by Hu Zhang (胡璋, courtesy name: Tiemei [铁梅]), and then taken over by Chen Fan (陈范, pseudonym: Mengpo [梦坡]). Its chief editors included Wang Wenfu (汪文溥, pseudonym: Langao [兰皋]) and Zhang Shizhao (courtesy name: Xingyan [行严]). The newspaper was under strict control in 1903 because it published a series of essays such as "Reading *The Revolutionary Army*" (《读〈革命军〉》) and "Introducing *The Revolutionary Army*" (《介绍〈革命军〉), for which Zhang Binlin (章炳麟, who later changed his name to Taiyan, 太炎) and Zou Rong (courtesy name: Weidan [慰丹]) were arrested and put into prison. Zou died in prison. This event was historically known as the "Su Newspaper Case"

"On Manchu-Hating" (《释仇满》), "To Conservatives, with Respect" (《敬告守旧诸君》), and "On Revolutionaries as the Pillar of Today's China" (《论中国当道者皆革命党》), etc., motivating people to initiate a "central revolution" to overturn "the Naras" and "Manchus." The newspaper strongly recommended Zou Rong's *The Revolutionary Army*, which became a trigger, and finally the Qing court counterattacked because it published Zou Rong's "Introduction" of his own book as well as the "Preface" written by Zhang Taiyan. As to how there were so many novels "criticizing officialdom," we may get an idea by reading Lu Xun's explanation of the historical background of "exposure novels." Lu Xun wrote:

> The Wuxu Reform failed, and two years later, in the year of Gengzi (1901), the Boxer Uprising broke out. People became aware that the government was not capable of building the country strong, and thus thought of denouncing the government. In novels, writers tried to expose the government's corruptions and evilness and became increasingly more critical of current affairs; somehow this extended to the entire society and became the custom.[4]

"Denouncing the government," to "expose" and be "critical" of it, could be seen as the background of exposure literature, as well as the social psychology, shared by authors and readers alike, of exposing the corruptions and evilness of the government. Together with revolutionary anger and aspirations, this also

---

[4]   Lu Xun: *A Brief History of Chinese Fiction* (《中国小说史略》), *Complete Works of Lu Xun*, Vol. 9, Beijing: People's Literature Press, 1981, p. 282.

5.6. Cover of *The Revolutionary Army* by Zou Rong

helps us to understand the origin of such motivational literary works as Zou Rong's *The Revolutionary Army* and Chen Tianhua's *Fiercely Looking Back*.

The Revolutionary Army was an extremely inspiring and motivating piece of literary propaganda, expounding the necessity of an anti-Qing revolution in quite a concise and pungent way. The book was divided into seven chapters, whose titles included "Reasons for Revolution," "Removing Servility Is Necessary for Revolution," "Principles of Revolution and Independence," etc. The following text talked about what was a "revolution":

Revolution is the general rule of evolution, the self-evident truth of the world and the principle to survive this transitional period. Revolutionaries are those following the way of the world, discarding the corrupt ways and retaining the good essence, and evolving from barbarians to civilized people. Indeed, revolutionaries are those who refuse to be enslaved and aspire to be their own owners.[5]

5.7. Scene of Chinese people being put on trial at the Cour Mixte Française (French Mixed Court) in Shanghai, published in *Dianshizhai Illustrated Magazine*

[5]   Zou Rong: *The Revolutionary Army*, Beijing: Zhonghua Book Company, 1971, p. 1.

The text was a bitter and angry plea for justice. Lu Xun once wrote about the writing style of Zou: "As for the influence of literary texts, perhaps nothing is as strong as *The Revolutionary Army* written by 'the revolutionary pioneer' Zou Rong, which was written in such a clear and understandable style."[6] Zou Rong was unreasonably sentenced to imprisonment for two years, and he died in prison in 1905. It was in the same year that Chen Tianhua drowned himself in a bay in Japan in order to protest against the "ban against Qing and Korean students studying in Japan" and to awaken the Chinese people. The texts he wrote before committing suicide, *Fiercely Looking Back* and *Alarm Bells*, were propaganda works trying to awaken people, with the mood being spirited and flaming.

5.8. Martyr Chen Tianhua, who committed suicide to awaken the Chinese people

Having discussed the revolutionary authors of motivating literary propaganda and urban novelists with a strong awareness to expose the evilness of society, we shall now look at those cultural figures who were ambiguous and thus caught in a dilemma regarding their attitudes toward the social phenomena of the times. They may have been high or low in social status, and their thoughts and viewpoints were extremely complex, but they were representatives of that specific period of time. Even these people demonstrated a kind of transitional feature, let alone other less conservative people. But examining their literary and living state is essential for us to get a better understanding of that turn-of-the-century literary accumulation period. They were Lin Shu (courtesy name Qinnan [琴南]), Zhang Taiyan (who once changed his name to Binglin, 炳麟), Su Manshu, and Wang Guowei.

In 1903, Lin Shu was fifty-one years old, the eldest of these four. This was quite an old age for the time, but Lin lived a long life, dying at the age of seventy-two. Back in 1903, Lin Shu was teaching in Fuzhou, Hangzhou, and Beijing successively, and though he failed several times in the Ministry of Rites examinations after passing the provincial civil service examination under the old-style Chinese examination system, he was quite good at writing classical Chinese essays. He cooperated with others in translating foreign literature, and his translation works, including *Stories of Paris's Lady of the Camellias* (《巴黎茶花女遗事》), *Uncle Tom's Cabin* (《黑奴吁天录》, the Chinese translation was entitled "Black Slaves Appeal to Heaven"), and

---

[6] Lu Xun: *Miscellanous Memories* (《杂忆》), *Complete Works of Lu Xun*, Vol. 1, Beijing: People's Literature Press, 1981, p. 221.

Aesop's Fables (《伊索寓言》), were extremely popular. The most important point of his literary career, the so-called Lin's translation novel, was still under development. His first published literary work was *The New Yuefu Poetry* (《闽中新乐府》). Hu Shi, a major figure of the May Fourth movement, after being "confronted with" Lin Shu for many years, once commented on Lin's *The New Yuefu Poetry*, saying that "Mr. Lin's 'new *yuefu*' poetry not only represented the shifting of his literary standpoint, but proved to us that such a reactionary leader of five or six years ago may have been an active participant of social reform thirty years earlier. Young people like me know Lin Qinnan the conservative, but we don't know Lin Qinnan the reformist. We hear that Lin Qinnan is opposed to vernacular literature, but we don't know that when he was young he also wrote very understandable vernacular poetry."[7] This comment of Hu Shi is quite typical, and helps us get a comprehensive understanding of our predecessors' "backwardness." Everybody has their own "turning point" in the development of thoughts and viewpoints. Lin Shu may have been a qualified reformist, but he could not accept the revolutionary thoughts so comfortably. He once said he wanted to end up as a "successful candidate of the imperial examinations of the Qing dynasty," showing his determination to be an "adherent" of the former dynasty, and thus became a major figure resisting the New Cultural movement.

Different from Lin Shu, being first a reformist and then a member of the United Allegiance Society, Zhang Taiyan had been at the core of the anti-Qing revolution. Earlier in Japan, he had taught *The Origin of Chinese Characters* (《说文解字》) to Lu Xun, Zhou Zuoren, and Qian Xuantong (钱玄同) for a short while, and was quite a well-known and influential scholar and revolutionary figure. Later, however, he was, as Lu Xun said, "content to be a peaceful scholar, living within the walls that were built by himself or built with the help of others."[8] Back in 1903, the year when the Su Newspaper Case occurred, Zhang Taiyan was thirty-four years old and was the news figure attracting attention from all over the country. He published "A Letter Opposing Kang Youwei's Views on Revolution" (《驳康有为论革命书》), reprimanding the emperor as "Zaitian the puppet who cannot distinguish rice from wheat." And he spared no effort in supporting the revolutionary literary work *The Revolutionary Army*. He was sentenced to three years' imprisonment because of the Su Newspaper Case, and once out of prison, he was invited by Sun Yat-sen to be the chief editor of the *People's Newspaper*, confronting Liang Qichao's *New Citizen*, hotly debating with the latter on whether China needed

---

[7]   Hu Shi: "Mr. Lin Qinnan's Vernacular Poetry" (《林琴南先生的白话诗》), first published in *The Sixth Year Anniversary Issue of the "Supplement of Morning Post"* (《晨报副刊六周年纪念增刊》) in December 1924.

[8]   Lu Xun: "A Few Things about Zhang Taiyan" (《关于太炎先生二三事》), *Complete Works of Lu Xun*, Vol. 6, Beijing: People's Literature Press, 1981, p. 545.

a "revolution" or a "reform." After the Republic of China was established, he was determined to launch a campaign against Yuan Shikai after Song Jiaoren (宋教仁) was assassinated. He used the Grand Metal awarded to him by Yuan as a fan decoration to show his contempt for the latter, and went to the gate of the presidential palace to condemn Yuan in public, exposing the latter's evil intentions. He was then put under house arrest by Yuan but refused to be bribed, and thus remained under house arrest until after Yuan died. Zhang Taiyan remained a determined revolutionary until this time, but again, he stopped being revolutionary at the turning point of the May Fourth movement. He gave no support to the New Cultural movement, but insisted on respecting Confucius and reading ancient Chinese classics, and gradually became dispirited. Later in his life, he resorted to Buddhism, and several times he intended to become a monk. An active advocate and participant of revolution thus became a die-hard conservative trying to reverse the trend of history. It was not uncommon at that time, and Zhang Taiyan was a man of two extremes.

In 1903, Su Manshu, who was only nineteen years old, became a member of the anti-Qing revolutionary group, and later he became a major poet of the South Society. He was a friend of Zhang Taiyan, Chen Duxiu, and their fellow revolutionaries, and was among the earliest to translate foreign literature into Chinese. He had been quite a radical intellectual and activist, and in Hong Kong he had once planned an independent assassination of Kang Youwei, supporter of the Qing emperor. Su Manshu's ambiguity showed in his cultural tendency, for it was in 1903 that he began to write six classical Chinese novels. His personal troubles came from the fact that he was born a half-Chinese, half-Japanese illegitimate child and was discriminated against because of this, and

5.9. Zhang Taiyan in kimono, taken when he was a promising young man

5.10. Zhang Taiyan in his later years, as he had gradually become dispirited

5.11. Su Manshu after he became a Buddhist monk

that he was entangled between revolution, romantic love, and Buddhist pursuit. His autobiographic novel *The Lone Swan* and other novels showed this entanglement: the narrator could not find a way out of worldly pains, so he finally converted to Buddhism as a way of detachment. It was this tragic personal experience of Su Manshu, as a transitional figure in that high-spirited revolutionary age, that made him what Sun Yat-sen called a "revolutionary monk." This was typical of a group of intellectuals, who sympathized with revolution but finally remained aloof from the exciting cultural movement. This also reminds us of Li Shutong (李叔同, whose Buddhist name was Hongyi, 弘一) from around the same time, as well as Li Shutong's student, a layman Buddhist Feng Zikai (丰子恺), both of whom had similar experiences and moods. They did not give utterance to their romantic temperament and were reserved about their brilliant talents in a number of artistic genres. Indeed, they might well have made even greater achievements in literature.

Only four years older than Lu Xun, Wang Guowei was twenty-six years old in 1903. He was a real scholar, and at that time his literary research career had just started. The greatest cultural mystery about Wang Guowei was that he could not truly face the reality of the collapse of the Qing and the upcoming new century, and drowned himself in Kunming Lake at the Summer Palace. Wang Guowei was the very first scholar in China who started his research by reading

5.12. Portrait of scholar Wang Guowei

original philosophical works of the West and reexamined traditional Chinese literature, in particular classical novels, poems, and dramas, etc., with evolutionary perspectives from the West and Western aesthetic viewpoints, thus fundamentally changing China's system of literary criticism. In 1903 he was still studying Kant and Schopenhauer and it wasn't until the next year that he began writing "Commentaries on *Dream of the Red Chamber*" (《红楼梦评论》). On the one hand, Wang Guowei's cultural and academic achievements represented a high point of Chinese scholars who became part of the global cultural landscape, and it seemed that part of him had already entered a modern world. On the other hand, Wang had quite conservative political and cultural views, and thus the other part of him seemed to remain forever in the years before the Xinhai Revolution and the May Fourth movement. Wang

Guowei was one of the four most renowned supervisors at the Tsinghua University Research Institute, the other three being Liang Qichao, Chen Yinke, and Zhao Yuanren. The first sentence of his will read: "I have no choice but to die at the age of fifty. I have experienced such tremendous changes in this world and my sense of honour makes any further humiliation unbearable to me." (五十之年，只欠一死，经此世变，义无再辱。) To quote Chen Yinke's explanation of the reason for his death in "Elegy for Mr. Wang Guantang, with a Foreword" (《王观堂先生挽词并序》): "Whenever a culture is declining, those who have been enlightened in this culture will surely feel the pain, and the more he is educated and enlightened, the more severe the pain he feels." Wang Guowei seemed to die as a martyr of the transitional period between the old and the new. He was quite different from Lin Shu, Zhang Taiyan, and Su Manshu, but they all had

5.13. *A History of the Song–Yuan Drama* (《宋元戏曲史》) by Wang Guowei

one thing in common, that is, as extremely ambiguous turn-of-the-century literary figures, they chose to remain in the past. The painful experience of these literary figures can be seen as an analogy of the difficult transition of Chinese literature into its modern era.

5.14. Wang Guowei's former residence in Haining, Zhejiang Province

5.15. Monument dedicated to Wang Guowei (courtesy name: Jing'an [静安]) within Tsinghua Garden, Beijing

SIX

THE RISE OF URBAN POPULAR FICTION IN AN EMERGING INTERNATIONAL TRADING CENTER

THE LITERARY MOVEMENTS OF *NEW FICTION* AND THE "fiction revolution" did not actually yield very fruitful results in terms of literary creation; rather, their major contribution lay in the fact that they created an atmosphere in which the novel was no longer a marginal literary genre but became a focus within the literary scene, and thanks to the circulation of newspapers and magazines, the reader base rapidly expanded from a few intellectuals to the mass public. Therefore, novels of the late-Qing period and modern cities actually emerged and developed together. Originally, the novels only told stories that took place in traditional cities such as Yangzhou and Suzhou, but later the focus shifted to the emerging metropolis, Shanghai. The development of commerce promoted the growth of the consumer market for publishing and cultural products, and thus specialized fiction journals began to appear and thrive in the large cities, as did a large number of professional novelists. These were something entirely new in China's literary history.

As an example, let's look at a variation of the late-Qing "scholar-beauty" (才子佳人) literature, the urban courtesan novels featuring brothels, prostitutes, and brothel visitors. By recounting the stories of male and female characters, full of twists and turns, these novels disclosed an emerging trend in Chinese society. *A History of Floral Treasures* (《品花宝鉴》, by Chen Sen [陈森]) was about prostitution and male homosexuality, and it was China's earliest full-length novel with prostitute characters as the focus. In *Traces of Flower and Moon* (《花月痕》, by Wei Xiuren [魏秀仁]), the author tried to liken himself to his characters, and tried to mirror his real-world experience by writing about the "failure" and "success" of his characters after their contacts with prostitutes. If we examine the novels by looking at the attitudes of the narrators toward prostitutes, there were three kinds of attitudes in these urban courtesan novels, namely "flattery," "belittlement," and "realistic" (see "On the Historical Evolution of Chinese Fiction" [《中国小说的历史的变迁》][1]). *A Brothel Dream* (《青楼梦》, by Yu Da [俞达]) fell into the first category, for the author tried to beautify prostitutes, writing about thirty-six prostitutes caring for an affectionate man of talent in the manner of young gentlewomen. This was doubtless a patriarchal ideal. In *Nine-Tailed Tortoise* (《九尾龟》, by Zhang Chunfan [张春帆]), all prostitutes were evil women cheating their customers and all brothel frequenters rascals, and their relationships were no less than the exposure of "hidden goings-on of evilness," so that fell into the second category. *A Dream of Romance* (《风月梦》, by Hanshang Mengren [邗上蒙人]) and *The Sing-Song Girls of Shanghai* (《海上花列传》, by Han Bangqing [韩邦庆]) were quite realistic novels, with their male and female characters (prostitutes and brothel frequenters) showing both good and evil traits, so they fell into the third category.

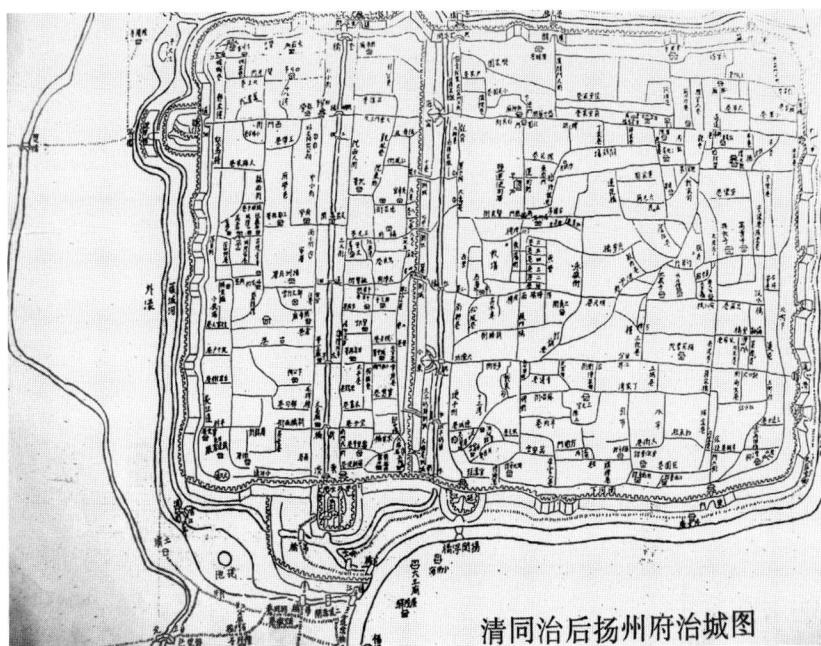

清同治后扬州府治城图

6.1. Map of Yangzhou, looking like a prosperous big city, after the Tongzhi period of the Qing dynasty

[1]   Lu Xun: "On the Historical Evolution of Chinese Fiction," collected in *Complete Works of Lu Xun*, Vol. 9, Beijing: People's Literature Press, 1981.

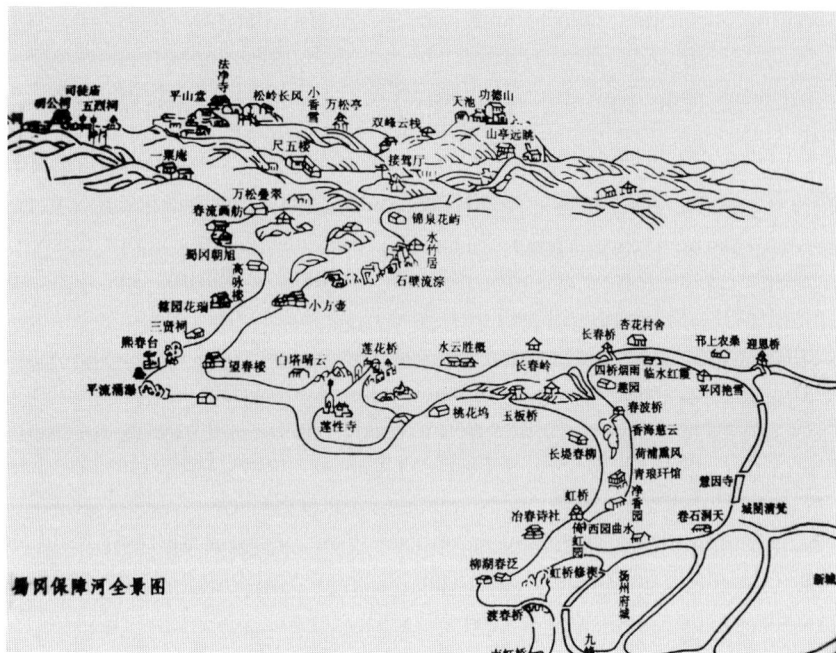

6.2. Panorama of Shu Hill (蜀冈) and Baozhang Lake (保障河, today's Shouxihu Lake)
(a partial reproduction of the *Gazetteer of the Hall of Pingshan* [《平山堂图志》]).
One may appreciate the beautiful scenery around the Twenty-Four Bridge (廿四桥)

As for the relationship between people and cities, we can see that *A Dream of Romance* wrote about Yanghzou; the story of *A Brothel Dream* happened in Suzhou, and the term "海上" ("on the sea") in the titles of *The Sing-Song Girls of Shanghai*, *Heartbroken Monument* (《海上尘天影》, by Zou Tao [邹弢]) and *Dreams in Shanghai* (by Sun Yusheng) referred to the city of Shanghai, which experienced tremendous changes during the late-Qing period.

A Dream of Romance told the story of protagonist Lu Shu going from Changshu to Yangzhou to buy concubines, where he pledged blood-brotherhood with Yuan You and three other local guys, and what happened between the four of them and Yuexiang, Shuanglin, Fenglin, Guilin, Qiaoyun, and other prostitutes. The story took place in Yangzhou when it was still a prosperous big Chinese city during the period under the reign of Jiaqing and Daoguang. At the very beginning of the story, Lu Shu came out from his aunt's house on Nanhexia Road, passing Chaoguan Gate (the South Gate) and the government offices on both sides of Changzhen Avenue, and walked along Gengzi Avenue to the crossroad outside the Small East Gate; after asking the way, he entered Daru Lane, then Nanliu Alley, and finally came to Yuan You's house in Beiliu Alley. These place names may be easily spotted on an ancient map of Yangzhou. Regarding the busy business streets inside Chaoguan Gate, the author wrote (in a lyrical parallel style, which was quite common before the May Fourth movement):

> The hotel lanterns are flickering to attract passing travelers, and the hanging shop signs show there are many businessmen in the city. People are coming in and out of the city, breathing the stale air, and carriers and shippers are sweating all the time. There is fragrance from flower stands and food stands, as well as unpleasant smells from stool and wastewater carriers. Vendors are competing with each other to sell their vegetables and fish and shrimps, and service providers enter and exit the city one after another. The shoulder poles of carriers clatter here and there, passed quickly by sedan chairs of salt merchants.[2]

In traditional Chinese cities, the busiest and liveliest time was during traditional festivals. In this story, Lu Shu hired a big boat and went to the "Rainbow Bridge" during the Dragon-Boat Festival to please Yuexiang, and while on the river, they watched the dragon boat performance and other people competing for targets (live ducks). And they also threw targets into the lake for people to race to get. Meanwhile, this was the scene described on the lakeside:

> On both banks of the lake there are many men and women, some holding boys and some carrying their daughters on their shoulders. Many village women are running here and there, wearing all kinds of decorations on their heads and makeup on their faces, with colorful shoes on their feet, shouting, pulling, and pushing their sisters or other women companions, sweating under the scorching sun. Then there are some drunkards smelling like a brewery, pressing and squeezing among the women. Various small vendors try to sell their products in the crowd, and it was quite a jolly scene.[3]

The "area from Little Gold Hill to the Lotus Bridge" was the central district of the well-known "area with beautiful sights around the Twenty-Four Bridge." And it was a long-used writing method to depict the city from the viewpoint of countrymen and countrywomen.

A Brothel Dream told the story of the affairs between Jin Yixiang, a man of literary talent from Suzhou, and thirty-six prostitutes, and how their loving affections eventually vanished without trace. The author tried to flatter these men and women of taste and talent, and let them embody everything wonderful that can be imagined in feudal society: "visiting gardens, accompanying beautiful women, picking up aromatic herbs, being selected as the highest in the public service examination, taking up government positions, returning

---

[2] Hanshang Mengren: *A Dream of Romance*, Beijing: Beijing Normal University Press, 1992, chapter 3, p. 14.
[3] Ibid., chapter 13, p. 94.

parents' love, making friends, playing musical instruments, and raising children." The author was very familiar with the sights and attractions in Suzhou, such as visiting Tiger Hill and going through Changmen Gate to the busy streets, and described them in great detail. In the scene where Jin Yixiang was roaming about the streets with others during the Lantern Festival, he wrote:

> The four roamed on the street and watched lanterns under the beautiful moon, and there were many men and women dressed grandly, so much so that they looked flowery from afar. The four walked leisurely and came to the front of Xuanmiao Taoist Temple. Here all different kinds of famous lanterns were hung on shop fronts, which was indeed a splendid and beautiful sight. And there were firecrackers spattering sparks here and there. At the entrance of the Zhusi Alley, they saw numerous visitors.[4]

These were the festival celebrations in Suzhou. The descriptions were not as rich and multidimensional as those of Yangzhou in *A Dream of Romance*, but both elaborated on the prosperity of traditional cities in a period when there was no strict boundary between urban and rural areas. After the rise of Shanghai as a trading port in the late Qing, however, the decline of traditional cities seemed inevitable. In *A Dream of Romance*, when visiting the North Hill of Yangzhou, the characters talked about what the area had looked like several decades ago: "[At that time] there were many sights, such as Doumu Palace, Wang's Garden, Little Rainbow Garden, Sunset Tower, Fist Stone Cave, West Sky Garden, Winding Lake, and Gathering Tower beside the Rainbow Bridge, but nowadays the towers and pavilions have all been torn down and the place is largely ruined,"[5] and all the characters felt sad about this. Similarly, in *A Brothel Dream*, the city of Suzhou was badly damaged by the war against the Taiping Heavenly Kingdom and showed a declining trend.

6.3. Map of the streets of Suzhou (formerly Wu County), 1913

On the other hand, *The Sing-Song Girls of Shanghai*, a masterpiece of urban courtesan novels that was highly praised by Lu Xun, Hu Shi, Mao Dun (茅盾), Zhang Ailing, and others, presented Shanghai as a thriving

---

[4]   Muzhen Shanren (慕真山人, Yu Da): *A Brothel Dream*, Changsha: Yuelu Press, 1988, chapter 9, p. 59.
[5]   Hanshang Mengren: *A Dream of Romance*, chapter 5, p. 31.

city full of temptations and evilness. The novel centered on the fall of Zhao Puzhai and his sister after they came to Shanghai, wrote about lots of different prostitutes, and portrayed various brothel frequenters in this bustling cosmopolitan city. The city life described in *The Sing-Song Girls of Shanghai* was quite rich and colorful. There was no need for festival celebrations to decorate citizens' lives, and everyday life scenes became the focus of the novel. Of them the most eye-catching was the introduction of Western novelties into Shanghai, such as enjoying Western cuisine in Yat Pang Heung Restaurant, visiting Arcadia Hall in Zhang Garden, and watching horse races, etc. The description of fire-fighting was especially spectacular:

> Just then, they heard a series of bells in the air. Xiaohong heard them first and said: "Are they alarm bells?" Liansheng immediately pushed open a window and shouted downstairs: "Alarm bells?" … They saw a foreign policeman at the corner of the street leading many people to arrange rubber pipes and connect them into one, put them on the ground along the street, open the water tap, and attach one end of the rubber pipe to the tap. One could not hear the sound of water, but the rubber pipe quickly swelled and became tightened. They walked along the rubber pipe near Fifth Avenue, where they were stopped by a policeman and were not allowed to continue until Liansheng spoke to him in a foreign language. The fire seemed to still be far away from them, but they could hear the strange sound of cracks, like thousands of firecrackers, and saw sparks over their head … Outside the gate many people chorused: "Good! Good!" Xiaoyun also came to see it, and said: "The chemical water pipe has been used and the fire is beaten down." Sure enough, the fire was lowered and gradually out of sight. Even the black smoke was increasingly thinner.[6]

This paragraph was about a novelty of that time: the earliest use of the Western mechanical fire-fighting system in Shanghai. They attached a rubber pipe to a water tap to spray the fire out instead of pouring basins and buckets of water on the fire. The "chemical water" flowing in the "chemical water pipe" referred to firewater mixed with extinguishing agent, quite a cutting-edge technology at that time. The author wrote in great detail about the "swollen" rubber pipe, implying that Shanghai citizens watched it quite closely with great interest. The sixth picture (Figure 6.4) from Volume 1, Issue 1 of *Dianshizhai Illustrated Magazine* (a lithographic pictorial launched in Shanghai in the tenth year of the Guangxu Era [1884], drawn by Wu Youru [吴友如] and others) was entitled "Watching a Fire but Meeting with a Disaster" (观火罹灾), which was a pictorial news report about foreigners fighting fire with fire truck hoses in Shanghai, and Chinese people rushing to a wooden bridge on the river to

---

[6] Han Bangqing: *The Sing-Song Girls of Shanghai*. Beijing: People's Literature Press, 1982, pp. 84–86.

watch the scene. The bridge was so crowded that it collapsed, and people fell into the river. This picture was evidence that people of the time took no less interest in watching fire-fighting than appreciating street performances. It is certainly belittling the author to say that he wrote about the fire-fighting scenes to show off the newly introduced machines and technological inventions. In *The Sing-Song Girls of Shanghai*, seeing Liansheng was worried that the fire may damage his own house, Chen Xiaoyun tried to comfort him, saying: "No need to rush. You have already had your house insured, so what's the fuss?"[7] We can see that, at that time, rich people in Shanghai had used fire insurance, so were aware that this Western social mechanism could be used to protect their private property. *The Sing-Song Girls of Shanghai* represented a very high achievement in its realistic portrait of characters and the mixture of Chinese and Western culture in city life, as well as plot structure in such a lengthy novel.

A short time later, exposure novels came onto the literary stage, becoming the climax of late-Qing novels. In terms of publishing media, most urban courtesan novels were published in woodblock print, while all exposure novels

6.4. News report "Watching a Fire" in *Dianshizhai Illustrated Magazine*, recording how Shanghai citizens scrambled to see the exotic sight of fire being fought in the foreign concession, and they remained in high spirits even after the bridge fell down because of the crowd

[7] Ibid., p. 85.

were first serialized in newspapers and magazines, then sent for mechanical printing to be published in separate editions (since *The Sing-Song Girls of Shanghai* was written a bit later than other urban courtesan novels, it was serialized in *Remarkable Books on the Sea* [《海上奇书》], edited by the author himself). This marked the beginning of novels being serialized in modern newspapers and magazines, which was around the 1890s. Exposure novels were published in the "four major fiction journals of the late Qing," including Liang Qichao's *New Fiction* (1902), Li Boyuan's *Illustrated Fictions* (launched in 1903), Wu Jianren's *All-Story Monthly* (launched in 1906), and Huang Moxi's *Forest of Fiction* (launched in 1907). Starting from its eighth issue, *New Fiction* began to publish Wu Jianren's *Bizarre Happenings Eyewitnessed over Two Decades*, one of the most important exposure novels, which, from the viewpoint of a character whose name was Jiu-si-yi-sheng (literally, "narrow escape"), mercilessly exposed the evilness of bureaucrats, the so-called men of talents and society as a whole. Also serialized in the same journal were Wu's *Annals of Sorrow* and *Nine Lives Mysteriously Wronged* (《九命奇冤》). Li Boyuan's *Officialdom Unmasked* (《官场现形记》) was published in the tabloid *World Vanity Fair*, but his other major works, such as *Short History of Civilization* and *Living Hell* (《活地狱》), were serialized in *Illustrated Fictions*. Part of Liu E's *The Travels of Lao Ts'an* was serialized in *Illustrated Fictions* (the ninth to eighteenth issues). Through the eyes of the narrator, a physician named Lao Ts'an, the story described the northern part of China, and such sections as "breaking ice on the Yellow River" and "the White Girl telling stories" were considered excellent realistic writings, with all characters and scenes portrayed multidimensionally. Zeng Pu's *A Flower in a Sinful Sea* sought to present the entire picture of social life through the story of Jin Wenqing (alluding to Hong Jun [洪钧], a diplomat of the late-Qing period) and Fu Caiyun (whose stage name was Sai Jinhua [赛金花]), and it was partly serialized (from chapter 21) in *Forest of Fiction*. Another novel by Wu Jianren, *Ashes after the Catastrophe* (《劫余灰》) was serialized in his own magazine, *All-Story Monthly*, under the Tragic Love Stories column. Both *Ashes after the Catastrophe* and *The Sea of Regret* (《恨海》) were Wu Jianren's literary works, which were kind of a combination of exposure novels with love stories, and can be seen as the beginning of the tradition of the Mandarin Duck and Butterfly school of the Republican period. We will come back to this later.

6.5. First issue of *Illustrated Fictions*, launched in 1903

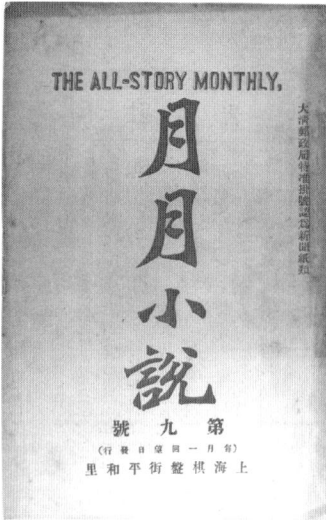

6.6. Cover of the ninth issue of
All-Story Monthly

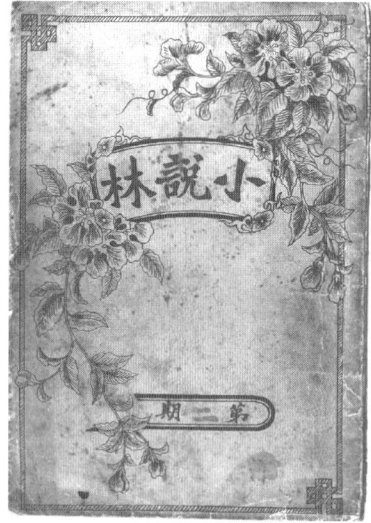

6.7. Cover of the second issue of *Forest of Fiction*

Of the "four major exposure novels," there were various descriptions of the half-Chinese, half-Western lifestyle in the earlier period of Shanghai, such as walking along the Bund, watching horse races, eating Western cuisine, playing billiards, etc. What is worth mentioning is that in *Bizarre Happenings Eyewitnessed over Two Decades*, like in *The Sing-Song Girls of Shanghai*, there was also a fire-fighting scene in Shanghai:

> Just then, it was suddenly quite noisy outside, and all were surprised. They stopped and listened, hearing that there was a fire somewhere, they rushed outside to have a look, only to see thick smoke rising high at the entrance of the alley. Jin Zi'an said: "Too bad, there is a fire over there!" … After a while they saw the smoke became red and sparks flew overhead. It was even noisier now and alarm bells screamed. Presently, the fire-fighting team arrived, and four or five water pipes sprayed the fire. Fortunately, there was no wind that night and the fire was not so big, so it was put out soon.[8]

Even the sentences of this paragraph were similar to those in *The Sing-Song Girls of Shanghai*, and in *Bizarre Happenings Eyewitnessed over Two Decades* there were details about policemen in Shanghai who did not allow people to save personal belongings from a fire, and the characters also talked about insurance:

> I said: "When there is fire, policemen prohibit us from moving our belongings, that's too much." Zi'an said: "There are two reasons for this

---

[8]   Wu Jianren: *Bizarre Happenings Eyewitnessed over Two Decades*, Beijing: People's Literature Press, 1981, p. 532.

6.8. New-style fire-fighting team established in Shanghai in the late-Qing period, imitating those in the foreign concession. Some of its members still had their hair in queues

rule; firstly, for fear that someone would take the chance to rob people of their belongings, and secondly, people moving things would become obstructions to the fire-fighting team. This sounds reasonable, but as far as I can see, most probably this is the idea of insurance companies." I said: "Why is that?" Zi'an said: "Only if you are not allowed to move your things out, could they make every one of you have your things insured."[9]

From the rule of "not moving things" during fire-fighting in Shanghai, the characters turned to the twofold nature of the way an emerging metropolis established its citizens' standard of conduct: on the one hand, the city rules had an absolute authority over people, exemplified by the enforcement of such rules on fire-fighting; and on the other hand, business networks were all pervasive in modern cities, which brought with them unfairness and fraudulence. Nearly every step in the progress of modern civilization meant the undulation and readjustment of traditional civilizations, in which some traditional aspects disappeared and some new ones were established. The exposure novels showed the earliest stage of this process in China in a realistic (albeit unconscious) manner.

At that time, the exposure novels contained detailed descriptions of streets in Shanghai, which were more meticulous than any there had been in Chinese novels before. That was because the Bund and the streets of Shanghai were indeed unprecedented in traditional Chinese cities. Bao Tianxiao, an author of the later-stage Mandarin Duck and Butterfly literary school, once recalled

[9] Ibid., pp. 532–533.

what he saw when he first came to Shanghai from Suzhou at the age of nine. He went to the Bund by carriage to see foreign ships: "I was shocked to see the big steam vessels several times higher than houses. The carriage took us around the busiest district at the sides of Big Avenue (Nanjing Road) and Fourth Avenue (Fuzhou Road), and as such it was a tourist attraction called 'Riding the Carriage.'"[10] His memory of Shanghai was exactly the same as descriptions by others in late-Qing novels. An example is the description of Jin Wenqing and his friends walking along the Bund in *A Flower in a Sinful Sea*:

> They got on the carriage waiting outside. The driver took the reins in hand and drove off at top speed toward the Bund of Huangpu River, and it seemed the yellow Arab horse kept flying. So they made to the north down the Bund, fast and secure, and out there on the Huangpu River they saw the water was glassy and motionless and there were many sailboats. Looking up, they could see the bronze statue of Gordon standing on the bank, and then they saw a stone tower just ahead, and knew it was the monument. Just as the two were talking with each other, the carriage stopped and they got off, entered the park, and saw bright pavilions and precious trees and flowers. The two sat within a pavilion, watching Chinese and Western ladies passing by, all dressed formally and beautifully … After a while, the sun began setting in the west, and the shadows of trees became darker and longer. They walked slowly out of the park and called a carriage, went back along the Bund to Big Avenue. As the carriage turned around Fourth Avenue, they saw many buildings on both sides were still under construction. Just as they passed Maijiaquan and came on to Baoshan Street, they saw the retainer of Wenqing, with an invitation in hand, shouting to them: "Lord Xue invites My Lord to go to Yat Pang Heung Restaurant immediately to enjoy the big feast in Booth No. 8."[11]

This driving route was exactly the same as that recalled by Bao Tianxiao of his childhood. They saw boats on the Huangpu River, instead of steam vessels. Gordon was the English general who had helped Li Hongzhang crack down on the uprising of the Taiping Heavenly Kingdom, and therefore the bronze statue was set up in his memory. The stone tower monument was also built to the memory of a foreigner. These traces of colonialism disappeared later. The park they entered was the Bund Park, which was known to discriminate against Chinese people by not allowing "Chinese and dogs" in, but that was what happened later. Jin Wenqing ranked No. 1 in the imperial examination of the Wuchen Year (1868), the year the Bund Park first opened. In this book the two Chinese characters entered the park proudly, and in the park they saw

---

[10] Bao Tianxiao: *Memoirs of the Bracelet Shadow Chamber*, Hong Kong: Dahua Press, 1971, p. 31.
[11] Zeng Pu: *A Flower in a Sinful Sea*, Shanghai: Shanghai Classics Publishing House, 1980, pp. 10–11.

6.9. Busy Fourth Avenue, Shanghai, during the late-Qing period, in which we can see the tall Qinglian'ge Teahouse building and the imposing sights around it

many "Chinese and Western ladies" passing by, which was true to reality, since at the time there was no prohibition against Chinese people, and it was only years later that foreigners began to discriminate against Chinese people on the basis of "hygiene." Out of the park one walked from Big Avenue to Fourth Avenue, both of which were well-known latitudinal roads, interconnected by a longitudinal road, the famous "Maijiaquan," also known as "Wangping Street" (Shandong Road). "Many buildings on both sides were still under construction" showed the fact that, as a business street, Nanjing Road was not as good as Fuzhou Road. Yat Pang Heung Restaurant, located on Fourth Avenue, was a reputable restaurant where people enjoyed Western cuisine. Thus along the road one could see what one wanted to see, most of which were exotic sights.

As Shanghai entered its modern era, the traditional mainstream members of Chinese society and their values were often put into an embarrassing situation, which we may get a glimpse of through exposure novels. There was a wonderfully written paragraph in *Officialdom Unmasked* about a provincial administration commissioner wanting to inspect an account at a foreign bank in Shanghai:

> Even before they got to the entrance of the bank, the footman was eager to rush inside with the official's visiting card, and climbing up the steps he shouted loudly: "Come and get the visiting card!" Luckily no foreigner saw him, and a houseboy at once waved and hinted at him to get out, then told him to go to the back of the building and come in through the back entrance. The footman came back down the steps and reported what he had been told to the commissioner, who had just got out of his

carriage. The commissioner was not happy, thinking: "I am a guest coming to visit them. Why are they telling me to come in through the back entrance?" In fact, at HSBC, all business with Chinese people, such as withdrawing foreign currency and cashing checks, had to be done with the cashiers and counters at the back of the building, which was why the houseboy was told to go to the back. Left with no choice, the commissioner had to go to the back of the building, following his footman. The people around were quite surprised to see his red cap, for it was not necessary to be so formally dressed to withdraw money, and if he was there to visit the comprador, he may as well be dressed casually because there was no need to show so much respect to him.

... They were unsure what to do, when suddenly they saw a Chinese man coming out, but they had no idea what he was doing at the bank. So the commissioner approached the man to consult him, saying that he, as the Jiangnan Provincial Administration Commissioner, had come to talk to foreigners and inspect an account under the order of the governor-general. Hearing that he was the Provincial Administration Commissioner, the man looked him up and down and replied: "The foreigners are busy in their offices upstairs, and they don't have time to see you right now." The interpreter who accompanied the commissioner said: "Is it all right to talk with the comprador if the foreigners are not available?" The man then said: "The comprador is busy, too. What exactly are you doing here?" The commissioner said: "A circuit intendant named Yu has deposited an amount with your bank, and I have come to check whether he actually did it or not." The man said: "I don't know any circuit intendant named Yu. Now I have to go because I have something to do outside. Go ask somebody else." Then he swept out of the back entrance.

6.10. The Bund at the turn of the twentieth century, where foreign banks and organizations were set up

6.11. Shanghai citizens from all walks of life looking at photographs from the West with great curiosity in the late-Qing period

> … As they tried to figure out what to do, suddenly the interpreter said: "Alas! It's half past twelve!" The commissioner asked: "What's the matter with that?" The interpreter said: "They will all leave at half past twelve." The commissioner said: "Very good. Then we can wait for them here. They will surely come out, and then I can approach to ask them." As soon as he said that, they saw many people rush outside through the back entrance, but it was impossible to tell who was the comprador, who was in customer services and who were the clerks. They saw many people rush out, but no foreigners. Why? Because foreigners exited the building through the front door. Therefore, the commissioner waited in vain. The building was in total silence after all the people had gone outside.[12]

A provincial-level Chinese official came to a British bank based in Shanghai, and while he wanted to show his authority, he eventually made a scene of himself. From beginning to end, the commissioner was simply unaware that the interpersonal relationships within a foreign bank were not a strictly hierarchical one as in a Chinese government office like his. Except for his janitor and interpreter, who had to listen to him, no one here was obliged to be humble and submissive to him. The reason why he was put in such an embarrassing situation, then, was that he had little knowledge about the outside world. At that time, Shanghai was quite "advanced" in many aspects, and maybe one could say that in becoming a Western colony Shanghai had developed into

---

[12] Li Boyuan: *A Revelation of Official Circles*, Beijing: People's Literature Press, 1979, pp. 557–559.

a modern metropolis, but what exposure novels showed us was the mud-dleheaded and shallow Chinese officials who were ruling the country. Surely these people could not lead China to be one of the most powerful countries in the world, but could only lead to the total destruction of the Beiyang Navy, despite having the most cutting-edge warships imported from Europe. This was the case of officialdom in Shanghai, not to say other parts of China. Therefore, these realistically depicted details retained by novels of the late-Qing period were extremely valuable as both historical sources and literary material.

SEVEN

EMERGING ELITES OF THE SOUTH SOCIETY

T‍HE IMPORTANCE OF THE S‍OUTH S‍OCIETY (南社) N‍OT only lay in its poetic creation, though its poetry was quite reputed for a time, and by carrying forward the tradition of "poetry revolution," it had had great political influence before the Xinhai Revolution; the importance of the South Society also lay in its unprecedented size and life-span: it attracted all the progressives of the time and carried out many activities beyond the realm of literature, it did not evade the impact of newly emerged urban culture upon literature, but instead took an active approach in a number of cultural and literary fields including publishing, news media, and education. After the Qing dynasty collapsed, the South Society rapidly declined and split up; its life cycle epitomizing the formation and evolution of a professional modern Chinese intellectual and author group, as well as its complex transitional nature.

The South Society, as its name implied, was founded to resist the "North (Qing) Court." The idea originated in 1903, and later, after frequent communication between people of similar purposes and interests, on November 13, 1909 (the first day of the tenth lunar month in the first year of the Xuantong Era), about nineteen young poets from Shanghai, Nanjing, Wujiang, and Jinshan held an elegant gathering at the memorial temple of the anti-Qing martyr Zhang Guowei (张国维; pseudonym: Dongyang [东阳]) on Tiger Hill in Suzhou, and the South Society was thus initiated and founded by Chen Qubing, Gao Xu, and Liu Yazi. As Tiger Hill had also been the site of a gathering of several thousand people from the Restoration Society (复社)

in the fifth year of Emperor Chongzhen's reign (1632), the site might easily inspire people's feelings of nationalism. Most of the earliest members of the South Society were also members of the United Allegiance Society (同盟会), so their anti-Qing aspirations were very clear. That year Liu Yazi was twenty-two years old, just in the heyday of youth, and later he became the "life and soul" of the South Society, its constant organizer and leader. Basically, the South Society organized its literary activities in traditional ways: the first was through elegant gatherings, at which people drank and recited poetry, exchanged views on art and literature, and discussed the rules and regulations of the Society. Originally they intended to hold two elegant gatherings each year, one in spring and one in autumn, but it turned out to be impractical. Altogether they held eighteen elegant gatherings in over a decade, which was not an easy job. The second was through publishing poetry and prose written by members in a journal called *Collection of the South Society* (《南社丛刻》), of which a total of twenty-two issues were published. Altogether more than 1,000 people from various professions joined the South Society, and its organization was quite loose. Apart from its three founders, there were other poets, including Ma Junwu, Ning Tiaoyuan (宁调元), Su Manshu, Gao Xie (高燮), Huang Moxi (黄摩西), and Huang Jie (黄节); propagandists, including Yu Youren, Shao Yuanchong (邵元冲), Ye Chucang (叶楚伧), Dai Jitao (戴季陶), and Shao Lizi (邵力子); scholars, including Wu Mei (吴梅), Huang Kan (黄侃), and Ma Xulun (马叙伦); and politicians, including Huang Xing, Song Jiaoren, Wang Jingwei (汪精卫), Chen Qimei (陈其美), and Zou Lu (邹鲁). According to the "Address Book of the South Society Members" published in January 1911, there were only 193 members then, which meant most members joined after the founding of the Republic of China. After the goal of overturning the Qing dynasty had become outdated, the South Society was still a cohesive organiztion for a period of time under the banner "Against (Feudal) Restoration" and "Against Yuan Shikai." In the "Address Book of the South Society" published in 1912, there were 321 members; in the "List of Names of the South Society" published in 1913, there were 403 members, and in the "Revised List of Names of the South Society" published in 1916, there were 825 members. After Yuan Shikai died and up until the New Cultural movement, the South Society, with its members coming from very different backgrounds, began to split up. According to the "List of Names of the South Society Members" attached to *A Brief Record of the South Society* (《南社纪略》) written by Liu Yazi after the Society dissolved, there were altogether 1,170 members, but they were such a medley of a crowd. The South Society also had various branches, such as the Yue Branch (越社) based in Shaoxing, of which Lu Xun became a member in the late spring of 1911. And at the invitation of Song Zipei (宋紫佩), founder of the Yue Branch, Lu Xun compiled the first issue of *Collection of the Yue Branch* (《越社丛刊》) and cofounded the *Yueduo Daily* (《越铎日报》), but Lu Xun always kept a distance from the South Society, as he did not like the elitist style of its members.

7.1. First formal gathering of the South Society in 1909, when Liu Yazi (front row, third from left), Chen Chaonan (陈巢南, who changed his name into Qubing), Huang Binhong (黄滨虹), Zhu Zhenzhuang (诸贞壮), and others took this group photo at the front of the memorial temple of Zhang Dongyang on Tiger Hill, Suzhou

7.2. Liu Yazi in his middle age

7.3. Liu Yazi, one of the founders of the South Society, before the Xinhai Revolution

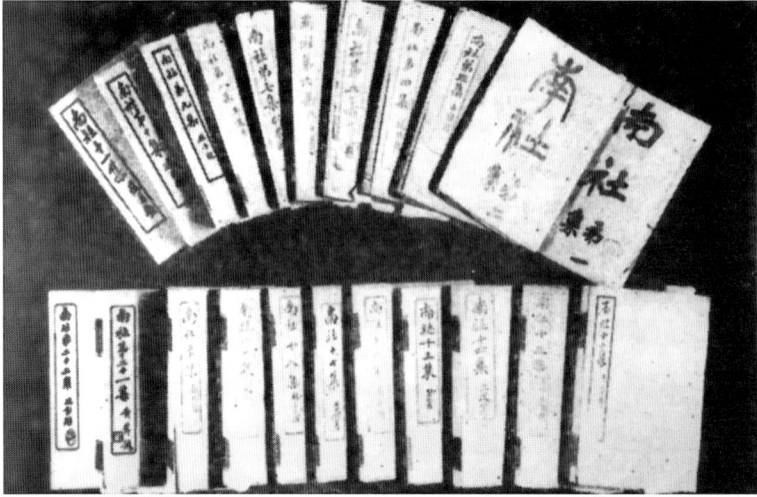

7.4. Issues of the *Collection of the South Society*

For such a huge and mixed group of intellectuals, it is very interesting to closely examine the geographic origins of the South Society's members. It is easy to see that its members came from China's nineteen provinces and areas, breaking the geographic barrier between Chinese intellectuals that had existed since ancient times, which certainly had something to do with the rise of Shanghai as a metropolis. Bao Tianxiao once said that the "members [of the South Society] came from all provinces across the country ... because it was based in Shanghai" and many of them were "living away from home in Shanghai" or "frequenting to and from Shanghai."[1] And it also had something to do with the fact that Tokyo was a gathering place for students and exiles from all provinces studying and living there. Many members of the South Society had been active in Japan. This was further evidence that Shanghai and Tokyo were the two literary centers of the late-Qing period. Another impressive feature was that a larger proportion of members came from certain provinces. Altogether 1,053 members came from just seven provinces, namely Jiangsu (including Shanghai), Zhejiang, Guangdong, Hunan, Anhui, Fujian, and Sichuan, more than ten times the total number of all the other twelve provinces combined. This can be attributed to the fact that it was easy for its initiators to contact people of the same origin, but the imbalance of geographic distribution of literary talents was actually caused by the imbalance of economic and cultural development between the northern and southern parts of China, and thus it was an issue with historical roots. If one looks closely at the flow of literary scholars (authors) from Song through Ming and then to the

---

[1]   Bao Tianxiao: *Memoirs of the Bracelet Shadow Chamber*, Hong Kong: Dahua Publishing House, 1971, p. 353.

Republican period when New Literature emerged, and examines the South Society against this historical context, it is not hard to see a long tradition behind this. Most members of the South Society came from the Yangtze River basin and Lingnan area, and later during the period of New Literature, there were Lu Xun and Mao Dun from Zhejiang and Ba Jin and Guo Moruo from Sichuan. These were not unrelated facts. This reminds us that when Lu Xun was in Beijing, in response to someone's attack that he belonged to some origin and some department, he wrote a wonderful essay entitled "My 'Origin' and 'Department'" (《我的"籍"和"系"》). Putting aside the specific context of this debate, it was an undisputable fact that at that time there were a great many talents of Zhejiang "origin" working in the Chinese Department of Peking University. And the fact that there were a

7.5. Chen Qubing, another founder of the South Society

large proportion of literary scholars of Zhejiang origin in the leftist, Beijing school, Shanghai school, and urban popular literary schools during the 1930s was probably a reason why the urban popular literature of modern China was so genteel. It was quite different from China's modern native-soil literature, which featured both the refinement and sophistication of authors from Jiangsu, Zhejiang, Hubei, and Hunan and the primitiveness and grandeur of authors from the Northeast. The rueful feelings toward the fate of the nation expressed in the poetic and prose writings of members of the South Society were also characteristic of the southern areas of China.

People of the South Society wrote poetry to enlighten others and promote the capitalist revolution, carrying forward the tradition of the "poetry revolution." But at first they were against the rule of an alien tribe (referring to the Manchus) and inherited the "positions of the Incipience Society (几社) and Restoration Society," and later they were against Yuan Shikai's attempt to restore feudal rule and supported the republic institution, thus they showed some progress compared to Liang Qichao's reformation stand. However, their progress ended there. Most members of the South Society wrote lyrical poetry with historical themes; before the Xinhai Revolution, they wrote poetry to the memory of anti-Mongolia and anti-Qing martyrs of the Song and Ming periods such as Yue Fei (岳飞), Xia Wanchun (夏完淳), Zhang Huangyan (张煌言), Shi Kefa (史可法), and Zheng Chenggong (郑成功), in order to express their anger and sorrows toward reality. Some poems were written with great force and energy, such as "At Yue Fei's Tomb" (《岳坟》) by Huang Jie:

> We have worshipped the Yue Fei Temple for ten years, / Only to see the mountains around the West Lake even greener. / The imperial majesty of the Great Han has faded off, / And thus its military strength has to

lurk for a long time. / Late crickets are sighing beside the tombs of Yue Fei and his son, / And their heroic stories are told within teashops in the autumn. / I am the only person who mourns the hero alone, / For loyalty and indignation always bring so much sorrow." (中原十载拜祠堂，不及西湖山更苍。大汉天声垂断绝，万方兵气此潜藏。双坟晚蟀鸣乌石，一市秋茶说岳王。独有匹夫凭吊去，从来忠愤使人伤。)

At the outbreak of the Xinhai Revolution, the poets of the South Society were excited and exhilarated, and thus Gao Xu wrote "The wild singing after wines is heartbreaking, / While the gatherings among revolutionaries are loud and strong." (酒后狂歌声激楚，楼头高会气豪雄。"An Impromptu on the Happy Encounter of Taiyi on the Sea" [《海上喜遇太一即赠》]) But after the Xinhai Revolution, many backsliding phenomena disappointed and confused the poets. Chen Qubing, for example, once wrote such sentimental lines as "One cannot but drink to excess when overwhelmed by sorrow, / For he has nowhere else to anchor his aspirations in this hopeless world." (事有难言唯纵酒，身无可托独含愁。"Autumn Sentiments" [《秋感》]) In his earlier days, Liu Yazi called himself "Rousseau of Asia," and changed his name to "Renquan" (meaning "human rights") and his courtesy name to "Yalu" (meaning "Asian Rousseau"), showing the brilliant talent and heroic spirit of a young man. "Singing Songs" (《放歌》) was a five-character-line poem to express his political views, and it was altogether 400 characters long. In 1905, Liu Yazi wrote two poems entitled "Mourning the Martyr Weidan" (《哭威丹烈士》) in which there were such lines as "The evil omen in the sky appeared before the death of a hero, / And our nation has lost such a great talent forever. / We don't sing marching songs but only lament the shortness of life, / Thus the barbarians are singing and dancing while the Han people are living in grief." (白虹贯日英雄死，如此河山失霸才。不唱铙歌唱薤露，胡儿歌舞汉儿哀。) And in 1907 he wrote four poems entitled "Mourning Ms. Qiu of the Mirror Lake" (《吊鉴湖秋女士》) in which he wrote "She has devoted her chivalric bones and flesh to the nation, / Which gained her a heroic reputation that spreads afar. / Her blood had been drained and dedicated to her motherland, / Which flows into the angry tides of Qiantang River sobbing and whimpering" (已拼侠骨成孤注，赢得英名震万方。碧血摧残酬祖国，怒潮呜咽怨钱塘) to show his bold and unrestrained indignation. Within the South Society, Liu Yazi advocated the Tang-tradition poetry, and insisted that poetry should be magnificent and elegant. He also thought highly of the *ci* (词) works by Xin Qiji (辛弃疾), for which he even changed his name into "Qiji," and thus his poetic style combined the magnificence and unconstrainedness of both. For a long time within the South Society, there had been disputes among members between those advocating the Tang tradition and those promoting the Song tradition. At their first gathering at Tiger Hill, Liu Yazi had a fierce debate with Cai Shou (蔡守) and other members who promoted the tradition of the Jiangxi poetic school. Liu Yazi had a stammering tongue, which became even more serious when he was anxious, and he thus cried out of anger. Liu Yazi, who respected the poetic tradition of the Tang dynasty, wrote impassioned and forceful poems, such as "Indignation" (《孤愤》), his well-known poem written to attack Yuan Shikai's attempt to proclaim to be emperor, which was quite characteristic of his style:

> *My indignation is so great that it spreads to the ends of the earth,*
> *And I cannot bear to see so many soulless bodies fawning to gain favor.*
> *The new regime has already been praised by Yang Xiong,*
> *And Ruan Ji's Memorandum has been heard to support the recovered monarchy.*
> *Who has seen a monkey wearing the crown and becoming an emperor?*
> *Now even rotten rats take advantage of the evil chance.*
> *I dream of defeating the despotic Qin every night,*
> *Hearing the mass pledge of the Northern Expedition troops.*

(孤愤真防决地维，忍抬醒眼看群尸？
美新已见扬雄颂，劝进还传阮籍词。
岂有沐猴能作帝？居然腐鼠亦乘时。
宵来忽作亡秦梦，北伐声中起誓师。)[2]

Apart from gathering and making friends through poetic writing and provoking "revolutionary" sentiments, another major characteristic of the South Society was that many of its members were newspapermen. Their original intention was to use mass media for revolutionary propaganda. It was a time when Chinese newspapers and magazines were burgeoning, and they made the most of the excellent opportunity to display their talents. According to the research of some scholars, there were altogether 128 members of the South Society who participated in launching newspapers and magazines, with more than forty newspapers and magazines involved.[3] This must be an underestimate, and "participating in" is quite an ambiguous phrase; does it mean being editor-in-chief, editorial writer, president, and founder, or does it also include working as editors and important authors? Obviously in the case of the latter, there should have been even more. And considering the frequent changes of presidents

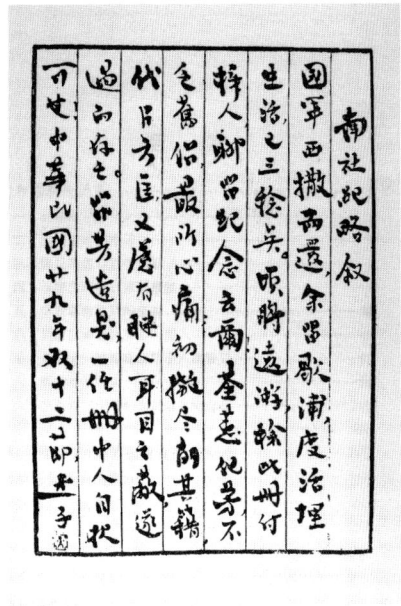

7.6. Liu Yazi's handwriting

---

[2] *Selected Poems of Liu Yazi* (《柳亚子诗词选》), Beijing: People's Press, 1959, p. 35.

[3] See Fang Hanqi: *History of China's Newspapers and Magazines in Early Modern Times*, Taiyuan: Shanxi People's Press, 1981.

and editors-in-chief of many newspapers and magazines, it was really hard to give the exact figures. I tried to draw a table of all newspapers and magazines launched by members of the South Society (see Table 7.1), and found there were as many as seventy involved. Taking the *Su Newspaper* for example, it was originally a newspaper of inferior content and quality, but in 1898, two years after it was launched, it was taken over by Chen Fan (whose later pseudonym was Tuian [蜕庵]), and Wang Wenpu (汪文溥) and Liu Yazi were invited to be its editorial authors, all backbones of the South Society. The newspaper shared the same causes as the China Education Society and Shanghai Patriotic Society (the members of the South Society were also quite active in both of these societies), and thus its image was quite different from before, supporting student unrests and publicly expressing anti-Qing viewpoints. In 1903, the *Su Newspaper* invited Zhang Binlin (Taiyan) and Cai Yuanpei to be contributing authors, propagated Zou Rong's *The Revolutionary Army*, and published Zhang Binlin's essays attacking Kang Youwei and promoting revolutionary ideals, so that the Qing government colluded with the Shanghai Municipal Council of the concession and arrested Zhang Binlin. Zou Rong gave himself up to the police, and both he and Zhang were put in the Western-style prison. The *Su Newspaper* was closed down. This was the "Su Newspaper Case," famous in China's modern history. The table (see Table 7.1) also listed twelve newspapers and magazines, including *Jiangsu*, launched in Tokyo by Chinese students. Some of them seemed to be published in Tokyo, but they were actually edited in Shanghai and printed in Tokyo and released both at home and abroad. From this we can see that members of the South Society had been active among students in Japan. Then there were the *Shenzhou Daily* and three related newspapers with their mastheads all starting with the character "*min*" (民, literally, "people"), written vertically, hence nicknamed "*shu-san-min*" (竖三民), launched by Yu Youren, a member of the South Society of Shaanxi origin. Most of these experiences epitomized the late-Qing intellectuals' struggles against the Qing court for national independence, free speech, and free press. According to historical records, the *Minhu Daily* pleaded on behalf of people and revealed the evilness of the governor-general of Shaanxi and Gansu who suppressed the news about the famine for three years and thus caused cannibalistic tragedies in the area. As revenge, the imperial government had Yu arrested by the authority of the concession and the newspaper, which had been launched less than 100 days before, was closed down and its release discontinued. Over a month later, Yu Youren launched another newspaper, called *Minyu Daily*. Later there were two explanations about why the Chinese character "呼" (*hu*) was changed to "吁" (*yu*). The first was that the two dots of the character "呼" were removed, making it "吁," as it looked like a person's eyes were removed. Another explanation was that "吁," before becoming the simplified style of the character "籲," was mainly used in an idiom to mean "sighing," while "呼" meant "calling loudly"; so the change meant that since it was impossible to call out loudly for people, the newspaper could not but sigh for Chinese people. By that time, Japan had sped up swallowing Manchuria and Mongolia, and when its prime minister Ito Hirobumi was assassinated by the Korean activist An Jung-geun in Harbin, people felt quite pleased, but all the newspapers in Shanghai kept silent about this out of fear for the Japanese government. The *Minyu Daily* was the only one that dared to report the news and commented on it vigorously. Therefore, forty-eight days after it had been launched, the newspaper was closed down. When *Minli Daily* (《民立报》) was launched several months later, its circulation quickly increased to 20,000 and it became the most popular newspaper in Shanghai. It was an event that made members of the South Society very proud,

7.7. Shao Piaoping, a member of the South Society and a famous newspaperman of the *Beijing Press* (京报), who was shot dead in 1926 by members of the Fengtian clique

and seeing this, they launched more and more newspapers, so many that Liu Yazi once made a public statement that "today's China is dominated by the South Society!"

Moreover, by engaging themselves in new professions such as launching newspapers, members of the South Society paved the way for their evolution into a new generation of professional intellectuals. In 1905, the Qing government was forced to announce the abolition of the imperial examination system. Of those who were to become members of the South Society a few years later, many naturally loathed the scholar-official career path, and now they were even more determined and came to Shanghai, making a living by launching and founding newspapers, publishing houses, schools, businesses, independent organizations, or political parties, and thus became editors, journalists, teachers, contributing authors, investors, and politicians. Certainly, they were somewhat bound by the new-style socioeconomic relationship, but compared with the past, they had much more intellectual independence and higher social status, and to a certain extent they enjoyed more freedom of expression and speech. This was because newspapers and magazines relied on the market, that is, general citizens, for their survival. Taking Yu Youren for example, one may get an idea of the multifaceted significance of members of the South Society founding newspapers and magazines: just look at how the success of his newspapers in turn gave him even stronger free speech, thus preparing him for his future political career. This said, there is little wonder why many newspapermen came from the South Society. Apart from Yu Youren, there were Ye Chucang, Shao Lizi, Lin Baishui (whose original name was Lin Xie), Shao Piaoping, Cheng Shewo (成舍我), etc. In 1926, because they insisted on free

7.8. *Beijing Press* office gate, looking as if it is trying to defend itself

press, Shao Piaoping and Lin Baishui were successively shot dead only three months apart by warlords of the Fengtian Clique (奉系军阀), so in their memory their contemporaries wrote the sorrowful line "The green duckweed and white water reunite after one hundred days" (青萍白水百日逢, since the character "萍" in Shao's name meant "duckweed" and Lin's name "白水" meant "white water").

Some members of the South Society later became authors of the Mandarin Duck and Butterfly literary school, which had something to do with the fact that apart from its political tendencies, this literary society was quite sensitive to market demands. Their experience as newspapermen enabled the intellectuals to understand the reading needs and tastes of urban citizens, and when novels quickly attained their prominence in modern newspapers and magazines, these authors, at a transitional period between old and new literature, chose to write in the tradition of linked-chapter novels. The literature of this school reached its peak after the Republic of China was established. Among these authors, some joined the South Society in its early stages, such as Bao Tianxiao, whose member account number was 104; Zhou Shoujuan's (周瘦鹃) account number

7.9. Funeral service held by people of the All-Zhejiang House (全浙会馆) for Shao Piaoping and Lin Baishui, both newspapermen shot dead for striving for free press, on Xiaxiejie Street, Beijing, 1928

7.10. The South Society's formal gathering held in Beijing in 1912, which was attended by Huang Keqiang (黄克强, that is, Huang Xing, Keqiang being his courtesy name), Chen Yingshi (陈英士), Ye Chucang, and Chen Taoyi (陈陶遗)

was 508 and Zhou Guisheng's (周桂笙) was 965. Other famous authors of the Mandarin Duck and Butterfly school who were also members of the South Society included Xu Zhenya (徐枕亚), Wang Xishen (王西神, aka Wang Yunzhang [王蕴章]), Wang Dungen (王钝根), Fan Yanqiao (范烟桥), Ye Chucang, and Zhao Shaokuang (赵苕狂), etc. These constituted the backbone of the Mandarin Duck and Butterfly literary school, and they were also experts in founding modern newspapers, magazines and literary supplements, hence they were pioneers in this field.

The South Society remained active until 1923, when the last issue of the *Collection of the South Society* was released. On the surface, the Society was disorganized because of disputes between members, while the true reason was that during a transitional period for literature and for culture as a whole, the Society could not bring most of its members up to date on social transformation, and thus it could do nothing but decline and fade away. In terms of its strong anti-imperialistic stand, the South Society was a revolutionary organization, while from the perspective of the May Fourth New Culture, the Society stood up for old literature. The debate between Liu Yazi and Zhu Yuanchu (朱鸳雏) on promoting Tang-style or Song-style poetry also involved Cheng Shewo, who approved the latter's viewpoint, and Liu Yazi, who could not even tolerate the academic disagreements on old-style poetry, dismissed Zhu and Cheng out of the organization in a patriarchal manner, which caused a big stir within the Society. Later Liu Yazi felt sorry for what he had done, but it was too late. Members within the South Society included Wu Yu (吳虞), a harsh critic of Confucius, and new-style intellectuals who had been studying in Europe and the United States, but most intellectuals still lived in an old cultural circle which conflicted with the New Cultural movement. Gao Xu, one of the initiators of the South Society, strongly held his anti-Yuan Shikai position after the Xinhai Revolution, while later he assisted Cao Kun to carry out bribery in the election and became a "piglet parliament member." There were as many as a dozen such "piglet parliament members" within the South Society. Some members went back to flattering poets of the Tongguang style, causing a further split in the organization. Later, in an attempt to save it from declining, Liu Yazi called for a "New South Society," making announcements and issuing rules and regulations, but it was hardly sustainable. The May Fourth New Cultural movement had become a strict criterion to distinguish new intellectuals from old ones, and history, like a high-speed train, would inevitably throw some people out at a sharp bend. This historical approach might need reconsideration, but it was, after all, a historical fact.

7.11. Group photo taken during a formal gathering of the South Society in Changsha in 1916

TABLE 7.1 *Newspapers and journals of the South Society*

South Society founder of newspaper or journal	Name of newspaper or journal launched	Time	Place
Chen Fan (pseudonym: Mengpo)	*Su Newspaper*	Taking over in 1898	Shanghai
Deng Qiumei (邓秋枚), Huang Jie (黄节)	*Politics and Arts Fortnightly* (政艺通报)	1902	Shanghai
Chen Qubing	*Jiangsu*	1903	Tokyo
Liu Chengyu	*Hubei Students*	1903	Tokyo
Huang Xing	*Translation Series of Overseas Students* (游学译编)	1903	Tokyo
Lin Xie (pseudonym: Baishui)	*China Vernacular Newspaper*	1903	Shanghai
Chen Qubing, Su Manshu	*China National Gazette* (国民日日报)	1903	Shanghai
Gao Xu	*Awakening Citizens*	1903	Songjiang
Lin Xie, Liu Shipei (刘师培)	*Alarming Bells Daily* (警钟日报, formerly *Alarming News about Russian Actions*)	1904	Shanghai
Chen Qubing	*Great Stage of the Twentieth Century*	1904	Shanghai
Bao Tianxiao, Shao Piaoping	*Eastern Times*	1904	Shanghai
Gao Xu, Chen Qubing	*Awakened Lion* (醒狮)	1905	Tokyo
Huang Jie, Deng Qiumei	*National Essence Journal* (国粹学报)	1905	Shanghai
Wang Jingwei	*Min Bao*	1905	Tokyo
Liu Yazi	*Autonomous Newspaper* (自治报, later changed to *Restoration Newspaper* [《复报》])	1906	Tokyo
Li Genyuan (李根源), Lü Zhiyi (吕志伊)	*Yunnan* (云南)	1906	Tokyo
Chen Jiading (陈家鼎), Ning Tiaoyuan	*Dongting Waves* (洞庭波)	1906	Tokyo
Lei Tieya (雷铁崖)	*Cuckoo Sounds* (鹃声)	1906	Tokyo
Bao Tianxiao	*News Supplement of Eastern Times*	1906	Shanghai

(continued)

TABLE 7.1 *(continued)*

South Society founder of newspaper or journal	Name of newspaper or journal launched	Time	Place
Fu Fu (傅尃)	*The Struggle* (published every ten days)	1906	Shanghai
Jing Dingcheng, Jing Yaoyue	*History of Shanxi*	1907	Tokyo
Yu Youren	*Shenzhou Daily*	1907	Shanghai
Zhao Shijue (赵世钰)	*Summer Sounds* (夏声)	1908	Tokyo
Lü Zhiyi	*Guanghua Daily* (光华日报)	1908	Rangoon
Wang Jingwei, Lei Tieya	*Guanghua Daily*		Pulau Pinang
Yu Youren	*Minhu Daily*	1909	Shanghai
Yu Youren, Jing Yaoyue	*Minyu Daily*	1909	Shanghai
Ning Tiaoyuan	*Empire Daily* (帝国日报)	1909	Beijing
Lei Tieya	*Yue Newspaper* (越报)	1909	Shanghai
Bao Tianxiao	*Fiction Times*	1909	Shanghai
Yu Youren	*Minli Daily*	1910	Shanghai
Chen Qubing, Liu Yazi	*Collection of the South Society*	1910	Shanghai
Wang Yunzhang (王蕴章, literary name Xishen)	*Fiction Monthly*	1910	Shanghai
Chen Qimei, Lei Tieya	*People's Sound* (民声丛报)	1910	Shanghai
Chen Qimei, Chen Qubing	*China Bulletin* (中国公报)	1910	Shanghai
Li Shutong, Dai Jitao	*Tianduo Bao* (天铎报)	1910	Shanghai
Li Jizhi (李季直)	*Kefu Academic Journal* (克复学报)	1911	Shanghai
Tang Qunying (female)	*Journal of the Society of Female Overseas Students in Japan* (留日女学会杂志)	1911	Tokyo
Jing Dingcheng, Tian Tong (田桐)	*National Customs Daily* (国风日报)	1911	Beijing
Tian Tong, Jing Dingcheng	*National Light News* (国光新闻)	1911	Beijing
Shao Piaoping	*Han People's Daily* (汉民日报)	1911	Hangzhou
Zhou Shoujuan, Wang Dungen	*Free Talk* (自由谈) column in *Shun Pao*	1911	Shanghai

(continued)

TABLE 7.1 *(continued)*

South Society founder of newspaper or journal	Name of newspaper or journal launched	Time	Place
Jing Dingcheng, Jing Yaoyue	*Jinyang Vernacular Newspaper*		Taiyuan
Lu Esheng (卢谔生), Shen Houci (沈厚慈)	*Mass Newspaper* (群报)		Guangzhou
Xie Yingbo (谢英伯)	*Journal of Current Pictorial* (时事画报)		Guangzhou
Xie Yingbo	*Oriental Daily* (东方报)		Guangzhou
Xie Yingbo	*Anti-Yuan Shikai Daily* (讨袁报)		Guangzhou
Xu Langxi (徐郎西)	*Life Daily* (生活日报)		
Chen Qubing, Song Zipei	*Collection of the Yue Branch*	1912	Shaoxing
Ye Chucang, Yao Yuping (姚雨平)	*Pacific Newspaper*	1912	Shanghai
Deng Jiayan (邓家彦)	*Chinese People's Newspaper*	1912	Shanghai
Dai Jitao	*Civil Rights Newspaper* (民权报)	1912	Shanghai
Wang Xuchu (汪旭初)	*Republican Times* (大共和日报)	1912	Shanghai
Shao Yuanchong, Chen Quanqing (陈泉卿)	*People's Republic News* (民国新闻)	1912	Shanghai
Song Jiaoren	*East Asian News* (亚东新报)		
Chou Liang (仇亮)	*Democracy* (民主报)		
Fu Fu	*Changsha Daily* (长沙日报)		Changsha
Xu Zhenya	*Thicket of Fiction* (小说丛报)	1914	Shanghai
Wang Dungen, Zhou Shoujuan	*Saturday* (礼拜六)	1914	Shanghai
Yao Yuanchu (姚鹓雏)	*Seven Stages* (七襄)	1914	Shanghai
Bao Tianxiao	*Fiction Miscellany*	1915	Shanghai
Shao Lizi, Ye Chucang	*People's Republic Daily* (民国日报)	1916	Shanghai
Yao Yuanchu	*Spring Sounds* (春声)	1916	Shanghai
Bao Tianxiao	*Illustrated Novel Magazine*	1917	Shanghai
Shao Piaoping	*Peking Press*	1918	Beijing

(continued)

TABLE 7.1 *(continued)*

South Society founder of newspaper or journal	Name of newspaper or journal launched	Time	Place
Zhou Shoujuan	*Spring and Autumn* (《春秋》), a *Shun Pao* supplement		Shanghai
Xu Zhenya	*Fiction Quarterly* (小说季报)	1918	Shanghai
Zhou Shoujuan, Zhao Shaokuang	*Recreation World* (游戏世界)	1921	Shanghai
Zhou Shoujuan	*Bi-Monthly* (半月)	1921	Shanghai
Bao Tianxiao	*Weekly* (星期)	1922	Shanghai
Zhou Shoujuan	*Violet Petals* (紫兰花片)	1922	Shanghai
Fan Yanqiao	*Stars* (星)	1922	Suzhou
Wang Dungen	*Aspirations* (心声)	1922	Shanghai
Fan Yanqiao	*Star Light* (星光)	1923	Shanghai
Zhou Shoujuan	*Violet* (紫罗兰)	1925	Shanghai

(*Source*: Sun Zhimei [孙之梅]: *Studies on the South Society* [《南社研究》], Beijing: People's Literature Press, 2003)

EIGHT

FROM SUZHOU AND YANGZHOU TO SHANGHAI

Literature of the Mandarin Duck and Butterfly Literary School

THE LITERATURE OF THE MANDARIN DUCK AND BUTTERFLY literary school originated in Shanghai at the turn of the late-Qing and the Republican period. Most of its early members were literary intellectuals from Suzhou, Yangzhou, and the surrounding Jiangnan area who had moved to Shanghai. This can be verified if one draws a map of the origins and domiciles of Mandarin Duck and Butterfly authors and the cities where the stories of their representative literary works took place. Xu Zhenxya (pseudonym: Zhenxia Gezhu [枕霞阁主], literally, "Owner of the Glow Pavilion") was a native of Changshu, and his novel *Jade Pear Spirit*, which was regarded as the beginning of the Mandarin Duck and Butterfly school, told a story that took place in Wuxi. Wu Shuangre (吴双热) was also a native of Changshu, and in his *Mirror of Evil Injustice* (《孽冤镜》) the story took place in Suzhou, with Changshu also mentioned. Li Dingyi (李定夷) was a native of Changzhou, and in *Lost Jade* (賈玉怨) the story took place in Shanghai and Suzhou. Li Hanqiu (李涵秋; pseudonym: Qinxiang Gezhu [沁香阁主], literally, "Owner of the Fragrance Pavilion") was from Yangzhou, and his lengthy one-million-Chinese-character novel *Tides of Yangzhou* (《广陵潮》) was about the history of Yangzhou over a period of thirty years. Bi Yihong (毕倚虹; pseudonym: Suopo Sheng [娑婆生]), was from Yizheng, a place near Nanjing, and he grew up in Hangzhou with his father, while his *Living Hell* (《人间地狱》) was about the brothels in Shanghai. Zhu Shouju (朱瘦菊; pseudonym: Haishang Shuomengren [海上说梦人], literally, "Dream Teller on the Sea") grew up in

Shanghai, and his *Huangpu Tides* (《歇浦潮》) was about the hidden tricks and goings-on in Shanghai. Zhou Shoujuan (pseudonym: Ziluolan Zhuren [紫罗兰主人], literally, "Violet Owner") was a native of Wu County and could be considered a native of Suzhou but was born in Shanghai; originally his major literary career was translation, with his three-volume *A Collection of Short Stories by Renowned European and American Writers* (《欧美名家短篇小说丛刻》) praised by Lu Xun. On behalf of the Popular Education Research Association (通俗教育研究会), Lu Xun applied for an award for this translation work with the Ministry of Education. Bao Tianxiao (pseudonyms: Tianxiao Sheng [天笑生] and Chuanying Louzhu [钏影楼主], literally, "Owner of the Bracelet Shadow Chamber") was also a native of Wu County, and his novels *Shanghai Records* (《上海春秋》) and *Redemption* (《补过》) were both about Shanghai, with which he was very familiar. At that time in Shanghai, the area around Fifth Avenue (Guangdong Road) and Fourth Avenue (Fuzhou Road) that led the cultural fashion of the city had passed the "smaller Suzhou" period depicted in urban courtesan novels. An urban society characteristic of the modern period had emerged in Shanghai, while Suzhou gradually became a sort of "smaller Shanghai," so much so that it was out of fashion for prostitutes in Shanghai to speak Suzhou dialect (like those in *The Sing-Song Girls of Shanghai*). Suzhou and Yangzhou became Shanghai citizens' memory of freshly bygone traditional cities. The Mandarin Duck and Butterfly authors who had moved from Suzhou and Yangzhou and settled in Shanghai occupied a very large share of the reading market in Shanghai. This is key to our understanding of the Mandarin Duck and Butterfly school: when the genteel and refined characteristics of the Jiangnan culture were combined with the modern popular culture and became commodities in a commercialized metropolis, and when Shanghai citizens began their conscious consumption of literature as a cultural commodity, the literature of the Mandarin Duck and Butterfly school appeared on the scene.

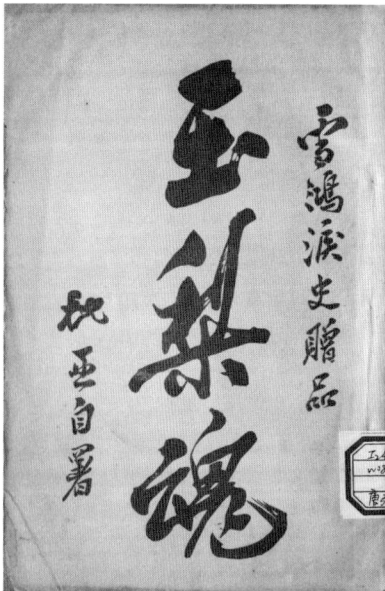

8.1. 1915 edition of Xu Zhenya's *Jade Pear Spirit*

The term "Mandarin Duck and Butterfly school" came from novels of that time, such as *Traces of Flower and Moon*, *Nine-Tailed Tortoise*, and *Lost Jade*, in which the authors used a poetic line "Thirty-six pairs of mandarin ducks share the same fate, / And a pair of butterflies are miserable lovers" (卅六鸳鸯同命鸟，一双蝴蝶可怜虫) to describe the love scenes of talented scholars and beauties. It was the authors of New Literature on the eve of the May Fourth movement who first

8.2. Cover of Li Hanqiu's *Tides of Yangzhou*, Vol. 1, which was about Yangzhou, a long-established commercial Chinese city

8.3. Portrait of Zhou Shoujuan

used this term to refer to this literary school of romantic fiction; examples include Zhou Zuoren, who called these novels "Mandarin Duck and Butterfly style" (鸳鸯蝴蝶体) in 1918,[1] and Qian Xuantong, who simply called them "novels of the Mandarin Duck and Butterfly school."[2] Later the term was widely used. Most authors of this literary school, however, refused to accept or pay attention to this, since their literary works were later identified by some with "obscenity" and "promiscuousness," and thus many authors of the Mandarin Duck and Butterfly school became a bit defensive about this term. It would have been easier for them to accept if it had been referred to as "old-style urban popular literature."

However, when this literary school first came to the foreground of the late-Qing literary scene, it was hardly "old-style" literature, but should be regarded as "new-style" to a certain extent. The Mandarin Duck and Butterfly authors did not write about rural society, but about the declining traditional cities

---

[1] See Zhou Zuoren: "The Development of Japanese Novels in the Recent Thirty Years" (《日本近三十年小说之发达》), collected in *Compendium of Chinese New Literature, Constructive Theories* (《新文学大系·建设理论集》), Shanghai: Young Companion Printing and Publishing Co., 1935.

[2] See Song Yunbin (宋云彬) and Qian Xuantong: "Of 'Hidden Goings-On'" (《〈黑幕〉书》), published in *New Youth*, Vol. 6, Issue 1, January 1919.

8.4. June 1917 issue of *Illustrated Novel Magazine*, whose editor-in-chief was Bao Tianxiao

8.5. Portrait of Bao Tianxiao

which still offered a luxurious and leisured lifestyle but had begun to be negatively impacted, as well as the rapidly developing modern metropolis. At that time, the stories happening in Suzhou and Yangzhou were mixed with those happening in Shanghai, and it can be seen as China's earliest modern urban popular literature. Their literary works were published via modern mass media, including newspapers, tabloids, and magazines, most of which were new-style newspapers and magazines launched by Mandarin Duck and Butterfly authors themselves. What's most interesting is that these literary intellectuals were by no means die-hard conservatives; traditional values had begun to decline, and although new values seemed a bit strange to them, they tried to understand and accept them. When *Tides of Yangzhou* was first serialized daily in the *Daily News on Public Opinion* (《公论新报》) in Hankou, its original title was "Transitional Mirror" (《过渡镜》), which was quite an intriguing title, and from this we can see that the Mandarin Duck and Butterfly authors were fully aware that they were writing in a transitional period and that they themselves were transitional writers.

Frequenting brothels, editing newspapers, releasing news stories, writing novels to be serialized in several newspapers and magazines simultaneously, and sometimes improvising in a hurry to be printed immediately, this constituted the everyday life and work of Mandarin Duck and Butterfly authors, and even Su Manshu, the "revolutionary monk," was no exception. Therefore, it makes sense that some people see Su Manshu's novels as the beginning of sentimental novels of the Mandarin Duck and Butterfly school (and it is also worth literary historians' attention that Chen Duxiu once commented that Su Manshu could "well be regarded as having laid the foundation for New Literature"[3]). The following text from *Living Hell* was surely a self-portrait of the author Bi Yihong, with the prototype of the character Ke Liansun being the author himself, and that of the character Su Xuanman being Su Manshu. Su Manshu did introduce a child prostitute to Bi Qihong when the latter first frequented brothels, and that child prostitute, Ledi, was the prototype of the prostitute character named Qiubo in the novel:

> Hearing what Xuanman said, both Qiwu and Liansun looked outside and saw a gentle, pretty young girl, 13 or 14 years old, entering the room with a smile, half reserved and half shy. She looked around the room with a pair of glittering and translucent eyes, and beamingly sat beside Xuanman, greeting him as "Master Su." Xuanman said laughingly: "How come you call me Master Su now?" Qiubo replied with a smile: "Oh

8.6. Frequenting the brothels on Fourth Avenue was the most common social activity in Shanghai during the late-Qing period, as was written in this bamboo twig ballad: "One can see the extravagant life in Changsan Shuyu brothel, where the silver pipes are decorated with eight kinds of precious stones. Making friends with the rich and nobles and liberal with money, they often show their social distinction by entertaining prostitutes in public." (长三书寓大排场，银水烟筒八宝镶。结纳王孙多阔绰，摆台花酒十三洋。)

---

3   See Liu Wuji, ed.: *Collection of Articles to the Memory of Master Manshu* (《曼殊大师纪念集》), Shanghai: Zhengfeng Press, 1944, p. 427.

I forget again! Mo … nk." Xuanman accepted this with a laugh … Then he pointed to Ke Liansun who sat next to him and said: "Look, Qiubo, a person as handsome as the third young master of the Ke's has so many tricks to play and cannot be as well-behaved as us monks." At this Qiubo turned to have a close look at Ke Liansun, while Ke was also staring at her, attracted to her delicate beauty. When their eyes met, Ke felt Qiubo was so charming and radiant, and Qiubo found him so handsome, dashing, and refined. Qiubo flushed and gently patted Su Xuanman on his shoulder, saying: "You are such a meddling monk. How can you know he has tricks to play." Su Xuanman quickly replied: "How strange! You don't even know the third young master of the Ke's. How come he did not oppose to my comments but you blame me as such on his behalf." To this Liansun cut in: "This is because 'where there is injustice, there is an outcry.'"[4]

From this we can get an idea of Mandarin Duck and Butterfly authors' style when writing love scenes, and about how literary intellectuals of that time frequented brothels. In cities and towns in the Jiangnan area near Suzhou and Yangzhou, living standards and cultural tastes had risen since the Song period, so there was this long-held tradition to spend money in wine shops, teashops, theaters, and storytelling places. Rich people surely bought higher-end luxuries, while ordinary people, too, spent money, even though they could only afford low-end services. This was the cultural tradition of the Jiangnan area. Now that Shanghai had become a metropolis, there was a sudden increase in demand for cultural commodities and services from a larger number of Shanghai citizens. Indeed, citizens needed to gossip, to entertain themselves by reading, and to have more to talk about at their social gatherings. Once novels stopped being overvalued as something to enlighten people and serve the social reformation, the renovated traditional teahouse Qinglian'ge and Yat Pang Heung Restaurant, where people followed the fashion to enjoy Western cuisine, began leading the cultural trend in this transitional scene. The Mandarin Duck and Butterfly authors were among the first to embrace this change; on the one hand, they went around sing-song houses and became familiar with lower-class citizens, and on the other hand, they publicly denounced such conventional principles as reading to govern the state and writing to convey truth, and upheld the banners to promote the role of literature as a consumer commodity and a way of entertainment. The most telling example of this was the magazine *Saturday*, a well-known magazine of the Mandarin Duck and Butterfly school that published 100 issues before the Xinhai Revolution and another 100 issues after. As the editor of this magazine, novelist Wang Dungen

---

[4] Bi Yihong: *Living Hell*, continued by Bao Tianxiao, Beijing: Yanshan Press, 1994, Chapter 20, pp. 192–193.

8.7. Cover of the 100th issue of *Saturday*

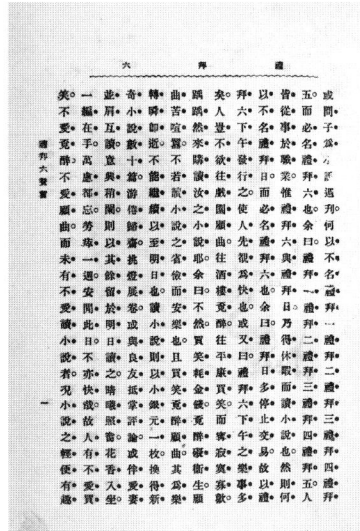

8.8. Wang Dungen's "Some Superfluous Words" in the inaugural issue of *Saturday*

asserted eloquently but in an argumentative style in "Some Superfluous Words on the Publishing of *Saturday*" (《〈礼拜六〉出版赘言》):

> Some may say: "On Saturday afternoons there is so much entertainment, why don't people go to the theater, drink in wine shops, or seek pleasure in brothels, but stay alone and come to buy your novels to read?" I said: "You are wrong. Visiting brothels costs a lot of money, drinking does harm to your health, and it is so noisy in the theater; all of these are not as money-saving and pleasant as reading novels. The pleasure of brothel visiting, drinking, and enjoying theater is fleeting and cannot last till the next day. However, it only costs a penny to buy a dozen new stories, and when you are tired of walking during the day, you may take the book back home to read at night, discussing it with your good friends, or reading aloud for each other with your beloved wife. If you feel tired, just put it aside and pick it up the next day. On a sunny

8.9. Photo of Wang Dungen, editor of *Saturday*, and his wife

> day when there are flowers blooming outside your window, sitting there with an issue in hand may take you away from all trivial worries, and you may have a good rest after a week's work. Isn't that true happiness?

8.10. Inaugural issue of *Element of People's Rights* (《民权素》), the earliest magazine of the Mandarin Duck and Butterfly school

8.11. Fiction journal *Fiction Miscellany* (《小说大观》), launched by Bao Tianxiao in Shanghai in 1915

Therefore, some people don't like to visit brothels or drink in wine shops or go to theater, but everybody likes reading novels. Moreover, is there any novel as portable and interesting as *Saturday*?"[5]

"Sitting there with an issue in hand may take you away from all trivial worries, and you may have a good rest after a week's work. Isn't that true happiness?" What a loud and clear announcement of the entertaining role of novels from this literary school! From this we can see the Mandarin Duck and Butterfly authors' conscious attitude toward the combination of literature and newspapers and magazines. "Money-saving and pleasant," "portable and interesting," and that you can put it aside and resume reading next time, all of these were advantages of "novels in *Saturday*" over other forms of entertainment, and this was brought about by nothing other than modern mass media, newspapers and magazines. The popularity of Mandarin Duck and Butterfly novels, most of which were published in newspapers and magazines, relied on a number of external conditions during the late-Qing and early-Republican period. As was recalled by some people, "It was very easy to launch a newspaper or magazine at that time. Firstly, there was no need to register; secondly,

---

[5] Dungen: "Some Superfluous Words on the Publishing of *Saturday*," collected in *Critical Material on Theories of the Twentieth-Century Chinese Novel*, Vol. 1, Beijing: Peking University Press, 1997, p. 484. "Dungen" refers to Wang Dungen.

the price of paper was very low; thirdly, postal delivery nationwide was fast and safe; and fourthly, it was not difficult to solicit contributions, and the payment for writing was quite low." It was a golden age for the publishing industry.[6] The circulation of newspapers and magazines publishing Mandarin Duck and Butterfly novels was quite large and they disseminated widely. Specialized fiction journals included *Fiction Times*, launched by Chen Jinghan and Bao Tianxiao (1909); the early-period *Fiction Monthly*, launched by Wang Yunzhang and Yun Tieqiao (1910); *Element of People's Rights*, launched by Liu Tieleng (刘铁冷) and Jiang Zhuchao (蒋箸超) (1914); *Thicket of Fiction*, by Xu Zhenya and Wu Shuangre (1914); *Eyebrow Talks* (《眉语》), by Gao Jianhua (高剑华) (1914); *Saturday*, by Wang Dungen and Zhou Shoujuan (1914); *New Bulletin of Fiction* (《小说新报》), by Li Dingyi (1915); *Fiction Miscellany*, by Bao Tianxiao (1915); *Illustrated Novel Magazine*, by Bao Tianxiao (1917); and *Fiction Quarterly*, by Xu Zhenya (1918), etc. Altogether there were over thirty fiction journals at that time, and some were well-known literary strongholds where many famous novelists gathered. Urban tabloids also emerged during the same period, and in Shanghai, a large number of tabloids were first launched by authors of exposure novels and then by Mandarin Duck and Butterfly novelists. The earliest tabloids were known to be *Entertainment* and *World Vanity Fair*, launched by Li Boyuan, and later there were Sun Yusheng's *Selected Rumors Daily* (《采风报》) and *Forest of Laughter Daily*; Xu Zhenya's *Fiction Daily* (《小说日报》); Zhou Shoujuan's *Eden* (《先施乐园日报》); and the famous *Jing Bao*, launched by Yu Daxiong (余大雄) and Bao Tianxiao on the eve of the May Fourth movement; most of the texts in all of these were written by Mandarin Duck and Butterfly authors. Unfortunately, because no one collected and preserved those tabloids, we aren't able to look at them, but for citizen readers of that time, these cultural products were quite readable and enjoyable, like refreshments in their everyday life. Major newspapers, on the other hand, had unignorable cultural impact due to their social status and large circulation, and Mandarin Duck and Butterfly authors had even won a prominent place in them. For example, Mandarin Duck and Butterfly authors played quite an important role in the literary supplements of three major newspapers, namely *Shun Pao*, *News Report*, and the *Eastern Times*. For twenty years, the Free Talk column in *Shun Pao* was edited by Wang Dungen, Wu Juemi (吴觉迷), Chen Diexian (陈蝶仙), Chen Lengxue (Jinghan), and Zhou Shoujuan, all Mandarin Duck and Butterfly authors; and the Forest of Pleasure (快活林) column in *News Report*, launched by Yan Duhe (严独鹤), and the Sideshows (余兴) column in the *Eastern Times*, by Bao Tianxiao, were very popular for a while. This is further evidence of the large reader base

---

[6]   Qiuweng (秋翁, aka Ping Jinya 平襟亚): "Journals and Magazines of Thirty Years Ago" (《三十年前之期刊》), *Phenomena* 《万象》, Vol. 4, Issue 3, 1944.

8.12. Issue 12 of *Entertainment*, a tabloid launched by Li Boyuan in June 1897

of Mandarin Duck and Butterfly novels, which spread widely via newspapers and magazines; and in order to cater for the cultural and aesthetic tastes of newspaper and magazine readers, authors of this literary school surely made deliberate arrangements in their novels in terms of moral implications, narrative twists, and their appeal to urban readers.

At that time, there were mainly three types of Mandarin Duck and Butterfly novels: romantic fictions, social novels, and detective stories. During the late-Qing and early-Republican period, the detective stories referred to translations of "Sherlock Holmes," for the earliest of the "Hawthorne Detective Stories" series translated by Cheng Xiaoqing (程小青) was not published until 1919. These detective stories were different from old-style Chinese legal cases. One distinction was that the latter promoted the punitive justice of the feudal system, while the former put more emphasis on collecting authentic evidence through scientific means. More full-blown Chinese detective stories and detective characters, like better-developed *wu-xia* (武侠, "martial arts") stories and heroes, would not be presented to readers until the mid-1920s. Therefore, the Mandarin Duck and Butterfly novels of this period were mainly romantic fictions and social novels, with major romantic works being *Jade Pear Spirit*, *Mirror of Evil Injustice*, and *Lost Jade*, and social works *Tides of Yangzhou*, *The Huangpu Tides*, and *Living Hell*, as well as *Private Records of Studying in Japan* by Pingjiang Buxiaosheng. These two types of novels inherited the tradition of urban courtesan novels and exposure novels, respectively, and expanded and enhanced the themes and narrative techniques of their respective antecedents.

Xu Zhenya's *Jade Pear Spirit* set a precedent for sentimental novels. First serialized in the *Civil Rights Newspaper* in Shanghai in 1912 (*Element of People's Rights* was its supplement before separating), it became an instant hit, and its stand-alone edition sold several hundred thousand copies, an incredible figure at that time. The novel was a tragic love story between He Mengxia, a talented scholar from Suzhou who had come to teach in Wuxi, and Bai Liying, the widowed daughter of the owner of He's dwelling place. In the end they could not break free of the conventional constraints imposed by society and by their own outdated concept of rules of etiquette, and both died a tragic death. There was quite an old-style moral admonition in this novel, and it was the so-called custom of "beginning with emotion and stopping at propriety" that smothered the love of its characters, but the story was told by a narrator sympathetic to the love between the young man and widowed woman. Its restrained awareness to pursue freedom, as well as its bold appreciation of love as a high value, showed that the Mandarin Duck and Butterfly novels were combinations of the progress of the modern world and the backwardness of the old one. This was inherited by other Mandarin Duck and Butterfly authors in their romantic fictions and gradually became a pattern of their writing. Another characteristic worth mentioning is that *Jade Pear Spirit* was written in the lyrical parallel style, which suited the fancy of intellectual readers of that time (the first group of general readers educated by new-style schools had not yet truly formed), while it was no less readable because it seldom used allusions and the narration was clear and smooth. Take Bai Liying's monologues for example: "Now I have to live alone in my private chamber and weep alone for my lot; looking in the mirror I can see nothing but a sorrowful and worried face, and lying in the bed I can do nothing but dream unrealizable dreams. The parrot under the decorated window is silent, and mandarin ducks at the clear pond leave me envious. It is so hard to taste such bitterness in life."[7] This style suited the fashion of a freer classical Chinese style, and it was easy to read and understand. Most importantly, the story of *Jade Pear Spirit* was partly based on the author's own life and emotional experiences, in which sense it was a modern novel. Xu Zhenya had a very similar experience to his character He Mengxia, and he, too, wrote poetry and letters to and fell in love with the widowed mother of a student of his. In the end, he listened to the woman's advice and married her sister-in-law instead. The couple had a good relationship, but they had to divorce and then live together in secret because Xu's mother maltreated her daughter-in-law. Because of this, Xu's wife died in a depressed state, and he then wrote 100 poems entitled "Mourning Ruizhu" (《泣珠词》, for his wife's name was Cai Ruizhu [蔡蕊珠]) in her memory. Who would have guessed that the story of *Jade Pear Spirit* extended into the real world? The novel and Xu's mourning poems moved Liu Yuanying (刘沅颖), a daughter of Liu Chunlin, who was No. 1 in the final imperial examination of Qing dynasty, and the girl insisted on being married to Xu Zhenya, a dozen years her elder, despite her father's disapproval.

Zhou Shoujuan, another Mandarin Duck and Butterfly author who specialized in tragic love stories, fell in love with a student from Wuben Girls' School (务本女校) when he was young, but had to break up with her because the girl's parents were snobbish and refused to marry their daughter to a poor scholar like Zhou. This sorrowful experience later became the inspiration for Zhou's lifelong literary creation. In remembrance of his first love, Zhou Yinping (周吟萍), he used the pseudonym "Violet Owner" because her English name was "Violet." This tells us the best Mandarin Duck and Butterfly authors of

---

7 Xu Zhenya: "Fragrant News" (芳讯), *Jade Pear Spirit*, Shanghai: Shanghai Popular Book Co., 1948, Chapter 5, p. 24. The original text was not punctuated.

8.13. *Entertainment Newspaper*, launched by Gao Taichi (高太痴) in the same year but a bit later than *Entertainment*

love stories were not making a fuss about nothing, but sought to record actual events and their own emotional experiences, which was one of the reasons why their love stories could be written and move so many readers. Certainly, this could not conceal the fact that there were many love stories with petty and vulgar subjects written simply to meet the increasing demands of the reader market.

There were two major social novels, and both had the Chinese character "潮" (*chao*, "tides") in their titles: Li Hanqiu's *Tides of Yangzhou* and Zhu Shouju's *Huangpu Tides*. *Tides of Yangzhou* was one of the better-organized lengthy linked-chapter novels and had better-constructed characters. With Yangzhou as the scene and the love triangle between Yunlin, Shuyi, and Hongzhu as the main plot, the story started with the occupation of Yangzhou by the British Army, exposing various hidden goings-on of the Republican government, and portrayed various characters including corrupted officials, degenerate scholars, and low-class rascals, of whom Fu Yuluan, a capitalist revolutionary, was a vividly rendered character. This was also the author's half-autobiographical character, and thus in this novel the author interweaved his own personal experience, the ups and downs of life in the city of Yangzhou, and historical anecdotes. For example, there was this appealing description of how a rascal named Wanggouzi (nicknamed Huang Tianba) recaptured Yangzhou, a farce during the dramatic history of the Xinhai Revolution:

> On the seventeenth of the ninth lunar month, when night had fallen, but not total darkness, rumor spread that the revolutionary party in Zhenjiang had sent people here to recapture Yangzhou. It spread quickly and soon everybody knew. The heads of those twenty-five neighborhoods, then, called on people from each neighborhood to line up at the entrance of the market and wait respectfully for the coming of the revolutionaries …
>
> They waited impatiently, until suddenly they saw several people running toward them with all speed, the lanterns in their hands crashing and clanking, shouting: "Welcome! Welcome! The revolutionary army has entered the city from the South Gate!" Hearing this, those from the neighborhoods were surprised, but feared that it was a groundless rumor, so they crowded around the several people and kept asking about details. Out of breath, they replied: "He who lies is a son of a bitch! We saw the army soldiers with our eyes, each had a white cloth strip wrapped around his arm. They have come straight into our city under a

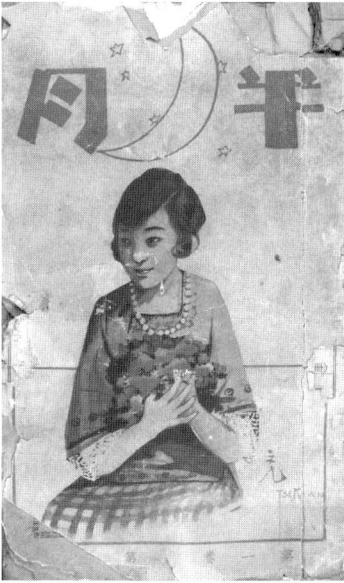

8.14. *Fortnightly*, launched on Dec. 20, 1911

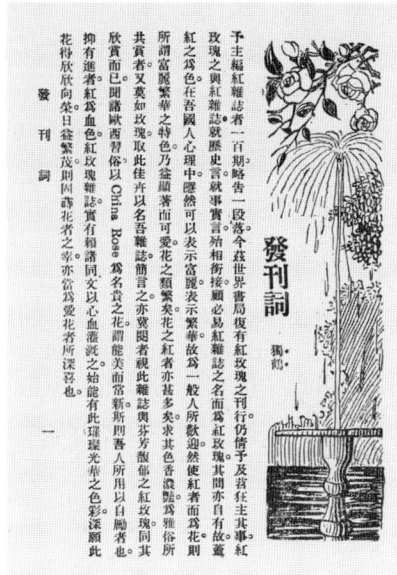

8.15. Editor's opening statement in the magazine *Red Roses* (《红玫瑰》)

leader who had white silk around himself." Hearing these details, people started to believe them. And soon they saw a team of foot soldiers coming, equipped with foreign rifles. One could not see what characters were written on their numbered uniforms, but the white cloth strip was wrapped neatly. At the head was a short brave man who shouted loudly: "I am the Revolutionary Governor! I am resolved to recapture Yangzhou today, even at the risk of my life!"

… At that moment, all people, whether vendors or residents, had a white cloth hanging over their door by mutual consent; those who could not afford white cloth paid three coins and bought some white paper to be posted over the door, in order to celebrate the victory of the revolutionary party. Thus the entire city of Yangzhou was suddenly recovered.[8]

This reminds us of Ah Q, who boasted about the revolutionaries, wearing "white helmets and white armor," moving cases, utensils, and the Ning-style bed out of the house of successful county candidate Zhao.[9]

[8] Li Hanqiu: "Huang Tianba Recovered Yangzhou by Himself, and Meng Haihua Was Committed to Attacking Pukou" (黄天霸只手陷扬州 孟海华一心攻浦口), *Tides of Yangzhou*, Tianjin: Baihua Literature and Art Publishing House, 1986, Vol. 2, chapter 57, pp. 762–763.

[9] Lu Xun: "The True Story of Ah Q" (《阿Q正传》), *Complete Works of Lu Xun*, Vol. 1, Beijing: People's Literature Press, 1981, p. 521. Ning-style furniture originated in Ningbo and the surrounding areas in the Qing dynasty. The high level of craftmanship and unique artistic style makes it popular among higher-class and wealthier people. – Translator's note

An extremely large number of Mandarin Duck and Butterfly novels were published, but we do not have an exact figure. According to relevant statistics, in 1912 alone, there were as many as 445 Mandarin Duck and Butterfly novels published in 162 journals in Shanghai.[10] And if one counts the overall number of their novels, "according to incomplete statistics, there were 949 full-length romantic fictions and social novels, 818 martial arts and detective fictions, and if one counts all the historical, court stories, comical novels, and other writings based on folklore, the total number should be over 2,000."[11] This does not include the short stories published widely in many newspapers and magazines. And one of the major contributions of Mandarin Duck and Butterfly novels to China's literary scene was that while catering to the general readers' reading habits by writing in the format of linked-chapter novels familiar to Chinese readers, they also helped readers develop new reading habits by integrating writing styles borrowed from foreign novels, which were unfamiliar to Chinese readers, thus unconsciously laying the foundation for May Fourth literature. Another sense in which the Mandarin Duck and Butterfly novels laid a foundation for May Fourth literature was that since they were popular stories of great influence and appealed to men and women alike, many of them were adapted into spoken drama plays and traditional operas. Take *Jade Pear Spirit* for example, it was adapted into a spoken drama play by the Shanghai Minxing Troupe (民兴社), and later there was a film based on this novel, adapted by Zheng Zhengqiu (郑正秋) from Mingxing Studio (明星公司). Then there was a spoken drama play based on *Mirror of Evil Injustice*, adapted and performed by the Minming Troupe (民鸣社). Bao Tianxiao's short story "A Strand of Flax" (《一缕麻》) was adapted into Peking opera, Shaoxing opera, and other traditional operas. The Mandarin Duck and Butterfly authors were indeed active in the field of drama. Most of them were excellent at writing playscripts based on novels, such as Bao Tianxiao, Chen Lengxue, Zhou Shoujuan, and Xu Zhuodai (徐卓呆; alias: Banmei [半梅]), who had been studying in Japan and was later famous for his comical stories, and in this way, they promoted the development of modern Chinese literature. The transitional nature of the literature of the Mandarin Duck and Butterfly school was once ignored, and people thought it was an enclosed literary genre of its own, but actually the transition process lasted for a long time, well into the prosperity of urban popular literature in the 1940s.

[10] See *The Encyclopedia of Twentieth-Century Chinese Literature, 1897–1929* (《二十世纪中国文学大典（1897－1929）》), Shanghai: Shanghai Education Press, 1994, p. 246.
[11] Liu Yangti (刘扬体): *The Changing Trends: A New Understanding of the Mandarin Duck and Butterfly School* (《流变中的流派——"鸳鸯蝴蝶派"新论》), Beijing: China Federation of Literary and Art Circles Publishing Corporation, 1997, pp. 8–9.

8.16. Stage photo of the sound film *Jade Pear Spirit*, adapted by Zheng Zhengqiu and first shown in 1924 in Shanghai

Certainly, throughout this long process the literature of this school changed to fit in with the trends of modern literature. With an increasing number of dramas and vernacular translations of foreign literature presented to readers, and with the radical transformation of people's literary concepts brought about by the literary enlightenment movement, modern Chinese literature in its real sense would finally come into focus.

PART II

The May Fourth Movement

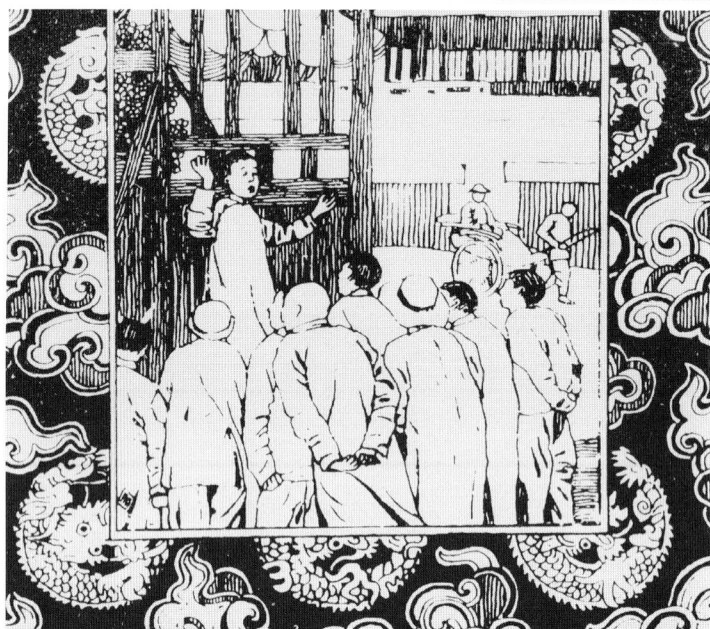

第二章

『五四』启蒙

NINE

INTRODUCTION OF SPOKEN DRAMA INTO CHINA

The Earliest Theater Performances

THE MODERN SPOKEN DRAMA (*HUA-JU*, 话剧), A TRULY imported art form, was introduced to China from two sources. In 1907, Chinese people performed *Black Slaves Appeal to Heaven* (《黑奴吁天录》) successively in Tokyo and Shanghai, the two literary centers at that time. The drama was adapted from Harriet Beecher Stowe's *Uncle Tom's Cabin*, which was known to Chinese people by the *Black Slaves* title, and translated by Lin Shu. The scripts for these two performances, however, were written by two people. This marked the birth of early Chinese spoken drama, a phylogeny related to the emerging New Literature style.

The first group to perform the drama *Black Slaves Appeal to Heaven* was the Spring Willow Society (春柳社), composed of Chinese students in Japan. The Society was formed by Zeng Xiaogu (曾孝谷), Li Shutong (later Monk Hongyi), and Huang Ernan (黄二难), all studying Western painting at the Tokyo School of Fine Arts at that time. At the end of 1906, they watched and were inspired by Japanese *shinpa* theater and founded the Spring Willow Art and Literature Research Society. (*Shinpa* theater was influenced by European Romantic theater; this kind of indirect influence of Western literature through Japanese literature remained throughout the development of modern Chinese literature.) The Society was divided into four departments, namely Arts, Literature, Music, and Drama. In February the following year, the Drama Department performed selected acts of *La Dame aux Camélias* by Alexandre Dumas *fils* in the Surugadai Chinese YMCA hall (whose building was just completed) in order to raise funds to aid people suffering from the flood in the Huai River basin area. One act they selected was Armand's father, Mr. Duval, visiting Marguerite to persuade her to leave his son, and the other act was Marguerite's death. Zeng Xiaogu played the role of Mr. Duval, and Li Shutong, Marguerite. The male impersonation of female roles suggested a historical period when no woman was allowed on the spoken drama stage. In order to play the female character Marguerite, Li Shutong had his specially grown artist-style moustache shaved off, prepared gorgeous dresses for himself, and missed several meals to get slim. The performance of *La Dame aux Camélias* was a great success, not only among Chinese students but even the famous Japanese *shinpa* actor Fujisawa Asajirō and eminent playwright and drama critic Matsui Shoyo watched the performance and went backstage to congratulate the actors. Matsui Shoyo also wrote a critical essay to praise Li Shutong's performance. Then in June that year there was a grand performance of *Black Slaves Appeal to Heaven* at the Hongo-za Arena in Tokyo by the Spring Willow Society. The five-act play was adapted by Zeng Xiaogu, and its plot quite suited the increasingly revolutionary atmosphere. Someone recalled that "the play had its own complete script and fixed dialogues, … the dialogues in the entire play were in spoken language. There was no reciting, singing, monologues, or asides. That is, the entire play was in the form of pure spoken

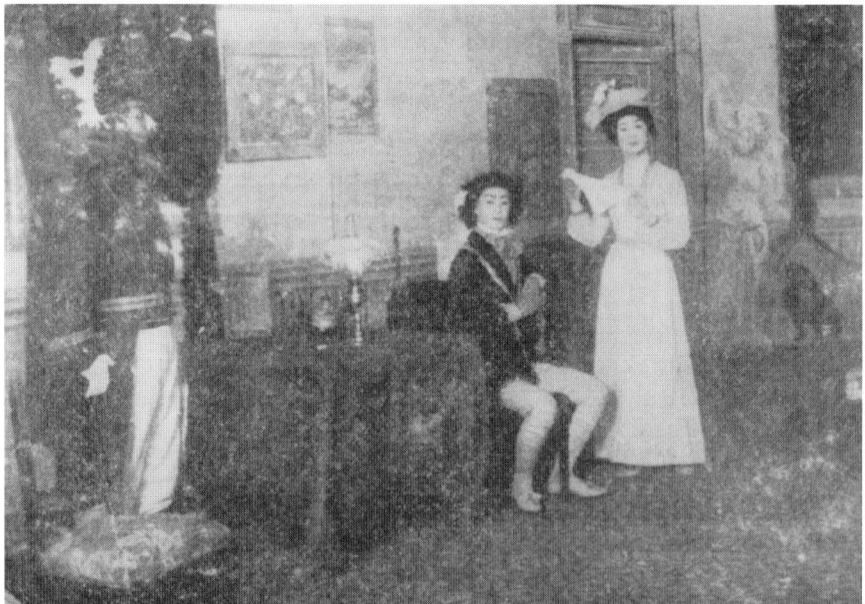

9.1. Stage photo of *Hot Blood* (《热血》), performed by actors of the Spring Willow Society in Tokyo, Japan. The three actors in this photo, from left to right, are Wu Wozun (吴我尊), Lu Jingruo (陆镜若), and Ouyang Yuqian (欧阳予倩), the latter playing a female character quite vividly

drama."[1] The word "pure" is very important here, for it highlighted the Spring Willow tradition that had existed since the very beginning of modern Chinese spoken drama: they would rather sacrifice some commercial interest in order to insist on the original style of Western drama introduced through Japan. It was quite different from the "new civilized drama" (*wen-ming xin-xi*, 文明新戏) or "civilized drama" (*wen-ming xi*, 文明戏), the later forms of early Chinese spoken drama, in which most dramatists took a step back and tried to adopt the performing style of traditional Chinese operas (this was surely justified by the need to win the mass audience).

It's a pity that the script for *Black Slaves Appeal to Heaven* is lost; however, the program of the original performance is in Waseda University's Tsubouchi Memorial Theater Museum collection, on which is written:

9.2. Li Shutong, dressed as Marguerite, a female character, and Zeng Xiaogu in *La Dame aux Camélias*, a major performance for the Spring Willow Society in 1907

> Theatrical performance is an important matter in human civilization, and therefore in founding this Society we established a special department to study new and old dramas, hoping to take the lead in our country's theatrical reformation. We performed at the YMCA earlier this spring to help raise funds, and so many peers and colleagues took the time to come and show their support. Having gained the support of intellectuals from home and abroad, the people of this Society didn't dare give up this career. It was decided that the Dingwei year Grand Performance would be held at the Hongo-za Arena on the first and second of the sixth lunar month, and the five-act *Black Slaves Appeal to Heaven* would be performed from one o'clock each afternoon. For each act, all plot outlines and names of characters and their respective performers are hereby listed on the left. It is our great honor to have you virtuous talents come and give your valuable advice.

The program (as well as stage setting) was designed by Li Shutong, from which we may get a clear idea of the title, plot outline, and characters in each act of the play. Since the play had grand scenes and a great many characters, almost all the actors, Zeng Xiaogu, Li Shutong, Zhuang Yunshi (庄云石), Wu Wozun, Ouyang Yuqian, Xie Kangbai (谢抗白), and Li Taohen (李涛痕), had to play

---

[1] Ouyang Yuqian: "Reminiscing about the Spring Willow Society" (《回忆春柳》), *Complete Works of Ouyang Yuqian* (《欧阳予倩全集》), Vol. 6. Shanghai: Shanghai Literature and Art Publishing House, 1990, p. 150.

9.3. Stage photo of *La Dame aux Camélias*, whose selected acts were performed by the Spring Willow Society in February 1907

9.4. Li Shutong starved himself to get slim enough to play Marguerite in *La Dame Aux Camélias* in 1907

9.5. Portrait of young Li Shutong

more than two characters each. By the day of the performance, there were no empty seats in the 1,500-seat Hongo-za Arena. "The balcony was full of people standing there, and hardly any room was left"[2]; "3,000 seats were reserved for the performance on June 2nd, but actually more than 3,000 people came,

---

[2] See *Hochi Shinbun,* No. 10833 (June 3 of the fortieth year of the Meiji period). Quoted from Huang Aihua (黄爱华): *China's Early Spoken Drama and Japan* (《中国早期话剧与日本》), Changsha:Yuelu Press, 2001, p. 61.

9.6. Poster for the performance of *Black Slaves Appeal to Heaven* at the Hongo-za Arena in Tokyo on the first day of the sixth lunar month, 1907. One can feel what a spectacular event it was

9.7. Stage photo of the second act of *Black Slaves Appeal to Heaven* performed by Chinese students in Tokyo. The actors included Ouyang Yuqian, Zhuang Yunshi, Li Shutong, and Huang Ernan. All female characters were played by male actors

and even the aisles were full of people standing there."[3] The performance was constantly interrupted by applause and cheers, and it was extensively reported on and praised by newspapers and magazines in both Japan and China. Japanese reporters went so far as to say that the performance was "far better than those of

---

[3] This was written by a renowned Japanese drama critic in an essay published in the 6923rd issue of *Miyako Shinbun* (June 3 of the fortieth year of the Meiji period). Quoted from Huang Aihua: China's Early Spoken Drama and Japan, p. 62.

our country's amateur troupes, and compared with the performance of *shinpa* dramas by Takada, Fujisawa, Ii Yōhō, and Takeo Kawai, not only it is more worth watching, but it had far greater force."[4] This was probably an exaggeration. According to records, during the three months the play was in rehearsals at the Dragon-Wave Hall (龙涛馆) in Tokyo, Fujisawa Asajirō, the renowned Japanese *shinpa* actor, had come on site over twenty times to give his advice. And it is certainly unimaginable that without the selfless help of Fujisawa, such a big theater as Hongo-za Arena would have been rented out to a Chinese students' amateur drama troupe at such a low price. All in all, it was a great achievement for Chinese spoken drama to have caused such a big stir.

Only a few months after that, the Spring Sun Society (春阳社), founded by Wang Zhongsheng (王钟声), performed *Black Slaves Appeal to Heaven* at the Lyceum Theater in the concession of Shanghai. The playwright was Xu Xiaotian (许啸天). We do not have strong evidence to suggest that seeing the success of the Spring Willow Society the Spring Sun Society chose to perform the same play, but Wang Zhongsheng had studied in Germany and Japan, and he clearly had a solid knowledge of the Western drama. When the performance of the Spring Willow Society in Japan was extensively reported on by major newspapers in China, Wang was entrusted by Ma Xiangbo and Shen Zhongli (沈仲礼) to found China's first drama school in Shanghai (Tongjian School, 通鉴学校), and he surely heard of the dramatic event in Japan. This performance of *Black Slaves Appeal to Heaven* was the result of three months of teaching at Tongjian School. According to Xu Banmei (that is, Xu Zhuodai, who wrote comical stories), who had watched the performance: "The play was divided into several acts, completely different from the incessant scene-after-scene performances of new Peking opera; ... sets were used on stage, ... and the lighting in the Lyceum was extremely well equipped, by which the audience was amazed." Interestingly, most of the student actors had only received short-term training and did not fully understand what spoken drama was about. The actors playing black slaves were unwilling to apply charcoal to their faces, so the stage was full of "nonblack black slaves," and the play became something like "*Non-Black Slaves Appeal to Heaven*." On the other hand, most students had some background in Peking opera, so their performance was "not different from Pihuang (皮簧) opera, in which gongs and drums were used, Pihuang were sung, and chanting, introductory recitals, or mixed rhythms were adopted to precede the entry of each character; what was most funny was that some characters entered with a horsewhip in hand."[5] Today we cannot trace the origin of the term "civilized drama," while if we use it as the general term

4   See *Tokyo Mainichi Shinbun*, No. 11482 (June 2 of the fortieth year of the Meiji period). Quoted from Huang Aihua: *China's Early Spoken Drama and Japan*, p. 62.

5   Xu Banmei: *Reminiscences of the Early Period of Spoken Drama* (《话剧创始期回忆录》), Beijing: China Theater Publishing House, 1959, p. 19.

to mean "early spoken drama," there shall at least be two schools, namely "pure spoken drama" and "impure spoken drama." However, actually there was not a clear demarcation between the two. The Spring Sun Society was similar to the Spring Willow Society, but even its first performance was very similar to traditional Chinese opera (impure), not to say other troupes and performances. Later, Ren Tianzhi (任天知), who claimed to have been a member of the Spring Willow Society, joined the Spring Sun Society. He cooperated with Wang Zhongsheng and produced the play *Joan Haste*,[6] breaking free from the tradition of traditional Chinese opera. Xu Banmei also watched *Joan Haste* and thought this performance finally "made it look like spoken drama."[7]

However, the performance by the Spring Sun Society, which blended Chinese and Western styles, actually had an origin dating back to the earliest emergence of Western drama in China, much earlier than 1907. With the entry of Western powers through the trading ports of China, the first amateur drama troupe was organized by foreign residents in the British Concession as early as 1850. They reconstructed the warehouse at the corner of today's Beijing and Guangdong roads into a shabby theater with bench seats, and called it "New Theater" (新剧院), and later "Empire Theater" (帝国剧院). From December 12 of that

9.8. Members of the Spring Sun Society after the performance of *Black Slaves Appeal to Heaven* in Shanghai in September 1907

---

[6] The Chinese title was "A Brief Biography of Jiayin" (《迦茵小传》), which was also the title of Lin Shu's translation of H. Rider Haggard's novel, *Joan Haste*.

[7] Xu Banmei: *Reminiscences of the Early Period of Spoken Drama*, p. 24.

9.9. Stage photo of the twentieth performance of *Victims of Opium* (《黑籍冤魂》) by the New Citizen Society (新民社). The performance was seen as carrying forward the tradition of *Black Slaves Appeal to Heaven* by the Spring Willow Society and Spring Sun Society

year, they performed Western plays, including *Diamonds Are the Only Cure* (《以钻攻钻》), *Gentleman on the Beam* (《梁上君子》), *Legitimate Inheritance* (《合法继承》), *Love, Law, and Medicine* (《爱情、法律和药品》), and *High Life Downstairs* (《楼梯下的高等生活》). In 1866, the Footpads Troupe and the Rangers Troupe, both founded by Westerners in Shanghai, merged and became the Amateur Dramatic Club of Shanghai, called ADC for short. The ADC then proposed to build the very first modern theater in Shanghai, the Lyceum Theater, a wooden structure located on Yuanmingyuan Road. The first public performance at the Lyceum was held in 1867; however, the theater was destroyed in a fire in 1871. In 1874 another Lyceum Theater, with two stories and a spacious stage, was built near the British Consulate. It was in this Lyceum Theater that the Spring Sun Society performed its version of *Black Slaves Appeal to Heaven*. (In 1929, the Lyceum Theater was sold to a Chinese owner at the price of 175,000 silver ingots, and in December that year, the ADC built a third Lyceum Theater, a concrete structure, on the corner of Rue Bourgeat and Route Cardinal Mercier in the French Concession, which is still standing today.) At that time, the Lyceum Theater was a kind of foreign residents' club, and it did not open to ordinary Chinese people. However, a few Chinese people, such as Xu Banmei, Zheng Zhengqiu, and Bao Tianxiao, etc., mingled with foreigners and entered the theater, and it was there that these people first saw what Western spoken drama was like. Japanese residents also built their own theater, the Tokyo Arena, in Hongkou, Shanghai, which had around 200 seats and was dedicated to *shinpa* theater; it was also frequented by Xu Banmei. These performances were held right in front of Chinese people, on a daily basis, and they showed Chinese people what Western drama should be like. The earliest Chinese practice of Western drama were the performances by Chinese students from mission schools in Shanghai. The earliest record of such a performance was that of the "performance to follow the Western philosophers' educational words and deeds" in "the eleventh lunar month in the winter of Jihai Year" by students of St. John College in 1898.[8] Other mission schools, such as Nanyang Public School and St. Ignatius School, also held performances of a similar nature. Most of these performances chose from a list of Western plays, and they were also considered a chance for students to

9.10. Lyceum Theater, rebuilt for the second time in a different location. Foreign residents performed spoken drama here and imported this art form into China

enhance their oral foreign languages. What's worth mentioning here is that during the Christmas of 1899, some students from St. John College wrote and performed *A Scandal in Officialdom* (《官场丑史》), the earliest attempt to integrate Chinese people's everyday life into the imported art form of spoken drama. Wang Youyou (汪优游), one of the earlier spoken drama artists, said that it was after watching *A Scandal in Officialdom* as a high school student that he decided to organize school performances and began his career in the field of spoken drama.

What coexisted with these imitation-style performances but had a greater influence among audiences was the reformed old-style traditional opera, that is, Shanghai-school Peking opera. As its name implies, Shanghai-school Peking opera was a Shanghai-style Peking opera, which could be seen as a more fashionable and Westernized form of Peking opera. The modernized, modern-dress operas were popular in Shanghai during the latter half of the nineteenth century. In 1893, a one-act play, *An Iron Rooster* (《铁公鸡》), was performed in Tianxian Tea Garden in Shanghai. It was a play about the Taiping Heavenly Kingdom, which had just been beaten. The Qing-costume play, with its twelve scenes presented nonstop under traditional Chinese colored lights and with its

[8] Quoted from Zhu Shuangyun (朱双云): *A History of New Theater: Spring and Autumn* (《新剧史·春秋》), Shanghai: New Drama and Fiction Press, 1914.

vivid military fighting, attracted a very large audience. The playwright Wang Xiaonong was a major figure in the opera reformation of this period; he wrote new plays and created new sounds, reformed the costumes and adornments of Peking opera that had been used for over 100 years, and even let the actors come on stage in fashionable dress and Western-style suits (the Shanghai-school Peking opera was the precedent of modern Peking opera). In 1904 he raised funds and cofounded China's first theatrical journal, *Great Stage of the Twentieth Century*, whose chief editors were Chen Qubing and Liu Yazi. The reformed new opera promoted by Wang Xiaonong and others had a great many fans among Shanghai citizens, which was one of the reasons why the spoken drama performed by the Spring Sun Society displayed some features of Peking opera. When students of the Spring Willow Society returned home to perform spoken drama and continued to introduce Western drama to China, they encountered a cultural environment in which pure Western drama had been encroached and penetrated by reformed Peking opera.

In 1908, Xia Yueshan (夏月珊), his brother Xia Yuerun (夏月润), and Pan Yueqiao (潘月樵), all renowned for their modern dress Peking opera performances, had the New Stage (新舞台) theater built at the former dock of south Shanghai's sixteenth pier (it was later rebuilt at Jiumudi [九亩地], in the northwest corner of the former walled city). At the New Stage, the reformation of traditional Chinese theater began. Instead of an old-style stage with pillars on three sides, the New Stage had a modern proscenium-arch stage, and a revolving stage was also attached; Japanese technicians and carpenters were invited to design and build stage sets, and with modern lighting and 2,000 seats, the theater was quite spectacular for the time. The theater performed Peking opera plays in modern dress, such as *Victims of Opium*, *New La Dame aux Camélias*, and *A Tragic History of Poland* (《波兰亡国惨》), using the Zhongzhou accent and Suzhou dialect, "with the emphasis on speaking instead of singing, despite its use of gongs and drums."[9] And it adopted the new system of selling tickets for performances and abolished the outmoded conventions of drinking tea, cracking melon seeds, and throwing towels. The New Stage later held a key position in the activities of new-style performances of traditional operas and traditional-style performances of new operas. The word "new" here is, indeed, quite significant.

With the return of members of the Spring Willow Society on the eve of the Xinhai Revolution, various dramatic societies and troupes were set up here and there, promoting new drama in the accomodating atmosphere. Most of these civilized drama troupes were located in Shanghai, including the Evolution Society (进化团), the New Dramatic Society (新剧同志会),

[9] Ouyang Yuqian: *Since I Became an Actor* (《自我演戏以来》), Beijing: China Theater Publishing House, 1959, p. 67.

the Shanghai Association of Theatrical Performance (上海演剧联合会), the Social Education Society (社会教育团), and others; more than twenty altogether. In Beijing there was the Enlightening People Society (牖民社); in Suzhou there was the Suzhou New Drama Society (苏州新剧行进社); and in Wuhu (芜湖) there was the Enlightenment New Drama Troupe (迪智群新剧团), etc. In Tianjin, students of Nankai School, under the guidance of Principal Zhang Boling (张伯苓), became the first to conduct campus theatrical activities, which had a great influence on the north and the entire country. Zhang Boling's younger brother, Zhang Pengchun (张彭春), studied dramatic art as a minor subject when he studied in the United States in the 1910s, and later he became the backbone of the Nankai spoken drama movement, meaning the earlier spoken drama in the north also enjoyed the direct influence of European and American drama. By that time, Lu Jingruo and Ouyang Yuqian had become core members of the Spring Willow Society. In their later days in Japan, they had cofounded the Shenyou Society (申酉会) and cooperated in the performance of *Strange Tale* (《电术奇谈》) and *Hot Tears* (《热泪》). Back in Shanghai, Lu Jingruo cooperated with the Spring Sun Society and held performances of *Fiercely Looking Back* and *Society Bell* (《社会钟》) at Zhang's Garden under the name of New Art Theater (文艺新剧场), and after the Xinhai Revolution, he cofounded the New Dramatic Society together with Ouyang Yuqian, Wu Wozun, and Ma Jiangshi (马绛士), who were collectively called the "Four Friends of Spring Willow." They performed *Love and Hate in a Family* (《家庭恩怨记》), *Better Go Home* (《不如归》), and other plays at Zhang's Garden. They also performed for other dramatic troupes; for example, sometimes they performed in Shanghai under the "Spring Willow Theater" name. *Love and Hate in a Family* had a complete script, but most other plays performed by the Spring Willow school were only based on plot outlines. Their plot outlines were minutely prepared, however, detailing the division of acts, giving a general outline of each act, and including important dialogues, etc. They had fewer act divisions, did not use intermission shows, and did not use speeches, slogans, or comic and acrobatic performances. The performing style they adopted was that of relatively pure

9.11. "Four Friends of Spring Willow": (left to right) Ouyang Yuqian, Wu Wozun, Ma Jiangshi, and Lu Jingruo. Lu Jingruo supported the Spring Willow Society until his death

Western drama, and thus the early Chinese spoken drama, an art form indirectly imported from the West, maintained its original style.

In 1910, Ren Tianzhi founded the Evolution Society (进化团) in Shanghai, which was China's first professional new drama group, and its members included Wang Youyou, Chen Jinghua (陈镜花), and Chen Dabei (陈大悲), etc. After their successful performances of *Long Live the Republic* (《共和万岁》), *The Yellow Crane Tower* (《黄鹤楼》), and *The Storms of East Asia* (《东亚风云》), they raised a "Tianzhi-School New Drama" banner in front of their theater and were quite popular for a time. It was the Tianzhi-school's strategy to take advantage of political propaganda theater to attract a larger audience and bring in more profit, but this strategy could not be sustained once the political situation changed. Its plays had more acts than others, and one of its major features was that the characters could deviate from the script and deliver impromptu speeches on stage, and gongs, drums, and singing were added at the entry and exit of characters and key points of dramatic development. These disguised speeches promoted revolution, which could win unexpected cheers and applause. Accordingly, the roles in the plays could be categorized into "old male role with long speeches," "young male role with long speeches," and "main female role with long speeches," etc., a step back toward the traditional operas that featured stereotyped roles. Once when Ouyang Yuqian was acting onstage with Ren Tianzhi, there were also two comic roles, played by Wang Youyou and Zha Tianying (查天影), who frequently interrupted Ren Tianzhi's speech on love, so much so that Ren leapt up in a great rage and waved his stick and said an impromptu line to Ouyang Yuqian: "My young girl, how come you have so many dogs? It seems I have to beat these dogs before speaking to you!"[10] It was shocking to see that "speeches" and "comic roles" could spoil the play to such a great extent.

Neither the Spring Willow Society nor the newly emerged civilized drama groups had a fixed performing venue, which was a sign that spoken drama had not become an independent art form in China. The so-called New Art Theater (文艺新剧场) was not a physical theater, and therefore the New Stage and other Peking

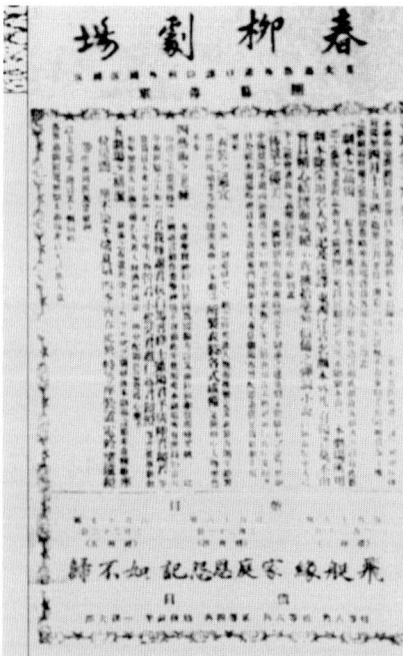

9.12. Poster of performances at Moudeli Theater in Shanghai by the Spring Willow Society in 1914, in which the plays included *Better Go Home*, *On the Aircraft* (《飞艇缘》), and *Love and Hate in a Family*

[10]   Ibid., p. 66.

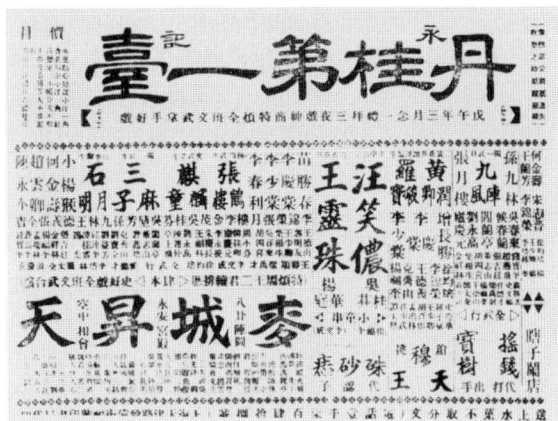

9.13. At that time, Peking opera theaters established in the late Qing in Shanghai also delivered Wang Xiaonong's reformed Shanghai-school Peking opera, which was interpenetrated with civilized drama

opera theaters that imitate the New Stage, such as the Singing and Dancing Stage (歌舞台), the Grand Stage (大舞台), and the Laughing Stage (笑舞台), became temporary venues for civilized drama. For a time some theaters allowed civilized dramatic plays to be performed before Peking opera evening shows, with the latter coming on as the last but best. But soon the Peking opera performers were complaining that the new drama players prolonged their performances at will. This practice of sharing performing venues showed that traditional Chinese operas were trying to resemble new drama, and that earlier spoken drama made concessions to reformed traditional opera. To illustrate this, such traditional opera plays as *The Tablet of Blood and Tears* (《血泪碑》) and *Family's Blood* (《杀子报》) were performed on the spoken drama stage without any reform, and such translated spoken drama plays as *Napoleon's Love Affairs* (《拿破仑艳史》) and *Sacrifice* (《牺牲》) were adapted into modern dress Peking opera plays. Many civilized drama plays began to backslide toward traditional Peking opera. Zheng Zhengqiu, one of the main figures of the so-called Resurgence of the Jiayin Year in the history of Chinese spoken drama, once promoted "adding singing to new drama" when he performed family drama, as a means of enhancing the box office earnings of civilized drama. And some civilized drama troupes were even more degenerate, going so far as to attract the mass audience with sexual shows or snake charming.

By that time, Moudeli Theater (谋得利剧场) located on Nanjing Road near the Bund gradually took shape as a theater specializing in early spoken drama. In Shanghai, entertainment facilities were concentrated around Fuzhou Road (Fourth Avenue), Fujian Road (Stone Road), and Hankou Road, while Moudeli Theater was located on the second floor of the warehouse of Moudeli Gramophone Company on Peking Road. The small theater with only 500–600 seats was known to few people, so much so that there were rumors that the theater was haunted on rainy nights. In 1914, Lu Jingruo and his New Dramatic Society, which had performed *Better Go Home*, *On the Aircraft*, and

Love and Hate in a Family in other cities, went back to Shanghai and began their performances at Moudeli Theater on April 15 under the signboard of "Spring Willow Theater." According to the "Statement for the Opening of Spring Willow Theater" published in *Shun Pao*, since its earliest performances in Japan, [all members of] Spring Willow Society "had been dedicated to the development of art and literature for ten years, and never cared about worldly gains."[11] On the flyer at the opening, it still insisted on such principles as "respectable scripts," "beautiful settings," "appropriate costumes," "sophisticated art expressions," and "clear and clean theater," and was "unwilling to adapt valueless lyric-type novels in order to cater for lower-class people."[12] This was the ideal of members of the Spring Willow Society, but actually their insistence on this ideal conflicted with the embarrassing realities in front of them. Some fans who had come to watch the opening performance complained that the drama was too solemn and difficult to understand. Market demands compelled them to change their repertoire, and later they had to perform plays adapted from popular novels such as *Heaven Rain Flowers* (《天雨花》) and *Phoenixes Flying Together* (《凤双飞》). Within a year, the Spring Willow Theater frequently changed their repertoire (with over 100 plays involved), and performing *Nora*, *Salome*, and *Resurrection* had virtually become dreams that would never come true. They had no pay, and had to live quite a meagre life, all sustained by Lu Jingruo with leverage. Once when they performed *La Dame aux Camélias* on a rainy night, there were only three people in the audience.[13] When their only supporter Lu Jingruo suddenly died of disease, the Spring Willow school had lost their mainstay and disbanded.

In 1913, Zheng Zhengqiu's New People Society also hired the Moudeli Theater as a venue, and performed *The Evil Family* (《恶家庭》). Originally, they intended to perform only two acts, but it was unexpectedly popular with the audience, so they wrote and performed a dozen acts, hence the upsurge of "family drama." But they, too, gradually declined. After insisting on performing on the Laughing Stage and failing, Zheng Zhengqiu abandoned spoken drama and published "Statement of Zheng Zhengqiu Abandoning New Drama," indignantly claiming that "seeing the growing popularity of extremely vicious bandit plays, absurdly unreasonable farces, happy-ending lyric plays, multiact plays selling gorgeous outfits and settings, how can I bear all this?"[14] He could not save civilized new drama from declining; and he was not aware that to

[11] See "Statement for Opening of Spring Willow Theater," published in the Free Talk column of *Shun Pao* on April 17, 1914.

[12] See "Flyer at the Opening of the Spring Willow Theater," quoted from Huang Aihua: *China's Early Spoken Drama and Japan*, p. 206.

[13] Ouyang Yuqian: *Since I Became an Actor*, p. 48.

[14] Quoted from Zhu Shuangyun: *Historical Material on Early-Stage Professional Spoken Drama* (《初期职业话剧史料》), Chongqing: Independence Press, 1942.

introduce spoken drama into Chinese cities, one must show great patience in enlightening its audience and sometimes had to make concessions to the latter, and one had to have scripts that could be easily accepted by Chinese audiences. He could do nothing but sigh and lament. This showed that it was not yet time for spoken drama to keep a foothold in China. At the same time, we should take note that in the north, the development of spoken drama was far behind that in the south, which can be attributed to the high political pressure in the north and the power of traditional opera. Once Wang Zhongsheng went to Beijing and Tianjin to perform the plays they had put on in Shanghai, but they were immediately banned. Then in 1911, Wang was assassinated in Tianjin because of his involvement in anti-Qing activities. And because of dramatic performances, the head of the Enlightening People Society, founded in Beijing in 1912, was also arrested the next year. Such a bad cultural environment surely led to the underdevelopment of spoken drama in the north. Therefore, when Lu Xun and his colleague Qi Zongyi (齐宗颐) from

9.14. Zheng Zhengqiu: after bringing about an upsurge of "family drama" during the period of civilized drama, he became one of the founders of Mingxing Studio, a pioneer of China's silent films

9.15. Playwright and director Zheng Zhengqiu (on the right, at the stern), lead actress Hu Die (胡蝶), and other actors shooting outdoor scenes for the film *Romance in Spring* (《春水情波》)

MAP 9.1. Locations of theaters where China's earliest spoken dramas were performed

the Department of Social Education of the Ministry of Education went to Tianjin to inspect the new drama in June 1912 and watched the current-affair drama *The Flood of North China* (《江北水灾记》) at Guanghe Theater on June 11, he recorded this in his diary: "they are courageous but greatly lack knowledge and skills."[15] One could predict that civilized drama could never be revived, and a new page would be turned for modern spoken drama after the May Fourth movement.

TABLE 9.1 *Theaters where China's earliest spoken dramas were performed*

Theater name	Date	Plays performed	Performing troupe and main actors	Notes
Guanghe Theater, Tongle Garden	1911	*Diary of a Pig* (《猪仔记》), *A Tragic History of Vietnam* (《越南亡国惨》), *New La Dame aux Camélias*	Enlightening People Society / Guan Tianseng (关天僧)	The head of the Society was arrested
Guangde Tower Theater	Jan. 1915	*A Blessing in Disguise* (《因祸得福》), *A Hating Old Woman* (《仇大娘》), etc.	Adapted by Nankai New Drama Troupe (南开新剧团)	
Nankai School	Sep. 1909	*Misplaced* (《用非所学》)	Adapted and directed by Zhang Boling (Principal)	
Nankai School	1915	*One Silver Dollar* (《一元钱》)	Nankai New Drama Troupe / students and teachers of Nankai School	
Nankai School	1916	*A Slight Error in Thought* (《一念差》)	Nankai New Drama Troupe / students and teachers of Nankai School	
Nankai School	1918	*New Village Head* (《新村正》)	Nankai New Drama Troupe / students and teachers of Nankai School	

(continued)

[15] "Renzi Dairies" (《壬子日记》), June 11, 1912, collected in Vol. 2, *Complete Works of Lu Xun*, Beijing: People's Literature Press, 1981, p. 5.

TABLE 9.1 *(continued)*

Theater name	Date	Plays performed	Performing troupe and main actors	Notes
Shengping Theater	Feb. 1911	*The Bloody Straw Rain Cape* (《血蓑衣》), *The Storms of East Asia*, etc.	Evolution Society / Ren Tianzhi, Wang Youyou, Chen Jinghua	China's first professional drama troupe
Soochow University	Sep. 1909	Western drama	Chaired by Chen Dabei	
Zhongjiang Grand Stage	Apr. 1911	*The Bloody Straw Rain Cape*, *The Sea of Regret*, etc.	Evolution Society / Ren Tianzhi, Wang Youyou, Chen Jinghua	
The Roaring-Heaven Spoken Drama Troupe (振天声剧社) at Peng's Garden, Lychee Bay (荔枝湾)	1908	*The Uprising Led by Xiong Fei* (《熊飞起义》), *Assassinating Emperor Qinshihuang with a Big Hammer* (《博浪椎击》), etc.	Roaring-Heaven Spoken Drama Troupe / Chen Tiejun	Performed in Cantonese
Hongo-za Arena	June 1–2, 1907	*Black Slaves Appeal to Heaven*	Spring Willow Society / Li Shutong, Ouyang Yuqian, etc.	A complete performance of spoken drama
Tokyo Arena	Around Mar. 1909	*Hot Tears*	Shenyou Society / Ouyang Yuqian, Lu Jingruo, etc.	Highly praised by Huang Xing of the United Allegiance Society
Tokiwa Hall (Yorozucho)	Apr. 14, 1908	*Pitying Each Other* (《生相怜》)	Spring Willow Society / Zeng Xiaogu, Li Shutong, Ouyang Yuqian	
Golden Hall (Kanda)	Jan. 1909	*Voice of Protest* (《鸣不平》)	Shenyou Society / Zeng Xiaogu, Ouyang Yuqian, Lu Jingruo	
Surugadai Chinese YMCA (Kanda)	Feb. 11, 1907	Two acts of *La Dame aux Camélias*	Spring Willow Society / Zeng Xiaogu, Li Shutong, Tang Ken (唐肯), etc.	Beginning of pure spoken drama
	May 5, 1908	*New Butterfly Dreams* (《新蝶梦》)	Li Taohen (李涛痕), a member of the Spring Willow Society	Anniversary of Chiba-ken Chinese Medicine Society

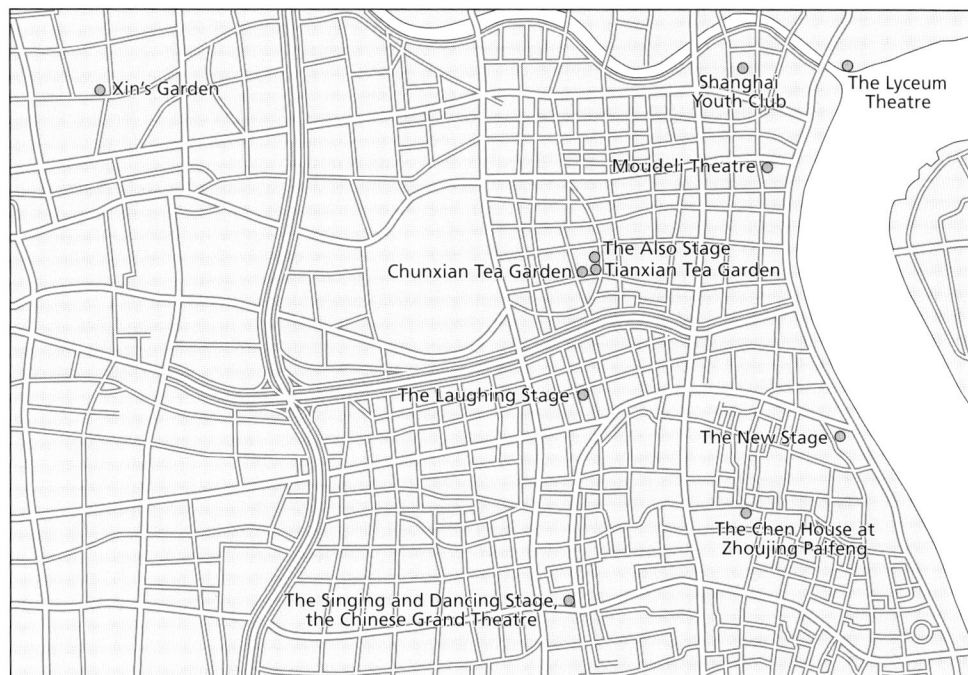

MAP 9.2. Performance venues for spoken drama in Shanghai (partial sketch)

TABLE 9.2 *Statistics of earliest performances of spoken drama in Shanghai (partial)*

Venue	Location	Date	Plays performed	Performing troupe and main actors	Notes
Nanyang Public School	North of Xujiahui Town (Today's Xuhui Campus, Jiaotong University)	Dec. 1900	*Six Gentlemen* (《六君子》), *The Boxer* (《义和拳》), etc.	Students of Class 2 of the secondary section of the school	Campus performance
St. Ignatius School	Xujiahui (Today's Xuhui Middle School)	1902	*Fleeing* (《脱难记》)	Students of the school	Campus performance
Yucai School	Today's Yucai Middle School	1903	*The Revenge of the Great Swordsman* (《张汶祥刺马》) and *The British Army Captured Ye Mingchen* (《英兵掳去叶名琛》)	Students of the school	Campus performance

(continued)

TABLE 9.2 *(continued)*

Venue	Location	Date	Plays performed	Performing troupe and main actors	Notes
Nanyang Second Public Middle School	Weihai Road	1904	New drama to celebrate Confucius's birthday	Students of the school	Campus performance
Chen's House at Zhoujin Paifang	At the crossing between Sanpaifang and Zhoujin roads	1905	*Capturing An Dehai* (《捉拿安德海》) and *The Church Case in Jiangxi* (《江西教案》)	Literary Fraternity (文友会) / Wang Zhongxian (汪忠贤, pseudonym: Wang Youyou [优游]) and his brother	Campus performances went public
Chunxian Tea Garden (春仙茶园)	Guangdong Road, opposite to Mantingfang on Fujian Road	Early 1908	*Joan Haste*	Spring Sun Society / Wang Zhongsheng, Ren Tianzhi	Civilized new drama in China formally took shape
Lyceum Theater, Xin's Garden, Weichun Garden (味莼园)	At the corner of Gaomen Road and Yuanmingyuan Road, near Xinzha Road and Taixing Road (formerly Medhurst Road), at the west end of Jing'an Temple Road	1908	*A Flower in a Sinful Sea* and *The Revenge of the Great Swordsman*, etc.	Spring Sun Society / Wang Zhongsheng, Wang Youyou, etc.	Weichun Garden was also known as Zhang's Garden
Tianxian Tea Garden	At the corner of Fujian and Guangdong roads	1908	*The Little Mirror* (《小镜子》)	Benevolent Society (仁社) / Shen Jinglin (沈景麟), Lu Shenlin (陆申麟)	
Weichun Garden	West end of Jing'an Temple Road	June 1910	*Waves in the Love Sea* (《爱海波》) and *Fiercely Looking Back* (adapted from *The Eternal Tides*)	New Art Theater / Wang Zhongsheng, Lu Jingruo, Xu Banmei	A Work of Koroku Sato; Weichun Garden was also known as Zhang's Garden

(continued)

TABLE 9.2 *(continued)*

Venue	Location	Date	Plays performed	Performing troupe and main actors	Notes
New New Stage (新新舞台)	At the corner of Jiujiang and Hubei roads	Dec. 1911	*An Unfortunate Girl* (《薄命花》)	Evolution Society / Ren Tianzhi, Wang Youyou, Chen Jinghua	Its name was changed to "Reformation Society" (改进团)
Weichun Garden, Yu Garden (愚园)	West end of Jing'an Temple Road, half a *li* from the north-eastern part of Jing'an Temple	1911	*Society Bell* (adapted from *Bell of the Cloud* 《云之响》)	Lu Jingruo	A work by Koroku Sato
Weichun Garden, Shanghai Youth Club	West end of Jing'an Temple Road; on the Sichuan Middle Road, in today's Puguang Middle School	Mar. 1912	*Love and Hate in a Family, Free Marriage* (《自由结婚》)	New Dramatic Society / Lu Jingruo, Ouyang Yuqian, etc.	Once coworked with the Chinese Performance Troupe (中华演剧团)
Grand Stage, Moudeli Theater	Hankou Road; East Nanjing Road near the Bund	Mar. 1912	*A Love-Sick Idiot* (《情痴》)	Illumination Society (开明社) / Li Junpan (李君磐), Zhu Xudong (朱旭东)	
New Stage	Near the former dock at the sixteenth pier of south Shanghai, leading to Lee Maloo Road at the back	May 1912	*Twin Stories* (《双编记》), *Red Pomegranate Blossom* (《榴花血》)	Students of Nanyang University (南洋大学)	
Minming Troupe		Apr. 1914	*Last Words* (《遗嘱》), *A Female Lawyer* (《女律师》), *Love-Hate* (《晴天恨》)	New Drama Association (新剧公会) / Xu Xiaotian, Wang Hanyang	An association of six dramatic groups including New People Society
Also Stage (亦舞台)	Huizhong Hotel on Daxin Street (大新街, Hubei Road)	1918		Yaofeng Drama Troupe (药风剧社) / Zheng Zhengqiu	

(continued)

TABLE 9.2 *(continued)*

Venue	Location	Date	Plays performed	Performing troupe and main actors	Notes
Singing and Dancing Stage, Chinese Grand Theater (中华大戏院)	French Concession, Third Avenue, the corner of Hubei and Hankou roads	Nov. 1913	*The Empress Dowager* (《西太后》)	Minming Society/ Jing Yingsan (经营三), Zhang Shichuan (张石川), and Gu Wuwei (顾无为)	
Singing and Dancing Stage	French Concession	July 1914		Minxing Society (民兴社) / Su Shichi (苏石痴)	The first group that promoted actors and actresses performing together on the stage
St. John College	Fanwangdu Ferry (梵王渡)	1899	*A Scandal in the Officialdom*	Students of the college	Campus performance
Laughing Stage	Guangxi Road	1916		Laughing Stage / Zhu Shuangyun, Wang Youyou, Xu Banmei	
Laughing Stage	Guangxi Road	1919		New Drama Department of Heping Society (和平社) / Zheng Zhengqiu became a member	
Moudeli Theater	East Nanjing Road near the Bund	July 1911	*A Shadow in the Mirror* (《镜中影》), *Xu Zhonglu* (《徐仲鲁》) and *Who's the First to Die* (《谁先死》), etc.	Social Education Society / Xu Banmei	
Moudeli Theater	East Nanjing Road near the Bund	1912	*Love and Hate in a Family* and *Better Go Home*, etc.	Spring Willow Theater / Lu Jingruo, Ouyang Yuqian, etc.	

(continued)

TABLE 9.2 *(continued)*

Venue	Location	Date	Plays performed	Performing troupe and main actors	Notes
Moudeli Theater	East Nanjing Road near the Bund	Aug. 1913	*The Evil family* and *Orchid of the Valley* (《空谷兰》)	New People Society / Zheng Zhengqiu	The first "family drama"
Daoqian Primary School	Renhe Alley, East Gate of the South Market	1906	Unknown	Illumination Dramatic Performance Society (开明演剧会) / Zhu Shuangyun, Wang Youyou	
New Stage	Near the former dock at the sixteenth pier of south Shanghai	1907	*New La Dame aux Camélias, The Red Shoes* (《红菱艳》) and *Napoleon's Love Affairs*	Peking opera troupes in Western-style dress	The first traditional opera garden that was changed into a dramatic stage
Lyceum Theater	Yuanmingyuan Road	Sep. 1907	*Black Slaves Appeal to Heaven*	Spring Sun Society / Wang Zhongsheng, Ma Xiangbo, etc.	Gongs and drums were still used in the drama

TEN

BUILDING A BRIDGE TO WORLD LITERATURE

TRANSLATION IN CHINA HAD ITS ORIGIN IN THE HAN and Tang dynasties when people began translating Buddhist scriptures. The literary elements of Buddhist scriptures had no small influence on classical Chinese literature, but the purpose of introducing Buddhist scriptures had nothing to do with literature. By the late-Qing period, there were extensive translation activities taking place throughout China. This was due to the fact that the country's doors had been forced open by imperialist powers; it was also an integral part of the efforts to reform and make the country rich and strong, and thus it was closely related to thoughts of enlightenment. And the translation activities of this period went further in both breadth and depth, made a greater breakthrough, and were deeply integrated into the "innovation" process of modern Chinese literature.

In this period, translation was regarded as a means of promoting modern civilization, enlightening ordinary people, and facilitating better communication with the outside world, so the first books to be translated were "scientific" books, including those about science and technology, and economic and military development of foreign countries. As for translation institutions, in 1860, the Interpreters' College (同文馆) was established with the approval of the imperial court. The college established four departments successively, namely English, French, Russian, and Japanese departments, and later it was incorporated into the Imperial University of Peking and became its Translation Academy. In Shanghai, Li Hongzhang founded the "Foreign-Language

School" (广方言馆) in 1863, and later Zhan Tianyou, one of the boys who went to study in the United States under the Chinese Educational Mission and who eventually became a renowned engineer, was once a student of this school. In 1866 the "Foochow Naval Dockyard School" (船政学堂) was established in Fujian, one of whose distinguished graduates was Yan Fu, who later went to the United Kingdom for naval studies. In 1867, a translation college was established under the Jiangnan Manufacturing Bureau (江南制造局) in Shanghai. Gradually, these institutions not only translated political, philosophical, and historical books, but began to translate and introduce foreign literature to China. Looking at Lu Xun's early literary translation works, we can also see this line of development: he first translated scientific fictions (*From the Earth to the Moon* and *Journey to the Center of the Earth*), then historical fictions (*The Ghost of Sparta*), and finally began translating pure literary fictions, cotranslating *Short Stories from Abroad* with his brother Zhou Zuoren. It was difficult for people of later generations to imagine how flourishing translation was at that time. According to statistics compiled by Ah Ying (阿英) in the *Catalogue of Operas and Novels in the Late Qing* (《晚清戏曲小说目》),[1] more than 600 novels were translated during the forty years from the first year of Emperor Guangxu's reign to the Xinhai Revolution, two thirds of all novels (original Chinese novels and translated novels) published during this time. And in "Survey of Novels Published in the Dingwei Year" (《丁未年小说界发行书目调查表》), Xu Nianci (徐念慈) observed that in 1907 alone, as many as eighty translated novels were published.[2] And then someone corrected him, saying the number

10.1. Entrance of the Interpreters' College (Translation Bureau) of the Imperial University of Peking

---

[1] Ah Ying: *Catalogue of Operas and Novels in the Late Qing*, Shanghai: Shanghai Joint Publishing House of Literature and Art, 1954.

[2] Juewo (觉我，Xu Nianci): "Survey of Novels Published in the Dingwei Year," published in Issue 9 of *Forest of Fiction*, Feburary 1908. Of the eighty novels, thirty-two were translated from novels published in the United Kingdom, twenty-two were published in the United States, nine in France, eight in Japan, two in Russia, and eight in other countries.

[3] See Chen Pingyuan (陈平原): *History of Twentieth Century Chinese Novels* (《二十世纪中国小说史》), Vol. 1, Table 3: "Statistics of Translated Novels Published in Various Countries" (《清末民初各国小说译作统计》), Beijing: Peking University Press, 1997, p. 50.

10.2. Well-dressed and well-known scholars (left to right) Xu Jianyin, Hua Hengfang (华衡芳), and Xu Shou (徐寿) at the Jiangnan Manufacturing Bureau's Translation College, established in 1867 at the petition of Zeng Guofan to the imperial court

should be 126.[3] These were not necessarily precise statistics, especially considering that a huge number of translated stories published in monthly fiction journals (which were thriving by then) were not taken into account.

The earliest translators were Liang Qichao, Yan Fu, and their peers. Liang was the first to promote translation and earnestly practice what he advocated. In 1896 he published an essay entitled "On Translation" (《论译书》) in his *Journal of Current Affairs*; during his life in exile after the failure of the Wuxu Reform, he launched the *Journal of Pure Critique*, in which he published "Foreword to the Publication of Political Novels in Translation" as well as the political novels he himself translated, including Shiba Shirō's *The Adventure of a Beauty* and Yano Ryukei's *Praiseworthy Anecdotes of Statesmanship* (《经国美谈》). By the time he launched *New Fiction* in 1902, he had already translated *An Account of the End of the World* (《世界末日记》), and he published a great many translated novels in *New Fiction*. Taking advantage of his great reputation, Liang Qichao introduced foreign political novels to China, in order to teach Chinese novelists how to write their own political novels (he himself wrote *A Future Record of New China*). For him, this was the ultimate purpose of translation, and it inspired many people in the following years. Yan Fu was the translator of excerpts of T. H. Huxley's *Evolution and Ethics* (Chinese

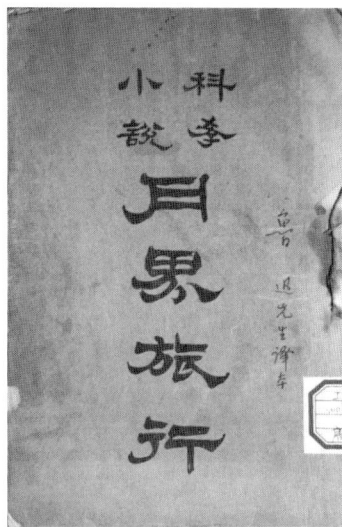

10.3. On the cover of Lu Xun's translation of Jules Verne's *From the Earth to the Moon* are the words "Science Fiction" (科学小说)

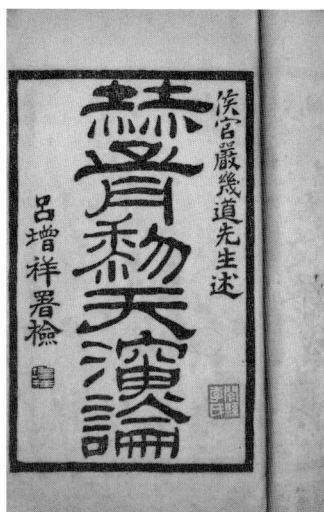

10.4. The Xinchou Year edition (under Emperor Guangxu's reign) of Yan Fu's translation of *Evolution and Ethics*

title: 《天演论》); when Huxley's work was first published in 1897, no one could have expected that its ideas and theories would cause such a huge impact on modern Chinese literature. Another achievement of Yan Fu's was that he put forward his own theories on translation. In the same year his translation of *Evolution and Ethics* was published, he coauthored and published "On the Origin of the Fiction Department of This Publishing House" with Xia Zengyou in the *National News Daily*, in which he noted: "I have heard that in Europe, America and Japan, novels played an important role in enlightening their people. And therefore I take painstaking efforts to collect and edit foreign novels and present them here in installments. Some of them are famous works by well-known authors, and some obscure works known to few."[4] Thus he became the first to expound the purpose of translating foreign novels in terms of the relationship between translated literature and enlightenment. At the very beginning of his "Translation Preface to *Evolution and Ethics*" (《〈天演论〉译例言》), Yan wrote: "There are three challenges in translation: faithfulness, expressiveness, and elegance."[5] These three words later

[4] Jidao (Yan Fu) and Bieshi (Xia Zengyou): "On the Origin of the Fiction Department of This Publishing House," published in the *National News Daily*, Oct. 16 – Nov. 18, the thirty-third year of Emperor Guangxu's reign (1897). Chen Pingyuan and Xia Xiaohong eds., *Critical Material on Theories of the Twentieth-Century Chinese Novel*, Vol. 1, Beijing: Peking University Press, 1997, p. 27.

[5] Yan Fu: "Translation Preface to *Evolution and Ethics*," *Collection of Yan Fu*, Vol. 5, Beijing: Zhonghua Book Company, 1986.

became a topic that has been repeatedly discussed by people right up until now. Though people have different understandings about their precise meanings, generally "faithfulness" means the translation should be faithful to the original text; "expressiveness" means the translation should fluently express the content of the original text, and "elegance" means the translation should be faithful and expressive with the use of elegant language that adheres to grammar rules. It was people's rigorous research and discussions about these three criteria that have constantly enhanced Chinese people's translation efforts.

However, it was "Lin's translated novels" (林译小说) that were real translation literature with a large readership. It is probably hard for people of today to understand why, at a time when classical Chinese had become freer in Liang Qichao's writings, the classical Chinese prose writer Lin Shu, who did not understand any foreign languages, could have translated more than 100 foreign fictions into classical Chinese. And the novels he translated made such a great impact on Chinese literature that later, when many great Chinese writers recalled their first encounter with world literature, they spontaneously talked about how reading Lin's translated novels at a young age had made a deep impression on them. Talking about the years he and Lu Xun were in Japan, Zhou Zuoren said: "We were so eager to read Lin's translated novels. Whenever there was one published and released in Tokyo, we would without fail rush to the Chinese bookstore in Kanda and buy it. After we finished reading, Lu Xun would bring it to the book binding service to add a hard cover as well as a bluish-gray cotton spine to it."[6] Guo Moruo once said: "The fictions translated by Lin Qinnan were extremely popular at that time, and they were my favorite readings, too. The first one I read was his translation of Haggard's *Joan Haste*. … This was probably the very first Western novel I ever read."[7] Ye Shengtao began reading Lin's translated novels when he was fourteen years old, and he still remembered them over sixty years later: "I remember borrowing Lin's translation of *The Talisman* from somewhere and reading it, which was my very first encounter with translated novels."[8] And Qian Zhongshu, who was a dozen years younger than the writers just mentioned, gave an even more vivid account of how Lin's translated novels had guided several generations (altogether three decades from the 1880s when Lu Xun was born till the 1910s when Qian Zhongshu was born) of Chinese people to get their first glimpse of

[6] Zhou Zuoren: "Lu Xun and the Literary Circle of Late-Qing Period" (《鲁迅与清末文坛》), *Lu Xun's Youth* (《鲁迅的青年时代》), Shijiazhuang: Hebei Education Press, 2002, chapter 7.

[7] Guo Moruo: *My Childhood.*

[8] See Shang Jinlin (商金林): *A Prolonged Chronology of Ye Shengtao* (《叶圣陶年谱长编》), Vol. 1. Beijing: People's Education Press, 2004, p. 29.

foreign language and the outside world: "It was after reading novels translated by him that I became more interested in learning foreign languages. The two small boxes of Lin's translation novels published by the Commercial Press were my grand discovery when I was eleven or twelve years old, and it led me to a brand new world, a world outside and beyond that of *Water Margin*, *Journey to the West* and *Strange Stories from a Chinese Studio*."[9] These words may help us know to what extent Lin Shu's translation promoted Chinese people's understanding of the world.

10.5. Portrait of Lin Shu

The first novel Lin Shu translated was *La Dame aux Camélias* by the French novelist Alexandre Dumas *fils*. In 1897, when Lin Shu's wife passed away, in order to get over the profound grief, he accepted the suggestion of his friend Wang Shouchang (王寿昌), who was proficient in French, and cotranslated it with him. The sentiment of this novel quite suited Lin's state of mind at that time. In their collaboration, Wang Shouchang interpreted the novel for Lin, and the Lin, who knew no foreign languages, wrote the translation in classical Chinese. The novel was published in 1899 and was extremely well received. After that, Lin Shu cooperated with Wei Yi

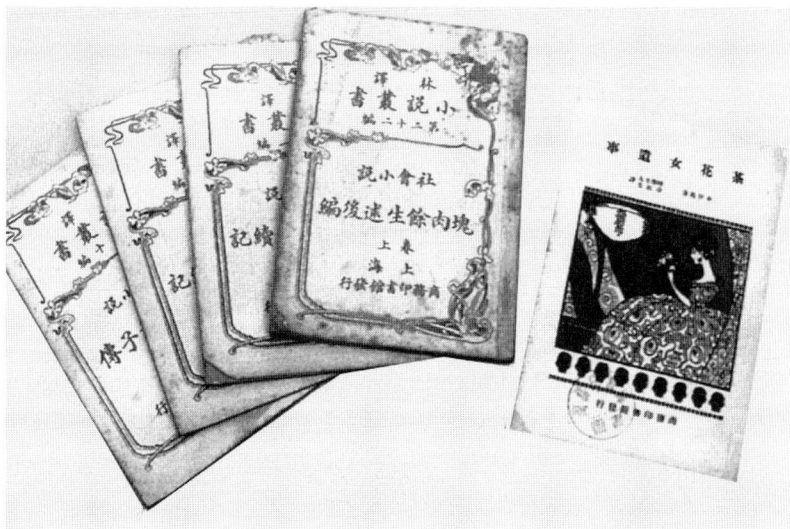

10.6. Five of Lin's translated novels, including *Stories of Paris's Lady of the Camellias* (the title of his translation of *La Dame aux Camélias*)

---

9   Qian Zhongshu: "Lin Shu's Translations" (《林纾的翻译》), *Four Essays Written in the Past* (《旧文四篇》), Shanghai: Guji Press, 1979, p. 66.

10.7. Lin Shu's translation of *Ivanhoe*, with the Chinese title 《撒克逊劫后英雄略》, literally, *The Legend of a Saxon Hero after the War*

(魏易), Chen Jialin (陈家麟), Zeng Zonggong (曾宗巩), and Li Shizhong (李世中), who all understood either English or French, and translated one novel after another. It was said that when he worked fast, he could produce 6,000 Chinese characters of translation within four hours, and altogether he translated more than 180 titles in over twenty years. Of them, forty were world-reknown masterpieces, including Mrs. Stowe's *Uncle Tom's Cabin* (the title of his translation was *Black Slaves Appeal to Heaven*), *Aesop's Fables*, Daniel Defoe's *Robinson Crusoe*, Sir Walter Scott's *Ivanhoe* (the title of Lin Shu's translated version was *The Legend of a Saxon Hero after the War* 《撒克逊劫后英雄略》), Jonathan Swift's *Gulliver's Travels* (translated version: *Account of Happy Journeys to Remote Nations* 《海外轩渠录》), Charles Dicken's *The Old Curiosity Shop* (translated version: *Biography of the Filial Daughter Nell* 《孝女耐儿传》), Charles Dicken's *David Copperfield* (translated version: *The Life Story of an Orphan* 《块肉余生述》), as well as the works of such great writers as Shakespeare, Cervantes, Hugo, Tolstoy, Alexandre Dumas *père*, Irving, and Sir Arthur Conan Doyle, etc. He also translated the works of some second- or third-rate foreign authors, which made up three quarters of all the novels he translated, and this was understandable in the context of the late Qing;

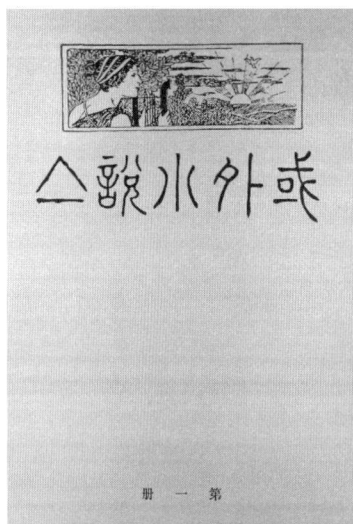

10.8. *Short Stories from Abroad* translated by Lu Xun and his brother

after all, this was when Chinese people were beginning to get to know world literature, and they still only had a rough understanding of it. Lin Shu and his partners chose quite a number of H. Rider Haggard's popular novels, who was among the better of the second-rate authors they chose to translate. In 1905, Lin Shu translated the entire book of Haggard's *Joan Haste*, differing from Yang Zilin (杨紫麟) and Bao Tianxiao, who had translated only excerpts of this novel and published them in the journal *Compendium of Translations to Encourage Learning* (《励学译编》) in 1901. Lin's translation was negatively criticized by conservatives Jin Songcen (金松岑) and Yin Bansheng (寅半生), among others, for the reason that in the version by Yang and Bao, the translators had omitted the plot of Joan Haste's premarital pregnancy with the excuse that the entire novel was not available to them, which was surely more agreeable for those conservatives.[10] Translations of the late Qing featured paraphrasing, and it was not rare for translators to omit or alter the original texts, so it was quite interesting that Lin Shu tried to remain faithful to the original text and did not omit the character's moral ambiguities in the novel.

Certainly, Lin Shu's translated novels, as well as the earlier translation works of Lu Xun and others, did not go against the practice of paraphrasing at the beginning. It wasn't until the Zhou brothers began to translate and introduce the novels of suppressed nations such as Russia, Northern European countries, and Poland, etc. and published *Short Stories from Abroad* in Tokyo in 1909 that they began to take "verbal translation" seriously and abandon the practice of paraphrasing. In Lin Shu's time, omission, addition, and incorrect translation, as well as the translator's addition of comments or arbitrary alterations of the narrative perspectives

10.9. Lin Shu's translation of *Tales from Shakespeare*, with the Chinese title 《吟边燕语》, literally, *An English Poet Reciting from Afar*

were all common practices. For example, Lin Shu omitted all the religious plots from *Black Slaves Appeal to Heaven*, and then in *An Unofficial History of Comics* (《滑稽外史》, his translation of *Nicholas Nickleby*), he embellished the plot of Dickens' novel, and translated Miss Knag's cries into an amusing jingle. Miss Knag, the forewoman of the fashion store, heard some customers murmuring something like "old thing" about her, and in jealousy of young and beautiful girls:

> she first laughed and finally cried, sounding more like a sing-song: "Hem! For fifteen years I have been here and for fifteen years I have been the credit and ornament of this room and the one upstairs."—As she sang this, she tromped her left foot: "Oh my God!" and then her right foot: "Oh my God! For fifteen years I have never been disgraced, but now these bitchy girlies come to me and dare to insult me like this! How heartbroken I am!"[11]

And this was a main feature of Lin Shu's translation. Thus Hu Shi once noted: "There is something very funny about classical Chinese, and it is amazing that

---

[10] In his "A Glimpse of Literature and Art in Shanghai" (《上海文艺之一瞥》), Lu Xun said that the "earlier translators" deliberately omitted the plot of "Joan's premarital pregnancy" in the first half of the novel, which proved to be his misunderstanding. See Luan Jianmei (栾建梅): *King of Popular Literature: Biography of Bao Tianxiao* (《通俗文学之王包天笑传》), Taipei: Yeh Chang Publishing Co., 1996, p. 46.

[11] Quoted from Qian Zhongshu: "Lin Shu's Translations," p. 68.

Lin Shu translated the works of Irving and Dickens into classical Chinese."[12] Quoting what Mao Dun had said in private, Zheng Zhenduo (郑振铎) praised Lin Shu that "except for a few minor errors, his translation of *Ivanhoe* preserved the aesthetic appeal of the original text."[13] According to Qian Zhongshu's research, in his translation, Lin Shu actually did not use the same "classical Chinese language" he used to write prose or that which he desperately insisted on during the May Fourth period as against vernacular Chinese. "Lin Shu did not translate novels into 'classical Chinese,' and it was impossible to translate novels into 'classical Chinese.'"[14] This was a significant discovery, for it established renewed ties between the language used in translation works of the late Qing and the vernacular language advocated during the May Fourth movement, showing that the classical Chinese used in earlier translation works was not necessarily in opposition to the May Fourth vernacular language. In analyzing Lin Shu's translation, Qian Zhongshu said:

> The literary form that Lin Shu employed for his translations was what he understood to be a relatively popular and informal form of classical Chinese that was rich in elasticity. Although it retained a certain number of elements from "ancient prose," it was nevertheless very much freer than "ancient prose." The rules that governed its diction and syntax were not at all strict. It proved an extremely capacious form of prose. Because of this, the "exquisite phrases" and "clever conceits" found in classical Chinese such as "the gentleman in the rafters" (*liang-shang jun-zi*, 梁上君子 – i.e. a thief), "five clusters of cloud" (*wu-duo-yun*, 五朵云 – i.e. one's signature), "earthen bun" (*tu-man-tou*, 土馒头 – i.e. a grave mound), or "a lady for passing the night" (*ye-du-niang*, 夜度娘 – i.e. a prostitute), and so on, all of which were certainly not permitted in "ancient prose," made their appearance within his translations in all sorts of guises. Colloquial vernacular expressions such as "precious little one" (*xiao-bao-bei*, 小宝贝), "Papa" (*ba-ba*, 爸爸), "God forsake thee, Blimber" (*tian-sha-zhi bo-lin-bo*, 天杀之伯林伯), and so on appeared in great profusion. Many of the foreign neologisms then much in vogue—what Lin Shu called the "neologisms of the Easterner" (*dong-ren xin-ming-ci*, 东人新名词) that "seem unrhymed in the lines at the first glance"—such as "common" (*pu-tong*, 普通), "degree" (*cheng-du*, 程度), "heat" (*re-du*, 热度), "well-being" (*xing-fu*, 幸福), "society" (*she-hui*, 社会), "individual" (*ge-ren*, 个人), "collective" (*tuan-ti*, 团体), "brains" (*nao-jin*, 脑筋), "brain bag" (*nao-qiu*, 脑球), "cerebral force" (*nao-qi*, 脑气), "reactionary force" (*fan-dong zhi-li*, 反动之力), "sweet dreams" (*meng-jing tian-mi*, 梦境甜蜜), "a lively spirit" (*huo-po-zhi jing-shen*, 活泼之精神), "coolie" (*ku-li*, 苦力), and so on make as

---

[12] Hu Shi: "Mr. Lin Qinnan's Vernacular Poetry."

[13] Zheng Zhenduo: "On Mr. Lin Qinnan" (《林琴南先生》), published in *Fiction Monthly*, Vol. 15, Issue 11, Nov. 1924.

[14] Qian Zhongshu: "Lin Shu's Translations," p. 83.

many appearances in his translations as is to be expected. His translations are also afflicted by the contemporary mannerism of substituting transliteration for translation. Words such as *ma-dan* (马丹, "Madame"), *mi-si-tuo* (密司脱, "Mr."), *an-qi-er* (安琪儿, "angel"), and *ju-le-bu* (俱乐部, "club") appear on every page of his translations, some such transliterations being employed quite unnecessarily, as in *lie-di* (列底, a respectful term of address for a woman) (in chapter 5 of his translation of *Ivanhoe*, a transliteration of "lady") or *de-wu-mang* (德武忙, which is akin to saying that one does as much as possible for one's friends) (chapter 10 of *La Dame aux Camélias*, a transliteration of "*du dévouement*"). Totally unexpected are the remarkable elements of "Europeanization" also found employed in Lin Shu's translations.[15]

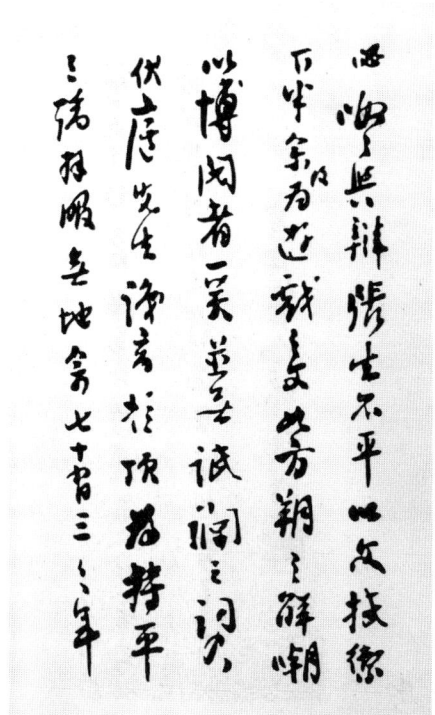

10.10. Example of Lin Shu's handwriting

In his analysis, Qian Zhongshu indicated the source of each word he chose from Lin Shu's translations as illustration, and used many other examples to prove that in Lin's translations in classical Chinese, he consciously or unconsciously incorporated "exquisite phrases," "clever conceits," and "loan words," making it a freer "Europeanized" classical Chinese. With its huge readership and cult appeal, Lin's translated novel had a great influence, which later contributed to the tendency to employ Europeanization of the vernacular after the May Fourth movement. This was probably not foreseen by Lin Shu himself.

It was the vernacular translation of foreign literature that truly introduced world literature to China, created a new atmosphere in the literary circle, and paved the way for vernacular literature to flourish during the May Fourth period. Su Manshu and Zhou Guisheng were among the earliest to translate foreign literature in vernacular, and their transitional position was obvious. Su Manshu was a major novelist writing in classical Chinese during the Republican period, but he translated Victor Hugo's *Les Miserables* in vernacular and published it in the *National Daily* with the title *Can Shehui* (《惨社会》, literally, "Miserable Society") in 1903, and when it was published as a separate edition the following year, the name Chen Youji (陈由己, an alias of Chen Duxiu) was added as a cotranslator. *Les Miserables* was also paraphrased, in

[15] Ibid., pp. 83–84.

which the translators added a French knight called Nande, who understood Chinese culture and made the following oft-quoted critical comments about Confucius:

> The messages about submissiveness by Confucius of China are only worshipped by those bitchy Chinese; why should we, the respected Frenchmen, listen to his bullshit, too?

And Su Manshu attacked the outdated Chinese culture in his translation through another character he created:

> Alas, I also heard that there was a country in East Asia called China, whose customs were extremely barbarous. Everybody spent a lot of money to burn incense paper and worship those earthy and wooden Buddhas. What's funnier is that women in that country would wrap their natural feet with a piece of white cloth and make it pointed like a pair of pig feet, and they could not even walk because of this. Isn't that funny?[16]

From these lively words, we can have a glimpse of the vernacular language used in the translated novels at that time. Of the earlier Mandarin Duck and Butterfly translators, Zhou Guisheng was an influential one who did most of his translations in classical Chinese. A literary school focusing on original creation, the Mandarin Duck and Butterfly school was also a school of literary translation. Many of its writers wrote and translated novels, spanning two periods, first translating in classical Chinese and then translating in vernacular Chinese. Zhou Guisheng was proficient in English and French, and once worked as the translation editor of *All-Story Monthly*. He preceded Lin Shu in translation, and was known for his translation of Sherlock Holmes. It is said that the term *zhen-tan xiao-shuo* (侦探小说, "detective stories") was coined by him. In 1903, he published a vernacular translation entitled *Circle of Poisonous Snakes* (《毒蛇圈》) in Issue 8 of *New Fiction*, which was also thought highly of.

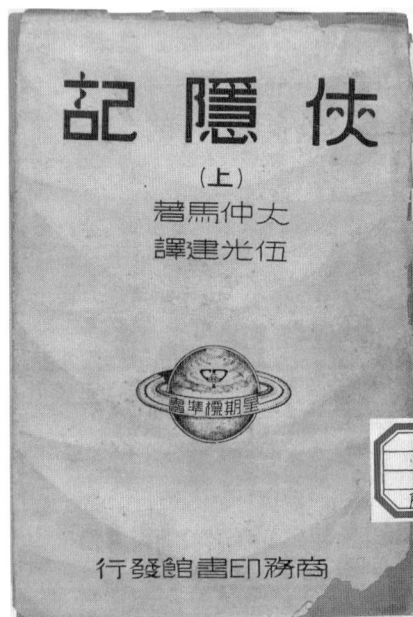

10.11. *Biography of a Secluded Hero* (i.e. *The Three Musketeers*) (Vol. 1), translated by Wu Guangjian

---

[16] The two quotations are from Wang Hongzhi (王宏志): *Reinterpreting Faithfulness, Expressiveness and Elegance: Studies on Chinese Translation of the Twentieth Century* (《重释"信达雅"：二十世纪的中国翻译研究》), Shanghai: Oriental Publishing Center, 1999, p. 157. "Miserable Society" was the title used for the Chinese translation when it was first published.

Wu Guangjian (伍光建) was the first to translate in vernacular Chinese during the period of "paraphrase." In 1907 he published his famous translation of *The Three Musketeers* by Alexandre Dumas *père*, with the Chinese title 《侠隐记》 (*A Biography of a Secluded Hero*). Even after the May Fourth movement, this translation was still praised by peers of *New Youth*, who severely criticized Lin Shu by quoting Wu's "clear and understandable" vernacular language. As late as 1934, Mao Dun was still enthusiastic about commenting on Wu Guangjian's vernacular translation by comparing it with the original text. Mao Dun took the translated text of the first chapter (entitled "A Letter Lost in a Hotel") of *The Three Musketeers* as an example:

> One day in April 1625, the town of Meung in France suddenly fell into a state of revolution. Women were flying toward the high street, and their children were crying at the open doors. Men hastened to don the cuirass and take a musket to rush to Jolly Miller.

According to Mao Dun's analysis, Wu Guangjian altered "On the first Monday of the month of April, 1625" in the original text into "One day in April 1625"; after "the town of Meung," he deliberately omitted the sentence "in which the author of *Romance of the Rose* was born," and after the "state of revolution," he deliberately omitted "as if the Huguenots had just made a second La Rochelle of it." Besides, in the original text the sentence about women and children was a subordinate clause: "Many citizens, seeing the women flying toward the High Street, leaving their children crying at the open doors," but in his translation, Wu Guangjian changed it into two parallel sentences: "Women were flying toward the high street, and their children were crying at the open doors," etc. From this we can see that in the vernacular translation of the late Qing, translators already considered cutting short and changing Europeanized sentences into clear and understandable vernacular Chinese, which was a smart practice that did not compromise the meaning of the original text. Due to the influence of "paraphrase" in the late-Qing period, there were certainly examples of improper omission, and Mao Dun quoted both good and bad examples from Wu Guangjian's translation.[17]

The early vernacular translations of the Mandarin Duck and Butterfly school had indeed made some achievements. There was Maupassant's short story "Volunteer Army" translated by Chen Lengxue, and then there was the *Series of Short Stories by Famous European and American Writers*, Vol. 1–3 (《欧美名家短篇小说丛刊》 （1－3卷）), which included fifty short stories written by forty-seven authors, all translated by Zhou Shoujuan. When Lu Xun was taking office in the Ministry of Education, he discovered this book

---

[17] See Mao Dun: "Wu's Translation of *The Three Musketeers* and *Vanity Fair*," *Complete Works of Mao Dun* (《矛盾全集》), Vol. 20, Beijing: People's Literature Press, 1990, pp. 26–27.

TABLE 10.1 *World literature translated by Lin Shu*

Title of Lin's translation	Title of today's general translation	Author	Country of origin of the author	Interpreter	Time of publication	Publisher	Notes
巴黎茶花女遗事 (*Bali Chahuanü Yishi*)	*Camille* (茶花女)	Alexandre Dumas *fils*	France	Wang Shouchang	1899	Weilu's Private Collection Edition	
黑奴吁天录 (*Heinu Yutianlu*)	*Uncle Tom's Cabin* (汤姆叔叔的小屋)	Mrs. Stowe	United States	Wei Yi	1901	Wulin Wei's Collection Edition	
伊索寓言 (*Yisuo Yuyan*)	*Aesop's Fables* (伊索寓言)	Aesop	Greece	Yan Peinan, etc.	1903	Commercial Press	
英国诗人吟边燕语 (*Yingguo Shiren Yinbian Yanyu*)	*Tales from Shakespeare* (莎士比亚故事集)	Brother and sister Charles and Mary Lamb	United Kingdom	Wei Yi	1904	Commercial Press	Mistakenly thought to have been written by William Shakespeare
迦茵小传 (*Jiayin Xiaozhuan*)	*Joan Haste* (迦茵小传)	Haggard	United Kingdom	Wei Yi	1905	Commercial Press	
撒克逊劫后英雄略 (*Sakexun Jiehou Yingxiong Lüe*)	*Ivanhoe* (艾凡赫)	Scott	United Kingdom	Wei Yi	1905	Commercial Press	
鲁滨逊飘流记 (*Lubinxun Piaoliu Ji*)	*Robinson Crusoe* (鲁滨逊飘流记)	Defoe	United Kingdom	Zeng Zonggong	1905	Commercial Press	
海外轩渠录 (*Haiwai Xuanqu Lu*)	*Gulliver's Travels* (格列弗游记)	Swift	United Kingdom	Zeng Zonggong	1906	Commercial Press	It was noted on the copyright page that it was interpreted by Dong Yi (董易)
红礁画桨录 (*Hongjiao Huajiang Lu*)	*Beatrice* (比阿特丽丝)	Henry Rider Haggard	United Kingdom	Wei Yi	1906	Commercial Press	

(continued)

TABLE 10.1 *(continued)*

Title of Lin's translation	Title of today's general translation	Author	Country of origin of the author	Interpreter	Time of publication	Publisher	Notes
鲁滨逊飘流续记 (*Lubinxun Piaoliu Xuji*)	*Robinson Crusoe* (鲁滨逊飘流流记)	Defoe	United Kingdom	Zeng Zonggong	1906	Commercial Press	
拊掌录 (*Fuzhang Lu*)	*The Sketch Book of Geoffrey Crayon* (见闻杂记)	Washington Irving	United States	Wei Yi	1907	Commercial Press	
十字军英雄记 (*Shizijun Yingxiong Ji*)	*The Talisman* (十字军英雄记)	Scott	United Kingdom	Wei Yi	1907	Commercial Press	
神枢鬼藏录 (*Shenshu Guicang Lu*)	*The Chronicles of Martin Hewitt* (马丁·海威特记事)	Arthur Morrison	United Kingdom	Wei Yi	1907	Commercial Press	
金风铁雨录 (*Jinfeng Tieyu Lu*)	*Micah Clarke* (迈卡·克拉克)	Conan Doyle	United Kingdom	Zeng Zonggong	1907	Commercial Press	It was noted on the copyright page that it was interpreted by Dong Yi (董易)
大食故宫余载 (*Dashi Gugong Yuzai*)	*Tales of the Alhambra* (阿尔宫伯拉)	Washington Irving	United States	Wei Yi	1907	Commercial Press	
旅行述异 (*Lüxing Shuyi*)	*Tales of a Traveler* (旅客谈)	Washington Irving	United States	Wei Yi	1907	Commercial Press	
滑稽外史 (*Huaji Waishi*)	*Nicholas Nickleby* (尼古拉斯·尼克尔贝)	Dickens	United Kingdom	Wei Yi	1907	Commercial Press	
剑底鸳鸯 (*Jiandi Yuanyang*)	*The Betrothed* (未婚妻)	Scott	United Kingdom	Wei Yi	1907	Commercial Press	

(continued)

TABLE 10.1 (continued)

Title of Lin's translation	Title of today's general translation	Author	Country of origin of the author	Interpreter	Time of publication	Publisher	Notes
孝女耐儿传 (Xiaonü Naier Zhuan)	The Old Curiosity Shop (老古玩店)	Dickens	United Kingdom	Wei Yi	1907	Commercial Press	
块肉余生述 (前编) (Kuairou Yusheng Shu, Vols. 1 and 2)	David Copperfield (大卫·科波菲尔)	Dickens	United Kingdom	Wei Yi	1908	Commercial Press	
歇洛克奇案开场 (Xieluoke Qi'an Kaichang)	A Study in Scarlet (血字的研究)	Conan Doyle	United Kingdom	Wei Yi	1908	Commercial Press	
幕刺客传 (Ran Cike Zhuan)	Uncle Bernac (伯纳克勇男)	Conan Doyle	United Kingdom	Wei Yi	1908	Commercial Press	
恨绮愁罗记 (Henqi Chouluo Ji)	"The Fugitive" (逃亡者)	Conan Doyle	United Kingdom	Wei Yi	1908	Commercial Press	
贼史 (Zei Shi)	Oliver Twist (奥列佛尔)	Dickens	United Kingdom	Wei Yi	1908	Commercial Press	
新天方夜谭 (Xin Tianfang Yetan)	New Arabian Nights (新天方夜谭)	Mr. and Mrs. Stevenson	United Kingdom	Zeng Zonggong	1908	Commercial Press	
电影楼台 (Dianying Loutai)	The Doings of Raffles Haw (拉弗尔斯·霍行实)	Conan Doyle	United Kingdom	Wei Yi	1908	Commercial Press	
钟乳骷髅 (Zhongru Kulou)	King Solomon's Mines (所罗门王的宝藏)	Henry Rider Haggard	United Kingdom	Zeng Zonggong	1908	Commercial Press	

(continued)

Title	Original title	Author	Country	Translator	Year	Publisher	Notes
蛇女士传 (She Nüshi Zhuan)	Beyond the City (城外)	Conan Doyle	United Kingdom	Wei Yi	1908	Commercial Press	
不如归 (Bu Ru Gui)	Hototogisu (The Cuckoo, 不如归)	Kenjirō Tokutomi	Japan	Wei Yi	1908	Commercial Press	
玉楼花劫 (Yulou Huajie)	The Knight of the Red House (红屋骑士)	Alexandre Dumas père	France	Li Shizhong	1908	Commercial Press	
冰雪因缘 (Bingxue Yinyuan)	Dombey and Son (董贝父子)	Dickens	United Kingdom	Wei Yi	1909	Commercial Press	
玉楼花劫(后编) (Yulou Huajie, Vol. 2)	The Knight of the Red House (红屋骑士)	Alexandre Dumas père	France	Li Shizhong	1909	Commercial Press	
玑司刺虎记 (Jisi Cihu Ji)	Jess (杰丝)	Henry Rider Haggard	United Kingdom	Chen Jialin	1909	Commercial Press	
黑太子南征录 (Heitaizi Nanzheng Lu)	The White Company (黑太子南征录)	Conan Doyle	United Kingdom	Wei Yi	1909	Commercial Press	
双雄较剑录 (Shuangxiong Jiaojian Lu)	Fair Margaret (美丽的玛格丽特)	Henry Rider Haggard	United Kingdom	Chen Jialin	Starting from July 1910	Fiction Monthly	Separate edition published in 1915
三千年艳尸记 (Sanqiannian Yanshi Ji)	She (她)	Henry Rider Haggard	United Kingdom	Zeng Zonggong	1910	Commercial Press	
古鬼遗金记 (Gigui Yijin Ji)	Benita (贝妮达)	Henry Rider Haggard	United Kingdom	Chen Jialin	1912	Guangyi Press	

(continued)

TABLE 10.1 (continued)

Title of Lin's translation	Title of today's general translation	Author	Country of origin of the author	Interpreter	Time of publication	Publisher	Notes
离恨天 (Lihen Tian)	Paul et Virginie (Paul and Virginia, 保尔和薇吉妮)	Bernardin de Saint-Pierre	France	Wang Qingji (王庆骥)	1913	Commercial Press	
罗刹因果录 (Luocha Yinguo Lu)	Two Old Men and Seven Other Short Stories (二老者论等短篇小说8篇)	Tolstoy	Russia	Chen Jialin	Starting from July 1914	Oriental Magazine	Separate edition published in 1915
哀吹录 (Ai Chui Lu)	Adieu and Three Other Short Stories (再会等短篇小说4篇)	Balzac	France	Chen Jialin	Starting from Oct. 1914	Fiction Monthly	Separate edition published in 1915
蟹莲郡主传 (Xielian Junzhu Zhuan)	The Regent's Daughter (摄政王的女儿)	Alexandre Dumas père	France	Wang Qingtong	1915	Commercial Press	
鱼海泪波 (Yuhai Leibo)	An Iceland Fisherman (冰岛渔夫)	Pierre Loti	France	Wang Qingtong	1915	Commercial Press	
鱼雁扶微 (Yu Yan Jue Wei)	Persian Letters (波斯人信札)	Montesquieu	France	Wang Qingji	After 1915	Oriental Magazine	Finished serializing in 1917
鹰梯小豪杰 (Yingti Xiao Haojie)	The Dove in the Eagle's Nest (鹰巢中的鸽子)	Charlotte Mary Yonge	United Kingdom	Chen Jialin	Starting from Jan. 1916	Sea of Fiction	Separate edition published in the same year
雷差得纪 (Leichade Ji)	Richard II (理查二世)	Shakespeare	United Kingdom	Chen Jialin	1916 年1月	Fiction Monthly	
亨利第四纪 (Hengli Disi Ji)	Henry IV (亨利四世)	Shakespeare	United Kingdom	Chen Jialin	Feb. 1916	Fiction Monthly	

(continued)

Title	Source	Author	Country	Translator	Date	Publisher
亨利第六遗事 (Hengli Diliu Yishi)	Henry VI (亨利六世)	Shakespeare	United Kingdom	Chen Jialin	1916	Commercial Press
香钧情眼 (Xianggou Qingyan)	Antonine (安东妮)	Alexandre Dumas fils	France	Wang Qingtong	1916	Commercial Press
凯彻遗事 (Kaiche Yishi)	Julius Caesar (裘利斯·恺撒)	Shakespeare	United Kingdom	Chen Jialin	Starting from May 1916	Fiction Monthly
血华鸳鸯枕 (Xuehua Yuanyang Zhen)	L'Affaire Clemenceau (克列孟梭的事业)	Alexandre Dumas fils	France	Wang Qingtong	Starting from Aug. 1916	Fiction Monthly
鸡谈、三少年遇死神 (Jitan, Sanshaonian Yu Sishen)	Two Tales from Chaucer in Prose (乔叟故事集 2篇)	Charles Cowden Clarke	United Kingdom	Chen Jialin	Dec. 1916	Fiction Monthly
格雷西达 (Geleixida)	A Tale from Chaucer in Prose (乔叟故事集 1篇)	Charles Cowden Clarke	United Kingdom	Chen Jialin	Feb. 1917	Fiction Monthly
林妖 (Lin Yao)	A Tale from Chaucer in Prose	Charles Cowden Clarke	United Kingdom	Chen Jialin	Mar. 1917	Fiction Monthly
天女离魂记 (Tiannü Lihun Ji)	Ghost King (鬼王)	Henry Rider Haggard	United Kingdom	Chen Jialin	1917	Commercial Press
烟火马 (Yan Huo Ma)	The Brethren (烟火马)	Henry Rider Haggard	United Kingdom	Chen Jialin	1917	Commercial Press

(continued)

TABLE 10.1 (continued)

Title of Lin's translation	Title of today's general translation	Author	Country of origin of the author	Interpreter	Time of publication	Publisher	Notes
社会声影录 (Shehui Sheng Ying Lu)	A Landlord in the Morning and Another Tale (一个地主的早晨等2篇)	Tolstoy	Russia	Chen Jialin	1917	Commercial Press	
路西恩 (Luxien)	Luzern (琉森)	Tolstoy	Russia	Chen Jialin	May 1917	Fiction Monthly	
死口能歌 (Si Kou Neng Ge), 公主遇难 (Gongzhu Yunan)	Two Tales from Chaucer in Prose	Charles Cowden Clarke	United Kingdom	Chen Jialin	June 1917	Fiction Monthly	
魂灵附体 (Hunling Futi)	A Tale from Chaucer in Prose	Charles Cowden Clarke	United Kingdom	Chen Jialin	July 1917	Fiction Monthly	
人鬼关头 (Ren Gui Guantou)	The Death of Ivan Ilych (伊凡·伊里奇之死)	Tolstoy	Russia	Chen Jialin	July 1917	Fiction Monthly	
决斗得妻 (Juedou De Qi)	A Tale from Chaucer in Prose	Charles Cowden Clarke	United Kingdom	Chen Jialin	Oct. 1917	Fiction Monthly	
恨缕情丝 (Hen Lü Qing Si)	The Kreutzer Sonata and Another Tale (克莱采奏鸣曲等2篇)	Tolstoy	Russia	Chen Jialin	Starting from Jan. 1918	Fiction Monthly	Separate edition published in 1919
鹦鹉缘 (前编) (续编) (Yingwu Yuan) (Vols. 1 and 2)	Les Aventures de Quatre Femmes et d'un Perroquet (四女和一鹦鹉的奇遇)	Alexandre Dumas fils	France	Wang Qingtong	1918	Commercial Press	

(continued)

Chinese Title	Original Title	Author	Country	Translator	Date	Publisher	Notes
鸚鵡緣（第三编）(Yingwu Yuan) (Vol. 3)	Les Aventures de Quatre Femmes et d'un Perroquet	Alexandre Dumas fils	France	Wang Qingtong	1918	Commercial Press	
现身说法 (Xianshen Shuofa)	Childhood, Boyhood, and Youth (幼年·少年·菁年)	Tolstoy	Russia	Chen Jialin	1918	Commercial Press	
铁匣头颅（前编）（续编）(Tiejia Toulu) (Vols. 1 and 2)	The Witch's Head (女巫的头)	Henry Rider Haggard	United Kingdom	Chen Jialin	1919	Commercial Press	
戎马书生 (Rongma Shusheng)	The Lances of Lynwood (林伍德的骑士)	Charlotte Mary Yonge	United Kingdom	Chen Jialin	Starting from Oct. 1919	Oriental Magazine	Separate edition published in 1920
蒙士述猎 (Hao Shi Shu Lie)	Maiwa's Revenge (梅娃的复仇)	Henry Rider Haggard	United Kingdom	Chen Jialin	Starting from Nov. 1919	Fiction Monthly	
伊罗理心记 (Yi Luo Mai Xin Ji)	La Boîte d'Argent (银盒)	Alexandre Dumas fils	France	Wang Qingtong	Starting from Jan. 1920	Fiction Monthly	
球房纪事 (Qiufang Jishi)	Memoirs of a Marker (一个台球房记分员的笔记)	Tolstoy	Russia	Chen Jialin	Starting from May 1920	Fiction Monthly	
乐师雅路白忒遗事 (Yueshi Yalubaite Yishi)	Albert (阿尔拜特)	Tolstoy	Russia	Chen Jialin	Apr. 1920	Fiction Monthly	
高加索之囚 (Gaojiasuo Zhi Qiu)	A Prisoner of the Caucasus (高加索的俘房)	Tolstoy	Russia	Chen Jialin	May 1920	Fiction Monthly	

(continued)

TABLE 10.1 *(continued)*

Title of Lin's translation	Title of today's general translation	Author	Country of origin of the author	Interpreter	Time of publication	Publisher	Notes
炸鬼记 (*Zha Gui Ji*)	*Queen Sheba's Ring* (示巴女王的戒指)	Henry Rider Haggard	United Kingdom	Chen Jialin	1921	Commercial Press	
洞冥记 (*Dong Ming Ji*)	*A Journey from This World to the Next* (冥府旅行记)	Henry Fielding	United Kingdom	Chen Jialin	1921	Commercial Press	
双雄义死录 (*Shuangxiong Yisi Lu*)	*Quatrevingt-treize* (九三年)	Victor Hugo	France	Mao Wenzhong	1921	Commercial Press	
沙利沙女王小记 (*Shalisha Nüwang Xiaoji*)	*The Island Mystery* (神秘岛)	George A. Birmingham	United Kingdom	Mao Wenzhong	1921	Commercial Press	
梅孽 (*Mei Nie*)	*Ghosts* (群鬼)	Ibsen	Norway	Mao Wenzhong	1921	Commercial Press	
魔侠传 (*Moxia Zhuan*)	*Don Quixote* (堂吉诃德)	Cervantes	Spain	Chen Jialin	1922	Commercial Press	

(*Main source:* Xue Suizhi [薛绥之] and Zhang Juncai [张俊才], eds.: *Research Material of Lin Shu* [《林纾研究资料》], Fuzhou: Fujian People's Press, 1982) and thought it "the sound of hope," and he wrote "Comments" together with Zhou Zuoren to praise this translation series. "In this book, for the first time we see translation of novels from Italy, Spain, Sweden, Holland, and Serbia, and most selected works are masterpieces," and he went even further to say that this series was "a dim light in the darkness, a sound in the silence."[18] But it wasn't until long after Lu Xun had passed away that Zhou Shoujuan became aware that he had been awarded for this translation series because of Lu Xun's high praise. This is considered a legend in modern Chinese literary history.

[18]   Quoted from *Chronological Biography of Lu Xun (enlarged revision)* (《鲁迅年谱（增订本）》), Vol. 1, Beijing: People's Literature Press, 2000, p. 367.

ELEVEN

THE INCUBATION OF A LITERARY REVOLUTION AT HOME AND ABROAD

I N 1917, HU SHI AND CHEN DUXIU PUBLISHED "SOME Modest Proposals for the Reform of Literature" (《文学改良刍议》) and "On Literary Revolution" (《文学革命论》) in *New Youth* successively; in 1918, in two issues of the same journal, were published Lu Xun's vernacular short story "The Diary of a Madman" (《狂人日记》) and vernacular poems written by Hu Shi, Shen Yinmo (沈尹默), and Liu Bannong (刘半农); and then in 1919, the May Fourth movement broke out and evolved into the New Culture movement. These are considered the hallmark events for the beginning of China's modern literature. However, the May Fourth literary revolution was by no means an accident. Tracing back a bit further, the preparations had already begun in the late-Qing period: Liang Qichao talked about a "new literary style" that shook off "the restraints of the old style, I always write in an easy and clear one, sometimes using slang, verses, and loan words, without constraints to my free expression of ideas,"[1] making preparations for a freer classical Chinese written style. A National Language movement was initiated to advocate vernacular language, for which more than 200 vernacular newspapers and magazines were launched and widely circulated; the position of novel as a literary genre was enhanced, thanks to Liang Qichao's promotion of "new fiction"

---

[1] See Liang Qichao: *Intellectual Trends in the Ching [Qing] Period*, a longer quotation of which has been used in Chapter 4 of this book.

and the launch of four major fiction journals, including *New Fiction*; poetry and prose were the Chinese literary genres most difficult to transform, but there were "poetry revolution" and "prose revolution"; Huang Zunxian claimed that "my pen should reflect what I say and what I think"; spoken drama, too, was introduced into China; and then translation works in freer classical Chinese and late-Qing vernacular language were extremely well accepted among readers. The immediate driving force for the outbreak of the May Fourth literary revolution was in fact all the preparatory efforts made by people at home and abroad who were ready to turn a new page for Chinese literature, including those studying in Japan, such as Lu Xun, Qian Xuantong, Zhou Zuoren, Guo Moruo, Yu Dafu (郁达夫), and Cheng Fangwu (成仿吾); those studying in the United States, such as Hu Shi and Mei Guangdi (梅光迪); and those who remained in China, such as Cai Yuanpei and Chen Duxiu.

Obviously, Chinese students studying abroad had already seen the modern civilization of the outside world with their own eyes, and thus it was not surprising that they became the vanguard of new thoughts and culture. Examining the timeline, we can see that the Qing court sent government-funded students to the United States earlier than to Japan; however, the earliest four batches of students to the United States were but little boys, and the project was abandoned halfway. It was not until 1909 that the Qing court selected and sent the first group of forty-seven students to study in the United States through the Boxer Indemnity, and Hu Shi, Zhao Yuanren, and Zhu Kezhen (竺可桢) belonged to the second group of seventy students sent in 1910. By 1924, there were no more than 689 government-funded students studying in the United States. On the other hand, it was in 1893 that the Qing court sent the first group of thirteen government-funded students to Japan; and by the time Lu Xun went to Japan in 1902 (eight years earlier than Hu Shi going to the United States), there were more than 1,000 Chinese students studying in Japan, and three or four years later, there were as many as 10,000; in 1906 and 1907, more than 10,000 Chinese students were going to Japan each year. When Hu Shi departed from Shanghai for the United States, Lu Xun had already been back home for a year.

Such a great number of Chinese students in Japan must have formed quite a multifarious mix. Excluding those pampered sons of wealthy families who enjoyed leisurely and wasteful lives, there were two kinds of students: those righteous individuals who were devoted to political revolution and tried to accumulate resources to overthrow the Qing dynasty,

11.1. Lu Xun took this photo after cutting off his queue in 1903 when he was twenty-three years old and studying in Tokyo

and those who wanted to learn some modern knowledge and contribute to making the country richer and stronger. It was sometimes not easy to make a clear distinction between these two categories, for some people were originally devoted to knowledge learning, but became resolute revolutionaries in that special atmosphere. An excellent example was Lu Xun. Hearing that Japan's rise after the Meiji Restoration started from its adoption of Western medicine, he originally went to Japan to study Western medicine in order to treat and cure those who, like his father, had died after mistreatment by quacks, and to treat and cure the weak people of China, and thereby the weak country, with the intention to serve as a medical doctor in the army during the war. In Japan, his life was similar to others, "besides studying Japanese and getting prepared to enter medical school, [I would] go to students' halls, bookstores, attend gatherings, and listen to speeches."[2] The "gatherings" and "speeches" mentioned here referred to the activities organized by revolutionaries and radical people such as Zhang Taiyan, Sun Yat-sen, Qiu Jin, and Tao Chengzhang. There were so many political events, and those Lu Xun get involved in and witnessed included: Gathering of the Commemorative Society for the 242nd Anniversary of the Loss of China; Anti-Russian movement; the Restoration Society organized by revolutionaries from Zhejiang; the grand debate between the royalist *New Citizen* and the revolutionary *People's Newspaper*; the nation-wide student strike to protest the Rules to Ban Students of the Qing dynasty from Studying in Japan by the Ministry of Education, Science, and Culture of Japan; Chen Tianhua's suicide by drowning himself in the sea; and Xu Xilin and Qiu Jin being executed in China, etc. In his second year at Sendai Medical School, while in a bacteriology class, Lu Xun saw some slides that had been taken during the Russo-Japanese War, and was deeply disillusioned seeing the dumb expressions on the faces of executed Chinese spies and of the Chinese onlookers. This made him aware that if ordinary Chinese people were not politically and ideologically awakened, no matter how strong they were physically, nothing could stop them from facing public shame or becoming ignorant onlookers. This was why he decided to give up his career in medicine for one in literature.

Lu Xun was by no means the only one to choose to do so, and of those who went to study science in Japan and later turned to writing, most had similar experiences. For example, Guo Moruo, who went to study medicine in Japan in 1914, also gave up medicine and started writing. Yu Dafu went to study medicine in Japan in 1913 and later turned to law, finally choosing to study economics at the Imperial University of Tokyo. Zhang Ziping (张资平, who

---

[2]   Lu Xun: "A Few Things Recollected in Connection to Mr. Taiyan" (《因太炎先生而想起
的二三事》), *Complete Works of Lu Xun*, Vol. 6, Beijing: People's Literature Press, 1981, p. 558.

went to Japan in 1913) and Cheng Fangwu (who went to Japan in 1910) were both students of the Imperial University of Tokyo, one studying geology and the other weapon manufacturing. These four people founded the Creation Society (創造社) after the May Fourth movement, and they all became writers later and did not practice what they had learned in Japan. Actually, the general trend of that time was to study science and get involved in industry, and people generally looked down on humanities. As Guo Moruo recalled: "Anyone with inspiration and interest would learn some practical knowledge to make

11.2. A Chinese person being beheaded by the Japanese army for being a spy for the Russian army, with Chinese onlookers in the background. This photo was taken outside the town of Kaiyuan in Northeast China, and it may help us imagine what Lu Xun saw at medical school

11.3. Slides taken during the Russo-Japanese War. Nowadays some foreign scholars doubt the truthfulness of the incident of Lu Xun seeing the slides at medical school, on the grounds that the slides Lu Xun mentioned cannot be found. However, it was Lu Xun's account of what happened, so it is not unfounded

our country stronger, and therefore there was a general dislike for literature."[3] Because of this, those who changed their studies to literature had to be really determined to do so, for there was no turning back.

Transferring from engineering and medicine, the earlier literary writings of these people were different from those who studied humanities in Europe and the United States, for the latter may have read literary works in the original languages, and some were even students of the authors of those works. Take Lu Xun for example, his literary career started with writing scientific essays such as "A Brief Outline of Chinese Geology" (《中国地质略论》) and "An Essay on the Instruction in History of Science" (《科学史教篇》); then he translated and commented on the historical novel *The Soul of Sparta* (《斯巴达之魂》) and science fiction novel *From the Earth to the Moon*; published literary essays "On the Power of Mara Poetry" (《摩罗诗力说》) and "On Cultural Extremes" (《文化偏至论》); set up to launch the literary magazine *New Life* (《新生》, which was later aborted); and cotranslated with Zhou Zuoren and published *Short Stories from Abroad*, etc. These were the results of the indirect influence (Lu Xun read the texts in Japanese and German) of Western science, literature and art, and philosophical ideas. But the modern thoughts grasped through indirect influences produced remarkable results in Lu Xun. For example, in one of his earlier theoretical essays, "On Cultural Extremes," he proposed to "accumulate material wealth to enhance national spirit, to promote individualism, and to repel group orientation," and that "the foremost task is to upbear the individual, and then everything could be conducted; as for the way to achieve this, one must respect individuality and encourage personal spirit."[4] Even today, these sentences still sound so relevant and impelling.

To overthrow the Qing dynasty and put an end to the feudal monarchy, the students in Japan made preparations in terms of ideology and talent cultivating, and after the Xinhai Revolution, they made preparations for the start of a new culture and new literature. Japanese left-wing thoughts were encouraged by the success of the October Revolution in Russia and held a strong position in the field of social sciences in Japan, so that it was somewhat easier for Chinese students in Japan to transform from historical evolutionists into revolutionaries, and radical talents emerged one after another who were active in putting revolutionary theories into practice. Different from those studying in Europe and the United States – who often studied a modern subject thoroughly and returned home to be engaged in a special academic field, then became

3   Guo Moruo: "School Days: A Decade of Literary Creation" (《学生时代 • 创造十年》), *Complete Works of Guo Moruo* (《郭沫若全集》), Literature, Vol. 12, Beijing: People's Literature Press, 1992, p. 65.

4   Lu Xun: "On Cultural Extremes," *Complete Works of Lu Xun*, Vol. 1, Beijing: People's Literature Press, 1981, pp. 46, 57, and 56.

famous scholars or professors and remained gentlemen all through this process, or those who entered officialdom and became technology-wise officials – many students from Japan did not think highly of the academic degree. Since 1901, Chen Duxiu had been to Japan four times; however, he never finished his studies at Tokyo Higher Normal School, but devoted all his time and energy to ideological propaganda activities. He was indeed a student studying in Japan, but his more important identity was as a revolutionary who edited the *China National Gazette* and ran the *Anhui Colloquial Newspaper* in China, organized activities for the Shanghai Patriotic Society and the Warrior Yue Society (岳王会) and was an active participant of the anti-Yuan Shikai campaign. After the anti-Yuan campaign failed, Chen Duxiu went in self-imposed exile to Japan to help Zhang Shizhao run the *Jiayin* (《甲寅》) journal, in which he published some radical comments that best reflected his political and cultural aspirations before *New Youth* was launched. Chen Duxiu never thought about completing his unfinished studies in Japan, which was typical of those who studied there.

11.4. Portrait of Zhang Yuanji (张元济), a late-Qing presented scholar who was once appointed as a Hanlin academician. This photo was taken in 1910, before his round-the-world travels. He was a leader in modern Chinese education and publishing

Back home, the backbone in preparing for a new culture and new literature was comprised of several generations. Liang Qichao, Zhang Taiyan, and Wang Guowei were all figures of the transitional period who could not see the true spirit of the May Fourth movement and thus could never be a part of it. Zhang Yuanji committed himself to the modern publishing cause as a presented scholar (*jin-shi*, 进士) and Hanlin academician, and became one of the founding members of the Commercial Press. He, too, was a transitional figure, for his reformist constitutional ideas would chain him to the old social system, while he became the choice of history to be one of the earliest figures of China's mechanical printing and modern publishing, and the modern publishing industry he built up had unbreakable ties with modern Chinese literature. On the other hand, Cai Yuanpei, who cooperated with Zhang Yuanji in editing the Commercial Imprint primary school textbooks and became the first Head of the Department of Translation and Editing of the Commercial Press earlier than Zhang, was far ahead of the latter to embrace new ideas and concepts. Cai Yuanpei, too, was a presented scholar and Hanlin academician, but he founded the China Education Society, Patriotic Society, organized the Restoration Society, joined the United Allegiance Society, championed the Republican cause, and finally became a "rebel" against the Qing court. When he went to study in Germany in 1907 at 39 years of age, he was already a celebrity in China, and thus he was different from most young students studying abroad.

11.5. Cai Yuanpei in 1920, when he was the chancellor of Peking University. The "compatible and inclusive" principles he initiated during that time are still compelling

11.6. Portrait of Cai Yuanpei in his youth

While he lived overseas, Cai Yuanpei gradually formed his theoretical system on modern education and aesthetics, thus making preparations for his later career as the minister of education for the Republic of China. In the interim government, he appointed Lu Xun and others to take office in the Ministry of Education and brought them to Beijing. In 1917, he initiated and founded the Research Society for National Language (国语研究会) and became its president, and the Society's "A Letter to Recruit New Members" made it clear that "all textbooks of national schools shall use vernacular language from now on."[5] This almost coincided in time with the vernacular movement initiated by Hu Shi, and therefore, as Li Jinxi (黎锦熙) said, in that year "the waves of 'literary revolution' and 'unification of national language' merged."[6] During the time Cai Yuanpei was the Chancellor of Peking University, he gave strong support to the New Culture movement, which was still in the preparation stages. He appointed another "rabbit," Chen Duxiu, who was twelve years younger than him, to be the dean of Humanities at Peking University, and Chen employed a third "rabbit," Hu Shi, who was another 12 years younger, to work as a professor in Peking University ("rabbit" being the zodiac sign of all these three).[7] It was the concerted efforts of these three generations of

[5] See *Chinese Times* (《中华新报》), Mar. 9 and 13, 1917.
[6] Li Jinxi: *An Overview of the National Language Movement* (《国语运动史纲》), Vol. 2, Shanghai: Commercial Press, 1935.
[7] The term "rabbit" is to quote Hu Shi, who once said that Peking University was famous for "three rabbits," namely Cai Yuanpei (born in 1867), Chen Duxiu (born in 1879), and himself (born in 1891), for they were all born in the Year of Rabbit, with twelve years in between. – Translator's note

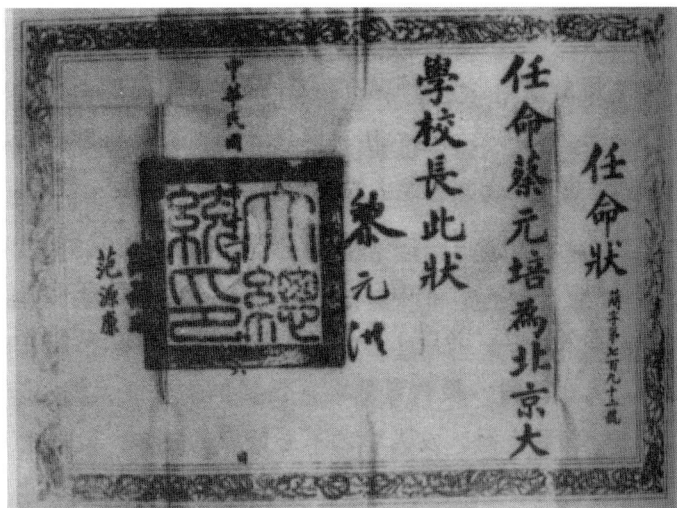

11.7. Appointment awarded to Cai Yuanpei by Li Yuanhong, president of the Republic of China, to be chancellor of Peking University in 1917

people that had started the tide of the New Culture movement, with its core being *New Youth* and Peking University. Ye Shengtao and Shen Yanbing were a generation younger – they were born at the end of the nineteenth century, as were Qu Qiubai, Zheng Zhenduo, Zhu Ziqing, Wen Yiduo (闻一多), and many others – but Ye and Shen had started working earlier due to their poor family backgrounds, and they had been working for the Commercial Press before the May Fourth movement. The others in the younger generation were still studying in new-style schools during the May Fourth period: Qu Qiubai was a student leader at the Russian Language Institute of the Ministry of Foreign Affairs (北京俄文专修馆); Zheng Zhenduo was a student representative of the Peking School of Railway Management; Zhu Ziqing was at the core of student unrest at Peking University, and Wen Yiduo was studying at Tsinghua School (the precursor of Tsinghua University) when he was elected as a student representative to attend the meetings of the National Student Association. They were all involved in this patriotic student movement, and it was the May Fourth movement that guided their first steps toward a literary career.

Qu Qiubai went to the USSR after learning Russian, and Wen Yiduo went to the United States after attending the preparatory school for students to be sent by the government to the United States, which meant even though both were active during the May Fourth movement, each took a very different path afterward. A brief comparison between those who studied in Europe and the United States and those who studied in Japan may reveal the difference. Those who studied in Japan were much greater in number, but few of them studied humanities; and even combined with those who eventually switched over to literary writing, the total number of those who studied humanities was no larger than those who studied humanities in Europe and the United States. This would be almost unbelievable were it not for the relevant facts and statistics. Those who studied in Europe and the United States, it seems, lived under less pressure in terms of everyday life and political atmosphere (except for those who went to Moscow to study political revolution, for they were attending short-term courses at the Communist University of Toilers of the East [东方大学] and Sun Yat-sen University [中山大学]). They could choose any humanities subjects they were interested in, and back home, most of them were teaching and writing in universities and were committed to introducing Western academic culture and ideas to China, so that the number of people engaged in humanities was actually larger. Hu Shi was a major figure within this group. In "Driven to Revolt" (《逼上梁山》) he recalled his experience of this time in his life, giving a detailed account of how he and his fellow Chinese students in the United States made preparations for the vernacular literary movement back in China in terms of ideas and theories. He was somewhat boastful on this account, for a cultural movement with profound historical influence was by no means initiated through several discussions of some young students, but such discussions were significant as triggers. Actually, Hu observed that at the time, everything was ready for the Chinese literary revolution and only a trigger was needed. According to Hu, when he was in the United States in 1915, each time he received the monthly allowance sent by Zhong Wen'ao (钟文鳌), secretary of the Tsinghua student supervision division, along with the check there were always some flyers that had been put in the envelope by Zhong in private. The flyers had various messages, such as "No marriage until twenty-five years old," "Abolish Chinese characters and adopt letters," "It is good to plant more trees," etc.

> One day I saw a new flyer sent by him, claiming that the Chinese language should employ the system of letters, for this was the only way to universal education. I was angry at this and wrote a brief letter to reprimand him. The general idea of my letter was that "you people know nothing about Chinese characters, so you are in no position to blab about reforming Chinese characters. Before talking about it, you should first spend some years to become proficient in Chinese, and until then you are not qualified to say whether Chinese characters should be abolished or not."[8]

Hu Shi immediately "regretted" writing this letter, and it was said that that was why he started to make serious efforts to examine closely the issue of

8   Hu Shi: "Driven to Revolt: The Beginning of the Literary Revolution" (《逼上梁山——文学革命的开始》), *Autobiography of Hu Shi* (《胡适自传》), Hefei: Huangshan Shushe Press, 1986, pp. 104–105.

reform of Chinese characters and literature: "I said Mr. Zhong was not qualified to talk about this issue, [so] we people who are qualified should spend some time and effort to conduct in-depth research on it."[9] From this anecdote we can get the feeling of the general atmosphere among students in the United States who were concerned about China's specific problems, so much so that even a clerk was influenced by the atmosphere and sent such flyers. Thus the conditions for the reform of Chinese characters and literature were indeed ripe by that time, and Hu Shi was but an epitome of this reform. We can also see that as discreet and sophisticated as Hu Shi was, he was also proud and felt superior to ordinary people; no wonder that later students returning from the United States did not get along well with literary authors who had returned from Japan, and Lu Xun found it hard to endure their condescending manner.

11.8. Hu Shi in 1914

From that point on, academic discussions became a part of Hu's student life. His first step was to found the Research Department of Literature and Science (文学与科学研究部) within the Chinese Student Union of the East Coast of America. At the first annual meeting held that year, he and Zhao Yuanren decided to hold a thematic seminar on the "issue of Chinese characters." Zhao Yuanren's title was "Whether and How Chinese Literature Can Employ the System of Letters" (《吾国文字能否采用字母制，及其进行方法》); and preparing his discussion on the theme "By What Means the Ancient Literary Chinese Can Get Easily Taught" (《如何可使吾国文言易于教授》), Hu Shi found that the ancient classical Chinese language had become a "dead language" or "half-dead language" just like Greek and Latin, while English, French, and the "vernacular of our country" was "living language" or "everyday language." This was the beginning of Hu Shi's comparison between classical and vernacular Chinese and of his disbelief in the former, which reflected a view of historical evolution: the fact that the everyday languages used in Europe and the United States actually took shape as modern languages by incorporating the colloquial language of each country (and eliminating Latin) assured him that the Chinese language could also incorporate vernacular in order to become a modern language. He also raised the issue of "language symbols" based on foreign languages.[10] In the same year, Hu Shi published his essay "On Sentences, Phrases, and Punctuation

---

[9] Ibid., p. 105.
[10] Ibid., p. 106.

11.9. Portrait of Hu Shi

Marks" (《论句读及文字符号》) and proposed ten punctuation marks, which were the earliest punctuation marks of modern Chinese language.

Then, in Ithaca, New York, where Cornell University is located, Hu Shi presented his idea that classical Chinese had become a "half-dead system of writing" to a group of Chinese students for discussion. In summer 1915, a number of people participated in the discussion, including Ren Shuyong (任叔永), Mei Guangdi, Yang Xingfo (杨杏佛), and Tang Yue (唐钺), among others, and the topic extended from Chinese language to Chinese literature, but nobody had expected that a hot debate had thus been started. Of them Mei Guangdi, an intimate friend of Hu Shi, was especially upset and highly critical of Hu's view that classical Chinese had been "dead."

After that, for over one year, their discussion continued by means of lake tours, farewell notes, correspondence, and poetry writings, and their frequent exchange of views was almost beyond imagination. According to Hu Shi, there was "a postcard sent every day and a long letter sent every three days."[11] In September, when Mei Guangdi went to Harvard, Hu Shi wrote a long poem for him, which seemed a summary of this prolonged discussion:

> My dear Mr. Mei, please have no self-contempt! // China's literature has been withering and decaying for a long time, / It is a hundred years since anyone vigorous has arisen. // There's a new tide that cannot be stopped, / It is time for a literary revolution! // You and I both have responsibility for it. // Let's call on several other young people, / And take the lead in the revolutionary army, / Let's whip and expel so many ghosts from China, / And embrace the coming of a new century! // This is not a slight way to serve our country: / We may propose to change the world with it. // My dear Mr. Mei, please have no self-contempt![12]

> 梅生梅生毋自鄙！神州文学久枯馁，百年未有健者起。新潮之来不可止，文学革命其时矣！吾辈势不容坐视。且复号召二三子，革命军前杖马箠，鞭笞驱除一车鬼，再拜迎入新世纪！以此报国未云菲：缩地戡天差可儗。梅生梅生毋自鄙！

It was the first time that Hu Shi's proposed idea of "literary revolution" had been recorded. In this 420-character-long poem (the above is but an

---

[11] Ibid., p. 126.
[12] Ibid., p. 108.

excerpt), Hu Shi used as many as eleven transliterations of foreign words. This was an old practice frequently used by Tan Sitong to Huang Zunxian during the period of "poetry revolution," but Ren Shuyong made a joke of Hu Shi with it by joining these transliterations into a nonsense verse and giving it to Hu when he went to Columbia University:

> Newton and Edison, Bacon and Calvin,
> Thoreau and Hawthorne, inspiration.
>   After whipping so many ghosts, fine poetry would be produced.
> In the literary revolution today, I compose this poem for Hu my friend.[13]

> 牛敦爱迭孙，培根客尔文，
> 索虏与霍桑，"烟士披里纯"。
> 鞭笞一车鬼，为君生琼英。
> 文学今革命，作歌送胡生。

Hu Shi knew this was a joke, ridiculing that his "revolution" was nothing but old-style poems spiced with some loan words. But Hu was quite serious about "literary revolution,"

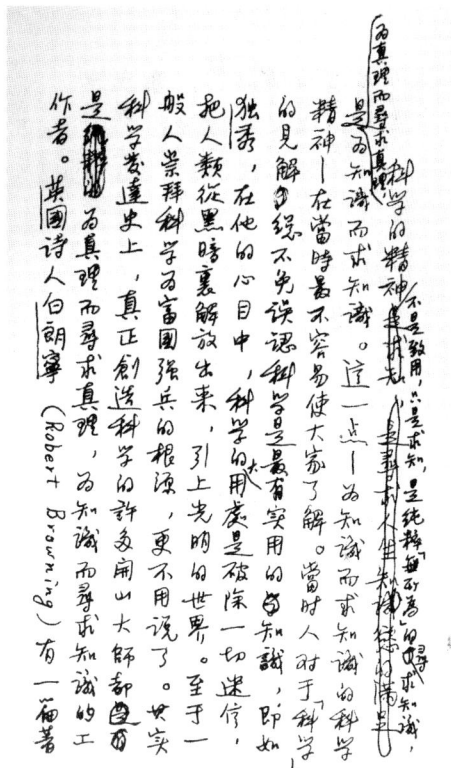

11.10. One of Hu Shi's manuscripts

so on the train to New York, he used the original rhyme of Ren Shuyong's to write a poem as his solemn reply to those who remained at Ithaca:

> From where shall the literary revolution start?
> We must start from writing poems like prose composition.
> A flowery and ornamental poem is lacking in energy,
> What sounds like a poem is not necessarily genuine.
> I am indeed bold in prose writing,
> While each of you is an outstanding talent.
> Wish we could make sincere efforts in this,
> We people are no longer a banal generation.[14]

> 诗国革命何自始？要须作诗如作文。
> 琢镂粉饰丧元气，貌似未必诗之纯。
> 小人行文颇大胆，诸公一一皆人英。
> 愿共僇力莫相笑，我辈不作儒腐生。

---

[13] Ibid., p. 108.
[14] Ibid., p. 109.

Mei Guangdi was not blindly opposing to writing in vernacular. In the debate, he accepted Hu Shi's view that the vernacular literature of the Song and Yuan dynasties was of value, and he agreed that vernacular language could be used to write novels and *ci* and *qu*, but he insisted it should not be used to write poems. In a letter to Hu Shi, he wrote:

> You said that the poetry revolution shall start from "writing poems like prose composition." This I cannot agree with. Ever since there were poem and prose (in China as well as in the West), the poetic diction has been quite different from the prose diction. As a pioneer in the poetry revolution, you may reform the poetic diction, but you cannot transplant the prose diction in poetic composition and call it "revolution."[15]

Hu Shi's point here was not merely writing poetry with "prose diction," and thus in his reply, he began to propose specific ways to avoid "writing without substance," from "three points" (firstly, what you say must be about something; secondly, pay attention to grammar; and thirdly, don't avoid colloquial words and phrases),[16] to "eight programs" (see Hu Shi's letter to Zhu Jingnong [朱经农], dated Aug. 19, 1916). Such repeated questioning and replying deepened Hu's understanding of the "literary revolution," and he finally found where to make a breakthrough to literary revolution: in terms of language, one must understand that language is a means to express what one thought. "The Chinese literary history is nothing but a history of new forms of language (as a means) superseding the old," and "a living literature shall use living language to express the emotions and thoughts of the writer's own age. If the language is fossilized, it shall be replaced by a new, living one, and this is literary revolution."[17] Then in terms of literature, one should start from writing vernacular poems. At this moment he came increasingly closer to the view expressed in his letter to Chen Duxiu and his essays. Both the students studying abroad and the revolutionaries remaining home had chosen a "radical" path in the field of cultural reform (even the students could not make any breakthrough if they were not radical) and would join hands to begin a grand and magnificent chapter in the history of modern Chinese literature.

[15] Ibid. p. 110.
[16] Ibid.
[17] Ibid., p. 111.

TABLE 11.1 *Writers studying in Japan around the May Fourth period (until 1929)*

Name	City	Starting from	Subject	Returning in
Su Manshu	Yokohoma / Tokyo	1898	Preparatory courses	1903
Lu Xun	Tokyo/Sendai	1902	Medicine	1909
Chen Duxiu	Tokyo	1902/1913	Army Department / English	1908/1915
Ouyang Yuqian	Tokyo	1902		1910
Shen Yinmo	Japan	1905		1906
Xia Mianzun	Tokyo	1905	Preparatory courses	1907
Li Shutong	Tokyo	1905	Fine arts	1910
Wu Yu	Japan	1905		1910
Qian Xuantong	Tokyo	1906	Literature	1910
Zhou Zuoren	Tokyo	1906	Humanities	1911
Tao Jingsun (陶晶孙)	Fukuoka	In Japan in 1906	Studied medicine in 1919	1927
Cheng Fangwu	Tokyo	1910	Weapon Manufacturing Department	1921
Luo Heizhi (罗黑芷)	Keio University	Before 1911	Humanities	1911
Xu Zuzheng (徐祖正)	Japan	1911		1922
Li Dazhao	Tokyo	1913	Politics	1916
Liu Dabai (刘大白)	Japan	1913		1915
Li Liuru (李六如)	Japan	1913	Politics / Economics	1918
Guo Moruo	Tokyo / Fukuoka	1913	Medicine	1923
Zhang Ziping	Tokyo / Kumamoto	1913	Geology science	1922
Yu Dafu	Tokyo	1913	Medicine / Economics	1922
Li Chuli (李初梨)	Tokyo	1915		1927
Tian Han (田汉)	Tokyo	1916	English Department	1922

(continued)

TABLE 11.1 *(continued)*

Name	City	Starting from	Subject	Returning in
Zheng Boqi (郑伯奇)	Tokyo / Kyoto	1917		1926
Bai Wei (白薇)	Tokyo	1917	Science / History	1925
Chen Dabei	Japan	1918		1919
Zhang Kebiao (章克标)	Tokyo		Mathematics Department	1925
Zhang Wentian (张闻天)	Japan / United States	1920	Philosophy	1924
Xie Liuyi (谢六逸)	Tokyo	1920	Humanities	1924
Mu Mutian (穆木天)	Kyoto / Tokyo	1920	Humanities	1926
Qian Gechuan (钱歌川)	Japan	1920		1926
Xia Yan (夏衍)	Tokyo / Fukuoka	1920	Electrical engineering	1927
Shen Qiyu (沈启予)	Tokyo / Kyoto	1920	Literature	1927
Feng Zikai	Tokyo	1921	Fine arts	1922
Liu Na'ou (刘呐鸥)	Tokyo	In Japan during his youth	Humanities	1925
Feng Naichao (冯乃超)	Kyoto / Tokyo	Born in Japan	Philosophy / Aesthetics	1927
Yang Sao (杨骚)	Tokyo	1921	Normal school	1924
Teng Gu (滕固)	Japan	Before 1924		1924
Yang Kui (杨逵)	Tokyo	1924	Literature	Returned to Taiwan in 1927
Sun Lianggong (孙俍工)	Tokyo	1924	German literature	1928
Liu Dajie	Tokyo	1926	European literature	1930
Ni Yide (倪贻德)	Tokyo	1927	Fine arts	1928
Zhou Yang (周扬)	Tokyo	1928		1930
Ren Jun (任钧)	Japan	1928		1932

(continued)

TABLE II.I *(continued)*

Name	City	Starting from	Subject	Returning in
Hu Feng (胡风)	Tokyo	1929	English Department	Expelled in 1933
Lou Shiyi (楼适夷)	Japan	1929	Russian literature	1931
Cai Yi (蔡仪)	Tokyo / Fukuoka	1929		1937
Gao Changhong (高长虹)	Japan / Europe	1929		1937

TABLE II.2 *Writers studying in Europe and the United States around the May Fourth period (until 1929)*

Name	City/Country	Starting from	Subject	Returning in
Cai Yuanpei	Germany	1907	Philosophy	1912
Li Qingya (李青崖)	Belgium	1907	Engineering	1912
Hu Shi	United States	1910	Agronomy, later changed to Philosophy	1917
Mei Guangdi	United States	1911	Literary criticism	1920
Chen Xiying (陈西滢)	United Kingdom	1912	From middle school until doctoral studies	1922
Hu Xiansu (胡先骕)	United States	1913/1923	Botany	1916/1925
Song Chunfang (宋春舫)	Switzerland	1914		1916
Ding Xilin (丁西林)	United Kingdom	1914	Physics / Mathematics	1920
Chen Hengzhe (陈衡哲)	United States	1914	History / Literature	1920
Yuan Changying (袁昌英)	United Kingdom	1916	British literature	1921
Hong Shen (洪深)	United States	1916	Dramatic literature	1922
Wu Mi (吴宓)	United States	1917	Literary criticism	1921
Xu Zhimo (徐志摩)	United States / United Kingdom	1918	History / Politics	1922

(continued)

TABLE II.2 *(continued)*

Name	City/Country	Starting from	Subject	Returning in
Lin Yutang	United States / Germany	1919	Literature / Linguistics	1923
Li Jinfa (李金发)	France	1919	Fine arts / Sculpture	1925
Li Jieren (李劼人)	France	1919	Literature	1924
Cao Jinghua (曹靖华)	Moscow, USSR	1920	Oriental University	1921
Xiao San (萧三)	France / USSR	1920	Oriental University	1924
Wang Jingxi (汪敬熙)	United States	1920		1924
Yang Zhensheng (杨振声)	United States	1920		1924
Zong Baihua (宗白华)	France / Germany	1920	Philosophy / Aesthetics	1925
Wang Duqing (王独清)	France	1920		1925
Luo Jialun (罗家伦)	United States / United Kingdom / Germany / France	1920		1925
Liu Bannong	United Kingdom / France	1920	Linguistics / Literature	1925
Fu Sinian (傅斯年)	United Kingdom / Germany	1920	Psychology / Philosophy	1926
Kang Baiqing (康白情)	United States	1920		1926
Jiang Guangci (蒋光慈)	Moscow, USSR	1921	Communist University of Toilers of the East	1924
Su Xuelin (苏雪林)	France	1921	Literature / Art	1925
Wen Yiduo	United States	1922	Fine arts	1925
Lin Ruji (林如稷)	France	1922	Law / Humanities	1930
Xu Dishan (许地山)	United States / United Kingdom		Religion / Philosophy	1926

(continued)

TABLE 11.2 *(continued)*

Name	City/Country	Starting from	Subject	Returning in
Fang Lingru (方令孺)	United States	1923		1929
Yu Shangyuan (余上沅)	United States	1923	Drama	1925
Shao Xunmei (邵洵美)	United Kingdom / France	1923	British literature	1927
Liang Shiqiu (梁实秋)	United States	1923	Literary criticism	1926
Gu Yiqiao (顾一樵)	United States	1923	Electrical engineering	1929
Bing Xin	United States	1923	Literature	1926
Lin Huiyin	United States	1924	Fine arts / Design	1928
Xiong Foxi (熊佛西)	United States	1924	Dramatic literature	1926
Liang Zongdai (梁宗岱)	Switzerland / France, etc.	1924	Language / Literature	1931
Lao She (老舍)	United Kingdom	1924	Language teaching	1930
Nie Gannu (聂绀弩)	Moscow, USSR	1925	Sun Yat-sen University	1927
Sun Dayu (孙大雨)	United States	1925	British literature	1929
Zhu Guangqian (朱光潜)	United Kingdom / France	1925	Literature / Philosophy	1933
Gao Shiqi (高士其)	United States	1925	Bacteriology	1930
Li Bozhao (李伯钊)	Moscow, USSR	1926	Sun Yat-sen University	1931
Lin Tongji (林同济)	United States	1926	International relations, etc.	1934
Zhu Xiang (朱湘)	United States	1927	Literature	1929
Wang Li（王力）	France	1927	Literature	1932
Li Liewen (黎烈文)	France	1927	Literature	1932
Fu Lei (傅雷)	France	1927	Art criticism	1931
Chen Xuezhao (陈学昭)	France	1927	Literature	1934

(continued)

TABLE II.2 *(continued)*

Name	City/Country	Starting from	Subject	Returning in
Chen Quan (陈铨)	United States / Germany	1928	Philosophy / Literature	1934
Ai Qing (艾青)	France	1929	Fine arts	1932
Luo Niansheng (罗念生)	United States / Greece	1929	Language / Literature	1934
Luo Shu (罗淑)	France	1929	Language teaching	1933

(*Source*: Zheng Chun [郑春]: *Overseas Educational Background and Modern Chinese Literature* [《留学背景与中国现代文学》], Jinan: Shandong Education Press, 2002)

TWELVE

THE RISE OF RADICALS FROM *NEW YOUTH* AND PEKING UNIVERSITY, AND CONSERVATIVES' COUNTERCLAIMS

BEFORE MAY FOURTH, THE NEW CULTURE MOVEMENT had already begun by seizing on the momentum of the "literary revolution." This was a significant turning point. On the surface, it appeared to rely on nothing but a journal and a university, while actually it had deep-rooted social and historical support. The journal was *New Youth*, which was to become very famous, and the university was Peking University, the stronghold of the New Culture movement. The year was 1917, and the venue was Beijing, the locus of the Beiyang warlord government, the political center where a slight move could affect the situation of the entire country.

On January 1, 1917, Hu Shi, who was still writing his PhD dissertation at Columbia University in New York, had his "Some Modest Proposals for the Reform of Literature" published in *New Youth* (Vol. 2, Issue 5). Chen Duxiu's "On Literary Revolution" was published in the next issue. Before that, the journal had already published the trans-Pacific correspondence between Chen Duxiu and Hu Shi in 1916, which conveyed the strongest message of cultural reform since the Republican period.

In the correspondence and "Some Modest Proposals for the Reform of Literature," Hu Shi proposed the well-known "eight matters" (八事). In a letter to Chen, he said: "It is my belief that those wishing to discuss literary revolution today should begin with eight matters." Later he changed the sequence of the eight matters and some of the wording, changing the words "literary

12.1. Students' parade through the streets of Beijing during the May Fourth movement

revolution" to "literary reform," which seemed milder, but what he meant was still "revolution." The "eight matters" were:

1. Writing should have substance.
2. Do not imitate the ancients.
3. Emphasize the technique of writing.
4. Do not moan without an illness.
5. Eliminate hackneyed and formal language.
6. Do not use allusions.
7. Do not use parallelism.
8. Do not avoid vulgar diction.[1]

Chen Duxiu, certainly an experienced revolutionary, proposed his "three great principles" (三大主义), which were not so profound in reasoning, but more distinctive in diction:

> As for the literary revolution, it has mushroomed for a not inconsiderable length of time, and the foremost in the vanguard, who first raised the revolutionary banner, is my friend Hu Shi. I am willing to brave the enmity of all the pedantic scholars of the country and hoist the great banner of the "Army of the Literary Revolution" in support of my friend. On this

[1] Hu Shi: "Some Modest Proposals for the Reform of Literature," *New Youth*, Vol. 2, Issue 5, (Jan. 1, 1917).

banner shall be written in big, clear characters my three great principles of the Revolutionary Army: To overthrow the painted, powdered, and obsequious literature of the aristocratic few, and to create the plain, simple, and expressive literature of the people; to overthrow the stereotyped and over-ornamental literature of classicism, and to create a fresh and sincere literature of realism; to overthrow the pedantic, unintelligible, and obscurantist literature of the hermit and the recluse, and to create the plain-speaking and popular literature of society in general.[2]

Almost each one of Hu Shi's "eight matters" was about the relationship between thoughts and feelings and words, and at the end he wrote: "Yet, from today's perspective of historical evolution, we can see with complete certainty that vernacular literature is really canonical and will be a useful tool for developing future literature."[3] This idea that vernacular should replace classical Chinese as

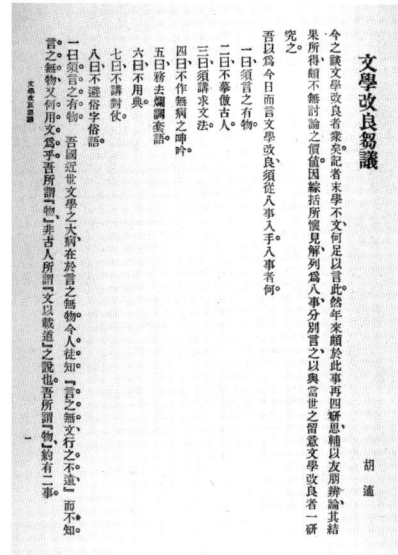

12.2. "Some Modest Proposals for the Reform of Literature" by Hu Shi, published in *New Youth* (Vol. 2, Issue 5) in January 1917

the "canonical" language later became a spiritual banner. Chen Duxiu, on the other hand, found "eighteen demons" (十八妖魔) from classical Chinese literature and listed positive examples from European literature, claiming: "Is there some outstanding writer in our own national literature who will take on the role of China's Hugo, Zola, Goethe, Hauptmann, Dickens, and Wilde? Is there anyone bold enough to make a public challenge to the 'eighteen demons,' ignoring the criticism of reactionary scholars? If so, I am willing to drag out the cannon of forty-two-centimetre bore to form his vanguard!"[4] What a magnificent declaration!

Once published in *New Youth*, these words caused a great stir; they were well received and responded to by intellectual

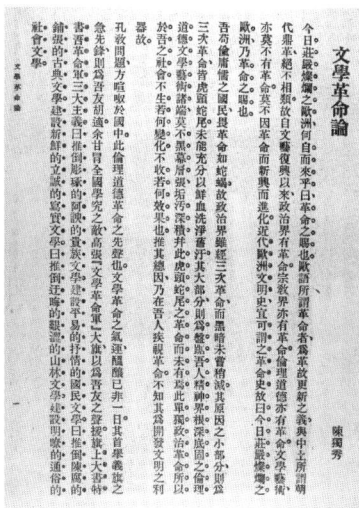

12.3. "On Literary Revolution" by Chen Duxiu, published in *New Youth* (Vol. 2, Issue 6), February 1917

[2]   Chen Duxiu: "On Literary Revolution," *New Youth*, Vol. 2, Issue 6, Feb. 1, 1917.
[3]   Hu Shi: "Some Modest Proposals for the Reform of Literature."
[4]   Chen Duxiu: "On Literary Revolution."

youths throughout the country, thus becoming the curtain raiser to the New Culture movement and "literary revolution."

It was by no means fortuitous that *New Youth* could assume such a great responsibility. *New Youth* was founded by Chen Duxiu, recommended by his friend Wang Mengzou (汪孟邹), boss of Shanghai East Asia Library, to Chen Zipei (陈子沛) and his brother Chen Zishou (陈子寿) of Qunyi Book Company, and published in Shanghai in 1915. It was originally named *Youth* (《青年杂志》) and Chen Duxiu himself assumed the position of editor-in-chief. This was something Chen Duxiu had always wanted to do during the years he was in exile and fled to and from Shanghai and Tokyo; with this journal, which specialized in political propaganda and was complemented by academic and literary discussions, he wanted to fulfill his aspiration to enlighten Chinese people. On the cover of Volume 1, Issues 1–6, there was a drawing of a row of young people dressed in black sitting and listening to a lecture, above which were the French words "LA JEUNESSE" (meaning "Youth"); on the right there was the Chinese name of the journal, the characters written vertically, and dominant on the cover was a portrait of one of six foreign figures (each issue had a different portrait), including US industrialist Andrew Carnegie, making it clear that the intention of this journal was to enlighten young Chinese people about Western civilization, including the revolutionary thoughts in France and the entrepreneurship of American people. At first the contributing authors were those from *Jiayin*, with whom Chen Duxiu had worked as an editor when he was engaged in the anti-Yuan Shikai activities in Japan, and the essays published concerned such sensitive topics as youth, education, nation, women, modern civilization, science, human rights, the national identity of Chinese and Western people, and modern European art and literature. In its typesetting *Youth* applied paragraphs and punctuation marks to ancient Chinese language, which made it quite a new-style journal. However, at that time a breakthrough had yet to be made in terms of cultural and literary reform, so *Youth* only had a print-run of around 1,000 copies per issue and had very limited influence. Its great opportunity came thanks to a series of incidents. After six issues had been published, the name of the journal was changed to *New Youth*. This happened by chance. Qunyi Book Company had received a letter of protest from Shanghai YMCA accusing *Youth* of adopting a similar name to their journal *Shanghai Youth* (《上海青年》). Chen Zishou then suggested to change the name to "New Youth," an idea Chen Duxiu agreed with, and he seized on this opportunity and wrote an essay entitled "New Youth," which was published in the first issue of Volume 2, after the name had been changed, in which he gave a lecture on "What makes youths new youths? They are different from old youths." From Volume 2, Issue 2, the correspondence between Chen Duxiu and Hu Shi started appearing in the journal. At the end of 1916, when Cai Yuanpei, who just returned from Europe and assumed the position of Chancellor of Peking University, was looking for talents to transform Peking University by reforming the humanities disciplines, Tang Erhe (汤尔和) recommended Chen Duxiu to him. In November that year, Chen Duxiu happened to come to Beijing with Wang Mengzou to raise funds for the merging of East Asia Library and Qunyi Book Company, and he stayed in a hotel just outside the Qianmen Gate. On December 26, Cai Yuanpei went to visit Chen Duxiu. The two became friends at that first meeting, and Cai decided to appoint Chen to be the dean of the Humanities Faculty at Peking University on the spot. As for the future of *New Youth*, Cai solved the problem by simply saying "just move the editorial office to Beijing." At the time this talk was going on, Hu Shi's "Some Modest Proposals for the Reform of Literature" was already typeset and printed and was due to be published on

12.4. *Youth* (Vol. 1, Issue 1; predecessor of *New Youth*)

New Year's Day, 1917. At that time Cai Yuanpei was 50, Chen Duxiu was 38, and Hu Shi only 26 years old, but nobody could ever imagine that these three people would make such a huge difference to history by linking Peking University and *New Youth*.

This historically significant linking between *New Youth* and the Humanities Faculty of Peking University was indeed an epoch-making event. Since its inception as the Imperial University of Peking in 1898, the year of the Wuxu Reform, nearly twenty years had passed. The Imperial University of Peking was the earliest Chinese university to introduce Western-style education, and when the new policies of the Wuxu Reform were abolished after the Reform failed, the university was the only survivor. It was closed when the Eight-Nation Alliance invaded Beijing, and reopened in 1902. The conservatives always wanted to make it an academy committed to ancient Chinese classics, but according to some students' recollection, at that time "modern science" courses still "accounted for the largest proportion," and some recalled how Zhang Zhidong listened to the psychological lectures by a Japanese lecturer when he came to inspect the university.[5] In 1912 its name was changed to Peking University, with Yan Fu being its first chancellor. At first its Humanities

---

[5] Zou Shuwen (邹树文): "Memories of the Earliest Days of Peking University" (《北京大学最早期的回忆》), *Old Photos of Peking University* (《北大老照片》), Beijing: China Foreign Economic Relations and Trade Publishing House, 1988, p. 2.

12.5. Gate of the former site of Peking University, located at the Fourth Princess's Mansion (四公主府) at Ma Shen Temple (马神庙), soon after its name was changed from the Imperial University of Peking to Peking University

12.6. Group photo of Cai Yuanpei (first row, fifth from the left), Lu Xun (second row, fifth from the left), and others at the opening of the Imperial Library of Peking in 1917. Lu Xun was designated by the Ministry of Education to be in charge of the library

Faculty was dominated by conservatives, including Ma Qichang (马其昶), Lin Shu, Yao Yonggai (姚永概), Yao Yongpu (姚永朴), among others, all members of the Tongcheng school. Later, Zhang Taiyan's students Ma Yuzao (马裕藻), Shen Jianshi (沈兼士), Qian Xuantong, and Huang Kan joined successively, so even before Cai Yuanpei became its chancellor, there were already conflicts between new and old styles at the university. Cai Yuanpei opened a new epoch for Peking University. He accepted German and European educational thoughts and strongly advocated the educational principles of "freedom of thoughts," "academic equality," and "all-embracing attitudes," and carried out reforms decisively. He appointed Chen Duxiu to be the dean of the Humanities Faculty and boldly employed young talents, so that Hu Shi, Liu Bannong, Zhou Zuoren, Wu Mei, and Chen Yinke all began working for Peking University in the year 1917. "All-embracing" meant they did not exclude conservatives like Gu

12.7. Cai Yuanpei wrote this inscription for the Special Issue of *New Youth* to Commemorate International Labor Day. The Chinese characters mean "laborers are sacred"

Hongming and Liu Shipei, but at that time, what's more significant about this principle was that it supported and protected the new-style group. After Chen Duxiu moved

12.8. One of the locations of the editorial office of *New Youth* after it was moved to Beijing: the office of the dean of the Humanities Faculty in the Red Building at Sha Tan (沙滩)

the editorial office of *New Youth* to Beijing, it published a series of essays written by Hu Shi and Chen Duxiu, and *New Youth* became increasingly more influential, with its print-run increasing to 6,000 copies per issue. Chen Duxiu was still the editor-in-chief, but actually, most of the lecturers from the Humanities Faculty, including Hu Shi, Qian Xuantong, Shen Yinmo, Li Dazhao, Zhou Zuoren, Liu Bannong, Lu Xun, and Wu Yu, gradually took part in the editing and discussion of the journal. By 1918, the journal adopted an alternate editor system, with its editors being six professors from Peking University, namely Chen Duxiu, Qian Xuantong, Gao Yihan (高一涵), Hu Shi, Li Dazhao, and Shen Yinmo. The close alliance between the National Peking University and *New Youth* made it possible for the new-style professors' intellectual thinking and accomplishments to complement social revolutionaries' political ideals and courage. By that time, *New Youth* had finally become a reputable journal, and its core editors were professors of Peking University, so there was no need to use external authors and pay for writing contributions, and it was promoting the new culture to people all over the country.

Promoting and actually using vernacular language was something that had actually been happening in literary translation and creation since the late-Qing period. Some regarded the text of vernacular academic speeches made by Zhang Taiyan in Tokyo as another origin of modern Chinese vernacular language, which makes some sense.[6] Cai Yuanpei thought otherwise. He said:

> But at that time people wrote in vernacular because it was easy to understand and thus could be used to promote common sense, not because they wanted to replace classical Chinese with it. It was since the age of *New Youth* that advocates of vernacular Chinese insisted on replacing classical Chinese with vernacular in writing and held high the banner of literary revolution.[7]

12.9. Hu Shi's inscriptions for the resumed *New Youth* in 1936

One might add that *New Youth* carried out language reform and intellectual enlightenment at the same time, so that it held two banners, namely intellectual revolution and literary revolution. Thus the radical writings in *New Youth* attacking outdated Confucian morality, old-style education, outmoded ethics, criticizing Confucianist views, idol worship, and cultural despotism, and debating on the topics of family system, European war, women's fidelity, Bertrand Russell's philosophy, sacredness of laborers, and scientific methods were linked with the reform ideas concerning evolution of national language, writing horizontally, new poetry writing, dramatic reform, and Esperanto, together with the Western humanism, evolution, and socialist theories it tried to introduce to China,

---

6   See Chen Pingyuan: "How to Formulate Knowledge: The Vernacular Writing of Zhang Taiyan" (学问该如何表述——以《章太炎的白话文》为中心), *Touches of History: An Entry into "May Fourth" China* (《触摸历史与进入五四》), Beijing: Peking University Press, 2005, chapter 4.

7   *Complete Works of Cai Yuanpei* (《蔡元培全集》), Vol. 6, Beijing: China Book Corporation, 1988, pp. 574–575.

greatly excited and inspired young Chinese readers. In 1918 Hu Shi published his "Toward a Constructive Theory of Literary Revolution" (《建设的文学革命论》) in *New Youth*, which equated vernacular movement to the creation of New Literature, making vernacular a means of literary creation, thus shifting the focus from promoting the "literature of national language" to creating a "literary national language."

The rise of *New Youth* and Peking University would inevitably lead to disputes between the old and new styles. At that time, one could easily feel the existence of opposing forces; as Lu Xun put it, "as far as I can remember, at that time *New Youth* was beset by enemies,"[8] but at first what they felt was forerunners' loneliness. For example, starting from Volume 4, Issues 1 and 2, published in January and February 1918, all the texts in *New Youth* were written in vernacular language, but it received neither praise nor criticism. Therefore, an act of criticism and countercriticism was staged in *New Youth*, in which Qian Xuantong, using the pseudonym of Wang Jingxuan (王敬轩) wrote a fake letter that represented all kinds of fallacies opposing New Literature and vernacular movement, which were then refuted by Liu Bannong one by one. This was the so-called duet letters event.[9] It was not until 1919, with the vernacular movement penetrating and gaining a foothold, that the real opponents began to appear. Lin Shu, the creator of "Lin's translated novels," stood out as a classical Chinese writer and bigot, and published an insinuating novel entitled "Master Jing" (《荆生》) in *New Shun Pao* (《新申报》). In the story, three young scholars by the names Tian Qimei (田其美, referring to Chen Duxiu, for originally in ancient China, the Chen's and Tian's were of the same origin), Jin Xinyi (金心异, referring to Qian Xuantong, with the three characters paired with the three characters of 钱玄同 according to explanations of Chinese characters in ancient books), and Di Mo (狄莫, referring to Hu Shi, who had returned from the United States, "狄" being a derogatory term of address for foreign countries in Chinese) drank at Taoran Pavilion in Beijing and made high remarks on overthrowing the Confucius and Mencius teachings and abolishing the classical Chinese language. Suddenly they heard a loud noise and from out of the wall came a giant called Master Jing, who made a speech full of thrusts at the three scholars, unsparingly letting off the author's resistance against the new culture.[10] Soon after that, Lin Shu published "A Letter to Cai Yuanpei" (《致蔡鹤卿太史书》) in *Public Speech Newspaper*, accusing Peking University of sheltering men who "stand against the five Confucian

---

[8] Lu Xun: "Foreword to *Hot Wind*" (《〈热风〉题记》), *Complete Works of Lu Xun*, Beijing: People's Literature Press, 1981, p. 291.

[9] See Wang Jingxuan and Liu Bannong: "Reverberations of the Literary Revolution" (《文学革命之反响》), *New Youth*, Vol. 4, Issue 3, Mar. 15, 1918.

[10] Lin Shu: "Master Jing," serialized in *New Shun Pao* from Feb. 17 to Mar. 20, 1919.

virtues and make too many absurd statements."[11] Cai Yuanpei answered Lin's letter with his own public letter, "Reply to Lin Qinnan" (《答林琴南书》), publicly expressing his open-minded position of "following the principle of freedom of thoughts with an all-embracing attitude."[12] Meanwhile, hearing all kinds of slanders and criticisms against them, Chen Duxiu published an essay entitled "A Self-Defense of Our Journal's 'Criminal Case'" (《本志罪案之答辩书》), solemnly publishing the declaration of advocates of the New Culture movement:

> Fundamentally, my comrades commit no crime, and these accusations just arise because they champion two gentlemen, namely Mr. Democracy and Mr. Science. If we support Mr. Democracy, we must oppose Confucianism, ritualism, laws, chastity, old ethics, and politics. If we endorse Mr. Science, we must oppose old arts and religion. To support Mr. Democracy and Mr. Science is to oppose the national essence and old literature.[13]

From the diction of this essay we can feel the great pressure felt by the forerunners and their determination to carry the revolution forward. Only by putting it into the context of China where "even moving a table would cause bloodshed," could we truly understand the radical attitudes of *New Youth*. Qian Xuantong, in particular, was radical in his statements. He was a student of the master of classical Chinese, Zhang Taiyan, so nobody could say he did not understand classical Chinese, and therefore his support for vernacular was even more significant. In his letter to Hu Shi, Qian Xuantong raised the slogans of "Scoundrels of the Tongcheng School" (桐城谬种) and "Demons of Wenxuan [parallel prose] School" (选学妖孽), which were similar to Chen Duxiu's "eighteen demons" and were disseminated widely.[14] He also said that "talking about good readings for young people, one can well say that among Chinese novels there is not a single good one worth reading."[15] In a letter he later wrote to Chen Duxiu, he talked about "the future Chinese writing system," in which he even proposed that

> in order to abolish Confucianism, Chinese characters have to be abolished. … Let me make this bold prediction: to abolish Confucianism and eliminate Taoism is a fundamental way to prevent the fall of China and to allow the Chinese to become a civilized nation in the twentieth century.

---

[11] Lin Shu: "A Letter to Cai Yuanpei," *Public Speech Newspaper*, Mar. 18, 1919.

[12] Cai Yuanpei: "Reply to Lin Qinnan," *Public Speech Newspaper*, Apr. 1, 1919.

[13] Chen Duxiu: "A Self-Defense of Our Journal's 'Criminal Case'," *New Youth*, Vol. 6, Issue 1, Jan. 15, 1919.

[14] For the letter from Qian Xuantong to Hu Shi dated July 2, 1917, see the Correspondence column of *New Youth*, Vol. 3, Issue 6, Aug. 1, 1917.

[15] See Hu Shi and Qian Xuantong: "On Novels and Vernacular Poems" (《论小说及白话韵文》), "Letter from Qian Xuantong to Hu Shi," *New Youth*, Vol. 4, Issue 1, Jan. 15, 1918.

But a more fundamental way than this is to abolish the written Chinese language, in which Confucian thoughts and fallacious Taoist sayings are recorded.[16]

These remarks were indeed startling, and even people within the group that advocated New Literature disagreed on "abolishing Chinese characters." But actually, its intention was to overthrow the old culture of the old world, and the slogan of abolishing Chinese characters was nothing more than an evolutionary viewpoint looking forward to the prospect of the "alphabetic writing of Chinese" and "Esperanto," so it was not as shocking as it sounded. Qian Xuantong was one of the initiators of the system of horizontal character writing that we use today, and it was Liu Bannong, who had played hardball during the prime period of *New Youth*, who invented the characters "她" ("she") and "牠" (whose simplified form is 它, mean-

12.10. Chen Duxiu, taken when he was dean of the Humanities Faculty at Peking University

ing "it"). These critics of Chinese characters did contribute constructively to the development of modern Chinese characters, which shall not be ignored.

12.11. Portrait of Hu Shi when he worked at Peking University

12.12. Portrait of Qian Xuantong, who urged Lu Xun to join the "New Youth" group

[16] See Qian Xuantong: "The Future Chinese Writing System" (《中国今后之文字问题》), "Letter from Qian Xuantong to Chen Duxiu," *New Youth*, Vol. 4, Issue 4, Apr. 15, 1918. The translation is quoted from David Moser: *A Billion Voices: China's Search for a Common Language: Penguin Special China*, Beijing: Penguin Books China, 2016. – Translator's note

The New Literature initiated by *New Youth* was doubtless even more pioneering and constructive. As for the achievements of New Literature, the most difficult and most important genre should be poetry. Since it was the orthodox genre of the old literature, poets regarded it essential to make a breakthrough in their writing of new-style vernacular poetry. Starting in Volume 2, Issue 6, *New Youth* published eight vernacular poems written by Hu Shi, thus opening a thorny path for the creation of new poetry. In contrast to vernacular poetry, the genre of vernacular short stories appeared to have a high standard from the very beginning. In May 1918, Lu Xun published his "The Diary of a Madman" in *New Youth*, which was so awakening and so enlightening that he could not stop writing, and successively published "Kong Yiji" (《孔乙己》), "Medicine" (《药》), "Storm in a Teacup" (《风波》), and "Hometown" (《故乡》), etc., laying a solid foundation for modern Chinese fiction writing. As for the Impromptu Reflections (《随感录》) column, political essays and letters, the authors were all *New Youth* colleagues, and the topics discussed were closely related to those addressed during the New Culture movement. Li Dazhao's "The Living Present" (《今》), Liu Bannong's "Bowing-out-ism" (《作揖主义》), and Lu Xun's "My View on Chastity" (《我之节烈观》) opened up a new world for modern Chinese essay writing. Lu Xun joined the "New Youth" group a bit later than others, and according to him, his old friend Qian Xuantong (who also used the pseudonym Jin Xinyi, given to him by Lin Shu) often came to Shaoxing Hall to urge him to contribute articles to *New Youth*, and they had repeated discussions about the "iron room." They thought China was like "an iron room with no windows or doors, a room it would be virtually impossible to break out of." Lu Xun raised the question of whether it was necessary to awaken some of the light sleepers, only to let them "go to a certain death fully conscious of what was going to happen to them," to which Qian Xuantong replied: "But since several people are awakened, one cannot say there is no hope of destroying the iron room."[17]

This was the mindset of people of the "New Youth" group at that time. They were indeed China's Prometheus. Besides literary creation, they also made efforts in the field of literary theories, holding discussions on vernacular poetry and dramatic reform, promoting the genre of short stories, and finally raising the issue of "human literature."[18] In translation, Zhou Zuoren translated Russian, Polish, and Danish novels and fairy tales; the "Special Issue on Ibsen" was published, of which there were Ibsen's representative works *Nora* (《娜拉》) and *An Enemy of the People* (《国民之敌》) translated by Luo Jialun and Hu Shi. All these were efforts to kindle the fire of modern civilization in order to destroy the iron room.

---

[17] Lu Xun: "Preface to *Call to Arms*" (《〈呐喊〉自序》), *Complete Works of Lu Xun*, Vol. 1, Beijing: People's Literature Press, 1981, p. 419.
[18] Zhou Zuoren: "Human Literature" (《人的文学》), *New Youth*, Vol. 5, Issue 6, Dec. 15, 1918.

New Youth was indeed a blazing fire. It inspired a series of advanced youth magazines including *New Tide*, *Dawn* (《曙光》), and *New Society* (《新社会》). It spread widely and had increasingly greater influence. Guo Moruo, who was still studying in Japan at that time, talked about the magazines in China when he was preparing to found the Creation Society with his literary friends, and they noted the "enlightening" nature of *New Youth*. Many years later, Ba Jin (巴金), in his novel *The Family* (《家》), wrote about how the three Gao brothers eagerly read *New Youth* and the *Weekly Review* (《每周评论》) in Chengdu: "Their words were like sparks, setting off a conflagration in the brothers' hearts. Aroused by the fresh approach and ardent phrases, the brothers found themselves in complete agreement with the writers' sentiments."[19] Thanks to the spreading of these advanced thoughts, Sichuan didn't seem to be such a remote province anymore. There were certainly different voices, such as the *Critical Review* (《学衡》), now regarded as a cultural conservative journal, which published a series of essays criticizing the New Culture movement, with its attacks directed at *New Youth*. This was another trend of the time, and its major contributors were those students who had debated with Hu Shi in the United States.

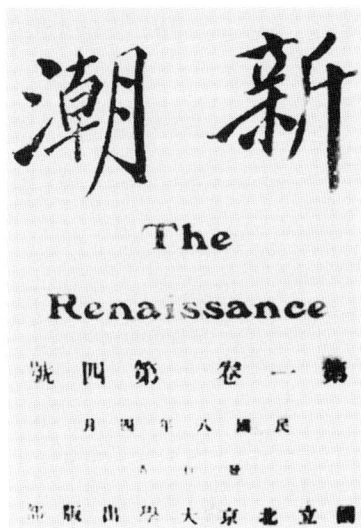

12.13. *New Tide* (《新潮》), another famous magazine launched at Peking University during the May Fourth period

New Youth represented radical cultural ideals, while the *Critical Review* represented conservative cultural thoughts in its modern visage. The *Critical Review* was launched later, that is, after the high tide of the May Fourth movement had already passed. It was launched in Nanjing in January 1922, but was printed and released in Shanghai. The founders and core authors of the *Critical Review* included Mei Guangdi, Wu Mi, and Hu Xiansu, all of whom had studied in the United States in the past and were then professors of the Southeast University in Nanjing. Hu Xiansu's major was forest botany and his research field was biology, so he was but a guest writer of the journal. Mei Guangdi and Wu Mi had both been students of Irving Babbitt when they studied in the United States. The principle they promoted by launching the *Critical Review* was to "debate and investigate learning, explain truth, promote national essence, and integrate new knowledge" (论究学术，阐求真理，昌明国粹，融化新知), which was based on the scholarly theories of New Humanism and the cultural concepts of the National Essence sect of the South Society. These theories surely had their argumentative strength when used to promote comparative

---

[19] Ba Jin: *The Family*, Beijing: People's Literature Press, 1978, p. 40.

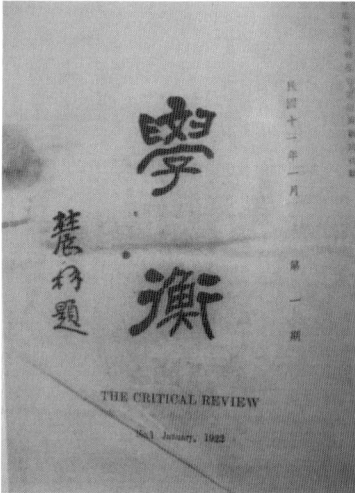

12.14. Inaugural issue of the journal *Critical Review*, published in January 1922. Those who are now regarded as culturally conservative men of letters centered around this journal

literature or criticize the excessive romanticism of May Fourth literature, but their holders were at a disadvantage in the debate when they chose the New Culture movement, which followed the general trend of history, as their target of criticism. Mei Guangdi's "A Commentary on Those Who Advocate the New Culture" (《评提倡新文化者》) was published in the inaugural issue, Hu Xiansu's "Review of *Collection of Experimental Writings*" (《评〈尝试集〉》) in the first and second issues, and Wu Mi's "On the New Culture Movement" (《论新文化运动》) in the fourth issue, all defending traditions and fiercely attacking "literary revolution," thus making the journal an opponent of *New Youth*. Hu Shi, Lu Xun, Zhou Zuoren, and Shen Yanbing fought back with their own essays (Lu Xun wrote a famous essay entitled "An Appraisal of the *Critical Review*" [《估〈学衡〉》]), but soon they simply ignored it. Later even Hu Xiansu thought that "The *Critical Review* has too many shortcomings, cherishes the outmoded, and preserves the outworn, thus it is not liked by new-style lecturers of Chinese classics."[20] From its inaugural issue until 1926 when the China Book Company refused to print it anymore (actually it lasted until 1933), for five years the average print-run had been no more than several hundred copies per issue, and its influence had become increasingly weaker. This showed that in theory, cultural conservatism could no longer receive response and support from intellectuals.

In June 1919, Chen Duxiu was arrested for distributing handbills entitled "Manifesto of the Citizens of Peking" at the New World Amusement Park in south Beijing. Before that, his conservative opponents had already

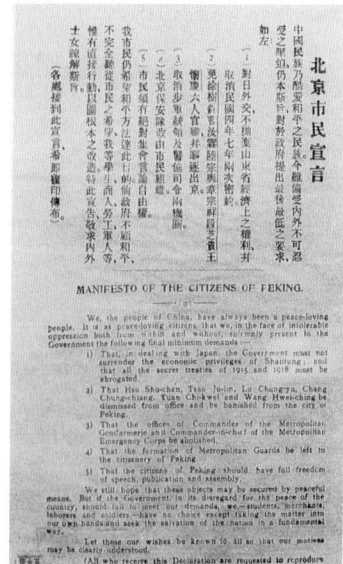

12.15. Copy of Chen Duxiu's bilingual handbills entitled "Manifesto of the Citizens of Peking" (《北京市民宣言》), which he distributed in the South-City Recreation Garden at Tianqiao and the New World Amusement Park in Beijing on June 11, 1919

---

[20] *Wu Mi's Diary* (《吴宓日记》), Vol. 3, Beijing: Joint Publishing, 1998, p. 437.

spread rumors accusing Chen of being "immoral privately," and compelled Peking University to dismiss him from the position of dean of the Humanities Faculty. Thus Chen Duxiu asked for long-term leave and left Peking University. Just over a month later, the May Fourth movement broke out, but on that day, neither Chen Duxiu nor Hu Shi was present, and the student leaders were Fu Sinian, Luo Jialun, and others from *New Tide*. Therefore, Chen and Hu were only the spiritual leaders of the May Fourth movement. Chen Duxiu was released on bail after three months' imprisonment and fled to Shanghai in disguise, where he contacted Li Da (李达), Chen Wangdao (陈望道), and others and was soon transformed into a communist in theory. Starting from Volume 8, Issue 1, at the request of Chen Duxiu, the editorial office of *New Youth* was moved back to Shanghai, where it gradually changed from an intellectual and cultural journal into a political one, and became the official organ of the Shanghai Communist Group. The politically oriented direction of the journal was sure to cause disagreement and division within the "New Youth" group: should it remain a coterie journal, or should it change into a political party journal? Should it put more emphasis on cultural and academic issues, or should it be part of political activities? Hu Shi was sensitive to this and responded quickly. In his letter to the editorial committee of *New Youth* in January 1922, he expressed his hope that the journal might continue to "put more emphasis on academic thoughts," and suggested launching another magazine specializing in discussions of art and literature, or moving the editorial office back to Beijing, or that the journal stop being politically oriented. Chen Duxiu did not agree with his suggestions. Lu Xun thought that it would be better for them to split than to cooperate reluctantly. They still had not resolved these issues (but division seemed inevitable) when the authorities in the French Concession banned *New Youth*. The fire stolen by Prometheus was never put out, but the torch of an era was extinguished.

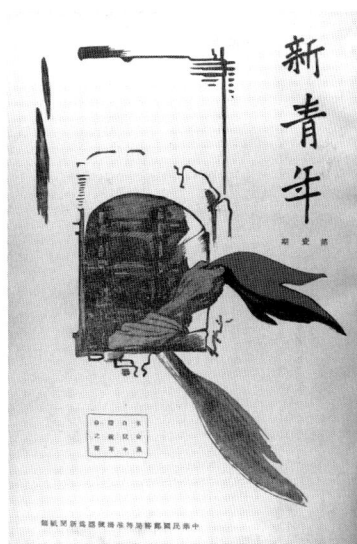

12.16. *New Youth,* which was later resumed and became a quarterly

THIRTEEN

A CHRONICLE OF LITERARY EVENTS IN THE YEAR 1921 (AN ERA OF LITERARY ENLIGHTENMENT)

SELECTING THE YEAR 1921 AS A TYPICAL YEAR TO SHOW the literary ecology of that period is fully justified. It was an important year when, after the outbreak and spread of the May Fourth literary revolution, the achievements of New Literature really began to come to light, and vernacular literature began to gain a firm foothold. By this time, the enlightening nature of May Fourth literature had become evident. It challenged feudal morality and ethics, the conservative family system, and the autocratic political institution; it tried to elevate the value of laborers, women, and children, as well as the significance of "human" equality, independence, and freedom; and it championed emancipation of the individual and ideological liberation. In literature, it advocated "human literature," "literature of the common people," and "vernacular literature," which was to play an important role in the coming years.

The two new literary societies that advocated "human literature," namely the Literary Research Society (文学研究会) and the Creation Society, were both established in this year, and this brought about the mushrooming of even more new literary societies. For the first time in history, Chinese literature began to adopt the mode of group organization. Actually, before the Literary Research Society and the Creation Society were founded, the *New Youth* and *New Tide* editorial offices had already shown some characteristics of a quasiliterary group; almost as if it had been rehearsed, they each published a

13.1. (left to right) Gao Mengdan (高梦旦), Zheng Zhenduo, Hu Shi, and Cao Chengying (曹诚英, 1902–1973, China's first woman professor of agronomy) during the May Fourth period

journal, and then likeminded people gathered around the journal. The cultural stance of *New Youth* and *New Tide* remained, and at this time, literary groups with distinctive features came into existence.

The Literary Research Society was established in Beijing, and its journal was at first edited in Shanghai. The most active members included Zheng Zhenduo, who was a student of the Peking School of Railway Management of the Ministry of Transportation during the time the society was prepared and established, and when he went for his internship at Shanghai's West Railway Station after graduation and soon began editing "Lamp of Learning" (《学灯》), the supplement of the *Shanghai China Times*, he became a very active member of the society; and Shen Yanbing (沈雁冰, aka Mao Dun) from the Commercial Press. By that time, the main locus of activities of the Literary Research Society had actually moved to Shanghai, taking the prevailing route of Chinese literature's migration.

As the idea of the Literary Research Society burgeoned, its founders were aware that they should seek to publish their own journal, and Zheng Zhenduo raised this issue when he met Zhang Yuanji, then general manager of the Commercial Press, and Gao Mengdan, head of the editorial office of the Press, when the two came to Beijing in November 1920. The Commercial Press did not immediately

13.2. Young Zheng Zhenduo in Shanghai. This photo was taken immediately after the Literary Research Society was established in Beijing, and one can see he was tall even though he was sitting down

promise to publish a new journal edited in Beijing, but expressed their willingness to restructure *Fiction Monthly* to incorporate works of New Literature. Therefore, Zheng Zhenduo and his fellow members decided to shift their focus to establishing the literary society. On November 29 of that year, they held a meeting at the office of the head of Peking University Library, "decided to actively prepare the initiation of the literary society, and Zheng Zhenduo was recommended to draft the constitution. The *Fiction Monthly* journal, in the name of an individual, promised to publish their writings, and to be a temporary makeshift literary journal of the society." On December 4 and December 30, they gathered in the house of Geng Jizhi (耿济之) in Wanbaogai Lane, Beijing, passed the constitution, decided that Zhou Zuoren would draft the manifesto, and decided on twelve founding members of the society, namely Zhou Zuoren, Zhu Xizu (朱希祖), Geng Jizhi, Zheng Zhenduo, Qu Shiying (瞿世英), Wang Tongzhao (王统照), Shen Yanbing, Jiang Baili, Ye Shaojun (叶绍钧, aka Ye Shengtao [叶圣陶]), Guo Shaoyu (郭绍虞), Sun Fuyuan (孙伏园), and Xu Dishan, as well as adopting its earliest members and various issues concerning the inaugural meeting.

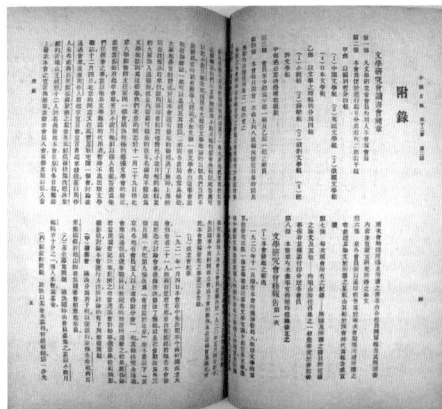

13.3. Memorandum of the Literary Research Society Reading Club and the First Report on the Work of the Society, published in *Fiction Monthly* (Vol. 2, Issue 2), February 1921

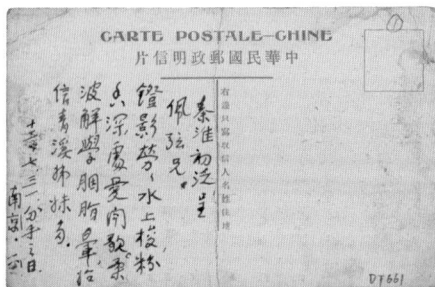

13.4. Postcard sent by Yu Pingbo (俞平伯), a member of the Literary Research Society, to Zhu Ziqing (朱自清), another member, around the time the two wrote prose essays with the same title after sailing on the Qinhuai River

TABLE 13.1 *Chronicle of literary events in 1921*

Date	Major literary event
Jan. 1	*New Voice* (《新声》), a magazine of the Mandarin Duck and Butterfly literary school, was launched in Shanghai, edited by Shi Jiqun (施济群) and Lu Dan'an (陆澹安), which later became *Red* (《红》), *Red Roses* (《红玫瑰》), etc.
Jan. 4	The Literary Research Society held its inaugural meeting in Laijinyu Pavilion (来今雨轩) within Central Park (today's Zhongshan Park) in Beijing, which was attended by twenty-one people, including Zheng Zhenduo
Jan. 6	*Lady Youlan* (《幽兰女士》), a drama written by Chen Dabei, was published in the *Morning Post*
Jan. 10	After being fully reformed, the new *Fiction Monthly* (Vol. 12, Issue 1) was published. Its editor-in-chief was Shen Yanbing (using the pseudonym Mao Dun), and the "Declaration of Reform of *Fiction Monthly*" (《〈小说月报〉改革宣言》) was published in this issue
Jan. 10	The literary theoretical essay "Relationship between Literature and Man, and Misunderstanding of the Writer's Identity since Ancient China" (《文学与人的关系及中国古来对于文学者身份的误认》) by Shen Yanbing (Mao Dun) was published in *Fiction Monthly* (Vol. 12, Issue 1)
Jan. 10	Xu Dishan's fiction "The Bird of Destiny" (《命命鸟》) was published in *Fiction Monthly* (Vol. 12, Issue 1)
Jan. 10	Geng Jizhi's translation of Nikolai Gogol's short story "Diary of a Madman" (《疯人日记》) was published in *Fiction Monthly* (Vol. 12, Issue 1)
Jan. 12	Lu Xun began his employment at Peking Higher Normal School (today's Beijing Normal University) and became a lecturer on Chinese Fiction History; he worked there until 1925
Feb. 1	Guo Moruo's poem "A Hymn to the Sun" (《太阳礼赞》) was published in "Lamp of Learning," the supplement of the *Shanghai China Times*
Feb. 10	Ye Shaojun (aka Ye Shengtao) published his short story "The Changeling" (《低能儿》) in *Fiction Monthly* (Vol. 12, Issue 2)
Feb. 10	Lang Sun (郎损, aka Mao Dun) published his literary theoretical essay "Responsibilities and Efforts of Scholars of New Literature" (《新文学研究者的责任与努力》) in *Fiction Monthly* (Vol. 12, Issue 2)
Feb. 10	Zheng Zhenduo's translation of Maxim Gorky's short story "On a Raft" (《木筏之上》) was published in *Fiction Monthly* (Vol. 12, Issue 2)
Feb. 14	Guo Moruo's poem "I Am an Idol Worshiper" (《我是个偶像崇拜者》) was published in "Lamp of Learning," the supplement of the *Shanghai China Times*
Feb. 15	Guo Moruo's poetic drama *Rebirth of the Goddesses* (《女神之再生》) was published in *Min Duo* (《民铎》) magazine (Vol. 2, Issue 5)
Mar. 5	Ye Shaojun (aka Ye Shengtao) began to have his literary theoretical column On Literary Arts (文艺谈) published in the supplement of *Morning Post*. It consisted of forty essays and the serialization ran until June 25 of the same year

(continued)

TABLE 13.1 *(continued)*

Date	Major literary event
Mar. 19	The weekly magazine of the Mandarin Duck and Butterfly school, *Saturday*, was resumed, with Zhou Shoujuan as its editor-in-chief. In total 100 issues had been published before the Xinhai Revolution, and now another 100 issues were being planned
Apr. 1	Guo Moruo's drama *The Entangled One of the Xiang River* (《湘累》) was published in *Learning Arts* (《学艺》) (Vol. 2, Issue 10)
Apr. 1	Shoujuan (Zhou Shoujuan) had his translation of Alphonse Daudet's short story "L'Enfant Espion" published in *Oriental Magazine* (Vol. 18, Issue 7)
Apr. 10	Bing Xin's short story "Superman" (《超人》) was published in *Fiction Monthly* (Vol. 12, Issue 4)
Apr. 10	Luo Huasheng (落华生, pseudonym of Xu Dishan) published his short story "The Merchant's Wife" (《商人妇》) in *Fiction Monthly* (Vol. 12, Issue 4)
Apr. 10	Lang Sun (Mao Dun) published his literary theoretical essay "Random Comments on the Spring Literary Creation Forum" (《春季创作坛漫评》) in *Fiction Monthly* (Vol. 12, Issue 4)
Apr. 24	Guo Moruo's poems "Sunrise Seen from a Boat" (《海舟中望日出》), "At the Mouth of the Huangpu River" (《黄浦江口》), and "Shanghai Impression" (《上海印象》) were published in "Lamp of Learning," the supplement of the *Shanghai China Times*
April	Chen Dabei's dramatic theoretical work *Amateur Theater* (《爱美的戏剧》) began to be serialized in the *Morning Post*
April	Zheng Zhenduo's translation of Anton Chekhov's play *The Seagull* (《海鸥》) was published by the Commercial Press in Shanghai
May 1	*Literary Ten-Daily* (《文学旬刊》) was launched in Shanghai by the Literary Research Society. Its name was later changed to *Literature* (《文学》) and *Literary Review* (《文学周报》)
May 1	Lu Xun's short story "Hometown" was published in *New Youth* (Vol. 9, Issue 1)
May 10	Luo Huasheng (Xu Dishan) published his short story "Phoenixes Exchanging Their Nests" (《换巢鸾凤》) in *Fiction Monthly* (Vol. 12, Issue 5)
May 31	The monthly *Drama* (《戏剧》) was launched in Shanghai. It was edited by the Masses Theater Society (民众戏剧社), and altogether six issues were published
May	Zheng Zhenduo invited Guo Moruo to meet with Mao Dun and others and invited Guo to join the Literary Research Society but he declined
May	Lin Shu and Chen Jialin's translation of Henry Rider Haggard's novel *Queen Shaba's Ring* was published by the Commercial Press in Shanghai

(continued)

TABLE 13.1 *(continued)*

Date	Major literary event
May	The Masses Theater Society was established in Shanghai, with its founding members being Wang Youyou (Zhongxian), Ke Yicen (柯一岑), Shen Yanbing, and Chen Dabei, among others
May	*Leisure Monthly* (《消闲月刊》) was launched in Suzhou, edited by Zhao Mianyun (赵眠云) and Zheng Yimei (郑逸梅)
June 1	"Discussions of the New Drama" (《新剧底讨论》) by Su Xiongrui (苏熊瑞) and others was published in *New Youth*, (Vol. 9, Issue 2)
June 8	Ziyan (子严, aka Zhou Zuoren) published his "Belles Lettres" (《美文》) in the *Morning Post*
June 10	Wang Tongzhao's short story "Night of Spring Showers" (《春雨之夜》) was published in *New Youth* (Vol. 12, Issue 6)
June 10	Yu Changyuan (俞长源) had his translation of O. Henry's short story "The Gift of the Magi" published in *Oriental Magazine* (Vol. 18, Issue 11)
June 10	Zhen Chang (真常) had his translation of Molière's drama *L'Avare* (《悭吝人》) serialized in *Fiction Monthly* (Vol. 12, Issues 6–9 and 11)
June 15	Tian Han's translation of Shakespeare's drama *Hamlet* was published in *Youth China* (《少年中国》) (Vol. 2, Issue 12)
June 20	Xi Di (西谛, aka Zheng Zhenduo) published his literary theoretical essay "Mission of Literature" (《文学的使命》) in *Literary Ten-Daily* (Issue 5)
June 25	The monthly *Recreation World* was launched in Shanghai. Its editors-in-chief were Zhou Shoujuan and Zhao Shaokuang
June 30	Zheng Zhenduo's literary theoretical essay entitled "Literature of Blood and Tears" (《血和泪的文学》) was published in *Literary Ten-Daily* (Issue 6)
June	Guo Moruo returned to Japan and discussed founding the Creation Society with Yu Dafu and Zhang Ziping
June	Zheng Zhenduo became editor-in-chief of "Lamp of Learning," the supplement of the *Shanghai China Times*
July 7	Yu Dafu's short story "A Silver-Grey Death" (《银灰色的死》) was published in "Lamp of Learning," the supplement of the *Shanghai China Times*
July 10	Lu Yin (庐隐) had her short story "Red Roses" (《红玫瑰》) published in *Fiction Monthly* (Vol. 12, Issue 7)
July 10	Ye Shaojun's drama *Reunion* (《恳亲会》) was published in *Fiction Monthly* (Vol. 12, Issue 7)
July 10	Lang Sun (Mao Dun) had his literary theoretical essay "Social Background and Literary Creation" (《社会背景与创作》) published in *Fiction Monthly* (Vol. 12, Issue 7)

(continued)

TABLE 13.1 (continued)

Date	Major literary event
July 10	Shen Yanbing (Mao Dun) had his literary theoretical essay "The Future of Literary Creation" (《创作的前途》) published in *Fiction Monthly* (Vol. 12, Issue 7)
July 10	Lu Xun's translation of Mikhail Artsybashev's short story "The Worker Shevyrev" (《工人绥惠略夫》) was serialized in *Fiction Monthly* (Vol. 12, Issues 7–9, 11, and 12)
First third of July	The Creation Society was founded by Chinese students in Japan, whose major members included Guo Moruo and Yu Dafu, and they decided to launch a quarterly titled *Creation* (《创造》)
July	(German author) Theodor's novel *Immensee* (《茵梦湖》), translated by Guo Moruo and Qian Junxu (钱君胥), was published by Taidong Press in Shanghai (上海泰东图书局)
July	Zhu Guangqian began his studies at the University of Hong Kong
Aug. 1	Zhou Zuoren's translation "Miscellaneous Translation of Japan's Top Thirty Poems" (《杂译日本诗三十首》) was published in *New Youth* (Vol. 9, Issue 4)
Aug. 5	Guo Moruo's anthology *Goddess* (《女神》) was published by Taidong Press in Shanghai
Aug. 10	Lu Yin's short story "Two Pupils" (《两个小学生》) was published in *Fiction Monthly* (Vol. 12, Issue 8)
Aug. 10	Zhu Ziqing's poems "The Journey" (《旅路》) and "In the World" (《人间》) were published in *Fiction Monthly* (Vol. 12, Issue 8)
Aug. 10	Lang Sun (Mao Dun) had his literary theoretical essay "On the Creations of April, May, and June" (《评四五六月的创作》) published in *Fiction Monthly* (Vol. 12, Issue 8)
Aug. 10	Song Chunfang's translation of Anton Chekhov's short story "The Death of a Government Clerk" (《那个可怜的办事员是怎样死去的》) was published in *Oriental Magazine* (Vol. 18, Issue 15)
Aug. 21	Zheng Boqi's literary theoretical essay "Criticism on Guo Moruo's First Anthology, *Goddess*" (《批评郭沫若的处女诗集〈女神〉》) was published in "Lamp of Learning," the supplement of the *Shanghai China Times*
Aug. 26	Guo Moruo's poem "Prologue to *Goddess*" (《〈女神〉序诗》) was published in "Lamp of Learning," the supplement of the *Shanghai China Times*
Autumn	Zhu Ziqing began to teach at Shanghai Wusong Chinese Public School (上海吴淞中国公学) and met Ye Shengtao
Sep. 6	*Semimonthly* (《半月》), the magazine of the Mandarin Duck and Butterfly school, was launched in Shanghai. Its editor-in-chief was Zhou Shoujuan and its writer-in-chief was Yuan Hanyun (袁寒云)

(continued)

TABLE 13.1 *(continued)*

Date	Major literary event
Sep. 10	Wang Sidian (王思玷) had his short story "In the Storm" (《风雨之下》) published in *Fiction Monthly* (Vol. 12, Issue 9)
Sep. 30	Pu Boying (蒲伯英) had his literary theoretical essay "I Insist on Promoting Professional Theater" (《我主张要提倡职业的戏剧》) published in *Drama* (Vol. 1, Issue 5)
September	Shanghai Taidong Press and other publishing houses began to publish the Creation Society book series (创造社丛书)
September	The extra issue of *Fiction Monthly*, Vol. 12, became a special issue on "Research of Russian Literature"
September	The monthly *Literary Art Magazine* (《文艺杂志》) was launched in Beijing. It was edited by Di Xingnan (狄杏南)
September	Qu Qiubai went to teach the Chinese class at the Communist University of Toilers of the East
Oct. 1	Yu Dafu's literary theoretical essay "Preface to *Immensee*" (《〈茵梦湖〉的序引》) was published in *Literary Ten-Daily* (Issue 15)
Oct. 10	A special issue on "The Literature of Damaged Nations" (《被损害民族的文学》) was published in *Fiction Monthly* (Vol. 12, Issue 10)
Oct. 10	The fortnightly *Double Voices* (《双声》) was launched in Hong Kong. Its editors were Huang Kunlun (黄昆仑) and Huang Tianshi (黄天石)
Oct. 12	The original section 7 of the *Morning Post* began to be published separately with the title "Supplement of the *Morning Post*" (《晨报副刊》)
Oct. 15	Yu Dafu's collection of short stories *Sinking* (《沉沦》) was published by Shanghai Taidong Press
Oct. 25	Victor Hugo's novel *Ninety-Three* (《双雄义死录》), translated by Lin Shu and Mao Wenzhong (毛文钟), was published by the Commercial Press in Shanghai
Oct. 27	Yan Fu, translator of *Evolution and Ethics*, passed away
Oct. 30	Wang Zhongxian's drama *The Good Son* (《好儿子》) was published in *Drama* (Vol. 1, Issue 6)
October	The monthly *New Tide of Novels* (《小说新潮》) was launched in Shanghai. Its editor-in-chief was Chen Tiesheng (陈铁生)
October	The monthly *Comic Newspaper* (《滑稽新报》) was launched in Shanghai. Its editor-in-chief was Ping Jinya
Nov. 1	Zhu Ziqing's poem "The Grasses" (《小草》) was published in *New Tide* (Vol. 3, Issue 1)
Nov. 20	The Tsinghua Literary Society (清华文学社) was established

(continued)

TABLE 13.1 *(continued)*

Date	Major literary event
November	The Commercial Press in Shanghai began publishing Library of World Literature (世界文学丛书)
November	The Beijing Experimental Theater Society (北京实验剧社) was established, which was organized by the Beijing Student Amateur Drama Troupe Association and presided over by Li Jianwu (李健吾)
Dec. 4	Ba Ren's (another pseudonym of Lu Xun) novel *The True Story of Ah Q* began to be serialized in "Supplement of the *Morning Post*," and the serialization was completed on February 12, 1922
Dec. 10	Mianzun (Xia Mianzun [夏丏尊]) had his translation of Kunikida Doppo's short story "Nyonan" (《女难》) published in *Fiction Monthly* (Vol. 12, Issue 12)
December	Tolstoy's *The Greatest Short Stories of Leo Tolstoy* (《托尔斯泰短篇小说集》), translated by Geng Jizhi and Qu Qiubai, was published by the Commercial Press in Shanghai
December	Vol. 1 of *Collected Essays of Hu Shi* (《胡适文存》) was published by the Shanghai East Asia Library
This year	Yu Pingbo's anthology *Winter Nights* (《冬夜》) was published by the Shanghai East Asia Library
This year	Wang Jingxi's collected short stories *Snowy Nights* (《雪夜》) was published by the Shanghai East Asia Library
This year	Ivan Turgenev's novel *On the Eve* (《前夜》), translated by Shen Ying (沈颖), was published by the Commercial Press in Shanghai
This year	Anton Chekhov's play *Uncle Vanya* (《万尼亚叔父》), translated by Geng Shizhi (耿式之), was published by the Commercial Press in Shanghai
This year	Ostrovsky's play *The Storm* (《雷雨》), translated by Geng Jizhi, was published by the Commercial Press in Shanghai
This year	The Shanghai Drama Association was established, founded by Huang Yanpei (黄炎培) and others; its earliest members included Wang Youyou and Ying Yunwei (应云卫), and later Ouyang Yuqian, Hong Shen, and others joined
This year	The World Journal Book Store (世界书局) was restructured and became a stock company, which first published Chinese martial arts fictions (*wuxia*), romantic fictions, and detective stories, and later shifted its focus to textbooks and academic works on traditional Chinese culture, etc.
This year	Liang Qichao's *Intellectual Trends in the Ching [Qing] Period* was published

13.5. The Literary Research Society was established in January 1921 in Beijing. This group photo of all members was taken in front of the Laijinyu Pavilion. Courtesy of National Museum of Modern Chinese Literature

The photo taken of members of the Literary Research Society in front of the Laijinyu Pavilion on January 4, 1921, is valuable literary material (see Figure 13.5). There were altogether twenty-one people present that day, but in the photo we can only see twenty, and it remains a mystery as to who was not in the photo. The society's founding was quite well-planned, with some senior celebrities being invited as a "sophisticated" gesture to seek moral support. The founding members who did not attend the meeting included Shen Yanbing, Zhou Zuoren, Ye Shaojun, and Guo Shaoyu, and those present who were not founding members included Huang Ying (黄英, aka Lu Yin) and her husband Guo Mengliang (郭梦良). Lu Yin and Bing Xin later became major writers of the Literary Research Society, and they were the earliest modern Chinese women writers. At the meeting that day, Zheng Zhenduo reported the founding of the society, and all members discussed and decided on the constitution, and elected Zheng Zhenduo to be the secretary general and Geng Jizhi the accounting secretary by ballot. After the photo (Figure 13.5) was taken, they discussed the issues of a reading club, fundraising, and the publication of book series, etc. The declaration and the Society's constitution were published in the *Morning Post*, "Awakening" (《觉悟》, the supplement of the *Republican Daily*

[《民国日报》]), *New Youth*, and *Fiction Monthly* either before or after the inaugural meeting.[1] The most significant sentence in the Society's constitution was: "The purpose of this Society is to study and introduce world literature, sort out the valuable traditional Chinese literature, and create new Chinese literature."[2] And the "enlightening" features shown in its activities involved its paying great attention to the social responsibility of literature and to the discrimination suffered by people of lower social status and complaints of the latter. Lu Xun's literary ideas were similar to those of the Literary Research Society. He did not join this group however, because he was a commissioner of the Ministry of Education and was subject to the Beiyang government's *Civil Service Act*, which made it clear that civil servants could not join societies and groups. Nevertheless, the Declaration of the society was drafted by Zhou Zuoren, and it was said that Lu Xun had read it as his brother was working on it. The Declaration listed three reasons why the Literary Research Society was founded, of which the third one is worth special attention:

> Thirdly, it will lay the foundation for establishing a writers' union. The time has passed when literature and art were regarded as a leisurely entertainment or a means to deal with disillusionment. We believe literary creation is a job of great importance to human beings; and people choosing this job shall make it their lifelong career, as farming to farmers. Therefore, we establish this society, hoping it not only to be an ordinary literary group, but to lay a foundation for the association of the writing profession, so as to seek the development of the literary profession as a whole: this may be a thing of the future, but it is a vital hope for us.

This paragraph helps us understand the nature of the historical "May Fourth" literary period, the ideas of people of that time, as well as the fundamental difference between modern literary groups and ancient-style elegant gatherings among men of letters. The literary ideas advocated by the Literary Research Society were later summarized as "literature for life," for it opposed recreational literature, claimed that literature as a profession was like that of workers and farmers, and that they were all equal. It was based on this concept that Zhou Zuoren later brought forward "human literature" and "literature of the common people" and Zheng Zhenduo proposed "literature of blood and tears." The Literary Research Society paid equal attention to literary creation and translation. In the former they created life stories, problem novels, native-soil fictions, short poems, and prose essays, and launched two literary journals, *Literary Ten-Daily* and *Poetry* (monthly); and in the latter they put special

---

[1]   They were published in the following order: *Morning Post*, Dec. 13, 1920; *Awakening*, a supplement of *The Republican Daily*, Dec. 19, 1920; *Fiction Monthly*, Vol. 12, Issue 1, Jan. 10, 1921, and finally, *New Youth*, January 1921.

[2]   "Constitution of the Literary Research Society" (《文学研究会简章》), *Fiction Monthly*, Vol. 12, Issue 1, Jan. 10, 1921.

emphasis on translating and introducing the literature of Soviet Russia and the weak nations in Northern and Eastern Europe. In literary theories and literary criticism they sought to promote a kind of realistic literature, in which process they introduced naturalism, realism, and symbolism of world literature and criticized the Mandarin Duck and Butterfly school and the Critical Review school, and held debates with the Creation Society. Thus the Literary Research Society gradually showed the characteristics of its own "style." As for the proposal of "establishing a writers' union," it can be seen as an effort by the Society to gather a number of professional writers based on their shared literary ideas, trying to protect their interest and operate a modern literary organization like a trade union. This is another point that deserves a mention.

The Creation Society was the only new-style literary group that could rival the Literary Research Society. Its initiation also started with seeking to launch its own journal, but except for this, the two groups were quite different, for the Creation Society was quite an individual-oriented group and was full of romantic sentiment. According to the recollection of the founding members of the Creation Society (presumably to compete with the Literary Research Society), in the summer of 1918, Guo Moruo and Zhang Ziping met in Fukuoka, Japan, and discussed launching a literary journal, which could be considered a period of incubation for this society. Later, these students were quite unorganized, and it was not until 1920 that they discussed it again in the students' dormitory building of the Imperial University of Tokyo, and Tian Han volunteered to make contact with Chinese publishing institutions back home. However, he was unsuccessful, so their plans were again aborted. Then in April 1921 Guo Moruo returned home to China, and while in Shanghai he went with Cheng Fangwu to visit Zhao Nangong (赵南公), the boss of Taidong Press. They finally agreed to launch a literary journal. In June that year, Guo went back to Japan and met Zheng Boqi and Mu Mutian in Kyoto. In the six-tatami-mat room of Yu Dafu at the University of Tokyo, the four of them, together with Zhang Ziping and Tian Han, discussed the details of publishing their literary journal and book series, which can be seen as the formal inception of the Creation Society. No ceremony was held, nor did they draft any constitution or declaration. Guo Moruo later said:

> That afternoon all of us had a talk in Dafu's room, and we all agreed to use the name "Creation." We decided to launch a quarterly for the moment, and that we might launch other publications when we were capable in the future. We thought the sooner the publishing of the journal, the better, and that the contributions to the inaugural issue should be prepared during the summer

13.6. Guo Moruo looking in high spirits, dressed in Japanese-style school uniform while he was studying in Japan

13.7. "Founders" of the Creation Society in Japan, including Guo Moruo (standing in the middle) and Yu Dafu (sitting)

vacation. That meeting might be seen as the formal establishment of the Creation Society, and it was in early July 1921, but I cannot remember the exact date.[3]

All members of this literary society were Chinese students in Japan who had not yet finished their studies. Therefore, the Creation Society was full of youthful vigour, but the founding members were young and impetuous, which meant they were often undisciplined and slack. The announcement of the inaugural issue of their *Creation* quarterly was not made until September that year, and the publication of that issue was delayed till March 15, 1922. However, it was an undisputable fact that the members of this new literary group were full of creativity, and they were a group of literary talents producing quite excellent literary works. Their rebellious desire for emancipation of the individual, bursts of emotions, and limited acceptance of the concept of "art for art's sake," as well as the I-novel (自我小说) and poetry they invented, no doubt echoed the revolting and aggressive spirit of the May Fourth period. In such an era, even the creative works of members of the Literary Research Society had some romantic elements, but in general, they tended to be realistic and critical, quite different from those of the Creation Society. These two literary groups acted as enlightening sources of their respective literary styles in modern Chinese literature, so that their respective foundings were indeed the most important literary events of the year 1921.

From that point, new literary groups mushroomed. Those established in the year 1921 included the Masses Theater Society of Shanghai, Shanghai Drama Association, and Dawn Literary Society of Hangzhou, all founded by young university teachers and students. By 1923, there were more than forty literary groups nationwide, and by 1925 there were even more. Each literary group had one or more journal(s), so that the number of literary journals throughout the country exceeded 100. The literary writers of these groups were quite different from those of the transitional period of 1903. In the aspect of knowledge base,

---

[3]   Guo Moruo: "School Days: A Decade of Literary Creation," p. 119.

these people had educational backgrounds in both old-style and new-style learnings. What deserves a special mention is that they were the earliest students to graduate from the new-style schools founded during the Reform movement, so they had the courage to break old conventions and embrace a new era, and they tried to know more about the trends of the world and proactively created vernacular literature. These people were determined to practice new literature. As for the geographic origins of members, it is very interesting if one makes a brief analysis of the places of origin of the Literary Research Society writers and compares the result with that of the South Society. The Literary Research Society had "no more than 172 formally registered members."[4] Of them it was found that 102 had membership numbers.[5] Of these 102, thirty-six Zhejiang natives made up the largest proportion (35 percent) and then there came twenty-four Jiangsu natives (23 percent), followed by eight Hunan natives, five Fujian natives, five Jiangxi natives, three Sichuan natives, and three Shandong natives. Certainly, this could be partly explained by the society's core founders' social and geographical relations, but from this one can gain a general idea of the distribution of Chinese literary talents during the past hundred years. The South Society was founded in the Jiangnan area, so that of its total 1,170 members there were 437 Jiangsu natives (37 percent), 226 Zhejiang natives (19 percent), followed by the natives of Guangdong, Hunan, Anhui, Fujian, and Sichuan, etc. The Literary Research Society was founded in the north, but the distribution of places of origin of its literary talents was generally the same as that of the South Society. This showed an inheritance of a cultural tradition; that is, the literary tradition of the Jiangnan area around the Yangtze River since the Ming and Qing dynasties had a direct impact on the composition of modern Chinese literary writers. In premodern times, people had little means of transportation and they seldom moved, so most people lived in their places of origin. For a writer, their homeland was their source of childhood memories and source of inspiration, the starting point of all their writings. But modern writers were different from those of the past. They were living in an era when modern transportation began to emerge; they gathered in cities through schooling and work, and considerably more people from the rural areas settled in cities after receiving their education there. The establishment of modern literary societies in cities and their reliance on the publication of journals and books, provided excellent soil for the emergence of literary talents throughout the country.

[4] Zhao Jingshen (赵景深): "A Secret Record of the Birth Date and Places of Origin of Modern Writers" (《现代作家生年籍贯秘录》), *Reminiscences of the Literary Circle* (《文坛忆旧》), Shanghai: Beixin Press, 1948, p. 203.

[5] See Su Xingliang (苏兴良), "Studies on Record of Members of the Literary Research Society" (《文学研究会会员考录》), *Material on the Literary Research Society* (《文学研究会资料》), Vol. 1, Zhengzhou: Henan People's Press, 1985, pp. 15–17.

13.8. Reissued inaugural issue of the quarterly *Creation*, which was not exactly the same as the original edition.It was popular among young readers of the time

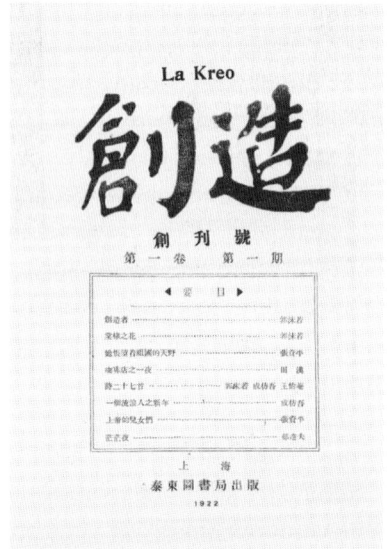

13.9. Cover of the inaugural issue of the original edition of the journal *Creation*, a quarterly of the Creation Society

13.10. *Creation Monthly*, one of the journals of the Creation Society

13.11. Group photo taken after Ye Shengtao (second from the left) and Zhu Ziqing (third from the left) of the Literary Research Society were employed as advisors by the Dawn Literary Society of Hangzhou in 1921. The first and second from the right are Wang Jingzhi (汪静之) and Cao Chengying

It was during this year that the journal *Saturday*, which had been discontinued after the Xinhai Revolution, was resumed. Some other major journals of the Mandarin Duck and Butterfly school also emerged, including *Recreation World* and *Semimonthly*, etc. From the chronicle of literary events of 1921, we can see that these writers of transitional nature were not totally inactive, for their recreational and entertaining literature still had a large reader base among urban citizens and had quite a large market demand. New Literature, on the other hand, was supported by radical young students, and represented the general trend of the times. The reform of *Fiction Monthly* carried out this year was of great significance and was the best evidence of the shift from old to new literature. *Fiction Monthly* was originally a long-standing magazine affiliated to the Commercial Press, launched in 1910. The editorial work was presided over by Wang Yunzhang and Yun Tieqiao, successively, both venerable editors. For a long time it had been a journal dedicated to the Mandarin Duck and Butterfly writers, and its development had been quite slow. This period witnessed an accelerated development of Chinese society however, and thus the circulation of *Fiction Monthly* decreased sharply, which lowered to a print-run of 2,000 copies per issue by the time Vol. 11, Issue 10 was published. Therefore, the

13.12. Mao Dun. This photo was taken in the library of his home when he was editor-in-chief of *Fiction Monthly* in 1921, shouldering a great responsibility at such a young age

former editors resigned and the management of the Commercial Press had to respond to the situation by restructuring the journal. They chose Shen Yanbing, then a new literary talent of the press, to be its editor. Only twenty-five years old, Shen Yanbing had a heroic spirit, with which he cast aside the writings bought by his predecessor (which were enough for publishing for an entire year), solicited new contributions, and completed typesetting and printing in a matter of two weeks. He sought help from Wang Jiansan (王剑三, aka Wang Tongzhao), who introduced him to Zheng Zhenduo. Zheng wrote a letter to him to express his willingness to contribute writings, and also invited Shen to join the proposed Literary Research Society. This was a great occasion for Chinese literature. A long-established magazine with a good reputation as it was, the *Fiction Monthly* was now fundamentally reformed by Shen Yanbing, who was still a nobody, and chance had it that it became a temporary makeshift journal of the Literary Research Society. After its reform, Vol. 12, Issue 1, of *Fiction Monthly* had a print-run of 5,000 copies and was immediately sold out. The branch bookstores of the Commercial Press throughout the country sent telegraphs to the headquarters and demanded that more copies be printed for the next issue. Therefore, the next issue had a print-run of 7,000 copies, and by the end of the year the issue had a print-run of 10,000 copies. It was a success for Shen Yanbing as well as a success for New Literature.

It was in this year that Lu Xun's *The True Story of Ah Q* was published. By pungently criticizing the inherent weakness of Chinese people's national character, this story pointed out that the main weakness of Chinese people lay in their spirit, and thus this should be the entry point for any reformation. Guo Moruo's *Goddess*, which called on people to embrace the rebirth of the country with a fully emancipated human spirit, was also published in 1921. Yu Dafu's *Sinking*, published this year, was fiercely attacked by conservatives for its bold sexual description, while it was unsparingly supported by people of the New Literature camp, including both Zhou Zuoren from the Literary Research Society and Guo Moruo from the Creation Society, who pointed out that the story was valuable at this period of time for it laid bare the bitter sentiments of a new generation of youth and described young people's mental and sexual experiences. In displaying what was "human," the enlightening New Literature reached an intensity and profundity that had been unprecedented by anything since 1840, and it showcased the truly unparalleled and convincing creativity of vernacular literature.

Thus the most representative masters of modern Chinese literature, Lu Xun, Shen Yanbing, Guo Moruo, and Yu Dafu, came to the foreground. Lu Xun was born in Shaoxing, Zhejiang Province, in 1881 and received his earlier education at the new-style School of Mines and Railways and Naval School in Nanjing, while it was in Japan, where he studied medicine in Sendai and studied literature in Tokyo, that he began to gain some knowledge about Western civilization. After participating in the New Culture movement and literary revolution initiated by *New Youth* and Peking University, he wrote "The Diary of a Madman," the first vernacular short story in its real sense in modern Chinese literary history, as well as "Impromptu Reflections" and other essays. These writings echoed the zeitgeist of democracy, science, and antifeudalism of the May Fourth period, and Lu Xun became increasingly influential. In 1921, Lu Xun's *The True Story of Ah Q*, the greatest novel of twentieth-century China, began to be serialized in the "Supplement of the *Morning Post*," and Lu Xun thus became an icon of modern Chinese literature.

In 1921, Mao Dun was still known as Shen Yanbing; the pseudonym "Mao Dun" was not used until the short story "Disillusion" (《幻灭》) was published [in 1927]. As is already noted, Shen Yanbing became known to people because of his independent efforts to fundamentally reform *Fiction Monthly*, and he was also known for his identity as the only founding member of the Literary Research Society living outside Beijing and as a literary theorist. Shen Yanbing was born in Wuzhen, Tongxiang, Zhejiang Province, in 1896. Since his homeland was the border area between the ancient Wu and Yue states and was close to Shanghai, which had been rising as an international metropolis, Shen Yanbing received his education in new-style schools, first at Huzhou Middle School and then at Jiaxing Middle School, at the time of the Xinhai Revolution. He was dismissed for

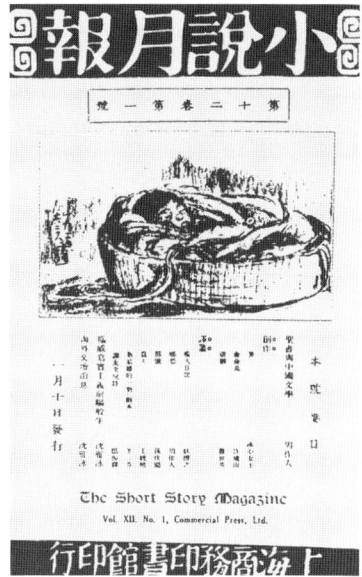

13.13. Cover of *Fiction Monthly* (Vol. 12, Issue 1), which emerged as a brand-new magazine in January 1921 after being fundamentally reformed by Mao Dun

13.14. First issue of *Fiction Monthly* from the Commercial Press, which was edited by members of the Mandarin Duck and Butterfly school. Readers who are interested in this may compare it with the first issue edited by Mao Dun

revolting against the superintendent and transferred to Anding Middle School in Hangzhou, which is where he graduated. Then he spent three years in the preparatory program of Peking University, and since his family could not support him to continue university education, he was referred to by his relatives to work at the Commercial Press, China's best modern publishing institution. At that time Shen Yanbing worked as an editor, and he also did some translation and wrote essays. In 1921, he wrote literary reviews while editing *Fiction Monthly*, and soon published such literary theoretical essays as "Responsibilities and Efforts of Scholars of New Literature" and "Naturalism and Modern Chinese Novels" (《自然主义与中国现代小说》). Referred by Li Hanjun (李汉俊), he had already secretly joined the Communist Group in Shanghai. Politically and literarily, Shen Yanbing had choices to make, but his major step in the field of literature started in the year 1921.

While he was still studying in Japan, Guo Moruo, with the help of Zong Baihua, began to publish his poems in "Lamp of Learning," the supplement of the *Shanghai China Times*. His poems attracted wide attention. Guo was born in 1892 and was a native of Shawan, Leshan, Sichuan Province. The imperial examination system was aborted when he was a young boy, and thus he continued his primary education in Leshan, where the Giant Buddha statue is

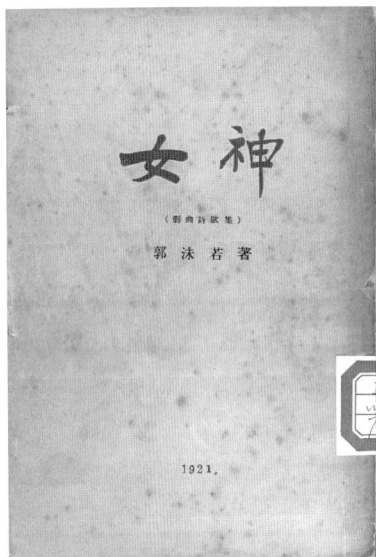

located. While attending Jiadingfu Middle School, he was dismissed for revolting against the superintendent, and went to Fenshe Middle School and Chengdufu Middle School in Chengdu until graduation. He read Walt Whitman's *Leaves of Grass* on the eve of the May Fourth movement, when he was still studying in Japan, and thus ushered in his most creative era of poetic writing. According to his own reminiscences: "During the several months between 1919 and 1920, I was immersed in poetry writing virtually every day. When I had the desire to write poems, I felt trembling like I had a fever, sometimes I was too excited to write a word."[6] It was in this condition that he wrote "Nirvana of the Phoenix" (《凤凰涅槃》), "A Heavenly Dog" (《天狗》), "A Burning Coal" (《炉中煤》), and "O Earth, My Mother!"(《地球，我的母亲！》). These poems had an imposing manner that paralleled the spirit of the May Fourth period, and were the earliest successful results of vernacular free verse. On

13.15. First edition of Guo Moruo's *Goddess*, which collected all of Guo's earlier poems. The publishing of this book was of epoch-making significance to the new poetry

6   Guo Moruo: "School Days: A Decade of Literary Creation," p. 68.

August 5, 1921, Guo Moruo's epoch-making anthology *Goddess* was published by Taidong Press of Shanghai as the first of the Creation Society book series. Hu Shi's *Collection of Experimental Writings* was but opening the path for new poetry, while the publishing of *Goddess* was the real burst of May Fourth new poetic creativity.

With the emergence of these literary masters and their masterpieces, the year 1921 became an important year in modern Chinese literary history.

TABLE 13.2 *Membership number, name, and native place of members of the Literary Research Society*

Membership no.	Name	Native place	Membership no.	Name	Native place
1	Zhu Xizu	Haiyan, Zhejiang	5	Guo Shaoyu	Wu County, Jiangsu
2	Jiang Baili	Haining, Zhejiang	6	Ye Shaojun	Wu County, Jiangsu
3	Zhou Zuoren	Shaoxing, Zhejiang	11	Geng Jizhi	Shanghai, Jiangsu
7	Sun Fuyuan	Shaoxing, Zhejiang	12	Qu Shiying	Wujin, Jiangsu
9	Shen Yanbing	Tongxiang, Zhejiang	25	Geng Shizhi	Shanghai, Jiangsu
21	Chen Dabei	Hang County, Zhejiang	38	Geng Mianzhi (耿勉之)	Shanghai, Jiangsu
27	Tang Xingtian (唐性天)	Zhenhai, Zhejiang	39	Shen Ying	Wuxing, Jiangsu
28	Jin Zhaozi (金兆梓)	Jinhua, Zhejiang	49	Liu Yanling (刘延陵)	Taixing, Jiangsu
29	Fu Donghua (傅东华)	Jinhua, Zhejiang	50	Teng Gu	Baoshan, Jiangsu
36	Liu Tingfang (刘廷芳)	Yongjia, Zhejiang	51	Gu Jiegang (顾颉刚)	Wu County, Jiangsu
45	Shen Zemin (沈泽民)	Tongxiang, Zhejiang	52	Pan Jiaxun (潘家洵)	Wu County, Jiangsu
48	Hu Yuzhi (胡愈之)	Shangyu, Zhejiang	59	Zhu Ziqing	Jiangdu, Jiangsu
53	Yu Pingbo	Deqing, Zhejiang	60	Liu Bannong	Jiangyin, Jiangsu

(continued)

TABLE 13.1 *(continued)*

Membership no.	Name	Native place	Membership no.	Name	Native place
55	Xia Mianzun	Shangyu, Zhejiang	69	Ma Guoying (马国英)	Jiangsu
64	Zhou Yutong (周予同)	Rui'an, Zhejiang	76	Wang Boxiang (王伯祥)	Wu County, Jiangsu
65	Zhou Jianren (周建人)	Shaoxing, Zhejiang	83	Zhang Chongnan (张崇南)	Jiading, Jiangsu
70	Le Sibing (乐嗣炳)	Zhenhai, Zhejiang	87	Gu Yiqiao	Wuxi, Jiangsu
78	Chen Wangdao	Yiwu, Zhejiang	100	Wu Qiubai (吴秋白)	Wu County, Jiangsu
79	Liu Dabai	Shaoxing, Zhejiang	105	Yan Dunyi (严敦易)	Dongtai, Jiangsu
80	Wang Renshu (王任叔)	Fenghua, Zhejiang	108	Su Zhaolong (苏兆龙)	Yancheng, Jiangsu
93	Xu Zhimo	Haining, Zhejiang	110	Gui Chenghua (桂澄华)	Wu County, Jiangsu
96	Fan Zhongyun (樊仲云)	Sheng County, Zhejiang	141	Su Zhaoxiang (苏兆骧)	Yancheng, Jiangsu
103	Sun Zhongjiu (孙仲久)	Shaoxing, Zhejiang	144	Xu Weinan (徐蔚南)	Wujiang, Jiangsu
106	Xu Tiaofu (徐调孚)	Pinghu, Zhejiang	148	Lu Kanru (陆侃如)	Haimen, Jiangsu
107	Zhu Dongjiao (诸东郊)	Yu County, Zhejiang			
121	Chen Yi (陈逸)	Sheng County, Zhejiang			
122	Wang Luyan (王鲁彦)	Zhenhai, Zhejiang			
124	Pan Chuitong (潘垂统)	Yuyao, Zhejiang			
125	Feng Zikai	Chongde, Zhejiang			
127	Zhang Xichen (章锡琛)	Shaoxing, Zhejiang			

TABLE 13.1 *(continued)*

Membership no.	Name	Native place	Membership no.	Name	Native place
128	Hu Zhongchi (胡仲持)	Shangyu, Zhejiang			
129	Xu Jie (许杰)	Tiantai, Zhejiang			
130	Wang Yiren (王以仁)	Tiantai, Zhejiang			
134	Gu Zhongyi (顾仲彝)	Jiaxing, Zhejiang			
155	Wu Wenqi (吴文祺)	Haining, Zhejiang			
168	Zhu Yingpeng (朱应鹏)	Hang County, Zhejiang			
20	Yi Junzuo (易君左)	Hanshou, Hunan	81	Zhao Jingshen	Yibin, Sichuan
68	Li Jinhui	Xiangtan, Hunan	137	Jin Mancheng (金满城)	Emei, Sichuan
82	Li Qingya	Xiangyin, Hunan	169	He Changqun (贺昌群)	Mabian, Sichuan
102	Sun Lianggong	Shaoyang, Hunan	8	Wang Tongzhao	Zhucheng, Shandong
139	Ouyang Yuqian	Liuyang, Hunan	136	Sui Yuwei (隋玉薇)	Shandong
142	Xie Xiaoyu (谢小虞)	Xiangxiang, Hunan	172	Yu Jianhua (俞剑华)	Licheng, Shandong
147	Li Liewen	Xiangtan, Hunan	56	Xu Yunuo (徐玉诺)	Lushan, Henan
170	Peng Jiahuang (彭家煌)	Xiangyin, Hunan	112	Cao Jinghua	Lushi, Henan
4	Zheng Zhenduo	Changle, Fujian	90	Zhu Xiang	Taihu, Anhui
10	Lu Yin	Minhou, Fujian	140	Wang Zhongxian	Wuyuan, Anhui
13	Bing Xin	Minhou, Fujian	104	Wang Shoucong (王守聪)	Tianjin, Hebei
74	Yu Xiangsen (余祥森)	Minhou, Fujian	167	Shu Qingchun (舒庆春, namely Lao She)	Beijing, Hebei

(continued)

TABLE 13.1 *(continued)*

Membership no.	Name	Native place	Membership no.	Name	Native place
91	Gao Junzhen (高君箴)	Changle, Fujian	24	Xie Liuyi	Guiyang, Guizhou
131	Wang Shiying (王世颖)	Minhou, Fujian	162	Jian Xian'ai (蹇先艾)	Zunyi, Guizhou
30	Ke Yicen	Wanzai, Jiangxi	160	Chen Xiaohang (陈小航)	Fengqing, Yunnan
71	Xiong Foxi	Fengcheng, Jiangxi	62	Xu Menglin	Kunming, Yunnan
72	Deng Yancun (邓演存)	Nancheng, Jiangxi	163	Li Jianwu	Anyi, Shanxi
150	You Guo'en (游国恩)	Linchuan, Jiangxi	153	Xu Dishan	Tainan, Taiwan
156	Luo Heizhi	Wuning, Jiangxi			
57	Yan Jicheng (严既澄)	Sihui, Guangdong			
86	Huo Yao (侯曜)	Fanyu, Guangdong			
88	Tang Chengbo (汤澄波)	Hua County, Guangdong			
92	Liang Zongdai	Xinhui, Guangdong			
149	Li Jinfa	Mei County, Guangdong			

(*Source*: Jia Zhifang [贾植芳], Su Xingliang [苏兴良], Liu Yulian [刘裕莲], Zhou Chundong [周春东], and Li Yuzhen [李玉珍], eds.: *Material on the Literary Research Society* [《文学研究会资料》], Zhengzhou: Henan People's Press, 1985)

FOURTEEN

THE LITERARY NICHE CREATED BY NEWSPAPERS, MAGAZINES, AND PUBLISHING HOUSES OF BEIJING AND SHANGHAI

FROM THE LITERARY EVENTS OF 1921, IT WAS CLEAR that literary societies and groups formed around newspapers and magazines had become a sign of literary modernity. In their initial stages, both the Literary Research Society and the Creation Society sought to publish their own journals and publications, and if independent publishing was impossible, they tried to find publishing institutions that were willing to cooperate with them. In editing and publishing these journals and publications, they tried to uphold their own literary ideals, styles, and methodologies, and with these, attract their own readers. The authors had already known that modern mass media could disseminate their literary works, and its width and speed had a direct impact on the "production" of literature. Both professional and nonprofessional modern writers had to rely on the large circulation of newspapers and magazines to survive, while at the same time, they tried to find the right balance between their literary ideals and the reading market.

The Commercial Press joining hands with literary journals to participate in the shaping of May Fourth literature can be seen as an example of the alliance of commercial publishing and distribution and literary innovation. Ten years after its launch, *Fiction Monthly*, produced by the Commercial Press, was fundamentally reformed by Shen Yanbing, and with Zheng Zhenduo and Ye Shaojun (Shengtao) being its chief editors successively, the magazine became one of the major strongholds of May Fourth authors. Apart from Lu Xun, the authors actively publishing their literary works in this magazine, including Xu Dishan, Bing Xin, Ye Shengtao, and Zhu Ziqing, formed the backbone of the

Literary Research Society. It was in this magazine that Shen Yanbing published his novella *Disillusion* using the pseudonym "Mao Dun" and thus became a major novelist. And it was also in this magazine that those authors younger than Mao Dun published their early literary works and became major players in the literary circle, including Lao She, who published his *Philosophy of Old Zhang* (《老张的哲学》) in 1926; Ding Ling (丁玲), who published her "Mengke" (《梦珂》) in 1927; and Ba Jin, who published his *Destruction* (《灭亡》) in 1929. Zheng Zhenduo launched the Literary Research Society's own journal, *Literary Ten-Daily* (《文学旬刊》, later changed to *Literary Weekly* [《文学周报》]) in Shanghai, which was originally affiliated to the *Shanghai China Times* and later became an independent journal, and was published by Kaiming Bookstore. This was a journal focusing on literary theories, powerfully criticizing the Mandarin Duck and Butterfly school, and debating with the Creation Society. The Literary Research Society paid much attention to literary criticism and regarded it as a means to establish itself as a literary school, which later became a tradition of modern Chinese literature. Besides these journals, the Society also cooperated with the Commercial Press and published the Literary Research Society book series (including two categories: original literary works and translation works), which included 125 titles published from 1921 through to 1937, and became the earliest and largest book series of modern Chinese literature. Later, other literary schools also adopted the form of book series to promote their literary endeavours and showcase their literary achievements. Meanwhile, writers also promoted literature by publishing advertisements in newspapers, an example of which was the monthly *Poetry* (《诗》) edited by Ye Shengtao and Liu Yanling, who published the poetic "Announcement of the Publishing of *Poetry*" (《〈诗〉底出版底预告》) before its publication:

> *The bones of dead old poetry had been carried to the widely opening tombs,*
> *While the new poetry, born three years ago, had not a chance to talk to people.*
> *But who has stronger instructing power than this lovely infant?*
> *And who shoulders more urgent consoling mission than this lovely infant?*
> *We build a little garden called Poetry to be his nursing ground,*
> *And those who love him, please do come and give him some candies and fruits!*[1]

> 旧诗的骸骨已被人扛着向张着口的坟墓去了，
> 产生了三年的新诗还未曾能向人说话呢。
> 但是有指导人们的潜力的，谁能如这个可爱的婴儿呀？
> 奉着安慰人生的使命的，谁又能如这个婴儿的美丽呀？
> 我们拟造了这个名为《诗》的小乐园做他的歌舞养育之场，
> 疼他爱他的人们快尽你们的力来捐些糖食花果呀！

---

[1] "Annoucement of the Publishing of *Poetry*," published in "Lamp of Learning," the supplement of the *Shanghai China Times*, on October 18, 1921.

Poetry was published by the Zhonghua Book Company, whose founder, Lubi Kui (陆费逵), as well as the founder of Kaiming Bookstore, Zhang Xichen, both started their careers at the Commercial Press. The Literary Research Society had always relied on major publishing institutions, and a large proportion of its readers were intellectuals and students, which gave this literary group a stronger foothold. Besides, though most of its active members were young, some of its founding members, Zhou Zuoren, Zhu Xizu, and Jiang Baili, as well as members such as Liu Dabai, Chen Dabei, Li Qingya, and Xia Mianzun, were in their middle age. Some of them were distinguished gentlemen holding a position in educational or publishing institutions. Taking supplements of newspapers, for example, the "Lamp of Learning" edited by Zheng Zhenduo, the "Supplement of the *Morning Post*" edited by Sun Fuyuan, and "Green Light" (《青光》), another supplement of the *Shanghai China Times*, edited by Ke Yicen, were all places where authors of the Literary Research Society published their works. Among these, the *Morning Post* had the longest history of running supplements. The *Morning Post* was originally a conservative newspaper focusing on academic research. In 1919, its manager Pu Boying accepted new ideas and radically reformed the genteel literary and art supplement page in its section 7 and showed an inclination toward the New Culture movement. In 1920 Sun Fuyuan became its editor, and with the help of Lu Xun he changed this supplement page into a separate supplement, which published Lu Xun's works, May Fourth problem novels, Zhou Zuoren's column My Own Garden (自己的园地), Bing Xin's "Letters to My Little Readers" (《寄小读者》) and

14.1. The Oriental Library (东方图书馆, also known as the Hanfen Building [涵芬楼]), which was unfortunately burnt to ashes in a Japanese air raid in 1932

14.2. Although Mao Dun's earliest three novels, *Disillusion*, *Waverings* (《动摇》), and *Pursuits* (《追求》), were not published in *Fiction Monthly* until a later stage (the periodical had been running for ten years before he published his first novel in it), one can see that this literary journal launched by the Commercial Press was among the best of the time. These are the separate editions of the novels

Chen Dabei's essays that promoted nonprofessional theater, "Amateur" (《爱美剧》). From 1923 to 1925, the *Morning Post* also had a supplement called *Literary Ten-Daily*, edited by Wang Tongzhao in the north, in cooperation with the journal of the same name launched in Shanghai. In October 1924, in order to protest against Liu Mianji (刘勉己), the deputy editor-in-chief of the *Morning Post*, for removing Lu Xun's poem "My Lost Love" (《我的失恋》) just before the magazine was printed, Sun Fuyuan resigned and turned to the *Beijing Press* to edit a new supplement. Thus the "Supplement of the *Beijing Press*" also became the venue where authors of the Literary Research Society published their works. The two major questionnaires in 1925, namely "Top Ten Books Young People Must Read" and "Top Ten Books Young People Love to Read," were both initiated by this supplement. Lu Xun was the tenth person to answer the questionnaire "Top Ten Books Young People Must Read," in which he did not list a single book, but made such astounding comment as "I believe that you should read very few, if any, Chinese books, and read more foreign books," and "There are some persuasions in Chinese books, but most of them are vampires' optimism; one can indeed find something depressing and pessimistic in foreign books, but those are living people's depression and pessimism."[2] Almost all of the journals and supplements mentioned here published works of authors of the Literary Research Society; no wonder that when authors of the Creation

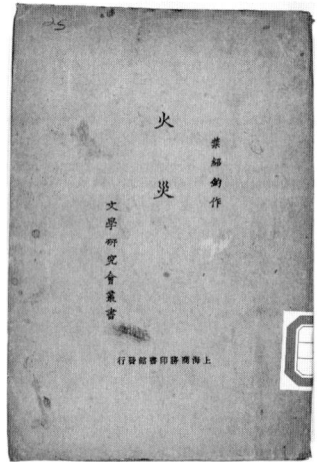

14.3. Front cover of Ye Shaojun's (Shengtao) *The Fire* (《火灾》), a title from the Literary Research Society book series

[2] Lu Xun: "The Books Young People Must Read" (《青年必读书》), *Complete Works of Lu Xun*, Vol. 3, Beijing: People's Literature Press, 1981, p. 12.

Society came onto the literary stage, they found it dominated by the Literary Research Society. The Creation Society might have been at a loss if it was not for the modern cultural atmosphere: the special advantages enjoyed by the May Fourth authors, as well as the huge literary capacity created by modern publishing and mass media industries, helped the Creation Society find its own foothold in a short time.

Most authors and readers of the Creation Society were rebellious modern-style young people (besides students, there were storekeepers and workers in the cities who had received some education), which itself made the group more precarious. Zong Baihua, who was the editor of the "Lamp of Learning" before Zheng Zhenduo, was the first person who perceived the poetic talent of Guo Moruo. Guo's earliest poems, "Temptation of Death" (《死的诱惑》) and "An Infant Bathing in Hakata Bay" (《抱和儿浴博多湾中》), as well as his major works like "Nirvana of the Phoenix" and "A Burning Coal," were all first published in the "Lamp of Learning." But the Creation Society intended to have its own publications, and joining hands with Taidong Press gave it an opportunity to become a self-reliant independent literary group. Later, most publishing institutions cooperating with the Creation Society were small- and mid-sized presses, which made its fate even more dubious. Then the quarterly *Creation* (1922), which focused on original creative works, and *Creation Weekly* (1923), which paid equal attention to literary theories and criticism and creative works, stood out with an avant-garde tinge, for they represented the style of the Creation Society that featured mixed romantic and aesthetic qualities. In July 1923, Zhang Jiluan (张季鸾), then the editor-in-chief of the *Chinese Times* in Shanghai, recognized the value of the Creation Society and offered to publish a daily

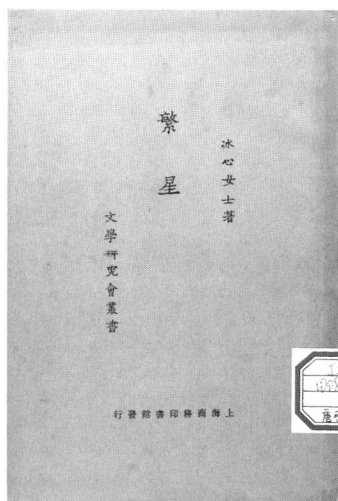

14.4. Bing Xin's *Myriad Stars*, a title from the Literary Research Society book series

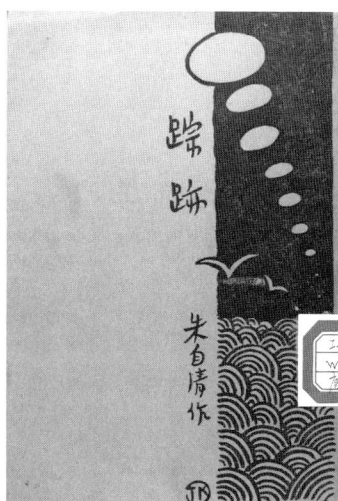

14.5. *Footprints* by Zhu Ziqing, an author from the Literary Research Society

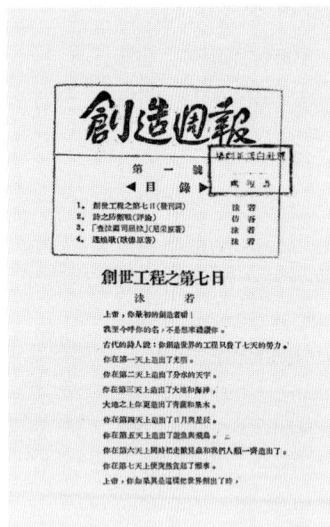

14.6. First issue of *Creation Weekly* (《创造周报》), another journal launched by the Creation Society

supplement for them, which was the "Creation Daily" (《创造日》). Later, we could see that none of the journals of the Creation Society lasted for a long time: the government found it difficult to deal with its rebellious nature and often issued bans against it. Members of the Creation Society often revolted against their publishers because they could not bear to be "exploited" by them, and the members disagreed on a number of issues. By 1924, the weekly *Flood* (《洪水》), which focused on literary theories and criticism, was published by Taidong Press, only to be closed down after one issue. The next year it was changed into a semimonthly and published by the Kwong Wah Book Store, and later its publisher changed again to the Publishing Department of the Creation Society, evidence of the instability of this literary group. The middle period of *Flood* witnessed a shift of focus for the Creation Society, and after it, the *Creation Monthly* (1926) and *Cultural Criticism* (《文化批判》, 1928) raised the banner of "revolutionary literature." Under the influence of the younger generation of Chinese students back from Japan (Li Chuli, Peng Kang [彭康], Feng Naichao, and others, who were collectively called the "young fellows of the late-stage Creation Society"), this literary school shifted its focus sharply from promoting avant-garde art and literature to aesthetic art and literature, and then to revolutionary art and literature. Meanwhile, some minor journals such as *A.11*, *Mirage* (《幻洲》), and *Quicksand* (《流沙》) were published, thus forming quite a multifarious publishing scene for the Creation Society. This literary society also edited and published its long-term book series, but they also featured diversification and disorderliness. Take the Creation Society book series for example, it had fourteen titles published by Taidong Press, five titles published by Kwong Wah Book Store, and forty-seven by the Publishing Department of the Creation Society, making a total of sixty-six titles. And there were many other book series of creative works, translation works, literary and art theories,

14.7. *Vase* (《瓶》), a collection of poems by Guo Moruo, published by the Creation Society in April 1927. There were no words on the cover, only a picture

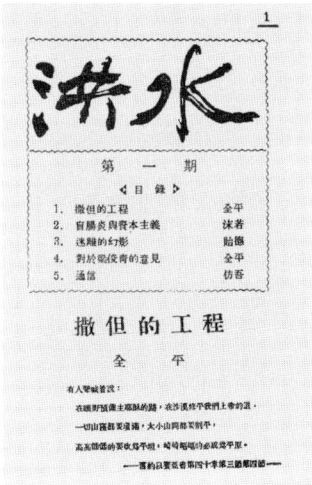

14.8. First issue of *Flood*, a journal of the later-stage Creation Society

and social science books, such as the Xinyi mini-book series, Fallen Leaves book series, Tomorrow mini-book series, Social Sciences book series, Selected World Masterpieces, etc. What's worth a special mention is the establishment of the Publishing Department of the Creation Society, which sought to bypass publishers and establish direct links between authors and readers, and its success and failure can be seen as an interesting record of how authors ran bookstores. Later, Lu Xun also ran his own publishing and distribution institution; small and independent as it was, its efforts paid off and it was much more surefooted.

Talking about the relationship between the Creation Society and Taidong Press, Zheng Boqi said it was a "super economic exploitation by the boss of Taidong Press of Moruo, Dafu, and Fangwu."[3] This was a somewhat harsh comment, and here are more objectively recounted details:

The Creation Society had Taidong Press be its publishing supporter, but the latter was quite poorly managed because its boss Zhao Nangong was muddleheaded and several of its managers were master cheaters … Taidong Press earned a high reputation and made a substantial profit by publishing earlier literary works by members of the Creation Society, but its bookstore was increasingly losing money, and authors' payments were simply out of the question. When Guo Moruo, Cheng Fangwu, and Yu Dafu went to Shanghai, they could eat and drink at the Peking Tongxing Restaurant on credit, and they could be reimbursed for their travel expenses, but their remuneration and royalties could never be cashed and were just passed off with empty promises. There were many people in the Literary Research Society who relied on payments from the Commercial Press, and quite a number of

14.9. The inaugural issue of *Mirage*, one of the journals of the later-stage Creation Society, which was distributed by the Publishing Department of the Creation Society located at A-11, Sande Alley, Baoshan Road, Shanghai

3 Zheng Boqi: "Recollections of the Creation Society" (《忆创造社》), quoted from Rao Hongjing (饶鸿竞) et al., ed., *Material of the Creation Society*, Vol. 2 (《创造社资料（下）》), Fuzhou: Fujian People's Press, 1985, p. 863.

14.10. Group photo of all the staff at Beixin Press when it (the distribution agency) was located in Qipu Road, Shanghai. The bosses of the press, Li Xiaofeng and Li Zhiyun (李志云), are in the front row, eighth and ninth from the left

14.11. Li Xiaofeng (on the right) with his elder brother Li Zhiyun (and an unknown person) when they ran Beixin Press in Shanghai

people in the Yu Si Society (语丝社) relied on Beixin Press, but not a single member of the Creation Society relied on Taidong Press in this manner, not even on their small allowances … People of the Creation Society could not live on the payments from Taidong Press and thus they were not restrained by the latter; on the contrary, they could even criticize the publisher, so they enjoyed much freedom in their writings and became bold in their speech.[4]

This surely had something to do with the unruly temperament of talented members of the Creation Society. The case was quite different with the Yu Si Society, the Wilderness Society (莽原社), and the Weiming Society (未名社), all of which enjoyed personal support from Lu Xun. Each of these literary societies had only one journal, namely *Yu Si* weekly (1924), *Wilderness* weekly (1925), and *Weiming* semimonthly (1926), all the fruits of cooperation between Lu Xun and people of the younger generation. These were smaller literary groups with Lu Xun at their core. The name of the journal *Yu Si* was chosen in quite an unusual way. According to the recollection of the people concerned, Sun Fuyuan and others gathered at Kaicheng Bean Restaurant within the Dong'an Market in Beijing and decided to publish a journal. The expences would be shared by Lu Xun and all seven people attending the meeting. As they could not decide on a name for the journal, Gu Jiegang randomly turned the pages of *Our July* (《我们的七月》), a small publication of the Literary Research Society edited by Yu Pingbo, and randomly pointed at two characters, which were "Yu Si" (语丝,

4   Zhou Yuying (周毓英): "The Later Stage of the Creation Society" (《记后期创造社》), quoted from Rao Hongjing et al., ed., *Material of the Creation Society*, Vol. 2, Fuzhou: Fujian People's Press, 1985, p. 792.

meaning "thread of language") in the first poem of "Little Poetry" (《小诗》) by Zhang Weiqi (张维祺), and they agreed to use these two characters as the name of their journal. This was in keeping with Lu Xun's comments on the style of essays published on *Yu Si*, "free and unrestrained." Soon after that, *Yu Si* was published by Beixin Press, located in Cuihua Lane, Beijing; and since Li Xiaofeng (李小峰), the boss of Beixin Press, was one of the seven founding members of the journal and the society, members of this literary society participated in the entire publishing process, which was a pattern later adopted by all journals related with Lu Xun. By the time *Weiming*, the successor of *Wilderness*, was published, Lu Xun decided to separate from Beixin Press, and seriously considered the pattern he often used later in Shanghai, which was to establish a press by himself, and young authors had to run all kinds of errands to get their books published. Indeed, Lu Xun had unsparingly sued Beixin Press for the reason that it refused to pay him due royalties of the books *Call to Arms* (《呐喊》) and *Wandering* (《彷徨》), but he still gave Beixin Press the publishing rights of his *Correspondence* (《两地书》). Lu Xun set an example for authors in cooperating with bookstores while refusing to be taken advantage of by them. He never spared efforts in protecting authors' rights and interests, and Lu Xun's writing and translating style became widely known with the wide distribution of these journals.

Other literary groups that received attention from Lu Xun, like the Low Grass Society (浅草社, and its successor the Sunken Bell Society, 沉钟社), the Mass Society (弥洒社), the Hurricane Society (狂飙社), etc., all had their own independent journals to publish the works of their members. The *Low Grass* quarterly was published by Taidong Press in 1923, but it became nonexistent except in name when its founder Lin Ruji went to study in France. By 1925, its original members Chen Weimo (陈炜谟), Chen Xianghe (陈翔鹤), and Feng Zhi (冯至) had a meeting in Beihai, Beijing, and discussed resuming the journal. They renamed their group the Sunken Bell Society, after the famous poetic play *The Sunken Bell* by Gerhart Hauptmann, wishing to inspire young Chinese people with the story of the perseverant bellfounder. The weekly and semimonthly *Sunken Bell*, published successively, were referred to Beixin Press by Lu Xun, who also showed his special treatment by asking Tao Yuanqing (陶元庆), his favorite avant-garde painter, to design the cover for the journal, and recommended foreign works he believed worth translating. This society lasted for nine years, and was "China's most persistent, honest and long-lasting literary group." Lu Xun praised their general style as "absorbing nutrition from the outside foreign literature and uncovering their soul's purpose from inside their heart," and "singing the songs of truth and beauty to lonely people."[5]

---

5   Lu Xun: "Preface to Fiction II of *Compendium of Chinese New Literature*" (《〈中国新文学大系〉·小说二集序》), *Complete Works of Lu Xun*, Vol. 6, Beijing: People's Literature Press, 1981, p. 242.

14.12. First issue of *Sunken Bell* weekly, published on October 10, 1925. It had a very simple design

Then there was the Mass Society, founded in Shanghai, which also had a tendency of "art for art's sake." In its *Mass* monthly, published in 1923, was its "Manifesto" ("The Mass"), written by Hu Shanyuan (胡山源), singing that "We are gods of art and literature; / We don't know where we come from, / Nor do we know why we have come."[6] The Hurricane Society, separated from the Wilderness Society, had the *Hurricane* weekly published by Kwong Wah Book Store in 1926. Gao Changhong, once a close follower of Lu Xun, pronounced his Nietzsche-style "superman" dictum in this "Manifesto," expressing his strong emotions and protesting against society. The Hurricane Society's book series were also printed by Taidong Press. All this reinforced the surrealistic aberrational and rebellious elements of the May Fourth literary niche. It deserves our special interest that the avant-garde literature of that time actually received much support from commercial publishing institutions.

The Crescent Moon club, which started its activities in Beijing in 1923, was different from the literary groups already mentioned in that it was formed by a group of gentlemen back from their studies in Europe or the United States. They met at gathering parties and social clubs, and had a strong interest in performing and watching theater. Besides men of letters, their members also included bankers, politicians, and celebrities of society, and at the core were such figures as Liang Qichao, Hu Shi, Xu Zhimo, and Lin Huiyin. This was the beginning of the Crescent Moon Society. At this time, their journal *Contemporary Critique* (《现代评论》, 1924) was a weekly focusing on a range of general topics of current affairs, and Chen Xiying and Wen

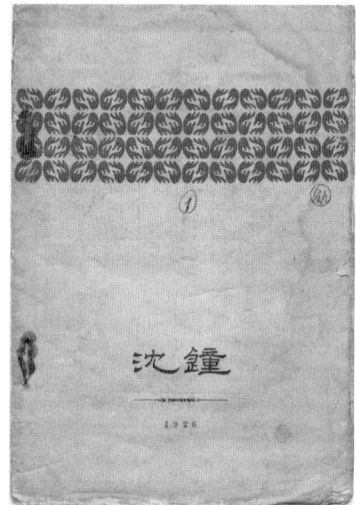

14.13. Cover of *Sunken Bell* weekly, designed by Tao Yuanqing at the recommendation of Lu Xun. As simple as it was, it displayed a distinct modern style

[6]   Ibid., p. 241.

14.14. Entrance of the former Songpo Library (松坡图书馆, located at 7 Shihu Lane), a venue where members of the earlier Crescent Moon club gathered

14.15. *Independent Review* was another journal of members of the earlier Crescent Moon club in which they criticized and commented on politics

Yiduo joined the club as literary authors. Chen Xiying (whose original name was Chen Yuan [陈源]) was widely known by contemporary Chinese readers for his debate with Lu Xun in the column Casual Talks (闲话) of this journal. The editorial office of the journal was located at Jixiang Lane in Beijing, and therefore its members were also known as the "Jixiang Lane clique." They printed the Contemporary Critique Society literary book series, which included Yang Zhensheng's novel *Yujun* (《玉君》), Ding Xilin's one-act comedy "A Wasp" (《一只马蜂》), and *Zhimo's Poems* (《志摩的诗》). By the time Xu Zhimo became the editor-in-chief of the "Supplement of the *Morning Post*" in 1925–1926, he started some new columns including Poetry (诗镌) and Drama (剧刊), promoting the new poetry and national drama movements. These can be seen as part of the May Fourth literary activities, and increased the reputation of the later Crescent Moon school.

14.16. Cover of the original version of *Temple of Flowers* (《花之寺》) by Ling Shuhua (凌叔华), a book from the Crescent Moon Society. It had quite a feminine style

Around the time such political events as the May Thirtieth movement and the March Eighteenth Incident happened, the Crescent Moon Society was not widely different from other May Fourth literary groups. Later, however, with the splitting of the New Culture movement, some intellectuals of the Crescent Moon school had increasingly heated disagreements with Lu Xun and others, and became a distinct liberal literary clique that promoted democracy

14.17. Cover of the 101st issue of *Saturday*. Another 100 issues were published after it was resumed after the May Fourth movement, evidence that it was still popular among urban resident readers

in China. The Crescent Moon school claimed to be undisciplined and unconventional, and to respect the independent will of each member, and they proudly boasted that leopards and tigers hunted alone, while dogs and wolves hunted in groups. By the end of the May Fourth period, around 1927, left-wing literary people gradually built up a major literary force to meet the trend of revolutionary literature, and meanwhile, the Crescent Moon intellectuals resumed their activities. With the opening of the Shanghai Crescent Moon Bookstore and the publishing of *Crescent Moon* monthly as a start, the Crescent Moon school came to the foreground.

What merits our equal attention is the author groups in direct opposition to May Fourth literature. An example of this is the Mandarin Duck and Butterfly school, which represented the old-style urban popular literature and had been dominating the reading market since the late-Qing period. The outbreak of the May Fourth movement suddenly deprived them of a large number of young student readers, and thus they tried to maintain their market niche by winning urban readers with their popular literature. After *Fiction Monthly* was taken over by authors of the Literary Research Society, the Mandarin Duck and Butterfly authors launched the weekly *Fiction World* (《小说世界》, 1923) relying on a group of editors of the same disposition within the Commercial Press. Their journal *Saturday* was launched in 1914, and because it was more advanced in its literary awareness than the Mandarin Duck and Butterfly school, some people thought that this genre of popular literature could be called "Mandarin Duck and Butterfly – Saturday literary school" to show its difference from the literary school of the late Qing, from which we can see the significance of the journal. *Saturday* was discontinued in 1916, but after the May Fourth movement, it was resumed in 1922. These two historical facts showed that the Mandarin Duck and Butterfly – Saturday literary school did not completely slip from view, but just lost its dominating role in the literary scene and became increasingly marginal. Looking at the list of literary journals launched by this literary school after 1921, one finds that besides the two journals just mentioned, there were also *Recreation World* monthly (1921), *Semimonthly* (1921), *Happiness* (《快活》, 1922) published every ten days, *Weekdays* weekly (《星期》, 1922), *Red Magazine* weekly

(《红杂志》, 1922), *Detective World* semimonthly (1923), *Red Roses* weekly (1924), *Violet* semimonthly (1925), and the earlier *Young Companion* (《良友 画报》, 1926), etc. And this list does not include the various tabloids of the Mandarin Duck and Butterfly – Saturday literary school. Indeed, this literary genre lasted throughout the entire development history of modern Chinese literature.

As for other authors uncongenial with the May Fourth spirit, such as the major figures of classical learnings, Liu Shipei and Huang Kan, who launched the monthly *National Heritage* (《国故》), formed an opposing group within the Chinese Department of Peking University. *Critical Review*, launched in 1922 by Hu Shi's friend Mei Guangdi and Wu Mi, Hu Xiansu and others who had studied in the United States and became professors of the Southeast University in Nanjing, was the only journal mentioned in this section that was not edited in Beijing or Shanghai but was published in Shanghai (by Zhonghua Bookstore). Intermittent as it was, *Critical Review* was not discontinued until 1933, and though some of its views can be seen as a balance of power for the avant-garde cultural trend, at that time it became quite a historical hindrance. In 1927, Wu Mi had to pay 100 silver dollars per issue to Zhonghua Bookstore for them to be willing to continue printing *Critical Review*. Wu Mi sighed in his diary that "China's new-style scholars not only enjoy high reputations, but earn a lot of money. For example, Zhou Shuren earned more than 10,000 silver dollars with his *Call to Arms* alone. And Zhang Ziping, Yu Dafu and others also earn a lot each month. The payment for their novels may be as high as over twenty silver dollars per 1,000 characters."[7] This meant that *Critical Review* had fallen into oblivion and most readers were on the side of Lu Xun, Guo Moruo, Yu Dafu, Zhou Zuoren, or even urban popular authors.

Thus a multilayered literary niche was formed through a number of newspapers and magazines, which is evidence that from its very beginning, modern Chinese literature was a complicated and polyphonic sphere.

[7]   *Wu Mi's Diary*, Vol. 4, p. 17.

HEILONGJIANG

OUTER MONGOLIA

JILIN

CHAHAR

LIAONING

JEHOL

SUIYUAN

Beijing

Tianjin

NINGXIA

HEBEI

SHANXI

Yellow R.

SHANDONG

Yellow
Sea

GANSU

SHAANXI

SHANXI

HENAN

JIANGSU

Nanjing

ANHUI

Shanghai

SICHUAN

HUBEI

Hangzhou

ZHEJIANG

East
China
Sea

Yangtze R.

HUNAN

JIANGXI

FUJIAN

GUIZHOU

Taiwan

GUANGXI

GUANGDONG

Guangzhou

VIETNAM

South China

Hainan

Sea

PHILIPPINES

KOREA

Sea
of
Japan

Tokyo

JAPAN

PACIFIC OCEAN

| 0 | 250 | 500 | 750 | 1000 km |
| 0 | 200 | 400 | 600 miles |

MAP 14.1. Distribution of major literary societies of the May Fourth period

TABLE 14.1 *Major literary societies of the May Fourth period*

Name of the literary society	Time of establishment	Founders and major members	Journals
Literary Research Society	Jan. 1921	Zheng Zhenduo, Zhou Zuoren, etc.	*Fiction Monthly* and others
Tsinghua Literary Society	Nov. 1921	Gu Yiqiao, etc.	
Beijing Experimental Theater Society	Nov. 1921	Chen Dabei, Li Jianwu, etc.	
Daylight Society (曦社)	Feb. 1922	Li Jianwu, Jian Xian'ai, etc.	"Supplement of the *National Customs Daily*" (《国风日报副刊》)
Crescent Moon Society (earlier)	Mar. 1923	Xu Zhimo, Hu Shi, etc.	*Poetry*, "Supplement of the *Morning Post*"
Hurricane Society	Sep. 1924	Gao Changhong, Gao Ge (高歌), etc.	*Hurricane* (weekly) and others
Yu Si Society	Nov. 1924	Lu Xun, Zhou Zuoren, etc.	*Yu Si* (weekly) and others
Wilderness Society	Apr. 1925	Lu Xun, Wei Suyuan (韦素园), etc.	*Wilderness* (weekly) and others
Weiming Society	Summer 1925	Lu Xun, Wei Suyuan, etc.	*Weiming* (semimonthly)
Sunken Bell Society	Oct. 1925	Yang Hui (杨晦), Chen Weimo, etc.	*Sunken Bell* weekly and others
Green Wave Society (绿波社)	May 1923	Zhao Jingshen, Jiao Juyin (焦菊隐), etc.	*Poetic Circle* (《诗坛》) and others
Critical Review School	Jan. 1922	Wu Mi, Mei Guangdi, etc.	*Critical Review*
Masses Theater Society	May 1921	Wang Zhongxian, Chen Dabei, etc.	*Theater* (《戏剧》) (monthly)
Shanghai Drama Association	1921	Ying Weiyun, Wang Zhongxian, etc.	
Low Grass Society	Jan. 1922	Lin Ruji, Chen Weimo, etc.	*Low Grass* (《浅草》) (quarterly)
Green Society (青社)	July 1922	Bao Tianxiao, Hu Jichen (胡寄尘), etc.	*Evergreen* (《长青》)
Mass Society	Mar. 1923	Hu Shanyuan, Qian Jiangchun (钱江春), etc.	*Mass* (monthly)

(continued)

TABLE 14.1 *(continued)*

Name of the literary society	Time of establishment	Founders and major members	Journals
Spring Thunder Literary Society (春雷文学社)	Nov. 1924	Jiang Guangci, etc.	
Dawn Literary Society	Oct. 1921	Wang Jingzhi, Pan Mohua (潘漠华), etc.	
Lakeside Poets' Society (湖畔诗社)	Apr. 1922	Wang Jingzhi, Pan Mohua, etc.	*Feburary in China* (《支那二月》) (monthly)
Orchid Society (兰社)	1922	Dai Wangshu (戴望舒), etc.	*Orchid Friends* (《兰友》) (published every ten days)
Guangzhou Literary Research Society (广州文学研究会)	Summer 1922	Liang Zongdai, Liu Simu (刘思慕), etc.	
Creation Society	July 1921	Guo Moruo, Yu Dafu, etc.	*Creation* and others

FIFTEEN

LEADING BREAKTHROUGHS IN MODERN VERNACULAR POETRY AND SHORT STORIES

After the banner of "literary revolution" was held high, the novel had indisputably become the foremost literary genre in twentieth-century Chinese literature, but it was modern vernacular poetry that showed the earliest achievements. Hu Shi's "Some Modest Proposals for the Reform of Literature" was published in *New Youth*, Vol. 2, Issue 5 (January 1917), and in the next issue, that is, Vol. 2, Issue 6 (February 1917), the journal published Hu Shi's "(Eight) Vernacular Poems," while it wasn't until more than a year later that Lu Xun published his "The Diary of a Madman" in *New Youth*, Vol. 4, Issue 5 (May 1917).

Why did the experiment with new poetry occur earlier? When Hu Shi discussed the issue with his fellow students in the United States, he said: "From where shall the literary revolution start? It must be to write poems like prose composition." Whereas Mei Guangdi insisted that "the case is different for different literary genres. One can use vernacular language to write novels and *ci* and *qu*, but cannot use it to write poems."[1] Mei was not opposing to vernacular language, but thought that the language used in poetry should be different from that in other literary genres. It was not proper to write poetry in prose diction, not to say vernacular language. This view of "poetic diction versus prose diction" seemed reasonable, but putting it back into the context of that time, his insistence that vernacular language should not be used in poetry,

---

[1] For the quotations of Hu Shi and Mei Jinzhuang (Guangdi), see Hu Shi: "Why Do I Write Vernacular Poems? Preface to *Collection of Experimental Writings*"(《我为什么要做白话诗？（〈尝试集〉自序）》), *New Youth*, Vol. 6, Issue 5, May 1919.

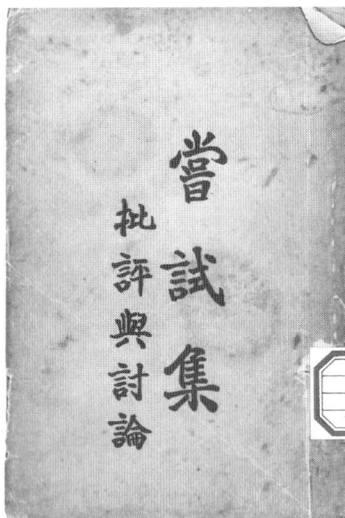

15.1. Original edition of Hu Shi's *Collection of Experimental Writings*, a pathbreaker for new poetry

the most established genre of old-style literature, was indeed his last resort to resist against writing in vernacular language. Seeing that empty talk was useless, Hu Shi decided to "conquer the difficulty," and thus made lonely but dedicated efforts in writing vernacular poetry. He was not afraid to be criticized for not having broken loose from the bondage of "old-style poetry" and "classical Chinese," nor was he afraid of mocking comments such as his poetry was nothing but "unbound bound feet." And Hu Shi knew his own limitations, so that by the time he published the very first vernacular anthology of modern China, he entitled it *Collection of Experimental Writings*.

Hu Shi was indeed experimenting with poetic writing. China had over a thousand years' tradition in poetic writing, and there were such unsurpassable peaks as Tang poems, Song *ci*, and Yuan *qu*, so vernacular poetry written at that time was nothing but an experiment. Apart from Hu Shi, there were others inspired by the radical journals *New Youth* and *New Tide* to write vernacular poetry, including Shen Yinmo, Liu Bannong, Yu Pingbo, Zhou Zuoren, Tang Si (唐俟, another pseudonym for Lu Xun), Liu Dabai, Kang Baiqing, Wang Jingzhi, Fu Sinian, and Zhu Ziqing, etc., and even Chen Duxiu and Li Dazhao wrote some of their own. Most of these were, as Lu Xun said about himself: "echoing to show our support to the lonely poetic writers; and [we] immediately stopped writing when real poets emerged."[2] They just fulfilled their duty to pave the way for new poetry.

The earliest vernacular poems were certainly unformed. Take the poem "Doves" (《鸽子》), with which readers are familiar, as an example: "Thin clouds in the high sky, / Late autumn glowing in the trees! / Overhead a flock of doves, / Playing games in the breeze. / Look at them in threes and twos, / Winding as they come and go, / Unhurried as they please, – / Suddenly, they turn their bodies in the sunlight, / With their white feathers against a blue sky, / How splendid!"[3] Simple and plain, but not without traces of *ci*, this poem agreed with the principles Hu himself had insisted upon: "trying to use vernacular characters, vernacular grammar, and the natural syllables of vernacular language" and writing "prose-style poetry," and we can feel the fresh spirit of youth of the May Fourth period. "Doves" was a simple poem expressing the

---

[2]   Lu Xun: "Preface to *Uncollected Works Beyond the Collection*" (《〈集外集〉序言》), *Complete Works of Lu Xun*, Vol. 4, Beijing: People's Literature Press, 1981, p. 4.

[3]   Hu Shi: "Doves," *Collected Poems of Hu Shi* (Expanded Edition) (《胡适诗存（增补本）》), Beijing: People's Literature Press, 1993, p. 175.

15.2. Fourth revised and enlarged edition of Hu Shi's *Collection of Experimental Writings* (with *Leaving the Country* attached)

15.3. Liu Bannong was another of the earliest vernacular poets of the May Fourth period

poet's feelings using the technique of comparison, and his later poems, includ-ing "A Predestined Star" (《一颗遭劫的星》), "Optimism" (《乐观》), and "Power" (《威权》), were written with more mature skills of symbolism. One stanza of "Power" reads: "Power sat on the mountain top, / Ordering a team of chained slaves to exploit a mine for him. / He said: 'Who of you dare not work hard? / I can do to you whatever I could!' // The slaves worked hard for ten thousand years, / The iron chains on their head gradually abraded. / They said: 'When the iron chains are broken, we will rebel!'"[4] Here I write more about Hu Shi's poems to correct the past practice of devaluing Hu's role in new poetry, and on the other hand, I want to draw the readers' attention to the ideas expressed in Hu's poetry; Hu Shi played a vital role in raising people's consciousness of equality and democracy.

Another type of poetry that was very popular during the May Fourth period was simple and straightforward, realistic poems showing sympathy to laborers. Examples of these included Hu Shi's "Rickshaw Coolie" (《人力车夫》), Liu Bannong's "Only One Sheet of Paper in Between" (《相隔一层纸》) and "An Apprentice's Hardships" (《学徒苦》), Zhou Zuoren's "Two Snow-Sweeping Men" (《两个扫雪的人》), and Liu Dabai's "Ballad of Selling Fabric" (《卖布谣》). "Only One Sheet of Paper in Between" was quite famous: "Inside, the fire crackles in the stove. / The old gentleman orders to open the window and buy fruit. / He says: 'It is not cold outside and the fire is too hot, / See that I'm not ill.' / Outside the house lies a beggar, /

4   Hu Shi: "Why Do I Write Vernacular Poems? Preface to *Collection of Experimental Writings*."

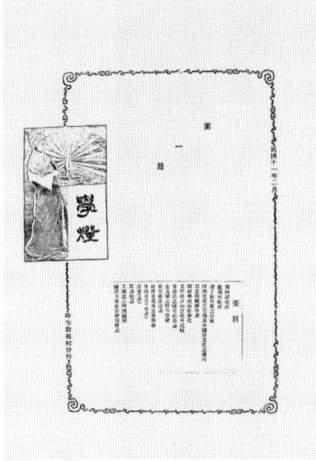

15.4. Guo Moruo's earliest poems were published in "Lamp of Learning"

He bites his teeth and moans toward the north wind: 'I want to die.' / Oh, for mercy, outside and inside, / Are separated only by a thin sheet of paper!" (A thin sheet of paper referred to the paper window. At that time, very few rich people in Beijing could afford glass windows.) Both this realism and the lyric expressions mentioned had an impact on the new poetry of later times.

Then came Guo Moruo. Guo was the leading figure of the Creation Society, and when he was studying in Japan, he felt the pulse of his times, was enlightened about world civilization, and with his own poetic talent he experienced an outburst of poetic creativity. He could not stop the pouring forth of the poetic lines and had to write them in the classroom. Hence, Guo Moruo the poet.

Goddess, Guo's anthology published in 1921, turned a passionate and romantic page in the history of China's new poetry. The poems in *Goddess* were significant in three ways. Firstly, they brilliantly prompted the rebirth of the Chinese nation. "The Nirvana of the Phoenix" cursed the old world, and after being tempered in fire, the "phoenix" was reborn, and so was the universe: "We are the harmony! / We are the harmony!" / One of all, harmony! / All of one, harmony! / Harmony be you, harmony be me! / Harmony be him, harmony be fire! / Fire be you! / Fire be me! / Fire be him! / Fire be Fire! / Soaring! Soaring! / Singing! Singing!"[5] Such repeated chanting swelled the emotions of celebrating the rebirth of China from its nirvana. And in "Coal in the Furnace—Emotion for My Motherland" (《炉中煤——眷念祖国的情绪》), the lyrical poet compared himself with

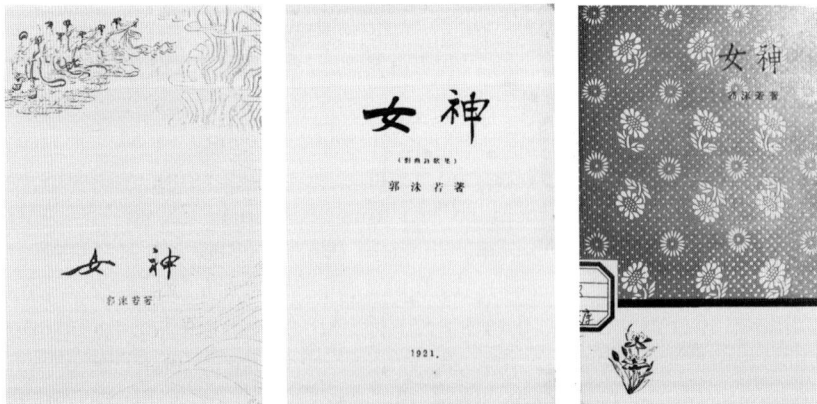

15.5. First edition (middle) and other editions of *Goddess*

[5] Guo Moruo, "The Nirvana of the Phoenix," *Complete Works of Guo Moruo*, Literature, Vol. 1, originally in the Appendix of the original version of *Goddess*, Beijing: People's Literature Press, 1982, p. 46.

the coal in the furnace, and his motherland to a beautiful woman, chanting: "I burn my heart to excess / For my dear lass!"[6] Secondly, the poems showed an openness of Chinese people to embrace world civilization. What was awakened and praised in "Good Morning" (《晨安》) included not only the Yangtze River, the Yellow River, and the Great Wall, but also "Good morning, Ganga, spiritual light flowing in the Ganges!" "Good morning! Washington's grave! Lincoln's grave! Whitman's grave! O Whitman! Whitman! The Pacific Ocean-like Whitman!"[7] Here he put special stress on Whitman because he owed a lot to this American poet when he wrote *Goddess*. "Earth, My Mother!" (《地球，我的母亲》) and "Shouting on the Rim of the Earth" (《立在地球边上放号》) were famous poems of Guo Moruo's, and the theme of "earth" simply showed the poet's aspiration to be a "man of the world." Thirdly, he gave unprecedented high praise to the rebellious and courageous quality of reformers. "In Praise of Bandits" (《匪徒颂》) praised all so-called bandits in "political revolution," "social revolution," and "religious revolution," from Lenin, Martin Luther, Copernicus, and Darwin through to Rousseau. The image of the "heavenly dog" in "Heavenly Dog" (《天狗》) was nothing but an incarnation of such a rebel: "I am a Heavenly Dog! / I swallow the Moon. / I swallow the Sun. … I am I now! / I am going to explode!"[8] Guo Moruo's May Fourth poems showed surging poetic power and extraordinary imagination, and had a grand and spectacular beauty and strength. His lines were free and unrestrained and totally broke free from the set patterns of old-style poetry. He drew from foreign experience and created the free-verse style of Chinese new poetry. Guo Moruo had showed quite different poetic modernity from that of the reformist poets of the late-Qing period.

Another poetic school that played a role in turning around Chinese poetry was the Crescent Moon school, whose major figures were Wen Yiduo and Xu Zhimo. They came into the literary circle a bit later than Guo Moruo, and the height of their creative power coincided with the ebb tide of the May Fourth movement. Due to the poets' literary educational background in Western European romanticism, the poems of the Crescent Moon school had a lot more content about individual dreams, love, mystery, and beauty, and later they even had a tinge of modernism.

Wen Yiduo (1899–1946) had been a student of Tsinghua University and actively participated in the May Fourth movement. Originally he studied fine arts in the United States, and back in China, he was recommended by Xu

---

[6] Guo Moruo, "The Coal in the Furnace," *Complete Works of Guo Moruo*, Literature, Vol. 1, Beijing: People's Literature Press, 1982, p. 58.

[7] Guo Moruo, "Good Morning," *Complete Works of Guo Moruo*, Literature, Vol. 1, Beijing: People's Literature Press, 1982, p. 65.

[8] Guo Moruo: "The Heavenly Dog," *Complete Works of Guo Moruo*, Literature, Vol. 1, Beijing: People's Literature Press, 1982, pp. 54–55.

15.6. "Before the Audience," an illustration drawn by Wen Yiduo for the *Tsinghua Annual* (《清华年刊》) in 1921, which showed a student making a speech in front of Tian'anmen. Wen was a painter and had studied fine arts in the United States

15.7. Wen Yiduo's first anthology, *Red Candle*, published by Taidong Press in September 1923

Zhimo and took the position of dean of Beiping Art School. Those who had been to his lodge found Wen painted his walls black with a golden rim, which showed his taste in fine arts. This was why he proposed that the goal of poetry should be to achieve three aspects of beauty, namely musical beauty, pictorial beauty, and architectural beauty. His poems were collected in the anthologies *Stagnant Water* (《死水》) and *Red Candle* (《红烛》). Seeing the living conditions of Chinese people in the United States, he was homesick and wrote "Remembering Chrysanthemum" (《忆菊》), full of meticulous emotions inherent to the Chinese culture. "Ballad of Washing" (《洗衣歌》) criticized social inequality. Back home in China, he saw the backwardness and desolation of the entire nation and shouted: "That's not you, that's not my favorite! / I ask closely the sky, question closely the wind all around, / I asked (fists beat the bare chest of the ground)."[9] He predicted that only reform could revive the nation of China: "There is one sentence that can light fire, / Or, when spoken, bring dire disasters. / Don't think that for five thousand years nobody has said it, / How can you be sure of a volcano's silence? / Perhaps one day, as if possessed by a spirit, / Suddenly out of the blue sky a thunder / Will explode: / 'This is our China!'"[10] Later Wen Yiduo became a modern scholar, and was

---

[9] Wen Yiduo: "Discovery" (《发现》), *Complete Works of Wen Yiduo* (《闻一多全集》), Vol. 3, Beijing: Joint Publishing, 1982, p. 188.

[10] Wen Yiduo: "One Sentence" (《一句话》), *Complete Works of Wen Yiduo*, Vol. 3, Beijing: Joint Publishing, 1982, p. 188. English translation courtesy of Hsu Kai-yu.

assassinated when he took part in democratic activities in the 1940s. His poems were refined and showed respect to forms and patterns, but they were by no means rigid.

Xu Zhimo (1897–1931) was the figure head of poetry in the Crescent Moon school. Having graduated from Peking University, he went to study in the United States and the United Kingdom, and claimed that only Cambridge University (which Xu translated as Kangqiao [康桥]) gave him a real valuable education: "My eyes were opened there, my thirst for knowledge was stirred up there, and my self-consciousness was born there."[11] In Xu's poems, to express his personal emotions the language had a soft and bright texture, and it was not too subtle even if the poet felt gloomy and at a loss. This can be seen in his "I Don't Know Which Direction the Wind Is Blowing" (《我不知道风是在哪一个方向吹》): "I don't know / Which direction the wind is blowing— / I am in a dream, / In the dream's gentle wave lingering. // I don't know / Which direction the wind is blowing— / I am in a dream, / Her tenderness, my ecstasy outbreaking."[12] Influenced by Western liberal ideas, Xu Zhimo also wrote some humanitarian works, such as "Serves You Right, Beggar!" (《叫化活该》), "Mister, Mister" (《先生，先生》), "It Is Not Easy to Live These Days" (《这年头活着不易》), and "Mount Lu Masonry Songs"

15.8. A photo of Xu Zhimo, which he gave to Hu Shi

15.9. The wonderful design of the cover of the original edition of *Poems of Zhimo*

[11] Xu Zhimo: "Smoking and Culture (Oxford)" (《吸烟与文化〈牛津〉》), quoted from *Autobiography of Xu Zhimo* (《徐志摩自传》), Nanjing: Jiangsu Literature and Arts Press, 1997, p. 34.

[12] Xu Zhimo: "I Don't Know Which Direction the Wind Is Blowing," *Complete Poems of Xu Zhimo* (《徐志摩诗全编》), Hangzhou: Zhejiang Literature and Arts Press, 1990, p. 204.

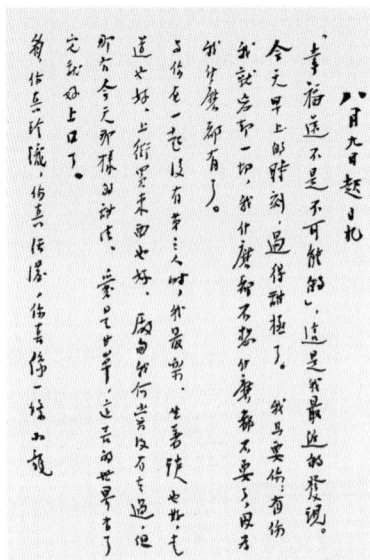

15.10. Page from Xu Zhimo's *Love Mei Notes* (《爱眉小札》) manuscript

15.11. "Special Issue Mourning Zhimo" from *Beichen Garden* (《北晨学园》)

(《庐山石工歌》), etc. But with his fine and delicate language and abundant imagination, Xu was better at writing farewell poems and love poems. "Taking Leave of Cambridge Again" (《再别康桥》) was the most well-known of his poems, in which the language had the free and elegant texture most typical of Xu: "Softly I am leaving, / Just as softly as I came; / I softly wave goodbye, / To the clouds in the western sky."[13] The entire poem created an artistic conception with its gentle and repeated chanting, and using clear and simple language, it gave full expression to the poet's sentiments. Of Xu's well-known short love poems there were "Chance" (《偶然》), "I Come to the Bank of the Yangtze River to Buy a Bunch of Lotus Pods" (《我来到扬子江边买一把莲蓬》), and "Sayonara" (《沙扬娜拉》), etc. Some of his love poems were thought to be not so elegant, although they were actually written from a more personal level, such as "Lovesickness from Far Away" (《两地相思》) and "Don't Pinch Me, Pain" (《别拧我，疼》). The title of the latter seemed a bit erotic, but it never went that far. Xu Zhimo published four anthologies, namely *Poems of Zhimo* (《志摩的诗》), *A Night in Florence* (《翡冷翠的一夜》), *Fierce Tiger* (《猛虎集》), and *Wandering About* (《云游》).

The Crescent Moon school was a poetic school that emerged after Guo Moruo's Whitman-style free verse, and one of its major contributions to China's new poetry was that just after the new poetry gained a foothold, it

---

[13] Xu Zhimo: "Taking Leave of Cambridge Again," *Complete Poems of Xu Zhimo*, Hangzhou: Zhejiang Literature and Arts Press, 1990, p. 317.

advocated such principles as "sensible control of emotions" within the camp of romantic poetry, was opposed to the direct expression of one's feelings, and brought up the matter of reestablishing forms and patterns for new poetry. Zhu Ziqing thus called the Crescent Moon clique a "Western metrical verse school." And some of the Crescent Moon poems featured refined language, neat grammatical structures, and harmonized tunes, which was later referred to as "dried bean-curd style." Some held different views on this poetic style, but it was generally agreed that it complied with the Chinese language system. In 1931 Xu Zhimo died in a plane crash when he took a mail plane from Nanjing to Beiping, and the plane hit a hill in Kaishan near Jinan, Shandong Province. Xu was the core of the Crescent Moon Society, and with his death, the Crescent Moon Society slowly fell apart and disbanded. The very first breakthrough for Chinese new poetry thus drew to a close: the vernacular poetry had found its feet, with free verse and new metrical verse emerging successively.

Almost immediately after new poetry, modern vernacular fictions came onto the literary stage even more aggressively, with short stories taking the lead.

From the late-Qing to the Republican period, the dominant type of fiction was the Mandarin Duck and Butterfly linked-chapter novel. Within this category there were some changes during this time. For example, they began to record the life of common people in large cities; they developed a sense of humanitarianism, began to use vernacular language, and even short stories emerged, but their structure was still that of linked-chapter novels in classical Chinese, and their narrative and composition quite outdated. According to Hu Shi:

> China's men of letters today probably don't understand what is a 'short story.' Nowadays it seems that all kinds of notes and compilations in newspapers and magazines that are not long enough can be called 'short stories.' Therefore, even the clichéd fictions starting with 'there was some guy from somewhere who was talented since his childhood … One day, this guy met a girl when he was visiting some garden; he glanced at her, and was stunned by her beauty …' call themselves 'short stories'![14]

The kind of fiction starting with "there was some guy" could be called "some-guy style" for short, with which today's readers are not so familiar, since we have been reading modern fictions (with elements borrowed from foreign novels) from the very start. If you open a short storytelling script from the Ming dynasty, such as *Tangchun Yu Encountering Adversity But Meeting Her Husband* (《玉堂春落难逢夫》) and *The Jest That Leads to Disaster* (《十五贯戏言成巧祸》), you can see all those stories start with the name, origin,

---

[14] Hu Shi: "On Short Stories" (《论短篇小说》), *New Youth*, Vol. 4, Issue 5, May 1918. The suspension points are quoted from the original text.

and identity of the main character, and there was no exception to this rule, so it had become China's long-standing storytelling and story-listening habit. In 1922, Shen Yanbing criticized that though the fictions of the Republican period used vernacular and "superficially adopted the structure of Western fictions, the narrative and descriptions are all those of old-style Chinese linked-chapter novels." And he also criticized this outdated "bookkeeping style": "In these fictions, each time a character enters for the first time, the author will surely use dozens or even hundreds of characters to describe in a bookkeeping style the features, stature, apparel, and manners of this character."[15] This was a view shared by new literary theorists and authors, and it was how they were determined to reform short stories and make them an entry point to reform Chinese fictions.

The novelists representing this May Fourth turnaround were Lu Xun, Yu Dafu, Ye Shengtao, and Xu Dishan. Lu Xun wrote "The Diary of a Madman," the modern short story in the real sense of this term. In "The True Story of Ah Q," he created an immortal character typical of the inherent weaknesses of Chinese people's national character. He took the lead to write the May Fourth "native-soil fictions," including his well-known works "Kong Yiji," "Hometown," and "Storm in a Teacup," etc. In fact, of all the May Fourth

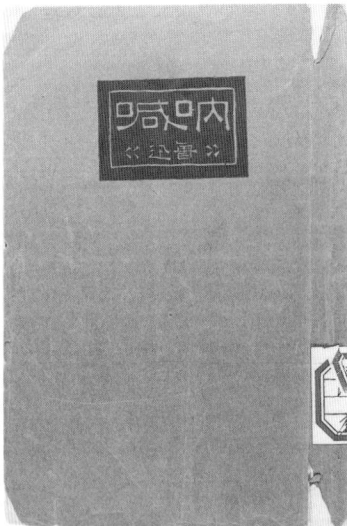

15.12. Original edition of *Call to Arms*, a collection of Lu Xun's short stories, published by Beijing New Tide Press in August 1923

15.13. Public shaming of a prisoner during the late-Qing period. If we look at this picture from Lu Xun's perspective in "A Public Example," we can indeed see the blank and numb faces behind the convict

[15] Mao Dun: "Naturalism and Modern Chinese Novels," *Complete Works of Mao Dun*, Vol. 18, Beijing: People's Literature Press, 1989, pp. 229 and 226.

novelists, Lu Xun experimented with the largest number of forms and styles of short stories, and he was the most creative novelist. In his three small collections of short stories, namely *Call to Arms*, *Wandering*, and *Old Tales Retold* (《故事新编》), there were diary fictions ("The Diary of a Madman"), fictions with prefaces ("The Diary of a Madman" and "The True Story of Ah Q"), documentary fictions ("A Public Example" [《示众》]), psychological fictions ("Soap" [《肥皂》]), fictions exploring Freudian theory ("Mending Heaven" [《补天》]), poetic fictions ("Regret for the Past" [《伤逝》]), prosaic fictions ("The Comedy of Ducks" [《鸭的喜剧》]), and fictions written as one-act Western-style plays ("Raising the Dead" [《起死》]), etc. Interestingly, various kinds of short stories were collected in the original edition of *Call to Arms*, and a dozen years later, when Xiao Hong (萧红) discussed the possibil-

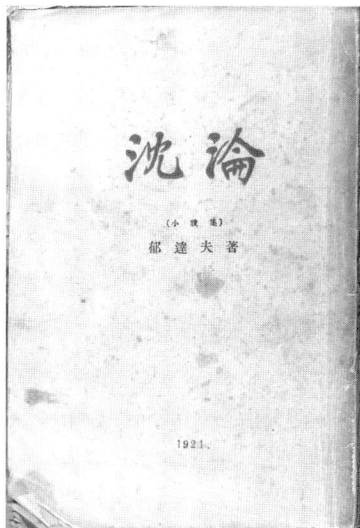

15.14. *Sinking*, a collection of Yu Dafu's short stories, which was published earlier than Lu Xun's *Call to Arms*

ity of "various kinds of fictions" with Nie Gannu in Hong Kong, she took Lu Xun as an example, and listed such miscellaneous fictions as "A Story about Hair" (《头发的故事》) and "The Comedy of Ducks."[16] Lu Xun was indeed the source of all types of modern Chinese fictions.

Yu Dafu (1896–1945) was the pioneer of romantic autobiographical novels. His most important work was "Sinking" (which was the name of the collection as well as of the most important short story in that collection), which told of the loneliness and depression of Chinese students in Japan, the discrimination they felt as nationals of a weak nation, as well as young people's worries and bewilderment concerning sexuality. Yu Dafu gave quite sincere expression to all these entangled political, economic, and physiological suppressions. Since these fictions were based on the author's personal experiences and one can see the author in his characters, it was called autobiographical fiction. His later fictions continued to tell the stories of these displaced people. Some had first-person narrators, as in "Wisteria and Dodder" (《茑萝行》) and "Blue Smoke" (《青烟》); some used omnipotent narrators and called the characters "that person" (伊人), as in "Journey South" (《南迁》); and in some the character was called "Yu Zhifu" (于质夫), as in "Misty Night" (《茫茫夜》) and "Homesick" (《怀乡病者》). Yu Dafu described sexual worries and the conflict between body and soul in his fictions, and was thus attacked by hypocritical moralists for his explicit descriptions. Zhou Zuoren's counterattacks

---

[16] Nie Gannu: "Preface to *Selected Works of Xiao Hong*" (《〈萧红选集〉序》), *Selected Works of Xiao Hong* (《萧红选集》), Beijing: People's Literature Press, 1981, p. 3.

against these conservatives deserve special attention. He refuted those who claimed Yu's fictions were "immoral literature," arguing that "Sinking" was totally different from *Private Records of Studying in Japan* from the late Qing, for the "obscene content" in the latter was "obviously subordinate and insignificant, and the author's attitude was insincere," while "'Sinking' is an artistic literary work."[17] This was the most obvious evidence that the modern turnaround during the May Fourth period was epoch-making, quite different from the accumulation of modernity during the late-Qing period. Yu Dafu was influenced by a complex set of ideas and ideologies, including traditional Chinese sentiments, liberal ideas, and socialism. He imagined himself having the honesty and straightforwardness and unconventionality of old-style men of letters and created the character Huang Zhongze (黄仲则), the ancient poet in "The Quarry" (《采石矶》); he had sympathy with laborers and wrote "A Humble Sacrifice" (《薄奠》, which was about rickshaw coolies) and "A Night in Intoxicating Spring Breeze" (《春风沉醉的晚上》, which was about women laborers). The mature works he wrote in his later years were "The Past" (《过去》) and "Late-Flowering Cassia" (《迟桂花》). A literary talent as he was, Yu Dafu was honest and sincere, which was why Lu Xun preferred Yu Dafu to other writers of the Creation Society.

Ye Shengtao (1894–1988) represented the realistic style of the Literary Research Society. There were a number of realistic novelists in the Literary Research Society following a similar path to Ye Shengtao, starting with the somewhat vague "love" and "beauty," which had something to do with the spirit of the earlier May Fourth period. Later they calmed down and began to perfect their stories based on the real-world life they were familiar with. Ye Shengtao was familiar with the urban citizen class in the cities and towns south of the Yangtze River, and in such short stories as "Food" (《饭》) and "The Headmaster" (《校长》), he revealed the humble life of lower intellectuals with his calm tone and plain description. Talking about Ye Shengtao, what was not given enough attention to in the past was that he combined the satire of reality with the satire of social customs. In "Records of a City" (《某城纪事》) and "Records of a Town" (《某镇纪事》), for example, he gave a vivid account of the absurdities after "revolutionary adventurers" entered the city and the town. Thanks to his mastery of satire, he later wrote such fables as "The Scarecrow" (《稻草人》). Originally Ye Shengtao contributed his stories to the urban literary journals of the Mandarin Duck and Butterfly school, while after he entered the May Fourth literary circle, he began to write about the selfishness and pettiness of urban citizens and established the new literature's long-standing tradition of criticizing urban society.

[17] Zhou Zuoren: "On *Sinking*," *My Own Garden*, Changsha: Yuelu Press, 1987, p. 62.

Xu Dishan (1893–1941) was also an author of the Literary Research Society, but he wrote romantic symbolic fictions. Within the Literary Research Society, these kinds of authors were different from Ye Shengtao in that their fictions were mostly narrations from a subjective point of view. Xu Dishan was a native of Zhangzhou, Fujian Province, and he was born in Taiwan and later returned to the mainland. He was raised in a religious atmosphere of Buddhism and Christianity, and therefore his fictions were rich in picturesque charm, religious experience, and philosophical reflection. Most of his love stories started with a realistic description while ending in a surrealistic realm. The young man and woman in "The Bird of Destiny" rebelled against social norms, and in the end they came to understand the truth in life and committed suicide by sinking in the lake out of frustrated love. The title of the short story "The Spider Hard at Work Making a Net" (《缀网劳蛛》) contained an outlook on life and moral principles, as well as a religious theme. The woman character in this short story held an enduring but persistent attitude toward the world and her sufferings. Xu's later story "Chuntao" (《春桃》) was about a ragpicking woman bravely embracing her disabled husband from whom she had been separated during the war and the man she had later fallen in love with, and there was an invisible religious influence in the woman's attitudes toward everything. Xu Dishan was not an ardent believer, but he studied religious teachings throughout his life. His romantic fictions were unique during the May Fourth period, showing that from its inception, this literary period featured diversity and inclusion.

These breakthroughs made by short story writers ran parallel with the theoretical imports made by Hu Shi, Zhou Zuoren, Shen Yanbing, and others. There were two main sources of literary theory in the May Fourth period: one was the US theories on fiction, the most important being *A Manual of the Art of Fiction* by Clayton Hamilton, which was once used as a popular textbook at Harvard University. Hu Shi's "On Short Stories" drew some viewpoints from this book. Yu Dafu's *On Novels* (《小说论》) drew immediate inspiration from *Sixteen Lectures on the Research of Fiction* (《小说研究十六讲》) by a Japanese writer called Kimura I, but he listed Hamilton's book in his bibliography. Wu Mi's lectures on fiction theories at the Southeast University, as well as the theories on fiction developed by Zhang Ziping, Qu Shiying, Sun Lianggong, and others, all showed some influence from this book. Chinese authors were indirectly enlightened about the principle of the three elements of fictions, namely the character, plot, and setting, and came to understand that fictions should not only tell stories, but should create characters, and it was from then on that they started consciously writing new fictions. Another source of theories on fiction was from France, especially those of Maupassant and Zola about "presenting a section of human life to readers," which began to influence Chinese authors through Shen Yanbing and others of the Literary

Research Society. The May Fourth authors understood the feature of short stories was to write "the most remarkable and extraordinary section or aspect of reality." Comparing the relationship between traditional short stories and modern short stories to their material, we can see that traditional short stories presented a vertically cut longitudinal section, so that "one could not see the entire picture until one read to the last page"; while modern short stories were a "cross-section" like that of a tree cut horizontally, and "if this section was cut in the right place, it could symbolize an individual character, country, or society." In saying this, Hu Shi took Daudet's "The Last Lesson" as an example, arguing that this short story used the last French lesson of primary school as a "cross-section" to show the big picture of a historical event: France losing the Franco-Prussian War and having to cede territory to Prussia.[18] Shen Yanbing said: "The purpose of short stories is to choose a section of life to show the entire human circumstance."[19] If readers had learned to appreciate modern short stories with their "cross-sections," *Short Stories from Abroad*, translated by Lu Xun and his brother, would not have been so poorly received. Chinese readers were used to reading "longitudinal sections," and at first they could not accept modern short stories that "ended immediately after the start." Nevertheless, thanks to the leading experiments of May Fourth authors, they would sooner or later change their habit of fiction reading. Indeed, the forming of the genre of the modern short story played a vital role in the shaping of modern Chinese literature.

[18] For all the quotations, see Hu Shi: "On Short Stories."
[19] Mao Dun: "Naturalism and Modern Chinese Novels," p. 230.

SIXTEEN

A HISTORY OF THE DISSEMINATION AND ACCEPTANCE OF *THE TRUE STORY OF AH Q*

A S THE HIGHEST PEAK OF MAY fourth literary creations, Lu Xun's magnum opus, *The True Story of Ah Q*, deserves its glory. By the end of the twentieth century, in various questionnaires on China's "One Hundred Years of Literary Works," among the general public as well as literary scholars, *The True Story of Ah Q* ranks No. 1 without exception. How this great literary work was gradually accepted by readers of the world is doubtless a living history of how readers become part of the shaping of literary canon.

The publication and dissemination of the Chinese edition of this fiction was not complicated. It was first serialized in the "Supplement of the *Morning Post*" on December 4, 1921 for the newly launched column Entertaining Remarks at the request of Sun Fuyuan (who was to become the editor-in-chief of this supplement after Li Dazhao), a student of Lu Xun

16.1. *The True Story of Ah Q*, first serialized in the Entertaining Remarks (开心话) column of the "Supplement of the *Morning Post*" on December 4, 1921

when he taught at Shaoxing Junior Teachers' School. At that time, it was published under the pseudonym "Ba Ren" (巴人), meaning "low-brow literature," or in Chinese, "下里巴人" (*xia-li-ba-ren*).[1] The novel was serialized as Lu Xun wrote it, which was quite a rare case for him. Originally neither the author nor the editor thought about the fate of the work, but soon after, the image of Ah Q changed and seemed to no longer be that of an ordinary lovable peasant. Sun Fuyuan saw that this literary work was not a humorous story in its usual sense, and from the second chapter, it was moved to the New Literature and Art column. Thus it was serialized every week or every two weeks, with the last installment published on February 12 the following year, in which the vagrant character Ah Q carelessly drew a circle in the grand hall and was executed by a captain of the "revolutionary party," hence the grand finale of the story. The characterization, structure, and narrative tone of *The True Story of Ah Q* were partly related to the way it was originally published. When Lu Xun's short story collection *Call to Arms* was published in 1923, *The True Story of Ah Q* was incorporated, and it was never removed from the various editions of *Call to Arms*. It was then included in the first *Complete Works of Lu Xun* published in Shanghai by the Restoration Society during the Isolated Island (孤岛) period in 1938, as well as in all kinds of complete works, selected works, and collections of Lu Xun since then. *The True Story of Ah Q* was a 20,000-character novella, not lengthy enough to be published as a separate edition (later there were separate editions with illustrations and phonetic symbols), but it excited the interest of readers and had a great impact on Chinese society even before its last installment was published. Lu Xun himself had noticed a story by Gao Yihan that appeared in the Casual Talks column of *Contemporary Critique*:

> I remember when each installment of *The True Story of Ah Q* came out, many people were full of fear. They were afraid that the reproach would later fall on their heads. Moreover, there was a friend who told me directly that one paragraph in yesterday's *True Story* seemed to be reprimanding him. Subsequently, he guessed that the author of *True Story* was so and so. How so? It was because only so and so knew about this private affair of his … When he found out the name of the author of *True Story*, he finally realized that they weren't acquainted in the least. He was suddenly enlightened by this and explained to everyone he met that the work wasn't rebuking him.[2]

Such a small bureaucrat-style self-exposing response was an essential part of the earliest history of readers' acceptance of *The True Story of Ah Q*, which certainly had something to do with the Chinese people's habit of taking it

---

[1]   Lu Xun: "How *The True Story of Ah Q* Was Written" (《〈阿Q正传〉的成因》), *Complete Works of Lu Xun*, Vol. 3, Beijing: People's Literature Press, p. 378.

[2]   Han Lu (涵庐, aka Gao Yihan): Casual Talks column, *Contemporary Critique*, Vol. 4, Issue 89, 1926. Lu Xun quoted some paragraphs of this essay in his "How *The True Story of Ah Q* Was Written."

personally when reading novels, but it also served as evidence of the impact of the image of Ah Q. The dissemination of *The True Story of Ah Q* after that point is tantamount to a history of how readers accepted the Ah Q type.

In the 1920s, once the image of Ah Q appeared in print, Lu Xun's contemporary authors immediately recognized his value. Mao Dun was the most sensitive to this, and he began discussing the story in the Correspondence column of *Fiction Monthly* just after the fourth chapter had been published in the *Morning Post*. Some readers felt that "the author's satire is quite biting, while it seems too sharp to be true," but Mao Dun was more far-sighted, saying: "When I read this fiction, I always felt Ah Q was so familiar. Yes, he is the crystallization of the moral character of Chinese people!"[3] Mao Dun saw that the image of Ah Q served as the epitome of Chinese people. Later in his "Reading *Call to Arms*" (《读〈呐喊〉》) and "On Lu Xun" (《鲁迅论》), he further argued that "Ah Q is the crystallization of 'deficient' Chinese people," and Ah Q's "method of spiritual victory" was shared by many;[4] he raised the important concept of the "Ah Q image" and further expanded this concept: "I also feel that the 'Ah Q image' is not necessarily a totally special fixture of the Chinese race. It seems to be a kind of universal weakness of humanity."[5] The analysis was somewhat shallow, but he unconsciously predicted the major points of bewilderment of people when they tried to understand this most important character type of modern Chinese literature in the years that followed. In the same year the novel was published, Hu Shi praised Lu Xun as an author to symbolize the fact that "the genre of short story has gradually formed" in Chinese vernacular literature (later it was considered a novella), and that "from 'The Diary of a Madman' published four years ago to *The True Story of Ah Q* published recently, [Lu Xun] has not written too much, but generally none of his works is poorly written."[6] At that time, it was not known to many that "Ba Ren" was Lu Xun, and Zhou Zuoren, claiming that he knew the author quite well, revealed the origin of *The True Story of Ah Q*, including its purpose of "irony" and "cold satire"; he regarded it "belonging to reasonable literature, a classical-style realistic work," "indeed a posture of idealism"; and he gave a preliminary analysis of its origin, saying it "lies in foreign short stories. Most obvious of these works are those by Russia's Gogol and Poland's Sienkiewicz, and the influence of Japan's Natsume Soseki and Mori Ogai is not small"; but the character of Ah Q "is a national type," and he pointed

---

[3]   Tan Guotang, Yanbing (Mao Dun): "Correspondence," *Fiction Monthly*, Vol. 13, Issue 2, Feburary 1922.

[4]   Fang Bi (方璧, Mao Dun): "On Lu Xun," *Fiction Monthly*, Vol. 18, Issue 11, November 1927.

[5]   Yanbing (Mao Dun): "Reading *Call to Arms*," published in "Lamp of Learning," supplement of the *Shanghai China Times*, October 8, 1923.

[6]   Hu Shi: "Fifty Years of Chinese Literature" (《五十年来之中国文学》), *Memorial Volume of the Fiftieth Anniversary of Shun Pao* (《申报五十周年纪念册》), March 1922.

out that the character was based on "a really lovable Ah Gui," who was still alive.[7] Even Lu Xun's political opponents, such as Chen Xiying with whom he had become enemies with during the "Peking Women's Normal College Event," said impartially in his "Ten Works Since the New Literary Movement" (《新文学运动以来的十部著作》) that: "Ah Q is not only a type, Ah Q is a lively person, a character as lively and interesting as Li Kui, Lu Zhishen, and Liu Laolao, and maybe will be as eternal as these."[8] These contemporaries of Lu Xun truly understood literature and had a historical perspective, and they all attached great importance to the symbolic significance of Ah Q.

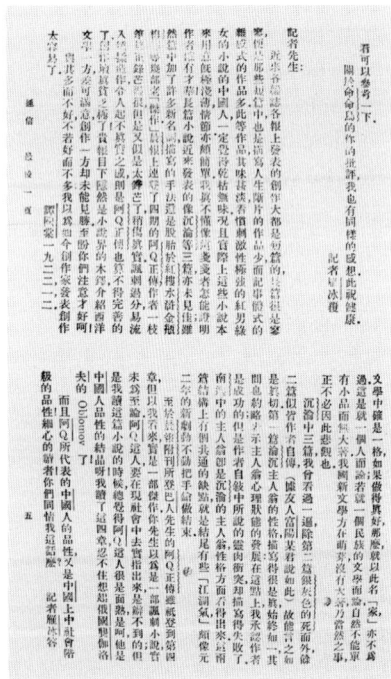

16.2. The correspondence between Yanbing and a reader called Tan Guotang on *The True Story of Ah Q*, published in *Fiction Monthly* (Vol. 13, Issue 2, Feb. 10, 1922). Mao Dun can be regarded as the first person to comment on *The True Story of Ah Q*

Between 1925 and 1926, the various commentaries on *The True Story of Ah Q* did not fall into silence, but became even more heated due to the response from the rest of the world. According to Cao Jinghua, it was he who introduced *The True Story of Ah Q* to a young Russian man called B. A. Vasilyev (Б. А. Васильев), who, after reading it, was eager to translate the work into Russian. Then "after the first draft of his translation was finished, he listed all his questions and difficulties in detail. I wrote a letter to Lu Xun, with Vasilyev's letter attached."[9] Today we can read the letter written by Vasilyev to Cao Jinghua in Chinese during the time he was translating the work, suggesting to ask Lu Xun to write a preface for Russian readers and provide a biographical sketch and photos, etc.[10] This was why Lu Xun wrote "Preface and Author's Commentary to the Russian Translation of *The True Story of Ah Q*" (《俄文译本〈阿Q正传〉序及著者自叙传略》).

Thus the author became a part of the trend to interpret his own work. Most importantly, he explained that his main purpose for writing the story of Ah Q was to "rouse the impenetrable

---

[7] Zhong Mi (仲密, Zhou Zuoren): "On the True Story of Ah Q," published in the "Supplement of the *Morning Post*," March 19, 1922.

[8] Chen Xiying: "Ten Works Since the New Literary Movement (Part 1)," *The Causeries of Xiying* (《西滢闲话》), Shanghai: Crescent Moon Bookstore, 1928, p. 339.

[9] Cao Jinghua: "Seems Like the First Swallow of Spring" (《好似春燕第一只》), *Flowers* (《花》), Beijing: The Writers Publishing House (作家出版社), 1964, p. 135.

[10] The letter written in Chinese by Vasilyev on April 17, 1925, was published in the "Supplement" of *Beijing Press* (《京报副刊》) on June 16 of the same year.

and silent spirit of the people of ancient China," and expressed his depression at not being understood by people when he wrote about "the Chinese life I have witnessed." He wrote:

> After my story was published, it first received the censure of a young critic; later some considered it sick, some considered it comical, some considered it satirical or perhaps ironical, and I even came to the point that I suspected that there lay hidden in my heart a terrible block of ice.[11]

This was Lu Xun's "loneliness." According to relevant research, the critics Lu Xun viewed negatively here were Cheng Fangwu, Zhang Dinghuang (张定璜), Feng Wenbing (冯文炳), and Zhou Zuoren (by this time the brothers had become enemies), among others. Later, Qian Xingcun (钱杏邨) stubbornly insisted that "Ah Q's image has already become extinct, as have the techniques used in *The True Story of Ah Q*," that Lu Xun's Ah Q was limited to the

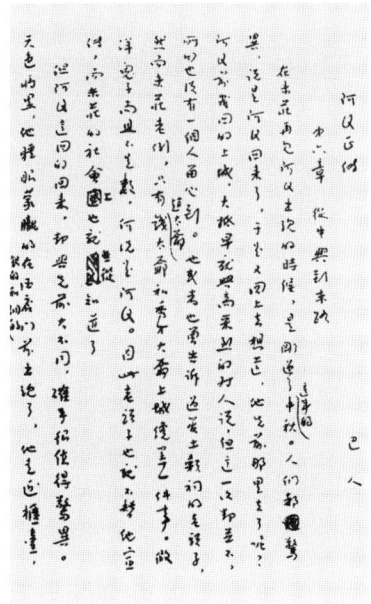

16.3. Page of the manuscript for *The True Story of Ah Q*

period from the late Qing to the Xinhai Revolution, and the image of Ah Q could not even represent the May Fourth period, let alone the time after the May Thirtieth movement.[12] For the left-wing revolutionaries, the image of Ah Q had a very short lifespan, which proved to be wrong in later history. These people only cared about their so-called revolution, and were so detached from China's peasants, land, and history. Lu Xun certainly hoped to be understood by "other" readers, which he expressed in his preface to Vasilyev's Russian translation (not published until 1929). By 1926, Lu Xun wrote at the end of his essay "How *The True Story of Ah Q* Was Written" that he had seen the French and English translations. The French translation was published in *Europe* in 1925, and the translator, Jing Yinyu (敬隐渔), had sent his translation to the great French writer Romain Rolland, whose comments, "a piece of realistic and ironic art" and "Ah Q's suffering face will always have a place in my memory" were no small praises.[13] The Japanese translation was published a bit later, but it was retranslated into Japanese many times afterward, showing how much attention the people of this neighboring country to China's east gave to Ah Q.

---

[11] Lu Xun: "Preface and Author's Commentary to the Russian Translation of *The True Story of Ah Q*," *Complete Works of Lu Xun*, Vol. 7, Beijing: People's Literature Press, p. 82.

[12] Qian Xingcun (Ah Ying): "The Bygone Age of Ah Q" (《死去了的阿Q时代》), originally published in the *Sun Monthly* (《太阳月刊》), March 1928.

[13] Bo Sheng (柏生): "*Romain Rolland's Critique of Lu Xun*," published in the "Supplement" of *Beijing Press*, March 2, 1926, which quoted Romain Rolland's words.

16.4. Illustration on the title page of the Russian edition of *The True Story of Ah Q*

16.5. An English–Chinese edition of *The True Story of Ah Q*

Within the Chinese border, meanwhile, more general readers began to see the importance of *The True Story of Ah Q*, and thus the adaptation of *The True Story of Ah Q* began. The documented earliest spoken drama adaptation was the six-act play adapted by Chen Mengshao (陈梦韶) in 1929. In 1934, when Yuan Muzhi (袁牧之) was editing "Theater" (《戏》), the weekly supplement of the *China Daily News* (《中华日报》), his script entitled *The True Story of Ah Q* was serialized in the weekly. These were multiple-act spoken drama plays, and they were very close to the original text, with few rewritings carried out on the plot. However, even before Lu Xun died, he had already found out what was wrong with these playwrights' understanding of the image of Ah Q. Then there were many people trying to create a portrait of Ah Q, and it became a chance for many young artists to demonstrate their artistic skills. Lu Xun was an active advocate of woodcut paintings, and some young woodcut artists began their career by producing illustrations for Lu Xun's literary works. Lu Xun himself had collected ten woodcut paintings of *The True Story of Ah Q* by Chen Tiegeng (陈铁耕) and once sent them to Yuan Muzhi to be used in the *Theater* weekly. These were well documented. Liu Xian (刘岘) was one of these woodcut artists; when he was young, he cut illustrations for *Call to Arms* and had planned to cut for *Midnight*. He was quite ambitious when he began to cut illustrations for *The True Story of Ah Q*, and wanted to cut 200 paintings, so as to "translate the text into pictures and help illiterates understand the character Ah Q."[14] As a left-wing artist advocating popularization, he obviously had a strong sense of purpose. What Liu Xian actually did was much

---

[14] Liu Xian: "Postcript to *Illustrations for The True Story of Ah Q*" (《〈阿Q正传〉插图后记》), *Illustrations for The True Story of Ah Q* (《〈阿Q正传〉插图》), Shanghai: Weiming Woodcut House, 1935.

less impressive, his *Illustrations for The True Story of Ah Q* published by Weiming Woodcut House (未名木刻社) in 1935 only had twenty paintings, and in his "Postscript" he mentioned his own problem, exactly the same with those who adapted the story into spoken drama plays. In fact, after seeing the first two paintings he cut, Lu Xun had written to him and told him: "The appearance of Ah Q is not good enough; it is more like Mr. Zhao." As Liu Xian began to cut illustrations for *Call to Arms*, Lu Xun had advised him: "In my mind, the appearance of Ah Q should be less bully-like. In my hometown such fierce-looking men could live like a parasite and there was no need for them to work. Mr. Zhao can look like this."[15] In both cases Lu Xun contrasted Ah Q with Mr. Zhao and made it clear that these two characters were fun

16.6. "Ah Q Being Executed," a woodcut painting by Liu Xian

damentally different, but the young Liu Xian did not get the point. Later, Lu Xun made this famous remark in his letter to the editor of the *Theater* weekly, giving his own insightful explanation of his character, Ah Q:

> I saw several portraits of Ah Q in your weekly and felt them too unusual, or even weird. In my opinion, Ah Q should be an ordinary-looking man around thirty years old, with peasant-style simplicity and dimwittedness, but had learned some shrewdness of idle layabouts. In Shanghai, one could easily see this kind of person among coachmen and rickshaw pullers, but he should not look like a bully, nor a tramp. Once you put a skullcap on his head, you lose the essence of Ah Q. I remember I gave him a felt hat.[16]

The person who painted Ah Q wearing a skullcap was Ye Lingfeng (叶灵凤), but even those who were so close to Lu Xun, like the young artist Liu Xian, would paint Ah Q as a person with a fierce look or looking like a bully, so it was not an easy task to get the essence of the character Ah Q. Actually, readers of the 1930s had already recognized Ah Q as a national type, and had begun to understand the significance of this peasant embodying the universal weaknesses of the human race. As for the inherent weaknesses of Chinese people, it was generally agreed that "servility" was the core of Ah Q's character traits. For example, Su Xuelin once listed in detail all "inherent weaknesses of Chinese people alluded to in *The True Story of*

---

[15] See Liu Xian: "Postcript to *Illustrations for The True Story of Ah Q*."

[16] Lu Xun: "Letter to the Editor of *Theater* Weekly" (《寄〈戏〉周刊编者信》), *Complete Works of Lu Xun*, Vol. 6, Beijing: People's Literature Press, 1981, p. 150.

16.7. Ah Q in a traditional Chinese painting by Jiang Zhaohe (蒋兆和)

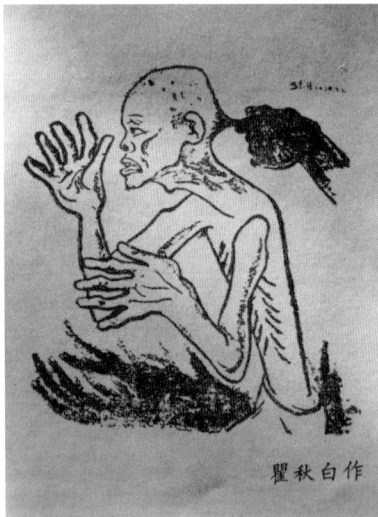

16.8. Cartoon of Ah Q by Qu Qiubai

Ah Q," including "cowardliness," "spiritual victory," "opportunism," "exaggeration mania and self-respect addiction," "sex mania," "shamanistic moralism," "full of taboos," "shrewdness," "dimwittedness," "miserliness and greed," "reliance on chance," "seeking pleasure in spectatorship," "muddleheadedness," and "apathetic," etc.[17] But the fact was generally ignored that Ah Q was a vagrant working for others; he was a poor peasant with vices, but not a bully. In understanding Ah Q, it was easier for most readers of that period to find his universality, but they had some doubts about the individuality of this specific peasant, and did not fully understand the author's sympathy and pity toward this character. Therefore, Lu Xun repeatedly said that "I believe *The True Story of Ah Q* hasn't the essentials to be adapted to the stage or cinema because as soon as it goes on stage, all that is left is the farcical."[18] It was because he saw the collective misunderstanding of the general public that Lu Xun had to express his own opinion, and hoped to correct such misunderstandings. He accurately predicted how his character would be accepted by the public in the future.

After Lu Xun died, under the guidance of the imported "theory of the type," the character of Ah Q as a type versus Ah Q as an individual had long been a focus of debate. In the late 1930s and 1940s, Lu Xun was remembered and his work garnered increasingly higher praise. *The True Story of Ah Q* was again popularized, and it became a major concern among intellectuals about how to interpret this "type." The Ah Q portrayed by Jiang Zhaohe (1938) was thin and there was nothing comic in him; Jiang tended to guide people to understand the helplessness of this peasant. Qu Qiubai created a cartoon of Ah Q that was published after both he

---

[17] Su Xuelin: "*The True Story of Ah Q* and Lu Xun's Creative Art" (《〈阿Q正传〉及鲁迅创作的艺术》), *National News Weekly* (《国闻周报》),Vol. 11, Issue 44, November 5, 1934.

[18] Lu Xun's letter to Wang Qiaonan on October 13, 1930, *Complete Works of Lu Xun*, Vol. 12, Beijing: People's Literature Press, 1981, p. 26.

16.9. Portrait of deceased Ah Q by Feng Zikai, which was closest to Lu Xun's original idea of this character

16.10. "An Illustrated Story of Ah Q" by Ding Cong (丁聪), who captured the complexity of this character

himself and Lu Xun had passed away (1939); in this portrait Ah Q had a skinny body and huge hands, which highlighted his identity as a suppressed farmworker, but this skeleton-like Ah Q also looked quite weird. Another cartoon of Ah Q, by Feng Zikai (1939), was the closest to Lu Xun's original idea about this character: the patchy clothes and girdle showed Ah Q's social status, that he had to make a living by working; his ringworm scars and thick lips, his posture of putting his hands on his back, his scolding expression showed not only his perverseness but also his rebellion, and the expression in his eyes revealed the dissatisfaction and fear deep in his heart. Feng Zikai seemed familiar with the appearance and psychology of peasants in the Zhejiang area. Later in the 1940s, Liu Jian'an (刘建庵), Guo Shiqi (郭士奇), and Ding Cong all created illustration strips of Ah Q, and each had its strengths and weaknesses: Liu and Guo gave more weight to Ah Q's vices, while Ding Cong's Ah Q had the appearance of a complex literary character with his anger, cowardice, brag, and depression (1946). On the first anniversary of Lu Xun's death, an excellent opportunity to adapt *The True Story of Ah Q*, there was a report from abroad that in 1937 a US playwright had adapted this short story and the play was performed in New York; back in China, Xu Xingzhi (许幸之) and Tian Han broke through the restriction of the story of Ah Q per se, and incorporated most characters in Lu Xun's earlier novels in the same scene. The spoken drama plays of the same title adapted by these two had some resonance in that year, including favorable and unfavorable comments. From the critiques we can see that compared with the time when the novel was first published, people had made some progress in their understanding of Ah Q, and had absorbed the opinions of Lu Xun himself. For example, some people pointed out that "Xu Xingzhi's Ah Q took part in the revolution for profit, which, like other parts of his adaptation, made Ah Q a sheer laughing stock, a fool. Ah Q was indeed greedy, but he knew the consequence of joining the revolutionary army would be the death of his whole family. The reason he welcomed revolution was that even the famous scholar-master in the area feared the revolution, and the panicked expressions on the face of petty men and women in Weichuang made him happy." Even by today's standard, this understanding of the relationship between Ah Q and revolution is insightful. As for the "biggest weakness" of Tian Han's script, it was that "he forgets about the spectators of the execution of Ah Q, which was extremely significant in the original text. The author of the original text never forgot that human beings can be cruel,"[19] a view of someone who had largely understood Lu Xun.

In the 1950s, the academic research of Lu Xun and his works began. There were debates between three camps on the image of Ah Q: that Ah Q was a "ideological type" represented by Feng Xuefeng (冯雪峰, see his "On *The True Story of Ah Q*"); the theory of "common name" represented by He Qifang (何其芳, see his "On Ah Q," insisting that Ah Q was the common name of all methods of spiritual victory); and the theory of "typical characters' zeitgeist and place in society" represented by Li Xifan (李希凡 his "Questioning New Theories of Typicality" [《典型新论质疑》], etc.) The debates went nowhere, but Li Xifan's view was the dominating ideology of that time, and thus there were two basic understandings of Ah Q; those who agreed with this view held a social class-oriented understanding, and those who did not totally agree with him, a human nature-oriented one. Most scholars may sympathize with the views of Feng Xuefeng and He Qifang, but whenever there was a political campaign and even self-preservation became an issue, when it was simply better to be more leftist than rightist, even Feng and He had no choice but to review their "mistakes," not to say their sympathizers. Under the influence of this atmosphere, there was an interesting phenomenon that showed through in the portraits of Ah Q from the mid-1950s to the 1960s: in Lu Xun's text, Ah Q was "listless and lean," and "as thin and weak as his opponent [young D]," and in the past Ah Q had been portrayed as skinny, but in Gu Bingxin (顾炳鑫) and Cheng Shifa's portraits, Ah Q became strong! They rendered Ah Q as a normal young peasant, walking on the road or in the market, but much younger and stronger; so much so that without reading the caption one could hardly recognize it was the same Ah Q. This was the prevailing "social class" approach to Ah Q as a representative of the poor peasant class, which tried to dig out a kind of revolutionary enthusiasm for farmers from the character Ah Q.

[19] For both quotations, see Ouyang Fanhai (欧阳凡海): "On Two Scripts of *The True Story of Ah Q*" (《评两个〈阿Q正传〉的剧本》), *Literature*, Vol. 9, Issue 2, August 1937.

During the past twenty years, people have made great progress in understanding Ah Q from a modern perspective. Some have analyzed the image of Ah Q with the system theory (see Lin Xingzhai [林兴宅]: "A System Analysis of Ah Q's Personality" [《论阿Q性格系统》]);[20] some have tried to explain the character from the relationship between Lu Xun and modernism (see Yan Zhen [阎真]: "Understanding Ah Q: Outside the Bounds of Modernism" [《理解阿Q：在现实主义界柱之外》]),[21] and some have tried to look at Ah Q from a broader perspective of world literature and have suggested that Ah Q was a spiritual archetype (see Zhang Mengyang [张梦阳]: *A New Interpretation of Ah Q: Ah Q and the Problem of Spiritual Archetype in World Literature* [《阿Q与世界文学中的精神典型

16.11. Illustration of *The True Story of Ah Q* by Cheng Shifa (程十发), in which Ah Q became stronger than he should be. Cheng had his own style, but was restricted by the ideology of that time

16.12. Stage photo of the spoken drama *The True Story of Ah Q*, directed by Yu Cun (于村) and Wen Xingyu (文兴宇), and first performed by the Central Experimental Modern Drama Theater on August 30, 1981. The script was written by Chen Baichen (陈白尘). Ah Q was played by Lei Kesheng (雷恪生)

16.13. Stage photo of the spoken drama *The True Story of Ah Q*, performed by the Drama Research Society of the National Southwestern Associated University (西南联大戏剧研究社) in 1940

[20] This is an article in *Lu Xun Research Monthly* (《鲁迅研究》) published by Lu Xun Museum, Issue 11, 1984.
[21] *Collection of Yan Zhen* (《阎真文集》), Vol. 5, Beijing: People's Literature Press, 2012.

16.14. Qiu Sha and Wang Weijun painted the most impressive Ah Q

16.15. Side-profile portrait of Ah Q by Zhao Yannian

16.16. Ah Q on his way to be executed, as portrayed by Yan Han

问题》]).[22] These were all attempts to make a clear break with the past analysis of "ideological type," but it was not an easy task. The overseas research has also attracted much attention, which has filled the gap in mainland China's interpretation of Ah Q in two respects: the first concerns the process of writing of this serialized novella, in which Lu Xun's purpose, mood, and method had changed and this had caused some defects; for example, the story of Ah Q started as a "comic episode" but ended with a "tragic destiny," and Lu Xun "apparently never bothered to correct the resultant incongruity of tone in his story" (literary critic Hsia Chih-Tsing's view, see his *A History of Modern Chinese Fiction* [《中国现代小说史》]).[23] The second analyzed the narrative technique of *The True Story of Ah Q* by expounding the relationship between tradition and modernity. By 1981, the 100th anniversary of Lu Xun's birth, various adaptations of this story in the form of film, spoken drama, ballet, and modern dance opera emerged and rendered this character extremely complex. In all these years, painters joined this trend of interpretation of Ah Q with even more enthusiasm and commitment. Take the painting of the execution of Ah Q by Yan Han for example; it paid special attention to the eyes of the character, which, as a window to his heart, showed everything inside Ah Q at that last moment: emptiness, fear, and absence of soul. Ah Q saw that the spectators (who did not appear in the painting but were felt by viewers) had the "wolf's eyes, fierce yet cowardly, gleaming like two will-o'-the-wisps," and "his whole body was being scattered like so much light dust." This was a painting

[22] Zhang Mengyang: *A New Interpretation of Ah Q: Ah Q and the Problem of Spiritual Archetype in World Literature*, Xi'an: Shaanxi Education Press, 1996.

[23] Hsia Chih-tsing: "Literary Revolution," *A History of Modern Chinese Fiction*, translated by Liu Shaoming (刘绍铭), Shanghai: Fudan University Press, 2005, chapter 1.

that penetrated into the soul, and was unprecedented in the paintings of Ah Q. Zhao Yannian's (赵延年) side-profile portrait of Ah Q showed a spiritual victory with its leering glare, but that was also a blank face, and his long queue accorded with Lu Xun's metaphor of the English letter "Q" in his name. The painting of Ah Q by Qiu Sha (裘沙) and Wang Weijun (王伟君) was indeed perfect in both form and spirit. His appearance was exactly that of a perverse vagrant peasant of the Xinhai period, and the pencil sketching conveyed the suppressive atmosphere of that time, showcasing the painters' broad point of view. Their painting showed that Ah Q "had never forgotten that wolf's eyes" before his death, and the fearful glaring eyes of Ah Q in that iron room just before his death were the expression of his real soul.

Such is a brief summary of the acceptance of *The True Story of Ah Q* over the past 100 years.

TABLE 16.1 *Major Chinese and foreign language versions and adapted and illustrated versions of* The True Story of Ah Q

Version	Author, adaptor, translator	Time of publishing	Publisher
First installment of *The True Story of Ah Q*	Ba Ren (Lu Xun)	Dec. 1921 to Feb. 1922	"Supplement of the *Morning Post*"
First publishing of *The True Story of Ah Q*	Lu Xun	Aug. 1923	In *Call to Arms*, by Beijing New Tide Society
French version of *The True Story of Ah Q*	Excerpts translated by Jing Yinyu (敬隐渔, aka J. B. Yn-Yu Kyn)	May 1926	*Europe* magazine, published by Rieder House in Paris
The True Story of Ah Q	Lu Xun	Oct. 1926	In *Call to Arms*, by Beijing Beixin Press
English version of *The True Story of Ah Q*	Translated by George Kin Leung	First published in 1926	Commercial Press in Shanghai
Russian version of *The True Story of Ah Q*	Translated by B. A. Vasilyev	1929	Leningrad High Wave Press
Russian version of *The True Story of Ah Q*	Translated by M. D. Kokin (взведенный)	1929	*Collection of Contemporary Chinese Novellas and Short Stories*, published by Molodaia Gvardia, Gosudarstvenaaja Biblioteka SSSR

(continued)

TABLE 16.1 *(continued)*

Version	Author, adaptor, translator	Time of publishing	Publisher
Script of a six-act spoken drama of *The True Story of Ah Q*	Script written by Chen Mengshao	Oct. 1931	Shanghai Hua Tung Book Company
Japanese version of *The True Story of Ah Q*	Translated by Lin Shouren (Yamagami Masayoshi)	Oct. 1931	Shiroku Shoin
Japanese version of *The True Story of Ah Q*	Translated by Koubai Inoue	Nov. 1932	The one-volume *Complete Works of Lu Xun*, published by Kaizosha
Spoken drama of *The True Story of Ah Q*	Adapted by Yuan Mei (袁梅, or Yuan Muzhi)	1934	*Theater* weekly
Japanese version of *The True Story of Ah Q*	Translated by Haruo Sato and Masuda Wataru	1935	*Complete Works of Lu Xun*, one title of the "Iwanami book series" published by Iwanami Shoten
English version of *The True Story of Ah Q*	Translated by Wang Jizhen (王际真)	1935	*China Press* monthly, New York, Vol. 2, Issues 2–4
Illustrations of *The True Story of Ah Q*	Painted by Liu Xian	1935	Twenty woodcut paintings, published by Weiming Woodcut House
Six-act play of *The True Story of Ah Q*	Script written by Xu Xingzhi	Apr. to May 1937	*Light* (《光明》), Vol. 2, Issues 10–12, published by Shanghai Bright Press in 1939
Five-act play of *The True Story of Ah Q*	Script written by Tian Han	May to June 1937	*Drama Times* (《戏剧时代》), Vol. 1, Issues 1–2, published by Hankou Times Press in 1937
Czech version of *The True Story of Ah Q*	Translated by Jaroslav Průšek	1937	*Call to Arms*, published by People's Culture Press, Bragg
The True Story of Ah Q collected in *Complete Works of Lu Xun* for the first time	Edited by Mr. Lu Xun Memorial Committee	Aug. 1938	Restoration Society in Shanghai, Complete Works of Lu Xun Press

(continued)

TABLE 16.1 *(continued)*

Version	Author, adaptor, translator	Time of publishing	Publisher
Script of the Japanese spoken drama of *The True Story of Ah Q*	Script written by Tian Han, translated by Lin Shouren (Yamagami Masayoshi)	Nov. 1938	*Kaizo* (Reconstruction) in Tokyo
Russian version of *The True Story of Ah Q*	Revised by Rodolfo(?) (Родольфо) Emi Xiao, and Springchin(?) (Сортированный Лин Цинь)	1938	Institute of Oriental Culture of the Social Academy of Sciences, Moscow
Cartoon strip of Ah Q	Painted by Shi Tie'er (史铁儿, aka Qu Qiubai)	1939	*The Contemporaries* (《现代》), Issue 7, 1939
Cartoon strips of *The True Story of Ah Q*	Painted by Feng Zikai	1939	Fifty-three cartoon strips, published by Shanghai Kaiming Bookstore
English–Chinese edition of *The True Story of Ah Q*	Lu Xun	Jan. 1941	Contemporary Comments Press, Hong Kong
Vietnamese version of *The True Story of Ah Q*	Translated by Đặng Thai Mai	1943	*Thanh Nghi* magazine
Portrait of Ah Q	Painted by Liu Jian'an	1943	Fifty woodcut paintings, published by Guilin Yuanfang Bookstore
Russian version of *The True Story of Ah Q*	Translated by Vladimir Kokovtsov	1945	*Complete Works of Lu Xun*, published by Moscow State Literature Publishing House
Pictorial story of Ah Q	Painted by Guo Shiqi	1946	Thirty cartoon strips, published by Qingdao Aiguang Press
Illustrations of *The True Story of Ah Q*	Painted by Ding Cong	1946	Twenty-four cartoon strips, published by Shanghai Publishing Company
Russian version of *The True Story of Ah Q* (illustrations painted by Ding Cong)	Translated by Vladimir Kokovtsov	1947	Moscow Times Press

(continued)

TABLE 16.1 *(continued)*

Version	Author, adaptor, translator	Time of publishing	Publisher
Seven-act Yunnan opera play of *The True Story of Ah Q*	Script written by Meng Jin (孟晋)	1949	Experimental Theater of the Education Department of Yunnan Province, Kunming
Japanese version of *The True Story of Ah Q*	Translated by Yoshimi Takeuchi	May 1953	Three-Volume *Selected Works of Lu Xun*, published by Chikuma Shobo, Tokyo
French version of *The True Story of Ah Q*	Translated by Paul Gamade	1953	Editeurs Francais Reunis
German version of *The True Story of Ah Q*	Translated by Erta Nann and Richard Rung	1954	Paul Lister Press, Leipzig
Russian version of *The True Story of Ah Q*	Translated and adpated by Aldrin(?) (Олдрин)	1955	*The True Story of Ah Q and Other Novels*, published by Soviet Union National Children's Publishing House
Farce version of *The True Story of Ah Q*	Script written by Nan Wei (南薇), costume designed by Zhang Leping (张乐平)	1956	Shanghai Ta Kung Farce Troupe, Ah Q played by Yang Huasheng (杨华生)
Spoken drama of the "Grand Finale of Ah Q"	Script written by Zuolin (佐临)	1956	Actor's Training Program by the Shanghai Film Studio, Ah Q played by Xiang Kun (项堃)
Filmscript of *The True Story of Ah Q*	Script written by Xu Yan (许炎) and Xu Chi (徐迟)	1958	Great Wall Pictorial Press, Shanghai
Illustrations of *The True Story of Ah Q*	Painted by Gu Bingxin	1959	Eight prints, published by Shanghai People's Fine Arts Publishing House
Four-act farce of *The True Story of Ah Q*	Script written by Lu Qun (陆群), costumes designed by Zhang Leping (张乐平)	1961	Shanghai Ta Kung Farce Troupe, Ah Q played by Yang Huasheng (杨华生)
Japanese version of *The True Story of Ah Q*	Translated by Masuda Wataru	1962	Kadokawa Book Series

(continued)

TABLE 16.1 *(continued)*

Version	Author, adaptor, translator	Time of publishing	Publisher
108 pictures of *The True Story of Ah Q*	Painted by Cheng Shifa	1963	108 prints, published by Shanghai People's Fine Arts Publishing House
Three-act Japanese spoken drama of *The True Story of Ah Q*	Script written by Miyamoto Ken	1969	*Tragedies and Comedies,* Issue 8, published by Hayakawa Publishing
Japanese version of *The True Story of Ah Q*	Translated by Noboru Maruyama	Nov. 1975	New Japan Book Series, published by New Japan Publishing House
French spoken drama of *The True Story of Ah Q*	Script written by Jean Jourdheuil	1975	Université Paris Diderot – Paris VII
Illustrations of *The True Story of Ah Q*	Painted by Fan Zeng (范曾)	1977	Five illustrations painted by Fan Zeng, in *Collection of Illustrations for Novels by Lu Xun*, published by Beijing Rong Bao Zhai
Eight-scene Shaoxing opera play of *The True Story of Ah Q*	Script written by Pan Wende (潘文德) and Wang Yungen (王云根)	1979	Shaoxing Opera Troupe
The True Story of Ah Q	Painted by Zhao Yannian (赵延年)	1980	Fifty-eight woodcut prints, published by Shanghai People's Fine Arts Publishing House
The True Story of Ah Q	Lu Xun	1981	Taipei Four Season Publishing Company (台北四季出版事业), edited by Chaling (茶陵)
Spoken drama of Xianheng Hotel	Script written by Mei Qian (梅阡)	1981	Beijing People's Art Theater, Ah Q played by Zhu Xu (朱旭)
Filmscript of *The True Story of Ah Q*	Script written by Chen Baichen	1981	Published by China Film Press, Ah Q played by Yan Shunkai (严顺开)
Seven-act spoken drama of *The True Story of Ah Q*	Script written by Chen Baichen	1981	China Theater Publishing House, Beijing

(continued)

TABLE 16.1 *(continued)*

Version	Author, adaptor, translator	Time of publishing	Publisher
Seven-act farce of *The True Story of Ah Q*	Script written by Mu Ni (穆尼) and Lu Qun, costumes designed by Zhang Leping	1981	Shanghai People's Farce Troupe, Ah Q played by Yang Huasheng
Modern dance opera of *The True Story of Ah Q*	Produced by the Creation Team of Chongqing Song and Dance Ensemble (重庆歌舞团创作组)	1981	Chongqing Song and Dance Ensemble, Ah Q played by Shan Fusheng
Ballet opera of *The True Story of Ah Q*	Script written by Qian Shijin (钱世锦)	1981	Shanghai Ballet, Ah Q played by Lin Jianwei (林建伟)
200 pictures of *The True Story of Ah Q*	Painted by Qiu Sha and Wang Weijun	1981	203 pencil sketches, published by People's Fine Arts Publishing House, Beijing

(*One of the sources*: Peng Xiaoling [彭小苓] and Han Aili [韩蔼丽], eds.: *Seventy Years of Ah Q* [《阿Q70年》], Beijing: Beijing October Literature and Arts Press, 1993)

SEVENTEEN

"YU SI," "CASUAL TALKS," AND VERNACULAR PROSE STYLE

JUST LIKE PEOPLE TEND TO TAKE FOR GRANTED WHAT IS most familiar to them, various modern Chinese literary histories often focus their attention on how modern prose per se evolved and transformed from its ancient forms, but generally ignore the fact that prose writing was the basis of various literary styles. Actually, the evolution of prose during the past 100 years was closely linked to the development of modern literary vernacular Chinese.

The authors back in the May Fourth period paid much attention to this link. Almost every one of them had reflected and commented on the issue from these two aspects. Hu Shi once said: "The vernacular prose has made great progress. That of lengthy argumentative essays is so obvious that there is no need to talk about it here. In recent years, the most noteworthy development in the field of prose is the familiar essays promoted by Zhou Zuoren and others. These familiar essays convey a profound message with their plain conversations; sometimes they may seem clumsy, but they are humorous. The success of these literary works may totally smash the myth that vernacular Chinese cannot produce elegant essays."[1] Lu Xun, who was also a member of the *New Youth* group and later disagreed with Hu Shi in social and political views, said in 1933: "It was not until the May Fourth movement that there was a new development: the success of the prose and familiar essay was almost more remarkable than that of fiction, drama, and poetry. Such essays certainly expressed their authors' struggles and battles, but since this genre was partly borrowed from the English essay, they were also written

---

[1] Hu Shi: "Fifty Years of Chinese Literature," *Fifty Years of Chinese Literature*, Taipei: Yuan-Liou Publishing, 1986, pp. 149–150.

with some humor and grace, and some of them had both style and substance. This was a gesture to display vernacular literature's strength to the old-style literature, for even in the field that the latter boasted to be strong, vernacular literature could make its own presence felt."[2] This comment was quite informative, and we will mention it later in this chapter. What's worth a mention here is that generally Lu Xun thought better of the prose of the May Fourth period, and in the end he almost totally agreed with Hu Shi, making it clear that the success of prose meant the success of vernacular literature.

Here the so-called struggling and battling summarized the attitudes and styles of all *New Youth*'s contributing writers, which were exemplified by the column Impromptu Reflections. Since the period of its predecessor, *Youth*, there had been a Correspondence column in *New Youth*, in which various social issues were discussed. Gradually such discussions became increasingly tense, and all major figures of the May Fourth period participated in them, literature and Chinese language becoming two of the main topics. In 1918, *New Youth* (Vol. 4, Issue 4) started a new column entitled Impromptu Reflections, focusing on intellectual and cultural critique, and the discussions were even fiercer. Impromptu Reflections was a collective literary project, in which each article carried the byline of the author, but most authors used pseudonyms. Most articles had no title; each was designated a number according to the order it was published. For example, Lu Xun, under the pseudonyms of "Si" (俟), "Tang Si," and "Lu Xun" (at that time, this last one was still strange to most readers), published a total of twenty-seven articles in Impromptu Reflections, with the first one called No. 25, and it wasn't until No. 56 and 57 that he gave them actual titles, namely: "It's Coming" (《来了》) and "The Butchers of Today" (《现在的屠杀者》). This can be seen clearly in the table of contents of *Hot Wind* (《热风》). The authors of these Impromptu Reflections were the earliest to write with vernacular Chinese, but their style was inherited from Liang Qichao's "New Citizen style," featuring a combination of classical and vernacular Chinese while expressing modern-day thoughts and feelings. It was the transitional period of modern vernacular; in Zhu Ziqing's words, most vernacular written Chinese formed in the texts of new-style writers after the late-Qing period was "a mixture of old-style novels, classical Chinese, and aphoristic style."[3] By the time of *New Youth*, Hu Shi's texts had the fewest classical Chinese elements, Qian Xuantong had probably tried to remove such elements from

---

[2] Lu Xun: "The Crisis of Familiar Essays" (《小品文的危机》), *Complete Works of Lu Xun*, Vol. 4, Beijing: People's Literature Press, 1981, p. 576.

[3] Zhu Ziqing: "On Vernacular Writings: Some Thoughts after Reading *North and South Poles* and *Little Peter*" (《论白话（读〈南北极〉与〈小彼得〉的感想）》), *Complete Works of Zhu Ziqing* (《朱自清全集》), Vol. 1, Nanjing: Jiangsu Education Press, 1988, p. 267.

his writings, and others showed varied degrees of classical Chinese style. We may call them the first generation of vernacular stylists of the May Fourth period. Great prose writings of this period included Li Dazhao's "Youth" (《青春》) and "The Living Present"; Chen Duxiu's "On the Smashing of Idols" (《偶像破坏论》) and "The Inferior Anarchic Party" (《下品的无政府党》); Qian Xuantong's "Impromptu Reflections No. 44" (《随感录四十四》); and Liu Bannong's "Bowing-Out-Ism" (《作揖主义》). Taking "The Living Present" by Li Dazhao (1889–1927) as an example, we can see his as well as Chen Duxiu's writing style:

> I remember Duxiu said in his "The Year 1916" (《一九一六年》) that in order to revitalize our nation, young people "must destroy 1915s young people and value 1916s young people." I once extended his idea and said the sole purpose in life, as well as young people's sole responsibility, should be "to establish the present young me, kill the past young me, and make room for the future young me. ... Not only urge the present young me to kill the present old me, but shall urge the present young me to kill the future old me."[4]

This was similar to Lu Xun's style, which used skillful combinations of vernacular and classical writing styles. Lu Xun also criticized that Chinese people always killed "the present," with his antithetical couplets written in lively vernacular, and he showed less classical elements than Li Dazhao and Chen Duxiu:

> As human beings they want to become immortals, and born on the earth they want to ascend to the sky; they are modern people inhaling modern air, but force everybody to cling to the corrupted moralities and dead language and spare no effort to insult the present. They are "butchers of the present." They have killed "the present" and so have killed "the future" – and the future is our children's and grandchildren's time.[5]

And in Lu Xun's "How We Should Father Now" (《我们现在怎样做父亲》) written around the same time as the Impromptu Reflections, the classical Chinese sentences were blended with his vernacular style without trace:

17.1. Table of contents, *New Youth* (Vol. 4, Issue 4, 1918) – the issue that published the first Impromptu Reflections

---

4   Li Dazhao: "The Living Present," *New Youth*, Vol. 4, Issue 4, 1918.
5   Lu Xun: "No. 57, 'The Butchers of the Present'" (《五十七 现在的屠杀者》), *Complete Works of Lu Xun*, Vol. 1, Beijing: People's Literature Press, 1981, p. 350.

17.2. Li Dazhao in his youth, with quite an impressive beard

Take China, my country, as an example. Filial sons were elected as civil officials as early as the Han dynasty. In Tang dynasty there was an honored position assigned to those with filial piety and fraternal love and who worked hard in the field. And in the late Qing there was an honored position for those who were filial and honest; such qualities could always be used in exchange for an official position. Parents' graciousness has always been ranked before royal favor, but in the end, few people cut their own flesh to save the life of their parents. This is sufficient evidence that China's ancient dogmas and measures actually yield very little, and their only effect seems to give evil people more hypocritical rhetoric and inflict more fruitless pain on good people.[6]

After the New Youth group split up, *Yu Si* became a major player in the literary circle, with Lu Xun being its core. While it insisted on the "struggling and battling" style, "some humor and grace" also flourished with *Yu Si*. The journal *Yu Si* was launched in 1924, and its major contributors included Lu Xun, Zhou Zuoren, Liu Bannong, Qian Xuantong, Sun Fuyuan, Chuandao (川岛), and Lin Yutang, among others, its prose pieces featuring such forms as random thoughts, comments on current affairs, familiar essays, and prose poems. Zhou

17.3. Cover of Lu Xun's *The Grave* (《坟》), designed in a depressing style

Zuoren (1885–1967) was a major contributor to *Yu Si*, who had participated in several fierce debates together with his elder brother, but gradually developed his own style. The Zhou brothers held similar views during the time of the "Beijing Women's Normal College Event" and "March Eighteenth Incident," while Lu Xun's greatness, achieved by such eternal prose works as "In Memory of Miss Liu Hezhen" (《记念刘和珍君》) and "Place of Death" (《死地》) that conveyed his depth and profoundness with extremely dismal and indignant sentences, could not be rivalled by his brother, who wrote on the same events works like "On Those Who Died on March 18" (《关于三月十八日的死者》) and "Women in New China" (《新中国的女子》). One cannot say that Zhou Zuoren was not fierce in these works; for example, he expressed his anger with such a couplet: "Redness, redness, even now

---

6   Lu Xun: "How We Should Father Now" (《我们现在怎样做父亲》), *Complete Works of Lu Xun*, Vol. 1, Beijing: People's Literature Press, 1981, p. 137.

some scholarly celebrities and journalists are framing the dead up. Futile, futile, in the end the so-called revolutionary government is the same with imperialism" (赤化赤化，有些学界名流和新闻记者还在那里诬陷。白死白死，所谓革命政府与帝国主义原是一样东西), but the passions expressed in the writings of the brothers were totally different. Moreover, Zhou Zuoren could not write great works on the topic of realistic political conflicts. By 1926, the prose writings characteristic of Zhou Zuoren's style began to emerge, including "Wild Herbs of My Hometown" (《故乡的野菜》), "*Chi Cha*" (《吃茶》), "Bitter Rain" (《苦雨》), and "Black Canopied Boats" (《乌篷船》).

Lin Yutang (1895–1976) was also from the *Yu Si* school. In his *Cutting and Dusting* (《翦拂集》), we can see no less of a "struggling and battling" spirit, and we can also see this in his essays "In Mourning of Ms. Liu Hezhen and Ms. Yang Dequn" (《悼刘和珍杨德群女士》) and "Gossip and Rumors" (《闲话与谣言》). He had some minor disagreement with Lu Xun on whether one should insist on fair-play and hit the dog that had fallen into the water, but they were generally of the same camp. After the "March Eighteenth Incident," he drew a picture entitled "Mr. Lu Xun Hitting a Dog" (《鲁迅先生打叭儿狗图》), and in his essays "Dispelling Doubts about Hitting a Dog" (《打狗释疑》), "Manifest against the Dog" (《讨狗檄文》), and "General Comments on Becoming Red and Homeless Dogs" (《泛论赤化与丧家之狗》), he made it clear that he was convinced that "one must chase the dog into the river and hit it." Interestingly, however, Lin Yutang did not show his unique style in *Cutting*

17.4. Original edition of *Wild Grass* (《野草》). This was a collection of Lu Xun's prose poems that he wrote from his own painful life experiences. Seen from the aspect of prose style, this was an outstanding collection characteristic of his unique style

17.5. On March 18, 1926, petitioners encountered armed police at the front of the Duan Qirui (段祺瑞) warlord government in Beijing, and shots were fired at unarmed petitioners. Lu Xun published very fierce essays about this event

17.6. Cover of *Yu Si* (Vol. 4, Issue 1). The authors formed the so-called *Yu Si* school, with Lu Xun being its core

and Dusting, in which one cannot find any outstanding text and impressive sentences. Therefore, we can regard Zhou Zuoren and Lin Yutang as members of the *Yu Si* school who tended to have "humor and grace," and thus later in their literary style these two came closer to that of *Contemporary Critique*, with which they originally had no common cause. The journal *Camel Grass* (《骆驼草》), launched in 1930, could be regarded as a landmark, as after Lu Xun went south and *Yu Si* was discontinued in Shanghai, Zhou Zuoren, Fei Ming (废名, aka Feng Wenbing), and Liang Yuchun (梁遇春) finally found their own "leisurely style" (*xian-hua-ti*, 闲话体), which was independent from the style of *Yu Si*. In 1932 Lin Yutang launched *Analects* (《论语》) in Shanghai, and later he launched *This Human World* (《人间世》) and *Cosmic Wind* (《宇宙风》), thus starting to write in his own style featuring "humor and grace."

According to Zhu Ziqing, Zhou Zuoren was a representative writer of second-generation vernacular prose writing. From his translation to his prose essays, "Mr. Zhou Zuoren's 'literal translation' had indeed created a brand new vernacular and a brand new style of writing. … In the field of writing, Mr. Zhou's new vernacular was very popular, an example of which was the so-called Europeanized vernacular. This was Chinese writing abiding by Western grammar rules, and it indeed revitalized the Chinese language to some extent."[7] This Europeanized vernacular, with obvious shortcomings as it was, became the general trend and finally became the official modern Chinese written language (that it was constantly adjusted by "colloquial Chinese" and improved was another question). Originally its style was simple and smooth, without any trace of classical elements, and was

17.7. "Mr. Lu Xun Hitting a Dog," drawn by Lin Yutang, collected in *Cutting and Dusting*, Beixin Press, 1928. Evidence that at that time they still agreed with each other

7   Zhu Ziqing: "On Vernacular Writings: Some Thoughts after Reading *North and South Poles* and *Little Peter*," pp. 267–268.

not as obscure as it later became. Take Zhou's "Tea Pastries of Beijing" (《北京的茶食》) as an example:

> Besides the everyday necessities, we must have some useless games and entertainments to make our life more interesting. It is equally necessary for us to watch the sunset, appreciate the autumn river, enjoy flowers, listen to raindrops, smell fragrance, drink wine when we are not thirsty, and eat pastries when we are not hungry – these are just unnecessary ornaments in our life, but they shall be as refined as possible. It's a pity that nowadays Chinese people's lives are extremely uninteresting and vulgar. Among other things, I have been wandering for a dozen years in Beijing but have never found any delicious tea pastries.

17.8. Portrait of Zhou Zuoren, owner of the Bitter Rain Studio, published in *This Human World*

Seen from the eyes of those who could barely survive, to eat pastries when one is not hungry may seem a need of the "leisured class," but actually, it was simply part of an urban lifestyle in the area to the south of the Yangtze River. Therefore we can see that in "*Chi Cha*" (literally, "Eating Tea," which was titled "Drinking Tea" [《喝茶》] when it was first collected in *Book of a Rainy Day* [《雨天的书》]), the vernacular language was used by Zhou Zuoren to express traditional Chinese ideas and style. Thus we shall not exaggerate the strangeness of Europeanized vernacular: actually it was localized from the very start:

> One should drink tea under the tile room and beside the paper window; the green tea should be brewed with clear spring water and shall be served with simple and elegant pottery tea ware. Drinking tea with a couple of friends and having a carefree afternoon may well relieve one from ten years' worries. After the tea, one may continue pursuing one's own worldly success, be it for honor or for profit; they are fine, but occasional leisure and pleasure are indeed necessary in life.

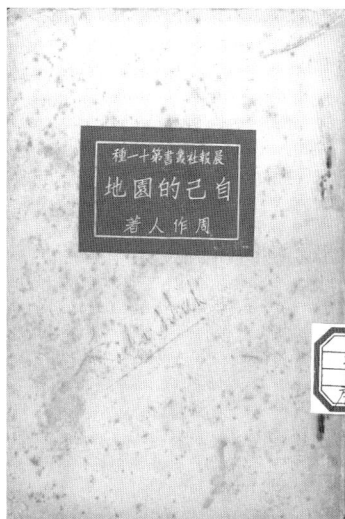

17.9. *My Own Garden* by Zhou Zuoren

So, Zhou Zuoren did make his own contributions to the combination of vernacular and the leisurely style.

The term *xian-hua* (闲话) had a long-standing history in China, but later it was used to refer to a literary style, that is the English familiar essay. This style was the orthodox school of European prose writings, and its simple and elegant taste was expressed in fireside chats and leisurely conversations. Sir

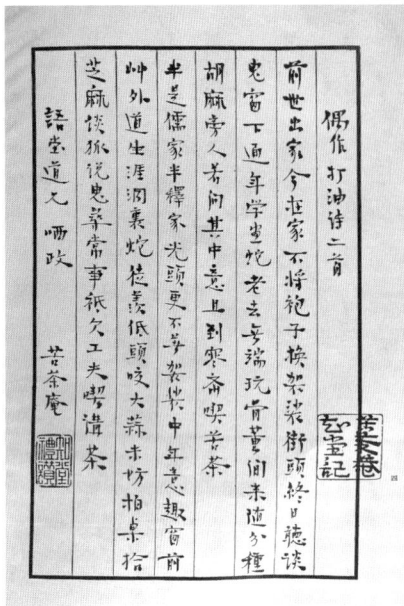

17.10. Zhou Zuoren's famous handwritten poem to celebrate his own birthday, published in Lin Yutang's *This Human World*, which was widely criticized

Richard Steele and Joseph Addison, recognized as inventors of this kind of familiar essay, had launched the single-page familiar essay journals *Tatler* and *Spectator*, with the former translated as *Xianhua Bao* (literally, "Tattling Newspaper") in Chinese by some. Such English familiar essays introduced into China during the May Fourth period were combined with Ming sketches and casual writings and became quite popular for a while. Many newspapers and magazines started their own *Xian-hua* column, of which the most famous was that of the *Contemporary Critique*, and its major contributor, Chen Xiying (1896－1970), later published a collection entitled "Causeries of Xiying" (*Xiying xian-hua*, 《西滢闲话》), a best seller of the Crescent Moon Bookstore. However, also due to the debate between Chen Xiying and Lu Xun, the "leisure style" had an ambiguous reputation. For a while, the prose pieces as "little ornaments" were indeed inferior to essays that were "daggers and spears." But if we examine them today with calmness and objectivity, we may find the "leisurely chats" and causeries had formed a style with "grace": putting their themes to one side, Lin Yutang's prose writings covered everything from "the big universe" to "tiny flies"; and putting each author's writing techniques to one side, this prose genre could be used to write about everything including cultural stories, anecdotes of famous figures, prefaces, and book reviews, as well as analects and aphorisms. Thus these familiar essays became distinct from the social and intellectual essays filled with strong combativeness and vehement criticism. They did have something in common, however; for example, both could be used to criticize civilization and society, but they were different styles, and the most obvious difference was that one featured "satire" and the other, "humor." Later, Lu Xun's miscellaneous essays and Zhou Zuoren's familiar essays represented the highest achievements of these two types of modern Chinese prose.

And in the writings of Chen Xiying, Xu Zhimo, and Liang Yuchun, the link between "familiar essays" and modern vernacular became even closer. Zhu Ziqing, who paid special attention to the development of the modern Chinese language, once praised them generously: "Mr. Chen Xiying's *Causeries* were written with calm plainness and clear argument, making them somewhat like newspaper reports. He was accurate in ideas, and therefore his writings were well organized. His language was, similar to that of [Hu] Shizhi, close to colloquial language. … The National Language style [国语体, referring to the style of Mr. Hu Shizhi, Chen Xiying, and others] is fundamental to our vernacular language."[8] This comment deserves our attention. Chen Xiying's familiar essays were somewhat Europeanized Chinese, but they were written with clarity and grace, and showed an easy free style. His writings were expressions of his gentleman-like character; he expressed his own ideas in those essays, sometimes made quite sparkling comments, with a uniquely skillful mastery of irony, sharp wit, and humor. For example:

> Having more dollars does not make one an artist, though sometimes some artists do have some dollars. If somebody makes a statue out of gold, or glues dollars onto a picture, such statue or picture shall not become art works because they are made of gold and dollars, though at least gold can be made into something with great artistic value. Thank God this is still believed by people; even the most extreme materialistic scholars, such as Dr. Scheidler, the German professor teaching in China recently, would probably not say no to this.
>
> But, danger is pending. Don't you see the advertisements of the US film companies? Their first sentence starts with "This film cost however many dollars" and their final sentence ends with "This film cost however many dollars." One hundred thousand! Two hundred thousand! Half a million! A million! Does this mean that the more it cost, the more valuable the film is? Dollars are thus identified with art, which has been acknowledged at least by the film production industry of the United States.[9]

These were Europeanized Chinese sentences, but they were as clear as day and the message very relevant even by today's standard. Within the Crescent Moon school, Xu Zhimo's texts were regarded as fluent, florid, and sentimental, but they were doubtless easy and fresh. "The Cambridge I Know" (《我所知道的康桥》) was one of his famous essays, in which he wrote about the Cambridge River, spring days spent on its banks and rowing on the river, as well as cycling in the countryside and watching sunsets, all of which were perfectly blended with the spirit of freedom of the University of Cambridge. "The morning was a wonderful time to watch the smoke from chimneys; the morning mist gradually rose, unfolding the grayish sky dome (it was better after some soft hail). The smoke from chimneys, near and far, in threads, in strands and in rolls, some light, some heavy, some dark gray, some light blue, and some pale white, gradually rose in the still morning air. Gradually it disappeared, like the prayers of people in the morning, one after another, becoming clouds in the heavens."[10] These

---

[8] Ibid., pp. 268–269.
[9] Chen Xiying: "Dollars and Art" (《洋钱与艺术》), *Causeries of Xiying*, Shanghai: Crescent Moon Bookstore, 1928, pp. 59–60.
[10] Xu Zhimo: "The Cambridge I Know," *Tidbits from Paris* (《巴黎的鳞爪》), 3rd ed., Shanghai: Crescent Moon Bookstore, 1931, pp. 61–62.

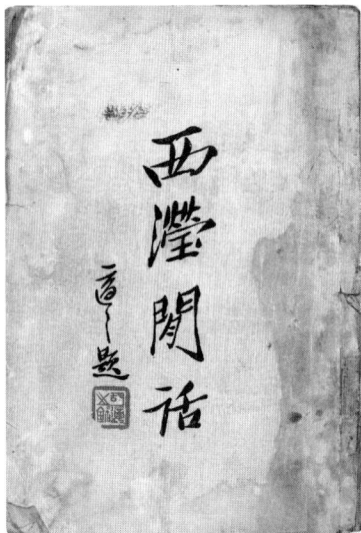

17.11. *Causeries of Xiying*. The title on the cover was inscribed by Hu Shi, and it was an important book published by the Crescent Moon Bookstore

were full and beautiful expressions of the serenity and freedom of spring mornings in Cambridge.

Liang Yuchun (1906–1932) had a very short creative life, but his familiar essays were elegant argumentative essays, as well as excellent examples of fresh and clear texts written in Europeanized vernacular. He wrote about his own experiences in his prose essays and liked to write antitheses and things not typically written about by others. While others wrote about the "outlook on life," he wrote "Outlook on Death" (《人死观》); while others respected teachers, especially professors, he wrote a critical essay entitled "On the Salesmen of Intellectual Shops" (《论智识贩卖所的伙计》); while others were opposed to sleeping late, he wrote an essay entitled "The Priceless Moments of a Spring Morning" (《〈春朝〉一刻值千金》) to praise sleeping late, and so on. He did not write on big topics, and thus the most solemn essay he ever wrote was one entitled "Firefighters" (《救火夫》), in which he gave sincere praise to firefighters. Most topics were drawn from his everyday life and readings, and he wrote in his unique style, as an honest person full of consciousness and prone to meditation. His writings read like a stream of consciousness, spreading out, never staying in one place for too long. His sentences were elegant and graceful; they were not harsh satires, but humor without hostility. Look at the following example:

> If you feel life is boring, just try to lie in bed for another half an hour (or better, an hour), then you will surely find you hardly have any time to do everything, and you had to be busy – being busy is the golden key to the palace of happiness, especially when that "busy" is caused by yourself. Being busy is the best way to exhaust our energy. Didn't Aristotle say for human beings, happiness came from the satisfaction that their abilities had been changed into efficiency. I always sleep until the last five minutes before the working hour, and finish face-washing, teeth-brushing, and

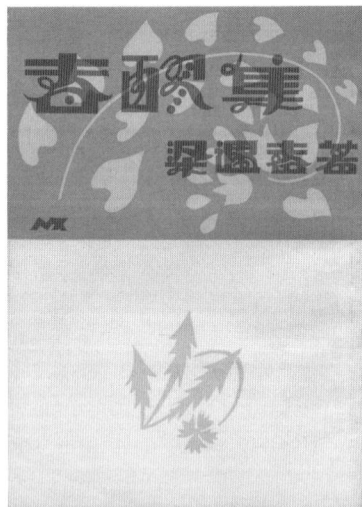

17.12. Liang Yuchun's collection of prose writings, *Spring Wine* (《春醪集》), was published in 1930 and showed his great writing talent. After his death, his friends helped publish another collection of his writings, *Tears and Laughter* (《泪与笑》)

breakfast at top speed, making all of them romantic moves. When the toothpaste sputters and water
splashes, when one combs one's hair and at the same
time is eating one's breakfast in front of the mirror,
who can say life is deprived of happiness?[11]

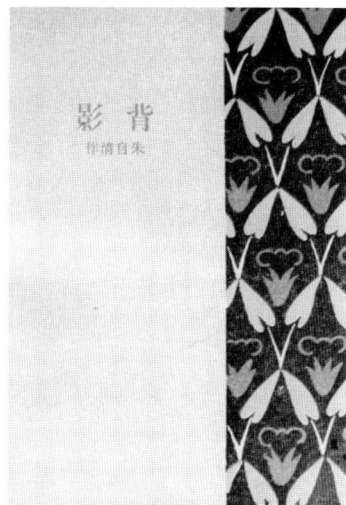

After the May Fourth cultural camp split apart, those
who did not take the socialist path and were close
to British and American liberalism showed a stronger
leisurely style, but among them were many who had
been angry fighters, an obvious example being the *Yu
Si* school. But it was the joint efforts of them all that
made modern vernacular language even more clear
and fluent. In his article "On the Modern Chinese
Familiar Essay" (《论现代中国的小品散文》) writ-
ten in 1928, Zhu Ziqing said:

17.13. *A View of My Father's Back*, a
collection of Zhu Ziqing's best prose
writings

> To discuss the prose as it stands, we shall say its devel-
> opment in the recent couple of years has been quite
> splendid; there are various styles and various literary schools that express
> and criticize the different aspects of human life; they spread and flow, and
> change with each passing day. In terms of ideas, they show characters of
> Chinese elites, Western gentlemen, recluses, and rebels. In terms of writ-
> ing techniques there are descriptive and ironic, roundabout and accurate,
> fierce and florid, concise and fluent, and reserved.

They all made their contribution to the diversity of modern vernacular language.
And Zhu Ziqing himself had written such florid pieces as "Oar-Splashing and
Lantern-Illuminating Qinhuai River" (《桨声灯影里的秦淮河》) and "Lotus
Pond by Moonlight" (《荷塘月色》), and such concise and simple pieces as
"A View of My Father's Back" (《背影》). In "A View of My Father's Back,"
he wrote extremely simple and clear sentences to describe the father climbing
up and down the platform to buy oranges for his son:

> I watched as my father, wearing a black cap, a black jacket, and a dark
> blue cotton robe, stumbled over to the platform and climbed down to
> the tracks. That wasn't the hard part. He still had to climb up on the other
> side of the tracks. Hands clinging to the edge of the platform, my father's
> legs contracted upward and his heavy body tilted to the left as he strug-
> gled to pull himself up. Looking at his silhouette, I felt tears streaming
> down my cheeks.[12]

---

[11] Liang Yuchun: "The Priceless Moments of a Spring Morning," *Spring Wine*, Shanghai: Beixin
Press, 1930, p. 233.
[12] Zhu Ziqing: "A View of My Father's Back," *Complete Works of Zhu Ziqing*, Vol. 1, Nanjing:
Jiangsu Education Press, 1988, p. 48.

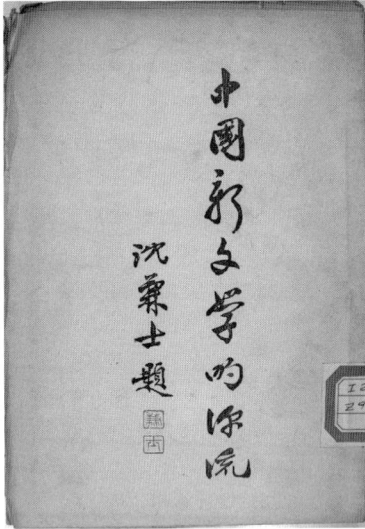

17.14. *On the Origins of China's New Literature* by Zhou Zuoren

While in "Lotus Pond by Moonlight" the style was totally different:

All over this winding stretch of water, what meets the eye is a silken field of leaves, reaching rather high above the surface, like the skirts of dancing girls in all their grace. Here and there, layers of leaves are dotted with white lotus blossoms, some in demure bloom, others in shy bud, like scattering pearls, or twinkling stars, or beauties just out of the bath. A breeze stirs … a tiny thrill shoots through the leaves and flowers, like a streak of lightning, straight across the forest of lotuses.[13]

But no matter how perfectly the styles of conciseness and floridity were blended in the writings of Zhu Ziqing, just as those of struggle and grace blended in the earlier and later writings of Lin Yutang, there was a higher "spirit" that was universal in the vernacular prose essays, a quality that was hardly seen in ancient literature and was characteristic of the modern times: the vigorous individuality of the authors, shown in their writings and their general attitudes toward life and the world (whether they were about major social events or about their personal trivialities).

The individualized writing and way of thinking with the presence of "I" is the quintessence of vernacular modern literature. Seeking the origin of blending this quintessence and style, people tried to look for it in foreign sources, which wasn't the wrong direction. Since the figurative huge "iron house" was made of the long-standing autocratic political system and institution, feudal conventions, and ideologies, only the advanced human civilization that not only came together with foreign firearms and grotesque skills but also was "actively grabbed" by the Chinese people had the strength to destroy it. Hu Shi, Lu Xun, and Zhu Ziqing all mentioned the effect of "English familiar essays" on the May Fourth prose writing. Not only did they produce a number of authors specializing in writing familiar essays, but who could say that an author who wrote such sentences as "they did not only destroy, but wiped out, shoutingly and aggressively, all obstructive old rails, partly or entirely" ("Another Discussion on the Collapse of Lei Feng Pagoda" [《再论雷峰塔的倒掉》]); "The feast of human flesh is still arranged now, and many want it to continue" ("Jottings by Lamplight" [《灯下漫笔》]); and "There should have been a brand new literary circle a long time ago, as well as some fierce fighters" ("On Looking Facts in the Face" [《论睁了眼看》]) was someone without

---

[13] Zhu Ziqing: "Lotus Pond by Moonlight," *Complete Works of Zhu Ziqing*, Vol. 1, Nanjing: Jiangsu Education Press, 1988, pp. 70–71. English translation courtesy of Professor Zhu Chunshen. – Translator's note

individuality and courage? Later Zhou Zuoren raised the concept of "new literary movement of the late Ming," arguing that vernacular literature and vernacular language also had their origins in ancient China: "Hu Shizhi's 'eight programs' actually revitalized what was advocated by the Gong'an school of the late Ming: 'uniquely express [one's] personality and innate sensibility without being restrained by convention or form' (独抒性灵，不拘格套), and 'good style comes naturally from sincerity in writings and honesty in sayings' (信腕信口，皆成律度)."[14] Once published, this was disapproved by many in the literary circle, but it is not difficult for us to accept today. Moreover, by saying this, Zhou Zuoren did not deny foreign influence or advocate reverting to old ways. In the same article, he made it quite clear that "if we remove the Western influence he received in terms of science, philosophy, literature, and Western ideas from Mr. Hu Shizhi's thinking, what remains is something very close to the most famous maxim of the Gong'an school."[15] Therefore, Zhou did not turn a blind eye to the "Western influence received" by Hu Shi. If we take this approach to trace the origin of modern Chinese prose, we could fully integrate literature and language, and examine and explore them as an organic whole.

[14] Zhou Zuoren: *On the Origins of China's New Literature*, Changsha: Yuelu Press, 1989, p. 54.
[15] Ibid., p. 22.

EIGHTEEN

DISCOVERY OF PEASANTS AND REGIONAL COLORS BY EARLIER NATIVE-SOIL LITERATURE

For the modernized Chinese literature, the very first successful trend was that of native-soil (乡土) literature. It was a literary event most characteristic of the May Fourth period when a large number of intellectuals began to turn their eyes to China's vast and backward countryside. This was because although the late-Qing novel had already begun its modernization process, it followed the tradition of writing about cities and urban citizens, never covering the countryside and rural peasants (when the latter were mentioned in traditional novels, they were only extensions of urban citizens, not major characters themselves). Traditionally, Chinese novels and operas originated among citizens and thrived in cities as a kind of cultural consumer product. The novels around the Republican period remained unchanged, and it was not until the May Fourth period that literature began its exploration of women and children, as well as peasants, as its subject matter.

Such exploration was different from the themes of "pitying farmers" and "sympathizing with farmers" of traditional Chinese poetry and prose, which was basically condescending pity for farmers shown by the official-scholar class. The May Fourth authors, on the other hand, wrote under the banners of "laborers are sacred" and "commoners' literature," and at least intended to, tried to, and hoped to, within the framework of modern democracy, establish an equal relationship with peasants, and be concerned with peasants' lives as well as their poverty, ignorance, and sufferings. It was true that in terms of economic position and spiritual pursuit, modern Chinese intellectuals were still in a privileged position, but at this time, the viewpoints and attitudes they took to examine the countryside and peasants were totally different from those of late-Qing intellectuals and the Mandarin Duck and Butterfly authors.

Just think about how the first-person narrator, "I," in Lu Xun's "Hometown" "shuddered" when hearing his childhood playmate Runtu addressing him as "Master" and realized "what a wretched thick wall now stood between us." And how "I" examined himself; on the one hand, he hoped the next generation, his own son Hongsheng and Runtu's son Shuisheng, would "never live like my generation with everyone cut off from everyone else," while on the other hand he harshly criticized himself: "When Runtu took the censer and candlesticks, I had laughed at him behind his back. 'Can't let go of that superstitious idol-worship of his for a single minute!' But what was this thing called 'hope' if not an idol that I had fashioned with my own hands."[1] This humanism expressed in the May Fourth native-soil literature was indeed unprecedented in China's literary history.

These authors who "explored peasants" were intellectuals who were born in the countryside but had, by the time of their writings, long been away from their hometown and were living in cities, or specifically, in Beijing and Shanghai. Lu Xun, Wang Luyan, Xu Qinwen (许钦文), Tai Jingnong (台静农), Jian Xian'ai, and Fei Ming were living in Beijing, while Xu Jie and Peng Jiahuang lived in Shanghai. Being influenced and trained by civilized urban life, they examined the country village where they were "born and raised" based on their memories and created literary works that represented peasants. Therefore, these were "wanderers from their native soil" in the modern sense and their memories of the countryside were those of rebels, mixed with their absolute disagreement with traditions, their indignation toward peasants for "pitying their misfortune while being angry at their unworthiness," and the nostalgia of rootless and displaced wanderers, all expressed with the spirit of social and cultural criticism. And due to the vastness of China's countryside (thanks to modern means of transportation, these intellectuals could travel from their resident cities to their hometowns in around one or two weeks, and thus their horizons were largely expanded), as well as the cultural difference between different parts of China, the picturesque regional colors and uneven development between different regions had always been a theme of modern Chinese literary works.

18.1. Illustration of "Hometown" (painted by Fan Zeng; "Brother Xun" felt that a thick wall now stood between himself and the peasant Runtu

---

[1] Lu Xun: "Hometown," *Complete Works of Lu Xun*, Vol. 1, Beijing: People's Literature Press, 1981, pp. 481–485.

18.2. Illustration on a translated version of Lu Xun's "Hometown"; "Brother Xun" was in meditation, as were native-soil authors

First of all, let's look at the native-soil fiction representing eastern Zhejiang Province, by a group of writers with Lu Xun at its core (including those of the Weiming Society, the Wilderness Society, and some young members of the Literary Research Society). It did not start very successfully, because most earlier works were written with a concept of "problem novels" in mind, and they tried to "exhibit" sufferings of peasants in the countryside, as if the most unbearable sufferings of the entire world could be epitomized by a single person or a single story. But, after all, Lu Xun was in this group, and his "Hometown," "Storm in a Teacup," and *The True Story of Ah Q* were surely far beyond ordinary. With the standard of modern national citizen in mind, and with the broad outlook to facilitate the reestablishment of peasant identity in modern times, Lu Xun spared no effort to write about the ugly and extremely ignorant character traits of peasants under the disguise of their simplicity. The criticism of the "Ah Q mentality" was naturally its peak. Another theme of Lu Xun's native-soil works was the in-depth analysis and harsh criticism of the returned intellectuals who had been "in exile," examples including "The Misanthrope" (《孤独者》) and "In the Wine Shop" (《在酒楼上》). In these works, the intellectuals sympathized with peasants, but facing the increasingly decayed countryside, they felt deeply disillusioned about their own passionate rebellions and idealism, and living in doubt and guilt, they became more and more dejected. Women, who were deeply hurt and insulted in the gloomy traditional marriage system, were another focus of authors of eastern Zhejiang Province, so we see such women as the widow who considered bringing bad luck to her husband in Lu Xun's "New Year's Sacrifice" (《祝福》), the ghost marriage in Wang Luyan's "Wedding of Juying" (《菊英出嫁》), and wife pawning in Xu Jie's "The Gambler Jishun" (《赌徒吉顺》). The Zhejiang countryside was actually the most developed rural area in China because it was located in the coastal area in the southeast and was so close to Shanghai, the commercial port witnessing rapid development in modern times; this was something largely ignored in our past research of literary history. Looking at the Zhenhai countryside in Ningbo in the novels of Wang Luyan (1902–1944), we can see two obvious differences between his fictional locations, namely "Wangjiaqiao" (王家桥), "Zhaojiaqiao" (赵家桥), "Chensiqiao" (陈四桥), and "Fujiazhen" (傅家镇), and "Weizhuang" (未庄) and "Luzhen" (鲁镇) in Lu Xun's novels. Firstly, there were many stores in the countryside and villagers did a lot of business. "People in Zhaojiaqiao always tended to do business, and few of them aspired to become officials."[2] In "Maybe It's Not Like That" (《许是不至于罢》), a wealthy man of Wangjiaqiao named Wang Ayu (王阿虞) had stores on Xiaoqitou Street "within a short walking distance" from his home, and business was flourishing:

> He now opened several small stores on Xiaoqitou Street: a rice store, a timber store, a brick and tile store, and a brick and tile factory. Apart from these stores, he had an interest in several big stores in Xiaoqitou, including Kefu Silk Store, Kaicheng Southern Goods Store, and Xinshichang Soy Sauce Store. – And he must have an interest in the newly opened Renshengtang Drugstore and Wenji Paper Shop! This store makes a good profit each year, and the business was even better last year, when it was said to have made 20,000, and some even said it was 50,000! Each of the assistants in his store could gain a dividend of sixty dollars; no wonder they were all beamed with joy. Even an apprentice whose surname was Chen gained fifty dollars! This year many tycoons recommended people to work for Wang Ayu; if there was no vacancy at a higher rank, they were willing to recommend apprentices to him.[3]

18.3. Cover of *Gold*, a collection of Wang Luyan's native-soil fictions. He was the earliest author to write about how the countryside was affected by cities

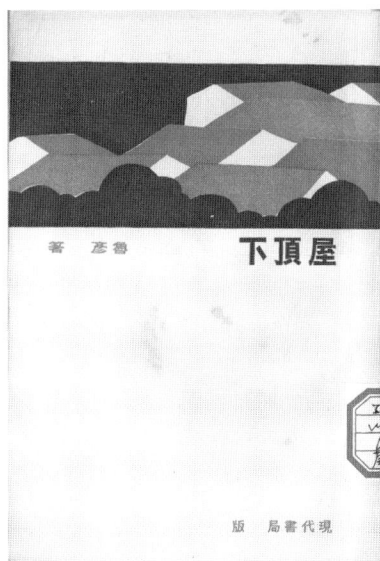

18.4. *Under the Roof*, another collection of Wang Luyan's short stories

The commerce in this rural town was thriving so much that it wasn't only young people who competed to become apprentices, and the stock system was adopted by so many businesses, which could not be matched by the inland rural areas. Secondly, increasingly more people left their hometowns to make a living as laborers. In *Gold's* Chensiqiao Village, which was surrounded by mountains, the son of Uncle Shi was working in the

---

[2] Wang Luyan: "The Last Victory" (《最后的胜利》), *Gold* (《黄金》), Shanghai: New Life Bookstore, 1929, p. 198.

[3] Wang Luyan: "Maybe It's Not Like That," *The Pomelo* (《柚子》), Shanghai: Beixin Press, 1926, p. 75.

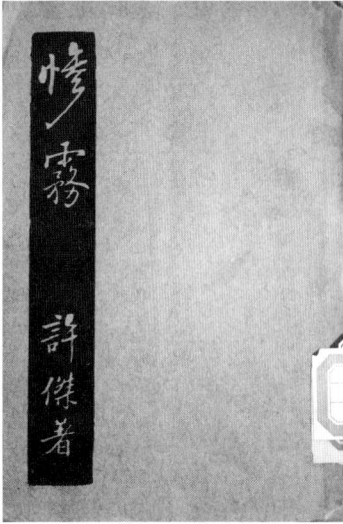

18.5. *Sad Fog*, a collection of Xu Jie's short stories, not only a book about the isolation of the countryside

city to earn money for his family. In *Under the Roof*, Granny Bende and her daughter-in-law were living in the countryside, while the major breadwinner of the family, Uncle Ah Zhi, was working as a waiter on a ship and regularly sent money back. Therefore, what made Wang Luyan's native-soil stories outstanding was not their exhibition of "unenlightened" and "backward" country life: he wrote about how a family whose family member was away working but had no money to send back was discriminated against by their fellow villagers, and thus it seemed that gold (money) had become a major criterion used by villagers in this area to look at others and their relationships with each other; he wrote about how a daughter-in-law listened to her husband, doing housework and respecting her in-laws, but there was constant conflict between her and her mother-in-law, who had been hard-working and thrifty all her life. In his stories, we can not only read about how peasants rapidly fell into poverty, but how wealthy people could also go bankrupt within a short time, and we read about the increasingly fierce infighting between people in the countryside ("Self-Reliance" [《自立》] and "The Last Victory"). The most outstanding thing about these stories was the fact that new concepts and values began to affect this small place in the southeastern part of China, and thus the traditional economic and moral value system began to disintegrate in a modern sense. Take "Self-Reliance" for example, the narrator's great-grandfather had lost a ninety-nine-*mu* piece of land and the room to the west of the main house because of his own cousin with whom he shared the same grandfather; this cousin accused him of occupying public space, and thus they had to spend a lot of money in a prolonged lawsuit, which finally benefited the county head. In the story we can read quite surprising views expressed in the discussions about this lawsuit by the great-grandfather's offspring, that "the betrayal of brothers was a way to seek 'self-reliance'" and that "it's not immoral that brothers oppose each other for their own interest … This is something like the theory of 'evolution via competition' you learn in school nowadays; if it were not like this, we human beings would go backward."[4] This was obviously a viewpoint of urban citizens that had taken root in the countryside.

The same could be seen in the stories of Xu Jie (1901–1993), who was born and raised in Tiantai, Zhejiang Province. Tiantai was located in the mountainous area in the eastern part of Zhejiang, and thus in "Sad Fog" (《惨雾》), he

4   Wang Luyan: "Self-Reliance," *The Pomelo*, Shanghai: Beixin Press, 1926, p. 72.

wrote about the cruel fighting between villagers for the boundary of a piece of land, which was depressingly backward. However, Xu Jie wrote about something else in "A Comedy among the Audience" (《台下的喜剧》) in which the lively scenes reflected the influence of modern civilization on the countryside. An adulterous affair occurred while an opera troupe was performing in Fengxi Village. Jinsha, who had been born in the village but had been married to a man in Mazhuang Village nearby, fell in love with the "young man" in the opera, and they were caught twice. Jinsha was not frightened, but "tried to cover the young man" when villagers beat them. All the villagers among the audience expressed different views about Jinsha, which was indeed a "real-life opera with various responses," much more heated and lively than the opera taking place on stage. Of them, the view of the wife of Brother Song was quite bold, seen in the context of the countryside at the beginning of last century:

> They were caught having an adulterous affair, but so what? Are they human beings? If I were her, I would say quite straightforwardly: please, it's none of your business, why on earth do you have to meddle in this? – One can say this, right? – As I have said: it's the Republic of People period, we all have freedom. You see, it's an accomplishment to have a lover, and there's nothing to be worried about if being caught. – It's not something about chastity, and it's OK if they two truly love each other and won't have adultery with others.[5]

Here we can see that some subtle changes had occurred in the country life of eastern Zhejiang Province. Under the impact of urbanization and commercialization, seeing people going out working, doing business, jostling and fighting, and committing adultery, the villagers' values changed accordingly. This was first sensed by the native-soil authors of the eastern Zhejiang Province, who tried to reflect the villagers' sensitivity, anxiety, and liveliness.

Now let's look at the native-soil fiction of the area around Guizhou and Anhui. This was an area far poorer than eastern Zhejiang Province, but we can see more striking regional characteristics in the associated literary works. Jian Xian'ai (1906–1994) was a native of Guizhou, and he had a calm and reserved narrative style. In "Water Burial" (《水葬》), on the surface he wrote about the savage custom in the Guizhou area, but digging deeper the author focused on the thief being water buried and Shuangshuang, the peasant on the river bank looking at this scene with absolute indifference. Exposing this national character in order to draw people's attention to its cure showed the obvious influence of Lu Xun. Tai Jingnong (1903–1990) was a native of Anhui, and he had a "cold harshness like the Russian writer Andreyev." In his short stories "Red Lantern" (《红灯》), "Second Elder Brother Tian" (《天二哥》),

5   Xu Jie: "A Comedy among the Audience," *Sad Fog*, Shanghai: Commercial Press, 1926, p. 202.

18.6. *Morning Fog*, a collection of
Jian Xian'ai's short stories

18.7. Cartoon of an old Jian Xian'ai,
drawn by Fang Cheng (方成) in 1986

"Candle Flame" (《烛焰》), and "Bowing at the Wedding" (《拜堂》), collected in *Son of the Earth* (《地之子》), he wrote about local customs set
against the dark social landscape: floating river lanterns on the fifteenth of the
seventh lunar month (referred to as the "Ghost Festival"); marriage in order
to cure ill relatives; a man marrying his sister-in-law and having to hold the
wedding at midnight; wife selling and wife pawning, etc.; all being part of the
lifestyle of the lower-class villagers of poverty-stricken areas. Actually, these
customs could be found all over the country, with different forms in different
places. Wang Luyan, for example, wrote about
ghost marriage in the eastern Zhejiang area in
"Wedding of Juying": he gave a detailed and
true-to-life description of the dowries and the
wedding parade, and he wrote it as a flashback,
so readers did not realize the bride was actually dead until the end of the story. Xu Jie had
written about wife pawning in "The Gambler
Jishun": the protagonist Jishun lost everything
at the gambling house, and thus had to sign
a contract and agree that within a prescribed
period, his wife and all his children would
belong to the owner of the pawnshop, which
was equally wretched. But Tai Jingnong was
more delicate in his description of local customs. Take "Bowing at the Wedding" for example: at the wedding between a younger brother
and his widowed sister-in-law, they kowtowed

18.8. *Son of the Earth*, a collection
of Tai Jingnong's short stories.
The description of local
customs within the stories has a
penetrating power

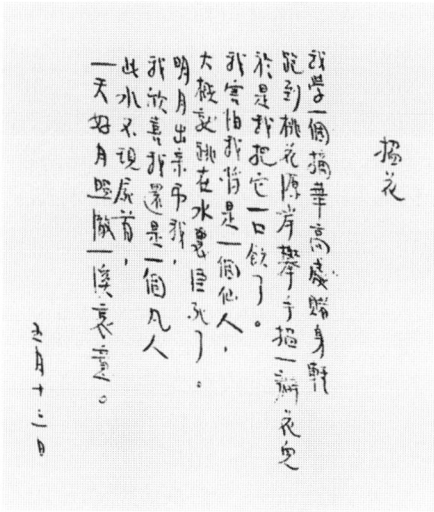

18.9. Fei Ming's handwritten manuscript of the poem "Picking a Flower" (《掐花》)

18.10. Fei Ming in a white gown, taken in Beijing in the 1930s

to Heaven and Earth, to the ancestors, to their living father (who was bad-tempered and claimed that he had already gone to bed, thus "let's just kowtow to him"), and their dead mother. All this went well, but suddenly,

> "Ah, I almost forgot … let's perform a kowtow to my dead brother."
> Suddenly the sister-in-law was all in tears, and she was trembling all over. The second son in the Wang's was standing there dumbfounded, his face as pale as the dead. The romantic atmosphere suddenly turned into ghastly dismay. Even the light of double candles became dim. All people were frightened and panic-stricken.

Readers are immediately transported to the scene of this regional custom. This was a charming description of a desolate region, and the style was solemn and serious.

And then there was the native-soil fiction representing the Hunan and Hubei areas. Hunan and Hubei are located in the middle reaches of the Yangtze River, which were rich but isolated areas at the beginning of last century. The area belonged to the Chu state in ancient times, so native-soil writers from this area were rich in imagination. Fei Ming (1901–1967) was one of them. He published a collection, *Tales of the Bamboo Grove* (《竹林的故事》, under his birth name Feng Wenbing), in which the characters were based on simple and honest people from his hometown, and both the imagery and writing style were fresh and clear. He was born in Huangmei

County, Hubei Province, and it seemed that everything in his hometown had long been ingrained in his memory. The laundress who was kind and diligent but was hurt by rumors ("Laundering Mothers" [《浣衣母》]), the gentle and quiet Third Girl from the vegetable-growing and fishing family ("Tales of the Bamboo Grove"), and the old actor who made a living through puppet-shows and loved the willows in front of his house ("Willows on the River" [《河上柳》]), all these formed the native-soil world of his earlier fictions. In these stories we can feel a delicate and withdrawn tone, and his narrative was poetic. Later, after his "Peach Garden" (《桃园》) and "Jujube" (《枣》), especially after his novel *The Bridge* (《桥》, also considered a collection of short stories) and *The Biography of Mr. Neverwas* (《莫须有先生传》) were published, his fictions became much less readable, and his style changed from freshness to obscurity. On the one hand, he adopted the foreign-style mul-tiple points of view and Chinese-style scattered points of view in his later fictions, and on the other hand, Zen Buddhism became a theme of his novels, and thus his focus shifted from storytelling to philosophical implications. All in all, he became engrossed in fantasy, while in his earlier writings, Fei Ming opened a lyrical tradition through his narrative about nature and human life on the native soil.

Peng Jiahuang (1898–1933) from Hunan was a master of comic narrative and description of regional colors. He was a native of Xiangyin, on the banks of Dongting Lake, and the location for all his major stories was a place called "Xi Town" (谿镇). He had a talent for using ridiculous local dialects and jargon to create comic characters from the countryside, and even tragic stories would become full of liveliness and humor, with a strong sense of irony. In "Living Ghost" (《活鬼》), "Ox of the Fourth Uncle Chen" (《陈四爹的牛》), "Enticing" (《怂恿》), and other stories, he depicted the comic carelessness of local bullies in the Hunan countryside. "Living Ghost" was not actually about a ghost, but about a long-standing practice of marrying older wives to younger husbands, and thus the wives were young women in their twenties while their husbands were mere boys; and therefore, within the huge family of a landlord who owned a property of land as large as 500 or 600 *mu*, peo-ple always performed the family farce of catching men in the rooms of their daughters-in-law and granddaughters-in-law. "Enticing" was Peng Jiahuang's most important work. It told the story of a shrewd landlord called Niuqi entic-ing his clansman Zhengping, who had suffered losses in selling his pigs, to take revenge on the boss of Yufeng Store (whose surname was Feng). Rich people played tricks on each other, while poor people suffered from rough luck, and in the end it turned out to be a farce in which the losses doubled. Zhengping's wife Erniangzi pretended to commit suicide in the house of the elder brother of Feng, but her pretense almost became true and she gained nothing but an insult, which was quite ironic. The rural characters Niuqi and Xibao were

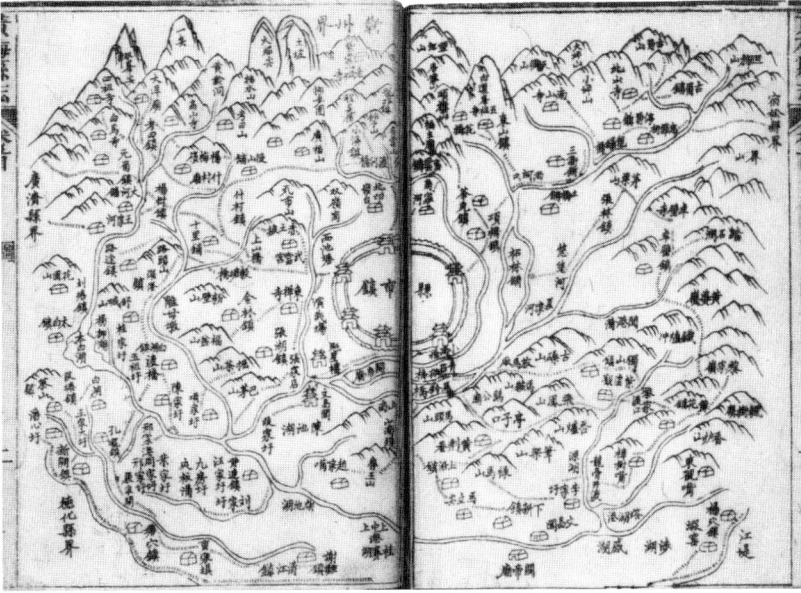

18.11. Map of Huangmei County from the *Annals of Huangmei County*. Throughout his life, Fei Ming wrote about his hometown in his stories, and the names of places in the northwest of this map, Tuqiaodun (土桥铺), Longxiqiao (龙锡桥), and Wuzusi (五祖寺), were all used in his stories

quite vividly depicted. Niuqi was a scoundrel in the town, and let's see how he cursed the young mediator Ri'nian:

> "Hem! He comes, so what? Ri'nian, I know him very well, he is the poor grandson of the cousin of Yufeng. His uncle was a thief, stealing stuff from others and was caught in public. The entire family was full of cripples and blindmen, and his mother probably had affairs with monks. He had been to school for so many years, and so? Still a little nuisance, worthless, fucking ignorant and good for nothing! Son of a bitch, I reckon he is nothing but a stupid jerk! … "[6]

(Note the use of local dialects and vulgar language in this dialogue; the speaker was a male in the countryside.) Xibao, an assistant working in Feng's store, was a shrewd businessman. The following paragraph is about how he bought pigs, and it gives another example of how vulgar language was used in the narrative:

> Xibao was an old hand at buying pigs, and Zhengping was not his match. For example, a business may seem impossible, but when he interfered, it would surely be accomplished. Facing a whole floor of pigs, just shouting and snapping his whip at the entrance of the house, he would immediately know how much each of the pigs was worth: how heavy that one with a big belly was, how much fat that one with a white neck had, that

---

[6] Peng Jiahuang: "Good News" (《喜讯》), *Enticing*, Beijing: People's Literature Press, 1984, p. 46.

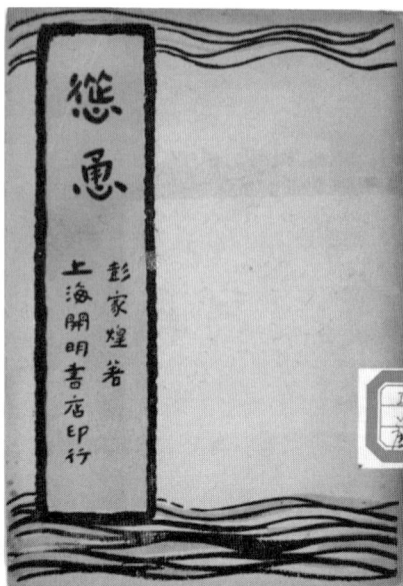

18.12. Cover of the first edition of Peng Jiahuang's *Enticing*, published in 1927, which had a strong taste of rural comedy

18.13. Cover of Xu Qinwen's *Hometown* (《故乡》); the character "Red Robe" was painted by Tao Yuanqing

the one with a black tail put on weight poorly, and even the tricks that the pigs were fed with rot food and had had weight added would be detected by him. He was a nice person, but he had such a glib tongue that whatever he said, it would be to others' ears like hot pepper chicken, fierce, but so delightful.[7]

In summary, the native-soil fictions of these three areas were largely realistic works without too much lyricism. However, May Fourth realism did not fully comply with the norms of modern world realism, which had just been introduced into China and was still being blended with the traditional Chinese realistic style. Romanticism often flowed out of the authors' pens. The mode of narrative adopted by native-soil authors was through memory, which also had something to do with traditional poetic sentiments and lyrical style. Xu Qinwen, another native-soil author from eastern Zhejiang, wrote a memoir-like work entitled "My Father's Garden" (《父亲的花园》), which was quite famous at the time. Most of his works were in prose style, and seen from today's standard, he was not very good at realistic characterization or depiction of scenes. His popularity largely lay in the fact that the sentiments he expressed were shared by most native-soil authors, whose hometowns had been lost forever.

[7]   Ibid., p. 32.

As we know, writers of the May Fourth period had the mindset of modern people, and though the native-soil literature initiated by them still had great room for development in the years that followed, the very first step they took was extremely important. From the perspective of "discovering peasants," the May Fourth authors examined peasants and commoners, the peasant spirit and the national spirit by putting them on the same dimension; they revealed the peasants' trauma inflicted by long-term spiritual slavery and treated it as an important part of the correction and cure of the Chinese national character. This opened a path for the later native-soil literature, all through to the July school (七月派) and the novels of Lu Ling (路翎). Mechanical copying was surely possible. For example, after *The True Story of Ah Q*, there were "Thief Ah Chang" (《阿长贼骨头》) by Wang Luyan, "The Gambler Jishun" by Xu Jie, "Snot Ah Er" (《鼻涕阿二》) by Xu Qinwen, and other works of the same type, all being more or less imitations of Lu Xun's work. As for the "discovery of local regions," we have already talked about fictions with the diversified regional colors of eastern Zhejiang, Anhui, Guizhou, Hubei, and Hunan. Literature with "regional colors" may be narrow-minded and conservative, but in depicting their "regional colors" the May Fourth native-soil authors had quite a conscious open mind, thanks to their broad outlook. They saw the decay and ugliness of their once beautiful hometown, and took a similar position with regional-color authors of other nations (especially those of small nations). Besides literary creation, there were also theoretical discussions. For example, Zhou Zuoren once said: "I look down upon traditional literature with fake patriotism, but I value native-soil art; I strongly believe that a strong local taste is an important part of 'world' literature."[8] He said this in 1923. Eleven years later, Lu Xun echoed his brother's statement, saying "now literature also has such a tendency, those works, whichever are filled with local colors, become more likely to be seen worldwide, i.e. to be noticed more easily by other nations."[9] It was this mode of examining and representing local characters of the native soil by putting them within the context of world literature that made May Fourth literature more ambitious than the traditional Chinese literature of the past.

[8] Zhou Zuoren: "Preface to *Old Dreams*" (《〈旧梦〉序》), *My Own Garden*, Changsha: Yuelu Press, 1987, p. 117.
[9] Lu Xun: "Letter to Chen Yanqiao on April 19, 1934" (《1934年4月19日致陈烟桥》), *Complete Works of Lu Xun*, Vol. 12, Beijing: People's Literature Press, 1981, p. 391.

NINETEEN

LITERARY SOLACE FOR URBAN CITIZENS

The reform of *FICTION MONTHLY* AND THE RESUMED PUBLICATION OF *Saturday* (see Chapter 13) were typical events signifying the replacement of the existing literature with New Literature after the May Fourth movement. However, the replacement wasn't simply of one for the other, as the old-style urban popular literature also "gradually improved itself" and held its ground. In other words, the Mandarin Duck and Butterfly – Saturday literary school, fiercely attacked by the New Literature camp, especially by Zheng Zhenduo, Shen Yanbing (Mao Dun), Zhou Zuoren, and other authors of the Literary Research Society, did not give up and step off the stage of history. The reason was simple: they still had their readers. Immediately after *Fiction Monthly* began publishing works of New Literature, some citizens complained that they could not understand them – and they were not a minority, instead making up a large proportion of urban citizens. Therefore, the Mandarin Duck and Butterfly – Saturday literary school's perseverance was definitely not short-lived, and the replacement process continued for a long time. For example, when *Young Companion* was first launched in 1926, its founder Wu Liande (伍联德) did some editing work himself, while the editor-in-chief he brought in was Zhou Shoujuan, a famous Mandarin Duck and Butterfly author. As one of the backbones of that literary school, Zhou certainly published charming pictures and serialized love stories in the magazine when took charge. The following year, by the time the thirteenth issue was published, the editor-in-chief was suddenly changed, and Liang Desuo (梁得所), who had graduated from Pui Ying Middle School in Guangzhou, took over the magazine. It turned out that Liang was a man of merit for *Young Companion*. He made considerable changes to the magazine, added a large number of pictures on current affairs and modern cities, reported scientific and technological news reports from around the world, and published the creative works of Mu Shiying (穆时英) of the New Sensationalist school and Yu Qie (予且), a new urban writer, as well as various paintings and artistic photographic works from China and abroad. Any hint of the Mandarin Duck and Butterfly school suddenly disappeared, and *Young Companion* became the earliest modern popular pictorial sold to the outside world (especially Southeast Asia). Another example was "Free Talk," a famous supplement of *Shun Pao*. Launched in 1911, "Free Talk" was an established supplement with a dozen-year history, and since its inception, it had always been one of the Mandarin Duck and Butterfly school's base camps. This was obvious if one looked at the list of its successive editors-in-chief: Wang Dungen, Wu Juemi, Yao Yuanchu, Chen Diexian, Chen Lengxue, and Zhou Shoujuan. As in the case of *Young Companion*, after Zhou Shoujuan, the magazine was taken over by Li Liewen, who had just returned home from overseas, on December 1, 1932. Thanks to the full support of Lu Xun, Qu Qiubai, and Mao Dun, the supplement became a well-known headquarters of New Literature. These examples, however, only showed the general trend of the time, while the old-style urban popular literature by no means collapsed at the outbreak of the May Fourth movement. Two years after *Fiction Monthly* became a magazine of New Literature, the Commercial Press launched a new magazine, *Fiction World*, for the Mandarin Duck and Butterfly school; similarly, just one month after the "Free Talk" had a new editor-in-chief, *Shun Pao* let Zhou Shoujuan launch another supplement, "Spring and Autumn" (《春秋》). The publishers were quite clear that before the new generation urban popular literature came into existence, the old-style urban popular fiction still had a large reader base, and it could be used to keep the balance between the reading markets of the old and new literature.

19.1. Successive editors-in-chief of *Young Companion* (right to left): Wu Liande (Issues 1–4), Zhou Shoujuan (Issues 5–12), Liang Desuo (Issues 13–79), and Ma Guoliang (马国亮, after Issue 80)

19.2. Cover of the first issue of *Young Companion*, launched in 1926, featuring the film star Hu Die

Why was the Mandarin Duck and Butterfly literature still needed by the general public? This is an interesting question. In order to urge authors of this literary school to write short stories for profit, He Haiming (何海鸣), a Mandarin Duck and Butterfly author, had expressed his view that in order to "sell" their novels, they should first "raise the value of fiction and let Chinese people know it is a very important literary genre, and that we should find solace in our life. When there are big market demands, the price of fiction will naturally rise."[1] Talking about the value of Mandarin Duck and Butterfly novels, Hsia Chih-tsing said: "It should be instructive to attempt a serious study of this fiction, if not to discover literary merit, at least to analyze the kinds of daydream and fantasy to which a large section of the reading public yielded during the Republican period."[2] The words "daydream" and "solace" both involved the true purpose of the literary creation of urban popular writers. They did not write solely to make money, but offered everyday reading material for urban citizens, so that they could anchor their hopes for peace and well-being in their private reading. If their lives were not peaceful, the need for literature was even more urgent, for evil was punished and the power of good was exaggerated in the fictional world, helping readers attain a kind of spiritual peace. These people made up a large proportion of urban citizens, and they formed the reader base of the Mandarin Duck and Butterfly literature.

19.3. The Mandarin Duck and Butterfly style of the "Free Talk" supplement of *Shun Pao*, published on Nov. 5, 1932, before its face-lift

19.4. "Free Talk," the supplement of *Shun Pao*, announces its face-lift

[1]   He Haiming: "Entreating the Owner of House of Happiness to Sell Novels" (《求幸福斋主人卖小说的话》), published in *Semimonthly*, Vol. 1, Issue 10, January 1922.
[2]   Hsia Chih-tsing: "Literary Revolution," *A History of Modern Chinese Fiction*, Bloomington: Indiana University Press, 1999, p. 25.

I will regard the period from the May Fourth movement until Zhang Henshui (张恨水) published *An
Unofficial History of Beijing* (《春明外史》) as a period
of modern Chinese urban popular literature. I believe it
will be very interesting to examine the literary works of
this period and their understanding of urban society and
citizens, focusing on their accounts of people's lifestyles
in Shanghai and Beijing, the most important Chinese
cities in modern China.

Following the tradition of *Dreams in Shanghai* by Sun
Yusheng (Haishang Shushisheng [海上漱石生]) and
writing about people and their stories in Shanghai, or on
the other hand, focusing the lens on the kaleidoscope-
like bustling scenes of this modern metropolis, had
become the distinctive characteristic of urban popular
novels of Shanghai at this time. Of these novels, some
influential ones included *Huangpu Tides* by Zhu Shouju

19.5. *Huangpu Tides* by
Zhu Shouju (aka Haishang
Shuomengren)

(Haishang Shuomengren), which began to be serialized in *New Shun Pao* in
1916 and finished five years later, with the separate edition published in 1921;
Living Hell by Bi Yihong (Suopo Sheng), whose first sixty chapters were serialized in *Shun Pao*'s "Free Talk" from 1922 to 1924 (after the author died at the
age of 35, the last twenty chapters were continued by his friend Bao Tianxiao);
Revelations of the Stock Exchange (《交易所现形记》) by Jiang Hongjiao
(江红蕉), which was serialized in *Weekdays* from 1922 to 1923; *Shanghai Records*
by Bao Tianxiao, which was serialized in the newspaper from 1924 to 1926,
until the eighty-chapter separate edition was published by Da Dong Press
(大东书局) in 1927 (the first part of the separate edition was published in
1924, the same year the novel was first serialized); and *Tides in the Human Sea*
(《人海潮》) by Ping Jinya (Wangzhu Sheng [网珠生]), published by New
Spring Book Society (新春书社) in 1927. These works were all about Shanghai,
much like biographies of the city. It was indeed quite rare for any Chinese city
to become the subject of biography in one or even more novels. In the late-
Qing period, in *The Sing-Song Girls of Shanghai* and *A Flower in a Sinful Sea*,
part of the story or the entire story may have happened in Shanghai, but the
city was no more than a context. Whereas although the novels mentioned
here also had a certain coherence of plot, they often detached themselves from
the specific stories and elaborated on the urban lifestyle and exposed various
crimes and swindling, allowing the authors to express their opinions on this
fascinating metropolis. Usually the authors expressed their opinions to answer
this question: what is a modern metropolis, and what is Shanghai?

Explaining why he wrote *Shanghai Records*, Bao Tianxiao (1876–1973)
started with this question, saying:

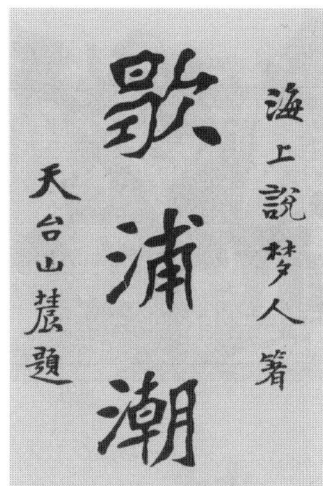

The so-called metropolis is a pool of civilization and a den of evilness. To get a glimpse of the culture of a nation, one has to look at its metropolis, where everything fascinating and grotesque is hidden or spread everywhere. Shanghai is the largest metropolis of our country. Having been away from my hometown and living here for nearly twenty years, I have some coarse understanding of all aspects of this city, and have put them together into a novel, entitled *Shanghai Records*, which has been serialized in the newspaper. After being serialized for a while, the novel becomes lengthy, and taking my friends' advice to publish a separate edition, I have divided the chapters and assigned a title for each chapter, and hereby publish it as a new book. The first part has already been printed, and I hereby write some redundant words. In general, the purpose of this book is nothing except writing about China's urban social conditions over the past decade, with Shanghai, China's largest market, being an example. There is nothing more significant.[3]

Making "the largest metropolis of our country," "China's largest market" the subject of his novel, trying to showcase the culture it represented, and more significantly, to expose its darkness, this was the purpose made explicit by Bao Tianxiao. But actually, compared with its being a "pool of civilization," these authors put much more attention on the aspect of the metropolis being a "den of evilness." However, fully aware that Shanghai's evil and wicked things were too numerous to be listed, people rushed to the city from all around, trying to make a living, and if lucky, to make a profit here, never daunted by the prospect of failure. Therefore, almost all these novels started with the pattern of describing the "first experience of country folks entering the city." Tracing this to its source, this pattern of narrative was initiated in *The Sing-Song Girls of Shanghai*. In that novel, the title of the first chapter was "Zhao Puzhai visits his uncle in Xiangua Street" (赵朴斋咸瓜街访舅), and this was how the story started: Zhao Puzhai and his younger sister went to Shanghai from the countryside and became associated with a brothel. In *Shanghai Records*, the story also started with a girl from the countryside in Dangkou, Suzhou, who became a prostitute in Shanghai (the author added a title to each chapter when the separate edition was published, and that of the first chapter was "Wearing gorgeous clothes, the poor girl prostitutes herself" [成罗衣贫女始投身]). *Living Hell* started with a girl called Ah Mei coming to Shanghai from Hangzhou, hoping to make a better living there. The first ten chapters of *Tides in the Human Sea* wrote about the countryside in Suzhou, and it was not until the eleventh chapter that the author began to write about how Suzhou natives went to Shanghai and were overwhelmed in the metropolis. This kind of writing, starting from "wanderers" and "drifters," was a realistic depiction, for we know that the population of Shanghai consisted of immigrants from the northern and southern parts of

---

[3]   "Redundant Words" (赘言), *Shanghai Records*, Shanghai: Guji Press, 1991, p. 3.

19.6. Bao Tianxiao in his youth

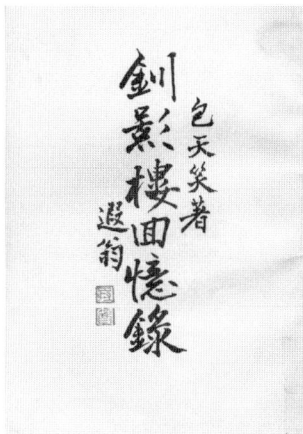

19.7. Bao Tianxiao's *Memoirs of the Bracelet Shadow Chamber* was an extremely comprehensive record of the everyday life of Shanghai citizens from the late Qing to the Republican period. The novel also had a sequel

Jiangsu, the northern part of Zhejiang, and all places through to Guangdong, who rushed to the city to make a living, and this narrative pattern was best for readers to have a good overview of the metropolis Shanghai.

Upon entering the city, the image of Shanghai in the mind of the country-folk and people from surrounding towns (some Shanghai citizens addressed all those who were not native of Shanghai as "countryfolk") was full of evilness and danger. This was usually the first impression of the modern metropolis in the mind of people from the farming community, and even today, many rural migrant workers still harbor a kind of enmity toward cities. Therefore, writing about every aspect of the evil city of Shanghai was a shared feature of these novels, and it was nothing new, but a tradition inherited from the late-Qing period. Success in cities was all about "adventures." Take the main character, Qian Ruhai, of *Huangpu Tides* for example – he first made his fortune by selling fake and inferior medicine, and then he opened an insurance company, doing all kinds of dubious businesses. *Revelations of the Stock Exchange* was certainly about speculators making fictitious transactions. *Tides in the Human Sea* and *Shanghai Records* were full of dark hidden secrets in the business circle, brothels, publishing, and entertainment industries. Those who failed in cities were cheated and would naturally sink afterward. Loaning money to do business was gross deception, while even consumption and entertaining, like eating and drinking, brothel visiting, gambling, and social activities, were full of snares and delusions. Sometimes people may have found true love in brothels, as in *Living Hell*, in which the author praised and sympathized with prostitutes, but it was extremely rare, as for most brothels cheating and swindling occurred every day. The superficial civilized life within the foreign concession concealed their ill deeds; in

19.8. In Shanghai's earlier years, a huge number of people from other places rushed to the city and lived on its borders, creating a special cultural landscape for the city

Huangpu Tides, seeing the hidden secrets within the legal profession was indeed shocking. The key point of a metropolitan drama was that every character was being cheated while at the same time cheating others. The moral bankruptcy of the city was recorded with a dazzling narrative, and this was a mindset generally held by people from the farming community who first entered the industrial and commercial world. Citizens had a love-hate attitude toward their city, for moral degradation was a result brought about by material civilization. The following comments on freedom of social activities and of love, made by the rich boys and girls of *Huangpu Tides*, who got to know each other when they watched spoken drama plays in the new-style theater in Shanghai, may well reflect the views and principles of the urban popular writers of that time:

> You people should know that since Western learning is flourishing in China, the boundaries between men and women have long been broken down. In ancient times, women had the bad habit of being shy and not facing men; actually, it was the same person before and after marriage, and if one did not have a face marked with smallpox or a head with favus, what on earth was there to be shy about? Such bad habits have been done away with since the reform; nowadays men can take a good look at women and women can watch men to their heart's content – isn't it a pleasure? But these are ordinary men and women. As for those in the new-style schools, they receive more education in Western learning and have naturally evolved more rapidly, and often there are men and women, who first meet and hardly know each other, talking happily in public, and some even have a child after a half or one year. You see, things will turn into their opposite, civilization in its extreme case will have something barbarian. It can be seen as a kind of physical cycle, and it's the way of the world.[4]

4   Haishang Shuomengren (Zhu Shouju): *Huangpu Tides*, Vol. 1, Shanghai: Guji Press, 1991, p. 187.

19.9. The swimming pools in Shanghai at the beginning of the twentieth century were so open that men and women shared the same swimming pool; but in terms of swimming suits, men also wore tops, so it was hard to distinguish men from women in the swimming pool

19.10. During the Republican period, men and women in large cities could enjoy freedom in social activities, and dancing was quite common

Isn't it a downright "love-hate" attitude? Therefore, some say that urban popular writers rejected modern civilization, which may be an exaggeration, but it was true that they were different from, and indeed, more conservative than new literary writers who praised "Nora leaving home" and at the same time, discussed "what happens after Nora leaves home." What was obvious here was a typical philistine mindset, and with this in mind, it is easy for us to imagine what kind of "daydream" was anchored in the urban popular novels of the time: that one could make a fortune by doing insurance business, buying and selling stocks, gambling, or helping others engage in a lawsuit, but one should be prudent; one could seek pleasure in watching operas, visiting brothels or loving women, but one should protect oneself from being harmed. Everything you did could possibly turn into its opposite, but it was safe and secure to seek solace by reading novels. The social novels and romantic fictions by urban popular writers functioned as textbooks on city life, teaching citizens how to hasten after wealth and avoid damage.

These novels that recounted all kinds of vices and foibles of life in Shanghai at the beginning of the Republican period act as a living fossil for scholars of history of folk customs and social history. A widely cited example of this is how literary critic Hsia Tsi-an felt after he read some novels he found in a hardware store in the United States. He "read *Huangpu Tides* and found it 'charming to the eye'; and then he read Bao Tianxiao's *Shanghai Records* and was rapt in admiration. It was a pity that there were only the first sixty chapters of Bao's novel, and he did not know where to borrow the remaining chapters. [He] wanted to write an article to talk about those novels on Shanghai."[5]

---

[5] Quoted from Hsia Chih-tsing: "Hsia Tsi-an's Views on Chinese Popular Literature" (《夏济安对中国俗文学的看法》), *Love, Society, and the Novel* (《爱情 • 社会 • 小说》), Taipei: Pure Literature Press, 1970.

And it confirmed Hsia Chih-tsing's assertion that it "should be instructive to attempt a serious study of this fiction."

On the other hand, these urban popular novels were about the personal experiences of intellectuals of the early Republican period, drawn from their everyday lives. Often, urban popular writers mixed their observations of Shanghai with their own life experiences. Pin Jinya was from a poor family and made a living by selling his articles, and finally became a well-known publisher in Shanghai. In his *Tides in the Human Sea*, he wrote about the literary circle and publishing and entertaining industries in Shanghai, with which he was extremely familiar. When Bi Yihong was a young boy, his father bought an official position for him and later he followed his father's advice to enter the political arena; he then became tangled in a lawsuit about his father's debt, opened a legal office, and fell in love with a prostitute, which was all in his mind when he wrote *Living Hell*. The same was true of Zhu Shouju, Bao Tianxiao, and others. Therefore, these novels were based on the range of vision of these "literary talents of glamorous Shanghai," which was generally the same as that of common citizens. Sometimes they would go so far as to make the relationship between known intellectuals and prostitutes the core thread of their novels (*Living Hell*), so that one could identify the characters of the novel with celebrities without having to conduct in-depth examination: in the novel Ke Liansun alluded to Bi Yihong, Yao Xiaoqiu to Bao Tianxiao, Monk Xuanman Shangren to Su Manshu, Hua Yafeng to Ye Xiaofeng (Ye Chucang), and Zhao Qiwu to Yao Yuanchu, etc. Some plots in the novels were almost a truthful record of what happened at that time; such as that of Ke Liansun getting to know Qiubo the singing girl through Xuanman Shangren, as well as the death of the latter. Making the celebrities in the Republican period visible in the glamorous Shanghai scenes was a reason why these urban popular novels were well accepted by readers. And then there was another kind of "truthful record," that is, some of these novels were based on "local news reports." Many urban popular novelists had worked as journalists and reported news on the spot in Shanghai, where the newspaper industry was quite thriving. According to Bao Tianxiao, he was lucky to hear Wu Jianren (Wu Woyao) teach him how to write novels: "I got to know Wu Woyao in the editorial office of *All-Story Monthly*, and knowing that he was the author of *Bizarre Happenings Eyewitnessed Over Two Decades*, I once asked his advice of novel writing. (He showed me a notebook, which was full of glued clips of news stories cut from newspapers, and stories told by friends that he had noted down. He said these were all raw material and, writing novels, you just need to link them together.)"[6] When he wrote *Shanghai Records*, Bao Tianxiao turned to the Local News section of

---

[6]   Bao Tianxiao: "Starting as a Magazine Editor," *Memoirs of the Bracelet Shadow Chamber*, Hong Kong: Dahua Press, 1971, p. 357.

the *China Times* to accumulate material and wrote the novel by linking the news stories together. These novels were less fictional and more like historical material, and part of their literary value lay in their historical value, thus inheriting the tradition of Chinese historical and biographic literature.

As if overwhelmed by the urban popular novels representing Shanghai, in the Republican period there were less outstanding urban novels representing Beijing. It was probably not until Zhang Henshui published his *An Unofficial History of Beijing* and *The Story of A Noble Family* (《金粉世家》), when the southern writer wrote excellent stories about this large city in the north, that one could say there was finally modern urban popular literature with Beijing as its subject. Such novels published before Zhang Henshui included Ye Xiaofeng's *So This is Beijing* (《如此京华》), whose first edition was published in 1921, and He Haiming's *Thick Smoke in Beijing* (《十丈京尘》), which was

19.11. Shanghai citizens of the early Republican period, who had just cut off their queues, were fond of eating Western food in the concession

serialized in *Semimonthly* for two years around the same time. It was after his *An Unofficial History of Beijing* was published that Zhang Henshui attracted attention as an urban popular writer. *An Unofficial History of Beijing* began to be serialized in "Night Light" (夜光), the supplement of *Evening World* (《世界晚报》), in 1924, with its last installment published in 1929, so we may regard it as a landmark literary work indicating the transition of the May Fourth urban popular novels turning a new page in the 1930s. Different from those depicting the rise of Shanghai as a commercial metropolis, these novels could not voice high-sounding words about what a modernized metropolis Beijing was. In these novels, Beijing was a political jungle that had a glorious past but was becoming corrupted, decaying and declining, but still stood erect. *So This is Beijing* told a story with the mansion of Grand General Fang (alluding to Yuan Shikai) as its main thread, depicting Beijing as a trafficking market of official positions. *Thick Smoke in Beijing* took the relationship between a disillusioned official and a prostitute as the thread of the story, writing about the ups and downs of southern officials in the political arena in Beijing. These novels made officialdom in Beijing their subject matter, while *An Unofficial History of Beijing* was a love story with the political situation of Beijing as its background. In a word, the city of Beijing could be identified with officialdom. Before Zhang

Henshui and Lao She of the New Literature camp came to the foreground, one could not see the colorful life of commoners living in *hutong* lanes. Even brothels were officialdom, and they represented high-rank officialdom (the so-called reception room of the State Department), which could best show what Beijing was like. In *So This is Beijing*, the author wrote a concise and vivid satire about the register of a brothel from a servant's point of view:

> The first entry was the clerk of some prince, then there was this chief and that supervisor, all big noblemen, and he looked at it, engrossed in the entries. Who could imagine, he thought, that in this small room there was such a register of the State Department?[7]

And in the same book, when a prostitute heard someone say they did not know anything about "state affairs," she made a very accurate and interesting comment about how the brothel could become the place of officialdom in a short time:

> "Come on! Who involved in state affairs has not use this brothel as a reception room? The day before yesterday, that secretary general entertained a feast here in my room, and his guests were either cabinet ministers or foreign ministers, and just in the interval between two dishes were served, they agreed on something about some minister of internal affairs or minister of foreign affairs. Later when my shoelace came loose, it took a longer while for that secretary general to tighten it for me. You see, the state affairs you guys talk about sound big, but they were not even as time-wasting as tightening a shoelace."[8]

Here we see the urban citizen laughing at officialdom, but she was also showing off how high-rank officials visited her room, which was a vulgar, philistine mindset. As in the urban popular novels representing Shanghai, these novels also focused on exposing evilness, and uncovering the adventures and fraudulent behavior of some high-rank figures in the officialdom in Beijing. Examples included Hao Xiaoze in *Thick Smoke in Beijing*, who made his fortune by gambling and found a shortcut to officialdom; Gong Jichuan (whose nickname was "Saturday"), who went to and from Beijing and Tianjin each week by train and went up the ladder by getting to know well-off people in the first-class carriage; and Quan Baoqing, who took an active part in official circles by cheating, etc. The difference between Beijing and Shanghai lay in their urban cultural background and different modernization process, each representing the characteristics of their respective geographic regions. The urban popular novels depicting Beijing often had anecdotes and stories of the past, full of daydreams recalling the city's glorious past, characteristic of the transition from the late Qing to the Republican period.

---

[7]   Quoted from Fan Boqun, ed.: *A History of Modern Chinese Popular Literature* (《中国近现代通俗文学史》), Vol. 1, Nanjing: Jiangsu Education Press, 2000, p. 365.

[8]   Quoted from ibid., pp. 366–367.

It seemed that martial arts (*wuxia*) fictions had nothing to do with urban culture, but actually the so-called *wuxia* world was the back street, the home base of each city. This was a grotesque venue, where there was no clear boundary between good and evil powers; honest commoners and local bullies were juxtaposed, the higher-level politics and lower-level resistance coexisted, and moral heroes in this imagined world sought good and justice on behalf of urban citizens who were treated unfairly, thus creating a half-fantasy, half-real miniature society in the jungle. The martial arts novels of the Republican period entered a new stage. There were two famous authors: "Xiang from the south and Zhao from the north." Xiang referred to Xiang Kairan (1890–1957, pseudonym: Pingjiang Buxiaosheng), author of *Marvelous Gallants of the Rivers and Lakes* (《江湖奇侠传》), which began to be serialized in *Red* magazine in 1923, with some chapters being continued by Zhao Shaokuang. Its separate edition began to be published by the World Journal Book Store in 1925,

19.12. He Haiming's *Thick Smoke in Beijing* manuscript, which was written on paper specially made for this novel

and altogether eleven volumes were published, with the last one published in 1929. "Zhao" referred to Zhao Huanting (赵焕亭), author of *The Valiant History of the Strange Knights-Errant* (《奇侠精忠全传》), whose eight volumes were published by Yixin Press from 1923 to 1927, and the entire novel totalled 1.35 million characters. Voluminous as it was, *The Valiant History of the Strange Knights-Errant* did not depart from the set pattern of the old-style legal case novels of the Qing dynasty, and the Yang brothers and other heroes in the novel were extremely loyal to the imperial court and helped the latter suppress unrests here and there, willing to be ruled and ordered by ministers of the feudal court. *Marvelous Gallants of the Rivers and Lakes* started with the armed fighting for a boundary of a piece of land between peasants of Pingjiang and Liuyang of Hunan, putting up a fight between swordsmen of the Kunlun Sect and Kongtong Sect. The swordsmen were no longer masters of martial arts, but became people with magic weapons and magic powers. The novel was richer in imagination and written more vivaciously through borrowing various local customs and folk legends, and the heroes were no longer loyal servants and cops taken advantage of by officials of the Qing court. Thus *Marvelous Gallants of the Rivers and Lakes* broke loose the bondage of the ideological framework of legal case novels and made martial arts fiction an independent literary genre, and Pingjiang Buxiaosheng thus became the founder of the martial arts fiction of the Republican period, which both Huanzhu Louzhu (还珠楼主)

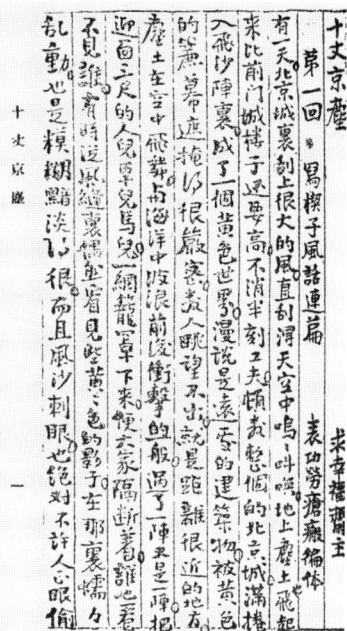

19.13. Portrait of Pingjiang Buxiaosheng (aka Xiang Kairan), the master of martial arts fiction

19.14. Cover of the first edition of Pingjiang Buxiaosheng's magnum opus, *Marvelous Gallants of the Rivers and Lakes*, with which he became the founder of the martial arts fiction of the Republican period

and Jin Yong (金庸) of the later ages recognized. Other novels that had been out of the old pattern of legal case novels included Yao Aimin's (姚哀民) *Ten Marvelous Gallants of the Country* (《南北十大奇侠传》), a *wuxia* novel serialized in *Red Roses* from 1926 to 1928. This novel wrote about the secret society under the cover of the "rivers and lakes," and was an antecedent for later secret society novels, in which the secret society was rich in the popular grassroots atmosphere. The narrative pattern of martial arts fictions was an endless cycle of reprisal and retaliation, with morals and justice surely winning in the end. Thus when ordinary urban citizens lived in a disadvantaged position and could not find an outlet for their resentment, reading martial arts fiction was a satisfying experience and a great solace for them, which was why these novels continued to be popular among readers.

Now it was time for Zhang Henshui to come to the foreground. It was when new readers educated in new-style schools became citizen readers and when writers of May Fourth New Literature turned to urban popular literature and reconciled it with Shanghai school literature, that a new page of modern urban popular literature was finally turned.

PART III

The Coexistence of Diverse Types of Literature

拓荒者

第四五期合刊

新月

第一卷　第一號

上海新月書店發行
民國十七年六月再版

文學雜誌

創刊號

商務印書館發行

現代
1932

創刊號

現代書局印行

TWENTY

TO THE SOUTH

The Return of the Literary Center

IN AUGUST 1926, LU XUN DEPARTED FOR THE SOUTH, which was a signal that the New Culture camp in the north had already split up and Beijing would soon lose its status as the source of the May Fourth literary revolution and thus as the country's literary center.

Many other intellectuals left Beijing around the same time, for which there were two reasons. Firstly, the Beiyang government under the Duan Qirui administration had strengthened its cultural control, censorship was increasingly prohibitive and freedom was more limited. After the March Eighteenth Incident and the death of Liu Hezhen and others, a blacklist of more than fifty intellectuals from the cultural and educational circle was published in the newspaper, which included Lu Xun and Lin Yutang (whose name appeared on the blacklist as "玉堂"). Lu Xun had to hide himself in the editorial office of *Wilderness*, the Yamamoto Clinic, and hospitals run by Germans and Frenchmen, with his safety in jeopardy. Secondly, the Northern Expedition had started in the south, attracting a large number of progressive literary writers. In March that year, Guo Moruo, Yu Dafu, Cheng Fangwu, Zheng Boqi, Wang Duqing, and Mu Mutian, all core members of the Creation Society, went to Guangzhou. In July, Guo Moruo dropped the pen and joined the Northern Expedition as deputy head of the General Political Department of the National Revolutionary Army (NRA). Yu Dafu was not so enthusiastic about joining the army, and he returned to Shanghai at the end of that year, probably because he felt that Shanghai suited literary authors better. Lu Xun was definitely not alone in leaving Beijing. Once the blacklist was published, Lin Yutang left Beijing first and went to Xiamen University to work as the dean of the Faculty of Arts. Then he asked Lu Xun to teach at the same university with him. After the Beijing Press was closed down, its editor Sun Fuyuan, one of Lu Xun's students, also went to Xiamen, so when Lu Xun arrived at Xiamen University, he was welcomed by Lin Yutang, Sun Fuyuan, and others, and he settled temporarily in the Department of Biology building. This started the southbound migration of members of the Yu Si Society, who would later move to and gather in Shanghai. To get an idea of the huge gap left in the literary world of the north after Lu Xun left Beijing, one may look at the examples of two young men, both of whom later became significant left-wing writers. One was Zhang Tianyi (张天翼), who had just passed the entrance examination to the prep school of Peking University in the summer of 1926. Seeing that Lu Xun, whom he regarded as his guide, had left Beijing, he felt he "could not learn what I wanted to learn at Peking University,"[1] and thus quit and returned to Hangzhou one year later. Zhang Tianyi did not give up his desire to follow Lu Xun, but started writing to him for advice at the end of 1928. Their earliest documented correspondence was made on January 24, 1929: Lu Xun wrote in his diary that day about replying to Zhang. It was a coincidence that another young man, Sha Ting (沙汀), also graduated from the First Provincial Teachers' Training College in Chengdu in the summer of 1926. He went all the way to Beijing to continue his studies, only to find that he had just missed the date of examination. He then considered listening to the lectures without credit, but knowing that Lu Xun had left, he returned disappointed to Sichuan in October. By 1930, Sha Ting was listening to Lu Xun's lectures in the classrooms of China Art University in Shanghai. These were

20.1. Liu Hezhen (second from the right in the second row from the back) and her fellow students from National Beijing Women's Normal College. Liu, who died at the young age of 22, was a student of the English Department and was chairperson of the Students' Council. Lu Xun wrote one of his most famous essays after her death in the March Eighteenth Incident

[1] Zhang Tianyi: "In the Writer's Own Words" (《作家自述》), *Studies on Modern Chinese Literature*, Issue 2, 1980.

passionate young people who would soon establish close literary relationships with Lu Xun, and we can imagine that if Lu Xun had not left Beijing, how many young people like them would have been attracted to the city.

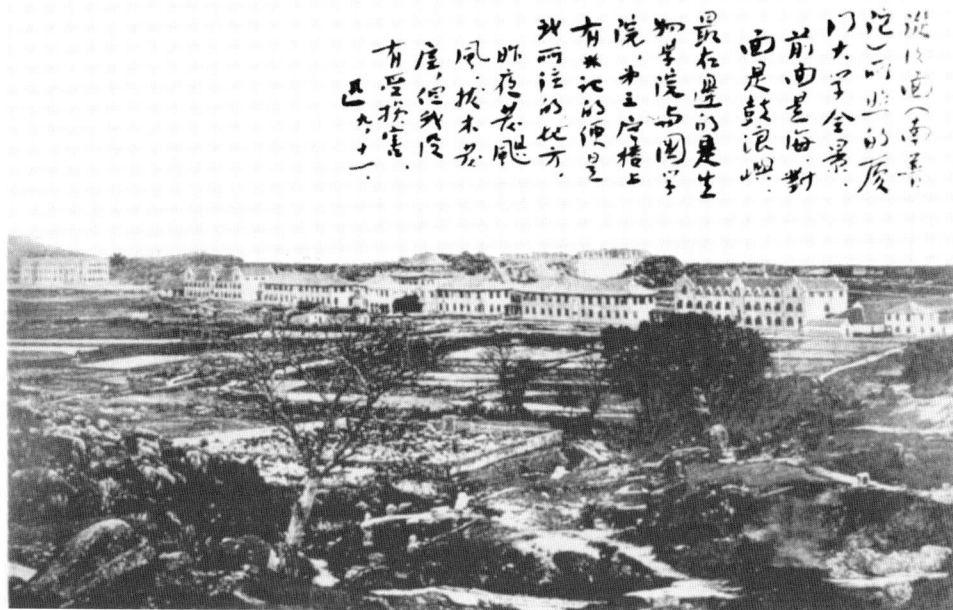

20.2. Upon his arrival in Xiamen in September 1926, Lu Xun sent this postcard of "Panorama of Xiamen University" to Xu Guangping (许广平), who had already arrived in Guangzhou. Lu Xun indicated the location of the Department of Biology building, where he settled, on the postcard

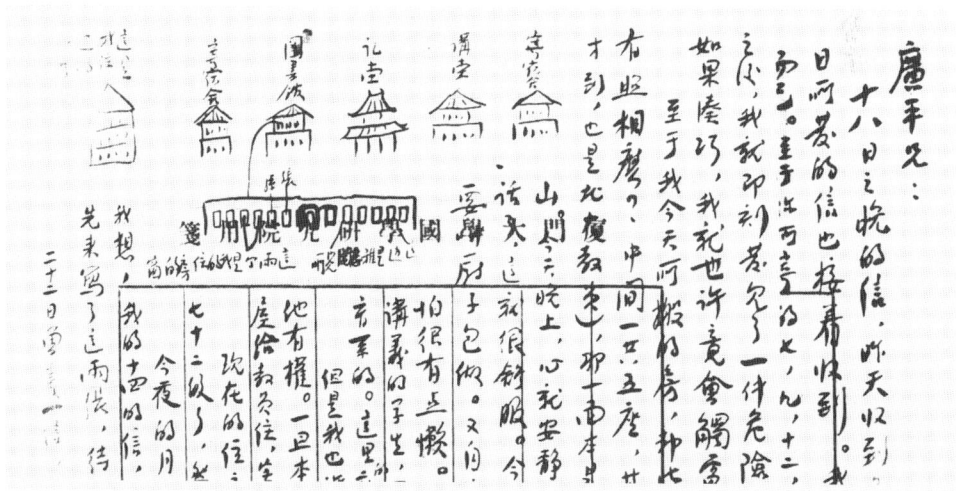

20.3. In this letter to Xu Guangping, Lu Xun drew a picture to show where he lived and worked at Xiamen University

At Sun Yat-sen University in Guangzhou, Lu Xun was deeply shocked to hear of the April Twelfth Incident. In October 1927, he decided to leave Guangzhou and went to Shanghai by boat together with Xu Guangping, where he lived until his death. In the same year, *Yu Si* magazine moved south, and in December the first issue of Volume 4 was published in Shanghai. According to Lu Xun:

> *Yu Si* had escaped being torn up by Duan Qirui and his toadies in Beijing, but was finally banned by Grand Marshal Zhang. The Beixin Press was also closed down. That was in 1927.
>
> In that year, Xiaofeng once came to my dwelling place and suggested that *Yu Si* would be printed in Shanghai soon and asked me to be its editor. Considering our closeness, I should not dodge this responsibility, and thus I became its editor.[2]

"Xiaofeng" referred to Li Xiaofeng, a member of the Yu Si Society and the boss of Beixin Press. "Closeness" was about the relationship between the press and May Fourth New Literature, and its close ties with Lu Xun. The center of May Fourth New Literature was Beijing, but most New Literature books were published in Shanghai. For example, most Literary Research Society books were published by the Commercial Press and Creation Society books by Taidong Press. If we say there was a famous publishing institution in Beijing publishing the works of New Literature, that was Beixin Press. One can see the significance of this middle-sized literary press by the fact that Lu Xun's *Call to Arms*, *Wandering*, *Hot Wind*, *Three Leisures* (《三闲集》), *False Freedom* (《伪自由书》)*, Unlucky Star* (《华盖集》), *Sequel to Unlucky Star* (《华盖集续编》), and *And That's That* (《而已集》), Bing Xin's *Letters to My Little Readers*, and Jiang Guangci's *The Moon Forces its Way through the Clouds* (《冲出云围的月亮》) were all published by Beixin Press. Li Xiaofeng had always known that Shanghai would surely resume its status as a literary center, as it had been in the late Qing, and therefore he had been busy opening the Shanghai branch of Beixin Press, publishing the Camel book series (骆驼丛书) and launching *Beixin* magazine. Now he simply took the opportunity to move the headquarters of the press to Shanghai (which was first located in Baoshan Alley along Baoshan Road and later moved to the basement of Yufengtai Restaurant at the corner of Fuzhou and Shandong roads), and finally moved the entire Beixin Press south.

---

[2] Lu Xun: "My Involvement with *Yu Si* from Beginning to End" (《我和〈语丝〉的始终》), *Complete Works of Lu Xun*, Vol. 4, Beijing: People's Literature Press, 1981, p. 169.

One of the reasons why Lu Xun left Xiamen University was because he felt that people of the Contemporary Critique clique were gathering there. This can be seen as another example of the total disintegration of the New Literature camp in Beijing. There was an affinity between the Contemporary Critique clique and the Crescent Moon clique that formed later. Most members were professors returning from Europe or the United States, with core members of both being Hu Shi, Xu Zhimo, and Chen Xiying (aka Chen Yuan). The *Contemporary Critique* weekly, launched in 1924, had its first 138 issues printed by the Publishing House of Peking University. The activities of members of the Crescent Moon clique at the Songpo Library, 7 Shihu Lane, Beijing, were more like dinner parties or those of a drama club or literary salon. By this time, these people also moved south. The first was Hu Shi, who had returned home when the Northern Expedition won one battle after another; he stayed in Japan for over a month and could not decide where to settle. His friends dissuaded him from going to Beijing, with his student Gu Jiegang being most vigorous. Hu Shi finally settled in Shanghai. He received an appointment at Kwang Hua University in 1927, and became principal of China Public School in 1928. By July 1927, the headquarters of the *Contemporary Critique* weekly moved to Shanghai and began publishing its last seventy issues, from No. 139 to No. 209. The Crescent Moon Society was also formally founded around this time in Shanghai:

> After the March Eighteenth Incident and the outbreak of the Northern Expedition War immediately after, some members of the Crescent Moon school moved south and some went abroad, so that their activities in Beijing discontinued. Upon Hu Shi's arrival in Shanghai in 1927, the old and new core members, including Xu Zhimo, Yu Shangyuan, Liang Shiqiu, Rao Mengkan (饶孟侃), Pan Guangdan (潘光旦), Wen Yiduo, and Ding Xilin, were quite happy and soon gathered around Hu Shi, seeking to revive their organization and let the light of "Crescent Moon" shine again. They established the Crescent Moon Bookstore, asked Hu Shi to be its chairman, and then launched the *Crescent Moon* monthly and the *Poetry* quarterly.[3]

The Crescent Moon Bookstore, established in spring 1927, and the *Crescent Moon* monthly, launched in March 1928, marked the establishment of the Crescent Moon Society in Shanghai, which later became one of the few literary groups in the city that could rival left-wing literature.

---

[3] Hu Ming (胡明): *A Biographical Account of Hu Shi* (《胡适传论》), Vol. 2, Beijing: People's Literature Press, 1996, p. 668.

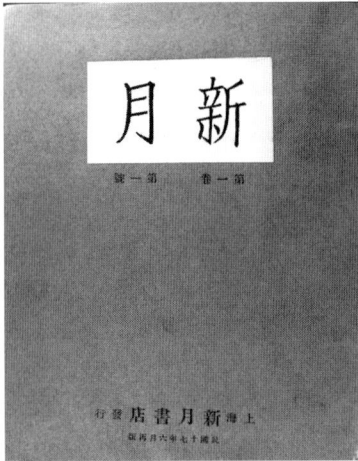

20.4. Inaugural issue of *Crescent Moon*, which marked the establishment of the Crescent Moon Society

The authors of the Literary Research Society had long since moved the center of their activities to Shanghai. Unlike the Creation Society (even Yu Dafu and Ye Lingfeng, who seemed to not take the same line as later left-wing writers, had actually joined the League of Left-Wing Writers at first, but both were expelled; Yu because he refused to attend the "flying assemblies,"[4] and Ye because he contributed to journals with "nationalist backgrounds"), these authors did not all turn left-wing after 1927, but split into two groups, left-wing and democratic, with Mao Dun being the representative of the former, and the latter consisting of the Lida (立达) school and Kaiming school. They all made Shanghai the center of their activities. Zhou Zuoren was the only one remaining in Beijing, and he became the founder of Beijing school literature (marked by his support of the launch of *Camel Grass* magazine). The Lida and Kaiming literary schools continued the tradition of the Literary Research Society. Ye Shengtao, Xia Mianzun, Feng Zikai, Zhu Ziqing, Zheng Zhenduo, Kuang Husheng (匡互生), Wang Boxiang, and Liu Xunyu (刘薰宇), among others, did not go backward from May Fourth literature, nor did they take a radical path. They went through the Chunhui Middle School period along the White Horse Lake in Shangyu of Zhejiang, the Lida Middle School and Lida Academy periods in Shanghai, and finally merged with editors from the Kaiming Bookstore and became an author group with their own characteristics in Shanghai. In 1930, Ye Shengtao quit his job at the Commercial Press and joined the Kaiming Translating and Editing Department. From then on, the creative achievements of this group of writers were even more brilliant. They focused on prose writing, and at the same time were devoted to the Chinese-language education of primary and secondary schools and of the general public; by linking together literature, education, and academic research, they established their own style featuring simplicity and honesty, sincerity and frankness, earnestness and elegance. This was especially outstanding in the frivolous atmosphere of Shanghai.

---

4   Flying assemblies (飞行集会) were tactics used by CCP members in the 1920s and 1930s when demonstrations and gatherings were restricted and forbidden in large cities. During these so-called flying assemblies, demonstrators who pretended they did not know one another gathered at a designated place where they delivered speeches, read protest announcement, and distributed leaflets, and then dispersed quickly after the protest. – Translator's note

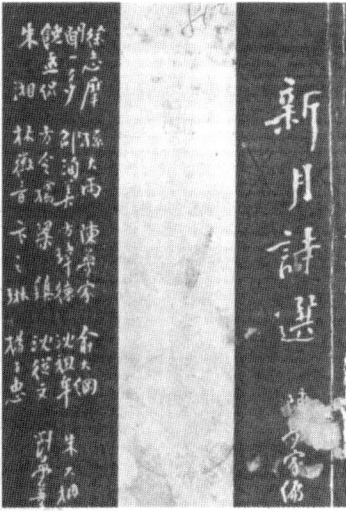

20.5. An anthology of the Crescent
Moon school: *Selected Crescent Moon
Poetry* (《新月诗选》), edited by
Chen Mengjia (陈梦家)

20.6. Chen Mengjia and Zhao Luorui
(赵萝蕤), both Crescent Moon poets, in
1935, within the west entrance of Peking
University

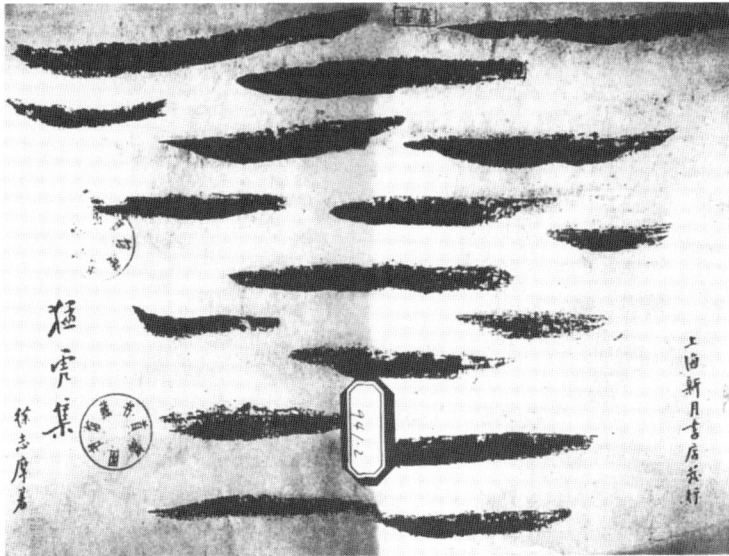

20.7. Xu Zhimo's *Fierce Tiger*, another book published by the Crescent Moon
Bookstore. The cover was designed by Wen Yiduo in 1931

Lin Yutang left the Yu Si group and launched *Analects* in Shanghai in
1932, and later launched several other famous magazines of a similar style,
including *This Human World* and *Cosmic Wind*. Echoing Zhou Zuoren in the
north, he raised the banner of "humorous literature" that championed innate

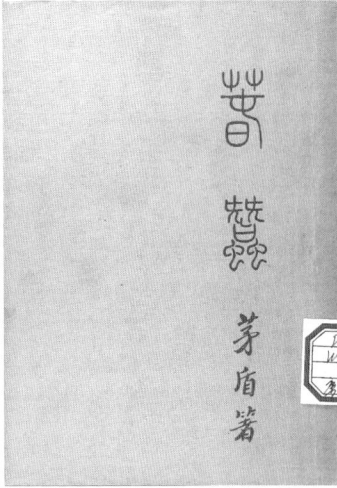

20.8. Kaiming Bookstore published a number of progressive books and magazines, such as Mao Dun's *Spring Silkworms* (《春蚕》); this was the edition published by the Kaiming Bookstore in May 1933

sensibility, self-expression, and a leisurely lifestyle. This was certainly different from the left-wing line, but it belonged to democratic literature, and in a sense promoted the urban popular culture. The authors of this group, including Tao Kangde (陶亢德) from the editorial office; Xu Xu (徐訏), who made outstanding achievements in literary creation later, and others, such as Shao Xunmei, Li Qingya, and Zhang Kebiao, were also Shanghai school authors. From Xiamen to Guangzhou through to Shanghai, Lin Yutang had always remained close to Lu Xun. After *Analects* was published, Lu Xun wrote an essay entitled "A Year of *Analects*" at Lin's request. They were close friends, but they were becoming increasingly different in literary and political stance. Still, humorous literature was another consumptive type of New Literature targeted at urban citizens (and it did not give up the "enlightenment" aim), and thus it gained a foothold in the urban citizen reading market.

The writers who chose the revolutionary path gathered in Shanghai. At that time the world ushered in the "Red Decade," socialist thoughts spread further among Chinese intellectuals, and many left-wing intellectuals who had to retreat underground after the April Twelfth Incident fled to the concession of Shanghai more than ever. Those returning from Japan and retiring from the revolutionary front became the vital force of the later-stage Creation Society, and they put forward the slogan of "Revolutionary Literature" marked by the "Revolution and Literature" (《革命与文学》) published by Guo Moruo in 1926 and "From Literary Revolution to Revolutionary Literature" (《从文学革命到革命文学》) by Cheng Fangwu in 1928. Those sharing the same slogan also included the Sun Society (太阳社), established in 1928, which consisted of Jiang Guangci, Qian Xingcun, and Meng Chao (孟超), and the Our Society (我们社) with generally the same members. In relevant discussions, the later-stage Creation Society and the Sun Society, influenced by the socialist ideology of the time, proposed to promote proletarian literature that was too radical for China's reality at the time, attempted to step over May Fourth literature and thus looked down upon it, and even criticized Lu Xun and Mao Dun for lagging behind the times. On the other hand, during this time Lu Xun closely examined and pondered over China's history and reality, learned about the experience and theories of proletarian revolutions in other countries, and translated the earlier literary and art theories of the USSR; thus as a left-leaning intellectual, he developed his own theories and essay writing style. All of this was not possible without the active cultural and intellectual

20.9. The first photo Lu Xun and Xu Guangping took with relatives and friends after arriving in Shanghai in October 1927. Front row (left to right): Zhou Jianren, Xu Guangping, Lu Xun; Back row (left to right): Sun Fuxi (孙福熙, Sun Fuyuan's brother), Lin Yutang, and Sun Fuyuan

20.10. This picture of Lu Xun wearing a sweater knitted by Xu Guangping showed that he had finally settled in Shanghai

20.11. Inaugural issue of *Sun Monthly* (《太阳月刊》)

exchanges and facilitating environment in Shanghai, which paved the way for the end of debate and the establishment of various groups of "left-wing writers" in 1930.

Meanwhile, facing the pressure of New Literature, the Mandarin Duck and Butterfly – Saturday literary school was entrenched in the field of urban popular literature. Their newspapers, magazines and publications had always been based in Shanghai, and by this time, they were even more concentrated on their commercial literary "production." The emergence of Zhang Henshui broke with the tradition that this kind of literature could only be produced in Shanghai. Zhang was a southerner, a native of Anhui, and at first was a newspaperman in the south, but it wasn't until after he came to Beijing as a newspaperman and serialized his *An Unofficial History of Beijing* and *The Story of A Noble Family* in *Evening World* (《世界晚报》) and *World Daily* (《世界日报》) that he became known. Interestingly, however, Zhang was not widely known to the entire country until he serialized *Fate in Tears and Laughter* (《啼笑因缘》) in the *Daily News* (《新闻报》) in Shanghai. Yan Duhe, a

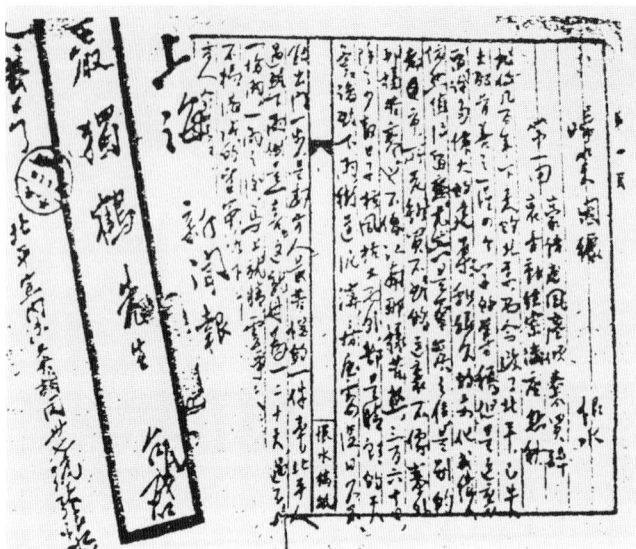

20.12. Manuscript of Zhang Henshui's *Fate in Tears and Laughter* and the envelope he used to send the manuscript to Yan Duhe. Later the novel was serialized in "Forest of Pleasure," the supplement of the *Daily News*, and caused a stir among urban citizens

famous newspaperman and Mandarin Duck and Butterfly author, invited Zhang to do this. A while later, Shanghai Mingxing Film Studio invited Yan Duhe, the facilitator of the publication of the novel, to adapt it for the screen, and in 1932 released a film of the same name starring Hu Die and Zheng Xiaoqiu (郑小秋), which caused a big stir throughout the country. It was later adapted for film and opera many times and had a great influence on urban citizens. Zhang Henshui became a household name in Shanghai, and even in cities in the inland areas.

It was by no means fortuitous that Shanghai resumed its status as a literary center and witnessed a renewed influx of authors. Taking the left-wing literature that thrived a while later as an example, it could only be based in Shanghai and nowhere else. In 1927 the Kuomintang (KMT) government was formed and made Nanjing its capital, changing the name of Beijing to "Beiping," which meant that Beijing had lost its status as the political center of the country. The KMT government promoted "literature obeying the Three People's Principles" and the Nationalist Art and Literature movement, while "left-wing literature" in Shanghai, which was so close to Nanjing, could thrive despite the pressure of the art and literary policies of the KMT, relying on the profit-oriented operation of newspapers, magazines, and publishing institutions, as well as the special status of the concession, which protected freedom of speech. At that time the publishing industry was prosperous in Shanghai, and it was quite a peculiar phenomenon that they rushed to publish "proletarian literature" and made it a new fashion in the metropolis. The Modern Book Company (现代书局), for example, was one of the active small- to mid-sized presses focusing on literature and art in Shanghai, which was jointly run by Hong Xuefan

20.13. *Pioneers*, a journal whose editor-in-chief was Jiang Guangci, was published by the Modern Book Company It was launched as the journal of the Sun Society and became an official journal of the League of Left-Wing Writers from the combined fourth and fifth issue, after which it was immediately banned

(洪雪帆), Zhang Jinglu (张静庐), and Lu Fang (卢芳) and had such first-class talented editors as Shi Zhecun (施蛰存) and Ye Lingfeng. It was not a left-wing press, but risked publishing three left-wing magazines one after another, namely *Popular Literature* (《大众文艺》) in 1928, which later became one of the official journals of the League of Left-Wing Writers; *New Tide Monthly* (《新流月报》) in 1929, which acted as a substitute of *Sun Monthly*, a journal of the Sun Society, after the latter was prohibited from being published by another press; and *Pioneers* (《拓荒者》) in 1930, which was a substitute of *New Tide Monthly* when it was jeopardized after four issues were published. When the League of Left-Wing Writers was established in March 1930, *Pioneers* became its official journal after the third issue, only to be banned by the government after the combined fourth and fifth issue was published. In one of his letters to a friend that recommended journals worth reading, Lu Xun mentioned several left-wing journals published by the Modern Book Company:

> As for art journals published in China, I don't think there are any that are truly worth reading. Proletarian literature has been quite fashionable recently, and it seems that publications are thought outdated if they do not raise this banner, but there are very few authors in this field. The magazines with a large circulation include *Pioneers*, *Modern Fiction* (《现代小说》), *Popular Literature*, and *Meng Ya* (《萌芽》), but I'm afraid they will soon be banned.[5]

20.14. Inaugural issue of *Vanguard Monthly* (《前锋月刊》) (Oct. 1930), which the Modern Book Company was forced to publish. It was a stronghold of nationalist art and literature

---

5   Lu Xun: "Letter to Li Bingzhong on May 3, 1930" (《1930年5月3日致李秉中》), *Complete Works of Lu Xun*, Vol. 12, Beijing: People's Literature Press, 1981, p. 15.

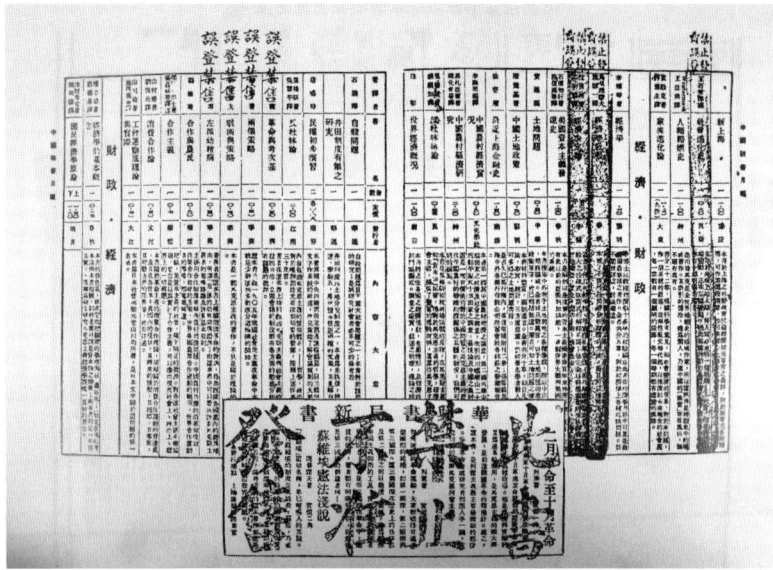

20.15. Banned books – an example of the KMT government banning the publication and release of progressive books and magazines

And when *Pioneers* was banned, the Modern Book Company was also closed down. The conditions proposed by the government to lift the ban were that the chief of the editorial office had to be appointed by the government and that the press must publish two nationalist art and literary journals sponsored by the government, namely *Vanguard Monthly* and *Modern Literary Review* (《现代文学评论》).[6] The press had no choice but to accept these conditions, but it did not stop publishing left-wing art and literary books. In one of his essays, Lu Xun recorded a piece of news published in the *Shanghai Evening Post and Mercury* (《大美晚报》) on March 14, 1934, which included a list of 149 books published by twenty-five presses banned by the KMT Shanghai Branch, of which as many as twenty-seven had been published by the Modern Book Company. On the list, literary works by famous left-wing authors included "Orchards" (《果树园》) translated by Lu Xun, *A Decade of Literary Creation* and *Research on Ancient Chinese Society* (《中国古代社会研究》) by Guo Moruo, "Night Meeting" (《夜会》) by Ding Ling, "Coal Miners" (《炭矿夫》) by Gong Binglu (龚冰庐), *Poems* (《诗稿》) by Hu Yepin (胡也频), "Seaside Commemoration" (《野祭》) and "The Sorrow of Lisa" (《丽莎的哀怨》) by Jiang Guangci, *Exile* (《流亡》) and *Homecoming* (《归家》) by Hong Lingfei (洪灵菲), (as well as Ba Jin's *Family* and other

---

[6] See Zhang Jinglu: *Twenty Years in the Publishing Industry* (《在出版界二十年》), Shanghai: Shanghai Magazine Company, 1938. The details may vary, but the general facts were true.

nonleft-wing but quite radical literary works).[7] Due to the profit-driven business operations of commercial publishing institutions that tried every means to meet the market demand, left-wing authors could thrive by insisting on writing revolutionary literature, despite the KMT government's life-threatening pressure. Left-wing literature was protected by the reading market, which was one of the reasons why it could develop and prosper in Shanghai and nowhere else.

To summarize, there were four reasons why Shanghai became the literary center of the country at that time. Firstly, it had a thriving publishing and printing industry, and newspapers and books enjoyed large market demand, so authors of various literary schools could make a living (or pursue their revolutionary goals) by selling their literary works. The established best-selling market mechanism (many books by Lu Xun, Guo Moruo, and Jiang Guangci were best-sellers) provided de facto protection for rebellious literature. Secondly, the reading market had its own regulating effect, which enabled young authors to compete against famous ones on equal terms. Lao She, Cao Yu, and Ding Ling all became famous overnight after their influential works were published in famous literary journals. And if Ba Jin, Ai Wu (艾芜), and Sha Ting had not left Sichuan for Shanghai, if Xiao Hong, Xiao Jun (萧军), and Duanmu Hongliang (端木蕻良) had not left the northeast and found residence along the Huangpu River, they would not have become so well known among readers within such a short time. Thirdly, at the intersection of Chinese and Western, ancient and modern cultures, Shanghai was extremely active in translating avant-garde literature from foreign countries and introducing spoken drama, film, Western painting, and woodcut painting, all being means of media that could be widely used by modern authors. And fourthly, the existence of the concession in Shanghai not only strengthened the authors' nationalist feelings, but protected the development of all types of literature. In this way, under the cultural rule of the despotic KMT government, it was still possible for various opposing political and nonpolitical literatures, including left-wing literature, Shanghai school literature, Beijing school literature, and the urban popular literature of the Mandarin Duck and Butterfly school, to be produced and spread, thus forming a literary landscape featuring diversity and coexistence. After its initial surge, New Literature had finally entered a new stage in which it was defined and redefined, deepened and transformed.

---

7   See Lu Xun: "Postscript of *Second Collection of Essays from a Semi-Concession*" (《且介亭杂文二集·后记》), *Complete Works of Lu Xun*, Vol. 6, Beijing: People's Literature Press, 1981, pp. 452–454.

TWENTY ONE

THE POPULARITY, DEVELOPMENT, AND DISPUTES OF LEFT-WING LITERATURE

O N   M A R C H   2 ,   1 9 3 0 ,   T H E   L E A G U E   O F   L E F T - W I N G   W R I T E R S (*Zuolian*, 左联) was established in Shanghai, the literary center of that time. This marked the end of the "debate over revolutionary literature" with the later-stage Creation Society and Sun Society on one side and Lu Xun and Mao Dun on the other (which also involved attacks against Yu Dafu and Ye Shengtao, and others) that had lasted for two years from 1928 to 1929. Left-wing writers were finally united and could resist the Kuomintang government's cultural rule with a new vigor. Meanwhile, the left-wing literature created by the League of Left-Wing Writers signalled, in a sense, the transformation of China's enlightenment literature.

The founding group of the League of Left-Wing Writers consisted of twelve people, namely Lu Xun, Zheng Boqi, Shen Duanxian (沈端先, aka Xia Yan), Qian Xingcun, Feng Naichao, Peng Kang (彭康), Yang Hansheng (阳翰笙), Jiang Guangci, Dai Pingwan (戴平万), Hong Lingfei, Rou Shi (柔石), and Feng Xuefeng, of whom only Lu Xun and Zheng Boqi (who was a member of the Creation Society) were not Communist Party of China (CPC) members.[1] Ending the debate and preparing for the establishment of *Zuolian* were results of the direct interference of the CPC Central Committee. Lu Xun was elected its undisputed "leader"; other initiators represented each of their own groups, and Xia Yan, who had not been involved in the previous debate, was appointed the organizer of its specific activities. The founding group met several times in the building of the Gongfei Café located on North Sichuan Road. When

---

[1] Xia Yan: *A Recollection of Old Dreams* (《懒寻旧梦录》), Beijing: Joint Publishing, 1985, p. 149.

21.1. China Art University: the site of the inaugural meeting of the League of Left-Wing Writers in March 1930

Lu Xun was asked for advice, he was strongly opposed to be appointed as the "chairman" or "secretary-general," and suggested that "Yu Dafu should be a member, for he is an excellent writer." At the inaugural meeting held at the China Art University on March 2, the three-person presidium consisted of Lu Xun, Qian Xingcun, and Xia Yan. The meeting was held in secret and was attended by forty or fifty people. It passed the program of the League and the outline of its action program, and elected an executive committee of seven members, including Lu Xun. Lu Xun made a famous speech at the meeting. Several days later, Feng Xuefeng wrote a draft of this speech from memory, which was revised by Lu Xun and published with the title "Thoughts on the League of Left-Wing Writers" (《对于左翼作家联盟的意见》).

Reading Lu Xun's speech today, we can see there were many problems at that time. For example, he talked about the solidarity of left-wing writers, but emphasized "a common aim is the prerequisite for a united front."[2] Here the "common aim" certainly involved resisting the KMT government, believing in the class basis of literature, and standing up for the masses of workers and peasants. Later, *Zuolian* and Lu Xun took the same stand in firmly criticizing the Western gentleman style of the Crescent Moon clique and the nationalist art and literature movement with its KMT background. However, Lu Xun said more than that, and he repeatedly emphasized the point that "it is very easy for 'left-wing' writers today to turn into 'right-wing' writers." He said: "if you simply shut yourself behind glass windows to write and study instead of keeping in touch with actual social conflicts, it is easy for you to be extremely

[2] Lu Xun: "Thoughts on the League of Left-Wing Writers," *Complete Works of Lu Xun*, Vol. 4, Beijing: People's Literature Press, 1981, p. 237.

radical or 'left.' But the moment you come up against reality, all your ideas are shattered. Behind closed doors it is very easy to spout radical ideas, but equally easy to become 'right-wing' if you do not understand the actual nature of revolution."[3] Lu Xun was obviously hinting at the issues remaining within the left-wing group, and it was later proved again and again that Lu Xun's harsh comments on the shortcomings of left-wing intellectuals were by no means groundless.

According to Mao Dun, from its foundation in 1930 to its voluntary dissolution in 1936, the League of Left-Wing Writers went through two stages:

> From its foundation until November 1931 was the earlier stage of *Zuolian*, when it gradually shook off the negative influence of ultraleftist errors; from November 1931 *Zuolian* entered its maturity, when it had generally broken away from the ultraleftist shackles and began thriving and hitting out in all directions.[4]

Many people concerned did not totally agree with Mao Dun. For example, some thought that the ultraleftist influence remained throughout, and some did not agree that November 1931 was the dividing line between stages; however, most at least agreed on the fact that *Zuolian* went through two stages. Mao Dun borrowed this view from Qu Qiubai. After being pushed out of the leadership of the CPC Central Committee by Wang Ming's ultraleftist line, Qu Qiubai had been a leader of *Zuolian* for two years. His friendship with Lu Xun led to a precious period when Lu Xun's views were in line with those of *Zuolian*. At that time, the executive committee of the League had passed a resolution titled "New Missions of the Chinese Proletarian Revolutionary Literature" (《中国无产阶级革命文学的新任务》), which was drafted by Feng Xuefeng under the leadership of Qu Qiubai. Mao Dun regarded it as a step to correct a series of errors of the League in its earlier stage caused by the leftist ideology that attached too much importance to politics and to unlawful resistance. For example, it made it important for writers to attend flying assemblies and distribute leaflets promoting "Armed Defense of the USSR," or told many writers to "organize the worker messenger movement" or "open night schools for workers" in factories all over Shanghai. The writers' association was managed like a political party, and little attention was paid to literary writing. If attention was paid to writing, it was only to subject matter, which was divided into significant and insignificant, directly concerning the resistance and life of workers and peasants, and trivial matters of petty bourgeoisie, with the latter being harshly attacked ("subject matter determinism" later became a long-term problem of the revolutionary art and literary theory). Therefore, when young

---

[3]   Ibid., p. 233.
[4]   Mao Dun: "The Earlier Stage of *Zuolian*" (《"左联"前期》), *Complete Works of Mao Dun*, Vol. 34, Beijing: People's Literature Press, 1997, p. 476.

Sha Ting and Ai Wu wrote to Lu Xun, they asked for his advice concerning subject matter. Both were troubled by their unfamiliarity with the material within the circle impacted by the "grand modern tides," but they could not write about the life they were familiar with outside that circle.[5] Certainly, since aspirational and passionate young people gathered around the League, even in its earlier stage, their devotion to writing about "isms" created sparks from time to time. A famous example of this occurred in January 1931, when five young left-wing writers were arrested as they held a meeting in the Shanghai Oriental Hotel. They were executed in secret in Longhua that February. Those who have read Lu Xun's "To Remember in Order to Forget" (《为了忘却的记念》) can never forget one of the young writers, Rou Shi, a short-sighted young man who did not believe the cases of deceit, friends betrayed, or blood-suckers, and who could shoulder his responsibilities by either old or new morality standards. The other four young writers were Li Weisen (李伟森), Hu Yepin, Yin Fu (殷夫), and Feng Keng (冯铿), and they were collectively known as the "Five Martyrs of the League of Left-Wing Writers.".

In its later stage, *Zuolian* paid more attention to lawful resistance and literary creation. Its literary activities involved editing left-wing literary journals, publishing literary works, and writing literary criticism. Within several years, there were a good few journals published by the League and its peripheral organizations. Those of its earlier stage, such as *Meng Ya*, *Pioneers*, *Baerdi Shan* (《巴尔底山》), and *Frontline* (《前哨》), only published articles with a clear-cut leftist stand, so they were often banned immediately after the inaugural issue was published. Those published in its middle stage, including *Literary News* (《文艺新闻》) and *Dipper*

21.2. Family photo of Lu Xun in 1930 when his son Haiying (海婴) was 100 days old. Lu Xun had resigned from his official position and began his "ten years in Shanghai" as a freelance writer

---

5   See "Correspondence on Subject Matters of Novels (with the letters of Y and T attached)" (《关于小说题材的通信（并Y及T来信）》), *Complete Works of Lu Xun*, Vol. 4, Beijing: People's Literature Press, 1981. "Y" referred to Yang Ziqing (杨子青), or Sha Ting, and "T" referred to Tang Daogeng (汤道耕), or Ai Wu.

21.3. Qu Qiubai and Yang Zhihua (杨之华), revolutionaries returning from the USSR who took on a fashionable appearance

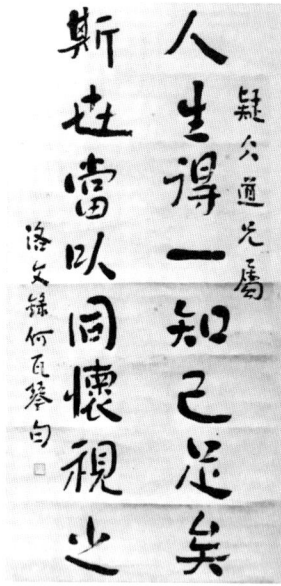

21.4. Calligraphy scroll Lu Xun wrote for and gave to Qu Qiubai. After retiring from the core leadership of the Communist Party, Qu Qiubai was a leader of the League of Left-Wing Writers for a short while and became close friends with Lu Xun

21.5. Shanghai Oriental Hotel: the site where the five left-wing martyrs were arrested

(《北斗》), lasted for a longer period of time because they also accepted contributions from nonleft-wing authors. And in its later stage, both *Crossroads* (《十字街头》) and *Literary Monthly* (《文学月报》) paid attention to strategies of resistance. The Northern Branch of the League of Left-Wing Writers (北方左联) launched *Literary Magazine* (《文学杂志》, edited by Wang Zhizhi [王志之] and others) and *Literature and Art Monthly* (《文艺月报》, edited by Zhang Panshi [张盘石] and others). More left-wing writers published their literary works in various centrist newspapers and magazines, including *Contemporaries*, *Literature*, and *Analects*, as well as *Literary Quarterly* (《文学季刊》) and, in the north, *Ta Kung Pao · Literature and Art*

(《大公报・文艺》). Lu Xun's last days coincided with this later stage, when he wrote not only essays about revolutionary resistance there and then, but also powerful essays recapitulating history. Mao Dun's *Midnight* (《子夜》), published in 1933, could be seen as a novel that embodied the significant literary achievements of the League. It was reprinted four times in three months after first being published, with the total copies printed exceeding 23,000. The League even held a secret victory meeting in an elementary school because of its great success. At that time, even those who never read works of New Literature, like grandmothers, young ladies and daughters of rich families, and taxi dancers, all rushed to read *Midnight*.[6]

The influence of left-wing literature was multifold. It exerted pressure on the "literature obeying the Three People's Principles" and the nationalist art and literature movement, which, despite the KMT government's sponsorship and support, had few readers and could not attract the best literary talents. The left-wing authors debated with the liberalist Crescent Moon clique over the class basis of literature and was championed by radical literary youths from the large cities. Some Shanghai school authors had once been left-leaning; for example, Shi Zhecun, who had joined the Communist Youth League and followed the fashion to write such proletarian novels as "Pursuit" (《追》) and "Ah Xiu" (《阿秀》). Later, however, when he wrote psychoanalytical literary works such as "At the Paris Theater" (《在巴黎大戏院》) and "Witchcraft" (《魔道》), he was immediately criticized by Lou Shiyi and Qian Xingcun.[7] Mu Shiying, a major writer of New Sensationalism, was also praised by the left-wing camp for his language of workers and clear and rhythmic narrative style in "North and South Poles" (《南北极》); a review of this short story was published in the inaugural issue of *Dipper*, and in Qian Xingcun's "Looking Back on the Literary Scene of 1931," published in Vol. 2, Issue 1 of the same journal, he mentioned this short story; praise was also to be found in *Literary News* (No. 43, 1932). However, when Mu's New Sensationalist work "A Man Treated as a Plaything" (《被当作消遣品的男子》) was published, he was fiercely attacked by Qu Qiubai and others. Shu Yue (舒月) published an article in *Modern Publishing World* (《现代出版界》, Issue 2, July 1932) titled "The Lumpen Proletarian of the Social Garbage and Mr. Mu Shiying's Literary Creation" (《社会渣滓堆的流氓无产者与穆时英君的创作》). Interestingly, despite all these criticisms and attacks, Mu Shiying continued to write in two styles alternatively, sometimes

---

6   See Mao Dun: "The Story of My Writing *Midnight*" (《〈子夜〉写作的前前后后》), *Complete Works of Mao Dun*, Vol. 34, Beijing: People's Literature Press, 1997, p. 516.
7   Lou Shiyi: "Shi Zhecun's New Sensationalism: Review of 'At the Paris Theater' and 'Witchcraft'" (《施蛰存的新感觉主义——读了〈在巴黎大戏院〉与〈魔道〉之后》), *Literary News*, Issue 33, Oct. 26, 1931. In his "Looking Back on the Literary Scene of 1931" (《一九三一年文坛之回顾》) published in *Dipper*, Vol. 2, Issue 1, Qian Xingcun also said that Shi Zhecun's new works represented the New Sensationalism "in declination."

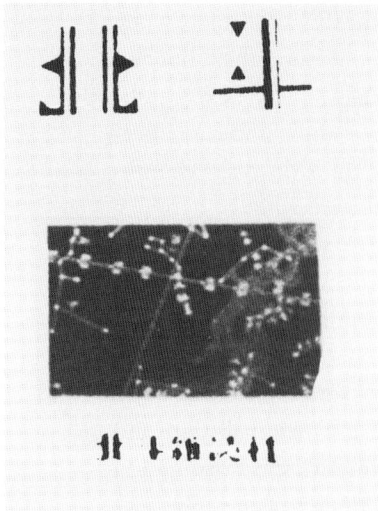

21.6. *Dipper*, a famous literary magazine of the League of Left-Wing Writers whose editor-in-chief was Ding Ling. Publishing quality left-wing literary works was its priority

21.7. *Baerdi Shan*, a left-wing literary journal

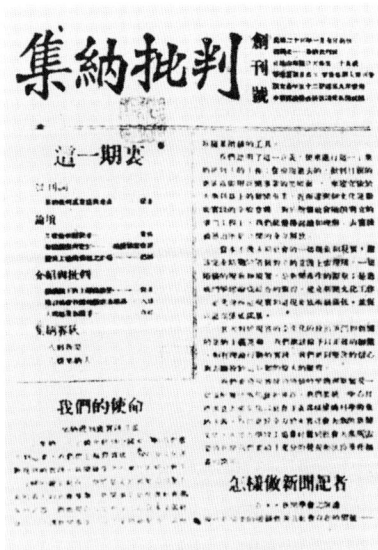

21.8. *Collective Critique* (《集纳批判》, monthly) was an official journal of the Federation of Chinese Left-Wing Journalists (中国左翼新闻记者联盟) expanded from "Collective" (《集纳》), a supplement of *Literary News*. It was launched on January 7, 1934 and was banned after four issues were published

imitating the left-wing writing style, sometimes writing in the New Sensationalist style. Examples of the former included "The Baker Who Stole Bread" (《偷面包的面包师》), "A Man with a Broken Arm" (《断了条胳膊的人》), and "Oilcloth" (《油布》), all included in the expanded edition of *North and South Poles* published in 1933. From the preface and postscript Mu Shiying wrote for that book, we can tell that he was impacted by and felt a bit uneasy about the criticism from the left-wing camp. As for the interactions between Beijing school authors and left-wing authors in the north, we can get an idea about them from the "debate between Beijing (school) and Shanghai (school)." Writing in the commercial hub of Shanghai, left-wing authors there also wrote literary works to cater for popular readers, and therefore the attacks against Shanghai school writers would sometimes get them involved. The Beijing school, on the other hand, had been more deeply penetrated by the left-wing camp, so that the liberal stance of Xiao Qian (萧乾) was for a while not so distinctive, and He

Qifang simply became a "leftist" during the Anti-Japanese War, and thus when people in the Nationalist-controlled area "implemented" the principles of Mao Zedong's "Talks at the Yan'an Forum on Literature and Art" (《在延安文艺座谈会上的讲话》), it was He Qifang who led members of the former *Zuolian* in their studies. This was an example of the mixture of left-wing and other literary schools.

The popularity of left-wing literature in Shanghai could be traced back to the late 1920s when "revolutionary literature" was first advocated. Before the League of Left-Wing Writers was associated, "revolutionary plus love" literary works, with the most famous being those by Jiang Guangci, were best-sellers for the bookstores. The "revolutionary plus love" literary works should not be regarded as merely following the fashion of left-wing writing, but were a true record of the bewilderment and pursuit of the young post-revolutionary generation. Their method of formularization and conceptualization certainly led to their decline. Paradoxically, reading these novels today, we pay more attention to the spiritual values shown in them about young intellectuals aspiring to be integrated into a kind of group and going through the process of "destruction of individuality." This can be seen as an inherent ambiguity of left-wing literature, for it stood opposite to individualism and thus departed from the May Fourth tradition. As already mentioned, one of the reasons why we say left-wing literature had surpassed nationalist literature was that it attracted many literary talents. The young writers gathered under the guidance of Lu Xun, such as Ding Ling, Zhang Tianyi, Sha Ting, Ai Wu, Wu Zuxiang (吴组缃), Xiao Hong, Duanmu Hongliang, Xiao Jun, and Ye Zi (叶紫), joined the left-wing camp, but somehow they all witnessed the infancy or exploratory stage of left-wing literature, and gradually matured after going through a series of theoretical and practical signposts from "revolution plus love" and "proletarian literature" to neorealism (based on the theory of Kurahara Korehito [藏原惟人] imported from Japan), "applying materialist dialectics to literary creation" (based on the theory imported from RAPP[8] of the USSR), "the New Novel" (which, according to the definition of Feng Xuefeng, should

---

[8]   RAPP, abbreviation of Rossiyskaya Assotsiatsiya Proletarskikh Pisateley, or in English, Russian Association of Proletarian Writers, was a so-called proletarian literary group of the USSR from 1925 to 1932. It was under the direct leadership of the Communist Party of the USSR, and thus got involved in the huge political and economic changes there. It changed direction during this process and finally dissolved. Factional struggles remained, like those between the "Positional Faction," "Literary Front Faction," and "Left-Wing Opposing Faction." China's left-wing literature was deeply influenced by the RAPP, which could be seen from its always regarding literature as a means to convey ideology and proposing that literature should serve current political purposes, and its active discussions of literary techniques, etc., and the views of the "Positional Faction" were used in the "debate over revolutionary literature" in 1928. Qu Qiubai, Feng Xuefeng, and Zhou Yang had all translated the theories of RAPP, which played an important role in criticizing "revolutionary romanticism" and promoting new "realistic literary techniques." – Translator's note

21.9. *Pioneers* was launched on January 10, 1930, and published by the Modern Book Company. A journal of the Sun Society, its editor-in-chief was Jiang Guangci. Later it became a journal of the League of Left-Wing Writers

21.10. *Crying for China* (《哀中国》) by Jiang Guangchi (蒋光赤, aka Jiang Guangci)

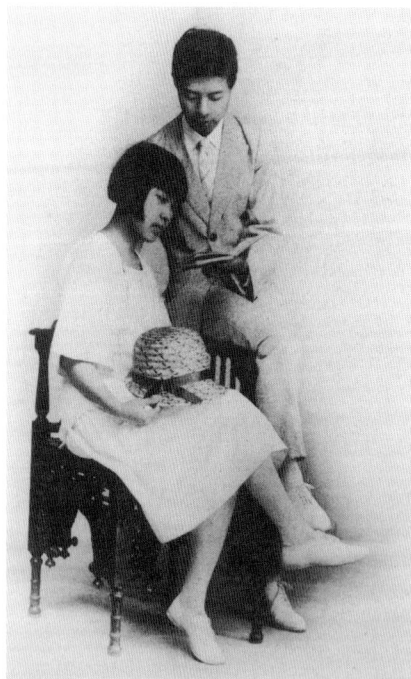

21.11. Ding Ling and Hu Yepin in Beijing in 1926

have the elements of choosing significant subject matters, portraying the masses, and changing from romanticism to neorealism, etc.) and through to "socialist realism" (based on the theories imported from the USSR after RAPP dissolved).

Ding Ling (1904–1986) was a talented woman writer. She outstandingly went through all stages of the mainstream writing of *Zuolian*, and wrote novels that represented each of these stages. But her creative brilliance could not be overshadowed by political dogmatism. "Wei Hu" (《韦护》) was a fiction representing the fashion of "revolution plus love" stage, which was based on the love story between Qu Qiubai and Wang Jianhong (王剑虹, who was Ding Ling's classmate and intimate friend) and was quite popular among readers for a while. "Flood" (《水》) was a short story based on the proposed concept of "the New Novel," for it painted with a rare, vigorous style a portrayal of the rebellious and awakening peasant public living in hardship after a flood had swept across sixteen provinces of China. "Night Meeting" could be regarded as an achievement of "revolutionary realism," for the author had been to factories in Shanghai in order to record the life of workers there. But it was "Miss Sophie's Diary" (《莎菲女士的日记》) that was most characteristic of Ding Ling's literary style. The short story attracted the attention of young readers immediately after it was published in *Fiction Monthly*. With unprecedented bold and detailed psychological descriptions, Ding Ling presented in front of us a female character, one of the post-revolutionary women intellectuals marginalized politically and caught in the conflict between bewilderment and rebellion, body and soul. These intellectuals maintained the independence gained from the May Fourth movement that championed liberation of individuality, and showed their rebellion through their dispirited, disillusioned lifestyle, indulging in sensuous enjoyment and toying with men's feelings. Morbid as it seemed, it was women's rebellion. Thus the character Sophie became immortal, and in the fiction, one could recognize some of the author's own experiences. Ding Ling integrated such personal emotional experiences into her fictional works, and established her own style of detailed descriptions and narrative techniques. And it became her long-term creative tendency to create "modern women" characters from different historical eras, expressing era-specific feelings from the women's perspective, full of new pursuits, new discoveries, and new fictional conflicts. During this period she also wrote the novel *Mother* (《母亲》), based on her

21.12. Ding Ling and her mother in Changde, Hunan, in 1923. At that time Ding Ling was still a literary youth, shy and bashful, and she probably never imagined she would write the novel *Mother* in the future

21.13. Advertisement for Ding Ling's *Mother*, published in *Young Companion* in 1933. The portrait was painted by Cai Weilian (蔡威廉), Cai Yuanpei's daughter, in 1929. On the day the book was launched at a bookstore on North Sichuan Road, all copies of the collectors' edition signed by the author before she was arrested immediately sold out

21.14. Portrayal of Ding Ling by a left-wing woodcut artist, made after Ding was arrested in 1933. The alleged artist was Renjun (纫君)

own mother, recording the thorny path taken by rebellious women who had just had their feet unbound during the Xinhai Revolution. She had planned to write lengthy novels to portray Chinese society and the characters living in it, but her dream was never fulfilled.

Zhang Tianyi and Sha Ting were satirists of the League of Left-Wing Writers. Zhang Tianyi (1906–1985) was a native of Hunan, but had been born in a city south of the Yangtze River, and in his literary works he criticized the lower-class citizen society with which he was very familiar. His earlier short story "Twenty-One Soldiers" (《二十一个》) was regarded as a landmark work that broke the pattern of "revolution plus love" with its recording of real life and its skillful use of colloquial language. The literary works that were particularly characteristic of his style were "The Father and the Son of the Baos" (《包氏父子》), "Laughter" (《笑》), and "The Breast of a Girl" (《脊背与奶子》), among others. In these short stories, he mocked hypocritical bureaucrats, low-class civil servants, petty intellectuals, and petty bourgeois. "The Father and the Son of the Baos" was the best of them. In this story, the father Lao Bao, a concierge, sought to raise his low social status and anchored all his hopes on his son, Xiao Bao, who was good for nothing but pretended to live like a young master. This was a tragic story comically told: both father and son tried to climb up the social ladder in their own shameful way. The best Xiao Bao could attain was a dependent and subservient position, while Lao Bao had lost everything even before his humble hopes were fulfilled. The story was told with comic language and rhythm and thus had an ironic twist, in which the author sympathetically ridiculed the vulgarity of urban citizens who had great expectations for their children and were willing to be enslaved, and the satire was powerful. Zhang Tianyi also wrote satirical novellas and novels including *Diary of a Ghost* (《鬼土日记》) and *At the Qingming Festival* (《清明时节》). "Big Lin and Little Lin" (《大林和小林》) was an exceptional left-wing fairy tale. With his rich and colorful ridiculing style of writing, the author told a story of two brothers taking different paths in life, one becoming rich, the other becoming poor. Later, during the Anti-Japanese War, Zhang Tianyi created even more masterpieces satirizing citizens and bureaucrats. Sha Ting (1904–1992) was raised in a remote area in Northern Sichuan, and thanks to his special family background and experience in life, he was familiar with the cruelty and carelessness of the grassroot-level government in rural towns and villages. He was a remarkable native-soil satirist. His earlier works tended to be exposés, and thus in such works as "Communal Compact" (《乡约》), "The Murderer" (《凶手》), "The Way of the Beast" (《兽道》), and "In the Ancestral Temple" (《在祠堂里》), we read barbaric stories of a big brother being forced to shoot dead his deserter younger brother, a mother-in-law asking the soldiers to rape her instead of her pregnant daughter-in-law, a warlord army commander nailing his rebellious wife alive in a coffin, but these were all things that actually happened in the chaotic rural towns and villages, and there was a shocking brutality and savage grotesqueness in them. Placing these stories in horrifying and helpless settings, the author told them with perfect grimness and composure. When "The Acting Magistrate" (《代理县长》) and "Master Gong's Entity" (《龚老法团》) were published, the author's character novels ridiculing those in power in rural towns and villages attracted great attention. It was Sha Ting's strength to treat the subject matters of corruption and in-fighting by rude and vulgar "rotten bureaucrats" with his downright comical language. Later he created satiric short stories and novels that portrayed the darkness of his native land, which occupied an important position in Anti-Japanese War literature. These achievements of young writers of the League of Left-Wing Writers showed the creative inheritance and further development of Lu Xun's satirical art.

Left-wing native-soil literature was even more prominent than May Fourth native-soil literature. The native soil of the 1930s was no longer somewhere for intellectuals to nostalgically seek their spiritual homeland, as it had become full of injustices and a field of life and death where the old was declining and the new rising. A number of young left-wing talents emerged writing

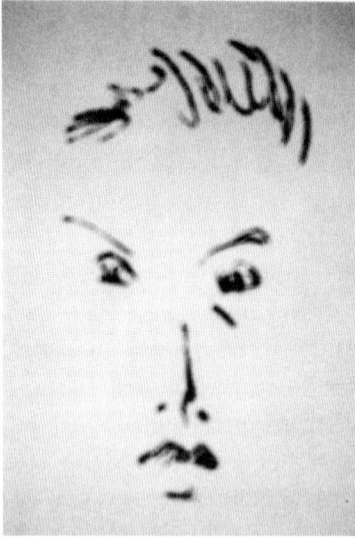

21.15. Zhang Tianyi's self-portrait in 1933

21.16. *Diary of a Ghost* by Zhang Tianyi, which painted a portrait of the dark human world and was imaginative and bizarre

21.17. Zhang Tianyi in Nanjing in 1934

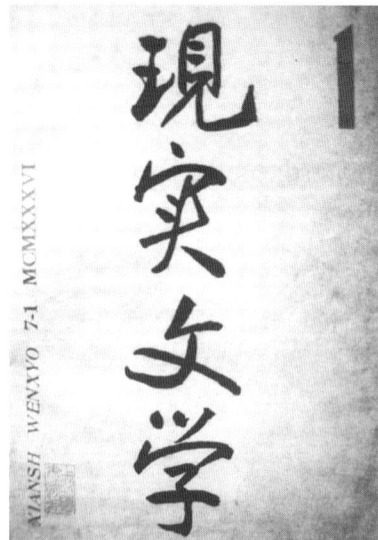

21.18. Cover of *Realistic Literature* (《现实文学》), a later-stage left-wing journal, handwritten by Zhang Tianyi. When Lu Xun died, Zhang Tianyi wrote a lot of the calligraphy used during his funeral

in this genre, such as Ai Wu, Sha Ting, Wu Zuxiang, Xiao Hong, Duanmu Hongliang, and Ye Zi, among others. Their literary achievements showed how the May Fourth realistic native-soil fictions were defined and then deepened over this period of time. Indeed, diverse as May Fourth literature was, there was always a romantic tone to it, which had been criticized by Liang Shiqiu from a neoclassicist point of view in his 1926 article "The Trend of Romanticism in Modern Chinese Literature" (《现代中国文学之浪漫的趋势》).[9] On the other hand, the League of Left-Wing Writers continued to import Marxist and Leninist art and literary theories and promoted various new forms of "realism," as a gesture to get rid of the earlier "revolutionary romantic" tendency. This facilitated the rapid development of realistic literature during this period. These achievements of young left-wing writers, so to speak, all followed the tradition of realistic May Fourth fictions. Since its inception, the League of Left-Wing Writers paid attention to the translation and introduction of "proletarian literary theories," but in its earlier stage, such attempts also brought in vulgar sociologism, which misled left-wing realistic literature for a while. It was after Qu Qiubai translated two letters by Engels on Balzac and Ibsen and two articles by Lenin on Tolstoy[10] based on documents newly discovered in the USSR in 1932 that left-wing writers began to read the original texts by the founders of Marxism and Leninism on art and literature. After long-term discussion and practice within the left-wing literary camp on the issue of realism – specifically, Qu Qiubai and Feng Xuefeng's praise of Lu Xun and Mao Dun as "the most sensitive realism" and "revolutionary realism," the debate between Hu Feng and Zhou Yang on the issue of "archetype," and later, the introduction and promotion of "socialist realism" – left-wing realistic literature developed and defined May Fourth realistic literature from the following three aspects. Firstly, it held that one should not embellish social reality, but should reveal its conflicts in an objective manner and try to examine them from both a historical and forward-looking perspective. For example, the struggle between comprador capitalists and national capitalists during the 1930s depicted in *Midnight*, was regarded as an exemplar of revolutionary realism, and contained true-to-life details. Secondly, it put characters at the core of literary works, and thus regarded the ability to create "typical characters"

---

[9] Liang Shiqiu's "The Trend of Romanticism in Modern Chinese Literature" was published in the "Supplement to the *Morning Post*" in 1926.

[10] Qu Qiubai, trans.: "Engels on Balzac – A Letter to Ms. Harkness" (《恩格斯论巴尔札克——给哈克纳斯女士的信》), "Engels on Ibsen – A Letter to Paul Ernst" (《恩格斯论易卜生的信——给爱伦斯德》), "Leo Tolstoy as the Mirror of the Russian Revolution" (《列甫•托尔斯泰像一面俄国革命的镜子》), and "L. N. Tolstoy and His Epoch" (《L.N.托尔斯泰和他的时代》), *Collected Works of Qu Qiubai (Literature)* (《瞿秋白文集（文学编）》), Vol. 4, Beijing: People's Literature Press, 1986.

as the highest goal of literary creation. Wu Sunfu in *Midnight*, Sophie in "Miss Sophie's Diary," Lao Bao in "The Father and the Son of the Baos," the bureaucrats of rural towns and villages in Sha Ting's works, and people living in the borderland in Ai Wu's writings were all examples of typical characters. Thirdly, it insisted on describing typical fictional settings. The towns in Hulan County in the northeast created by Xiao Hong, the Khorchin Grassland written by Duanmu Hongliang, the mountainous areas by Wu Zuxiang, and the rural villages around Dongting Lake in Hunan written by Ye Zi, were all settings in which typical characters were created. The description of settings was regarded as an integral part of characterization. Thus by the 1930s, realistic literature, which had been shaped under the influence of ancient Chinese vernacular literature and French and Russian literature since the May Fourth period, evolved into a left-wing realistic literature that attached great importance to the relationship between characters and their settings and to the description of details. And from the perspective of nonleft-wing literary writers, left-wing literature that formed the general trend of the era exerted pressure on them, so Shi Zhecun called it "orthodox" from his own perspective as a marginalized Shanghai school author.[11]

21.19. Group photo of Sha Ting and other members of the League of Left-Wing Writers. Back row, left to right: Ai Wu, Sha Ting, and Yang Sao (杨骚); front row, left to right: Bai Wei, Du Tan (杜谈), and Wang Mengye (王梦野). They were indeed a group of vibrant young people

[11] Shi Zhecun: "Dialogues in Fiction" (《小说中的对话》), *Cosmic Wind*, Issue 39, April 16, 1937.

21.20. Advertisement for the Scientific Theories of Art book series (科学的艺术论丛书) published by Kwong Wah Book Store in *Meng Ya* (Vol. 1, Issue 1, 1930). The book series included fourteen titles, whose translators included Lu Xun, Feng Xuefeng, Xia Yan, Su Wen (苏汶), Feng Naichao, and Lin Boxiu (林伯修), among others

Even in the grand tide of left-wing literature, "orthodox" realistic literature was opposed by people from various nonrealistic literary schools, and itself experienced some healthy changes in the process of development. According to Nie Gannu, Xiao Hong once said this in a casual conversation with him:

> There is a theory outlining the set rules and necessary elements for fiction writing, as if one has to write something like those of Balzac or Chekhov. I don't believe in that. For me there are various kinds of authors and thus various kinds of fictions. If fiction writing had to meet some set rules, some of Lu Xun's are not fictions, like "A Story about Hair," "An Incident" (《一件小事》), and "The Comedy of Ducks."[12]

This was the driving force to seek changes from the perspective of literary forms within the left-wing literary camp. Indeed, all literary works written by Xiao Hong (1911–1942) during this period of time, the novel *The Field of Life and Death* (《生死场》) and the short story "On the Ox Cart" (《牛车上》), broke away from the set rules that centered around characters and plots. Her exceptional fictions presented in front of us the folk custom paintings of the blood-tainted dark soil in the north of China and people's tenacious survival like animals. The temporal and spatial stillness caused by social and cultural stagnancy, as well as the author's narrative that freely traveled back and forth between the present and her memories of the past, between reality and her dreams, had given rise to a new literary form that crossed the boundaries between fiction, prose, and poetry, which was in line with her writing about the suffocating state of the nation. Xiao Hong died when she was only 31 years old, and her later writings were even more brilliant, but

[12] Nie Gannu: "Preface to *Selected Works of Xiao Hong*," *Selected Works of Xiao Hong*, Beijing: People's Literature Press, 1981, pp. 2–3.

they were never purely realistic works. Then there were other authors, like Ai Wu (1904–1992), who was a classmate of Sha Ting at the Teachers' School. He wrote about his own experience of walking from Sichuan to Yunnan and then crossing the national border to Myanmar, Malaysia, and Singapore, and collected these writings in *A Journey to the South* (《南行记》). Some stories in the collection, like "In the Mountain Gorge" (《山峡中》), "Straw Land" (《茅草地》), and "I Curse You For Laughing Like That" (《我诅咒你那么一笑》), wrote about the fate of various refugees such as opium traffickers, sedan chair carriers, horse thieves, and vagrants, and there was a romantic tone in his realistic writings. Wu Zuxiang (1908–1994) incorporated unrealistic elements in his native-soil social realistic works written in a style similar to that of Mao Dun. In his famous piece "Eighteen Hundred Piculs of Rice" (《一千八百担》), the absolute realistic style was brought into full play in that he only used simple and straightforward dialogues to portray a vivid picture of a dozen characters of the Song's family scrambling for the family wealth. But in "Fan Family Village" (《樊家铺》), he created an abnormal setting in which a peasant woman killed her loan shark mother. In "Bamboo Mountain Hut" (《菉竹山房》) he wrote a story about an old woman who had been a widow for most of her life peeking at her newlywed niece, and the gloomy and ghastly atmosphere was not characteristic of realistic writings. Wu Zuxiang was an extremely creative author, writing about the bankruptcy of rural areas in Anhui through to the inner changes of human relationship. As for Duanmu Hongliang and Xiao Jun, both were authors from the northeast, and both could integrate their own personal and creative energy into their descriptions of the tough and vast land in the northeast. In his *Village in August* (《八月的乡村》), Xiao Jun (1907–1988) used a simple, realistic narrative, but his tone throughout was loud and passionate. Duanmu Hongliang (1912–1996), in particular, hid his deep sorrow and indignation in the lyrical scenic description in his first well-known piece "Sorrows of Egret Lake" (《鹭鸶湖的忧郁》), a story about peasant women trying to seduce the men coming to guard the immature crops. His other writings, such as "Faraway Wind and Sand" (《遥远的风砂》), were also written with great narrative power. He started writing his novel *The Khorchin Grassland* (《科尔沁旗草原》) quite early on, but it was such a grand epic that it was not published until the Anti-Japanese War broke out. These novelists were not realistic writers in the pure sense, and are evidence that in the middle and late stage of *Zuolian*, authors began to write in their own individual styles.

These left-wing writers, such as Xiao Hong and Xiao Jun who were close to Lu Xun, never actually joined the League of Left-Wing Writers, which implies that there was a rift within the League. Examining the history of the League, we can see that from the "debate over revolutionary literature" during its foundation until the "debate over two slogans" ("两个口号论争") at its

21.21. First picture given to Lu Xun by Xiao Hong and Xiao Jun. Their look was fashionable for Harbin at that time

21.22. Entrance of Xiao Hong and Xiao Jun's dwelling in Harbin, located at 25 Market Street

21.23. Cover of the first edition of Xiao Hong's *Field of Life and Death*

dissolution, various disputes actually remained throughout its lifespan. The conflict between Lu Xun and Zhou Yang (who worked as the secretary of the Party Branch of the League and was its de facto leader) showed a disagreement between the Independent Sect and the Mainstream Power Sect within the left-wing camp. The latter called Lu Xun a "flagman," but actually regarded him as nothing but a "fellow traveler" outside the CPC. Sectarianism and closed-doorism did exist. An obvious example was that just before the League voluntarily dissolved to suit the new situation of the anti-fascist and anti-Japanese united front, Zhou Yang and Lu Xun successively raised the slogans of "national defense literature" and "mass literature of national revolutionary war." But behind the disagreements between different sects, there were also differences in left-wing art and literary theories that were still evolving. To put it simply, on the relationship between literature and politics, Lu Xun referred to world art and literature and emphasized that literature should have independence and should absolutely not be subservient to politics, and he was always alert to the existence of leftist mechanisms and vulgar sociologism. This was one of their differences. When the League criticized the "free man" Hu Qiuyuan (胡秋原), a poem by Yunsheng (芸生) entitled "Testimony of a Traitor" (《汉奸的供状》) was published in its official journal, *Literary Monthly*, in which there were lines such as "Watch out! Your head will become a halved watermelon," and Lu Xun seriously pointed out that "insults and threats are certainly not fighting the good fight"![13] Another difference concerned the relationship between the authors' worldviews and their literary creations. It was true that since the May Fourth period, Lu Xun had always said his literary creations "obey the General's order" and were "literature written to order," but he strongly opposed the practice to equate authors' political stands with their literary creations, and he respected literary writers' freedom of creation. For this he had been persistently resisting against the despotic cultural rule of the KMT government, and he was sensitive to the excessive subordinate relationships or even slavery between people in his own literary organization. These differences involved different assessments of the May Fourth enlightenment tradition, and they were not issues of Chinese left-wing literature alone. They concerned the history of acceptance of Marxist and Leninist art and literary theories throughout the world and remained well after Lu Xun's death, extending to the "liberated region" in Yan'an, to the Hu Feng Incident, and through to a series of literary critical campaigns launched by leftists. Therefore, people of later generations could learn lessons from both sides.

21.24. Portrait of Wu Zuxiang in 1933

21.25. Duanmu Hongliang was one of the young left-wing writers with a higher education, having been a student at Nankai and Tsinghua

[13]   See Lu Xun: "Insults and Threats Are Certainly Not Fighting the Good Fight" (《辱骂和恐吓决不是战斗》), *Complete Works of Lu Xun*, Vol. 4, Beijing: People's Literature Press, 1981.

TABLE 21.1 *Left-wing journals during the Zuolian period*

Name	Type	Editor-in-chief and editors	Time and place of launch	No. of issues published	Time and reason for discontinuance	Publisher
Meng Ya (*New Land*)	Monthly	Lu Xun as editor-in-chief, Feng Xuefeng as editor	Jan. 1, 1930	1 volume, 6 issues	Banned on June 1, 1930	Kwong Wah Book Store
Pioneers	Monthly	Jiang Guangci as editor-in-chief	Jan. 10, 1930	5	Banned on May 1, 1930	Modern Book Company
Art (艺术)	Monthly	Shen Duanxian (aka Xia Yan)	Mar. 16, 1930	1	Banned immediately after it was launched	Beixin Press
Literary and Art Lectures (文艺讲座)	Nonperiodic	Feng Naichao as editor-in-chief	Apr. 10, 1930	1	Banned immediately after it was launched	State Light of the Divine Land Press
Baerdi Shan	Published every ten days	Lu Xun, Li Yimang (李一氓), etc.	Apr. 11, 1930	1 volume, 5 issues	Banned on May 21, 1930	Editorial office of *Baerdi Shan*
Sha Lun (沙仑)	Monthly	Shen Duanxian (aka Xia Yan) as editor-in-chief	June 16, 1930	1	Banned after one issue was published	Beixin Press
World Culture (世界文化)	Monthly	Editors of the *World Culture* monthly	Sep. 10, 1930	1	Banned immediately after it was launched	Editorial office of *World Culture* monthly
Literary Life (文学生活)	Monthly	Yao Pengzi (姚蓬子) as editor-in-chief	Mar. 1, 1931	1	Banned after one issue was published	Lianhua Bookstore
Literary News	Weekly	Yuan Shu (袁殊) as editor-in-chief	Mar. 16, 1931	75	Banned on June 20, 1932	Editorial office of *Literary News* magazine
Frontline (aka *Literary Guide* [文学导报])	Semimonthly	Lu Xun, Feng Xuefeng, etc.	Summer 1931	1 volume, 8 issues	Nov. 15, 1931	Hufeng Press

(continued)

Name	Type	Editor-in-chief and editors	Time and place of launch	No. of issues published	Time and reason for discontinuance	Publisher
Dipper	Monthly	Ding Ling as editor-in-chief, Yao Pengzi and others as editors	Sep. 20, 1931	2 volumes, 8 issues	Banned on July 29, 1932	Hufeng Press
Crossroads	Semimonthly; later published every ten days	Lu Xun as editor-in-chief, Feng Xuefeng as editor	Dec. 11, 1931	3	Banned on Jan. 5, 1932	League of Left-Wing Writers
Literary Monthly	Monthly	Yao Pengzi, Zhou Qiying (周起应, aka Zhou Yang)	June 10, 1932	6	Banned on Dec. 15, 1932	Kwong Wah Book Store
Cultural Monthly (文化月报)	Monthly	Chen Lefu (陈乐夫)	Nov. 15, 1932	1	Banned immediately after it was launched	Editorial office of *Cultural Monthly*
Anonymous Literature (无名文艺)	Published every ten days	Ye Zi as editor-in-chief	Feb. 5, 1933	Only 2 can be found	Reformed on Feb. 15, 1933	Editorial office of *Anonymous Literature*
New Poetry (新诗歌)	Published every ten days; later monthly	Mu Mutian, Ren Jun, and Yang Sao, etc.	Feb. 11, 1933	2 volumes, 11 issues	Dec. 1, 1934	China Poetry Society
Art News (艺术新闻)	Weekly	Xia Lujiang (夏芦江)	Feb. 17, 1933	4	Mar. 11, 1933	Editorial office of *Art News*
Literary Magazine	Monthly	Wang Zhizhi, Gu Wanchuan (谷万川), and Pan Xun (潘训), etc.	Apr. 15, 1933 (Beiping)	1 volume, 4 issues	July 31, 1933	Northwest Book Company
Literature and Art Monthly	Monthly	Zhang Panshi and Chen Beiou (陈北鸥) as editors-in-chief	June 1, 1933 (Beiping)	1 volume, 3 issues	Banned on Nov. 1, 1933	Lida Book Company

(continued)

Title	Frequency	Editor	Launch date	No.	End/ban	Publisher
Anonymous Literature (文云)	Monthly	Ye Zi and Chen Qixia (陈企霞) as editors-in-chief	June 1, 1933	1	Discontinued after one issue was published after being reformed	Beixin Press
Art and Literature (文艺)	Monthly	Zhou Wen (周文) and Liu Dan (刘丹)	Oct. 15, 1933	1 volume, 3 issues	Banned on Dec. 15, 1933	Hua Tung Book Company
New Poetry	Monthly	Wang Yaping (王亚平) and others	Spring 1934 (Beiping)	4	Summer 1934	Hebei branch of China Poetry Society
Spring Light (春光)	Monthly	Zhuang Qidong (庄启东) and Chen Junye (陈君冶)	Mar. 1, 1934	1 volume, 3 issues	Banned on May 1, 1934	Spring Light Bookstore
Contemporary Literature (当代文学)	Monthly	Wang Yuqi (王余杞)	July 1, 1934 (Tianjin)	1 volume, 5 issues	Nov. 1, 1934	Tianjin Bookstore
New Forest of Language (新语林)	Semimonthly	Xu Maoyong (徐懋庸) and Zhuang Qidong as editors-in-chief	July 5, 1934	6	Banned in Sep. 1934	Kwong Wah Book Store
Oriental Tide (东流)	Monthly	Lin Huanping (林焕平) and Chen Daren (陈达人) as editors-in-chief	Aug. 1, 1934 (Tokyo)	14	Nov. 15, 1936	Editorial Office of *Oriental Tide* monthly
Translation (译文)	Monthly	Lu Xun as editor-in-chief, Huang Yuan (黄源) as editor	Sep. 16, 1934	28	June 16, 1937	Editorial Office of *Translation*
Literary New Land (文学新地)	Monthly	Editors of the *Literary New Land* magazine	Sep. 25, 1934	1	Banned immediately after it was launched	Editorial Office of *Literary New Land*
New Fiction	Monthly	Zheng Jumping (郑君平, aka Zheng Boqi)	Feb. 15, 1935	6	July 1, 1935	Young Companion Book Company

(continued)

Name	Type	Editor-in-chief and editors	Time and place of launch	No. of issues published	Time and reason for discontinuance	Publisher
New Literary Compilation (文学新辑)	(Not clear)	Editors of the Literary New Compilation magazine	Feb. 20, 1935	1	Banned immediately after it was launched	Editorial Office of Literary New Compilation
Essays (朵文 or 质文)	Monthly	Du Xuan (杜宣) and Xing Tonghua (邢桐华) as editors-in-chief	May 15, 1935 (Tokyo)	8	Nov. 10, 1936	Editorial Office of Essays
Petrel (海燕)	Monthly	Nie Gannu, Hu Feng, and Xiao Jun, etc.	Jan. 20, 1936	2	Feb. 20, 1936	Editorial Office of Petrel
Nightingale (夜莺)	Monthly	Fang Zhizhong (方之中) as editor-in-chief	Mar. 5, 1936	4	June 15, 1936	Editorial Office of Nightingale
Literary Gazette (文学丛报)	Monthly	Wang Yuanheng (王元亨) and Ma Zihua (马子华) as editors-in-chief	Apr. 1, 1936	5	Aug. 1, 1936	Editorial Office of Literary Gazette
Ling Ding (令丁)	Monthly	Editors of the Literary Branch of Ling Ding monthly	Apr. 1, 1936 (Beiping)	1 volume, 2 issues	Banned on May 15, 1936	Editorial office of the Literary Branch of Ling Ding monthly
Literary Circle (文学界)	Monthly	Dai Pingwan, Yang Sao, and Sha Ting, etc.	June 1, 1936	4	Banned in Nov. 1936	Kwong Wah Book Store
Realistic Literature	Monthly	Yin Geng (尹庚) and Bai Shu (白曙)	July 1, 1936	2	Banned on Aug. 2, 1936	Editorial office of Realistic Literature
Novelists (小说家)	Monthly	Ouyang Shan (欧阳山) as editor-in-chief	Oct. 15, 1936	2	Banned on Dec. 1, 1936	Editorial office of Novelists

Note: All left-wing journals in the table were published in Shanghai unless otherwise noted.

(Source: Tang Yuan [唐沅] et al., eds.: Catalogue and List of Modern Chinese Literary Journals [《中国现代文学期刊目录汇编》], Tianjin: Tianjin People's Press, 1988; and Yao Xin [姚辛], ed.: A Dictionary of the League of Left-Wing Writers [《左联词典》], Beijing: Guangming Daily Press, 1994)

TWENTY TWO

NOVELS STRONGLY CHARACTERISTIC OF THE ERA

Since the 1930s were a time when the May Fourth literature was defined and enriched, after a period of incubation, the novel, which marked the maturity of modern Chinese literature, became increasingly important. Generally speaking, novels first came to the fore in the mid-1920s, and after Zhang Ziping, Wang Tongzhao, Lu Yin, Yang Zhensheng, and others published their relatively immature novels of some length, excellent works began to emerge in the late 1920s, and the genre became fully developed in the mid-1930s. Listing them in chronological order according to the publication of their separate editions, in 1929 there was Ye Shengtao's *Ni Huanzhi* (《倪焕之》); in 1930 there were Mao Dun's *Eclipse* (《蚀》, a trilogy consisting of *Disillusion*, *Waverings*, and *Pursuits*) and Zhang Henshui's *Fate in Tears and Laughter*; in 1931 there was nothing (*The Family* began to be serialized in 1931, but if we take the time of serialization into account, *Disillusion* began being serialized in 1927, even before *Ni Huanzhi*, which began being serialized in January 1928); in 1932 there was Fei Ming's *The Bridge*; 1933 saw the publication of Mao Dun's *Midnight*, Ba Jin's *The Family*, and Lao She's *Divorce* (《离婚》); in 1934 there was Shen Congwen's *Border Town* (《边城》); in 1935 there were Li Jieren's *Ripples on Stagnant Water* (《死水微澜》), Xiao Jun's *Village in August*, Xiao Hong's *The Field of Life and Death*, and Zhang Henshui's *The Story of a Noble Family*; in 1936 there was Li Jieren's *On the Eve of the Storm* (《暴风雨前》) (it deserves a mention that Lao She's *Camel Xiangzi* [《骆驼祥子》] began to be serialized in *Cosmic Wind* in 1936, and although its separate edition was not published until 1939 due to the war, it shall be regarded as a pre-war novel); in 1937 there were Zhou Wen's *In the Town of Baisen* (《在白森镇》), Li Jieren's *The Great Wave* (《大波》, three volumes), and Xiao Jun's *The Third Generation* (《第三代》). *The Third Generation* was meant to be part of a lengthier novel, but Xiao Jun was interrupted by the war and never resumed writing it, even when he stayed in the countryside of Yan'an – further evidence that the war destroyed culture. Novels, however, had their own course of development, so we can get a clear idea about why so many excellent novels emerged in the mid-1930s.

The novels of this period could be roughly divided into realistic ones and poetic ones. The poetic novels will be discussed later when we talk about Beijing school literature; here we will focus on realistic novels strongly characteristic of the 1930s era, when left-wing literature had become the general trend. The native-soil literature, promoted during the May Fourth period, was still one of the important literary achievements of the 1930s, which formed an intersection with the era-specific literature; that is, for some native-soil works, like those of Fei Ming and Shen Congwen, their charm was not era specific, whereas for some other works, like Xiao Hong's *The Field of Life and Death*, life in the native lands was multifaceted and vividly described, and the historical background was no less impressive in the latter half of the novel, but since the novelist focused her attention on the countryside, the field of vision seemed more or less limited. It was after writing *Ni Huanzhi* (which described the protagonist's family and school life up to the period when he entered society and threw himself into the May Thirtieth movement and the Grand Revolution) that Ye Shengtao began to gain a broad perspective, and when his *Disillusion* was published under the pseudonym "Mao Dun," a brand-new era-specific novel with a vast field of vision came to the foreground. And it proved that its influence was profound and far-reaching.

The era-specific novels were written from the authors' personal experiences and struggles, combined with their motives to make sense of such experiences from the perspective of social history. The literary creations of Mao Dun (1896–1981) were the best examples of this. He fled back to Shanghai in secret after the split of the KMT and CPC in 1927 and lived in Jingyun

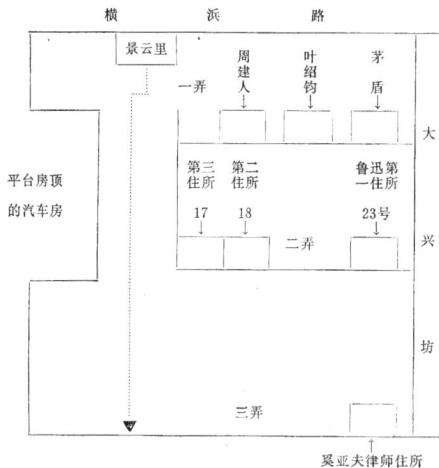

横 浜 路

景云里

一弄

周建人 ↓   叶绍钧 ↓   茅盾 ↓

平台房顶 的汽车房

第三住所   第二住所   鲁迅第一住所

17 ↓   18 ↓   23号 ↓

二弄

大兴坊

三弄

▽

裘亚夫律师住所

22.1. Map of the dwelling places of Lu Xun and Mao Dun in Scenic Clouds Alley (Jingyun Alley, 景云里). They once lived opposite each other, and it was here that Mao Dun wrote *Disillusion* and other works in secret (Source: *Chronological Biography of Lu Xun* [Expanded Edition], Vol. 3, compiled by Lu Xun Museum)

22.2. Lu Xun moved to No. 23, Lane 2, at the end of Jingyun Alley, Shanghai, in the latter half of 1927. Xu Guangping later wrote something like "in the depth of scenic clouds was my home"

22.3. Present-day entrance of Jingyun Alley. Back in 1927 both Mao Dun and Lu Xun lived here

Alley, Hongkou, where the back door to his dwelling was opposite the front door of the house Lu Xun moved into two months later. Soon after he moved there, Lu Xun asked his second younger brother Jianren to accompany him to visit Mao Dun, because the latter was hiding there and was not free to move about. Living in seclusion for ten months allowed this well-known editor and literary critic of the May Fourth period some time to ponder the grand history he had just experienced. According to his recollections, several "new women of the Republican era," with whom he was acquainted in Wuhan during the Northern Expedition War, often came to his mind. One day, after attending a secret meeting and walking back home in the rain, a "new woman" walking beside him suddenly inspired his creative passion. Therefore, when we reread the story in the "Eclipse" trilogy about several women pursuing the revolutionary ideal and then becoming disillusioned, which was the mental state of young intellectuals of that specific era, we find that although its grand concept and historical outlook were similar to those of *Midnight*, what made it different was the vivid portraits of the professional women in the Political Department of the Northern Expedition army, the male–female relationships in such settings, the complex relationships within the left-wing camp, and the true record of the initiation scenes before the Northern Expedition in Wuhan. The author perfectly combined scenes of everyday life with those of historical events, which was not often seen in his later novels. Somehow *Eclipse* was written as a way of emotional venting, but *Midnight* was not; it had a clear and reasonable motive for writing. According to Mao Dun's recollection, it originated from the large-scale polemic among Chinese intellectuals on the nature of Chinese society at the end of summer 1930. He himself agreed with the view that China was reduced to a half-feudal, half-colonized society, and in order to show his opposition to the view that China had been a capitalist society, he wanted to write a novel to show that imperialists would never allow China's national capitalists to stand up independently. However, Mao Dun did not only have a keen sense of social analysis, but also had a huge amount of material about real social life. Many of his relatives and old acquaintances were capitalists and business people, and his uncle Lu Xuepu, who had been supporting his studies in Beijing, helped him find a job at the Commercial Press, and who was a banker and had been the head of the National Debt section in the Beiyang government, was the person he paid special attention to. This uncle later became the model on whom he based Wu Sunfu, the protagonist of *Midnight*. In the autumn of 1930, Mao Dun could not read or write due to his eye disease, so he took the opportunity to sit in his uncle's living room and talk extensively with various business people, went to the Shanghai Stock Exchange to experience the hustle and bustle among speculators (he wrote essays on this), and thus wrote his magnum opus in just over one year from 1931 to 1932.

The era-specific characteristics of *Midnight* can be summed up in four points. Firstly, it was not only a story of Wu Sunfu the national capitalist, but a synchronized record of the history of the entire Chinese society in the 1930s

22.4. First page of the manuscript for *Midnight* (original name: *Sunset*). Mao Dun had quite elegant and refined handwriting (Source: Courtesy of the National Museum of Modern Chinese Literature)

connected by Wu Sunfu. The selection of significant subject matter, the panoramic outlook, and the real-time examination were unprecedented in Chinese
novels. The novel covered complex human relationships involving all classes
and social statuses in the special economic, political, and cultural environment
in 1930s Shanghai, including the confrontation and compromise between the
national capitalist and comprador capitalist (Zhao Botao); the coalition and
division between large national capitalists (Wu Sunfu and his close relative Du
Zhuzhai); the joining and merging between big and smaller capitalists (including Zhu Yinqiu who opened a silk factory, Chen Junyi who had a silk weaving
factory, and Zhou Zhongwei who ran a match factory, etc.); the capitalists'
exploitation, repression, bribing and splitting of workers; the penetrating and
detaching relationship between capitalists and their subordinates (Tu Weiyue
and Mo Gancheng) as well as their friends; the loving and unloving relationship
between capitalists and their relatives and friends; their relationship with the
landlords, usurers, and peasants back in their homeland, and even the capitalists'
intermediate relationship with underground CPC members and the different guidelines within the CPC through workers' strikes and their counter-
strike measures, etc. Such a huge social network was the grand stage where
characters lived and developed, faced their destiny, and acted out a drama of
human history. Mao Dun himself had once explained: "I thought those 'historical events' could only be fully recorded and developed within a novel of
at least 100,000 characters in length."[1] He thus developed a gigantic structure
to match these grand events. Secondly, the author reestablished a tragic hero
character. The May Fourth literature had promoted writings with commoners
and ordinary people as the center, but this rule was overthrown in a new sense.
Mao Dun sought to resume the link with the literary tradition of the romance
of ancient Chinese heroes and at the same time borrowed the concept and
technique of French and Russian roman-fleuve, and highlighted all the complex character traits of Wu Sunfu the national capitalist. The author sympathetically and critically portrayed Wu Sunfu as a "hero" of the industrial kingdom
of the 1930s, and by putting him at the core of all the complex conflicts in
the novel, unfolded this shrewd and cruel character who was tough-looking
but weak and cowardly inside, as well as his doomed failure. Wu Sunfu was a
spiritual brother of modern Western capitalists and the backbone of China's
industrial society, and thus he was totally different from his father (his father
died immediately after arriving in Shanghai, which was referred to figura-
tively by a minor character as "the dead body of the feudal society decayed
upon arriving in Shanghai"). His ambition was to develop national industry;
he had the knowledge and skills to manage modern enterprises, and he was an

---

[1]   Mao Dun: "My Memoirs" (《我的回顾》), *Complete Works of Mao Dun*, Vol. 19, Beijing:
      People's Literature Press, 1991, p. 408.

iron-handed man with determination and decisiveness. On the other hand, he was haunted by the ghost of feudalism, and his relationships with his subordinates, family, and wife, and peasants often revealed tyrannical isolation. He was born at the wrong time, and had to fight his way out of the pressures from all sides, but finally failed under the suppression of the comprador economy and imperialist economy. Besides Wu Sunfu, the author also constructed personality traits for minor characters, like the foreman Tu Weiyue, who was portrayed as a tough and resourceful character as shown in the multilayered conflicts with his superiors, fellow scabs, and workers. This was obviously different from the way Beijing School literary works treated their minor characters and their lyrical descriptions of local customs. Thirdly, the author had great narrative power and was skilled in sculpture-like multidimensional descriptions. We can get a strong sense of the atmosphere of the modern metropolis from the novel, from the ever-changing scenes of workers' strikes and speculations on the stock market, the protests and flying meetings. And he spared no efforts in telling the stories of Zhao Botao, who excelled in manipulating finances and dallying with women; Zhu Yinqiu, the smaller capitalist who was taken over by Wu Sunfu; the rich man Feng Yunqing, who came to Shanghai from a rural town to probe the stock market but lost everything; and modern metropolitan women such as Xu Manli. And fourthly, in writing this era-specific novel, the author showed an unremitting spirit to explore the root causes and future prospects of social conflicts. Therefore, like Ye Shengtao said when he talked about Mao Dun, with whom he was very familiar: "I have the impression that in writing *Midnight*, he had both a literary author's creative genius and a scientist's rigorous accuracy."[2] This may be the strength as well as the weakness of this novel.

22.5. Original edition of *Midnight* (hardback), which was quite well designed by the standards of that time

---

2   Ye Shengtao: "A Brief Discussion of Yanbing's Literary Work" (《略谈雁冰兄的文学工作》), *Prose Essays of Ye Shengtao* (《叶圣陶散文》), Chengdu: Sichuan People's Press, 1983, pp. 495–496.

22.6. First edition and manuscript of Mao Dun's *Rainbow* (《虹》), another excellent era-specific novel

Mao Dun wrote era-specific novels throughout his literary career. In the 1940s, he wrote *Red Leaves Are as Beautiful as Spring Flowers* (《霜叶红似二月花》) when he stayed in Guilin. In the novel he chose a small county in Jiangnan as the standpoint from which to unfold the turbulent history of modern Chinese society, which involved all social classes including national capitalists, impoverished aristocrats, and ameliorated landlords (Qian Liangcai), and their families. The female character Zhang Wanqing predicted that the best of the old-style higher-class Chinese women would soon become China's "new women" of the modern age. Mao Dun's novels were often too grandly designed and could not be fully realized, so he had many unfinished novels. *Red Leaves Are as Beautiful as Spring Flowers* was intended to cover the period from after the Xinhai Revolution till 1927 (end to end with the start of *Eclipse*), but he stopped in the middle. His earlier novel *Rainbow* started from the time the female protagonist Mei Xingsu went out of her home in Sichuan during the May Fourth period and ended with the May Thirtieth period in Shanghai, but careful readers may notice that the end was written quite perfunctorily. Actually, the author admitted this in the "Postscript": "I was too ambitious at that time, wishing to chronicle China's grand history of the last decade. Then the novel was discontinued due to moving, and after that, I could never find a time to resume writing." The novel *Tempering* (《锻炼》), written in 1948 (what we read today was only its first volume), began with the August Thirteenth Incident in Shanghai and continued until the fall of Shanghai into Japanese hands. The author intended to write five volumes, with the following volumes covering defending Wuhan and China's "bitter victory" against Japanese and the assassination of Li Gongpu (李公朴) and Wen Yiduo (see the "Small Preface" of the novel), but they were never written. Such was Mao Dun the novelist, who took the standpoint of a spokesman for the history of his time to deal with strongly era-specific and political subject matters. In his novels he could combine his grand historical ideas with detailed descriptions of everyday life, and he was especially good at portraying two kinds of characters, "new women of the Republican era" and national capitalists, so that his novels had the historical and aesthetic strength of socioanalytical novels, but their artistic value was somehow jeopardized by his essentialist mindset. However, Mao Dun's era-specific novels had a profound influence on the development of the novel genre and on revolutionary realism in Chinese literature. In his realistic writings, Mao Dun creatively used the technique of "creating typical characters in typical settings," and he paid attention to learning from world literature, so that they were in themselves not a closed ring. But later, under China's literary and artistic policies, which revered realism exclusively, they gradually showed the limits of self-enclosure.

Li Jieren (1891–1962) was not a left-wing writer but borrowed the technique of French roman-fleuve and wrote a chronicle for Sichuan. His most important works were the trilogy *Ripple on Stagnant Water*, *On the Eve of the Storm*, and *The Great Wave*, all published by Zhonghua Book Company before the outbreak of the Anti-Japanese War in 1937. Each of them told its own separate story and had its own characters, but some characters remained throughout the trilogy, and the three novels shared the same subject matter. *Ripple on Stagnant Water* was the best of them. It took Tianhui Town, which was close to Chengdu, as the setting, and took the relationship between Askew-mouth Luo (Luo Waizui, who was a member of the Elder Brother Society) and Sister-in-Law Cai (Cai Dasao) as the main plot, presenting the fatal fights between the two powers, namely believers and the Elder Brother Society, in the hinterland of China during the period from 1894 to 1901 due to the interference of imperialists and local government forces. By the standards of feudal morality, the "love" between Luo Waizui and Cai Dasao was aberrant, but it was described by the author with sympathy and praise. The image of Cai Dasao was especially lovely, alive with the wilderness of lower-class people. This was a woman with a poor family background but who was full of passionate desire for life and full of courage and responsibility. When the local Elder Brother Society lost the fight, she decided to remarry herself to the landlord in order to save the lives of her lover and her husband, manifesting her great courage to ignore the old convention of chastity and her unwillingness to live life as in the past. *On the Eve of the Storm* was about the reformation in Chengdu from 1901 to 1909. With the half-official, half-gentleman family of Hao Yousan as the main thread, the story covered the activities of You Tiemin and other reformists who returned from Japan, interposed with other plots, such as the relationship between Hao Yousan and a commoner woman, Wu Dasao. *The Great Wave* described the Railway Protection movement in Sichuan on the eve of the Xinhai Revolution. With the plot about Huang Lansheng's family in Chengdu and related characters, the story linked a series of historical events such as the association of the Railway Protection Comrades League, the resistance against the Qing court nationalizing the railway and being suppressed, as well as the love affairs between Chu Zicai and the wife of his uncle, Mrs. Huang. The author was five years older than Mao Dun and was familiar with Sichuan. As a real Chengdu-pro, he knew almost everything about the city, including how the city and its surrounding towns and cities took form, the historical development of its streets and lanes, the layout of its stores and teashops, and its citizens' lifestyles. Therefore, his novels were not only strongly characteristic of the era, but were permeated with local culture in every detailed description of scenes, the relationships between characters, dresses and appearances, and the layout of houses and yards. The novel depicted the colorful and picturesque local scenes like the market fairs on the Chengdu Plains (called "Chuanxi Ba" by local people), the lantern festival in the first lunar month on Dongda Street in Chengdu, visiting Qingyang Palace in the second lunar month, the life of commoners at Xialiangchi, and the sports meeting of all schools from the entire province. Like Mao Dun, Li Jieren also integrated the history of that specific era, of Chinese society and of the local customs in his novels, but he had his own distinctive style. In the structure and narrative of novels, on the other hand, both were masters of grand era-specific novels, but Mao Dun's were more like a cross-sectional record of history, whereas Li Jieren was better at longitudinal-sectional records and he showed more composure and objectivity. Both were good at creating "new women" characters of that special era, and both were objective, but Mao Dun would express his personal feelings more frequently than Li. Since he had returned from France, Li Jieren had lived exclusively in Sichuan, and it was a pity that he did not make remarkable progress in novel writing, for the pace of *The Great Wave* was not well-controlled and there was too much intermediate recounting. For a long time, not enough attention was paid to Li Jieren and he did not gain the praise he deserved, but Guo Moruo quite appreciated his fellow countryman's roman-fleuve, and it was said that each time he read Li's novel, Guo would be engrossed in it for several days, and he might be seen as a soulmate of Li.

Of the era-specific novels, there was another genre, family saga. This literary genre actually had elements of "history" and "society," but they were presented through the stories of one or several families, unfolding the big picture from small details, thus divulging the complex stories and fates of several generations. Often, the collapse of big families epitomized the radical changes of a historical era, and the decline of the older generation heralded a new beginning of the later and younger generation. Traditionally, China was a feudal society with family as its basic unit, which is why family sagas were especially popular among era-specific novels. In the 1930s there were Ba Jin's *The Family,* which was extremely influential, and Duanmu Hongliang's

22.7. Li Jieren in 1922, still sporting the appearance of a student from France

22.8. First edition of *Ripple on Stagnant Water* by Li Jieren, published in 1936

The Khorchin Grassland, and in the 1940s there were *Four Generations under One Roof* (《四世同堂》), *Moment in Peking* (《京华烟云》), and *Rich Men's Children* (《财主底儿女们》), created one after another by either left-wing or nonleft-wing authors.

The Family by Ba Jin (1904–2005), and *Spring* (《春》) and *Autumn* (《秋》), collectively known as the "Torrent Trilogy" (激流三部曲), were extremely prominent. The latter two were not as well-written as *The Family*, but the three were novels followed each other in sequence. *The Family* was based on the author's own family, and at that time, Ba Jin was a passionate young man who believed in anarchism. From 1931 to 1932 *The Family* was serialized in the *Times* (《时报》) in Shanghai. During that time Ba Jin's eldest brother, the model for the character Juexin, committed suicide in Chengdu. *The Family* was serialized in the newspaper for a whole year, but it was not so well received among readers, so much so that the newspaper almost decided to stop serializing it, and it only carried on after Ba Jin offered to not take any remuneration for the novel. However, the separate edition of the novel, published by Kaiming Bookstore the following year, was extremely well received and rapidly spread among readers, evidence that the readers of separate editions of books were totally different from those of novels serialized in newspapers. This is also a good example that both reader groups drove the development of different types of modern Chinese literature. *The Family*'s plot covered the stories of several generations of the Gao Family in Changdu, starting on the eve of the May Fourth movement. The big feudal family had already become a spent force, with the fourth and fifth uncles, both wastrels, dismantling the physical and spiritual buildings of the family, but Master Gao insisted on managing family affairs with old-style family ethics, and still held the supreme power in the family. Juexin, the eldest grandson born to the eldest son in the family, was the most successfully created character in the novel. He was influenced by new ideas, but his status in the family and his education in feudal ethics left him with a weak personality, giving in and compromising over everything. He gave up his love for his cousin of the Qians (Cousin Mei), sacrificed his opportunity to study at university, and married someone he did not love at his family's orders. When his wife Ruijue was giving birth to his child, she was driven to a place outside the city to avoid the "bloody disaster" that could affect the grandfather, and she died during labor. His brothers and all his own experiences finally changed Juexin, and he began supporting his brothers' rebellion, with the idea that "we need a rebel in this family." Juehui was the first to have awakened in the family, actively participating in various student movements. He fell in love with the maid Mingfeng, but Mingfeng, being given by Master Gao to some other master as a concubine, drowned herself in the lake, after which Juehui became fully aware of the evilness of his own family. After helping his second elder brother Juemin oppose an arranged marriage, Juehui left home and went afar. This story about the May Fourth generation breaking free from their feudal family and entering society to get control of their own lives inspired many generations of young people. Indeed, "leaving home" became a synonym of rebellion, awakening, and pursuing one's own ideals, so much so that when the revolutionaries pursued their socialist ideals and went to Yan'an, they would set out on the long journey with a copy of *The Family* in their backpack. In this regard, Ba Jin's era-specific novels insisted on the enlightenment spirit of the May Fourth tradition, which made them somewhat different from those of Mao Dun and Li Jieren. The characters rebelled against old social norms based on the ideals of humanism, democracy, and freedom, and thus the novels paid more attention to the value of "individuality." Ba Jin always had obvious subjective tendencies in his narrative, and the emotional and passionate descriptions gave the novels a strong spirit of youth, making them more to the taste of young people. Ba Jin attracted a huge number of readers to era-specific novels and expanded the social influence of this literary genre. This proved that modern Chinese literary readers had quite a strong social sensitivity, though some citizens were satisfied with being entertained by literature. *The Family* then became a must-read for one generation after another of radical young people as they entered society, and it was the most-printed masterpiece of twentieth-century modern Chinese literature.

22.9. Entrance of Ba Jin's own family residence, the prototype for his novel *The Family*. It still existed at the end of the 1950s, but later disappeared

22.10. Ba Jin in 1927, looking gentlemanly yet determined

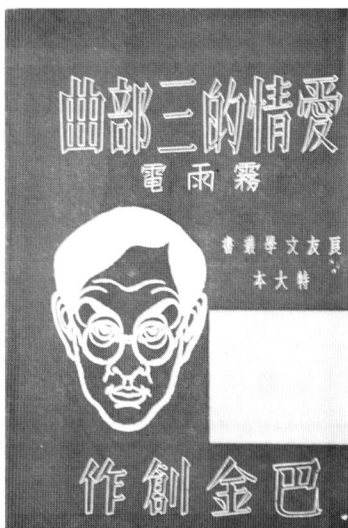

22.11. Large print edition of one of Ba Jin's earlier novels that influenced young readers, "Love Trilogy" (《爱情的三部曲》), published by the Young Companion Book Company

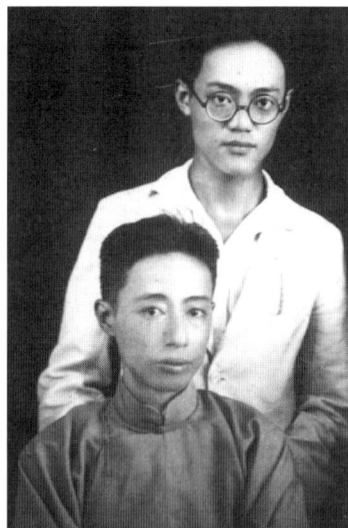

22.12. Ba Jin and his eldest brother (the model for his character Juexin) in Shanghai in 1929. Soon after, before *The Family* was published, his brother committed suicide

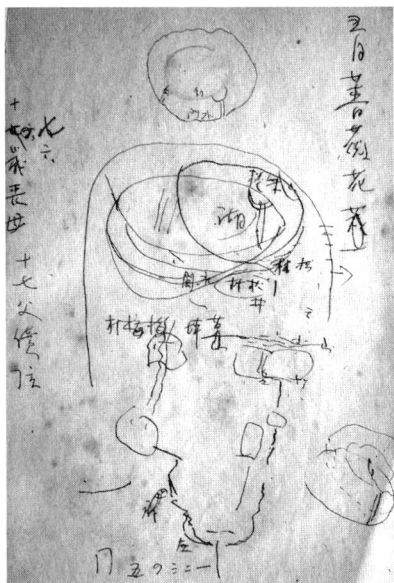

22.13. On a blank page of the fourth edition of *The Family*, published by Kaiming Bookstore, there was a floor plan of Ba Jin's own family home, drafted by Ba Jin himself, which would be further revised later

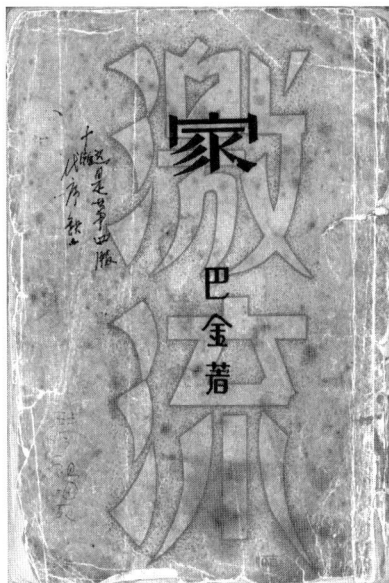

22.14. On the fourth edition of *The Family*, published by Kaiming Bookstore, was an inscription by Ba Jin to give the copy as a gift. He attached great importance to the revisions of his own books

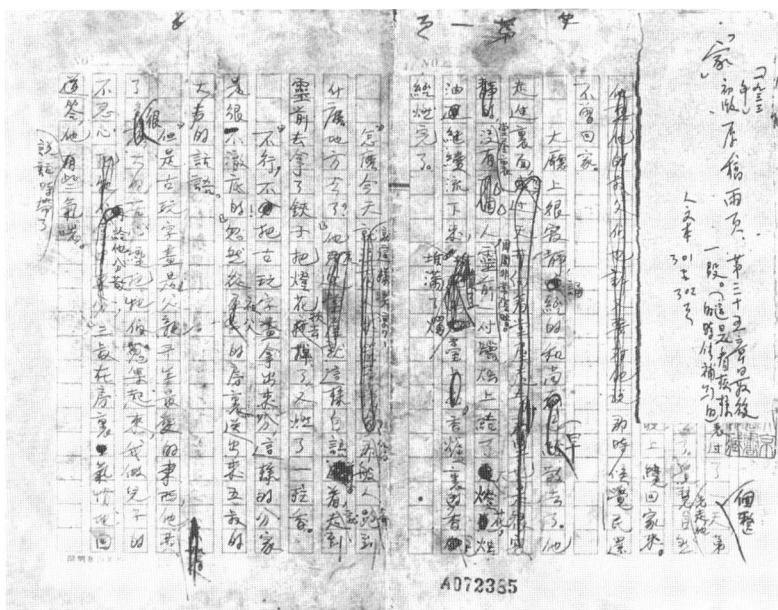

22.15. Manuscript of Ba Jin's *The Family*

22.16. Illustration in *The Family*: family
feast during the Lunar New Year

22.17. Cover of a translated edition
of *The Family*

From the viewpoint of literary history, we can say that the era-specific novels of the 1930s laid the foundation for the future development of modern Chinese novels.

TWENTY THREE

THE SUCCESSIVE BOOM OF ERA-SPECIFIC AND INDIVIDUALIZED LITERARY WRITINGS

THE SUCCESS OF ERA-SPECIFIC WRITINGS IN THE 1930S was due to it being a decade of struggle and the special composition of the readership. In Chapter 22 we mentioned the incident where Ba Jin's *The Family* was almost discontinued from being serialized in the *Times* in Shanghai, for which two explanations were given by the authors of Ba Jin's biography. The first was that after the September Eighteenth Incident in the northeast, news about national calamities increased sharply and there was limited space for novels and literary works in newspapers. The second explanation was that editors complained that the novel was too long. Actually, neither of these explanations makes sense. For the first explanation, we can see that the novel resumed serialization on January 26, 1932, just two days before the January Twenty-Eighth Incident occurred in Shanghai. National emotions were extremely strong among citizens in Shanghai, but it did not affect the serialization of the novel. To cite another example for the second explanation, from September 1931 to March 26, 1933, Zhang Henshui's lesser known novel *Flower of Peace* (《太平花》) was serialized in the *Daily News* in Shanghai; its length was 300,000 characters, exactly the same as *The Family*, and the novel was serialized without interruption even though the period witnessed an increase in national calamities from the September Eighteenth Incident to the January Twenty-Eighth Incident. The true reason for the discontinuance, then, was that readers of the serialized novel in the newspaper were people who were happy to read several hundred characters of popular works each day, even if that meant they would not finish reading it until several years later. *The Family* failed to interest them, and therefore it was not well received. While the separate edition of *The Family* was an immediate success; its readers were different from the readers of novels in newspapers, and its high-pitched style characteristic of the era was appreciated and well responded to by young readers of that era. Ba Jin was not a left-wing writer, so the reader group of era-specific writings was not necessarily left-leaning; it was a larger group, which we might want to call the "radical urban reader group." They had some literary taste, and certainly did not spend their money on reading political lectures. By supporting writers, readers also affected the choice of theme and style of literary writings. It was easy for era-specific writings to become politically conceptualized, but thanks to the effect of readers and to the individualized literary creations of excellent authors of the 1930s, the New Literature showed signs of progress by continuously overcoming this tendency.

23.1. Bookstalls were very common in Shanghai. They were always frequented by people, and were a means of cultural consumption for urban citizen readers

23.2. Shanghai citizens looking at anti-imperialist posters on the street during the May Thirtieth movement, evidence that they were also concerned with politics

When he praised the poet Bai Mang (白莽, aka Yin Fu), one of the "Five Martyrs of the League of Left-Wing Writers," Lu Xun poetically expressed his view toward era-specific poetry:

> This book is a glimmer in the east, an arrow whistling through the forest, a bud emerging at the end of winter, the first step of an army's advance, a banner of love for pioneers, and a monument of hate for despoilers. This collection cannot be compared with any so-called polished, concise, serene, or lofty works; for these poems belong to an utterly different world.[1]

Here "these poems" referred to the revolutionary poems expressing emotions of the specific era of the 1930s, which belonged to a poetic school different from the Crescent Moon clique and the Expressionist clique. The revolutionary poems had their own course of development. Before the China Poetry Society was established in 1932 under the leadership of *Zuolian*, the first signs of "proletariat poetry" came from poet Jiang Guangci (who was also a novelist). *New Dream* (《新梦》) was Jiang's major collection of poems, which inherited the "commoner" tradition of earlier vernacular poetry, but abandoned the subjectivity and individuality of May Fourth poetry, maintaining instead that poets should throw themselves to and become one of the masses and extol political ideals. In "Poems of Moscow" (《莫斯科吟》), for example, he sang loudly: "October Revolution, is like a soaring torch, / Leaving behind it the wreckage of the past, / And illuminating in front of it the new way to the future." And in "Self Portrait" (《自题小像》) he claimed: "Only from the waves of the masses, could a true self of me emerge." These poems often set the individual against the era and expressed the poets' new feelings and ideas.

The main poets of the China Poetry Society included Yin Fu, Pu Feng (蒲风), and others. The Society launched *New Poetry* and other journals, vigorously promoting realistic poetry that reflected the real changes of the era and the struggles of workers and peasants. The political lyrical poems of Yin Fu (1909–1931) were high-spirited and passionate and full of loaded language, for example, "On May First, 1929" (《一九二九年的五月一日》), and "Characters in Blood" (《血字》). In "Characters in Blood" he wrote: "O May Thirtieth! / Stand up, and go to Nanjing Road! / Illuminate the horizon with your shining blood, / Let your unyielding attitude be reflected in the Huangpu River, / And let your loud prediction resound in the universe!"[2] The style was vigorous, with both narrative and critic elements in the poetic

---

[1] Lu Xun: "Preface to Bai Mang's *The Children's Pagoda*" (《白莽作〈孩儿塔〉序》), *Complete Works of Lu Xun*, Vol. 6, Beijing: People's Literature Press, 1981, p. 494.
[2] Yin Fu: "Characters in Blood," *Selected Poetry and Prose of Yin Fu* (《殷夫诗文选集》), Beijing: People's Literature Press, 1954.

lines. Yin Fu was from a rich family, and his elder brother was a high-rank official of the Kuomintang, so devoting himself to revolution had given him some painful personal experiences. We can see this from his poem "Farewell, Brother!" (《别了，哥哥！》), whose subtitle was "Something Like Saying Goodbye to a 'Class'" (《算作是向一个"阶级"的告别词吧》). In dealing with the relationship between the individual and a social class, his self was often seen in grand historical scenes in such era-specific poems, but it was not his "individual self," but a larger and higher self that had been tempered in battles. Thus the lyrical subject of his poetry was often the collective "we." In "On May First, 1929," for example, the poet was walking with all people in the "May First parade" and melted into the masses; he realized he had become a spokesperson for a newly born class that could make history:

> I rushed into the crowd and cried:
> "We ... We ... We ..."
> The colorful paper scraps, white and red,
> Flying in the morning light like a flock of pigeons.
> Oh, echo, echo, echo,
> All streets resounded with our cries!
> I melted into a wave of sounds,
> And we became one great heart.
> All streets were crowded with workers, comrades, we,
> All streets resounded coarse cries,
> All streets were full of joyful laughter and cries,
> And the silence of night was wiped out.[3]

23.3. Lively scene of a parade on the streets of Shanghai

---

[3]   Yin Fu: "On May First, 1929," *Selected Works of Yin Fu* (《殷夫选集》), Shanghai: Kaiming Bookstore, 1951.

23.4. Advertisement for Pu Feng's collection of poems, *Endless Nights* (《茫茫夜》), in *Spring Light* (《春光》, Vol. 1, Issue 3, May 1, 1934). The collection was published in April that year by Spring Light Bookstore

Not only parades, but also secret meetings could be written into poems. In "Resolution" (《议决》) Yin Fu wrote: "In the dim light of the oil lamp, / We became endless infinity – our shadows melted into one, / We inhaled the same rotten smell, / We shared the same bigger heart."[4] When the individual took on the traits of the group and seemed to be expanding infinitely, it resembled and shared some features with the May Fourth lyrical protagonist in Guo Moruo's poems. Another major poet of the China Poetry Society was Pu Feng, who wrote quite bold and grand poems about peasants' struggles, such as "Endless Nights," and "Fire in the Sixth Month." In "Endless Nights," the young peasant that had joined the "poor people's army" talked with his mother, using the wind as their messenger: "Why is that we labored days and nights, year after year / But still suffer hunger and cold, insult and abuse? / Why is that they are satiated and entertained for all their life, / And we shall bow to them forever?"[5] These are tough and unyielding poetic lines. This poetic school also proposed writing in "ballad style" and put it into practice. The result was not desirable, but it became part of the "massification of poetry" process throughout the "Red 1930s," and one could feel its influence in the poetic movement during the earlier Anti-Japanese War period and in the "liberated region" in the 1940s, even in the political lyrical poetry of Guo Xiaochuan (郭小川).

The voice of era-specific poetry was by no means weak, but even it had a tendency to extend outside the left-wing camp. The best evidence of this was Zang Kejia (臧克家, 1905–2004), who had earlier been strongly influenced by the Crescent Moon clique, so much so

23.5. First edition of Zang Kejia's anthology, *Branding*, whose cover was designed with simplicity and composure, hence a contrast to the passionate poems inside

[4]   Yin Fu: "Resolution," *Selected Poetry and Prose of Yin Fu*, Beijing: People's Literature Press, 1954.
[5]   Pu Feng: *Endless Nights*, Shanghai: International Institute of Compilation and Translation, 1934.

that when his first anthology *Branding* (《烙印》) was published, the preface was written by Wen Yiduo. Later he gradually became left-leaning and became one of the poets most expressive in reflecting the sufferings of peasants and the realities of the countryside. His famous poem "The Old Horse" (《老马》) was indeed well written: "The cart had to be loaded come what may. / He had no word of complaint. / The burden bore down into his flesh, / He lowered his laden head. // No moment betrayed what the next would bring, / His tears were swallowed, not shed. / The whip shadow flitted before his eyes. / He looked up and started ahead."[6] These lines described an old horse that carried heavy burden, but it was also a portrait of Chinese peasants of that time. It inherited China's long-standing tradition of poetry in praise of particular objects, but endowed it with the emotions and language of that specific era, and was written with sculpture-like vigor: rough and tough as they were, the lines also showed exquisiteness. This was unique of Zang Kejia's poetic style.

A national poet who maintained and gave full play to his individual originality in creating era-specific poems was Ai Qing (1910–1996). He shocked the poetic circle in 1933 with a poem written in prison entitled "Dayanhe – My Nurse" (《大堰河——我的保姆》). Dayanhe was a workwoman, who was in reality the nurse of Ai Qing, the son of a landlord. The poem was written with deep emotions: "I am the son of a landlord, / But I am also the son of Dayanhe, / Brought up on her milk. // By nursing me, Dayanhe fed her family, / I was raised on the milk of your breast, / O Dayanhe, my nurse."[7] Here was the revolutionary poet's hidden willingness to change his original purely intellectual stance. Ai Qing had been studying painting in China and in France, and his poems were influenced by European symbolistic and expressionistic poetry (both were modernist poetry), and he had read the best works of the nineteenth-century Russian realistic masters. He was hailed as a "poet blowing reed pipe," with the "reed pipe" being European style. Thus it is easy for us to understand why, even after he actively participated in revolutionary activities and later

23.6. Ai Qing in Paris in 1929

---

6   Zang Kejia: "The Old Horse," *Branding*, Shanghai: Kaiming Bookstore, 1934.
7   Ai Qing: "Dayanhe – My Nurse," *Dayanhe* (《大堰河》), Shanghai: Shanghai Cultural Life Press, 1939.

went to Yan'an and became an outstanding modern poet, he was less prone to the flaw of conceptualization than other realistic authors, but could combine what he had learned from world modern poetry and his own poetic genius to write about Chinese peasants and China's vast land.

Ai Qing's era-specific lyrical poems were intense and vehement, and attained a very high artistic level. "Snow Falls on the Chinese Land" (《雪落在中国的土地上》) was one of his famous poems about the land, in which he linked his own fate with that of common "peasants" who drove their carts, a "disheveled and dirty-faced young woman" and an "old mother," lamenting "The pain and agony of China / Are as wide and long as this snowy night."[8] And here is his "I Love This Land" (《我爱这土地》):

> *If I were a bird,*
> *I would sing with my hoarse voice*
> *Of this land buffeted by storms,*
> *Of this river turbulent with our grief,*
> *Of these angry winds ceaselessly blowing,*
> *And of the dawn, infinitely gentle over the woods …*
> *— Then I would die*
> *And even my feathers would rot in the soil.*
> *Why are my eyes always brimming with tears?*
> *Because I love this land so deeply …*[9]

23.7. Ai Qing (second from right) was studying fine arts in Paris with his friends in 1930

[8]   Ai Qing: "Snow Falls on the Chinese Land," *The North* (《北方》), Shanghai: Shanghai Cultural Life Press, 1942.
[9]   Ai Qing: "I Love This Land," *The North*, Shanghai: Shanghai Cultural Life Press, 1942.

The language here is simple and clear, people and the soil blending together, making this short poem so touching. For Ai Qing, he did not feel the necessity to divide "I" from "we." His "The Announcement of the Dawn" (《黎明的通知》) gave a message of "brightness" and "warmth": "through the lips of a good man, / Please bring them the message. // Tell those whose eyes smart with longing, / Those distant cities and villages steeped in sorrow, … Let all people prepare to welcome me, / I shall come when the cock crows for the last time, … as night is nearly over, please tell them / That what they have been waiting for is coming."[10] This should be the hope of all good people who have had nightmares, and the poet expressed his feelings in one stretch, giving free vent to peasants' love of the land. Ai Qing's poems "The Sun" (《太阳》) and "Toward the Sun" (《向太阳》) expressed people's relentless pursuit of a bright future, using the symbolic image of the "sun" to capture the feeling of the moment and refine it into thoughts and emotions. This was what he had learned from the Western modernist arts, which paid more attention to subjective feelings and impressions, and he integrated it into his own realistic poetry. In "The Trumpeter" (《吹号者》) he wrote about the most common reality in the army, and he linked the entire poem with the "reveille," "starting call," and "bugle call"; when the trumpeter was hit by a bullet, the poet caught the last moment before the trumpeter's death and condensed his feelings and impressions into these poetic lines: "On the smooth bronze surface of the trumpet, / Reflected the blood of the dead / And his pale face; / And reflected the crowd that / kept running ahead shooting, / And the whining horses, / The booming carts … / And the sun, the sun, / Shone the trumpet and made it glitter … /" (the suspension points in both places were by the poet himself).[11] This was something like cinematography, but one feels the charm of poetic language that cannot be found in films. Growing into a revolutionary poet, Ai Qing did not narrow his artistic field of vision, but integrated the significance of that specific era with a highly individualized realistic and symbolic style. He added many masterpieces to the canon of free verse, and provided useful theories and practices to the prose style of

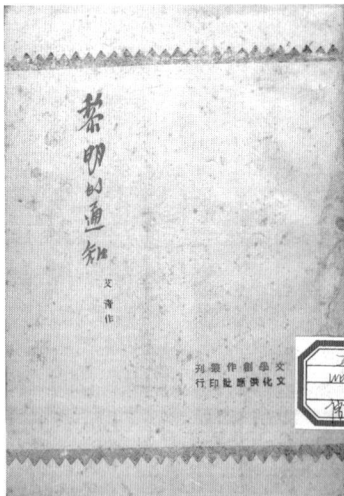

23.8. *The Announcement of the Dawn* by Ai Qing

---

[10]   Ai Qing: *The Announcement of the Dawn*, Guilin: Guilin Cultural Press, 1943.

[11]   Ai Qing: "The Trumpeter," *He Died the Second Time* (《他死在第二次》), Shanghai: Shanghai Magazine Company, 1946.

poetry. Throughout the twentieth century, Ai Qing was the Chinese writer of era-specific poems with the most individualized originality.

As in the case of poetry, entering the 1930s, spoken drama was also involved in the rising tide of era-specific writing. A brief review of the development of spoken drama in China from its beginning – that is, since the May Fourth period when Ibsen's theater and his theatrical theories were introduced to China by *New Youth*; Hu Shi wrote his drama *The Greatest Event in Life* (《终身大事》); and Chinese society became concerned with the destiny of Nora – revealed that so far it had taken a rugged path, including its criticism of the traditional Chinese opera, its practice of amateur (nonprofessional) theater as a correction of excessive commercialism and professionalism of the civilized drama, and in practice, it gradually set learning from Western drama as a basic principle. Indeed, disagreements on how to deal with the relationship between traditional Chinese opera and Western drama always remained, and even initiators of the New Literature could not agree on this issue. In 1924, Hong Shen (1894–1955), who had received systematic education in drama in Europe and the United States, directed *The Young Lady's Fan* (《少奶奶的扇子》), whose script was adapted from Oscar Wilde's *Lady Windermere's Fan*. He changed the "star-oriented system" into a "director-oriented system," and promoted the Chinese spoken drama to become a standard "theater drama." In 1928, Hong Shen translated the term "drama" into "*hua-ju*" (话剧, literally, "spoken drama"), and finally established the terminology. It was then that Tian Han (1898–1968) came to the fore in the circle of theater as a playwright, organizer, and educator of spoken drama, and his experience represented a tendency to change from individualized to era-specific drama writing. Tian Han's early plays, *A Night in a Café* (《咖啡店之一夜》) and *One Evening in Suzhou* (《苏州夜话》), were typically aesthetic and romantic works. *The Death of a Famous Actor* (《名优之死》) was the story of an honest performer written in a more realistic style, but its tone was sentimental and without a grand outlook. Later the Tian Han-led Southern China Society (南国社) was united with other left-leaning dramatic societies, including the Xinyou Drama Society (辛酉社), Modern Society (摩登社), and Shanghai Artistic Drama Association (上海艺术剧社) to become the League of Left-Wing Dramatists (左翼戏剧家联盟). Tian Han was inspired by dramatists of the younger generation within the Southern China Society, and published an article entitled "Our Self-Criticism" (《我们的自己批判》) in *Southern China* (《南国》, monthly) in 1930, publicly announcing a turn to "proletariat drama." The plays written after that, such as *The Flood* (《洪水》), *The Death of Gu Zhenghong* (《顾正红之死》), *Disorderly Bell* (《乱钟》), and *Seven Women in the Storm* (《暴风雨中的七个女性》), among others, tended to write about struggles between different social classes and characterize heroes of the era, but they were not so finely written. Not only Tian Han, but even Hong Shen, who was not a left-wing dramatist, experienced the same transformation and wrote his representative works "Trilogy of the Countryside" (《农村三部曲》, which included three plays about the countryside, namely *Wukui Bridge* [《五奎桥》], *Fragrant Rise* [《香稻米》], and *Black Dragon Pond* [《青龙潭》]). *Wukui Bridge* touched upon the reality of life in the countryside at that time by presenting the sharp conflicts between peasants and landlords around the "bridge." When the "national defense drama" was promoted and there were collectively created plays such as *Smuggling* (《走私》, written by Hong Shen) and *The Posterity of Traitors* (《汉奸的子孙》, written by You Jing [尤兢]), the entire dramatic circle became the stage for era-specific plays. Xiong Foxi (1900–1965), who had been studying drama in the United States and was not a left-wing dramatist, was influenced by this tide and practiced the "peasant experimental drama" (农民戏剧实验) in Zhengding County, Hebei Province, from 1932 to 1935. The performance of Xiong Foxi's *River Crossing* (《过渡》) in a village square in the countryside was an exemplary event of the nationwide Mass Drama movement around that time. His representative street-theater piece *Put Down Your Whip* (《放下你的鞭子》), which spread widely in the "great hinterland" during the Anti-Japanese War, was actually written before the September Eighteenth Incident, but it was not influential until the war broke out in 1937. However, of these era-specific drama writings, few were masterpieces, since their propaganda function was overemphasized, and pieces written hastily to catch up with the situation were often not well-honed artistic works, but they had their own means of improvement. Take Tian Han's *Spring Returns* (《回春之曲》) written in 1935 for example, it combined the subject matter

23.9. Tian Han in Shanghai in 1930

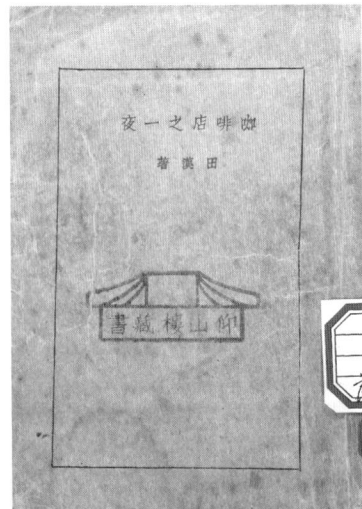

23.10. *A Night in a Café* was Tian Han's major romantic play created earlier in his career

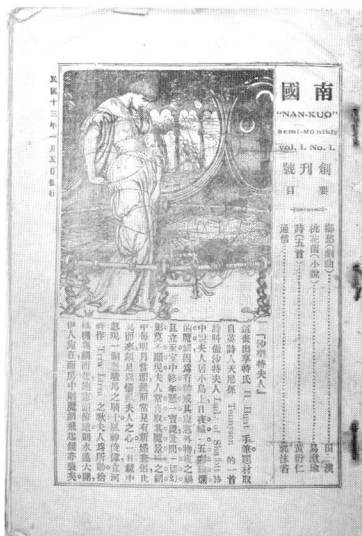

23.11. Inaugural issue of *Southern China*; the Southern China Society was part of Tian Han's earlier dramatic career

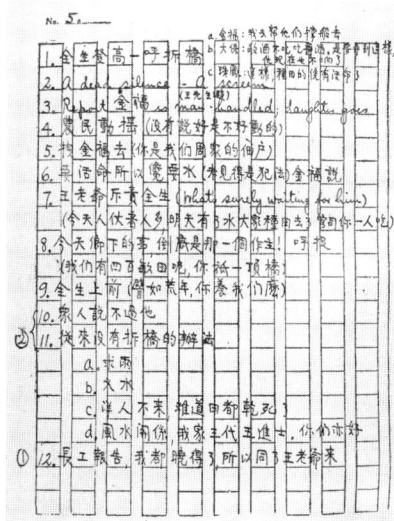

23.12. Synopsis of Hong Shen's *Wukui Bridge*

of national defense with a love story involving the female protagonist, Mei Niang, and found the right balance between the era-specific subject matter and the playwright's individual dramatic lyrical and romantic style. But in the end, era-specific plays were not as successful as era-specific novels and era-specific poetry. The script of *Spring Returns* could only be categorized as a "revolution plus love" play, and it was remembered mostly because of the theme song sung by Mei Niang.

Lu Xun's essay writing during his last ten years in Shanghai represented the real masterpiece of individualized era-specific literary writing. From the "Impromptu Reflections" of the May Fourth period to the Yu Si period, Lu Xun had developed his own sharp and trenchant criticism that fought on two sides: resisting against the violent rule of the Beiyang warlord government, and in-depth analysis of the revolutionary literary camp as well as analysis and criticism of himself. In the 1930s, Lu Xun's essays showed even stronger

23.13. Stage photo of *River Crossing*, performed in an outdoor theater in the countryside. Note that it was difficult to distinguish the actors on the stage from the peasant audience

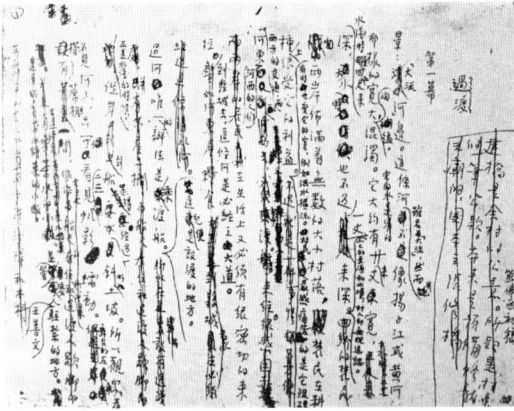

23.14. Page of Xiong Foxi's script for *River Crossing*, a representative work of peasant spoken drama in Ding County

era-specific characteristics. Those essays went deep into all aspects of modern life in China, and gave profound political, ideological, cultural, and aesthetic responses to them, trying to summarize the historical experience and reality of the Chinese nation. Lu Xun had the consciousness to keep a detailed record of the era in his essays, which could be seen from the way he edited his essays in a chronological order. From *Three Leisures*, compiled after 1927, to *The Final Essays from the Semi-Concession Pavilion* (《且介亭杂文末编》) of 1936, these nine collections were all compiled in strict chronological order, and the two addenda, *Uncollected Works beyond the Collection* (《集外集》) and *Gleanings of Uncollected Works beyond the Collection* (《集外集拾遗》), were also edited chronologically from 1903 to 1936. Often, Lu Xun's essays started with a piece of news from that time to attack the despotic ruling of the authorities and analyze the spiritual strength of Chinese people ("Have Chinese People Lost Their Self-Confidence?" [《中国人失掉自信力了吗》] and "A Brief Discussion of the Chinese Face" [《略论中国人的脸》]), or to analyze and satire the servility and flattery of modern urban citizens ("A Playboy" [《吃白相饭》], "Title Undecided, A Draft" [《题未定草》], and "Ah Jin" [《阿金》]), as well as the servile character of Chinese intellectuals ("The Art of the Number-Two Clown" [《二丑艺术》] and "Estrangement" [《隔膜》]). And he also used the method of a "collection of news reports," as in "September Eighteenth" (《九一八》), in which he listed eight news stories published on the second anniversary of the September Eighteenth Incident by the Central News Agency, Associated Press of Japan, Reuters, *Shanghai Evening Post and Mercury, Evening News* (《大晚报》), and *Life Weekly* (《生活周刊》) about how the government strengthened its control on the anniversary of national humiliation to prevent people from gathering and taking part in parades.[12] In the seemingly noncombative prefaces and postscripts, he used the method of collecting a huge amount of material from newspapers "F.Y.I.," which produced quite a strong effect of social criticism. The postscript of *False Freedom*, for example, was a 20,000-character essay,

---

[12] Lu Xun: "September Eighteenth," *Complete Works of Lu Xun*, Vol. 4, Beijing: People's Literature Press, 1981, pp. 578–581.

a record-breaking lengthy postscript for Lu Xun, in which he copied and quoted twenty-four comments with references, titles, and names of authors attacking Lu Xun's texts published in "Free Talk," *Shun Pao*, as a way to expose the ugliness of some intellectuals.[13] The postscript of *Quasi-Romances* (《准风月谈》) was also famous, including copies of around eighteen articles to show the cultural siege of that time, and the postscript of *Second Compilation from the Semi-Concession Pavilion* (《且介亭杂文二集》) just copied the list of books banned by the national government. Lu Xun made no comment in these, but showcased the harsh reality faced by people of the time. These newspaper clippings and postings were material of social, cultural, literary, and ideological history recorded from the standpoint of ordinary people.

The essay genre had had a long history in China since the ancient times, but it was fully developed by Lu Xun with his creative genius, and became a genre of prose with great capacity and remarkable expressiveness. Even during Lu Xun's time, many young writers inherited his style, including Tang Tao,

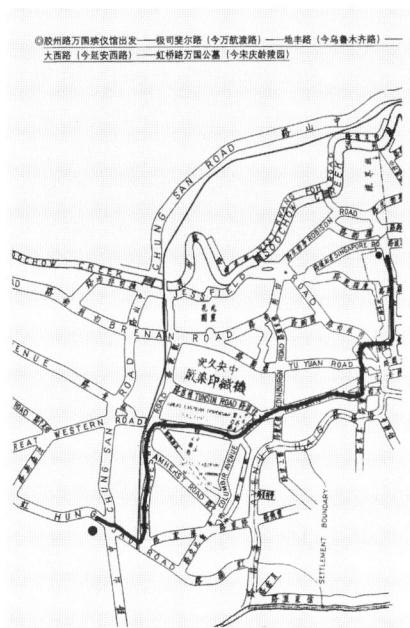

23.15. Route of Lu Xun's funeral procession in Shanghai (see Kong Haizhu [孔海珠], *Bereavement of Lu Xun* [《痛别鲁迅》]). Before Lu Xun, only Sun Yat-sen's funeral had motivated such a great number of people

23.16. Lu Xun's funeral procession on October 22, 1936 (the banners in front of the procession were written by Zhang Tianyi)

---

[13] Lu Xun: "Postscript of *False Freedom*," *Complete Works of Lu Xun*, Vol. 5, Beijing: People's Literature Press, 1981, pp. 152–186.

Nie Gannu, and others, and until now, essays are still written by many, but no one has ever surpassed Lu Xun. Lu Xun's essays were extremely individualized. Firstly, his essays had an argumentative quality and battling style strongly characteristic of Lu Xun. In order to avoid censorship, Lu Xun used numerous pseudonyms, but discerning readers would immediately recognize if a work had been written by him. His criticism was sharp and trenchant, and he often caught the tender point of his opponents in the debate and dealt them a fatal blow; even a casual comment could make his opponents uncomfortable. As Lu Xun said: "Familiar essays that exert life force must be daggers, spears, must be able to kill and fight out a bloody road of existence together with the readers" ("The Crisis of Familiar Essays"). Some people accused his essays of being "spiteful," but Lu Xun straightforwardly said that he had no "personal enemies," only "public enemies." Secondly, Lu Xun's essays repulsed and attacked current affairs and analyzed national psychology, and his analysis went deep into China's profound cultural accumulations. He read between the lines of official history and found reversed meanings in them, and he tapped into unofficial history for the historical truth that was covered or distorted in official history. "Skimming" (《随便翻翻》) was about how reading unofficial history could prevent one from being cheated. "On Buying *Complete Works of Detailed Research on Language*" (《买〈小学大全〉记》) and "Miscellaneous Talk after an Illness" (《病后杂谈》) used past history to satirize the present, made a detailed record of all kinds of literary inquisition of the Qing dynasty and the practice of torture at the end of Ming dynasty, seeking to inspire readers and refusing to forget the past and the present. He reflected and interpenetrated historical criticism and the critique of current reality, which functioned as a telescope and microscope through which he observed the world's past and present. Thirdly, Lu Xun's essays excelled at generalizing the archetype. In the postscript of *Quasi-Romances*, Lu Xun replied to the criticism that his *False Freedom* was printed "solely for a tail – the 'Postscript,'" saying that "this is actually a misunderstanding. My essays usually write about a nose, a mouth, a feather, but combined they may almost form the entirety of an image and seem all right even if nothing is added. But it looks even more complete when a tail is added."[14] And he also said: "My vice is that I don't save face for anybody when commenting on current affairs. I often use the type to expose social problems, and this seems especially inappropriate. Writing about the type, for social problems, is like the rendering of pathology; if there is an ulcer or gangrene, the pathological rendering is like a specimen of all kinds of ulcer and gangrene, so that it may look like the ulcer of this person, or it

---

[14] Lu Xun: "Postscript of *Quasi-Romances*," *Complete Works of Lu Xun*, Vol. 5, Beijing: People's Literature Press, 1981, pp. 382–413. For the quotations, see pp. 382–383.

may look like the gangrene of another."[15] Here he made it clear that what he criticized was the ulcer and gangrene of this or that person, but not the person themselves. This suggested how to read his essays; that is, each of his essays started from his comments on somebody or something at a specific time, but it formed an "entirety" of the era when "combined"; it looked like he was writing about Shao Xunmei, Zhang Kebiao, or Liang Shiqiu, but when "combined," he actually talked about a cultural type; he expanded his perspective beyond a specific point, but his comments did not constitute a generalization of this somebody or something. Rejecting traditional Chinese medicine was his way to criticize the nonscientific mysticism of Chinese culture, and by satirizing Mei Lanfang, he actually criticized the Chinese scholar-official culture that tried to elevate Mei up from the popular culture and then cover him with a glass enclosure. This is something that readers living after Lu Xun's era should pay special attention to.

Lu Xun's essays were considered "encyclopedic" since they covered almost every aspect of that era, including the cultural autocracy of the nationalist government, the rise of left-wing culture, the alternate success of various literary schools, the leftist line within the CPC, the profit-oriented cosmopolitan social atmosphere in Shanghai, and all kinds of deceiving and self-deceiving in society. Starting from commenting on the social phenomena, he went deep into

23.17. Lu Xun's desk on the day he died (Source: Kong Lingjing's [孔另境] private collection)

[15] Lu Xun: "Preface of *False Freedom*," *Complete Works of Lu Xun*, Vol. 5, Beijing: People's Literature Press, 1981, p. 4.

23.18. Lu Xun's tomb in the International Cemetery of Shanghai; the tombstone was built later. Later the tomb was moved to Hongkou Park, which is today's Lu Xun Park (Source: Kong Lingjing's private collection)

all cultural and ideological aspects and dug into the root cause of the spiritual slavery and enslavement of those with power, accomplices, intellectuals, and weak people, demonstrating his tenacious fighting spirit and his grand outlook in historical and civilization criticism. In opposing the prose of Zhou Zuoren and that of Lin Yutang in *Analects*, he developed a style of essay with artistic and combative characteristics that sought to "immediately respond to and fight against harmful things, be the sensitive nerve and the fighting and defending hands and feet" ("Preface to *Essays from the Semi-Concession Pavilion*"). After Lu Xun died, the disputes over whether we should inherit the legacy of Lu Xun's essays and whether we still need "Lu Xun-style essays in this era" have never stopped, while one after another generation of people with insights who share the same spirit as Lu Xun can understand this kind of literature written in and for a specific era and space, which will surely become eternal and universal. When Lu Xun died in Shanghai in October 1936 at the age of fifty-five, thousands of young students and urban citizens voluntarily went to pay their respects and to attend his funeral procession. It was in Lu Xun's essays that era-specific writing reached its peak, which would surely have been impossible without Lu Xun's literary genius.

TWENTY FOUR

THE GRACEFUL BEAUTY OF BELLES LETTRES BY BEIJING SCHOOL AUTHORS

IN OCTOBER 1933, SOON AFTER SHEN CONGWEN AND Yang Zhensheng returned to Beiping from Tsingtao University and began taking charge of the Literary Supplement of the Tianjin *Ta Kung Pao*, Shen published an article entitled "The Attitudes of Authors" (《文学者的态度》) in the supplement for which he himself was the editor-in-chief, which caused a stir among some intellectuals in Shanghai. What Shen Congwen criticized in his article was, of course, a frivolous "attitude," but it incurred a counter-argument by Su Wen (aka Du Heng [杜衡]), who published an article entitled "Writers in Shanghai" (《文人在上海》) in *The Contemporaries*. This started a debate between the Beijing school and Shanghai school literature that spanned over years, and it involved many people, including Lu Xun and Cao Juren (曹聚仁), who were originally not related to either literary school. Then, in February 1934, Lu Xun published an article "Beijing School versus Shanghai School" (《〈京派〉与〈海派〉》); but it seemed that he still had a lot to say, as he published "Beijing School and Shanghai School" (《〈京派〉和〈海派〉》) a year later, putting forward the view that "writers in Beijing tend to be cozy with government officials, whereas writers in Shanghai are beholden to business interests," which was frequently quoted later. In fact, both sides of the debate referred to different people when they mentioned the term Beijing school or Shanghai school, and they did not agree on definitions of the terms, let alone the literary camps involved. The Beijing school in Lu Xun's mind was the "intellectual circle" in Beijing after the May Fourth New Literature camp split up, including "those who have 'achieved success and won recognition and retired from the battlefront,' those who have 'secured their

24.1. Shen Congwen and Zhang Zhaohe (张兆和) at Dayuan Garden (达园) in Beijing in the spring of 1934, soon after their wedding. Around that time Shen was the editor of the Literary Supplement of *Ta Kung Pao*

position,' and those who have even 'risen in social status,'"[1] insinuating those of the Crescent Moon clique and the *Independent Review*. On the other hand, talking about some intellectuals of the Shanghai school, Shen Congwen said they were "sentimental leftists, brave as lions, who recant the moment the wind shifts and turn in their friends for profit – these are the so-called *Hai Pai* (Shanghai school),"[2] which seemed to have included some left-wing intellectuals. One of the long-term side effects of this debate was that it reified and further spread the concepts of the Beijing school and Shanghai school which were nothing but a parlance among people, and it fully related these concepts with the literary circle of that time.

That Beijing school authors were "cozy with government officials" was a general comment on the political and regional culture of Beijing, and there is no need to do any fact-checking. And when we mention the Beijing school in modern Chinese literary history today, we actually borrow this term to refer to, generally, the liberal intellectuals who remained in Beiping or in the north after the literary center moved southward, those who had been members of the Literary Research Society, Yu Si Society, and Crescent Moon Society. Most of these intellectuals were teaching in universities such as Peking University, Tsinghua University, or Yenching University, and some of their students also became well-known writers, so the Beijing school consisted of several generations of authors within the academic circle who had teacher–student relationships. Except for the fact that they did not form an association and put up a banner of a literary group, they could be seen as a clearly-defined literary school. The Beijing school had a solid team of authors, who gathered within certain intellectual circles, such as the two famous literary salons in Beiping of that time: one being the residence of Lin Huiyin at 3 Beizongbu Lane in the eastern part of Beijing, referred to as "Our Lady's Salon," where they exchanged the latest literary information, made wise

[1]   Lu Xun: "'Beijing School' versus 'Shanghai School,'" *Complete Works of Lu Xun*, Vol. 5, Beijing: People's Literature Press, 1981, p. 432.
[2]   Shen Congwen: "On '*Hai Pai*'" (《论〈海派〉》), *Collected Works of Shen Congwen* (《沈从文文集》), Vol. 12, Guangzhou: Huacheng Press, 1984, p. 159.

and witty comments, and enjoyed the delicious Western-style pastries baked by the beautiful hostess; the other was the residence of Zhu Guangqian and Liang Zongdai at 3 Cihuidian, Houmenqiao, which was a place where young intellectuals gathered regularly to recite and discuss poems and was therefore referred to as the "Poetry Recitation Society." And they published their literary works in certain journals or in their own literary journals, such as *Camel Grass*, *Mercury* (《水星》), the Literary Supplement of *Ta Kung Pao*, *Learning Literature* (《学文》), and *Literary Magazine*. Therefore, they were also referred to, collectively, as the "northern authors" or "*Ta Kung Pao* authors," but the catchiest appellation was the "Beijing school." Certainly, what's most important was the literary ideas and ideals shared by these authors: without cutting off the close ties between literature and social life, they chose to stay away from the left-wing and right-wing sectional and political literature; without cutting off the ties between literature and the reading market, they advocated giving full play to originality and literary exploring spirit of individual authors, and opposed the commercial and market literature that gave in to readers' tastes and profit. These were what made the Beijing school stand out in China's literary world in the 1930s.

There was a strong lineup of authors in the Beijing school; of the older generation, there were Zhou Zuoren, Yang Zhensheng, and Ye Gongchao (叶公超). Around the time he launched *Camel Grass*, the earlier journal of the Beijing School, together with Yu Pingbo and Fei Ming, Zhou Zuoren began to make himself the core of the Beijing school and laid the theoretical foundation for this literary school. In its later stage, it was Zhu Guangqian who carried out the influential theoretical work in the Beijing school. As a prestigious

24.2. One of the Beijing school's salons: Lin Huiyin's "Our Lady's Salon," located at 3 Beizongbu Lane, Beiping. The ambience was modern, blending Western and traditional Chinese flavors

24.3. Zhu Guangqian in his youth

author of the May Fourth period, Yang Zhensheng wrote less later, but he taught literature at university for a long time, so he acted as a major organizer within the Beijing school. Thanks to his own achievements in literary creation, and the fact that the Literary Supplement of *Ta Kung Pao* he took charge of became the headquarters of the Beijing school literature, Shen Congwen gradually became the new core within the literary clique, which further expanded, incorporating an abundant supply of literary talents. This included novel writers such as Shen Congwen, Ling Shuhua, Yang Zhensheng, Fei Ming, Lu Fen (芦焚), Lin Huiyin, and Xiao Qian; prose writers such as Zhou Zuoren, Shen Congwen, Fei Ming, He Qifang, Liang Yuchun, Li Guangtian (李广田), Lu Fen, and Xiao Qian; poets such as Feng Zhi, Bian Zhilin (卞之琳), Lin Geng (林庚), He Qifang, Lin Huiyin, Sun Dayu, Sun Yutang (孙毓棠), Liang Zongdai, and Fei Ming; dramatists such as Li Jianwu; and theoretical critics such as Liu Xiwei (刘西渭, pseudonym: Li Jianwu), Liang Zongdai, Li Changzhi (李长之), Chang Feng (常风), and Zhu Guangqian. Generally speaking, this literary school started with the launch of *Camel Grass* in 1930, its middle period was when Shen Congwen was editing the Literary Supplement of the Tianjin *Ta Kung Pao*, and it was fully developed when Zhu Guangqian became the editor-in-chief of *Literary Magazine* in 1937 before the outbreak of the Anti-Japanese War. The war interrupted its extremely promising development.

As one of the three literary pillars of the 1930s, the other two being the left-wing literature and Shanghai school literature, the Beijing school maintained its independence. It insisted on the May Fourth literary tradition that focused on human life, individual liberation and freedom, and thus drew a demarcation line with the left-wing literature on era-specificity and political functions of literature. Certainly, the best left-wing authors also had their originality, but writing under the general principle that emphasized the priority of a specific era and class basis over individuals, their individuality in literary creation had to be compromised. Not

24.4. Zhu Guangqian in front of his residence at Cihuidian, a place where Beijing school writers gathered: the Poetry Recitation Society

only did they detach themselves from era-specific themes, the Beijing school writers also insisted that literature was not utilitarian, and that it was related to, but not "for the sake of" human life and human nature. Back in 1922, Zhou Zuoren, who held that literature was concerned with life (*rensheng pai*, 人生派), had already shown that he was different from other members of the Literary Research Society. In his "My Own Garden," he argued that "art for art's sake" is "subordinating life to art," while "'art for life's sake' is subordinating art to life, which makes art a means to change life and not an end in itself, and thus isn't it another practice to separate art from life?" This view that took art as the ultimate purpose in itself and not as a means to somewhere else could be seen as arguing for belles lettres. Therefore, what he said next about his original understanding of "art related with life" can be seen as the general instruction of literature that was later followed by authors of the Beijing school:

> Art has its independence, but it should in the first place be related to human nature, so that it should not be separated from human life, nor should it be for the sake of human life, just let it be an integrated art related to life. The literature "concerned with art" makes the individual a maker of art, while that "concerned with life" makes art a slave of human life; the correct understanding is that the individual should be the owner of art and express their emotions and thoughts in art, so as to provide the reader with artistic enjoyment and understanding of human life, and therefore the latter's spiritual life is enriched, which can be of practical use in their real life; this is the key point of art related to life, which maintains its independent artistic beauty and at the same time has imperceptible practical use.[3]

The literary concepts expressed by people of this literary school were similar to this. Take Zhu Guangqian for example: in *Literary Magazine*, of which he took charge, he made the statement that "paying attention to the close ties between literature and cultural ideas shall not necessarily lead to the narrow approach of 'literature as a vehicle of moral instruction.'" He argued against "regarding art and literature as a tool to propagate some moral, religious, or political dogma," and disagreed with the "unhealthy view of literature and art" that held "art for art's sake."[4] He

24.5. Literary Supplement of *Ta Kung Pao*, edited by Shen Congwen. This page was dedicated to the discussion of Cao Yu's *Sunrise* (《日出》)

---

[3] Zhou Zuoren: *My Own Garden*, Changsha: Yuelu Press, 1987, pp. 6–7.
[4] Zhu Guangqian: "My Hopes for This Magazine" (《我对于本刊的希望》), published in the inaugural issue of *Literary Magazine* in May 1937.

loudly declared that literature was "the expression of the entire life cycle of a nation."[5] This indeed echoed Zhou Zuoren's view. Therefore, the Beijing school authors pursued "belles lettres," including "pure poetry" and "pure prose" styles. Around the time He Qifang wrote *Painted Dreams* (《画梦录》), he had said something like "I am in pursuit of pure softness, pure beauty."[6] Chinese society in the 1930s witnessed constant social confrontations, which challenged these literary views and upset them, so that they sometimes had to look outside the windows of their academic world or "our lady's salon," but insisting on such belles lettres ideals and pursuing a literature advocating sincerity, humanity, and beauty, was indeed what distinguished the Beijing school from other literary schools.

Thus we can see the major achievement of Beijing school novels did not lie in interpreting Beijing (Beiping), but in seeking to represent the native soil and the life-

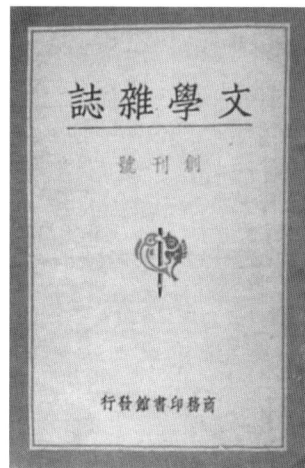

24.6. Inaugural issue of *Literary Magazine*, edited by Zhu Guangqian. It was a later-stage journal of the Beijing literary school, edited in Beijing and published by the Commercial Press in Shanghai. The design on the cover was chosen by Lin Huiyin

style of China's remote and primitive borderland areas, but it inherited the tradition of May Fourth native-soil literature and was totally different from that of the left-wing school. The poetic and culture-oriented native-soil fictions of Shen Congwen, Fei Ming, Lu Fen, and Wang Zengqi (汪曾祺) represented a peak of modern Chinese literature.

Fei Ming (1901–1967) was a major author contributing to *Camel Grass* and he began literary creation earlier than other Beijing school authors. He was a student of Zhou Zuoren at Peking University and was recommended by the latter to teach at the university after graduation, and thus his teacher Zhou Zuoren wrote the preface for almost all his published books. When Shen Congwen talked about his own native-soil narratives, he admitted being deeply inspired by Fei Ming's fictional works (published under his real name, Feng

24.7. *Mercury*, one of the journals of the Beijing school, launched in October 1934

---

5   Zhu Guangqian: "Foreword to the Resumed Magazine" (《复刊卷首语》), *Literary Magazine*, Vol. 2, Issue 1, June 1947.

6   He Qifang: "Preface to *Notes from a Visit Home*" (《〈还乡杂记〉代序》), *Collected Works of He Qifang* (《何其芳文集》), Vol. 4, Beijing: People's Literature Press, 1984.

Wenbing) about the farming families and ordinary people in Huangmei (黄梅, Fei Ming's hometown) in Hubei Province. Here Shen referred to those works collected in *Tales of the Bamboo Grove*, in which the working people the author wrote about were not representatives of a social class, but real people living in harmony with nature; the environment his characters lived in was serene and solitary, which gave the stories a pastoral air. The hard-working, benevolent, and sorrowful laundering women ("Laundering Mothers"), the beautiful girl Sanguniang (三姑娘) who made a living by fishing and selling vegetables ("Tales of the Bamboo Grove"), the old puppet-show performer who loved the willow tree in front of his house ("Willows on the River"), and the

24.8. Fei Ming in the 1930s

father and daughter of the peach garden who relied on each other for life ("The Peach Garden") were all characters who were intimate with the native soil far from modern civilization. They lived within the tranquil landscape and their tenacity and suffering had a sense of dignity about it. Here Fei Ming had given up realistic native-soil literature and had begun his lyrical and poetic writings.

In the 1930s, Fei Ming planned to "hone" a novel in a decade, namely *The Bridge*; however, in the end he only finished the two parts of Volume 1 and a few chapters of Volume 2. This was a novel written with Fei Ming's unique style, in which he paid little attention to plot and characters, and the final work was something between novel and prose. He wrote about the scenes in the countryside outside the southern gate of the small county town he lived in during his childhood and thus was very familiar with. He wrote about Xiao Lin's childhood life when he went to the old-style private school within the city gate and when he and Qinzi from Shijiazhuang spent time together (Part I of Volume 1); when Xiao Lin returned after studying far from home, he played happily with his fiancée Qinzi and his cousin Xizhu (细竹, Part II of Volume 2). The loosely structured plots were scattered throughout the novel like sparkling and crystal-clear pearls, and it was the fragments of scenes that remained in readers' minds long after reading this novel: his happy truancy after the dull time at school, the boy and girl practicing calligraphy together, the interesting shadow plays and peeping at the dim light, the scenes of young girls laundering in the river and combing their hair under the trees, the beauty of sunset and night flowers, and the local customs of giving ox to get engaged and sending ghost lamps as gifts during festivals. All these poetically described scenes contained metaphors, symbols, and zen wisdom that were difficult to trace. Fei Ming was indeed humble in his attitude while "unrestrained in writing" (to quote Bian Zhilin). And he studied Buddhism, recited Buddhist scriptures, and practiced meditation, and even lived

24.9. *Camel Grass*, a Beijing school journal launched on May 20, 1930, which published most literary works of the Beijing school authors in its earlier stage

a secluded life in Haidian, Beiping, where it was as remote as the countryside at that time. Legend goes that he once discussed Buddhism with Xiong Shili (熊十力), who was his colleague at Peking University and his fellow countryman, and they got into such a fierce debate that they began wrestling with each other. In writing novels, Fei Ming sought to express his poetic ideas with prose-style sentences, and was quite bold in his choice of diction, use of metaphors, creation of imagery, and blank space to facilitate the flow of thoughts and feelings. Just as Fei Ming himself said, he was writing novels as painstakingly as people of the Tang dynasty wrote quatrains. The novels *The Biography of Mr. Neverwas* and *After Mr. Neverwas Rides a Plane* (《莫须有先生坐飞机以后》, written after the Anti-Japanese War) were both based on Fei Ming's personal experiences, and they should have been chapters of a lengthier book. "Mr. Neverwas" was Fei Ming speaking of himself, and the novels were about what the Chinese Don Quixote saw and experienced when he wandered freely in the countryside of China. Obviously different from *The Bridge*, in the "Mr. Neverwas" series there was more introspection, more irony, and more ridiculing, with the mockery of local customs and sympathetic

24.10. Cover of the first edition of Fei Ming's novel *The Bridge*, published in June 1932

24.11. *The Peach Garden*, a collection of short stories by Fei Ming

24.12. Young Shen Congwen in Baojing, Hunan, before he left for Beijing in 1922

teasing being targeted at both peasants and intellectuals alike. The comicality of the series added to the revelatory significance of the character "Mr. Neverwas." Fei Ming persistently explored a national style of literature, but that's exactly what made him hard to understand.

Shen Congwen (1902–1988) was one of the most important Beijing school authors. He was born in the remote and beautiful town of Fenghuang, Hunan, and was a hybrid of Miao, Tujia, and Han nationalities. He only completed his primary school education, but was extremely familiar with and carefully examined the land of western Hunan and the river of Yuanshui (he dedicated a series of articles to the relationship between his literary creation and rivers), as well as the people living there. Influenced by the May Fourth ideas, he went to Beijing alone in 1922 but could not find anybody to teach him, so he had to practice writing in extreme poverty. We can see this from Yu Dafu's famous essay entitled "A Public Letter to a Literary Youth" (《给一位文学青年的公开状》) written after he visited Shen Congwen in the latter's narrow and moldy residence. Shen Congwen gradually emerged as a talented writer and entered the literary circle with the support of people of the Crescent Moon clique.

The most attractive element in Shen Congwen's fictions was, certainly, the local color of western Hunan. Some may attribute Shen's success among readers to the latter's curiosity about the world outside civilization, which was indeed an oversimplification. With his rich experience in the real world, literary talent, artistically crafted emotions, and memories, as well as his ability to catch small details of everyday life, Shen Congwen created a literary "western Hunan world" with his entire corpus of texts. And the ensemble of real people in his hometown, consisting of peasants, soldiers, sailors, shop boys, boatmen, and prostitutes, as well as their unique "form of life," constituted his inexhaustible source of inspiration. At first he was not fully aware of his own strength, so in the collections such as *Ducks* (《鸭子》), *Sweet Mandarins* (《蜜柑》), *After the Rain and Others* (《雨后及其他》), and *The Romance of a Shaman* (《神巫之爱》), the theme of "western Hunan" had emerged, but his literary thoughts were not fully developed and his language still not very refined. Entering the 1930s, the publication of the collections *The Marble Carrying Boat* (《石子船》), *Long Zhu* (《龙朱》), *The Tiger Cub* (《虎雏》), *Under Moonlight* (《月下小景》), *A Portrait of Eight Steeds* (《八骏图》), *The New and The Old* (《新与旧》), and *Novel Compositions of Congwen*

(《从文小说习作选》), especially his masterpieces in novel and prose writing, *The Border Town* and *Discursive Notes on Traveling Through Hunan* (《湘行散记》), established Shen Congwen as an excellent modern Chinese writer. He created an honest and simple atmosphere of western Hunan, in which lower-class people lived in hardship, still struggling for survival; in "The Cypress Tree" (《柏子》) he wrote about the rather primitive love between a sailor and a prostitute living in a stilt house, and a deep-felt sorrow was shown from the contrast between the unscrupulous sexual relationship and the toughness of risking beaching each month to make a living. "Xiaoxiao" (《萧萧》) was a story of a child bride. She was seduced by someone other than her husband, but because she gave birth to a son, she was not victimized by her husband's family. This story had quite a profound ending: her illegitimate son was to be married to an older child bride, and thus one could predict the lives of generations after generations of "Xiaoxiao's." "The Husband" (《丈夫》) went a step further in describing the complexity of human feelings. In the borderland areas, a peasant husband seemed accustomed to the fact that his wife was a prostitute who entertained sailors, but his primitive masculinity was aroused once when he went to visit the sailors' boat, which could be seen as an awakening of human nature. The husband remained silent but had deep-felt sorrow in his heart. *The Border Town* represented the peak of such narratives about the landscape and people of western Hunan, and was categorized into a kind of "almost eventless tragedy." *The Border Town* was about the simple life of an old ferryman and his granddaughter Cuicui, and embedded in the tragic love story between Cuicui and the sons of the local captain was the sorrowful love story of Cuicui's mother. Like the other young female characters created by the author, such as Sansan in "Sansan" (《三三》) and Yaoyao in "The Long River" (《长河》), Cuicui was a gentle, beautiful, and quiet girl. Deep in their ancient and self-contained lifestyle was planted the seed of love, and the scene of the songs sung by her grandparents before she went to sleep each night appeared in Cuicui's dreams. All of this conveyed the beauty of nature and human feelings in western Hunan. It was a remote area, but people there were kind, honest, and unsophisticated, and had simple and persistent beliefs in life, from which we can see the liveliness of the ethnic people living in the borderland areas. Wang Zengqi once said: "*The Border Town* is a work of love and warmth, but the author concealed behind it a deep sense of tragedy. ... The life described in *The Border Town* is real, but it is also idealized, making it an idealized reality."[7] This made it totally different from the left-wing native-soil literature. The natural and spontaneous lifestyle of Cuicui and other characters was both sorrowful and full of vitality,

---

7   Wang Zengqi: "Reading *The Border Town* Again" (《又读〈边城〉》), *Collected Works of Wang Zengqi* (《汪曾祺文集》), Literary Criticism volume, Nanjing: Jiangsu Literature and Arts Press, 1993, p. 100.

and Shen Congwen's literature was the literature of life.

Sensitivity to cultural conflicts gave Shen Congwen a special perspective in novel writing. He was aware that he stayed detached from the people of cities and their culture. In 1934, soon after his wedding, Shen Congwen heard that his mother was seriously ill, and he hurriedly returned to his hometown along the Yuanshui River; eleven years had passed since he had left. After a twenty-five-day journey, he remained at home for three days to stay with his mother. It was a visit home, but also a chance for him to revisit the culture along the road. On the journey, he jotted down what he saw, recalling the cultural conflicts between the city and the countryside, and wrote thirty-four long letters to his newlywed wife, hence the collection *Discursive Notes on Traveling through Hunan*. It was during this journey that he met a woman, Xiaocui (小翠), from a yarn shop in Luxi County,

24.13. Shen Congwen's hometown, Fenghuang County in western Hunan, vividly portrayed by Huang Yongyu (黄永玉)

24.14. North gate of the town of Fenghuang, Shen Congwen's hometown, taken in the past

24.15. Shen Congwen standing outside the north gate of the town of Fenghuang when he returned home in May 1982. One can compare this picture with Figure 24.14

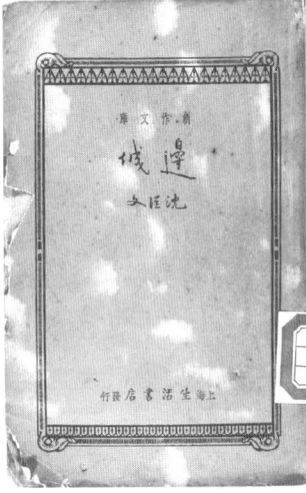

24.16. First edition of Shen Congwen's masterpiece *The Border Town*, published in October 1934

who had a white string in her hair to remind her of her late mother Cuicui, and he was shocked by the difference between things here and those in the cities: in the countryside life seemed to fall to a standstill and destiny seemed to repeat itself. It was then that he was inspired to continue writing *The Border Town*, which he had only just started, and settled on the name for the female protagonist. Writing about this contrast, Shen Congwen established his unique western Hunan narrative, and he also had a satirical (antilyrical) narrative of city life, like the hypocritical high-class men and women in "The Gentry Wives" (《绅士的太太》), the cultural castration of university professors in "A Portrait of Eight Steeds," and the wasteful lifestyle of literary youths from the countryside in the metropolis in "Mr. Huanhu" (《焕乎先生》). He recorded the differences and contrasts between, for example, the city and the countryside, the modern and the traditional, the areas where modernity had made rapid progress and those with less development, the central areas dominated by the Han culture and those marginalized ethnic areas. As a "countryman" from western Hunan who had bumped into a modern metropolis and became an intellectual, he deconstructed modern Chinese life from a historical and cultural perspective, and writing on the theme of the confrontation between rural and urban areas, he criticized the complex "normalcy" and "changes" brought about by the intrusion of modern civilization into China. Shen Congwen proposed the solemn goal of "reconstructing" the Chinese nation and national culture. This seemed too large a goal for belles lettres, but all the same it was put forward, evidence that even authors of belles lettres did not turn a blind eye to the overall social and cultural conditions, which could be seen as a characteristic of the Beijing school writers.

Shen Congwen was recognized as one of the finest Chinese "stylists," and though this was not considered praise for a certain period of time, we can look at it with more objectivity now. As for the form of fiction writing, Shen Congwen gave up the Fei Ming-style obscurity and narcissism, and his modern

24.17. "A Corner of My Cabin," drawn by Shen Congwen when he returned to western Hunan by boat in 1934

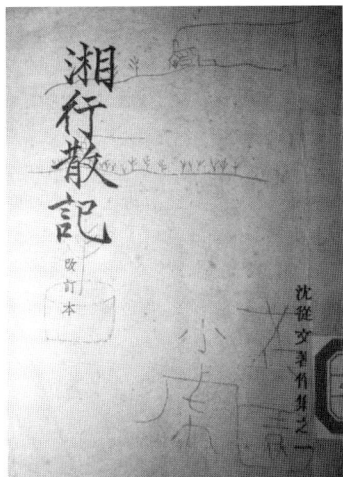

24.18. One of Shen Congwen's major collections of prose writings, *Discursive Notes on Traveling through Hunan*

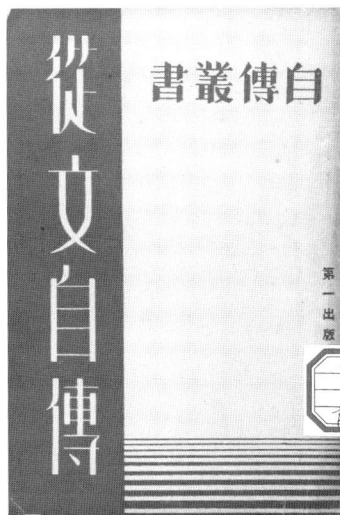

24.19. Another major work of Shen Congwen's, *Autobiography of Congwen* (《从文自传》), which was beautifully written and full of life

poetic native-soil fictions were full of vitality and had their cultural heritage and their own path. He paid more attention to feelings and emotions in narrative, or we can say he added his intuition to the scenes and characters, paying attention to establishing the narrative subject, portraying innocent characters, creating atmosphere, and unifing descriptions of human characters and their stories, so that the narrative was flowing and lively. He attached less importance to characterization or deliberate arrangements of plot, but made "atmosphere creation" the priority in his narrative writings. These poetic fictions emphasized elaborating the cultural environment at the beginning. When he taught narrative writing at university, Shen Congwen gave full play to his literary talent and listed the beginnings of several fictions he had written and compared them in class. Some novels started with descriptions of the docks and river streets, some with the introduction of local culture and history, some with lengthy dialogues, and some without any dialogue. He flexibly used his pen to describe, recount, compare, hint, and comment, exploiting emotions, images, and cultural implications from narratives, creating an artistic conception that combined reality and drama. He gradually threw off obscurity in his language, using colloquial language on the one hand, and absorbing concise words and sentences from classical Chinese language on the other. He promoted naturalness and clarity, but also paid attention to diction and speech polishing, likening the practice to a "workout": "A workout that 'condenses the emotion into depth and expresses it straightforwardly' and that 'distorts the language to test

24.20. Stilt houses along the Jianjiaxi River, Taoyuan, western Hunan, drawn by Shen Congwen. He noted that it was a pity he could not copy the sound, how beautiful the sound was! There was the sound of scullers singing, water flowing, and the sound of voices within the stilt houses

its tenacity and punches it to test its hardness.'"[8] This style of language could be used to express emotions, satire, and write fairy tales and legends, as well as Buddhist stories. The novels were written with a simple prose style and a poetic quality, conveying the author's warm and deep sympathy toward human beings of the world. Shen Congwen's native-soil lyrical narrative had a far-reaching influence on the literature of later times.

Lu Fen (1910–1988) used another pseudonym, Shi Tuo (师陀), in the 1940s, and both pseudonyms were known to people. The collection of short stories, *The Valley* (《谷》), which he wrote under his original name Wang Changjian (王长简), won the literary prize of *Ta Kung Pao*, a magazine dominated by Beijing school authors, in 1937, and he also wrote other major works that described his hometown, Henan, such as *Forgotten Events from Old Home* (《里门拾记》). Similar to Fei Ming and Shen Congwen, he did not evade his native-soil cultural background but made painstaking efforts to create native-soil lyrical images of his own; but what distinguished him from the others was his unique ethos of the Central Plains area, and the deserted cities, gardens, land, and houses were all his recollections and emotional expressions about China's decline from the perspective of "a returning intellectual." He was sharper in his satire of local customs, as in "Baishun Street"

---

[8]   Shen Congwen: "An Exercise of Emotions" (《情绪的体操》), *Collected Works of Shen Congwen*, Vol. 11, Guangzhou: Huacheng Press, 1984, p. 159.

24.21. Portrait of young Shi Tuo (aka Lu Fen)

(《百顺街》), when he wrote about a grotesque market street in a rural Chinese town, mocking at the arrogance of those who were in power and foolish submissiveness of ordinary people, the atmosphere quite ridiculous and the meaning allegorical. Symbolism had been another strength of Lu Fen's, as represented in "Crossing the Mountains" (《过岭记》), in which the mountain journey was a symbol of human life. We will discuss Lu Fen again later when talking about the literature of the 1940s, when he wrote the even more outstanding short story series *Records of Orchard City* (《果园城记》), the novella *A Master in the Village of No Hope* (《无望村的馆主》), and a number of prose writings, and established his important position in the poetic native-soil literature of the Beijing school.

In the autumn of 1935, Xiao Qian (1910–1999) graduated from Yenching University and started working at *Ta Kung Pao* assisting Shen Congwen to edit the literary supplement and later he participated in the preparation and editing work of the Shanghai *Ta Kung Pao* and its supplement. As a young writer and new member of the Beijing school, Xiao Qian was full of energy, and apart from his work as an editor and journalist, he also wrote short stories and novels. His earlier fictions, like those in the short story collections *Under the Fence of Others* (《篱下集》) and *Chestnuts and Other Stories* (《栗子》), revealed his uniqueness brought about by his lower urban class background. From "The Galloping Legs" (《印子车的命运》) and "Deng Shandong" (《邓山东》), one could see he was quite sensitive to the gap between rich and poor in the cities. His poor and humble childhood had left a lasting mark on him, which could be felt through his awareness of civilians (shared by almost all Beijing school authors) and the fact that he often took a "child's perspective" in his literary writings. The criticism of religion in "The Conversion" (《皈依》), "Dense Clouds" (《昙》), and "Lucifer and Orien" (《参商》) was unique to him. Xiao Qian's Beijing school poetic quality was especially obvious in his love stories. In "Silkworms" (《蚕》), he linked the life cycle of silkworms with the twist and turns of the love story of a young couple, and it was said that this creative conception was

24.22. Xiao Qian worked as a journalist and editor for *Ta Kung Pao* immediately after he graduated from Yenching University in 1935. This spiky-haired appearance quite matched his character

praised within "Our Lady's Salon." *The Valley of Dreams* (《梦之谷》) was his autobiographic novel, in which he wrote a love tragedy in a poetic style. Xiao Qian's most important achievement in his later career was his correspondent accounts written from Europe during World War II.

Lin Huiyin (1904–1955), who praised Xiao Qian, was not very productive in literary creation, but she wrote excellent pieces in each literary genre, including poetry, prose, fiction, and drama. In her collection of short stories, *Scattered Text of Faint Reflections* (《模影零篇》), "Zhong Lü" (《钟绿》) was about a rare beauty; "Jigong" (《吉公》) was the story of a mechanical enthusiast from an old-style family who received a new-style education but was of lower status in the family, and "Wenzhen" (《文珍》) was the story of a runaway maid, all tragic stories beautifully written. "In Ninety-Nine Degree Heat" (《九十九度中》) described the lives of people in the extreme heat of the lanes of Beiping. This awareness of civilians was also shown in the writings of authors of higher social standing, which was common among Beijing school writers. The narrative of "In Ninety-Nine Degree Heat" was structured with crosscut sections of the kaleidoscope of human life, which Liu Xiwei considered to have been influenced by modern English novels, "structureless but structured, disorderly but organized, plotless but full of stories," and the narrative represented the principle to "regard life as a piece of wood that cannot be encircled by both arms," which was "modernist in its truest sense."[9] In fact, the Beijing school authors did draw a great amount from avant-garde world literature, just like Shen Congwen in the 1940s when he wrote *The Candle Extinguished* (《烛虚》), which will be discussed later in this book. Those who should be discussed in detail among authors from the National Southwestern Associated

24.23. Lin Huiyin and her father Lin Changmin in London in 1920, when she was only sixteen years old

[9] Liu Xiwei: "'In Ninety-Nine Degree Heat' by Ms. Lin Huiyin" (《〈九十九度中〉——林徽因女士作》), *Selected Literary Works and Critical Essays of Li Jianwu* (《李健吾创作评论选集》), Beijing: People's Literature Press, 1984, p. 454.

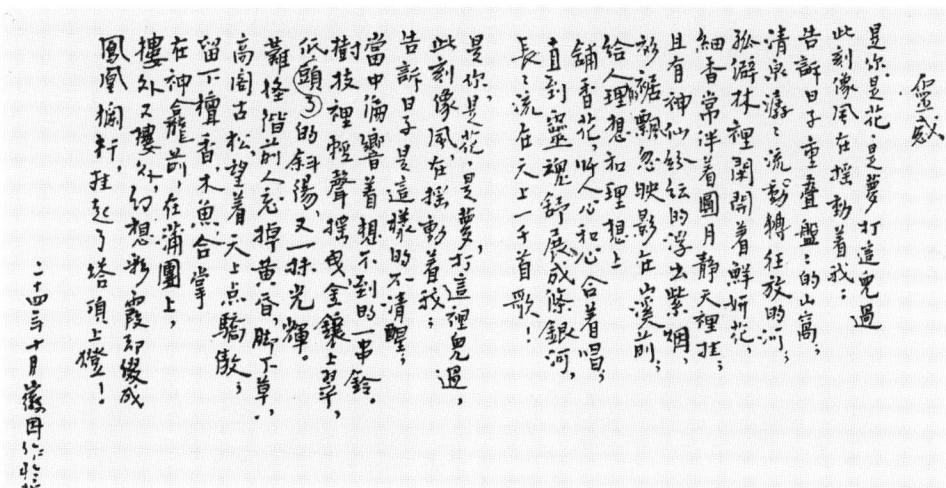

24.24. Lin Huiyin was talented in many fields, and this was the manuscript of one of her poems

University, such as Wang Zengqi, a later-stage member of the Beijing school, also had a clear link with modernism.

Compared with their fictions, the modernist features of Beijing school poetry were obvious. Bian Zhilin of the "Han Garden Trio" (汉园三诗人, with the other two being He Qifang and Li Guangtian), as well as Fei Ming, Lin Geng, and Lin Huiyin, among others, were closely related to the romantic metrical poetry of the Crescent Moon school, but later they echoed Dai Wangshu and other poets around *The Contemporaries*, giving up sentimental self-expression, finally forming the new scene of modern Chinese poetry. From the time when Li Jinfa started to practice Chinese modernist poetry in the 1920s, to Dai Wangshu launching *New Poetry* in Shanghai in 1936 and inviting Bian Zhilin, Sun Dayu, Liang Zongdai, and Feng Zhi to be its coeditors, Chinese modernist poets were finally gathering together. Of the Beijing school poets, Bian Zhilin (1910–2000) was especially talented. He blended French symbolist techniques with the aesthetic taste of traditional Chinese poetry, and from around 1935 until the eve of the Anti-Japanese War, he wrote a number of philosophical verses that tried to express a modern poet's complex poetic ideas through clusters of imagery with intellectuality, such as those in *Fish Eyes Collection* (《鱼目集》) and *Poems of a Decade* (《十年诗草》). Interestingly, the poem "Round Treasure Box" (《圆宝盒》), which appeared in *Fish Eyes Collection*, due to the dense web of increasingly irrelevant images, even Beijing school poets and critics disagreed on its interpretation, so much so that Liu Xiwei had discussed the poem repeatedly with its author.[10] Such ambiguity of

[10] See Liu Xiwei "*Fish Eyes Collection*" (《鱼目集》) and its appendices: "On *Fish Eyes Collection*" (《关于〈鱼目集〉》) by Bian Zhilin, "Answering the author of *Fish Eyes Collection*" (《答〈鱼目集〉作者》) and "On 'You'" (《关于〈你〉》) by Bian Zhilin, all collected in Liu Xiwei's *A Collection of the Finest Essays* (《咀华集》), Shanghai: Shanghai Cultural Life Press, 1936.

24.25. Bian Zhilin at Peking University in the 1930s

24.26. Bian Zhilin when he joined the army in Shanxi in 1939

meaning was caused by the interactions between sense and sensibility, and the dense web of images, as well as temporal and spatial interlocking and alternations, which made Bian's poems extremely obscure and difficult to understand. On the other hand, this was exactly the artistic conception preset in modernist poetry, so that readers could have the aesthetic satisfaction of interpretation in their close reading. As a love story, "The Ichthyolite" (《鱼化石》) was rather peculiar:

I want to have the shape of your embrace,
I am always dissolved into the lines of water.
Just like a mirror, you truly love me. Both you and I
Have gone into the distance and the ichthyolite emerges.

The subtitle of this poem was "Said a Fish or a Woman" (《一条鱼或一个女人说》), which means the "I" who said this was not clearly defined, and the "you" who was addressed to changed accordingly and thus entailed multiple interpretations. "The ichthyolite" was a primary metaphor of this poem on the theme of love, and thus the meanings of loving embrace, being dissolved into the water, and becoming mirrors for one another were all easy to perceive and understand, but the image of (a blended couple) going into the distance and forming the ichthyolite was quite unintelligible. Here there was a leap of ideas: one did not truly understand the value of blending until there was a distance in between, and thus the ichthyolite became the token of eternal love. Other major poetic works of Bian Zhilin written in this period included the extremely well-known "Fragment" (《断章》): "While you watch the scenery from the bridge, / The sightseer watches you from the balcony," which conveyed the idea that everything in this world is linked to everything else.

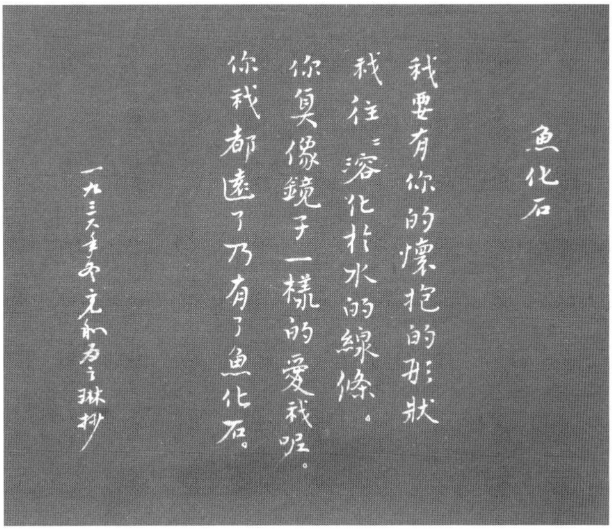
魚化石
我要有你的懷抱的形狀
我往往溶化於水的線條。
你真像鏡子一樣的愛我呢。
你我都遠了乃有了魚化石。

24.27. Bian Zhilin's poem "The Ichthyolite," handwritten by Zhang Chonghe (张充和), the young sister of Shen Congwen's wife, Zhang Zhaohe

"The Composition of Distances" (《距离的组织》) conveyed the twofold sense of distance with the lines that broke the distance of time and space: "Mount a high tower alone to read *The Rise and Decline of the Roman Empire*, / Rome's comet suddenly appears in the newspaper." This poem had ten lines, and at first the author annotated for three lines, but later he added notes for altogether seven lines, evidence of how difficult the poem was. These poems were by no means written in a freely flowing style, but they were very much cultured and restrained, and were considered the major works of Bian Zhilin's innovative poetry, widely different from the easy and simple era-specific poems written around the same time. When the Anti-Japanese War broke out, Bian Zhilin had been to Yan'an with He Qifang and others, but he later returned to teach and write in the Nationalist-controlled area, and one can see his influence in the works of the Nine-Leaves poetic school (九叶诗派) of the 1940s.

Fei Ming was not productive in poetry writing, but his poems were similar to some of Bian Zhilin's in that they were equally profound and abstruse. In "The Barber Shop" (《理发店》) one reads: "The soap foam of the barber shop / has nothing to do with the universe, / But it is like the fish forgotten in rivers and lakes." Comparing the trivial soap foam with the vast universe and comparing the small fish with the large rivers and lakes, such strings of seemingly unrelated images constituted the author's poetic conception. The image of a "mirror" in "Vanity Desk" (《妆台》) echoed that of Bian Zhilin's "The Ichthyolite," but Bian's poem contained an understanding of Western relativism, while Fei Ming's idea reflected an oriental philosophy and zen wisdom, for his mirror was empty. In "On the Street" (《街头》), the narrator was in a trance-like state on the bustling street, and the combination of images led to an epiphany: "Walking on the street there are cars passing, / there are

24.28. Lin Geng in his youth

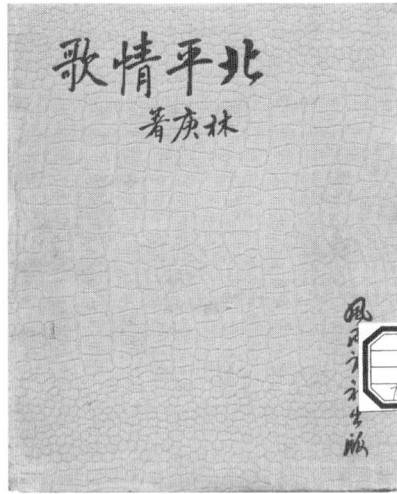

24.29. Lin Geng's anthology, *Love Songs of Beiping* (《北平情歌》)

mailboxes solitude." No wonder when Fei Ming talked about the history of Chinese poetry, he said the poems of Yuan Zhen (元稹) and Bai Juyi (白居易) were easy to understand and those of Wen Tingyun (温庭筠) and Li Shangyin (李商隐) were difficult. He did not criticize the latter, but said that the poems of Wen and Li "seemed to show the trend of today's new poetry,"[11] which was the pursuit of the Beijing school imagist lyrical poems.

We can see that the Beijing school poems were quite avant-garde in their exploration of poetic forms. Lin Geng (1910–2006), who was a graduate of Tsinghua University, also sought to break away from the restraint of the Crescent Moon clique and wrote free verse in his earlier stage, and "The Spring Field and Windows" (《春野与窗》) was written in this period of time. Those written after 1935, most of which are collected in the anthologies *Love Songs of Beiping* and *The Sleepsong and Others* (《冬眠曲及其他》), however, showed his attention had returned to metrics (he emphasized the rhythms of the Chinese language) and to matching the rhythms of poetic language with those of modern life. For example, his seven-character poems written during this period of time did not consist of three-feet lines but of two-feet lines: "Raindrops fall at the foot of the mountain / The road at the mountain front is covered with mud / Tomorrow the wind will blow from the northwest / Where is the traveler will he return home or not" ("Raindrops" [《雨丝》], which was not punctuated by the poet). And "Deep Autumn" (《秋深》), which consisted of fifteen-character three-feet lines, was not punctuated either: "In the autumn of Beiping I dream of my hometown as soft as a

[11] Fei Ming: "On New Poetry: New Poetry Shall be Free Verse" (《谈新诗·新诗应该是自由诗》), *Selected Works of Feng Wenbing* (《冯文炳选集》), Beijing: People's Literature Press, 1985, p. 436.

piece of gauze / In the remote border town my friends have gone and left the blowing wind / The moonlight shines since the ancient times on the dreams of lovers in the sound of midnight trumpet / Homesickness remains sentiments thicken with the wind entering homes." This was closely related to the "nine-character two-feet lines" (with five characters in the first foot and four in the second) he later promoted. Like other Beijing school poets, Lin Geng was also an advocate of pure poetry, but did not approve of obscurity. Another Tsinghua graduate, Sun Yutang, was a historian and an amateur poet, and he also changed from Crescent Moon to modernist poetic style. In 1937, he won that year's *Ta Kung Pao* Literary Prize for his 763-line epic "Ferghana Horse" (《宝马》), which was about the war launched by Emperor Wu of the Han dynasty to plunder Ferghana horses from the Western Regions, but the poet added the soldiers' and ordinary people's modern-style understanding of this event.

Beijing school prose inherited and developed the elegant and melodious Bing Xin-style of the May Fourth period (epitomized by *Letters to My Little Readers* [《寄小读者》]) and the Zhu Ziqing-style that featured simple and refined vernacular language (epitomized by "A View of My Father's Back" and "Lotus Pond by Moonlight"). We can see the same spirit of poetic ideas expressed with the beautiful prose style in Shen Congwen's *Discursive Notes on Traveling through Hunan, Western Hunan* (《湘西》), and *Autobiography of Congwen*, and language that could be used in both novels and prose in the writings of Fei Ming and Lu Fen's *Yellow Flowering Moss* (《黄花苔》) and *Collection of Rivers and Lakes* (《江湖集》). *Painted Dreams*, written by He Qifang (1912–1977) during his period as a Beijing school writer, represented the peak of this beautiful poetic prose style, which seemed to be unprecedented and insurmount-

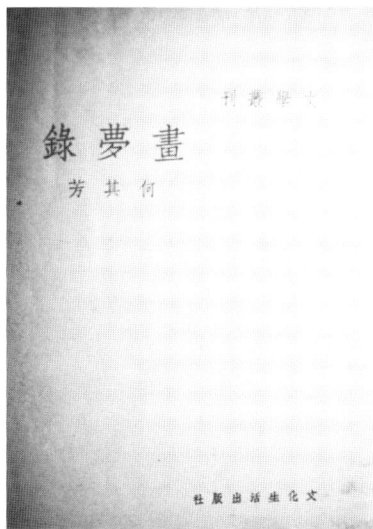

24.30. First edition of He Qifang's *Painted Dreams*

able. This also stemmed from his pursuit of belles lettres. The articles collected in *Painted Dreams* did not insert lyrical self-expression into reasoning and narration, but gave the former a position independent of the latter, and thus the author gave vent to his constrained youthful emotions and passions with a series of daydream-like symbolic expressions: "The Tomb" (《墓》), "Elegy" (《哀歌》), and "Strings" (《弦》) showed his beautiful dream world dilapidated; "Dusk" (《黄昏》) was a collage of many color blocks; and "Before the Rain" (《雨前》), in which the scenes before the rain in the north and that in his hometown in the south were treated like a duet, and his imagined raindrops trickled on his pining, homesick dreams, was easy to understand. Generally, *Painted Dreams* expressed the author's beautifully decorated emotions (sometimes they may seem a bit overblown); the author tried to create a hazy aesthetic effect, and blanks were left for readers to fill with their creative close reading. Later He Qifang went to Yan'an and became a left-wing writer, and these pursuits in *Painted Dreams* seemed to have disappeared forever. Li Guangtian (1906–1968) was the prose writer of the "Han Garden Trio," and since he always had a northern native-soil style of Shandong, the texts in his *Gallery Collection* (《画廊集》) and *Silver Fox Collection* (《银狐集》) were much simpler and clearer than those discussed earlier. In "Mountains and Rivers" (《山水》), which appeared in the *Birds and Straw Collection* (《雀蓑集》), in particular, the author expressed his homesickness through cherishing the memories of his hometown on the plains where there was neither mountain nor river. This awareness of civilians, gentle human sympathy, and lyrical language were all features of Beijing school literature.

Now we should talk a little about Liang Yuchun, whom we mentioned earlier as being a talented young writer. He died of scarlet fever at the age of twenty-six, but was considered a major writer of Chinese leisurely-style prose. At first glance, one may think his prose pieces imitate English famil- iar essays, but they actually had the quintessence of classical Chinese casual writings. His close friend Fei Ming once said that Liang's writing style was "Six-dynasty-style prose among New Literature," and "he would have great success in the future."[12] Liang Yuchun inherited the tradition of the Yu Si Society's "civilization criticism," wrote freely and brilliantly about the trivialities of everyday life – reading, dreaming, wandering, tears, and laughter, life and death – and added his own life experience, associations of knowledge, and understanding of life. Liang only published one collection of prose pieces, *Spring Wine*, while he was alive, and after his death, his friends published the collection *Tears and Laughter* for him. He also translated many English familiar essays. Liang's writings showed a graceful and humorous manner, in which one can see his extremely rich imagination and broad-mindedness. His humorous language was gentle and harmless, with which he took

24.31. Liang Yuchun, who died young, at the age of twenty-six

12 Fei Ming: "Preface to *Tears and Laughter*" (《〈泪与笑〉序》), *Selected Works of Feng Wenbing*, Beijing: People's Literature Press, 1985, p. 327.

various "vantage points" to examine living creatures, pretending to be an idiot, a lovelorn man, or even the shadow of himself. These beautiful commentary essays were full of love, humor, sympathy, and humanity – a branch of Zhou Zuoren's leisurely style prose. It was a pity that he died so young and didn't have the chance to give full play to his literary talent.

The Beijing school dissolved when the Anti-Japanese War broke out, but soon after, signs of its reemergence gradually appeared at the National Southwestern Associated University. Shen Congwen, Feng Zhi, Bian Zhilin, and others not only continued to write, but also led and cultivated a number of young novelists and poets, such as Wang Zengqi and Mu Dan (穆旦), among others. In June 1947, Zhu Guangqian took the lead again and resumed *Literature Magazine*, which showed even more obvious features of the Beijing school than before, and continued and carried forward the tradition of Beijing school literature.

TWENTY FIVE

NEW PERCEPTIONS OF THE SHANGHAI SCHOOL IN THE MODERN METROPOLIS

I T WAS BY NO MEANS A COINCIDENCE THAT A DEBATE occurred between the Beijing and Shanghai literary schools between 1933 and 1934. These two literary schools were based in China's two major cities at that time, and their cultural links with their respective cities broke through the territorial restrictions and became even more extensive. At that time, Beijing was associated with "rural China," not "urban China," and the literary world created by Beijing school authors was largely based on native-soil imaginings; whereas Shanghai school writers took root in Shanghai, the leading modern Chinese metropolis that most obviously demonstrated the duality of capitalism and colonialism.

Developing through the late-Qing dynasty, the earlier Republican period, and the 1920s, Shanghai took on an unprecedented modern look in the 1930s. Since its opening as a trading port in 1843, the twenty-third year under Emperor Daoguang's reign, the concession gradually rose and the city gradually became one of the major metropolises of the world. If we take the financial district along the Bund as the epitome of the city, we can see that its development roughly went through three stages. The first stage was the 1850s. At that time a dozen British and French banks had just set up their offices here and the buildings were not very high, so one could still see the outer gate of the Chinese government agency, Chinese Imperial Customs, from afar. This was a time when imperialist powers dumped opium into China and the door of the country was forced open. The second stage started in the 1890s, when banks from the United Kingdom, France, Germany, Japan and Russia began to erect buildings in the city, and foreign countries expanded their trade with China, money flew in and out, with which the buildings became higher and higher. Even the building for China's first commercial bank, the Imperial Bank of China, founded by Sheng Xuanhuai (盛宣怀) of the Self-Strengthening movement, was a Western-style building. At that time, the busiest street in Shanghai was Fourth Avenue (Fuzhou Road), within the concession, and people adopted a hybrid consumption style that incorporated traditional Chinese and Western cultures. Chinese people ate grand feasts (Western-style cuisine) and went to billiard saloons, but it was not the mainstream. Instead, their major entertainment involved going to Qinglian'ge Teahouse and other teahouses (where Western-style tea pastries had begun to be served and silent movies were shown), as well as restaurants and opera theaters, bookshops and brothels, which constituted the scenes described in the novels written from the late-Qing period (such as *The Sing-Song Girls of Shanghai* and *A Flower in a Sinful Sea*) until the Mandarin Duck and Butterfly school. The third stage started from the 1920s, when a new round of dismantling and construction began along the Bund: the HSBC Bank building was finished in 1923, Sassoon House at the corner of Nanjing Road in 1928; the modernist-style Broadway Mansions along the Suzhou River at the northern end of the Bund in 1934; and it was not until 1936 that the Bank of China building, the only building along the Bund designed by a Chinese designer, was finished. This was basically the skyline of the old Bund that we see today. At the same time, Big Avenue (aka Nanjing Road) in the international concession and Avenue Joffre in the French Concession became China's well-known modern commercial business and cultural entertainment streets, where world-class department stores, race clubs, cinemas, dance halls, and restaurants opened one after the other. Their influence extended to each avenue and alley around Shanghai and changed the everyday life and views of Shanghai citizens. By the mid-1930s, the largest modern metropolis built by importing the Western model but rooted in Chinese culture took shape at the mouth of the Yangtze River, and it was at this time that Shanghai school literature and left-wing literature began to take Shanghai as their subject matter from their respective perspectives.

25.1. The Bund just after Shanghai was opened as a trading port. The traditional Chinese-style Chinese Imperial Customs building stood out among the Western-style buildings

25.2. The financial district along the Bund during its second stage of development

Since the late-Qing period, all literature with Shanghai as its theme had focused on the evilness and abnormality of the city. Even those talking about the technological progress that was happening might imply that it was no more than wicked trickery. In the late 1920s, writers of the Creation Society became the first to construct a modern-style narrative of Shanghai from the perspective of class conflict, or the conflict between the rich and the poor. Later, left-wing literature, with Mao Dun as the leader, began to show Shanghai as an economically and politically powerful arena. For example, the first chapter of *Midnight* started with Wu's father dying immediately after he arrived in Shanghai from the countryside, which was referred to as the dead body of the feudal society decaying upon arriving in the dazzling and shocking modern scenes of Shanghai, which was treated as a modern-day allegory. In the ninth chapter, the author presented Nanjing Road on the eve of the May Thirtieth movement from the viewpoint of a young intellectual wearing Western-style

25.3. By the 1930s, the Bund had taken shape; this picture was taken from exactly the same viewpoint as Figure 25.2, but here one can see the new Shanghai Customs House, Sassoon House, and Broadway Mansions

clothes, and the tense atmosphere thus created used the noncommercial cityscape as the setting of confrontation between classes. And in the eleventh chapter, the author wrote about the constantly changing and unpredictable Shanghai Stock Exchange from the viewpoint of Liu Yuying, which was a totally different scene from the one just described: "The stock exchange is even more noisy than the farmers' market. There are layers upon layers of people, and the smell is unbearable. … Those who rap the gavel on the platform and those who hold the telephone receivers all blush, waving their hands in the air and shouting loudly, but their voices are totally inaudible. There are around seventy or eighty stock brokers and over 100 assistants and innumerable speculators shouting numbers, which is as loud as thunder and everybody's ears are turned deaf."[1] This was the sheer commercial cityscape of Shanghai, where the market was like a battlefield. With its multisided narrative, *Midnight* presented an image of Shanghai with conflicting dimensions of modernity. Certainly, *Midnight* was not a novel about workers, but focused on national capitalists; however, Mao Dun expressed his view in his novel *Rainbow*: "The real veins of Shanghai beat in the low honeycomb-like houses in areas like Xiaoshadu, Yangshupu, Lannidu, and Zhabei!"[2] Mao Dun showed a clear-cut left-wing stand in these writings. Then we can see how Yin Fu, one of the "Five Martyrs of the League of Left-Wing Writers," conveyed the same message in his poem entitled "A Tribute to Shanghai" (《上海礼赞》): "Shanghai, I saw your dead body in my dream, / Laid bare at the bank of the Huangpu River, / At the foot of Longhua Pagoda, /

25.4. Nighttime view of the Paramount Dance House in the 1930s

On which there were thousands of white maggots crawling, / But you did not let out a groan of grief or doubt."[3] The image was extremely striking. The city presented in the writings of left-wing literature, however, was still full of evilness. Therefore, it was in Shanghai school literature that the city finally shook off the label of "evil metropolis."

---

[1]   Mao Dun: "Midnight," *Complete Works of Mao Dun*, Vol. 3, Beijing: People's Literature Press, 1984, p. 317.
[2]   Mao Dun: "Rainbow," *Complete Works of Mao Dun*, Vol. 2, Beijing: People's Literature Press, 1984, p. 253.
[3]   Yin Fu: "Characters in Blood: A Tribute to Shanghai," *Selected Poetry and Prose of Yin Fu*, Beijing: People's Literature Press, 1954.

25.5. Inaugural issue of *The Contemporaries*, whose editor-in-chief was Shi Zhecun. It was a journal that marked the independence of Shanghai school literature and its inclusiveness and openness

Let's see how people on the streets of Shanghai were described in Shanghai school literature:

A cashmere scarf, two scarves actually, came near, wrapping the soft and smooth skin of two teenage girls. In the shade of their bangs, unsettled feelings were deeply hidden in their clear eyes. A bachelor man, who took a cane like the arm of his wife, rubbed shoulders with them. His nose and beard were almost inside his pipe. The mailbox in green stood at the roadside, opening its mouth, a hungry look.[4]

And a dance hall in Shanghai:

The azure blue dusk shrouded the entire hall. A saxophone was extending its neck and opening its big mouth, wooing them. On the smooth floor at the center, there was fluttering dresses, fluttering robe ends, delicate high heels, heels, heels, heels. Fluffy hair and men's faces. White collars of men's shirts and women's smiling faces. Extending arms, emerald earrings dangling to the shoulders. Tables were well arranged, but the chairs were disorderly. White boys stood in the dark corners. There was the smell of wine, fragrance, English-style ham and eggs, and smoke …[5]

This was an unprecedented writing style, no longer just exposing the "darkness" and "evil-doings" of the metropolis, but also focusing on its "contemporariness." The authors writing in this style constituted a group, but they were not associated, and they were not only characterized by living in Shanghai and writing about Shanghai. What they wrote was not left-wing political literature, nor was it Beijing school belles lettres, but the market-oriented literature that catered to the aesthetic taste of white-collar urban citizens of Shanghai in the 1930s. The Shanghai school was a group of authors from the New Literature camp who gained a sense of modernity from the modern metropolitan lifestyle.

What is "modernity"? Shi Zhecun once tried to answer this question when, as an editor, he replied to the question of what was "modern poetry" raised by readers of *The Contemporaries*, which still seems to make sense now. He said:

The poems published in *The Contemporaries* are poems, and they are purely modern poems. They express the modern emotions felt by modern

---

4   Liu Na'ou: "Flowing" (《流》), *Urban Shanghai Landscape* (《都市风景线》), Shanghai Shuimo Bookstore, 1930, p. 45.

5   Mu Shiying: "Shanghai Foxtrot" (《上海的狐步舞》), *Cemetery* (《公墓》), Shanghai: Modern Book Company, 1933, pp. 201–202. The ellipsis dots are quoted from the original text.

people in modern life, and these emotions are arranged in modern poetic forms with modern diction.

The so-called modern life consists of all kinds of individual features: a harbor packed with ships, a factory filled with loud noise, a mine pit deep under the ground, a dance hall with jazz music, a department store within a high building, the air battles by planes, the huge racecourse … even the natural scenery is different from that of the past. How could our poets' emotions endowed by this kind of life be the same as those gained from their life by poets of the previous generation?[6]

We may take this as a statement about the literary concept of the Shanghai school. Certainly, several points could be added: firstly, such modern life and emotions in this machine civilization were first felt by the white-collar class inside those office buildings in Shanghai, and only then extended to the general public to be regarded as "modern." Therefore, the earliest readers of Shanghai school literature were fashionable young people of the metropolis. Their cultural tastes, their metropolitan style of consumption, and their admiration for Western civilization determined the aesthetic taste of Shanghai school literature. Secondly, the fact that this literature was popular because it was fashionable ensured that its avant-garde nature (partly borrowed from the world modernism of that time) could also gain some market share among general public readers in Shanghai. The reading market could be occupied through both avant-garde and popular aspects; this became a unique feature of Shanghai school literature. That "Mu Shiying-fever" emerged later, however, had something to do with the entertainment consumption of urban citizens. Thirdly, popularity brought with it a tendency for vulgarization. Therefore, Shanghai school literature had this two-sidedness from its beginning. The left-wing and Beijing school authors emphasized its vulgarity and commercial nature. For example, Shen Congwen once said Mu Shiying "borders on perverse," that the latter was "good at creating new sentences, new tones, and new conceptions, but his weakness lies in his affectation," and that Mu's "literary works are like romances (he mainly writes about men and women in modern metropolises, and they can be seen as romances of Shanghai). Thus it is good for him to write for pictorials, for decoration magazines and entertainment magazines about women, films, and games. The 'metropolis' is the subject of the author's writings but it also limits his field of vision."[7] Shen Congwen made this comment from the viewpoint of a native-soil author, and the left-wing authors surely made harsher comments about Mu from a

---

[6] Shi Zhecun: "And About the Poems Published in This Magazine" (《又关于本刊中的诗》), *The Contemporaries*, Vol. 4, Issue 1, Nov. 1, 1933.

[7] Shen Congwen: "On Mu Shiying" (《论穆时英》), *Collected Works of Shen Congwen*, Vol. 11, Guangzhou: Huacheng Press, 1984, pp. 203–204.

25.6. *Trackless Train* (《无轨列车》), one of the earliest journals of Shanghai school authors

political point of view. But neither denied that Shanghai school authors were strong in writing on the subject of "metropolis." Before Shanghai school literature came into being, the metropolis was only the setting where characters lived and stories happened, but it was in the writings of Shanghai school authors that the modern metropolis first became a separate body of literary imagination and a totally independent aesthetic object.

The earliest Shanghai school authors were those who split from the Creation Society and other aesthetic literary associations of the May Fourth period, and it was thus a branch of New Literature. In its early stage, the Creation Society had the agenda of revolutionary romanticism and "art for art's sake," and in the 1930s, when other members championed "revolutionary literature" and became left-wing, Zhang Ziping and Ye Lingfeng (Ye once joined *Zuolian* but was expelled; as part of the emerging literature, the Shanghai school was not totally isolated from the left-wing authors) led other members along a winding path to the cause of urban popular literature. Shanghai school authors had the habit of exaggerative self-boasting. For example, in his novels, Mu Shiying often let his characters talk about their favorite books and authors, which included himself and his writer friends. In *Seasonal Dreams of Shanghai* (《上海的季节梦》), his character Xu Zulin recalled "the days I read 'Taili' (《苔莉》) secretly in class." In his personal diary dated 1927, Liu Na'ou also noted that he did not like the tendency of *Fiction Monthly* leaning toward the Literary Research Society, but preferred such writings as "Zhang Ziping's 'Taili,' Yu Dafu's 'The Past' (《过去》), and others" published in *Creation Monthly*. He said that Zhang Ziping could "describe Chinese society, especially the sexual desire of Chinese people, in quite a carefree manner."[8] This unconsciously revealed the relationship between Zhang and New Sensationalist literature, which emerged later. One of the founding members of the Creation Society, Zhang Ziping (1893–1959) was the author of the very first modern Chinese novel, *Fossils in the Age of Alluvial Clays*

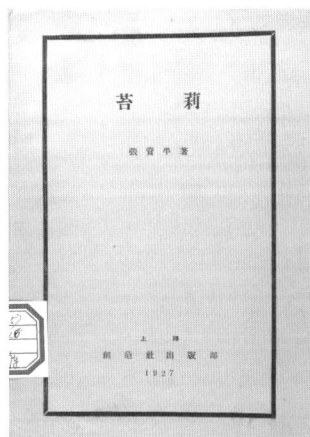

25.7. Zhang Ziping's "Taili." Afterward, Zhang began writing exclusively for the popular reading market

---

8   Kang Laixin (康来新) and Xu Qinzhen (许秦蓁), eds., *Complete Works of Liu Na'ou: Diaries* (《刘呐鸥全集——日记集》), compiled and translated by Peng Xiaoyan (彭小妍) and Huang Yingzhe (黄英哲), Tainan: Bureau of Culture of Tainan County, 2001, pp. 424, 316.

25.8. Cover of Zhang Ziping's *Children of God*

25.9. Title page of Zhang Ziping's *Children of God*

(《冲积期化石》), and was praised by Li Changzhi as "the person who began to write new novels in fluent national language."[9] "Taili" was one of Zhang's representative works. Later he experienced a period when he could write and publish several urban popular novels every year. He opened the Lequn Bookstore (乐群书店) to publish nothing but his own best-selling books, so that some said he opened a "fiction factory." During this period, he gave full play to his ability to integrate the passions and sexual desires of men and women into metropolitan settings, and his better novels included *Last of Happiness* (《最后的幸福》), *Long Journey* (《长途》), and *Children of God* (《上帝的儿女们》), among others. Since his literary creations were increasingly market- and profit-oriented, he repeatedly wrote about the same theme of love triangles and polyamories, and the sexual, psychological descriptions became vulgar and even perverse. He was thus criticized by Lu Xun and Shen Congwen. The example of Zhang Ziping showed how the profit-oriented writings of Shanghai school authors could degenerate in taste and style.

Ye Lingfeng (1905–1975) was a member of the later-stage Creation Society, and he was talented in many fields, including painting, writing, book collection, ex-libris making and collection, journal editing, and art editing. In the field of fiction writing, he wrote sentimental fantasies and romances in his earlier stage, including "The Sin of *Nüwa*" (《女娲氏之遗孽》), "Jiu Lümei" (《鸠绿媚》), and "Luoyan" (《落雁》). He was also one of the earliest Chinese authors trying out Freudian psychoanalytical writings, including "The Night of Wedding of the Elder Sister" (《姊嫁之夜》) and "The Temptation

---

[9]   Li Changzhi: "Examinations of Zhang Ziping's Romantic Fictions" (《张资平恋爱小说的考察》), *Tsinghua Weekly* (《清华周刊》), Vol. 41, Issue 3.

of Mojia" (《摩伽的试探》). After 1932, he followed the fashion of modern-ism and changed his own writing style, writing and publishing "The Purple Violet" (《紫丁香》), "Woman No. 7" (《第七号女性》), and "Anatomy of Melancholy" (《忧郁解剖学》), among others, which marked the beginning of his New Sensationalist writings. Reading these new literary works published in *The Contemporaries*, Dai Wangshu was very happy and wrote to Ye from Paris, saying that he "liked 'Woman No. 7' in particular."[10] Examining how Ye Lingfeng presented modern metropolitan female characters and his descriptions in this much praised "Woman No. 7," we can see that the tie between Ye and Mu Shiying was obvious. The metropolitan male character in this short story assigned a number to each woman he met on the bus and wrote it down in the notebook he took with him every day. In Mu Shiying's *Seasonal Dreams of Shanghai*, the male character Xu Shijie also recorded "Woman No. 9," "Woman No. 11," and "Woman No. 12" and had a memo about their ratings like "A+," "A," and "A−," which was hardly a coincidence. A bit later, Ye Lingfeng made a complete U-turn and began serializing urban popular novels in newspapers. In around two years, he wrote three tragic Shanghai stories, namely *A Girl of the Times* (《时代姑娘》), *The Unfinished Confession* (《未完的忏悔录》), and *Forever Woman* (《永久的女性》). Some friends tried to dissuade him from wasting his literary talent on writing such popular novels, to which Ye replied in each separate edition of these novels, saying that his only "intention" was to "lead the general readers into the garden of New Literature through my popular novels,"[11] "in order to attract those general readers who have just turned from old-style novels to New Literature," that he wrote for those "general readers of newspapers who were isolated from high-brow literary works."[12] These clearly stated the view of readership of the Shanghai school authors at that time. Firstly, these authors wrote for readers, who were the lifeblood of their writings. This made them totally different from authors of belles lettres who "write for themselves." Secondly, they did not think that New Literature could be isolated from popular writings, but wanted to put "high-brow" literary elements into popular literature through their own writings. The three urban popular novels by Ye

25.10. Ex libris made by Ye Lingfeng

---

[10] See "Letter by Dai Wangshu to Ye Lingfeng on March 5, 1933," collected in Kong Lingjing, ed., *Letters of Modern Writers* (《现代作家书简》), Guangzhou: Huacheng Press, 1982.

[11] Ye Lingfeng: "Self-Preface to *A Girl of the Times*" (《时代姑娘·自题》), *A Girl of the Times*, Shanghai: Si She Publishing, 1933.

[12] Ye Lingfeng: "Preface to *The Unfinished Confession*" (《未完的忏悔录·前记》), *The Unfinished Confession*, Shanghai: Jindai Bookstore, 1936.

Lingfeng, for example, were not mere repetitions of the form of linked-chapter novels in the late Qing, but integrated elements of romantic novels and New Sensationalist novels. Thirdly, they were aware of the transition of urban readers in Shanghai in the 1930s, which included both "readers who have just turned from old-style novels to New Literature" and many "general readers of newspapers who were isolated from highbrow literary works," that is, swing readers. Ye Lingfeng's aims were threefold: to gain the readers of romantic fictions, modernist fictions, and popular fictions. Retrospectively, from the development path of Shanghai school literature in the 1940s, we can see he was quite prescient in this.

This was a period when New Sensationalism was the fashion. The pioneer who introduced this literary genre to China from Japan was Liu Na'ou (1905–1940), a native of Taiwan who was more

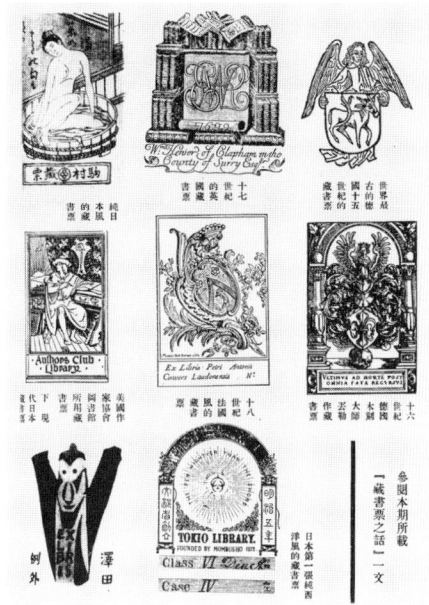

25.11. Bookplates from various countries collected by Ye Lingfeng, about which he wrote an essay in *The Contemporaries* (Vol. 4, Issue 2, Dec. 1933)

proficient in Japanese than in Chinese. In 1926 he entered the special class of Aurora University to learn French from Pere Tostan, a famous missionary of the times, and one of his classmates was Dai Wangshu. The next year, Dai Wangshu's friends Shi Zhecun and Du Heng were admitted to the special class, too, which was the reason why these people later gathered in the three-story house rented by Liu Na'ou located at Gongyuan Alley, Jiangwan Road, Hongkou, and began writing literature, launching journals, and opening bookstores, gradually forming an author group. Liu Na'ou was familiar with the latest literary trends in Japan, which included USSR literature after the October Revolution and modernist literature in Europe. He translated a collection of short stories by Japanese New Sensationalist writers and entitled it *Exotic Culture* (《色情文化》, which was often held by characters of Mu Shiying' novels), and Japanese New Sensationalist writers actually learned from the expressionist, futurist, surrealist, and stream of consciousness literature and integrated these into their own writings. Liu Na'ou not only introduced this new literary trend to China, but took the lead in writing New Sensationalist fictions and publishing them in his own journal, *Trackless Train*, which increased the popularity of this literary trend in the years that followed.

Liu Na'ou was not very productive in fiction writing, and his short stories were collected in a thin book, *Urban Shanghai Landscape*, whose title had unexpectedly become extremely popular in Chinese cities by the 2000s. Those

25.12. Liu Na'ou, the pioneer of
New Sensationalist literature

25.13. *Urban Shanghai Landscape* by Liu
Na'ou, whose title almost became syn-
onymous with modern urban literature

stories collected in *Urban Shanghai Landscape* were about men and women in
Shanghai, but it set the keynote for narratives of urban life in modern times:
the suppression of speed and machines on human beings, as well as the spiritual
sensations and physical enjoyment brought about by excessive and corrupt
cultural consumption. In "Landscape" (《风景》) he wrote about a man and a
woman who met each other on a train. Once in the countryside, they felt that
even their clothes were a burden put on them by modern civilization:

> Not only the clothes were machine-like, even the houses we lived in
> became mechanical. All the architecture and utensils inside were com-
> prised of lines and angles. There were electric wires, water pipes, heating
> pipes, gas pipes, and the square shed was built on the roof. Didn't human
> beings live in the center of a mechanical world?[13]

And taking modern women as a central image and symbol of the modern
metropolis later became a distinctive feature of novels of this genre. These
women had stepped out of the melancholic and chaste settings of old-style love
stories and had become playgirls in the public space of the metropolis. "Games"
(《游戏》) was about an "eel-like woman" who managed to flirt with two
men and could "love and break up with them freely and happily." The woman's
body was described through the lustful eyes of men: "What else is it if it's not
a product of modernity? He thought about how her body moved when she

---

[13] Liu Na'ou: "Landscape," *Urban Shanghai Landscape*, Shanghai: Shuimo Bookstore, 1930, p. 31.

walked on the street and her agile movement under the waist. Her highly protruding breasts, and her soft and smooth eel-like eggs." Later, in Mu Shiying's writings, this kind of woman was given even more brilliant descriptions.

Mu Shiying (1912–1940) made his name known through *The Contemporaries*, edited by Shi Zhecun, and Mu was referred to as the "great master of New Sensationalist literature." He demonstrated the best techniques and the significance of Shanghai school literature of the 1930s. At the time when he published his short stories about workers' fierce resistance against capitalists, which were later collected in *North and South Poles,* he was regarded as a new proletarian author; but at the same time, he also wrote a number of New Sensationalist fictions that focused on the lives of the white-collar class in the metropolis. These two subject matters were integrated into a structure consisting of desire, abreaction, and destruction. And when he went deeper into the texture of metropolitan life, as in such writings as *Cemetery* (《公墓》) and "A Platinum Statue of the Female Body" (《白金的女体塑像》), he finally found the modern nature of urban objects and all aesthetic sensations of urban subjects, from body to soul. In "Shanghai Foxtrot", for example, one finds his best language describing the metropolitan space:

> The white-painted legs of roadside trees, the legs of electric line poles, the legs of all still-life objects … all these were like a revue, the girls who extended their crossed white-powdered legs … the lines of white-painted legs. Along that quiet avenue, from those windows of residential houses, lamplights would peep through the window screenings, pink, purple, green, from everywhere, like eyeballs of the metropolis.[14]

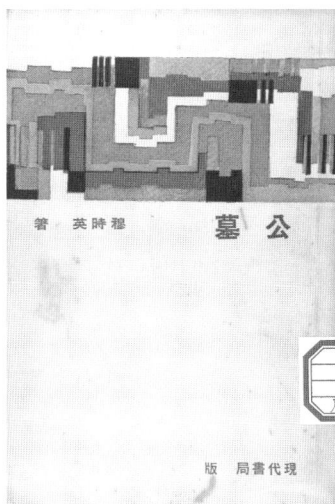

25.14. *Cemetery* by Mu Shiying

25.15. Mu Shiying's first collection of short stories, *North and South Poles*

[14] Mu Shiying: "Shanghai Foxtrot," *Cemetery*, Shanghai: Modern Book Company, 1933, p. 197. The ellipsis dots were quoted from the original text.

It was a city built on wheels, which had its special lights, colors, shadows, and flavors. The "legs" on the streets and "lamplights" from the windows formed a gorgeous image; the narrative was like a movie camera moving along, showing us the speed, rhythm, and dynamics, as well as the temporal and spatial crossing and superposition of the city. Everywhere we see the streamlined texture of the urban city, its material prosperity, its vulgar sexual message, the temptation of money, people's relaxation during the quiet and still night after a busy day, and its multiplicity as a heaven-and-hell. Here we can feel the unfathomable depth of city life, and it was the Shanghai lived in and understood by Mu Shiying. Thanks to his great literary talent, he could impress the sensation of the subject on the description of objects in the urban city, to achieve the compounding and distillation of various sensations. Take his description of the Huangpu River under the moonlight for example: "From east to west, on the surface of the river, the moonlight extended for several miles, and a large round moon was dragging behind the ship. A pulling-boat came near on the moonlit surface, the boatman's hair silver."[15] His description of the neon lights: "'Evening Post!' The newsboy opened his blue mouth, one could see his blue teeth and blue tongue tip; in front of him, the tip of that giant high-heel shoe in the blue neon light just directed at his mouth. // 'Evening Post!' Suddenly he had a red mouth, a tongue tip extended from the mouth, for that giant wine bottle was now pouring red wine." The illusions of city life were fully integrated into its lights and colors; Mu Shiying invented the narrative language and technique of New Sensationalist literature.

And Mu Shiying certainly excelled at fully conveying the openness of the women in cities. In "Craven 'A,'" the narrator read a map of the body of a social butterfly, an objectification of women through the lustful male gaze. The lady in "A

25.16. Wedding photo of Mu Shiying and Qiu Peipei. Qiu was a dance girl who had long featured in Mu's fictions as various characters. It was said that Mu could improvise novels in the dance hall. Even their marriage had a kind of literary symbolic meaning

---

[15] Mu Shiying: "Night" (《夜》), *Cemetery*, Shanghai: Modern Book Company, 1933, p. 177.

Platinum Statue of the Female Body" presented a seemingly lifeless nude body in front of us: "an inorganic statue without a sense of shame or morality, and even deprived of human desire. A metallic and flowing gaze seemed to slide through the lines of that nude body."[16] But it was this female body deprived of desire due to excessive sexual activities that stimulated Dr. Xie's desire. Here one could see the overall fatigue of modern people. Mu Shiying went beyond Liu Na'ou's "magic women" characters and presented his female characters who were "pressed flat" by their everyday life. In "Black Peony" (《黑牡丹》) there was the dance girl who had fled to the country house, and the author described her dancing movements in this way: "Under the blue lamplight, her slender black-gaze high-heel shoes floated on the floor with the music, as beautiful as a dream, like a pair of crows flying under the rainbow over the horizon." Her own account of her story was: "I live in luxuries, and without the jazz music, foxtrot dance, cocktail, fashionable colors of the fall, eight-cylinder sports car, and Egyptian tobacco, I will become a soulless person." And the conclusion: "Life is as trivial as ants. // So many ants, one after another, line as the number 3. // Here it is! Here it is! // Here I see 333333333333 … crawling toward me endlessly from all directions, unavoidable and inescapable."[17] Through these writings Mu Shiying expressed his own understanding of life and people in the modern metropolis, which was not so very profound, but there was a grain of truth in it.

The New Sensationalist literature was a writing style with a great sense of formality, so it had been commented on by Beijing school authors as form overwhelming content. Shen Congwen, for example, once said that Mu Shiying was hollow in his heart. But indeed, hollowness was part of modern and postmodern city life. Mu Shiying's innovative narrative matched the rhythm of urban life. He deployed all kinds of techniques to create an urban world that was dynamic, vital, and full of life but where everything was decaying so quickly, including the alternate use of long and short sentences (with the long ones like neverending threads and short ones like a breathless breath), meticulously organized paragraphs, deliberate punctuation (especially brackets and ellipsis dots), frequently changed points of view, refrains, and variants of refrain. In his writings we can see, at least in part, the spiritual price human beings had to pay for the progress of material civilization.

Shi Zhecun (1905–2003) was also an author pursuing an avant-garde artistic sensibility. He was one of the pioneers of modern Chinese

---

[16] Mu Shiying: "A Platinum Statue of the Female Body," *Complete Works of Mu Shiying* (《穆时英全集》), Beijing: October Literature and Arts Press, 2008, p. 10.

[17] Mu Shiying: "Black Peony," *Cemetery*, Shanghai: Modern Book Company, 1933, pp. 216, 218, and 233. The ellipsis dots were quoted from the original text.

25.17. Shi Zhecun in Shanghai in 1934

psychoanalytic novels, and taking the approach of Freudian theory, he wrote such works employing stream of consciousness as "One Rainy Evening in the Spring" (《梅雨之夕》) and "At the Paris Theater" without borrowing much from Japanese New Sensationalists. In "One Rainy Evening in the Spring" there were the various fantasies and associations of a man toward a woman he met in the rain. "At the Paris Theater" was about a married man's sexual imagination and his release of sexual desire toward his female companion sitting beside him in the darkness of the cinema. There was a paragraph about the man smelling the woman's handkerchief, in which the author gave full details of the man's sensations about the mixed smell of fragrance and sweat, the salty smell of sweat, even the fishy smell of spit and mucus, so much so that he suddenly felt sexual satisfaction, like he was hugging the nude body of a woman. Later, in the collection of short stories *Exemplary Conduct of Virtuous Women* (《善女人行品》), he gave a more in-depth analysis of the psychology of women in urban cities: in "A Comet in the Sign of Leo" (《狮子座流星》), the thoughts of a young woman looking forward to pregnancy were written in quite a fluid manner; "Spring Sunshine" (《春阳》) was a significant story about a rich woman, Auntie Chan, who had sacrificed her youth, and felt the stirring of love and sexual desire in the urban atmosphere in the spring. In *Small Treasures* (《小珍集》) there was a story entitled "Seagulls" (《鸥》), which was about a low-rank bank clerk, Xiao Lu, sitting behind the bank counter boringly day after day, thinking about the seagulls at the beach in his hometown and the girl who was his first love. Due to his boring book-keeping work and lovesickness, one day he saw this scene before him:

> The still sunshine suddenly trembled a bit, and Xiao Lu had the experience that this meant someone was walking past the window. If it was a dark tremble, it meant that person wore some dark clothes, and if it was bright, it simply meant the person was in some light color.
>
> But what surprised Xiao Lu was the exceptional brightness and continuous trembles of sunlight on his account book. He could not help raising his head, and he saw the white caps of a group of four or five nuns walking past the window. If he could liken the black-painted area on his window to a deep blue ocean, these white caps were so much like fluttering seagulls.[18]

[18] Shi Zhecun: "Seagulls," *Fog, Seagulls, and the Comet* (《雾·鸥·流星》), Beijing: People's Literature Press, 1991, pp. 175–176.

25.18. (left to right) Shi Zhecun, Mu Shiying, Dai Wangshu, and Du Heng on the deck of the Datean Cruise before Dai Wangshu departed to study in France

Unlike Mu Shiying, who was fascinated by the superficial showy lights and colors of the urban city, Shi Zhecun paid more attention to the inner psychological workings of people living in the metropolis. And thanks to his close ties with districts around Shanghai – Songjiang, Suzhou, and Hangzhou – his stories often presented a combination of urban and rural landscapes through the viewpoint of his characters who entered the metropolis from a rural town in the Jiangnan area. In this way, he could somehow avoid the weakness of Mu Shiying and Liu Na'ou, whose descriptions of city life seemed, vivid as they were, to be skimming over the surface. (Later Zhang Ailing went even further by writing about old-style families in Shanghai.)

25.19. Shi Zhecun in Hangzhou in 1936

This tendency to explore the psychologies of love and sex had been used by Shi Zhecun in the historical psychoanalytic fictions he invented. In "Kumarajiva" (《鸠摩罗什》) we can see the bewilderment of confusion about religious commandments and human nature within the protagonist, an eminent monk of the Later Qin Kingdom. "The General's Head" (《将军底头》) was about the dilemma between race, rules and discipline, and sexual desire through General Hua Jingding, who was beheaded in the battlefield. "Shi Xiu" (《石秀》) was a rewriting of the story of Shi Xiu, a hero from *Water Margin*, helping his sworn brother Yang Xiong to kill Pan Qiaoyun and Monk Pei

25.20. *One Rainy Evening in the Spring* by Shi Zhecun

25.21. Shi Zhecun's collection of historical stories, *The General's Head*, was also known for its in-depth psychoanalysis

25.22. Paris Theater, an entertainment venue in Shanghai, on which Shi Zhecun based his avant-garde fiction

Ruhai, in which the author explored Shi Xiu's hidden sexual abuse tendency. These were adaptations and rewritings of histories and past historical stories, and they were paid attention to by Shi's contemporaries because they explored human nature by rereading the inner life of ancient people viewed through modern-time moral standards. Besides applying psychoanalysis to historical subject matters, Shi Zhecun also made multiple experiments in the form of fiction, including combining descriptions of subconsciousness with fantasies, as in "Witchcraft" and "Yaksha" (《夜叉》); combining descriptions of hidden psychology with detective elements, as in "Haunted House" (《凶宅》); and rewriting folklore from a modern approach, as in "Master Huangxin" (《黄心大师》). Shi Zhecun made constant efforts in avant-garde literary experimentation.

Other talented young writers of this literary school included Hei Ying (黑婴), who wrote such works as "Pelota Lines" (《回力线》), "A 1,000-Chi Cartoon Strip" (《一〇〇〇尺卡通》), "Depression in the Café" (《咖啡座的忧郁》), and "A Man with Misogyny" (《女性嫌恶症患者》). Then there was He Jin (禾金); just looking at the titles of his literary works, such as "Subtype Depression" (《副型爱郁症》), "Mold Dynamics" (《造形动力学》), and "Like Butterflies" (《蝶蝶样》), we can feel his close relationship with the genre of New Sensationalism. None of them, however, ever surpassed the level attained by Mu Shiying.

New Sensationalist literature marked the rise of the metropolis and of metropolitan literature in the 1930s, and it was the most successful reinvention of modernism by local Chinese writers since modernist literature had been introduced to China during the May Fourth period. Shanghai school literature was similar to left-wing literature in its radical exploration of urban feelings toward city life and modern women, but left-wing literature integrated these feelings into a modern imagination guided by the "revolutionary discourse." In a recently discovered lost text by Mu Shiying, people found four fragments of a novel published during his lifetime, entitled "The March of China" (《中国行进》, also known as "China in 1931" [《中国1931》]). Combining them together, plus "Shanghai Foxtrot," which has been proved to be a part of this same novel, one can see this novel had a grand structure that could well match Mao Dun's *Midnight*, containing such threads as the strategies used by national capitalists of textile and shipping industries against the economic invasion of Japan through workers' strikes, the cooperation of intellectuals and national capitalists, the workers' organized strike movement, and peasants' rent strikes. It is certainly beyond our expectations that a Shanghai school author, excelling at "fashionable writing," could have such a "grand and comprehensive" literary outlook.

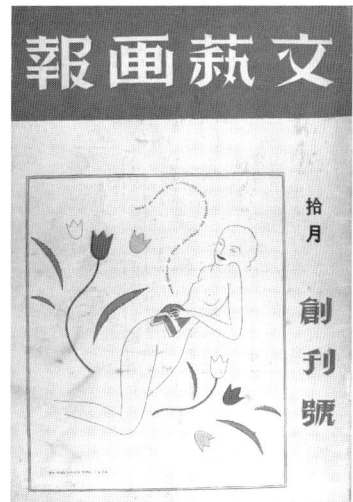

25.23. *Literary Pictorial* (《文艺画报》), coedited by Ye Lingfeng and Mu Shiying and launched on October 10, 1934. The modernist style of its cover was quite obvious

TABLE 25.1 *Literary journals related to Shanghai school literature*

Name	Type	Launched in	Discontinued in	Editor-in-chief or major editors	Remarks
Pearl Necklace (瓔珞)	Published every ten days	Spring, 1925	Spring, 1925	Shi Zhecun, Dai Wangshu, and Du Heng	Only four issues were published
The Young Companion	Pictorial monthly; later semimonthly	Feb. 1, 1926	Oct. 1, 1945	Wu Liande, Zhou Shoujuan, Liang Desuo, and Ma Guoliang, etc.	Continued in Hong Kong
Truth, Virtue, and Beauty (真善美)	Semimonthly; later monthly, etc.	1927	1931	Zeng Pu and his son Zeng Xubai (曾虛白)	
Literary Workshop (文学工场)	(Not known)	Spring, 1928	Aborted even before the inaugural issue was published	Shi Zhecun, Dai Wangshu, Du Heng, and Feng Xuefeng	The proof copy was printed by Kwong Wah Book Store
Modern Fiction	Monthly	Jan. 1, 1928	Mar. 1, 1930	Ye Lingfeng and Pan Hannian (潘汉年)	
Trackless Train	Semimonthly	Sep. 1, 1928	Dec. 1, 1928	Liu Na'ou	Closed down
Lequn (乐群)	Semimonthly; later monthly	Oct. 1, 1928	Mar. 1, 1930	Zhang Ziping, Chen Shaoshui (陈勺水), and Zhou Yuying	
Furnace (熔炉)	Monthly	Dec. 1, 1928	Dec. 1, 1928	Xu Xiacun (徐霞村)	Only one issue was published
Gold Chamber Monthly (金屋月刊)	Monthly	Jan. 1, 1929	Sep. 1, 1930	Shao Xunmei and Zhang Kebiao	
New Literature (新文艺)	Monthly	Sep. 1, 1929	Apr. 1, 1930	Liu Na'ou, Shi Zhecun, and Dai Wangshu	Closed down
New Age (新时代)	Monthly	Aug. 1, 1931	Discontinued in February 1934	Zeng Jinke (曾今可)	Renewed in 1937, and four issues were published
Jieqian Monthly (絜茜)	Monthly	Jan. 1, 1932	Sep. 1, 1932	Zhang Ziping and Ding Ding (丁丁)	

(continued)

TABLE 25.1 *(continued)*

Name	Type	Launched in	Discontinued in	Editor-in-chief or major editors	Remarks
The Contemporaries	Monthly	May 1, 1932	May 1, 1935	Shi Zhecun, Du Heng, and Wang Fuquan (汪馥泉)	
Chats on Literature and Art (文艺茶话)	Monthly	Aug. 1, 1932	May 1, 1934	Zhang Yiping (章衣萍), Xu Zhongnian (徐仲年), Hua Lin (华林), and Sun Fuxi	
Literature and Arts Spring and Autumn (文艺春秋)	Monthly	July 1, 1933	June 1, 1934	Zhang Yiping and Xu Zexiang (徐则骧)	
Verses (诗篇)	Monthly	Nov. 1, 1933	Feb. 1, 1934	Shao Xunmei	Journal of the Green Society (绿社)
Fiction (小说)	Monthly; later semimonthly	May 1, 1934	Mar. 1, 1935	Liang Desuo, Bao Kehua (包可华), Li Ni (丽尼), and Huang Miaozi (黄苗子)	
Literary Pictorial	Featuring literary texts	1934	1935	Ye Lingfeng and Mu Shiying	
Literary Landscape (文艺风景)	Monthly	June 1, 1934	July 1, 1934	Shi Zhecun	
Literary Vignettes (文饭小品)	Monthly	Feb. 1, 1935	July 1, 1935	Edited by Kang Siqun (康嗣群) and distributed by Shi Zhecun	
Six Arts (六艺)	Monthly	Feb. 1, 1936	Apr. 1, 1936	Gao Ming (高明), Yao Sufeng (姚苏凤), Ye Lingfeng, Mu Shiying, and Liu Na'ou	
Miscellaneous Record (杂志)	Semimonthly	May 10, 1938	Aug. 10, 1945	Lü Huaicheng (吕怀成) and Wu Chengzhi (吴诚之)	
Fiction Monthly	Monthly	Oct. 1, 1940	Nov. 25, 1944	Gu Lengguan (顾冷观)	
Phenomena (万象)	Monthly	July 1, 1941	July 1, 1945	Chen Dieyi (陈蝶衣) and Ke Ling (柯灵)	

(continued)

TABLE 25.1 *(continued)*

Name	Type	Launched in	Discontinued in	Editor-in-chief or major editors	Remarks
The Popular (大众)	Monthly	Nov. 1, 1942	July 1945	Qian Xumi (钱须弥)	
Spring and Autumn	Monthly; later semimonthly	Aug. 1, 1943	Mar. 25, 1949	Chen Dieyi and Wen Zongshan (文宗山)	
Heaven and Earth (天地)	Monthly	Oct. 10, 1943	June 1, 1945	Su Qing (苏青, aka Feng Heyi [冯和仪])	

TWENTY SIX

THE LITERARY HORIZON OF TWO TYPES OF CIVIL SOCIETY

SHANGHAI SCHOOL AUTHORS' "NEW PERCEPTIONS" OF Shanghai the modern metropolis were unprecedented events in Chinese literary history. The image of the city in Chinese literature before that, from Kaifeng of the Song dynasty through to Yangzhou and Suzhou, was traditional, and presented in the form of linked-chapter novels. When late-Qing novels and Mandarin Duck and Butterfly novels emerged, the narrative seemed well able to record the Beijing of the times, but it did not suffice to present Shanghai, which featured a mixed combination of Chinese and Western elements. It wasn't until the late 1920s and 1930s that authors of the New Literature camp began to deploy a brand-new narrative to write about the increasingly modernized Shanghai. Around the same time, an author from the New Literature camp who began a new narrative of Beijing, which took a bit longer to be modernized, also came to people's attention. This author was Lao She.

Beijing and Shanghai represented two types of modern Chinese cities, within which there were two types of civil societies. One was characterized by a sudden and massive implantation of Western culture, which experienced some mutations during this process and was somehow localized; and the other evolved from the civil society of ancient times, so that it accepted modern culture at a steady pace and tried to maintain the self-esteem of an ancient nation. Although both cities were within the same Chinese cultural system and both had the characteristics of secularity, materiality, and profit-orientedness, the two cities showed large discrepancies due to their different degrees of modernization. And thus the external appearance and internal character of their respective citizens' everyday lives were quite different.

In the year 1934, Lao She, who wrote literary works while teaching in Jinan, Shandong, strongly felt that it was time for him to write a masterpiece (he had had his first novel, *The Philosophy of Old Zhang*, serialized in *Fiction Monthly* as early as 1926), but he did not have enough spare time to do so. He had a long-term cooperation with journals and publishing institutions in Shanghai, so in June of that year, he made a bold decision: he quit his teaching job at Cheeloo University and went to Shanghai alone in August, and spent a dozen days in the city to see whether he could become a professional writer there. He returned in disappointment, feeling that Shanghai was not the right place for him. After that, he accepted a job offer from National Shandong University and went to Qingdao, thus remaining in the north. Soon afterward, some of his most important works, "Crescent Moon" (《月牙儿》), "Deadly Spear" (《断魂枪》), and *Camel Xiangzi* were published one after the other. Lao She did not talk publicly about his impression of Shanghai, but later when talking about the similarities between Chengdu and Beijing, he said: "I don't like Shanghai, for I cannot capture the character of that city, and I am not sure what it is exactly."[1] I suppose many people shared the same feelings as Lao She, for they were not sure whether, in this international metropolis without a long history as a traditional city but rising straight from the ground, its material luxuries were decadent or advanced, its citizens' tastes and interests refined or vulgar, and its fashionable culture admirable or confusing. But it seemed not so difficult to understand Beijing. Beijing was already the world's largest city in the 1600s (during Emperor Kangxi's reign) and remained so until it was surpassed by London in terms of population, size, and economic output in 1800. Located at the northern frontier of China, it was originally a city of strategic political and military importance; after being a capital for several dynasties, it became a city with royal magnificence, and since it remained wealthy until very late, even commoners were not willing to relinquish their pride. When the regime changed after the Xinhai Revolution, the city's name was changed to Beiping in 1928, and then it became an abandoned capital, lost its position as a political center, and became a site of cultural relics. When Shen Congwen first arrived in Beijing in 1923, he saw a heap of historic rubble, where the feather pipe affixed to the top of a Qing official's ceremonial hat, worth 800-liang silver ingots each in the past, was sold for only four silver dollars at the time. Past officials, down and out from the Qing government and the Beiyang government, remained, as well as a huge number of bannermen who had lost their high social and economic status after the Nationalist government abolished the banner status of Manchu people. Therefore, old-style citizens filled

---

[1]   Lao She: "Lovely Chengdu" (《可爱的成都》), *Collected Works of Lao She* (《老舍文集》), Vol. 14, Beijing: People's Literature Press, 1989, p. 232.

this city. Later, the living standards of ordinary people would be far lower than those of Shanghai, but the cost of living was low and people lived quite a leisurely life. Life was quite slow in Beijing, with the old and new coexisting, and one could see cars, trolleys, rickshaws, donkey carts, camels, and flocks of sheep simultaneously on the streets. On the other hand, Beijing boasted the best universities in China, as well as cultural groups with long-term traditions. It attracted knowledgeable Chinese intellectuals and thus became a city with a unique cultural vitality. The civil society in this city could trace its history and step into the future in a leisurely and graceful manner.

26.1. Old image of the semi-circular enclosure at the Beijing Front Gate, which has now been largely destroyed

26.2. Dongsi Archway of Beiping, where one could see various modes of transportation: trolleys, rickshaws, carts, and bicycles; the only thing missing is camels

26.3. In the 1920s, Lao She, who was familiar with the city of Beijing, frequented the library at the School of Oriental Studies, University of London when he taught there. He spent his time reading and writing there, trying to cure his spiritual "jet lag"

It was in this city of Beijing that Lao She (1899–1966) was born to a Manchu bannerman family in the Plain Red Banner, and like most Manchu people who had lost their privilege, he was raised in a commoners' district in the northwestern corner of the ancient city. He lived together with poor citizens in the compounds where many families lived and was quite familiar with folk customs, folk speech and singing, and classical Chinese operas. He tried to avoid all radical politics and thus remained detached from all revolutionary currents. It wasn't until 1924 when he got a chance to be recommended to teach in London that he began to read world literature (including Charles Dickens, who was good at writing about the slum areas in London) and began his own literary creation using civil society in Beijing as his subject matter. Lao She took a clear-cut stance as a new literary author, and from the very first day of his writing, the moral gray zone of civil society became the target for his humorous mockery and irony. He wrote most and best about old-style citizens, such as Mr. Ma Sr. in "The Two Ma's" (《二马》), Elder Brother Zhang in "Divorce," and the old man Qi in *Four Generations under One Roof*, which was published a bit later. Conventional, kind-hearted, having a sense of shame, enthusiastic, careless, easily content with everything, withering, moderate, cowardly, and insisting on the philosophy of reconciliation, all this formed the cultural characteristics of these people. Niu Tianci in *Biography of Niu Tianci* (《牛天赐传》) was a foundling adopted by an impoverished gentle merchant with the surname of Niu. As a man without any background, he became a lifeless good-for-nothing in a decayed civilian family, a "bamboo-pipe," a hollow man. The official clerk, Elder Brother Zhang, in "Divorce," was a character devoted to only two things in his life: matchmaking and opposing divorce.

He made a match for whoever could possibly make a couple, and tried every means possible to persuade couples to get along (instead of getting divorced). Therefore, in the fiction Lao She wrote: "Life consists of compromising and muddling along, of leading an aimless life totally different from one's ideals," which was a theme of Lao She's fictions, which criticized the old-style civil society.

Certainly, there were some bright spots in this gray zone of Lao She's old-style civil society. He admitted that he was not good at writing about women, love, or marriage, which perhaps had something to do with the fact that he was influenced by the moral ideas of civilians; however, he did write about the lives of three kinds of old-style civilian women: The first type were low-class women who were harshly insulted and hurt, such as the young wife of Wang who could not but hang herself in "The Liu's Compound" (《柳家大院》); Little Fuzi, who went downhill, became a low-class prostitute, and committed suicide in *Camel Xiangzi*; and the mother who was a prostitute herself and whose daughter was also a prostitute in "Crescent Moon." Lao She expressed his indignation toward the injustice in the human world through these women characters and showed his deep-felt compassion and humanitarianism. The second type were women who were suppressed but also cheated and tried to oppress others, such as Huniu in *Camel Xiangzi*; and the religious woman, "the one from the Willow Village," in "The One from the Willow Village"

26.4. Before departing for Jinan after the winter vacation of 1931, Lao She gave this photo to Hu Jieqing (胡絜青). It was the first photo he gave to her

26.5. Young Lao She. He gave this photo to Guan Shizhi (关实之), his classmate and friend at Beijing Normal School, in May 1923. From the inscription we can see that Lao She had already developed his own style of calligraphy

26.6. First edition of *Divorce* by Lao She

(《柳屯的》). In writing these characters Lao She used profound irony for human weaknesses. The third type were ideal women in his mind, such as Xiuzhen and Young Lady Ma in "Divorce," and Yunmei in *Four Generations under One Roof*, a better representative of traditional Chinese women. In them, Lao She found endurance and righteousness, the beauty of traditional Chinese women. Certainly, he also extolled the male characters' championing of righteous principles, such as Li Jingchun, who tried to prevent the Temple of Heaven from being sold in *Thus Speaks Master Zhao* (《赵子曰》); Second Lord Ding, who killed Xiao Zhao to save Xiuzhen in "Divorce"; Lord Hu, who tried to help Niu Tianci out of his predicament in *Biography of Niu Tianci*; and the chivalrous poet Qian Moyin in *Four Generations under One Roof*. Lao She may have criticized their overall attitude toward life, but he approved of their moral integrity. It was Lao She's uniqueness to hold a critical attitude mixed with profound love and compassion toward traditional civilians. This position could also be seen in his symbolic novel *A Record of the City of Cats* (《猫城记》). The characterization of *A Record of the City of Cats* was not very successful, but the author expressed his observations and reflections about the future of his own ancient country in the modern era.

Lao She also wrote about the new-style citizens of Beijing, and showed his individual style in such writings. While he criticized the moral gray zone of old-style citizens with his humorous irony, which was not short of sympathy and love, his criticism of new-style citizens used cartoon-style satire. These were young shallow intellectuals who regarded "new style" as fashion and thus often blindly followed the fashion without understanding the core truth of "new style." Examples included Dr. Mao in "The Sacrifice" (《牺牲》), who had studied at Harvard and was described by the author as "like something in between," "he seemed rootless, not like a native Chinese, but not like a foreigner either." And the left-wing student in "New Hamlet" (《新韩穆烈德》), who always wanted to "emancipate" the tenants and salesmen of his father's grocery store. He had an idea that "boarding [the third-class carriage] occasionally may show some proletarian taste," but finally used his father's money and went in the second-class carriage. Having gained the benefit of "new style," he enjoyed the advantage of "old style" with a clear conscience. Lao She, looking at these citizens from a unique point of view, thought those who were devoted to nothing but political speculation and the pursuit of profit were even more unworthy. This may sometimes seem one-sided, but it did present the embarrassing situation faced by modern Chinese civic culture. This was probably commonly seen in Beijing as the city slowly began its modernization process: "the old and new are mixed together; the old is not abandoned, and the new is gradually accepted. In this compromising spirit one seems to see the weakness of our nation" (*The Electorate* [《选民》]). When looking at the issue from the perspective of the modern transformation of national culture, one can see that Lao She had actually pointed out that old ideas and culture might obstinately erode the new with the power of "the Monkey King drilling into the belly of Princess Iron Fan." Those old ideas and culture had a great killing power, indescribable but as omnipresent as the air – wasn't that alarming enough?

When Lao She's masterpieces *Camel Xiangzi*, *My Whole Life* (《我这一辈子》), and others were published, the tragedies of the urban poor, including for example rickshaw pullers and lower-rank police officers, presented themselves in the form of

26.7. Illustration of *A Record of the City of Cats*, drawn by Gao Rongsheng (高荣生)

ridiculous comedies in everyday life in Beijing, which increasingly became Lao She's focus of attention. Xiangzi in *Camel Xiangzi*, a diligent young man who came to the city from the countryside, had the energy and willingness to

work hard, and dreamed of buying a rickshaw of his own and living a peaceful life in the city. His dream seemed humble, but it was serious for an ordinary citizen; he failed despite all efforts, and in the end he slid into total destruction. If such a handsome rickshaw puller as Xiangzi was doomed, what hope was there for people of his class? In the novel, the author made it quite clear that Xiangzi was victimized by the entire society, through all kinds of plunder by the rickshaw owner, armed marauders, detectives, and others; even Huniu, his wife, became a part of this destructive social force. Huniu trapped him with sex, then cheated him into marriage by faking pregnancy. She may have loved him, and bought a rickshaw for him, but they had different ideals in life, and Huniu's purpose in life was to live in luxurious enjoyment, so that day after day, she corrupted Xiangzi and deprived him of his hope to live peacefully with his own hard work. And

26.8. Illustration of *Camel Xiangzi*, drawn by Ding Cong: "Because he had never thought of her as a woman, the sudden sight of her red lips made him feel rather embarrassed"

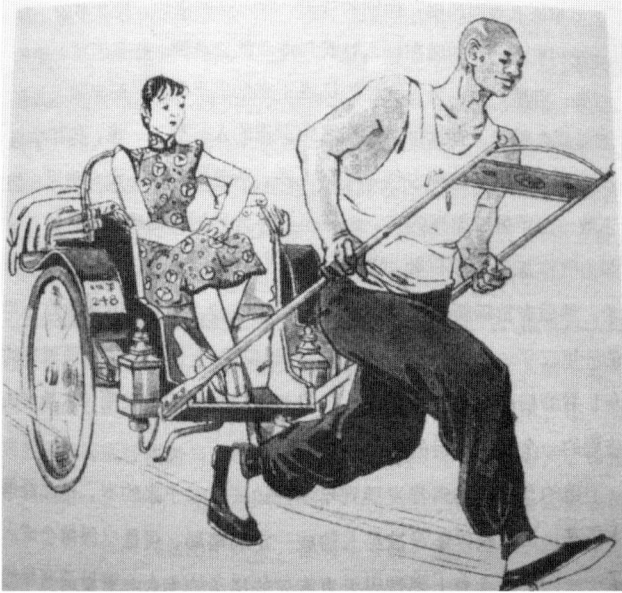

26.9. Illustration of *Camel Xiangzi*, drawn by Sun Zhijun (孙之僎): "Belonging to the category of those who owned their vehicles, he was master of his own fate, a high-class puller"

the difference between *Camel Xiangzi* and old-style novels was that Lao She had the perspective that Xiangzi himself was part of the corruptive forces of his own life. At first Xiangzi tried to resist this destiny, refused to get on with others, but it was his selfishness and vulnerability that drove him deeper into the social abyss. This, combined with the social circumstances, made him a lazy, apathetic, fraudulent, mischievous, and treacherous person, a walking corpse. Let's look at Xiangzi at the beginning of the novel:

> … a man with an ingenuous face and a hint of mischief about him. Watching those high-class pullers, he planned how to tighten his belt to show off his sturdy chest and straight back to better advantage. He craned his neck to look at his shoulders: how impressively broad they were! His slender waist, baggy white trousers and ankles bound with thin black bands would set off his "oversize" feet. Yes, he was surely going to be the most outstanding rickshaw puller in town …[2]

At the end of the novel, however, Xiangzi, who "had he been a spirit in hell, would probably have made the best of his surroundings," had become this:

> Xiangzi, so decent, willing, fond of day-dreaming, self-serving, solitary, strong, and admirable, had been an attendant at countless funerals, but he has no idea when and where he will be buried himself, where his despairing ghost, the product of a sick society, degenerate, selfish, unfortunate, and individualistic will finally be laid to rest.[3]

---

[2]   Lao She: *Camel Xiangzi* (Illustrated Edition), Beijing: People's Literature Press, 2004, p. 6.
[3]   Ibid., p. 361.

In this way, Xiangzi changed from being a simple peasant who entered the city with the hope of making a living through his hard work to being a self-abandoned philistine without any moral principles (luckily, not a rogue philistine like those in "Taking Office" [《上任》]). There was something shocking in this process, and thus the author felt that he could not use humor in a perfunctory way. Compared with his previous works, he used less mockery and added an element of tragedy in this novel. Lao She incorporated the Beijing dialect's qualities of dexterity, liveliness, and humor into his writing language and created a genuine local (non-Europeanized) vernacular Chinese language, fully displaying the great expressiveness of modern written language.

26.10. Full-length photo of Lao She after visiting the editorial office of *The Young Companion*, which was published in Issue 76 of the pictorial

Overall, by portraying various civilian characters of Beijing, Lao She depicted the decay of traditional society and presented his criticism of Chinese people's national character. Since the late-Qing period, Chinese writers had been obsessed with Chinese people's national character (i.e. inherent weaknesses), which was rooted in their sense of crisis and concern for the survival of the entire nation after the country had been defeated and colonialized. Lu Xun laid particular stress on enlightening Chinese people by harshly attacking "servility," while Lao She emphasized criticism of culture and human nature. On the one hand, Lao She continued his in-depth analysis of the hideous lifestyle and customs of civilians of Beijing, including such cultural phenomena as conformism and conventionality, personal bondage, worldly wisdom, and cannibalistic ethics; on the other hand, he was fully aware that the Beijing he loved so deeply had two sides: it was "dirty but beautiful, old but lively, chaotic but leisurely and lovely."[4] In his excellent short stories "The Time-Honored Brand" (《老字号》) and "Deadly Spear," the characters maintained their independent identity in the waves of "the new" replacing "the old," which made them outstanding old-style civilians. The author did not hide the truth of their decadence or blindly advocate maintaining the old. The business of "time-honored brand" was no match for new-style department stores that offered discounts every day, and Sha Zilong (沙子龙), the kungfu master who refused to teach "five-tiger deadly spear," could not prevent the decline of the bodyguarding business, but they maintained their fundamental moral principles. This doubtless suggested

---

[4]   Ibid., p. 351.

how this ancient nation could maintain its independent identity during an era of rapid social transformation, so as not to lose its soul when encountering the outside world. Lao She created many other novels and characters later in his life, but he insisted on this principle in his depiction of civil society in Beijing where he was born and raised.

Almost at the same time, Zhang Henshui (1895–1967) also portrayed civil society in Beijing, not with New Literature, but with urban popular literature. Lao She's earliest works about Beijing, *The Philosophy of Old Zhang* and *Thus Speaks Master Zhao*, were written between 1926 and 1928. Zhang Henshui started earlier. His *An Unofficial History of Peking* began to be serialized in the newspaper in 1924, *The Story of A Noble Family* in 1927, and *Fate in Tears and Laughter* in 1930, with its separate edition published in the same year. These three novels were all about Beijing. Zhang Henshui was a native of Anhui, and he only became familiar with the life and language of Beijing after coming to the city, so he could not create a genuine atmosphere in his novels like Lao She. But he had been a journalist for a long time, and taking advantage of his career he gained an even more all-encompassing picture of Beijing from direct or indirect sources, and thus he could write from the lower-class civil society up to higher-class people, while Lao She never wrote about the higher-class life in Beijing. Zhang Henshui was extremely prolific, creating more than 110 novels during his life, of which these three were his best. *An Unofficial History of Peking* still had traces of the old-style linked-chapter novel, with its plot being threaded by the protagonist Yang Xingyuan, who was well capable of doing this because he was a journalist. "Chunming" was a nickname for Beijing the capital, and this journalism-style novel of social denunciation targeted its criticism against high-rank officials and warlords of the Beiyang government in the city. The other two were typical love stories, whose chapter-based structures were organized through the love stories of their male and female protagonists: in *The Story of A Noble Family*, it was between Leng Qingqiu, who had a commoner family background, and Jin Yanxi, who was from a powerful, wealthy family; and in *Fate in Tears and Laughter* it was between Shen Fengxi, a female performer of popular drum-songs at Tianqiao, and Fan Jiashu, from a rich family. The author denounced extravagant, rich families and domineering warlords, whose evilness was treated from the viewpoint of lower-class citizens. Righteousness was the criterion used by citizens in their moral judgment, and here we can see the similarity between Zhang Henshui and Lao She. Generally, when an author tried to expose overbearing social power in fictions, they tended to oversimplify the issue, but what made *The Story of A Noble Family* outstanding was that Prime Minister Jin's family, on which the author focused a lot of writing, was quite open-minded and liberal. The prime minister, Jin Quan, for example, was a liberal high-rank official of the Nationalist government, and he agreed to his son marrying a woman whose family had been in decline for a long time and said the following about the wedding:

> I have never intervened in my children's marriages, but sometimes I think about their marriage decisions and give my opinions on them. Miss Leng is from a scholar-gentry family, and she herself reads a lot, so actually Yanxi has married up. But seen from the surface, since I am taking office in the government now, it seems there is a gap in the social status between our families. For those who have a sense of decency, one side would think a family like mine is too powerful to be married to, and the other side would seek a family with similar social status, and thus it seemed not easy for them to form alliance through marriage. But I don't think this way. Therefore I give my full approval to Yanxi and his wife for breaking free from the class restrictions. I dare not say I am an egalitarian, but I do want to correct people's stereotyped impression of rich families, and on the other hand, I do hope real rich families might think about this idea of mine.[5]

It was indeed rare for an author of popular novels to write about bureaucrats without defaming them, but in the end, Jin Yanxi separated from Leng Qingqiu because of the class rift, or because his family was "too powerful to be married to." Raised in the Jin family, it was easy for Yanxi to become a playboy, and he was not alone. The eldest son of Jin Quan was also like this, doing business in his father's name, paying a lot to flirt with opera performers, and taking concubines, indulging in a life of debauchery. Therefore, Jin Quan once said that it was the "big family system" that brought about his children's playful habits. This was a modern-style reflection on the entire Chinese society, and it was certainly more profound than other novels exposing and denunciating bureaucrats and warlords.

As for lower-class citizens, Zhang Henshui held different attitudes toward different people. For example, he gave the highest praise to Leng Qingqiu, who was well bred, moral, and disdained money. When Jin Yanxi's playful habit got the better of him, she devoted herself to raising their child and to Buddhist learning. Afterward, she ran away from the Jin family

26.11. Picture of Zhang Henshui in his youth, published in the newspaper

---

5   Zhang Henshui: "The Story of a Noble Family," *Selected Works of Zhang Henshui* (《张恨水选集》), Vol. 2, Hefei: Anhui Literature and Arts Press, 1985, p. 574.

26.12. Cover of the first edition of Zhang Henshui's *Fate in Tears and Laughter*

with her child during a big fire, living peacefully in seclusion and poverty. Leng Qingqiu had ideal qualities that satisfied the civilian norms. Shen Fengxi in *Fate in Tears and Laughter*, on the other hand, gave in to the power and wealth of warlords, and as a member of the oppressed, she took the path of self-destruction. Serialized in the *Daily News* in Shanghai, *Fate in Tears and Laughter* caused a sensation among readers. To meet the requirements of citizen readers, the newspaper requested the author add some *wuxia* elements, so Zhang made the father and daughter of the Guan's, who were lower-class citizens, swordspeople who trapped and killed General Liu at the West Hill in the end. Thus he championed the righteous, and one could see this kind of arrangement in Lao She's novel, too.

Most interestingly, in his *An Unofficial History of Peking*, Zhang Henshui harshly criticized the new things that had emerged in Beijing earlier in the Republican era, including students' performances of amateur drama in order to raise funds to relieve disasters, painting nude models, launching societies of new poetry, and establishing women's associations. These were all closely related with May Fourth cultural activities, but they were presented in Zhang's novels as a mess and therefore a laughing stock at a time when social divisions between men and women were blurred. Most typical of this view of his was found in chapter 67, when Yang Xingyuan was discussing with his friends the qualities of women in a perfect marriage. They thought women should be good at housekeeping like old-style women, while at the same time they

26.13. Advertisement for the second part of the film adapted from *Fate in Tears and Laughter*, published in *Shun Pao* on November 27, 1932

should know how to comfort their husbands like new-style ones: "she should be gentle, and should not be excessively emancipated."[6] Here "should not be excessively emancipated" was indeed the crucial point of the issue. Therefore, the new-style people in this book were similar to the fashionable left-wing young people in Lao She's novels. On certain occasions, Yang Xingyuan expressed his own understanding of these phenomena. For example, he once said: "Nowadays men and women cannot communicate with or contact each other in a totally open manner, so they have to do so in the name of research institutions or literary societies, which function as the matchmaking agencies."[7] Thus we can see Yang Xingyuan himself was a man caught between the old and new, as was the civil society of Beijing in which he lived, where transition and transformation from the old to the new was by no means an easy task. On this focal point, Lao She the new literary author and Zhang Henshui the urban popular author surprisingly agreed with each other.

Looking back at the narrative adopted by Shanghai school literature about Shanghai's civil society discussed in Chapter 25, we can see their remarkable and significant difference. The works of New Sensationalist authors showed a brand-new tendency of modern urban citizens. Traditional moral standards collapsed without being clung to (being clung to or not was by no means insignificant), and a new moral and cultural standard based on personal freedom and enjoyment began to prevail in the metropolis. New-style citizens were not looking back as frequently as old-style ones, for they had experienced the duality of modern civilization well ahead of others: Shanghai was a heaven as well as a hell. This did not only lie in the huge gap between the rich and poor, but in the suppression and alienation of human beings by dazzling material progress and technologies, and in the gradual obliteration of human nature. Hence Shanghai's civil society in the writings of New Sensationalist authors was presented as novel and changeful. As for the uncertainty of living in the city, one could feel it immediately from the stories of meetings between men and women in the city, which was the subject matter they wrote about the most, and from the transient, distressing, and bewildering relationships between the male and female characters and the city.

Xu Xu (1908–1980) was a Shanghai school writer who came to prominence in the 1930s. His masterpiece novel *Whistling Wind* (《风萧萧》) was written later, during the Anti-Japanese War, but its theme was the duality of Shanghai as heaven and hell. His first well-known piece, *The Love of a Ghost* (《鬼恋》), was a novella published before the war, and this thrilling and mysterious love story was so well received among urban citizen readers that it was printed as many as nineteen times in a period of seven years. The novel started with the

---

6   Zhang Henshui: *An Unofficial History of Peking*, Vol. 2, Beijing: China Journalism Press, 1985, p. 1059.
7   Ibid., p. 1328.

26.14. Xu Xu's self-portrait of himself as a youth

鬼
戀

徐
訏

26.15. Xu Xu's first well-known piece, *The Love of a Ghost*, was printed nineteen times in seven years. This was the nineteenth edition published by Shanghai Night Window Bookstore in 1947

encounter between the male character and a female ghost in a cigar shop on Nanjing Road, Shanghai, and ended with the female ghost's disappearance. After that, the man would go to the cigar shop whenever he missed her. The encounter happened in the modern metropolitan setting, and the man was amazed by the female ghost's cool beauty at his first sight of her: "[she] reminded me of a silver three-dimensional female artificial model in a window of some shop along the Avenue Joffre. I suddenly realized where that feeling of déjà vu in the cigar shop came from."[8] From this we can see that even love emotions were fortuitous and uncertain in the modern metropolis of Shanghai, and it was amazing that even an artificial model in a shop window could function as a link between two strangers. And having experienced all vicissitudes of life, the female would rather be a "ghost" than a human being, but she, too, clung to the love between herself and the man. The rich and eventful life she had lived formed a sharp contrast with the somber yet loving relationship between the two, symbolizing the fact that human beings were like ghosts in the metropolis. In this way, the uncertainty of Shanghai in Xu Xu's writings was linked to the city in those of New Sensationalist writers.

Urban popular authors took another approach to represent the city of Shanghai. Yu Qie (1902–1989) had quite a long literary career, and his novels *Xiaoju* (《小菊》) and *The Ruyi Pearl* (《如意珠》) and collections of short stories *The Art of Wifehood* (《妻的艺术》) and *Two Rooms* (《两间房》) were published as early as the mid-1930s, but the peak of his literary creation was in the 1940s. Yu Qie was an intellectual with a mixed style, and it was hard to say whether he represented the old or the new. In depicting the civil society of Shanghai, he presented the life of citizens living in alleys of *shikumen*-style buildings. The Shanghai in his writings was by no means

---

8   Xu Xu's *The Love of a Ghost* was serialized in *Cosmic Wind*, Issues 32 and 33, January 1937. Here the author quoted from the separate edition (Xu Xu: *The Love of a Ghost*, Shanghai: Shanghai Night Window Bookstore, 1947, p. 5).

26.16. Yu Qie's handwritten fortune-telling text. He wrote it for someone under the pseudonym "Owner of the House with a Flowery Pond" (水绕花堤馆主)

"uncertain," but quite real and lively thanks to his observation of the trivialities of its citizens' everyday lives. He did not write tragedies, and most of his writings were light-hearted stories. Young men and women from the alleys would fall in love simply because of and through "real stuff in everyday life," as in the light comedies "Photo Taking" (《照相》) and "An Umbrella" (《伞》), where the stories originated from nothing but real photo taking and an umbrella. The young men and women in love benefited from the progress of material civilization. Life was surely not perfect and not short of conflicts, but imperfections and conflicts were part of the characters' lives and could be mended. Therefore, most of Yu Qie's love stories happened after the characters' marriage, and according to him, men should be tolerant and kind in the family (they could maintain their independence in smoking, drinking, and social activities, but at the same time they should consider how their wives felt about it), and he praised the marriage between an older man and a younger woman because he thought that kind of marriage would remain constant, and he insisted that women should be self-reliant (which was the key to their happy life). His stories in *The Art of Wifehood* and *Two Rooms* showed that at that time in Shanghai, among other things, common citizens had already begun to respect women's interests. Thus romantic love was deconstructed in everyday life, and "love is just so so" became a motto of his literary characters. But marriage was not "just so so," and he tried to make a point that marriage was more important than love (a mind-set of middle-aged civilians) and love was not significant if it was not attached to everyday life. It seemed that Yu Qie's love and marriage stories unveiled and demystified romantic love, not as a gesture of desperation but as a way to be down to earth in real life. This was the Shanghai seen by its citizens with certainty. In striking contrast to the fact that Lao She and Zhang Henshui agreed so much in the way they treated the civil society of old-style Beijing, the aesthetic taste of new literary authors and urban popular authors were totally different in representing how Shanghai citizens thought and lived. During the "isolated island" and "occupied" period in the 1940s, the situation was even more complex because Zhang Ailing came to the foreground. This will be discussed later.

TWENTY SEVEN

THE MATURE STAGE OF PROFESSIONAL SPOKEN DRAMA IN THEATERS

Since its introduction into China, modern spoken drama went through a period of "civilized drama" and then a period of "amateur drama." Thanks to the efforts by such pioneers as Tian Han, Hong Shen, Ouyang Yuqian, Ding Xilin, and Xiong Foxi to practice and promote spoken drama, by the 1930s a new wave of professionalism of modern spoken drama in theaters emerged under multiple driving forces, including era-specific writings and increasing demands for cultural consumption by urban citizens.

This came a bit later than the demand for fiction, poetry, and prose, and there was a good reason for this. Traditional Chinese opera had been a low-brow art form in China, which peasants watched openly in squares, and in theaters of cities, a majority of citizen audience members watched plays as entertainment. Facing this relatively unenlightened audience, soon after Western drama was introduced to China in the late Qing, it was localized into a vulgar form of entertainment for citizens. Basically, the decline of "civilized drama" was caused by the gradual decrease of "modern civilization" in this "vulgar" form. It was only after dramatic literature by and for intellectuals was produced during the May Fourth cultural movement that intellectuals and young students began to read and watch plays. The market, consisting of both ordinary citizens and intellectuals, would have a long-term impact on modern spoken drama, which would have no true vitality without "performances." This is indeed a paradox. Amateur performances could help maintain the purity of this inherently popular art form, but they could not gain a solid market share for spoken drama. Without high-level performances of spoken drama in theaters, it was impossible to sustain a professional spoken drama troupe. Finely honed spoken drama scripts and commercial performances that would attract urban audiences to the theater, therefore, became the goal of Chinese spoken drama; and the key to achieving this goal was the emergence of talented playwrights who could help shape the market for reading plays and for watching real Chinese spoken drama performed in theaters.

The summer of 1933 was quite sultry, and it was when Cao Yu (1910–1996), then a student of the Department of Western Literature at Tsinghua University, created his maiden dramatic work, *Thunderstorm*, at the very young age of 23. Prior to that, he had learned a lot from May Fourth New Literature and at Nankai School in Tianjin, an important city for spoken drama in the northern part of the country. Listed here are the plays he had performed in under the guidance of Zhang Pengchun of the Nankai New Drama Troupe: Ding Xilin's *Oppression* (《压迫》), Tian Han's *The Night the Tiger Was Caught* (《获虎之夜》), and Ibsen's *An Enemy of the People* and *A Doll's House* (in which he impersonated Nora). When *Thunderstorm* was finished, Cao Yu gave it to his middle school classmate Jin Yi (靳以), who coedited the *Literary Quarterly* with Ba Jin at that time. Perhaps to avoid arousing suspicion, the play was put aside in a drawer of the editorial office for some time before it was given to Ba Jin. Finding himself in tears after reading the drama, Ba Jin immediately made the decision to publish all four acts in one installment, and thus the play was finally put into print in July 1934. Soon after that, the teachers and students of White Horse Lake Middle School in Zhejiang Province premiered *Thunderstorm*. Then in April 1935, Chinese students in Japan staged a more influential performance in Tokyo, which brought to mind the time when Li Shutong and his friends established the Spring Willow Society in Tokyo in 1907. The plays they performed back then, *La Dame aux Camélias* and *Black Slaves Appeal to Heaven*, were stories of foreign countries, while this time it was the heartbreaking tragedy of a Chinese family. Soon after that, other amateur student troupes, such as the Lone Pinetree Drama Troupe (孤松剧团) of Tianjin Municipal Normal School and Fudan Drama Troupe of Fudan University in Shanghai, joined White Horse Lake Middle School in rehearsing and performing this play. It seemed like an afterglow of the brilliant history of amateur dramatic activities. Meanwhile, the Chinese Traveling Troupe, the very first performing troupe of modern Chinese spoken drama, led by Tang Huaiqiu (唐槐秋), decided to rehearse *Thunderstorm*. The troupe had China's best acting and directing talents in spoken drama, and now with a brilliant playscript, their performances in Beiping and Tianjin, both cities

27.1. Cao Yu, taken at the Lotus Pond, Tsinghua Garden in 1933, when he was a student at Tsinghua University

27.2. Nankai Drama Troupe's performance of *Craze for Riches* (《财狂》), adapted from Molière's *L'Avare*. The person stooping (second from right) is Wan Jiabao (万家宝, aka Cao Yu). The stage designer was Lin Huiyin

with a solid foundation in cultivating the audiences of spoken drama, were a commercial success. On May 6, 1936, at the Carlton Theater in Shanghai, then China's literary center, the performance of *Thunderstorm* by the Chinese Traveling Troupe was a great hit. The misfortune of Shiping (aka Lu Ma) and her daughter, the fierce love and hatred of Fanyi, the tragic deaths of Zhou Chong and Sifeng, both the most innocent youths in the play, Zhou Ping's suicide, and Zhou Puyuan's cruel and grave remarks, all this went straight to the heart of each radical intellectual and general audience member. The theater

27.3. Cao Yu's former residence in Tianjin, from which one can feel the atmosphere in *Thunderstorm*

27.4. In a public performance of *Thunderstorm* in Nanjing in 1936, Cao Yu performed the role of Zhou Puyuan

responded quickly to the success of the performance, and for the first time ever, it was willing to extend the term of its contract with a troupe from ten days to three months and changed the original 7/3 profit split to 3/7. The performance was such a sensation that it drew sellout crowds for three consecutive months. When the performance was staged again in September, Shanghai citizens queued up to buy tickets overnight and it enjoyed a good box-office run. The Carlton Theater seized this opportunity and made the following announcement: "From 1937, the theater will be devoted to spoken drama and no film will be shown, and the name of this theater will be changed to the Shanghai Arts Theater (上海艺术剧院)."[1] Soon after that, the advertising for the separate edition of *Thunderstorm* claimed: "It is *Thunderstorm* that sustained the Chinese spoken drama stage," and "only after *Thunderstorm* was performed, did the Chinese spoken drama stage have its own script."[2] With its repertory of plays including *Thunderstorm* and others, the Chinese Traveling Troupe had finally stopped performing like traveling players. Mao Dun immediately realized the significance of all this to the cause of modern Chinese spoken drama and said: "The professional performing troupes and theaters that stage performances of spoken dramatic plays in a regular manner, the public appeal of grand performances to the audience of traditional Chinese operas and the civilized drama, ... all of these are the preconditions for spoken drama to gain a foothold in our society and expand its influence," and it was something that "should occur

27.5. Nobody had ever expected that the performance of *Thunderstorm* by the Chinese Traveling Troupe, after its premiere on May 6, 1936 at the Carlton Theater in Shanghai, would enjoy huge success for three consecutive months. This theater thus became a famous site for modern Chinese spoken drama

---

[1]   See "Carlton Changed into a Spoken Drama Theater" (《卡尔登改为话剧场》), published in *Stage and Screen Monthly* (《舞台银幕月刊》), Vol. 1, Issue 3. The theater didn't actually change its name in the end, but it became the best spoken drama theater in Shanghai.

[2]   This advertisement was published in the *Drama Times*, Vol. 1, Issue 2, June 1937.

27.6. Lone Pinetree Drama Troupe's performance of *Thunderstorm* in Tianjin in 1935, a bit later than the performance in Japan shown in Figure 27.7

27.7. Chinese Spoken Drama Club of Chinese Students in Japan's performance of *Thunderstorm* at the Hitotsubashi Premiere Auditorium in Kanda, Tokyo, on April 27, 1935. Compare the stage in this picture with that in Figure 27.6

when spoken drama enters its mature stage and changes from an art form for intellectuals within universities into one for ordinary citizens and the general public."[3] Here lies the importance of Cao Yu.

Thunderstorm was obviously an outstanding dramatic work compared to any Chinese spoken drama play that had been written before. This was a polyphonic literary work: on the one hand, the playwright spared no effort to expose the evilness of a feudal-style family of a capitalist, and on the other hand, he examined his characters, who tried to find a way out of the evil social web but failed, with sympathy and compassion. *Thunderstorm* was a tragedy of personality that was disconcerting and gloomy. There were fierce conflicts between people of different classes and backgrounds. In the plot where Shiping and Zhou Puyuan meet again thirty years after she had been abandoned by the latter, Zhou Puyuan was presented as a tyrannical and selfish "Master," hypocritical but showing a least bit of remorse and finally took a cruel stance. In the relationship between Fanyi and Zhou Puyuan, where she was insulted and suppressed by the latter (especially in the scene where she was forced to take medicine), Fanyi showed all her rebellion and retribution in her resistance. In the dubious relationship between Fanyi as a stepmother and Zhou Ping, one could see her desperate need for love and her final piece of revenge (she sent for Zhou Puyuan just as the half-brother and -sister, Zhou Ping and Sifeng, were going to leave, which led to the final act of the play that unveiled the truth about their identities), and thus brought the play to its climax. The introduction of the character Fanyi was an excellent piece of writing that helped us understand the depth of Cao Yu's characterization and how this play explored society and human nature. It was one of the most brilliant paragraphs of all literary works throughout modern Chinese literary history:

> She is obviously a woman of ruthless determination. The faint red of her lips is the only touch of color in her otherwise pale face. Her large, dark eyes and straight nose give her face a certain beauty, though a beauty with a sinister cast to it. The eyes beneath her long, steady lashes betray her unhappiness. Sometimes, when the smoldering fires of misery in her heart blaze into life, these eyes will fill with all the anguish and resentment of a frustrated woman. The corners of her mouth are slightly drawn back, revealing her to be a repressed woman controlling herself with difficulty. Whenever she coughs in her quiet way, her slender, delicate white hands press against her flat, emaciated chest, and when the coughing is over, leaving her panting for breath, they will go up to feel her face, now flushed with coughing. With her delicate health, her secret sorrows, her intelligence, and her love of poetry and literature, she is a woman of old

---

3   Mao Dun: "Critique on the Dramatic Movement" (《剧运平议》), *Literature*, Vol. 9, No. 2, August 1937.

China; yet there is a primitive wildness in her which shows in her courage, in her almost fanatical reasoning, and in her sudden, unaccountable
strength in moments of crisis. The sum impression which one gains of
her is of a crystalline transparency, as if she is the sort of woman who
can offer a man no companionship but the platonic kind, and her broad,
unclouded forehead is expressive of a subtle intelligence; but when, lost
in sentimental reverie, she breaks into a sudden smile of happiness, or
when, at the sight of someone dear to her, a flush of pleasure suffuses her
face and dimples appear on her cheeks, one feels for the first time that
it would be possible to love her and that she does indeed deserve to be
loved – one realizes, in fact, that she is a woman after all, a woman no different from all the others. When she loves, she loves with a fiery passion,
and when she hates, she hates fiercely, with a hatred which can destroy;
yet on the surface she appears quiet and wistful, and when she stops
beside you, it is like a leaf falling by your side on a late autumn afternoon.
She seems to feel that the summer of her life is now over, and that the
shade of evening is falling around her.[4]

Cao Yu once said that Fanyi had the "stormiest" personality, which means
understanding this character was key to understanding the entire play. Like
a thunderstorm, she set the entire play in motion, and became the driving
force of each plot line of the play. In this vortex of dramatic conflicts, we
see other characters such as Zhou Ping, who was a coward and remorseful;
Shiping (Lu Ma), who was self-respecting and enduring; Zhou Chong, who
was innocent and aspiring; Sifeng, who was kind-hearted and eager for love;
Lu Dahai, who was a rugged worker; and Lu Gui, who was a vulgar, malevo-
lent, and greedy manservant of a wealthy family; all this was presented in
front of the audience in minutest detail. *Thunderstorm* was also a tragedy of
fate. Besides the material gains and passions and desires, fate seemed to take
control of all its characters with a supernatural power and bring them into
a "secret realm": Shiping's daughter worked as a maidservant at the Zhou's;
Zhou Puyuan's son organized a strike in the mine against him; and Zhou
Ping was entangled simultaneously in two incestuous affairs; while Zhou
Chong, the most innocent boy in the play, ran into an unrepaired electric
wire in the heavy rain. According to Cao Yu, apart from his social experience,
including that with his father and his own family, he wrote *Thunderstorm*
out of an emotional impulse. "I have nothing but pure feelings of happiness
toward *Thunderstorm*, something like a mother seeing her own baby for the
first time. It is a passion for life itself. … In the play, the universe is like a cruel
well. Anyone falling into it has no chance of escaping from this dark abyss,

---

[4]   Cao Yu: *Thunderstorm*, Beijing: China Theater Press, 1957, pp. 23–24. The translation is quoted
      from Cao Yu: *Thunderstorm* (Echo of Classics Series), translated by Wang Zuoliang and A. C.
      Barnes, Beijing: Foreign Languages Press, 2001. pp. 63–65.

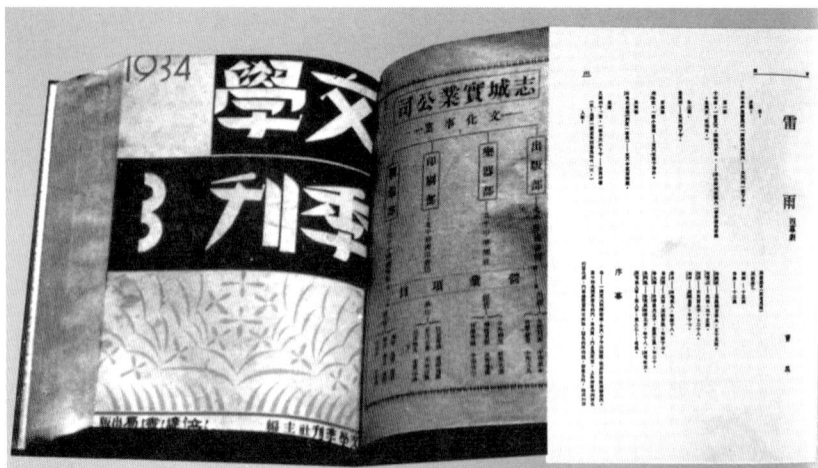

27.8. *Literary Quarterly* (Vol. 1, Issue 3), in which *Thunderstorm* was first published. As can be seen, there was a "Prologue" (and an "Epilogue") in the original playscript

no matter how hard one cries for help."[5] And Cao Yu had his own design for how to interpret this play. He added a "Prologue" and an "Epilogue" to the play, which he wrote many years later, in which Zhou's house became a hospital and accommodated two mad women, Shiping and Fanyi; the culprit of the tragedy, Zhou Puyuan, old, shaky and repentant, came to see them; and music from the church was heard from afar. Such an arrangement showed the author's intention to guide his readers and make it clear to them that *Thunderstorm* was not only a social tragedy but a tragedy of life. As the author once said: "I regarded *Thunderstorm* as a poem and a story, and I added the 'Prologue' and 'Epilogue' to extend the temporal space of a complicated evil to somewhere in the infinite. ... The scenes in the 'Prologue' and 'Epilogue' thus created a kind of 'aesthetic distance'." This was how *Thunderstorm* went beyond the reality and entered the realm of symbolism and religious sentiments, and the author "wished the audience could have a birds'-eye view of the characters, while keeping a compassionate eye."[6] Thus we can see that Cao Yu did not write this play to ignite his readers' hatred or vengeance, which made him somehow similar to some Beijing school authors, but it did not follow the fashion of era-specific literary writing of that time. Therefore, ever since the very first performance of *Thunderstorm*, whether to include the "Prologue" and "Epilogue" in the performance and whether to highlight its nature as a social problem play or as a tragedy of fate, became the key to how *Thunderstorm* was read and understood. For example, Tian Han once pointed

[5] Cao Yu: "Introduction to *Thunderstorm*" (《〈雷雨〉序》), *Thunderstorm*, Shanghai: Shanghai Cultural Life Press, 1936.

[6] Ibid.

out that the era *Thunderstorm* was performed in "was no longer 'breezy' but a 'stormy' one," and therefore he "agreed with Mr. Yuqian about revising this 'tragedy of fate' that was a bit 'behind the times' into something like a 'social tragedy,' and disapproved of performances of this play that showed no criticism of society."[7] This was a typical viewpoint of the left-wing camp, outside the ordinary citizen audience, and it turned out to have a far-reaching influence on Cao Yu that can not be ignored.

The influence was gradual. Before the Anti-Japanese War broke out, at least when Cao Yu wrote his second and third spoken drama plays, *Sunrise* and *The Wilderness*, he seemed to combine "presenting social problems" and "presenting life issues." *Sunrise* told the tragedy of a playgirl, Chen Bailu, who was not a total degenerate but was finally destroyed by her social environment. The play paid special attention to the social causes of Chinese people's state of mind in the 1930s, when a capitalist economy developed in some parts of the country. Fang Dasheng, Chen Bailu's former classmate and lover, wanted to drag her out of the dark world consisting of Pan Yueting, Zhang Qiaozhi, Gu

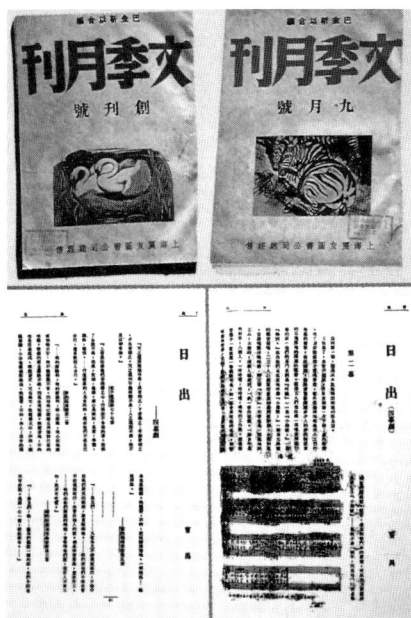

27.9. *Literary Season Monthly* (《文季月刊》), the inaugural issue and the September issue, in which *Sunrise* was first published

27.10. Performance of *Sunrise* at the Hitotsubashi Premiere Auditorium in Tokyo in March 1937, organized by the International Association for the Advancement of Drama by Chinese Students in Japan. This scene is from Act Three, with the character Chen Bailu (on the right) played by Fengzi (风子), who was invited to Japan for the performance

---

[7] See Tian Han: "A Glance of the Art Circle of Nanjing in the Storm" (《暴风雨中的南京艺坛一瞥》), quoted from Qian Liqun: *Between the Big and Small Stages* (《大小舞台之间》), Hangzhou: Zhejiang Literature and Arts Press, 1994, p. 54.

27.11. Spoken drama play *The Wilderness* was prohibited for a long time. The wide-screen feature film *The Wilderness* was not totally taboo-breaking, but it was a courageous new start. The film was produced by the South Sea Film Company (南海影业公司) in 1981 and starred Yang Zaibao (杨在葆) and Liu Xiaoqing (刘晓庆)

Banainai, Hu Si, and others (as well as Jin Ba, who was not present in the play but represented the power of wealth behind all these evil characters) but failed. The character Pipsqueak (*xiao-dong-xi*) took audiences to have a look at the low-class brothels, which were in sharp contrast to the luxury hotels. It was said that in order to write about the low-class brothels in the third act, Cao Yu had been to such places for field research. Chen Bailu had empathy for those whose social status was lower than her own, but she could not even save herself. To the sound of work songs sung by workers, she killed herself, but not before she recited this poem: "The sun rises, leaving the darkness behind. But the sun is not ours, for we now sleep." This gave the play a symbolic significance, which quite clearly showed the author's political tendencies. *Sunrise* was more like a social problem play, but one could still see Cao Yu's unique style in it. *The Wilderness* was nothing less than a poetic play, in which the playwright explored the theme of how a peasant's high-spirited revenge could lead him into a predicament. It was the story of a peasant's resistance against his landlord, but it was distorted because the playwright presented the resistance as a "primitive force." Qiu Hu's family members were all savagely murdered by the local tyrant Jiao Yanwang, himself put into prison with broken leg, and his fiancée Jinzi forced to marry Jiao Yanwang's son Jiao Daxing, a coward and good-for-nothing. Eight years later, Qiu Hu finally escaped from prison and sought revenge, only to find that the target of his revenge, Jiao Yanwang, had already died, so he had to change his objective. He first won back the love of Jinzi, and then killed Jiao Daxing by tricking Jiao's mother, which led to the tragic death of the completely innocent Xiao Heizi. This revenge was by no means fair, as Jiao Daxing had been Qiu Hu's kind-hearted playmate when they were young and there was no hatred between them. Frightened by the horrifying soul-summoning words and acts of Jiao's mother, Qiu Hu's pain and fear became increasingly unbearable. It was here that the playwright broke free from literary realism by highlighting his characters' psychological illusions and creating a mysterious atmosphere. During their escape, Qiu Hu and Jinzi got lost in the black forest, where ghosts appeared with their memories, and they were tortured by their conscience, and the use of symbolism became increasingly more elaborate and evocative. It was the consensus of critics that here the influence of O'Neill's *The Emperor Jones* was obvious, and thus *The Wilderness* became a brilliant drama with the most profoundly used symbolism and expressionism in China. And for this same reason, while *Sunrise* was widely praised for its social significance, *The Wilderness* was largely slighted because it explored abstract human nature, and that modernism was still a far cry from the taste and interest of audiences of that time. This also had something to do with the fact that mainstream literature in the 1930s tried to reshape May Fourth literature into realism. Cao Yu's achievements in dramatic creation were widely recognized, but the limitations of that era were obvious. It was not until the 1980s, when the film *The Wilderness* was shown, that the spoken drama play finally gained the attention it deserved.

Back in the mid-1930s, the "grand performances" mentioned by Mao Dun were in full swing in Shanghai. This referred to the Theatrical Art movement planned and launched by left-wing dramatists, through which national defense dramas were somewhat promoted, but they were not the mainstream. The concentrated performances in "grand theaters" included the historical allegorical play *Sai Jinhua* (《赛金花》) premiered at the Jincheng Grand Theater (金城大戏院) in November 1936 (the major characters were played by Jin Shan [金山] and Wang Ying [王莹]); meanwhile, three foreign plays were performed at the Carlton Theater, namely Ostrowski's *The Storm* (the major performer being Zhao Dan [赵丹]), Leo

27.12. Tao Jingsun (left) and Xia Yan performing *All Quiet on the Western Front* at the Shanghai Artistic Drama Association in March 1930

Tolstoy's *The Power of Darkness*, and Seán O'Casey's *Juno and the Paycock*; in February 1937 *Sunrise* was performed at the Carlton Theater; by March 1937 when the spoken dramatists in Shanghai organized joint performances, they attracted huge audiences for twenty consecutive days at the Carlton Theater, and most of the plays performed were by foreign playwrights. In April that year, the most reputable drama group, the Shanghai Amateur Drama Association (业余剧人协会), received funding and turned professional. It was restructured into the China Amateur Experimental Theater (中国业余实验剧团), evidence that spoken drama had won a large number of citizen audience members and had gained a foothold in grand theaters. It was China's second professional spoken drama troupe, after the Chinese Traveling Troupe, was even bigger than the latter, and largely consisted of left-wing dramatists. Soon after it was restructured, the troupe performed *Romeo and Juliet* (《罗密欧与朱丽叶》) at the Carlton Theater in June 1937, and then, showing the actual achievements of China's spoken dramatists, it performed *Wu Zetian* (《武则天》) by Song Zhidi (宋之的); the first part, *Jintian Village* (《金田村》), of Chen Baichen's *The Taiping Heavenly Kingdom* (《太平天国》); and Cao Yu's *The Wilderness* (in which Jinzi was played by Shu Xiuwen [舒绣文]). If it were not for the outbreak of the August Thirteenth Incident in Shanghai, the troupe would also have performed Xia Yan's *Under Shanghai Eaves* (《上海屋檐下》), as they had already been rehearsing the play.

27.13. Xia Yan in 1930, around the time *Zuolian* was established

From these performances that laid the foundation for the maturity of China's spoken drama in theaters, we can see that Cao Yu had made a great contribution to the development of Chinese spoken drama with his three earlier plays. Besides Cao Yu, there was also Xia Yan (1900–1996), an outstanding left-wing dramatist who created *Sai Jinhua* and *Under Shanghai Eaves*. As for left-wing criticism of drama, an article written by Zhou Yang about *Sunrise* represented the left-wing views, which, while affirming the "anti-feudalist" positive effect of Cao's play and labeling him as a "realist" dramatist, analyzed Cao's "incomplete realism" and thus created a pattern of criticism of Cao Yu that attached more importance to social reflection.[8] But the dramatists of that time enjoyed more freedom in their relationships with each other. Xia Yan's earlier plays, *Sai Jinhua* and *The Biography of Qiu Jin* (《秋瑾传》, also known as *The*

---

[8]   Zhou Yang: "On *Thunderstorm* and *Sunrise*" (《论〈雷雨〉和〈日出〉》), *Light*, Vol. 2, Issue 8, March 1937.

27.14. Xia Yan's play *Sai Jinhua* was based on the story of a famous prostitute in Beijing named Sai Jinhua

27.15. Xia Yan's *Under Shanghai Eaves*, published by the Theatrical Times Press in November 1937

Spirit of Freedom [《自由魂》]), had quite an obvious tendency of political propaganda with the use of historical material. According to Xia's recollection, it was after reading Cao Yu's plays that he began to understand the importance of characterization and creation of typical settings. His masterpiece written in 1937, *Under Shanghai Eaves*, presented the audience with the everyday life and fate of five ordinary families living in a Shanghai alley by skillfully cutting and linking within the same space on the stage. The story happened during rainy days in the spring, with the love triangle between Lin Zhicheng and two other characters as the main plot. Xia Yan created dramatic scenes and sustained dramatic tension by portraying the personalities of a dozen characters and painting the trivial life scenes of ordinary people who seemed to live like that forever, while on the other hand, conflicts loomed anytime, anywhere. Xia Yan had his unique style of plainness, simplicity, and reservedness, and instead of confronting the dark forces in an aggressive manner like a revolutionary, he had a kind sympathy and compassion toward his imperfect characters and their tragic fate, and thus integrated humanism into his revolutionary emotions. This was because Xia Yan learned from Chekhov's style, which featured plainness and simplicity, smiles in tears and warmth in chill. Cao Yu also mentioned the influence of Chekhov's plays on himself, but it did not show until after the Anti-Japanese War, when Cao Yu had some social experience. The dramatic conflicts in *Thunderstorm*, after all, were too intense. In China, Xia Yan was the playwright who had gained the best experience in learning from Chekhov.

As for the maturity of spoken drama in theaters and its relationship with street theater, Chinese spoken drama still had a long way to go after the Anti-Japanese War. And it was not surprising that Cao Yu, who had made such a great contribution to the development of modern Chinese spoken drama in theaters, wrote such outstanding plays as *Peking Man* (《北京人》) and *The Family*, which were even more poetic and gave an even more in-depth analysis of the cultural spirit of Chinese people, but also directed street performances and took the lead in writing propaganda plays such as *National Mobilization* (《全民总动员》, whose name was later changed to *Twenty-Eight in Black* [《黑字二十八》]). But no doubt the spoken drama in theaters had always been the backbone in innovating and promoting China's spoken drama. One can see this clearly just by considering the fact that during the warring period, in addition to street theater, *Thunderstorm* was constantly being performed in Yan'an, in the "great hinterland," and in the base areas.

MAP 27.1 Locations of performances of *Thunderstorm* during the 1930s–1940s

TABLE 27.1 *Performances of* Thunderstorm *during the 1930s–1940s*

Performing troupe	Date	City and venue	Director	Major actors
Lone Pinetree Drama Troupe	Aug. 1935	Auditorium of Tianjin Normal School	Lü Yangping (吕仰平)	Tao Yi (陶一), Yan Ru (严如), and Li Lin (李琳)
Chinese Traveling Troupe	Oct. 1935	Tianjin New New Dramatic Movie Theater (天津新新影戏院)	Tang Huaiqiu	Dai Ya (戴涯), Zhao Huishen (赵慧深), and Tang Ruoqing (唐若青)
Chinese Traveling Troupe	Feb. 1936	Tianjin New New Dramatic Movie Theater	Tang Huaiqiu	Same as the performance in Tianjin in Oct. 1935
Chinese Traveling Troupe	Oct. 1936	Hankou Star Movie Theater (汉口明星影戏院)	Tang Huaiqiu	Same as the performance in Tianjin in Oct. 1935
Chinese Traveling Troupe	After July 1937	Hankou	Tang Huaiqiu	
Chinese Traveling Troupe	May 1936	Nanjing World Grand Theater (南京世界大戏院)	Tang Huaiqiu	Same as the performance in Tianjin in Oct. 1935
Chinese Dramatic Society (中国戏剧学会)	Jan. 1937	Nanjing World Grand Theater	Cao Yu and Ma Yanxiang (马彦祥)	Cao Yu, Zheng Yimei (郑挹梅), and Yu Zhenru (于真如), etc.
Fudan Drama Troupe	Autumn 1935	Association of Natives of Ningbo in Shanghai (上海宁波同乡会)	Ouyang Yuqian	Fengzi, Li Lilian (李丽莲), and Wu Tieyi (吴铁翼), etc.
Chinese Traveling Troupe	May and Sep. 1936	Shanghai Carlton Theater	Tang Huaiqiu	Same as the performance in Tianjin in Oct. 1935
Blue Bird Drama Troupe (青鸟剧社)	Jan. 1938	Shanghai		Organized by Yu Ling (于伶), Ouyang Yuqian, Xu Xingzhi, and Ah Ying, etc.

(continued)

TABLE 27.1 *(continued)*

Performing troupe	Date	City and venue	Director	Major actors
Students of Chunhui Middle School	Dec. 1934	Chunhui Middle School on the bank of White Horse Lake	Jing Jincheng (景金城)	Hu Yutang (胡玉堂) and Chen Weihui (陈维辉), etc.
National Drama School	June 1938	Chongqing	Under the guidance of Cao Yu	Cheng Yongliang (陈永倞), etc.
National Drama School	July 1938	Chongqing Cathay Theater (重庆国泰大戏院)	Wang De (汪德)	
Chengdu Drama Troupe	Mar. 1938	Chengdu Zhiyu Cinema (成都智育电影院)	Shi Chao (施超) and Xie Tian (谢添)	Yan Qun (燕群), etc.
Sichuan Traveling Drama Team	Mar. 1938	Chengdu Chunxi Grand Stage	Chen Guang (陈光)	Li Enqi (李恩琪), Zhang Xilian (张西莲), and Xiang Airu (项爱如), etc.
Shanghai Filmmakers' Drama Troupe (上海影人剧团)	Mar. 1938	Chengdu Sullivan Theater (成都沙利文剧场)	Cao Zao (曹藻)	Cao Zao, etc.
Shanghai Association of Amateur Dramatists	June 1938	Chengdu Zhiyu Cinema	Shi Chao and Xie Tian	
Chinese Spoken Drama Club (中华话剧同好会)	Apr. and May 1935	Hitotsubashi Premiere Auditorium in Kanda, Tokyo	Wu Tian (吴天) and Du Xuan	Jia Bingwen (贾秉文), Chen Qianjun (陈倩君), and Qiao Junying (乔俊英), etc.

(*Major source*: Qian Liqun: *Between the Big and Small Stages*)

TWENTY EIGHT

A CHRONICLE OF LITERARY EVENTS
IN THE YEAR 1936 (AN ERA
OF DIVERSIFICATION)

IN FEBRUARY 1936, THE *COMPENDIUM OF CHINESE NEW Literature: Index of Historical Material* (《新文学大系 • 史料索引集》) edited by Ah Ying (aka Qian Xingcun), the left-wing author who was very scholarly and had a strong interest in collections, was published. Then, from the earliest volume, *Fiction I* (《小说一集》), all ten volumes of the *Compendium of Chinese New Literature*, whose editor-in-chief was the young editor Zhao Jiabi (赵家璧) and which was published by the Young Companion Printing and Publishing Company, were published within a period of less than two years. The subtitle of the *Compendium* was "The First Decade: 1917–1927" (《第一个十年：1917–1927》), and its intention was to review the achievements of New Literature. Therefore, literary works included in the *Compendium* were those of the May Fourth literary period, mostly the best works of the May Fourth literary period that had just passed, but its editors, including Cai Yuanpei, who wrote the "General Preface"; Hu Shi, who edited *Constructive Theories* (《建设理论集》); Zheng Zhenduo, who edited *Literary Contentions* (《文学论争集》); Mao Dun, who edited *Fiction I*; Lu Xun, who edited

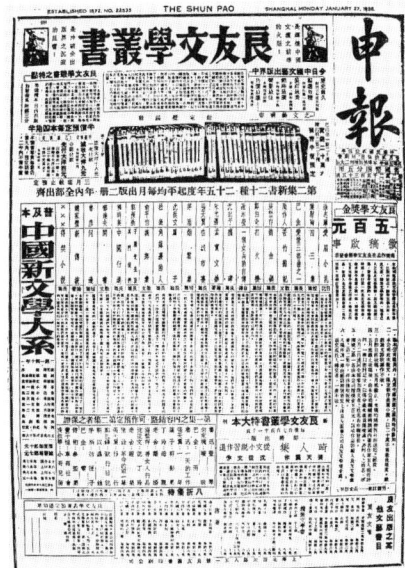

28.1. Large advertisement for the *Compendium of Chinese New Literature* and the Young Companion literary series published in *Shun Pao* on January 27, 1936

Fiction II; Zheng Boqi, who edited *Fiction III*; Zhou Zuoren, who edited *Prose I* (《散文一集》); Yu Dafu, who edited *Prose II*; Zhu Ziqing, who edited *Poetry* (《诗集》); Hong Shen, who edited *Drama* (《戏剧集》); and Ah Ying, who edited *Index of Historical Material*, in spite of their open and impartial attitude, were all looking back from the perspective of the mid-1930s, or were looking at this literary period as a continuous period of history from May Fourth up to the 1930s. Most of these editors were left-wing writers, including Lu Xun. Mao Dun's "Preface" highlighted the earlier Marxist critical views and methods. Originally the editor of *Poetry* was intended to be Guo Moruo, but at that time Guo was in political exile in Japan and the censors regarded Guo as too left-leaning, and thus Zhu Ziqing was appointed as its editor. Among the other editors, Hu Shi had become a representative of liberal intellectuals; he emphasized the value of vernacular language as a revolution of literary tool, and his evolutionary literary view was consistent with that expressed in his "Fifty Years of Chinese Literature." As the one who laid the theoretical foundation for Beijing school literature, in his "Introduction" to *Prose I*, Zhou Zuoren adopted a dichotomy between two prose genres, namely prose as a vehicle to express ambitions and prose as a vehicle of moral instruction, which was also consistent with his views shown in *On the Origins of China's New Literature*. Shanghai school writers were not yet qualified to criticize May Fourth literature, but according to Zhao Jiabi's recollection, Shi Zhecun, who was then editing *The Contemporaries* and who was a fellow townsman of Zhao from Songjiang, had exerted great influence on the design of this ten-volume compendium through many decisions on specific details, such as his strong support of the term "Compendium" in the title, as well as his suggestion to change the original system of "selected works" into a new pattern that laid equal stress on literary theories, literary works, and historical material.[1] Here we can feel the general literary atmosphere of that era; since the splitting and restructuring of the May Fourth literary camp, a uniform literary landscape no longer existed. Diversity had become the feature of the literary scene of the 1930s, hence the *Compendium of Chinese New Literature* sought to look back and review the literary scene of the previous decade.

In this diversified literary scene, one could see four major constituent parts: the first part was left-wing literature. When it was first promoted in China it was called "revolutionary literature," and due to the rise of this "revolutionary literature," the authors of the Literary Research Society, Creation Society, and other literary associations split apart. The radical members among them gathered around *Zuolian* and Lu Xun under the banner of Marxism and the leadership of the CPC, and became left-wing authors with a strong political bias.

---

[1]　See Zhao Jiabi: *An Editor's Recollections of the Past* (《编辑忆旧》), Beijing: Joint Publishing Company, 1984.

TABLE 28.1 *Chronicle of literary events in 1936*

Date	Major literary event
Jan. 20	Lu Xun's historical fiction "Leaving the Pass" (《出关》) was published in the inaugural issue of *Petrel* monthly
Jan. 20	*Petrel* monthly was launched in Shanghai, edited by Nie Gannu, Hu Feng, and Xiao Jun. It was discontinued in February of this year after two issues had been published
Jan. 20	Zhang Tianyi's collection of short stories, *The Eccentric* (《畸人集》), was published by the Young Companion Printing and Publishing Company
January	Lu Xun's collection of historical fiction, *Old Tales Retold*, was published by Shanghai Cultural Life Press
January	Cao Yu's spoken drama play *Thunderstorm* was published by Shanghai Cultural Life Press
January	Li Changzhi's collection of literary criticism, *Critique of Lu Xun* (《鲁迅批判》), was published by Shanghai Beixin Press
January	The Association of Shanghai Dramatists was formed, which actively launched the National Salvation Drama movement
Feb. 15	*Compendium of Chinese New Literature: Index of Historical Material*, edited by Ah Ying, was published by the Young Companion Printing and Publishing Company
February	Zhou Zuoren's collection of prose essays, *Bitter Bamboo Miscellanies* (《苦竹杂记》), was published by the Young Companion Printing and Publishing Company
February	The League of Left-Wing Writers was dissolved
Mar. 5	*Nightingale* monthly, whose editor-in-chief was Fang Zhizhong, was launched in Shanghai, which was a left-wing literary journal edited by members of *Zuolian* after it was dissolved. It was discontinued in the June of this year after four issues had been published
Mar. 5	*Book of Leisure* (《逸经》) semimonthly was launched in Shanghai, whose president was Jian Youwen (简又文) and editor-in-chief was Xie Xingyao (谢兴尧) and Lu Danlin (陆丹林), successively. It was discontinued in August 1937 after thirty-six issues had been published
March	Yu Dafu's collection of prose essays, *Travel Notes of Dafu* (《达夫游记》), was published by Shanghai Literary Creation Press
March	Shen Congwen's collection of prose essays, *Discursive Notes on Traveling through Hunan*, was published by the Commercial Press in Shanghai
March	The correspondence between Xu Zhimo and Lu Xiaoman (陆小曼), *Love Mei Notes*, was published by the Young Companion Printing and Publishing Company
March	Tang Tao's collection of miscellaneous essays, *Collection of Dissuasion* (《推背集》), was published by Shanghai Tianma Bookstore
March	The collection of poems by Bian Zhilin, He Qifang, and Li Guangtian, *The Han Garden Collection* (《汉园集》), was published by the Commercial Press in Shanghai

(continued)

TABLE 28.1 *(continued)*

Date	Major literary event
March	The collection of Chen Mengjia's poems, *Remaining Poems of Mengjia* (《梦家存诗》), was published by the Shanghai Times Book Company
March	Fang Weide's (方玮德) *Collection of Poetry and Prose of Weide* (《玮德诗文集》), edited by Chen Mengjia, was published by the Shanghai Times Book Company
March	Zhu Ziqing's collection of prose and poetry, *You. Me.* (《你我》), was published by the Commercial Press in Shanghai
March	Xiao Qian's collection of short stories, *Under the Fence of Others*, was published by the Commercial Press in Shanghai
March	Zhao Jingshen's collection of prose essays, *Sketch of Intellectuals* (《文人剪影》), was published by Shanghai Beixin Press
Apr. 1	Lu Xun's "Preface to Bai Mang's *The Children's Pagoda*" was published in *Literary Gazette*, Issue 1
Apr. 1	Xie Bingying's (谢冰莹) autobiographical novel, *Autobiography of a Female Soldier* (《一个女兵的自传》), began to be serialized in *Cosmic Wind* (Issue 14), with its separate edition published by the Young Companion Printing and Publishing Company in June of this year
Apr. 1	Xia Yan's play *Sai Jinhua* was published in *Literature* (Vol. 6, Issue 4), with its separate edition published by Shanghai Life Bookstore in November of this year
Apr. 1	Zhou Yang's literary critical article "Typicality and Individuality" (《典型与个性》) was published in *Literature* (Vol. 6, Issue 4)
Apr. 1	*Literary Gazette* monthly was launched in Shanghai, whose editors-in-chief included Wang Yuanheng, Ma Zihua, and Nie Gannu. The journal was discontinued in August of this year after five issues had been published
Apr. 1	*Ling Ding* monthly was launched in Beiping, edited by the Ling Ding Monthly Editorial Office. The journal was discontinued in May of this year after two issues had been published
Apr. 15	Xiao Hong's short story "Hands" (《手》) was published in the inaugural issue of *Writers* (《作家》)
Apr. 15	*Writers* monthly was launched in Shanghai, edited by Meng Shihuan (孟十还). The journal was discontinued in November of this year after eight issues had been published
Apr. 16	The Association of Shanghai Dramatists held a symposium on *Sai Jinhua*, at which all attendees agreed that the play was the first achievement after the slogan of "national defense drama" was raised
Apr. 25	The CPC Central Committee sent Feng Xuefeng as an emissary to Shanghai from Wayaobao of Northern Shaanxi to set up the United Front of Shanghai Literary and Art Circle through Lu Xun and others
April	Ba Jin's "Love" trilogy (《爱情三部曲》, including *Fog* [《雾》], *Rain* [《雨》] and *Lightning* [《电》]) was published by the Young Companion Printing and Publishing Company

(continued)

TABLE 28.1 *(continued)*

Date	Major literary event
April	Zhu Guangqian's collection of art and literary criticism, *Essays of Mengshi* (《孟实文钞》), was published by the Young Companion Printing and Publishing Company
April	Shao Xunmei's anthology, *Twenty-Five Poems* (《诗二十五首》), was published by the Shanghai Times Book Company
April	*On Writers* (《作家论》), by Mao Dun and others, was published by Shanghai Literature Press (上海文学出版社), in which there were comments on Xu Zhimo, Lu Yin, Zhou Zuoren, Lin Yutang, Bing Xin, Shen Congwen, and Zhang Tianyi, among others
April	Hu Feng's first collection of literary criticism, *Essays on Literature and Art* (《文艺笔谈》), was published by Shanghai Literature Press
May 1	Shu Qun's (舒群) short story "Child without a Fatherland" (《没有祖国的孩子》) was published in *Literature* (Vol. 6, Issue 5). A collection of short stories with the same title was published by Shanghai Life Bookstore in September of this year
May 15	Lu Xun's health worsened, with him suffering from asthma and high fever
May	Mao Dun's novella *Multifaceted Relations* (《多角关系》) was published by Shanghai Literature Press
May	The collection of short stories by Shi Tuo (aka Lu Fen), *Valley* (《谷》), was published by Shanghai Cultural Life Press under his original name, Wang Changjian. It was awarded the literary prize of *Ta Kung Pao* the following year
May	Shen Congwen's *Novel Compositions of Congwen* was published by the Young Companion Printing and Publishing Company
June 1	Lu Yan's novel *Wildfire* (《野火》) began to be serialized in *Literary Season Monthly* (Vol. 1, Issue 1), with the separate edition published by the Young Companion Printing and Publishing Company in May the following year with the title "The Angry Countryside" (《愤怒的乡村》)
June 1	*Literary Season Monthly* was launched in Shanghai, whose editors-in-chief were Jin Yi and Ba Jin. This major literary journal was a continuation of *Literary Quarterly* and was discontinued after seven issues had been published
June 1	Cao Yu's spoken drama play *Sunrise* began to be serialized in *Literary Season Monthly* (Vol. 1, Issue 1), with the separate edition published in November of this year by Shanghai Cultural Life Press
June 1	Hu Feng published his article "What Do the Masses Demand of Literature?" (《人民大众向文学要求什么？》) in *Literary Gazette* (Issue 3), in which he raised the slogan of "mass literature of national revolutionary war"
June 5	*Literary Circle* monthly was launched in Shanghai, with its editors including Dai Pingwan, Yang Sao, and Sha Ting; the journal was discontinued in September of this year after four issues had been published
June 5	Sha Ting's short story "In the Ancestral Temple" was published in the inaugural issue of *Literary Circle*

(continued)

TABLE 28.1 *(continued)*

Date	Major literary event
June 7	The Union of Chinese Writers and Artists (中国文艺家协会), whose thirty-four founders included Wang Renshu, Zhou Libo (周立波), Sha Ting and Huang Mei (荒煤), held its inaugural meeting in Shanghai and they delivered the "Manifesto of the Union of Chinese Writers and Artists"
June 9	Lu Xun dictated his "Reply to a Letter from the Trotskyists" (《答托洛斯基派的信》) on his sickbed, which was recorded by O.V. (Feng Xuefeng)
June 10	Lu Xun dictated his "On Our Literary Movement at Present" (《论现在我们的文学运动》) on his sickbed, in which he explained the slogan of "mass literature of national revolutionary war," which was recorded by O.V. (Feng Xuefeng)
June 10	Xia Yan's piece of reportage *Indentured Laborers* (《包身工》) was published in the inaugural issue of *Light*, and later, in 1938, a collection of pieces of reportage of the same title was published by Guangzhou Lisao Press
June 10	*Light* semimonthly was launched in Shanghai, whose editors-in-chief were Hong Shen and Shen Qiyu (沈起予). The journal was discontinued in October, 1937 after twenty-nine issues had been published
June 16	Lao She's prose writing "Thinking of Beiping" (《想北平》) was published in *Cosmic Wind* (Issue 19)
June 18	Maxim Gorky, the world-renowned Soviet writer, died, who was widely commemorated by left-wing Chinese authors and people of the progressive literary and art circle
June 27	Zhang Henshui's novel *Deep in the Night* (《夜深沉》) began to be serialized in the *Daily News* in Shanghai, running until March 7, 1939. The separate edition was published by Sanyou Press in June 1941
June	Lu Xun's collection of miscellaneous essays, *Fringed Literature* (《花边文学》), was published by Shanghai Lianhua Press
June	Ye Lingfeng's *The Unfinished Confession* was published by Jindai Bookstore
June	*Muddy Loess* (《黄土泥》), a collection of short stories by Lao Xiang (老向), was published by Shanghai Human World Bookstore
June	Hong Shen's collection of spoken drama plays, "Trilogy of the Countryside" (*Wukui Bridge*, *Fragrant Rice*, and *Black Dragon Pond*) was published by Shanghai Magazine Company
June	Chen Baichen's spoken drama play, *Shi Dakai at the End of His Life* (《石达开的末路》), was published by Shanghai Life Bookstore
June	*Secret China*, written by Egon Erwin Kisch, was translated by Zhou Libo and was partly published in *Literary Circle* (the specific issue may be found in the *Catalogue and List of Modern Chinese Literary Journals*, Vol. 2, p. 1860)
June	*Smuggling*, a collectively created spoken drama play written by Hong Shen, was published in the inaugural issue of *Light*

(continued)

TABLE 28.1 *(continued)*

Date	Major literary event
June	Tian Jian's (田间) anthology, *Chinese Pastoral Songs* (《中国牧歌》), was published by Shanghai Poets Press
July 1	"Manifesto of the Chinese Workers on Literature and Art" (《中国文艺工作者宣言》) was delivered by sixty-three people including Lu Xun, Ba Jin, Cao Yu, Wu Zuxiang, Zhang Tianyi, Cao Jinghua, and Xiao Jun
July 1	Guo Moruo's memoir, *On the Road of the Northern Expedition* (《北伐途次》), began to be serialized in *Cosmic Wind* (Issue 20), with its separate edition published by Shanghai Chaofeng Press in January the following year
July 1	*Realistic Literature* (《现实文学》) monthly was launched in Shanghai, whose editors-in-chief were Yin Geng and Bai Shu. It was discontinued in August of the same year after two issues had been published
July 10	*The Posterity of Traitors*, a collectively created spoken drama play written by You Jing (aka Yu Ling), was published in *Light* (Vol. 1, Issue 3), with its separate edition published by Shanghai Life Bookstore in January of the following year
July	Li Jieren's novel *Ripples on Stagnant Water* was published by Shanghai Zhonghua Book Company (some sources claim it was published in July 1935)
July	He Qifang's collection of prose writings, *Painted Dreams*, was published by Shanghai Cultural Life Press
July	Tian Jian's lengthy narrative poem, "The Story of China's Countryside" (《中国农村的故事》), was published by Shanghai Poets Press
July	Zhu Guangqian's work on aesthetics, *The Psychology of Literature and Art* (《文艺心理学》), was published by Shanghai Kaiming Bookstore
July	Lao She quit his job at Shandong University and devoted all his time and energy to writing
Aug. 1	Duanmu Hongliang published his short story "The Sorrows of Egret Lake" in *Literature* (Vol. 7, Issue 2)
Aug. 1	Lu Xun published "Reply to Xu Maoyong and on the Issue of United Anti-Japanese Front" (《答徐懋庸并关于抗日统一战线问题》) in *Writers* (Vol. 1, Issue 5)
August	Li Ni's collection of prose writings, *Songs of Hawk* (《鹰之歌》), was published by Shanghai Cultural Life Press
August	Lu Li's (陆蠡) collection of prose writings, *Starfish* (《海星》), was published by Shanghai Cultural Life Press
August	Xiao Hong's collection of prose writings, *Market Street*, was published by Shanghai Cultural Life Press
Sep. 1	Luo Shu's short story "A Stranger's Wife" (《生人妻》) was published in *Literary Season Monthly* (Vol. 1, Issue 4). A collection of short stories with the same title was published by Shanghai Cultural Life Press in 1938
Sep. 5	*Mainstream* (《中流》) semimonthly was launched in Shanghai, whose editor-in-chief was Li Liewen. Twenty-two issues were published before it was discontinued in 1937

(continued)

TABLE 28.1 *(continued)*

Date	Major literary event
Sep. 16	Lao She's novel *Camel Xiangzi* began to be serialized in *Cosmic Wind* (Issue 25), with its separate edition published by Shanghai Human World Bookstore in March 1939
Sep. 18	Ding Ling fled from Nanjing to Shanghai with the protection of the underground CPC organization and later passed through many places to Northern Shaanxi in secret
September	The collectively created street play *Put down Your Whip*, which was rewritten by Chen Liting (陈鲤庭) based on the one-act play adapted by Tian Han, was published in *Guide to Everyday Life* (Vol. 2, Issue 9)
September	The lengthy collection of works of reportage, *One Day in China* (《中国的一日》), compiled by Mao Dun, was published by Shanghai Life Bookstore. It collected nearly 500 works that reflected the life of Chinese people on the day of May 21
September	Shi Zhecun's collection of short stories, *Small Treasures*, was published by the Young Companion Printing and Publishing Company
Oct. 1	"Manifesto of Artists and Writers on Solidarity against Aggression and for Freedom of Speech" (《文艺界同人为团结御侮与言论自由宣言》) was jointly delivered by twenty-one people including Lu Xun, Mao Dun, Guo Moruo, Ba Jin, Lin Yutang, Bao Tianxiao, and Feng Zikai
Oct. 1	Xiao Hong's short story "On the Ox Cart" was published in *Literary Season Monthly* (Vol. 1, Issue 5)
Oct. 1	*Poetry Magazine* (《诗歌杂志》), the journal of the Chinese Poem Writers' Association (中国诗歌作者协会), was launched in Shanghai and its editors-in-chief were Meng Ying (孟英) and others
Oct. 5	Lu Xun's essay "The Ghost of a Hanged Woman" (《女吊》) was published in *Mainstream* (Vol. 1, Issue 3)
Oct. 15	*Novelists* monthly was launched in Shanghai, whose editor-in-chief was Ouyang Shan. It was discontinued in December of this year after two issues had been published
Oct. 16	*New Poetry* monthly was launched in Shanghai, whose editors included Bian Zhilin, Sun Dayu, Liang Zongdai, Feng Zhi, and Dai Wangshu
Oct. 17	Lu Xun wrote his last, unfinished essay, "A Few Things Recollected in Connection to Mr. Taiyan"
5:25 a.m., Oct. 19	Lu Xun died in his residence at Continental Village in Shanghai at the age of 56. On the same day, a funeral committee was organized by Cai Yuanpei, Song Qingling, and others, and an "Obituary of Mr. Lu Xun" was delivered
16:30 p.m., Oct. 22	Lu Xun's funeral was held in Shanghai International Cemetery
October	Mao Dun's collection of prose writings, *Impressions, Reflections, Recollections* (《印象·感想·回忆》), was published by Shanghai Cultural Life Press
October	Zhou Zuoren's collection of prose writings, *Talks of Wind and Rain* (《风雨谈》), was published by Shanghai Beixin Press

(continued)

TABLE 28.1 *(continued)*

Date	Major literary event
October	Du Yunxie's (杜运燮) anthology, *Forty Poems* (《诗四十首》), was published by Shanghai Cultural Life Press
October	Wang Yaping's anthology, *Songs of the Petrels* (《海燕之歌》), was published by Shanghai Joint Press
Nov. 1	The Preparatory Meeting of the Mr. Lu Xun Memorial Committee was organized in Shanghai, which consisted of seventeen people including Cai Yuanpei, Song Qingling, Kanzo Uchiyama, Mao Dun, Xu Jingsong (许景宋, aka Xu Guangping), and Zhou Jianren
Nov. 10	Ai Qing published his anthology *Dayanhe* at his own expense, which was entrusted to be sold by Shanghai Mass Magazine Company
Nov. 10	Bian Zhilin published the poem "The Ichthyolite" in *New Poetry* (Issue 2)
Nov. 22	The Association of Writers of Beiping (北平作家协会) was established, whose first executive committee consisted of eleven people including Sun Xizhen (孙席珍), Cao Jinghua, Li Helin (李何林), Lu Kanru (陆侃如), and Wang Xiyan (王西彦)
Nov. 22	The Chinese Literary and Artistic Association (中国文艺协会) was established in Bao'an (保安) in Northern Shaanxi, whose first council consisted of fifteen people headed by Ding Ling
November	Lao She's collection of short stories *Clams and Seaweed* (《蛤藻集》) was published by Shanghai Kaiming Bookstore
November	Xiao Hong's collection of short stories and prose writings, *The Bridge*, was published by Shanghai Cultural Life Press
November	Li Guangtian's collection of prose writings, *The Silver Fox Collection*, was published by Shanghai Cultural Life Press
Dec. 25	Zhou Libo's literary criticism, "Review of Fiction Creation in 1936" (《一九三六年小说创作的回顾》), was published in *Light* (Vol. 2, Issue 2)
December	Li Jieren's novel *On the Eve of the Storm* was published by Shanghai Zhonghua Book Company
December	Ye Zi's novella *Stars* (《星》) was published by Shanghai Cultural Life Press
December	The collection of literary criticism by Liu Xiwei (aka Li Jianwu), *Relishing Flowers* (《咀华集》), was published by Shanghai Cultural Life Press
December	Zhang Ziping's novel *Love between Young People* (《青年的爱》) was published by Shanghai Hezhong Bookstore
This year	The novel *The Paperboy* (《送报伕》), written by Taiwanese author Yang Kui, was published by Shanghai Cultural Life Press
This year	The collection of news stories by Fan Changjiang (范长江) entitled *The Northwest Corner of China* (《中国的西北角》) was published by the editorial office of Tianjin's *Ta Kung Pao*

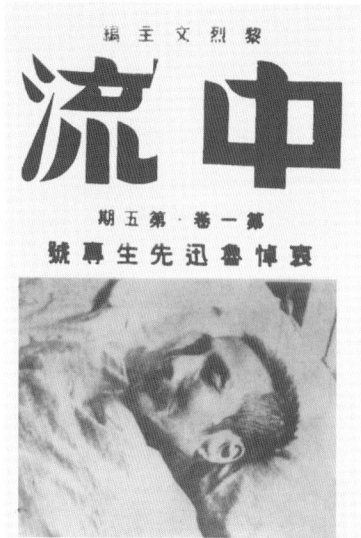

28.2. *Mainstream*'s Lu Xun Memorial Issue; the photo on the cover was taken by Sha Fei (沙飞)

28.3. *Life Weekly*'s Lu Xun Memorial Issue; the photo on the cover was taken by Sha Fei

Its opposition was the high cultural pressure from the Kuomintang government and authors promoting "nationalist literature" who had connections with the government. The achievements of left-wing literature in 1936 included Lu Xun's collection of historical stories, *Old Tales Retold*, which was the last collection published before he died. Then he also published his last miscellaneous essays, including "Reply to Xu Maoyong and on the Issue of United Anti-Japanese Front," "Death," "The Ghost of a Hanged Woman," and "A Few Things about Zhang Taiyan," as well as his unfinished essay "A Few Things Recollected in Connection to Mr. Taiyan." Zhang Tianyi published his important collection *The Eccentric*; Xiao Hong published her short stories "Hands" and "On the Ox Cart"; and Ai Qing wrote his maiden poem "Dayanhe." Xia Yan's play *Sai Jinhua* was considered a major achievement of the "national defense drama," and was well received when it was performed. The "national defense drama" was a slogan raised by Zhou Yang, the actual leader of *Zuolian*, and others. Later, on behalf of Lu Xun who was on his sickbed, Hu Feng raised the slogan of "Mass Literature of National Revolutionary War" to oppose Zhou Yang, which was known as the debate over "two slogans" within *Zuolian*. When Feng Xuefeng went to Shanghai from Northern Shaanxi, he was sent by the CPC Central Committee to set up a united anti-Japanese front of the literary circle, but he was disapproved of by people of Zhou Yang's sect who claimed that he was too close to Lu Xun. Despite Lu Xun's will, however, *Zuolian* was finally dissolved for the need of the "united front." In October of this year Lu Xun died after exhausting all his energy, so much so that he only weighed 38.7 kg before his death. Lu Xun's death brought about the Chinese people's largest memorial ceremony to mourn the "spirit of the nation."

The second part was Beijing school literature, whose influence was second only to left-wing literature. Based on May Fourth realistic literature, the left-wing authors learned from the literature of the

USSR and explicitly experimented with various avant-garde writings in the name of "revolutionary realism," seeking to bring all genres of modern literature into the "discipline" of realism. It was a group-oriented literature full of ambitions and dreams. Approaching literature with a rigid sociological understanding as it was, its resistant nature gave it a kind of spiritual twist. Beijing school authors, on the other hand, gathered in the north with a shared passion for academic culture and literary beauty as well as a conscious detachment from politics and political sects. They championed individuality and spiritual independence. Believing that the collectivity promoted by left-wing authors would surely stifle individuality, they consciously combined human nature, commoners, and individuality in their literature. Beijing school literature was more avant-garde in literary styles and forms. The year 1936 saw prolific literary works by Beijing school authors, and they could well match left-wing authors. In prose writing, there were Zhou Zuoren's *Bitter Bamboo Miscellanies*, Shen Congwen's *Discursive Notes on Traveling through Hunan*, and He Qifang's *Painted Dreams*, which represented three different styles respectively, and were all books of far-reaching influence. In novel writing, there was Xiao Qian's *Under the Fence of Others*, and in poetry there was *The Han Garden Collection*, coauthored by Bian Zhilin, He Qifang, and Li Guangtian, as well as Bian Zhilin's famous poem "The Ichthyolite." Bian's poems had a kind of intellectual obscurity characteristic of modernist poetry, making them interesting and thought-provoking, and they have become more and more appreciated and loved by people of later ages. In literary criticism, there was Liu Xiwei's *Relishing Flowers*, in which almost every critical essay was a finely written piece, making it an excellent book of Beijing school impressionist literary criticism. These only formed a small part of the achievements of Beijing school authors, but show the strength of this literary school.

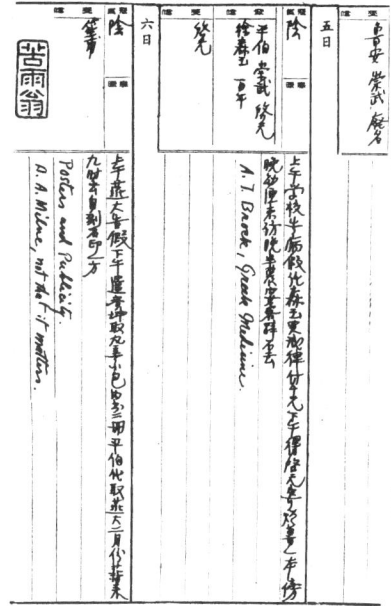

28.4. Page from Zhou Zuoren's handwritten diary, March 5–6, 1930

28.5. Dai Wangshu in Madrid, Spain, in 1934

The third part was Shanghai school literature. If we see left-wing literature as politically utilitarian and Beijing school literature as detached from worldly gains, Shanghai school literature was a profit-oriented literature that viewed literature as a means of entertainment and leisure. Led by the former members of the Creation Society, Shanghai school authors, as part of New Literature, plunged into this "commercial world." This year, Zhang Ziping continued writing his popular novels about polyamory (such as *Love between Young People*). Ye Lingfeng practiced writing New Sensationalist novels and at the same time had his popular novels serialized in newspapers (his *Unfinished Confession* was published this year). Later, both of them left the Creation Society. New Sensationalism was close to its end at this time, except that Shi Zhecun's *Small Treasures* could be seen as a new trend, in which such works as "Seagull" and "The Spiritual Response of the Pagoda" broke the barriers between modernism and realism and between the countryside, civil society, and the metropolis, juxtaposing the evilness and beauty of the urban city, contrasting it against the countryside while avoiding absolute antagonism. When he was editing *The Contemporaries* magazine, Shi Zhecun cooperated with Dai Wangshu and promoted modern poetry writing. Dai Wangshu's earlier poem "Rainy Alley" (《雨巷》) was written within the framework of romantic poetry, so Bian Zhilin once said it "seemed an extended or 'diluted' vernacular version of the old-style verse 'The Lilac Could Nurse Sorrows of the Rain' (丁香能结雨中愁)."[2] It was not until the period when he wrote "The Cut Finger" (《断指》), "My Memories" (《我的记忆》), and "Bird of Paradise" (《乐园鸟》) that he finally absorbed what he had learned from the later-stage Western symbolistic poetry and raised the banner of Chinese symbolistic poetry. This was similar to the case of New Sensationalist authors, who had learned from Japanese authors and then wrote brilliant Chinese New Sensationalist works. Dai's later poems "Inscribed on the Prison Wall" (《狱中题壁》) and "With My Injured Hand" (《我用残损的手掌》) were once exaggerated as the best of his poems, but they were actually no more than symbolistic poems written with a realistic tinge, something like Shi Zhecun's *Small Treasures*. In the end, Dai Wangshu was a Shanghai school poet.

The fourth part was Mandarin Duck and Butterfly literature, an urban popular literary genre. Popular

28.6. Cover of Zhang Henshui's *Deep in the Night*, published by Sanyou Press in 1941

---

[2]   Bian Zhilin: "Preface to *Poetry Anthology of Dai Wangshu*" (《戴望舒诗集·序》), *Poetry Anthology of Dai Wangshu*, Chengdu: Sichuan People's Press, 1981.

literature had always been an important part of modern Chinese literature that kept a watchful eye on avant-garde literature, but different literary schools defined the term "popular" differently. Left-wing literature had the popular readers of political literature, and throughout its lifespan *Zuolian* was discussing the problem of how "proletarian literature" could access the masses, and they also tried, but failed, to write popular novels. In the CPC-controlled Soviet area in Jiangxi, writers practiced massification of drama and poetry, which laid the foundation for literary massification in the "great hinterland" and Yan'an during the Anti-Japanese War, and it was also a path toward the modern "popularization" of literature. While practicing avant-garde writing, Shanghai school authors also tried popularization, which could be seen as a kind of compromise in order to win over new-style citizen readers. However, the Mandarin Duck and Butterfly school had been completely about urban popular literature from the very beginning, but as urban citizens changed with the times, this group adapted itself to the modern era, in order to keep pace with its urban popular readers. Zhang Henshui could best represent this process of popularization. In writing and innovating the genre of linked-chapter novels, he learned and borrowed from New Literature, trying to enhance the expressiveness and widen the readership of this traditional literary genre. In 1936, while his masterpieces *The Story of A Noble Family* and *Fate in Tears and Laughter* had already been published and his Anti-Japanese War novels had not yet taken shape, in June his *Deep in the Night* began to be serialized in the *Daily News*, which, totally different from his earlier novels about the tragic love between people from different classes and backgrounds, was a soul-stirring love story between Yang Yuerong, a street performing girl, and Ding Erhe, a cart driver, both lower-class citizens. *Deep in the Night* was thus an important work for Zhang Henshui and he became a master of popular novels in modern Chinese literary history.

Once they were formed in the 1930s, these four literary "parts" had an enormous and profound influence on the landscape of modern Chinese literature. Afterwards, emerging genres might alternatively dominate the literary scene for a while, avant-garde literature might gradually become commonly seen, but the avant-garde status and popular status of political literature, belles lettres, and profit-oriented literature, the penetration and interactions between the statuses of these three kinds of literature, became a fundamental motif of modern Chinese literature for quite a while. It was a period that saw the mixture of modern group-oriented literature and modern individual-oriented literature. Such a vast mixture may accommodate the transformation between diverse kinds of literature. The "*Analects* sect" led by Lin Yutang, for example, was a literary clique lingering somewhere between left-wing, Beijing school, and Shanghai school. Deriving from the "Yu Si sect," these authors originally wavered between Lu Xun and Zhou Zuoren (on whether one must chase the

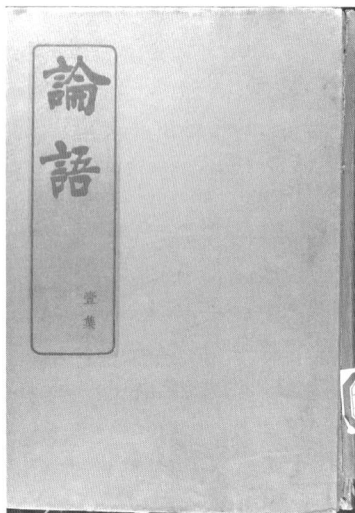

28.7. *Analects* was well received because it promoted humor. It had a circulation of 30,000–40,000 urban citizens

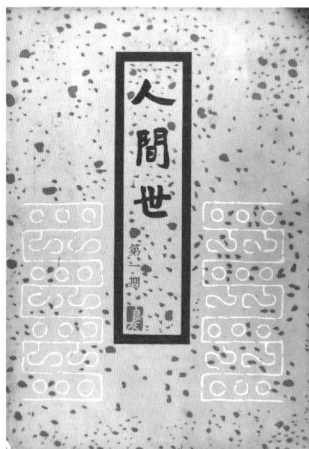

28.8. Another journal of casual essays, *This Human World*, was launched by Lin Yutang a year after *Analects* was published, due to the disagreement between Lin and Shao Xunmei. Its editor-in-chief was Tao Kangde

dog into the river and hit it or whether one should insist on fair play), but soon began to promote humor, leisure, innate sensibility, and punctuating Ming sketches and casual writings, becoming more in concert with Zhou Zuoren of the Beijing school. At first Lu Xun contributed articles to Lin's *Analects* magazine, and when he wrote "A Year of *Analects*" at Lin's request, he made it clear in the opening that: "I often disapprove of what he promotes. First it was 'fair play' and now it is 'humor'."[3] After *Analects* semi-monthly came *This Human World* and *Cosmic Wind*, which collectively constituted a series of Lin Yutang-style popular cultural journals for urban citizens. When *This Human World* was launched in April 1934, Lin asked for Zhou Zuoren's handwritten poem to celebrate his own birthday, and printed it in the magazine with a large-size photo, which caused a stir among intellectuals. Lin Yutang's frequent interactions with such May Fourth veterans as

28.9. Feng Zikai and his third elder sister Tingfang (庭芳), taken after he cut her hair, which shows the taste of people of his generation

---

3   Lu Xun: "A Year of *Analects*," *Complete Works of Lu Xun*, Vol. 4, Beijing: People's Literature Press, 1981, p. 567.

28.10. Lin Yutang's handwriten poem in response to Zhou Zuoren's poem to celebrate Zhou's own birthday, published in *This Human World*

Qian Xuantong, Hu Shi, and Cai Yuanpei outraged Hu Feng and other young authors, and they began debating on newspapers. This, actually, meant it was an era when liberal authors and left-wing authors coexisted. And we could regard the "Kaiming sect" authors (thus called because these authors, including Xia Mianzun, Ye Shengtao, and Feng Zikai, gathered in Shanghai Kaiming Bookstore) as Beijing school authors based in Shanghai. Living and writing in this business world and editing books and magazines for profit, these authors were honest and righteous and naturally amiable. They worked as writers, editors, and educators at the same time, giving up political sectarianism, and had a strong sense of responsibility; they were from the Literary Research Society, but they were modest and self-disciplined gentlemen without the unruly temperament of Shanghai school talents or combativeness of left-wing authors. Feng Zikai's literary achievements could best represent the style of this sect, and he deserved a higher position in the history of modern Chinese prose writing. Overall, examining the "Kaiming sect" from the broader perspective of the 1930s when four literary constituent parts coexisted, we could see the unique characteristics of this sect quite distinctively. And this was also true for other literary phenomena.

Generally, these four constituent parts of literature contained three kinds of literary views: the left-wing authors' utilitarian view of literature, the Shanghai school and Mandarin Duck and Butterfly authors' view of literature as entertainment, and the Beijing school authors' position of detachment and distance. This is key to our understanding of the literary trends, movements, and theoretical criticism of the 1930s. In the compilation of the *Compendium of Chinese New Literature* mentioned at the beginning of this chapter, we can see that since the series was taken charge of by May Fourth literary veterans, the

《鲁迅杂感选集》序言·

（一九三三年四月八日）

自己背着因袭的重担，肩住了黑暗的闸门，放他们到宽
阔光明的地方去……

——鲁迅：《坟》

象牙塔里的绅士总会假清高的笑骂："政治家，政治
家，你算得什么艺术家呢！你的艺术是有倾向的！"对于
这种嘲笑，革命文学家只有一个回答：

你想用什么来骂倒我呢？难道因为我要改造世界的那种
热诚的巨大火焰，它在我的艺术里也在燃烧着么？

——卢那察尔斯基①：《高尔基②作品选集序》

革命的作家总是公开地表示他们和社会斗争的联
系；他们不但在自己的作品里表现一定的思想，而且时常
用一个公民的资格出来对社会说话，为着自己的理想而
战斗，暴露那些假清高的绅士艺术家的虚伪。高尔基
小说戏剧之外，写了很多的公开书信和"社会论文"（Pu-
blicist articles），尤其在最近几年——社会的政治的斗争

28.11. "Preface to *A Selection of Lu Xun's Random Thoughts*" by Qu Qiubai (see *Collected Works of Qu Qiubai*)

sharp oppositions between different literary groups were invisible or hidden against the vast panoramic backdrop. Actually, of the literary criticisms of the 1930s, there were two loud voices, namely left-wing criticism and Beijing school criticism, from which we can gain some in-depth understanding of this literary era.

There were many typical characters and events in left-wing literary criticism. Lu Xun's criticism was diversified, and when he mentioned Russian literature and the literature of weak and small European nations, when he analyzed Xiao Hong's extremely original style that often deviated from conventional rules, he did not identify with the social utilitarian and social reflective critical views held by Mao Dun and Zhou Yang. He expressed his liberal and open-minded acceptance of the excellent cultural heritage of human civilization, and did not restrict himself to the Marxist views on literature and art that had just been introduced to China and preliminarily interpreted. Mao Dun focused his attention on literary and art criticism earlier in his career, and influenced by French literature and literary theories, he emphasized that literature should reflect the social life and the specific era, as well as the enlightening and educating purpose of literature, and analyzed literary forms based on this view. By the 1930s, influenced by Marxist literary theories, Mao Dun adopted the discussion on writers as his major literary critic style, and set an example for left-wing literary criticism. In all his "discussions on writers" that we can read today, including those on Lu Xun, Wang Luyan, Xu Zhimo, Ding Ling, Lu Yin, Bing Xin, and Luo Huasheng (aka Xu Dishan), we can see that these were all well-known "petty bourgeoisie authors" who had been indiscriminately denied by left-wing political literary criticism during the period "revolutionary literature" was promoted. This was somehow an act of correction. In analyzing authors and their works, Mao Dun departed from the requirements of society and the specific era, clung tightly to the authors' class and ideological position, and pointed at the political leaning of the literary works. As for the form of the work, he adopted the criterion of "unification of content and form" to see whether these two were consistent. There were elements of leftist mechanism here, but since Mao Dun was well read in world literature and could appreciate art, the flaws caused by his ignorance of the authors' artistic core may be somehow offset. And he was especially insufficient in his "qualitative" analysis of the authors who did not pay much attention to social reflection, such as Xu Zhimo. The "social-historical literary criticism" established by Mao Dun within the left-wing camp had a strong long-term influence on literary creation. The epochal, epic, social, and ideological nature became important concepts that should be valued by literary authors, and dominated literary creation until the 1980s. Qu Qiubai's criticism of Lu Xun was no less important than the literary criticism of Mao Dun, represented by his "Preface to *A Selection of Lu Xun's Random Thoughts*" written in 1933. Qu Qiubai adopted an authoritative style in bringing the entire cultural and ideological revolution into the field of "class analysis" and bringing the drawbacks, splitting, and transformation of May Fourth New Literature and New Culture into the perspective of "proletarian revolution," which was quite advanced at that time and achieved precision and incisiveness. It was not only regarded as a peak in the history of Lu Xun research, but as a good example of how dialectical materialism and historical materialism could be applied to sociohistorical literary criticism.

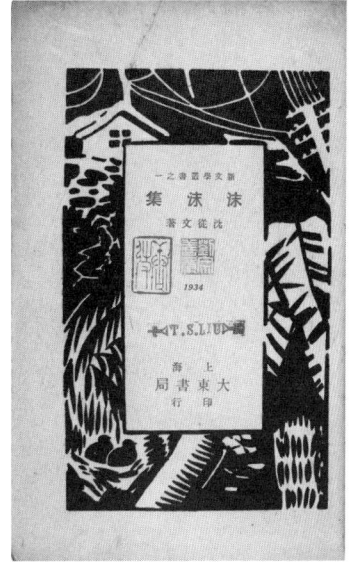

28.12. Title page of the 1934 edition of Shen Congwen's collection of literary criticism, *Collection of Foam* (《沫沫集》)

28.13. Inaugural issue of *Six Arts* (《六艺》) magazine, launched in 1936. This cartoon entitled "Tea Chart of the Literary Circle" was about a gathering of literary writers and critics from different schools and sects

Beijing school literary criticism was important in that it inherited the May Fourth tradition and sought to combine Western theories and traditional Chinese literary criticism. It adopted Zhou Zuoren's guideline literary historical work *On the Origins of China's New Literature* as the basic theoretical pattern, which was carried forward by Fei Ming and Yu Pingbo of the same sect. The literary criticism of Liu Xiwei (aka Li Jianwu) and Zhu Guangqian could be seen as integrating Western and traditional Chinese styles. Shen Congwen's comments on writers were aimed directly at literature for profit and literature for political purposes. The core of these literary criticisms was "human beings." Beijing school authors wrote "individual literature," and its judgment of literature was naturally based on the creation and expression of "individuals" and how "individuals" were explored. It opposed the suppression of "individuals" by collectivity and literature as a vehicle of moral instruction.

It is within the entanglement and conflicts between diversified literature that we see a real world: the Chinese literary world of the 1930s.

TWENTY NINE

INTERACTIONS BETWEEN CINEMATOGRAPHIC ART AND LITERATURE

Inside the Eastern China Hotel –

Second floor: white-painted rooms, the fragrance of bronze opium pipes, Mahjong tiles, the sound of *The Fourth Son Visits His Mother*, the high-class prostitute calling the low-class one a bitch, the cologne perfume and smell of lust, the waiters in white, prostitutes and middlemen, kidnappers, schemes and trickeries, Russian rogues …

Third floor: white-painted rooms, the fragrance of bronze opium pipes, Mahjong tiles, the sound of *The Fourth Son Visits His Mother*, the high-class prostitute calling the low-class one a bitch, the cologne perfume and smell of lust, the waiters in white, prostitutes and middlemen, kidnappers, schemes and trickeries, Russian rogues …

Fourth floor: white-painted rooms, the fragrance of bronze opium pipes, Mahjong tiles, the sound of *The Fourth Son Visits His Mother*, the high-class prostitute calling the low-class one a bitch, the cologne perfume and smell of lust, the waiters in white, prostitutes and middlemen, kidnappers, schemes and trickeries, Russian rogues …

The lift disgorged him on the fourth floor, and Mr. Liu Youde, humming the tune of *The Fourth Son Visits His Mother*, stepped into a room full of the sound of Mahjong tiles.[1]

Written by the New Sensationalist writer Mu Shiying in the 1930s, these sentences were much like film scenes. Reading the lines, you seemed to be brought

---

[1] Mu Shiying: "Shanghai Foxtrot," *Cemetery*, Shanghai: Modern Book Company, 1933, pp. 206–207. The ellipsis dots are quoted from the original text. In order to avoid confusion, the ellipsis dots are omitted at the end of the final quoted paragraph.

inside a lift (which were quite rare things in those days) and taken to the higher floors of a building. The camera shot swept over each floor, on which there were scenes of the "corrupt" lives of rich people in Shanghai, and you were brought into very specific (visibly and audibly) detailed scenes. This was a typical example of how the modern art form of film affected the narrative of Chinese novels, and we can see that modern material life, together with modern art, had largely penetrated the domain of literature in this 1930s metropolis. Such penetration and reverse penetration were not limited to film and literature, however; other art forms, such as painting, music, drama, journalism, and pictorials, were all closely related with literature. Literature was not an isolated art form, but was inextricably linked with other cultural media and environments. Here I want to take the emerging film art of the twentieth century as an example and try to put this interrelationship into the context of literary history.

From the perspective of Chinese film history, during the period of silent films, it was literature that influenced film and not vice versa. Film, as an art form, was introduced to China quite early on. The world's first film was shown in Paris in 1895, and it was shown in the teahouses and entertainment places in Shanghai the following year. An article entitled "Watching American Shadow Play" (《观美国影戏记》) in *Entertainment* wrote about watching film, instead of slide shows, in the public places in Shanghai, and the date was 1897.[2] By 1907, a Spanish man called Ramos had built Hongkou Cinema, the first cinema in Shanghai. Later a number of foreign-funded cinemas were built, which showed foreign films, and the audiences were largely foreigners or higher-class Chinese people who could afford the tickets (the price of a cinema ticket was as high as two or three silver dollars, which was not affordable for ordinary people). The production of Chinese domestic films didn't start until later; 1905 is generally set as the date. That year, a section of Tan Xinpei's (谭鑫培) Peking opera documentary *Dingjun Mountain* (《定军山》) was shot in Fengtai Photo Place (丰泰照相馆) of Dashilan Street near the Front Gate of Beijing. The first Chinese feature film, however, was not shot until 1913, when the film *A Couple in Difficulty* (《难夫难妻》) was shot in the foreign-funded Asian Film Company (亚细亚影片公司) in Shanghai. The crew of this feature film included Zheng Zhengqiu as the screenwriter (who had watched spoken drama plays performed by foreigners in the Lyceum Theater and had played the lead role in the civilized drama *Resurgence of the Jiayin Year*) and Zhang Shichuan as the director, both closely related with civilized drama and had initiated the New People Society and Minming Troupe. At that time, they adopted a plot outline system to shoot films, in which the director explained the story of each plot to the actors and then shot their improvisation. This

[2] Fan Boqun, ed.: *A History of Modern Chinese Popular Literature*, Beijing: Peking University Press, 2007, pp. 393–394.

29.1. Exterior of Hongkou Cinema, the very first cinema built in China

showed the influence of spoken drama on film at its earlier stage. Later, when filmmakers began adapting their filmscripts based on published novels or translated novels, or even mobilized literary writers to create special stories for filmmaking, the filmmaking industry was dominated by Mandarin Duck and Butterfly authors.

It was easy to understand why the Mandarin Duck and Butterfly literature was closely related with filmmaking. Zheng Zhengqiu, Zhang Shichuan and others established Mingxing Studio in 1922, which was one of China's earliest commercial filmmaking institutions, and we may take it as an example to have a look at Mandarin Duck and Butterfly films. In 1923, *The Orphan Rescues Grandfather* (《孤儿救祖记》), produced by Mingxing Studio and based on the Mandarin Duck and Butterfly-style love story, was an immediate success. This was regarded by film historians as the landmark showing the earliest artistic pursuit of Chinese feature films. From this time until 1933, when Mao Dun's *Spring Silkworms* was produced by Mingxing Studio, Chinese films almost had nothing to do with New Literature. The audiences in the cities were mostly urban citizens, who liked to watch popular plots and characters from the films. Writers of New Literature simply turned up their nose at the vulgar and coarsely made domestic films, and therefore these two were not related at that time. In 1924, Zheng Zhengqiu adapted a filmscript based on a famous literary work, from the earliest Mandarin Duck and Butterfly literature, Xu Zhenya's *Jade Pear Spirit*. According to Bao Tianxiao, another famous Mandarin Duck and Butterfly author, when these films were first produced in China, "Mingxing Studio stopped suffering from lack of good stories, but were in want of good filmscripts," so they asked him

29.2. "Produced by Mingxing Studio," China's first martial arts film, *The Burning of Red Lotus Temple*, starring Hu Die (on the left), was extremely popular; Zheng Xiaoqiu is on the right

to adapt two of his novels, *Orchid in an Empty Valley* (《空谷兰》) and *The Fall of the Plum Blossom* (《梅花落》), into filmscripts. Later they produced another film based on Bao's short story "A Strand of Flax," and changed its name to *A Couple in Name* (《挂名夫妻》), which was the very first film starring Ruan Lingyu (阮玲玉).[3] After 1928, Zheng Zhengqiu and Zhang Shichuan continued their cooperation at Mingxing Studio and adapted part of the story of the martial arts fiction by Pingjiang Buxiaosheng (Xiang

29.3. After the film of *The Burning of Red Lotus Temple* was shown, its popularity continued for a long time, and could still be felt through the advertisement for the Peking opera version in *Shun Pao* on January 1, 1936

3   Bao Tianxiao: "The Film and I (Part 1)" ("我与电影（上）"), *Sequel to Memoirs of the Bracelet Shadow Chamber* (《钏影楼回忆录续编》), Hong Kong: Dahua Press, 1973, pp. 95–96, 104.

Kairan), *Marvelous Gallants of the Rivers and Lakes*, into an eighteen-episode film entitled *The Burning of Red Lotus Temple* (《火烧红莲寺》), starring Zheng Zhengqiu's daughter, Zheng Xiaoqiu, and Hu Die, who would later become an extremely popular film star. The film started an upsurge of Chinese martial arts film. The popularity of this film shocked left-wing writers. Mao Dun, for example, had written about the spectacle in the cinema: "Upon stepping inside any cinema when this film was shown, you could see the magic power of *The Burning of Red Lotus Temple* to lower-class urban citizens. Applause and cheers are not forbidden in those cinemas; you are surrounded by frenetic fans, and whenever the swordsmen characters were fighting each other, the cheers of the audience were as loud as the battles in the film. … It was *The Burning of Red Lotus Temple* that first had strong emotional effects on ordinary people."[4] Mao Dun took a critical view toward this, but what he said recorded the atmosphere among audiences of that time. Quite a number of Mandarin Duck and Butterfly authors participated in filmmaking, including Zhou Shoujuan, Cheng Xiaoqing, Zheng Yimei, Yao Sufeng, Xu Zhuodai, Gu Mingdao (顾明道), and Wang Dungen. Yan Duhe, in particular, participated in the production of China's first sound film, *Sing-Song Girl Red Peony* (《歌女红牡丹》), in 1931, and after inviting Zhang Henshui to write *Fate in Tears and Laughter* for "Forest of Pleasure," a supplement of *Shun Pao*, seeing its popularity, he adapted this novel into an influential and widespread filmscript.

Such a close interrelationship between Mandarin Duck and Butterfly literature and film production surely had a positive effect. It lent real support to domestic filmmaking, and thus domestic films, coarsely made as they were, could rival imported foreign films and gain a market share with their advantages of lower costs and ticket prices. Since Mandarin Duck and Butterfly literature already occupied a share of the urban cultural market and had helped to develop a group of urban citizen readers with certain reading habits and preferences, the filmmakers could easily gain the readers of the Mandarin Duck and Butterfly stories, who in turn became the mid- and lower-class urban citizen audience of domestic Chinese films (surely a negative effect was that these films catered to the low and vulgar tastes and interests of urban citizens). And the well-developed typology of Mandarin Duck and Butterfly novels could be transplanted to earlier Chinese films, such as romantic films and martial arts films. Its other effects included the literary characteristics of the camera narrative of Chinese films, the moral pattern of film stories, the relative weakness of audio and visual features, and the importance of "captions" during the period of silent films.

---

[4] Mao Dun: "Feudal Philistine Art and Literature" (《封建的小市民文艺》), *Complete Works of Mao Dun*, Vol. 19, Beijing: People's Literature Press, 1991, pp. 369–370.

The article by Mao Dun quoted earlier revealed the long-term contempt by authors of left-wing New Literature toward Mandarin Duck and Butterfly films. Mao Dun not only criticized *The Burning of Red Lotus Temple*, but at the end of the same article, he also criticized the film *Fate in Tears and Laughter*. This situation did not change until after 1932, and its reason had something to do with the January Twenty-Eighth Incident in Shanghai. Due to the deepening national crisis caused by the invasion of imperial Japan, urban citizens had unprecedented patriotic emotions, and the filmmakers engaged in producing Mandarin Duck and Butterfly films were sensitive to the change of sentiments among their audiences, and thus invited left-wing writers to participate in their films. The most seasoned left-wing filmmaker (who was also a playwright), Xia Yan, had recalled how Hong Shen suggested Mingxing Studio should "change its direction" and "invite some left-wing authors to be screenwriters and consultants." Receiving their invitation, Xia Yan was very cautious, and did not decide on infiltrating the filmmaking circle until several discussions were held during the meetings of the "Cultural Committee" chaired by Qu Qiubai.[5] That year, Xia Yan, Qian Xingcun, and Zheng Boqi worked for Mingxing Studio using aliases, and Mingxing shot Mao Dun's *Spring Silkworms* the following year. After the Team of Film Critics was established by the Shanghai Association of Theatrical Performance, the Film Team that directly reported to the Cultural Committee was established and chaired by Xia Yan, evidence that the left-wing camp was determined to occupy the

29.4. Left-wing film literature was extremely popular, and thus its critical journal *Film Art* (《电影艺术》) was published

29.5. *Sha Lun* was the earliest left-wing journal about films, which integrated film, theater, and literature

[5]   See Xia Yan: "Infiltrating the Filmmaking Circle" (《进入电影界》), *A Recollection of Old Dreams*, Beijing: Joint Publishing, 1985, pp. 224–237.

popular art domain of film. Besides Mingxing, Tian Han, Yang Hansheng, and Xia Yan also worked for Yihua Film Company (艺华电影公司) in 1933. Tian Han's *Light of Motherhood* (《母性之光》) and *Three Modern Women* (《三个摩登女性》), Xia Yan's *Spring Silkworms, Twenty-Four Hours in Shanghai* (《上海二十四小时》), and *The Torrents* (《狂流》), Qian Xingcun and Zheng Boqi's *Salt Tide* (《盐潮》), Yang Hansheng's *A Tale of Red Tears* (《铁板红泪录》), Zheng Boqi's *Children of the Times* (《时代的儿女》, in cooperation with Xia Yan and Qian Xingcun), and other films were produced and shown successively and were well received by urban citizens. A period of left-wing films thus started.

Generally, these left-wing authors involved in filmmaking were playwrights. They abandoned the preliminary shooting techniques and relied heavily on stories and began to use screen scripts. Not trained in filmmaking as he was, Xia Yan helped Cheng Bugao (程步高), a director of Mingxing Studio, to complete the shooting script of *The Torrents*, which was the first one in China's film history. This became an important factor of the standardization and high quality of film screenwriting and direction. Left-wing literature also brought a strong sense of social responsibility into films, seeking to reflect the sufferings of ordinary people and strengthening the theme of social critique in their films. Left-wing literature, on the other hand, also learned an important lesson from film, so that during this popularization practice targeted at urban citizens, left-wing authors had a deeper understanding of the real popular art

29.6. Mao Dun's *Spring Silkworms* was adapted into a film by Cai Shusheng (蔡叔声, aka Xia Yan). It was produced by Mingxing Studio and directed by Cheng Bugao

29.7. The stage setting of Xia Yan's *Under Shanghai Eaves*, whose cross-section, split-screen technique showed the influence of film

and literature. Film, as an emerging modern art, offered such new techniques of using cameras, temporal and spatial expressions, and the special technique of montage, which became sources of inspiration for authors who expressed themselves in words. The creative stage management of left-wing playwrights was obviously borrowed from the film shooting technique of shifting between a long shot, medium shot, and close shot. The stage setting of *Under Shanghai Eaves* by Xia Yan was a typical example of this. In this play, a common town-house in a Shanghai alley was cut at a cross-section, so that the kitchen and living room on the first floor, the small room between the first and second floors, and the front room and attic on the second floor became the living and performing space of the five families presented in front of the audience. This stage setting conformed to the actual situation of the limited living space of ordinary Shanghai citizens. As for the narrative speed and rhythm of novels, the bouncing rhythm of the language in Zhang Tianyi's novels easily reminded one of the movement of camera shots. Hu Feng once talked about the "dynamic effect" of Zhang Tianyi's narrative,[6] taking the opening of his short story "The Last Train" (《最后列车》) as an example:

> The city is panting. The earth's pulse beats rapidly.
> The bed bug-like armored car. Shrapnel. 42-calibre gun muzzle. Bomber. The blood and flesh of a colonized nation. A proud flag, on which the pattern is like a cross profile of a salt duck egg.
> A dozen bold characters appeared at the entrance of the arsenal:
> "… enter … shot dead …"

---

[6]   Hu Feng (written as 胡丰, but referring to 胡风): "On Zhang Tianyi" (《张天翼论》), *Literary Quarterly*, Vol. 2, Issue 3, Sep. 1935.

Some have the component of three-dot water, or that of one-person, a vertical line and a dot, those weird characters.

Dead bodies are piled on the street. Blood flows in ditches and trenches. The wind blows the smell of blood to each city and each country village. Ordinary people are ready to flee. The army officers have a severe look.[7]

This writing style had never been tried by Chinese writers before. The description of settings was an array of words and phrases, looking very much like the sweeping motion of a film camera. Zhang Tianyi adopted the same technique in writing about people, as in "Laughter": when Jiuye (the Ninth Master) was going to rape the farming woman Faxin Sao, one seemed to see the camera shifting quickly between these two characters, sometimes it was a close shot and sometimes an enlarged close-up:

Thus Jiuye targeted his eyeballs at Faxin Sao – closer and closer. There were blood streaks on his eyeballs, and his left eye was only half the size of the right one.

Faxin Sao dared not look at his face, only focused her eyes on the button of his silk coat.

But a hand caught hold of her shoulder. And then a cold tongue was on her chin – like a chisel.

"No ... No ... "[8]

We cannot specifically point out which films inspired Zhang Tianyi to adopt this narrative style, but apart from Hu Feng's comment about the "dynamic effect" of his language, everyone interested in Zhang's writing style would mention his "intense representation of human life and ability to get to the focus of struggles" (to quote Qu Qiubai), or his "most efficient descriptions and narrative arrangement" and "agile narrative style" (to quote Hsia Chih-tsing), all of which were actually about his interconnection with the "moving art" and "visual narrative" of the film art form. Of all the novelists of the 1930s, however, those who evidently borrowed most from the art of film were New Sensationalist writers.

Immediately after *Spring Silkworms* was adapted into a film in 1933, the New Sensationalist writers

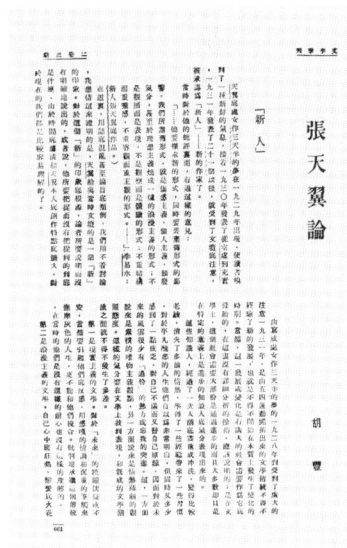

29.8. Page of Hu Feng's "On Zhang Tianyi," published in *Literary Quarterly*, in which Hu mentioned Zhang's narrative style with "dynamic effect"

---

7 For this paragraph quoted by Hu Feng, see Zhang Tianyi: "The Last Train," *Collected Works of Zhang Tianyi*, Vol. 1, Shanghai: Shanghai Literature and Arts Press, 1985, p. 280. This short story was published in 1932. "Some have the component of three-dot water, or that of one-person, a vertical line and a dot" – these referred to Japanese characters.

8 Zhang Tianyi: "Laughter," *Collected Works of Zhang Tianyi*, Vol. 2, Shanghai: Shanghai Literature and Arts Press, 1985, p. 109.

29.9. Ye Lingfeng and friends in Shanghai in the 1930s. (left to right) Ye Lingfeng, Liu Na'ou, and others. Liu Na'ou was a novelist who advocated soft film literature and theory

started a debate with left-wing writers over "soft film" (purely entertaining) versus "hard film" (political propaganda), and the debate lasted for two or three years. Liu Na'ou and Mu Shiying of the New Sensationalist literary sect published lengthy theoretical essays to declare their position favoring the "soft film." Left-wing writers started their critique of the New Sensationalist writers by quoting this simple sentence: "The film is ice-cream for the eyes and a sofa for the soul." This was actually a direct confrontation between the view of literature as entertainment and as a political tool. The New Sensationalist writers had finally made it clear what Mandarin Duck and Butterfly authors had long wanted to say but could not articulate due to their lack of theoretical training. Actually, there was no domestic soft film masterpiece; the Hollywood musicals and light comedies imported from the United States during the 1930s represented the best of soft film. But Shanghai school authors were always ready to try avant-garde literary experiments. They borrowed from the latest modern art form of film in their avant-garde literary writings, which could in a way corroborate their theories on film, and vice versa, so that we can see they were the ones who truly interconnected film and literature. As Leo Ou-fan Lee said: "If print culture served as a crucial aid in this process of appropriating visuality, the popularity of this visual medium soon triggered a reversed process—of the visual entering into the written and of film providing the key source for fictional technique. Needless to add, the writers who specialized in such new cinematic modes of fiction writing – Liu Na'ou and Mu Shiying in particular – were themselves avid film spectators."[9]

---

[9]   Leo Ou-fan Lee: *Shanghai Modern: The Flowering of a New Urban Culture in China, 1930–1945* (《上海摩登——一种新都市文化在中国1930–1945》), translated by Mao Jian (毛尖), Beijing: Peking University Press, 2001, p. 135.

An example of a New Sensationalist novel that explicitly claimed to be related with film was Ye Lingfeng's "Flu" (《流行性感冒》). This short story adopted a streamlined narrative and in the end, there was a paragraph that simply wrote about the female protagonist, Zhenzi (蓁子), like an interlined filmscript: "D. The Dark space, and the comet's tail that had swept like electricity. / D. I Zhenzi's face emerged gradually from the light. / A close-up of Zhenzi's eyes, from which stretched octopus-like tentacles. A captive animal. Struggling. (F. O) / Captions: I am not 'her,' but I feel the possibility of falling in love with you."[10] This paragraph is full of hints about the theme of the short story. Then there were "Mold Dynamics" and "Like Butterflies" by He Jin, which both explicitly adopted shifting camera shots and the insertion of pictures. But it was Mu Shiying and Liu Na'ou who integrated the paradigm of filmmaking into most of their fictions. Besides Mu Shiying's "Shanghai Foxtrot," quoted at the beginning of this chapter, there were his "Five Characters in a Nightclub" (《夜总会里的五个人》) and "Street Scenes" (《街景》), and Liu Na'ou's "Games" (《游戏》) and "Two People Impervious to Time" (《两个时间的不感症者》), in all of which one could find camera-like rhythms and bouncing water-like narratives. Here I try to summarize the relationship between these novels and films. Firstly, these novels were somehow inspired by films from their images of the metropolis to their female characters. In most modern metropolises there were high and peculiar building complexes, which needed to be examined from a certain point of view. Seen from a higher point of view, or a bird's-eye view, it was like taking an aerial photograph: "Two large patches of cloud that were tired of floating, sweating

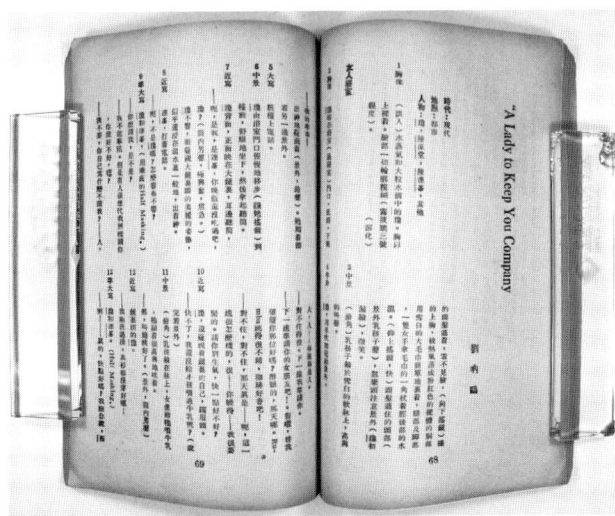

29.10. Liu Na'ou's fiction, which took on the format of a filmscript, published in 1934 in *Literary Landscape*, whose editor-in-chief was Shi Zhecun

[10] Ye Lingfeng: "Flu," *Purple Violet* (《紫丁香》), Beijing: Economic Daily Press, 2002, pp. 28–29.

glitteringly, stopped on the top of the mountain ranges composed of high buildings at the opposite side. Overlooking the walls within the metropolis from afar, just below there was a large platform that overlooked a large patch of grassland, which had been packed with a huge crowd of people who were eager to gamble, making it look like an ant nest."[11] This was describing the racecourse. And when only various kinds of "legs" were seen, it had to be from an extremely low point of view, as if looking out at the lower level of the metropolis from a car window: "The white-painted legs of roadside trees, the legs of utility poles, the legs of all still-life objects ... like a revue, the girls who extended their crossed white-powdered legs ... the lines of white-painted legs."[12] These views of the metropolis were usually a quick glance, making it like a camera sweeping through what was in front, colorful and dynamic. The following writing style, which had a strong sense of camerawork, could be seen everywhere in the novels of New Sensationalist writers: "The revolving door of the office building was like a windmill, and that of the restaurant like a crystal pillar. People were standing on the street, with waves of red light shining from behind them; cars swept across just in front of their noses. When the crystal pillar-like revolving door stopped, the crowd flew in like fish."[13] As for female characters, some literary scholars pointed out that in one of his essays on film, Mu Shiying classified the most popular Hollywood female film stars into "cool" and "hot" types, and in his novels, the female patient in *A Platinum Statue of the Female Body* belonged to the former while the female protagonist Yu Huixian in "Craven 'A'" belonged to the latter. Moreover, Mu Shiying went so far as to model his descriptions of female characters on Hollywood film stars, so that in his essay on film, his portrayal of a woman combining the features of "Greta Garbo, 'Marlene' Dietrich and Joan Crawford" was: "a 5x3-type face, below her feature-like long eyelashes there were a pair of half-closed big eyes, like waterlilies blossoming in a clear pond at midnight, which seemed to always be weaving cloudy dreams of the season of May!"[14] In his own short story "A Girl in Dark Green" (《墨绿衫的小姐》), he used these expressions to describe the female protagonist: "Below her feather-like long eyelashes, it seemed that pair of eyes could not even bear the soft sorrows of her own melodies." He simply confused the Hollywood film stars with his own characters.

---

[11] Liu Na'ou: "Two People Impervious to Time," *Urban Shanghai Landscape*, Shanghai: Shuimo Bookstore, 1930, p. 91.

[12] Mu Shiying: "Shanghai Foxtrot," p. 197. The ellipsis dots were quoted from the original text. "Revue" means light musical play.

[13] Mu Shiying: "Five Characters in a Nightclub," *Cemetery*, Shanghai: Modern Book Company, 1933, pp. 69–70.

[14] Mu Shiying: "Strolling in Films: Sexual Attraction and Mysticism" (《电影的散步 • 性感与神秘主义》), *Complete Works of Mu Shiying*, Vol. 3, Beijing: October Literature and Arts Press, 2008, p. 178.

Secondly, in term of narrative techniques, New Sensationalist novels were inspired by films and also made some innovations. The shifting of narrative points of view, in particular, became even freer, which can be seen in the examples given earlier about the "metropolis." And the leaping and bouncing connections and changes of rhythm were directly borrowed from the montage technique of film shooting, and thus superimposition and juxtaposition were most commonly used in the narratives of New Sensationalist writers. Such connections could produce new meanings; an example can be seen in "Shanghai Foxtrot," in which the juxtaposition of scenes of the mother-in-law pimping for her daughter-in-law and that of incest in a luxury room, as well as the juxtaposition of ballrooms, cars, restaurants, and manual

29.11. By the 1940s, such journals as *Mercury Lamp* (《水银灯》) and *Western Films* (《西影》), which introduced Hollywood films, emerged one after another, and were directly related with Shanghai school literature

laborers, representing a new interpretation of what Shanghai was like. The temporal and spatial structure of the novel were thus changed, breaking free from the fixed causal link of characters and settings, and became as broken, chaotic, and fragmentary as modern city life, which could never be condensed into a clearly defined organic whole.

If we examine all this from the perspective of the 1930s, when May Fourth New Literature was defined, we can say that the left-wing writers were determined to unify realism and revolutionary literature, which was indeed an act of defining. But then we immediately find the vulnerability of this attempt at defining. Just looking at the relationship between literature and modern film art, we can see the definition was often blurred and broken through. Taking

29.12. Old Shanghai film advertisements tried to introduce progressive ideas against the background of metropolitan merriment

the novel as an example, left-wing realistic novels inherited the core of the "cross-section" feature (which was a major innovation of May Fourth novels), and thus influenced left-wing films with their three-dimensional characterization and characters' complex connections with their environment, as well as the originality of fictional language. Almost at the same time, however, New Sensationalist novels learned from films and broke the simple "cross-section" structure, presenting a fragmented modern world with multiple viewpoints, simultaneously involving different points in time and space. This was not the only source of Chinese modernism, but learning from the art of film and carrying out new explorations in understanding and expressing the modern world had indeed constituted a major aspect of Chinese modernist literature. China's realism and modernism were thus both closely related to the emerging art form of film.

THIRTY

A TIMELY EMBRACE OF WORLD LITERATURE

THE TRANSLATION OF WORLD LITERATURE INTO CHINESE started gaining ground as early as the late-Qing period, but it was not a systematic activity at that time. Looking closely at the catalogue of all 180 titles of fiction translated by Lin Shu, one can see that Lin and a dozen of his oral translation assistants picked original texts simply based on their own tastes and market demand. Of all his translation works, only a few were first-class novels, such as *La Dame aux Camélias*, which was praised by Yan Fu: "the pitiful story of *Camélias* has broken the hearts of numerous people in China." Lin also translated over twenty novels written by the second-class English novelist Henry Rider Haggard, who was not even included in the list of 180 reputed English authors in *Encyclopedia of China – World Literature*, so much so that even Lu Xun, who had read Lin's translation novels widely in his younger years, said ironically: "Later, Lin Qinnan translated a large number of novels by Haggard, and we again read about sentimental ladies in London and weird savages in Africa."[1] Such an indiscriminate selection of original texts, the lack of quality translators of foreign languages, the casual adaptation and rewriting during translation, and the Mandarin Duck and Butterfly style of the final translations, all shows that this was simply the earliest stage of modern translation. And it wasn't until the period of *New Youth* that specialized translation organizations, teams, and journals began their systematic translation of world literary classics with the intention of promoting New Literature in China.

---

[1] Lu Xun: "Celebrating the Exchange of Language between China and Russia" (《祝中俄文字之交》), *Complete Works of Lu Xun*, Vol. 4, Beijing: People's Literature Press, 1981, p. 459. Lu Xun wrote the Chinese for Africa, "非洲," as "菲洲."

Since it was launched in 1915 (when its name was still *Youth Magazine*), *New Youth* began serializing Turgenev's *Torrents of Spring* and *First Love*, translated by Chen Gu (陈嘏), and Oscar Wilde's comedy *The Ideal Husband*, translated by Xue Qiying (薛琪瑛), but these were not these authors' major works. In 1918, *New Youth* launched a Special Issue on Ibsen (Vol. 4, Issue 6), and published Hu Shi's article "Ibsenism" (《易卜生主义》) and three plays by Ibsen – namely *Nora*, cotranslated by Luo Jialun and Hu Shi; *An Enemy of the People*, translated by Tao Lügong (陶履恭); and *Little Eyolf*, translated by Wu Ruonan (吴弱男) – and thus the Norwegian playwright was immediately known to intellectuals of even remote areas in China. Ibsen advocated women's liberation, and his heroine, Nora, realized one day that "she was simply a puppet of her husband's and her children were her puppets. So she left home, and one could only hear the sound of the door closing, and that was the end of the play."[2] It was not a loud sound, but it resonated deeply in China's intellectual and literary circle.

30.1. Special Issue on Ibsen, *New Youth* (Vol. 4, Issue 6, June 1918), which caused an "Ibsenism" craze among intellectuals in China

From that time until 1949, according to the *General Catalogue of Modern Chinese Literature* (《中国现代文学总书目》), there were altogether 13,500 modern Chinese literary books, and translation books totaled 3,894 titles, representing 29 percent of the total, meaning for every four separate editions of modern Chinese literature, one was a translation of a foreign literary work.[3] Here we can see the importance and significance of translation. One of the features of the history of translation literature started by *New Youth*'s Special Issue on Ibsen was its nature of enlightenment. In translating the plays of Ibsen, the main purpose of the translators within the *New Youth* group was to promote Ibsenism, not to disseminate literature. Its influence on the writing of social problem plays, such as Hu Shi's

---

[2]   Lu Xun: "What Happens after Nora Leaves Home" (《娜拉走后怎样》), *Complete Works of Lu Xun*, Vol. 4, Beijing: People's Literature Press, 1981, p. 158.

[3]   Jia Zhifang and Yu Yuangui (俞元桂), eds.: *General Catalogue of Modern Chinese Literature*, Fuzhou: Fujian Education Press, 1993. The statistics are quoted from Li Jin (李今): *On the Chinese Translation of Russian Literature during the 1930s and 1940s* (《三四十年代苏俄汉译文论》), Beijing: People's Literature Press, 2000, in which the number of translated literary books totaled 3,900 titles, generally the same as the statistics "over 4,400" quoted in "Notes on the Edition of this Volume" of *General Catalogue of Modern Chinese Literature (Volume of Foreign Literature)*, and the difference lay in the number of translation of literary theories and literary criticism.

30.2. Page of original paintings of Ibsen in the Special Issue on Ibsen, *New Youth* (Vol. 4, Issue 6)

30.3. *Fiction Monthly*, Special Issue on Translation: The Literature of Weakened Nations

The Greatest Event in Life, and its influence on later social problem novels, were simply side effects. Such a translation spirit that put ideology in front of literature was also obvious when Lu Xun and Zhou Zuoren recommended the Japanese author Mushanokoji Saneatsu in *New Youth*. Lu Xun translated Mushanokoji's play *A Young Man's Dream* (《一个青年的梦》) and Zhou Zuoren translated his "To Unknown Chinese Friends" (《与支那未知的友人》). Zhou Zuoren also wrote a review of *A Young Man's Dream* (published in Vol. 4, Issue 5) and the articles entitled "The New Village in Japan" (《日本的新村》, Vol. 6, Issue 3) and "The Spirit of New Village" (《新村的精神》, Vol. 7, Issue 2), which all focused on the idea and practice of the New Village movement in Japan instead of on literature. At that time, the New Village movement promoted by Mushanokoji was full of communist anarchistic spirit, following the trend of socialism, and it was valuable as an emerging idea.

During this period, translation of world literary masterpieces strengthened and the selection broadened, but it could still not be regarded as systematic translation of world literature. The journals of the New Culture movement, such as *New Youth*, mainly introduced French and Russian realistic authors; translators led by Lu Xun focused their attention on the literature of weakened nations in Eastern and North Europe; *Fiction Monthly*, chaired by Shen Yanbing, had launched special issues on "Research on Russian Literature," "Research on French Literature," and "Special Issue on Literature of Weakened Nations," but these were just following the new cultural trends of the May Fourth period. Most translators of that time were literary authors who translated world literature with the intention of creating new Chinese literature. The origin of the loud call for "art concerned with life" could be found in Russian literature. Lu Xun once said: "Since the period of Nicholas II, Russian literature was concerned with life, no matter whether it sought to explore it or to deal with it; sometimes it got engaged in mysteries or reduced life to dejection, but its mainstream was, always, concerned with life."[4] Looking back retrospectively, this view may not represent the entirety of the great spirit of classical Russian literature, but it represented the significance understood by Chinese authors of that time. Chinese intellectuals borrowed the essence of foreign cultures from all directions during the May Fourth period, so that within a short period of time, Chinese literature had traversed the road of Western literature of over a hundred years, including romanticism, realism, naturalism, and symbolism, but in the end, each literary school established their own tendency based on their own preference and practice of the trio of literary creation, translation, and criticism. For example, people of the Literary Research Society translated the works of Russian and French realistic authors including Turgenev, Leo Tolstoy, Chekhov, Gorky, Andreyev, Maupassant, Ibsen, and Sienkiewicz. Those in the Creation Society translated European romantic, symbolistic, futuristic, and expressionist authors including Goethe, Heine, Byron, Shelley, Keats, Hugo, Romain Rolland, Whitman, and Wilde. The Yu Si Society focused their attention on the folk literature and satires of Russia, Eastern Europe, and Japan. The Low Grass Society and Sunken Bell Society were devoted to the works of Hauptmann, Nietzsche, Rolland, Wilde, and Allan Poe from Germany and other Western countries. The Weiming Society, which became a literary society mainly engaged in translation with the support of Lu Xun, spared no effort in importing Russian literature, especially the literature of the USSR after the October Revolution (besides literary works such as *Tobacco Pouch* [《烟袋》] and *The Forty-First* [《第四十一》], they also translated, among others, *Literary Disputes in Soviet Russia* [《苏俄文艺论战》] and Trotsky's *Literature and Revolution* [《文学与革命》]). During the start-up period of the Crescent Moon Clique, Xu Zhimo translated the novels of Katherine Mansfield, the female impressionist writer from the United Kingdom. Before Mansfield died of lung disease, Xu went to her residence to visit her for what would be the first and last time, which became his lasting memory. Thus we can see people of the time had a broad vision of world literature, and from this we can feel what the full opening up of the May Fourth period was like. As for translation, there was no disagreement within the camp of New Literature on the combination of "translating and commenting on well-known Western authors," "explaining the trends and tendencies of world

---

4   Lu Xun: "Preface to *Harp*" (《〈竖琴〉前记》), *Complete Works of Lu Xun*, Vol. 3, Beijing: People's Literature Press, 1981, p. 432.

literature," and "discussing how Chinese literature could be reformed and make progress" (see "Manifesto of Reform of *Fiction Monthly*" [《〈小说月报〉改革宣言》》]). But, personal feelings aside (picking holes in each other's translations), they disagreed on such issues as whether realism and naturalism should be introduced, whether translation should focus on "essential content" or should be "systematic," and whether such importance should be given to the literature of weak nations. Mao Dun wrote "My Views on the Systematic and Efficient Introduction of Western Literature" (《对于系统的经济的介绍西洋文学底意见》), and proposed two similar lists of books for translation, one involving forty-four works by twenty authors, and the other forty-six works by twenty authors, in his articles "My Views on the Introduction of Western Literature" (《我对于介绍西洋文学的意见》) and "Manifesto of the 'New Tides of Fiction' Column" (《〈小说新潮〉栏宣言》).[5] He seemed to have a plan for a complete and systematic translation of world literature into Chinese. A close look at his lists, however, would reveal

30.4. The Literary Research Society paid great attention to translation. This was the Russian literary work *Sanin* (《沙宁》), translated by Zheng Zhenduo, which was included in the Literary Research Society book series

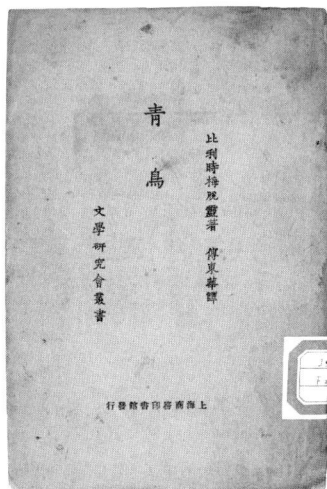

30.5. 1923 edition of the translation of *The Blue Bird* (《青鸟》), one title of the Literary Research Society book series

30.6. *The Sorrows of Young Werther*, translated by Guo Moruo, was extremely popular for a while

---

5   These three articles are all collected in *Complete Works of Mao Dun*, Vol. 18, Beijing: People's Literature Press, 1989.

30.7. Illustration from *Dead Souls*, a major translation work of Lu Xun's in his later years; he combined translation with collections of literary illustrations

30.8. One of Kravchenko's woodcut illustrations from *And Quiet Flows the Don*: the scene is of Aksinia and Grigori going fishing in the River Don on a stormy night

that they included no more than realistic and naturalistic literature and social problem plays and novels. Therefore, they were immediately questioned after being published, and Mao Dun justified his lists by the standard of "essential content." In the end, his "systematic" translation was basically that of "essential content."[6] This debate continued for a long time, and by the time Lu Xun published "'As Yet Untitled,' A Draft" (《〈题未定〉草》) in 1935, Lin Yutang criticized this idea by saying ironically in his "Eight Sicknesses of Today's Literature" (《今文八弊》): "As for literature, they import Polish poets today and introduce Czech literary masters tomorrow, but reject well-known English, American, French, and German intellectuals as out-of-date, refusing to explore them in depth." By that time, Lin Yutang had separated from the Yu Si Society, and his tone was very much like those of the Crescent Moon clique. This view that looked down upon the "timely" translation of literature from Poland, Czechoslovakia, and other weakened nations and deliberately placed it in opposition with English, American, French, and German

---

6   Huang Housheng (黄厚生): "My Thoughts after Reading 'Manifesto of New Tides of Fiction'" (《读〈小说新潮宣言〉的感想》) and Mao Dun's article entitled "Reply to Mr. Huang Housheng's 'My Thoughts after Reading "Manifesto of New Tides of Fiction"'" (《答黄君厚生〈读《小说新潮宣言》的感想〉》), *Complete Works of Mao Dun*, Vol. 18, Beijing: People's Literature Press, 1989.

30.9. Address of the Weiming Society: Weisu Garden, 5 Xinkai Road, opposite the
Red Building, Shatan, Beijing. Established in 1925, the Society was led by Lu Xun and
engaged in introducing world literature to China

literature obviously infuriated his old friend Lu Xun. Therefore, they began
settling old scores of translation from the May Fourth period. Lu Xun claimed
to be the first to promote Polish literature since he had written "On the Power
of Mara Poetry" thirty years earlier, and he asked in return: "Even now, how
can introducing Polish poets and Czech literary masters be seen as 'flattering'?
Don't these nations have well-known intellec-
tuals?"[7] Neither Lu Xun nor Mao Dun was
opposed to the systematic translation of world
literature, but both of them gave priority to
the necessity of "timely" translation.

By the 1930s, left-wing intellectuals were
very active in translating. The cultural context
both in China and abroad promoted left-wing
literature and cultivated a group of left-wing
readers in the cities, and thus introducing and
translating Soviet–Russian literature became a
major feature of this period. According to relevant statistics, of the 3,894 translated literary
books in the thirty years of the Republican
era, from 1917 to 1927 only 93 were translated
from Soviet–Russian works (with only two

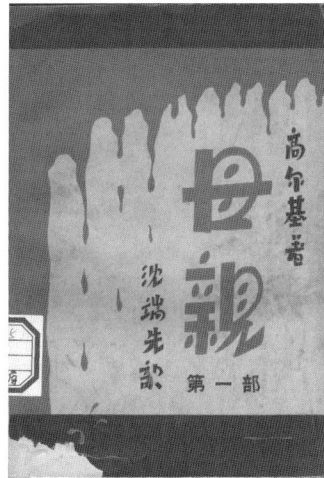

30.10. Chinese edition of Gorky's
The Mother, translated by Xia Yan

---

[7] For quotations of both Lin Yutang and Lu Xun, see "'As Yet Untitled', A Draft," *Complete
Works of Lu Xun*, Vol. 6, Beijing: People's Literature Press, 1981, pp. 355–356.

30.11. Later edition of Gorky's *The Mother*, translated by Xia Yan and published by China Youth Press in 1954

from the USSR), approximately one sixth of the total 530 titles that decade; from 1928 to 1938 the number increased to 327 (167 of which were from the USSR, slightly more than those from Russia), slightly less than one fourth of the total number of 1,619 during that time; and from 1939 to 1949, the number rose further to 577 (425 of which were from the USSR, three times the number from Russia), over one third of the total number of 1,689 during that period.[8] We can tell a lot from these numbers. For example, Xia Yan was among the first to translate Gorky's *The Mother* (《母亲》), which was regarded as the start of socialist realistic literature. *Destruction* (《毁灭》) by Fadeyev, translated by Lu Xun, occupied an important position in Soviet literature. Cao Jinghua (1897–1987) was an important translator who had translated Serafimovich's *The Iron Flood* (《铁流》) and Lavrenyev's *The Forty-First* (the latter was a controversial literary work as to how revolutionary literature should reflect human nature, but it was appreciated by Lu Xun). The translation and publishing of these works experienced great difficulty at that time, and some had to be published by Lu Xun's Three Leisures Bookstore (三闲书屋) at his own expense, which was referred to as a Promethean act. Other books that were translated in the 1930s and became increasingly more influential red classics were Sholokhov's *And Quiet Flows the Don*, translated by He Fei (贺非, another translated edition by Jin Ren [金人] appeared in the 1940s); and another work by this author, *Virgin Soil Upturned* (《被开垦的处女地》), translated by Zhou Libo; as well as Ostrovsky's *How the Steel Was Tempered* (《钢铁是怎样炼成的》), translated by Duan Luofu (段洛夫) and Cheng Feihuang (陈非璜) (the translated edition that was popular in the 1940s was by Mei Yi [梅益]). Besides literary works, the translation of Marxist art theories was also considered to be of great importance at that time. In his debate with the Creation Society, Lu Xun translated

30.12. Literary works of the USSR became popular among progressive young people in China during the 1930s and 1940s. This is *How the Steel Was Tempered*, which was extremely influential

[8]   Li Jin: *On the Chinese Translation of Russian Literature during the 1930s and 1940s*, p. 3.

30.13. Hardback copy of the World Library book series (《世界文库》), with all books designed in a unified style

30.14. Table of contents of the World Library, including "Chinese Literature" and "Foreign Literature" volumes

(from versions in other languages) *On Literature and Art* (《艺术论》) by Lunacharsky and *Art and Social Life* (《艺术论》) by Plekhanov. Feng Xuefeng translated Plekhanov's *Art and Social Life* (《艺术与社会生活》) and Lenin's "The Party's Organization and the Party's Literature" (《党的组织和党的文学》, which has since been retranslated and entitled "The Party's Organization and the Party's Publications" (《党的组织与党的出版物》), quite a major revision). Lu Xun and Feng Xuefeng paid more attention to the results of relatively loosely controlled and active theoretical activities of the USSR during the 1920s, which were not much eroded by leftist mechanisms and vulgar sociologism. Qu Qiubai translated directly from Russian, including the collection of Soviet art theories, *Reality* (《现实》); Lenin's articles on Leo Tolstoy, "Leo Tolstoy as the Mirror of the Russian Revolution" (《列甫·托尔斯泰像一面俄国的镜子》) and "L. N. Tolstoy and His Epoch" (《托尔斯泰和他的时代》); and two letters by Engels on the realism that had just been revealed in the USSR, all of which were left-wing theoretical documents that were later retranslated again and again. In the formation of Chinese left-wing literature, many other left-wing theoretical works from the USSR and Japan were also translated (including infantilistic left-wing art and literature policies and resolutions). After 1932, for example, Zhou Yang (aka Zhou Qiying) took the lead in introducing the "socialist realistic" creation method (named by Stalin) with his article entitled "On 'Socialist Realism' and Revolutionary Romanticism: The Denial of the Materialist Dialectical Creation Method" (《关于"社会主义的现实主义与革命的浪漫主义"——"唯物辩证法的创作方法"之否定》)

published in *The Contemporaries* in 1933. Just looking at this lengthy title one could feel the urgency and complexity of the repeated introduction of left-wing literary theories. This was the start of Zhou Yang's career, in which he would become an authority in interpreting the art and literary theories of Mao Zedong.

The overall and systematic translation efforts of the 1930s did not completely give way to the timely efforts, which could be seen from both left-wing and nonleft-wing camps, and an example of this was the publication of various translation book series. The book series of the 1920s were often mixtures of literary translation and creation. The Literary Research Society book series, Literary Review book series, Fiction Monthly series, and others compiled by the Literary Research Society and published by the Commercial Press included a large number of translation books, as did the Creation Society book series, Xinyi mini-book series, and Tomorrow mini-book series published by the Creation Society at its own expense or together with Taidong Press and other publishing institutions. After the Northern Expedition failed, progressive intellectuals gathered in Shanghai, where one of the few things they could do was to open bookstores, and translate and edit book series on social sciences and art theories, such as the Scientific Theories of Art book series published by Shuimo Bookstore, whose editor-in-chief was Feng Xuefeng, and the Art Theories mini-book series published by Dajiang Bookstore. All of these were part of the planned efforts to introduce left-wing literary and art theories. For the translation of literary works, there were the Modern Art and Literature book series published by State Light of the Divine Land Press, which included *Armored Train* (《铁甲列车》) and *October* (《十月》) from the USSR; the Emerging Literature book series by Shuimo Bookstore, which included *All Quiet on the Western Front* (《西部前线平静无事》) by Remarque and *The Money Changers* (《钱魔》) by Upton Sinclair; and the World Drama Translation series published by the Modern Book Company. These, however, were not large-scale book series. By the 1930s, some major publishing institutions with ample funds began translating and editing large-scale translation series, such as the World Literary Classics book series (世界文学名著丛书),[9] which was organized by the Commercial Press and translated and edited by authors of the Literary Research Society; and another book series with the same title published by Zhonghua Book Company. By 1935, Shanghai Life Bookstore asked Zheng Zhenduo to be the editor-in-chief of World Library, which was an extremely ambitious plan; it intended to publish one title of approximately 400,000 characters each month, and the first volume included as many as 60–80 titles; the intended "Foreign Literature" volume had nearly 400 titles of literary

---

[9]   This series included fourteen titles of translated books. See *Material on the Literary Research Society*, Vol. 2, Zhengzhou: Henan People's Press, 1985, pp. 1348–1353.

30.15. *Complete Plays of Shakespeare* (《莎士比亚戏剧集》), translated by Zhu Shenghao (朱生豪); this was published by the Writers Publishing House in March 1954

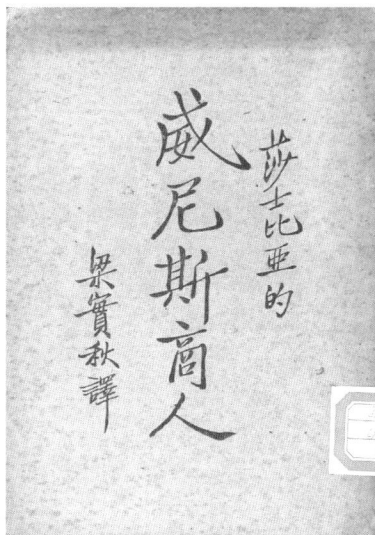

30.16. Liang Shiqiu was another major translator of Shakespeare, no less important than Zhu Shenghao; he started later but did an even better job. This was his translation of *The Merchant of Venice* (《威尼斯商人》)

masterpieces from the ancient times through the nineteenth century. The editorial and translating committee formed for this book series consisted of more than 100 well-known writers and translators, including Lu Xun and Hu Shi, most of whom were nonleft-wing intellectuals, but it did not exclude left-wingers. By 1936 over 100 masterpieces from twelve countries, including the USSR–Russia, France, the United States, and the United Kingdom, were published, including *Dead Souls*, translated by Lu Xun, and *Don Quixote*, translated by Fu Donghua. The project was discontinued because of the Anti-Japanese War. This was quite different from the case of *Translation* (《译文》) magazine (which was chaired by Lu Xun and Huang Yuan and was repeatedly suppressed by the authorities due to its leftist tendencies), for one was a large-scale systematic translation project, and the other was an ambitious translation journal (which had published over 100 translation works in nearly three years), but both showed the aspirations of the translation circle during the 1930s.

By the 1940s, translation efforts had resumed after being discontinued due to the war in 1937 and 1938, and the translation of Western literary classics was largely completed. Specialized translating masters emerged, and it had become standard practice for each of them to focus on translating a certain foreign literary master. Zhu Shenghao (1912–1944), for example, translated the plays of Shakespeare in the most difficult times during the Anti-Japanese War. He left Shanghai under gunfire, lost all his wealth and properties, but took with him the original text of the complete plays of Shakespeare and his own translation manuscript. He fled to the countryside to his hometown, Jiaxing of Zhejiang, and continued translating Shakespeare until his death at the young age of thirty-two. He had translated thirty-one of Shakespeare's plays and left another one unfinished, twenty-seven of which were published by the World Journal Book Store in 1947. Another mark of the maturity of the translation of world classics was the practice of multiple translations of the same text. This was the case for the translation of Shakespeare's plays: besides Zhu Shenghao, Cao Weifeng (曹未风) translated a dozen of Shakespeare's plays from 1931 to 1949; Liang Zhiqiu began his translation of Shakespeare with *Macbeth* in 1936, and later became the only Chinese author who finished translating all of Shakespeare's works; and Cao Yu, as a playwright, retranslated *Romeo and Juliet*. The translators of Turgenev, namely Ba Jin, Li Ni, and Lu Li from the Cultural Life Press, also translated new editions, different from the translations of the May Fourth period. The translator of Flaubert and Molière was Li Jianwu, a translator and scholar of French literature. Most novels by Leo Tolstoy and Dostoyevsky had their own Chinese editions. There were translation masters devoted to translating Balzac, namely Li Jianwu, Gao Mingkai (高名凯), and Fu Lei. Fu Lei (1908–1966) translated *Le Père Goriot* (《高老头》) in 1946, and thus began his career as a translator specializing in Balzac. And with the change of situation from the Anti-Japanese War to the civil war, preparation efforts began to be put into place for the literary era of the People's Republic of China. For example, the imported literature from the USSR after the October Revolution, especially works on the theme of the Patriotic War, were popular in both the Nationalist-controlled area and the "liberated region." Xiao San translated Korneichuk's *The Frontline* (《前线》) and had it serialized in the *Liberation Daily* in Yan'an in 1944. The *Liberation Daily* went so far as to publish an editorial entitled "What Can We Learn from Korneichuk's Play *The Frontline*" (《我们从考纳丘克的剧本〈前线〉里可以学到些什么？》) and tried to connect it with the Anti-Japanese War, which had not yet ended. Such "timely" translation efforts persevered because they made sense at the time. Sometimes the selection of one country's literature was too lopsided. For example, American literature was given more attention during the 1940s, but under the influence of the progressive ideology, Chinese translators attached more importance to such authors as Upton Sinclair, Theodore Dreiser, Mark Twain, and Jack London, but were not so enthusiastic about translating Sinclair Lewis, Pearl Sydenstricker Buck, and William Faulkner, who had been awarded the Nobel Prize in Literature. Within the special literary atmosphere of the National Southwestern Associated University, modernism was much more popular than in Chongqing and Yan'an, and therefore Feng Zhi, Bian Zhilin, and Mu Dan absorbed the modernism of Rainer Maria Rilke and T. S. Elliot, albeit in a reserved manner. And the translated works of *The Young Guard*

(《青年近卫军》), *Days and Nights* (《日日夜夜》), and *Report from the Gallows* (《绞刑架下的报告》) would become popular readings in the near future.

An overview of the history of Chinese translation during these thirty years reveals that it was a gradual process toward completion and systematicity, and in each stage priority was given to translation for immediate and urgent use. There was an interdependence between the dissemination of new ideas and constructing Chinese literature. After the method of oral translation and rewriting of the late Qing was abandoned, debates continued between the views of verbal translation, paraphrase, and adaptive translation, each of which had its own reasonings and specific applications. Those who put expressiveness in front of faithfulness certainly advocated paraphrase, and those who put faithfulness first insisted on verbal translation. Lu Xun always insisted on verbal translation, holding that the Western

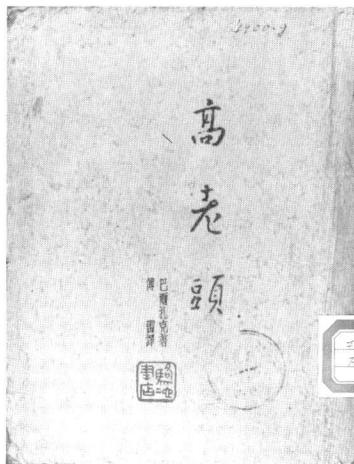

30.17. *Le Père Goriot*, translated by Fu Lei; this was published by Camel Bookstore in June 1947. Fu Lei later became a translation master devoted to translating Balzac

civilization should be presented to Chinese people as it were, in which process no distortion should be made. Later, the general trend was to seek a better integration of faithfulness and expressiveness, by learning the syntax, grammar, and new expressions of foreign languages to reform, enrich, and enhance modern Chinese vernacular language, and to learn from foreign literature to create Chinese literature. Thus translation became an integral part of modern Chinese literature, and finding the source of foreign literature that Chinese authors learned from, including the countries of origin and specific foreign authors, became an important part of research on the history of modern Chinese literature.

We may get a general idea about the countries of origin of foreign literature that influenced modern Chinese literature from several sets of statistics. According to the "General Catalogue of Translation" of the *Compendium of Chinese New Literature*'s "Index of Historical Material," during the eight years after the May Fourth movement, there were 187 translated works published, of which 65 were from Russia, 31 from France, 24 from Germany, 21 from Britain, 14 from India, and 12 from Japan.[10] In terms of journals publishing translated works, such as *Fiction Monthly*, from Volume 12, Issue 1 (published in January 1921) to Volume 17, Issue 12 (published on December 10, 1926), of all the translated works first published in this journal, there were 33 from Russia, 27 from France, 13 from Japan, 8 from Britain, and 6 from India.[11]

---

[10] Quoted from Chen Yugang (陈玉刚), ed.: *A History of Translated Literature in China* (《中国翻译文学史稿》), Beijing: China Translation and Publishing Corporation, 1989, p. 126.

[11] Quoted from ibid., p. 119.

30.18. After the 1950s, an increasing number of major modern Chinese literary works were translated into foreign languages. These are some foreign language translations of Ba Jin's *The Family*

According to the *General Catalogue of the Republican Period (Foreign Literature)* (《民国时期总书目（外国文学）》), of the translated works from 1911 to 1949, there were 952 titles from Russia and the USSR (262 from Russia and 690 from the USSR), 740 from the United Kingdom, 571 from France, 450 from the United States, 231 from Japan, 203 from Germany, and 38 from India.[12] And according to the statistics from 1917 to 1949 cited in the *General Catalogue of Modern Chinese Literature*, of the translated works there were 1,011 titles from Russia and the USSR (409 from Russia and 602 from USSR), 577 from the United Kingdom, 522 from France, 452 from the United States, 192 from Germany, and 199 from Japan.[13] From these somehow incomplete statistics, we can see that of all the foreign countries, the literature of Russia and the USSR certainly had the greatest influence on modern Chinese literature. Many scholars had proved that this source of influence had something to do with the fact that China and Russia had similar situations, their cultural attractiveness to each other, and that Chinese intellectuals chose to follow the path of the USSR after the October Revolution. The literature of the United Kingdom, France, and Germany had been a steady source of influence, and that of the United States increased later on. During the May Fourth period, the United States had little influence on the modernization of Chinese literature, whereas by the 1940s, its influence could not be ignored.

[12] National Library, ed.: *General Catalogue of the Republican Period (Foreign Literature)*, Beijing: Catalogue and Documentary Press, 1987.
[13] Li Jin: *On the Chinese Translation of Russian Literature during the 1930s and 1940s*, p. 3.

30.19. Foreign language editions of Lao She's *Camel Xiangzi*

As for Asian countries, Indian literature had some influence in the 1920s, such as on Bing Xin and Xu Dishan, and over time, especially during the "Red 1930s," Japanese literature had historical significance on the changing course of modern China.

Examining the influence of specific foreign authors, we may look at the "Index of Foreign Names" (《外国人名索引》) appended to a large-scale book on the relationship between world literature and thirty major modern Chinese authors, including Lu Xun, Mao Dun, Yu Dafu, Lao She, Fei Ming, Shen Congwen, Ba Jin, Shi Zhecun, Lu Ling, Guo Moruo, Xu Zhimo, Wen Yiduo, Feng Zhi, Dai Wangshu, Ai Qing, Bian Zhilin, Zhou Zuoren, Feng Zikai, Liang Yuchun, Tian Han, Xia Yan, and Cao Yu. The Index showed there were in total fifty-seven foreign authors who appeared over four times in the book, namely Natsume Soseki and Tayama Katai from Japan; Tagore from India; Ibsen from Norway; Pushkin, Gogol, Herzen, Lermontov, Turgenev, Dostoyevsky, Leo Tolstoy, Chekhov, Gorky, Blok, Mayakovsky, and Yesenin from Russia and the USSR; Sienkiewicz from Poland; Petőfi from Hungary; Goethe, Schiele, Heine, and Nietzsche from Germany; Rilke from Austria; Verhaeren and Maeterlinck from Belgium; Shakespeare, Richardson, Stern, Wordsworth, Scott, Byron, Shelley, Keats, Dickens, Hardy, Wilde, Conrad, Wells, Dowson, and Eliot from the United Kingdom; Yeats from Ireland; Rousseau, Balzac, Hugo, Baudelaire, Flaubert, Zola, Mallarmé, Verlaine, Maupassant, Romain Rolland, Valéry, and Barbusse from France; Dante from Italy; Allan Poe, Whitman, and

Pound from the United States.[14] This was a much simplified list of foreign authors, and the Chinese writers influenced by them covered the entire modern Chinese literary history. As for the scale of influence, the exchange between Chinese and world literature had reached an unprecedented level, which was evidence of the awakening of national literature during the modern era. As for the depth of influence, these foreign authors had a great influence on Chinese authors' understanding of human beings and their imagination of the emancipation of individuals, personal freedom and independence, and putting people first, which were elements of modernity of literature per se. We heard May Fourth poets' passionate recitals of the poetic lines by Byron, Shelley, Goethe, and Whitman; we saw the intellectuals of the National Southwestern Associated University climbing the hills with the poems of Rilke and Eliot in their hearts, for they had integrated their experience in the war as part of their life experience; and we knew the marches against hunger and for democracy moved forward to the beat of Keats and Mayakovsky. In *Midnight*, the mourning hall of Grandfather Wu reminded us of the grand parties in *Ivanhoe*, and Lu Ling's *Rich Men's Children* reminded us of the structure and description in *War and Peace*. Lu Xun opened the greatest free and unrestrained space for us, from the Western Romantic poets in "On the Power of Mara Poetry" through the Soviet–Russian, Eastern European, Northern European, and Japanese realism represented by Gogol, Sienkiewicz, and Natsume, to the psychoanalysis and symbolism of Nietzsche, Freud, and Kuriyagawa Hakuson. This was a door truly open to the outside world, which had lasting appeal to young people of one generation after another. Later a two-way exchange began, involving translating and introducing modern Chinese literary masterpieces to the outside world. Naturally, this process will never end.

[14] Zeng Xiaoyi (曾小逸), ed., "Index of Foreign Names," *Marching Toward World Literature (Modern Chinese Authors and Foreign Literature)* (《走向世界文学（中国现代作家与外国文学）》), Changsha: Hunan People's Press, 1985, Appendix 2, pp. 653–666.

TABLE 30.1 *Translated world literary classics in the thirty years of the Republican era*

Title of the translated text or name of the translation activity	Country of origin	Original author	Translator(s)	Date published	Publisher	Influence on Chinese literature
Special Issue on Ibsen: 《娜拉》 (*Nora*), etc.	Norway	Ibsen	Luo Jialun, Hu Shi, etc.	1918	*New Youth*	Promoted Ibsenism, which influenced Chinese realism and problem novels
卖火柴的女儿 (*The Little Match Girl*)	Denmark	Hans Christian Andersen	Zhou Zuoren	1919	*New Youth*	Later *New Youth* published a "Special Issue on Andersen"
华伦夫人之职业 (*Mrs. Warren's Profession*)	United Kingdom	George Bernard Shaw	Pan Jiaxun	1919	*New Tide*	This play had an earlier influence on the shaping of Chinese spoken drama
甲必丹之女 (*Captain's Daughter*)	Russia	Alexander Sergeyevich Pushkin	An Shouyi (安寿颐)	1921	Commercial Press	A major novel by Pushkin, and the translation was later entitled 《上尉的女儿》
海鸥 (*The Seagull*)	Russia	Anton Chekhov	Zheng Zhenduo	1921	Commercial Press	This play was poetic and not so dramatic, which had an influence on Chinese spoken drama
哈孟雷特 (*Hamlet*)	United Kingdom	William Shakespeare	Tian Han	1921	*Youth China*	An earlier introduction of *Hamlet*, with another edition published by Zhonghua Book Company the following year
工人绥惠略夫 (*Worker Shevyren*)	Russia	Mikhail Artsybashev	Lu Xun	1921	*Fiction Monthly*	Reflected the effect of anarchism on society and people
茵梦湖 (*Immensee*)	Germany	Theodor Storm	Guo Moruo, Qian Junxu	1921	Taidong Press	Promoted romanticism in China
沙乐美 (*Salome*)	United Kingdom	Oscar Wilde	Tian Han	1921	*Youth China*	Had a far-reaching influence on Chinese aesthetic and romantic literary schools
巡按 (*Revizor*)	Russia	Nikolai Vasilievich Gogol	He Qiming (贺启明)	1921	Commercial Press	*The Government Inspector* was a satirical play that had a great influence in China

(continued)

TABLE 30.1 (continued)

Title of the translated text or name of the translation activity	Country of origin	Original author	Translator(s)	Date published	Publisher	Influence on Chinese literature
前夜 (On the Eve)	Russia	Ivan Sergeyevich Turgenev	Shen Ying	1921	Commercial Press	As for the earliest influence of Russian literature in China, Turgenev was second only to Leo Tolstoy
托尔斯泰短篇小说集 (Collection of Short Stories by Tolstoy)	Russia	Leo Tolstoy	Qu Qiubai, Geng Jizhi	1921	Commercial Press	An earlier translation of Tolstoy that spread widely in China
被损害民族的文学号 ("Special Issue on Literature of Weakened Nations")	Poland, etc.	(many writers)	Zhou Zuoren, Lu Xun, etc.	1921	Fiction Monthly	Started the tendency of translating and introducing the literature of weak nations during the May Fourth period
少年维特之烦恼 (The Sorrows of Young Werther)	Germany	Johann Wolfgang von Goethe	Guo Moruo	1922	Taidong Press	A romantic love story that intrigued and inspired young people of the May Fourth period
阿丽思漫游奇境记 (Alice in Wonderland)	United Kingdom	Lewis Carroll	Zhao Yuanren	1922	Commercial Press	Influenced the development of Chinese fairy tales
我的叔父虚勒 ("My Uncle Jules")	France	Guy de Maupassant	Chen Sheng (陈生)	1922	Youth China	Earlier translation and introduction of French literature and Maupassant
飞鸟集 (Stray Birds)	India	Rabindranath Tagore	Zheng Zhenduo	1922	Commercial Press	Zheng Zhenduo also translated Gitanjali (《吉檀迦利》) and The Crescent Moon (《新月集》), which influenced Bing Xin's poetry
复活 (Resurrection)	Russia	Leo Tolstoy	Geng Jizhi	1922	Commercial Press	A major novel of Tolstoy's
史特林堡戏剧 (Strindberg's Plays)	Sweden	August Strindberg	Zhang Yugui (张毓桂)	1922	Commercial Press	Strindberg's symbolism had influenced Chinese dramatists and novelists

(continued)

Title	Country	Author	Translator	Year	Publisher	Notes
少奶奶的扇子 (*The Young Lady's Fan*)	United Kingdom	Oscar Wilde	Hong Shen	1923	*Oriental Magazine*	A famous adapted translation of Oscar Wilde's *Lady Windermere's Fan*
悭吝人 (*L'Avare*)	France	Molière	Gao Zhenchang (高真常)	1923	Commercial Press	An earlier influence on the creation of Chinese comic spoken drama
青鸟 (*The Blue Bird*)	Belgium	Maurice Maeterlinck	Wang Weike (王维克)	1923	Taidong Press	This play of Maeterlinck was called a "fairy tale" or "fantasy" during the May Fourth period
套中人 (*Man in the Case*)	Russia	Anton Chekhov	Zhao Xizhang (赵熙章)	1923	*Fiction Monthly*	Chekhov's "almost eventless" satirical style and typicality
爱弥儿 (*Émile*)	France	Jean-Jacques Rousseau	Wei Zhaoji (魏肇基)	1923	Commercial Press	An education novel that influenced the child-oriented thinking of the May Fourth period
苦闷的象征 (*Symbol of Anguish*)	Japan	Kuriyagawa Hakuson	Lu Xun	1923	Editorial Office of *New Tide*	An influence of modernism on the interpretation of art and literature
侠隐记 (*A Biography of a Secluded Hero*)	France	Alexandre Dumas *père*	Wu Guangjian	1924	Commercial Press	The reviser of this book was Mao Dun (signed with his original name, Shen Dehong [沈德鸿]), and it influenced popular literature
神曲一脔 (*Divine Comedy*)	Italy	Dante	Qian Daosun (钱稻孙)	1924	Commercial Press	*Divine Comedy* had been highly praised by Guo Moruo, and this was a translation in classical Chinese
三姊妹 (*The Three Sisters*)	Russia	Anton Chekhov	Cao Jinghua	1925	Commercial Press	One of Chekhov's major plays, which Chinese dramatists who promoted poetic plays paid great attention to

(continued)

TABLE 30.1 (continued)

Title of the translated text or name of the translation activity	Country of origin	Original author	Translator(s)	Date published	Publisher	Influence on Chinese literature
格尔木童话集 (*Grimms' Fairy Tales*)	Germany	The Grimm brothers	Wang Shaoming (王少明)	1925	Education Bureau of Henan Province	The earliest translation of the Grimm brothers' fairy tales
出了象牙之塔 ("Out of the Ivory Tower")	Japan	Kuriyagawa Hakuson	Lu Xun	1925	Weiming Society	Another translation of Kuriyagawa Hakuson by Lu Xun
马丹波娃丽 (*Madam Bovary*)	France	Gustave Flaubert	Li Jieren	1925	Zhonghua Book Company	Flaubert's *Madam Bovary* was known for its psychological description and characterization
棉被 ("The Quilt")	Japan	Tayama Rokuya	(Xia) Mianzun	1926	*Oriental Magazine*	The earliest introduction of psychoana-lytical novels
若望·克利司朵夫 (*Jean-Christophe*)	France	Romain Rolland	Jing Yinyu	1926	*Fiction Monthly*	The personal strivings of Jean-Christophe were an inspiration for Chinese intellectuals
雪莱诗选 (*Selected Poems of P. B. Shelley*)	United Kingdom	Percy Bysshe Shelley	Guo Moruo	1926	Taidong Press	Had a great influence on Chinese romantic poetry
劳苦世界 (*Hard Times*)	United Kingdom	Charles Dickens	Wu Guangjian	1926	Commercial Press	There were many translation editions of Dickens and Scott by Lin Shu during the late-Qing period and there were fewer at this time
穷人 (*Poor Folk*)	Russia	Fyodor Dostoyevsky	Wei Congwu (韦丛芜)	1926	Weiming Society	One of Dostoyevsky's most important novels

(continued)

Title	Country	Author	Translator	Year	Publisher	Notes
外套 (Joseph Had a Little Overcoat)	Russia	Nikolai Gogol	Wei Shuyuan (韦漱园)	1926	Weiming Society	Had an influence on the realistic satires of Chinese writers after Lu Xun
福尔摩斯探案大全集1—13册 (The Case-Book of Sherlock Holmes, 1–13)	United Kingdom	Conan Doyle	Cheng Xiaoqing, etc.	1927	World Journal Bookstore	This was a punctuated edition in vernacular Chinese, following the tradition of Chinese detective stories of the late-Qing period
曼殊斐尔小说集 (Collection of Short Stories by Katherine Mansfield)	United Kingdom	Katherine Mansfield	Xu Zhimo	1927	Beixin Press	Had a deep influence on Xu Zhimo and the Crescent Moon school
(爱伦·坡和霍夫曼）特刊 (Special Issue on Edgar Allan Poe and Gerhart Hauptmann)	United States, etc.	Edgar Allan Poe, etc.	Yang Hui, Chen Weimo	1927	*Sunken Bell*	The Sunken Bell Society was influenced by the decadent aesthetic style of Edgar Allan Poe and Gerhart Hauptmann
妄想 ("Daydreams")	Japan	Mori Ogai	Huashi (画室, aka Feng Xuefeng)	1928	Human World Bookstore	Influenced Lu Xun and others
富美子的脚 ("Fumiko's Legs")	Japan	Tanizaki Junichiro	Shen Duanxian (aka Xia Yan)	1928	*Fiction Monthly*	An earlier translation of Tanizaki, which had an influence on Chinese aestheticism
浮士德 (Faust)	Germany	Johann Wolfgang von Goethe	Guo Moruo	1928	Publishing Department of the Creation Society	Influenced a whole generation of writers after Guo Moruo
卢骚忏悔录 (The Confessions)	France	Jean-Jacques Rousseau	Zhang Jingsheng (张竞生)	1928	Beauty Bookstore	A literary autobiography of a great Enlightenment thinker

(continued)

TABLE 30.1 *(continued)*

Title of the translated text or name of the translation activity	Country of origin	Original author	Translator(s)	Date published	Publisher	Influence on Chinese literature
显克微支小说集 (*Short Stories of Sienkiewicz*)	Poland	Henryk Sienkiewicz	Wang Luyan	1928	Beixin Press	One of the authors from weak European nations that had the greatest influence in China
色情文化 (*Erotic Culture*)	Japan	Kataoka Teppei, etc.	Liu Na'ou	1928	First Line Bookstore	Japanese New Sensationalism had a great influence on Chinese New Sensationalism
草枕 ("Grass Pillow")	Japan	Natsume Soseki	Cui Wanqiu (崔万秋)	1929	Truth Virtue and Beauty Bookstore	A Japanese author who had a great influence on Lu Xun and other Chinese writers who had been studying in Japan
西线无战事 (*All Quiet on the Western Front*)	Germany	Erich Maria Remarque	Hong Shen, Ma Yanxiang	1929	Equality Bookstore	Influenced Chinese writers' descriptions of modern wars
茶花女 (*La Dame aux Camélias*)	France	Alexandre Dumas *fils*	Xia Kangnong (夏康农)	1929	Spring Tides Book Company	Continued its influence in China after Lin Shu's translation into classical Chinese
格里佛游记 (*Gulliver's Travels*)	United Kingdom	Jonathan Swift	Wei Congwu	1929	Weiming Society	This was a fairy tale with worldwide influence, especially the tales of the "Kingdom of Giants" and "Kingdom of Dwarfs"
屠场 (*The Jungle*)	United States	Upton Sinclair Jr.	Yi Kanren (易坎人, a pseudonym of Guo Moruo)	1929	Nanqiang Book Company	A good example of the description of workers for left-wing writers

(continued)

Title	Country	Author	Translator	Starting from	Publisher	Description
母亲 (The Mother)	Soviet Russia	Maxim Gorky	Shen Duanxian (aka Xia Yan)	1929	Dajiang Bookstore	Later referred to as the first major work of socialist realistic literature
艺术论 (Art and Social Life)	USSR	G.V. Plekhanov	Lu Xun	1930	Kwong Wah Book Store	Spread Plekhanov's earlier Marxist theories on art and literature
当代英雄 (A Hero of Our Time)	Russia	Mikhail Yuryevich Lermontov	Yang Hui	1930	Beixin Press	Magnum opus of Lermontov, whose title and characters had influenced Chinese writers
蟹工船 (Crab Cannery Ship)	Japan	Kobayashi Takiji	Pan Nianzhi (潘念之)	1930	Dajiang Bookstore	Japanese left-wing literature was one of the sources of inspiration for Chinese left-wing literature
加力比斯之月 (The Moon of the Caribbees)	United States	Eugene O'Neill	Gu Youcheng (古有成)	1930	The Commercial Press	O'Neill's The Emperor Jones had an immediate influence on Cao Yu's The Wilderness
多惹情歌 (The Love Poems)	United Kingdom	George Gordon Byron	Zhang Jingsheng	1930	World Journal Bookstore	The poetry of Byron, Shelley, and some of their peers influenced May Fourth romantic poetry
波多莱尔散文诗 (Prose Poems of Baudelaire)	France	Charles Pierre Baudelaire	Xing Pengju (邢鹏举)	1930	Zhonghua Book Company	Baudelaire was a pioneer of symbolism and his "Les Fleurs du Mal" had a great influence in China
十日谈 (The Decameron)	Italy	Giovanni Boccaccio	Huang Shi (黄石), Hu Zanyun (胡簮云)	1930	Kaiming Bookstore	The Decameron was a world-renowned masterpiece
毁灭 (Destruction)	USSR	Alexander Fadeyev	Sui Luowen (隋洛文, a pseudonym of Lu Xun)	1931	Dajiang Bookstore	A famous work of socialist literature from the USSR, which had an increasing influence later

(continued)

TABLE 30.1 (continued)

Title of the translated text or name of the translation activity	Country of origin	Original author	Translator(s)	Date published	Publisher	Influence on Chinese literature
铁流 (The Iron Flood)	USSR	Alexander Serafimovich	Cao Jinghua	1931	Three Leisures Bookstore	Another socialist literary work of great influence
静静的顿河 (And Quiet Flows the Don)	USSR	Mikhail Aleksandrovich Sholokhov	He Fei	1931	State Light of the Divine Land Press	Later there was an edition translated by Jin Ren, and Sholokhov had a great influence on Chinese revolutionary literature
夜店 (The Lower Depths)	Soviet Russia	Maxim Gorky	Li Yi (李谊)	1931	Hufeng Press	During the Japanese occupation period in Shanghai, this play was performed after being adapted by Ke Ling and Shi Tuo
少年哀史 (Les Misérables)	France	Victor Hugo	Ke Pengzhou (柯蓬洲)	1931	World Journal Bookstore	Victor Hugo's world-renowned classic
战争与和平 (War and Peace)	Russia	Leo Tolstoy	Guo Moruo	1931	Literature and Art Book Store	Had a great influence on Chinese novels, and later there was an edition translated by Gao Zhi (高植) and Dong Qiusi (董秋斯)
被侮辱与被损害者 (Humiliated and Insulted)	Russia	Fyodor Dostoyevsky	Li Jiye (李季野)	1931	Commercial Press	An important novel by Dostoyevsky
吉诃德先生 (Don Quixote)	Spain	Miguel de Cervantes	He Yubo (贺玉波)	1931	Kaiming Bookstore	Cervantes's character Don Quixote had a world-wide influence
夏娃日记 ("Eve's Diary")	United States	Mark Twain	Li Lan (李兰)	1931	Hufeng Bookstore	An earlier translation of Mark Twain's work

(continued)

Title	Country	Author	Translator	Year	Publisher	Notes
妇心三部曲 (*Trilogy of Women's Hearts*)	Austria	Arthur Schnitzler	Shi Zhecun	1931	State Light of the Divine Land Press	Schnitzler's influence on Chinese psychoanalytical novels started from this translation
旧根 (*Old Hatred*)	Japan	Nagai Kafū	Fang Guangtao (方光焘)	1931	*Oriental Magazine*	Influenced Zhou Zuoren and the Lion's Roar Society (狮吼社)
大街 (*Main Street*)	United States	Sinclair Lewis	Bai Hua (白华)	1932	Publishing Department of *Ta Kung Pao*	Lewis's work was introduced to China after he was awarded the 1930 Nobel Prize in Literature
大地 (*The Good Earth*)	United States	Pearl Sydenstricker Buck	Hu Zhongchi	1933	Kaiming Bookstore	She was awarded the 1938 Nobel Prize in Literature, but the left-wing intellectuals denied that she was writing about the reality in Chinese society
娜娜 (*Nana*)	France	Émile Zola	Wang Liaoyi (王了一)	1934	Commercial Press	Zola's masterpiece was known to be a naturalist work
双城记 (*A Tale of Two Cities*)	United Kingdom	Charles Dickens	Xu Tianhong (许天虹)	1934	Beiping and Tianjin Bookstore (平津书店)	Dickens's compassionate satirical style influenced Lao She, Zhang Tianyi, and other writers
奥德赛 (*Odysseus*)	Greece	Homer	Fu Donghua	1934	Commercial Press	One of the great Greek epics, this was known to have lasting charm
苔丝姑娘 (*Tess of the d'Urbervilles*)	United Kingdom	Thomas Hardy	Lü Tianshi (吕天石)	1934	Zhonghua Book Company	Hardy's compassion for the poor had a great influence on Lao She
阴谋与爱情 (*Intrigue and Love*)	Germany	Friedrich von Schiller	Zhang Fusui (张富岁)	1934	Commercial Press	Schiller's masterpiece, and his style was referred to as Schillerism

(continued)

TABLE 30.1 (continued)

Title of the translated text or name of the translation activity	Country of origin	Original author	Translator(s)	Date published	Publisher	Influence on Chinese literature
红字 (The Scarlet Letter)	United States	Nathaniel Hawthorne	Zhang Menglin (张梦麟)	1934	Zhonghua Book Company	One of Hawthorne's works with the greatest influence in China
失乐园 (Paradise Lost)	United Kingdom	John Milton	Zhu Weiji (朱维基)	1934	No. 1 Publishing House	An epic and world-renowned classical masterpiece
吉姆爷 (Lord Jim)	United Kingdom	Joseph Conrad	Liang Yuchun, Yuan Jiahua (袁家骅)	1934	Commercial Press	Magnum opus of Joseph Conrad; Liang Yuchun did not finish translating it before he died and Yuan Jiahua completed the translation
高龙芭 (Colomba)	France	Prosper Merimee	Dai Wangshu	1935	Zhonghua Book Company	The romanticism and exotic atmosphere had a great influence
野性的呼唤 (The Call of the Wild)	United States	Jack London	Liu Dajie, Zhang Menglin	1935	Zhonghua Book Company	Jack London was widely received by left-wing intellectuals as a great writer after this translation
真妮姑娘 (Jennie Gerhardt)	United States	Theodore Dreiser	Fu Donghua	1935	Zhonghua Book Company	Another literary work favored by left-wing intellectuals because it exposed the darkness of capitalist society
傲慢与偏见 (Pride and Prejudice)	United Kingdom	Jane Austin	Yang Bin (杨缤)	1935	Commercial Press	A world-renowned masterpiece by Jane Austin
死魂灵 (Dead Souls)	Russia	Nikolai Gogol	Lu Xun	1935	Shanghai Cultural Life Press	A grave realistic satire that had a great influence on Lu Xun and writers after him

(continued)

Title	Country	Author	Translator	Year	Publisher	Notes
泰绮思 (*Thaïs*)	France	Anatole France	Wang Jiaji (王家骥)	1936	Qiming Book Store	Its description of the charm of increased desire for material enjoyment had an influence on Chinese romantic writers and Shanghai school writers
马克白 (*Macbeth*)	United Kingdom	William Shakespeare	Liang Shiqiu	1936	Commercial Press	Later Liang Shiqiu became a translator who translated all of Shakespeare's plays
查泰莱夫人的情人 (*Lady Chatterley's Lover*)	United Kingdom	D. H. Lawrence	Rao Shuyi (饶述一)	1936	Beixin Press	Its bold literary description of sexual life made it controversial and attracted a lot of attention
欧也尼·葛朗台 (*Eugénie Grandet*)	France	Honoré de Balzac	Mu Mutian	1936	Commercial Press	Balzac's *The Human Comedy* was seen as a world masterpiece of realism
被开垦的处女地 (*Virgin Soil Upturned*)	USSR	Mikhail Sholokhov	(Zhou) Libo	1936	Life Bookstore	A great epic that had a lasting influence on revolutionary literature
庐贡家族的家运 (*The Fortune of the Rougons*)	France	Émile Zola	Lin Ruji	1936	Commercial Press	*The Fortune of the Rougons* and the series influenced Ba Jin and other Chinese writers
安娜·卡列尼娜 (*Anna Karenina*)	Russia	Leo Tolstoy	Zhou Jian (周笕), Luo Jinan (罗稷南)	1937	Life Bookstore	One of Tolstoy's major works (Zhou Jian was a pseudonym of Zhou Yang), and there was another Chinese edition translated by Gao Zhi
第四十一 (*The Forty-First*)	USSR	Boris Lavrenyev	Cao Jinghua	1937	Young Companion Printing and Publishing Company	This work was controversial within the left-wing camp and was denied several times, in which process their understanding was deepened
钢铁是怎样炼成的? (*How the Steel Was Tempered*)	USSR	Nikolai Ostrovsky	Duan Luofu, Chen Feihuang	1937	Shanghai Chaofeng Press	Later an edition translated by Mei Yi was published, which was the most fashionable "textbook on everyday life" in the 1950s

(continued)

TABLE 30.1 *(continued)*

Title of the translated text or name of the translation activity	Country of origin	Original author	Translator(s)	Date published	Publisher	Influence on Chinese literature
秘密的中国 (*Secret China*)	Czechoslovakia	Egon Erwin Kisch	Zhou Libo	1938	Shanghai Tianma Bookstore Press	Created a craze of reportage writing during the Anti-Japanese War period
西行漫记 (*Red Star Over China*)	United States	Edgar Snow	Wang Changqing (王厂青) and eleven other people	1938	Restoration Society	The Chinese edition was originally entitled "红星照耀中国," which was known as the first literary work about the Liberation Area
在俄罗斯谁能快乐而自由 ("Who Is Happy in Russia")	Russia	Nikolai Nekrasov	Gao Han (高寒, aka Chu Tu'nan [楚图南])	1939	Commercial Press	A famous epic known for the poet's complex love and passion for his motherland
保卫察里钦 (*Tsaritsyn Defense*)	Soviet Russia	Aleksey Nikolayevich Tolstoy	Wang Chuliang (王楚良)	1939	Pearl Forest Bookstore	One of A.Tolstoy's literary works that was introduced to China earlier than others
茨冈 (*Tsygany*)	Russia	Alexander Pushkin	Qu Qiubai	1940	New Literary Trend Press	A narrative epic of Pushkin's was published as a separate edition after Qu Qiubai's death
卡拉马佐夫兄弟 (*The Brothers Karamazov*)	Russia	Fyodor Dostoyevsky	Geng Jizhi	1940	Young Companion Printing and Publishing Company	Dostoyevsky's last and most profound novel, an earlier modernist literary work
战地春梦 (*A Farewell to Arms*)	United States	Ernest Hemingway	Lin Yijin (林疑今)	1940	West Wind Press	The title of this novel of Hemingway's is now translated as "永别了，武器"

(continued)

Title	Country	Author	Translator	Year	Publisher	Notes
飘 (*Gone with the Wind*)	United States	Margaret Mitchell	Fu Donghua	1940	Longmen Book Store	A popular novel from the United States that was widely read by Chinese intellectuals during the Anti-Japanese War period
愤怒的葡萄 (*The Grapes of Wrath*)	United States	John Steinbeck	Hu Zhongchi	1941	Great Times Book Store	Steinbeck was given attention by Chinese writers for his writing about workers' resistance in the United States
叶甫盖尼·奥涅金 (*Yevgény Onégin*)	Russia	Alexander Pushkin	Su Fu (甦夫)	1942	*Poetic Creation* (《诗创作》)	The source of the Russian literary concept "superfluous man"; there was another edition translated by Lü Ying (吕荧)
穿裤子的云 ("A Cloud in Trousers")	USSR	Vladimir Mayakovsky	Lin Xiao (林啸)	1942	*Poetic Creation*	The passion and style of Mayakovsky's revolutionary poetry was widely imitated by Chinese poets
阿尔达莫诺夫家的事业 (*The Artamonov Business*)	Soviet Russia	Maxim Gorky	Ru Long (汝龙)	1942	*Free China* (《自由中国》)	An era-specific novel about a three-generation family of the farming capitalist class
呼啸山庄 (*Wuthering Heights*)	United Kingdom	Emily Brontë	Liang Shiqiu	1942	Commercial Press	The title is now translated as "呼啸山庄", and is still popular in China
罗米欧与朱丽叶 (*Romeo and Juliet*)	United Kingdom	William Shakespeare	Cao Weifeng	1943	Wentong Bookstore	Cao Weifeng also translated the complete plays of Shakespeare
父与子 (*Fathers and Sons*)	Russia	Ivan Turgenev	Ba Jin	1943	Shanghai Cultural Life Press	One of the representative works of Turgenev
非洲大雪山 (*The Snows of Kilimanjaro*)	United States	Ernest Hemingway	Xie Qingyao (谢庆尧)	1943	*Time and Tides Literature and Art* (《时与潮文艺》)	The title is now translated as "乞力马扎罗的雪", and it is one of Hemingway's major works

(*continued*)

TABLE 30.1 *(continued)*

Title of the translated text or name of the translation activity	Country of origin	Original author	Translator(s)	Date published	Publisher	Influence on Chinese literature
蝴蝶与坦克 ("The Butterfly and the Tank")	United States	Ernest Hemingway	Feng Yidai (冯亦代)	1943	Aesthetics Press	A collection of short stories by Hemingway that was translated into Chinese earlier than others
铁木儿及其伙伴 (*Timur and His Gang*)	USSR	Arkady Gaidar	Fu Ming (桴鸣)	1943	New Knowledge Bookstore	This work of Gaidar had a great influence on children's literature after the founding of the People's Republic of China
红与黑 (*The Red and the Black*)	France	Stendhal	Zhao Ruihong (赵瑞蕻)	1944	Writers' Bookstore	Demonstrated the influence of French novels
大路之歌 ("Song of the Open Road")	United States	Walt Whitman	Gao Han (aka Chu Tu'nan)	1944	Reading Press	Whitman's *Leaves of Grass* had influenced Guo Moruo and poets after him during the May Fourth period
前线 (*The Frontline*)	USSR	Aleksandr Korneichuk	Xiao San	1944	*Liberation Daily* (《解放日报》)	This novel was serialized in Yan'an and had a great influence; later there was an edition translated by Jiang Chunfang (姜椿芳), which was entitled "战线"
简·爱 (*Jane Eyre*)	United Kingdom	Charlotte Brontë	Li Jiye	1945	Shanghai Cultural Life Press	The two novels by the Brontë sisters enjoyed almost equal popularity in China
高老头 (*Le Père Goriot*)	France	Honoré de Balzac	Fu Lei	1946	Camel Bookstore	Later Fu Lei had famous translated editions including those of the works of Balzac and *Jean-Christophe*
团的儿子 (*Son of the Regiment*)	USSR	Valentin Kataev	Mao Dun	1946	Wanye Bookstore	Kataev also wrote a great work entitled *Time, Forward!*

(continued)

Title	Country	Author	Translator	Year	Publisher	Notes
日日夜夜 (*Days and Nights*)	USSR	Konstantin Simonov	(Xu) Leiran (［许］磊然)	1946	Times Books and Newspapers Press	Had a great influence on Chinese novels about the war, until the publication of *Western Route*
康特波雷故事 (*The Canterbury Tales*)	United Kingdom	Geoffrey Chaucer	Fang Zhong (方重)	1946	Cloud Sea Press	The earliest Chinese translation of Chaucer's *The Canterbury Tales*
钟楼怪人 (*The Hunchback of Notre Dame*)	France	Victor Hugo	Yue Yi (越裔)	1946	Qunxue Bookstore	Later Chen Jingrong's (陈敬容) translation, entitled "巴黎圣母院," was published in 1949
谁之罪 (*Who Is to Blame?*)	Russia	Alexander Herzen	(Lou) Shiyi (［楼］适夷)	1947	Dayong Books	Herzen became even more famous in China thanks to Ba Jin's translation
青年近卫军 (*The Young Guard*)	USSR	Alexander Fadeyev	(Ye) Shuifu (［叶］水夫)	1947	Times Books and Newspapers Press	This novel was very popular during the 1950s as a revolutionary literary work
莎士比亚戏剧全集1－3辑 (*Complete Plays of Shakespeare, 1–3*)	United Kingdom	William Shakespeare	Zhu Shenghao	1947	World Journal Bookstore	Included twenty-seven tragedies, comedies, and miscellaneous plays by Shakespeare and a chronicle of Shakespeare's life
原野与城市 (*The City from a Field*)	Belgium	Emile Verhaeren	Ai Qing	1948	Xinqun Press	Verhaeren's poems influenced Ai Qing and China's modernist poetry
俄国人的性格 (*The Character of Russian People*)	Soviet Russia	Aleksey Nikolayevich Tolstoy	Wen Shan (文姗)	1948	*Fiction* (《小说》)	Regarded as a typical work of an old-time author writing about characters of the new society
绞索勒着脖子时的报告 (*Report from the Gallows*)	Czechoslovakia	Julius Fucik	Liu Liaoyi (刘辽逸)	1948	Kwong Wah Book Store	A revolutionary work of the 1950s, whose title was later translated as "绞刑架下的报告"

(continued)

TABLE 30.1 (continued)

Title of the translated text or name of the translation activity	Country of origin	Original author	Translator(s)	Date published	Publisher	Influence on Chinese literature
两姐妹 (The Sisters)	USSR	Aleksey Nikolayevich Tolstoy	Zhu Wen (朱雯)	1949	Wenfeng Press	One title of "The Ordeal: A Trilogy," and it had a great influence in the 1950s
唐璜 (Don Juan)	France	Molière	Li Jianwu	1949	Kaiming Bookstore	Li Jianwu, a translator of Gustave Flaubert, translated and published five of Molière's comedies
真正的人 (Tale of a True Man)	USSR	Boris Polevoy	(Xu) Leiran	1949	Times Press	It was hard to distinguish Polevoy's news report from his novels based on real people; his work was popular in the 1950s

(Source: The Encyclopedia of Twentieth-Century Chinese Literature, The Encyclopedia of Chinese Literature [《中国文学大典》], and General Catalogue of the Republican Period ("Foreign Literature"), etc.)

Except for those first published in journals and magazines and the following:

Main Street was published by the Publishing Department of Ta Kung Pao in Tianjin
Secret China was published by Hankou Tianma Bookstore
The Grapes of Wrath was published by Chongqing Great Times Book Store
Wuthering Heights was published by the Commercial Press in Chongqing
Romeo and Juliet was published by Guiyang Wentong Book Store
Fathers and Sons was published by Guilin Cultural Life Press
"The Butterfly and the Tank" was published by Chongqing Aesthetics Press
Timur and His Gang was published by Chongqing New Knowledge Bookstore
The Red and the Black was published by Chongqing Writers' Bookstore
"Song of the Open Road" was published by Chongqing Reading Press
Jane Eyre was published by Chongqing Cultural Life Press
Report from the Gallows was published by Dalian Kwong Wah Book Store
All other books were published in Shanghai

Under the Clouds of War

THIRTY ONE

FORMATION OF MULTIPLE LITERARY CENTERS UNDER THE CLOUDS OF WAR

THE ANTI-JAPANESE WAR DID NOT END CHINESE literature's modernization process, but it did dramatically change the life of Chinese writers. It caused a fundamental spiritual, as well as material, change of human conditions. The pattern of a single literary center was broken, and writers gathered in different places in occupied and unoccupied areas around the country. The writing and publishing models changed with the realities of unrest, while the most profound change was people's experiences, reflections, and expressions of life in the harsh and cruel environment of war.

After Beiping, Shanghai, and Nanjing were lost to the Japanese army, writers began migrating all over the country. Seeing that the national conflict between China and Japan ranked top of the national agenda and that the KMT and CPC had begun to cooperate for the second time in history, all writers, no matter what their political views were, became consciously aware that they were part of the same great national community and thus voluntarily made up and shared a sense of solidarity. As early as October 1, 1936, while the shadow of Japanese militarism hovered over China, the "Manifesto of Artists and Writers on Solidarity against Aggression and for Freedom of Speech" was published in Shanghai; Lu Xun signed it before his death, together with writers of other political leanings, including the Mandarin Duck and Butterfly authors Bao Tianxiao and Zhou Shoujuan, attracting the attention of the whole country. Immediately after that, many intellectuals that followed the government to migrate to the interim capital Wuhan began to consider reestablishing their own organization. The All-China Resistance Association of Writers and Artists (for short, the Association of Writers and Artists) and the Third Office of the Political Department of the Military Commission of the National Government (for short, the Third Office) were established almost at the same time, and were the most important cultural events in Wuhan at that time. When Yang Hansheng, a former leftist writer, and Wang Pingling (王平陵), a major member of the Chinese Literary Society (中国文艺社) under the direct leadership of the former Propaganda Department of the KMT, proposed to establish the Association of Writers and Artists, it received quite a resounding response. They met and exchanged ideas at Shuzhen Restaurant and the office of the Chinese Literary Society at 20 Yongkangli in Hankou. When Lao She went south to Wuhan, since he was a prestigious writer and respected by people of all political leanings, he was recommended to continue the preparation work together with Mao Dun, Wang Pingling, Feng Naichao, Hu Feng, and Zeng Xubai. Important figures from both the KMT and the CPC, including Feng Yuxiang (冯玉祥), Ye Chucang, Shao Lizi, Zhang Daofan (张道藩), and Zhou Enlai (周恩来), gave their support to the organization. By March 27, 1938, the inaugural meeting of the Association of Writers and Artists was held in the auditorium of the General Chamber of Commerce of Hankou, and was attended by over 300 writers, artists, and guests. The banners at either side of the stage read "Use a pen as a gun to win national independence" (拿笔杆代枪杆，争取民族之独立) and "Use cultural strategies to promote human glory" (寓文略于战略，发扬人道的光辉). Shao Lizi, Zhou Enlai, Guo Moruo, and others delivered passionate speeches, and the Articles of Association was passed. Of the forty-five directors and fifteen candidate directors elected at the meeting, there were writers of all parties, styles, and political leanings, as well as avant-garde and popular writers. At that time, Zhang Henshui had arrived in

31.1. Artists of the Third Office in Luojiashan, Wuhan, in 1938, including Guo Moruo (front row, fourth from left) and Zhou Enlai (third from left)

31.2. Group photo taken outside the auditorium after the inaugural meeting of the Association of Writers and Artists was held on March 27, 1938, including Feng Yuxiang, Zhou Enlai, Zhang Daofan, Lao She, Hu Feng, and Tian Han.

Chongqing to take charge of the editorial work of the supplement of the *New Citizen* newspaper, and he was elected as director of the first session of the Association, though he did not attend the inaugural meeting, which made compelling news in those days. Later, Lao She was elected as director of the General Affairs Department of the Association, and became its de facto leader. Just before Wuhan was lost, the general office of the Association was moved to Chongqing, the provisional capital in wartime. And after its office at 33 Side Street, Linjiangmen, was destroyed in bombings, it was moved to 65 Zhang's Garden. During the war, branches of the Association were established in all provinces throughout unoccupied areas, which, together with the Association per se, made great contributions to uniting writers against external enemies, promoting "going to the countryside," "going to the army," and supporting the creation of literature of resistance.

The Association of Writers and Artists was a government-funded civil society organization,[1] while the Third Office was a government department in

---

[1] The Association of Writers and Artists was approved by the Society Department of the KMT Central Committee, filed with and partly led by the Department. It was also funded by the KMT government, receiving a monthly amount of 500 yuan from the Propaganda Department, 500 from the Political Department of Military Committee, and 200 from the Ministry of Education, which was later raised slightly. Source: Ni Wei (倪伟): *The Imagination of "Nation" and the "State" Governance* (《〈民族〉想象与国家统制》), Shanghai: Shanghai Education Press, 2003, p. 244.

charge of propaganda.[2] In July 1937, Guo Moruo secretly returned home from Japan, where he had been in exile, and was invited by the head of the KMT Political Department, Chen Cheng (陈诚), to be head of the Third Office, and he agreed with the persuasion of Zhou Enlai (deputy head of the KMT Political Department due to the KMT–CPC cooperation). Around him were former members of the Creation Society, namely Tian Han, Yang Hansheng, and Feng Naichao, and important intellectual figures Hong Shen, Ying Yunwei, Shi Dongshan (史东山), Ma Yanxiang, Xian Xinghai (冼星海), and Zhang Shu (张曙), who were collectively nicknamed a "cabinet of celebrities," and who formed a group of progressive writers and artists that became an important force at the United Cultural Front in the Nationalist-controlled area. Focusing on propaganda with drama, film, and other forms of art and literature, the group reorganized the National Salvation Performing Troupe and Children's Theater Troupe (both formed in Shanghai) into ten resistance theater troupes, four resistance propaganda teams, and a children's theater troupe, and later it formed the Instruction Theater Troupe (教导剧团), which became the backbone of the anti-Japanese drama movement. At the end of 1938, the Third Office moved to Chongqing from Changsha and Guilin, and after being dissolved in 1940, it was transformed into the Cultural Work Committee (CWC) led by Guo Moruo. At that time, in Chongqing, the most active and productive novelists and dramatists were Mao Dun, Lao She, Ba Jin, Guo Moruo, and Cao Yu. The "fog performing season," with Guo's political historical play *Qu Yuan* (《屈原》) as the major play, was very popular in the mountainous city. There were various novel and poetry recitations held here and there. The gatherings to celebrate the fiftieth birthday of Guo Moruo and the twenty-fifth anniversary of his literary creation; the fiftieth birthday of Hong Shen; the twenty-fifth anniversary of the publishing career of Zhang Jinglu; the twenty-fifth anniversary of Lao She's literary creation; the fiftieth birthday and thirtieth anniversary of literary creation of Zhang Henshui; and the fiftieth birthday and twenty-fifth anniversary of literary creation of Mao Dun became important

31.3. Inaugural issue of *Resistance Literature and Art*, the official journal of the Association of Writers and Artists

---

[2]   As a department under the direct leadership of the Political Department of the Military Committee, the Third Office could be funded as much as 60,000 silver dollars each month. Different documents and personal memoirs disagree on this figure, but it was probably more than 60,000 silver dollars. Certainly, the funds granted to both the Association and the Third Office could often be embezzled or delayed. See Ni Wei: *The Imagination of "Nation" and the "State" Governance*, p. 242.

activities supported by the CPC to review the achievements of the Chinese literary movement and Chinese authors. And there were influential journals, including *Literary Front* (《文艺阵地》),whose editor-in-chief was Mao Dun, and *July* (《七月》) and *Hope* (《希望》), both edited by Hu Feng. Deserving a special mention is *Resistance Literature and Art* (《抗战文艺》), edited by the Association of Writers and Artists, whose editing and publishing persisted in spite of all the hardships from its inauguration in May 1938 until it was discontinued in May 1946. Thanks to the authors gathering around the Association and the Third Office (and CWC) and their literary creation achievements, Chongqing the provisional capital also became the literary center of the Nationalist-controlled area.

31.4. Lao She in Chongqing in 1939. During the Anti-Japanese War he was the director of the General Affairs Department of the Association of Writers and Artists and was its de facto leader. He always shouldered responsibility for the Association

Dropping the pen and joining the army was an objective for many writers at the beginning of the war, but actually, very few of them could join the army and engage themselves in cultural work, mainly because the conditions in the army were not fit for writers to live and write for a long period of time.

Zang Kejia was among the few. He joined the Youth Corps of the Fifth War Zone led by Li Zongren (李宗仁) in 1938–1939, interviewed those who had participated in the Battle of Taierzhuang (and wrote the lengthy reportage piece *On the Bloody Battle along the North Jinpu Railway* [《津浦北线血战记》]); then he joined Yu Heiding (于黑丁), Tian Tao (田涛), and Zou Difan (邹荻帆) to form the fourteen-member Cultural Troupe of the Fifth War Zone and walked around Henan, Hubei, and Anhui provinces (when he wrote the epic *The Dabie Mountains* [《大别山》]); and then he joined the Eighty-Fourth Army in Guangxi together with Yao Xueyin (姚雪垠) and participated in the Battle of Sui County and Zaoyang. It was a rare opportunity for him to have such a chance. Even so, Zang later left the army because he was not welcomed there. A group of

31.5. Special issue of the *Xinhua Daily* (《新华日报》) to celebrate Guo Moruo's fiftieth birthday in Chongqing. Those whose birthdays were celebrated also included Mao Dun and Lao She

31.6. In November 1941, the writers and artists in Chongqing celebrated the fiftieth birthday of Guo Moruo and the twenty-fifth anniversary of his literary creation; Guo was presented with a giant rafter-like pen as a gift, on which were inscribed four characters "扫清妖孽," meaning "Eliminate all evildoers"

31.7. Ding Ling, a female soldier, in 1938. She led the Service Group of the Northwestern Battle Area to many places in Shanxi and Shaanxi

young authors, mainly authors from the northeast, including Xiao Jun, Xiao Hong, and Duanmu Hongliang, and young intellectuals including Ai Qing, Tian Jian, and Nie Gannu, went to Linfen together in 1938 to join the Shanxi National Revolutionary University (山西民族革命大学) founded by Yan Xishan (阎锡山). They were seemingly teachers at the university, but actually lived a military life (as many as 10,000 students came to the university from all over the country), and thus their yearning for the army was partly fulfilled. In Linfen, they met Ding Ling, who had led the Service Group of the Northwestern Battle Area. We might regard the three groups, namely Ding Ling's Service Group, the Writers' War Area Interview Group led by Wang Lixi (王礼锡), and the Northern Consolation Group of the National Army Consolation Association, which Lao She had joined and which had been to Yan'an, as cultural consolation groups that had come close to the battlefront. Wang Lixi even died of exhaustion in Luoyang on the way to console and entertain the army. In November 1938, Sha Ting and He Qifang, as teachers of Lu Xun Arts College of Yan'an, led students of literature and drama from the college to march to northwestern Shanxi with He Long's

31.8. Qiu Dongping, a July school author who later died in battle as a soldier of the New Fourth Army

(贺龙) 120th Division and then marched to central Hebei at the beginning of the following year, which could be seen as a short-term military life. On this battlefield, Sha Ting wrote *Discursive Notes on the Journey with the Army* (《随军散记》, also known as *About He Long* [《记贺龙》]). In contrast to these superficial military experiences, July school authors Qiu Dongping (丘东平), Ah Long (阿垅), Cao Bai (曹白), Peng Baishan (彭柏山), and others had been truly living with the army, participating in battles as soldiers, and had written excellent literary works on military themes. Back in 1932, when the January Twenty-Eighth Incident occurred in Shanghai, Qiu Dongping had already been a soldier of the Nineteenth Route Army and published a number of battlefield works, from novels to newsletters, such as *The Seventh Company* (《第七连》). Later he participated in the August Thirteenth Songhu Battle and wrote novels such as *A Company Commander's War Experience* (《一个连长的战斗遭遇》), which were full of real-life descriptions of the battlefield, and conveyed a sense of tragic heroism without avoiding the plight and darkness of war. Later, Qiu Dongping went to the base area of the New Fourth Army in northern Jiangsu Province and died during the battle to smash the enemy's "mopping-up" campaign in Yancheng in 1941. This was the most typical example of authors dropping the pen and joining the army. Certainly, due to the mobility of armies and the scattering of authors, a fixed cultural center was impossible at this time.

Then there were authors who moved to the hinterland alongside educational institutions. Cao Yu, for example, moved west to Changsha, then to Chongqing, and then to Jiang'an of Sichuan with the National Drama School. In the small city of Jiang'an, he wrote such masterpieces as *The Metamorphosis* (《蜕变》) and *Peking Man*. Since Jiang'an was a remote corner of the province, Cao Yu's *Peking Man* had to be sent to the dramatic center, Chongqing, for the premiere. Later Cao Yu also went to Chongqing. Another example was Feng Zhi, who moved to Jiangxi and then to Guangxi with his whole family following Tongji University, and later he was employed by the National Southwestern Associated University and arrived in Kunming in 1939. At that time, most major universities throughout the country were moved to the hinterland: Fudan University was moved via Lushan to Huangjue Township,

Beibei, Chongqing; Zhejiang University was moved via Ji'an, Jiangxi, to Zunyi, Guizhou; the Central University of Nanjing was moved to Chongqing; Wuhan University was moved to Leshan; Beiyang University and Beiping Normal University and others were moved out of Beiping and Tianjin and later were merged and became Xi'an Associated University before moving to Chenggu, Shaanxi, and changing its name into the National Northwestern Associated University (国立西北联合大学). All these universities were moved with their professors and writers, and some even employed writers to be their professors; some examples include Hu Feng, who was invited by Wu Lifu (伍蠡甫) of Fudan University; and Ye Shengtao, who was invited by Chen Xiying of Wuhan University. An even larger team was that of Beijing school authors following Peking University and Tsinghua University southward. On the morning of August 12, 1937, Shen Congwen, Yang Zhensheng, Zhu Guangqian, Liang Zongdai, Zhao Taimou (赵太侔), and others departed from Beiping's Zhengyang Gate railway station with assumed identities of secretaries and typists of foreign firms, changed their plan in Tianjin and went to Yantai by ship, then went to Nanjing via Jinan by train. At that time, Shanghai had become an isolated island, and thus the Ministry of Education decided to move Peking University, Tsinghua University, and Nankai University to Hunan and establish a temporary university there, so that these people went to Wuhan and then to Changsha. But soon after that, the temporary university had to be moved to Kunming, and these professors could no longer stay in Hunan. Shen Congwen's younger brother, who was an army officer then, once invited Mei Yiqi (梅贻琦), Yang Zhensheng, Jin Yuelin (金岳霖), Zhang Xiruo (张奚若), Wen Yiduo, Zhu Ziqing, Liang Sicheng, Lin Huiyin, and Xiao Qian to a dinner on behalf of his elder brother. Wen Yiduo joined the teachers and students to walk to Yunnan, having lived in Shen's home in Yuanling for a while before departure. Shen Congwen himself went to Kunming via other places by bus. The name of the temporary university was then changed to the National Southwestern Associated University (the College of Arts, Law School, and Business School were first located in Mengzi). Other people whose destination was the National Southwestern Associated University, including many female students and those who were weak, old, sick, or disabled, first went to Hai Phong, Vietnam, through Guangzhou or Hong Kong, then went to Yunnan via the Yunnan–Vietnam railway or the Yunnan–Burma Road, as did Shen Congwen's wife Zhang Zhaohe and their children.

31.9. Cao Yu in 1938

31.10. Former site of the Academic Affairs Office of the National Drama School. In April 1939, the school moved to Jiang'an under orders. Cao Yu was the teaching fellow and dean of Academic Affairs

Bian Zhilin went to Yan'an from Chengdu together with Sha Ting and He Qifang, and later he returned alone from there and went to Kunming. Thanks to Kunming's advantageous location as a remote unoccupied area, as well as the cultural advantages brought by university teachers and students, the Southwestern Associated University writer group gradually took shape. Young writers grew up on this piece of land, among people including the Nine Leaves poet Mu Dan and the "last Beijing school writer" Wang Zengqi. Kunming thus became one of the major base areas of wartime Chinese literature.

For many writers whose homeland was Sichuan or Hunan, their first choice was to return home. Zhang Tianyi, whose ancestral home was in Xiangxiang, Hunan, was born in Nanjing and had never been to his native place. He then left Shanghai for his native place together with another writer of Hunan origin, Jiang Muliang (蒋牧良). It was in Changsha that he keenly observed some speculative intellectuals and philistines who were busy holding meetings for "national salvation," and wrote his famous "Mr. Huawei" (《华威先生》). Tian Han was a native of Changsha, but as a dramatist, he decided to go to Chongqing and Guilin for the sake of his career. Writers of Sichuan origin, namely Sha Ting, Ai Wu, Zhou Wen, and He Qifang, returned to Sichuan and gathered together with local writers, including Li Jieren, to establish the Chengdu Branch of the Association of Writers and Artists, which later became one of the best organized branches of the Association and made some outstanding achievements. This was different from the case of Hunan, which soon became a war area, so writers could not stay there and had to move to the mountainous areas. For this reason, Zhang Tianyi later went to the Wartime Academy in Tangtian, Shaoyang, and met Wang Xiyan, and then he went to the Republican University of Beiping, which had been moved to Datan, Xupu County. Sichuan, on the other hand, remained an unoccupied area for a long time, and Chengdu thus became a major cultural city second to Chongqing.

31.11. Tsinghua University president Mei Yiqi (front row, third from the right) and professors who went to Kunming on foot; Wen Yiduo is in the second row, third from the right

31.12. Wen Yiduo's sketch of the chain bridge over the Chong'an River, which showed his high-level training in painting

31.13. Chengdu Branch of the Association of Writers and Artists, established on January 14, 1939: (front row, first on left) Feng Yuxiang, (second from left) Xiao Jun, (fourth from right) Li Jieren, (fifth from right) Chen Xianghe, (sixth from right) Lao She, and (eighth from right) Zhou Wen

Thanks to the rich resources of this area and to the enthusiastic support from Li Jieren, who was quite a rare local writer and businessman (he ran a paper factory in Leshan), the Chengdu Branch of the Association of Writers and Artists was quite well-organized and held various activities.

Taking advantage of the KMT–CPC cooperation, left-wing intellectuals turned a corner of Yan'an into a new land that enjoyed relative independence even though it had limited material resources. A number of influential progressive writers moved from their garrets in Shanghai to the cave dwellings on the Loess Plateau in the northwest. Ding Ling was the first of them. Escaping from illegal home arrest under the KMT government in September 1936, she secretly went to Bao'an in northern Shaanxi and later went to Yan'an. Zhou Yang, Ke Zhongping (柯仲平), and Wang Shiwei (王实味) were among the earliest, going there in 1937, followed by Chen Huangmei (陈荒煤), Liu Baiyu (刘白羽), and Ma Jia (马加), who went in 1938. Xiao San returned home from the USSR and went to Yan'an in 1939. The CPC had planned to break through the barrier between the left and right and solicit writers from all over the country, and writers known to be invited included Mao Dun, Ba Jin, Lao She, Cao Yu, Shen Congwen, and Xiao Qian. Hearing this, Shen Congwen, Cao Yu, Xiao Qian, and Sun Fuyuan had visited Xu Teli (徐特立) at the Changsha Office of the Eighth Route Army and asked him whether they would be welcomed in Yan'an and got positive responses from Xu. Most of them, however, did not make it for various reasons. He Qifang traveled around the unoccupied areas and finally decided to go to Yan'an in 1938, where he remained and transformed from a Beijing school writer into a left-wing one. Xiao Jun went to Yan'an in 1940 after stopping in Wuhan and Linfen, and Ai Qing arrived in the same year after stopping in Wuhan, Linfen, Guilin, and Chongqing. Yan'an became increasingly attractive to progressive literary youths all over the country, and from Xi'an to the north of Shaanxi, one after another group of young people broke through the blockade and went to the revolutionary destination on foot. The Shaanxi, Gansu, and Ningxia Border Area Association of the Cultural Circle to Resist Japan and Save the Nation (陕甘宁边区文化界抗日救亡协会), founded in 1937; the Lu Xun Arts College (whose name was later changed to the Lu Xun College for Art and Literature [鲁迅艺术文学院]), founded in 1938; and the Yan'an Branch of the Association of Writers and Artists, founded in 1939 (whose predecessor was the Border Area Association of the Cultural Circle to Resist Japan [边区文化界抗战联合会]), were important cultural and literary organizations that cultivated a number of literary youths, a number of whom would later become well-known, including He Jingzhi (贺敬之), Kang Zhuo (康濯), Kong Jue (孔厥), Ma Feng (马烽), and Xi Rong (西戎). From the "liberated region" around the revolutionary literary center of Yan'an, were Zhao Shuli (赵树理) from the border area of Shanxi and Suiyuan, and Sun Li (孙犁) from the border area of Shanxi, Hebei, and Chahar.

Guilin, which had an advantageous location between Chongqing and Hong Kong, was another center where many intellectuals gathered during the Anti-Japanese War. As an area under the direct jurisdiction of the local military forces of Guangxi, it was never fully obedient to the central Nationalist government, and therefore, the cultural control by the central government was relatively loose in this beautiful scenic spot, making it a sanctuary within the Nationalist-controlled area. Hong Kong, too, was a cultural buffer strip. Xu Dishan was among the earlier to move there and teach at Hong Kong University, although he died quite unexpectedly there in 1941. Other intellectuals, such as Mao Dun, Zou Taofen (邹韬奋), Xia Yan, Xiao Hong, Duanmu Hongliang, Luo Binji (骆宾基), and Dai Wangshu, all went to Hong Kong because, as a colony of the United Kingdom, it was out of the strict cultural control. As for Yu Dafu and other people who went to the southwestern part of China or Southeast Asia, they regarded Hong Kong as a place to ensure safe transfer. These writers brought the cultural progress started by the May Fourth period to the south, which, combined with the local culture of Hong Kong, nourished this piece of land that had become too commercially focused. After the Wannan Incident occurred in 1941, the CPC had planned to evacuate left-wing intellectuals from Chongqing to Hong Kong, but they had to be moved after the Japanese army occupied Hong Kong in 1942, this time the destination being Guilin. Mao Dun's *Miscellaneous Record on the Escape* (《脱险杂记》) was about how he and his wife assumed aliases, disguised themselves as vendors, and broke through the blockade under the protection of guerrilla forces, and finally made it back safely to the mainland through Kowloon, Ton Kiang, and Lao Long. It took them two full months to arrive in Guilin from Hong Kong. Those who settled in Guilin after the war broke out included Wang Luyan (who died there out of poverty and illness in 1944), Ouyang Yuqian, Ai Wu, Sima Wensen (司马文森), and Shao Quanlin (邵荃麟). And those who moved there from Chongqing, Guangzhou, and Hong Kong for refuge included Mao Dun, Xia Yan, Tian Han, An E (安娥), Luo Binji, Duanmu Hongliang, Hu Feng, and Nie Gannu. In the peak period there were as many as a thousand intellectuals living in Guilin. It was in this city that Mao Dun wrote the major novels of his later period. There were many dramatic activities in Guilin, almost as good as the theatrical performances in Chongqing. A dozen newspapers and magazines were edited and published in the city. And, according to Zhao Jiabi, up to 80 percent of the literary books in the entire Nationalist-controlled area were published in Guilin. Guilin remained a cultural center during the Anti-Japanese War until 1944, when the war situation in Hunan and Guilin became tense and intellectuals had to evacuate again.

The flow between these wartime literary centers was inevitable as well as necessary. Taking Mao Dun and Ba Jin for example, they traveled to almost

31.14. Ouyang Yuqian (front row, in the middle), who fled to the southwest, took this photo in 1940 with young people of the Guangxi Opera Troupe, of which he was a cofounder

31.15. Inaugural issue of *Call to Arms* weekly, from whose table of contents one can see the note explaining it was a temporary merger of four journals, and the title of the Inaugural Message: "Taking Up Our Respective Posts"

every city in the southwestern and northwestern part of the country because they edited newspapers and books and were closely linked to constantly moving editorial offices and publishing houses. Before Shanghai was occupied by the Japanese army, its four largest literary journals launched before the war, namely *Literature*, *Mainstream*, *Literary Season*, and *Translation*, were temporarily combined into one magazine, *Call to Arms*, which was later moved to Guangzhou with its name changed to *Beacon Fire* (《烽火》) and existed for a while. When *Call to Arms* was launched, Mao Dun was its editor and Ba Jin its publisher; Mao Dun wrote the Inaugural Message for the journal, entitled "Taking Up Our Respective Posts" (《站上各自的岗位》). And during the eight years after the war broke out, Mao Dun and Ba Jin indeed wandered from one place to another and endured many hardships, but they always took up their posts as responsible intellectuals. In order to edit *Literary Front* and "Language Forest" (言林), a supplement of the *Li Newspaper* (《立报》),

Mao Dun first went to Guangzhou and Hong Kong, and later traveled to Xinjiang to escape danger, then left Yan'an for Chongqing for the united cultural front, and then fled between Hong Kong, Guilin, and Chongqing. He published *Corrosion* (《腐蚀》) in Hong Kong, *Red Leaves Are as Beautiful as Spring Flowers* in Guilin, and wrote *Before and After the Qingming Festival* (《清明前后》) in Chongqing. Ba Jin remained in the isolated island of Shanghai to finish *Spring*, the second of his "Torrent" trilogy; and in order to resume the publishing of *Beacon Fire*, and to edit and publish *Literary Series*

31.16. Three Zhangs of the Chongqing *New Citizen* newspaper in the 1940s: (left to right) Zhang Huijian (张慧剑), Zhang Henshui, and Zhang Youluan (张友鸾). All fled to the unoccupied area in Sichuan from the lower reaches of the Yangtze River

(《文丛》) and the series books and journals of the Cultural Life Press, he traveled between Hong Kong, Guangzhou, Wuhan, and Guilin, then returned to Shanghai to finish *Autumn*, the last of the "Torrent" trilogy; and with the freshly published 500-page *Autumn*, he went to Kunming to see his fiancée Xiao Shan (萧珊), who was studying at the Southwestern Associated University. It was on his way to Kunming that he stopped in Jiang'an to visit Cao Yu, which was the beginning of their friendship, and later his novel *Family* was creatively adapted by Cao Yu. After his wedding, Ba Jin wrote *Garden of Repose* (《憩园》) in Guiyang and *Ward Four* (《第四病室》) in Chongqing. Migrating between different literary centers, he kept writing as a patriotic intellectual.

31.17. Cartoon strip drawn by Zhang Henshui during the Anti-Japanese War, published in *New Citizen*, which satirized traitors of the Chinese people

During the isolated island period and the occupation period, Shanghai had long lost its position as a literary center. The writers who lived in seclusion in the city at that time expressed their resistance with their silence. On the other hand, the outflow of left-wing writers and radical young student readers left plenty of room for the development of popular literature and the popularization of literature. At this time, in Shanghai as well as other occupied areas in the northeastern and northern parts of the country, a number of writers who blended the old and new styles and appealed to both refined and popular tastes came to the foreground, including Zhang Ailing, Su Qing, Yu Qie, Dongfang Didong (东方蝃蝀), and Mei Niang. Meanwhile, there was a trend of commercialized drama for urban citizens in Shanghai. Examples included the performance of *Qiu Haitang* (《秋海棠》), a popular drama jointly adapted by the former novelist Qin Shouou (秦瘦鸥), the playwright Gu Zhongyi, and film directors Huang Zuolin (黄佐临) and Fei Mu (费穆); and then there were adaptations of foreign plays into local popular plays, such as Li Jianwu's *Wang Deming* (《王德明》, adapted from Shakespeare's *Macbeth*), Shi Tuo's *The Big Circus* (《大马戏团》, adapted from Andreyev's *He Who Gets Slapped*), and Shi Tuo and Ke Ling's *The Night Inn* (《夜店》, adapted from Gorky's *The Lower Depths*). All these were good efforts that took advantage of the unique market situation in Shanghai during this time. The literary journal *Phenomena* (《万象》), edited and transformed by Ke Ling, also displayed the trend of urban popular literature blending the old and the new. Thus, in the 1940s, a literary ecology took shape featuring the diversification and coexistence of multiple literary centers, including Chongqing, Yan'an, Guilin, and Kunming. This had never happened before the war, but it was a new literary landscape that had origins everywhere.

MAP 31.1. Direction of migration of some writers during the Anti-Japanese War period, 1936 to 1945.
Mao Dun

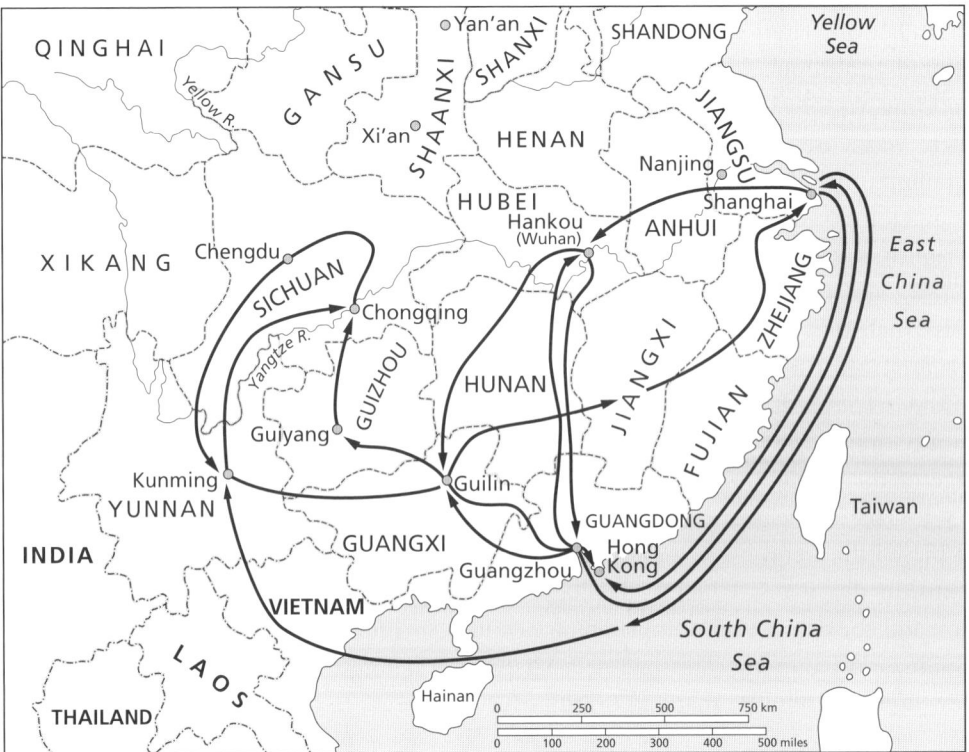

Ba Jin

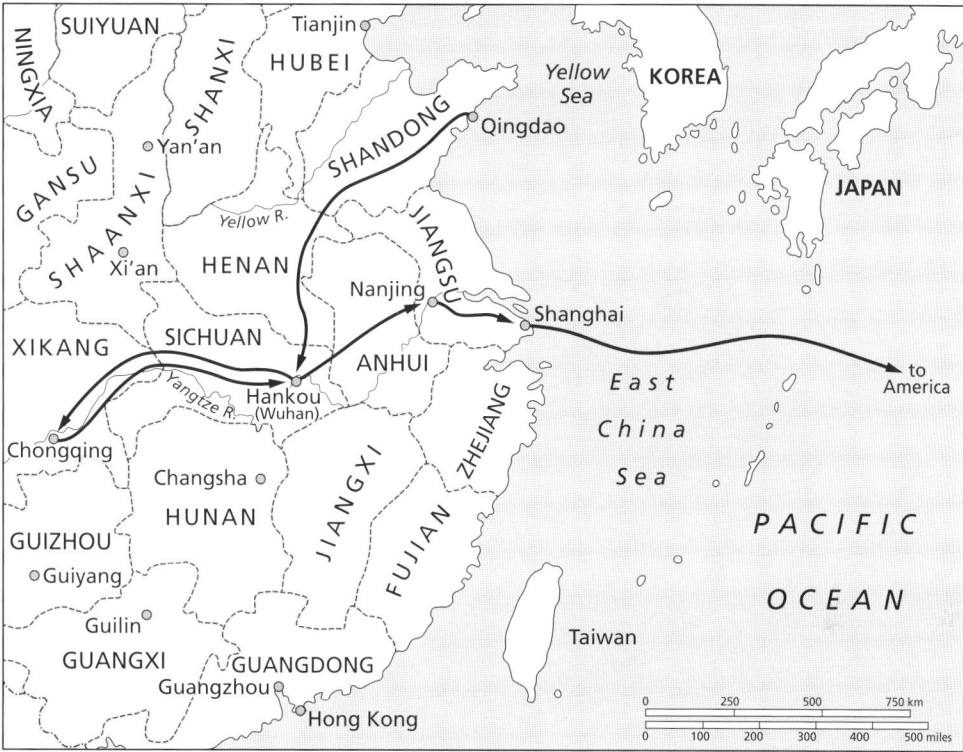

Lao She

Tian Han

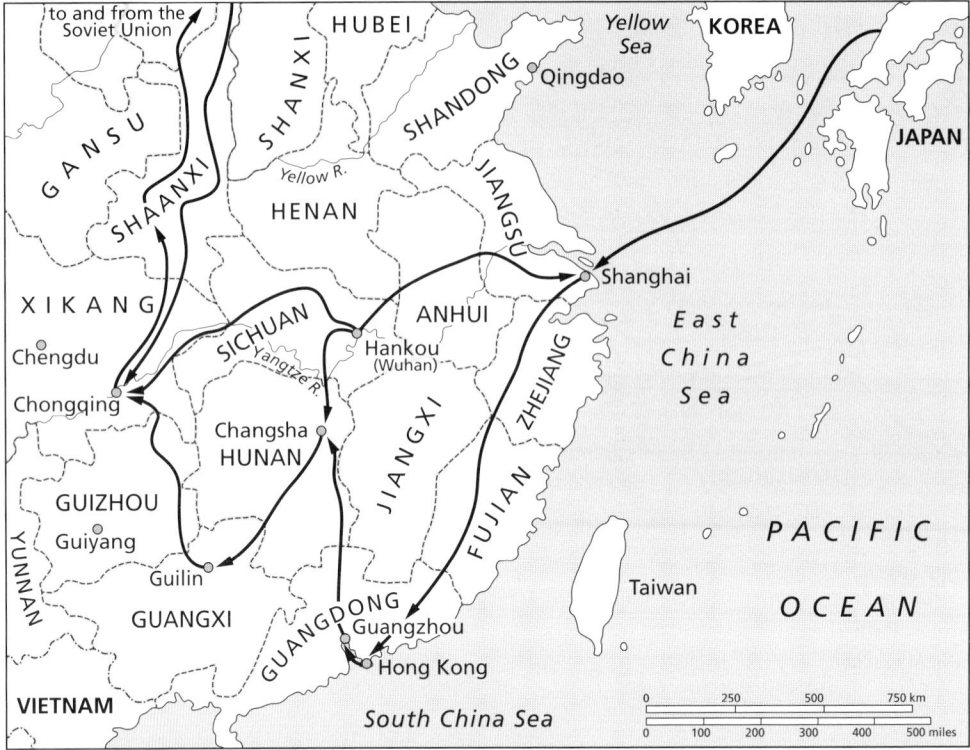

Guo Moruo

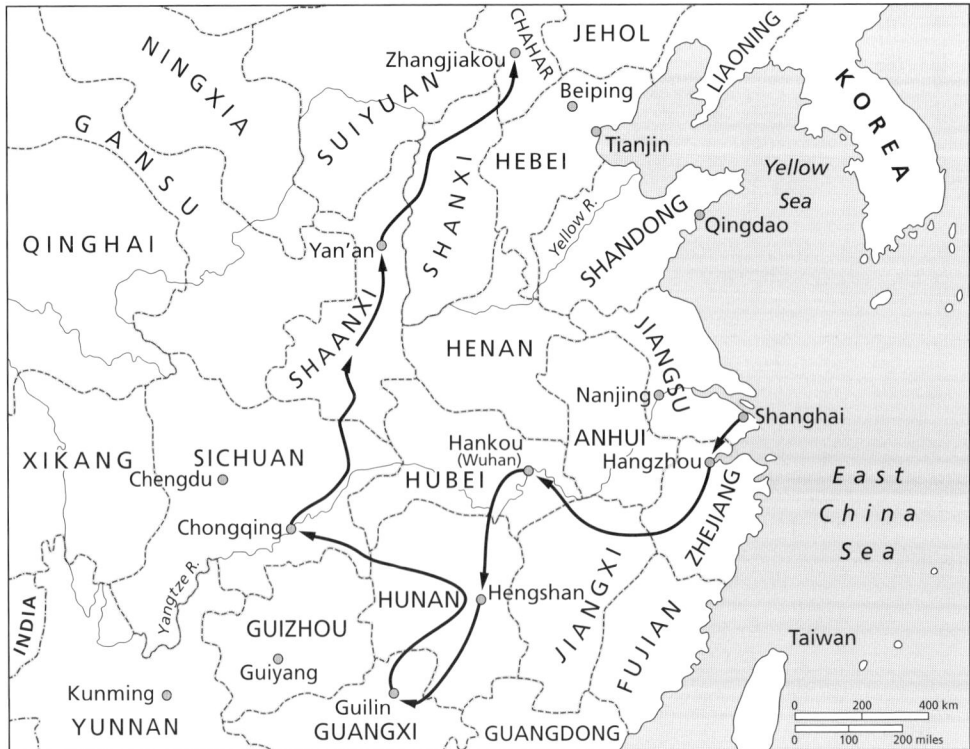

Ai Qing

TABLE 31.1 *Direction of migration of some writers during the Anti-Japanese War period*

Name	Whereabouts in July 1937	Whereabouts in October 1938 when Wuhan was lost	Whereabouts in January 1941 when Wannan Incident occurred	Whereabouts in December 1941 when Hong Kong was occupied by the Japanese Army	Whereabouts in November 1944 when Guilin fell	Whereabouts in August 1945 when Japan surrendered
Mao Dun	Shanghai	Hong Kong, later went to Xinjiang	Chongqing, then returned to Hong Kong	Hong Kong, later retreated to Guilin	Remained in Chongqing	Chongqing, returned to Shanghai the following year
Lao She	Qingdao	Wuhan, went to Chongqing in July	Chongqing	Remained in Chongqing	Still remained in Chongqing	Chongqing, went to the United States from Shanghai the following year
Guo Moruo	Ichikawa, Japan	Wuhan, went to Guilin	Chongqing	Remained in Chongqing	Still remained in Chongqing	In USSR, returned to Chongqing and then went to Shanghai the following year
Bing Xin	Beiping	Kunming	Chongqing	Remained in Chongqing	Still remained in Chongqing	Chongqing, returned to Beiping the following year
Ye Shengtao	Suzhou	Chongqing, later went to Leshan	Chengdu	Remained in Chengdu	Still remained in Chengdu	Chengdu, later went to Shanghai from Chongqing
Ding Xilin	Shanghai	Shanghai, later went to Kunming	Hong Kong	Hong Kong, later went to Guilin	Went to Chongqing before the fall of Guilin	In USSR, returned to Chongqing and then went to Shanghai

(continued)

TABLE 31.1 (continued)

Name	Whereabouts in July 1937	Whereabouts in October 1938 when Wuhan was lost	Whereabouts in January 1941 when Wannan Incident occurred	Whereabouts in December 1941 when Hong Kong was occupied by the Japanese Army	Whereabouts in November 1944 when Guilin fell	Whereabouts in August 1945 when Japan surrendered
Cao Yu	Tianjin	Chongqing, later went to Jiang'an	Jiang'an	Jiang'an, later went to Chongqing	Remained in Chongqing	Chongqing, went to the United States from Shanghai the following year
Ba Jin	Shanghai	Witnessed the fall of Wuhan and Guangzhou	Chengdu, later went to Chongqing	In Guilin for most of the time, went to the border of Guizhou and Sichuan	Remained in Chongqing	Chongqing, returned to Shanghai at the end of the year
Bai Wei	Beiping	Wuhan, later went to Guilin	Chongqing	Remained in Chongqing	Still remained in Chongqing	Chongqing, went to Shanghai the following year
Hu Feng	Shanghai	Went to Chongqing after Wuhan fell	Chongqing, later went to Hong Kong	Hong Kong, later retreated to Guilin	Remained in Chongqing	Chongqing, returned to Shanghai the following year
Zhang Henshui	Nanjing	Chongqing	Chongqing	Remained in Chongqing	Still remained in Chongqing	Chongqing, returned to Anqing the following year
Feng Zikai	Shimen Town, Chongde County	Guilin	Zunyi	Remained in Zunyi, later went to Chongqing	Chongqing	Chongqing, returned to Shanghai and Hangzhou the following year

(continued)

Zhang Tianyi	Shanghai	Shaoyang, later went to Xupu	Xupu, later migrated to Ningxiang	Ningxiang	Went through a tough journey to Chongqing	Chengdu, returned to Shanghai three years later
Sha Ting	Shanghai	Yan'an, later went to Jizhong	Chongqing, later returned to An County	Lived in seclusion in his hometown, Jushui Town, An County	Was called to Chongqing for Rectification	Still lived in seclusion in Jushui Town, An County
Wu Zuxiang	Nanjing	Wuhan, later went to Chongqing	Chongqing	Remained in Chongqing	Still remained in Chongqing	Chongqing, went to the United States and then returned to Nanjing
Lu Ling	Nanjing	Returned to Chongqing from Hechuan	Chongqing	Chongqing	Remained in Chongqing	Chongqing, returned to Nanjing the following year
Zang Kejia	Returned to Linqing from Beiping	The Fifth War Zone, including Henan, Hubei, and Anhui	Resident of the Thirtieth Division of the National Revolutionary Army	Sizhuang Village, Ye County, Henan, later went to Chongqing	Remained in Chongqing	Chongqing, went to Nanjing and Shanghai the following year
Xia Yan	Shanghai	Retreated to Guilin after Guangzhou fell	Guilin, then took refuge in Hong Kong	Retreated to Guilin after the fall of Hong Kong	Remained in Chongqing	Chongqing, went to Shanghai in September of this year
Tian Han	Nanjing	Wuhan, later went to Changsha	Chongqing, later went to Guilin	Remained in Guilin	Guilin, later went to Guiyang	Kunming, went to Chongqing and Shanghai the following year
Wen Yiduo	Beiping	Migrated to Hunan from Beiping and then walked to Kunming	Chenjiaying, in the northern suburbs of Kunming	Sijiaying, in the northeastern suburbs of Kunming	Remained in Kunming	Kunming, was assassinated the following year

(continued)

TABLE 31.1 *(continued)*

Name	Whereabouts in July 1937	Whereabouts in October 1938 when Wuhan was lost	Whereabouts in January 1941 when Wannan Incident occurred	Whereabouts in December 1941 when Hong Kong was occupied by the Japanese Army	Whereabouts in November 1944 when Guilin fell	Whereabouts in August 1945 when Japan surrendered
Zhu Ziqing	Beiping	Migrated to Mengzi from Beiping and then returned to Kunming	Chengdu	Settled in Sijiaying after returning to Kunming	Went between Chengdu and Kunming	Chengdu, returned to Beiping through Chongqing the following year
Feng Zhi	Shanghai	Went to Guangxi through Hunan from Jiangxi	Yangjiashan, in the eastern suburbs of Kunming	Returned to Kunming	Kunming	Kunming, returned to Beiping through Chongqing the following year
Shen Congwen	Beiping	Went to Kunming from Yuanling	Long Street in Chenggong, near Kunming	Chenggong	Chenggong	Chenggong, returned to Beiping the following year
Bian Zhilin	Yandang	Yan'an, visited the Taihang mountain areas	Kunming	Remained in Kunming	Still remained in Kunming	Kunming, returned to Shanghai, and then went to Tianjin the following year
Ding Ling	From Bao'an to Yan'an	Returned to Yan'an from Xi'an	Yan'an	Remained in Yan'an	Remained in Yan'an for a total of eight years	Yan'an, later went to Zhangjiakou
Ai Qing	From Shanghai to Hangzhou	Hengshan, later went to Guilin	Chongqing, later went to Yan'an	Remained in Yan'an	Remained in Yan'an for four years	Yan'an, later went to Zhangjiakou

(continued)

Xiao Jun	Shanghai	Chengdu, later went to Chongqing	Yan'an	Remained in Yan'an, once participated in farmwork in the countryside	Yan'an	Yan'an, went to the northeast through Zhangjiakou
He Qifang	Liaoyang	Yan'an, went to Jizhong and then returned	Yan'an	Remained in Yan'an	Chongqing, later returned to Yan'an	Yan'an, later went to Chongqing
Xiao Hong	Shanghai	Went to Chongqing after the fall of Wuhan	Hong Kong	Passed away in a hospital in Hong Kong during the war		
Shi Zhecun	Songjiang, Shanghai	Went to Hong Kong and then returned to Kunming	Yong'an	Yong'an	Changting	Changting, returned to Shanghai the following year
Yu Dafu	Returned from Shanghai to Fuzhou	Fuzhou, later went to Singapore	Singapore	Went to Sumatra after Singapore fell	Hid and assumed an alias in Sumatra	Murdered in Sumatra in September

THIRTY TWO

INTELLECTUALS' ECONOMIC CONDITIONS AND THEIR WRITING LIFESTYLE

W HAT'S WORTH A SPECIAL MENTION ABOUT THE WARTIME literary scene was writers' state in exile and their general poverty. Destitution and homelessness, combined with specific political and cultural factors, as discussed in Chapter 31, had reinforced people's sense of insecurity and given rise to multiple literary centers. But poverty was a threat that was faced even more frequently and helplessly. Or we might say that it was under the double shadow of poverty and death that intellectuals had profound experiences of life amid homelessness and the life-threatening danger of war, which may be seen as the twofold effect of this double-edged sword of the literary environment. In February 1941, Hong Shen, the well-known dramatist living

in Chongqing, the largest literary center during the war, attempted suicide with his entire family, and he wrote these as his intended last words: "I am totally helpless, in such hard political, career, family, and economic conditions. It would be better to return." Fortunately they were all rescued from danger. Even such a prestigious writer who had studied in the United States was stuck in such a plight, not to mention the untimely deaths of Ye Zi and Wang Luyan, and the total helplessness of Zhang Tianyi after falling seriously ill. Therefore, activities were organized in the hinterland to save and help poor and sick writers, to discuss ways to increase writing income and

32.1. Hong Shen, who attempted suicide with his whole family during the war

drama royalties and improve writers' living conditions, and the slogan "1,000 characters shall be worth a deca-litre of rice" (meaning the writing income for 1,000 characters should be enough to buy a decalitre of rice, and the price to buy the copyright should be double this amount) was devised. Due to soaring prices and the collapse of the currency, writers had to evaluate their writings with material objects like this. Here I want to conduct a brief review of the living and economic conditions of three generations of intellectuals from the late Qing to the 1940s, as well as how these conditions affected their writing lifestyle.

From the late-Qing period to the early Republican era was the first stage of modern transformation of Chinese literature. Intellectuals of this period may be represented by the Mandarin Duck and Butterfly authors, that is, the first generation of modern professional writers, of whom Bao Tianxiao was typical. Bao was born into a merchant family, which had come to poverty, in Suzhou in 1876, the second year under Emperor Guangxu's reign. Being only five years older than Lu Xun, Bao had participated in the imperial examinations twice and was a full-time student of the old-style education system; he became a lowest-level scholar after passing the national civil service examination. Intellectuals of his generation, however, after receiving formal education in the old-style system, became the earliest professional

32.2. Special page published by *The Contemporaries* to commemorate Zhu Xiang, who committed suicide before the war. The ultimate reason for most writers to commit suicide was their spiritual predicament

32.3. The earliest royalty agreement in China, signed between Yan Fu and the Commercial Press in 1903 for the book *A Full Account of Society* (《社会通诠》). Writers' incomes were closely related to their living conditions

writers who made a living by writing for modern publishing and newspaper industries because their families had become impoverished, and Bao was indeed not alone. Bao Tianxiao launched the *Suzhou Vernacular Newspaper*, participated in the founding of the Shanghai Jinsuzhai Translation Agency (金粟斋译书处), began writing novels as a newspaperman and editor of the *Shanghai Times* and *Forest of Fiction*, and became famous after publishing "A Strand of Flax," "Shine Forever" (《留芳记》), and *Shanghai Records*, etc. If he had not entered the newspaper and publishing industries in Shanghai, Bao could only have made a living by teaching as a lower-level scholar within the imperial examination system, and the monthly salary of the old-style private school was three silver dollars. But as an editor of the *Shanghai Times* who also wrote news comments and fictions, he could earn as much as 80 silver dollars per month, with another 40 silver dollars earned by editing *Forest of Fiction*, and then he also had other sources of writing income. Bao Tianxiao was such a quick hand in writing that he could write as many as 4,000–5,000 characters each day. According to relevant documents, the writing income of that time was, as claimed by the "Notice on Contributing Paintings" (see Chapter 1, Figure 1.18), "two silver dollars (for each painting)," which was the earliest published promise of remuneration for works to be published. According to Liang Qichao's recollection, when he launched *New Citizen* and *New Novel* in Japan in 1902,

> the remuneration for news comments and critique writings may be fixed to three silver dollars per 1,000 characters. That for treatises may be a bit more (according to the value of the specific article), with the highest as much as four silver dollars, while for the average ones, three silver dollars. As for news stories or accounts of events, it is two silver dollars per 1,000 characters. This is a general rule of remuneration.[1]

This was not very different from Bao Tianxiao's account:

> the standard rate was two silver dollars per 1,000 characters, and fictions of this level needed no revision. … Later they raised the rate of remuneration for my fictions to three silver dollars per thousand characters, and the increase was because the Commercial Press asked me to write education novels for their education magazines. … By that time Mr. Lin Qinnan had been translating and writing fictions for the Commercial Press and other publishing institutions, and the Commercial Press paid him five silver dollars per thousand characters.[2]

Certainly, these were the best of all professional writers. Bao Tianxiao mentioned that for the writings that needed revision, the remuneration could be

---

[1] Ding Wenjiang: *A First Draft of the Long Version of Master Liang Rengong's Chronological History, Volume I*, p. 229.
[2] Bao Tianxiao: *Memoirs of the Bracelet Shadow Chamber*, Hong Kong: Dahua Publishing House, 1971, pp. 324–325.

as little as half a silver dollar per 1,000 characters, and he then took Pingjiang Buxiaosheng (aka Xiang Kairan) as an example, saying that Xiang did not have any business connections when he returned from Japan, so that even for his novel *Private Records of Studying in Japan*, which brought a huge amount of wealth for the publisher, the remuneration was only half a silver dollar per 1,000 characters. Therefore, if a mediocre writer could write 50,000 characters per month, he could earn twenty-five silver dollars, barely enough for supporting a family but ample for a single person. If a writer could sell his writings for two silver dollars per 1,000 characters, according to Bao Tianxiao's memoir, his monthly writing income often exceeded his fixed income, and the two income sources combined may well exceed 200 silver dollars per month. The cost of living in Shanghai was higher than in other places during the late Qing, and he rented a wing-room of a *shikumen*-style building for seven silver dollars per month, and the general purchase power of one silver dollar was equivalent to seventy yuan today; therefore, the "living expenses and small expenses [of a three-member family] were at most fifty or sixty silver dollars."[3] Thus Bao Tianxiao was transformed into a successful profit-making modern writer.

By the time of *New Youth*, Chen Duxiu, Lu Xun, and Zhou Zuoren, who had all studied in and returned from Japan, as well as Hu Shi and others who had studied in and returned from the United States, became the pioneers and pathbreakers of the literary revolution. In 1916, Chen Duxiu fixed the remuneration for writings published in *New Youth* as "two silver dollars (for translation) to five silver dollars (for original writings) per 1,000 characters," and at that time, the magazine had a circulation of 1,000 copies per issue. By the following year, the circulation of the magazine suddenly soared to 10,000–20,000 copies. In 1918, however, this extremely popular magazine published a notice, saying that "the article contribution rules have been abolished. All writing and translating will be done by staff members of the editorial office, and no articles or translations from external sources will be collected." According to relevant research, apart from the editing payment of 200 silver dollars for the alternate editor-in-chief of each issue, staff members of the magazine were indeed not paid for their contributions. Even Lu Xun published his fictions and essays such as "The Diary of a Madman" and "Impromptu Reflections" in *New Youth* without being paid. The key point here was that most writers for *New Youth* were teaching staff members of the Faculty of Humanities of Peking University, and their main source of income was teaching instead of writing. For them, it was possible and worthy to compromise their remuneration in order to maintain the purity of the magazine and avoid spending time and energy revising contributions from external sources. Thus they became the earliest examples of professor-writers and university writers. In the 1910s,

---

[3] Bao Tianxiao: *Memoirs of the Bracelet Shadow Chamber*, p. 324.

the living expenses in Beijing were quite low: a well-off family of four or five could sustain themselves with twelve silver dollars per month, and for a wealthy family of intellectuals, eighty silver dollars was sufficient for all their meals, rent, and commuting expenses. While in 1919 the monthly income of those at Peking University was as follows: Cai Yuanpei was paid 600 silver dollars as the president; Chen Duxiu, 300 silver dollars as the dean of Humanities; Hu Shi, 280 as a professor; Qian Xuantong, 240, professor; Zhou Zuoren, 240, professor and the director of the National History Compilation Office; Wu Mei, 220, professor; Liu Bannong, 200, professor; and Li Dazhao, 120, curator of the Peking University Library.

Outside Peking University, staff members of other public education institutions were also well paid. Lin Qinnan, for example, was paid as much as 500 silver dollars as a professor of Beijing Zhengzhi School (北京正志学校) thanks to his seniority in age and experience. Lu Xun was also well paid as a commissioner for the Ministry of Education, 300 silver dollars per month, and he had other sources of income as a part-time teacher at universities in Beijing.[4] We can see that these May Fourth writers were quite well-off, living a middle-class life. From Lu Xun's diaries one can get a glimpse of their everyday lives, which consisted of reading, teaching, writing, meeting friends, attending dinner parties, visiting antique shops, going to the theater, and watching movies. Compared with Bao Tianxiao and other talented newspapermen in Shanghai, they did not need to do night shifts or live the night life, and they did not spend so much on entertainment. Some professors of Peking University also entertained themselves with prostitutes, but they were only a few. Under the rule of the Beiyang government, Lu Xun and other professor-writers and civil servant-writers were sometimes troubled by inflation or back pay, but their life was generally secure. Therefore, for accomplished writers, they enjoyed fairly good economic conditions for literary creation. As for the hardships faced by literary youths in Beijing – such as Shen Congwen, who was penniless when he first came to Beijing in 1923 – it was another matter; as was the case of literary youths in Shanghai, who lived in the garret and

32.4. Left-wing writers usually gathered in modern venues in Shanghai, such as the Gongfei Café, where plans for setting up the League of Left-Wing Writers were made

---

4   This material is quoted from Chen Mingyuan: *Economic Life of Intellectuals*, pp. 87–90.

could either find no one to buy their writings or were seriously exploited by publishers. However, once Shen Congwen was able to have his writings published in newspapers and magazines, his living conditions were greatly improved – evidence that one could sustain a family with writing income at that time.

By the 1930s, a generation of young writers who had been born at the beginning of the twentieth century and received new-style education rose to fame, and several groups of writers began to take shape, such as the left-wing, Shanghai school, Beijing school, and Mandarin Duck and Butterfly school. The liberal writers in Beijing followed the tradition of university writers: with Hu Shi and Zhou Zuoren at Peking University and Zhu Ziqing, Wen Yiduo, Yu Pingbo, and Chen Yinke at Tsinghua University. Students from these two universities who later became excellent writers included Fei Ming, He Qifang, Li Guangtian, Bian Zhilin, Lin Geng, Cao Yu, Wu Zuxiang, and Qian Zhongshu. The salary for professors was a bit higher than that in the May Fourth period. After graduation, the students could remain at the university to be teaching assistants or teach in middle schools, and thus they could, like their predecessors, have a teaching job but also write for another source of income. Those who were less qualified to become professors in Beijing could start at universities in other places. Lao She, for example, had been a professor in Shandong for a long time. He had attempted to quit teaching and become a professional writer in 1934, but failed. He mentioned this in the preface of *Cherries and the Sea* (《樱海集》), saying that it seemed that "I cannot sustain myself by writing." Shen Congwen, who had not even finished his primary school education in his native town, later published a number of books in Shanghai. Hu Shi recommended him to teach at the China Public School, and it was only after he had gained teaching experience at the college that he was able to teach at Shandong University in Qingdao and later teach in Beijing. Interestingly, a "debate between Beijing and Shanghai schools" occurred in 1933, in which an article written by Su Wen (aka Du Heng) entitled "Writers in Shanghai," in response to Shen Congwen's argument, boiled the issue down to economic conditions:

> It is not easy to make a living in Shanghai, which naturally affected writers, and thus writers in Shanghai, like those in every other profession, have to make money. Further, it is not easy for writers in Shanghai to find a side occupation (or I shall call it a "full-time occupation"). They could not even find a job to make a living, not to say a job as a professor, and writers in Shanghai are certainly more eager to make money. As a result, naturally, they are more prolific; they finish writing more quickly and are eager to submit it. They cannot leave the draft in the drawers and revise it again and again.[5]

---

[5] Su Wen: "Writers in Shanghai," *The Contemporaries*, Vol. 4, Issue 2, Dec. 1, 1933.

32.5. Liu Bannong and his family in their residence in Paris when he studied there in 1924. The stove and soy sauce bottle showed that they lived a meagre life there, but it also showed they were happy together

32.6. Tian Han, who was transformed by the influence of the younger generation during the period of the Southern China Society and was a dramatist who lived a bohemian-style life

Putting aside the reasons Su Wen mentioned, this passage vividly presented the physical and psychological state of Shanghai writers, who struggled to make a living from writing. Except for professor-writers and official-writers (who were officials in charge of cultural and educational affairs), most Shanghai school writers and left-wing writers, who lived in extreme poverty and did not write popular literature but worked as freelance writers in the metropolis, would encounter such difficult situations in the 1930s. Of them, Lu Xun was a famous writer who was not in poverty, but he gave up his teaching job at Xiamen University (which paid him 400 silver dollars per month) and at Sun Yat-sen University (which paid him 500 silver dollars per month) in the 1920s and changed dramatically from a professor-civil official to a freelance writer. Lu Xun did write to make a living, but his writings sold well and were well paid in the market in spite of his political leanings. Writing for "Free Talk," the supplement of *Shun Pao*, Lu Xun's remuneration was six silver dollars per 1,000 characters, and he was even paid as much as ten silver dollars per 1,000 characters in Shanghai. All his books, from *Call to Arms* to *Correspondence*, were enduring best sellers. Ba Jin was another well-known freelance writer who was well paid; with his best-selling novels and good reputation as a journal editor, he could live well among young readers without having to rely on any political party. Lu Xun took a liking to him because of this. In the left-wing camp, prestigious and well-educated writers such as Tian Han, Xia Yan, and Hu Feng were generally well-off with the payments they received for their writings, drama performances, and translation works. Tian Han was sometimes an exception because of his profession and his personality. A native of Hunan, he was nicknamed "Boss Tian" by people in the dramatic circle, for he was born romantic and unconstrained. He could have well sustained himself and supported his family if he just made a living by selling his plays, but he founded dramatic troupes and launched journals like a wasteful boss, and would help others generously whenever they were in difficulty, so he often could not make ends meet. And then there were left-wing garret writers such as Ding Ling, Sha Ting, Ai Wu, Rou Shi, Ye Zi, Xiao Jun, and Xiao Hong. They were from different family backgrounds, but all struggled as lower-class urban citizens when their works did not sell in the market. The League of Left-Wing Writers did not pay them salaries, but assigned revolutionary work to them without considering how they could make a living. After Ai Wu was expelled to Shanghai from Myanmar, he joined *Zuolian* and was sent to Yangshupu by the Committee of Mass Literature and Art to organize the correspondent movement and teach at the workers' night school in a factory without any payment. Therefore, he had to borrow money from his former classmate Sha Ting (at that time, six silver dollars was enough for him to sustain himself each month), until he was arrested at the factory. These people had high ideals and hope for the future, without which it was impossible for them to live such an extremely poor semiclandestine life.

The New Sensationalist writers, mostly from the Jiangsu and Zhejiang areas, formed a relatively special group. Liu Na'ou was from a wealthy Taiwanese family, and others were from impoverished middle-class families. But they took an interest in the latest fashions in Shanghai, were fascinated by avant-garde art and literature, and pursued an unrestrained lifestyle as modern young people. After graduating from university, Mu Shiying lived alone in an apartment in Hongkou, and went dancing in the nearby Moon Palace Ballroom every night, sometimes even writing his fictions in a corner of the ballroom. Liu Na'ou opened up his house in Park Alley, Jiangwan Road, to his friends Mu Shiying, Dai Wangshu, Ye Lingfeng, Du Heng, and Gao Ming, and let them live there without charging rent. They wrote and read fictions or poetry during the daytime, and took walks in the garden, or

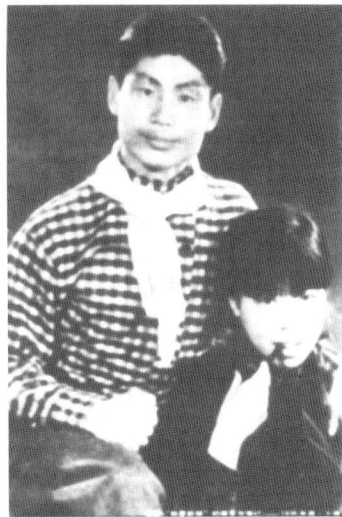

32.7. In order to visit Lu Xun at his home in 1934, Xiao Hong spent a whole day making a Western stand-up collar shirt for Xiao Jun, and the pipe was a prop from the photo shop. Both were typical left-wing garret writers

went for bike rides, or went swimming, dancing, and betting on ball games at dusk, and returned to "sit on the doorstep in the mild breeze, watching the moon and talking freely" at night.[6] It felt like a settlement for Chinese modernist writers. However, their economic conditions could not sustain such a lifestyle, for they were, ultimately, freelance writers, different from Beijing school university writers. Theirs, therefore, was no more than a short-term literary summer camp.

From the outbreak of the Anti-Japanese War until the 1940s, as the war progressed, writers' living conditions deteriorated. Those in the Nationalist-controlled area felt it most strongly (though people's feelings sometimes could not reflect their actual situations; in the "liberated region," writers, like other people, lived in a free supply system, and did not feel as though they were in great poverty). Freelance writers were the most vulnerable, and even the best-known writers felt it necessary to find other sources of income. Examples include Lao She, who worked in the Association of Writers and Artists, and Guo Moruo, who was paid by the Third Office. The income must have been one of Mao Dun's chief considerations when he thought of working in Xinjiang. Cao Yu, who was from a rich family and was not capable of making a living by himself, had to attach himself to the drama school. Ba Jin, who was most vigorous in literary creation, had finished 400,000 characters in six months when he wrote *Autumn* in the isolated island Shanghai, during which time he wrote from nine o'clock in the evening until three or four o'clock in the morning. But even he could not make a living with his writing income, but had to take some shifts with Cultural Life Press. Even the professor-writers lost their advantage of high salaries due to the inflation of wartime legal currency and price rises, and the gap between them and freelance writers narrowed, gradually disappearing, so much so that their living conditions became even worse than lower-class working people. This could be seen as the largest inverse wage disparity between intellectuals and blue-collar workers in the last century. Economists and sociologists of the National Southwestern Associated University published an academic report entitled "Estimates of Minimum Living Expenses of Professor Families in Kunming" (《昆明教授家庭最低生活费的估计》). According to their estimates, before the war, the minimum living expenses for a family of five of a professor or associate professor was fifty silver dollars, while the average monthly salary of a professor or associate professor was 350 silver dollars; with an expense–income ratio of 1:7, they led quite a well-off life before the war. By October 1941, the minimum living expenses increases to 1,800 silver dollars, while the monthly salary only increased to 600 silver dollars, leading to an expense–income ratio of 3:1,

---

[6] Mu Shiying: "Letter to Ye Lingfeng" of June 7, 1935, *Complete Works of Mu Shiying*, Vol. 2, Beijing: Beijing October Literature and Arts Press, 2008, p. 38.

32.8. Young left-wing writers who migrated from Shanghai and met in Xi'an: (left to right): Sai Ke (塞克), Tian Jian, Nie Gannu, Xiao Hong, and Duanmu Hongliang; (back row): Ding Ling

which deteriorated further to 5:1 by November 1942, when the minimum living expenses increased to 7,500 silver dollars and the monthly salary was only increased to 1,400 silver dollars. Another source suggested that in 1945, the average monthly salary of a professor of the National Southwestern Associated University was 113,000 silver dollars, but the actual purchasing power of such a huge currency value was equivalent to that of 18.6 silver dollars before the war, less than the salary of a dustman.[7] With such dramatic changes, one can imagine the poor living conditions of professors. No wonder the wives of the professors of the National Southwestern Associated University began to pawn their clothes, open booths on the street, or open restaurants. Things were even worse for Zhu Ziqing and Wen Yiduo who had a lot of children to raise. During a vacation, Zhu Ziqing sent his family to Chengdu, where the prices were lower; to pay for their traveling expenses, he had to sell his gramophone

32.9. Ba Jin, while he was devoting all his time to writing *Autumn* in the isolated island of Shanghai

[7]   This material is quoted from Chen Mingyuan: *Economic Life of Intellectuals*, pp. 219–220, 246.

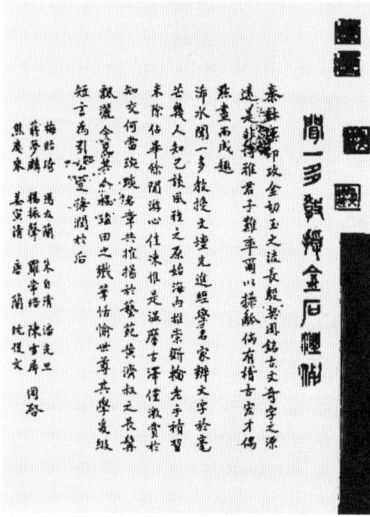

32.10. "Standard of Payment" written by Pu Jiangqing of the Department of Chinese at the National Southwestern Associated University for Wen Yiduo, when the latter began cutting seals for profit. Quite a few famous professors of the Department signed their names on a "Standard," which became a bitter story, well-known among professors and scholars

and two phonograph records, the only luxuries in his home, to the junk shop. Many people remembered the "bizarre clothing" worn by Zhu Ziqing during winters in Kunming, which was a Yunnan caravan coarse felt throw (called a "bell"), which he draped over his shoulders during the daytime and which he used as bedding at night. It indeed took some courage for a professor to act like this. Wen Yiduo excelled at seal cutting, and he had long been cutting seals for others as a source of income. See Figure 32.10 for the "Standard of Payment for the Inscriptions of Professor Wen Yiduo" (《闻一多教授金石润例》) written by Pu Jiangqing (浦江清), a professor of the same department, when Wen Yiduo began cutting seals for profit. The "Standard" was signed by twelve professors, including Mei Yiqi, Feng Youlan (冯友兰), Zhu Ziqing, Yang Zhensheng, and Shen Congwen. From this we can get some idea about why Wen Yiduo, as a professor-writer who enjoyed excellent living conditions in the 1930s and an assiduous scholar who was nicknamed "owner of the Why Not Coming Out Building" (because Wen was diligent in his studies and seldom went outside the building), later joined the democratic movement and was assassinated after delivering his "Last Speech."

Here we shall also give some consideration to the living conditions of female writers during the war. Bai Wei's soul-stirring experience to escape marriage during the 1920s was unforgettable, while talented Xiao Hong died in Hong Kong in 1942 at the age of 30 because of poverty and illness. Her last words were: "I will live with the blue sky and green water forever, and have to leave the unfinished half of *Dream of the Red Chamber* for others to write."

The economic conditions of intellectuals in the "liberated region" were quite different: the conditions were indeed poor, but there was no big gap between superior officials and lower-rank soldiers, and the military free supply system covered students and teachers of the Lu Xun

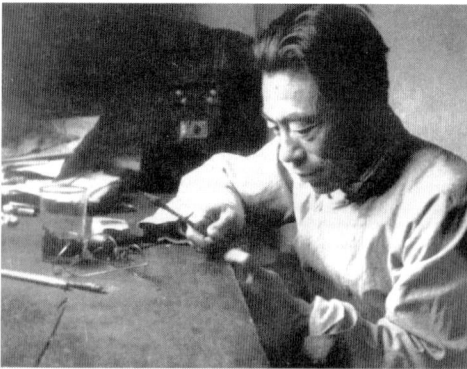

32.11. Wen Yiduo cutting seals for others as a source of income to make ends meet

Arts College. This egalitarian system was a relief and brought hope to writers, especially before the Rectification began.

Thus under the severe living conditions of the war, modern Chinese writers began to explore their personal experiences or the destiny of certain social classes, and the entire nation and human race, with an unprecedented historical perspective. Feng Zhi, the May Fourth lyrical poet, returned home after studying in Germany for five years and migrated to the unoccupied area with his wife and children at the beginning of the war. When he came to teach at the National Southwestern Associated University, he had already experienced a spiritual transformation. What he had learned from Western modernist poetry and existentialist philosophy greatly enhanced his personal experience of the war, the historical era, and life per se. On a winter's afternoon, Feng Zhi walked on a path among the Yangjiashan Woods outside the city of Kunming and saw several silver aeroplanes passing in the blue sky; he was reminded of a dream of a huge mythical bird from ancient times. It was a moment of revelation for him, and he improvised a variant of a sonnet entitled "An Ancient Dream" (《一个旧日的梦想》). Hence the beginning of his masterpiece, *Sonnets* (《十四行集》).

These circumstances also offered a rare opportunity for writers to come close to peasants and lower-class urban citizens, live like them, and gain knowledge of their hardships, and material and spiritual needs. Lu Ling, who lived near Chongqing during the war, took the chance to get to know how the

32.12. Students of the Lu Xun Arts College listening to lectures in the open air, under tough circumstances

32.13. After arriving in Yan'an from Shanxi on foot in 1938, Xiao Jun designed this image of a hiker for himself in a photo studio, which was quite original

lower-class miners, mariners, deserters, performers, and peasants lived, and wrote his "Under the Coal-Unloading Platform" (《卸煤台下》), "Hungry Guo Su'e" (《饥饿的郭素娥》), and "The Hero's Dance" (《英雄的舞蹈》), and his profound reflection on himself and the historical era led to the lengthy novel *Rich Men's Children*. It wasn't until this point in time that writers from cities in the "liberated region" had had a chance to get in touch with the coarse culture, personality, and feelings of peasants and understand their psychological changes. And it was by living with lower-class citizens that writers in the occupied region gained a deeper understanding of human nature among the air-raid sirens. Thus we see the political and cultural stage in Chongqing, the emerging urban popular literature in Shanghai, and the popularization of Yan'an literature that featured the peasant class seeking to face the world, as well as the development and inner conflicts of all these literary landscapes. A full-length literary landscape of the 1940s thus unfolded.

THIRTY THREE

CHONGQING

National Salvation Literature, from Rise to Fall

F ROM WUHAN TO CHONGQING, THE LITERATURE AT THE beginning of the Anti-Japanese War was national salvation literature strongly characteristic of the united anti-Japanese front.

In this unprecedented war of national defense, it became the top priority of patriotic intellectuals to try their best to simply make literature "a means of propaganda." It was against this background that short and efficient art forms were thriving. For example, street theater flourished as the market share of theater plays shrank, because it could easily be used to motivate people to do their best. From the street theater, teahouse plays, and skits that had become popular since the January Twenty-Eighth Incident in Shanghai several years before, to the great number of new plays created after the August Thirteenth Incident, various troupes performed them in urban and rural areas all over the country, including *Put Down Your Whip*, *How Wonderful Are the Three Rivers* (《三江好》, referring to the Heilong River, the Songhua River, and the Yalu River), and *The Last Stratagem* (《最后一计》, these three plays were collectively referred to as "What a Wonderful Stratagem of Whipping" [好一计鞭子]), as well as *Eight Hundred Heroes* (《八百壮士》), *Shedding Blood for the Marco Polo Bridge* (《血洒卢沟桥》), *The Posterity of Traitors* (《汉奸的子孙》), *The Zhang' Inn* (《张家店》), and *Rear Defense* (《后防》). The most famous among these was *Put Down Your Whip*, in which Jin Shan and Wang Ying played the role of the father and daughter respectively, and it was even performed in Southeastern Asia, and Xu Beihong painted an oil painting based on this anecdote (Figure 33.2). Other famous performers of this play, who were no less influential, were Yuan Muzhi and Chen Boer (陈波儿), Ling Zifeng (凌子风) and Ye Zi (叶子), and Cui Wei (崔嵬) and Chen Boer. In poetry, the boundary between era-specific poetry and poetry to express personal emotions, which was clear before the war, blurred. The mass popular poetry advocated by Pu Feng and Ren Jun was greatly promoted; street poetry, leaflet poetry, and poetry for recitation became widely read, and popular poems filled with national sentiments that were adapted from old-style folk ditties, drum lyrics, and sing-song clapper lyrics became extremely popular. Poets involved in this poem recitation movement included Guang Weiran (光未然), Feng Naichao, Xu Chi, and Gao Lan (高兰), the latter even publishing his *Collection of Recitation Poems of Gao Lan* (《高兰朗诵诗集》). As for the well-known poets, their anthologies published during this time, such as Guo Moruo's *Collection of Triumph* (《战声集》), Zang Kejia's *A Soldier at the Front* (《从军行》), Xu Chi's *The Strongest Voice* (《最强音》), and Hu Feng's *Singing for the Motherland* (《为祖国而歌》), also featured swift, masculine, and battle-like qualities. The most outstanding of them was Tian Jian (1916–1985), who was praised by Mao Dun, Wen Yiduo, and Hu Feng and was referred to as the "drummer of the times." It seemed that his poetic lines were written to echo the drumbeat of the Anti-Japanese War:

> *My Dear*
> *People!*
> *Let's grab*
> *Whatever arms*
> *From timber plants,*
> *Wall corners*
> *And*
> *The muddy ditch*
> *Let's throw out*
> *Our scorched,*
> *Weathered,*
> *And badly whipped*
> *Chest,*
> *And let's fight back!*
> *In fighting,*
> *We win*
> *Or die*[1]

Such an outburst of sonorous poetic lines was perfect for motivation. As for narrative works, the situation seemed too urgent for writers to create fictional narratives, so there was a fashion for novelists to write war reports (feature stories) like journalists. Well-known examples included *A Company Commander's War Experience* (by Qiu Dongping), *Here, Life Is Also Breathing* (《这里，生命也在呼吸》, by Cao Bai), *A Battle Is on the Way in Zhabei* (《闸北打了起来》, by Yi Men [亦门]), *A Commando in the Eastern Battlefield*

---

[1]   Tian Jian: "To Fighters" (《给战斗者》), *July*, Vol. 1, Issue 6, 1938.

33.1. Stage photo of Zhang Ruifang (张瑞芳) and Cui Wei (崔嵬) when they performed *Put Down Your Whip* to console and entertain the army in Gubeikou in 1937

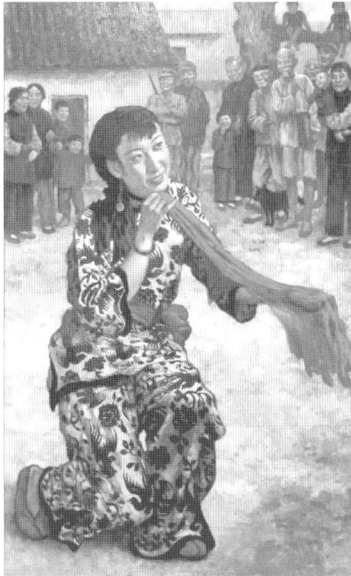

33.2. Oil painting by Xu Beihong (徐悲鸿) of the actress Wang Ying (王莹) performing *Put Down Your Whip*

33.3. Tian Jian (first on left), dressed like a peasant, and friends

(《东战场别动队》, by Luo Binji), *Impressions of the Border Area among Shanxi, Chahar, and Hebei* (《晋察冀边区印象记》, by Libo), *A Sketchy Account of General Peng Dehuai* (《彭德怀将军速写》, by Ding Ling), *Discursive Notes on the Journey with the Army* (《随军散记》, by Sha Ting), *Three Days in Tanggu*

(《塘沽三日》, by Jian Xian'ai), *Four Eggs* (《四个鸡蛋》, by Wang Xiyan), and *Restoration of Humanity* (《人性的恢复》, by Shen Qiyu). Even Bian Zhilin, who was known for his obscure and abstract poetry writing, wrote *The 772nd Regiment along the Taihang Mountain Range* (《第七七二团在太行山一带》).

For a time, the massification and popularization of literature, and the promotion of nationalism and heroism, became two major tasks for literary writers, which was unprecedentedly agreed upon by intellectuals of various groups and even became the government authorities' guiding principle of art and literature. The All-China Resistance Association, for example, had once been entrusted by the propaganda department of the Kuomintang to organize writers to compile guidance regarding Chinese people's recreational activities and entrusted by the Ministry of Education to hold popular art workshops.[2] And the "theory of art of resistance and reconstruction" proposed by the Kuomintang in 1941 included "putting the nation first" and "putting the country first," which was nothing short of raising the old banner of "nationalist literature" of the Nanjing government in the name of "resistance and reconstruction." Certainly, under the pressing circumstances of nationwide resistance, during the period when the KMT government moved its capital to Wuhan and then to Chongqing, nobody voiced any disagreement with this (disputes were raised later, however). Writers devoted their time and energy to the massification and popularization of literature. Lao She, for example, had enthusiastically written drum lyrics, popular song lyrics, traditional opera, cross talks, and popular novels, and compiled and then published the collection of his popular works, *Three, Four, One* (《三四一》). He also gave

33.4. Many authors moved from Chongqing to Beibei after large-scale air bombings, including intellectuals from the All-China Resistance Association and those from Fudan University. This was Liang Shiqiu's Elegant House (雅舍), which he later wrote famous essays about

---

[2]   Ni Wei: *The Imagination of "Nation" and the "State" Governance*, Shanghai: Shanghai Education Press, 2003, p. 244.

his support to the launch of popular journals such as *Resisting Till the End* (《抗到底》), and participated in the editing of popular readings. Tian Han took the lead in adapting local operas that were already familiar to people, putting anti-Japanese resistance elements into the Hunan opera play *Grabbing Umbrella* (《抢伞》), and performed the adapted play entitled *Fellow Travelers* (《旅伴》). He also wrote a thirty-six-act new opera *Jiang-Han Fishermen's Song* (《江汉渔歌》) with a Peking opera format. All these could be seen as efforts in the popularization of literature. It seemed natural, then, for Zhang Henshui to change from writing his familiar social novels to writing resistance novels. Of all the novelists, he was the one who wrote the most novels on the theme of the Anti-Japanese War, including *A Night of Street Fighting* (《巷战之夜》), *The River of No Return* (《大江东去》), and *Long Live Huben* (《虎贲万岁》), evidence that even writers of urban popular novels were actively and consciously reinforcing nationalism.

Certainly, even in the initial stages of this trend, there were some dissonances that had profound implications. The inaugural issue of *Literary Front* (published in April 1938), whose editor-in-chief was Mao Dun, published Zhang Tianyi's short story "Mr. Huawei," in which Zhang presented a character who was enthusiastic about attending meetings and seeking to grab power for his personal gain. This immediately triggered a dispute about whether the art of resistance should focus on exposure and how to expose. In the following year, "Mr. Huawei" was translated into Japanese, which again triggered a debate about whether this would quench Chinese people's fighting spirit. The debate lasted for a long period of time, and had direct bearing upon the position of satire in the literature of resistance. Yao Xueyin's (1910–1999) first well-known piece, "The Half-Baked" (《差半车麦秸》), was published in the third issue of *Literary Front*, which also caused a considerable stir. In this short story, the author presented how a peasant guerrilla character who was simple and selfish and nicknamed "Half-Baked" (because he picked up whatever was useful and took it home from the battlefield) awakened and grew up in the cruel national war. Thus the topic of "rebuilding [peasants'] national character" and remaking "new people" was raised and attracted the world's attention. Both literary works actually predicted the direction of the development of national salvation literature: the negative exposure of social problems and positive reconstruction of the national character had gradually evolved into an introspective literature of national salvation. And by and by, it reignited the various traditions within the literature of the united anti-Japanese front that had been broken by the war, including the left-wing tradition, Beijing-school tradition, and Shanghai-school tradition, as well as the tradition of urban popular literature. This actually linked the literature of resistance with that of the 1930s and made the literature of the 1940s even more complicated, and eventually, gave rise to the post-May Fourth commonality shared by all the literature from these two decades.

In the third or fourth year after the war broke out, the persistence of the war became notable, and faced with extreme poverty and spiritual pressure, the blind optimism of the earlier period of the war abated, and anguish, memories of the past, and somber thoughts began to prevail in literature. In particular, with the "tightness in the front and looseness in the rear," that is, with the increasingly severe political and social corruption, especially the Wannan Incident in 1941 that marked the ongoing conflict between the KMT and CPC, the honeymoon of united anti-Japanese front literature came to an end.

This was particularly true with novel writing. In terms of external conditions, this literary form required the devotion of a great amount of time and energy as well as cultural and artistic accumulations, but in the latter half of the Anti-Japanese War, despite the hard times, Chinese writers were able to focus and reflect on various social and historical issues, and therefore, the 1940s saw the height of maturity of modern Chinese novels. Firstly, authors showed great enthusiasm about writing narrative works that exposed the dark side of the Anti-Japanese War, satirized the inherent weak spots of national character, and presented a historical review of the modern national culture. Sha Ting's *The Gold Diggers* (《淘金记》, one of his three works of social and historical records), for example, exposed the hidden secret of the dog fights in a remote town of Sichuan, and revealed the power structure of Chinese society and its basic pattern of operation. Through the fighting over the Shaojibei goldmine in Beidou Town, the novel presented the tussle between the gentleman class, underworld gangs, and landlord class in the local political arena, and gave the stage to the "old-style" performance of despotism, violence, conspiracy, and political trickery under the new context of war profiteering. This was indeed a much more in-depth exposure. Lao She's *Four Generations under One Roof* (including three parts, namely *Bewilderment* [《惶惑》], *Ignominy* [《偷生》], and *Famine* [《饥荒》]), turned our eyes from the rural areas back to equally old-aged urban society. Through the various behaviours of his characters, including Old Man Qi, Qi Ruixuan, Yunmei, and Qian Moyin, living in Beijing during the Japanese-occupied period, the novel reflected the weaknesses of the Chinese national character, such as conservativeness and being content with momentary ease and comfort, as well as the specific process by which the national spirit was encouraged, and hinted at the frustrations encountered by Chinese people in the modern history and their possibility of regeneration. These weaknesses and frustrations coexisted with the hope that Chinese people's national character could be rebuilt in their gradual awakening. Often, thanks to the self-consciousness and special perspective adopted by writers, this theme was shown in their narrative of the predicament of intellectuals during wartime. Ba Jin, for example, had changed his characteristic vehement exposure into profound reflection in his masterpiece created after the outbreak of the war, *Freezing Nights* (《寒夜》). The smothering experiences of intellectuals during the wartime, poverty, sicknesses, unemployment, marriage breakups, and social chaos, etc., were compressed in the conflicts between the couple Wang Wenxuan and Zeng Shusheng, and the entry of Wang's mother added even more complicated human and ethical conflicts to this family, which consisted of a generation of intellectuals who went backward despite the May Fourth movement. The author showed sympathy toward his characters and called attention to the tragedies of common people, but his tone was no longer "Ba Jin-style" boldness and ebullience, but became cool and somber, and his criticism became more reserved. Other examples included Ai Wu, whose *My Native Land* (《故乡》) was about the dark realities faced by university students who returned to their hometowns during the war; Sha Ting, whose *Caged Animals* (《困兽记》) was about the ever-changing political atmosphere and the anguish felt by a group of rural intellectuals before and after their theatrical performances; Wang Xiyan, whose "Pursuit Trilogy" (追寻三部曲), consisting of *The Old House* (《古屋》), *The Lost God* (《神的失落》), and *Dream Pursuers* (《寻梦者》), was about his reflections on the fate of rural intellectuals during the war; Jin Yi, whose *The Night Before* (《前夕》) tried to depict the era through an in-depth analysis of a bureaucratic family; Li Guangtian, whose *Gravity* (《引力》) was about how idealistic women turned their eyes from personal emotions to the broader world; and Xia Yan, whose *Love in Chilly Spring* (《春寒》) was about how personal happiness would eventually rely on the liberation of the entire Chinese nation. All these were lengthy novels, and though some were not as good as the others, they wrote seriously about Chinese intellectuals' baptism of fire during this national war. The classical masterpiece among these was doubtless Lu Ling's grand work of nearly one million characters, *Rich Men's Children*.

Secondly, their personal experience of the hardships of war, as well as their awareness that the war was a huge driving force of history, stimulated writers' frequent recollection and retrospection. It then became a fashion to create novels

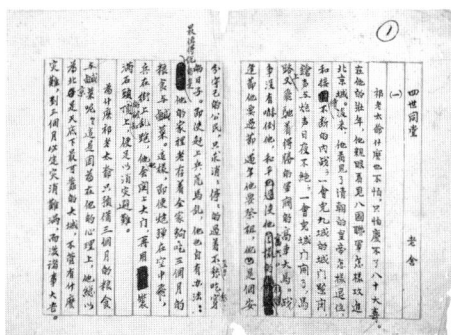

33.5. First page of Lao She's manuscript for *Four Generations under One Roof*, which he began writing in Beibei, Chongqing

33.6. Two volumes of the first part of *Four Generations under One Roof: Bewilderment*

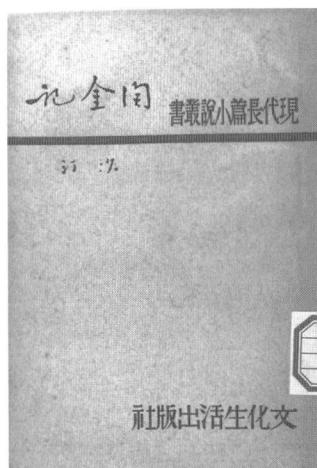

33.7. Sha Ting's *The Gold Diggers* featured his criticism of the Chinese-style despotic power structure

that "examined history in retrospect." In *Red Leaves Are as Beautiful as Spring Flowers,* Mao Dun tried to recollect the complicated process of modern revolution through the vicissitudes of the rural areas of Zhejiang (a small fictional town in the Jiangnan area), where the economy developed faster than other areas of China had in modern times. He borrowed from world literature and created the form of the modern Chinese national novel. Ba Jin's *Garden of Repose* could be seen as the continuance of *The Family*, which had brought him great fame, and it was an elegy for the big feudal family and several generations of owners. Even the war could not stop but indeed precipitated the decline of this old-style family, but the war had deepened the author's reflection on such issues as nationality and universal humanity. Thus for the first time, Ba Jin showed his compassion for the lost old world. Although Wu Zuxiang was not satisfied with his *Mountain Torrent* (《山洪》, aka *Duckbill Waterlog* [《鸭嘴涝》]), it was actually his retrospection and reconstruction of the experiences of the people in his hometown during the war. Perhaps because the northeast had been occupied by Japan earlier than any other part of the country, those talented northeastern authors who had come through the Shanhaiguan Pass, such as Xiao Hong, Duanmu Hongliang, Xiao Jun, and Luo Binji, with their painful experience as exiles, happened to write their respective family novel masterpieces, like a collective traveling back in history. Since all of them were originally left-wing writers, these literary works

33.8. First edition of *Freezing Nights*, Ba Jin's major novel of the 1940s

highlighted a kind of class-based nationalism. *Tales of Hulan River* was undoubtedly Xiao Hong's (1911–1942) masterpiece that deviated from left-wing literary conventions. In her "memories of childhood," her remote hometown was so beautiful, full of the fragrance of her back garden and the stables, while the people there were living and dying like animals ("surviving" forever), kind-hearted but benighted, they allowed and even prompted the flowery lives (like that of the child bride) to die and rot (in the gap between men and women, the rich and poor). Xiao Hong's poeticized stories echoed the innovative narratives of Beijing school novelists, but in presenting the lifestyle of the ordinary people of her hometown, she reminded one of Lu Xun in her serious record of the spiritual trauma of the Chinese nation, and at the same time, as a woman, she presented her unique experience of temporal eternity and spatial depth. She caught the minutest details of reality and expressed them in a sadly moving, affectionate, and brightly beautiful tone, thus created her own narrative style that lay between poetry and prose, and combined rich imagination and freedom of thought. Other northeastern writers were also sensitive to the era and full of poetic charms. Xiao Jun (1907–1988) was among the more dynamic of them. He continued his *The Third Generation*, whose first and second parts had been published in 1937, at this time, and later he changed the title to "The Past Generation," making it a grand epic of rural and urban life in the northeast, covering both the countryside and the city (Changchun), both bandits and revolutionary intellectuals. *The Khorchin Grasslands* by Duanmu Hongliang (1912–1996) was an epic of the grasslands. With his poetic narrative, the author wrote this novel based on his own family, and in it he thoroughly recorded the vicissitudes of the Ding's as well as

33.9. *Garden of Repose* was its author Ba Jin's favorite novella; the cover design of the book was based on his family's house

the different fates of several generations of people in the family. In his autobiographic fiction, *Childhood* (《幼年》, also known as *Chaos: Jiang Buwei's Family History* [《混沌——姜步畏家史》]), Luo Binji (1917–1994) wrote about his hometown, Huichun, from the perspective of a child, and in the scenes of the multinational border area one could still see the decline of the family and the different destinies of several generations of people.

The emergence of so many excellent literary works in a short period of time pushed the creation of modern Chinese novels to a new high. These novelists were also prose writers and poets, and were highly skillful in writing short stories. Sha Ting's "In the Fragrant Chamber Teahouse" (《在其香居茶馆里》) and "An Autumn Evening" (《一个秋天晚上》), Xiao Hong's "Cry in the Wilderness" (《旷野的呼喊》) and "Spring in a Small Town" (《小城三月》), and Luo Binji's collection, *Spring in the North-Facing Garden* (《北望园的春天》), were all outstanding short stories. It was their sentimental nostalgia for their hometowns during the war that had contributed to literary writers' profound reflection on traditional Chinese family society in their literature. More or less, all these works combined the era and the authors' personal life and feelings. Some were better at portraying characters while others at depicting scenes and atmosphere, but all of them shared people's spiritual experience of the war and cultural themes, and the lyrical and critical presentation of this specific era was thus more compassionate and humane than that of the literature of 1930s, with a historical outlook on both class and national aspects.

Due to the special conditions during the war, the most flourishing form of spoken drama was no longer street theater, but theater plays in Chongqing, the provisional capital, represented by the "fog performing season" (so called because Chongqing was draped in fog each year from October to the following May). After Wuhan was lost to the enemy, talented dramatists gradually gathered in Chongqing. In October 1938, twenty-five performing troupes held a twenty-two-day "drama festival" in Chongqing, obviously a sign of transformation. The festival went through three phases: for the first three days the dramatists performed on the streets in urban and suburban areas; during the following half month, they held a dozen "five-penny" public performances in the Social Auditorium of Martial Arts Performing Hall in Chongqing (with the purpose of promoting theater plays); at the end of the month, the festival reached its climax with the public performance of the four-act spoken drama play, *National Mobilization*, participated in by over 200 performers.[3] Also known as *Twenty-Eight in Black*, *National Mobilization* was adapted by Cao Yu and Song Zhidi based on a playscript about capturing a Japanese spy, entitled *Mobilization* (《总动员》). As well as the famous actors and actresses Zhao Dan, Bai Yang (白杨), Shu Xiuwen, and the rising star Zhang Ruifang, even Zhang Daofan, then director of the propaganda department of the Kuomintang, Yu Shangyuan, then principal of the National Drama School, the playwright Song Zhidi, and the director Ying Yunwei all participated in the performances. Such grand performances characteristic of the united front have seldom been equalled, before or since.

From 1939 to 1941, stage productions saw a resurgence in both the creation of plays and the cultivation of audiences. Plays praising Chinese people's resistance and endurance of hardships included *Within One Year*

33.10. Stage photo of the premiere of *Peking Man* by the Central Youth Drama Troupe (中央青年剧社) on October 24, 1941

[3] Ge Yihong (葛一红), ed., *General History of Chinese Spoken Drama* (《中国话剧通史》), Beijing: Cultural and Arts Press, 1997, p. 212.

(《一年间》) by Xia Yan and *The Nation Above All* (《国家至上》), cowritten by Song Zhidi and Lao She. Cao Yu's *The Metamorphosis* went so far as to create aspirational bureaucratic characters. Plays satirizing corruptive realities included Chen Baichen's *Men and Women in Wild Times* (《乱世男女》), Hong Shen's *Bao De Xing* (《包得行》, the title was a Sichuan dialect idiom meaning "It Will Do"), and Ding Xilin's *Three Dollars of National Currency* (《三块钱国币》). Despite their different styles, they were all delightfully written comedies. Those in between but also reflecting the wartime social reality included Song Zhidi's *Chongqing in the Fog* (《雾重庆》, originally entitled *The Whip* [《鞭》]), which recorded the experience of young people in exile in the Nationalist-controlled area, their wandering, and in the end their spiritual collapse. The playwright gave up cheap optimism, but sought to reflect the harsh reality of life. Cao Yu's *Peking Man*, another of his masterpieces, seemed to span an even larger temporal and spatial range. Cao Yu finally went beyond the fierce conflicts of personalities and fates of his characters, and went deep inside. For the protagonist Zeng Wenqing, his heart had been hollowed out in his feudal scholar-official family, through old-style education and outdated traditional culture, so he could not break free from his shackles and could not find his happiness. Sufang, who seemed weak on the surface, took a decisive step out of all this. In a sense, *Peking Man* answered the question of how one can break out of the spiritual and cultural shackles and seek rebirth in a national crisis. The vitality of the ancient "Peking Man" called out to his descendants, Beijingers of the time, and their predicament; the theme was inspiring and evocative. *Peking Man* later became part of the repertoire of spoken drama.

The first "fog performing season" was held in Chongqing from October 10, 1941 until May of the following year, during a break in the Japanese army's air bombings, and it then became a routine. The annual "fog performing season" contributed to the restoration of spoken drama in the "great hinterland." A dozen dramatic troupes performed altogether twenty-nine plays during the first festival. Realistic plays included Chen Baichen's *Spring Returns to the Earth* (《大地回春》), which was about how national capitalists in the textile industry survived the difficulties, and was the very first play to be performed by the Chinese Dramatic Arts Society (中华剧艺社) after it was founded. A new genre suddenly coming to the fore this year was historical drama. Guo Moruo's newly written play *Twin Flowers* (《棠棣之花》) was performed by the Long Live China Drama Troupe (中国万岁剧团), which emphasized the importance of unity and fighting against the national enemy by telling the ancient story of Nie Zheng, who gave up his life for justice in the Spring and Autumn period. The Chinese Dramatic Arts Society also performed *The History of the Taiping Rebellion* (《天国春秋》), written by Yang Hansheng, which insinuated the current state of affairs through the words of historical characters. Each time the character Hong Xuanjiao cried out on stage: "The enemy is coming, and we cannot kill each other!" she would receive a lengthy applause from the audience. The success of these plays inspired Guo Moruo, who completed his five-act historical drama *Qu Yuan* in a matter of ten days in January 1942 (while the first "fog performing season" was still on). By writing about the last day before the patriotic poet Qu Yuan drowned himself, the play showed the fierce conflict between the resistance group and the surrendering group within the royal court of Chu State. The premiere of this play by the Chinese Dramatic Arts Society became a big political and cultural event in Chongqing. Jin Shan and Zhang Ruifang, the actor and actress portraying Qu Yuan and Chanjuan, fully revealed the significance of their historical characters. In the play, the imprisoned Qu Yuan cried out the following startling words (monologue):

> Oh, how I long for Dongting Lake, the Yangtze River, and the East China Sea. How assailing and boundless are those raging waves and magnificent forces. They are freedom, dances, music, and poems.
>
> Oh, magnificent poems of the Universe! All of you – Thunder, Lightning, and Wind, you roar in darkness and gleam on each and every thing. All of you are poems, music, and dances. You are magnificent performing artists of the Universe. Let's see how you push your power to the max and let go your infinite rage. Just blow up this dark and gloomy Universe. Let it blow up! Let it blow up!

This was the famous "Ode to Thunder and Lightning" (《雷电颂》), the voice representing Chinese people's anger toward the fact that cracks appeared everywhere within the united front when the Anti-Japanese War was persisting. No wonder each time this scene was performed, feelings of excitement were evoked and echoes heard throughout the theater. The cries reminded one of *Goddess*, and even their diction and sentences were so alike. Certainly, here Guo's purpose of using the past to disparage the present was quite obvious, targeting the acts of the ruling party that brought grief to its own people and gladdened the national enemy. In a sense, these formed the object of attack of almost all historical plays created during the Anti-Japanese War. These included the "Warring States plays" about resisting against the Qin State, such as *Tiger Seal* (《虎符》) and *Gao Jianli* (《高渐离》, aka *Zhu* [《筑》]), both written by Guo Moruo; the "late Ming dynasty plays" that criticized surrendering and insisting on principles, such

33.11. Stage photo of *The History of the Taiping Rebellion* performed by Fengzi and Shu Xiuwen in 1946

as *The Peach Blossom Fan* (《桃花扇》) by Ouyang Yuqian and *The Grass in the South* (《南冠草》) by Guo Moruo, and the "Taiping Rebellion plays" against the national split, such as *The Death of Li Xiucheng* (《李秀成之死》) by Yang Hansheng, *Li Xiucheng the Loyal King* (《忠王李秀成》) by OuyangYuqian,and *TheDaduRiver*(《大渡河》, aka *Shi Dakai, the Assistant King* [《翼王石达开》]) by Chen Baichen. The choice of these three themes was deliberate. With an eye on the reality of national war, these plays promoted the Chinese people's historical experience of firm and unyielding resistance, unity, and fighting against the national enemy, and therefore they had the effect of motivating and organizing people in the theaters. Inheriting the left-wing tradition and fully developing the fighting role of literature, these historical plays that hinted at and disparaged the current realities were written with high spirits and poetic charm, and their influence was far-reaching.

33.12. *Qu Yuan*, written by Guo Moruo and directed by Chen Liting, was performed in Chongqing in 1942, with Jin Shan as Qu Yuan and Zhang Ruifang as Chanjuan. The "Ode to Thunder and Lightning" scene made a great impact

The second, third, and fourth "fog performing seasons" were all held in the wartime atmosphere. According to relevant statistics, there were as many as 118 spoken drama plays performed during these four or five years,

33.13. Group photo of the author, director, and actors of *Qu Yuan* after its performance in Chongqing in April 1942

33.14. Wu Zuguang and his father in Chongqing in 1942; at the time he was writing *Returning from a Stormy Night*

which was a huge scale and an amazing achievement.[4] During the "fog performing season" starting in October 1942, the major play was Xia Yan's *The Fascist Bacillus* (《法西斯细菌》), performed by the Chinese Dramatic Arts Society, which told the story of a bacteriologist stepping out of his laboratory into reality, and the play was characteristic of Xia Yan's left-wing perspective and his detailed representation of characters' psychology. Then there was *Returning from a Stormy Night* (《风雪夜归人》), the play that marked Wu Zuguang's (吴祖光) rise as a literary figure; and Yu Ling's famous realistic work, *Long Night's Journey* (《长夜行》). The China Art and Drama Society (中国艺术剧社) performed Song Zhidi's *The Motherland Is Calling Us* (《祖国在呼唤》) and Cao Yu's *The Family*. In the following seasons there were *Annals of Theater* (《戏剧春秋》), coauthored by Xia Yan and others, which recorded the history of Chinese spoken drama and dramatists; *A Fragrant Flower on the Horizon* (《芳草天涯》) by Xia Yan, which deviated from left-wing conventions and thus caused debates among critics; *Exemplar of Teachers for Myriad Ages* (《万世师表》) and *The Story of a Small Town* (《小城故事》) by Yuan Jun (袁俊, aka Zhang Junxiang [张骏祥]); *Peaches and Plums in the Spring Wind* (《桃李春风》), coauthored by Lao She and Zhao Qingge (赵清阁); *The Wedding March* (《结婚进行曲》) and *A Tale of Winter* (《岁寒图》) by

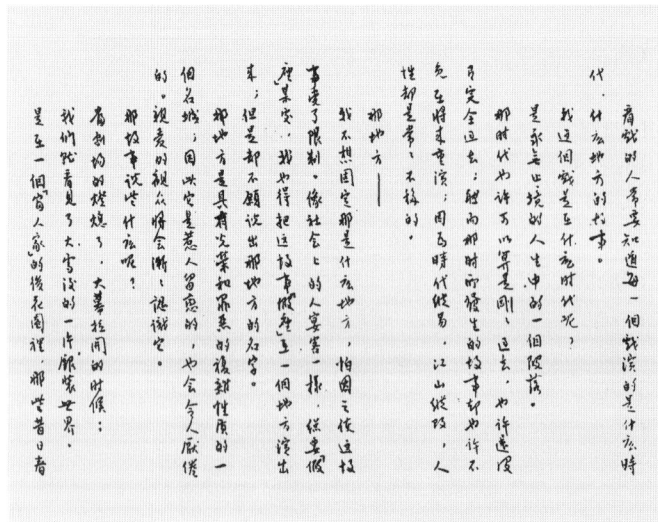

33.15. Manuscript of Wu Zuguang's *Returning from a Stormy Night*

4   This part of the material can be found in Ge Yihong, ed., *General History of Chinese Spoken Drama*, pp. 216–228.

33.16. *July*, edited by Hu Feng. Other journals edited by Hu Feng's clique included *Hope*, *Soil* (《泥土》), and others, but the clique was known by the name of this journal

33.17. Inaugural issue of *Hope*, launched by Hu Feng

Chen Baichen; and *Twenty-Four Hours in Chongqing* (《重庆二十四小时》) by Shen Fu (沈浮). These fell into two categories: realistic plays reflecting the depression, dignity, and rise of intellectuals, and satirical comedies exposing the corrupt life in the Nationalist-controlled area. These almost echoed the two styles of novel creation during the latter half of the war, and both could be references for each other.

In order to understand the richness and extensiveness of literature in the Nationalist-controlled area in Chongqing, one should pay special attention to the July and Zhanguoce literary cliques.

The July clique borrowed its name from the literary journal *July*. In September 1939, when most journals published in Shanghai disappeared in the war, Hu Feng (1902–1985) launched this weekly on his own. The title of the journal was taken from Lu Xun's words "*qi-yue*" (July), and it later turned out that it followed the direction pointed out by Lu Xun. With the war going on, the journal was resumed in Wuhan as a fortnightly in December 1937, and then resumed as a monthly in Chongqing in July 1939, but by then it could hardly be published regularly. By the time it was discontinued in September 1941, altogether thirty-two issues had been published over a period of four years. As for the significance of *July*, it was commented by people of the times that:

> In my opinion, the unyielding attitude of *July* showed that literature refuses to step down. When the national army failed at the eastern battlefront and the *Beacon Fire* was discontinued, it seemed that literary and

art activities were effectively silenced, but *July* could stand up alone in extremely difficult times, which is the most outstanding achievement of this journal.[5]

By that time, the July clique began to form, and Hu Feng established his position as the head of this literary clique. The journal then published the works of excellent reportage authors such as Qiu Dongping, Cao Bai, and S. M. (aka Ah Long), whose works were discussed in Chapter 31. The team of poets was even larger and stronger, for Hu Feng himself was a poet. The earlier major poems of Ai Qing and Tian Jian (both of them later went to the "liberated region" and separated themselves from the July clique), such as "Snow Falls on the Chinese Land," "The North," and "To Fighters," were all published in this journal. Other poets included Ah Long, Zou Difan, Peng Yanjiao (彭燕郊), and Sun Tian (孙钿). When *July* was discontinued, the members of the clique gathered around *Cultivated Land of Poetry* (《诗垦地》) in Chongqing, and *Fortnightly Literature* (《半月文艺》), *Poetic Creation* (《诗创作》), and other journals in Guilin. Hu Feng began to edit the July book series, including approximately twenty titles under the categories of "Poetry," "Prose," and "New Books," and it was through this book series that Lü Yuan and other poets came to the fore with their anthologies. In January 1945, Hu Feng launched *Hope* despite all difficulties, of which eight issues from two volumes had been published by October 1946, which was like the resurrection of *July* with another title. *Hope* showed even more obvious characteristics of the clique, publishing the works of new writers such as Lu Ling, Shu Wu (舒芜), Lu Li (鲁藜), Ji Fang (冀汸), Lu Dian (芦甸), Lu Mei (鲁煤), and Niu Han (牛汉). When *Hope* was discontinued, the literary clique continued to launch other journals with its characteristics, such as *Breathing* (《呼吸》), *Soil*, *Small Collection of Ants* (《蚂蚁小集》), and *Small Collection of Ominous Cock-Crowing* (《荒鸡小集》), and another twenty or so titles of the July book series were published, with the last ones edited in 1948 and published in the 1950s, when the regime had changed.

The July clique paid equal attention to novels, poetry, and literary theory. Hu Feng was able to launch literary journals to help form a literary clique, and he was even better at promoting the effective interactions between theoretical exposition and literary creation. In this regard, the July clique differed from the other modern Chinese literary schools. The July poetic clique became the most influential group of poets in the Nationalist-controlled area, including Ai Qing and Tian Jian in their early period, Lü Yuan, Ah Long, and Niu Han, among others. Like the left-wing literature that had been developing since the 1930s, their poems sought to reflect the reality of the Anti-Japanese War and passionate life, to "link poetry with human beings, link the struggles in

---

5   Lou Shiyi's speech. See "Current Literary and Art Works and *July* (Symposium Minutes)" (《现时文艺活动与〈七月〉（座谈会记录）》), *July*, Issue 15, April 29, 1938.

the aesthetic sense embodied in poetry with the social responsibility and struggling tasks of human beings, and thus they were affirmation and inheritance of the modern Chinese free verse tradition."[6] Certainly, the "free verse tradition" here referred to the May Fourth and left-wing tradition, but what made the literature of this clique valuable was that it consciously tried to break free from the shackles of leftist mechanistic views, vulgar sociologism, and doctrinairism and to avoid the banalization, utilitarianism, and rigidness of realism. Instead, it promoted realism with the subjective fighting spirit at its core. Thus the poetry of the July clique was full of era-specific originality and passions, and the images creatively used in its poetry, such as wind and snow, storm and soil, and the symbolic meanings of lyrical subjects, were not short of historical implications and dynamics; its dictions and sentences were serious and pertinacious, all this showed its exploration in the form of prose-style poetry. One representative poet of the July clique was Lü Yuan (1922-2009),

33.18. *Fairy Tales* (《童话》), the earliest anthology of Lü Yuan's work, published as part of the July book series

whose famous political lyrical poems included "To the Naive Optimists" (《给天真的乐观主义者们》), "Galileo Facing the Truth" (《伽利略在真理面前》), and "The Destination, and Starting Point" (《终点，又是一个起点》). In these poems he sought to apply his subjective passions to social events and historical details and thus achieved the strength and beauty of critical thinking.

33.19. A handsome and confident-looking Lu Ling in 1948, when he had just completed his novel *Rich Men's Children*

One of the best novelists within the July clique was Lu Ling (1923–1994). As an excellent heir of the left-wing novel, his novellas *Hungry Guo Su'e* and *A Snail in Thorns* (《蜗牛在荆棘上》), as well as a number of short stories, were about lower-class people, such as poor farmers, miners, street performers, deserters, prostitutes, scoundrels, vendors, and young students, their material as well as spiritual state of "hunger" and life in exile, and their strong rebellious acts and minds. Nevertheless, his novels were different from the past revolutionary realism in the following aspects: Firstly, in the historical context of national salvation, he did not forget the intellectuals' responsibility for

---

[6] Lü Yuan: "Preface to *White Flowers*" (《〈白色花〉序》), in Lü Yuan and Niu Han ed., *White Flowers*, Beijing: People's Literature Press, 1981, p. 2.

enlightenment, and thus his novels integrated liberation of the nation with that of individuality, which was not completed during the May Fourth period. Therefore, the peasant and worker characters in Lu Ling's novels were not automatically the embodiment of justice and hope just because they were suppressed, but were souls that needed to be transformed because they were distorted and benighted, and thus their resistance seemed convulsive. The author "explored the personalities at the root of his characters hidden under the surface of social structure,"[7] such as Guo Su'e, who resisted after being cruelly tortured; Luo Dadou, who was, like Ah Q, a young man from an impoverished family and idling around doing nothing (*The Life of Luo Dadou* [《罗大斗的一生》]); the old female sugar vendor Liu Ertaipo, who tried to cheat small customers (*The Old and the Small* [《老的和小的》]); the storyteller who was no match for the popular singer of "Drizzles" ("The Hero's Dance" [《英雄的舞蹈》]); and Guo Zilong, who was called "half rich young master and half heroic hooligan" (*The Burning Waste Land* [《燃烧的荒地》]). By digging at this root, Lu Ling, like Lu Xun, brought to light the "trauma of spiritual enslavement" (that is, the servility) of people (especially peasants), and at the same time displayed their "primitive brutal force" (blind resistance and natural vitality), and thus revealed the strong and weak, good and evil, bright and dark sides of human nature within the class in an exciting manner, full of ups and downs. Secondly, his depiction of the historical era and of modern intellectuals adhered to the realistic principles and methods with the subjective fighting spirit at the core; that is, he "embraced" and "wrestled with" historical content with his passions. In his novel *Rich Men's Children*, Lu Ling "plunged into" the family history of Jiang Jiesan, the richest family in Suzhou, showcasing different paths of life of descendants of this feudal family, including Jiang Weizu; Jiang Shaozu, who was reduced from being an awakened May Fourth youth to a bureaucrat; and Jiang Chunzu, a progressive young man who was devoted to the national liberation cause but escaped in confusion in the end. With an overwhelming force, he presented the psychology, personality, and spiritual state of each major character against the historical background, and presented their fates as both the result of social forces and that of personal choice. It seemed those characters were going back and forth along the historical channel from the ancient times till the present, experiencing both sublimity and abjection, sensibility and violence, resistance and recession, brightness and darkness, but could not find a way out in the modern Chinese history except through destruction and death. This subjective generalization was an exploration of each individual in the modern chaotic world rather than of "historical laws," and it was a depiction in a tragic and agonizing tone, with a mode

---

7   Hu Feng: "Preface to *Hungry Guo Su'e*" (《〈饥饿的郭素娥〉序》), *Hungry Guo Su'e*, Shanghai: Hope Editorial Office, 1946, p. 2.

of discourse that highlighted the vitality of human beings and a highly original narrative style. We may well feel the freshness of the literature of the July clique; as part of the left-wing mainstream tradition, it consciously sought to deviate from the mainstream (it criticized the trend of deviating from Lu Xun's path, and criticized putting the label of "idealism" on writers who tried to maintain their subjectivity).

The emergence of the July clique revealed the split within the left-wing camp. This literary clique complied with but deviated from the mainstream of left-wing literature, which was both its uniqueness and its limitation. This could have contributed to the revision and perfection of left-wing literature, but unfor-

33.20. First edition of Lu Ling's *Hungry Guo Su'e*, published by *Hope* editorial office in January 1946

tunately, the attacks against Hu Feng and other members of this clique by those insisting on mainstream left-wing literature were pushed to the height of ideological struggle and political interference, so that the history of the July clique ended up a tragedy. Seen from Hu Feng's theoretical perspective, we could clearly see the conflicts and development within left-wing literature. Before the war, facing the conflict between Lu Xun and Zhou Yang within *Zuolian*, Hu Feng took part in the debate over typicality and "two slogans." After the war broke out, during the discussion on "national forms" in the literary circle of the Nationalist-controlled area in 1939, Hu Feng wrote the book *On the Issue of National Forms* (《论民族形式问题》), in which he opposed the view of Xiang Linbing (向林冰) that only the folk form could be the central fountainhead of Chinese literature's national form, and held that the massification of literature should not deviate from the May Fourth tradition, and that in the end, national forms were "the May Fourth realistic tradition trying to find new paths in the new historical context." He criticized the hidden trends of populism and revivalism. When Mao Zedong's "Talks at the Yan'an Forum on Literature and Art" was disseminated in the Nationalist-controlled area in 1944, members of the left-wing camp learned Mao's speech and rectified themselves accordingly. Hu Feng thought it was difficult to implement Mao's guiding principle of writing about and for the proletariat class, citing the reason that the state of affairs in the Nationalist-controlled area was different from that in the "liberated region." In 1945, Shu Wu's "On Subjectivity" (《论主观》) and Hu Feng's "Situating Ourselves in the Struggle for Democracy" (《置身在为民主的斗争里面》), published in the inaugural issue of *Hope*, caused a great uproar within the left-wing literary camp. The mainstream faction attacked

33.21. Hu Feng, Mei Zhi (梅志), and their son Xiaogu (晓谷) in front of Zhang's Garden in Chongqing, the headquarters of the All-China Resistance Association, in October 1945

them by confusing ideological "subjectivity" and "idealism" with Hu's subjective fighting spirit. In 1947, left-wing intellectuals set off a new surge of criticism aimed at Hu Feng and Lu Ling, to all of which Hu Feng replied with his "On the Path of Realism" (《论现实主义的路》) in 1948. By this time, the July clique had been fiercely attacked by its friends within the left-wing camp in the fields of literary theory and creation, and in these conflicts it developed even more systematic literary theories and literary creation with more individuality. However, it seemed impossible to insert the subjective fighting spirit within the framework of revolutionary realism.[8] Nobody had expected that these debates and conflicts could have influenced the development of Chinese literature for the latter half of the twentieth century.

The Zhanguoce clique was a totally different case. Looking back retrospectively, it was more evidence that the united front literature was no longer in existence. This clique was originally formed by several professors from the National Southwestern Asso ciated University and Yunnan University in Kunming, including Chen Quan from the Department of Foreign Languages, Lin Tongji from the Department of Economics, and Lei Haizong (雷海宗) from the Department of History. In April 1940, they launched a fortnightly called *Zhanguoce* (《战国策》), literally, "Stratagems of the Warring States," in Kunming, and later, at the end of 1941, Chen Quan launched a supplement of *Ta Kung Pao* entitled "Zhanguo" (战国, literally, "Warring States"), elaborating on their cultural views. At the core, they held that the world had entered a "period of great warring states," in which weak nations and countries, if they did not want to be swallowed up by powerful countries, should admire "force," "heroism," and "collectivism," and oppose the "individualism" promoted in the May Fourth movement. Then Chen Quan (1903–1969) wrote several plays, including *The Wild Rose* (《野玫瑰》), *The Blue Butterfly* (《蓝蝴蝶》), and *The Golden Ring* (《金指环》). The three-act spoken drama play *The Wild Rose*, in particular,

8   Quoted from Hu Feng: *On the Issue of National Forms*. See Zhou Yanfen (周燕芬): "Ideological and Theoretical Foundation of the July Clique" (七月派思想理论基础), *Standing Fast, Repelling and Surpassing: History of the July Clique* (《执守·反拨·超越——七月派史论》), Beijing: Zhonghua Book Company, 2003, pp. 75–158.

was premiered during the first "fog performing season" in Chongqing in 1942, and with its well-organized plot and well-portrayed characters, this spy play was quite popular among ordinary citizen audiences. It was then vehemently attacked by left-wing dramatists and literary writers, who criticized his "worship of power" and fascism (with Nietzsche as the intermedium) in cultural theory and accused Chen Quan of beautifying traitors in the creation of spoken drama plays. Actually, these were more or less distorted views, because if we put the theories of the Zhanguoce clique within the institution of higher learning, its nationalist position and insistence to transform the national character of Chinese people could find their origin in the views of Lu Xun, Hu Feng, and the Beijing school, which also championed "primitive brutal force." *The Wild Rose*, like Cao Yu's *National Mobilization* and Xu Xu's novel *Whistling Wind* (《风萧萧》, a representative work of the Shanghai school in the Nationalist-controlled area after the war broke out), told a love story with twists and turns about spies within the government agency. Indeed, at first Chen Quan and his friends in this literary clique had no political leanings or official background. Once their theories moved outside the intellectual circle, however, they had consequential social effects: the KMT government welcomed them, so much so that Zhang Daofan even appeared personally in organizing the premiere of *The Wild Rose*, and after that it was awarded a prize by the Ministry of Education. Chen Quan was then transferred and appointed as a professor of the Central Political School (中央政治学校) in Chongqing, director of the China Youth Troupe, and editor-in-chief of Zhengzhong Book Company. Pan Gongzhan (潘公展), then director of the Central Review Board of Books and Magazines, even said that *The Wild Rose* "should be promoted instead of being banned; it is the playscript of *Qu Yuan* that is 'an issue.'" This certainly stirred up even more criticism from the left-wing camp, which soon became a kind of political struggle, "a battlefield between the left-wing camp and KMT authorities."[9] Thus during the latter half of the Anti-Japanese War, the united front literature had ceased to exist except in name.

[9] See "The Play *The Wild Rose* is Still Performed in the Rear Area" (《〈野玫瑰〉一剧仍在后方上演》), *Liberation Daily*, section 2, June 28, 1942. The material is quoted from Ni Wei: *The Imagination of "Nation" and the "State" Governance*, pp. 280–281.

THIRTY FOUR

YAN'AN

From Wartime Art and Literature for the Masses to the Guiding Principle of Art and Literature for Workers, Peasants, and Soldiers

THE LITERATURE OF ALL ANTI-JAPANESE BASE AREAS under the leadership of Yan'an could be seen as the shifting of focus of 1930s left-wing literature from urban Chinese cities to the poor countryside in the northwest, from Shanghai garrets to cave dwellings, accessing the broad masses. This was not a conscious literary development, but was more or less caused by the political situations of that time. In Yan'an there was plenty of literary source material available: its predecessor was the art and literature of the Soviet areas, especially the literary experience of the Central Soviet Area in Jiangxi. That was literary propaganda that served the war and the Soviet areas, so literary forms that were short and efficient for motivating the public, such as opera plays and folk ballads, were better developed, making it like a prelude of the literature and art of resistance. The August First Drama Troupe (八一剧团) had been founded in Ruijin earlier, as had the Blue Shirt Theater Troupe (蓝衫剧团), which was affiliated to Li Bozhao's Gorky Drama School (高尔基戏剧学校). Qu Qiubai made much painstaking efforts to found the Soviet Drama Troupe after arriving in the Soviet area, and the plays performed by these troupes were all highly motivational. Then there was *Zuolian* art and literature, which was another predecessor of Yan'an art and literature. With the tradition of art and literature serving politics, *Zuolian* had been promoting art and literature for the masses of workers and peasants since its early stages, although the goal could not be achieved at that time. It took the literature of Soviet Russia and world literature as references, and had a rich heritage inherited from Lu Xun, which needed to be fully understood and digested later in history. And there was original folk art, especially that of northern Shaanxi, as well as the Shanxi and Hebei areas, which had a major effect on Yangko opera, new folk opera, long poetry in the form of northern Shaanxi love songs, and on the shaping of the Potato literary school and the Lotus Lake literary school.

It was after Ding Ling and Zhou Yang arrived in Yan'an that well-known writers began to gather there. Famous intellectuals came to Yan'an with the Red Army through the Long March, such as Cheng Fangwu, a former member of the Creation Society, but by this time, most of them were doing organizational work instead of literary creation. Therefore, when the first literary organization of the "liberated region," the Chinese Literary and Artistic Association (which was also referred to, in short, as "the Association," *Wenxie*) was founded in Bao'an in November 22, 1936, Ding Ling, who had just arrived a dozen days before, became head of the Association. We can easily understand why Ding Ling was warmly welcomed by the CPC's top leaders. Before her arrival, most freely associated literary groups in Yan'an were small-scale poets' clubs, and there were two major literary societies with official backgrounds. One was the Lu Xun Arts College, founded in April 1938 (whose name was later changed to the Lu Xun College for Art and Literature), or in short, "Lu Xun College." When planning the college, Mao

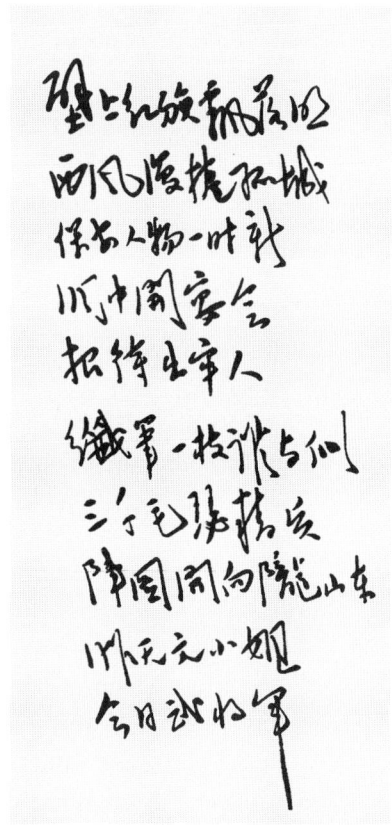

34.1. "Poem to the Tune of Lin Jiang Xian" (《临江仙》), written by Mao Zedong for Ding Ling when she first arrived in Bao'an, northern Shaanxi, in 1936

Zedong had repeatedly raised the issue of "blending the mountain tops in northern Shaanxi with the garrets in Shanghai," which was quite a resounding slogan, and accorded with the principle of the united anti-Japanese front.[1] The earliest head of Lu Xun College was Sha Kefu (沙可夫), and then Zhou Yang became its deputy principal and principal, and thus was in charge of the college for a long time. Its original site was outside the northern gate of Yan'an, and later was moved to Qiao'ergou, over ten *li* away from the town. At that time, a number of literary writers came to work as cadres or lecturers at Lu Xun College, such as Xiao San, He Qifang, Chen Huangmei, Zhou Libo, and Yan Wenjing (严文井) (plus the musician Xian Xinghai and the painter Cai Ruohong [蔡若虹]), and Mao Dun and Sha Ting worked as short-term lecturers at the college. Many young writers

---

[1] See Wang Peiyuan (王培元): "Preface," *Lu Xun College in Yan'an during the Anti-Japanese War* (《抗战时期的延安鲁艺》), Guilin: Guangxi Normal University Press, 1999, pp. 2, 10–11.

who grew up in Yan'an were graduates of the Department of Literature of Lu Xun College, such as Kong Jue, Kang Zhuo, He Jingzhi, and Feng Mu (冯牧). Another literary society was the Shaanxi–Gansu–Ningxia Border Area Association of the Cultural Circle to Resist Japan (陕甘宁边区文化界 抗战联合会, which was called "*Wenkang*" for short), launched in September 1938, and it elected Ding Ling and other executive members. In the following year, in order to strengthen its relationship with *Wenxie* under the leadership of Lao She in Chongqing, its name was changed into the Yan'an Branch of the All-China Resistance Association, but it was still called *Wenkang* for short. When Ai Qing, Luo Feng (罗烽) and his wife Yan Chen (严辰), and Zhang Ding (张仃) arrived in Yan'an together, Luofu (洛甫, alias of Zhang Wentian) and Kaifeng (凯丰) had asked for their opinion on their work arrangements, and whether they wanted to work at Lu Xun College or at *Wenkang*. Hearing that the leader of *Wenkang* was Ding Ling, Ai Qing chose to work there without hesitation. Many years later, Zhou Yang admitted that "there were two factions in Yan'an," and that "people in Lu Xun College [under him] advocated eulogizing brightness"[2] while "those in *Wenkang* [under Ding Ling] were devoted to exposing darkness." No matter how accurate this statement was, it was obvious that agreements and disagreements coexisted within the literary circle in Yan'an. The existence of different literary factions was evidence of diversity and richness, just as there was Lu Xun within *Zuolian* and

34.2. Lu Xun College was moved from the West Hill outside the northern gate of Yan'an to Qiao'ergou; this was its panorama, which looked quite magnificent against the background of the old cathedral

---

[2]   Quoted from Cheng Guangwei (程光炜): *Biography of Ai Qing* (《艾青传》), Beijing: October Literature and Arts Press, 1999, p. 340.

Hu Feng within the Nationalist-controlled area. In the later literary development in Yan'an, the interaction between these literary factions was an important element that played a role from time to time.

At first, the literature in Yan'an, like that of the entire country, took the path of national salvation literature. Similar to the case of the Nationalist-controlled area, there was a surge of street poems, street theater, and news reports; but in contrast, when progressive writers had just arrived in Yan'an, they felt a greater freedom in terms of both content and form. On August 7, 1938, for example, the first "Street Poetry Movement Day" was launched in Yan'an, when the street poems written by more than thirty people, including Ke Zhongping, Tian Jian, and Shao Zinan (邵子南), were posted on walls along all streets and avenues, which was quite a spectacle in the town. According to Tian Jian's recollection, "there were indeed many national guardsmen holding red-tasseled spears standing there to read the poems on the wall."[3] This literary form that was close to and accessible by the masses gradually diminished in the Nationalist-controlled area, but it remained popular in Yan'an, albeit without a formal literary status. In 1938, Mao Zedong told students and teachers at Lu Xun College: "Your Lu Xun College is nothing but a garden with a limited view … your garden with a grand view is located in the Taihang mountains and Lüliang mountains," encouraging writers to step out of the small literary circle and get closer to the masses.[4] At the beginning of 1939, people of the Shanxi–Chahar–Hebei border area raised the slogan "realism of the Three People's Principles," which was characteristic of the united anti-Japanese front (in the same year, Mao Zedong's inscription for the one year anniversary of Lu Xun College was "anti-Japanese realism and revolutionary romanticism"). After Mao Zedong published his "On New Democracy" (《新民主主义论》) in 1940, the slogan was changed accordingly into "realism of the New Democracy,"[5] but it was not loudly shouted. Thus, at that time, the guiding principle of the CPC in the field of art and literature was not very clear.

At that time, an increasing number of writers gathered in Yan'an; they came from cities to pursue social progress and their own ideals, and many of them were communist party members. However, it was by no means easy for them to truly fit in with the regime of the "liberated region." Ding Ling was quite enthusiastic about revolution after arriving in Yan'an, so much so that she had gone to the battlefront as a "Red Army soldier" several times and wrote the reportage piece *A Sketchy Account of General Peng Dehuai* and the novel *An Unfired Bullet* (《一颗未出膛的枪弹》), eulogizing both high-rank generals

---

[3] Quoted from Liu Zengjie (刘增杰): *History of Literature in the Liberated Region* (《中国解放区文学史》), Kaifeng: Henan University Press, 1988, pp. 221–222.

[4] He Qifang: "A Song in Praise of Mao Zedong" (《毛泽东之歌》), *Collected Works of He Qifang* (《何其芳文集》), Vol. 3, Beijing: People's Literature Press, 1983, p. 48.

[5] Quoted from Liu Zengjie: *History of Literature in the Liberated Region*, pp. 38–39.

34.3. Entrance of Lu Xun Arts College in Yan'an

34.4. Mao Dun teaching at Lu Xun Arts College after he escaped from danger in Xinjiang and arrived in Yan'an in the autumn of 1940

and ordinary soldiers. She led the Service Group of the Northwestern Battle Area of the Red Army in fights in several places for half a year, and then returned and remained in Yan'an to study and work. She had a great sense of freedom, although due to the influence of the May Fourth enlightenment of individualism and anti-feudalism, she often felt unfit for the complicated political life in the border area. In 1940, Ding Ling wrote *When in the Hospital* (《在医院中时》) based on her own experience in hospital. The protagonist was a female doctor called Lu Ping who came from a large city to Yan'an full of passion. In Yan'an, she saw chaotic and backward management, neglect of patients, and vulgar interpersonal relationships, and when she finally plucked up the courage to make suggestions to her superiors, all that was waiting for her were negative comments such as "petty-bourgeois sentiments" and "heroism." In this novel, Ding Ling reversed the mainstream theme of transformation of intellectuals, and wrote about the habitual mindsets of intellectuals and small farming producers, a theme least favored by the bureaucracy. According to recently published documents, Ding Ling faced such great pressure after

34.5. Ai Qing's poem "Into the Snow" (《雪里钻》)

this novel was published that she even wrote a piece of self-criticism, but she eventually gave up, seeing that she could not justify herself to the satisfaction of her critics. When she wrote "When I Was in Xia Village" (《我在霞村的时候》) in 1941, the influence of the May Fourth movement again manifested itself within her. She wrote about a peasant woman, Zhenzhen, who was forced to become a prostitute to entertain the Japanese army, and later endured humiliation and shouldered the task of doing intelligence work for the Red Army. When she returned to the village in the base area, however, she was discriminated against and blamed by her family and fellow villagers. The writer clearly took Zhenzhen's side and showed great sympathy for this woman who had endured so much humiliation but never yielded, and delivered unspoken criticism against the deep-rooted feudal concept of chastity among peasants

34.6. Ai Qing (on the left) and a peasant in Yan'an in the winter of 1944

34.7. After arriving in the "liberated region," Ding Ling worked as the head of the Service Group of the Northwestern Battle Area; she looked quite valiant and heroic in men's uniform

in the "liberated region." In September of the same year, Ding Ling became the editor-in-chief of the "Literature" supplement of *Liberation Daily* in Yan'an. With her complex feelings toward the reality in Yan'an as a writer of New Literature, and with her sensibility of multiple oppressions on women, she had a number of essays published in the supplement, including her own "We Need Critical Essays" (《我们需要杂文》) and "Thoughts on March Eighth" (《三八节有感》);Ai Qing's "Understanding Writers, Respecting Writers" (《了解作家，尊重作家》); Luo Feng's "It's Still an Era of Critical Essays" (《还是杂文的时代》);Wang Shiwei's "Wild Lilies" (《野百合花》); and Xiao Jun's "On 'Love' and 'Forbearance' between Comrades" (《论同志的"爱"与"耐"》). The responses to these essays had a direct bearing on the issue of whether literature could still criticize the political reality it championed and whether literature had limited independence and freedom. And disputes arose in Yan'an. Each time Ding Ling showed her unruly ideas she would review herself with self-criticism, and she also criticized others (she criticized Wang Shiwei, for example, and such criticism of others may be considered another form of self-criticism), but the next time

34.8. *Literature and Art Attack* (《文艺突击》), a literary journal in Yan'an, published on May 25, 1939

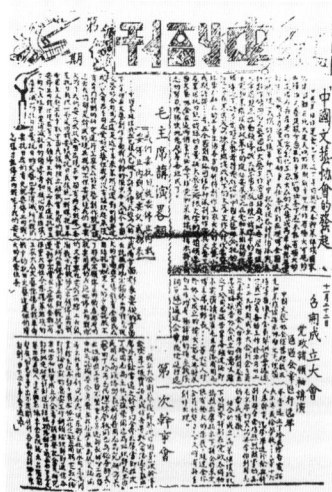

34.9. "Red China Supplement" (《红中副刊》) of the journal *Red China* (《红色中华》), launched by the Chinese Literary and Artistic Association

the profound influence of May Fourth ideals would again manifest themselves. This inner conflict always remained within her.

This was the situation before Mao Zedong delivered his "Talks at the Yan'an Forum on Literature and Art" (hereinafter referred to as "Talks"). Ideological debates were heard everywhere in cultural and ideological circles, not only in the field of literature and art. The broader context also involved the leadership within the CPC striving to eliminate the effect of Wang Ming's ultraleftist line and the upcoming party-wide Rectification movement. Wang Shiwei (1906–1947) was a special research fellow of the Central Research Institute in Yan'an. Before "Wild Lilies," he had already published an essay entitled "Politicians, Artists" (《政治家、艺术家》), criticizing the dark side of Yan'an by contrasting politicians and artists. Later in the mobilization meeting of the Rectification, he took the lead in showing open disapproval against the Research Institute's practice of arbitrarily deciding on leaders, and in the end, in a vote by a show of hands, three quarters of attendees at the meeting agreed to decide on the leaders by voting. This was one of extremely few democratic events in Yan'an. The wall newspaper of the Central Research Institution, called "Arrow and Target" (《矢与的》), was as well-known as the "Light Brigade Team" (《轻骑队》) launched by the Youth Committee, in which they published democratic opinions and caused quite a sensation in the town. Several issues were not even posted on the wall, but posted on a piece of cloth to be hung in the busy street outside the south gate of Yan'an, attracting so many people that even Mao Zedong heard of this and told his security guards to read the articles on the wall newspaper holding lanterns and torches late at night. It was probably impossible for Wang Shiwei to blend in with the mainstream of Yan'an; instead, he was a target of the Rectification movement and was labeled a "Trotskyist." He was tortured and later executed when the army marched during the war (the case was not redressed until 1991). Wang Shiwei's views were seen as the most extremist ones during the Forum.

However, at that time, most intellectuals in Yan'an were not in the style of Wang Shiwei; instead, the typical style was that of the writer He Qifang (1912–1977) of Lu Xun College, who changed from a Beijing school writer into a left-wing intellectual and became a eulogist of Yan'an.

34.10. Portrait of Wang Shiwei

34.11. Wang Shiwei's article "Politicians, Artists" published in *Grain Rain* (《谷雨》, the handmade paper edition)

34.12. He Qifang, who came to Yan'an with Sha Ting, remained there and later became head of the Department of Literature at Lu Xun College

When He Qifang wrote *Painted Dreams* in Beijing, he was nothing but a literary youth raving about his daydreams. It was after he graduated from university that he saw the real life of peasants in Shandong and Sichuan, and recorded his own earliest changes in *Miscellanies on Homecoming* (《还乡杂记》). After the war broke out, he wrote the poem "Chengdu, Let Me Wake You Up" (《成都，让我把你摇醒》), which was also his own self-awakening, and in the poem one could see such words as "like a blind man who has eventually opened his eyes." The reality definitely opened his eyes. He came to Yan'an following Sha Ting, a *Zuolian* writer, but he felt even more freedom than the latter. This was shown in his "I Am Singing for Yan'an" (《我歌唱延安》), written two months after his arrival. He Qifang wrote sincerely in this poem: "I am deeply moved, but the first thing I want to sing about is the air in Yan'an. / It is the air of freedom. Air of generosity. Air of happiness. / Entering the town, the first thing I did was breathe, inhaling this air, full of satisfaction."[6] This was prose instead of poetry, but he could not help writing it on separate lines. When he first worked at Lu Xun College, he continued to eulogize the brightness of Yan'an by expressing his sincere personal emotions, which could be seen in "Night Song" (《夜歌》). There we could see the conflicts between his old self and his new self, and the process of his change from an individualist into a collectivist. He also wrote a number of colloquial poems that were easy to understand and liked by young readers, such as "The Dawn" (《黎明》), "I Am Singing for Young Men and Women" (《我为少男少女们歌唱》), and "How Vast Life Is" (《生活是多么广阔》), totally giving up his past obscure style. When Sha Ting came out of the mountain areas where his hometown was located and was ordered to attend the "Rectification Studies" in Chongqing in 1944, He Qifang was already a guiding cadre appointed by top leaders of Yan'an.

Different from Ding Ling, Wang Shiwei, and He Qifang, Xiao Jun was another type of writer in Yan'an. Apart from his status as a left-wing writer

34.13. Xiao Jun rewrote his *The Third Generation* in a cave dwelling in Yan'an in the summer of 1945

---

6   He Qifang: "I Am Singing for Yan'an," *Selected Works of He Qifang*, Chengdu: Sichuan People's Press, 1979, p. 242.

of the 1930s, he also enjoyed a reputation as Lu Xun's "intimate student." Therefore, when he arrived in Yan'an in 1938 and 1940, respectively, Mao Zedong received him with courtesy, paying personal visits to him, and wrote as many as ten letters to him. Xiao Jun was a man of extremely strong character, straightforward and unrestrained. When Zhou Yang published his article "Talks on Literature and Life" (《文学与生活漫谈》) in Yan'an in 1941, Xiao Jun read it and exchanged views with Ai Qing, Luo Feng, Bai Lang (白朗), and Shu Qun, and wrote an article entitled "Collection of Talks after Reading 'Talks on Literature and Life' and Discussions with Comrade Zhou Yang" (《〈文学与生活漫谈〉读后漫谈集录并商榷于周扬同志》), which was submitted to *Liberation Daily* only to be rejected. Xiao Jun was furious about this; and also being unhappy with some other matters, he went to say good-bye to Mao Zedong in July that year. Mao persuaded Xiao Jun to stay, and on the eve of the Yan'an Forum on Literature and Art, Mao tried to find out the views of writers from other regions through Xiao's outspoken conversation and letters. At the Forum, Xiao Jun was the one who made a bold keynote speech, without considering the possibility of offending others. Later at the meeting in the Central Research Institute to criticize Wang Shiwei, Xiao Jun stood up and asked for the criticized's right to speak, not fearing that he would be labeled as "sympathizing with the Trotskyist." This was not only a matter of personality, but his open demanding for accommodating the universal democratic spirit and inheriting the May Fourth enlightening tradition within the Chinese-style Marxist–Leninist system. Later Xiao Jun was unreasonably criticized due to the so-called Northeast Cultural Gazette Incident during the Civil War, but that is a later story. At this time, he became one of the most outstanding intellectuals in Yan'an with the quality of an unrestrained, independent intellectual.

The Yan'an Forum on Literature and Art in 1942 marked the entrenchment of the CPC's guiding principles on literature and art. Before the Forum, Mao Zedong paid special attention to collecting adverse opinions in advance through Xiao Jun, Shu Qun, Ouyang Shan, Cao Ming (草明), Ai Qing, Ding Ling, Liu Baiyu, Hua Junwu (华君武), and Cai Ruohong, among others, and then he invited He Qifang, Yan Wenjing, and Zhou Libo from Lu Xun College for personal talks. On May 2, around 100 people from the literary and art circle attended the first meeting, at which Mao Zedong delivered a speech that later became the "Introduction" part; and Xiao Jun and others also spoke at the meeting. The second meeting was held on May 16, at which Ke Zhongping, Ouyang Shanzun (欧阳山尊), and others spoke during the discussions. The third meeting was scheduled on May 23, when Zhu De (朱德) delivered a speech in the afternoon, and Mao concluded the Forum with a speech, which later became the "Conclusion" part of the Talks. It was late in the afternoon, and so many people came to hear his speech after dinner that it had to be moved out into the open air, outside the meeting room, lit

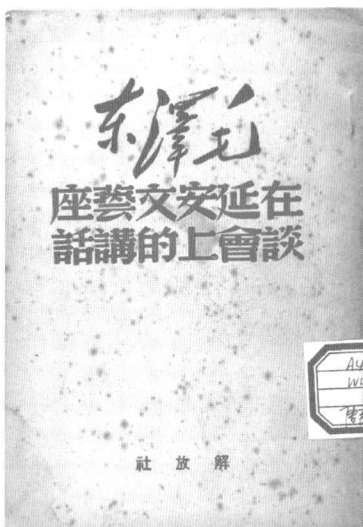

34.14. Earlier edition of Mao Zedong's "Talks at the Yan'an Forum on Literature and Art"

by a gas lamp. The official text of the Talks was published in *Liberation Daily* on October 19, 1943. Taking into consideration the different situations in the base area and the Nationalist-controlled area, and starting from the purpose of literature and art for the masses of people, the Talks further emphasized that literature and art were "in the first place for the workers, peasants, and soldiers; they are created for the workers, peasants, and soldiers and are for their use." And the way to realize this path of "for the workers, peasants, and soldiers" was that writers should go into the passionate life of workers, peasants, and soldiers and change their stand; as for the relationship between the raising of standards and popularity, Mao made it clear that popularity was the more urgent task at that time. These views seemed necessary from the perspective of the warring situation and the fact that the base area was located in China's poorest rural region in the northwest. And they later proved helpful for motivating and educating peasants, presenting peasants in literature and art, and creating national literary and artistic forms favored by the masses. But from the perspective of art and literature per se, the Talks obviously paid little attention to the special features of literature and art. In theory, it required that art and literature should absolutely serve politics, and political standards should be the top criterion for literary criticism (followed by artistic standards), and it corrected the so-called incorrect views of the "theory of human nature," that "literary and artistic works have always laid equal stress on the bright and the dark" and "this is still the period of critical essays," which all proved to be half-truths. Therefore, in the "liberated region" of the 1940s, the positive effects of the Talks as the text of guiding principles were greatly enhanced, but when the CPC entered the

34.15. Attendees of the Yan'an Forum on Literature and Art (full view, taken from the front)

34.16. After the Yan'an Forum on Literature and Art had been brought to a close, Mao Zedong had this photo take (partial) with attending literary writers and artists; this was the moment when everyone felt relaxed

city in the 1950s, it seemed increasingly ineffective to use the Talks as the only text guiding art and literature. This has been proved true by history.

After the Yan'an Forum on Literature and Art, with the Rectification movement within the literary and art circle, the guideline of literature and art "for the workers, peasants, and soldiers" was forcefully implemented. Writers rushed to the countryside and to the battlefront. Ai Qing went to Nanniwan and three border areas (namely Dingbian, Jingbian, and Anbian in northern Shaanxi); Chen Huangmei and Ouyang Shan went to Yan'an County successively; and Liu Qing (柳青) went to eastern Gansu. Ding Ling and Ouyang Shan immediately wrote the reportage writings *Tian Baolin* (《田保霖》) and *Living in the New Society* (《活在新社会里》), respectively, in praise of heroes among workers, peasants, and soldiers, and Mao Zedong wrote to them as an encouragement, saying: "I could not help reading your writings in one sitting after bathing and before sleeping. I celebrate the new writing style of both of you on behalf of Chinese people!"[7] Ai Qing was also quite active in "self-correction": he went to visit one after another model workers in the border area to interview them; wrote the long poem "Wu Manyou" (《吴满有》),

7   Quoted from *Selected Letters of Mao Zedong* (《毛泽东书信选集》), Beijing: People's Press, 1983.

34.17. Another perspective of the group photo of Mao Zedong, Zhu De, and attendees of the Yan'an Forum on Literature and Art

which was easy to understand; and devoted himself to the Yangko movement in Yan'an by voluntarily working as the deputy head of the Yangko Team of the Party School of the Central Committee of the CPC, and thus was elected as a first-class model worker of the border area. The new Yangko was the first artistic activity of the masses started after the Talks, and during the Spring Festival of 1943 and 1944, the entire Yan'an town boomed with Yangko dances. It was the Yangko Team of Lu Xun College that modified this traditional festive folk art, eliminating the vulgar entertainment elements and developing it into the new-style Yangko dance. Later dramatic plots were added and hence the upsurge of the creation and performance of the new-style Yangko opera.

Looking back at the drama genre in Yan'an, at first the major form was spoken drama performances. At that time, most dramatists were staying in the Nationalist-controlled area and there were few scripts written in the "liberated region," but there was no lack of public drama troupes: the Experimental Drama Troupe of the Department of Theater of Lu Xun College was a professional drama troupe, but some students performed in the troupe as intern practice; others included the Resistance Drama Troupe of the Propaganda Department of the CPC and the Education Department of the Border Area, the Beacon Fire Drama Troupe of the Political Department of the Rear Headquarters of the Eighth Route Army, the Fighting Drama Troupe of the Anti-Japanese

Military and Political University (抗日军政大学), the Northwestern Youth
National Salvation Drama Troupe of the Northwestern Youth National
Salvation Society (which was later changed to the Yan'an Youth Art Troupe
[延安青年艺术剧院]), and the Literature and Arts Working Team of Northern
Shaanxi Public School (whose name was later changed to the Northwestern
Literature and Arts Work Group [西北文艺工作团]). These were not profit-
seeking performing troupes, but propaganda organizations whose major aim was
self-entertainment and self-education. From 1939 to 1942, these public drama
troupes performed a number of famous Chinese and foreign plays, including
Cao Yu's *Sunrise*, *Thunderstorm*, and *The Metamorphosis*; Xia Yan's *Under Shanghai
Eaves* and *The Fascist Bacillus*; *The Inspector General* by Nikolai Gogol; *A Marriage
Proposal* and *An Avenger* by Anton Chekhov; *L'Avare* by Molière; *The Man with
a Gun* by Pogodin; *Armored Train* by Ivanov; and *Professor Mamlock* by Friedrich
Wolf. These high-level performances created a queer phenomenon: they claimed
to be for the masses, but their audiences were not workers, peasants, and soldiers
but many intellectual audience members gathering in Yan'an. Therefore, after the
Talks were delivered, this practice of performing high-brow theatrical plays was
criticized as "closing the door and raising standards." The writing and performing
of spoken drama plays thus declined (after that there were very few major spoken
drama plays created, except for *Comrade, You Are on the Wrong Road* [《同志，
你走错了路》]). And the general trend of going out of "the small garden of
Lu Xun College" into the "grand garden" contributed to the emergence of the
New Yangko Opera movement. Ai Qing, as head of the Yangko Team, witnessed
and participated in the entire process. He observed the creation, performance,
and viewing of the new Yangko opera plays and reflected on his own past literary
activities: "too obsessed with new forms and blindly admired the Western literature, and as a result, we were separated from the reality and from the masses –
the working people. Thus our literature and art became a decoration of culture,
something seeking to satisfy the taste of a small number of high-brow intellectuals."[8] One-sided or not, this was at least what Ai Qing truly felt at that moment.

A number of excellent plays were created during the thriving development
of new Yangko opera that started in 1943, including *Brother and Sister Clear
Wasteland* (《兄妹开荒》, written by Wang Dahua [王大化], Li Bo [李波], and
Lu You [路由]) about the Great Production movement; *The Couple Learning
to Read* (《夫妻识字》, written by Ma Ke [马可]) about peasants wishing
to be educated; *Liu'er Building a Fortune* (《刘二起家》, written by Ding Yi
[丁毅]) about changes of idlers in the countryside; and *The Wounded Soldier
Niu Yonggui* (《牛永贵挂彩》, written by Zhou Erfu [周而复] and Su Yiping
[苏一平]) about the new-style relationship between the army and people. These

8   Ai Qing: "On Massification and Old Forms" (《论大众化与旧形式》), *Complete Works of
Ai Qing*, Vol. 3, Shijiazhuang: Huashan Literature and Arts Press, 1994, pp. 235–236.

34.18. Later edition of the Yangko opera *Brother and Sister Clear Wasteland*

plays showed the writers' attention to ordinary peasants, soldiers, and cadres, as well as their moves to go beyond the small circle of personal feelings and devote themselves to the struggle and describe new characters, new subjects, and new themes. In the field of art, they consciously sought what was valuable from folk art heritage, trying to go a step further based on the May Fourth experience, and created brand new national forms and mass forms of literature. *The White-Haired Girl* (《白毛女》), the new opera emerging from 1944 to 1945, was the achievement of these efforts. The "white-haired female immortal" was a folklore character in the border area of northern China; the original story, which spread orally, was a traditional one about betrayal and abandonment, karma and the revenge of ghosts. When the story spread to Yan'an through the Service Group of the North-Western Battle Area, some people considered adjusting it into a playscript on the theme of breaking down superstitions among the masses. Later, through repeated discussions among the work group of Lu Xun College, He Jingzhi (1924–) and Ding Yi (1921–1998) did the actual writing, fully developing the relationship of oppression and resistance between the landlord Huang Shiren and the poor peasant Yang Bailao and his daughter Xi'er. Xi'er fled to the mountains, waited for her opportunity for revenge and became a "white-haired girl." Finally, the CPC led peasants to defeat the despotic landlord, and Dachun and other Eighth Route Army soldiers saved Xi'er and her hair turned black again, hence the new theme of "the old society turning people into ghosts and the new society turning ghosts into people." This was an attempt to integrate the subjects of emancipation of an entire class, emancipation of human beings, and the establishment of a new regime that brought happiness to ordinary people and condense them into a new literary theme. *The White-Haired Girl* was created within the broad framework of Western opera, in which Ma Ke, Zhang Lu (张鲁), and other musicians designed lyrical tunes based on folk songs (such as Hebei folk songs "Little Cabbage" [《小白菜》] and "The Tale of Qingyang" [《青阳传》], *bangzi* opera, flower drum tunes, and Yangko tunes) and integrated elements of traditional Chinese opera into it, creating a new form of opera with strong era-specific

34.19. Cover of the handmade paper edition of *The White-Haired Girl*, published by the Xinhua Bookstore in June 1946

34.20. After Yangko was developed into new Yangko opera, even more people got involved in this art form in Yan'an. This was *Carry Flower Baskets on Shoulder* (《挑花篮》), performed by the Yangko team, in which the carriers included Yu Lan (于蓝) and Jiang Yuheng (蒋玉衡)

34.21. Yangko dance performed by people from Lu Xun College in front of the General Office of the Central Committee of the CPC at Yangjialing (杨家岭)

34.22. Stage photo of *The White-Haired Girl* performed jointly by the Northern China Literary and Art Work Group (华北文艺工作团) and the Resistance Opera Troupe of the Hebei-Chahar-Shanxi Military Region (晋察冀军区抗敌剧社) at Zhangjiakou People's Theater in the autumn of 1945

characteristics and unique Chinese style. This play was a great success and ran for thirty consecutive performances in Yan'an. Peasants and peasant soldiers were deeply moved by the play and its characters, so much so that they wanted to punish the actor playing Huang Shiren as a real landlord. After watching the play, many people rushed to fight against despotic landlords, join the army, and support the front, and thus the performances became disguised motivation of the masses. In modern Chinese theatrical history, *The White-Haired Girl* opened the path for such a close dialogue between the imported modern literary and art genre and Chinese peasants. The play won the second-grade Stalin Art Prize within the socialist camp in 1951. New opera plays created after that, such as *Liu Hulan* (《刘胡兰》, written by Wei Feng [魏风] and others) and *Red Leaf River* (《赤叶河》, written by Ruan Zhangjing [阮章竞]), were all widely accepted by audiences of workers, peasants, and soldiers. Later during the Civil War, these plays were performed wherever the CPC army went.

The transformation of old opera went together with the creation of new opera. The Yan'an Pingju Opera Research Academy (延安平剧研究院), founded in 1942, was an institution whose mandate was to reform old Peking opera and create new national forms. With renovation as the guideline, people in the Academy collectively created *Driven to Revolt* (《逼上梁山》), based on the traditional opera *Water Margin* (《水浒传》), in 1943 (Yang Shaoxuan [杨绍萱] and Qi Yanming [齐燕铭] did the actual writing), as a representative work of the Academy. Later they also created *Occupying the Zhu's Village by Three Attacks* (《三打祝家庄》) with the new theme of "examination and

34.23. Stage photo of *Driven to Revolt*, performed by the Central Party School Club in Yan'an in 1943

research." This was the predecessor of modern Peking opera of the 1960s. Reform of Shaanxi opera of the same nature also achieved some success, whose excellent plays included *A Hatred of Blood and Tears* (《血泪仇》, by Ma Jianling [马健翎]).

Poetry in the "liberated region" showed two trends at this time, and the first insisted on writing new poetry to serve new audiences. Ai Qing was an example of this. Apart from "Wu Manyou," he also wrote the long poem "Into the Snow," which praised soldiers of the anti-Japanese resistance through the image of a battle steed. Lu Li and Ah Long, July clique poets who had lived in Yan'an for a while, also wrote some poems about the new life in the "liberated region," such as Lu Li's "Song of Yan'an" (《延安散歌》) and "I Love Winter" (《我爱冬天》). The second insisted on combining new realistic poetry with folk ballads, creating new folk song-style poetry, which became a new trend after the Talks. In 1945, Li Ji (李季, 1922–1980), who had lived in the three border areas for four or five years, wrote a new-style narrative poem that assimilated the Shaanxi folk art form *xintianyou* (信天游, short, improvised pastoral songs), entitled "Wang Gui and Li Xiangxiang" (《王贵与李香香》). This narrative poem closely combined the love of young peasants in the countryside with class struggles, and it made use of the *xintianyou* style featuring techniques of analogy and evocative images, and each two-line stanza built on a single rhyme, making a narrative poetic style with strong lyricism. (Examples: "The lucidum grass at both sides of the road, / No one is as good as my girl!" [大路畔上的灵芝草，/ 谁也没有妹妹好！]; "Picking up the best one with four silver hooves from all horses, / Choosing my love from all men and you are the best!" [马里头挑马四银蹄，/ 人里头挑人就数哥哥你！]; "Lighting the lantern with pipe bowl and half the room is illuminated, /

Measuring the rice with a small wine cup but I don't despise you because of poverty!" [烟锅锅点灯半炕炕明，/ 酒盅盅量米不嫌哥哥穷。]). In fact, the May Fourth new poetry also tried to assimilate elements of folk ballads, but was not very successful. They were truly blended into poetry through the blending of poets of the "liberated region" and peasants. Similar poems based on folk songs also included "The Zhang River" (《漳河水》) by Ruan Zhangjing; "Biography of a Cart Driver" (《赶车传》) by Tian Jian; and "Wang Jiu Making Complaints" (《王九诉苦》) and "Cannot Die" (《死不着》) by Zhang Zhimin (张志民).

As for the innovation of forms and blending with the masses of workers, peasants, and soldiers, the success achieved by Yangko opera, new opera, and folk song-style long poetry was unprecedented. But they were generally plain in manifesting the historical significance of ordinary people (peasants). It was the novel, the most fully developed literary genre since modern times, that achieved really profound results in the "liberated region." In the field of short stories, Kong Jue and Kang Zhuo, young writers who had graduated from Lu Xun College, showed their shockingly profound understanding of "liberated" peasants. Kong Jue's (1914–1966) "The Suffered" (《受苦人》) was an outstanding literary work. In the colloquial dialect of northern Shaanxi, "the suffered" referred to hard-working farm laborers, and here it referred to the "ugly man" who was crippled and prematurely senile from overwork at the age of 30, as well as the sixteen-year-old female protagonist Guinü'er, a child bride who was given to the ugly man at the age of three. Guinü'er was the narrator of this short story. And at the time of the story, she had been protected by the act of the "liberated region" and could break away from this "old" evil contract, but she knew that the "man" had been loving and raising her for thirteen years and was now just waiting to consummate their marriage. She called him "brother" to show her affection, but being his wife would destroy her whole life. She was grateful to him, but was afraid and delayed that moment, until she finally pretended to get married to him but refused to have sex with him, and he wounded her with an axe. In the story, Guinü'er's last words were: "My good comrades, it is better for me to be killed, I, the suffered who cannot die, what can I do with him in the future? But I don't blame him! He is so wretched! So … wret … ched …." The author left this open-ended for readers. Since a new marriage system had replaced the old one, women were awakened first because of their own interest, but they were bogged down in a tangle of sense, ethics, and feelings. Thus the author wrote about the deep and painful spiritual experience of peasants (especially women) in the "liberated region" and what's moving about this novel was that it sought to explore human conditions in a transitional period. Kang Zhuo's (1920–1991) *My Two Landlords* (《我的两家房东》) was written in a lyrical and reserved style, reflecting the happiness of young people in the border areas who had shaken off forced marriage. But his *The Morrow of Disaster* (《灾难的明天》) was written with a heavy heart. The story was about a famine in the "liberated region," and peasants were faced with a choice between fleeing from the famine, as in the old days, and staying and saving themselves through production. Xiangbao's family had its special circumstances: his mother was a child bride and grew into an aggressive woman because of her sufferings, but then she married a thirteen-year-old girl called Chunni to her twenty-year-old son Xiangbao, and Chunni was also full of hatred. The unnatural marriages of both generations formed unexpected tensions in this story, and the theme of this story, peasants' new life among the residue of the old social system, was highlighted, and thus it was much more profound than literary works of the same kind. It was during the period he studied and worked at Lu Xun College in Yan'an that Sun Li (1913–2002), who grew up in the middle of Hebei, wrote his novel of enduring charm, *The Lotus Lake* (《荷花淀》). After that, Sun Li always showed his unique style was different from other left-wing writers. It is said that when this novel was published in *Liberation Daily* in Yan'an, it was criticized by some as "full of petty-bourgeois sentiments" and "lacking the difficult and battling atmosphere of the rear area."[9] But it was Sun Li's aesthetic pursuit to explore the beauty of young women in the watery region of North China against the cruel background of war, so his approach was unique: in his writings, there were battle

34.24. Kong Jue, one of the young novelists who graduated from Lu Xun College

34.25. Illustrations of Kong Jue's "The Suffered," painted by Gu Yuan (古元)

9 See the article "We Need Literary Criticism" (《我们需要文艺批评》), *Liberation Daily*, June 4, 1945.

34.26. Kang Zhuo, who was another young writer of the "liberated region"

34.27. Sun Li at his Baiyang Lake and Lotus Lake

scenes covered up by a peasant woman's home visit, and in their complaints, the women expressed their love toward their husbands who joined the guerrilla forces and became soldiers. His language was pure and clear, with an opening like this:

The moon had risen and the little courtyard was delightfully fresh and clean. The rushes slit during the day were damp and supple, just waiting to be woven into mats. A woman was sitting in the yard plaiting the long soft rushes with nimble fingers. The thin, fine strands leaped and twisted in her arms.[10]

This was a bright and clear poetic narrative style with strength as well as grace. Sun Li had his own aesthetic ideal, which was to describe the beautiful souls among peasant women of the new era who were principled, enduring, optimistic, and devoted by portraying a group of young women in the countryside, such as Shuisheng's wife in *Lotus Lake* and *Exhortation* (《嘱咐》), the young girl in *Reed Flowers Lake* (《芦花荡》), the nun called Huixiu in *The Bell* (《钟》), the seventeen-year-old young woman Wang Zhenzhong in *After Leaving* (《走出以后》), and Ermei in *Wheat Harvest* (《麦收》). The author surely experienced and knew the material hardships and spiritual pressures faced by people in the national war, but he sought to tap into the poetic beauty from them. It was just like women in Hebei, with which he was very familiar, who had this habit: "No one knows where this custom originates. Women in the middle of Hebei, whenever they get out of home, as long as they form a group, no matter if it is going to attend meetings or going to school, going to block the road or to cut the wires, they will always get fully dressed, like they are going to some ceremonies."[11] Sun Li's philosophy of beauty came

[10] Sun Li: "Lotus Lake: A Record of Baiyang Lake" (《荷花淀——白洋淀纪事之一》), *Selected Works of Sun Li, Novels* (《孙犁选集 • 小说》), Xi'an: Shaanxi Normal University Press, 2003, p. 39.
[11] Sun Li: "Wheat Harvest," *Selected Works of Sun Li, Novels*, Xi'an: Shaanxi Normal University Press, 2003, p. 49.

from life, which later became representative of the Lotus Lake clique of the romantic lyrical literature of the "liberated region."

After the mid-1940s, perhaps thanks to the effects of the post-May Fourth literary pattern, both the Nationalist-controlled area and the "liberated region" witnessed a peak of novel creation. Driven by the Talks, it was popular for writers in the "liberated region" to write about workers, peasants, and soldiers, and there were two categories of such writings: those written in the literary forms favored by peasants and to be read by peasants; and those trying to represent peasants. The most outstanding writer of the first category was Zhao Shuli, whose style in such novels as *The Rhymes of Li Youcai* (《李有才板话》) and *Changes in Li Village* (《李家庄的变迁》) were the results of reforming the New Literature novel genre by internalizing the peasant mindset and peasants' language (which will be discussed in detail later). Ke Lan's (柯蓝) *The Story of an Iron Bucket* (《洋铁桶的故事》, 1944), Ma Feng and Xi Rong's *Heroes of Lüliang* (《吕梁英雄传》, 1945), and especially Kong Jue and Yuan Jing's (袁静) *New Tale of Heroes and Lovers* (《新儿女英雄传》, 1949) represented a restoration and reformation of the linked-chapter novel tradition. Revolutionary linked-chapter novels had a wide circulation, evidence that peasants liked their romantic style and style of speaking and singing literature that was easy to understand. And those trying to write about workers, peasants, and soldiers in a style more familiar to intellectuals (albeit with some colloquial and storytelling adjustments) included Liu Qing's *The Tale of Planting Rice* (《种谷记》, 1947), written from his own experience of working in the countryside in Mizhi County, which reflected the complex struggles of the countryside after all peasants were turned into farming workers; Ouyang Shan's *Gao Ganda* (《高干大》, 1949), the earliest novel written about the cooperative economy in the countryside; Cao Ming's *Motive Power* (《原动力》, 1948), about workers who tried to restore the hydroelectric plant; Liu Baiyu's *Flames at the Yangtze River* (《火光在前》, 1949) about the army and soldiers. Of these novels, Ding Ling's *The Sun Shines on Sanggan River* (《太阳照在桑干河上》, 1948) and Zhou Libo's *The Hurricane* (《暴风骤雨》, 1948–1949), which were both about the dramatic changes in the countryside brought about by the land reform, were doubtless representative works of the "liberated region." In 1951, these novels won the second-grade and third-grade Stalin Art Prize, respectively. *The Sun Shines on Sanggan River* enjoyed higher literary prestige, and was more valuable for historical analyses. It was in the "liberated region" that the Europeanized novel of the May Fourth period had the opportunity to truly assimilate the nutrients of folk art and be integrated with the latter, hence the multiple formats of novel created by Ding Ling, Sun Li, and Zhao Shuli, among others, which had a far-reaching influence on novels after the 1950s. Even the revolutionary linked-chapter novels had their continuance later, with examples including *Armed Working Team Behind Enemy Lines* (《敌后武工队》) and *Tracks in the Snowy Forest* (《林海雪原》, though the latter did not take the form of linked-chapter novel).

Overall, the blending of literature and peasant life in the "liberated region" was a historic high in terms of both scale and experience of peasants' lives by writers from urban cities and those from the base area. The advanced nature of May Fourth literature was not necessarily in agreement with the needs of massification of literature at this time, but the revolution and modernization of literature, as well as new creative styles thus incurred, continued. In the "liberated region," the guideline of literature serving politics was further strengthened. Thus it became a fashion for writers to merge with peasants and make writing a concentrated effort that should be finished quickly, and the general rule of literary creation per se was sometimes ignored. Undoubtedly this would continue in the following literary period.

TABLE 34.1 *Chinese People's Art and Literature book series* (中国人民文艺丛书)

Title	Genre	Author
The White-Haired Girl	New opera	Collectively created by people of the Lu Xun College of Art, written by He Jingzhi and Ding Yi
Wang Xiuluan (王秀鸾)	New opera	Fu Duo (傅铎)
Liu Hulan	New opera	Wei Feng and Liu Lianchi (刘莲池)
Red Leaf River	New opera	Ruan Zhangjing
The Invincible Militia (无敌民兵)	New opera	Ke Zhongping
Don't Kill Him (不要杀他)	New opera	Collectively created by people of the North China Resistance Opera Troupe (华北抗敌剧社), written by Liu Jia (刘佳)
Driven to Revolt	New Pingju opera	Collectively created by people of the Yan'an Pingju Opera Research Academy
Occupying the Zhu's Village by Three Attacks	New Pingju opera	Collectively created by people of the Yan'an Pingju Opera Research Academy, including Ren Guilin (任桂林), etc.
A Hatred of Blood and Tears	New Shaanxi opera	Ma Jianling
Everybody Is Happy (大家喜欢)	New Shaanxi opera	Ma Jianling
Hatred of the Poor (穷人恨)	New Shaanxi opera	Ma Jianling

(continued)

TABLE 34.1 *(continued)*

Title	Genre	Author
Defending Peace (保卫和平)	New Shaanxi opera	Ma Jianling
Li Guorui (李国瑞)	Spoken drama	Du Feng (杜烽)
Song of the Red Flag (红旗歌)	Spoken drama	Liu Canglang (刘沧浪), Lu Mei, and Chen Huai'ai (陈怀皑), etc.
Be Far-Sighted (把眼光放远点)	Spoken drama	Jizhong Battlefront Drama Troupe (冀中火线剧社), Hu Danfei (胡丹沸), Cheng Yin (成荫), etc.
Grow Up in Battles (战斗里成长)	Spoken drama	Rewritten by Hu Ke (胡可)
How Were the Bullets Made? (炮弹是怎样造成的)	Spoken drama	Chen Qitong (陈其通)
Li, the Roaming King (李闯王)	Spoken drama	Ah Ying
Passing a Barrier (过关)	(Not known)	Collectively created by people of the Shandong Experimental Drama Troupe, written by Jia Ji (贾霁) and Li Xia (李夏)
The Red Lantern (红灯记)	(Not known)	Liu Yi (柳夷)
Brother and Sister Clear Wasteland	Yangko opera	Wang Dahua and Ma Ke, etc.
Winning Honor by a United Effort (团结立功)	Yangko opera	Lu Yi (鲁易) and Zhang Jie (张捷)
The Wounded Soldier Niu Yonggui	Yangko opera	Zhou Erfu and Su Yiping, etc.
Wang Keqin Squad (王克勤班)	Yangko opera	Shanxi–Hebei–Shandong–Henan Military Region Literature and Arts Work Group (晋冀鲁豫军区文艺工作团), etc.
Baoshan Joining the Army (宝山参军)	Yangko opera	Wang Xuebo (王血波), Wang Shen (王莘), etc.
Street Vendor's Shoulder Pole (货郎担)	Yangko opera	Collectively created by people of the Mass Yangko Team of Qiaozhen Township of Yan'an (延安桥镇乡群众秧歌队)
Making Changes to the Old Style (改变旧作风)	(Not known)	Collectively created by people of the Taihangwu Township Light Opera Troupe (太行武乡光明剧团), written by Gao Jieyun (高介云)
Liu Qiao United with Her Family (刘巧团圆)	Folk art	Han Qixiang (韩起祥)

(continued)

TABLE 34.1 *(continued)*

Title	Genre	Author
A Little Girl in the Shanxi–Chahar–Hebei Border Area (晋察冀的小姑娘)	Folk art	Wang Zunsan (王尊三), Zhao Shuli, etc.
The Sun Shines on Sanggan River	Novel	Ding Ling
The Hurricane	Novel	Zhou Libo
Gao Ganda	Novel	Ouyang Shan
The Tale of Planting Rice	Novel	Liu Qing
The Story of an Iron Bucket	Novel	Ke Lan
Motive Power	Novel	Cao Ming
Heroes of Lüliang	Novel	Ma Feng and Xi Rong
The Upheaval (地覆天翻记)	Novel	Wang Xijian (王希坚)
The Rhymes of Li Youcai	Novel	Zhao Shuli
Changes in Li Village	Novel	Zhao Shuli
Minefields (地雷阵)	Collection of short stories	Shao Zinan, Sun Li, and Qin Zhaoyang (秦兆阳), etc.
The Invincible Trio (无敌三勇士)	Collection of short stories	Liu Baiyu and Liu Shi (刘石), etc.
A Story of a Woman Whose Life Turned Around (一个女人翻身的故事)	Collection of short stories	Kong Jue, Shu Wei (束为), and Fang Ji (方纪), etc.
A Sunny Day (晴天)	Collection of short stories	Wang Li (王力), etc.
Laozhao Going to the Countryside (老赵下乡)	Collection of short stories	Yu Lin (俞林), etc.
Double Red Flags (双红旗)	Collection of short stories	Lu Mei, etc.
Wang Gui and Li Xiangxiang	Long poem	Li Ji
Biography of a Cart Driver	Long poem	Tian Jian
Tenant Lin (佃户林)	Collection of poems	Xiao San, Ai Qing, Wang Xijian, etc.
A Trap (圈套)	Collection of poems	Ruan Zhangjing, Zhang Zhimin, etc.
The East is Red (东方红)	Collection of poems	Workers, peasants, and soldiers

(continued)

TABLE 34.1 *(continued)*

Title	Genre	Author
Heroic October (英雄的十月)	Reportage writing	Hua Shan (华山)
A Bomb without Fuse (没有弦的炸弹)	Reportage writing	Ding Fen (丁奋), etc.
The Flying Soldiers are on the Yimeng Mountain (飞兵在沂蒙山上)	Reportage writing	Han Xiliang (韩希梁) and Hong Lin (洪林), etc.
A Section of Norman Bethune's Life (诺尔曼·白求恩断片)	Reportage writing	Zhou Erfu and Shi Tianshou (师田手), etc.
The Light Illuminates Shenyang (光明照耀着沈阳)	Reportage writing	Liu Baiyu
Rescue (解救)	Reportage writing	Zhou Yuanqing (周元青), etc.
Hero Gully (英雄沟)	Reportage writing	Zheng Du (郑笃), etc.

Presided over by Zhou Yang in Pingshan County, Hebei, in late spring 1948; Ke Zhongping and Chen Yong (陈涌) were appointed editors and later Kang Zhuo, Zhao Shuli, and Ouyang Shan participated in the editing work.

Published successively by the Xinhua Bookstore since May 1949, and the editing agency appearing on the series was "Chinese People's Art and Literature Book Series Press." At first there were fifty-five titles (actually fifty-seven titles were published by the end of 1949).

In 1950, apart from those already published and successively revised and reprinted in a new format, the newly edited *Flames at the Yangtze River*, *The Zhang River*, and *Zhao Qiao'er* (《赵巧儿》) were published. The editing agency appearing on the series was changed into the "Editorial Committee of Chinese People's Art and Literature Book Series."

New titles added to the series in 1950:

Zhao Qiao'er by Li Bing (李冰) (poem)

Marching Forward Forever (《永远前进》) by Liu Baiyu and Sheng Mu (生木), etc. (novel)

The First Company Marching Toward Victory (《走向胜利的第一连》) by Dong Yanfu (董彦夫) (reportage writing)

Sixty-Eight Days (《六十八天》) by Han Xiliang (reportage writing)

This book series represents the achievements of implementation of the Talks by writers of the "liberated region." (Main source: Liu Zengjie: *History of Literature in the Liberated Region*)

THIRTY FIVE

GUILIN

The Upsurge of Theater and the Publishing Phenomenon of the Wartime "Cultural City"

BEFORE THE WAR BROKE OUT, SUILIN, LIKE KUNMING, which will be discussed in detail in Chapter 36, was nothing but a strategic town in the border province of the hinterland, and was not comparable to coastal cities in terms of economy and culture. For both cities, however, it was thanks to their special position during the war that they had such a close relationship with literature. Guilin's importance certainly did not lie in its beautiful landscape, but in its position as a political and cultural buffer strip during the Anti-Japanese War. Guangxi's local government had long been at odds with the central government, and now that the central government had retreated to the hinterland and had to rely on local forces, the local government suddenly gained a drastically larger share of administrative power. And even though it was the period of the second KMT–CPC cooperation, the competition between the two political parties under the cover of the united anti-Japanese front was intensely fierce in Guangxi. As for the cultural division away from the frontline, some intellectuals remained in Chongqing and some went to Yan'an; Kunming became the headquarters of Beijing school literature because a number of famous universities moved there, and Guilin became the gathering place of intellectuals from other cliques. This transportation hub that connected the southeast and southwest thus became an ideal place for cultural exchanges between the southern and northern parts of the country. For example, when Xia Yan received the order to move the *National Salvation Daily* (《救亡日报》) out of Shanghai, his first choice was Guangzhou, but then at the last moment before Guangzhou was occupied and the Japanese army was only a dozen miles from the city, he left Guangzhou for Guilin. When the Wannan Incident occurred in 1941, left-wing intellectuals evacuated to Guilin.

And when the Attack on Pearl Harbor took place at the end of the same year and Hong Kong was occupied, a large number of progressive intellectuals and citizens again retreated to Guilin. Some took a left-wing approach to explain the cultural prosperity of Guilin after March 1942: "Chongqing was a Fascist den of monsters; the atmosphere in Kunming was not very good, either. Yan'an had been blocked, and thus comparatively, Guilin seemed more safe and secure."[1] In terms of being an environment for literary creation, the difference between Kunming and Guilin was that in Kunming one had time to reflect on and think about the war, whereas Guilin kept an ambiguous distance from the war, where the war seemed around the corner, but one could still write literary works leisurely and calmly there. Therefore, Ai Qing and Dai Wangshu, who belonged to different poetic cliques before the war, cooperated and launched the journal *Pinnacle* (《顶点》) in Guilin, for which their intended purpose was different from, and broader than, that when they were in Wuhan. On the one hand, it "should become a force of resistance," while on the other hand, "the poetic works closely connected with the anti-Japanese resistance are not poetry of resistance in the narrow sense of the term."[2] Another example was that after Mao Dun retreated from Hong Kong to Guilin, he finished his "Pieces Picked Up after the Calamity" (《劫后拾遗》) about the war, and began to write *Red Leaves Are as Beautiful as Spring Flowers*, a novel about a small town in the lower Yangtze River in the beginning of the twentieth century. He had been deliberating on the novel for a long time, and attached many personal feelings and memories to the novel, making it a uniquely Chinese-style epic. After he left Guilin, where the landscape could match that of the watery towns in Jiangnan, he never finished the novel (certainly there were other reasons). Thus with its unique environment, Guilin, referred to as a "cultural city" at that time, rose to the fore.

This was a very extraordinary wartime urban cultural scape. Guilin's population increased drastically, from 70,000 in 1936, when it just became a provincial capital, to over half a million in 1944. A large number of national institutions were moved to take refuge here. Of the research institutes of the Nanjing Central Academy, those moved to Guilin included the Physics Research Institute, whose director was Ding Xilin (he was also a famous playwright); the Geography Institute, whose director was Wang Jingxi; and the Geology Institute, whose director was Li Siguang (李四光). More than

---

[1] Lin Huanping (林焕平): "Achievements and Significance of the Literature and Art of Resistance in Guilin: Preface to *Overview of Literature and Art of Resistance in Guilin* by Li Jianping" (《桂林抗战文艺的成就和意义——李建平著〈桂林抗战文艺概观〉序言》), *Overview of Literature and Art of Resistance in Guilin*, Guilin: Lijiang Press, 1991, p. 3.

[2] See "Editors' Miscellaneous Notes" (《编后杂记》) in the inaugural issue of *Pinnacle*, July 1939. Quoted from Xie Zhixi (解志熙): *The Modern and the Modern Era* (《摩登与现代》), Beijing: Tsinghua University Press, 2006, p. 6.

twenty banks also moved here, including the Central Bank and provincial banks. Many cultural and educational institutions were moved to the hinterland, including the National Association of Vocational Education of China (中华职业教育社), the Wuxi National Studies Training Institute (无锡国学专修馆), the International News Agency (国际新闻社), the Research Association for the Chinese Rural Economy (中国农村经济研究会), the Jiangsu Institute of Education (江苏教育学院), the Beiping School of Journalism (北平新闻专科学校), and the Association of Young Journalists in China (中国青年记者协会). The people from these institutions, together with students and teachers of Guangxi University and Guilin Normal Institute (桂林师范学院), formed quite a high-level educated population. A local audience for spoken drama was thus formed, as well as a group of readers of newspapers and magazines with higher tastes. Later an increasingly large number of newspapers and magazines were published and released from Guilin. Taking newspapers for example, apart from the local *Guangxi Daily* (《广西日报》), there were national major newspapers such as *Ta Kung Pao* (Guilin Edition), the *National Salvation Daily*, *Lihpao Daily* (《力报》), and *Mopping Up News* (《扫荡报》). A most surprising sight in Guilin was that bookstores and newspaper stands could be seen everywhere in the streets, as many as restaurants. The area around Guixi Road (桂西路) became a cultural street in Guilin, like Fourth Avenue in Shanghai. Many major publishing houses opened their branches along this street. The core literary organization was the Guilin Branch of All-China Resistance Association, whose inaugural meeting was held in October 1939, after nearly one year's preparation. Li Renren (李任仁) and Li Wenzhao (李文钊) acted in their own capacity as locals, and elected directors included such writers from outside as Xia Yan, Wang Luyan, Ouyang Yuqian, Huang Yaomian (黄药眠), Sun Ling (孙陵), Ai Wu, Hu Yuzhi, Jiao Juyin, and Shu Qun, and Wang Luyan was in charge of general affairs of the branch. After writers from all over the country gathered together with local intellectuals, Guilin began to occupy a key position in terms of culture. Of the writers, those living in the city for more than two years (accumulated) included Ouyang Yuqian, Meng Chao, Sheng Cheng (盛成), Sima Wensen, Qin Si (秦似), Ai Wu, Wang Luyan, Peng Yanjiao, Xiong Foxi, Shao Quanlin, Ge Qin (葛琴), Nie Gannu, Ba Jin, Liu Yazi, Luo Binji, Tian Han, Duanmu Hongliang, and Xia Yan. Those living in the city for a short time but having a great influence included Mao Dun, Ai Qing, and Hu Feng. In 1938, Guo Moruo led people of the Third Office to retreat from Wuhan and Changsha and stayed in Guilin for only twenty days, but he organized some of his people into the Third Unit of the Political Department at the field headquarters in Guilin. This was later referred to by locals as "the small Third Office," evidence of its effect in Guilin.

In the field of theater, Guilin had the advantages of its advanced local opera and its open attitude. When they came to Guangxi, the foremost motive of

35.1. Many newspapers, magazines, and bookstores were moved to Guilin from all over the country during the Anti-Japanese War, making it a wartime cultural city. This photo, taken by the Guilin Office of *Ta Kung Pao*, includes: (second row, fourth from the left) Hu Zhengzhi (胡政之), (fifth from the left) Xu Zhucheng (徐铸成), and (sixth from the left) Zhang Jiluan

Ouyang Yuqian and Tian Han, both leading authorities within the theater circle, was to help reform traditional Guangxi opera. Ouyang Yuqian (1889–1962) arrived in Guilin in 1938 at the invitation of the provincial government and Guangxi Society for Theatrical Improvement (广西戏剧改进会). Upon arrival, he adapted his Peking opera script, *Liang Hongyu* (《梁红玉》), whose performance had achieved success in Shanghai, into Guangxi opera, had it rehearsed by the Guangxi Opera Troupe of Guilin South China Theater (桂林南华戏院), and invited the four greatest female performers of that time, namely Xie Yujun (谢玉君), Li Huizhong (李慧中), Fang Zhaoyuan (方昭媛), and Yin Xi (尹羲), to alternately play the lead role, the national heroine Liang Hongyu. This caused quite a stir in the town. He came to Guilin again in 1939 and settled here, when the provincial government entrusted all matters concerning the reform of Guangxi opera to him, and he was appointed director of the Guangxi Society for Theatrical Improvement, then as curator of the Guangxi Provincial Institute of Art (省立艺术馆) and manager of the Experimental Troupe of Guangxi Opera (桂剧实验剧团). He established the stage director and rehearsal systems for traditional Guangxi opera, cultivated new-style theatrical talents, and brought his advanced experience

35.2. Ouyang Yuqian's *Li Xiucheng the Loyal King* was another major play following the trend of historical play performances in Guilin

of spoken drama into the art of local opera. He wrote, adapted, and collected as many as fourteen playscripts, of which the best was the Peking opera script and Guangxi opera script of his representative work in spoken drama, *The Peach Blossom Fan*. The premiere of the Guangxi opera play *The Peach Blossom Fan* set a historical record of thirty-three performances, from which we can see the large theater audience in the city.

Another dramatist, Tian Han, came to Guilin in 1939 at the invitation of Guangxi University and the Guangxi Society for Theatrical Improvement, and he led a Pingju opera propaganda team to perform the Peking opera *New Yanmenguan Pass* (《新雁门关》), adapted by himself, at the New World Theater. Tian Han had quite a different style from his close friend Ouyang Yuqian. He was more aggressive and always took the public audience into consideration, and thus brought the new trend of historical plays of resistance to Guilin, including his bold changes to the stage setting: embroidering the characters "抗战必胜" (WE WILL WIN THE WAR) and "救国必成" (WE WILL SAVE THE COUNTRY) on the curtain of the entrance door through which actors went onto the stage; and substituted the pattern of dragons on the tablecloth on the operatic stage with his own four-line poem that had a very clear theme: "We have 400 million actors, / We have 10,000 *li* battle lines. / We have the whole world as our audience, / Who watch our grand historical plays." He created a strong atmosphere of resistance by making the most of the political motivational effect of the left-wing theatrical tradition.[3] And Tian Han completed the scripts of his two grand Peking opera plays, *New Tale of Heroes and Lovers*, which was

35.3. In Guilin in 1942: (front row, left to right) Tian Han, Wang Ying, and Xia Yan

---

[3]   Quoted from Dong Jian (董健): *Biography of Tian Han* (《田汉传》), Beijing: October Literature and Arts Press, 1996, pp. 558–559.

about Chinese people resisting against Japanese occupation during the Ming dynasty; and *Jiang-Han Fishermen's Song*, which was about Han people resisting against the Jin nationality during the Song dynasty. After hurried rehearsals, the plays were put on public show at the Jincheng Grand Theater, and were equally enthusiastically received by the audience. Tian Han began writing the play *Jiang-Han Fishermen's Song* in Wuhan and completed it in Guilin, and it became the most frequently performed and the most influential of all his theatrical works adapted from traditional opera. In order to understand how the reform of traditional opera blended so well with the popularity of spoken drama and their mutual promotion, we may just look at the headline used in one of the local newspapers to welcome Tian Han: "A harbinger that all traditional operas shall serve the anti-Japanese war; people from the Pingju opera, Hunan opera, Guangxi opera, Guangdong opera, and spoken drama circles united to welcome Tian Han."[4] When Tian Han arrived in Guilin for the third time in 1941, he settled and lived in the city for three years, writing plays of spoken drama, Peking opera, and Hunan opera, and had an even greater influence.

Thus Guilin quickly became a theatrical center in the "great hinterland," second only to Chongqing, and a performing circle was formed with the National Defense Art Troupe (国防艺术社), New China Drama Group (新中国剧社), and Experimental Spoken Drama Troupe of Guangxi Provincial Institute of Art at its core. Of these, the National Defense Art Troupe was founded the earliest by local progressive intellectuals and was supported by the provincial government. In expansion, they invited Meng Chao and Jiao Juyin as management successively, and incorporated famous actors such as Fengzi, Chen Erdong (陈迩冬), and Tang Ruoqing. Many famous directors had directed performances for the troupe, such as Ouyang Yuqian, who directed *Behind the Green Curtain of Tall Crops* (《青纱帐里》, written by himself) and *The Devil's Den* (《魔窟》, written by Chen Baichen); Hong Shen, who directed *Luminescent Cup* (《夜光杯》, written by You Jing [尤竞], aka Yu Ling); Jiao Juyin, who directed *Thunderstorm* (by Cao Yu); Xiong Foxi, who directed *Peking Man* (by Cao Yu); and Zhang Min (章泯), who directed *The Flying General* (《飞将军》, written by Hong Shen) and participated in the performance of such famous plays as *The True Story of Ah Q* (adapted by Tian Han) and *The Wilderness* (by Cao Yu). Before it was disbanded in 1942, this performing troupe mainly performed realistic plays. The New China Drama Group was a civil performing troupe founded at the end of 1941 by organizing members of all theater troupes scattered around the southwestern part of the country, and it was infiltrated by communist party members. It was managed by Du Xuan and Qu Baiyin (瞿白音),

---

[4] See the news story in *National Salvation Daily*, April 24, 1939. Quoted from Dong Jian: *Biography of Tian Han*, p. 558.

successively, with Tian Han as its honorary president, who quickly wrote the spoken drama *Rhapsody on the Sound of Autumn* (《秋声赋》) for this performing troupe. Of all the spoken drama plays of resistance written by Tian Han, this play was based on his own family and love, and he wrote with both emotions and rationality about how an intellectual should choose between serving his country and his personal life and love. This troupe performed both domestic and foreign plays, such as *Farewell, Hong Kong!* (《再会吧，香港！》, written by Tian Han and others), *Annals of Theater* (written by Xia Yan and others), *Twenty-Four Hours in Chongqing* (written by Shen Fu), and the Russian plays *The Inspector General* and *The Storm*, and it took an active part in various theatrical activities in the southwest. The last theatrical institution was the Provincial Institute of Art, which was founded by the local government, but its management was entrusted to Ouyang Yuqian, who was proficient in both spoken drama and traditional operas. In terms of spoken drama, it paid equal attention to historical plays and realistic plays. The five-act play *Li Xiucheng the Loyal King* was another representative work written by Ouyang Yuqian during this period on top of *The Peach Blossom Fan*. This tragic play about the Taiping Heavenly Kingdom focused on Li Xiucheng's failed attempt to save Tianjing (Heavenly Capital), and its lament about the split within the group of peasant uprisings moved audiences from all over the city. The play ran for twenty-three performances to packed houses and total audience numbers allegedly exceeded 30,000. Ouyang Yuqian also directed *The History of the Taiping Rebellion*, written by Yang Hansheng in Chongqing, which was about the infighting between Wei Changhui and Yang Xiuqing, both important leaders of the Taiping Heavenly Kingdom, with Hong Xuanjiao and Fu Shanxiang involved in the fighting. This play caused an upsurge of Taiping Heavenly Kingdom plays in Guilin with its clear-cut characters, intense dramatic conflicts, and extremely strong stage effects. In July 1942, Tian Han invited people from the theatrical circle to attend a symposium on historical plays in the Seven-Star Cave of Guilin, at which they showed the outstanding achievements of historical plays of resistance. In terms of realistic plays, Ouyang Yuqian directed Xia Yan's *On the Defense* (《心防》) and *City of Sorrows* (《愁城记》); Lao She and Song Zhidi coauthored *The Nation Above All*; and there were performances of Cao Yu's *Sunrise*, Lao She's *The Problem of Face*

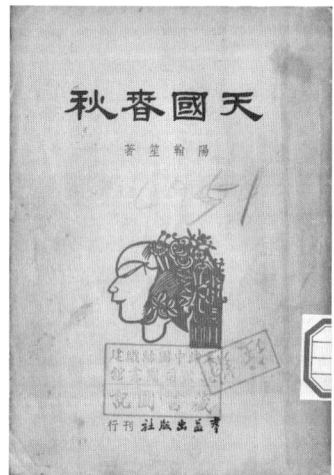

35.4. Yang Hansheng's spoken drama play *The History of the Taiping Rebellion*, one of the major historical plays about the uprisings of the Taiping Heavenly Kingdom

(《面子问题》), Chen Baichen's *The Wedding March*, and Ding Xilin's *Miaofeng Mountain* (《妙峰山》) directed by others (instead of the play-wrights themselves), and the achievements could match those of historical plays. *On the Defense* was an important play written by Xia Yan when he lived in Guilin in 1940, which was about how intellectuals staying in Shanghai, the isolated island, defended the spirituality of five million citizens with their literary works. Apart from the three performing troupes already mentioned, there were performances by the Petrel Theater Troupe (海燕剧艺社), the Lequn Theater Troupe (乐群剧团), the July Seventh Amateur Theater Troupe (七七业余剧社), the Xin'an Traveling Drama Troupe (新安旅行团), the Ninth Resistance Theater Troupe under the Third Office, and a number of students' theater troupes from universities and middle schools.

With the three famous dramatists Ouyang Yuqian, Tian Han, and Xia Yan at the core, these performing troupes cooperated well in the hard times and organized many influential theatrical activities. An example was the fundrais-ing performances organized by Xia Yan in 1939 as an emergency measure to raise funds for the *National Salvation Daily*, which was participated in by many colleagues in the theatrical circle in Guilin. The play performed was *Within One Year*, which Xia wrote in as little as three weeks. The play was about the spiritual chaos experienced by a country gentleman's family during the war, and reflected the ordeal experienced by people during that one year. Apart from Jiao Juyin, who was the chief director, Sun Shiyi (孙师毅), Ma Yanxiang, Tian Han, and Xia Yan also participated in the direction of the performances. The play was rehearsed by three operatic teams, with the Guangxi opera team assisted by Ouyang Yuqian and Ma Junwu, and the Guangzhou opera team guided by the linguist Chen Yuan, making it a grand meeting of people of both spoken drama and local operas. The play ran for nine performances in Guilin with a total audience of more than 10,000, and together with perfor-mances in Chongqing, altogether an amount of more than 17,000 silver dollars was raised, quite high box office takings at that time. When Xia Yan and other people returned to Guilin from Hong Kong in 1942, Hong Shen suggested that they collectively write a play based on this experience. They decided on the general framework of the play the following day, and according to their division of work, Xia Yan wrote the first act, Hong Shen the second and third acts, and Tian Han the fourth. The first draft was completed within one year, and after the final touching up by Xia Yan, it was submitted to be directed by Ouyang Yuqian, and was rehearsed and ready for performance by the New China Drama Group within one week. This was *Farewell, Hong Kong!*, another cooperative effort among the people of the theatrical circle. The play had been granted permission to go ahead, but it was stopped by military police during the performance of the first act during the premiere. Many people in the audi-ence refused to leave, and tore their tickets into pieces to show their respect for the dramatists and their unyielding resistance against the forces prohibiting the performance.[5]

These were incidents that reflected the wartime and popular feature of theatrical development in Guilin. Performances were frequent, and new theatrical works and performing troupes emerged constantly, but there were no new dramatists coming forth (unlike in Chongqing and Yan'an). This was because Guilin was nothing but a newly established arena for theatrical activities. The situation here was similar to Shanghai before the war and Chongqing during the war: there were a large number of theatrical intellectuals (though they moved frequently), and quite a large portion of the citizen audience who had the habit of cultural consumption and could afford it. Therefore, an audience base for theater performances was formed. The past historical resources paid too much attention to the moving and gathering of progressive intellectuals and ignored the large-scale immigration of ordinary citizens after the 1938 Changsha Fire and the occupation of Hong Kong by the Japanese army. Having an audience base consisting of receptors (readers) of theater was at least as important as the dramatists. The development reached its climax in 1944 with the Southwest Drama Exhibition held in Guilin, a grand theatrical event somewhat like a "public festival."

Held in the poor conditions during the war, the Exhibition was nearly a miracle. It was initiated as an event to celebrate the completion of the new Guangxi Institute of Art building, for which Ouyang Yuqian raised funds by himself so that dramatists had their own venue for professional activities, and it then became a grand event to review the achievements of plays of resistance. Under the leadership of Ouyang Yuqian, Tian Han, Xiong Foxi, Qu Baiyin, and others, the event lasted for three months, from February 15 until May 19. Twenty-nine performing organizations from eight provinces participated in the event, including the Fourth, Seventh, and Ninth Resistance Theater Troupe, the Experimental Spoken Drama Troupe of Guangxi Provincial Institute of Art, the New China Drama Group, the Training Brigade of the Political Department of the Fourth War Zone (四战区政治部教导大队), the Art Propaganda Brigade of the Political Department of the Seventh War Zone (七战区政治部艺宣大队), the Spoken Drama Group and Pingju Opera Team of the Delegation of Theatrical Workers in Jiangxi (江西戏剧工作者代表团),

35.5. Southwest Drama Exhibition poster

---

5   For all the above materials, see Chen Jian (陈坚): *Biography of Xia Yan* (《夏衍传》), Beijing: October Literature and Arts Press, 1998, pp. 310, 354.

the Siwei Pingju Opera Troupe (四维平剧社), the Experimental Guangxi
Opera Troupe of Guangxi Society for Theatrical Improvement, the Drama
Troupe of Guangxi Society for Theatrical Improvement, and the Spoken
Drama Troupe of Sun Yat-sen University, with nearly 1,000 performers and
126 plays, of which there were 31 spoken drama plays, 28 Pingju opera plays, 9
Guangxi opera plays, 7 skits, and 1 opera.[6] There were over 100,000 visits to the
Exhibition. Meanwhile, the Conference of Theatrical Workers in the Southwest
was held, at which the *Convention of Dramatists* (《剧人公约》) was drafted
and passed. A large-scale exhibition of theatrical material was held, showcasing
1,029 items, including documents, photos, tables and figures, operatic masks,
stage models and designs, manuscripts, works and letters, from a dozen theatrical troupes, and the surprisingly rich content attracted 36,000 visits. Looking at
the thirty-one spoken drama plays, we find that the Exhibition per se did not
produce major works, and it was indeed just a review of past achievements. It
was a strong manifestation of the confidence of Chinese dramatists to defend
Chinese culture and insist on literary creation during wartime, as well as their
belief that theater should serve the public. Ouyang Yuqian and Tian Han represented two different styles among progressive dramatists: Ouyang was more
professional and calm, paying much attention to artistic details in writing and
directing plays; while Tian was passionate and romantic, more energetic and
politically aggressive in his literary creation. During this Exhibition, however,
both tried to cooperate with each other, showing the progress of dramatists.
And the Exhibition was by no means an isolated event: Guilin maintained the

35.6. Attendees of the Conference of Theatrical Workers held at the same time as the Southwest Drama
Exhibition. The chairmen of the conference were Ouyang Yuqian and Tian Han

[6] For the specific plays participating in the Exhibition, see *Overview of Literature and Art of
Resistance in Guilin*, Guilin: Lijiang Press, 1991, p. 126.

35.7. *Wild Grass*, a famous monthly journal of prose writings, was launched in Guilin in 1940

good state of its grand stage and there were frequent performances during those four or five years. According to relevant statistics, the performances of spoken drama alone had 265 showings in 1939, 131 in 1940, 164 in 1941, and 228 in 1942. This meant that in 1939, there was an average of 22 showings per month, and in 1942 the number was 19.[7] No wonder when Tian Han wrote to Guo Moruo in 1942, he said that thanks to the theatrical movement in Guilin, it was nearly "possible to watch spoken drama plays every day. This year may be called a 'year of spoken drama.'"[8] These performances lasted until the end of 1944, when Guilin was occupied. Even then, when the government army gave the first order of evacuation, the New China Drama Group was still on stage performing the grand spoken drama play, *Shout Out Your Anger, Guilin!* (《怒吼吧，桂林！》), at the Provincial Institute of Art.

Other literary achievements of Guilin during the war are to be discussed by genre. Prose writing was especially thriving in Guilin thanks to the Wild Grass clique, a group of writers gathered around the specialized essay journal *Wild Grass* (《野草》, whose editor-in-chief was Xia Yan) launched in August 1940. It had been four years since Lu Xun died, and though there were various commemorative activities held all over the country, as for whether Lu Xun's style in essay writing was still relevant, one could see the response from society in *Wenhui Daily – Century Wind* (《文汇报·世纪风》) in 1938.[9] The title and style of *Wild Grass*, like those of *Century Wind* (《世纪风》) and *Lu Xun Wind* (《鲁迅风》) in Shanghai, the isolated island, showed its self-asserted mission to carry on Lu Xun's literary legacy. The article "Wild Grass (in lieu of The Foreword)" (《野草（代发刊语）》) written by Qin Si showed the position of the journal:

> Some of us claim to be good at looking forward to a better future, but they are also good at forgetting disasters. On the frontline and in the

---

7   See Liu Shoubao (刘寿保): "Achievements and Contributions of Guilin the Cultural City" (《桂林文化城的成就和贡献》), in Wei Hualing (魏华龄) et al., ed., *Proceedings on the Resistant Culture of Guilin* (《桂林抗战文化研究文集》), Guilin: Lijiang Press, 1992, p. 87.

8   Tian Han's letter to Guo Moruo, see "Correspondence" section of *Annals of Theater*, Vol. 2, Issue 2, quoted from *Overview of Literature and Art of Resistance in Guilin*, Guilin: Lijiang Press, 1991, p. 28.

9   The article "Our Opinions on Lu Xun's Essays" (《我们对于鲁迅杂文的意见》) by Ba Jin and others published in *Wenhui Daily – Century Wind* on December 18, 1938, showed the writers' views on the debates about whether Lu Xun's satirical style had been out of date and irrelevant.

enemy-occupied area people are fighting against the enemies, whereas away from the frontline some live a luxurious life, enjoying themselves and making a profit by smuggling. They talk about resistance and building the country, but what they think about or even what they do is resistance and making their own fortune.

Thus the purpose of essays in *Wild Grass* was to criticize the unjust realities, but it did not necessarily criticize them explicitly, sometimes they also adopted the implicit style. For example, Nie Gannu (1903–1986), a representative writer of this clique, was good at writing about women, ethical issues, and historical anecdotes, but all were written to criticize the ugly sides of the national character and national culture. "If I Were King" (《我若为王》) listed all the scenarios if "I" had become the "king," denouncing the despotic and autocratic rule and the social foundation of servility. "Mr. Rabbit's Speech" (《兔先生的发言》) exposed subservience as an inherent weakness in Chinese people's national character. In "Han Kang's Drugstore" (《韩康的药店》), Ximen Qing seized Han Kang's drugstore but could not monopolize the market, an analogy to assert the author's belief that the despotic rulers tried to suppress democracy but could not dominate the popular sentiment. Nie Gannu's essays showed his strong political leanings and philosophical ideas, and they were humorously written and had profound significance. When "Han Kang's Drugstore" was first published, popular readers of the time were deeply moved and excited, and even now, his social critique is still relevant. His collections of essays included *The Secret of History* (《历史的奥秘》), *The Snake and Tower* (《塔与蛇》), and *Waking Up Early* (《早醒记》). Among the Wild Grass clique, there was also Xia Yan, whose essays on international affairs were pungent and whose cultural essays were incisive, all collected in his collections *Now and Here* (《此时此地集》) and *Long Journey* (《长途》). Qin Si was a rising young essayist in the literary circle, but his reviews and small notes on current affairs were full of cultural spirit, their content biting, and their structure lively. His essays were included in the collections *The Sounds of Feel* (《感觉的音响》) and *Love of Time* (《时恋集》). Meng Chao published his collections *Collection of Long Nights* (《长夜集》) and *Grass Still Growing* (《未偃草》); loosely structured as they were, the miscellaneous essays and drama reviews showed the writer's extensive knowledge on life. Song Yunbin's *Transgressing Grass* (《破戒草》) and *Collection of Fishbones* (《骨鲠集》) were collections of his comments on current affairs; he had a simple but solemn style, and always showed an edge in his reviews and comments on history. As the combating characters of *Wild Grass* became recognized by readers, its print run increased drastically, from 3,000 to 10,000, and reached 30,000 at its peak. It was said that Mao Zedong heard about *Wild Grass* in Yan'an and asked the editors to send two copies to him of each issue published. No wonder when it was discontinued by the government authorities in 1943, it was moved to Hong Kong and immediately resumed. But *Wild Grass* was not the only journal of essays; in Guilin alone, there were many supplements of newspapers and journals publishing essays, such as "Cultural Position" (文化岗位) of the *National Salvation Daily* in its earlier stage, "Li River" (漓水) and "The South" (南方) of the *Guangxi Daily*, and "Little Armed" (寸铁) of the *Citizens Public Forum* (《国民公论》). Qin Mu (秦牧) was an essayist who emerged by publishing in these newspapers and magazines, and later published his first collection, *Essays by Qin Mu* (《秦牧杂文》), most of which were written in Guilin. Just looking at the titles of his essays, "Lynch, Market, and Appreciation of Blood" (《私刑·

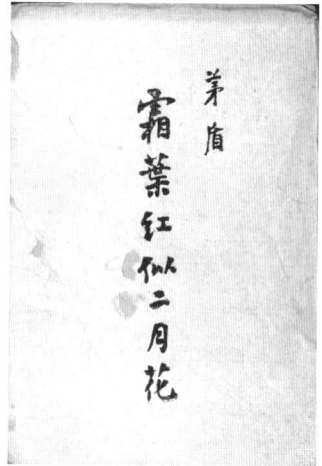

35.8. *Red Leaves Are as Beautiful as Spring Flowers* was Mao Dun's major novel written in the 1940s

人市·血的赏玩》) and "Evening Talks on Ghosts" (《鬼魅一夕谈》), one could feel his cultural and critical spirit that paid equal attention to emotions and knowledge, which laid a solid foundation for his future literary career.

As for fiction writing, a number of era-specific novels, novels of resistance, and native-soil novels were written in Guilin during this period. The first and foremost was Mao Dun's *Red Leaves Are as Beautiful as Spring Flowers*; apart from his reportage writings, essays, and short stories, this was his most important achievement during the nine months he lived in Guilin after he

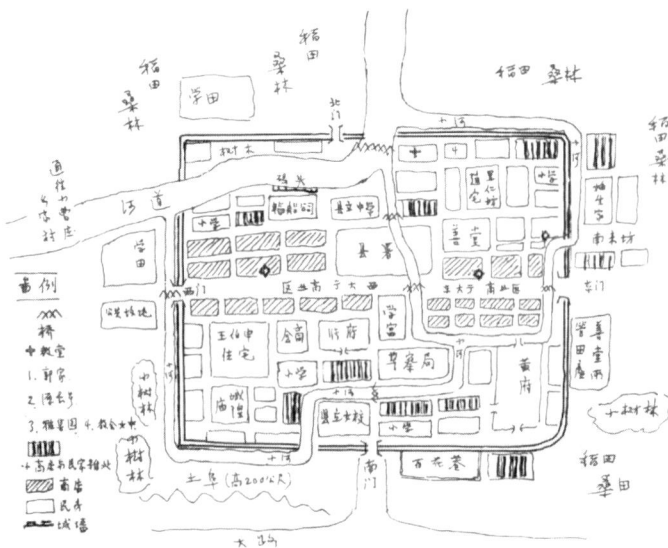

35.9. Map of the town in *Red Leaves Are as Beautiful as Spring Flowers*, drawn by Mao Dun himself when he wrote the novel

escaped from Hong Kong in 1942. At that time he lived temporarily in the kitchen of a house rented by Shao Quanlin, and on that table full of jars and bottles, he started writing one of his era-specific novels whose story happened the earliest (before the May Fourth movement). The grand historical scenes, dramatic social changes, and the author's imposing manner to look back and summarize a specific historical era were as grand as those in *Midnight*, but it was painted very accurately, with great attention given to details. Wang Boshen, general manager of a shipping company who represented the emerging capitalists in the beginning of the Republican era; Zhao Shouyi, who represented the feudal local tyrants and despotic gentry; Qian Liangcai, who was a capitalist reformist landlord and intellectual; these people, with farmers behind them, shaped the complex era-specific conflicts in this small town in the lower Yangtze River area. These conflicts showed themselves in serious tangles on the matters of opening channels for steam cutters and submerging farmland, but also in the marriage relationships of Zhang Wanqing, Huang Heguang, and Qian Liangcai, as well as in the family lives of Zhao Shouyi, Wang Boshen, and Zhu Xingjian, all big families in the town. As the description of the Jiangnan town gradually unfolded, the author did not give too much attention to the reformist nature of Qian Liangcai, but praised his compassion for peasants, and showed sympathy for his character and personal experience, so that the characterization was much more complex than that in other realistic novels. And then the author adopted an extremely elaborate style in describing in great details of the family life of Zhang and Huang, like those in *Dream of the Red Chamber*, and showed his classical Chinese aesthetic taste. Mao Dun only finished 150,000 characters of the first part of *Red Leaves Are as Beautiful as Spring Flowers*, which was very well received by readers after its publication.[10] It wasn't until 1974 that the author tried to resume writing, but it was never finished. From the remaining chapters and the outline, we can see that the focus of the novel still involved the cooperation and splitting of the KMT and CPC during the Northern Expedition, the wavering of left-wing members of the KMT, and the complicated process of an old-style woman's evolution into a modern woman. The detailed description of the higher-class family of a small town in Zhejiang as well as the marriage relationships between people of that class, and Mao Dun's nationalizing attempt to integrate the narrative of traditional Chinese love stories into a grand historical structure, were the most outstanding successes of this novel.[11]

[10] See "Summary of Discussions on Part I of *Red Leaves Are as Beautiful as Spring Flowers*" (《〈霜叶红似二月花〉第一部座谈纪要》), *Self-Study* (《自学》), Vol. 2, Issue 1, February 1944.

[11] See Mao Dun: *Red Leaves Are as Beautiful as Spring Flowers* (Continued), *Harvest* (《收获》), Issue 119, May 1996.

Ai Wu was a diligent and prolific novelist. He lived in Guilin for nearly five years, during which time he wrote two native-soil novels, *My Native Land* and *Wild Life* (《山野》), as well as a number of short stories. *My Native Land*, in particular, was a novel of half a million characters with a remote town in Sichuan as the setting. It was about twenty days of university student Yu Jun's life, when he passionately returned to his hometown during wartime but left there full of disappointment and disillusionment. Ai Wu totally gave up the romantic style shown in his *A Journey to the South*, but explored the corrupt and dark life in the feudal countryside to its rotten root. Ba Jin lived in Guilin for altogether two years, when he was busy working for Guilin Cultural Life Press. Here he wrote the third part of his novel *Fire* (《火》), and published one of his major novellas, *Resurrection Grass* (《还魂草》). Sima Wensen wrote a number of novels of resistance, including novels *The Rainy Season* (《雨季》) and *Hope of People* (《人的希望》), and novellas *Hope* (《希望》) and *The Flightless Bird* (《折翼鸟》). Both northeastern left-wing writers Duanmu Hongliang and Luo Binji moved from Hong Kong to Guilin. By this time, Duanmu Hongliang had already finished his major novels *The Sea of Earth* (《大地的海》) and *The Khorchin Grassland*. His short stories completed in Guilin, including "The *First Kiss*" (《初吻》) and "Early Spring" (《早春》), were his memories about young women in his native land; they were written with a gloomy and nostalgic sentiment, and adopted a child's perspective. Not coincidentally, Luo Binji (1917–1994) also took a similar perspective in his nostalgic native-land novels, for they were about a longer period of his characters' lives. In his "The Fellow Villager Kang Tiangang" (《乡亲——康天刚》), for example, he recollected the unyielding attitude of a ginseng digger. His

35.10. Title page of *Spring in the North-Facing Garden*

35.11. 1946 edition of *Spring in the North-Facing Garden*, a collection of Luo Binji's short stories

Chaos, Jiang Buwei's Family History, an autobiographical novel that was written from a child's point of view, was a family story about the downfall of a group of people who lived in the border area of China, Korea, and Russian. Luo Binji was destined to experience the peak of his literary creation in Guilin. Here he wrote a group of short stories, collected in *Spring in the North-Facing Garden*, about a group of intellectuals who lived humbly in the North-Facing Garden of Guilin, in which he gave a detailed account of the "desolate" psychology of intellectuals in that turbulent era. In poverty and under great spiritual pressure, human communications became difficult, and even the bright spot in his life (the young woman Lin Meina, who chatted with her son and dug earthworms to feed the chickens) was overshadowed by the general darkness in life. Nothing stood out here, and one anecdote after another was explored with the author's insightful eyes, so that the stories were filled with the tough and rugged lyrical emotions of a writer from the northeast, together with Luo Binji's deep and detailed understanding of the true nature of life. These were written by an author who attempted to pierce through the surface and explore the truth of life in the harsh conditions during the war, representing the high level reached by left-wing literary writers.

As for poetry, Ai Qing had been living in Guilin for nearly one year, and edited a number of literary supplements and poetry journals. It was in Guilin that he wrote his famous poems "I Love This Land" and the long poems "The Trumpeter" and "He Died the Second Time" (already covered in Chapter 23). The torch parade held in 1939 to commemorate the second anniversary of the July Seventh Incident inspired him to write another long poem, "The Torch" (《火把》). And in that same year, he published his *On Poetry* (《诗论》), making a theoretical summary for poetry. From the very beginning, Ai Qing was a poet integrating symbolism into realism, and therefore his wartime realistic poetry was far better than ordinary political propaganda poetry. The July clique and "Lingnan poets" (岭南诗人群) were representatives of new left-wing poetry in the area away from the frontline. Another member of the July clique who was active in Guilin was Peng Yanjiao, whose better poetic works written in Guilin included long poems "Calling from Here" (《在这边，呼唤着》, written in memory of Qiu Dongping, a writer of the July clique who died as a soldier of the New Fourth Army) and "The Half-Bare Cottage" (《半裸的田舍》), and the short poem "Little Calf" (《小牛犊》). Hu Feng, leader of the July clique, had retreated from Hong Kong and lived in Guilin for one year, when he wrote long poems "A Journey on the Sea" (《海路历程》) and "An Unwritten Poem" (《记一首没有写的诗》), and was busy publishing July anthologies (七月诗丛) in Guilin. For several of the twelve-volume July anthologies, each was the very first collection of poems of the respective poet, and when these collections full of idealist dreams of young poets were published, they opened a new chapter for the July clique in Guilin. Lingnan poets included Huang Ningying (黄宁婴), Lu Di (芦荻), Hu Mingshu (胡明树), and Ou Waiou (鸥外鸥), who were the backbone of poetic journals *China Poetry Forum* (《中国诗坛》) and *The Poetry Mass* (《诗群众》) in Guangzhou; they later moved to Guilin and stayed there for a long time, and became closely connected with the Guilin journals *China Poetry Forum* and *Poetry* (《诗》). Most of these poets were swinging between realism and modernism during the 1930s, and after the war broke out, they chose to face the reality with a positive attitude and paid attention to exploring poetic techniques. Huang Ningying's long poem "Defeated" (《溃退》) was about the shockingly agonizing retreat from Hunan and Guangxi. Lu Di's "A Long Song: To the Memory of Qu Yuan the Poet" (《长歌——纪念诗人屈原》) expressed his anger about the high political pressure. What deserves a special mention was a group of poets gathering around the journal *Poetry*, edited by Hu Mingshu and Ou Waiou, for they had quite a talent for avant-garde poetry. They consciously laid aside the "lyrical" function of new poetry and gave up the penchant for purity of modernism, but assimilated its strength of intellectuality, abstract thinking, and creation of unique images, writing left-wing modernist poetry. Some called these "antilyrical" intellectual poems, and quoted Hu Mingshu: "Nonlyrical poems should exist, for lyricism may not be a determinant of poetry. / Nonlyrical poems look 'emotionless,' but one should know the emotions within are cold steel that has been tempered in extremely hot temperatures."[12] This meant that the "cold steel" of poetry could also be used as a weapon in fighting and resistance. And it was Lu Xun who had learned from modernists and made critical poems into cold steel. In his "Theory of Digestion" (《肠胃消化的原理》), for example, Ou Waiou wrote about the hungry feelings of the poor, but he wrote it in cold blood as a "problem of digestion": "I sit on the toilet for a day / Without anything / Stool closed end, and urine refuses to flow / I have a digestion problem, … I have nothing in my stomach / Nothing is put in, surely nothing out / No deposit, no withdrawal / I have nothing to

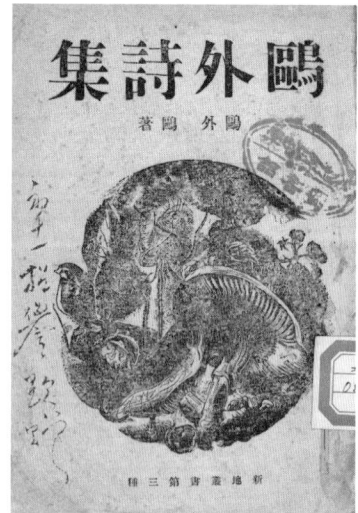

35.12. Cover of the *Ouwai Anthology* (《鸥外诗集》)

---

[12] Hu Mingshu: "On Issues of Creation of Poetry" (《诗之创作上的诸问题》), *Poetry*, Vol. 3, Issue 2, June 1942. Quoted from Xie Zhixi: *The Modern and the Modern Era*, pp. 30–31. The concept of "nonlyrical poetry" was raised in the book, which I choose to categorize as an achievement of the "Lingnan poets."

被開墾的處女地

山 山
山
東面望一望
東面一眷
山啊
南面望一望
西面望一望
山
山
西面一眷
北面一眷
山
都是山
又是山
山啊
山啊
屋前屋後都是山
街頭巷尾又是山
四周圍都站着突兀的山
駝耗耗的背的山
重重疊疊
包圍住了4十萬人的桂林
獵犬的蟄伏的尖的山啊

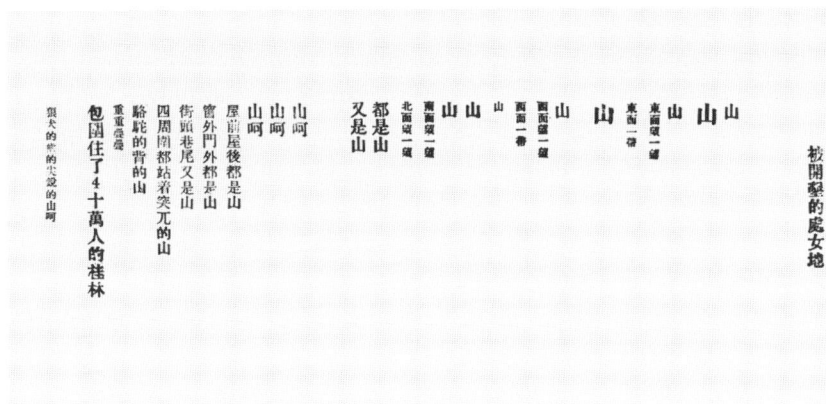

35.13. Page featuring the poem "Virgin Soil Upturned" in the *Ouwai Anthology*

let off / Nothing to let off / The current account of me / Has nothing to overdraw."[13] The bizarre ideas expressed in a monotonous and dry tone created quite a bitter incisiveness. And the poem "Virgin Soil Upturned" (《被开垦的处女地》) was about the pollution suffered by the beautiful town of Guilin after a huge crowd of citizens and merchants from Hong Kong came here to develop business. The author was extremely sensitive to this "modern" theme. He wrote about the pure and clean mountains: "Mountain / Mountain / Mountain / Looking in the east / The east is / Mountain / Mountain / Mountain / Looking in the west / The west is / Mountain / Mountain / Mountain / Looking in the south / Looking in the north / All mountains / Still mountains / Mountains / Mountains / Mountains." And about the pollution caused to the town surrounded by mountains: "The primitive town / Raised one hand after another to prevent / All strange modern guests from the outside world / But the raised hands, the mountains / Have their fingers / Between which all pervasive modern things from the outside / Sneak in."[14] (This poem was printed in letters of different sizes, creating a sense of oppression for its readers [see Figure 35.13].) This was a modernist poem in terms of both theme and poetic form, and it represented the highest level that could be reached by young left-wing poets in the 1940s.

In a sense, the thriving of literature in Guilin during the Anti-Japanese War depended on the publishing industry. It was the "publishing city" that supported the "cultural city."[15] Taking the publishing of poems as an example, and

---

[13] Quoted from Cai Dingguo (蔡定国), et al., *History of Literature of Resistance of Guilin* (《桂林抗战文学史》), Nanning: Guangxi Education Press, 1994, p. 598.

[14] This poem is quoted from *The Modern and the Modern Era*, p. 28, combined with the text of *History of Literature of Resistance of Guilin*, pp. 596–597.

[15] This was an appellation of Guilin adopted in the 1940s, evidence of which is the title of an article written by Zhao Jiabi and published in Shanghai's *Da Kung Pao* on May 18, 1947, "Memories of Guilin: the Wartime 'Publishing City'" (《忆桂林——战时的"出版城"》).

taking supplements of newspapers and general literary journals out of consideration, the specialized poetic journals published in Guilin included *Pinnacle* monthly, edited by Ai Qing and Dai Wangshu; *Poetry* monthly, edited by Hu Mingshu and Ou Waiou; *China Poetry Forum*, by Huang Ningying; the large poetry journal *Poetry Writing* (《诗创作》), by Yang Taiyang (阳太阳) and Hu Weizhou (胡危舟); and *Picking up Leaves* (《拾叶》), by Meng Chao and Chen Erdong. And there were also twenty titles of the specially published Poetry Writing book series, including the anthology of Tian Jian and others, and eight titles of July school anthologies, including that of Ai Qing. The total number was quite incredible.

Publishing institutions mushroomed: at that time, over 200 bookstores and publishing houses opened in Guilin. In 1942 alone, 79 publishing institutions formally registered with the Book Industry Association.[16] Of these, major publishing institutions included Life Bookstore, the New Knowledge Bookstore (新知书店), Reading Publishing (读书出版社), the Guilin Branch of *Xinhua Daily*, Guilin Cultural Press, Sanhu Bookstore (三户图书社), Xueyi Press (学艺出版社), Zhiyong Bookstore (致用书店), New Light Bookstore (新光书店), Yuanfang Bookstore (远方书店), Shixue Book Company (实学书局), Zhengzhong Book Company, Qiandao Book Company (前导书局), Bati Bookstore (拔提书店), Youth Bookstore (青年书店), National Defense Bookstore (国防书店), China Cultural Services Association (中国文化服务社), Huahua Bookstore (华华书店), Archival and Manuscript Press (文献出版社), Cultural Life Press (文化生活出版社), Kaiming Bookstore, the Young Companion Printing and Publishing Company, Dagong Bookstore (大公书店), Wenguang Bookstore (文光书店), Plowing Publishing Company (耕耘出版社), Flint Fire Press (石火出版社), Cubic Press (立体出版社), National Light Press (国光出版社), Kuang Ming Book Company (光明书局), Readers Bookstore (读者书店), Southern Press (南方出版社), Jimei Bookstore (集美书店), Baihong Bookstore (白虹书店), Today Press (今日出版社), Nantian Publishing Company (南方出版社), and Shanghai Magazine Company. The

35.14. Ding Ling's collection of short stores, *When I Was in Xia Village*, was also sent from the "liberated region" to Guilin to be printed, evidence that the literary publishing and printing industries of Guilin had quite a huge market

---

[16]   See Qiu Biao (秋飙): "The Publishing Cause in Guilin" (《桂林的出版事业》), published in Chongqing's *Xinhua Daily*, September 25, 1942.

printing capacity of these publishing institutions was also surprising. At the beginning of the war, there were no more than thirty handmade printing houses in Guilin, none of which could print books. By 1943, according to statistics, there were 109 large and small printing houses, of which eight were large printing houses; six could do book printing and colorful printing; twelve could do book printing and magazine printing; five were specialized in colorful printing, two specialized in typecasting, and three in binding. The paper needed each month amounted to 10,000 to 15,000 reams, and each month as many as thirty to forty million characters were typeset.[17] With such great printing, publishing, and releasing capacities, no wonder even Zhao Jiabi, the famous editor, marveled at the publishing industry in Guilin: "Each day an average of twenty new book and journal titles were published; the circulation of an ordinary journal may reach nearly 10,000 copies; that of a specialized journal on new poetry may reach 7,000, and a more popular journal may have as many as 20,000 printings. For separate editions, the first edition would have at least 5,000 printings."[18] These figures showed that the publishing and distributing industries' target market was the entire country and even Hong Kong and Southeast Asia, and their capacities were much larger than those of other industries.

According to Zhao Jiabi, at that time, of all the books in the country, "80 percent were produced and supplied by it (i.e. Guilin – author's note)."[19] The total number exceeded 1,000. From Table 35.1, one can see how many literary classics of anti-Japanese resistance were first published in Guilin, such as *Red Leaves Are as Beautiful as Spring Flowers* (by Mao Dun), *When I Was in Xia Village* (by Ding Ling), *Resurrection Grass* (by Ba Jin), *Hungry Guo Su'e* (by Lu Ling), *Spring in the North-Facing Garden* (by Luo Binji), *North China* (by Ai Qing), *The Announcement of the Dawn* (by Ai Qing), *To Fighters* (by Tian Jian), *Song of the Soil* (《泥土的歌》, by Zang Kejia), *Sonnets* (by Feng Zhi), and *Poems of a Decade* (by Bian Zhilin). This did not include the several hundred titles of over fifty sets of book series, such as the Monthly book series, whose editor-in-chief was Zheng Boqi; the Literary Creation book series, whose editor-in-chief was Shao Quanlin; the Wild Grass book series, whose editor-in-chief was Qin Si; the Literature minibook series, whose editor-in-chief was Ba Jin; the Poetry Writing book series, whose editor-in-chief was Hu Weizhou; the Cultural Life book series, whose editor-in-chief was Sima Wensen; the Young Companion Literature book series, whose editor-in-chief was Zhao Jiabi; and the July anthologies, whose editor-in-chief was Hu Feng. Later, most of these became modern Chinese literary classics. If an average of twenty book or magazine

---

[17] See Xi Wen (洗文): "The Printing Industry in Guilin" (《桂林的印刷工业》), published in *Chinese Industry* (《中国工业》), Issue 19, September 1943. Quoted from Wei Hualing et al., ed., *Proceedings on the Resistant Culture of Guilin*, p. 262.

[18] Zhao Jiabi: "Memories of Guilin: the Wartime 'Publishing City.'"

[19] Ibid.

35.15. Publication produced in Guilin: Ai Wu's two-volume novel *My Native Land*

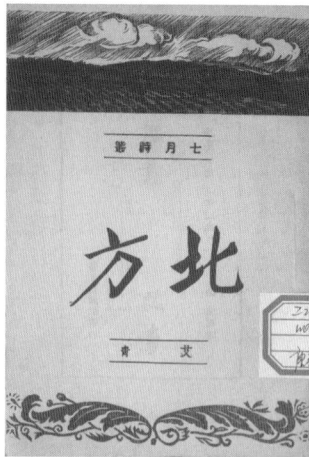

35.16. Publication produced in Guilin: Ai Qing's major collection of poems, *The North*

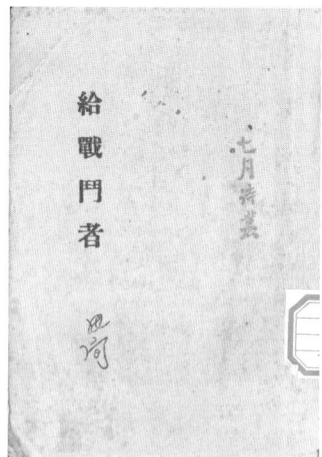

35.17. Tian Jian's representative collection, *To Fighters*, was also published in Guilin

titles were produced daily, no doubt over half of them were literature. This was obvious from a survey on the journals and magazines published in major cities of the Nationalist-controlled area from October 1938 to September 1944, which showed that among the thirty-nine journals published in Guilin, twenty-two were literary journals. And strikingly, in this survey, although Chongqing ranked No. 1 in the total number of journals and magazines published, there were only nineteen literary journals, fewer than in Guilin.[20] The large number of poetic journals published here, as already mentioned, was evidence of this. Other specialized theatrical, translation, and literary critic journals included *Annals of Theater*, *Literature in Translation* (《文学译报》), and *Literary Criticism* (《文学批评》). Among the reputed journals of literary creation, Jin Yi's *Literary Miscellany* (《文丛》) published Ba Jin's *Fire* in installments; Ye Shengtao's wartime fortnightly *Middle School Students* (《中学生》) published Ai Qing's poem "Our Land" (《我们的土地》); Sun Ling's *Writing Army* (《笔部队》) published Zang Kejia's epic *The Dabie Mountains*; Sima Wensen's *Literary Life* (《文艺生活》) published Xia Yan's five-act six-scene spoken drama play *The Fascist Bacillus* and Tian Han's five-act play *Rhapsody on the Sound of Autumn*; Wang Luyan's *Literary Art Magazine* published a number of novels including Ba Jin's *Resurrection Grass*, Sha Ting's *Destiny* (《奈何天》, aka *Caged Animals*), Ai Wu's *My Native Land* and Duanmu Hongliang's *The Khorchin Grassland (Part II)*, as well as Lao She's three-act play *Land Snakes*

[20] See Li Jianping: "On the Position and Effect of 'Guilin the Culture City' in the Art and Literary Activities of Resistance in the KMT-Ruled Area" (《论〈桂林文化城〉在国统区抗日文艺运动中的地位和作用》), in Wei Hualing et al. ed., *Proceedings on the Resistant Culture of Guilin*, Guilin: Lijiang Press, 1992, p. 38.

35.18. Inaugural issue of *Literary Life*, launched in Guilin in 1941

35.19. Inaugural issue of *Literary Creation*, launched in Guilin in 1942 during the Anti-Japanese War

(《大地龙蛇》); Xiong Foxi's *Literary Creation* (《文学创作》) published most literary works by Mao Dun and Ai Wu during the war, as well as Guo Moruo's four-act historical play *Peacock's Gall* (《孔雀胆》); and *Human World* (《人世间》), edited by Fengzi and Zhou Gangming (周钢鸣), published Xiao Hong's "A Tale of Red Glass" (《红玻璃的故事》) and Luo Binji's *Childhood*. What was comparable to the fact that there were over 200 publishing institutions founded here in Guilin, was the fact that around 200 literary journals and magazines were published here successively. The publishing of these literary works laid the foundation for this wartime "cultural city."

The highly centralized publishing industry in Guilin had a great reputation and a large market share. It attracted many newspapers and magazines from other wartime literary centers to gather here. When Guo Moruo's historical play *Zhu* was prohibited in Chongqing, Tian Han brought it to Guilin and had it published in *Annals of Theater* with the title changed to *Gao Jianli*. There were also many nationally known literary journals edited in other places that had to be printed and published in Guilin for various reasons, such as *Chinese Language and Literature Monthly* (《国文月刊》), edited by people of the National Southwestern Associated University in Kunming; *Chinese Language Magazine* (《国文杂志》), edited by Ye Shengtao in Chongqing; and even *Literary Battle Line* (《文艺战线》), edited by Zhou Yang in Yan'an; all were sent from afar to be published in Guilin, which is evidence of the close relationship between literature of resistance and publishing. Thus the literary world in Guilin was created not only by writers staying in the city, but also by writers from all over the country. Those who settled in Guilin would eventually leave, but Guilin would always be their unforgettable starting line.

TABLE 35.1 *Major literary works first published in Guilin during the Anti-Japanese War*

Title of the work	Genre	Author	When the work was written in Guilin	First published in Guilin by or in the newspaper of	When the work was first published in Guilin or in the newspaper in Guilin
Red Leaves Are as Beautiful as Spring Flowers	Novel	Mao Dun	1942	Huahua Bookstore	May 1943
Ode to a White Poplar (《白杨礼赞》)	Collected essays	Mao Dun	Self-edited in Guilin in 1942	Mild Grass Press	Feb. 1943
Miscellaneous Notes on What I See and Hear (《见闻杂记》)	Collected essays	Mao Dun	Self-edited in Guilin in 1942	Wenguang Bookstore	Apr. 1943
Pieces Picked Up after the Calamity	Reportage writing	Mao Dun	1942	Xueyi Press	June 1942
Self-Selected Collection of Mao Dun (《茅盾自选集》)	Collected essays	Mao Dun		Tianma Bookstore Press	May 1942
The Problem of Face	Spoken drama	Lao She		Zhengzhong Book Company	Apr. 1941
Tiger the King (《王老虎》, or *Roaring of the Tiger* [《虎啸》])	Spoken drama	Coauthored by Lao She, etc.		*Literary Creation*, Issue 6, Vol. 1	Apr. 1943
Discussions on 'National Forms' (《〈民族形式〉商兑》)	Collection of critical essays	Guo Moruo		Southern Press	Aug. 1940
Wild Life	Novel	Ai Wu	Starting from 1941	Serialized in ten issues of *Free China* (《自由中国》)	

(continued)

My Native Land	Ai Wu	Novel	Starting from 1940	Serialized in *Literary Art Magazine*	Starting from around 1940
Waste Land (《荒地》)	Ai Wu	Short story (collection)		Cultural Press	Jan. 1942
The Dusk (《黄昏》)	Ai Wu	Short story (collection)		Archival and Manuscript Press	May 1942
Harvest in Autumn (《秋收》)	Ai Wu	Short story (collection)	1939 to 1940	Archival and Manuscript Press	May 1944
Literary Manual (《文学手册》)	Ai Wu	Literary theories	1940	Cultural Press	Mar. 1941
A Tour of the Fifth War Zone (《第五战区巡礼》)	Xie Bingying, etc.	Collection of reportage writings		Life Bookstore (Guilin)	Sep. 1938
When I Was in Xia Village	Ding Ling	Short story (collection)		Yuanfang Bookstore	Mar. 1944
A Cry in the Wilderness (《旷野的呼喊》)	Xiao Hong	Short story (collection)		Shanghai Magazine Company (in Guilin)	1940
The Country Well (《乡井》)	Wang Xiyan	Short story (collection)		Sanhu Bookstore	Jan. 1942
Melancholy (《惆怅》)	Wang Xiyan	Short story (collection)		Today Literary and Art Press	Dec. 1942
The Old House	Wang Xiyan	Novel		The first three parts were serialized in *Literary Art Magazine*	Feb. 1942 to Jan. 1944
The Big River (《大江》)	Duanmu Hongliang	Novel		Companion and Renaissance Book and Printing Company	Apr. 1944

(continued)

TABLE 35.1 (continued)

Title of the work	Genre	Author	When the work was written in Guilin	First published in Guilin by or in the newspaper of	When the work was first published in Guilin or in the newspaper in Guilin
The Khorchin Grassland (Part II)	Novel	Duanmu Hongliang	1943	The first five chapters were serialized in Vols. 2 and 3 of *Literary Art Magazine*	Mar. to Dec. 1943
Empire of Golden Ducks (《金鸭帝国》)	Fairy novel	Zhang Tianyi		*Literary Art Magazine*	Jan. 1942 to Nov. 1943
Wu Feiyou (《吴非有》)	Novella	Luo Binji	Completed in 1941	Cultural Press	Jan. 1942
On the Border Line (《边陲线上》)	Novella	Luo Binji		Cultural Life Press	Oct. 1939
"Spring in the North-Facing Garden"	Short story	Luo Binji	1943	*Literary Creation*	1943
Hatred (《仇恨》)	Novella	Luo Binji	Completed in 1943	Shuiping Bookstore	1943
Jiang Buwei's Family History, Part 1: Childhood	Novel	Luo Binji		Sanhu Bookstore	May 1944
Ah Jin (《阿金》)	Short story (collection)	Shen Congwen		Kaiming Bookstore	July 1943
Black Phoenix (《黑凤集》)	Short story (collection)	Shen Congwen		Kaiming Bookstore	July 1943
Lamp of Spring (《春灯集》)	Short story (collection)	Shen Congwen		Kaiming Bookstore	Sep. 1943
Magnet (《磁力》)	Short story (collection)	Sha Ting		Sanhu Bookstore	Sep. 1943

(continued)

Title	Genre	Author	Notes	Publisher	Date
Collection of Short Stories by Dongping (i.e. *The Seventh Company*)	Short story (collection)	Qiu Dongping		Nantian Publishing Company	Feb. 1944
Resurrection Grass	Novella	Ba Jin	1941	Inaugural issue of *Literary Art Magazine*	1942
Fire (Part II, also known as *Feng Wenshu* [《冯文淑》])	Novel	Ba Jin	(Completed in Chongqing)	Kaiming Bookstore	Nov. 1941
Fire (Part III, also known as *Tian Huishi* [《田惠世》])	Novel	Ba Jin	1943	(later published by Shanghai Kaiming Bookstore)	
Collection of Short Stories by Ba Jin (Vol. 3)	Short story (collection)	Ba Jin		Kaiming Bookstore	June 1942
Untitled (《无题》)	Collected essays	Ba Jin		Cultural Life Press	June 1941
Correspondences on the Journey (《旅途通讯》)	Collected essays	Ba Jin	Parts of it were written in Guilin	Cultural Life Press	Apr. 1939
The Fishermen (《渔家》)	Novella	Shu Qun		*Cultural Position*, supplement of the *National Salvation Daily*	Oct. to Nov. 1939
New Water Margin (《新水浒》)	Popular novel	Gu Sifan (谷斯范)		Cultural Press	May 1940
A Symphony of April (《四月交响曲》)	Collection of reportage writings	Yao Xueyin		Frontline Press	Oct. 1939
The Story of the Red Lantern (《红灯笼故事》)	Short story (collection)	Yao Xueyin		Dadi Book Company	Oct. 1942

(continued)

TABLE 35.1 (continued)

Title of the work	Genre	Author	When the work was written in Guilin	First published in Guilin by or in the newspaper of	When the work was first published in Guilin or in the newspaper in Guilin
Hungry Guo Su'e	Novella	Lu Ling		Nantian Publishing Company	Apr. 1942
Country Girls (《乡下姑娘》)	Novella	Yu Feng (于逢)		Science Bookstore	Feb. 1943
Companions (《伙伴们》)	Novel	Yu Feng and Yi Gong (易巩)		Baihong Bookstore	Sep. 1942
Shanliao Village (《杉寮村》)	Novella	Yi Gong		Dadi Book Company	Apr. 1943
The North	Anthology	Ai Qing		Printed and published at the author's own expense in Guilin	Feb. 1939
He Died the Second Time	Anthology	Ai Qing	1938 to 1939	Shanghai Magazine Company (in Guilin)	Nov. 1939
The Announcement of the Dawn	Long poem	Ai Qing		Cultural Press	1943
On Poetry	Literary theory	Ai Qing	1939	Sanhu Bookstore	Sep. 1941
Sonnets	Anthology	Feng Zhi		Tomorrow Press	1942
She Also Wanted to Kill (《她也要杀人》)	Long poem	Tian Jian		Editorial Office of Poetry Writing	1943
To Fighters	Anthology	Tian Jian		Nantian Publishing Company	Nov. 1943

(continued)

Title	Type	Author	Notes	Publisher	Date
A Journey to Sui County and Dongyang (《随枣行》)	Collection of reportage writings	Zang Kejia		Frontline Press	Oct. 1939
Toward the Motherland (《向祖国》)	Anthology	Zang Kejia		Sanhu Bookstore	Apr. 1942
Song of the Soil	Anthology	Zang Kejia		Today Press	May 1943
The Prophecy	Anthology	He Qifang		Work Press	1944
Homecoming (《还乡记》)	Collected essays	He Qifang		Work Press	Feb. 1943
Poems of a Decade	Anthology	Bian Zhilin		Tomorrow Press	1942
Spring: Lure of the Earth (《春天——大地的诱惑》)	Long poem	Peng Yanjiao	Some of it was written in Guilin	Editorial Office of Poetry Writing	May 1942
A Battling Season in Jiangnan (《战斗的江南季节》)	Anthology	Peng Yanjiao		Shuiping Bookstore	Sep. 1943
First Love (《第一次爱》)	Anthology	Peng Yanjiao		Shanshui Press	1946
Fairy Tales (《童话》)	Anthology	Lü Yuan		Nantian Publishing Company	Dec. 1942
The Flag (《旗》)	Anthology	Sun Tian		Nantian Publishing Company	Aug. 1942
Gambler of Will (《意志的赌徒》)	Anthology	Zou Difan		Nantian Publishing Company	1942
When Waking Up (《醒来的时候》)	Anthology	Lu Li		Nantian Publishing Company	July 1943

(continued)

TABLE 35.1 (continued)

Title of the work	Genre	Author	When the work was written in Guilin	First published in Guilin by or in the newspaper of	When the work was first published in Guilin or in the newspaper in Guilin
An Enlivened Night (《跃动的夜》)	Anthology	Ji Fang		Nantian Publishing Company	1942
Ditties in the Rear (《后方小唱》)	Anthology	Ren Jun		Shanghai Magazine Company (in Guilin)	Apr. 1941
The Strongest Voice	Anthology	Xu Chi		Baihong Bookstore	Oct. 1941
Now and Here	Collected miscellaneous essays	Xia Yan		Archival and Manuscript Press	May 1941
Long Journey	Collected essays	Xia Yan		Jimei Bookstore	Dec. 1942
The Lofty Blue (《崇高的忧郁》)	Collected miscellaneous essays	Lin Lin (林林)		Archival and Manuscript Press	July 1941
A Small Collection of Long Essays (《长笔短辑》)	Collected miscellaneous essays	Ouyang Fanhai		Archival and Manuscript Press	May 1942
Winds from Everywhere (《西北东南风》)	Collected miscellaneous essays	Comrade (Товарищ, aka Jian Youwen)		Companion and Renaissance Book and Printing Company	June 1943
The Sounds of Feel	Collected miscellaneous essays	Qin Si		Archival and Manuscript Press	July 1941
Love of Time	Collected miscellaneous essays	Qin Si		Spring Grass Bookstore	June 1943

(continued)

Title	Genre	Author	Publisher	Date
The Secret of History	Collected miscellaneous essays	Nie Gannu	Archival and Manuscript Press	June 1941
The Snake and Tower	Collected miscellaneous essays	Nie Gannu	Archival and Manuscript Press	Aug. 1941
Transgressing Grass	Collected miscellaneous essays	Song Yunbin	Creation Press	Aug. 1940
Collection of Fishbones	Collected miscellaneous essays	Song Yunbin	Archival and Manuscript Press	Sep. 1942
Collection of Smoking (《冒烟集》)	Collected miscellaneous essays	He Jiahuai (何家槐)	Archival and Manuscript Press	Sep. 1941
Love and Thorn (《爱与刺》)	Collected miscellaneous essays	Lin Yutang	Tomorrow Press	Nov. 1941
Grass Still Growing	Collected miscellaneous essays	Meng Chao	Jimei Bookstore	Feb. 1943
Collection of Long Nights	Collected miscellaneous essays	Meng Chao	Archival and Manuscript Press	Oct. 1941
Collection of Skeletons (《骷髅集》)	Short story (collection)	Meng Chao	Archival and Manuscript Press	Aug. 1942
Record of Breakout (《突围记》)	Collection of short stories and essays	Sun Ling	Creation Press	Sep. 1940

(continued)

TABLE 35.1 *(continued)*

Title of the work	Genre	Author	When the work was written in Guilin	First published in Guilin by or in the newspaper of	When the work was first published in Guilin or in the newspaper in Guilin
Coming from the Northeast (《从东北来》)	Collection of reportage writings	Sun Ling		Frontline Press	July 1940
Company Commander Xiao (《萧连长》)	Short story (collection)	Wu Xiru (吴奚如)		Sanhu Bookstore	Aug. 1941
Infants (《婴》)	Short story (collection)	Sima Wensen		Cultural Life Press	Oct. 1941
An Idiot (《蠢货》)	Short story (collection)	Sima Wensen		Cultural Press	Jan. 1942
Transformation (《转形》)	Novella	Sima Wensen		Archival and Manuscript Press	Apr. 1942
Hope	Novella	Sima Wensen		National Light Press	Dec. 1942
The Rainy Season (Vols. 1, 2, and 3)	Novel	Sima Wensen		Archival and Manuscript Press	Sep. 1943
Tale of an Ox (《牛的故事》)	Short story (collection)	Tian Tao		Huaqiao Bookstore	June 1942
Sudden Change (《突变》)	Novella	Huang Mei		Weiming Society	July 1942
The Thorny Threshold (《荆棘的门槛》)	Short story (collection)	Han Beiping (韩北屏)		Baihong Bookstore	Sep. 1942
Talon Li San and Others (《鹰爪李三及其他》)	Short story (collection)	Chen Xianghe		Siwen Press	Oct. 1942

(continued)

Title	Author	Genre	Publisher	Date
The Fertile Soil (《肥沃的土地》, Part 1 of Flood of the Yellow River [《黄汛》])	Bi Ye (碧野)	Novel	Sanhu Bookstore	1943
Iron Seedling (《铁苗》)	Xiong Foxi	Novel	Intellectual Press	Dec. 1942
Impressions on the Landscape and People (《山水人物印象记》)	Xiong Foxi	Collected essays	Contemporary Press	May 1944
Victories (《战果》)	Ouyang Shan	Novel	Xueyi Press	Dec. 1942
A Couple of the Great Times (《大时代的夫妇》)	Bao Tianxiao	Novel	China Traveling Press	June 1943
The Mill (《磨坊》)	Ge Qin	Short story (collection)	Gengyun Press	June 1943
Echo (《回声》)	Li Guangtian	Collected essays	Editorial office of Torrents of Spring	May 1943
Double Happiness (《双喜团》)	Li Guangtian	Short story (collection)	Cultural Work Press	Oct. 1943
Collection of Partings (《离散集》)	Jian Xian'ai	Collected essays	Today Literary and Art Press	Sep. 1941
Travel Log (《旅程记》)	Yiqun (以群)	Collected essays	Jimei Bookstore	Dec. 1942
A Journey to the Southeast (《东南行》)	Yang Gang (杨刚)	Collected essays	Literature and Art Press	Jan. 1943
Camouflage (《保护色》)	Fang Jing (方敬)	Collected essays	Work Press	Feb. 1943

(continued)

TABLE 35.1 (continued)

Title of the work	Genre	Author	When the work was written in Guilin	First published in Guilin by or in the newspaper of	When the work was first published in Guilin or in the newspaper in Guilin
Raindrops (《小雨点》)	Collected essays	Lun Sun (罗荪)		Jimei Bookstore	July 1943
A Spring without Blossoms (《不开花的春天》)	Collected essays	Chen Mengjia		Companion and Renaissance Book and Printing Co.	Jan. 1944
On Lu Xun and Others (《鲁迅论及其他》)	Collection of literary theories	Feng Xuefeng		Chongshi Press	1941
Journey to Southwestern Sichuan (《川西南记游》)	Collected writings	Feng Yuxiang		Sanhu Bookstore	Aug. 1944
Self-Selected Collection of Twenty-Nine Writers (《二十九人自选集》)	Collected essays	Mao Dun, etc.		Yuanfang Bookstore	1943

(Sources: Li Jianping, ed.: Literary Activities in Guilin during the Anti-Japanese War Period [《抗战时期桂林文学活动》], Guilin: Lijiang Press, 1996;Volumes of Novel, Prose, etc., Dictionary of Modern Chinese Literature [《中国现代文学词典》], Guilin: Guangxi People's Publishing House, 1989–1990)

THIRTY SIX

KUNMING

Reflections on Personal Experiences of the Era

SINCE KUNMING WAS LOCATED AT THE MARGIN OF THE Nationalist-controlled area, the literature there should have deserved no special attention, but a combination of various conditions gained it prominence. And retrospectively, the inner quality of literature developed here has had an unexpectedly far-reaching influence, explicit or implicit, on the modernization process of Chinese literature throughout the past century.

Before the war broke out, the local literature and art of Kunming was quite unworthy. The city was located in a remote border area where people of the Han nationality and other ethnic people lived together; the local warlords were subject to, but estranged from or even resisted against, the central government, and the cultural development lagged behind other parts of the country despite its rich folk art resources. Not many newspapers were launched in Kunming, and by 1939, only two of them were still circulating: the *Republican Daily News* (《民国日报》), launched in 1924; and the *Yunnan Daily*, launched in 1934. All other newspapers that had launched earlier had been discontinued and gave way to those launched in culturally developed areas such as the *Nanjing Morning News* (《南京朝报》) and the *Central Daily News* (《中央日报》, Kunming Edition)[1]. As for literary societies, the Yunnan Forum of Resistance by Art and

---

[1] See "The Publishing Cause in Kunming" (《昆明出版事业》), published in *Kunming Weekly* (《昆明周刊》), Issue 15, Nov. 28, 1942. There was another newspaper, *Social Welfare* (《益世报》), which was launched in and moved from Tianjin, but it was moved to Chongqing after being run in Kunming for one year. Quoted from Yao Dan (姚丹): *Literary Activities in the Historical Context of the Southwestern Associated University* (《西南联大历史情境中的文学活动》), Guilin: Guangxi Normal University Press, 2000, p. 227.

Literary Workers (云南文艺工作者抗敌座谈会) was renamed the Yunnan Branch of the All-China Resistance Association in May 1938, working in concert with the All-China Resistance Association in Chongqing. Over sixty people attended the meeting to change its name, and its chairmen, Zhang Kecheng (张克诚) and Yang Jisheng (杨季生), were barely known outside Kunming. Half a year later, by January 1939, on the list of attendees of the meeting to reelect board members, were the names Mu Mutian, Zhu Ziqing, Shi Zhecun, Shen Congwen, and Feng Zhi, among others, meaning the Association was actually dominated by intellectuals from outside. And the culture brought to the area by these outside newspapers, writers, and educational institutions, such as the National Southwestern Associated University, associated with Peking University, Tsinghua University, and Nankai University, as well as a dozen universities that moved to Yunnan from other places, including the Chinese-French University (中法大学), Sun Yat-sen University, and Tongji University, had made Yunnan much closer culturally to other parts of the country. It was later proved that the group of writers consisting of teachers and students from the Southwestern Associated University was absolutely central to the literary creation of Kunming during the Anti-Japanese War. Evidence of this was that Shi Zhecun, the important Shanghai school writer and editor, actually came to Kunming much earlier than others, at the invitation of Xiong Qinglai (熊庆来), a former professor of Tsinghua University who was now president of Yunnan University, but this period of his literary career was largely ignored since he did not belong to the Southwestern Associated University group, and he himself seldom talked about his experience in Kunming. However, if one knows that the Yunnan–Myanmar Highway (there was also a plan to construct the

36.1. The Democratic Wall on both sides of the entrance to Southwestern Associated University was a place of interest in Kunming at that time

36.2. Library of the Southwestern Associated University; the shelves were made of wooden gas tanks, but they were filled with books

36.3. The teahouse frequented by students from the Southwestern Associated University; according to the recollections of Wang Zengqi, it was a place of origin for many literary youths

Yunnan–Myanmar Railway but it was not fulfilled; and the Yunnan–Vietnam Railway was blocked for a while) was the only channel to connect the area away from the frontline with other countries in the world during the war, it is easy to understand that the literature in Kunming was by no means isolated or outdated, and the campus literature of the Southwestern Associated University, which was based on academic culture, was literature that faced the world and faced the future.

Campus literature originated in the May Fourth period, when politically radical people from the humanities departments of Peking University were editors of *New Youth*, and the introduction and survival of spoken drama was impossible without the support of campus audiences. After the May Fourth movement faded away, teachers and students of Peking University, Tsinghua University, and Yenching University formed a group of Beijing school intellectuals, whose core writers later became teachers of writers at the Southwestern Associated University. But times had changed, and thus the spirit of Beijing school belles lettres did not simply migrate with these middle-aged writers when they moved to the border area in Yunnan. Those intellectuals originally enclosed in their own studies and creating refined literature while showing sympathy to ordinary people now became a group of cultural exiles fleeing major cities due to the war. Suddenly they had a spiritual encounter with survivors of upheavals of past dynasties with whom they were very familiar from books. The barrier between these intellectuals and ordinary people and peasants was breached. When the National Temporary University decided to move further west from Changsha, 200 teachers and students, including Wen Yiduo and Zeng Zhaolun (曾昭抡), traveled over 3,000 *li* on foot to Kunming, which could be considered an example of academic intellectuals consciously getting close to ordinary people. From its name of "Hunan-Guizhou-Yunnan Journey Group," however, we can see that their original intention was probably to make it a research trip, to examine and reflect on the living conditions and future of people in the border area from the viewpoint of outsiders, but some of them eventually integrated this experience as an exile into their own life experience. Seen from a broader perspective, the so-called experience as an exile included the different routes of migration of various institutions of learning and research (Lin Huiyin, Liang Sicheng, and their children went to Yunnan with the Society for the Study of Chinese Architecture [中国营造学社]); the drastic deterioration of living conditions of university professors, as well as the experience of "running off at the sound of an alarm" as recorded in Wu Mi's diaries and Wang Zengqi's essays; and the country life of most teachers in the villages near Kunming, such as Shen Congwen, who settled his family on Long Street in Chenggong County, the families of Lin Huiyin and Wang Li in Longtou Village in the northeastern suburb of Kunming, and those of Wen Yiduo and Zhu Ziqing in Sijiaying Village. Their channel to get close to ordinary people was indeed different from writers in the "liberated region" who "dug food" together with peasants in the Great Production movement, but circumstances were generally similar. Therefore, what intellectuals in Kunming tried to do was to find the right balance between the patriotic concern facing the reality of war and their intellectual sense of mission to transcend realities.

36.4. During their journey to Yunnan on foot, Wen Yiduo (left) and Professor Li Jidong (李继侗) agreed to grow beards and not shave until China won the Anti-Japanese War

36.5. Southwestern Associated University teachers' dormitory, where they lived as poor peasants

Most bright young writers were students or teaching assistants who had just graduated, and they were cultivated in the many campus literary societies. They were young and energetic, and few of them were willing to be enclosed in their studies to do scholarly research. The Southwestern Associated University adopted a liberal education system, in which "National Language 101" was a compulsory course for all students, using a textbook edited by Yang Zhensheng. This course inherited the tradition of New Literature teaching started by Zhu Ziqing at Tsinghua University, with the ratio of classical Chinese and vernacular Chinese being 15:11, paying great attention to the achievements of vernacular Chinese of the May Fourth period, and a large number of literary works of Lu Xun, Zhou Zuoren, Bing Xin, Xu Zhimo, and Fei Ming were collected in the textbook. There was a "Reference for Composition Exercises of National Language 101" showing that a larger proportion of reference books were written by Crescent Moon school and Beijing school authors.[2] And since many teachers of the Associated University were masters of New Literature, there was a strong atmosphere of free literary creation among students, not only for those of the departments of Chinese and foreign languages, but also for those of the departments of philosophy, sociology, economics, or even chemistry. Earlier, when the College of Humanities and Law was still in Mengzi, Liu Zhaoji (刘兆吉), Mu Dan (pseudonym of Zha Liangzheng [查良铮]), Zhao Ruihong, Liu Shousong (刘绥松), Lin Pu (林蒲, aka Lin Zhenshu [林振述]), and other students had established the South Lake Poetic Society (南湖诗社), whose name was changed to the Highland Literary Society (高原文艺社) when the college was moved back to Kunming. Later some larger poetic societies were formed, including the Wintergreen Society (冬青社), whose *Wintergreen Poetry Journal* (《冬青诗刊》) had a certain circulation outside the university. Then there was the Literary Gathering Association (文聚社), whose members were generally the same as the Wintergreen Society, such as Lin Yuan (林元), Du Yunxie, Liu Beisi (刘北汜), Mu Dan, and Wang Zengqi. Those young poets and novelists who later became well-known Southwestern Associated University intellectuals had already risen to the fore. The campus literary journal *Literary Gathering* (《文聚》), launched in 1942, had the longest lifespan and was not discontinued until 1946. Yuan Kejia (袁可嘉) was in the Plowing Literary Society (耕耘文艺社), founded in 1943 and dominated by Nankai Middle School graduates who had entered the Southwestern Associated University; and members of the Literary and Art Society (文艺社), founded in the same year, including Peng Peiyun (彭珮云), criticized the modernist tendency of the Plowing Literary Society and other literary societies and advocated realism. Zhu Ziqing, Wen Yiduo, Feng Zhi, Bian Zhilin, and Li Guangtian were all willing to work as tutors for these lively student societies. William Empson, the contemporary English poet, went from Changsha and Nanyue to Kunming (and later to Peking University after it resumed) to teach Modern English Poetry and other courses and brought the fresh wind of modernist philosophy and poetry to these talented students. Zhao Ruihong once wrote about their experience of listening to the lectures of Empson:

> Before them there was the mysterious, symbolistic, and fanciful Irish poet
> Yeats, master of poetry of that time. On their road, they saw a piece of

[2]   According to "Reference for Composition Exercises of National Language 101 of the Southwestern Associated University," published in *Chinese Language and Literature Monthly*, Issue 33, May 1945. In this reference, besides those of Lu Xun, others were works written by Hu Shi, Xu Zhimo, Zong Baihua, Zhu Guangqian, Liang Zongdai, Lin Huiyi, and Ding Xilin. Quoted from Yao Dan: *Literary Activities in the Historical Context of the Southwestern Associated University*, p. 136.

vast and barren Wasteland. The profound and robust T. S. Eliot was glittering and shining afar. In the poetic temple built by Eliot, these young poets found their own spiritual home and their enthusiastic confidence. However, the wasteland was eventually too desolate and too far. Their generation returned from the wasteland to the society and to factories, from the aphelion to the hot perihelion. What's more, they saw the inevitable pathetic killings among human beings. The shadow of war had always been in their poetic lines.[3]

The words here implied that the modernist generation during World War II, Chinese or foreign poets, were different from their former generations in that they did not turn their eyes away from the cruel realities of war. In the difficult environment, teachers and students had such a close relationship that teachers often contributed their writings to the original literary journals launched by students. Outside the university, teachers and students contributed their writings to "Daybreak" (平明), a supplement of the Kunming edition of the *Central Daily News*; "Revolutionary Army Poetry Journal" (革命军诗刊), a supplement of the *Guizhou Daily*; *South Central Tridaily* (《中南三日刊》); and the "Literary" supplement to *Ta Kung Pao* in Hong Kong, Guilin, and Chongqing (which were later resumed as the Tianjin and Shanghai *Ta Kung Pao*). By 1943, when student unrest started welling up in Kunming, Wen Yiduo suddenly devoted much of his Tang Poetry class to talking about Tian Jian and poetry for recitation, evidence that intellectuals in Kunming were not only scholars and writers, but had the temperament of social practitioners. But teachers and students in Kunming had always been concerned with the realities of the Anti-Japanese War. The year 1943 thus became a dividing line for writers in Kunming to gradually change from Beijing school modernism to a modernist writing style closer to that of ordinary people. This was a by-product of their time.

Poetry was the literary genre with the most outstanding achievements. As early as

36.6. Members of the Highland Literary Society went for an outing in Kunming; the third from the right is Mu Dan

---

[3] Zhao Ruihong: "Remembering the British Modern Poet Mr. Empson" (《回忆诗人燕卜荪先生》), *Time and Tide Literature and Art* (《时与潮文艺》), Vol. 1, Issue 2, May 1943.

36.7. *Northern Journey and Other Poems* (《北游及其他》), an earlier collection of Feng Zhi's

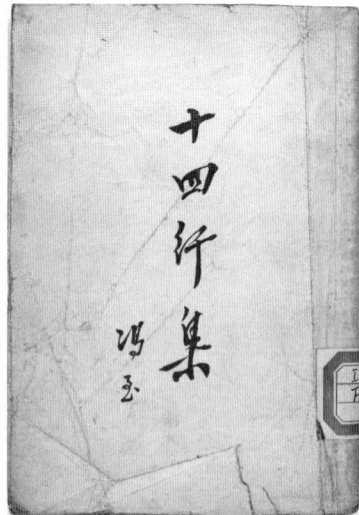

36.8. *Sonnets*, a representative collection of Feng Zhi's during the Anti-Japanese War period

the 1920s, Feng Zhi (1905–1993) was praised by Lu Xun as "China's most distinguished lyrical poet" from the Low Grass Society and Sunken Bell Society. Around the time he graduated from Peking University, Feng had already published several collections of poems, including *Songs from Yesterday* (《昨日之歌》) and *Northern Journey and Other Poems*. He then studied in Germany for five years, where he listened to the philosophy lectures of Karl Jaspers at Heidelberg University and read Rilke's poems intensively (in 1926 when he was still at home, he read the German edition of Rilke's major poem "The Lay of the Love and Death of Cornet Christopher Rilke" and felt the electric sparks of genuine attraction, and now he did a systematic close reading), and studied Nietzsche, Goethe, Kierkegaard, and Du Fu (杜甫). He was deeply influenced by Western existentialist philosophy and poetry, and integrating them into his research of the ancient and present, the Western and Chinese, he seemed to have experienced a spiritual transmutation. At that time, he had not been writing poetry for a while. Back home, since the war was still on, he took his family across the country to seek refuge, getting to know the life of ordinary people from his own perspective, and finally blended the experience of his own life and that of the era. Then, on a winter's afternoon in 1941, Feng Zhi walked on a path in the Yangjiashan tree farm outside the city of Kunming, looking up at several silver planes flying across the blue sky, and associated the scene with the dream of Chuang Tzu about changing and becoming a bird whose name was Peng. He was suddenly inspired and recited a variant of the sonnet format. This was the beginning of a series of twenty-seven poems of the same format, in which this first one was later numbered "18," and entitled

"An Ancient Dream," and the collection was later printed in Guilin as *Sonnets*. This rewriting of poetry in an imported format was thus considered the landmark of the maturity of Chinese modernist poetry. The modernist sentiments of these poems were somewhat uncertain and abstract, and their theme was the poet's experience of life, but the origin of each poem was quite clear: a blade of grass, a tree, an insect, a nameless peasant child or farm woman, a historical figure, or a famous city, a storm, or a high peak. All were events happening in China. The poet said: "I wrote a poem for everything that is deeply linked with my own life, from a small part of my own life to the circumstances shared by many."[4] Therefore, poetic lines full of the poet's personal experience of life and existentialist reflections were highly combined with various realistic events. Ordinary readers might not find them too obscure, and might have found the meaning of life and death from the theme of the "courage to assume responsibilities": "It was only in the transitional dawn and dusk / That we know you are Venus and you are the morning star, / While in the midnight you are no different / from all other stars; so many young people / Are living and dying rightly / By your serene enlightenment" (No. 10, "Cai Yuanpei" [《10 蔡元培》]; this poem was not titled until much later, and the same is true for the poems quoted later). Here the spirit of greatness was not hard to understand. If the reader had some background, he would, on a philosophical level, explore the meaning of existence of an individual and raise the question of ultimate concern: "The bronze incense burner is yearning for the mines in the deep mountains, / The porcelain teapot is yearning for the clay at the riverbank, / They were like the birds in the winds and rains / Going in their own directions. We are holding life tightly, / Like we cannot decide on our own. / The fierce wind throws everything into the sky, // And the heavy rain washes everything into the soil, / All we have is this dim red light / That may prove our temporary stay in this life." (No. 21, "We Listen to the Heavy Rain among the Fierce Wind" [《21 我们听着狂风里的暴雨》].) Here the poet revealed to us his questioning about the loneliness and helplessness of involuntary human life, and he showed the true meaning of life through "this dim red light." As for his understanding of the form and format of sonnet, he explained it quite vividly in his last sonnet, No. 27, "From a Flow of the Shapeless Water" (《27 从一片泛滥无形的水里》):

> From a flow of the shapeless water
> The water-carrier fills his oval pitcher,
> Thus so much water possesses a definite shape;
> Look, how the vane flutters in the autumn wind
> Holding an object that can't be held.

---

[4] Feng Zhi: "Preface to *Sonnets*" (《〈十四行集〉序》), *Sonnets*, Shanghai: Shanghai Cultural Life Press, 1949, p. 2.

This was almost a manifesto on the format of modernist poetry, in which he subtly explained that the real world, spiritual world, and emotional world were like formless water, which ultimately "can't be held"; but one could use the "pitcher" (like the metrical patterns of poetry, and finding the right image through one's own experience) to try to hold some images and philosophical thoughts. It was like in the erratic lines and color blocks of modernist sculptures and paintings, one could find something with deeper and richer meanings than concrete lines and color blocks. The sonnet form, which was transliterated into "*shanglai ti*" (商籁体) during the May Fourth period, "seemed to still have its vitality today" because it was "closest to the seven-character regulated verses of China."[5] Therefore, under the pen of Feng Zhi, who was trained in classical Chinese poetry and could understand Western poems in their original languages, this form was like a piece of enchanted mud, with which he could shape his own modernist poems full of emotions, symbols, and intellectual meanings. Thus Feng Zhi raised the flag of modernist poetry for other poets in Kunming.

Bian Zhilin (1910–2000) had a unique experience of poetry writing. Before 1937 he had already written his most obscure modernist poems, namely "Round Treasure Box," "Fragment," and "Ichthyolite," which were covered earlier when I talked about the poetry of Beijing school writers (see Chapter 24). The Anti-Japanese War started a new era, and when he returned from the Taihang Mountains to Yan'an, Bian Zhilin began writing "Letters of Consolation" in a bright and clear poetic style. These letters were addressed to sharpshooter soldiers, workers in the coal mines, young people opening up wastelands, children on watch, and even to the general of an army and author of "On Protracted War" (《论持久战》). At first glance, these were written in a realistic style totally different from that of his past poetry. In 1941, Bian Zhilin published his old poems in a collection entitled *Poems of a Decade*, which included the poems that were so difficult and obscure that each line would need a note for readers to understand it (such as "The Composition of Distances"), but they were profoundly meaningful when read carefully and almost proved Empson's theory that "obscurity shall be the basic element of excellent poetry," explained by the latter in the class of contemporary English and American poetry at the Southwestern Associated University. What surprised those students further was that the "Letters of Consolation," included in this collection, were not as easy as they seemed to be. The reality of the Anti-Japanese War could be put against the poet's personal feelings, which made them modernist poems that had integrated local objects of China:

<hr>

[5]   Bian Zhilin: "Author's Preface to *Carving of Insects*" (《〈雕虫纪历〉自序》), *Carving of Insects*, Beijing: People's Literature Press, 1979, p. 17.

After you shoot a bullet,
You may see, when you look back
Old men laugh with their beards moving,
Children laugh with their dimples deepened,
And women laugh with their teeth shining.
Before you shoot a bullet,
You knew, without looking back
Old men were looking at the sight bead on your gun,
Children were looking at the sight bead on your gun,
And women were looking at the sight bead on your gun.
No bullet would be shot in vain,
All men and women behind you put their trust in you,
When a series of bullets are about to go,
Please have another nip of that shining little thing,
On behalf of those passionate men and women, old and young.

("To a Sharpshooter at the Front" [《前方的神枪手》][6])

These lines were clear and easy to understand, but they left a lingering after-taste. The poet was not present in the poem, but from his perspective as a poet at the frontline, one felt that he was among the people "who are looking at you," that is, among those who were looking at the sight bead and bullet. Some "Letters of Consolation" had a sense of humor and wit. An example of this was the lovely image of a recruit who tried to stop the bullet with his straw hat, written in a lovely tone: "Now remember not to stop / (Like you always did when it was raining) / These bullets! These are bullets! / Lay down, on the earth that has raised you up!" ("To A New Recruit of the Local Armed Forces" [《地方武装的新战士》]) "Letters of Consolation" was a positive result from Bian Zhilin's attempt to "more consciously accept the influence of the young English poet W. H. Auden to represent the revolutionary content with modernist expressions," to "deal with the serious theme of struggling through ordinary life and characters" but to "still pay attention to the importance of the personal state of mind and emotional experience for poetic expressions."[7] W. H. Auden had visited China in the flames of war in 1938, and Bian Zhilin had translated the poems Auden wrote in China and had them published. According to the recollection of young poets of the Southwestern Associated University, the poems of Bian Zhilin and Auden had greatly inspired the students, and helped them understand how to bridge the gap that should not have been there between modern poetry and poems of resistance.

---

[6] Bian Zhilin: "To a Sharpshooter at the Front" from "Letters of Consolation," *Modern Poems of Southwestern Associated University* (《西南联大现代诗钞》), Beijing: China Literature Press, 1997, p. 4.

[7] Sun Yushi (孙玉石): *A Historical Review of Modernist Poetic Trends in China* (《中国现代主义诗潮史论》), Beijing: Peking University Press, 1999, p. 278.

36.9. First edition of Bian Zhilin's *Letters of Consolation*

In Kunming, where the atmosphere was good for exploring modernization of new poetry, the fruit of the New Chinese Poetry school (aka Nine Leaves school)[8] finally ripened, marking the start of a new generation modernist poetic school. This poetic school consisted of two groups, one included those gathering around the journal *Poetry Writing* (《诗创造》), such as Xin Di and Hang Yuehe (aka Cao Xinzhi [曹辛之]), and the other included those young poets of the former Southwestern Associated University who continued writing poems after returning to Beiping and Tianjin at the end of the war. One of the key links of the founding of this poetic school was in Kunming, and its poets Du Yunxie, Zheng Min, and Mu Dan were collectively called the "Three Rising Stars of the Associated University." Later, when talking about their tendency to write modernist new

36.10. Teachers and students of the Department of Chinese Language and Literature at the Southwestern Associated University in May 1946. Those sitting in the second row, from left to right, are: Pu Jiangqing, Zhu Ziqing, Feng Youlan, Wen Yiduo, Tang Lan (唐兰), You Guo'en, Luo Yong (罗庸), Xu Weiyu (许维遹), Yu Guanying (余冠英), Wang Li, and Shen Congwen

8   The name "New Chinese Poetry school" was taken from the journal *New Chinese Poetry* (《中国新诗》), which launched in 1948, and the name "Nine Leaves school" was taken from the *Collection of Nine Leaves* (《九叶集》) published by Jiangsu People's Press in 1981. Poets of this school included Xin Di (辛笛), Chen Jingrong, Hang Yuehe (杭约赫), Tang Qi (唐祈), Tang Shi (唐湜), Du Yunxie, Zheng Min (郑敏), Yuan Kejia, and Mu Dan.

poetry, Yuan Kejia said: "This new tendency originated from their inner psychological need and ended up a tradition integrating realism, symbolism, and metaphysics."[9] The so-called metaphysics may be considered borrowing from both Chinese and Western ancient metaphysical poetry, and here it meant the meditative, witty, and intellectual qualities of poetry. "Realism," "symbolism," and "metaphysics" may seem conflicting elements to many other poetic schools, but they were now integrated into one and became a conscious pursuit of a literary school, which was indeed an innovation.

The poetry of young poets from the Southwestern Associated University sought to represent people. Du Yunxie (1918–), who was once praised by Zhu Ziqing, wrote a poem entitled "The Burma Road" (《滇缅公路》) and declared this was a highway constructed with human blood and flesh and "loaded" with national spirit. It was hard to imagine how people built it: "It was they, facing the dangers of hunger, cold, and malarial mosquitos / (Malnutrition, half-naked, struggling to stay alive) / Each day they tried to precede the Sun, coming out of / Their hastily built earthen caves and straw huts, waving their primitive / shovels and pickaxes, sparing no blood and sweat, and inch by inch / Struggling for a smooth highway, for freedom of breathing, for the nation."[10] The poet joined the army and went to the battlefield when he was still studying at the university. He had been to Myanmar and India, where people called Western soldiers "leather-shoe soldiers" while Chinese soldiers were called "straw-sandal soldiers." Writing about Chinese soldiers, the poet started with the line "You miserable Chinese peasants, carrying the decayed old tradition, / Dying and struggling silently under the accelerating footsteps of history" ("Straw-Sandal Soldiers" [《草鞋兵》]). This is no great heroic image, but a group of suffered and enslaved people; however, they dominated this framed painting of history. Mu Dan (1918–1977) had taken part in the journey on foot with other students and teachers from Changsha to Kunming, and later he had joined the Chinese Expedition Force for Burma. The Chinese peasants he saw on such a long journey naturally entered his poetry. He saw the peasant "always turning and turning wordlessly after the plough," the hungry children and old woman in "the thatched hut which gathers darkness"; "When I pass by, and loiter on the road, / I loiter for the many years of humiliation, / And I am still waiting in the boundless mountains and rivers; / Waiting, our wordless affliction is too heavy to bear. / But a nation has stood up, / But a nation has stood up" ("Glorification" [《赞美》]). This repeated line "a nation has stood up" brought the poet and his nation so much closer

9 Yuan Kejia: "Modernization of New Poetry: Pursuit of a New Tradition" (《新诗现代化——新传统的寻求》), "Weekly Art and Literature" (星期文艺) of Tianjin's *Ta Kung Pao*, March 30, 1947.
10 All poems by Du Yunxie, Mu Dan, and Zheng Min are quoted from *Modern Poems of Southwestern Associated University*, Beijing: China Literature Press, 1997.

psychologically, and his personal consciousness was thus blended with that of
people. Certainly, "representing people"
should not be oversimplified as just picking
the thematic subject about the life of ordinary people. Young poets of the Associated
University chose the other way around
and expressed their personal experience of
reality as a psychological experience. Take
Zheng Min (1920–) for example, living in
the small world of the campus, this woman
poet may not have had a rich experience
of social life, but she excelled at watching, associating, and speculating, extracting
her message from the details in everyday
life and thus opened a path toward profoundness. She saw the ripe crops at the
sides of the road and associated them
with a "mother" who was "shouldering so
much weariness": "Golden rice stands in

36.11. Mu Dan in May 1938, after
making a journey to Kunming on
foot with students and teachers of
Southwestern Associated University

sheaves / In the newly cut autumn field. / I think of many exhausted mothers,
/ I see rugged faces along the road at dusk. / On the day of harvest, a full moon
hangs / Atop the towering trees, / And in the twilight, distant mountains /

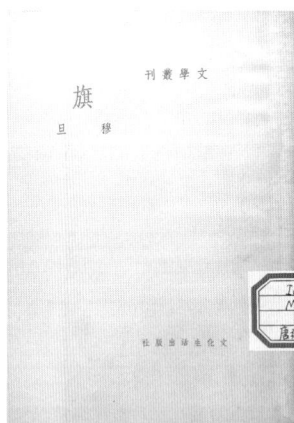

36.12. *The Flag* (《旗》),
published by Cultural Life Press
(1948 edition)

Approach my heart. / Nothing is quieter than
this, a statue" ("Golden Rice Sheaves" [《金黄
的稻束》]). What did this mother do? What was
her appearance like? These things did not matter.
What mattered was that she was given the image
of "golden rice sheaves," which was beautiful
and had been exhausted for the beauty in the
autumn. It was a golden "statue" of people and
"statue" of life. These poems written by young
poets of the Associated University were totally
different from those of refined modernist poets
who sought a kind of detachment from reality or
focused on their own personal feelings.

As for how to express modern sentiments
through poetry, young poets of the Southwestern
Associated University obviously had more avant-
garde views than their predecessors. Giving the images an intellectual touch,
making them representational as well as speculative, giving insinuating hints
more importance than metaphors, and seeking to bring associations into an

infinite realm, these were key elements of how the philosophical quality of Zheng Min's poems (she was a student of philosophy) did not violate their representational quality. The philosophical meditation had a detached grace, and it was anti-romantic and antilyrical. In the meditation, "a lotus stem" shouldered solemn burdens and contained multiple meanings about "life" ("Lotus Flower: On Viewing a Painting" [《荷花（观张大千氏画）》]); even the cracking of mountains, falling of huge trees, and lying down of soldiers were inadequate to exhaust the meaning of "death" ("Death" [《死》]); "dancing" was "the silent falling of a ripened apple, / Which sinks into the yellowing soft grass" ("Dancing" [《舞蹈》]); for life, "loneliness" perhaps meant "Nothing but the two big trees planted / In the yard and cannot move, / Even if they are hand in hand, / Their hairs entangled; / Nothing but the two panes on / A glass window, /

36.13. Zheng Min, looking full of vigor when *Anthology 1942–1947* (《诗集1942–1947》) was published in the 1940s

Always standing there, at their own positions." Loneliness, then, was both isolation and closeness, an integral part of the meaning of life. And loneliness had its aspect of "dignity": "I think of someone who suffered in the fire / But sought the last repose in 'faith,' / And I will also in the biting pain of 'loneliness' / Seek the most solemn meaning of life." And she understood that "life is eventually a running river" ("Loneliness" [《寂寞》]). The poetic speculation of these poems by Zheng Min indeed created a metaphysical beauty of poetry.

The meditations of Mu Dan, who was referred to as a "broad explorer" by his peer poet Tang Shi, had an even more extensive link with the outside world, even fiercer sentiments, and thus even more complex poetic images and implications. One of Mu Dan's meditations was to seek the ultimate answer. He turned his eyes toward both reality and history, but saw nothing but the evilness of feudal lords, and thus he asked loudly where to find his China. Then he got to know it was in the "sufferings of our mother," and we must "help our mother grow up." But this was unlikely, and one could not find a cheap, fast pass, "Falling in meditation, I am doubtful, / It is hope that links us together. Hope / In the power of no hope, no doubt" ("Where is China?" [《中国在哪里》]). This was quite a grave reflection on the destiny of the country, which contained the big question of "resisting against despair" raised by Lu Xun. When he turned his eyes toward the real-world countryside, in "In a Cold Night of a Winter Month" (《在寒冷的腊月的夜里》), the reader could feel the coldness from the title per se, not to mention in the North China village: "Our ancestors have been sleeping, sleeping not so far from us, / All stories have

been told, and only ashes are left." Then he turned his eyes to the people of ancient times – in "The Temptation of the Snake" (《蛇的诱惑》) the poet warned his readers that the snake changed by Satan in paradise would appear "for the second time": "On the people who are exiled for the second time, / Another whip will be raised above us." We have been reduced to "empty shells that have withered and fallen": "Am I alive? Am I alive? Why / Am I living?" These fully modernist questions made readers breathless. Another of Mu Dan's meditations was his anxiety, tension, and self-reflection in front of this impotent world. Or let's say under the material oppression, our spirit would "drift in the dustnet," "becoming a hollow shell after eight hours' work," and eventually became "pigs in the sludge" ("Reduction" [《还原作用》], an even more peculiar short poem). Here we can see the self-reflection of an intellectual as a forerunner. "A circle, how many years' human labor / Our despair will make it full. / Destroy it, my friend! Let ourselves / Be its incompleteness. … Because we are the besieged, / Only if we turn, should new soil awaken" ("The Besieged" [《被围者》]). Breaking out of an enclosure meant resistance. In a number of poems about revolting against reality written in a grave tone, the words "live on" and "destroy it" had their significance:

> Hope, disillusionment, hope, and live on
> Overwhelmed by infinite waves
> Who knows the heavy groans of time will fall at the banks formed in curses
> But being bathed in sunshine
> My children, see how we in the darkness give birth
> To the hard-to-bear holy feelings.
>
> ("Live On" [《活下去》])

The Europeanized language had a penetrating intellectual power. Here was something shared by young poets of the Associated University represented

36.14. Mu Dan and his wife on the boat returning to China from the United States in 1952. Mu Dan looked full of confidence in the future

by Mu Dan, consciously integrating the harsh reality of war and the creative spirit of meditative modernist poetry. In their repeated inquiries and hints about the meaning of life, their exploration of the winding path toward a philosophical realm and their strict self-criticism as intellectuals, these poets indeed surpassed the symbolist poets of the 1930s (albeit were related to them) and pointed to the style of the New Chinese Poetry school that emerged soon after.

By then, Kunming had become a new experimental field of modernist literature, which was not a coincidence. In fiction writing, this was the tendency implied by several literary events, consciously or unconsciously, like the poet Feng Zhi starting to write fictions, Shen Congwen's change, and the rising of Shen's student, Wang Zengqi. The historical novella by Feng Zhi, *Wu Zixu* (《伍子胥》), published in 1946, could be seen as the extension of his *Sonnets*. The story of Wu Zixu of the Wu and Yue region during the Spring and Autumn period was widely known in China. He sought revenge for his father's death and fled to the state of Wu, and in Zhaoguan, the last pass to the state of Wu, his hair turned completely white in one night due to the extreme pressure. Feng Zhi had wanted to write about this story since he was young. As time passed by, he read Rilke, saw the sudden death of his close friend Liang Yuchun, experienced hardships during the Anti-Japanese War, and reread "Cornet," one of the representative works of Rilke revised by Bian Zhilin, and finally felt it was time to reconstruct the story of Wu Zixu with his narrative. In Feng's novella, one could read the romantic stories of the fisherman on the river and the gauze-washing girl by the Li River giving food to Wu Zixu (Guo Moruo seemed to be good at writing this in his poetic plays), and one could read the author's satire of the present by alluding to the past by writing about the betrayal of Prince Jia, the chief witch of the state of Chen who provided military supplies to the enemy, and the professor who made a profit by peddling his shallow knowledge of the ancient rites and music in the market of Wu (which reminded the reader of Lu Xun's *Old Tales Retold*), but generally, it was neither a realistic satire nor a romantic psychological fiction. With his modernist approach, the author highlighted Wu Zixu's personal experience of life and death on the run, in which he integrated his own experience as an exile during the war, and thus described the possible state of being "thrown" in human life: having to make choices in times of danger, persevering despite interruptions, and overcoming the temptation to give up. This was a novella combining history, reality, and meditation. Therefore, in the section about Zhaoguan, in contrast to the legends and operatic plays that emphasized Wu Zixu's anxiety, Feng Zhi chose to highlight how his protagonist became a molting silkworm in one night and had the experience of being reborn. As in *Sonnets*, *Wu Zixu* was also about the unique and infinitely open experience of

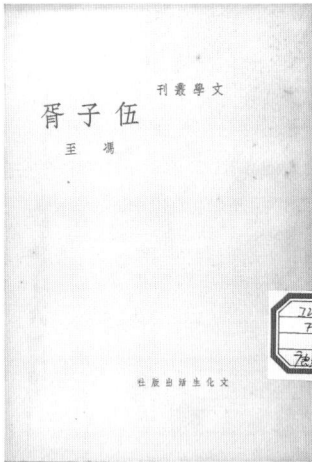

36.15. In his historical novella *Wu Zixu*, Feng Zhi integrated his own experience as an exile during the war into the fiction

human life, to which readers might respond by resorting to their own life experience.

Two months after he arrived in Kunming, Shen Congwen began to write *The Long River*, his last unfinished novel. The idea of this novel originated from his new knowledge about his native land, and it was an extension of his earlier lyrical piece, "The Border Town." He wanted to write about what happened after "the modern" began to enter western Hunan. It was a story about Lüjiaping and Luoboxi in the central section of Chenhe River, which abounded in tangerines and pomelos, a story of the owner of a tangerine orchard and his youngest daughter Yaoyao. Shen Congwen finished the first volume (altogether 140,000 characters, and he wanted it to be a three-volume, 300,000-character novel), but when it was sent to Guilin to be published, it caused much trouble because it described the New Life movement (新生活运动), officials from outside the town, and the captain of the special police brigade. After repeated censoring by the authorities and repeated revisions on Shen's part, it was abridged to 110,000 characters and finally published. There is no hard evidence about what hardships Shen Congwen had suffered during this process, but he simply stopped writing *The Long River*, which could have been his best literary work. After that, Shen Congwen turned to an "abstract lyrical style" (he said ambiguously in "Water and Cloud" [《水云》]: "In the past month my writing has been detained by the book censorship authority three times because it is about 'people,' which means my reflections and writing style of this human world are obviously not in agreement with this new age. Therefore I try to look into the 'temporal depth.'"[11]) For two years he seldom wrote, and the writings published after that were a kind of meditative psychological accounts that mixed true stories with his fabrications, narratives added in prose writing, and poetic implications in narratives, together with large paragraphs of monologues and commentaries, making them a montage of abstract impressions. These were "The Candle Extinguished" (《烛虚》), "Deep Abyss" (《潜渊》), "Venus" (《长庚》), and "Life" (《生命》), collected in *The Candle Extinguished*; "Water and Cloud," "Green Nightmare" (《绿魇》), "White Nightmare" (《白魇》), "Black Nightmare" (《黑魇》), and "Blue Nightmare" (《青色魇》), intended to be included in *The*

---

[11] Shen Congwen: "Water and Cloud," *Selected Works of Shen Congwen*, Vol. 1, Chengdu: Sichuan People's Press, 1983, pp. 383–384.

36.16. Shen Congwen in 1938, when he wrote *The Long River* in Yunnan and spent time gazing at beautiful clouds

Seven-Color Nightmares (《七色魇集》),[12] as well as *Gazing at Rainbows* (《看虹录》). The intellectual texture of these pieces was different from that of Shen's earlier works, and besides, the fragmentary and temporary qualities of these pieces somewhat reminded one of Lu Xun's *Wild Grass*. They discussed various matters such as women, genders, modern education, and modern civilization, as well as various matters since the May Fourth period, but finally boiled down to the themes of "beauty" and "life." "I find this 'I' who has survived in the city has become nothing but a hollow shell" (which echoed the sentiments of young poets of the Southwestern Associated University).[13] But the author wrote literature, and the literature he wrote in turn led to his redemption: "The greatest meaning of life is that it can be used to admire the grand nature or perfect artwork."[14] "We can transcend worldly emotions, explore the deep innermost recesses and marginal consciousness of human souls and find 'human beings,' which means there may be many new forms of 'love' and 'death.' This work will surely expand that 'I,' so that 'I' may occupy a larger space or a longer time."[15] However, due to his disillusionment with real life, this life that admired and created "beauty" seemed to exist only in his abstract meditations, and was torn into pieces in front of harsh realities. Therefore he said: "I see some symbols, some forms, a string of thread, silent music, a wordless poem. I see life in its most complete form. All these exist perfectly in abstraction, but they disappear in the real world."[16]

[12] *The Seven-Color Nightmares* was not published at that time, but each piece intended to be included in the collection was published separately. Of these pieces, "Red Nightmare" (《赤魇》) and "Orange Nightmare" were, respectively, part of his short stories "Clearing after the Snow" (《雪晴》) and "Fengzi" (《凤子》), so that they were quite different from the other pieces. Therefore, in editing the *Complete Works of Shen Congwen* (《沈从文全集》), the title *The Seven-Color Nightmares* was adopted but "Red Nightmare" and "Orange Nightmare" were not included in this collection. Only these five pieces were included.

[13] Shen Congwen: "The Candle Extinguished," *Collected Works of Shen Congwen* (《沈从文文集》),Vol. 11, Guangzhou: Huacheng Press, 1984, p. 276.

[14] Shen Congwen: "Deep Abyss," *Collected Works of Shen Congwen*, Vol. 11, Guangzhou: Huacheng Press, 1984, p. 284.

[15] Shen Congwen: "The Candle Extinguished," *Collected Works of Shen Congwen*, Vol. 11, Guangzhou: Huacheng Press, 1984, p. 281.

[16] Shen Congwen: "Life," *Collected Works of Shen Congwen*,Vol. 11, Guangzhou: Huacheng Press, 1984, p. 295.

These works of Shen Congwen's were more closely related with modernism. The stream of consciousness and description of sex and psychoanalysis showed the influence of Freud. With this solid background of modernist philosophy, his critical understanding of modern civilization seemed to become boundless and uncertain. He believed most people in society wanted nothing more than to survive and thus refused beauty. "I want to shout, but don't know to whom I can shout out."[17] "Human beings created a thrilling civilized world with their hands and head, but civilization is suddenly being destroyed by human hands."[18] He analyzed Qu Yuan and Chuang Tzu from a modernist perspective, and concluded that these two, one indignant and the other wise as they were, were actually "equally desperate."[19] Therefore, Shen Congwen meditated with his literature but did not give any clear answers to readers. Seen from a political point of view, these seemed like crazy talk, and may have been his way of escaping. Shen himself explained: "I have to flee into a kind of music, so as to highlight my confusion about this chaotic world."[20] Here "music" was an art that represented human life in an even more abstract form than literature, and this proved that in engrossing himself in "abstraction," Shen Congwen's purpose was to show his confusion about realities. And expressing this confusion in a modernist way was a kind of intellectual persistence. Different from his students, who could use modernist themes and techniques consciously, Shen Congwen just turned his eyes from the real-world life to meditation and abstraction; his modernism was a random choice, partly stimulated by the modernist atmosphere of the Associated University.

When he was a student at the Associated University, Wang Zengqi (1920–1997) had listened to Shen Congwen's lectures in three courses, namely "Composition in Various Styles," "Literary Creation Exercises," and "History of Chinese Fiction." Shen was by no means a good teacher, but Wang Zengqi bore his teacher's words in mind: "try to get close to your characters when you write." However, he did not write in the same style as his teacher when he first wrote fictions, but followed the fashion of that time and attempted writing modernist fictions. In "Under the Light" (《灯下》), "The Chimes of the Primary School" (《小学校的钟声》), and "Green Cat" (《绿猫》), which were not included in any collection, and "Revenge" (《复仇》), which was included in *Encounter* (《邂逅集》), his only collection of short stories published in

---

[17] Shen Congwen: "Black Nightmare," *Selected Works of Shen Congwen*, Vol. 1, Chengdu: Sichuan People's Press, 1983, p. 424.

[18] Shen Congwen: "Deep Abyss," *Collected Works of Shen Congwen*, Vol. 11, Guangzhou: Huacheng Press, 1984, p. 282.

[19] Shen Congwen: "Venus," *Collected Works of Shen Congwen*, Vol. 11, Guangzhou: Huacheng Press, 1984, p. 290

[20] Shen Congwen: "White Nightmare," *Selected Works of Shen Congwen*, Vol. 1, Chengdu: Sichuan People's Press, 1983, p. 419.

the 1940s, he adopted the techniques of scatter of sight and stream of consciousness. "Revenge" was the story of a sword carrier who was born a posthumous child and obeyed his mother's wish to revenge the death of his father; the story was similar to that of Lu Xun's "Forging Swords," but the writing technique and the author's concept were totally different. When the sword carrier lived in a monastic room by himself, his imaginations, consisting of sounds, colors, and smells, came out in close succession. And when he finally found the old monk, his foe, he was moved by the latter's act of waiting for death calmly and with an unyield-

36.17. Young Wang Zengqi and Shi Songqing (施松卿) in 1948

ing spirit, and they finally reconciled with each other (one cannot imagine Lu Xun would have reconciled with anyone). His "Wretchedness" (《落魄》), "Carpenter Dai" (《戴车匠》), "Men Famous for Chicken and Ducks" (《鸡鸭名家》), and "Special Talent" (《异秉》), also included in *Encounter*, were all excellent pieces in which he tried to combine modernist techniques with the style of traditional Chinese brush note novellas, and created an earlier form of modern novel about townspeople which he inherited from Shen Congwen but which was different from that of the latter. The literary world of Gaoyou town was created, where the urban citizens were simple and honest, giving spiritual integrity more weight than monetary consideration. Wang Zengqi showed his outstanding literary talent in his detailed description of the beauty of human souls, his plentiful account of the cultural atmosphere, his poetic representation of working skills, and his recollection of the past with deep emotional implications. Wang Zengqi's language was clear and simple; he tried to avoid Europeanized and classical Chinese, and his vernacular written language represented a high level of the 1940s. Indeed, when "Danao," the name of the lake from his "Men Famous for Chicken and Ducks" reappeared in his "A Tale of Danao" (《大淖纪事》), Wang's masterpiece published in the 1980s after he came back to the literary fore, people felt the lasting vitality of Beijing school literature.

36.18. Wang Zengqi's only collection of earlier short stories, *Encounter*, published by Cultural Life Press in April 1949

In the relatively freer atmosphere, various literary genres gained an opportunity to develop themselves in Kunming during the war. In novel writing, Bian Zhilin's novel *Mountains and Rivers* (《山山水水》) also deserves a mention. The novel, which was an account of the ideological development of young intellectuals from multiple points of view, was completed, but the writer set his manuscript on fire, and thus only some fragments that had been serialized in newspapers and magazines remain. After the war ended in 1946, Li Guangtian's *Gravitation* (《引力》) and Qian Zhongshu's *Fortress Besieged* (《围城》, Qian taught at the Associated University for a short time) began to be serialized in *Literary and Artistic Renaissance* (《文艺复兴》) in Shanghai. Both were written by professors, and the scenes described in *Fortress Besieged* were certainly more suitable to be placed in the setting of the occupied area. *The Unfinished Song* (《未央歌》) by Lu Qiao (鹿桥, a pseudonym of Wu Nesun [吴讷孙]), then a student of the Associated University, was a passionate piece of lyrical writing, in which one could feel the youthful passions of campus life within the Southwestern Associated University. The Zhanguoce clique (see Chapter 23) was also a cultural phenomenon that emerged from the Associated University, for there was dramatic literature represented by Chen Quan; I included it in the discussion of Chongqing purely because the center of the Zhanguoce clique moved out, and the performance of *The Wild Rose* and the debates it entailed were more closely related with Chongqing, the provisional capital and political and cultural center of the Nationalist-controlled area. Chen Quan could be seen as an example of the academic-centeredness and diversity of literature in Kunming, and left-wing realism was another example, but it was generally weak here. The significance of modernist literature of this time surpassed that of the New Sensationalist literature, modernist literature, and Beijing school literature of the 1930s in that it was not an imitation of Western modernism focusing on the rhythms of urban life and sketches of urban cities, but tried to get close to the core of modernist literature by representing the personal experience of the warring era and of human life. With the Southwestern Associated University at its core, the influence of its academic culture on literature was especially prominent. It was during this time that the Western existentialist philosophy was imported, multiple modern Chinese philosophical systems took shape (represented by Feng Youlan and Jin Yuelin, etc.), and contemporary world literature began to show its direct influence. These elements combined and affected literature, so that writers elevated their concerns with reality to an abstract level and transformed the entire Chinese nation's experience of war into their personal experience of reality. With the deepening of the Anti-Hunger and Democratic movement in Kunming and throughout the country, teachers responded to the call of the era and to their students' passions, and showed a left-wing ideological tendency. At first, Wen Yiduo influenced his students with his modern spirit and mythologies shown in his research of

36.19. The site where Wen Yiduo was assassinated in Kunming, not far from the entrance to the Associated University's faculty residence at Xicangpo

ancient mythology, the *Book of Changes*, the *Book of Songs*, and the *Songs of Chu* (Wang Zengqi remembered that Wen integrated symbolist and impressionist paintings into his lectures about Tang poetry), but after 1943, he publicly took the side of patriotic students and participated in the Democratic movement. The year 1945 saw the December First Incident, when military police forces entered universities to suppress student strikes and four people died. After Li Gongpu was assassinated the following year, Wen Yiduo, indignant, rushed to the front of parades, public memorial ceremonies, and public speeches. He was assassinated by special agents several days later. This will be mentioned again in my discussion of literature from 1946 to 1948. And this event was a demarcation line that marked the beginning of postwar Chinese literature.

THIRTY SEVEN

SHANGHAI AND OTHERS

The Pain of Homelessness and the Roundabout Development of Urban Popular Literature

T HE LITERATURE OF THE JAPANESE-OCCUPIED REGION was certainly not limited to any single city. Since the times and locations of occupation were different, the Japanese colonists adopted slightly different military and cultural ruling policies in the occupied territories in the northeast, North China, and Shanghai, and there was obvious literary misplacement in these three occupied areas. In Shanghai, the period was divided into two halves with the outbreak of the Pacific War on December 8, 1941 as the demarcation line: the semioccupied isolated island period, and the period when even the concession was occupied by the Japanese army. As the "Manchuria writer group" entered North China and gathered in Beiping, there were two centers for the literature of the Japanese-occupied region: Beiping and Shanghai. Therefore, focusing on these two places, and with a consideration of others, we can give a brief and clear account of the general trend of literature of the Japanese-occupied region.

Whichever city it was, the national literature would be suddenly discontinued upon being occupied and colonized. The Japanese and puppet state of Manchuria exerted high military pressure in the northeast and north of China, and there was thus a period of quiet for one or two years. The circumstances were disastrous in the northeast, where after the entire region was occupied, the puppet state of Manchuria issued the Publishing Act in 1932, and as many as 6.5 million Chinese books and magazines with national consciousness were burned, and many others were destroyed in other ways.[1] It was not until 1933

[1] See Xu Naixiang (徐乃翔) and Huang Wanhua (黄万华): *Literary History of the Japanese-Occupied Region during China's Anti-Japanese War* (《中国抗战时期沦陷区文学史》), Fuzhou: Fujian Education Press, 1995, p. 40.

that new literary journals and societies began to emerge. The same was true for North China and Beiping; when these areas were occupied by the Japanese army, the literary circle kept still and silent for over a year, and it was not until early summer 1939 that the belles lettres journals *The Hedge* (《篱树》, whose editor-in-chief was Wu Xinghua [吴兴华]) and *Literary Garden* (《文苑》, edited by Zhang Xiuya [张秀亚] and others) emerged in the campuses of Yenching University and Fu Jen Catholic University. However, during this time, within the isolated island of Shanghai, or the foreign concession, literature could still make its voice heard despite the fact that the British, American, and French concessions kept compromising with the Japanese invader. For example, in 1938, *Translation Report* (《译报》) could report news about the Anti-Japanese War indirectly by translating news stories by foreign news agencies; "Everybody Talks" of *Translation Daily* (《每日译报 • 大家谈》), whose editor-in-chief was Wang Renshu (aka Ba Ren) could serialize the popular novel *The New Water Margin* (《新水浒》) about the New Fourth Army written by Gu Sifan; and in 1939, the *Wenhui Daily − Century Wind*, whose editor-in-chief was Ke Ling, and the *Lu Xun Wind* weekly (which was later changed into a fortnightly), whose editor-in-chief was Feng Mengyun (冯梦云), could advocate writing critical essays. But by the time Wang Jingwei's puppet government went on the political stage and the foreign concession yielded even more to the Japanese invader, and by the time Shanghai was totally occupied by the Japanese army at the end of 1941, all remaining publishing institutions and over thirty newspapers and magazines were closed down and discontinued overnight, and literary development was suddenly stopped. Then there was a long period of roundabout development of literature in the Japanese-occupied region. During this period, on the one hand, there was the ruling of colonial culture: the literature written by traitors emerged under the banner of "peaceful literature" and "Great East Asian Renaissance," but few writers were engaged in this besides Zhou Zuoren and a few others who surrendered to the enemy. On the other hand, those who wrote roundabout literature chose to represent the national consciousness in a subtle and secret manner, hiding and implying this consciousness in various literary opinions. For example, they proposed to resume "May Fourth literature," championed "native-soil literature" and "popular literature," translated "Soviet Russian literature," and assimilated Western "modernist literature" through Japanese translations; all could be seen as implicit forms of resistance literature under the colonial cultural rule. They called for returning

37.1. In the 1940s isolated island period in Shanghai, the *Lu Xun Wind* insisted on carrying forward the spirit of Lu Xun's critical essays

37.2. Inaugural issue of *Translation Report*. After the KMT government army retreated in November 1937, Shanghai became an isolated island. *Translation Report* was launched in January 1938, and its editors-in-chief were Mei Yi (梅益) and Wang Renshu; and in the same year, *Translation Report Weekly* was launched. Both were forced to discontinue in 1939

home because they were homeless; such a roundabout development certainly had its elements of continuation and extension, though at first it might be a kind of compromise and concession. For example, in the northeast, members of the Cold Fog Society (冷雾社) launched the journal *New Youth* in the name of government officials (another roundabout act), in which earlier works of Yuan Xi (袁犀), Qiuying (秋萤), and Jue Qing (爵青) were published. They not only used the title of the famous May Fourth journal, but tried to resume the tradition of May Fourth literature. In 1937 there were debates about native-soil literature in the northeast, and in 1940 there were debates in the literary circle in North China after the slogans of "constructing new art and literature" and "renaissance" were raised by *Chinese Arts* (《中国文艺》) and other journals and magazines. All these could not be analyzed superficially, for they contained the significance of "persistence." For those who promoted critical realism and those who made a disguised attempt at writing modernist literature, no matter how complicated the literature of the

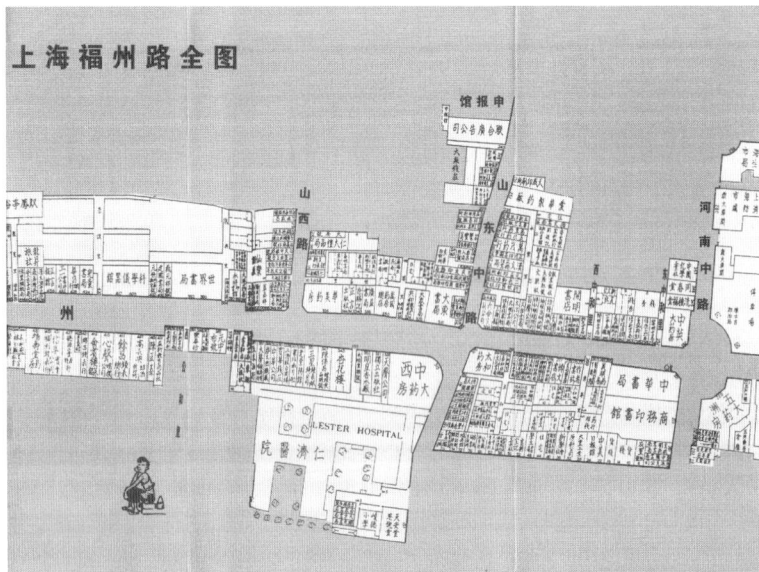

37.3. Map of Fourth Avenue (Fuzhou Road) in the 1940s, where publishing houses and cultural agencies were concentrated; from *Fourth Avenue* (《四马路》) by Hu Genxi (胡根喜), published by Xuelin Press

Japanese-occupied region was, they had their special route of development. The urban popular literature of the Japanese-occupied region became a major arena in which writers and readers tried to survive through the roundabout development and to maintain the national cultural tradition. Some writers were certainly better than others, and Zhang Ailing represented the highest level of literature in the entire Japanese-occupied region.

Native-soil literature was an important aspect of literary development in the occupied areas of the northeast and north of China. From the May Fourth period to the 1930s, Chinese native-soil literature had showed great achievements. Each of the three branches of native-soil literature, namely May Fourth native-soil literature, left-wing native-soil literature, and Beijing school native-soil literature represented by Lu Xun, Sha Ting, Ai Wu, Shen Congwen, and Fei Ming, among others, could not be rivalled by that of the Japanese-occupied region. When Xiao Hong and Xiao Jun published their collection *Arduous Journey* (《跋涉》), they were still in the northeast, just after it had been occupied, but by the time their important native-soil novels *The Field of Life and Death* and *Tales of Hulan River* were published, they had left the northeast. By emphasizing the native-soil literature of the entire Japanese-occupied region, I focus on its significance as a special literary form. Firstly, repeated discussions on native-soil literature started even before native-soil literature took form, which implied the importance of the "significance" of this literary form. The above-mentioned discussions in the northeast in 1937 were initiated by Shan Ding (山丁) and Wang Qiuying (王秋萤), members of the literary schools later referred to as the "Literary Selections" and "Literary Miscellany" cliques. At that time, there was an opinion that literature should go through three stages of development, namely native-soil literature, national literature, and world literature, but the "national literature" was that of Manchukuo, and the world literature here meant the imported literature characteristic of colonial culture. In response to this opinion, the intellectuals of the northeast promoted the primary form of these three, "native-soil literature," which could be seen as a gesture to resist against all foreign elements imposed on Chinese people by representing "the real life of a large part of us, our native soil."[2] It was around 1939, however, that these ideas were actually translated into literary creations. And the discussion in 1942 started because many well-known Manchurian writers moved to North China, wrote literary works with strong local colors of the northeast, and attracted the attention of North China writers. This time the discussions lasted for an even longer time, involving some literary journals in North China, such as *Chinese Arts*, *Chinese Public Opinion* (《中国公论》), and *Art and Life*

---

[2]   Shan Ding: "Native-Soil Literature and 'Shanding Flower'" (《乡土文学与〈山丁花〉》), *Mingming* (《明明》), Issue 7, 1937.

37.4. *Mountain Wind* (《山风》) by Shan Ding

37.5. *A Sail Fishing Boat* by Guan Yongji

(《艺术与生活》). By 1943, Shangguan Zheng (上官筝, a pseudonym of Guan Yongji [关永吉]) raised his opinion that "the 'native-soil' does not simply mean the countryside, but means 'my native place and my soil'; it shall include the entire society in which we writers are raised up and educated, and therefore a writer should be true to his own life in his literary creation, and thus achieve his realism," and opposed the trend of Mandarin Duck and Butterfly literature in the Japanese-occupied region.[3] The expression of "my native place and my soil" highlighted the national consciousness, and in extending the boundary of "native soil," he was raising the national consciousness of "my nation and my people," so that this almost became the best summary of the significance of native-soil literature throughout the Japanese-occupied region. Guan Yongji's representative native-soil literary work was not published until around 1945, evidence of the fact that literary discussions preceded literary creation.

Secondly, the achievements of native-soil literature of the northeast influenced and inspired the subsequent native-soil literature in North China. Their interactions not only lay in the fact that writers from the northeast became the backbone of the group of northern writers (Bi Jichu [毕基初], Yuan Xi, and Mei Niang were all exiles from the northeast who settled in North China), but also because their "native soil" had been further extended from steep mountain forests to vast plains. Shan Ding's novel *The Green Valley* (《绿色的谷》) contrasted the primitive world of the northeast with the rising business world of the South Manchurian Station, and described the fatal fights among comprador businessmen, local tyrants, armed peasants, and young intellectuals from landlord families because of the construction of a railway on the peasants' farmland. In the Postscript to this book, the author wrote: "Writing about the life of peasants in Manchuria should be the highest mission of literary writers of the northeast."[4]

3 Quoted from Xu Naixiang and Huang Wanhua: *Literary History of the Japanese-Occupied Region during China's Anti-Japanese War*, p. 332. Shangguan Zheng: "Some Additional Comments" (《再补充一点意见》), *Chinese Public Opinion*, Vol. 9, Issue 3, 1943.

4 Quoted from Xu Naixiang and Huang Wanhua: *Literary History of the Japanese-Occupied Region during China's Anti-Japanese War*, p. 123.

Wang Qiuying's *Bottom of the River* (《河流的底层》) was about the unsettled souls of young intellectuals who moved from the countryside to urban cities. Guan Monan's (关沫南) *Two Boatmen* (《两船家》) was about the personal and national hatred of peasants and boatmen and their gradual awakening. These literary works were quite well written. When Bi Jichu moved from the northeast to North China, he became a pioneer of North China native-soil literature. His representative work *The Twenty-Fifth Division* (《第二十五支队》) was about the unyielding spirit and loyalty of peasant soldiers who fought in one place after another. Guan Yongji, who rose to prominence later as a writer of North China, had a deeper understanding of the native soil. *A Sail Fishing Boat* (《风网船》) was about the displaced life of young peasants who struggled to survive rigorous living conditions. His novel *The Ox* (《牛》) was an account of the history of a family in a rural town on the North China plains, and he showed his great indignation toward the miseries of peasants who lived like oxen. Similar to those created by Lu Ling, the peasant characters in Guan Yongji's novels were all brutally humiliated by but stubbornly resisted against suppressors. In a word, most of these native-soil literary works avoided head-on confrontation with the Japanese and the puppet government, but vividly presented the image of peasants of the north who were simple and honest, full of primitive brutal force, and suffering historical trauma. The strong and broad minds of people in the north, and their stately, free, and unrestrained disposition resulting from long-time suffering, were intriguing and revealing in many aspects.

But some writers went beyond their "native soil." They were not just clinging to realism, but explored the creative depth of this literary genre, such as Jue Qing and Yuan Xi (a pseudonym of Li Keyi [李克异]). Indeed, the "Chronicle of the Arts" clique was different from the "Literary Selections" and "Literary Miscellany" cliques that championed the native-soil realism in that it assimilated diversified literary elements from outside. Jue Qing was referred to as a "genius" and the "writer of writers" because he paid attention to Western modernist literature, loved to read Edgar Allan Poe, and imitated the latter's mysterious, eccentric, and grotesque style to write bizarre Chinese stories. The novella *People of the Ouyang's* (《欧阳家底人们》) was his more influential work, written in a rather realistic style. The conflicts and destinies of three generations of an old-style family were threaded together through the image of "collapsed ruins," from which one could feel his "intellectually implicative" style. In other works, such as the short stories "Book of Ruins" (《废墟的书》) and "Defeated" (《溃走》) and the novel *Wheat* (《麦》), he sought to gain an insight of the secret psychology of his characters with bizarre, horrifying, and thrilling stories, so as to express his own anxiety and explore the meaning of life through literature. Everything in life was fortuitous ("The Gamble" [《赌博》]), and human destiny was as insolvable as a "lock" ("The Demon," [《恶魔》]), and then he raised the ultimate question: what is the tangible quality of life ("Testament" [《遗书》])? Jue Qing showed quite an obvious modernist style, and some of his works reminded one of Shi Zhecun's "Haunted House" and "Yaksha," but his style was not yet fully formed. Another writer who experienced multiple peaks in his long literary career was Yuan Xi (1920–1979). When he left the northeast and went to Beiping in 1942, he was still in his earlier literary period, which featured a mixture of realism and modernism. He lost his mother and was out on the street as a little boy, and was dismissed by the school of the Japanese-occupied northeast because he refused to speak Japanese in the classroom, which was why he could give a vivid and lively description of life in the urban slums, and boldly wrote about the lower-class people's yearning for books that might enlighten them under the high pressure of the Japanese and puppet Manchurian government. In two other novels, which formed a kind of series, *The Shell* (《贝壳》) and *The Veil* (《面纱》), the author actually analyzed the era-specific anxiety and confusion of young intellectuals of the Japanese-occupied region. In the chaotic and confusing modern civilization, Li Mei and her sister Li Ying swung back and forth, only to find that they were nothing but shells left on the beach after the waves ebbed. The most significant work of Yuan Xi was his collection of short stories, *Time* (《时间》), published in 1945, which included five short stories, namely "The Cane" (《手杖》), "The Spider" (《蜘蛛》), "The Unrivalled Beauty" (《绝色》), "The Dark Spring" (《暗春》), and "The Red Skirt" (《红裙》). With each title used as a metaphor, the author tried to combine concrete stories with intellectual abstraction and broaden his theme through narrative arrangements, so as to describe his emotional and aesthetic experience of human life. In "The Unrivalled Beauty," in order to avenge his mother's death, the "beautiful" boy destroyed himself and became "ugly," but it was actually hard for the reader to draw a clear distinction between beauty and ugliness, happiness and sorrow. In "The Cane," the cane of the protagonist seemed to have magic powers and could expose the crazy desires of possession, concealing, and destruction hidden in human nature and the uncontrollable morbid state. The illusion of human life described here helped readers feel the fragmentariness and evilness of the reality in the Japanese-occupied region; and the modernist techniques of symbols and metaphors showed the suffering and reflection of intellectuals living in the warring 1940s. Here the author combined his personal experience of life and of modernity of that time.

Even when native-soil realistic literature was the fashion of the Japanese-occupied region, there were modernist literary works by Jue Qing and Yuan Xi; this reminds us that literary development could sometimes (but not always)

37.6. Yuan Xi as a middle-school student

transcend the political divisions in China. Modern Chinese writers had been influenced by Western modernist literature since the May Fourth period, but different geographical areas showed uneven development for various reasons. In the 1930s there were modernist attempts at New Sensationalist novels and symbolist poetry in response to modernism, but after 1937, realistic literature was greatly promoted and made some achievements in the warring atmosphere. But as the war protracted, many people understood modernism from their respective perspectives, and began to use modernism to express their imaginations of China. This was also true for Jue Qing and Yuan Xi of the Japanese-occupied region. This literary exploration happened all over the country and affected Ai Qing in Guilin and Yan'an, Feng Zhi and

37.7. Cover of *The Shell* by Yuan Xi

Mu Dan in Kunming, as well as Wu Xinghua, the campus poet of Yenching University in the Japanese-occupied region. It seemed that even during the war, there was an experimental trend of Chinese literature that assimilated and artfully imitated ancient classical Chinese and European literary styles; writers broke out of the limitations of exclusive realism and exclusive aestheticism, and entered an explorative stage that combined reflections on Lu Xun, Baudelaire, Rilke, and T. S. Eliot.

Thus Wu Xinghua (1922–1966) revealed to us what really happened to the campus literature of the northern Japanese-occupied area. He was not only engrossed in reading extensively about the ancient and the modern, but was a poet who integrated ancient Chinese and European poetic elements into his poetic creation. Before Wu Xinghua wrote his modern pentametric quatrain: "My heart breaks at the partridge's melodies in the late spring / Departing the tree the fallen blossoms are reluctant to see the forest of their native mountain / I am a guest from the south coming to visit the north / Who cannot bear to think of the hometown where it is now cold and raining."[5] Lin Geng of Beijing literary school had experimented with a similar poetic format, and the older generation of Yenching student Lu Zhiwei (陆志韦) also practiced "miscellaneous pentametric poems" for a long time, and they were collectively referred to as "neo-classic" poets.[6] But Wu Xinghua was an even more outstanding

---

[5] Wu Xinghua: "A Quatrain" (《绝句》), *Yenching Literature* (《燕京文学》), Vol. 2, Issues 5 and 6, 1941.

[6] Lu Zhiwei's "Miscellaneous Pentametric Poems" (twenty-three poems) were published in *Literary Magazine*, Vol. 2, Issue 4, 1947, which was resumed and edited by Zhu Guangqian, but actually, he started writing these poems as early as 1936. See Xie Zhixi: *The Modern and the Modern Era*, p. 51.

rising star (his debut poem "Silence of the Forest" [《森林的沉默》] was published at the age of sixteen), and he attempted a more comprehensive innovation of modern poetry. Besides "A Quatrain," which tried to reconstruct classical Chinese poetry, he also wrote "Liu Yi and the Dragon Girl of Dongting Lake" (《柳毅和洞庭龙女》); "The Xian Mountain" (《岘山》); "Xiaoyu, Daughter of Fuchai, the King of Wu" (《吴王夫差女小玉》); "Four Poems on Ancient Tales" (《演古事四篇》), which focused on reconstructing Chinese historical stories as well as the sonnet that used the imported poetic form to express modern poetic thoughts; and "Xi Jia" (《西珈》), which attempted almost every Chinese and foreign poetic form, including ballads, Spenserian stanza, and hendecasyllabic and hexametric verses. Therefore, Bian Zhilin once commented: "He is obviously influenced by Eliot's theories on tradition and turned to 'anti-romanticism' and to modernism. This, actually, opened a door to the eighteenth century classical didactic and satirical poetry which were intellectual and bright in style on the one hand, and got closer to traditional Chinese poetry on the other."[7] This was quite an accurate and prudent comment. Here I give a special mention to Wu Xinghua not because I think him perfect, but because he represented the trend of the 1940s to integrate ancient Chinese and European elements into literary creation. However, he was more enclosed within the scholarly world and paid less attention to the wisdom and experience of his era, which was why Ai Qing was somewhat superior to him.

In the Japanese-occupied region of North China, there was a vast guerrilla zone that constantly made the situation unstable, but with the two major northern cities Beiping and Tianjin as their foundation, refined campus literature and urban popular literature survived and did not stop their advance into modernity. In the refined literature of university intellectuals, apart from the experimental poets represented by Wu Xinghua, Zhou Zuoren published his essay collections *Talks by Candlelight* (《秉烛谈》) and *Taste of Medicine* (《药味集》) around the time he surrendered, which had some influence in the literary circle. Most of these were essays on reading, intellectual familiar essays, and cultural treatises, which reflected Zhou Zuoren's complicated changes, inner conflicts, and pursuit of inner peace in the process of changing from a hermit to a traitor. As his cultural and intellectual system gradually took form, he paid increasingly more attention to explaining "Confucian humanism," which was evidence of his ambiguity involving appealing to the ruling culture of invaders and seeking to surpass them.

As for the range of influence of literature, the northern-school martial arts fiction and romantic fiction that tended to combine the refined and popular

---

7   Bian Zhilin: "Wu Xinghua's Poetry and His Translation of Poetry" (《吴兴华的诗与译诗》), *Studies on Modern Chinese Literature*, Issue 2, 1986.

tastes became major readings of urban citizens. During this period, the popular social novel developed into critical realism, represented by Zhang Henshui in the Nationalist-controlled area, while in the Japanese-occupied region, due to the external pressure, writers sought to greatly promote the modernity of two major popular literary genres, martial arts fiction and romantic fiction. Generally, the "five masters of the northern school" or "four masters of the northern school," referred to: Huanzhu Louzhu, whose literary achievements spanned the 1930s and 1940s, and Bai Yu (白羽), Zheng Zhengyin (郑证因), Wang Dulu (王度庐), and Zhu Zhenmu (朱贞木), who rose later. Huanzhu Louzhu (1902–1961) was the pseudonym of Li Shoumin (李寿民). Among his over forty works, *Swordsmen in Sichuan Mountains* (《蜀山剑侠传》) and *Nineteen Knights-Errant of Qingcheng* (《青城十九侠》) belonged to the category of fairy tale martial arts fiction. *Swordsmen in Sichuan Mountains* was his most important and widely known work, which began to be serialized in the *Tianfeng Newspaper* (《天风报》) in Tianjin from 1932, and continued during the Anti-Japanese War, with altogether fifty-five books published by 1949, making it an unprecedented lengthy martial arts novel (the author naturally drew out the structure and length of the novel, but the urban citizen readers who kept reading it every day in the newspaper probably couldn't get enough of it). Its most important characteristic was that it gave up the past patterns of martial arts fiction that featured conflicts between right and wrong, good and evil, and instead portrayed an extremely grand picture of the *wuxia* world that blended the human world, the wilderness, mythology, philosophy, and poetic sentiments. It was a genius depiction of a world of imagination, "for natural phenomena, sea water might be boiled; the earth overturned, mountains moved, human beings morphed, the sky might disappear and the continent sink. … As for human life, the soul might be separated from the body, objects incarnated, dead bodies resurrected, self-killing a way of flight; human beings might practice asceticism to become immortal while immortals may encounter some fatal disaster."[8] Thus he made "humanities and objects" splendid imageries "known" to his readers, and integrated the colorful national culture into his *wuxia* world, making literature an all-encompassing interpretation of the entire universe. In the book, all immortal swordsmen and demons of martial arts fought to escape the apocalypse that happened once every 490 years, an analogy of the modern theme that human beings had to "resist against" their destinies. For the author of this book, the martial arts and chivalry, immortals and demons were not used just to criticize the unjust, but he endowed modern meanings to *wuxia*, thus transforming the old-style martial arts fiction in which

8   Xu Guozhen (徐国桢): *On Huanzhu Louzhu* (《还珠楼主论》), Shanghai: Zhengqi Book Company, 1949, pp. 12–13.

37.8. Book V of *Swordsmen in Sichuan Mountains* by Huanzhu Louzhu, a super lengthy modern novel

readers could give vent to their grievances in the real world through the fictional jungle society within the *wuxia* world (which had already declined in modern society) into a new-style one in which *wuxia* became an externalization of human beings' internal experience of life. Huanzhu Louzhu thus became the first person to actualize this transformation. He surpassed Pingjiang Buxiaosheng (aka Xiang Kairan) and influenced the northern-school martial arts fiction by infusing a modern spirit into the *wuxia* world, and his literary concept and techniques could be seen in the post-1950s new martial arts fictions of Taiwan and Hong Kong, thus greatly and positively inspired the latter.

Bai Yu (1899–1966), whose original name was Gong Zhuxin (宫竹心), had some ties with Lu Xun and Zhou Zuoren during the May Fourth period; he later gave up New Literature and began writing popular literature, but it was not until his *Twelve Deadly Darts* (《十二金钱镖》) was published in 1938 that he became well known. He consciously put "chivalry" into a modern-time real world, and while presenting outstanding armed bodyguards and boxers who championed justice and had matchless martial arts skills, he revealed the dilemma of the chivalrous spirit in the modern era. In *Twelve Deadly Darts*, the bodyguard business was bullied and oppressed by feudal officials and local authorities, which was the true situation of martial arts in the real world. In *Account of Associated Bodyguards* (《联镖记》), the master of martial arts, Lin Tingyang, pardoned the defeated but was then killed by the latter in a surprise attack. In *Stealing Boxing Arts* (《偷拳》), Yang Luchan suffered a lot in order to learn martial arts, but had met many "fake masters." Later he pretended to be a mute beggar for many years and finally learned Master Chen's "ultimate void" tai chi method. When he finished his apprenticeship and listened to the instructions of Master Chen, the latter forwent his usual aloofness and warned him to "be modest and strict with yourself, never be proud and frivolous. Remember to visit as many famous masters as you can and try to confirm what you've learned. Respect members of other sects and avoid disputes and conflicts, … don't follow my suit."[9] This introspective writing style showcased the author's modern spirit. Zheng Zhengyin (1898–1960) learned martial arts and understood it; he learned tai chi from trainers at the Beiping National Martial

---

[9] Bai Yu: *Stealing Boxing Arts*, Tianjin: Zhenghua Publishing Department, 1940, p. 135.

Arts Academy and was able to use the nine-ringed saber. He became widely known after his *King of Eagle Claw* (《鹰爪王》) was serialized in *Three, Six, Nine* (《三六九》), a famous pictorial in Tianjin, in 1941, and later he wrote sequels that formed the King of Eagle Claw series. He was familiar with the hidden secrets of the Tianjin underworld, and in his martial arts fictions he seldom wrote about chivalrous sentiments, but chose to write about pure martial arts skills in detail. In contrast to Huanzhu Louzhu, he tried to write about martial arts realistically. His artistic conception was achieved by integrating these realistically described martial arts skills into his fictional plots, and thus had an influence on the later hard-style martial arts novels. Wang Dulu (1909–1977), on the contrary, was a writer of chivalrous sentiments, and most of his works were tragic stories. After 1938, he wrote five *wuxia* novels whose characters were related but each had their own story lines, collectively called the "crane-iron series," including *The Crane Startles Kunlun* (《鹤惊昆仑》), *Precious Sword, Golden Hairpin* (《宝剑金钗》), *Sword Force, Pearl Shine* (《剑气珠光》), *Crouching Tiger, Hidden Dragon* (《卧虎藏龙》), and *Iron Knight, Silver Vase* (《铁骑银瓶》). There were three tragic plot lines contained in these five novels. The tragic story between Jiang Xiaohe and Ah Luan originated in the fact that Ah Luan's grandfather, Bao Kunlun, killed his disciple, Jiang Xiaohe's father. The second plot line was that Meng Sizhao sacrificed his own life to bring his friends, Li Mubai and Yu Xiulian, together, while Li and Yu had to carry the moral burden of "chivalry" and could not set themselves free from it, and the friendship between the three was finally broken into pieces because of this. Here one saw the author's vigor of style in adding his profound insights of human nature to a popular *wuxia* story, and his psychological depiction was as meticulous as that in Liu Yunruo's (刘云若) *Unfaithful Love* (《红杏出墙记》), which will be discussed in the next paragraph. The third plot line was the love story between Luo Xiaohu and Yu Jiaolong. Luo and Yu were forced to separate due to sectarian prejudice, and their son was swapped for a daughter, but later, this son and daughter also fell in love with each other. The son was looking for his parents in the desert, only to see his father and mother die in front of him. With love, friendship, and kinship entangled together, the emotional conflicts and pain felt by these characters created a great sense of tragedy, and from this novel, the

210826 致 宫 竹 心

竹心先生:

昨天蒙访,适值我出去看朋友去了,以致不能面谈,非常抱歉。此后如见访,先行以信告知为要。

先生进学校去,自然甚好,但先行辞去职业,我以为是失策的。看中国现在情形,几乎要陷于无教育状态,此后如何,实在是在不可知之数。但事情已经过去,也不必再说,只能看情形进行了。

小说[1]已经拜读了,恕我直说,这只是一种 sketch[2],还未达到结构较大的小说。但登在日报上的资格,是十足可以有的;而且立意与表现法也并不坏,做下去一定还可以发展。其实各人只一篇,也很难于批评,可否多借我几篇,草稿也可以,不必誊正的。我也极愿意介绍到《小说月报》去,如只是简短的短篇,便绍介到日报上去。

先生想以文学立足,不知何故,其实以文笔作生活,是世上最苦的职业。前信所举的各处上当,这种苦难我们都受过。上海或北京的收稿,不甚讲内容,他们没有批评眼,只讲名声。其甚者且骗取别人的文章作自己的生活费,如《礼拜六》[1]便是,这些主持者都是一班上海之所谓"滑头",不必寄稿给他们的。两位所做的小说,如用在报上,不知用什么名字? 再先生报考师范,未知用何名字,请示知:

肋膜炎是肺与肋肉之间的一层膜发了热,中国没有名字,他们

...

37.9. Gong Baiyu (Zhuxin) worked at the Beijing Post Office before he began writing martial arts fictions. He had frequently communicated with Lu Xun between 1921 to 1922, who recommended his writings to newspapers and magazines

37.10. *Beiyang Pictorial* (《北洋画报》), the largest pictorial in the north, was the stronghold of urban popular culture

popular martial arts fiction deserved to become part of the modern "human literature" started during the May Fourth period. The last of the "four masters of the northern school" was Zhu Zhenmu, whose dates of birth and death are unknown. His representative work *The Tablet That Registers Seven Kills* (《七杀碑》) was not finished; it was a story between Yang Zhan, a successful candidate who passed the imperial examinations for choosing military officers in the late Ming, and four women, which was famous for its romantic chivalrous narrative. Zhu Zhenmu's depiction of human emotions was not as profound as Wang Dulu's, but his stories were full of twists and turns, and thus formed his own distinctive style. These northern martial arts novels by Huanzhu Louzhu, Wang Dulu, and others brought the modernity of this genre to an unprecedentedly high level. The martial arts skills, chivalry, and chivalrous sentiments strongly characteristic of the Chinese national cultural spirit could, after these authors' creative transformation, be used to express part of the emotions and psychology of modern people. The linked-chapter novel narrative format with the perspective of urban citizens showed a kind of openness. The title of each chapter, and (more importantly) the use of lively vernacular Chinese language, as well as the narrative, description, and fictional structure used to write about "human beings," all these represented the highest level of popular martial arts fiction of the 1940s.

In the northern-school romantic fiction, there was Liu Yunruo (1903–1950), a major novelist who, like Zhang Henshui, narrowed the gap between popular literature and New Literature. Liu Yunruo had had his novels serialized in newspapers in Tianjin since the 1930s, and he was very familiar with the urban citizen life in the north. In the 1940s he published several novels, including *The Setting Sun of the Old Lane* (《旧巷斜阳》) and *The Operatic*

37.11. Liu Yunruo, one of the masters of romantic fiction in the north

37.12. Cover of *If Only We'd Met Earlier* (《恨不相逢未嫁时》) by Liu Yunruo

Tunes (《粉墨筝琶》), with *Unfaithful Love* being recognized as a masterpiece. And it was because of this rarely excellent popular literary work that Zheng Zhenduo personally thought Liu Yunruo's "artistic attainments were far above Zhang Henshui."[10] What was special about *Unfaithful Love* was its mixture of popular and nonpopular elements. It was a fascinating story; the protagonist Lin Baiping found that his wife, Li Zhihua, had fallen in love with his close friend, Bian Zhongying, and so he chose to leave them both, thus entailing even more complicated relationships between even more characters. An intriguing story was certainly the basic element of a popular fiction, but in this novel, many characters – including Li Zhihua's close friend Fang Shumin, the ugly girl Longzhen, the famous prostitute Liu Rumei, the young lady from an official family Yu Lilian – emerged successively and formed a huge complicated web of loving relationships, threaded through the characters' repeated avoidance, entanglement, and repentance, so that the psychological turmoil between the characters was far more complicated than that of ordinary popular novels. In the dramatic conflict between characters, the arrangement of coincidences and misunderstandings was indeed something necessary for popular novels, but what was not common in this novel involved the presentation of the complicated psychological and emotional aspects of loving and sexual relationships, the in-depth analysis of good and evil in human nature, and the catastrophic destruction of major characters

[10] This was certainly Zheng's personal thought. Zheng said this to Xu Zhucheng, see Zhang Gansheng (张赣生): *Studies on Popular Fiction of the Republican Period* (《民国通俗小说论稿》), Chongqing: Chongqing Press, 1991, p. 227.

and tragic ending of the entire story. Overall, like works of New Literature, this novel explored the complexity and profundity of human nature, and in some respects, it even outdid the former, thus showcasing the author's high artistic skills to deploy elements of New Literature in a popular novel.

Another type of writer in the Japanese-occupied region in the northeast and north of China were those who started their career as writers of New Literature but later wrote popular literature, such as Mei Niang (1920–). Mei Niang's characters and stories were modelled on her own family background, and her lasting theme was the predicament of young women in big merchant or official families. In her novels of the "aquatic animal series," namely *Clam* (《蚌》), *Fish* (《鱼》), and *Crab* (《蟹》), she used symbolic titles to imply the destinies of her women characters: they were at first placed at the mercy of others, then had a little freedom and could swim a little in the web of feudal society. So many years after the slogans of "emancipation of women" and "emancipation of the individual" were raised during the May Fourth period, women still had no freedom in their love and marriage. *Crab* was better written. It was a tragic story about a girl named Lingling, who grew up in a big feudal family that was full of conflicts between each nuclear family and when her Third Uncle competed for the family fortune, along with an equally sad story of Xiaocui, daughter of Wang Fu, a long-term follower of Lingling's family. The author's skillful characterization and description of dialogues and scenes were not inferior to those of New Literature. But the author chose the urban citizens' perspective to see and evaluate the world. When Lingling and Xiaocui discussed their future marriages, Lingling said she was "going to drown myself in the sea and be wife to the sea god," while Xiaocui said "I've made up my mind, one can only rely on herself. I am doing needlework and learning to read just to learn something to survive. You see, if my dad is going to sell me, how can my mother stop him?"[11] Even so, she was still sold by her mean father, but from this small character, we could get a glimpse of the ideas of urban popular literature. Mei Niang was a writer of best-selling books in the north at that time, and her collection of stories, *Fish*, was reprinted in eight editions within half a year, just because urban citizen readers were attracted by her well-written stories of women characters. She was not as successful as Zhang Ailing, but both showed a high level in their writings and both succeeded in spreading New Literature among urban citizen readers.

In Shanghai, the actual situations were "simpler" than in other Japanese-occupied areas. It was the literary center of the 1930s, and then it had a buffer period as an isolated island, when its population did not decline but drastically

---

[11] Mei Niang: "Crab," collected in *Mei Niang's Collected Fictions and Essays* (《梅娘小说散文集》), Beijing: Beijing Press, 1997, p. 155.

increased to over five million, and profit-seeking cultural businesses resumed quickly and experienced distorted prosperity. Therefore in Shanghai, there was no need for a roundabout development in the name of May Fourth literature or native-soil literature; the outflow of avant-garde writers and readers indeed caused the shrinking of the market share taken by left-wing literature and experimental literature, but it was a great opportunity for the development of Shanghai school urban popular literature. Ke Ling was fully aware of this when he said "I think about it over and over again and find that even in such a big literary world, there was not one phase that would have accommodated a Zhang Ailing: the occupation of Shanghai was her only opportunity."[12] Writers had some freedom during the earlier isolated island period, and there was some residue of progressive literature, like the *Lu Xun Wind* and *Southeastern Wind* (《东南风》) magazines in the late 1930s, *Essay Series* (《杂文丛刊》) at the beginning of the 1940s, and var-

37.13. Mei Niang and her two daughters at Sun Moon Lake in Taiwan in 1948

ious supplements and columns of essays taken care of by Ba Ren, Zhou Muzhai (周木斋), and Ke Ling in newspapers, in which they promoted Lu Xun-style critical essays. At that time, it was so rare and praiseworthy to be a patriotic intellectual, like Zheng Zhenduo, who protected the national culture by means

37.14. *Records of Orchard City* by Shi Tuo

of teaching, launching journals, and saving classical documents, and insisted on writing literary works at the price of living in seclusion. Shi Tuo (1910–1988) was the most prolific of all writers living in seclusion. He had been writing under the pseudonym "Lu Fen" in the past and was an earlier Beijing school writer who was influenced by left-wing ideas but still maintained his independence in literary creation. During the Japanese occupation period in Shanghai, he worked as an editor with the Soviet radio station in Shanghai, and then entered the golden period of his literary career when he wrote about the native soil from a retrospective viewpoint and exposed city life in a romantic

---

[12] Ke Ling: "Sent to Zhang Ailing" (《遥寄张爱玲》), *Reading* (《读书》), April 1985.

satirical style. This "native soil–city" structure was Shi Tuo's best point of view as a secluded writer: he could either recall the declination of the native soil (somewhat like reflecting on the root cause of why China was invaded), or look at the frivolity of city life (the reality). His representative work of this period was the collection of short stories *Records of Orchard City*, novella *A Master in the Village of No Hope* (《无望村的馆主》), and novel *Marriage* (《结婚》), all high-level literary works. *Records of Orchard City* was a short story series, in which the author wrote the tragic lyrical stories of intrinsically related characters living in a small town of Henan to epitomize the entire native soil of China, which had been declining and stagnant. *Marriage* was a lively scene of people's moral decay in Shanghai during the war. His writings of this period featured both the use of complicated narrative skills as in *A Master in the Village of No Hope*, and the addition of "popular" elements in urban stories in order to appeal to urban citizen readers, and he also tried to adapt literary works into popular plays. After all, in the Japanese-occupied region, only popular fictions and popular operatic plays could be widely spread and become the cultural products bought by urban citizens. Writers of New Literature who turned to popular literature due to the influence of such an urban atmosphere not only included Zhang Ailing of the Japanese-occupied region, but also included Xu Xu, who wrote *Whistling Wind*, and Wu Ming Shi (无名氏), who wrote *Lady in the Tower* (《塔里的女人》) and *Landscape of the North Pole* (《北极风情画》) in the Nationalist-controlled area; these three best-selling books set records for being reprinted in over 100 editions. Thus a market pull in opposite directions

37.15. Inaugural issue of *Literary and Artistic Renaissance*, which began to serialize *Fortress Besieged* from Volume 1, Issue 2

37.16. Separate edition of Qian Zhongshu's novel *Fortress Besieged*, published by Dawn Press after the war, which was a portrayal of city life and Chinese intellectuals during the war

formed between these best-selling novels and the peak of belles lettres novels of the latter half of the 1940s: in the Nationalist-controlled area, Sha Ting's *The Gold Diggers*, Lu Ling's *Rich Men's Children*, Lao She's *Four Generations under One Roof*, and Ba Jin's *Freezing Nights* were all literary works that later enjoyed high prestige, but they did not have the same effect on readers as these best sellers. Even Qian Zhongshu's *Fortress Besieged*, which was serialized in *Literary and Artistic Renaissance* in Shanghai in 1946 after the city had recovered and was published the following year as a separate edition, quite an outstanding witty work written as a metaphor of the spiritual predicament of Chinese intellectuals during occupation, was not such a success at that time. This certainly had something to do with the fact that they did not follow the fashion of urban popular literature in wartime Shanghai and North China.

Some writers turned from refined to popular literature, while at the same time, some turned in the opposite direction. Some writers of New Literature were engaged in popular literature, and some old-style writers wrote works of New Literature. Yu Qie, whose original name was Pan Xuzu (潘序祖), was a new-style urban writer who had never published traditional novels before. It was said that he had written some old-style novels when he was a student, but his *Xiaoju, The Ruyi Pearl*, and the short story collection *Two Rooms*, all published before the war, were Western-style popular fictions. He catered to the taste of urban citizens and wrote about characters and stories that happened in the alleys of *shikumen*-style buildings. Around the Japanese occupation period in Shanghai, Yu Qie wrote an increasing number of novels, including *The Headmistress* (《女校长》), *The Tune of Nanny* (《乳娘曲》), *Golden Phoenix* (《金凤影》), the short story "Book of Seven Women" (《七女书》), as well as his citizen "Records" published separately in such magazines as *Popular* (《大众》) and *Miscellaneous Record*, such as "Record of Rejecting Marriage" (《拒婚记》), "Record of Trying New Son-in-Law" (《试婿记》), and "Record of Burying Love" (《埋情记》), all easy and readable stories. His originality could be seen in several aspects. Firstly, he was good at writing about the relationships between couples within a family. Secondly, he did not avoid writing about the material temptations faced by urban citizens and could analyze "romantic love" from an economic point of view. Thirdly, he applied avant-garde literary elements such as psycho-analysis and descriptions of sexual morbidity to his urban popular narratives and thus contributed to the moderni-zation of urban popular culture. He was an example of the narrowing gap between old- and new-style literature, which featured not a change of old-style literature but a kind of backward turn of new literature, so as to meet the increasing demand of urban citizen readers.

37.17. Yu Qie

37.18. Su Qing, whose reputation matched Zhang Ailing's during the Japanese occupation period

37.19. Cartoon portrait: "Su Qing, A Busy Editor" (by Wen Ting [文亭])

Those who followed this trend included Su Qing, as well as young women authors who were graduates of the aristocratic Dongwu University, such as Shi Jimei (施济美). These female Shanghai writers received a high education and were familiar with Chinese and foreign literature, and they obviously learned New Literature first and then wrote for popular newspapers and magazines, so they showed characteristics of both New Literature and popular literature. The representative work of Su Qing (1917–1982), *Ten Years of Marriage* (《结婚十年》), was a major best seller, with eighteen reprint editions during the four years after it was first published in 1944. Based on her own experience, Su Qing transformed her own love and marriage history into a fictional popular story and reflected on how difficult it was for women to make a living outside the domestic sphere. The novel was written in a clear and bright tone, and there was simply no pretention or affectation in her style, and there were few traces of old-style novels. Then Su Qing wrote a number of novels and essays, including *Sequel to Ten Years of Marriage* (《续结婚十年》), *A Beauty on the Wrong Path* (《歧途佳人》), *Waves* (《涛》), and *Washing Brocade* (《浣锦集》); her pragmatic literary style, which did not try to avoid personal interest, gained her the favor of urban citizen readers. Shi Jimei's (1920–1968) *Phoenix Garden* (《凤仪园》) and *Lane of No Sorrow* (《莫愁巷》) had some influence in the literary circle. The author was good at creating a "nostalgic" atmosphere in which she represented the futile and tragic loving relationship between men and women, and the sentimental tone of these stories suited the taste of female citizens. As a young female university student, the author had a lyrical and refined style that detached her from popular vulgarity, and the sentimental tone agreed with the unsettling and upsetting state of mind of urban citizens in the chaotic era. Other female writers who graduated from the aristocratic Dongwu University included Tang Xuehua (汤雪华), Yu Zhaoming (俞昭明), and Cheng Yuzhen (程育真). Then there was Pan Liudai (潘柳黛), who wrote *The Autobiography of a Wife Who Quit* (《退职夫人自传》). Writing about a certain type of woman making a living in society from the viewpoint of a professional woman, she gained some popularity among readers.

Zhang Ailing (1920–1995) came to the fore in the literary circle in 1943, the Japanese occupation period, with a fictional work strongly characteristic of her unique style, *Aloe Ashes: First Burning* (《沉香屑：第一炉香》), and she became a phenomenon in the literary circle within a few years, with her fame overshadowing any other woman writer of urban popular literature. She was raised in an environment where Chinese and Western cultures mixed, typical of Shanghai citizens of that time: she was from an impoverished aristocratic family, was educated in Western-style schools (St. Maria Girls' School and the University of Hong Kong), read *Dream of the Red Chamber* at the age of eight, and was familiar with *The Sing-Song Girls of Shanghai*. In order to practice English, she wrote nothing in Chinese during her three years of education in Hong Kong, and her writings covered various topics, such as films, Peking opera plays, dances, paintings, music, and fashion, all focusing on women. She submitted her writings to English monthly

37.20. Zhang Ailing in 1939, when she was studying at the University of Hong Kong

magazines first, then to Zhou Shoujuan's *Violet*, but claimed that her imaginary readers were "Shanghainese." Zhang Ailing could seamlessly integrate the old and new in her writings, which was fundamental to her becoming a new-style urban popular writer. Soon after her rise, Fu Lei acclaimed *The Golden Cangue* (《金锁记》), so much so that he compared the novella with "The Diary of a Madman," but harshly disparaged *Chain of Rings* (《连环套》) as a clichéd old-style novel; however, this was from the perspective of elite literature and ignored Zhang's true colors as a urban popular writer. It was, then, not surprising that she continued to write half new-, half old-style novels such as *Tulip* (《郁金香》) and *Eighteen Springs* (《十八春》, aka *Half a Lifelong Romance* [《半生缘》]).

37.21. Table of contents of *Miscellaneous Record* (Vol. 12, Issue 2, 1943), in which *The Golden Cangue* was published

The novel that represented Zhang Ailing best was *The Golden Cangue*. In this novella, she portrayed modern city life and the destiny of women with bitter incisiveness. In the bustling, cosmopolitan city of Shanghai, aristocratic families had long been in a disastrous state, and what mattered in the family and in relationships was nothing but money. The wife of the second son of the Jiang's, Cao Qiqiao, was a beautiful woman who, as the daughter of a sesame oil shopkeeper, was married to her crippled husband. Her life was a nightmare, among cheatings between people in the big family, her brother-in-law Jiang Jize's flirtation and deception, and her own weak and incapable children. She used the golden cangue as a way to mutilate others psychologically, while the instrument ironically stands for her own exploitation. When she became disillusioned with love because her brother-in-law just tried to exploit her financially, when she tried to alienate her daughter-in-law to destroy her son's marriage, when she implied to the suitor of her daughter that the latter was still addicted to opium (who had actually given up opium for a good marriage opportunity), her brutal and cruel nature hidden under her stubborn personality was completely unmasked. It was the unfortunate who inflicted so many sufferings on others, a shocking exposure of the cruelty of Chinese women and their perverse history. Other women characters in her novels, such as Bai Liusu in *Love in a Fallen City* (《倾城之恋》), who was discriminated against in her own family and was uncertain about her love and marriage with the rich merchant Fan Liuyuan, Tong Zhenbao's mistress Wang Jiaorui and his wife Meng Yanli in *The Red Rose and White Rose* (《红玫瑰与白玫瑰》), all seemed typical examples of women in the city, with their irreconcilable split of personality as wives, mothers, and mistresses. In these stories, Zhang Ailing refused to gain readers' sympathy for her characters with sad drama, but chose to examine the characters by putting them into the circumstances faced by "modern people."

The most peculiar text of Zhang's was *Blockade* (《封锁》), which showed how far she could have gone in her expression with modernist novels. This was a metaphor of the metropolis and human beings in the modern times: a streetcar stopped when an air raid alarm bell sounded (blockade), and a man and a woman had a chance encounter on the stopped streetcar. A spatial and temporal context deprived of normality became an excellent opportunity to show one's "realness," and thus Lü Zongzhen and Wu Cuiyuan got to know each other and fell in love, both feeling the other was a "real person." They were all kinds of people at other times: "At home she is a good daughter and at school she is a good student," "Usually, he is an accountant, the father of his children, a parent, a passenger in the car, a customer in the shop, a citizen," but not a real person. But their love came to nothing; when the blockade was lifted, it seemed the city of Shanghai suddenly woke up from a nap, and the two immediately disappeared into the crowd, and the city became a temporary and unfamiliar hollow shell. Connecting this modernist-style urban narrative with Zhang Ailing's other texts that integrated the old and new, leaves one amazed by her profundity in exploring human nature in modern times.

In terms of literary form, Zhang Ailing started by pursuing her own taste for urban popular literature (in the preface of *So Much Regret* [《多少恨》),

37.22. Cao Qiqiao, the heroine of *The Golden Cangue*, painted by Zhang Ailing

37.23. Jiang Jize, a character in *The Golden Cangue*, painted by Zhang Ailing

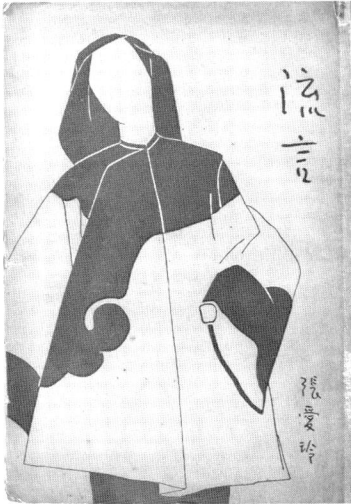

37.24. First edition of Zhang Ailing's collection of essays, *Written on Water* (《流言》), published in December 1944

37.25 The most important collection of short stories by Zhang Ailing, *Romances* (《传奇》)

she wrote: "I have always had a special fondness for popular novels"), and finally attained the high excellence to be part of Chinese national literature. Indeed, by trying to dissolve every literary element in her novels, elegant and popular, ancient and modern, Chinese and Western, she offered a modernist method of Chinese narrative. Part of her characters, stories, and language were borrowed from classical Chinese novels, but her free deployment of rich sentiments, psychological description, and associations was quite modern; the images of her novels were so gorgeous and well written that they conveyed an in-depth experience of life. Zhang Ailing's writings were Chinese as well as modern, and she was a writer trained in modern Chinese culture

37.26. Dongfang Didong's *Love Owed* (《补情天》), a novella recently discovered in a Shanghai tabloid and not included in his *A Painting of Gentlemen and Ladies* (《绅士淑女图》)

who could proudly stand alongside the world's best authors. She was certainly a gifted writer, but it seemed that modern Chinese fiction had developed since the late Qing and through the May Fourth period, and Zhang Ailing was a natural fruit of this development ripening in the 1940s. Many of

37.27. *Qiu Haitang*, Qin Shouou's representative popular novel

her peers also attained this achievement, such as Xu Xu and Wu Ming Shi, who were popular in both the Nationalist-controlled area and the isolated island of Shanghai, for their seamless integration and smooth use of popular and avant-garde literary elements in novels were unimaginable before this literary period. The cultural environment of the Japanese-occupied region was dangerous, but it could not prevent writers from sublimating modern novels from the perspective of a "citizen public." Dongfang Didong (aka Li Junwei [李君维]), Zhang Ailing's peer and a like-minded writer, published *A Painting of Gentlemen and Ladies*, in which he wrote about the frustration of descendants of old-style families in the metropolis based on his own experience, and created a "desolate" image among prosperity with a new form of urban popular novel. Then there was the university student writer

Linghu Hui (令狐彗, aka Dong Dingshan [董鼎山]), whose collection *Soil of Illusion* (《幻想的地土》) included urban popular novels about somewhat fashionable young men and women in Shanghai. Zhang Ailing's far-reaching influence has been visible in later writers in Hong Kong and Taiwan and even in today's mainland writers, for example Bai Xianyong (白先勇) and Wang Anyi (王安忆).

The trend of urban popular novels could also be seen from novelists whose fictions were serialized in old-style newspapers and magazines in Shanghai. The resurgence of southern-school romantic fiction was represented by Qin Shouou's *Qiu Haitang*. Qin Shouou (1908–1993) wrote *Waves of the Bitter Sea* (《孽海涛》) and translated *Two Years in the Forbidden City* (whose translated Chinese title was 《御香缥缈录》) earlier in his career, and one could feel his Mandarin Duck

37.28. Part of *Qiu Haitang*, drawn by Zhao Hongben (赵宏本), a comic-strip artist in Shanghai

and Butterfly taste just from his pseudonym and these titles. *Qiu Haitang* caused a sensation after being serialized in *Shun Pao* in 1941, but it did not attract citizen readers with its story. The story was a clichéd one: An actor called Qiu Haitang was disfigured after falling in love with a concubine of a warlord; he spent eighteen years raising their daughter, and finally died

37.29. Yu Ling in Beiping in 1931

tragically on stage because he could only play a bit role. As a "modernist" rewriting of an old-style novel, the author made use of the original tragic news story but did not rely too much on the "faithful report"; instead, he highlighted the humanistic content with the "fictional part," and sublimated the protagonist's value of enduring humiliation to shoulder his responsibilities. The novel was a mixture of old and new styles, but the sensation it caused lasted for a long time, so much so that there was a trend to adapt the novel into film, drama, and plays of various local operas, which could only be matched by the craze for Zhang Henshui's *Fate in Tears and Laughter* a dozen years before. What deserves a mention is Zhou Tianlai's (周天籁) tabloid story *Backroom Sister-in-Law* (《亭子间嫂嫂》), which was popular because it depicted the mutual help and relief between low-class prostitutes and poor intellectuals in Shanghai, and had the dual characters of courtesan novels and exposure novels. Certainly, it was probably a fact that some citizen readers read it as a courtesan novel.

Since plays were performed and could avoid being examined by the censorship authorities more easily than books and magazines, they could survive in Shanghai, a city with a glorious history of spoken drama. In the isolated island period, the plays created by Yu Ling (1907–1997), who had used the pseudonym You Jing before the war, may be seen as inheriting the legacy of left-wing literature. He wrote *Shanghai Night* (《夜上海》), a famous play of national salvation, which, through the drifting experience of the family of a country gentleman among the gunfire, vividly depicted people of all classes after the Battle of Shanghai on August Thirteenth. Then there was the realistic play *Apartment for Ladies* (《女子公寓》), the symbolic play *The Women's Kingdom* (《女儿国》), and the historical play *Legends of Heroes in the Ming Dynasty* (《大明英烈传》), among others. Ah Ying (1900–1977) focused on historical plays. He wrote plays on the late-Ming dynasty, *Royal Blood Flower* (《碧血花》, also known as *Hatred of the End of the Ming Dynasty* [《明末遗恨》], which was about Ge Nenniang, a famous Qinhuai courtesan, trying bravely to save the country) and *Zheng Chenggong: A Maritime National Hero* (《海国英雄——郑成功》), as well as the play on the Taiping Heavenly Kingdom, *Hong Xuanjiao* (《洪宣娇》), criticizing the ruling government by alluding to history. These plays had their political implications, and the performances achieved some success. By the time the entire city of Shanghai was occupied and political pressure increased, profit-seeking and professional theater performances became the mainstream, and popular spoken drama plays outshone all other operatic forms. There were several types of popular plays. Yao Ke's (姚克) *Sorrows of the Manchu Palace* (《清宫怨》; the critical film *Secret History of the Manchu Palace* [《清宫秘史》] of the 1960s was adapted based on this play) was a representative work of historical popular plays of this period, which focused on the relationship between historical figures, such as the conflicts between Emperor Guangxu, Imperial Concubine Zhen, and Empress Dowager Cixi, in which citizen audiences were interested. Of the realistic popular plays, the one with the highest box-office value was *Qiu Haitang*, coadapted by Qin Shouou and Gu Zhongyi, which was a success because it gave full play to the joys and sorrows of the characters and the emotional effect. The number of inferior entertainment plays also began to increase around this time, but what deserves attention is the rapid rise of a type of urban light comedy in the special conditions of occupation, a satirical comedy that appealed to both refined and popular tastes. These plays were written by intellectuals in universities, who were well educated and smartly ridiculed various ugly deeds of the urban society but did not fiercely attack them, for they showed some understanding of the weaknesses of low-class citizens and their need to survive. These comedies were well received among both intellectual and common citizen audiences, and some examples include *Professional Women* (《职业妇女》) by Shi Huafu (石华父, aka Chen Linrui [陈麟瑞]), and *Heart's Desire* (《称心如意》) and *The Deception Becomes Truth* (《弄真成假》) by Yang Jiang (杨绛). Another special feature of the dramatic circle in the Japanese-occupied region was the performance of adapted plays. Many famous playwrights were engaged in this work, transplanting foreign plays or novels onto the Chinese stage and changing them into Chinese plays by adopting Chinese characters, settings, and stories. Li Jianwu

37.30. Playwrights Ah Ying (left) and Yu Ling in Shanghai in 1938

adapted the French playwright Victorien Sardou's play *Tosca* into *Jin Xiaoyu* (《金小玉》) and adapted Shakespeare's *Macbeth* into *Wang Deming*. Shi Tuo (Lu Fen) adapted *He Who Gets Slapped* by the Russian playwright Andreyev into *The Big Circus*, and cooperated with Ke Ling and adapted the famous play by Gorky, *The Lower Depths*, into *The Night Inn*. All these were very successful. Some talented actors, such as Shi Hui (石挥), who played the character Murong Tianci in *The Big Circus* and was in his prime at that time, reached the summit of their careers by performing these adapted plays. With these adapted plays, playwrights made use of foreign stories to express their own indignation, and said something that was not allowed in the Japanese-occupied region, making them excellent for indirect criticism. And the theatrical practice of Chinese adaptation and popularization of foreign literature became a practical method to "enhance" the taste of citizen readers and audiences.

Thus the general trend of the Japanese-occupied region became quite clear, and could boil down to "new urban popular literature." This is obvious if we examine the discussions during those dozen years. As early as 1934, writers from the northeast had discussed creating popular novels; in 1942, *Citizens' Magazine* (《国民杂志》) in Beiping conducted a written interview on the "issue of content and form of novels," which labeled its respondents as "new literary writers" and "popular writers" and paid attention to the

---

[13] Shangguan Zheng (Guan Yongji), Chu Tiankuo (楚天阔) et al.: "'On the Issue of Contents and Forms of Novels' (Zhishang Discussions)" (《〈小说的内容与形式问题〉（志上丛谈）》), *Citizens' Magazine*, October 1942.

37.31. Stage photo of *The Big Circus* adapted by Shi Tuo; the second from the left is Murong Tianci, played by Shi Hui

37.32. Stage photo of *The Night Inn* performed by the Struggle Company (苦干剧团) in Shanghai in 1945; all these efforts were to enhance the taste of urban citizens

insights from both sides;[13] from 1942 to 1943 the two magazines in Shanghai, ghai, namely *Phenomena* and *Miscellaneous Record*, initiated a discussion on the topics of "popular literature" and "new literary style," which covered a wide range of issues, and the participants were made up of a larger variety of writers than before. The fact that such discussions continued for so many years was evidence that the question was far from being solved and was very important. Meanwhile, it showed that urban popular literature was eager to improve itself, which could be proved by the magazine *Phenomena*, whose average yearly circulation was as high as 30,000. The publisher of this magazine was the famous writer, author of *Tides in the Human Sea*, Ping Jinya, and the four years it existed coincided with the complete occupation of Shanghai by the Japanese army; for the first two years the editor-in-chief was the old-style writer Chen Dieyi, and for the latter two years, the new-style writer Ke Ling. Even when Chen Dieyi was in charge of the magazine, it was not conservative, and on its list of contributing writers, following Gu Mingdao, Xu Zhuodai, and Zhang Henshui, one could see Yu Qie, Shi Jimei, and even Wei Ruhui (魏如晦, another pseudonym of Ah Ying) and Li Jianwu, but the general trend was the old school assimilating the new style and paying attention to "breaking down the barrier between new and old literature."[14] When Ke Ling took charge, on the other hand, *Phenomena* did not become a stronghold of New Literature, but continued suiting the needs of citizen readers. The magazine incorporated both the old and the new; while the old-style authors of detective stories such as Sun Liaohong (孙了红) and Cheng Xiaoqing were still actively contributing their writings, the novels it serialized included *Wilderness* (《荒野》) by Shi Tuo (the short stories collected in Shi Tuo's masterpiece, *Records of Orchard City*, were also published in this magazine), *Chain of Rings* by Zhang Ailing, and *Rouge Tears* (《胭脂泪》) by Zhang Henshui, but the general trend was the new school incorporating the old. Here writers of different types had their own proper place and influenced and interacted with each other, and it was a strategy adopted to create new urban popular literature. In the past, the literary circle of Shanghai was dominated by left-wing literature and Shanghai school literature; now that left-wing literature had temporarily retreated to Chongqing, Yan'an, and Guilin, what was left in the Japanese-occupied Shanghai was the urban popular literature with its Shanghai school background. *Phenomena* marked the perceptiveness of this urban popular literature, that is, the popular aspect of literature was constantly influenced and driven by its avant-garde aspect and thus bore the fruit of the modern urban popular narrative. Its highest achievement was, as discussed, represented by Zhang Ailing.

---

[14] Chen Dieyi: "Popular Literary Movement" (《通俗文学运动》), *Phenomenon*, Issue 4 of the second year, October 1942.

MAP 37.1. Distribution of major literary supplements and journals launched in the Japanese-occupied region

TABLE 37.1 *Major literary supplements and journals launched in the Japanese-occupied region*

Name of the literary supplement or journal	Type	Editor-in-chief and editors	Date of launch	Date of closure	Notes
Supplement of *Morning Post* (resumed)	Daily, later published every two days	Xue Feibai (薛飞白) and Wang Senran (王森然)	Dec. 1, 1937	Nov. 8, 1939	Published the works of Chen Shenyan, Wu Xinghua, and Yao Tang (药堂)
Desert Pictorial (《沙漠画报》)	Weekly	Jiang Hansheng (江汉生) and Zhang Tiesheng (张铁笙), etc.	Apr. 16, 1938	Nov. 16, 1943	A general pictorial that paid attention to literature and art
Literary section of *New Beijing Daily* (《新北京报》)	Daily	Wang Yiren	June 1, 1938	Aug. 31, 1940	*Nineteen Knights-Errant of Qingcheng* by Huanzhu Louzhu, etc.
Literary section of *Morning Post*	Weekly	Fang Jisheng (方纪生)	Nov. 12, 1938	Mar. 25, 1939	Published the works of Yao Tang, Wen Guoxin (闻国新), and Wang Xindi (王辛笛)
Northern Wind (《朔风》)	Monthly	Fang Jisheng and Lu Li (陆离)	Nov. 14, 1938	Apr. 15, 1939	The belles lettres journal that was resumed earliest in North China
Family (《全家福》)	Monthly	Lü Ren (吕人), Xiao Quan (萧全), and Feng Yi (冯一)	Jan. 1, 1939	Sep. 1, 1944	A journal that lasted for a long period of time, paying equal attention to popular literature and new literature
Special literary page of *News Report* (《实报》)	Weekly	Zhang Tiesheng and Wang Shizi (王石子)	Jan. 29, 1939	Feb. 19, 1940	Published the works of Yao Tang and Wu Xinghua
Great Wall (《长城》)	Fortnightly pictorial	Gao Xubo (高绪伯) and Wang Jiefu (汪介夫)	Mar. 15, 1939	June 15, 1940	Published the translated text of Lin Yutang's *Moment in Peking*
Chinese Public Opinion	Monthly	Chen Zaiping (陈宰平) and Zhang Yuning (张域宁), etc.	Apr. 1, 1939	Jan. 1, 1944	An important general journal about literature and art

(continued)

Name of the literary supplement or journal	Type	Editor-in-chief and editors	Date of launch	Date of closure	Notes
Three, Six, Nine	Published three times a week	Wang Tailai (王泰来) and Geng Xiaodi (耿小的), etc.	Apr. 1, 1939	Oct. 6, 1945	Base of northern-school *wuxia* fiction and love stories
Fu Jen Literary Garden (《辅仁文苑》)	Irregular, quarterly	Li Jingci (李景慈) and Zhang Xiuya, etc.	Apr. 15, 1939	Apr. 30, 1942	A well-known campus journal whose original name was *Literary Garden*
Chinese Arts	Monthly	Zhang Shenqie (张深切), Zhang Tiesheng, and Lin Rong (林榕)	Sep. 1, 1939	Nov. 1, 1943	The most important literary journal in North China
Overturned Vase (《覆瓿》)	Monthly	Li Xiyu (李戏鱼)	Oct. 1, 1939	May 1, 1940	Published the works of Zhou Zuoren and Guo Shaoyu, etc.
Weekly literary supplement of *Morning Post*	Weekly	Lu Li	Oct. 23, 1939	July 29, 1940	Published the works of Zhang Kebiao and Shao Xunmei
Yenching Literature	Fortnightly, later monthly	Lu Zhiwei	Oct. 20, 1940	Nov. 10, 1941	Published the works of Lu Zhiwei and Wu Xinghua
Citizens' Magazine	Monthly	Wang Junshi (王君实) and Ito Sachio, etc.	Jan. 1, 1941	Dec. 1, 1944	An important later-period general journal with contents of literature and art
Ten-day literary supplement of *Popular Newspaper* (《民众报》)	Published every ten days	Liang Shanding (梁山丁)	Jan. 10, 1943	Mar. 1, 1944	Published the works of Mei Niang and Yuan Xi, etc.
Artistic and Literary Magazine (《艺文杂志》)	Monthly	You Bingqi (尤柄圻), Chen Mian (陈绵), and Fu Yunzi (傅芸子)	July 1, 1943	May 1, 1945	One of the most important literary journals in North China
Literary supplement of *Yong Newspaper* (《庸报》)	Published every ten days	You Bingqi	Sep. 1, 1943	Apr. 20, 1944	The supplement that deserved most attention in Tianjin
Literary Journal (《文学集刊》)	Irregular	Shen Qiwu (沈启无)	Sep. 1943	Apr. 10, 1944	Published Fei Ming's poetic theories and works of Yuan Xi, etc.
Chinese Literature (《中国文学》)	Monthly	Liu Longguang (柳龙光) and Zhang Tiesheng, etc.	Jan. 20, 1944	Nov. 20, 1944	The last important literary journal in North China

(continued)

Title	Frequency	Editor	Start	End	Description
Youth Taiwan (《少年台灣》)	Monthly	Zhang Wojun (張我軍)	Mar. 1, 1927	Closed down in 1928 after nine issues had been published	Launched by a mainland intellectual who was a native of Taiwan
Modern Poetry (《現代詩》)	Irregular	Liu Rong'en (劉榮恩)	Mar. 1, 1944	May 1, 1947	Discontinued once, and altogether thirteen issues were published
Miscellaneous Record	Fortnightly	Lü Huaicheng and Wu Chengzhi, etc.	May 10, 1938	Aug. 10, 1945	Managed by CPC members, discontinued and resumed twice
Southern Wind (《南風》)	Monthly	Lin Weiyin (林微音) and Wu Shangzhi (吳尚志)	May 15, 1939	Feb. 15, 1940	Published the works of Lin Weiyin and Fu Yanchang (傅彥長), etc.
Fictional Monthly (《小說月刊》)	Monthly	Liu Longguang and Yu Kangyong (俞亢詠)	Nov. 15, 1939	July 15, 1940	Published the works of Zhou Lengjia (周楞伽) and Yu Qie, etc.
Fiction Monthly	Monthly	Gu Lengguan	Oct. 1, 1940	Nov. 15, 1944	A journal that lasted for a long period of time, paying equal attention to popular literature and new literature
Phenomena	Monthly	Chen Dieyi, Ping Jinya, and Ke Ling	July 1, 1941	July 1, 1945	A journal that published both popular literature and new literature
Female Voice (《女聲》)	Monthly	Lin Junzhi (李俊堃) and Guan Lu (關露)	May 15, 1942	July 15, 1945	The literary section was edited by Guan Lu, an underground CPC member
Spoken Drama Circle (《話劇界》)	Weekly, later fortnightly	Wang Yun (王筠), Xia Yun (夏云), and Zheng Jun (鄭俊)	Aug. 20, 1942	Apr. 10, 1943	In all Japanese-occupied areas, only Shanghai had journals on spoken drama
Popular	Monthly	Qian Xumi (aka Qian Gongxia [錢公俠])	Nov. 1, 1942	July 1945	Published popular novels and Shanghai school spoken drama plays

(continued)

Name of the literary supplement or journal	Type	Editor-in-chief and editors	Date of launch	Date of closure	Notes
Chinese supplement of *China Daily News*	Monthly	Yang Zhihua	Nov. 22, 1942	Aug. 1945	Majoring in publishing articles about debates in the literary circle
Human World (《人间》)	Monthly	Wu Yisheng (吴易生)	Apr. 15, 1943	Oct. 1943	Majoring in publishing works of famous prose writers
Violet	Monthly	Zhou Shoujuan	Apr. 1943	Mar. 1945	Majoring in publishing popular literary works, sometimes also published new urban popular literature
Chats of Winds and Rains (《风雨谈》)	Monthly	Liu Yusheng (柳雨生)	Apr. 1, 1943	Aug. 1, 1945	An important literary journal in Shanghai after it was occupied by the Japanese army
Literary Friends (《文友》)	Fortnightly	Zheng Wushan (郑吾山)	May 15, 1943	July 15, 1945	A general journal that paid more attention to literature
Spring and Autumn	Monthly, later fortnightly	Chen Dieyi, Shen Ji (沈寂), and Yu Yang (余扬)	Aug. 1, 1943	Mar. 25, 1949	A journal that published both popular literature and new literature
Heaven and Earth	Monthly	Feng Heyi (Su Qing)	Oct. 10, 1943	June 1, 1945	Published the prose writings of authors other than Zhang Ailin, Yu Qie, and Su Qing
Literary Tides (《文潮》)	Monthly	Ma Boliang (马博良)	Jan. 1, 1944	Mar. 1, 1945	Jointly launched by writers from Shanghai and North China
Literature and Arts Spring and Autumn	Serial journal, monthly	(With the name "Yongxiang Book Printing Agency" [永祥印书馆] affixed)	Oct. 10, 1944	May 15, 1949	An important journal that lasted until the Civil War

(continued)

Title	Frequency	Editor(s)	Start date	End date	Notes
Six Arts	Monthly	Kang Yue (康月)	Feb. 1, 1945	Apr. 1, 1946	A journal that published both popular literature and new literature
"Buds" (《蓓蕾》) of International Gazette (《国际协报》)	Weekly	Kong Luosun (孔罗孙), etc.	1928	Feb. 1, 1932	Discontinued for a while after the September Eighteenth Incident
Dabei Newspaper (《大北新报》) pictorial	Weekly	Jin Jianxiao (金剑啸)	Aug. 1, 1931	June 1, 1936	Paid equal attention to pictures and text
"International Park" (《国际公园》) of International Gazette	Daily	Lin Lang (林朗) and Liu Li (刘莉, aka Bai Lang)	Oct. 1, 1931	Oct. 31, 1938	Published the works of Chen Di (陈隄), Lin Jue (林珏), and Xiao Hong, etc.
"Literature and Art" (《文艺》) of International Gazette	Weekly	Liu Li (aka Bai Lang)	Jan. 18, 1934	Feb. 1, 1935	Published the works of Xiao Hong, Xiao Jun, and Jin Jianxiao etc.
"Dabei Literature" (《大北文学》) of Dabei Newspaper	Weekly	Tan Tiezheng (谭铁铮) and Wang Guangdi (王光迪)	Feb. 1934	Apr. 1, 1945	Published the works of Chen Di and Guan Monan, etc.
Dabei Winds Series of Dabei Newspaper	Weekly	Tan Tiezheng, etc.	Sep. 24, 1939	Dec. 1, 1941	Including "Song River" (《松水》), "The Masses" (《群黎》) and "Dabei Literature and Art" (大北文艺)
"Night Watch" (《夜哨》) of Datong Newspaper (《大同报》)	Weekly	Chen Hua (陈华, aka Chen Huaquan [陈华权])	Aug. 6, 1933	Dec. 24 of the same year	Published the works of Jin Jianxiao, Xiao Hong, and Xiao Jun, etc.
Chronicle of the Arts (《艺文志》)	Quarterly, later semiyearly	Xiao Song (小松)	Oct. 18, 1939	June 13, 1940	A large journal, 200–400 pages long
Literary Serial Journal (《文艺丛刊》)	Irregular	Liang Shanding, etc.	Nov. 1, 1939	Jan. 24, 1941	Altogether four collections of short stories were published

(continued)

Name of the literary supplement or journal	Type	Editor-in-chief and editors	Date of launch	Date of closure	Notes
Learning Arts	Serial journal	Li Wenxiang (李文湘)	Feb. 22, 1941	Jan. 1942; altogether two issues had been published	Published Jue Qing's *People of the Ouyang's*
Poetic Season (《诗季》)	Serial journal	Shanding, Ge He (戈禾, aka Zhang Woquan [张我权])	June 1, 1941	Sep. 1941; altogether two issues had been published	A poetic journal
Youth Culture (《青年文化》)	Monthly	Zhang Fengxi (张凤墀) and Li Shoushun (李寿顺)	Aug. 1, 1943	Feb. 1, 1945	A cultural journal with more content of literature
Literary Serial Journal (resumed)	Monthly	Zhao Mengyuan (赵孟原)	Nov. 1, 1943	Oct. 1, 1944	Published the works of Gu Ding (古丁), Qiuying and Jue Qing
Mingming	Monthly	Saku Kokichi and Gu Ding, etc.	Mar. 1, 1937	Sep. 1, 1939	Published the literary criticism and creation of Gu Ding and Shan Ding
Literary Section of *Shengjing Times* (《盛京时报》)	Daily, later weekly	Wang Qiuying	Earlier 1932	Early summer of 1944	*Literature* was split from it on Dec. 7, 1940
Phoenix (《凤凰》)	Monthly	Zhou Dongjiao (周东郊) and Zhao Xianwen (赵鲜文)	1934	1937	Published the works of Shan Ding and Xiao Ran (萧然), etc.
New Youth	Published every ten days, later monthly	Cheng Xuezhu (成雪竹) and Jiang Lingfei (姜灵菲), etc.	Oct. 1, 1935	Dec. 1, 1941	Published the works of Jue Qing, Yuan Xi, and Wang Qiuying, etc.
Xingya (《兴亚》)	Monthly	Gao Xiang (高翔) and Zhang Xinshi (张辛实)	June 1, 1936	Dec. 1, 1943	Later became a large journal of 200 pages
Selected Literary Works (《文选》)	Irregular	Wang Qiuying	Dec. 20, 1939	Aug. 1, 1940	A major journal that matched *Chronicle of the Arts*

(continued)

Name	Editor/Author	Frequency	Start date	End date / issues	Notes
Style (《作风》)	Tian Bing (田兵)	Serial journal	Jan. 1, 1940	Only one issue was published	A large journal with over 360 pages
Literary supplement of *Taidong Daily* (《泰东日报》)	Wu Tiankui (吴天喟), etc.	Weekly	Winter 1929	1944	Including "Sounding Waves" (响涛), "Pioneering" (开拓) and "Seven-Day Talks" (七日谭), etc.
Learning Arts supplement of *Taiwan Nichinichi Shinpo*	Nishikawa Mitsuru (Japanese)	Daily	1920s	Mar. 1, 1944	Incorporated into *Taiwan Shinpo* (《台湾新报》)
Literature and Art (《文艺》)	Lin Jinfa (林进发)	Special issue	May 21, 1924	Only one issue was published	The first literary journal launched by Taiwanese
Supplement of *Taiwan New Citizen*	Lin Chenglu (林呈禄) and Lin Haiyin, etc.	Weekly, later daily	Mar. 29, 1930	Feb. 21, 1941	Changed to *Xingnan News* (《兴南新闻》)
Taiwan Battlefront (《台湾战线》)	Yang Kepei (杨克培) and Xie Aru (谢阿女)	Monthly	Aug. 1, 1930	December of the same year; altogether four issues had been published	The first proletariat literary journal in Taiwan
Taiwan Literature	Bessho Koji (Japanese)	Monthly	Sep. 1, 1931	Feb. 1932; altogether six issues had been published	The official journal of *Taiwan Literary Writers Association*
Southern Tone Stories	Guo Qiusheng (郭秋生)	Fortnightly	Jan. 1, 1932	Nov. 8 of the same year; altogether 12 issues had been published	Majoring in the works of writers from South Taiwan

(continued)

Name of the literary supplement or journal	Type	Editor-in-chief and editors	Date of launch	Date of closure	Notes
Frontline Troops (《第一线》)	Special issue	Guo Qiusheng and Zhu Dianren (朱点人), etc.	July 15, 1934	Only one issue was published	Changed to *Frontline*
Frontline (《第一线》)	Special issue	Liao Yuwen (廖毓文)	Jan. 6, 1935	Only one issue was published	Changed from *Frontline Troops*
Winds and the Moon (《风月报》)	Special issue	Jian Hesheng (简荷生) and Zhang Wenhuan (张文环)	July 1, 1937	June 1, 1941	Changed into *The South* (《南方》)
Taiwan Literature and Art (《文艺台湾》)	Bimonthly, later monthly	Nishikawa Mitsuru (Japanese)	Jan. 6, 1940	(Not known)	Only Vol. 6, Issue 5 can be found
Taiwan Literature	Quarterly	Zhang Wenhuan	May 27, 1941	Dec. 25, 1943	Discontinued after Vol. 4, Issue 1 was published
"Learning Arts" of *Taiwan News* (《台湾新闻》)	Published every three days	(Not known)	Around 1923	Mar. 1, 1944	Incorporated into *Taiwan Shinpo*
Taiwan Literature and Art	Monthly	Zhang Shenqie	Nov. 5, 1934	Aug. 28, 1936	Lasted for the longest period of time during the Japanese-occupied period
New Taiwanese Literature	Monthly	Loa Ho (赖和) and Yang Kui	Dec. 28, 1935	July 15, 1937	A journal enjoying equal popularity with *Taiwan Literature and Art*
Taiwan Literature Collective Journals (《台湾文艺丛志》)	Irregular	Zheng Runan (郑汝南)	Jan. 1, 1919	1923; altogether six volumes had been published	Published old-style prose and poetry

(*Source*: Qian Liqun and Feng Shihui [钱世辉], eds., *Compendium of the Literature of China's Japanese-Occupied Territories: Historical Material* [《中国沦陷区文学大系·史料卷》], Nanning: Guangxi Education Press, 2000)

THIRTY EIGHT

HONG KONG AND TAIWAN

Separation, Autonomy, and the Growth of New Literature

A T T H A T T I M E, H O N G K O N G A N D T A I W A N W E R E G E N E R A L L Y in a special state of "isolated island" and "total occupation." Their literature was, on the one hand, separated from the parent culture of the mainland and existed independently, and on the other hand, there were various explicit and implicit forms of blending, extending, and complementing between them. Hong Kong was ceded to the British under the unequal Treaty of Nanjing, and became a colony located outside the Pearl River Delta, just 100 or so kilometers away from Guangzhou. After Guangzhou was occupied by the Japanese army at the beginning of the war, Hong Kong became an "isolated island of concession" surrounded by Japanese-occupied areas. After the Pacific War broke out in December 1942, the Japanese army occupied the concession of Shanghai on December 8 and occupied Hong Kong on December 18, meaning both cities fell into the enemy's hand in the same month. Taiwan was ceded to Japan and became a colony after the Qing government lost the First Sino-Japanese War in 1895 and had to sign the Treaty of Shimonoseki. When the Anti-Japanese War broke out, the period of Japanese rule over Taiwan had almost come to an end, and it was recovered by the KMT government in 1945 after its retrocession. Putting the dangerous political environment aside, language itself, almost the lifeblood of literature, was an issue. At that time, people in Hong Kong used English and Chinese simultaneously, while in Taiwan, the ruling government abolished and forbade Chinese and forced Chinese people to use Japanese as the "national language." From this we can imagine how Chinese literature was distorted and suppressed in these colonies. However, people in Hong Kong and Taiwan had never severed cultural ties with the mainland. During the Ming and Qing dynasties and modern times, there were records of exchanges between classical-style "local" intellectuals and mainland intellectuals, and entering the modern times, the exchanges between their local literature and mainland literature had never stopped. May Fourth New Literature occurred in these colonies as well, just a bit later than on the mainland. We have seen the coexistence of native-soil literature, avant-garde literature, and popular literature in the Japanese-occupied regions of Beiping and Shanghai, and amazingly in Hong Kong the colony, we can also find the coexistence of left-wing literature, modernist literature, and popular literature (martial arts fiction), while in Taiwan, if a longer period is taken into consideration, the literature of nostalgia, modernist literature, and popular literature (romantic fiction) came to the fore successively. These happened at different times and each literary genre may have different formats and contents, but having studied the development of modern Chinese literature on the mainland, we seemed to know what would happen in these colonies.

Hong Kong witnessed a peak inflow of "southbound authors" after the war broke out, which greatly stimulated local literature, and to a certain extent, it made Hong Kong the national center of resistance culture in place of Shanghai after the latter sank. After the August Thirteenth Incident in Shanghai, the population of Hong Kong soared from 600,000 before the war to one million in a matter of two months. Since modern times, Hong Kong had always been the refuge of the weaker side after each major political conflict, but this time the city experienced the most significant swelling so far. Most people migrating to and gathering in Hong Kong were exiled intellectuals from Shanghai. In April 1938, Sa Kongliao (萨空了) published an article in the *Li Newspaper*, which had moved from Shanghai to Hong Kong, predicting that "for at least a period of time, China's cultural center will be Hong Kong."[1] But this could not be achieved through Hong Kong's advantageous geographical position and economic conditions or its relatively greater freedom of speech alone. After all, looking at the cultural environment of Hong Kong, we can see that by the mid- and late 1920s, the modernization process of literature in Hong Kong still lagged behind other areas. Lu Xun had been to Hong Kong several times in 1927, where he delivered speeches entitled, respectively, "Silent China" (《无声的中国》) and "Already Finished Singing the Old Tune" (《老调子已经唱完》), criticizing the outdated Chinese culture and advocating reformation. These topics originated in his experience in Hong Kong, for it was a weird phenomenon in Hong Kong that British rulers spared no effort in championing old Chinese learnings. In his "A Brief Talk about Hong Kong" (《略谈香港》), he copied the entire text of the speech made by Sir

---

[1] Liaoliao (了了, Sa Kongliao): "Building a New Cultural Center" (《建立新文化中心》), published in "The Small Teashop" (小茶馆), a supplement of the *Li Newspaper*, April 2, 1938.

Cecil Clementi, then governor of Hong Kong, that "China's national quintessence must be preserved and promoted," and it was noted down how Lu Xun was repeatedly impeded by conservative forces during his speech in Hong Kong: "At first it was interfered with by them, then there were opponents sending for the tickets so that others could not be admitted; later the speech was not allowed to be published in the newspaper, and after negotiations, the speech finally published was much abridged and distorted."[2] This helps us to understand why New Literature happened later in Hong Kong than in Taiwan, though both were colonies close to the mainland.

In terms of modern material conditions for literature, one should say at first Hong Kong was superior to Shanghai (it was only later that Shanghai surpassed Hong Kong, but this situation came to an end in the 1950s). That was why all newspapers printed in Chinese in modern times originated in Hong Kong (and Malacca), such as *China Serial* (《遐迩贯珍》), the earliest Chinese monthly, published in 1853; *The Chinese Daily* (《华字日报》) published in 1872, and the first Chinese newspaper launched and edited by a Chinese national (edited by Wang Tao) and to contain a literary supplement-style column; *Universal Circulating Herald*, the famous newspaper launched by Wang Tao independently in 1874. However, these newspapers and magazines could only prove Hong Kong's rapid adoption of modern technology, but had nothing to do with new ideas.

What Lu Xun saw in Hong Kong was an outdated and decayed cultural atmosphere; Zhang Shizhao, Lin Shu, and Zheng Xiaoxu (郑孝胥) all settled here, and the literary circle of Hong Kong was dominated by these old diehards of the late Qing who found refuge here after the Xinhai Revolution and old-style local intellectuals. The colonial government obviously adopted the policy to rule the colony with old-style Chinese culture, and the education system focused its attention on cultivating employees for foreign firms whose English was better than their Chinese. New Literature had been written for many years, but it did not have any influence here. Among local people, the literature with the most solid foundation was the profit-seeking popular literature that inherited the tradition of "comic

38.1. First issue of *Companions*, acclaimed as "the first swallow of New Literature in Hong Kong," launched in August 1928. It was easy to mistake it as a journal of the Mandarin Duck and Butterfly school

---

2   Lu Xun: "A Brief Talk about Hong Kong," *Complete Works of Lu Xun*, Vol. 3, Beijing: People's Literature Press, 1981, pp. 430–432.

readings" (humorous texts that made readers laugh) and suited the taste of newspaper supplements. For quite a while, these readings even shouldered the responsibility of introducing new ideas and new culture. This was indeed the special characteristic of Hong Kong literature. For example, the earliest literary journals in Hong Kong, *Fiction World* and *Collection of New Fiction* (《新小说丛》), launched in 1907, advocated anti-imperialism and anti-Qing ideas and used freer and easier classical Chinese styles, but they were nothing but popular literary journals. *Double Voices*, launched in 1921, was the earliest literary journal in Hong Kong to use semivernacular and vernacular Chinese, whose editors-in-chief were Huang Kunlun and Huang Tianshi, young local intellectuals with new ideas. It began publishing antifeudal literary works that showed sympathy toward commoners and the weak, but it was largely a Mandarin Duck and Butterfly journal, and published a large number of works by Mandarin Duck and Butterfly authors such as Xu Zhenya, Zhou Shoujuan, and Wu Shuangre from Shanghai. It wasn't until the late 1920s that the literary journal *Companions* (《伴侣》), acclaimed as "the first swallow to herald the spring of New Literature in Hong Kong," came into existence, and from that point Hong Kong writers began to write New Literature in pure vernacular Chinese. *Companions* cultivated the earliest writers of New Literature in Hong Kong, such as Lü Lun (侣伦), Zhang Wenbing (张吻冰), Cen Zhuoyue (岑卓云), and Chen Linggu (陈灵谷), but it still took the path of urban popular literature. It was the year 1928.

Such was the situation in Hong Kong before the war broke out, where New Literature had barely gained a foothold at the crossroad between the old to new styles. Gathering around major literary journals, local writers assimilated the latest literary progress in Shanghai and influenced, in turn, those in the Guangzhou and Lingnan areas. The major literary journals in Hong Kong at that time included *Iron Horse* (《铁马》), launched in 1929 by members of its first modern literary society, Society on the Island (岛上社); *Spring Thunder* (《春雷》) and *Small Gear* (《小齿轮》), launched in 1933 under the influence of proletarian literature of the mainland; and the belles lettres journal *Red Beans* (《红豆》), launched in 1933, which existed for three years (a rare achievement for a belles lettres literary journal). Among the readers of *Red Beans* were those who later became well-known writers in Hong Kong, such as Lü Lun, Li Yuzhong (李育中), Lu Di, and Lu Yishi (路易士). And Xu Dishan, who had taught at the University of Hong Kong since 1935, was one of the writers contributing to *Red Beans*.

As mentioned, during the war, Hong Kong literature was almost totally dominated by southbound authors. Among them, some made greater achievements in literary creation in Hong Kong, including Guo Moruo, Mao Dun, Ba Jin, Xiao Hong, Duanmu Hongliang, Xia Yan, Lin Yutang, Dai Wangshu, Ye Lingfeng, Xu Chi, and Xiao Qian. Most left-wing writers belonged to the Hong

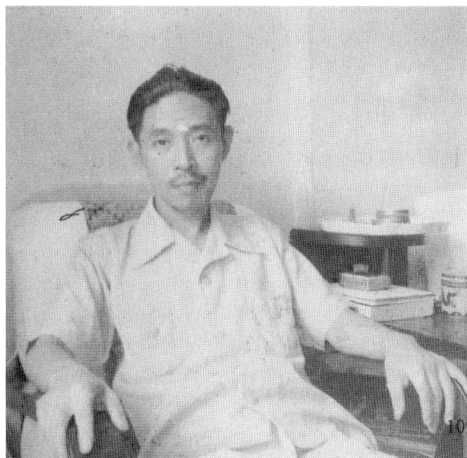

38.2. Mao Dun had been to Hong Kong and stayed there to write several times during the Anti-Japanese War; this photo was taken in 1948 when he was waiting in Hong Kong to go to the "liberated region"

Kong Branch of the All-China Resistance Association, while liberal writers belonged to the Chinese Cultural Advancement Association (中国文化协进会), and between them there was both friction and cooperation. The literary supplements to newspapers and journals launched by the southbound authors were far better than those that had been launched locally before, thanks to their broader outlook and the support of writers all over the country. Examples included *Literary Front* and "Language Forest" of the *Li Newspaper*, edited by Mao Dun; *Sing-Tao Daily – Constellations* (《星岛日报·星座》), edited by Dai Wangshu; *Hua Shang Daily – Lighthouse* (《华商报·灯塔》), by Xia Yan; and Literary Supplement of *Ta Kung Pao*, edited by Xiao Qian. *Literary Front* could not be considered a Hong Kong journal, for it was circulated throughout the country. Dai Wangshu and Xiao Qian themselves were avant-garde writers, and the supplements they edited were quite liberal, with progressive writers of the entire Southeast Asian region offering their support. Mao Dun's "Language Forest" and Xia Yan's "Lighthouse," on the contrary, leaned toward popular literature (which was probably influenced by local culture in Hong Kong). Mao Dun wrote a popular novel *Where Are You Running?* (《你往哪里跑》, also known as *The Story at the First Phase* [《第一阶段的故事》]) about business people and intellectual families at the beginning of the war and published on

38.3. Xiao Hong wrote *Tales of Hulan River* and other works during her last years in Hong Kong; she passed away soon after

38.5. Portrait of Xu Dishan by Situ Qiao (司徒乔)

38.4. Xu Dishan in the living room of his house in Hong Kong during the last days of his life

"Language Forest," which was an unsuccessful but valuable attempt. Another novel written by Mao Dun, *Corrosion*, was serialized in *Mass Life* (《大众生活》), a popular journal whose editor-in-chief was Zou Taofen; it was a diary novel exploring the soul of a young woman who was deeply entangled in a web of special agents. This was a novel showing Mao Dun's artistic talent and became a masterpiece of Hong Kong literature during this period of time. Xiao Hong, Duanmu Hongliang, and other exiled writers from the northeast were discussed in previous chapters. Deserving a special mention is Xiao Hong, who lived in poverty and illness in Hong Kong, but it was here that she wrote her most beautiful novella *Spring in a Small Town* and her best novels *Tales of Hulan River* and *Ma Bole* (《马伯乐》), a near-miracle. The Hong Kong period was also Xu Dishan's last period in his literary career. He was a senior May Fourth writer, and in his earlier works *The Bird of Destiny* and "Chuntao," his explorations of religion, life, and ethics were at first explicit and then implicit, evidence that he was a novelist with a unique style. In Hong Kong, he wrote a novella, *Yuguan* (《玉官》), which was different from other left-wing novels because he tried to reflect the true value of life from the perspective of a widow. "The Iron Fish with Gills" (《铁鱼的鳃》), in particular, was written under the inspiration of the resistance sentiment during the Anti-Japanese War. It was a tragedy about a submarine scientist conducting his lonely research during the war, only to be destroyed together with his experiment submarine, which featured quite an unusual approach. Xu Dishan took charge of the Hong Kong Branch of the

38.6. Woodcut portrait of Dai Wangshu

38.7. Dai Wangshu, the symbolist poet, in his youth

All-China Resistance Association and his health broke down through over-work. He was deeply mourned after he passed away in Hong Kong. One of the southbound writers, Dai Wangshu (1905–1950), was a well-known symbolist poet who stayed in Hong Kong for over ten years. He gained his reputation with the poem "Rainy Alley" early in his career, and in the 1930s he became a major poet attempting modernist poetic writing, such as "Bird of Paradise." During the Anti-Japanese War, after being tempered by his personal ordeal in that specific era, his mental horizon was enlarged and he began integrating symbolic poetic art with his own experience of reality, and thus wrote more mature poetic works. He was arrested by Japanese military police during the time Hong Kong was occupied and was tortured in prison. This experience inspired him to write "Inscribed on the Prison Wall," a resounding poem with brilliant imaginations:

> One of you died.
> In the prison of the Japan-occupied place,
> He harbored deep hatred,
> Which you should always bear in mind.
> When you return and
> Dig his damaged body from the earth,
> You should elevate his soul highly
> With your cheers of victory,
> Then you should place his white bones at the peak,
> Let them bathe in the sun and blow in the wind
> Which was his only beautiful dream,
> In that dark and wet cell.[3]

---

[3] Dai Wangshu: "Inscribed on the Prison Wall," *Collected Poems of Dai Wangshu* (《戴望舒诗 集》), Chengdu: Sichuan People's Press, 1981, pp. 125–126.

The literary creation of so many southbound writers constituted a characteristic of Hong Kong literature. Just as immigrants bring colorful cultural diversity to a country, writers from the mainland brought with them their rich writing experience as left-wing, Shanghai school, and popular writers. They gathered together with local Hong Kong writers, expanded the influence of New Literature in Hong Kong, and helped cultivate local writers. After the Anti-Japanese War was over, many intellectuals returned to the mainland, but they did not expect that the civil war would break out in 1946, and thus another wave of writers came to the south in order to escape the chaos and political prosecution. According to relevant statistics, this time the number was even larger than that during the Anti-Japanese War. These included Guo Moruo, who wrote his autobiographical *Great Wave Melody* (《洪波曲》); and Mao Dun, who had his *Tempering* serialized in the *Wenhui Daily* in Hong Kong; as well as Huang Guliu (黄谷柳), who had his *The Story of Xiaqiu* (《虾球传》, which consisted of three volumes, namely *Breeze and Rain* [《春风秋雨》], *Clouds and Sea* [《白云珠海》], and *Mountains and Rivers* [《山长水远》]) published in Xia Yan's *Hua Shang Daily* and caused a sensation in Hong Kong.

Discussing the question of whether Huang Guliu (1908–1977) was a southbound writer or a local writer may help us gain an understanding of Hong Kong literature from a historical point of view. Huang Guliu had quite a history of relations with Hong Kong. His native place was Guangdong, and he was born to a poor family in Vietnam. In the late 1920s, when working as a proofreader for *Universal Circulating Herald*, he became acquaintances with Lü Lun, Zhang Wenbing, and other writers, and published his first novel, *Exchanging Tickets* (《换票》). In the 1930s, however, he had been working in the army on the mainland for a long time, where he experienced many hardships; he witnessed the fall of Nanjing, went to explore the mines and railways, and got to know some communist party members. He returned to write in Hong Kong after the war ended, and it seemed that he had dual statuses as both a local and southbound writer. If we look at the novel *The Story of Xiaqiu* alone, however, it was the adventure of a Hong Kong guttersnipe. It was a narrative of the society of Hong Kong, Guangzhou, and the Pearl River Delta written through two plot lines, the vagrant orphan Xiaqiu, and the rascal money-seeker Eyutou. The author was extremely familiar with people of all walks of life in the urban society of Hong Kong: pickpockets, hardened gamblers, martial arts trainers, slaves and maid-servants, prostitutes, smugglers, local despots, and military and government officials. And he gave an even more vivid description of the customs and habits of low-class Hong Kong citizens and their vulgar language. Geographically, Hong Kong was part of the Pearl River Delta, and thus the upper-class Hong Kong

38.8. Huang Guliu's *Biography of Xiaqiu*, *Breeze and Rain* (Vol. 1); it aroused great interest among general readers in Hong Kong and Guangdong

people used English, while a majority of its mid- and lower-class citizens always used Chinese as their everyday language, and the Lingnan subculture dominated this part of Hong Kong. *The Story of Xiaqiu* was a biography of lower-class people, and at the end of the story, the protagonist, Xiaqiu, joined the South China guerrilla forces. The structure and characterization of the novel showed the influence of New Literature and left-wing literature, while the narrative, description of local customs, and imitation of the colloquial language of Hong Kong were characteristic of folk art and old-style linked-chapter novels. If we insist that writers born in Hong Kong did not gain a foothold in Hong Kong literature until the 1960s, Huang Guliu, who had internalized highly political higher-level New Literature and integrated it with the popular literary elements of local literature, should be considered a "real" Hong Kong writer.

A major literary work of another typical Hong Kong writer during this time was Lü Lun's *A Destitute Neighborhood*. Lü Lun (1911–1988) was born in Hong Kong and had been living there all his life except for a short period during the occupation when he fled to Guangdong. He was a member of the Society on the Island and had been engaged in writing New Literature since the 1920s, and his description of the Western-style society in Hong Kong showed an avant-garde style. He was an intimate friend of Ye Lingfeng, the Shanghai school writer on the mainland, and his novel *Dark Lila* (《黑丽拉》) was a romantic and sentimental Shanghai-style story that happened in Hong Kong between the protagonist and a café waitress. His later works, *Eternal Song* (《永久之歌》) and *Endless Love* (《无尽的爱》), were both moving romantic tragedies, in which loyalty always brought about tragic losses, and the sentimental stories full of twists and turns became best sellers in the Hong Kong reading market. *Endless Love* added content about social life during the occupation of Hong Kong to an ordinary romantic story. By the time

38.9. Self-portrait of Lü Lun

38.10. Lü Lun in the spring of 1948

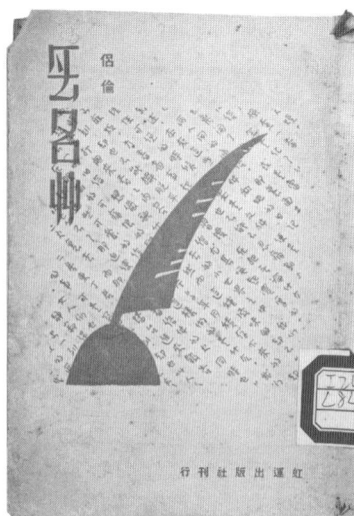

38.11. Cover of *Nameless Grass* (《无名草》) by Lü Lun

his *A Destitute Neighborhood* was serialized in the *Hua Shang Daily* in 1948, it was considered a work that broke "the solitude of the postwar new literary circle" in Hong Kong. This novel wrote about a destitute lane in Kowloon. Four men shared a room, and then there was a woman who attempted suicide but was rescued, which then gave rise to various dramatic plots such as employment and disappointment in love. The novel epitomized the life of

38.12. Zhang Wojun in 1933

lowest-class citizens struggling to survive. Lü Lun wrote about the "human world of Hong Kong" with the style and techniques of New Literature; he partly corroborated what Zhang Ailing said, "Hong Kong is a splendid but sad city,"[4] and partly echoed Yao Ke, a writer from Shanghai, who wrote about the low-class streets full of drug addicts in Kowloon. Yao Ke's play was titled *The Confined Alley* (《陋巷》).[5] Lü Lun represented the landmark when belles lettres finally gained a foothold in Hong Kong. And it was through this "dialogue" with New Literature in an environment that could not be totally separated from the mainland, and through the development of

[4] Zhang Ailing: "Jasmine Tea" (《茉莉香片》), *Romances*, Shanghai: Shanhe Book Company, revised and enlarged edition, 1946, p. 191.

[5] *The Confined Alley* was published after it was performed, and the final edition was not published until April 1968, when it was published in *Pure Literature* (《纯文学》) in Hong Kong.

popular literature based on the city's status as a business and commercial community, that Hong Kong literature became independent and autonomous.

Taiwan literature, too, showed some features of a wartime period. The Japanese-occupied period had almost come to an end; on the one hand, the Japanese colonial government continued to promote the Kominka ("conversion into dutiful imperial subjects") movement, while on the other hand, local writers in Taiwan (modern writers from the mainland did not go to Taiwan in large groups until after the retrocession in 1945) continued to write native-soil and resistance literary works. This originated in its tradition of New Literature, which could be traced back to the *Taiwan Youth* (《台湾青年》) magazine launched in Tokyo by Taiwanese students in Japan in 1920, and the *Taiwan People's News* (《台湾民报》) published in Tokyo in 1923. An analysis of the place of origin, editors, and major contributors of these publications would remind us of the relationship between the origin of New Literature of mainland China and the progressive

38.13. Page of the *Taiwan People's News*. Zhang Wojun once brought this newspaper when he visited Lu Xun in Beijing

38.14. Zhang Wojun and his wife in Taipei in 1925

literary circle in Japan, as well as the journals run by Chinese students in Japan in which Lu Xun earlier published his articles, such as *Henan* (《河南》) and *Zhejiang Tide*. *Taiwan Youth* was a new cultural journal launched by the organization of Taiwan students, New People Association (新民会), imitating *New Youth* of the mainland, which is obvious from their names. The inaugural issue published "Literature and Its Function" (《文学与职务》), an article written by Chen Xin (陈炘) to criticize the dead literature that resulted from the imperial examination system, and raised his view that only vernacular literature was lively literature, also reminding one of Hu Shi's views.[6] After the name *Taiwan Youth* was changed to *Taiwan* (《台湾》), the journal published Huang Chengcong's (黄呈聪) "The New Mission of Promoting the Vernacular" (《论普及白话文的新使命》) on January 1923, making its literary claims even more clear. The *Taiwan People's News* was hailed as the "cradle of Taiwan New Literature," and it was in this newspaper that Zhang Wojun, who was recognized as the one who had sown the seed of May Fourth New Literature in Taiwan, published his challenging articles, "A Letter to Taiwan Youth" (《致台湾青年的一封信》) and "The Awful Literary Scene in Taiwan" (《糟糕的台湾文学界》), in 1924, which caused strong repercussions around the entire island of Taiwan. As early as 1923, modern Chinese vernacular was adopted by this newspaper for all its text, five years earlier than *Companions* in Hong Kong. However, it wasn't until August 1927 that the *Taiwan People's News* was moved from Tokyo to Taiwan. Obviously, the environment on the island was very difficult for the development of modern literature, and progressive literature on the mainland and Japan constituted important external conditions for its growth.

The local New Literature in Taiwan was stronger than that in Hong Kong. Zhang Wojun (1902–1955) was born to a poor family in Banqiao district, Taipei. When he studied at Beijing Normal University on a half-study, half-work basis, he published articles in the *Taiwan People's News* introducing mainland May Fourth literature, and started debates on old-style and new-style literature with his theoretical essays. Apart from the already-mentioned essays, Zhang Wojun also wrote "Weeping for the Literary Scene in Taiwan" (《为台湾的文学界一哭》) and "Please Help Dismantle this Old Tumble-Down House in the Thicket of Weeds" (《请合力拆下这座败草丛中的破旧殿堂》). Just looking at these titles, one could feel his valor in opposing the old literary camp that was based in the Chinese column of the *Taiwan Nichinichi Shinpo* (*Taiwan Daily News*, 《台湾日日新报》). In 1925, Zhang Wojun published "The Significance of the New Literature Movement" (《新文学运动的意义》), in which he raised two important claims that came

---

6   Chen Xin: "Literature and Its Function," published in the inaugural issue of *Taiwan Youth*, July 1920.

to the point of opposing the old-style literature: building vernacular literature, and reforming Taiwan language, fulfilling his responsibility as a "street cleaner" and "daring vanguard." In the summer of 1926, he brought a copy of the *Taiwan People's News* and visited Lu Xun, who was going to leave Beijing, and he was the "Mr. Zhang Woquan" mentioned by Lu Xun in his essay, for he said sadly to the latter: "Chinese people seem to have forgotten Taiwan."[7] In terms of literary creation with vernacular Chinese, the first verse of new poetry in Taiwan was his "Still" (《沉寂》, published in the *Taiwan People's News* (Vol. 2, Issue 8), and the first collection of new poetry was his *Love in a Turbulent City* (《乱都之恋》, published in Taipei in 1925). With his *Buying Lottery Tickets* (《买彩票》), he was one of the earliest Taiwanese writers of vernacular fiction, writing realistically about the straitened circumstances of a Taiwan youth on the mainland. These vernacular literary works were still immature, but the path had been opened.

Loa Ho (1894–1943) was another pathbreaker and wrote the first vernacular novel in Taiwan, *Festival High Jinks* (《斗热闹》, published in the 1926 New Year Issue of the *Taiwan People's News*). He was born in Changhua, Taichung, and studied and practiced medicine for poor people. In 1926 he became the editor-in-chief of the literary column of the *Taiwan People's News*, was arrested and put into prison twice for participating in the cultural movement against colonial rulers, and was hailed as the "Father of Modern Taiwanese Literature." At that time, under the influence of Japanese and mainland left-wing literature, progressive literary societies and journals mushroomed in Taiwan, most of which were related with Loa Ho. Examples included the Taiwan Literary Writers Association (台湾文艺作家协会), founded in 1931, which was related with the Japanese Proletarian Arts Federation and launched *Taiwan Literature* (《台湾文学》); and the *Southern Tone Stories* (《南音》), a semimonthly which was later strongly characteristic of local colors. In 1934, the Taiwan Literary Arts Alliance (台湾文艺联盟) was established, whose official journals were *Taiwan Literature and Art* (《台湾文艺》) and *Frontline Troops* (《先发部队》), and Loa Ho was elected as the first chairman of the Alliance. Loa Ho's "The Steelyard" (《一杆秤仔》), "Making Trouble" (《惹事》), "The Harvest" (《丰作》), and "It's a Pity She Died" (《可怜她死了》) were the earliest native-soil literary works in Taiwan, showing his sympathetic affections for peasants. "The Harvest" was about how cane-growing peasants had harvested but were exploited by Japanese sugar manufacturing companies, very similar to the mainland stories of "Spring Silkworm" and "The Harvest Bigger by a Bushel" (《多收了三五斗》) about harvests turning into disaster, but this one was obviously attacking the colonists. This piece was translated by Yang

[7] Lu Xun: "A Few Words on 'The Question of Labor'" (《写在〈劳动问题〉之前》), *Complete Works of Lu Xun*, Vol. 3, Beijing: People's Literature Press, 1981, p. 425.

38.15. Loa Ho

Kui into Japanese in 1936 to be published in a progressive journal in Tokyo, evidence that before the war, there was room for left-wing literature, which was impossible without the support of Japanese left-wing intellectuals.

Now we come to the Taiwanese literature during the war. The environment here was harsher than in any other Japanese-occupied areas: in 1937 Taiwan adopted the "wartime system," and the colonial government took high-handed policies, including prohibiting Chinese courses in schools and prohibiting Chinese newspapers, so that writing in Chinese was totally impossible. Meanwhile, the Taiwan Literature Patriotic Association (台湾文学奉公会) was founded to befriend writers and fabricate Kominka literary works. For a while, most Chinese literary journals were closed down, and what remained that came at all close to literature was nothing but Japanese leisurely literature and art-for-art's-sake literature. The Japanese quarterly *Taiwan Literature* (《台湾文学》), launched in 1941, was the only journal dominated by Chinese writers during this period of time. The editor-in-chief of this journal was Zhang Wenhuan, and a few Japanese writers (those with integrity and courage) living in Taiwan contributed writings to the journal; it lasted for two years before being closed down by the colonial authorities. Most writers of *Taiwan Literature* followed the tradition of native-soil literature, like Yang Kui, Wu Zhuoliu (吴浊流), Lü Heruo (吕赫若), and Long Yingzong (龙瑛宗). This was a period when Taiwan literature experienced the most special roundabout development: a group of local writers wrote, sharply or vaguely, a number of literary works in Japanese to resist against the colonial ruling and against being internalized by colonial literature. Yang Kui (1905–1985) was a native of Sinhua in central Tainan. Before the war, he was a member of the Taiwan Literary Arts Alliance, launched the monthly *New Taiwanese Literature* (《台湾新文学》), and wrote the socialist fiction *Shinbun Haitatsu* (*The Paperboy*) in Japanese. He had studied Marxism when he was young, was arrested in Japan for joining a parade, and was then arrested a dozen times in Taiwan for organizing peasant protests; on his wedding night he was put into prison together with his wife, and he was imprisoned for twelve years from 1949 by the KMT government for supporting the February Twenty-Eighth movement. He was called "an uncrushable rose" for his unyielding

38.16. Portrait of young Yang Kui

38.17. Yang Kui in 1937–1938

and persevering spirit in spite of so many adversities. *The Paperboy* was based on Yang's own experience when he sent newspapers for a Tokyo dispatch office in Japan. He submitted the short story to Loa Ho to be serialized under the pseudonym "Yang Da" (杨达), and it was Loa Ho who changed the pseudonym to "Yang Kui," reminding one of the character Li Kui in *Water Margin* who was famous for resisting against injustice. The novel was prohibited before its seri-alization was completed, and with the sup-port of Japanese writers Tokunaga Sunao and others, it was elected as an excellent work by *Bungei Jihyo* (*Literary Review*) in Tokyo, and thus was fully published. During the war, in 1942, he published his famous "Mama Goose Gets Married" (《鹅妈妈出嫁》), contrasting the beau-tiful illusions of intellectuals studying in Japan with the cruel reality back home. Wu Zhuoliu (1900–1976) was a native of Xinpu, Hsinchu, and he was born to a rich intellectual family with national integ-rity. His Japanese novels were expressions of his repressed indignation and fierce national consciousness. "The Doctor's Mother" (《先生妈》) was published in 1944. Set against the background of

38.18. Wu Zhuoliu in 1975, shortly before his death

"Kominka" and "speaking national language (Japanese) at home" promoted by the colonial rulers, the story was about the incompatible conflict between two generations, the mother and her son. The son was enslaved easily, while the mother refused to speak Japanese and wear kimono, and she insisted on tearing the kimono into pieces before she died, so that she could see her ancestors clean and neat. Wu Zhuoliu risked his life writing during the war, and after the retrocession, he published his Japanese novel *Orphan of Asia* (《亚细亚的孤儿》), which was translated into Chinese, an epic novel that reflected the entire society through an individual's personal experience. The protagonist, Hu Taiming, was a young intellectual born to an old-style landlord family in Taiwan, and traveled between Taiwan, Japan, and the mainland. At first, he accepted the Japanized education, but one case after another of stimulation, sinking, and awakening finally made him a "madman" in Taiwan who turned the entire colonial society in Taiwan upside down. There were many complicated characters in this novel, showing the author's excellence in organizing the structure. The novel created a nostalgic atmosphere, and the concept of "orphan of Asia" was a metaphor of the huge predicament of the Taiwan people who were separated from their motherland. Wu Zhuoliu always maintained the courage to expose the evilness of society; after the war was ended, he saw the hidden secret of the KMT taking over Taiwan and exposed them in his satirical works "Potsdam Section Chief" (《波茨坦科长》) and "Cunning Ape" (《狡猿》). Lü Heruo (1914–1947) was good at writing the history of Taiwan peasant families, and his representative works included "The Oxcart" (《牛车》) and "Peace with the Whole Family" (《合家平安》). These writers learned from Loa Ho and had a strong national consciousness. Enduring colonial suppression, they were extremely sensitive and sharp, and became the backbone of realistic writers concerned with life.

Another group of writers gathering around *Taiwan Literature* had their special artistic styles. Zhang Wenhuan (1909–1978), founder of the journal, did a lot of work to unite the writers of Taiwan. He was born to a merchant family in Meishan Township, Chiayi County. He dealt with the colonial authorities during the occupation period, but as can be seen from his works, he was quite aware of the overall national interest. In his stories about the countryside, even those about the conflicts within rich families, such as "Capon" (《阉鸡》), he explored the subtleties of human nature. "The Geisha House" (《艺旦之家》) was about the mishaps of a geisha who was a foster daughter and her unfortunate love stories, as well as her complicated relationships with society and her own family. The author had great sympathy for common people. One could not see sharp class conflicts in Zhang's realistic pieces, and he was good at detailed and layered psychological descriptions, showing a high artistic style through his deliberate and skilled narrative. Long Yingzong (1911–1999) had read extensively about Western literature in Japanese when he was a student. In 1937 he published his maiden work, "A Small Town with Papaya Trees"

(《植有木瓜树的小镇》), expressing the disillusionment of young intellectuals in Taiwan. The piece attracted attention from critics for its obvious Western influence in terms of plot arrangement and narrative skills. "The White Mountain Chain" (《白色的山脉》) did not have a clear-cut plot or subject matter, but was about a homeless scholar imagining other people's homes and identities and his sentimental feelings aroused by revisiting an old haunt. Long Yingzong's literary works were his reflection and analysis on the pathologies of modern people, such as wandering and hesitation, internal weakness and lack of action, from a modernist perspective. Thus his fictions showed an obvious modernist tendency, in which characterization gave way to psychological exploration and a coherent plot to the creation of atmosphere and images, and they could be considered the beginning of aesthetic modernist literary writings in Taiwan.

After the war and the retrocession of Taiwan, the entry of the KMT government brought about a series of political changes. After the "national language," namely Japanese, was abolished, there was a gap in Taiwan literature due to the "loss of language." Many old writers had to learn Chinese to start writing again. For example, Yang Kui learned Chinese from his little daughter who was at primary school, and wrote his first Chinese piece "Spring Light Cannot Be Shut Out" (《春光关不住》) as late as 1957. The retrocession also attracted many mainland writers to Taiwan, such as Xu Shouchang, Tai Jingnong, Li Liewen, and Xie Bingying. They could not dominate the literary circle in Taiwan, however; this did not happen until a group of southbound writers came to Taiwan after the retreat of the KMT in 1949. One writer spanning the occupation period and the 1960s was Zhong Lihe (钟理和, 1915–1960), a major writer of native-soil literature. He was a native of Pingtung County, southern Taiwan,

and had gone to Shenyang to resist against a forced marriage, and had been living in Beiping for a while. Therefore in 1945, he published *Oleander* (《夹竹桃》) in Beiping, which was the only collection of short stories published during his lifetime and recorded his impressions of the everyday lives of ordinary people on the mainland. From the retrocession until the 1950s, Zhong Lihe completed most of his native-soil literary works in the countryside of southern Taiwan in spite of great difficulties in the form of poverty and illness and his son's death. Only a few of his works were published in the literary supplement of the *United Daily News* (《联合报》), edited by Lin Haiyin (林海音), and his novel *Li Mountain Farm* (《笠山农场》), written with painstaking

38.19. A signed photo of Zhong Lihe, from which we can see he was a simple literary youth from the foot of Li Mountain

38.20. Insisting on an independent marriage to his wife, Zhong Taimei, Zhong Lihe had left his hometown and gone to the northeast

38.21. *Oleander*, Zhong Lihe's only literary work published during his lifetime was a collection of short stories, published in Beiping

effort, was not published until his death at the age of forty-five (his *Complete Works* was not published until the 1970s). He wrote with pure vernacular and new literary style, and his simplicity and sincerity typical of the Hakkas of southern Taiwan was probably blended with the resolution of northerners. He wrote a short story entitled "Old Country Folk" (《原乡人》). The concept of "old country folk" was perhaps different from that of "orphan" raised by Wu Zhuoliu in their implications, but both expressed the indignation of the Taiwan people about the fact that they belonged to nowhere. For his entire life, Zhong Lihe was an intellectual exile on both sides of the Taiwan Strait, and his cries that "the blood of old country folks could only stop boiling after they return to their old country," still linger on.

In the 1950s, the literature of Hong Kong, Taiwan, and mainland China were all shrouded in the dark clouds of the Cold War. The mainland confronted Taiwan due to political reasons, and within Hong Kong there was conflict between left-wing and nonleft-wing elements. After the 1960s, modernist literature and new popular literature in Hong Kong and Taiwan prospered. But back at the end of the 1940s, Hong Kong again served its historical function as a "refuge": a number of left-wing elite intellectuals were gathering there and conducted special literary critical activities. Seen from a historical point of view, the conflicts inherent to these critical activities would later become an opportunity and lay preparations for the literature of the "People's Republic." This will be discussed in Chapter 40.

THIRTY NINE

FROM PEASANTS TO URBAN CITIZENS

New Momentum for the Development of Popular
Literature

I N T H E 1 9 4 0 S , N O M A T T E R I N W H I C H P O L I T I C A L A R E A , popularization of literature changed from empty talks among scholars into a concrete reality, and thus brought vigor and vitality to literature during the Anti-Japanese War.

A brief review of the historical evolution of popular literature of the past several decades would be helpful here. Originally late-Qing urban popular literature was the absolute mainstream of Chinese literature as modern Chinese cities began to emerge, but soon after that, New Literature, which was an elite literature, proudly came to the foreground in the literary circle, and native-soil enlightenment literature, which took the transformation of the Chinese national character as its mission, gained a footing. Thus urban popular literature, while making its progress toward modernity, was gradually marginalized as a nonintellectual literature. The May Fourth literature that spread new ideas and created new forms made educating and representing people its responsibility, raised the banner of "commoners' literature," and intellectuals from Peking University did not avoid any obscene lyrics when they publicly gathered ballads from the common people; at the same time, intellectuals began translating the literature of weak nations and folk literature of foreign countries, and folklore studies and cultural anthropology were introduced to China; all these helped new literary writers turn their eyes to ordinary people. However, this was not enough to achieve the "May Fourth popular literature" promoted by writers of New Literature, for they never took the reception and response of ordinary people into consideration, but just forged ahead with determination.

Things changed in the 1930s. From the very beginning, left-wing literary writers put on their agenda the important goal of building "popular art and literature." With the establishment of the League of Left-Wing Writers, a Research Society of Popularization of Literature and Art (文艺大众化研究会) was founded within the League, and the journal *Popular Literature* was launched. Multiple discussions on popularization and popular language were held, and the creation of popular art and literature was actively promoted. During this process, the comments on popularization by Qu Qiubai and Lu Xun were especially significant. By 1932, Qiu Qiubai had written and published a series of articles, including "The Real Questions of Proletarian Popular Literature and Art" (《普洛大众文艺的现实问题》), which led to continuous discussions. Qu made several points on this issue. Firstly, he reiterated that the importance of "popular art and literature" was "a central issue of proletarian literary movement, and it is a concrete task to be accomplished in order to seize the leadership of literary revolution."[1] This was the fundamental standpoint of Qu Qiubai, that this issue should be considered from the viewpoint of proletarian politics and the purpose was to seize political power, and thus they should first win over less-educated people. The purpose of popularization was to "enlighten people!" Secondly, he fiercely attacked the most serious flaw of the May Fourth literary movement, "Europeanization," criticizing it as detaching itself from the masses. Therefore, on the issue of literary language, he thought, up to the time he wrote the article, the situation still featured a split, "Chinese Europeanized young people read May Fourth-style vernacular, while commoners read old-style vernacular," so that "one more linguistic revolution is needed."[2] In this regard, he commented that the "Europeanized New Literature" had been reduced to a "new classical Chinese language," and he spared no effort in expounding how to create "new-style vernacular," "really clear and smooth modern Chinese language," and "new linguistics of standard modern Chinese language."[3] Thirdly, one should distinguish two totally different types of "popular

39.1. Since the League of Left-Wing Writers was established in the 1930s, the left-wing literary writers made "popular literature" their major goal, but the cover of the left-wing journal *Popular Literature* adopted quite a Westernized pop style

---

[1]   Qu Qiubai: "Europeanized Literature and Art" (《欧化文艺》), *Collected Works of Qu Qiubai (Literature)*, Vol. 1, Beijing: People's Literature Press, 1985, p. 492.

[2]   Qu Qiubai: "The Real Questions of Proletarian Popular Literature and Art," *Collected Works of Qu Qiubai (Literature)*, Vol. 1, Beijing: People's Literature Press, 1985, p. 465.

[3]   These wordings were found all over Qu Qiubai's articles, such as in "The Real Questions of Proletarian Popular Literature and Art" and "Europeanized Literature and Art."

literature." He was strongly against the "reaction-ary popular literature" that featured philistine mar-tial arts or immortal swordsmen or those mistaking robbers as upright magistrates, but actively pro-moted creating "revolutionary popular literature." Talking about the revolutionary popular literature in its earlier period, he thought one could use old forms to present revolutionary and class-oriented content. Qu Qiubai practiced what he preached, and took the lead to create popular literary and art works with folk art forms from as early as the September Eighteenth Incident in the northeast and the January Twenty-Eighth Incident in Shanghai. Examples of this included his "Battling Scenes in Shanghai" (《上海打仗景致》), imitating the tunes of "Wuxi Scenery" (无锡景), and his stories written in vernacular storytelling style, "A Man from the Upper Yangtze River Broke Up with His Mistress" (《江北人拆姘头》) and "The Hero's Clever Strategy to Offer Shanghai (to the Japanese Invaders)" (《英雄巧计献上海》). He also wrote the lyrics of "The Japanese Sending Troops" (《东洋人出兵》) in a Shanghai dialect edition and a northern dia-lect edition. The Shanghai dialect edition opened like this:

39.2. Important article by Qu Qiubai to promote proletarian popular literature

> Talking about the Japanese sending troops to Manchuria,
> Let's first ask what happened.
> It's because there is a group of rich Chinese people,
> Who are cruel and brutal like wolves.
> They rob the poor days and nights,
> And at last lost their heads.
> Their knives are used to kill workers,
> Their guns are used to kill peasants.
> When Japanese troops occupied three provinces in the northeast,
> They were cowards like turtles retracting their heads,
> The commander-in-chief ordered to withdraw,
> And the Kuomintang is as calm as they are.
> They just press us the ordinary people,
> Offering the lives of 400 million people as a favor.[4]

Obviously, when Qu Qiubai, who had not yet gone to the Central Soviet Area in Jiangxi but still remained in Shanghai, wrote these literary works, his imagined audiences (readers) were not peasants but Shanghai citizens

[4]   Qu Qiubai: "The Japanese Sending Troops," *Collected Works of Qu Qiubai (Literature)*, Vol. 2, Beijing: People's Literature Press, 1985, p. 376. This poem was first published in *Literary Guide*, Vol. 1, Issue 5, September 28, 1931, and it was printed on propaganda leaflets for distribution.

39.3. Manuscript of "In Defense of Comic Strips" (《〈连环图画〉辩护》), an article written by Lu Xun in 1932 as he participated in the discussions on popularization of literature and art

(including workers who were less educated). It is safe to say that the "popularization" at this time was actually citizenization, for the center of proletarian revolution was not yet transferred from the city to the countryside. Lu Xun's views on popularization were in general similar to those of Qu Qiubai. Lu Xun, too, was keenly aware of the flaw of New Literature, and he agreed on building "popular linguistics" by adopting such old forms as comic strips, and he agreed to achieve popularization of New Literature with the help of political support. But within the left-wing literary camp, Lu Xun was not as one-sided as others, and the biggest difference between him and Qu Qiubai was that he took an analytical approach to "Europeanization" and did not deny it as worthless. He agreed to create a new-style vernacular language with people's lively language, but did not reject strict and precise Europeanized language, saying that one should still "give support to the precise 'Europeanized' language, for the grammar of Chinese language lacked 'precision,' and surely the popular Chinese language will not be ambiguous forever. For example, the word 'Europeanization' mentioned by those opposed to Europeanization is not an inherent Chinese word."[5] This entailed his major disagreement with Qu Qiubai on the issues of "liberal translation" and "paraphrase." Lu Xun's view on "liberal translation" is unfamiliar to today's readers. He not only had the intention to import Europeanized grammar to China, but wanted to steal fire from foreign countries to cook his meat, with the intention of making some people in power feel uncomfortable.[6] Lu Xun advocated adopting old forms not just to "enlighten people," and he was even more strongly opposed to making folk culture the center; he insisted on maintaining ties with the progressive art and literature of the world, in order to create modern Chinese literature and art. He said adopting old forms was "at the same time the beginning of new forms and the transformation of the old," and that "when old forms are adopted, certain things must be removed while others must be added, resulting in a new form, a change."[7] In all these comments, Lu Xun sought to affirm and perfect May

[5]   Lu Xun: "Letter in Reply to Mr. Cao Juren" (《答曹聚仁先生信》), *Complete Works of Lu Xun*, Vol. 6, Beijing: People's Literature Press, 1981, p. 77.

[6]   For details of this view, see Lu Xun's "'Hard Translation' and the 'Class Character of Literature'" (《〈硬译〉与〈文学的阶级性〉》), collected in *Two Hearts* (《二心集》), Beijing: People's Literature Press, 2006.

[7]   Lu Xun: "On the 'Adoption of Old Forms'" (《论〈旧形式的采用〉》), *Complete Works of Lu Xun*, Vol. 6, Beijing: People's Literature Press, 1981, pp. 22, 24.

Fourth New Literature. Indeed, after Lu Xun's death, in all discussions on national forms and art and literature for workers, peasants, and soldiers held in the 1940s, there was an antithesis between the standpoints of participants concerning how to evaluate world literature and May Fourth literature.

The ambiguity concerning whether the intended readers of popularized literature should be citizens or peasants remained until the eve of the Anti-Japanese War. May Fourth New Literature had radical young urban students as its readers, and Mandarin Duck and Butterfly literature occupied the market share of citizens' readings. This was the real literary scene of that time; just as Qu Qiubai had said, "Europeanized young people read May Fourth-style vernacular, while commoners read old-style vernacular." Nobody cared about what peasants, the majority of the Chinese population, read. The thriving modern native-soil literature represented the countryside, but it was not to be read by peasants, who could only pick up the leftovers of urban popular literature from the songbooks sold in temple fairs or country fairs, outdoor opera performances and teashops and storytellers in nearby towns, mostly stories of the Three Kingdoms and romantic stories. "Peasant literature" simply did not exist. Citizens could read literary works written by urban popular writers, but they were for a long time marginalized by New Literature. According to Lu Xun, there was no "commoners' literature" in the real sense of the term. He said: "Somebody writes novels or poetry with commoners – workers or peasants – as their subjects, and we call it commoners' literature, but actually it is not commoners' literature, … it is just written by someone who look down upon commoners' lives and writes in the name of commoners."[8] The "literature written to represent the citizens' society" from the vantage point of New Literature that overlooked the crowd, then, was certainly not "citizens' literature." From Ye Shengtao to Zhang Tianyi, they formed a new literary tradition that criticized small private owners and small intellectuals. And the situation became even more complicated when Lao She rose in the literary standings with his novels *The Philosophy of Old Zhang* and *Thus Speaks Master Zhao*, serialized in *Fiction Monthly*, the authoritative belles lettres journal. Lao She abandoned the purely critical attitude of New Literature toward civil society. He reflected the inevitable decline of traditional civil society through the images of old-style Beijing citizens, but was even harsher in his criticism of new-style citizens and intellectuals, especially their blind following of new fashions and the profit-seeking characteristics of a business-oriented society. Lao She's criticism of civil society featured attacks on both sides, but what deserved more attention was that in his writings, the poor lower-class civilian characters had gradually played the "leading role." The everyday tragedies of poor citizens

---

[8] Lu Xun: "Literature of a Revolutionary Period" (《革命时代的文学》), *Complete Works of Lu Xun*, Vol. 3, Beijing: People's Literature Press, 1981, p. 422.

were put on show in a comedic form, and female citizens deserved more respect and sympathy. The author's temperament was similar to that of old-style citizens: quiet, honest, loyal, kind-hearted, and reasonable. Lao She did not agree on everything with citizens, but he obviously took dual perspectives to look at them, as both a new literary writer and a member of civil society. Therefore, his best works sung elegies for the old-style civil society while at the same time praised the self-respect of decent civilians, so that they were like multivoiced ensembles. Shanghai school literature, rising in Shanghai in the 1930s, also reflected the bustling, cosmopolitan city from a different perspective than Mandarin Duck and Butterfly literature. Mu Shiying's "Shanghai Foxtrot" was a story of city women of the upper bourgeois class or those as subsidiaries of the latter and "North and South Poles" was about the lumpenproletariat of the lower-class Wujiao Chang area, both manifesting the difference between the civil society in Shanghai and that of the north. By far, representative new literary writers representing the civil society of both the north and the south had emerged, as had the landmark of the modern transformation of the urban popular literature per se, which was Zhang Henshui, a master of urban popular novels. From the late 1920s to the early 1930s, Zhang Henshui's *The Story of A Noble Family* and *Fate in Tears and Laughter* won successes among civilian readers in the north and south simultaneously, but a native of Anhui as he was, his major achievement was to represent the society of Beijing. This was the general situation of modern urban popular literature and New Literature representing the civil society in Beijing and Shanghai. The literary works were certainly not "mass literature," but had countless ties with it (for example, Lao She was always associated with "mass literature" and "popular literature").

Chinese literature of the 1940s developed in a war of national defense, and facing the need to motivate millions of people, discussions on mass literature and national forms almost spanned the entire war. Before the League of Left-Wing Writers dissolved, Lu Xun raised the slogan of "mass literature of national revolutionary war" to contend with that of "national defense literature" within the organization. It certainly remained an empty slogan before Lu Xun's death, but after he died, it seemed possible that it could come true. The emergence of gun barrel poems, leaflet poems, street theater, civilian opera plays, popular novels, and various literary experiments to "put new wine in old bottles" (Lao She, for example, had adapted the form of drum lyrics), brought about new

39.4. Lower-class civil society always featured in Lao She's literary works. This was one of the illustrations of *Camel Xiangzi*: Xiangzi and Huniu (painted by Sun Zhijun)

opportunities for the development of mass literature. The second cooperation between the KMT and CPC and the fact that the CPC found its footing in northern Shaanxi, laid the foundation for the left-wing's literary massification in new situations. Mao Zedong's report on the Sixth Plenum of the Sixth Session in 1939 made it clear that "we can put Marxism into practice only when it is integrated with the specific characteristics of our country and acquires a definite national form," and that "foreign stereotypes must be abolished, there must be less singing of empty, abstract tunes, and dogmatism must be laid to rest, they must be replaced by the fresh, lively Chinese style and spirit that the common people of China love."[9] In 1940 Mao Zedong reiterated in "On New Democracy" that: "Chinese culture should have its own form, its own national form. National in form and new-democratic in content – such is our new culture today."[10] This entailed long-term discussions on the issue of "national forms" in Yan'an and Chongqing. In 1939, Zhou Yang, Xiao San, He Qifang, and Ai Siqi (艾思奇) of the "liberated region" published articles to show their approval and agreement with Mao's views. In 1940, *Ta Kung Pao* of the Nationalist-controlled area published Xiang Linbing's article entitled "On the Central Fountainhead of National Forms" (《论〈民族形式〉的中心源泉》), in which he emphasized the way to create new "national forms" was to use "folk art forms," and insisted that the May Fourth literature was a "lopsided development of literature that substitutes Chinese style and spirit with transplanted Europeanized and Japanized forms," and May Fourth art and literature were thus a "product of lopsidedly developed cities," and it was not the mainstream, but should take a subordinate role.[11] This caused debates, the key to which was whether the mass literature of the national war should inherit the May Fourth New Literature and assimilate the experience of world progressive literature to innovate modern Chinese "national forms." Guo Moruo, Mao Dun, and others expressed their significant viewpoints, and Hu Feng published the articles "May Fourth in Literature: In Memory of the May Fourth Movement" (《文学上的五四——为五四纪念写》) and "On the Origins and Main Issues of the Problem of National Form" (《论民族形式问题的提出和重点》) and the book *On the Issue of National Forms* to defend the May Fourth tradition of looking to the outside world that should not be distorted, and at the same time, he put forward his own views on the May Fourth literary revolution, which were different from those in "On

9 Mao Zedong: "The Role of the Chinese Communist Party in the National War" (《中国共产党在民族战争中的地位》), *Selected Works of Mao Zedong*, Vol. 2, Beijing: People's Press, 1966, pp. 499–500.

10 Mao Zedong: "On New Democracy," *Selected Works of Mao Zedong*, Vol. 2, Beijing: People's Press, 1966, p. 667.

11 Xiang Linbing: "On the Central Fountainhead of National Forms," published on the "Frontline" supplement of Chongqing's *Ta Kung Pao*, March 20, 1940.

New Democracy": "the May Fourth literary revolutionary movement of the Chinese people with civilians as its leader was nothing but a new outgrowth of global progressive literary tradition that had accumulated for several hundred years since the rise of civil society."[12] Hu Feng's view that integrated the May Fourth, the mass, and the civilians was the minority point of view within the left-wing camp, but it directly inherited Lu Xun's legacy.

By that time, the Rectification movement in Yan'an in 1942 had begun. In the field of art and literature, the purpose of the Rectification movement involved disciplining Ding Ling, Ai Qing, and the elites within the left-wing camp who tended to criticize the base area, containing the tendency of closing the door and raising standards at Lu Xun College, educating Xiao Jun who took a liberal way of life, and waging a severe campaign against Wang Shiwei. In May that year, Mao Zedong delivered two speeches at the Yan'an Forum on Literature and Art, which were integrated into the "Talks at the Yan'an Forum on Literature and Art" that later had a far-reaching influence. The "Talks" raised two points: that the revolutionary art and literature should "serve the masses" and "how to serve the masses." As for the issue of "for whom," art and literature should first serve workers, peasants, and soldiers, and then it should serve urban petty-bourgeois working people and intellectuals. This was the "worker–peasant–soldier orientation" of art and literature, which had its rationality in the context of the base area of the CPC, but the political and class base of literature and art thus emphasized was, seen retrospectively, one-sided and oversimplified. As for "how to serve the masses," it emphasized that writers should shift their stand and remold their thinking. This almost overthrew the historical identity of intellectuals as forerunners and enlighteners of people, and became the source of many problems in later years. Other discourses on this issue involved the relationship between popularization and raising standards: "the raising of standards is based on popularization, while popularization is guided by the raising of standards," quite a dialectical expounding of the guiding principle of massification; but the inherent law of art and literature was ignored, and the conclusion to "put the political criterion first and the artistic criterion second" was not rational, but took politics alone into account and confused art and literature with propaganda. In all, as the programmatic

39.5. Third edition of Hu Feng's *On the Issue of National Forms*, published by Petrel Bookstore in December 1950

---

[12] Hu Feng, "On the Issue of National Forms," *Collected Criticism of Hu Feng* (《胡风评论集》),Vol. 2, Beijing: People's Literature Press, 1984, p. 234. The emphasis marks are quoted from the original text.

document of the CPC's art and literary policies, the "Talks" played a major role in the special conditions in the wartime countryside for the purpose of creating literature loved by the people as well as serving, educating, and mobilizing the masses. Under the guidance of this principle, the mainstream literature in the "liberated region" for the first time became "mass literature for peasants." The "Talks" thus established their own theoretical and policy-related authority in the forming of literature in the "liberated region" and in the literary development of the New China.

The mass art and literature in Yan'an indeed became a wartime spectacle. The Yangko opera *Brother and Sister Clear Wasteland* and *The Couple Learning to Read* and the new folk opera *The White-Haired Girl*, the new Peking opera, street poetry, wall newspapers, popular stories, and especially Zhao Shuli's novels (which went so far as to be awarded a title "the Zhao Shuli direction" in 1947), were considered the literary achievements after the principles established in Mao Zedong's "Talks" were put into practice. In fact, Zhao Shuli's "Blackie Gets Married" (《小二黑结婚》) was written and published before the "Talks," and it drew the conclusion almost simultaneously that art and literature should serve "workers, peasants, and soldiers," especially "peasants" in the base area and "peasants in military uniforms." This principle of "massification" was not groundless, but taking a step forward from the popularization of literature and modern vernacular literature started several decades before. Zhao Shuli was educated in a new-style school and was influenced by May Fourth literature, but he harshly attacked the latter for its tendency of being detached from the masses. He ridiculed the literary works after the May Fourth movement, saying: "Most of the people who really like to read these kinds of things are those who are learning to write them, and when they

鲁艺演出秧歌剧《兄妹开荒》之一。扮演者王大化、李波。

39.6. Yangko opera *Brother and Sister Clear Wasteland* performed by the Lu Xun Arts College; the actors are Wang Dahua and Li Bo

39.7. *Brother and Sister Clear Wasteland* performed by Xing Ye (邢野) and others around 1942

39.8. *Brother and Sister Clear Wasteland* performed by the Lu Xun Arts College in Yan'an in 1943

become somebody in the literary arena, what they wrote will actually be read by someone new, so that they will, in turn, learn this and become somebody in the literary arena."[13] Therefore, he resolved not to become a "writer of the literary arena," but to be a "writer of the bookstall." "The intended readers of most of my works are literate people in the countryside, and I want them to present my works to illiterate people around them."[14] His inclusion of illiterate peasants as his indirect readers was certainly meaningful. He wrote about peasants in the "liberated region," and even for such a lengthy novel as *The Rhymes of Li Youcai*, one could see the label "a popular story" on its cover. Between the ideological intention of political writing and the reality of peasant life, he seemed to have found a niche for which he himself, as a peasant writer, was particularly suited, and it involved the "problems" in the "countryside" where the "peasants" lived, the subjects he claimed to write about. "I myself often call my works 'problem novels.' Why? Because my novels are all about the problems I saw when I went to work in the countryside, and I feel those problems, if left unsolved, will become obstacles for our work. I feel obligated to raise them."[15] This concept of "problem novel" originated in the May Fourth period, but Zhao's novels were certainly different from the enlightening novels of that period. The problem addressed in the May Fourth period was a broad and ultimate problem about the entire human life, arising out of people's perplexity and exploration as they witnessed an entirely new modern society replacing

---

[13] Quoted from Li Pu (李普): "Impressions of Zhao Shuli" (《赵树理印象记》), published in the inaugural issue of *Changjiang Literature and Art* (《长江文艺》), June 1949.

[14] Zhao Shuli: "Some Words on Writing 'The Sanliwan Village'" (《〈三里湾〉写作前后》), *Collected Works of Zhao Shuli* (《赵树理文集》), Vol. 4, Beijing: Chinese Workers' Press, 1980, p. 1486.

[15] Zhao Shuli: "Several Issues on My Current Literary Writing" (《当前创作中的几个问题》), *Collected Works of Zhao Shuli*, Vol. 4, Beijing: Chinese Workers' Press, 1980, p. 1651.

39.9. Zhao Shuli's "Blackie Gets Married" started a literature "for peasants"

39.10. Sanxiangu and Erzhuge in Zhao Shuli's "Blackie Gets Married," a woodcut illustration by Gu Yuan

the old one. Zhao Shuli's "problem" was a much narrower one, about concrete political work, but it was a practical question closely related to peasants. As a new regime brought about huge changes in its jurisdiction, it also brought various people, new tendencies, and new conflicts to the countryside. Zhao Shuli was a eulogist, but he found many "problems" from his own perspective as a political worker living in the "liberated region" for a long time, such as young peasants' freedom of marriage being throttled by evil forces or outdated conventions ("Blackie Gets Married" and "Marriage Registration" [《登记》]); the disagreement between the cadres who were separated from peasants and led by evildoers in the mobilization of the masses on the one hand, and those who became a harmonious whole with peasants and served the latter wholeheartedly and worked in their interests on the other (*The Rhymes of Li Youcai*); and the widespread problem of infringing on the interests of middle peasants by enlarging the scope of attacks in order to distribute movable property in the early stage of land reform (*The Just Prevails* [《邪不压正》]). These findings were penetrating, and some were very timely. Just imagine what obstructions he would meet writing about evil cadres and backward cadres in his novels; we know that simply finding and raising these problems was not a clear path to a new world. In the countryside after "liberation," Zhao Shuli gradually changed from a "political worker" to a "countryside goer," and he continued finding "problems," such as the numerous conflicts between the production of agricultural cooperatives and rectification ("Practice, Practice" [《锻炼锻炼》]) and the problems of the grandiose working style in the countryside caused by the Great Leap Forward movement ("The Honest-to-Goodness Worker Pan

Yongfu" [《实干家潘永福》]), but he was harshly criticized again and again, and finally died for raising these "problems," which was indeed a tragedy. Zhao Shuli's direction of writing about "peasants' problems" was in the end denied by the power that promoted the "Zhao Shuli direction." For all his life, he insisted on working and writing in the interests of peasants, showing the good conscience of an intellectual.

In terms of fictional style and language, Zhao Shuli's massification involved restoring the folk tradition after assimilating and understanding the May Fourth experience and his reinvention of folk art. With the intended readers being peasants, he restored the tradition of storytelling and innovated the national storytelling narrative form. Based on the colloquial language of peasants, he integrated modern political discourses and local everyday language (he did not use too much local dialect) and created a written vernacular Chinese easily understood by peasants from the north and south. Here are some examples of his language:

> In Yanjiashan there is a Li Youcai, whose nickname is "Never Die."
>
> The person is around fifty and without land, living on grazing cattle for his fellow villagers, and sometimes guards crops during summer and autumn seasons. He is a bachelor living alone and without family. He often likes to say some funny things, like "when I am fed, nobody is hungry in my family; locking the door, I don't care to starve the little bench."[16]

This was the opening of *The Rhymes of Li Youcai*. The author made flexible use of traditional narrative techniques, presenting the major character of the story at the very beginning. The small words he used were simple and smooth, like "a bachelor living alone"; "when I am fed, nobody is hungry in my family" is an expression understood by both northerners and southerners, and the "little bench" made the language even more lively and fresh. The nickname "Never Die" was not immediately explained but left there for readers to think about: how could such an unremarkable person be nicknamed "Never Die"? Please read on. Let's see another paragraph:

> Young people claim they want to consult the heavenly oracle, but what they really want is to view the heavenly image. San Xiangu secretly guesses what's on their minds, so she is dressed more gorgeously, her hair combed more smoothly, her jewelry polished brighter, and the powder on her face spread more evenly. The young people cannot help following her here and there.
>
> …

---

[16] Zhao Shuli: *The Rhymes of Li Youcai, Collected Works of Zhao Shuli*, Vol. 1, Beijing: Chinese Workers' Press, 1980, p. 17.

Xiaoqin is eighteen years now. Frivolous villagers say she is much prettier than her mother was when she was young. Young lads are always finding something to say to Xiaoqin. Xiaoqin goes washing clothes, young lads immediately rush to wash their own; Xiaoqin goes to pick wild vegetables, young lads immediately rush to pick their own.[17]

These are the paragraphs of "Blackie Gets Married" that explain that San Xiangu and her daughter Xiaoqin were both beauties. The author used four parallel sentences to write about San Xiangu, which was not peasants' language, but an occasional use brought no harm. Here we see the mother still needed to be dressed up, and there were artificial elements in her beauty. Writing about Xiaoqin, in contrast, the author did not use a single word

39.11. Li Youcai, a character from *The Rhymes of Li Youcai*, a woodcut illustration by Gu Yuan

about her appearance or clothes, but used the rhetorical device of foil; simple and clear as the description, every reader would immediately see that Xiaoqin was prettier. During the May Fourth period, Hu Shi had talked about his ideal: "We champion the literary revolution in order to create a national-language literature in China. Only with a national-language literature can there be a literary national language. Only with a literary national language can there be a real national language."[18] Thirty years later, the goal of "literary national language" proposed in 1918 had, at least partly, been achieved in Zhao Shuli's novels.

When "Blackie Gets Married" broke through obstruction and sold 40,000 copies in a short time in the rural base area, it was hard to ignore Zhao Shuli's significance. He managed to find a balance between political writing and writing for peasants, between the Western form of novel and traditional Chinese storytelling. His concept of "masses" was not a rigid one. He said: "When I wrote 'Blackie Gets Married,' it was common that the peasant masses were illiterate, and thus I had to think about whether they could understand when they read or heard the story. I don't know if you have noticed the fact that I did not use such words as 'however' and 'therefore' in 'Blackie Gets Married,'

---

[17] Zhao Shuli: "Blackie Gets Married," *Collected Works of Zhao Shuli*, Vol. 1, Beijing: Chinese Workers' Press, 1980, pp. 2–3.

[18] Hu Shi: "Toward a Constructive Theory of Literary Revolution," *New Youth*, Vol. 4, Issue 4, April 15, 1918.

39.12. *Changes in Li Village* by Zhao Shuli, published by New Knowledge Bookstore at the beginning of 1946

why? Because these were formulaic expressions used by intellectuals, and if I used them in my writings at that time, the peasant masses would not understand or feel comfortable." Then he said later there were more peasants who received middle school education and thus he would not avoid using such words as "however" and "therefore."[19] Zhao Shuli was fully aware where "mass literature" led to, and that it was ever-changing and boundless.

If "peasant literature" was a literary creation for the masses independent of market mechanisms and supported by political manipulation, the fashion of "civilian literature" in the Japanese-occupied region and Nationalist-controlled area represented by Zhang Ailing and Xu Xu, then, was a kind of urban popular literary creation under market mechanisms. In the latter case, a number of extremely successful popular literary works emerged in the market in the 1940s, including *Landscape of the North Pole* and *Lady in the Tower* (both by Wu Ming Shi), *The Love of a Ghost* and *Whistling Wind* (by Xu Xu), *Romances* (by Zhang Ailing), and *Ten Years of Marriage* (by Su Qing). And there were such left-leaning literary works that reflected the life and sentiments of urban citizens as *The Story of Xiaqiu* (by Huang Guliu) and *Hill Songs of Ma Fantuo* (by Yuan Shuipai [袁水拍], whose passages were often recited in the squares during the Anti-Hunger and Democratic movement later, and was as popular among urban citizens as the above-mentioned best sellers). This trend of popular literature was by no means an isolated incident, but an inevitable phenomenon in the wartime context that abided by the inherent laws of literature. Shanghai school literature, for example, having experienced New Sensationalist avant-garde writing, now showed the tendency to shift its focus from white-collar readers of office buildings to ordinary citizen readers, and thus became truly "popular." According to the documents uncovered so far, in the 1940s, Shao Xunmei, Mu Shiying, Yu Qie, Zhang Ailing, Su Qing, Dongfang Didong, and Shi Jimei and her fellow young women authors graduating from the aristocratic Dongwu University, had all contributed to urban tabloids. And Zhang Ailing was undoubtedly the best of them.

---

[19] Zhao Shuli: "Be the Hero of Your Own Life: Talks at the Forum on Literary Creation in the Zhuang Autonomous Region of Guangxi" (《做生活的主人——在广西壮族自治区文艺创作座谈会上的发言》), *Collected Works of Zhao Shuli*, Vol. 4, Beijing: Chinese Workers' Press, 1980, p. 1731.

Zhang Ailing was the spokesperson for the modern urban society of Shanghai. She claimed to write for Shanghainese, just like Zhao Shuli claimed to write for peasants. She said: "When I wrote this, I always thought of Shanghainese," that "only Shanghainese could understand the meaning behind my words."[20] She had a bone-deep love for Shanghai, where any of the apartment buildings, bustling noises on the street, streetcars, small grocery markets, pastry shops, and shaded avenues could arouse her strong sense of metropolis. Since her girlhood, she had liked reading *The Huangpu Tides* and *The Sing-Song Girls of Shanghai*, Zhang Henshui's novels, and Shanghai tabloids, and was extremely familiar with traditional urban popular literature. Therefore, when she herself began writing, she did not linger around the fashionable avenues, foreign-style buildings, and entertainment venues of Shanghai, but went deep into the families of civilians in Shanghai, from the impoverished old-style aristocratic families to the love stories and romances of ordinary house-wives, female clerks, marriage-seeking girls, and maidservants. She also wrote purely popular romances, such as *Chain of Rings*, *Eighteen Springs*, and *Xiao Ai* (《小艾》). She once said: "I have always had a special fondness for popular novels, especially for the characters whom the author does not need to explain, and for their sadness, happiness, separations, and unions. Some may say that popular novels are too superficial and lack depth, but no one can deny that bas-relief is still art."[21] She could see through the material-oriented philistine life of urban citizens, "once you cut through the waffle, only two things appear to remain: food and sex."[22] She wrote about these two things, but the "waffle" she wrote was by no means trivial. In *Love in a Fallen City*, the "waffle" was the contingency of human destiny in the wartime context; in *The Golden Cangue*, it was how money could diminish humanity; in all her stories about women she made serious inquiries about the sheer existence of women. Therefore, her romances about citizens had a sort of metaphysical exploration, which was why she was superior to Su Qing and Yu Qie. And it was for this reason that her urban popular literature appealed to both higher and lower tastes and had both new and old styles, so that both white-collar and blue-collar citizens understood and liked her novels.

Citizens certainly had a stronger faculty of understanding than peasants. Zhu Ziqing always attached importance to the status and future of post-May Fourth modern literary language, and thus when Mu Shiying and Zhang Tianyi rose in the literary circle, he paid attention to them with great enthusiasm, eager

[20] Zhang Ailing: "Shanghainese, After All" (《到底是上海人》), *Written on Water*, Shanghai: China Science Company, 1944, pp. 58, 59.

[21] Zhang Ailing: "So Much Regret" (《多少恨》), *Complete Works of Zhang Ailing* (《张爱玲典藏全集》), Vol. 9, Harbin: Harbin Press, 2003, p. 98.

[22] Zhang Ailing: "From the Ashes" (《烬余录》), *Written on Water*, Shanghai: China Science Company, 1944, p. 55.

39.13. First page of Zhang Ailing's work, *Tulip*, not included in any of her collections, which was serialized in *Small Daily* (《小日报》) in May 1947. Many Shanghai school writers contributed to tabloids

to see where the May Fourth vernacular language would lead.[23] Mu Shiying and Zhang Tianyi had different political leanings, but the civilian language they used highly agreed with their subjects. Qu Qiubai criticized Mu Shiying's political stands shown in his literary creation, but at first, he, too, paid equal attention to Zhang Tianyi and Mu Shiying.[24] Zhang Ailing was also outstanding in integrating modern civilian language into China's national language in her writings. She extracted words and expressions from civilians' spoken language, and like Zhao Shuli, she did not choose to use local dialects (she did not, like some tabloids, use the Shanghai vernacular), but created a refined and flexible written language suited to describing psychological activities, creating atmosphere, and innovatively using images. One may get a sense of the charming quality of Zhang's ingenious mixture of Europeanized language and traditional Chinese style:

> Shanghai thirty years ago on a moonlit night … maybe we did not get to see the moon of thirty years ago. To young people the moon of thirty years ago should be a reddish-yellow wet stain the size of a copper coin, like a teardrop on letter paper by To-yun Hsuan, worn and blurred. In old people's memory the moon of thirty years ago was gay, larger, rounder, and whiter than the moon now. But looked back on after thirty years on a rough road, the best of moons is apt to be tinged with sadness.[25]

This was the well-known opening of *The Golden Cangue*. The author used the conventional method of storytelling by making clear the time and venue of the story at the very beginning. The moon was a typical Chinese image, but it was depicted with a Europeanized long sentence. The stain size of a "copper coin,"

[23] See Zhu Ziqing: "On Vernacular Writings: Some Thoughts after Reading *North and South Poles* and *Little Peter*," p. 267. *North and South Poles* and *Little Peter* were, respectively, Mu Shiying and Zhang Tianyi's collections of short stories.

[24] "Just Painting Dogs" (《画狗吧》, an article on Zhang Tianyi) and "Red Radish" (《红萝卜》, an article on Mu Shiying), both collected in *Collected Works of Qu Qiubai (Literature)*, Vol. 1.

[25] Zhang Ailing: "The Golden Cangue," collected in *Romances*, enlarged and revised edition, Shanghai: Shanhe Book Company, 1946, p. 110. The ellipses are quoted from the original text.

the teardrop on "letter paper," these were vague imaginings of young people; "larger, rounder, and whiter" were words from colloquial language, plain but strong. No matter how bright old people's memories were, they were desolate, and desolation was the lingering tone set by Zhang Ailing at the beginning of her novel. Let's see another example:

> She was not a bird in a cage. A caged bird can still fly away when the trap is released. She was a bird sewn onto a screen – a white bird in clouds of golden thread, sewn on a satin screen of a depressing purple. After months and years, its feathers would start to fade, become moldy and rot. Even when it died, it would only die on the screen.[26]

This was the unusual imagination of Nie Chuanqing, the protagonist of "Jasmine Tea," when he was looking for his real father and conjecturing the destiny of his late mother (she): the bird on the screen was dead, but it used to be the vibrant life of a girl. The author used the ornate words and expressions

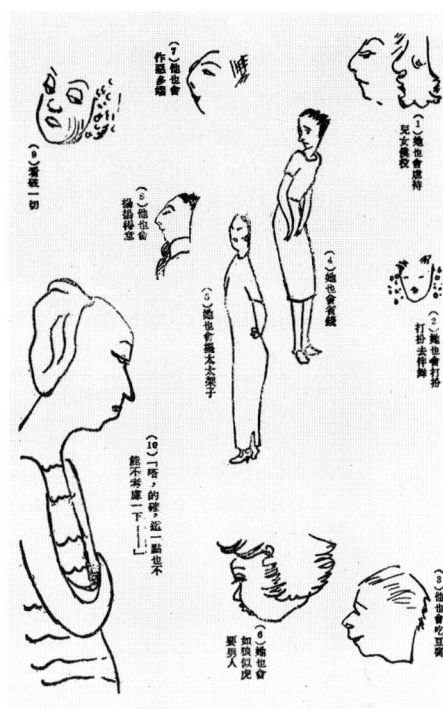

39.14. Zhang Ailing's sketches entitled "Little People," showing her understanding and criticism of the urban petty bourgeoisie

often used in old-style novels to describe gorgeous adornments: the purple, golden, and white colors, and clouds of golden thread sewn on satin, and birds, but all these could not conceal the sadness. Then she used many lively colloquial-style sentences ending with "*liao*" (了, an auxiliary word signifying "the end," which was also frequently used by Xiao Hong) to help deepen the chilly atmosphere. This writing style was more easily understood and accepted by Chinese readers, and the national language used deserved high praise.

Zhang Ailing's popular literature was about urban citizens of the metropolis; it raised the standard after gaining popularity, and on the other hand, it was closely related with world literature. By the 1950s, this literary genre was discontinued for historical reasons, while seen retrospectively today, its vitality is by no means inferior to the peasants' "popular" literature represented by Zhao Shuli, which had been the mainstream for a long time but suddenly disappeared after reaching its glorious peak. Is the persistence of Zhang Ailing-fever just proof of fashion going round in circles? Or is it because peasants would eventually enter cities and thus the narrowing of difference between cities

---

[26] Zhang Ailing: "Jasmine Tea," *Romances*, enlarged and revised edition, Shanghai: Shanhe Book Company, 1946, p. 200.

and the countryside would end up with urban citizens being the main body (instead of "peasants being the main body" proposed by the people's communes)? Is it that the day will come when the popular nature of peasants and urban citizens becomes one given the advanced development of the economy? I still remember there was a short story harshly criticized in the 1950s entitled "Between Me and My Wife" (《我们夫妇之间》), written by Xiao Yemu (萧也牧), about the conflict between the peasant wife and her citizen husband after they both entered the city. The wife raised a sharp question: "Are we coming here to reform the city, or are we to be reformed by the city?" At that time, this question could only be solved by suppressing citizens and enhancing the image of peasants. Even so, this short story was accused of "vilifying worker and peasant cadres." But the marriage between senior cadres from the countryside and young women from the city has become the most fashionable pattern in today's TV dramas, and nowadays nobody would call this a serious comparison between the proletariat and capitalist classes (actually, even according to theories of that time, most conflicts between peasants and citizens were conflicts between the proletariat and the petty bourgeoisie). In this regard, the massification for peasants and popularization for citizens of New Literature in the 1940s had accumulated their respective historical experience in integrating the literature of the late-Qing and May Fourth periods, in order to lead Chinese literature down a more modernized path with stronger national characteristics, and this was indeed significant.

FORTY

A CHRONICLE OF LITERARY EVENTS IN THE YEAR 1948 (AN ERA OF TRANSITION)

THE YEAR 1948 WAS ONE OF TRANSITION THAT WITNESSED[*] a tremendous change in China's political situation. During this year, decisive battles were waged between the KMT and the CPC, of which the Liaoshen Battle had come to an end while the Huaihai and Pingjin battles had started. In the north, the Land Reform movement was rapidly spreading across the vast countryside. The balance between the two political parties had obviously tilted, and it became apparent which party had gained people's support. In literature, this situation, first and foremost, brought about great changes in the general look of literary creation. We can see clearly from the Chronicle of Literary Events in 1948 (Table 40.1) that the summary publishing of "resistance literature" (whose creation had ended not long before) continued. The outstanding achievements of left-wing literature, such as Xiao Hong's *Spring in a Small Town* and Lu Ling's *Rich Men's Children*, were presented to readers, and at the same time, those writers who seemed to be detached from political influence, such as the symbolist poet Dai Wangshu, also published his *Years of Disaster* (《灾难的岁月》), a collection of poems more concerned with social realities. Meanwhile, the urban popular literature in cities, both martial arts fiction and romantic fiction, maintained its market share among its traditional readers. However, the literary achievements of the "liberated region" were increasingly more outstanding. Many new publishing institution names, which were unfamiliar to people and seemed uniform, such as the Xinhua Bookstore in Taiyue, south Shanxi, and south Hebei, the Northeast Bookstore

---

[*] Some material in this chapter is quoted from *Great Changes in 1948* (《1948：天地玄黄》) by Qian Liqun (钱理群).

in Kiamusze, the Harbin Guanghua Bookstore jointly instituted by relevant agencies of the "liberated region" in the north and northeast, began to come into view. These newly emerged publishing institutions obviously represented a rising power, and during this year, they published a number of literary works with great historical significance, including *The Sun Shines on Sanggan River*, *The Hurricane*, *The Just Prevails*, *Liu Hulan*, and *Motive Power*. The literature of newly "liberated" areas was coming to the fore with great strength. Such a massive cruel war, seldom seen in human history, with millions of casualties, should have been unfavorable for literary writers in terms of their state of mind, creative atmosphere, and basic material conditions, but a literature strongly characteristic of the "struggle of the era," evolving from the left-wing literature of the 1920s, did not decline but thrived at the turning point of 1948.

When talking about the significance of *The Sun Shines on Sanggan River*, Feng Xuefeng thought it was "a notable victory of socialist realism in reality."[1] We could say that, together with other literary works produced in 1948 in newly "liberated" areas, they provided a model for socialist realistic literature, which would later become the mainstream Chinese literature from the 1950s to 1970s in three aspects, namely creating, publishing, and structuring of literary works. The authors of these works went to the countryside with specific duties to meet, and they often went there multiple times and their literary works were based on their real-life experiences. They went to the countryside not as writers, but as social workers sent by the CPC. Ding Ling first went to Xinzhuang and Dongbali Village of Huailai County, Hebei, and then went to Wenquantun of Zhulu County to mobilize peasants to participate in the Land Reform movement. In Xinzhuang, she saw a pretty girl with shiny black hair woven into a thick braid, who later became the prototype of the character Heini. In Dongbali Village, she faced the problem of how to deal with middle peasants and rich peasants. Once at a mass meeting, there was a rich peasant who was not willing to "donate his land"; he stood there trembling, with a rugged strip of cloth tied around his waist, and this was the image in her mind when she later created the character Gu Yong, the old man. And the Sanggan River and Pingguoyuan of Wenquantun had the landscape of her imagined Nuanshuitun in her novel, whose first draft she had already finished in the villages of Hongtushan and Taitouwan of Fuping County of Hebei during the half year after she spent there with the army that autumn. After that, the novel was revised again and again, and in the process Ding Ling had to stop writing to do specific land reform work many times. In May and June 1947, when she went to the counties on both sides of the Beiping–Hankou railway line,

---

[1]   Feng Xuefeng: "The Significance of *The Sun Shines on Sanggan River* on Our Literary Development" (《〈太阳照在桑干河上〉在我们文学发展上的意义》), *Literary Gazette* (《文艺报》), Issue 10, 1952.

the leftist tendency of the Land Reform movement had already emerged. In her letter to her son, Ding Ling wrote:"I went around Jizhong and now have returned to Taitouwan. Tremendous changes have occurred in the review of land property during the past month, but I have to hurry back for my writing."[2] Then she went to Song Village in the surburb of Shijiazhuang to do more land reform work. She wrote in her letter before revising the entire novel: "Last year we held a border area land reform meeting in Fuping, and then … I have been to the countryside of Huolu County until now; another half month is needed for me to complete the novel."[3] It was not until May and June 1948 that she finally sat down in the North China Associated University in Zhengding County, Hebei, to revise her first draft, adding new chapters, and finally completed the novel. If the intellectual elites did not go to the countryside so many times, that is, to implement the principle of "moving their feet over to the life of masses" raised by Mao Zedong in his "Talks," it was certainly impossible for writers to truly write about peasants. The same was true for Zhou Libo. Like Ding Ling, he was also a native of Hunan and did not understand the northeast dialect, and he also went to participate in the land reform work as a social worker. He worked there as a member of the CPC Committee of Yuanbao District, Zhuhe County, which later became the fictional Yuanmaotun at the side of the Songhua River in his novel. His old friends, who had known Zhou Libo when he taught "World Literary Classics" in the Lu Xun Arts College, could not believe that he could use the northeast dialect and peasant's colloquial language so fluently. When he discussed *The Hurricane* in Harbin, for example, Cao Ming had shown his amazement at this.[4]

The Land Reform movement was carried out in both established and newly "liberated" areas, and covered a large range of territory. The movement was started successively, and there was big cultural difference in different places. Even so, there were many similarities between *The Sun Shines on Sanggan River* and *The Hurricane*: they both took a similar point of view, were about the major event of the era, and reflected the entire process of the event; after all, from mobilizing the masses to combating landlords, and then to the distribution and defense of the spoils of victory, the process was generally the same everywhere. No matter whether in Hebei or in the northeast, the thoughts and tendencies of peasants at various levels were generally the same. Those peasants who were brave and active in the Land Reform

---

[2] Ding Ling's Letter to Jiang Zulin on June 6, 1947, published in *New Materials on the History of Literature* (《新文学史料》), Issue 4, 1993.

[3] Ding Ling's Letter to Jiang Zulin on April 18, 1948, published in *New Materials on the History of Literature* (《新文学史料》), Issue 4, 1993.

[4] See "Summary of Memo of the Symposium on *The Hurricane*" (《〈暴风骤雨〉座谈会记录摘要》), published in *Northeast Daily* (《东北日报》), June 22, 1948.

TABLE 40.1 *Chronicle of literary events in 1948*

Date	Major literary event
Jan. 3	Shen Congwen published his prose "The Xiong's Mansion in Zhijiang County" (《芷江县的熊公馆》) on Tianjin *Ta Kung Pao*, which was later criticized by an article published on *Mass Literature Serial Journal* (《大众文艺丛刊》) in Hong Kong
January	Shi Tuo's novel *Ma Lan* (《马兰》) was published by Shanghai Cultural Life Press
January	Ai Wu's novel *Wild Life* was published by Shanghai Cultural Life Press
January	Xiao Hong's novella *Spring in a Small Town* was published by Hong Kong Ocean Bookstore
January	Zhou Erfu's collection of short stories, *Years of Standing Up* (《翻身的年月》) was published by Hong Kong Ocean Bookstore
January	Zheng Dingwen's collection of short stories, *Elder Sister* (《大姊》), was published by Shanghai Cultural Life Press
January	Xin Di's collection of poems, *Palms* (《手掌集》), was published by Shanghai Xingqun Press
January	Zang Kejia's collection of poems, *Winter* (《冬天》), was published by Shanghai Plowing Publishing Company
January	Song Zhidi's collection of playscripts, *Monkeys* (《群猴》), was published by Harbin Guanghua Bookstore
January	Feng Xuefeng's *Collected Works of Xuefeng* (《雪峰文集》), which collected his poems, prose writings and fables, was published by Shanghai Chunming Bookstore
Feb. 18	Xu Shouchang, Lu Xun's close friend and dean of the Chinese Department at the University of Taiwan, was assassinated in Taipei
February	Lu Ling's novel *Rich Men's Children* (Vols. 1 and 2) was published by Shanghai Hope Press
February	Huang Guliu's popular novel *The Story of Xiaqiu* (Vol. 1, *Breeze and Rain*) was published by New Democracy Press in Hong Kong
February	Zheng Zhengyin's martial arts novel, *Iron Lion King* (《铁狮王》), was published by Shanghai Sanyi Bookstore
February	Mu Dan's collection of poems, *The Flag*, was published by Shanghai Cultural Life Press
February	Dai Wangshu's collection of poems, *Years of Disaster*, was published by Shanghai Xingqun Press
February	Jin Yi's collection of prose writings, *Portraits of the Human World* (《人世百图》), was published by Shanghai Cultural Life Press
February	Ruan Zhangjing's opera *Red Leaf River* was published by Taihang Mountains Mass Bookstore

(continued)

TABLE 40.1 *(continued)*

Date	Major literary event
February	Zhou Yang's collection of literary criticism, *Portraying the Age of the New Masses* (《表现新的群众的时代》), was published by Hong Kong Ocean Bookstore
Mar. 1	*Mass Literature Serial Journal* was launched in Hong Kong, whose editors included Shao Quanlin and Feng Naichao. There were altogether six issues published, the first entitled "The New Direction in Literature and Art" (《文艺的新方向》)
Mar. 1	Shao Quanlin's "My Comments on the Current Literary Movement" (《对于当前文艺运动的意见》) was published in the first issue of *Mass Literature Serial Journal*
Mar. 1	Guo Moruo's "Debunking Reactionary Literature" (《斥反动文艺》) was published in the first issue of *Mass Literature Serial Journal*
Mar. 1	Hu Sheng's "A Critique of Lu Ling's Short Stories" was published in the first issue of *Mass Literature Serial Journal*
March	*Ode to Mao Zedong* (《毛泽东颂》), written by Ai Qing and others and edited by Feng Naichao, was published by Hong Kong Ocean Bookstore
March	Liu Baiyu's collection of short stories, *Political Commissar* (《政治委员》), was published by Northeast Bookstore in Kiamusze
March	Chen Xuezhao's novel *It's Beautiful to Be Working* (《工作着是美丽的》) was published by Northeast Bookstore in Kiamusze
March	Zhu Guangqian's literary theories *On Poetry* was published by the Shanghai Zhengzhong Book Company
March	*Small Collection of Ants* edited by Zhuang Yong and others, one of the continuous journals of the July school, was launched in Nanjing and published in the name of the Ants Society (蚂蚁社) of West China University and Sichuan University; altogether seven issues were published
March	The serial journal *China Poetry Forum* was launched in Hong Kong, which was edited and distributed by the China Poetry Forum Editorial Office; altogether three issues were published
March	Tian Han went to the North China "liberated region"
April	Mao Dun's reportage writing *Travels in the Soviet Union* (《苏联见闻录》) was published by Shanghai Kaiming Bookstore
April	Zhu Ziqing's collection of prose writings, *Standards and Criteria* (《标准与尺度》), was published by Shanghai Wenguang Bookstore
April	Zhou Libo's novel *The Hurricane* (Vol. 1) was published by Northeast Bookstore in Harbin. Volume 2 of the same novel was published by the same publishing house in May of the following year
April	Shen Ji's novella *Salt Mine* (《盐场》) was published by Shanghai Huaizheng Culture Press

(continued)

TABLE 40.1   *(continued)*

Date	Major literary event
April	Qin Shouou's popular novel *Record of the Beleaguered City* (《危城记》) was published by Shanghai Huaizheng Culture Press
April	Zhao Jingshen's collection of prose writings, *Reminiscences of the Literary Circle*, was published by Shanghai Beixin Press
May 15	The symposium on *The Hurricane* (Vol. 1) was held by the Northeast Literary Work Committee (东北文学工作委员会); Zhou Libo attended the symposium and talked about the creation of this novel
May	"Literary Creation and Subjectivity" (《文艺创作与主观》) by Qiao Mu (乔木, aka Qiao Guanhua [乔冠华]) was published in the second issue of the *Mass Literature Serial Journal*, "People and Art" (人民与文艺)
May	Shao Quanlin's "On the Question of Subjectivity" (《论主观问题》) was published in the second issue of *Mass Literature Serial Journal*
May	Zhu Ziqing's collection of literary criticism, *On Appealing to Both Refined and Popular Tastes* (《论雅俗共赏》), was published by Shanghai Observation Press
May	The collection of poems by Chen Jingrong, *Symphony* (《交响集》), was published by Shanghai Xingqun Press
May	The collection of poems by Hang Yuehe, *The Burned City* (《火烧的城》), was published by Shanghai Xingqun Press
May	The collection of poems by Fang Jing, *Melodies of the Suffered* (《受难者的短曲》), was published by Shanghai Xingqun Press
May	The collection of poems by Tang Qi, *Poems, Volume 1* (《诗第一册》), was published by Shanghai Xingqun Press
May	The collection of poems by Tang Shi, *The Heroic Grassland* (《英雄的草原》), was published by Shanghai Xingqun Press
May	Ai Wu's autobiographical prose writing, *My Youth* (《我的青年时代》), was published by Shanghai Kaiming Bookstore
May	Li Guantian's collection of essays, *Essays under the Sun* (《日边随笔》), was published by Shanghai Cultural Life Press
May	Cao Yu's playscript *Bright Sunny Days* (《艳阳天》) was published by Shanghai Cultural Life Press
May	Gu Sifan's novel *The New Peach Blossom Fan* (《新桃花扇》) was published by Shanghai New Era Press (上海新纪元出版社)
May	Shi Jimei's collection of short stories, *The Ghost Moon* (《鬼月》), was published by Shanghai Earth Press (上海大地出版社)
May	*Iron Knight, Silver Vase* (Vols. 1–6), Wang Dulu's representative work of martial arts fiction, was published by Tianjin Lili Press

(continued)

TABLE 40.1 *(continued)*

Date	Major literary event
May	*Literary and Art Work* (《文艺工作》) monthly was launched in Shanghai, edited by Sun Ling, and published by the Shanghai Literary and Art Work Editorial Office
May	Zhou Yang began his work on the Chinese People's Art and Literature book series, a collection of literary works created in the "liberated region," and editors participating in it included Ke Zhongping, Ouyang Shan, Zhao Shuli, Kang Zhuo, and Chen Yong
May	The new opera *The White-Haired Girl* was put on show for one month jointly by the Central Plains Dramatic Troupe (中原剧社), the Nation Building Dramatic Troupe (建国剧社), and the New Music Troupe (新音乐社), and the issue of the relationship between nationalization and modernization was discussed
June 18	Zhu Ziqing signed the declaration of professors of universities in Beiping to resist against the US aid policy to Japan and refuse claiming the US aid flour
June 22	"Summary of Memo of the Symposium on *The Hurricane*" was published in the *Northeastern Daily* (《东北日报》)
June	Cao Ming's novel *Motive Power* was published by South Shanxi Xinhua Bookstore
June	Wang Xiyan's novel *Dream Pursuers* was published by Shanghai Central Plains Press
June	Liu Baiyu's collection of short stories, *The Invincible Trio*, was published by Northeast Bookstore in Kiamusze
June	Shao Zinan's collection of short stories, *Li Yong Planning a Minefield* (《李勇大摆地雷阵》), was published by Hong Kong Ocean Bookstore
June	*The Big Circus*, a spoken drama play adapted by Shi Tuo, was published by Shanghai Cultural Life Press
June	*Discourses on Art* (《谈艺录》), a collection of literary theories by Qian Zhongshu, was published by Shanghai Kaiming Bookstore
June	*Poetry Writing* published the critical reviews of poems of Yuan Kejia, Tang Shi, and Chen Jingrong in the twelfth issue of the first year, with the issue entitled "Serious Stars" (严肃的星辰们)
June	Hang Yuehe and others withdrew from *Poetry Writing* and launched *New Chinese Poetry* in Shanghai with Fang Jing, which was published by Forest Press
July 1	*Fiction* (《小说》), the monthly whose editor-in-chief was Mao Dun, was launched in Hong Kong; its editor-in-chief was changed to Jin Yi from the third issue, and altogether twelve issues were published
July	*Literary Battlefront* (《文学战线》), whose editor-in-chief was Zhou Libo, was launched in Harbin
July	Sha Ting's novel *Returning Home* (《还乡记》) was published by Shanghai Cultural Life Press
July	Huang Guliu's popular novel *The Story of Xiaqiu* (Vol. 2, *Cloud and Sea*) was published by New Democracy Press

(continued)

TABLE 40.1 *(continued)*

Date	Major literary event
July	Xiao Qian's collection of essays, *Pearl Rice* (《珍珠米》), was published by Shanghai Dawn Press
July	Zhou Libo, living on the Sun Island of Harbin, started writing his novel *The Hurricane* (Vol. 2), with the entire novel completed in December of the same year
July	*Literary and Art Work* semimonthly was launched in Chengdu, edited by the Literary and Art Work Editorial Office, and altogether six issues were published
Aug. 12	Zhu Ziqing died of disease in Beijing
Aug. 15	*Mass Art and Literature* (《群众文艺》) monthly was launched in Yan'an, edited by the Editorial Committee of the Mass Art and Literature of Shaanxi, Gansu, and Ningxia Border Areas Association and published by Xinhua Bookstore; altogether twelve issues were published
August	Ding Ling's collection of sketchy essays, *Landscape in Northern Shaanxi* (《陕北风光》), was published by Northeast Bookstore in Kiamusze
August	Sha Ting's collection of short stories, *Small Scenes in Kamchatka* (《堪察加小景》), was published by Shanghai Cultural Life Press
August	*A Painting of Gentlemen and Ladies*, a collection of short stories by Dongfang Didong, was published by Shanghai Zhengfeng Cultural Press
August	*Complete Works of Wen Yiduo* (《闻一多全集》), edited by Zhu Ziqing and other members of the Committee of Collection of Mr. Wen Yiduo's Posthumous Works, was published by Shanghai Kaiming Bookstore
August	*On Joseph's Jacket* (《论约瑟夫的外套》), a collection of Huang Yaomian's literary criticism, was published by Hong Kong Human World Bookstore
August	A campaign against Xiao Jun and *Cultural Gazette* was waged by the entire literary circle of the northeast under the leadership of the propaganda department of the CPC Northeast Bureau
Aug. 19 or Sep. 7	The literary associations of the Shanxi–Chahar–Hebei and Shanxi–Hebei–Shandong–Henan border areas were combined into the Association of the Literary Circle of North China (华北文艺协会), with Zhou Yang being its director and Xiao San being its supervisor; Ouyang Shan and others edited its official journal, *North China Literature and Art* (《华北文艺》)
Sep. 9	Mao Dun's novel *Tempering* began to be serialized in the *Wenhui Daily* in Hong Kong, and the serialization was completed on December 29 of the same year
September	Ding Ling's novel *The Sun Shines on Sanggan River* was published by Harbin Guanghua Bookstore
September	*Crescent Moon and Other Stories* (《月牙集》), a collection of short stories by Lao She, was published by Shanghai Dawn Press

(continued)

TABLE 40.1 *(continued)*

Date	Major literary event
September	*Strange Stories in the Clouds* (《云海争奇记》), a martial arts novel by Huanzhu Louzhu, was published by Shanghai Zhengqi Book Company
September	*Love between Leopard and Phoenix* (《豹凤缘》), a popular novel by Feng Yuqi (冯玉奇), was published by Shanghai Guangyi Book Company
September	*Cicada* (《蝈蟖集》), a collection of poems by Guo Moruo, was published by Shanghai Qunyi Press
September	Hu Feng's literary theory *On the Path of Realism* was published by Shanghai Qinglin Press
September	Sun Li attended the Literary and Art Work Meeting of North China held in Shijiazhuang, and then he was transferred to Shen County (深县) as the deputy director of the propaganda department of the CPC County Committee
Oct. 1	Zhang Tianyi published his fable "The Tiger Problem" (《老虎问题》) in Issue 4 of the newly resumed Vol. 1 of *Fiction* monthly in Hong Kong, the first time he had published any literary works since he had fallen sick six years before
Oct. 13	Zhao Shuli's *The Just Prevails* began to be serialized in the *People's Daily* published in the "liberated region" in North China, and it was serialized until Oct 22. It was a literary work about how the mistakes made during the land reform could be corrected
Oct. 19	*Literature and Art Monthly* was launched in Jilin, edited by Wu Boxiao (吴伯箫) and others and published by the Jilin Society of Literature and Art (吉林文艺协会). It was the literary journal published in the early stages after the "liberation" of the northeast, and altogether four issues were published
October	A new edition of Zhang Henshui's popular novel, *Swallow Returns* (《燕归来》, including the novel per se and its sequel) was published by Shanghai Zhenghua Press
October	*Lower a Sail* (《落帆集》), a collection of essays by Tang Tao, was published by Shanghai Cultural Life Press
October	*Muttering* (《沉吟》), a collection of essays by Nie Gannu, was published by Guilin Cultural Press
October	Hu Feng, as well as Lu Ling and his wife, went to Hangzhou to visit Fang Ran (方然), Ji Fang, Luo Luo (罗洛), and Zhu Guhuai (朱谷怀), which was a rare gathering for them all
October	Ding Ling went to Budapest through Harbin to attend the Second Congress of Women International Democratic Federation as a member of the Chinese delegation, and she took her newly published book, *The Sun Shines on Sanggan River*
October	*Poetry Writing* was closed down by the KMT government after the fourth issue of this year was published

(continued)

TABLE 40.1 *(continued)*

Date	Major literary event
Nov. 1	*The Plains* (《平原》) fortnightly was launched in Heze, Shandong by the Literary Federation of the Hebei–Shandong–Henan Border Area (冀鲁豫边区文联)
Nov. 2	*Cultural Gazette*, edited by Xiao Jun, was attacked and then discontinued
Nov. 14	The memo of the symposium on the topic of "Direction of Today's Literature" attended by professors of Peking University including Shen Congwen, Feng Zhi, Zhu Guangqian, and Fei Ming, was published in Tianjin's *Ta Kung Pao*
Nov. 23	Guo Moruo departed Hong Kong by ship for the "liberated region" in the northeast and arrived in Beiping the following February to participate in the preparation of the National Congress of Literature and Art Workers and the new Chinese People's Political Consultative Conference (CPPCC)
November	Zhao Shuli's novella *The Just Prevails* was published by South Hebei Xinhua Bookstore in Wei County (威县)
November	Ai Wu's novel *Nostalgia* (《乡愁》) was published by Shanghai Zhongxing Press (上海中兴出版社)
November	Wang Xiyan's novel *The Lost God* was published by Shanghai Zhongxing Press
November	*A Knife for Cutting Dreams* (《切梦刀》), a collection of essays by Li Jianwu, was published by Shanghai Cultural Life Press
November	Lu Ling's playscript *The Lark* (《云雀》) was published by Shanghai Hope Press
November	*Overflow* (《盈盈集》), a collection of poems by Chen Jingrong, was published by Shanghai Cultural Life Press
November	*New Chinese Poetry* was closed down by the KMT government after five issues had been published
November	The comedy *Blackie Gets Married*, adapted from Zhao Shuli's novel with the same title, was performed by the Southern Dramatic Troupe (南方剧团) in Hong Kong
Dec. 9	Hu Feng, whose name was included on the blacklist, received the order to depart Shanghai for Hong Kong, and later he left Hong Kong for the north and arrived in Beiping in March the following year
Dec. 21	Two different articles, one positively commenting on and the other harshly attacking Zhao Shuli's *The Just Prevails* by Han Beisheng (韩北生) and Dang Ziqiang (党自强), respectively, were published in the *People's Daily* simultaneously
Dec. 31	Mao Dun, Hong Shen, and more than twenty others left Hong Kong on board a ship for Dalian in secret on the last day of this year; they arrived in Beiping in February the following year to participate in the preparation of the National Congress of Literature and Art Workers and the new CPPCC

(continued)

TABLE 40.1 *(continued)*

Date	Major literary event
December	Su Qing's novella *A Beauty on the Wrong Path* was published by Shanghai Sihai Press (上海四海出版社)
December	*The Tiger Shooter* (《射虎者》, also known as *The Tiger Shooter and His Family* [《射虎者及其家族》]), an epic by Li Yang (力扬), was published by Hong Kong New Poetry Press
December	*Collected Essays about England* (《英国采风录》), a collection of essays by Chu Anping (储安平), was published by Shanghai Observation Press
December	*Collection of Plays by Lao She* (《老舍戏剧集》) was published by Shanghai Dawn Press
December	*Liu Hulan*, the opera collectively created by members of the Northwestern Fighting Dramatic Troupe (西北战斗剧社) and written by Wei Feng and Liu Lianchi, etc., was published by Taiyue Xinhua Bookstore
December	At the invitation of Sun Yat-sen University, Liang Shiqiu left Beijing and went to Guangzhou by sea, where he left for Taiwan in June the following year
December	Zhu Guangqian decided to remain in Beiping when the city was besieged
December	Chen Huangmei went to Tianjin to work as the director of the Art and Literature Unit of the Military Control Commission
December	*Complete Works of Lu Xun*, edited by the Mr. Lu Xun Memorial Committee, was published by Shanghai Complete Works of Lu Xun Publishing House
This year	Huang Guliu's popular novel *The Story of Xiaqiu (*Vol. III, *Mountain and Water)* was published by New Democracy Press in Hong Kong
This year	Lao She wrote his novel *The Drum Singers* (《鼓书艺人》) in the United States (the only extant Chinese edition is translated by Ma Xiaomi [马小弥] from the English edition)
This year	Lao She completed the third volume, *Famine*, of his novel *Four Generations under One Roof* in the United States; he translated and helped his American friend translate *Divorce, Four Generations Under One Roof* and his other literary works into English
This year	At the end of this year, Cao Yu accepted the arrangement of the CPC and departed Shanghai for Hong Kong and then went to the "liberated region," and arrived in Beiping in February the following year

(*Sources*: Chen Shumin, ed.: *The Encyclopedia of Twentieth-Century Chinese Literature*; Yu Kexun and Ye Liwen, eds.: *Chronicles of Chinese Literature* [《中国文学编年史》], Changsha, Hunan People's Press, 2006; and *One Hundred Years' Literary Compendium* [《百年文学总系》], Taiyuan: Shanxi Education Press, 1998)

40.1. Editions published by the Xinhua Bookstore were coarsely produced, but they represented the fresh blood of the publishing industry. This was the edition of *The White-Haired Girl* published by Northeast Literature and Arts Press in September 1946

40.2. Edition of *The White-Haired Girl* published by Taiyue Xinhua Bookstore in January 1947

40.3. Title page of the Northeast Bookstore edition of *The Hurricane* (Vol. 1), published in April 1948

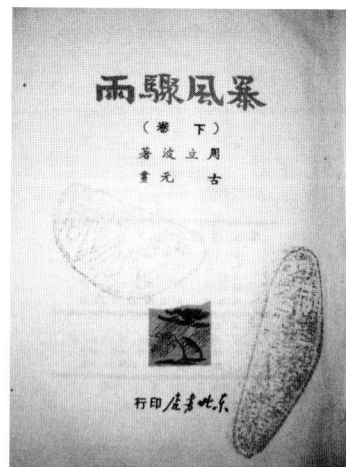

40.4. Title page of the Northeast Bookstore edition of *The Hurricane* (Vol. 2), published in May 1949

movement would certainly become heroes in their novels, while those wavering peasants were given a proper status correspondent to their positions. Most importantly, though this unprecedented historical transformation was rooted in the requirement of "land to the tiller" for many generations of peasants, the land reform was carried out in a top-down style, meaning the CPC sent working groups to make painstaking but effective efforts at mobilizing the masses and calling upon them to respond. The reason why the conception of these two novels happened to be similar was simple: both authors were writing under the unified guiding theory; that is, the analysis of the real-life raw material with ideological policies played a decisive role in the creation of these two literary works. This was the continuance of the left-wing tradition of the 1930s when Mao Dun created *Midnight*.

40.5. Ding Ling (front left) returned to Zhuolu County from Wenquantun by carriage in 1947; she told her fellow travelers that the concept for her novel *On Sanggan River* had been finished

Even Ding Ling, who had extremely strong individuality in literary creation and may present to her readers a complex setting in which land reform policies and personal experience coexisted, would try her best to lean toward the policies when there were conflicts between the two. Ding Ling first submitted her first draft to Zhou Yang, but there was no response from the latter for a long while; and then she heard that some senior leader had been critical about the fact that some novels on land reform, without naming any particular person, had the tendency to sympathize with landlords and rich peasants in terms of both emotional expression and literary description. The character Heini was originally the daughter of a landlord, but when Ding Ling revised the novel, she sensitively changed her status into a poor niece of the landlord Qian Wengui who lived as a maidservant in the Qian's. When Zhou Libo wrote *The Hurricane*, he devoted even more time and energy to repeated studies of the documents on land reform issued by the Northeast Bureau and CPC Central Committee, and claimed that his task was to "unify ideological policies with artistic images."[5] This was why in some places his *The Hurricane* was distributed among new members of the working group on land reform as a "semiguiding document." Thus the reality reflected in literature became the reality under the guiding policies, the "reality higher than life per se, more concentrated

---

[5] Zhou Libo: "On Literary Writing" (《关于写作》), *Literary Gazette* (《文艺报》), Issue 7, June 1950.

40.6. Woodcut illustration by Gu Yuan for the Northeast Bookstore edition of *The Hurricane* published in April 1948: "About the character Laosuntou"

40.7. Another woodcut illustration by Gu Yuan for the Northeast Bookstore edition of *The Hurricane* published in April 1948: "Combating the landlord Hanlaoliu"

and closer to the core." All these later became important elements of socialist realistic literature.

The dramatic process of publishing *The Sun Shines on Sanggan River* showed that the CPC had finally established its position as the direct leader in the field of literature and art. At first, "Zhou Yang expressed disagreement at publishing *The Sun Shines on Sanggan River* on the grounds that the love between Cheng Ren and Heini was anti-class."[6] A few days later, Ding Ling came across Mao Zedong at Xibeipo (whose name was later changed into Xibaipo [西柏坡]), and they had dinner together after a walk. Mao Zedong reiterated repeatedly that "history involved several decades, so that a person should be examined retrospectively for a period of several decades," and then talked about Lu Xun, Guo Moruo, and Mao Dun, and put Ding Ling "on par with Lu, Guo, and Mao"; "both Chairman Mao and Jiang Qing (江青) expressed their willingness to read my writings."[7] Ding Ling was greatly encouraged and submitted the copy of this novel to Hu Qiaomu (胡乔木), secretary of Mao Zedong, the next day and then submitted it to Ai Siqi and

[6]   Mei Zhi: "Biography of Hu Feng" (《胡风传》), *Collected Works of Mei Zhi* (《梅志文集》), Vol. 2, Yinchuan: Ningxia People's Press, 2007, p. 390.

[7]   See the diary of Ding Ling entitled "Some Fragments of Life Forty Years Ago: From Zhengding to Harbin" (《四十年前的生活片断——从正定到哈尔滨》), published in *New Materials on the History of Literature*, Issue 2, 1993. Later the son of Ding Ling, Jiang Zulin, pointed out that the text was revised and was not Ding's original wording. This text about Ding Ling coming across Mao Zedong was restored by Jiang Zulin according to Ding's diary and it was in the correspondence published in *New Materials on the History of Literature*, Issue 1, 1995.

40.8. Cover of the first edition of *The Sun Shines on Sanggan River* published by Northeast Guanghua Bookstore in September 1948

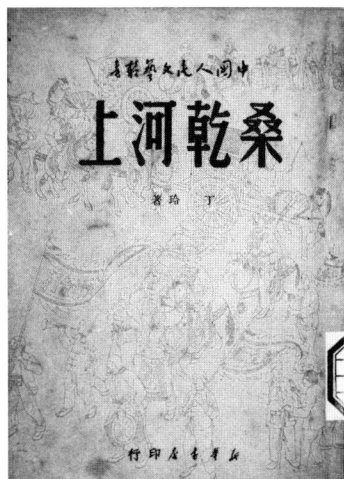

40.9. Edition of *On Sanggan River* (another title of Ding Ling's novel) published by Xinhua Bookstore in May 1949

Xiao San, but all this could not dispel Zhou Yang's prejudice against the novel. It was a while after that, when Hu, Ai, and Xiao discussed the matter with Mao, that the conclusion of timely publishing was drawn.[8] After that, the publishing process went quite smoothly: immediately after the decision was made in July, Ding Ling went to Dalian through Shandong to go abroad to attend the Congress of Women International Democratic Federation; she arrived in Harbin in August and in September saw the hardcover edition of her novel beautifully bound in black silk with a golden blocked title; in October the symposium on this book was held in Harbin, which Zhou Libo attended; and in November Ding Ling went to Europe to attend the Congress with her book. At the time the civil war was still on and people were suffering from material deprivation, the publishing of this book was as rapid as magic. In 1949 it was included in the Chinese People's Art and Literature book series, for which the title was changed to "On the Sanggan River" because the original title was too long. In the same year, the novel was serialized in *Znamya* (meaning "Banner"), an authoritative literary journal of the USSR, and was published in Moscow. In 1952, the novel, with its original title restored, won second prize in the Stalin Literary Prize Contest. These experiences of the novel, contrary to its earlier bad luck, would have been impossible without the interference of top CPC leaders. It had been made clear in Mao Zedong's "Talks" that the literary cause was part of the CPC's

---

[8]   See the memory of Gan Lu (甘露), wife of Xiao San, who was present at the discussion. Gan Lu wrote "A Few Things about Ding Ling and Chairman Mao" (《丁玲与毛主席二三事》), published in *New Materials on the History of Literature*, Issue 4, 1986.

political work, and now it was truly implemented through the publishing and distributing mechanisms. This practice and system of the "political party taking charge of literature and art" would become an important part of the guiding pattern in the development of literature after the People's Republic of China was founded.

Soon after that, the CPC strengthened the integration of literature into its political work. Those dissidents within the left-wing literary camp who failed the duties of "unity of thought" and "concert of action" were certainly the first group of people to be disciplined. The poetry, novels, and literary theories of the July clique led by Hu Feng actually had made great achievements among left-wing literary groups. This year, Lu Ling lost the manuscript of his novel but rewrote it with great perseverance and had it published. Hu Feng's literary works were published one after another. Another literary journal with the July school style, *Small Collection of Ants*, was launched under cover despite the high pressure of the KMT government. But the literary activities of Hu Feng and his people had led to opposition within their own literary camp. As early as the period of *Zuolian*, Hu Feng, standing together with Lu Xun, had debated with Zhou Yang based on different literary theories and sects. By 1944, when the "Spirit of Rectification" of Yan'an and Mao Zedong's "Talks" were communicated to the left-wing camp in the Nationalist-controlled area, Hu Feng refused to take a stand on the grounds that the "environment and mission" of the Nationalist-controlled area were different. In 1945, Shu Wu's article "On Subjectivity," published in the inaugural issue of *Hope*, and Lu Ling's article to criticize the "objectivity" of literary creation aroused opposition from the authors of the CWC and Talents clique in Chongqing, including Feng Naichao, Qiao Guanhua, Chen Jiakang (陈家康), and Hu Sheng, who deliberately confused "subjectivity" with "subjective fighting spirit" and accused the writers of Hu Feng's sect of ignoring the masses and writers' ideological remolding and of speaking contrary to Yan'an's opposition of "subjectivism," though some of them were attacked as "idealists" themselves shortly before that. Zhou Enlai talked with Hu Feng personally with good intentions to remind him that "on theoretical issues, only Chairman Mao's instructions are right," and told him to "change [his] attitudes toward the Party,"[9] but it proved that Hu Feng did not truly understand what Zhou had said to him. After that dispute, He Qifang was sent from Yan'an to the Nationalist-controlled area as a member to implement the spirit of the "Talks," and later he seemed to draw a conclusion in his lengthy article entitled "On Realism" (《关于现实主义》), relating the realistic literary theories with Mao's "Talks," pointing out that it was "our integration with the masses of the people" instead of "integration of the

---

[9] Mei Zhi: "Biography of Hu Feng," p. 352.

subjective spirit with objective matters" emphasized by Hu Feng that should be "the central issue of art and literature in today's 'great hinterland.'"[10] By May 1948, the *Mass Literature Serial Journal* was launched in Hong Kong, most of whose editors and contributors were Shao Quanlin and others who had criticized Hu Feng in their last disputes, together with influential writers such as Guo Moruo and Mao Dun, and thus another unprecedentedly harsh criticism campaign against Hu Feng and the so-called wrong tendency in literary creation in the Nationalist-controlled area was waged.

According to documents uncovered so far, one cannot prove whether the launch of the *Mass Literature Serial Journal* was the decision of top CPC leaders. At that time, Hong Kong again became a venue for left-wing intellectuals to gather and gain momentum. Most of those intellectuals were members of the Hong Kong Work Committee of the CPC South China Bureau or the Cultural Work Committee, including Quanlin (Shao Quanlin), Xiao Kai (萧恺, Pan Hannian), Hu

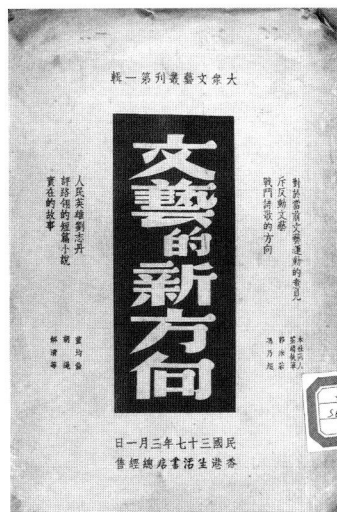

40.10. "The New Direction in Literature and Art," one issue of the *Mass Literature Serial Journal* published in Hong Kong, waged a criticism campaign against Hu Feng's ideas on art and literature

Sheng, Naichao (Feng Naichao), Lin Mohan (林默涵), Qiao Mu (Qiao Guanhua), Zhou Erfu, and Xia Yan, but it was certainly a journal organized by the top level of the CPC. Altogether six issues were published, each of which had a central topic, so that each had its own separate title. The first issue was entitled "The New Direction in Literature and Art"; the second, "People and Art" (May 1948); the third, "On the United Front of Art and Literature" (论文艺统一战线, July 1948); the fourth, "On Criticism" (论批评, alternative title: "The Path of Lu Xun" [鲁迅的道路], September 1948); the fifth, "On the Question of Subjectivity" (alternative title: "How to Write Poetry" [怎样写诗], December 1948), and the sixth, "The New Situation and Literature and Art" (新形势与文艺, alternative title: "On Films" [论电影], March 1949). All these were published within one year, but the journal's influence spanned a far longer time. It was a landmark event to correct right-wing ideas on literature and art that departed from the mainstream (Mao Zedong's "Talks at the Yan'an Forum on Literature and Art," which was published in Hong Kong in 1948 with the title "Problems of Art and Literature" [《论文艺问题》]) in the form of literary criticism, so as to achieve the goal of unity of thoughts within the united front of literature and art even before the decisive victory of the civil war was won. And it set the precedence for planned and large-scale ideological purge. Shao Quanlin's "My Comments on the Current Literary Movement"

[10] He Qifang: "On Realism," published in the Chongqing *Xinhua Daily*, February 13, 1946.

represented the guideline views of the CPC leaders at this level on the issue of art and literature. The "reactionary art and literature" he listed in the article included the "obscene arts" and "US cultural aid to China," "the accessory and toady literature serving landlords and big capitalists," and he mentioned the names of Zhu Guangqian, Liang Shiqiu, Shen Congwen, Gu Yiqiao, Xiao Qian, and Zhang Daofan. In his article "Debunking Reactionary Literature," Guo Moruo vividly categorized "reactionary literature" into five colors: red, yellow, blue, white, and black. "Shen Congwen is pink, Zhu Guangqian blue, tabloids yellow [obscene], and finally I want to say Xiao Qian is black." The three persons harshly attacked here, Shen Congwen, Zhu Guangqian, and Xiao Qian, were all Beijing school writers. They were "domestic liberal intellectuals" and indeed had proposed "the third road" or "the fourth organization" between the KMT and the CPC, but they were not political practitioners and did not belong to any political party, so that what they said was nothing but empty talk among intellectuals (interestingly, all three of these writers later chose to remain in mainland China). However, at least within the literary circle, by that time, they were already regarded as chief enemies instead of neutral wavering friends. Literary criticism seemed even harsher than political struggles, which later took a huge toll on the New China's historical development.[11] And this serial journal then published a number of articles to wage a concentrated criticism campaign against Hu Feng and the Hu Feng clique, including Hu Sheng's "A Critique of Lu Ling's Short Stories" (《评路翎的短篇小说》, Issue 1), Qiao Mu's (Qiao Guanhua) "Literary Creation and Subjectivity" (Issue 2), and Shao Quanlin's "On the Problem of Subjectivity" (Issue 5). Meanwhile, making use of the serial journal and other journals, these critics expressed severe comments on Yao Xueyin's *Spring Blossoms* (《春暖花开的时候》), Luo Binji's *Spring in the North-Facing Garden*, Zang Kejia's *Song of the*

40.11. A gathering of Hu Feng clique writers in Hangzhou in 1948: (front row, left to right) Jia Zhifang (贾植芳), Ren Min (任敏), Ji Fang, and Hu Feng; (back row) Zhu Guhuai, Yu Mingying (余明英), Lu Ling, and Luo Luo

[11] These two articles of Shao Quanlin and Guo Moruo, respectively, were published in *Mass Literature Serial Journal*, Issue 1, March 1948.

Soil, Li Guangtian's *Gravitation*, and Qian Zhongshu's *Fortress Besieged*. By the standards of today's readers, these were excellent literary works produced in the Nationalist-controlled area during the Anti-Japanese War. Hu Feng replied to all these criticisms with his theoretical book, *On the Path of Realism*. The ideas on art and literature of the Hu Feng clique were developed following the traditions of the May Fourth movement and Lu Xun, which were based on the enlightenment of people, clinging to reality, and fully developing the realistic fighting spirit of individual writers. Thus they stood opposed to the thoughts on art and literature that attached more importance to political purpose than reflecting life and championed collectivity and obliterated individuality. The conflict between these two could have enhanced the vitality of the left-wing camp, but it finally evolved into a tragedy of intolerance due to the general environment of China, which was in want of a tradition of democracy and had long emphasized "unity" but suppressed "diversity."

Meanwhile, in the new "liberated" areas in the northeast, on the one hand, new literary works that represented the masses of workers and peasants, such as *The Hurricane* and *Motive Power* were produced, and on the other hand, criticism campaigns were also waged, the typical event being the *Cultural Gazette* Incident concerning Xiao Jun. Xiao Jun was criticized much later than Hu Feng, but he was immediately disposed by the Party. This was because Hong Kong was a place where some CPC cultural workers with political backgrounds gathered, and thus they could only criticize others with their writings; while in Xiao Jun's case, it was the CPC Northeast Bureau, an integrated Party and government agency with both ideological and economic power, that waged the campaign against him. And Xiao Jun's problem was much easier to deal with than that of Hu Feng. No disagreement on literary thoughts within the complex realistic theoretical system was involved here; it was only the conflict between two newspapers: *Cultural Gazette*, launched by an intellectual championing the freedom and individuality of the May Fourth tradition, and *Life Post* (《生活报》), launched by the propaganda department of the CPC Northeast Bureau that required unity of thoughts and blind obedience to CPC's leadership. Such issues as sectarianism and individual personality were certainly involved. Xiao Jun, who claimed to be a student of Lu Xun, gave lectures everywhere, which alone displeased the propaganda department. *Life Post* seized on Xiao Jun's isolated words and expressions, elevated them to the question of principle and published one after another collectively written editorial to attack him as "anti-USSR," "anti-land reform," "anti-people," and "anti-Party," trying their best to put exaggerated labels on him. Xiao Jun, left to his own devices, published a series of articles (numbered I, II, III, etc.) with the same title "Sounds from the Ancient Pond" (《古潭里是声音》) to publicly "Denounce the Nonsense of *Life Post*" (the subtitle of his articles) in his own

40.12. Xiao Jun, vigorous in his old age, during the Fourth National Congress of Literature and Art Workers

Cultural Gazette, quite a rare spectacle back then! Thinking of the fact that back in Yan'an, at the public meeting criticizing Wang Shiwei, Xiao Jun, who did not even know Wang personally, had the courage to show his opposition, one could see that he was the one within the left-wing camp who had always insisted on freedom, independence, and integrity and never regretted it his whole life. The documents extant today, "Conclusions on the Mistakes made by Xiao Jun (*Cultural Gazette*)" (《关于萧军〈文化报〉所犯错误的结论》) written by the Northeastern Literature and Art Association and "Decision on Problems of Xiao Jun" (《关于萧军问题的决定》) by the Northeast Bureau, were historical documents that deserve profound reflection. Xiao Jun, then, was "demoted" to the coal mines in Fushun, but who could have imagined that this dauntless left-wing writer could survive this ideological suppression until the day it came to an end?

As for those nonleft-wing literary writers, they also found themselves in a delicate position at this historical moment of regime change. The political and literary choices of Beijing school intellectuals, who had already been harshly attacked by left-wing writers who would soon gain the ideological power, were shown from the speeches of Professors Shen Congwen, Fei Ming, Feng Zhi, and Zhu Guangqian of Peking University at a symposium held by the Direction Society (方向社), a students' literary society. The topic of the symposium was "Direction of Today's Literature." The situation urged these Beijing school writers who attached much importance to literature per se (belles lettres) to become concerned with political leanings, and when the discussion turned to the question of "literature as a vehicle of moral instruction," there was the following dialogue:

FEI MING: Throughout history, was there any literary writer writing to obey others' orders to write this or that? I know it very well that literature is a propaganda, but that could only be a propaganda of the writer himself, and no writer should write for others. Literary writers must have their own way, which might not necessarily be permitted by the society they live in … All good literary writers should be opposed to the reality. Even if they are not publicly doing so, they are not welcomed by society, like Shakespeare. Which talent, hero, or sage was not despised by society?

SHEN CONGWEN: Drivers must obey the police's commands, but can they ignore the traffic lights?

FENG ZHI: The traffic lights are good, and it is certainly wrong to ignore them.

SHEN CONGWEN: How about if someone is manipulating the traffic lights?

FENG ZHI: Anyone on the road should obey the traffic lights.

SHEN CONGWEN: Maybe some people think it is better without the traffic lights?

WANG ZENGQI: This is an incorrect metaphor. When you recognize his right to manipulate the traffic lights, you accept that right as legal and right. Then you have to obey the traffic lights on the road. But what if this is not the case? I hope to listen to the valuable experience of you, our predecessors.[12]

The discussions here on whether one should obey the traffic lights and challenge the legitimacy of the manipulator of traffic lights had shown the difference between individual writers within the Beijing school. But the ambiguity of this literary school did not represent the position of its members, some of whom did take a liberal political stand. The discussion also involved the issue of the assimilation of Western modernism by avant-garde literature of the time, which was of common concern for two generations of Beijing school writers and literary youths from the Southwestern Associated University attending the meeting. The moderator of the symposium attended by professors of Peking University was Yuan Kejia. When the journal *Poetry Writing* was launched in 1947, it became a gathering place for writers who were more deeply influenced by modernist poetry gathered by Hang Yuehe (Cao Xinzhi) and left-wing poets led by Zang Kejia; together with the poets from the July school, they constituted the majority of young Chinese poets of the 1940s. However,

---

[12] See "Direction of Today's Literature," published in the "Weekend Arts" supplement of the Tianjin *Ta Kung Pao*, November 14, 1948.

since they had different views on the experimental writing style of modernist poetry, the future Nine Leaves poets eventually split from the other poets of *Poetry Writing*. That was how *New Chinese Poetry* was launched in June that year, whose committee of editors included Fang Jing, Xin Di, Hang Yuehe, Chen Jingrong, Tang Shi, and Tang Qi. Certainly, its major contributors were Yuan Kejia, Du Yunxie, Zheng Min, and Mu Dan. The New Chinese Poetry Group (or Nine Leaves school) advocated, by refusing to make poetry a political tool, the integration of poetry with politics, reality, historical era, and people, seeking to create modernist Chinese poetry and pursuing modernization of poetry, which was consistent with the trend for belles lettres to make some changes to suit the wartime situation. From the Chronicle of Literary Events in 1948 (Table 40.1), one finds that this year saw the peak of poetic creation of this poetic school. But even so, due to the general atmosphere of that time, these poets were still criticized by left-wing poets. Then, by the end of that year, the KMT government was so shameless that it could not tolerate any literature related with "reality" and thus closed down both *Poetry Writing* and *New Chinese Poetry*.

Actually, the KMT government, which would soon collapse in mainland China, had already anticipated its destiny. Seeing the increasingly deteriorating financial crisis, inflation, and high political and cultural pressure, it had become an irresistible trend for liberal and democratic intellectuals to "turn left." In 1946, the assassinations of Li Gongpu and Wen Yiduo occurred in Kunming. Wen Yiduo, a famous poet of the Crescent Moon clique and liberal scholar, stood alongside students in the student democratic movement. Then in the

40.13. *Poetry Writing*, which was later disbanded

40.14. *New Chinese Poetry*, a journal of the Nine Leaves school, was launched in 1948

same year, before Zhu Ziqing died of poverty and illness, the well-known liberal and scholarly intellectual and writer showed his position close to "people" and his "national integrity" in his old age. With this, he approved of the academic research that "appealed to both refined and vulgar tastes" and the "massification of art and literature," and participated in the resistance campaign against the US policy to aid Japan, and signed his name on the declaration to refuse the flour aided by the United States. On the day of signing, he wrote in his diary: "Signing it will cost six million legal currency per month and it will surely negatively impact my family, but I still decided to sign. We people are opposed to the US policy to aid Japan, and we should start with ourselves. It is a spiritual opposition, but we have to shoulder our personal responsibilities."[13] For a poor professor who had to raise seven children in a period of inflation and lack of essential goods, these were words from the depths of his heart. And even two days before he died, Zhu Ziqing still remembered to tell his family that since he had signed the declaration, nobody in the family should buy the US flour rationed by the government. In 1948, this attitude toward the United States was obviously a "left turn." When these details were revealed by Wu Han, his colleague at Tsinghua University, during his mourning of Zhu, it received a great response and support from the entire society, and even high praise from Mao Zedong.

What was the future for literature and literary writers? Should they leave or remain in the mainland in the year 1948? The choice of Liang Shiqiu and

40.15. Funeral hall of Zhu Ziqing

[13] Quoted from Ji Zhenhuai (季镇淮): *Chronicles of Wen and Zhu* (《闻朱年谱》), Beijing: Tsinghua University Press, 1986, p. 176.

Hu Shi was to leave, which was understandable. Their political tendencies dictated them to go. Liang Shiqiu was a native of Beijing and he had properties in Beijing. Earlier he had been teaching in Qingdao for four years, and then his father ordered him to return to Beijing, citing in a letter that their yard in the Interior Ministry Street was so deserted that weasels were found loitering. From this we can see the home property was not a small one.[14] Liang did not leave until the last moment, when the Liberation Army strategically besieged Beiping in December of this year. "On the day I went southward in panic," he took nothing but a box of books.[15] He arrived in Guangzhou in January of the following year and went to Taiwan in June. Shen Congwen, who had just been given the label of "pink literature" and talked about "command of traffic lights," was living at Peking University's faculty dormitory building in Zhonglao Lane. People from the KMT government came to mobilize him to depart for Taiwan and even offered him the plane tickets to Taiwan, and his own students who were underground CPC members came to convince him to remain. Shen Congwen, in fact, would never throw himself into the KMT's lap. He was always detached from political parties and claimed to be a "countryman" from the remote western Hunan area, but he had many friends who were famous communist party members. However, just as Shen Congwen was waiting for the peaceful liberation of Beiping at Jin Yuelin's residence at Tsinghua, troubles ensued. Some radical students from Peking University posted large-sized slogans within the campus on which were written "Strike Down Shen Congwen of the Crescent Moon Clique, Contemporary Critique Clique Who Chooses the Third Road." Then the following year, he was not invited as a representative to the First All China Congress of Literature and Art Workers. This was followed by him attempting suicide, going to be "brainwashed" at the Central Revolutionary University, and being transferred from the literary circle to the Museum of Revolutionary History.[16] Shen Congwen still had a long way to go, but his "smart" plan of retreat helped him escape one political storm after another in the literary circle after the 1950s. For those literary writers gathering in Hong Kong, the case was totally different. Guo Moruo, Mao Dun, and others went northward on a ship to the "liberated region" in November and December this year, and the ship was full of vitality and full of the joy of victory. They would become

[14] See Liang Wenqian (梁文茜): "In the Memory of Liang Shiqiu, My Father," *Memories of Liang Shiqiu* (《回忆梁实秋》), Changchun: Jilin Literature and History Press, 1992, p. 203.

[15] Liang Shiqiu: "Books Basking in the Sun" (《晒书记》), *Collection of Prose of Liang Shiqiu* (《梁实秋散文》), Beijing: China Radio and Television Press, 1989, p. 250.

[16] Ling Yu (凌宇): "A Lonely Boat in the Hurricane" (《飓风孤舟》), *Biography of Shen Congwen* (《沈从文传》), Beijing: October Literature & Arts Press, chapter 9, 1988.

leaders in the field of literature and art in the upcoming New China. Lao She and Cao Yu were still in the United States, and they, too, would be successively welcomed into the arms of the new regime. Ba Jin was waiting for the "liberation" with quiet happiness in Shanghai. This writer who was always tolling the bell for old society, certainly had no fear of a new one. Meanwhile Hu Feng, who came to Hong Kong later than others, was most upset at this time. He had not arrived in Hong Kong from Shanghai through Guangdong until December this year, and had thought that he, like other left-wing intellectuals, should wait there for plans to be made to go to the "liberated region"; but little did he know, he had to solve his ideological problems first. He had arranged a meeting with the main figures of the *Mass Literature Serial Journal*, but the meeting was immediately ended due to their disagreement. Indeed, others were waiting for Hu Feng's self-criticism, but maybe Hu Feng was waiting for other people's introspection. The year 1949 would soon come, and the New Year Address of the Xinhua Press, "Carry the Revolution through to the End" inspired Hu Feng with enthusiasm. On January 6, Hu Feng, together with Du Xuan and others, boarded a Norwegian freighter and departed for the northeast "liberated region." What awaited him was bright sunshine, but indeed, there were also unforeseen storms.

A literary transition was coming. May Fourth literature had been a transition from the late-Qing period, and now there came another turning point. The success of one literary format meant a low tide, not the end, of other

40.16. On July 2–17, 1949, a group of literary writers and artists gathered for the First All China Congress of Literature and Art Workers in Beiping, of whom there were authors and artists familiar to many

40.17. Writers standing under the new national flag that had just been decided on at the CPPCC in 1949: (from third on the left) Hu Feng, Ding Ling, Ai Qing, Zhao Shuli, and Tian Han. They all looked quite high-spirited, but different destinies awaited them

literary formats. Conflicts would now occur within the literature of New China. Indeed, each step forward that modern Chinese literature was to take was destined to be accompanied by pain.

Completed to the sounds of firecrackers
on the fifth of the first lunar month, January 30, 2009
The revision before the second printing of the mainland edition
was completed on February 18, 2015,
The New Year's Eve of the Lunar Calendar

SELECT BIBLIOGRAPHY

COMPLETE WORKS, CATALOGUES, AND ENCYCLOPEDIAS

Collected Works of Ding Ling (《丁玲文集》, 10 vols.). Changsha: Hunan Literature and Arts Press (湖南文艺出版社), 1982–1995.

Collected Works of Feng Zikai (《丰子恺文集》, Literature, 3 vols.). Hangzhou: Zhejiang Literature and Arts Press, Zhejiang Education Press (浙江文艺出版社、浙江教育出版社), 1992.

Collected Works of Qu Qiubai (Literature, 6 vols.). Beijing: People's Literature Press (人民文学出版社), 1985–1988.

Collection of Fei Ming (《废名集》, 6 vols.). Beijing: Peking University Press (北京大学出版社), 2009.

Complete Works of Ba Jin (《巴金全集》, 26 vols.). Beijing: People's Literature Press, 1986–1994.

Complete Works of Guo Moruo (Literature, 20 vols.). Beijing: People's Literature Press, 1982–1992.

Complete Works of Lao She (《老舍全集》, 19 vols.). Beijing: People's Literature Press, 1999.

Complete Works of Lu Xun (16 vols.). Beijing: People's Literature Press, 1981.

Complete Works of Mao Dun (43 vols. including appended and [2] addendum vols.). Beijing: People's Literature Press, 1984–2006.

Complete Works of Shen Congwen (33 vols. including appended vols.). Taiyuan: Beiyue Literature and Arts Press (北岳文艺出版社), 2002–2003.

Selected Works of Xiao Hong. Beijing: People's Literature Press, 1981.

Tang, Yuan et al., eds. *Catalogue and List of Modern Chinese Literary Journals* (2 vols.). Tianjin: Tianjin People's Press (天津人民出版社), 1988.

Yu, Kexun and Ye, Liwen, eds. *Chronicles of Chinese Literature (Modern Period).* Changsha: Hunan People's Press, (湖南人民出版社) 2006.

Qian, Liqun and Feng, Shihui, eds. *Compendium of the Literature of China's Enemy-Occupied Territories: Historical Material.* Nanning: Guangxi Education Press (广西教育出版社), 2000.

Yan, Jiayan et al., eds. *Critical Material on Theories of the Twentieth-Century Chinese Novel* (5 vols.), Beijing: Peking University Press, 1997.

Encyclopedia of China: Chinese Literature (《中国大百科全书·中国文学》)(Vols. 1, 2). Beijing: Encyclopedia of China Publishing House (中国大百科全书出版社), 1986.

Encyclopedia of China: World Literature (《中国大百科全书·外国文学》) (Vols. 1, 2). Beijing: Encyclopedia of China Publishing House, 1982.

Chen, Shuming, ed. *The Encyclopedia of Twentieth-Century Chinese Literature, 1897–1929.* Shanghai: Shanghai Education Press (上海教育出版社), 1994.

Jia, Zhifang and Yu, Yuangui, eds. *General Catalogue of Modern Chinese Literature.* Fuzhou: Fujian Education Press (福建教育出版社), 1993.

General Catalogue of the Republican Period (1911–1949) (Foreign Literature). Beijing: Catalogue and Documentary Press (书目文献出版社), 1987.

Wang, Xiaoming, ed. *Historiography of Twentieth Century Chinese Literature* (《二十世纪中国文学史论》, Vols. 1–3), Shanghai: Oriental Publishing Center (东方出版中心), 1997.

Kong, Lingjing, ed. *Letters of Modern Writers.* Guangzhou: Huacheng Press (花城出版社), 1982.

Rao, Hongjing et al., eds. *Material of the Creation Society* (2 vols). Fuzhou: Fujian People's Press (福建人民出版社), 1985.

Jia, Zhifang et al., eds. *Material on the Literary Research Society* (3 vols). Zhengzhou: Henan People's Press (河南人民出版社), 1985.

Bao, Tianxiao. *Memoirs of the Bracelet Shadow Chamber*. Hong Kong: Dahua Publishing House (大华出版社), 1971.

Bao, Tianxiao. *Sequel to Memoirs of the Bracelet Shadow Chamber*. Hong Kong: Dahua Publishing House, 1973.

Cheng, Wenchao. *1903: Overnight Surge* (《1903：前夜的涌动》). Jinan: Shandong Education Press (山东教育出版社), 1998.

Wang, Yao. *A Draft History of New Chinese Literature* (《中国新文学史稿》, 2 vols.). Shanghai: Shanghai Literature and Arts Press (上海文艺出版社), 1982.

Ge, Yihong, ed. *General History of Chinese Spoken Drama*. Beijing: Cultural and Arts Press (文化艺术出版社), 1997.

Qian, Liqun. *Great Changes in 1948*. Jinan: Shandong Education Press, 1998.

Ren, Fangqiu (任访秋), ed. *A History of Early Modern Chinese Literature* (《中国近代文学史》). Kaifeng: Henan University Press (河南大学出版社), 1988.

Liu, Denghan, ed. *History of Hong Kong Literature* (《香港文学史》). Hong Kong: Hong Kong Writers Press (香港作家出版社), 1997.

Yang, Yi. *A History of Modern Chinese Fiction* (Vols. 1–3). Beijing: People's Literature Press, 1986–1991.

Wen, Rumin (温儒敏). *History of Modern Chinese Literary Criticism* (《中国现代文学批评史》). Beijing: Peking University Press, 1993.

Fan, Boqun, ed. *A History of Modern Chinese Popular Literature* (2 vols.). Nanjing: Jiangsu Education Press (江苏教育出版社), 2000.

Fan, Boqun. *History of Modern Popular Chinese Literature* (illustrated ed.) (《中国现代通俗文学史》[插图本]). Beijing: Peking University Press, 2007.

Liu, Denghan, ed. *History of Taiwan Literature* (《台湾文学史》, 2 vols.). Fuzhou: Straits Literature and Arts Publishing Company (海峡文艺出版社), 1991–1993.

Qian, Liqun, Wen, Rumin, and Wu, Fuhui. *Thirty Years in Modern Chinese Literature* (rev. ed.). Beijing: Peking University Press, 1998.

REFERENCES

Ai, Xiaoming (艾晓明). *The Origin of Chinese Left-Wing Literary Thoughts* (《中国左翼文学思潮探源》). Changsha: Hunan Literature and Arts Press, 1991.

Archives Bureau of Huangpu District of Shanghai Municipality, ed. *The Cultural Street on Fuzhou Road* (《福州路文化街》). Shanghai: Wenhui Press (文汇出版社), 2001.

Chen, Mingyuan. *Economic Life of Intellectuals*. Shanghai: Wenhui Press, 2005.

Chen, Pingyuan. *The Changes in Narrative Modes in Chinese Fiction* (《中国小说叙事模式的转变》). Shanghai: Shanghai People's Press (上海人民出版社), 1988.

Chen, Pingyuan. *History of Fiction: Theories and Practice* (《小说史：理论与实践》). Beijing: Peking University Press, 1993.

Chen, Sihe. *A Total View of New Literature in China* (rev. ed.) (《中国新文学整体观》). Shanghai: Shanghai Literature and Arts Press, 2001.

Chen, Zishan (陈子善). *The Lost Pearl* (《遗落的明珠》). Taipei: Yeh Chang Publishing (业强出版社), 1992.

Fan, Jun (樊骏). *On Studies of Modern Chinese Literature* (《论中国现代文学研究》). Shanghai: Shanghai Literature and Arts Press, 1992.

Hu, Ming. *A Biographical Account of Hu Shi*. Beijing: People's Literature Press, 1996.

Hu, Ming. *Chen Duxiu, A Cross-Current of Right and Wrong: An Interpretation of His Thoughts and Cultural Critique* (《正误交织陈独秀——思想的诠释与文化的评判》). Beijing: People's Literature Press, 2004.

Huang, Aihua. *China's Early Spoken Drama and Japan*. Changsha: Yuelu Press (岳麓书社), 2001.

Huang, Ziping (黄子平). *Revolution, History, Fiction* (《革命·历史·小说》). Oxford: Oxford University Press, 1996.

Lan, Dizhi (蓝棣之). *Modern Literary Classics: A Symptomatic Reading* (《现代文学经典：症候式分析》). Beijing: Tsinghua University Press (清华大学出版社), 1998.

Lee, Leo Ou-fan. *Shanghai Modern: The Flowering of a New Urban Culture in China, 1930–1945.* Mao, Jian, trans. Beijing: Peking University Press, 2001.

Li, Jianping, ed. *Literary Activities in Guilin during the Anti-Japanese War Period.* Guilin: Lijiang Press (漓江出版社), 1996.

Li, Nan. *Tabloids in Shanghai During the Late Qing and Early Republican Period* (illustrated ed.). Beijing: People's Literature Press, 2006.

Ling, Yu. *Biography of Shen Congwen.* Beijing: October Literature and Arts Press (十月文艺出版社), 1988.

Liu, Na (刘纳). *Evolution* (《嬗变》). Beijing: China Social Sciences Press (中国社会科学出版社), 1998.

Ni, Wei. *The Imagination of "Nation" and the "State" Governance.* Shanghai: Shanghai Education Press, 2003.

Peng, Xiaoling and Han Aili, eds. *Seventy Years of Ah Q.* Beijing: October Literature and Arts Press, 1993.

Qian, Gurong (钱谷融). *On the Characters in "Thunderstorm"* (《〈雷雨〉人物谈》). Shanghai: Shanghai Literature and Arts Press, 1980.

Qian, Liqun. *Between the Big and Small Stages: New Thoughts on Cao Yu's Plays* (《大小舞台之间——曹禺戏剧新论》). Hangzhou: Zhejiang Literature and Arts Press, 1994.

Qian, Liqun. *The Exploration of the Heart* (《心灵的探寻》). Shanghai: Shanghai Literature and Arts Press, 1988.

Shu, Wu. *An Overview of Zhou Zuoren* (《周作人概观》). Changsha: Hunan People's Press, 1986.

Sun, Yushi. *A Historical Review of Modernist Poetic Trends in China.* Beijing: Peking University Press, 1999.

Sun, Zhimei. *Studies on the South Society.* Beijing: People's Literature Press, 2003.

Tang, Xiaobing (唐小兵), ed. *A Reinterpretation: The Mass Literature and Ideology* (expanded ed.) (《再解读：大众文艺与意识形态》). Beijing: Peking University Press, 2007.

Tian, Benxiang (田本相). *Biography of Cao Yu* (《曹禺传》). Beijing: October Literature and Arts Press, 1988.

Wang, Furen (王富仁). *A Tortured Soul: Cultural Changes and Literary Changes* (《灵魂的挣扎——文化的变迁与文学的变迁》).

Changchun: Time Literature and Arts Press (时代文艺出版社), 1993.

Wang, Hongzhi (王宏志). *Reinterpreting Fidelity, Fluency and Elegance: Twentieth-Century Chinese Translation Studies* (《重释〈信达雅〉：二十世纪中国翻译研究》). Shanghai: Oriental Publishing Center, 1999.

Wang, Hui (汪晖). *Resisting Despair: A Study on Lu Xun's Mental Structure and His Collections "Call to Arms" and "Wandering"* (《反抗绝望——鲁迅的精神结构与〈呐喊〉〈彷徨〉研究》). Shanghai: Shanghai People's Press, 1991.

Wang, Xiaoming (王晓明). *Underflow and Vortex: On the Psychological Disorder of Twentieth-Century Chinese Novelists in Literary Creative* (《潜流与漩涡——论二十世纪中国小说家的创作心理障碍》). Beijing: China Social Sciences Press, 1991.

Wu, Fuhui. *Shanghai School Fiction in the Urban Vortex.* Changsha: Hunan Education Press (湖南教育出版社), 1995.

Xia, Xiaohong. *Awakening and Transmission: Liang Qichao's Literary Path.* Shanghai: Shanghai People's Press, 1991.

Xie, Zhixi. *The Modern and the Modern Era: A Historical Analysis of Modern Chinese Literature* (《摩登与现代——中国现代文学的实存分析》). Beijing: Tsinghua University Press, 2006.

Xu, Zidong (许子东). *A Preliminary Study of Short Stories of Hong Kong* (《香港短篇小说初探》). Hong Kong: Cosmos Books (天地图书有限公司), 2005.

Yan, Jiayan. *On Modern Fiction and Literary Thoughts* (《论现代小说与文艺思潮》). Changsha: Hunan People's Press, 1987.

Yang, Lianfen (杨联芬). *From Late Qing to May Fourth: The Advent of Chinese Literary Modernity* (《晚清至五四：中国文学现代性的发生》). Beijing: Peking University Press, 2003.

Yao, Dan. *Literary Activities in the Historical Context of the Southwestern Associated University.* Guilin: Guangxi Normal University Press (广西师范大学出版社), 2000.

Yuan, Guoxing (袁国兴). *The Birth of Chinese Spoken Drama* (《中国话剧的孕育与生成》). Beijing: China Theater Press (中国戏剧出版社), 2000.

Zhang, Xinying. *A Close Reading of Shen Congwen* (《沈从文精读》). Shanghai: Fudan University Press (复旦大学出版社), 2005.

Zhao, Yuan (赵园). *A Difficult Choice* (《艰难的选择》). Shanghai: Shanghai Literature and Arts Press, 1986.

Zhao, Yuan. *On the Ten Novelists* (《论小说十家》). Hangzhou: Zhejiang Literature and Arts Press, 1987.

Zhou, Yanfen. *Standing Fast, Repelling, and Surpassing: History of the July Clique.* Beijing: Zhonghua Book Company (中华书局), 2003.

INDEX

Please note: page numbers in *italic type* indicate illustrations or tables.